MW00679408

Handbook of Human Resource Management

Blackwell HRM Series
Edited by Myron Roomkin
J. L. Kellog Graduate School of Management

Handbook of Human Resource Management
Edited by Gerald R. Ferris, Sherman D. Rosen, and Darold T. Barnum

Forthcoming

Employment Law
Richard N. Block and Benjamin Wolkinson

Human Resource Strategies for Managing Diversity
Ellen Kossek and Sharon Alisa Lobel

Strategic Leadership Development
Albert A. Vicere

Human Resource Effectiveness
John W. Boudreau

Strategic Management Selection
Craig J. Russell

Handbook of Human Resource Management

Edited by Gerald R. Ferris,
Sherman D. Rosen, and Darold T. Barnum

BLACKWELL
Business

Copyright © Blackwell Publishers, 1995

First published 1995

Blackwell Publishers Inc.
238 Main Street
Cambridge, Massachusetts 02142, USA

Blackwell Publishers Ltd
108 Cowley Road
Oxford OX4 1JF
UK

Library of Congress Cataloging-in-Publication Data has been applied for.

ISBN 1–557–86719–4

British Library Cataloguing in Publication Data

A CIP catalogue record for this book is available from the British Library.

Commissioning Editor: Richard Burton
Desk Editor: Paul Stringer
Production Controller: Pam Park

Typeset in 10 on 12 pt Baskerville
by Graphicraft Typesetters Ltd., Hong Kong
Printed in the United States of America

This book is printed on acid-free paper

Contents

CONTENTS

Figures

Tables

Biographical Sketches of Contributors

THE EDITORS

Gerald R. Ferris is Professor of Labor and Industrial Relations, of Business Administration, and of Psychology, and Caterpillar Foundation University Scholar at the University of Illinois at Urbana-Champaign. He also is Director of the Center for Human Resource Management at the University of Illinois. He received a Ph.D. in Business Administration from the University of Illinois at Urbana-Champaign and subsequently served on the Department of Management Faculty at Texas A & M University. Ferris has research interests in the areas of interpersonal and political influence in organizations, performance evaluation, and strategic human resources management. He is the author of numerous articles published in such journals as *Journal of Applied Psychology, Organizational Behavior and Human Decision Processes, Personnel Psychology, Academy of Management Journal,* and *Academy of Management Review,* and he serves as editor of the annual series, *Research in Personnel and Human Resource Management.* He has authored or edited a number of books including *Strategy and Human Resource Management, The Employment Interview: Theory, Research, and Practice, Method & Analysis in Organizational Research, Personnel Management,* and *Human Resource Management: Perspectives, Context, Functions, and Outcomes.* Ferris has consulted on a variety of human resources topics with companies including ARCO, Borg-Warner, Eli Lilly, and PPG, and he has taught in numerous management development programs and lectured in Austria, Greece, Hong Kong, Japan, Taiwan, and Singapore, in addition to various U.S. universities.

Sherman D. Rosen recently retired from the post of Vice President of Human Resources at Hartmarx Corporation, a leading apparel manufacturer and retailer. Prior to joining Hartmarx in 1977, he was a management consultant with Cresap McCormick and Paget Inc., and Hay Associates, and a manufacturing executive in two metalworking firms. Currently, he is Adjunct Professor, Management Education Program, Institute of Labor and Industrial Relations, University of Illinois at Urbana-Champaign. He also serves as Deputy Director of the University of Illinois Center for Human Resource Management. He has taught a graduate course in human resources in the

College of Business Administration at the University of Illinois at Chicago. Rosen continues his human resources activities as a consultant to Deloitte & Touche, a leading accounting and consulting firm, in its human resources consulting practice. He received an M.A. in Labor and Industrial Relations at the University of Illinois at Urbana-Champaign, and a B.S. in Industrial Psychology from the same institution. He has served on the boards of several organizations, including The Human Resources Management Association of Chicago and the Midwest Business Group on Health.

Darold T. Barnum is Professor of Management at the University of Illinois at Chicago (UIC). He was a Founding Director of the University of Illinois Center for Human Resource Management, and the Founding Director of the Texas Tech University Public Employee Relations Project. He has served as Head of the UIC Department of Management, and Associate Director of the Indiana University Institute for Urban Transportation. He received his Ph.D. and M.B.A. from the Wharton School, University of Pennsylvania. His current research centers on the application of quantitative decision theory to management, human resources, and labor relations issues. He has published in journals such as *Industrial and Labor Relations Review, Management Science, Interfaces, Monthly Labor Review, Labor Law Journal, Human Resource Planning, Public Personnel Management, Transportation Research Record, Review of Public Personnel Administration, Risk, Journal of the American Medical Association, Transportation Research, Socio-Economic Planning Sciences,* and *Computers, Environment and Urban Systems.* He teaches in management development seminars on human resources, labor relations, strategic management and finance; has had grants from the National Academy of Sciences and the U.S. Departments of Labor, Transportation, and HEW; and has consulted for federal, state and local government units as well as for private sector organizations. He recently has served as a consultant and facilitator to federal government units and public transit systems that are restructuring themselves as high-performance organizations.

THE CONTRIBUTING AUTHORS

Robert G. Adams is Vice President – Personnel Services for Delta Air Lines at its corporate headquarters in Atlanta, Georgia. He is responsible for managing all of Delta's personnel services activities, including matters related to employment, compensation, training, equal opportunity, and international labor relations. Prior to joining Delta in January 1992, Mr. Adams served as Vice President of Personnel at Pan American World Airways. Over his twenty-six year career he has worked in both union and nonunion companies and has extensive experience in all aspects of international personnel management and employee relations. Mr. Adams holds a Master's degree in Industrial Management from Xavier University.

R. Wayne Anderson is Senior Vice President of Amoco Corporation, overseeing all human resources functions worldwide. From 1986 through 1992 he served as Vice President of Human Resources for Amoco, and during his 28 years with Amoco he has held various other human resources positions in the corporation. He is an officer of the Amoco Corporation and is a member of the strategic planning, human resources, crisis management and investment committees. In addition, he serves on the Metropolitan Life Insurance Customer Advisory Board, National Council of La Raza, and the Atlanta-based American Institute for Managing Diversity. He has a Bachelor's degree in Psychology from Southern Methodist University, earned his Master's degree in Labor and Industrial Relations from the University of Illinois at Urbana-Champaign, and completed the Executive Management Program at the University of Chicago. He is a partner in the University of Illinois Center for Human Resource Management, and is chair of the Center's executive board.

Timothy T. Baldwin is Associate Professor of Business Administration at the School of Business, Indiana University. He received a Ph.D. in Business Administration and an M.B.A. from Michigan State University. Baldwin has research interests in the areas of training and management development and he is the author of numerous journal articles and book chapters and has won several national awards for his research work. He has designed and delivered management development programs for organizations worldwide including a recent program in Eastern Europe. He is currently faculty director of the Indiana Service Partnership, a consortium of Indiana University and four large Indiana service firms, designed for the purpose of creating innovative management development programs for service-sector organizations.

P. B. Beaumont is Titular Professor in the Department of Social and Economic Research at the University of Glasgow. He received his Ph.D. from the University of Glasgow. Beaumont has research interests in the areas of union organization, public sector industrial relations, industrial relations in multinational companies, and strategic human resource management. He is the author of numerous journal articles, book chapters, and books, has directed a number of major research projects, consulted with a number of organizations on a variety of industrial relations and human resources issues, and taught courses in universities in Australia, Canada, and the U.S.

Michael Beer is Professor of Business Administration at the Harvard Business School where his research and teaching has been in the areas of organization effectiveness, human resource management, and organization change. He received a B.A. from Queens College in New York City, an M.S. from North Carolina State University, and a Ph.D. in organizational psychology and business from Ohio State University. Prior to joining the Harvard faculty, he was Director of Organization Research and Development at Corning Glass Works, where he managed internal consultants who worked with managers to improve the effectiveness of their organizations. He has authored or co-authored several books and many articles. *The Critical Path to Corporate Renewal,* his most recent book, written with Russell Eisenstat and Bert Spector, deals with the problem of large-scale corporate change. It won the Johnson, Smith & Knisely award for best book on executive leadership in 1990. Professor Beer has served on the editorial board of several journals, the board of governors of the Academy of Management, and has consulted with many Fortune 500 companies.

H. John Bernardin is University Professor of Research in the College of Business at Florida Atlantic University. He is former Chairman of the Division of Personnel and Human Resources of the National Academy of Management. He received his Ph.D. in Industrial Psychology from Bowling Green State University in 1975. Dr. Bernardin is the co-editor of the journal *Human Resource Management Review.* His research interests are performance measurement and personnel selection. He is the author of six books and over 100 articles in industrial-organizational psychology.

Robert L. Berra is Adjunct Professor of Labor and Industrial Relations at the University of Illinois at Urbana-Champaign. As Senior Vice President of Administration for the Monsanto Company, he provided leadership for the integration of human resource management decisions with corporate strategy. Mr. Berra also is past President of the Society for Human Resource Management and is a Fellow in the National Academy of Human Resources. He received his M.B.A. from the Harvard Graduate School of Business, and has authored many articles on management.

E. Ralph Biggadike is Vice President, Strategic Management at Becton Dickinson and Company, and is responsible for the strategic planning, business development, and organizational effectiveness activities for this manufacturer of medical supplies, devices, and diagnostic systems. His most recent responsibilities included the worldwide management of the Company's Drug Delivery System businesses. Mr. Biggadike was formerly the Paul M. Hammaker Professor of Business Administration at the Darden Graduate Business School, University of Virginia, where he headed the Business Policy and Political Economy Area. He joined Becton Dickinson in 1984 as Vice President, Planning and Development. Human Resources and Organization Development were added to his responsibilities in 1985, and in 1987, he was given the worldwide operating responsibilities referred to above. Mr. Biggadike received his M.B.A. from the University of Virginia, and D.B.A. from Harvard University.

Irving Bluestone, since 1980, has been University Professor of Labor Studies at Wayne State University. From 1986 to 1989, he served as Director of the Master's Degree Program in Industrial Relations. As UAW Vice President from 1972 to 1980 and Director of the UAW's General Motors Department, he led the union's activities related to the negotiation and administration of the UAW-GM national labor agreement, covering approximately 400,000 workers. From 1977 to 1980, he also chaired the UAW's Michigan Community Action Program, which is the political and legislative arm of the union in Michigan. Among his recent activities, he served from 1984 to 1990 as labor member of the board of directors of the employee-owned Weirton Steel Corporation. He also served from 1986 to 1989 on the board of directors of the employee-owned Copper Range Company. Currently he serves on the boards of numerous community organizations. Bluestone has published numerous articles and in 1992 he co-authored with his son, Barry Bluestone, the book, *Negotiating the Future.*

Richard Buckles is an internal consultant in Organizational Effectiveness in the Human Resources Department of Amoco Corporation. He has worked with many large, progressive organizations, including: Atlantic Richfield Company as Manager of Human Resources Development; Hughes Aircraft Company as Manager of Management Development; and Beatrice company as Director of Management and Organizational Development. He received his B.A. and M.A. in Industrial Psychology from California State University at Los Angeles, a Ph.D. in Organizational Psychology from California Western University, was an Assistant Professor of Management and Behavioral Sciences at the University of La Verne, and is the author of journal articles.

Douglas A. Cairns joined Dow Canada in 1970 as a chemist. Beginning in 1982 he served in a number of plant superintendent positions with the company. In 1989 he became Compensation and Benefits Manager for Dow Canada and in 1993 assumed his present role as Human Resources Director for R&D, Dow North America. He received a B.S. degree in chemistry from the University of Saskatchewan in 1970.

Janet M. Canavan began her career at Dow Chemical in sales in 1980. In 1983 she became a Senior Training Coordinator and subsequently held positions as Senior Employee Relations Administrator, Training Manager in Commercial Development, and Human Resources Manager in the Corporate Administration Department. She currently is Human Resources Manager in Administrative Services.

Patrick J. Canavan is Vice-President of Leadership and Organizational Development, Motorola, Inc., and a Motorola Director. Previously, he served as Head of Organization Development for Motorola in the Europe,

International, and Global divisions, as well as for Digital Equipment Corporation – Europe. He holds a Master's degree in Organizational Development from Yale University. Prior to working in industry, he was Assistant Professor of Organizational Behavior at Antioch College, Southern Methodist University, and the University of New Hampshire. He has both scholarly and applied interests in such areas as history, anthropology, diversity, empowerment, and spirituality. He is a partner in the University of Illinois Center for Human Resource Management, and is vice-chair of its Executive Board.

Dan R. Dalton is the Dow Chemical Company Professor of Management and Associate Dean, Graduate School of Business, Indiana University. Formerly with General Telephone & Electronics (GT & E) for thirteen years, he received his Ph.D. from the University of California. He is the editor of the *Journal of Management,* and *Methods and Analyses in Organizational Studies,* and consulting editor for the *Journal of Applied Psychology.* Widely published in business, ethics and psychology, his articles have appeared in the *Academy of Management Journal, Academy of Management Review, Academy of Management Executive, Administrative Science Quarterly, Journal of Applied Psychology, Journal of Business Ethics, Business Ethics Quarterly, Journal of Law and Public Policy, Strategic Management Journal, Journal of Business Strategy, Behavioral Science,* and *Human Relations,* as well as others. He was co-principal investigator for a five-year grant of personnel policy funded by the General Motors Foundation. Professor Dalton has received a series of awards for teaching excellence at the undergraduate, M.B.A., and doctoral levels.

Joseph L. Downey is a Senior Vice President of the Dow Chemical Company and chairman of DowBrands, Inc. and DowElanco. As a member of the board of directors of the Dow Chemical Company, he serves on the executive, finance, investment policy and public interest committees, as well as the corporate management board. He has responsibility for Human Resources, Employee Development and Quality Performance, Corporate Travel and Facilities Management and Information Systems. He began his career in 1961 and held various sales and marketing positions. In 1989, Downey was appointed to Dow's operating committee and in September 1989, he was elected to the board of directors and to the board's executive committee. He was elected a Senior Vice President of Dow in May, 1991. He holds a B.S. degree in chemical engineering from Kansas State University.

Richard D. Drankoski is a Human Resources Management Consultant for Xerox Corporation. He has fifteen years of experience in the human resource management field and has had the opportunity to work with all levels of line management in a number of operations and staff assignments. He has worked in partnership with various business functions, ranging from research and development to field selling, customer service, and administration. Rick has a B.S. in Industrial and Labor Relations and an M.S. in Human Resources Management and Organizational Behavior, both from Cornell University.

George F. Dreher is a Professor of Business Administration, Department of Management, Indiana University at Bloomington. Before joining the Indiana School of Business, Professor Dreher served as Assistant and Associate Professor of Business at the University of Kansas and was a staff industrial psychologist with Southern California Edison Company. His Ph.D. is from the University of Houston. Professor Dreher's specific interests focus on the design and evaluation of employee selection procedures and the administration of salary and benefit systems. Current research addresses the role of race, ethnicity, age, and gender in accounting for selection, promotion, and retention decisions. He has published papers in the *Journal of Applied Psychology, Academy of Management Journal, Indus-*

trial Relations, Personnel Psychology, Journal of Management, and *Journal of Organizational Behavior.* He has co-authored two books.

James H. Dulebohn is currently a doctoral candidate at the Institute of Labor and Industrial Relations at the University of Illinois at Urbana-Champaign. He has a Master's degree in Labor and Industrial Relations and a Master's degree in English as a Second Language. Prior to graduate school, he was employed for five years in the field of information management and worked for several organizations including IBM. During the last two years, he has been employed by the State Universities Retirement System of Illinois, where he has conducted research in areas of public pension funds and compensation. His research interests include performance evaluation, compensation, and organizational justice.

Russell A. Eisenstat is an independent consultant specializing in the management of large-scale organizational change and innovation, strategic human resources management, and strategy implementation. He is also the Director of the Senior Human Resources Executive Forum. The Forum's mission is to promote an ongoing dialogue among senior human resources executives on the management processes needed to develop strategically aligned and adaptive organizations. His prior work experience includes six years on the teaching faculty of the Harvard Business School. Eisenstat's most recent book, *The Critical Path to Corporate Renewal,* written with Michael Beer and Bert Spector, received the Johnson, Smith & Knisely Award for New Perspectives on Executive Leadership. Eisenstat earned a Ph.D. in organizational psychology from Yale University. His dissertation focused on the creation and diffusion of plant-level human resource innovations. He has a B.A. from Harvard College.

Peter Feuille is Professor of Labor and Industrial Relations, and Director of the Institute of Labor and Industrial Relations, at the University of Illinois at Urbana-Champaign. He received his Ph.D. in Industrial Relations/Organizational Behavior from the School of Business Administration at the University of California, Berkeley, and was formerly on the faculty at the University of Oregon and the State University of New York at Buffalo. He has published many articles in industrial relations and organizational behavior journals, book chapters, and books on various labor relations and dispute resolution topics, with a particular focus on grievances/complaints and arbitration in a wide variety of workplace disputes. His professional associations include the Industrial Relations Research Association, American Arbitration Association, and the National Academy of Arbitrators. He has also served as a mediator and arbitrator in many labor disputes.

J. Benjamin Forbes is a Professor of Management, and chair of the Department of Management, Marketing and Logistics, at John Carroll University. He was formerly the Director of the M.B.A. Program at John Carroll. His Ph.D. is from the University of Akron in the area of Industrial/Organizational Psychology. Forbes has research interests in the areas of management careers and promotion patterns, managerial skills development and assessment, and motivating for both performance and creativity. He is the author of numerous journal articles and a recent book on corporate mobility. He has recently helped design and taught in a management development program for executives, faculty, and labor representatives from the Czech Republic.

Allan Fowler has served as Director of North American Compensation and Benefits at Dow North America since 1993. After joining Dow in 1969, he served in a number of research positions, attaining the position of Laboratory Director of Analytical and Engineering Sciences in 1986. In 1989 he was named Director of Human Resources and Administrative Services, R&D. He earned a bachelor's degree in chemical engineering from Tri-State University.

Gregory M. Freiwald is Dow North America's Human Resources Director for Corporate Training, Law, Tax, Auditing and the Executive Department. He joined the company in 1979 as a salary administrator for Dow Latin America and occupied several successively responsible human resources positions in the U.S. and Argentina. Immediately prior to his present position he was Human Resources Manager for Marketing and Administration, Chemicals and Performance Products, Dow North America. He received a Bachelor's degree in Business Administration from Central National University in Buenos Aires.

Dwight D. Frink is visiting assistant professor of management at the University of Oklahoma. He holds a B.S. in Management from the University of South Alabama, and A.M. and Ph.D. degrees in Labor and Industrial Relations from the University of Illinois at Urbana-Champaign. His research interests include accountability mechanisms and processes in organizations, vertical and horizontal employment relationships, and the social and contextual influences on behavior, and the impact of those influences on human resources management systems. He has worked extensively in production, systems design, supervision, and management in the construction industry, and in operations in the chemical industry.

Maria Carmen Galang is an assistant professor at the School of Business, University of Victoria, British Columbia, Canada. She holds a B.S. in Psychology and a Master's in Industrial Relations from the University of the Philippines, and a Ph.D. from the Institute of Labor and Industrial Relations at the University of Illinois at Urbana-Champaign. She has had experience in organizing and managing human resources departments in the garment, construction, and non-life insurance industries in the Philippines, as well as designing and conducting training programs on a consulting basis. Her current research interests include power and politics in organizations, from both a macro and micro level of analysis, and cross-cultural aspects of human resource management.

Barry Gerhart is Associate Professor at the Center for Advanced Human Resources Studies, School of Industrial and Labor Relations, Cornell University. His work is in the areas of compensation/rewards and staffing. Professor Gerhart has worked with a variety of organizations, including TRW, Corning, and Petroleos De Venezuela. His research has appeared in the *Academy of Management Journal, Industrial and Labor Relations Review, Journal of Applied Psychology, Personnel Psychology,* and *Handbook of Industrial and Organizational Psychology.* Professor Gerhart is also co-author of the book, *Human Resource Management: Gaining a Competitive Advantage.* He serves on the editorial boards of the *Academy of Management Journal, Industrial and Labor Relations Review* and the *Journal of Applied Psychology.* He was a co-recipient of the 1991 "Scholarly Achievement Award," Human Resources Division, Academy of Management. Professor Gerhart received his Ph.D. in human resource management and industrial relations from the University of Wisconsin-Madison in 1985.

Luis R. Gomez-Mejia is Professor of Management at Arizona State University. He received his Ph.D. in Industrial Relations from the College of Business, University of Minnesota. He has 60 publications, including three books, mostly focused on macro compensation issues.

Allain Gosselin is an Associate Professor of Human Resource Management at the Ecole des Hautes Etudes Commerciales (HEC), the business school of the University of Montreal, where he is responsible for the HRM major in the M.B.A. program. Professor Gosselin has also been a Visiting Associate Professor at the University of South Carolina (1992–93). He received his B.B.A. from the University of Sherbrooke, his M.S. degree in HRM from HEC, and a Ph.D. in HRM from the University of Maryland. Prior to joining the faculty at HEC, he worked for several years as a labor relations specialist and a consultant in HRM. His principal areas of teaching and research are human resources strategies in different organizational contexts, including mergers and acquisitions, control in HRM, and performance management. Currently he is completing a book on the human factor in the competitiveness of the firm. He also serves on the editorial board of *Gestion, Revue internationale de gestion* and is a member of the executive board of the Association of Human Resource Professionals of the Province of Quebec as well as of the Administrative Sciences Association of Canada.

Arden Grabke is a doctoral student in the Management Department, Arizona State University. She had several years of work experience in the compensation area prior to joining the doctoral program.

Kathy A. Hanisch is Assistant Professor of Industrial and Organizational Psychology at Iowa State University. She received her Ph.D. from the University of Illinois at Urbana-Champaign. Her primary research interests are employees' multiple and patterned behaviors resulting from their attitudes including work satisfaction, stress, co-worker satisfaction, and organizational commitment. Her other research and applied interests include organizational safety programs, design and training of systems, organizational stressors, and health issues as they are enmeshed in the relations among employees' attitudes and behaviors. Dr. Hanisch has published in the *Journal of Applied Psychology, Current Directions in Psychological Science, Personnel Psychology, Journal of Vocational Behavior,* and *Ergonomics.* She has also contributed the definitions of "Organizational Withdrawal" and "Retirement" for the *Blackwell Dictionary of Organizational Behavior.*

Robert L. Hildebrand is the former Vice President of Employee Relations for the R. R. Donnelley & Sons Company in Chicago, Illinois. He retired in 1993 and has continued as a consultant for the Company since that time. He received his undergraduate degree from Illinois Wesleyan University at Bloomington, Illinois and in 1958 completed the General Electric Company Management Development Program, specializing in Employee Relations. He is past President of the Human Resource Management Association of Chicago, and has served on the Board of Directors of the Master Printers Association of the Printing Industry of America. He serves on the CUE/NAM Board of Directors, is a Deputy Director of the University of Illinois Center for Human Resource Management, and is an Adjunct Professor of Labor and Industrial Relations at the University of Illinois at Urbana-Champaign. Before his retirement, he was a partner in the University of Illinois Center for Human Resource Management.

Lawrence P. Holleran is Corporate Vice President, Human Resources, of FMC Corporation. He joined FMC in January 1972 as the Director of Personnel for its 30,000 employee Machinery Group. Prior to joining FMC, Holleran held management positions in manufacturing, marketing, and human resources with a specialty materials manufacturer, and a manufacturer of consumer electronics. Holleran has a B.S. degree from the University of Pittsburgh and an M.B.A. from the University of Chicago. He is a member of the Business Advisory Council of the College of Commerce at the University of Illinois at Urbana-Champaign; the Conference Board's Human Resource Advisory Council; Manufacturer's Alliance for Productivity and Innovation: Human Resource Planning Society; and past President and a member of the board of the Human Resource Management Association of Chicago. He is a partner in the University of Illinois Center for Human Resource Management, and a member of the Center's executive board.

Heidi Hopper is a graduate student in organizational behavior and human resources management at the University of Washington. Her interests are motivation, attributions, accountability, and decision making. She has recently published in the *Journal of Applied Psychology* and has presented papers at the Academy of Management and Association of Management national meetings.

Susan E. Jackson is Professor of Psychology at New York University. She received her Ph.D. from the University of California at Berkeley. Previously she held faculty appointments at the University of Maryland (Psychology) and the University of Michigan (Management), and has twice been a Visiting Professor of Management at Ecole des Hautes Etudes Commerciales, in France. She has published over 50 articles and chapters on a variety of topics, including top management team composition, strategic human resource management, job stress and burnout, and organizational approaches to managing workforce diversity. Her book, *Diversity in the Workplace: Human Resources Initiatives*, was published in 1992. An active member of the Academy of Management, she serves as editor for the *Academy of Management Review* as well as President for the Organizational Behavior Division. She is a Fellow of the Society for Industrial and Organizational Psychology and the American Psychological Association, and serves as a member of the board of governors for the Center for Creative Leadership.

Maddy Janssens is an Assistant Professor in Organization Behavior and Human Resource Management at Katholieke Universiteit Leuven. She received an M.B.A. and a Ph.D. degree in Organizational Psychology at Katholieke Universiteit Leuven, Belgium, and an M.S. degree from Northwestern University. She has published recently in the area of international relocations. Her current research topics include the transferability of HRM practices across cultures, cross-geographical and transnational teams, language in international management, and the social identity of employees in multinational companies.

Dennis L. Johnson is President of Behavior Analysts & Consultants, Inc. (BA & C), a management consulting firm based in Stuart, FL which has clients in 42 states and several foreign countries. Dr. Johnson received his Ph.D. in Clinical Psychology from Virginia Polytechnic Institute and State University. BA & C, which provides professional services in test development and validation, pre-employment screening, attitude/climate surveys, behavioral observation systems, and supervisory training, has evaluated more than 250,000 individuals since it was established in 1982. Prior to establishing BA & C, Dr. Johnson served with the U.S. Department of Justice, Federal Bureau of Prisons, where he was both a national chief psychologist, and chief instructor for hostage negotiation and tactical response interventions.

Preston Johnson, Jr. is Human Resources Manager, Administrative Services, Dow North America. He joined the firm in 1977 as an accountant and has served in a number of human resources positions. He also spent three years as Supervisor of Epoxy Planning and Shipping Services in Dow's Texas Operations. He earned a Bachelor's degree in Accounting from Sam Houston State University and a Master's in Business Administration from the University of Houston.

Timothy A. Judge is Assistant Professor of Human Resource Studies at the Center for Advanced Human Resource Studies, School of Industrial and Labor Relations, Cornell University. He received his Ph.D. from the Institute of Labor and Industrial Relations, University of Illinois at Urbana-Champaign. His primary research interest is applying individual differences and dispositions to work attitudes and behaviors. His other research interests are in the areas of job attitudes, careers, and social and political influences in human resource management.

Hervey A. Juris is Professor of Human Resources Management at the Kellogg Graduate School of Management, Northwestern

University and Associate Director of Northwestern University's Newspaper Management Center. He chaired Kellogg's Department of Management and Strategy and was associate dean for academic affairs. His research and teaching center on strategy in human resources management and labor–management relations, and he is particularly interested in the management of professional, managerial and white-collar workers. He has published extensively in academic journals and co-edited three books. He is a consultant to business, government, and professional associations. He has served as a director on the Chicago and national executive boards of the Industrial Relations Research Association, and has been president of the Human Resources Management Association of Chicago. He received an A.B. from Princeton, and an M.B.A. and Ph.D. from the University of Chicago.

Jeffrey S. Kane is an Associate Professor of Management at the University of North Carolina at Greensboro. He is also the founder and co-editor of *Human Resource Management Review,* a journal devoted to conceptual contributions to the field of HRM. He received his Ph.D. in Organizational Psychology from the University of Michigan in 1974. Dr. Kane has specialized in performance appraisal for over twenty years and has made numerous contributions to the subject. He is perhaps best known for the development of the distributional assessment model of appraisal and its operationalization in the form of APPRAISE!, a performance appraisal system for networked computing environments.

Bruce Kaufman is Professor of Economics and Senior Associate, and former Director, of the W. T. Beebe Institute of Personnel and Employment Relations at Georgia State University. He has published five books and numerous articles on labor economics and industrial relations topics, including *The Origin and Evolution of the Field of Industrial Relations*, which was awarded the 1992 Richard A.

Lester prize for best book in labor economics and industrial relations. Professor Kaufman is immediate past President of the University Council of Industrial Relations and Human Resources Programs, co-chair of the Industrial Relations Theory Study Groups of the International Industrial Relations Association, and editor of the bimonthly newspaper *HR Atlanta*. He graduated in 1978 from the University of Wisconsin-Madison with a Ph.D. in Economics.

John D. Keiser is a doctoral candidate in Organizational Behavior at the University of Illinois at Urbana-Champaign. He earned his B.S. degree from the Pennsylvania State University. Besides human resources issues related to downsizing, his research interests include career mobility and labor markets. Prior to beginning his graduate studies, he worked as a human resource manager for approximately seven years in the Washington, D.C. area.

Daniel W. Kendall is Senior Vice President and Chief Human Resource Officer with The Associated Group. He is responsible for all HR programs and strategic initiatives for this diversified and highly decentralized insurance, financial services, and managed health care company. He graduated from Indiana University School of Business with a B.S. degree. Prior to joining The Associated Group in 1990, he held numerous HR-oriented positions with Rohm and Haas Company, concluding his 20 years of service with Rohm and Haas as Group HR Director – in North America. He is a past national Vice President of the Society for Human Resource Management and has published articles in *Business Horizons* and *Personnel Administrator*.

Harriet F. King is Director of Personnel Resources at Dow. She joined Dow in 1969 in Dow U.S.A. Michigan Division Psychology and Training Resources. After being named psychologist and senior psychologist, she became salary administrator in Michigan Division Compensation and Benefits in 1975, and in 1977, joined Dow U.S.A. Compensation

Planning as a senior compensation analyst. She was named Personnel Manager, Marketing, in Marketing Personnel Services, 1979, Director of Compensation, Dow U.S.A. in 1981, and Director of Human Resources for Research and Development in 1984. She was named Director of Executive Compensation Administration in 1989. Ms. King received a Bachelor's degree in Psychology from the University of Louisville and a Master's degree in Clinical Psychology from Central Michigan University. She is a partner in the University of Illinois Center for Human Resource Management.

George M. Krawiec is General Manager, WFS Workforce Solutions, with overall responsibility for providing human resources programs and services to IBM's businesses and to outside organizations. Mr. Krawiec joined IBM in 1968 and has held positions covering all aspects of human resources, including management positions in the field, plant, division, and corporate headquarters. He has been IBM's Corporate Manager of Resource Assessment and Planning, responsible for all elements of worldwide operational and strategic human resource planning for the corporation. In 1987, he was named Director of Personnel Resources for IBM's U.S. manufacturing and development organizations, numbering approximately 100,000 employees. He became Director of Personnel for IBM's Personal Systems business in April 1988. In July 1991, Mr Krawiec was appointed Resource Programs Director, IBM United States Personnel, where he was responsible for overseeing all resource-related matters for the U.S. company, including policy and program development, staffing levels, skill utilization and deployment, employment and recruiting activities, and IBM's restructuring activities. George joined WFS at its inception and was a key architect in its design and implementation. He was appointed to his current position in October 1993. He holds an M.S. degree in Business Policy from Columbia University.

Frank LaFasto is the Vice President of Organization Planning and Development for Baxter International, Inc. where he is responsible for organization effectiveness, for the development of executive talent, and for working with customers of Baxter in the area of management process. He received his Bachelor's and Master's degrees from Bradley University and his Ph.D. from the University of Denver. Author and lecturer, he has conducted research in the areas of feedback, interpersonal competencies, selection criteria, diversity, work relationships, and teamwork, the subject of his co-authored book, *Teamwork: What must go right/What can go wrong*. As an applied researcher, his primary interest is in building collaborative processes within organizations.

Robert Lambertucci is currently Vice-President of Human Resources and Industrial Relations for Molson Breweries Quebec Division (Molson O'Keefe). His 25-year human resources career has spanned some of Canada's leading companies including Northern Telecom, Dominion Textile, Corby Distilleries, Frito-Lay and, for the last five years, he has been involved in merger planning and executing, and postmerger activities with the Brewery. He has acquired first-hand experience in dealing with mergers, acquisitions, and various restructurings, right sizings, downsizings, facility ownership transfers or closures. He is also experienced in developing industrial relations strategies and human resources plans. A native Montrealer, Mr. Lambertucci graduated with a B.A. from Sir George University in 1969.

Delmar L. (Dutch) Landen is chairman at Landen, Wells & Associates, a Florida-based consulting and training organization. He is also an Adjunct Professor of Labor and Industrial Relations, University of Illinois at Urbana-Champaign. From 1965 to his retirement in 1982, Landen was Director of Organizational Research and Development, General Motors Corporation. During his 25 years with GM, he was involved in numerous research projects, ranging from studies on absenteeism to a three-year, four-plant study done in collaboration with Rensis Likert and the Institute for Social Research at the University of Michigan, contrasting autocratic and participative management styles and their effects on operating performance and employee attitudes. In the 1970s he worked with Irving Bluestone in helping to launch QWL in GM and other organizations and communities throughout the U.S. He is the author of numerous articles, a frequent lecturer at national and international conferences, and a consultant to both for-profit and non-profit organizations.

Fred Lane is Human Resources Vice President at AT&T Global Business Communications Systems. He is responsible for all human resources activities including HR business strategy and planning, associate communications, diversity planning, education and training, labor planning, and associate services. He has held several positions in business planning finance operations and service management in New Jersey Bell and AT&T. He has a B.A. degree in Sociology from Colgate University and an M.S. in Management from Pace University. He has participated in the Bell Advanced Management and the Dartmouth Tuck Executive Program.

Edward E. Lawler III is Professor of Management and Organization at the University of Southern California. In 1979, he founded and became Director of the University's Center for Effective Organizations (CEO). He has consulted with more than 200 organizations and four national governments on such issues as employee involvement, organizational change, and compensation. As the author of more than 200 articles and 20 books, he is widely recognized as a contributor to the fields of organizational development and organizational behavior. His most recent books include *High Involvement Management* (Jossey-Bass, 1986), *Strategic Pay* (Jossey-Bass, 1990), *Employee Involvement and Total Quality Management* (Jossey-Bass, 1992), and *The Ultimate Advantage* (Jossey-Bass, 1992).

John J. Lawler is Associate Professor at the Institute of Labor and Industrial Relations at the University of Illinois at Urbana-Champaign. He previously taught at the University of Minnesota. In addition to his interest in human resource management and organizational effectiveness, his research includes information technology in HRM and international HRM. He received his Ph.D. from the University of California at Berkeley.

Tom E. Lawson is President and founder of Lawson International Ltd. which specializes in human resource management and organizational development consulting. He received a Ph.D. in Industrial Psychology from the University of Illinois and holds an M.S. in Industrial Relations from the University of Wisconsin. Prior to forming his own consulting organization, Lawson served in several executive positions including President of a human resource management consulting firm, Corporate Director of Management and Organization Development for Pillsbury Co., and Organization and Management Development Specialist for 3M Company. Lawson has designed management development strategies and programs for numerous US-based multinational corporations in Europe, the Pacific Rim, and Latin America and he recently completed work on a development project in Bhopal, India sponsored by the United States Agency for International Development.

Michael H. LeRoy is Assistant Professor of Labor and Industrial Relations, and is an adjunct member of the College of Law, at the University of Illinois at Urbana-Champaign. He received his J.D. from the University of North Carolina. He also serves as an arbitrator in the coal, electric utility, transportation, and communications industries. LeRoy's research interests include labor law and public policy, dispute resolution, and the American labor movement. He has published numerous law review and social science articles, and recently authored a labor–management report for the State of Illinois.

David Lewin is Professor in the Anderson Graduate School of Management, Vice-Dean and Faculty Director of the M.B.A. Program, Director of the Institute of Industrial Relations, and Chairman of the Human Resources Round Table at UCLA. He has published 12 books and more than 125 scholarly and professional articles on human resources and employee relations topics, including the 1994 *Human Resource Management* (with J. B. Mitchell), the 1992 research volume *Research Frontiers in Human Resources and Industrial Relations* (co-edited with Peter Sherer and Olivia Mitchell), and is co-editor of *Advances in Industrial and Labor Relations* and is an editorial board member of *Industrial Relations* and the *California Management Review.* Professor Lewin has received numerous research grants from organizations such as the National Science Foundation, Ford Foundation, and U.S. Department of Labor and has provided consulting services to several dozen major American corporations. He graduated from UCLA with a Ph.D. in Business Administration in 1971.

Robert C. Liden is Associate Professor of Management at the University of Illinois at Chicago. After completing his Ph.D. at the University of Cincinnati, he completed a year of postdoctoral research at the University of Washington in Seattle. He has been conducting research on leadership and related topics such as feedback and performance appraisal for over fifteen years. His research has been published in such journals as the *Academy of Management Journal, Academy of Management Review, Journal of Applied Psychology, Organizational Behavior and Human Performance, Personnel Psychology, Group & Organization Studies,* and *Human Relations.* He has received funding for several research projects sponsored by the Center for Human Resource Management

dealing with group process, evaluation, compensation, and leadership issues in the implementation and management of empowered groups.

Robert W. Lincoln, Jr., Director of Human Resources for Chemicals, Plastics and Hydrocarbons, joined Dow in 1977 in the Minneapolis Sales Office. In 1979 he moved to the human resources function in Texas. He received a J.D. from the University of Houston in 1986. In that year he relocated to Michigan where he has continued serving in successively responsible human resources positions.

Joseph J. Martocchio is Assistant Professor of Labor and Industrial Relations at the Institute of Labor and Industrial Relations, University of Illinois at Urbana-Champaign. He holds an M.L.I.R. degree and a Ph.D. in human resources management, from Michigan State University's School of Labor and Industrial Relations. Professor Martocchio's's research interests include employee absenteeism and employee training. His articles have appeared in the *Academy of Management Journal, Human Relations, Human Resource Development Quarterly, Human Resource Planning, Journal of Applied Psychology, Journal of Management, Organizational Behavior and Human Decision Processes,* and *Personnel Psychology.* Recently, Martocchio co-authored a comprehensive critique of the employee absenteeism literature, "To be there or not to be there? Questions, theories and methods in absenteeism research," *Research in Personnel and Human Resources Management,* 11 (1993), 259–329. He presently serves on the editorial review board of the *Journal of Management,* and is a member of the national research committee of the American Society for Training and Development.

Harvey Minkoff is the Director of Compensation for TRW Inc., based in Cleveland, Ohio. In his current position, he has companywide responsibility to develop programs and coordinate policies and practices regarding all employee reward systems. He also supervises the Human Resources Information Systems function. In his 18-year career with TRW, he has held positions as Corporate Manager of Compensation, Director of Human Resources for TRW's Castings Division, Compensation and Benefits Manager for the Industrial and Energy Sector, and Regional Human Resources Manager for the Information Services division. He has been active in the American Compensation Association and Cleveland Compensation Association. He received his B.B.A. degree from the New York College of Insurance in 1971 and earned the Certified Compensation Professional (CPP) designation from the American Compensation Association in 1990.

Terence R. Mitchell is Edward E. Carlson Professor of Business Administration and Professor of Psychology, University of Washington. He has an Advanced Diploma in Public Administration, University of Exeter; and M.A. and Ph.D. degrees from the University of Illinois at Urbana-Champaign (Social Psychology). Professor Mitchell's interests are decision making, leadership, and social responsibility. He has recently published articles on these topics in *Organizational Behavior and Human Decision Process, The Academy of Management Review, The Journal of the Academy of Management*, and the *Journal of Applied Psychology*. He is co-author (with J. Larson) of *People in Organizations* (McGraw-Hill, 1987) and a joint author of Birnbaum, Scott and Mitchell, *Organization Theory: A Structural and Behavioral Analysis* (Irwin-Dorsey, 1977). Mitchell is a fellow of the American Psychological Association, and the American Academy of Management. He is also a member of the Society for Organizational Behavior. He was Burlington Northern Scholar of the Year in 1981.

Nancy K. Napier is Associate Dean and Professor of Management at Boise State University, which she joined in 1986. Before that, she was a research scientist at Battelle Memorial Laboratories (Columbus, Ohio) and a Professor at the University of Washington's Business School (Seattle, Washington). She received her Ph.D. from The Ohio State University. Her areas of interest for research and teaching include strategic management, international human resource management, and merger and acquisition implementation. Her research and consulting has included working with such organizations as Mitsubishi Research Institute, Hitachi Steel and Nippon Metal Mining in Japan, Bekaert Steel (Belgium), Schott Glass (Germany) and the former Brown Boveri (Switzerland) in Europe. She also has worked with IBM, GE, First Interstate Bank of Washington and Idaho, and various public and non-profit groups in the United States. She is the co-author of *Strategy and Human Resources Management* and has published in such journals as *Strategic Management Journal, Human Resource Planning, Journal of Management Studies, Journal of Management Inquiry*, and *Asia-Pacific HRM*. Napier is also Boise State's Project Coordinator of the first market oriented MBA program in Vietnam, at the National Economics University in Hanoi, conducted in partnership with the University of Hong Kong and funded by the Swedish Development Authority.

Sandra K. Nellis currently is the Human Resource Strategy and Business Planning Director at AT&T Global Business Communications Systems, and has been with AT&T for 20 years. She has held a wide variety of positions at both the planning and operational levels, in customer service, marketing, sales, and human resources. Her experience in HR has centered around her involvement with various human resource initiatives, which include aggressive hiring programs, leadership development, force planning, strategic planning, and organizational change. She has a B.S. in English and Math, and is co-author of a recent article in *Organizational Dynamics* on facilitating organizational change by linking HR with the business.

Nigel Nicholson is Professor of Organizational Behavior and Director of the Center for Organizational Research at London Business School. He started his working life as a journalist, before reading Psychology, and subsequently conducting his doctoral research at University College, Cardiff. He then joined the Social and Applied Psychology Unit at Sheffield University, where he was a research team leader. Moving to London Business School in 1990, he is currently Chairman of the OB subject area. His research interests have embraced a wide variety of topics including absenteeism, organizational change, business ethics, union organization, innovation and company performance, employee relocation, graduate recruitment, human resources systems, and managerial career development. In these fields he has published widely, including the *Social Psychology of Absenteeism* and *Managerial Job Change,* and is currently editing the *Blackwell Dictionary of Organizational Behavior.* He has held visiting appointments at American, Canadian, and German universities, and was co-recipient of the Academy of Management "new concept award" for contribution to theory and method in Organizational Behavior.

Ray Olsen is currently Vice President, Compensation and Benefit Systems for TRW Inc., a diversified company of $8 billion sales, which employs 61,000 employees worldwide. Mr. Olsen has been with TRW for 28 years. He has companywide responsibility to develop programs and coordinate policies and practices with regard to all employee benefits. He also supervises the health, safety, security, and human resources information systems functions. Prior to joining TRW, Mr. Olsen held various personnel positions with the Los Angeles School Districts and the California State Personnel Board, where he served as a consultant to local public agencies. He has been active and held offices in various academic, professional, and civic organizations. Currently, Mr. Olsen serves on the Ohio Olympic Committee, the Council on Compensation of the Conference Board, the Center for Advanced Human Resources Studies of Cornell University, and several other national organizations.

George Paulin has been a consultant specializing in the area of executive compensation for 20 years, and is nationally known as an advisor to management and board compensation committees. Since 1982, he has been a partner and member of the board of directors of Frederic W. Cook & Company. He is currently President of the firm and head of Cook's West Coast office, located in Los Angeles, which he started in 1987. He is a member of the American Compensation Association's Executive and Variable Compensation Committee, and task force on FASB accounting rules for employee stock plans. He is a graduate of the University of Illinois at Urbana-Champaign with a Master's degree in Labor and Industrial Relations, and his undergraduate degree is in economics from Aurora College in Aurora, Illinois.

Patricia R. Pedigo is an Organizational Psychologist with IBM Consulting Group's Business Transformation Services practice, where she specializes in organization assessment and change management. She has 15 years' practical experience in organizational analysis and intervention. Pat is an expert in organizational behavior and survey research, with extensive experience in using customer and employee data to develop and deploy effective intervention strategies and plans, including job design, team development, training, performance measurement, and employee motivation systems. Previously, she has held management and staff positions in personnel research, quality, customer satisfaction, marketing, business process analysis, and human resource management. Pat has a Ph.D. in Industrial/Organizational Psychology from the University of South Florida and is an Adjunct Professor of Management in the Lubin School of Business at Pace University.

Ronald C. Pilenzo has over thirty-five years of experience in the field of human resources management. His private sector experience includes 23 years with several Fortune 200 companies and consulting firms. Prior to his present position, he served as the President and CEO of the Society for Human Resource Management (SHRM) for over ten years before retiring in 1991. He then joined Personnel Decisions Inc., an international management consulting firm, where he is a Senior Vice President of the firm and President of the International group. He has been an Adjunct Professor with the Institute of Labor and Industrial Relations at the University of Illinois at Urbana-Champaign since 1991, and is editor in chief of *HR Horizons.* He has a B.B.A. with a dual major in Industrial Relations and Economics, and an M.B.A. from the University of Detroit. He was recognized by the World Federation of Personnel Management Associations in 1990 when he was given the Georges Petitpas award.

Martin Plevel is Channels Director, Voice Processing Markets Group at AT&T Global Business Communications Systems, where he is responsible for the planning, business development, and channel management for the company's voice processing products. In his career with AT&T, he has held various sales, marketing reengineering, and channel management positions. He received an M.B.A. in management from New York University and a B.S. degree from the School of Engineering at the University of Pittsburgh.

Michael F. Pugh is Head of Human Resources at Sony Manufacturing Company, United Kingdom, located in Bridgend, South Wales. This is the biggest Sony manufacturing complex in Western Europe employing 3,000 people producing color televisions and graphic display monitors, of which 85 percent are exported to the mainland. After graduating in pure science from the University of Dundee in 1971, he took a postgraduate diploma in management studies from Swansea University in 1976 while working in the engineering industry. Pugh worked for the U.K. Engineering Employers' Federation for seven years in the 1970s specializing in industrial relations before moving back into industry and human resources management. He has been in his current post with Sony for seven years during which the manufacturing and development complex has doubled in size.

Darryl T. Rapini is a Senior Human Resources Consultant and EEO Officer for Miles Inc., Pharmaceutical Division, where he serves on the division's diversity advisory group and facilitates work-force diversity training. During his six years with Miles, he has also held positions in labor and employee relations. Previously, at General Electric and RCA, he held various specialist and generalist positions in human resources in both union and non-union locations. Additionally, at General Electric, he was in the RMP (General Electric's Relations Management Program). He is certified as a Senior Professional in Human Resources (SPHR) from the Society for Human Resource Management. He holds a Bachelor's degree in Economics from the Wharton School of the University of Pennsylvania with a dual concentration in organization behavior and labor relations.

Thomas F. Reed is Professor of Enterprise, Employment, and Public Policy at the University of Limerick, and Associate Professor of Urban, Labor, and Metropolitan Affairs, and Director of the Graduate Program in Industrial Relations, at Wayne State University. Reed received the Ph.D. and M.Phil. degrees from the Graduate School of Business at Columbia University. He also holds a Master of Public Health from Columbia University and a B.A. from the New School for Social Research. He has published widely in the fields of industrial relations, human resources, and public policy on topics such as union organizing, employee layoffs, and redevelopment of the inner city. His research has appeared in two monographs and the *Industrial and Labor Relations Review, Industrial Relations, Journal of Labor Research, Relations Industries/Industrial Relations, Research in Personnel and Human Resources Management Journal, Journal of Experimental Social Psychology, Administrative Science Quarterly,* and the *Strategic Management Journal.* Along with these academic activities, Dr. Reed has served in a senior policy position in the government of the City of New York, and consults with labor leaders and local and state/provincial governmental officials in Canada and the United States.

Myron Roomkin is a Professor of Human Resource Management at the J. L. Kellogg Graduate School of Management at Northwestern University in Evanston, Illinois. He also is a Research Fellow at Northwestern's Center for Urban Affairs and Policy Research. His expertise is in the area of strategic human resource management and industrial relations. His current research deals with new forms of voice and governance in employment relations. For 25 years he has served as a resolver of employment disputes through mediation and arbitration and as a consultant on human resources issues to both public and private organizations. The Blackwell series on Human Resource Management, including this handbook, are under his general editorial supervision.

Susan Ross is a Ph.D. candidate in strategic management at Florida Atlantic University. She received a B.A. from the University of Florida and an M.B.A. from Florida Atlantic. She spent eight years in retail management and was district manager for The Limited. Her research interests are strategic human resource management and globalization.

Randall S. Schuler is Professor, Stern School of Business, New York University. His interests are international human resource management, human resource strategy, strategic human resource management, entrepreneurship and the integration of business needs and human resource management. He has

authored or edited over 30 books and has published over 100 articles in professional journals and academic proceedings. Presently, he is associate editor of the *Journal of Business and Economic Studies* and is on the editorial boards of the *Academy of Management Review, European Management Journal, Journal of Organizational Behavior, Organizational Dynamics, Human Resource Planning, Human Resource Management, The International Journal of Human Resource Management, Asia Pacific Journal of Human Resources,* and *Journal of High Technology Management Research.* He is a Fellow of the American Psychological Association. He is past editor of the *Human Resource Planning Journal.* In addition to his academic work, he has conducted numerous executive and management development workshops in the United States, Europe, and Australia. His current consulting work focuses on realigning the structure of human resources departments to better serve the needs of the business, and developing HR vision statements and action strategies for human resources departments to pursue into the twenty-first century.

James M. Schultz is Director of Employee Development for Walgreen Company. He is responsible for the areas of: human performance analysis, human resources planning, human resources information systems, instructional design and development, systems usability and training, management and executive development, and media and meeting services. He attended the University of Denver, receiving a B.S. in Business Administration in 1969, and an M.B.A. in 1971. Currently he serves as the President of the Board of Directors for the Chicago Jewish Vocational Service, a provider of career development, skills training, and rehabilitation services. He was appointed to the State of Illinois Director of Education's Skills Standards Committee, representing the Illinois Retail Merchants Association, to aid in the development of national skills standards in support of President Clinton's "Goals 2,000 Educate America Act."

David M. Schweiger is a Professor of Management in the College of Business at the University of South Carolina. He is also affiliated with Groupe ESC Lyon, in France. David received his B.S. and M.S. from the Polytechnic Institute of New York and his D.B.A. from the University of Maryland. He is a consultant, researcher, and teacher in Strategic Management, focusing on mergers and acquisitions, international strategy, and strategic change. He has consulted and researched extensively on these topics with international firms and has published in several practitioner and academic journals. He is on the editorial boards of a number of journals and is past editor of *Human Resource Planning*.

Valerie I. Sessa is a Research Associate at the Center for Creative Leadership. Prior to her position at the Center, Valerie worked as both an adjunct instructor at New York University, Yeshiva University, and Marymount Manhattan College as well as a human resources and organizational research consultant. She received her B.A. in Psychology from the University of Pennsylvania and her M.A. and Ph.D. in Industrial and Organizational Psychology from New York University. Her research interests include work-force diversity, team conflict and effectiveness, and executive selection. She has published several articles and book chapters on the topics. She is a member of the Academy of Management, the Society for Industrial and Organizational Psychology, and the American Psychological Association.

Scott A. Snell is Associate Professor of Management in the Smeal College of Business Administration at Pennsylvania State University. He also serves as Director of Penn State's Institute for the Study of Organizational Effectiveness (ISOE). He received his Ph.D. in Business Administration from Michigan State University. His research and teaching interests are centered on the strategic aspects of human resource management. Most recently he completed a study of HR issues relating to the development of transnational teams in network organizations. He has written numerous journal articles and book chapters, and is co-author of *Managing Human Resources* (Southwestern Publishing). As a consultant to industry, Professor Snell has worked with companies such as AT&T, General Motors, IBM, Shell Chemical, and Weyerhauser redesigning human resources systems to cope with changes in the competitive environment. Professor Snell is actively involved in executive education and serves as Faculty Director for Penn State's Strategic Leadership Program.

James D. Spina is a manager with the Tribune Company in the area of management training and program development. He received his Ph.D. in Educational Administration from the University of Connecticut and also holds certification as Senior Professional in Human Resources. Spina has research interests in leadership theory and performance management and team-building activities.

James Stodd is a Partner with Furst Transitions, a human resources management consulting firm specializing in corporate outplacement, organization change, and management development. He has served as Vice President of Human Resources for Our Lady of the Lake Medical Center in Baton Rouge, LA, Vice President of Human Resources for BroMenn Healthcare in Bloomington-Normal, IL, and as Senior Consultant with Ernst & Young. He holds a Bachelor's degree in Psychology from Saint Louise University, a Master's degree in Industrial/Organizational Psychology from Illinois State University, and has completed significant graduate work towards a Ph.D. in Industrial Relations at the University of Minnesota. Stodd is accredited as a Senior Professional in Human Resources (SPHR).

Thomas W. Tewksbury recently retired as the Senior Vice President of Human Resources and Administrative Operations at Allstate Insurance Company. He holds a Bachelor's degree from Springfield College in Massachusetts and an M.S. from Pennsylvania State

University in University Park, Pennsylvania. He has 39 years of human resources experience with both Sears and Allstate Insurance Company. He has played an active role of support and leadership in cultural change and in the migration to an empowered work force at Allstate. He has been active in supporting research projects and in the overall development of the Center for Human Resource Management, where he was a partner and served as a member of the Center's executive board.

Martha L. Thornton recently retired as Senior Vice President Human Resources at Ameritech, a position she assumed in 1989. She started her career with Michigan Bell in 1963 and held various line, operations assignments including Department Head of Operation Services. In 1983, prior to the AT&T-Bell system divestiture, she joined Ameritech to establish the Human Resources and Benefits functions for the new company. She held various Human Resources Vice Presidential assignments prior to her promotion to Senior Vice President. She has been active in the Human Resource Management Association of Chicago, the Midwest Business Group on Health and the U.S. Chamber's Employers' Council on Health Care. Health care and the health-care system are her major areas of professional interest. Before her retirement, she was a partner in the University of Illinois Center for Human Resource Management.

Jacques Tibau is Corporate Management Development Manager of Interbrew (Belgium), Europe's fifth largest brewing company. He holds a university degree in Law from Katholieke Universiteit Leuven, Belgium. He has a postgraduate degree in Applied Economics from Universiteit Antwerpen and participated in the International Management Program at INSEAD, Fountainbleau (France) in 1992. He has lectured at several universities in Belgium, the Netherlands, and Italy and is a member of the Advisory Board of the Department of Applied Economics, Katholieke Universiteit Leuven. His primary responsibility is to develop a common value system for Interbrew, which has made several mergers and acquisitions in Western and Eastern Europe in the last five years.

David O. Ulrich is Clinical Professor at the School of Business at the University of Michigan. He received his undergraduate degree from Brigham Young University and his doctorate from UCLA. He has taught M.B.A., Ph.D., and executive education courses on how organizations compete through strategic change, organization design, culture change, human resources practices, and leadership. At Michigan, he is on the core faculty of the Michigan Executive Program, the Academic Director of Michigan's Human Resource Executive Program, and the co-director of the Advanced Human Resource Executive Program. His research assesses how organizations change, formulate strategies for competitive advantage, and integrate human resources into strategic goals. He has generated an award-winning national data base on organizations which assesses how strategies match human resources practices for improved financial performance. He has published over fifty articles and book chapters in *Academy of Management Review, Human Resource Management, Human Resource Planning, Organizational Dynamics, Human Relations, Journal of Management, New Management, Planning Review,* and *Sloan Management Review.* He is co-author of *Organizational Capability: Competing from the Inside/Out* and *Human Resources as a Competitive Advantage: An Empirical Assessment of HR Competencies and Practices in Global Firms.* He has served on the board of directors for the Human Resource Planning Society, is the editor of *Human Resource Management,* and serves on the editorial board of five other journals. He has consulted and done research with over half of the Fortune 200.

Thomas F. Urban combines 25 years of industry and academic experience as a consultant in executive development, organizational transitions, and strategic human resource management. He has been a speaker, trainer, and consultant for a number of industry, govern-mental, and non-profit organizations. Pre-viously, he was an internal consultant with ARCO Oil and Gas Company, an operating company of Atlantic Richfield, where he designed, developed, and implemented a number of organizational transition processes. His background includes being a tenured faculty member of the Colleges of Business at Texas A & M and Miami University (Ohio), a Visiting Professor at the University of Iowa, and Adjunct Professorships at the University of Texas-Dallas and the University of Dallas. He has published an extensive number of books, articles, and cases in the area of organizational change and is a frequent presenter on panels at professional conferences. His educational background includes a D.B.A. and M.B.A. from the Graduate School of Business, Indiana University and a B.S. from the College of Commerce, University of Detroit.

James W. Walker is a partner in The Walker Group, a human resources strategy and management effectiveness consulting firm based in Phoenix, Arizona. Prior to establishing the firm in 1986, he was Vice President at Towers Perrin, a New York consulting firm. He has served on the business faculties at Indiana University, San Diego State University, and Arizona State University. He is author of many articles and eight books. He was a founder of The Human Resource Business School Consortium, a group of fifty companies working together to develop human resources staff capabilities. He earned an M.A. in Labor and Management and a Ph.D. in Business Administration from the University of Iowa.

Sandy J. Wayne is Associate Professor of Management at the University of Illinois at Chicago. She received a Ph.D. in Management from Texas A&M University. Her research interests include power and politics, empowerment, group dynamics, leadership, job design, and motivation. She has published articles in

the *Academy of Management Journal, Journal of Applied Psychology, Organizational Behavior and Human Decision Processes*, and *Journal of Management*. She has been a consultant to Texas Instruments, Caterpillar, FMC, Allstate Insurance, and the law firm of Rosenthal & Shanfield.

Stanley E. Wertheim retired in 1990 as Vice President – Administration of Centerior Service Company formed as part of the Centerior Energy Company created from the affiliation of the Toledo Edison and Cleveland Electric Illuminating (CEI) companies. His responsibilities included human resources, information systems, procurement, office services, and strategic planning. He joined CEI's Technical Studies element in 1949 after receiving his B.S. in Electrical Engineering and later his M.S. in Engineering Administration from Case, now part of Case Western Reserve University. In 1956 he launched and subsequently managed the CEI's computerization program until he became Corporate Planner in 1981. He subsequently headed the System Planning Department and participated in the affiliation process as assistant to the President before becoming Vice President. During his career and at present he has been active in many community and religious organizations as a board member and president. Since retirement he has done major consulting assignments, first at Towers-Perrin and then at United Way. He is currently a part-time lecturer at John Carroll University, primarily in Strategic Management.

David A. Whetten is the Jack Wheatley Professor of Organizational Behavior, and Director of the Center for the Study of Values in Organizations, at Brigham Young University. His research has appeared in the leading professional journals in his field. In addition, he is the co-author of three research books: *Interorganizational Relations, Organizational Effectiveness*, and *Organizational Decline*. He is also co-author of *Developing Management Skills* and a variety of companion learning tools, for which he and his co-author were awarded the David Bradford Distinguished Educator Award by the Organizational Behavior Teaching Society. He has been editor of the *Academy of Management Review* and an associate editor of *Administration and Society*. He has served as a member of the Board of Governors of the Academy of Management, and in 1994 received the Academy's Distinguished Service Award.

David T. Whitford is Associate Professor of Finance, College of Commerce and Business Administration, and of Labor and Industrial Relations, University of Illinois at Urbana-Champaign. Professor Whitford's research specialities include risk analysis via cash flow patterns, and capital market efficiency and its implications for small firms. In 1990 and 1994 he received the Outstanding Teaching Award from the University's Executive M.B.A. Program. In addition, he currently serves as a Director of the Midwest Finance Association. Dr. Whitford received his Ph.D. from Georgia State University.

Foreword

The 1990s may be known as "The Decade of Human Resource Management." While business leaders have long claimed that human resources were our most important assets, only the exceptions have been willing to act according to that maxim. However, today, there seems to be a spreading acceptance by companies and societies that effective and appropriate people management can contribute to achieving and sustaining competitive advantage.

The elevation of human resources management as a function has been due to several factors. Partly it is attributable to greater competition in product markets domestically and internationally; partly it is due to the introduction of new technologies in the workplace; and partly it is due to changing demographics and diversity of the work force, especially with regard to gender, ethnicity, and race.

But along with these changes in the context facing today's managers, contemporary managers are much more accepting of human resources concerns. Increasingly, managers are exposed to the behavioral side of business in university training courses as well as the popular management press. The field of human resource management itself has been professionalized and specialized into subfields in which scientific and practical information is expanding rapidly.

Recognizing the new stature and complexity of human resources issues, Blackwell Publishers has begun a series, on "Human Resource Management," under my general editorship. The goal of the series is to be relevant at the intersection of practice and research by providing analyses of current issues in human resource management, by informing practitioners and other managers of current practices, and by helping to sharpen academic discussions and future research. Human resources practices sometimes have lagged behind research findings, while in other instances, theory and research ultimately confirms what practitioners always knew to be true. The Blackwell series endeavors to close these gaps.

I am very pleased to introduce this *Handbook of Human Resource Management* by Gerald R. Ferris, Sherman D. Rosen, and Darold T. Barnum as the initial volume in the series. As the reader can see, it is truly a handbook of the field. It provides guidance and information on a variety of topics. It covers the traditional subjects comprehensively and offers discussion at the cutting edge of the discipline. Moreover the book seeks to link academic researchers with human resources practitioners and vice versa. The editors' concern for linkage is apparent in the topics they have included and the authors they have selected (most of whom are teams of academics and practitioners). The *Handbook* itself is the product of a new applied human resource management research center at the University of Illinois, which encourages exchanges between university-based scientists and the practicing community. The *Handbook* is a very appropriate way to anchor the series. I anticipate it will be a useful reference for students and managers.

Myron Roomkin

Preface

Human resource management (HRM) involves acquiring, developing, utilizing, and retaining employees. It is practiced in some form in all organizations, by both HRM professionals and by general managers, among others. It also is the subject of extensive scientific study, mainly by academics housed in universities or research institutes.

Since the late 1930s, however, the science and practice of HRM have become largely disconnected. Practitioners often feel that theory and research on HRM issues is of little value to them. This lack of value may be partially because of topic selection by researchers. Another factor may be that practitioners have limited access to and difficulty comprehending reports of HRM research results published in scholarly journals. Journal articles often emphasize sophisticated theory or statistical analyses, and are usually not concerned with practical applications.

Academic researchers, on the other hand, frequently have little interest in or understanding of the problems that are dealt with by practitioners. There are several possible reasons for this situation. Academics sometimes feel that an applied research agenda

would be dictated by the ever-changing problems that organizations are facing, and hence would be less focused and less likely to contribute to the advancement of scientific knowledge. And, because many academic researchers have limited contact with real organizations and the people in them who practice HRM, they often have difficulty identifying and responding to problems encountered in the real world of work. Indeed, new problems in the workplace sometimes are not addressed in the academic literature for many years after they have appeared, because those dealing with the problems don't publish, and those publishing are not aware that the problems exist.

Many of us believe that bringing the practice and science of HRM closer together would be beneficial to both. Indeed, it was this objective that stimulated our interest in putting together this handbook. We had no desire to develop yet one more book on HRM which adopted the same perspective as all the others, but the thought of doing something new and different generated enthusiasm and piqued our interest.

We decided that a way to bring the science

and practice of HRM closer together, and develop a unique perspective in its own right, would be to have each chapter co-authored by at least one academic and one practitioner. Their task was to collaborate on the topic of their chapter, and integrate the theory, research, and practice concerning it. We chose topics for the book that covered traditional and contemporary HRM subject matter, in addition to future issues and challenges.

We are pleased, therefore, to introduce you to the *Handbook of Human Resource Management*, whose authors include many of the top HR scholars and prominent HR managers, executives, and consultants. Some books are too theoretical, others are too applied. We feel that the fruits of our authors' collaboration are an interesting blend of theory, research, and practice, and we hope that it will be seen by academics and practitioners alike as providing added value.

We feel that there are several groups that will find this book of interest. We see the *Handbook* as appropriate for adoption in advanced undergraduate and graduate HRM courses. We also believe the book could be of considerable use in management development programs. Finally, we hope that practitioners will use it as a reference, as they search for advanced state-of-the-art theory and practice.

We should mention that our interest in bringing the science and practice of HRM closer together did not originate with this book. All three of us have been actively involved in the pursuit of this mission for the several years that we have been directing the Center for Human Resource Management at the University of Illinois. The Center is a human resources research partnership between the University of Illinois and business organizations. It is concerned with promoting research that has the potential to improve HRM practice in organizations. So, we have spent much time, as directors of the Center, facilitating the collaboration of academic researchers and HR executives in a manner designed to result in the articulation, design, and conduct of research projects that both parties believe contributes value. Working with the Center's partner firms and academic faculty has convinced us that the collaboration of science and practice can lead to the more effective practice of HRM, as well as to more relevant and organizationally grounded theory and research.

Similiar joint ventures also are occuring elsewhere. For example, successful centers are in operation at universities such as Cornell University and the University of Southern California, and flourishing business–university human resources relationships exist in universities such as the University of Michigan, Boston University, the University of North Carolina, and Texas A & M University.

We would be remiss if we failed to acknowledge the many people who contributed meaningfully to making the *Handbook of Human Resource Management* "the best that it could be." First, and foremost, we would like to express our sincere appreciation to the contributing authors. They worked very hard at helping us to realize our vision for a book that integrated the theory, research, and practice of HRM, by effectively blending perspectives that don't always fit cleanly and neatly together. To the extent that this book is well received, it will be due to the efforts of our contributing authors.

Second, we would like to thank Blackwell Publishers for offering us the opportunity to develop a different type of book. Our good friend and colleague, Myron Roomkin, in his role as series editor for Blackwell, first approached us with the handbook idea, and he has effectively facilitated the interactions with our publishers. Rolf Janke and Richard Burton from Blackwell provided strong support and encouragement throughout the entire project. To all of you, we would like to express our gratitude.

Third, we thank the people involved in and supportive of the Center for Human Resource Management at the University of Illinois. The *Handbook of Human Resource Management*, in many respects, embodies the very essence and spirit of the Center. Of particular note is Dr. Walter H. Franke, retired Director of the Institute of Labor and Industrial Relations at the University of Illinois at Urbana-Champaign. From its inception, Walt provided strong support for the Center in both concept and in practice. And, he has been there to lend a hand, both financially and emotionally, when we have needed him. It is with mixed emotions that we write these comments about Walt, because he has recently retired. Our mixed emotions stem from our genuine happiness for Walt and his wife Pat, who embark upon a new and interesting part of their lives, along with our sense of sadness at missing a good friend, colleague, and leader. Let us simply say, thanks, Walt, we miss you.

Fourth, we would like to acknowledge Cindy Dodds Lusk and Penny Cole, and thank them for the clerical assistance they provided in getting this book manuscript ready for publication.

Finally, we would like to express a personal note of appreciation to our families, who tolerated the long hours that we put in on this project, and generally put up with us over the 16 months that we worked on putting together the *Handbook*. Jerry thanks his wonderful wife, Dr. Gail Russ, and his two beautiful daughters, Emily and Elizabeth. Sherm thanks his wife Sarene, and his children, Marianne, Jim, and Claire. Darold thanks his wife Phyllis and his sons William and Peter; he's happy and proud to be a member of their family!

We believe the *Handbook of Human Resource Management* is a unique volume, and we hope you enjoy it.

Gerald R. Ferris
Sherman D. Rosen
Darold T. Barnum

☐ Chapter 1 ☐

Toward Business–University Partnerships in Human Resource Management: Integration of Science and Practice

Gerald R. Ferris, Darold T. Barnum, Sherman D. Rosen,
Lawrence P. Holleran, and James H. Dulebohn

INTRODUCTION

Human resource management (HRM) is an important area for both organizational science and business practice. However, bridges are infrequently crossed between those who are involved in managing human resources and those who conduct research about HRM. The results of HRM research are not well communicated, understood, nor effectively utilized in the working world of human resource management. HRM researchers need to understand and involve themselves in the activities of real organizations, and human resource managers need to understand and appreciate the nature and outcomes of HR research.

In this chapter, we review current trends in the practice and the science of HRM. We suggest ways to integrate theory and research with practice. A framework is presented that shows the interrelationships of a multitude of issues that bear on the HRM field, and that serves to organize the material in this book.

DEFINITION OF HRM

The utilization of people within an organization is a function of a broad range of dynamic factors. These include the leadership, culture, and objectives of the organization; the environment in which people are expected to perform; and the diversity and self-management of the people themselves.

Human resource management, its concept, definition, study, and application have become more complex at a rate at least equal to societal change. Any definition that does not recognize these dynamics risks early obsolescence. However, the purposes of human resource management are more constant: getting and keeping the optimal quantity and quality of people needed to achieve the objectives of the organization; insuring those people have a work environment that is healthy, productive, and safe, and which provides the opportunity to perform and develop; and achieving these purposes with effectiveness and efficiency. We define human resource management as follows:

Human resource management is the science and the practice that deals with the nature of the employment relationship and all of the decisions, actions, and issues that relate to that relationship. In practice, it involves an organization's acquisition, development, and utilization of employees, well as the employees' relationship to an organization and its performance.

This broad definition encompasses industrial relations, as well as topics and issues that might conventionally be included under the rubrics of organizational psychology, organizational sociology, and strategic management. Thus, our definition casts the net rather widely, but we believe such inclusiveness is not only functional, but necessary to accurately reflect the current scope of the field.

During this century different yet generally equivalent labels have been used to refer to human resource management, personnel management having been the most commonly used label. Despite the labels used, HRM always has emphasized management's side of the employment relationship (Kaufman, 1993). The relatively recent adoption of the term "human resource management" by most U.S. organizations and academic scientists in place of personnel management indicates not only the awareness of the critical importance of the human element in organizational management, but also the extent to which the success of an organization must be balanced with the ability of the individuals in it to develop to their full potential.

THE PRACTICE OF HRM TODAY

The term HRM reflects the evolution of a science and practice distinct from its predecessor label, personnel management. Personnel management implied that employees were an organizational expense. On the other hand, HRM emphasizes the potential of employees as organizational assets. Concurrent with this shift from the usage of the term personnel management to human resource management has been a transformation of the responsibilities and prominence of the field.

The evolution of HRM has resulted in an enlarged scope and increased importance for HRM. The responsibilities of yesterday's personnel managers were characterized as maintenance activities, primarily at the operational (short-term) and secondarily at the managerial (medium-term) levels of the organization. In contrast, today human resources managers need to function successfully at three organizational levels: operational, managerial, and strategic (long-term) (Schuler, 1993). That is, the transformation of HRM has resulted in the inclusion of functions at the strategic level as well as expanded managerial-level activities. The new roles of today's human resources manager include: strategic business partner, employee advocate, diversity manager, maintainer of organizational culture, facilitator of organizational change, and internal consultant (Pettigrew, 1973; Schuler, 1993; Dyer & Holder, 1988).

The competencies demanded of successful HRM practitioners today are different from those required in the past. Whereas in earlier times practitioners primarily needed expertise for functional activities at the operational level, it is now crucial for them to have the skills necessary to operate at the managerial and strategic levels as well (Schuler, 1993). The skills required include a broad and general knowledge and understanding of business functions (e.g., accounting, finance, marketing, management), human resources functional skills and knowledge, communication skills, and planning skills (Sears, 1984). Finally, requisite competencies include change-management capabilities, such as influence and political skills (Ferris, 1993; Bender et al., 1995).

THE SCIENCE OF HRM: RESEARCH AND THEORY

Recent trends in HRM research

HRM researchers have, in the past, typically utilized theories from the social sciences (Dyer

& Schwab, 1982). HRM research has been characterized by the behavioral science approach and the principal level of analysis in HRM research has focused on micro (i.e., individual level of analysis), rather than macro (i.e., organizational level of analysis). Consequently, until recently, the primary focus of HRM researchers has been on separate HRM activities, resulting partially from former roles of HRM.

While HRM scholars continue to do micro-oriented research, some have begun to investigate HRM issues from a macro level of analysis. For instance, Jackson, Schuler, and Rivero (1989) examined the relationship between organizational characteristics and personnel practices using data obtained from 267 organizations. In addition, Russell, Terborg, and Powers (1985) examined organizational training as it related to firm performance using data from 62 stores. A final example is Gerhart and Milkovich (1990) who examined the differences in managerial compensation decisions across 200 organizations, and the effect of these differences on firm performance.

The widening scope of HRM also has resulted in the development of strategic human resource management (Butler, Ferris, & Napier, 1991). Strategic human resource management represents an effort to link HRM activities to a firm's business strategy (Lengnick-Hall & Lengnick-Hall, 1988). The perspective is representative of the assumptions that HRM activities are organizational in scope (Schuler, 1990), that HRM issues need to be considered in the formulation and the implementation of organizational strategy (Dyer, 1985), and that HRM practice influences the organization's performance (Ferris, Russ, Albanese, & Martocchio, 1990).

In addition to the general strategic human resource management approach, there have been efforts to place HRM in a broader context and at a higher level of analysis. These include the political perspective (Ferris & Judge, 1991), the economic/utility perspective (Lazear, 1993; Jones & Wright, 1992), and the international perspective (Butler et al., 1991; Kochan, Batt, & Dyer, 1992; Dowling & Schuler, 1990).

Theory building in HRM

To date, the focus of researchers on individual HRM functions and activities has resulted in a failure to develop an integrative theory of HRM (Mahoney & Deckop, 1986). The adoption of appropriate theories from other disciplines, while useful, is inadequate to integrate HRM research and practice (Wallace, 1983). Therefore, while the evolution of the practice of HRM – from a maintenance function to one of increasing organizational and strategic importance – has resulted in an integration of activities in HRM practice, the science of HRM has been marked by an absence of an integrative theory or general conceptual system.

Components of good theory

A theory helps make sense of the observable world by ordering relationships among observed elements (Klimoski, 1991). A theory specifies relationships among constructs (i.e., unobservable units) and variables (i.e., observable units) in the empirical world (Bacharach, 1989; Heneman, 1969). The two primary criteria upon which any theory may be evaluated are its falsibility and utility (Bacharach, 1989). Falsibility allows empirical refutation; utility refers to the ability of a theory to explain the substantive meaning of constructs, variables, and their linkages, while prediction empirically tests the explanation of that meaning (Bacharach, 1989).

Researchers have specified the components that a good theory needs to include. First, it should provide a delineation of major constructs and independent and dependent variables (Thompson, 1991). Second, it should define major relationships among the variables, which can generate hypotheses that can be tested (Wallace, 1983, Heneman, 1969). Third, a good theory should be generalizable, have clear implications for practice, and should direct future research (Miner, 1984). Fourth, it should be parsimonious and provide the simplest explanation to account for the phenomena observed (Landy & Vasey, 1984). Fifth, a good theory should be value-added and contribute to what is currently known (Whetten, 1989).

An additional consideration is a theory's scope. Attempts at grand or very broad theory development in HRM have resulted in theories stated at high levels of abstraction at which it has not been possible to deduce hypotheses that could be tested (Meltz, 1991). An alternative to theories that are so general that they provide little predictive accuracy and are not testable are "middle range theories" (Bobko & Russell, 1991). Middle range theories are concerned with one or a few phenomena, tend to be linkable to each other, and are concrete enough to generate testable hypotheses (Moore, Johns, & Pinder, 1980, 1–2).

Finally, researchers have emphasized that value orientation is a significant influence in perceptions of what constitutes a good theory (Klimoski, 1991; Boehm, 1980; Dubin, 1976). The separation that often exists between the science and practice of HRM contributes to different perceptions held by HRM scholars and practitioners. Whereas the objective of HRM practice is to devise rules and models for administering organizations, the objective of the science of HRM is to describe and predict phenomena at a very general level (Tullar, 1991). Academic research, and the theories behind the research, are often viewed by HRM practitioners as being inapplicable to the real world or organizational environment (Klimoski, 1991). This is understandable since the tendency of scientific research, based on the traditional model, is controlled observation which often results in research that

does not fit the real world of the practitioner (Boehm, 1980).

A description of the characteristics of good theories for HRM needs to include the components discussed above as well as take into account the applied nature of the field. The applied nature of HRM signifies the crucial importance of HRM research in organizations. It also suggests that productive research is dependent on cooperation between science and practice of HRM. HRM academicians need to be able and also willing to incorporate their research into organizations (Boehm, 1980), and practitioners need to expand their perception and definition of research to include the systematic examination of organizational problems, and thereby view it as a process from which they can benefit.

DEVELOPMENT OF A SCIENCE–PRACTICE PERSPECTIVE

The foregoing discussion examines the distinctions between the science and the practice of HRM. In this section, we suggest how the science and practice of HRM can be brought closer together, in an effort to effectively integrate theory, research, and practice. Some optimism for this effort comes from recent work on theory building. Wright and McMahon (1992) suggested that theory is important whether one's orientation is toward research or practice. In fact, Bacharach (1989) recently discussed the similarity of interest between researchers and practitioners in the development of good theory. He suggested that consultants serve to clarify and reduce the ambiguity of the world for clients. Because good theory intends to diminish the complexity of the world through prediction and explanation, sound theoretical development should benefit both researchers and practitioners.

Designing and conducting useful research

Several approaches have been proposed to bring science and practice closer together by "doing research that is useful" (Lawler, Mohrman, Mohrman, Ledford, & Cummings, 1985; Hakel, Sorcher, Beer, & Moses, 1982; Boehm, 1980). Hakel et al. were concerned with the design and execution of research when the interest is in implementation of the findings. Therefore, their focus is shared equally between research and implementation, and they have suggested that scientific research be designed so as to yield applied products, and that implementation or practical projects be designed in a way that contributes to gains in scientific knowledge.

Boehm (1980) suggested that progress in the organizational sciences has been limited by many scholars' strict adherence to the "scientific method" in the design and conduct of research, which often does not fit the realities of "real world" settings. She recommended that academics should not insist on choosing settings that fit their methods, but instead should consider altering their research design to fit the setting or environment being investigated. Doing this could have interesting and important implications for both research and practice.

Research on organizations can contribute to our scientific knowledge base as well as to practitioners who are interested in the effectiveness of organizations, according to Lawler and his colleagues (Lawler, 1985; Lawler et al., 1985), who have directed considerable effort toward doing "useful" research. Indeed, Lawler (1985, 2) has established two fundamental criteria that all research projects must meet: The project must help practitioners understand organizations in a way that will improve practice, and it must contribute to a theoretically and scientifically useful body of knowledge about organizations.

Business–university research partnerships

Concurrent with the evolution of HRM, there have been efforts to encourage cooperation between the science and the practice of HRM. Central to these efforts has been the establishment of business–university partnerships. The recent formation of a number of these partnerships has occurred in the context of a general growth of cooperative efforts between education and industry. For the field of HRM, these partnerships represent a movement toward the close and productive relationship that existed earlier in the century between the science and practice of HRM.

The idea of business–university partnerships is not new but can be traced back to the Morrill Act in 1862 that established land grant institutions and encouraged business–university partnerships (Powers et al., 1988). What is new is the growth in numbers, scale, and scope of business–education partnerships since the late 1970s. The decade of the 1980s witnessed an unprecedented move towards cooperative programs between U.S. business and public schools, private and public vocational and technical schools, community colleges, and public and private colleges and universities (Carnevale, Gainer, Villet, & Holland, 1990). Such cooperation has been viewed as an important means for increasing the United States' competitive position in the global marketplace (Morrison, McGuire, & Clarke, 1988). During the 1980s, the value of linking university and corporate research and development to increase competitiveness became widely recognized by many government, business, and educational leaders (Morrison et al., 1988). This recognition resulted in the emergence of many cooperative R&D programs between American businesses and educational institutions (Fairweather, 1988).

In the field of human resource management, a number of business–university partnerships have been formed between university HRM programs and various corporations.

5

Most of these HRM partnerships were established in the late 1980s or early 1990s. Typically the partnerships are called centers, are organizational units of educational institutions, and have a number of corporate sponsors who provide funding for research and other activities (Dulebohn, Ferris, & Day, 1994).

The predominant purpose of the HRM partnerships is to generate applied research (Dulebohn et al., 1994). Other activities include joint meetings of HRM researchers and practitioners, training and development programs and conferences, and recruiting of HRM students by the sponsors. HRM centers provide an unparalleled opportunity to bring researchers and practitioners together to address problems facing the HRM field. Similar to business–education partnerships in general, HRM centers provide faculty members (i.e., those involved in the science of HRM) with an increased awareness of real-world problems and opportunities to conduct research that will contribute to both the science and the practice of HRM (Dulebohn et al., 1994). For HRM practitioners, HRM centers provide access to faculty expertise, and opportunities to be involved in, and directly benefit from, innovative research.

One example that is not atypical of such centers is the Center for Human Resource Management at the University of Illinois. We discuss it here as a case study of how these centers are formed and function. In the late 1980s, the HRM faculties from the University of Illinois' campuses in Chicago (UIC) and Urbana-Champaign (UIUC) independently developed plans for forming university–business partnerships. Initial activity was centered in the Management Department at UIC, and in the Institute for Labor and Industrial Relations at UIUC. At that time, a vice president of human resources at a well-known corporation was closely involved with HRM faculty from both campuses. He brought the two faculty groups together, and strongly encouraged them to form a single center for the University of Illinois. (Interestingly, not only were the two faculty groups unaware of each other's efforts, but the involved faculty on the two campuses did not even know each other personally.) With strong support for a single University of Illinois center from another HR vice president as well, the first vice president facilitated the negotiation of a set of bylaws to govern the two-campus operation. These bylaws were approved by the faculty and administrations on both campuses, as well as by the HRM practitioners involved at the time. The Center was officially established on July 1, 1991.

Thus, from its very beginning, the Center was a joint venture of HRM practitioners and faculty, and was geared to meet the needs of both groups. The initial goals of the Center, which still were intact in 1994, reflect their joint interests:

- Support research that is future-oriented and intellectually rich, and that will result in new knowledge, approaches and techniques which can serve as the foundation for improved human resource management.
- Effectively transfer supported research to the workplace in a variety of ways, such as briefings and reports to Partners, Partner roundtable discussions, conferences, newsletters, journal articles, books, training, technical assistance, and other appropriate methods.
- Provide forums in which academics, and senior human resource executives whose firms are Center Partners, can meet and examine important human resource issues.
- Encourage the intellectual growth of University of Illinois students in the theory and practice of human resource management, through such methods as: (a) continual improvement of academic programs resulting from the feedback of experiences and research of faculty engaged in the work of the Center, and (b) the direct participation of students in the research,

educational, and other activities of the Center. Further, provide opportunities for financial assistance to students as they engage in the work of the Center.

- Develop close collaborative relationships between senior human resource executives and Center faculty, in order to better identify and study critical human resource issues, and to more successfully implement improved methods of human resource management growing out of the research.

The Center seeks to accomplish these goals in several ways. Perhaps most important are its governance, and its process for selecting research projects.

The Center is headed by two faculty directors with equal power and duties, one on each campus. (Interestingly, many university faculty and administrators felt that this joint leadership arrangement would not work, although HRM practitioners were not concerned. In fact, the joint leadership structure has worked well, and achieved its goal of keeping faculty on both campuses fully involved in the Center.)

The Center is governed by an executive board consisting of three representatives from partner firms, the two directors, and one faculty member from each campus, for a total of seven members. More votes are held by university professors, which is necessary for an organizational unit of the university. However, it is the strong norm and in actual practice no action is taken that does not have the support of the business partners on the board. Further, as spelled out in detail in the Center's bylaws, true control of the Center resides in this board. The board meets frequently on a wide variety of issues. Its discussions have been open and frank, with real attempts to meet the interests of all parties. As a result, all decisions to date have been made with the agreement of the business members as well as the members from each campus.

The process by which research projects are chosen for funding also reflects the joint interests of the parties. Here is how the process has worked for the first three years. First, a call for research suggestions is sent to all business partners. Often, partner suggestions have been developed in phone conversations between a center director and the partner involved, but they always are reduced to writing. Second, a call for brief one-page proposals is sent to faculty. This call includes the partner ideas, and faculty proposals based on partner ideas are strongly encouraged. Brief proposals are evaluated by the executive board, primarily for the acceptability of the topic. The purpose of the brief proposal evaluation is to provide responses to faculty before a substantial amount of effort is utilized in developing a full proposal. For those brief proposals evaluated favorably by the executive board, full-length proposals are requested. When developing a full proposal based on a partner idea, it is required that the proposal be developed in close consultation with the partner involved. This is especially important because most of the proposals entail doing research involving one or more partner firms.

The full proposals are first evaluated for scientific merit by faculty reviewers. Typically, two selected faculty members, one from each University of Illinois campus, review each proposal, with outside reviewers used when internal resources are not available. Faculty evaluations of each proposal are attached to it. The executive board then reviews the full proposals, which include the faculty evaluations of their scientific merit, and selects those proposals that will be funded.

About two-thirds of the funded proposals have been based on partner ideas, and the other third on faculty ideas. What they share in common, however, is that they are of interest to both the faculty members and the partners involved, that they have scientific merit (as determined by the faculty reviewers), and that they have practical value to partner firms (as determined by the executive

7

board review). As already noted, almost all research has been conducted at partner firms, so the link between faculty and partner interests becomes even stronger. Indeed, the primary value to faculty of having a proposal accepted has been access to the partner organization, not the money involved.

Although we certainly would expect the topics that are funded to change over time, we feel that research proposals approved will continue to reflect cutting-edge issues that are of mutual interest to business partners and academic scientists. Some of the projects funded in the first two years are listed below, as an indication of the issues that both groups agreed were important in the mid-1990s:

- Empowered work teams: Composition, process, rewards and effectiveness.
- Determinants of employee career success.
- Measuring the added-value of human resource management practices.
- Linking training practices with competitive strategy.
- Gap between theory and practice: Comparative study of diversity programs.
- Worker empowerment, team reward systems, and work group productivity.
- Validating a scale for measuring the climate for women in corporations.
- Empowered work groups: Measurement of leader behavior.
- Value-added analysis in human resource management.
- A multimedia computerized assessment system for evaluating managerial talent.
- Determinants of union and management commitment to participative management.
- Leading large and empowered work groups.
- Relations between individual and contextual factors and employees' creative behavior.
- Effects of value incongruity within organizations: Implications for managing diversity.

- Implications of downsizing for human resource management.

Finally, reproduced below are comments by a few of the business partners, showing the characteristics of the Center that they find of value. We expect that not only this Center, but the other centers built on the same philosophy, would receive the same type of responses. That is, these comments are included here to indicate the types of behaviors and activities that practitioners say have value in joint ventures with academic scientists.

The unique value of the Center comes from the direct involvement of active business partners. Partners play a central role in determining issues for research, providing sites for research, and analyzing research findings. The payoff is research that has real world application for the partners. The Center offers practitioners a unique opportunity to enhance the human resources function in corporate America. (R. Wayne Anderson, Senior Vice President, Amoco)

The CHRM provides an open forum for multi-disciplined academics and HR heads to challenge today's human resource practices and mutually develop tomorrow's, via objective research and spirited dialogue. (Lawrence P. Holleran, Vice President, Human Resources, FMC Corporation)

The Center for Human Resource Management provides its business partners with the opportunity to get in on the ground floor of exciting research. I have been very impressed with the openness of the Illinois faculty in forging close partnerships with the member companies. The Center does research on issues that are of interest to the partner companies, and that involve projects in which the partner companies can participate. It is operated as a true partnership, in that there is a close collaborative relationship between faculty and business partners. This is a unique opportunity to get involved with other leading companies to discuss, evaluate, and research human resources issues of mutual interest. (Fosten A. Boyle, Vice President, Human Resources, Honeywell)

After three years of existence, the Center is evaluating changes that it should make to continue its progress. However, what the preceding case study shows is that it is possible for practitioners and academic scientists to work closely together to produce results that both groups find of value.

Collaborative research and publication

We feel that a natural product of the growing relationships between HRM academics and practitioners will be an increase in joint research and publication. At the University of Illinois Center for Human Resource Management, we have witnessed a growing ability and desire of professors and managers to jointly conduct research projects.

This handbook itself provides evidence that the once-separated camps are coming together to produce products superior to what either group could produce alone. That is, the science–practice perspective introduced in this chapter is carried through the entire book. Almost all chapters are co-authored by at least one HRM researcher and one HRM practitioner, in an effort to provide both perspectives on each topic. Also, usually, chapters contain reviews of theory, research and practice, and make an effort to integrate them.

Collaborative research and publication is still in its infancy in HRM. We expect such relationships to mature over the next decade, and thereby produce results that make truly significant contributions to both the practice and the scientific body of knowledge of managing humans in organizations.

A HRM ORGANIZING FRAMEWORK

Earlier in the chapter we defined HRM as the organizational science and practice that deals with the employment relationship, encompassing all decisions, actions, and issues concerning that relationship. Now we specifically identify the topics involved. The model of HRM in figure 1.1 identifies and relates the subjects, as well as serving as an organizing framework for the book.

All employment relationships occur within social, economic, and political environments, and most certainly are influenced by them. That is, a relationship between a particular employee and employer always occurs within a context that includes laws and regulations, technology, international events, ethics and accountability norms, and an organization's culture. In the decade of the 1990s, at least in the United States, external influences on an employee–employer relationship also include the diversifying work force as well as organizational downsizing, restructuring, reorganizing, mergers, and acquisitions. Thus, as shown by the arrows on the chart, these contextual events have important influences on the nature of the employee–employer relationship.

The employee–employer relationship itself can be divided into two distinct parts: those elements that concern employee influence and work systems, and those that deal with reward mechanisms and the flow of human resources through the organization (Beer, Spector, Lawrence, Mills, & Walton, 1984). Employee influence and work systems include such subjects as empowerment, teamwork, dispute resolution, work-force governance, and high involvement and industrial democracy. Reward and human resources flow systems often are the functional concerns of HRM departments, and include such issues as planning, development, staffing, promotion, succession, performance evaluation, and compensation.

The consequences of these employee–employer interactions result in many outcomes. From the perspective of the organization, perhaps the most important general outcome concerns organizational effectiveness. Although there are a variety of specific

Figure 1.1 Human resource management framework

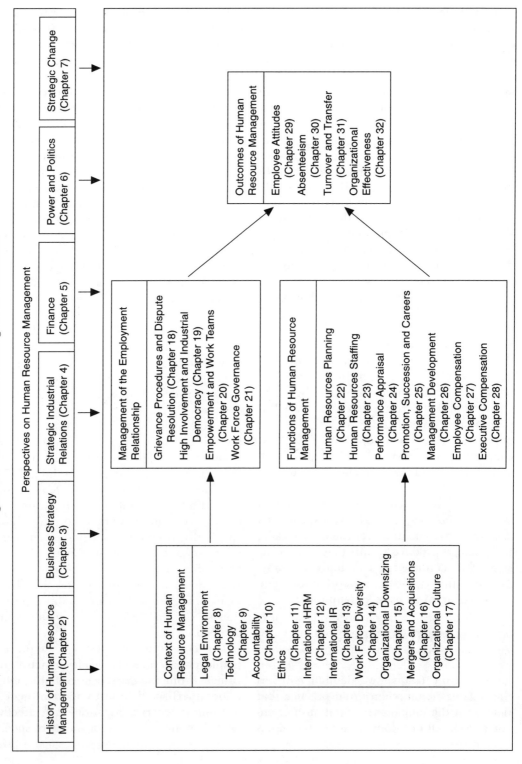

outcomes contributing to organizational effectiveness, three interesting ones that we have chosen to examine include employee attitudes, absenteeism, and turnover.

Finally, there are many general perspectives from which to view employer–employee relationships. The perspectives we have chosen to examine are shown at the top of the chart. They include history and evolution, business strategy, strategic industrial relations, finance, organizational power and politics, and strategic change.

As noted earlier, this chart serves both to identify the relationships between the topics, and as an organizing framework for the handbook. As shown on the chart, a chapter is devoted to each topic. And, the topics grouped together in each rectangle constitute a separate section of the book. This chart is reproduced at the beginning of each section, with the section under consideration being shaded, in order to reiterate the system binding the topics together.

SUMMARY AND CONCLUSIONS

The field of human resource management has undergone considerable change over time, and the relationship between the science and practice of HRM has as well. As discussed in Chapter 2, science and practice were closely connected in the early days of HRM, when researchers primarily investigated real-world HRM problems in organizations. Over time, the science and practice of HRM became disconnected as researchers turned their attention away from applied problems and focused on theory building and more esoteric issues. We feel that the science and practice of HRM need to be brought more closely together again, and we suggest vehicles like business–university research partnerships as mechanisms to help accomplish this.

When HRM researchers turned their attention away from applied problems to focus on theory development, it may have been in reaction to critics who labelled HRM a "problem driven" field, virtually without theory (Rowland & Ferris, 1982). However, today we see that this is not the limitation it was portrayed to be. In fact, respected scholars now suggest that an application or "problem driven" focus can be quite useful for the advancement of science. Hackman (1985) argued that applied research is perhaps more useful in generating advances in knowledge than basic research is in developing applications. Indeed, he suggested that doing problem-focused research is the best way to generate advances in basic theory.

The integration of science and practice has been promoted actively in the field of industrial-organizational psychology for some time (Dunnette, 1990; Murphy & Saal, 1990) and integration needs to be encouraged in other fields as well, including human resource management. We believe that a useful mechanism for accomplishing this objective is embodied in business–university partnerships. Such collaborative efforts should not only bring science and practice closer together, but also they should create a greater comfort level between researchers and practitioners. As has been suggested, we agree that an essential requirement for greater integration between science and practice is increased interactions between researchers and practitioners.

REFERENCES

Bacharach, S. (1989). Organizational theories: Some criteria for evaluation. *Academy of Management Review*, 14, 496–515.

Beer, M., Spector, B., Lawrence, P. R., Mills, D. Q., & Walton, R. E. (1984). *Managing Human Assets*. New York: Free Press.

Bender, J. M., Urban, T. F., Galang, M. C., Frink, D. D., & Ferris, G. R. (1995). Developing human resources professionals at ARCO Oil and Gas Company. In G. R. Ferris & M. R. Buckley (eds.), *Human Resources Management: Perspectives, context, functions, and outcomes*, 3rd ed. Boston: Allyn & Bacon.

Bobko, P., & Russell, C. (1991). A review of the role of taxonomies in human resources management. *Human Resource Management Review*, 1 (4), 293–316.

Boehm, V. R. (1980). Research in the "real work" – A conceptual model. *Personnel Psychology*, 33, 495–503.

Butler, J. E., Ferris, G. R., & Napier, N. K. (1991). *Strategy and Human Resources Management*. Cincinnati: Southwestern.

Carnevale, A., Gainer, L. J., Villet, J., & Holland, S. L. (1990). *Training Partnerships: Linking employers and providers*. Alexander, VA: American Society for Training and Development.

Dowling, P. J., & Schuler, R. S. (1990). *International Dimensions of Human Resource Management*. Boston: PWS-Kent.

Dubin, R. (1976). Theory building in applied areas. In M. D. Dunnette (ed.), *Handbook of Industrial and Organizational Psychology*, 1–46. Chicago: Rand McNally.

Dulebohn, J. H., Ferris, G. F., & Day, D. (1994). *Business–University Human Resources Research Partnerships*. Working paper, University of Illinois at Urbana-Champaign.

Dunnette, M. D. (1990). Blending the science and practice of industrial and organizational psychology: Where are we and where are we going? In M. D. Dunnette & L. M. Hough (eds.), *Handbook of Industrial and Organizational Psychology*, 2nd ed., vol. 1, pp. 1–28. Palo Alto, CA: Consulting Psychologists Press.

Dyer, L. (1985). Strategic human resources management and planning. In K. M. Rowland & G. R. Ferris (eds.), *Research in Personnel and Human Resources Management*, vol. 3, pp. 1–30. Greenwich, CT: JAI Press.

Dyer, L., & Holder, G. W. (1988). A strategic perspective of human resource management. In L. Dyer & G. W. Holder (eds.), *Human Resource Management: Evolving roles and responsibilities*, 1–46. Washington, DC: Bureau of National Affairs.

Dyer, L., & Schwab, D. P. (1982). Personnel/human resource management research. In T. A. Kochan, D. J. B. Mitchell, & L. Dyer (eds.), *Industrial Relations Research in the 1970s: Review and appraisal*, 187–220. Madison, WI: Industrial Relations Research Association.

Fairweather, J. S. (1988). *Entrepreneurship and Higher Education: Lessons for colleges, universities, and industry*. ASHE-ERIC Higher Education Report No. 6. Washington, D.C.: Association for the Study of Higher Education.

Ferris, G. R. (1993). *HR as a Strategic Business Partner*. Invited keynote address at the Fall Meeting of the Human Resource Advisory Board, School of Business, Indiana University, Bloomington, IN.

Ferris, G. R., & Judge, T. A. (1991). Personnel/human resource management: A political influence perspective. *Journal of Management*, 17, 447–88.

Ferris, G. R., Russ, G. S., Albanese, R., & Martocchio, J. J. (1990). Personnel/human resource management, unionization, and strategy determinants of organizational performance. *Human Resource Planning*, 13, 215–27.

Gerhart, B., & Milkovich, G. T. (1990). Organizational differences in managerial compensation and financial performance. *Academy of Management Journal*, 33, 663–91.

Hackman, J. R. (1985). Doing research that makes a difference. In Lawler et al. (eds.), *Doing Research that is Useful*, 126–48. San Francisco, CA: Jossey-Bass.

Hakel, M. D., Sorcher, M., Beer, M., & Moses, J. L. (1982). *Making it Happen: Designing research with implementation in mind*. Beverly Hills, CA: Sage.

Heneman, H. G., Jr. (1969). Toward a general conceptual system of industrial relations: How do we get there? In G. Somers (ed.), *Essays in Industrial Relations Theory*, 1–25. Ames, IA: Iowa State University Press.

Jackson, S. E., Schuler, R. S., & Rivero, J. C. (1989). Organizational characteristics as predictors of personnel practices. *Personnel Psychology*, 42, 727–86.

Jones, G. R., & Wright, P. M. (1992). An economic approach to conceptualizing the utility of human resource management practices. In G. R. Ferris & R. M. Rowland (eds.), *Research in Personnel and Human Resources Management*, vol. 10, pp. 271–99. Greenwich, CT: JAI Press.

Kaufman, B. E. (1993). *The Origins and Evolution of the Field of Industrial Relations in the United States*. Ithaca, NY: ILR Press.

Klimoski, R. (1991). Theory presentation in human resource management. *Human Resource Management Review*, 1 (4), 253–71.

Kochan, T. A., Batt, R., & Dyer, L. (1992). International human resource studies: A framework for future research. In D. Lewin, O. S. Mitchell, & P. D. Sherer (eds.), *Research Frontiers in Industrial Relations and Human Resources*, 309–37. Madison, WI: Industrial Relations Research Association.

Landy, F. J., & Vasey, J. (1984). Theory and logic in human resources research. In K. M. Rowland & G. R. Ferris (eds.), *Research in Personnel and Human Resources Management*, vol. 2, pp. 1–34. Greenwich, CT: JAI Press.

Lawler, E. E., III (1985). Challenging traditional research assumptions. In Lawler et al. (eds.), *Doing Research that is Useful*, 1–17. San Francisco, CA: Jossey-Bass.

Lawler, E. E., III, Morhrman, A. M., Jr., Mohrman, S. A., Ledford, G. E., Jr., & Cummings, T. G. (eds.) (1985). *Doing Research that is Useful for Theory and Practice*. San Francisco: Jossey-Bass.

Lazear, E. P. (1993). Compensation, productivity, and the new economics of personnel. In D. Lewin, O. S. Mitchell, & P. D. Sherer (eds.), *Research Frontiers in Industrial Relations and Human Resources*, 341–81. Madison, WI: Industrial Relations Research Association.

Lengnick-Hall, C. A., & Lengnick-Hall, M. L. (1988). Strategic human resources management: A review of the literature and a proposed typology. *Academy of Management Review*, 13, 454–70.

Mahoney, T. A., & Deckop, J. R. (1986). Evolution of concept and practice in personnel administration/human resources management (PA/HRM). *Journal of Management*, 12, 223–41.

Meltz, N. H. (1991). Dunlop's *Industrial Relations Systems* after three decades. In R. J. Adams (ed.), *Comparative industrial relations*, 10–20. London: HarperCollins Academic.

Miner, J. B. (1984). The validity and usefulness of theories in an emerging organizational science. *Academy of Management Review*, 9 (2), 296–306.

Moore, L. F., Johns, G., & Pinder, C. C. (1980). Toward middle range theory: An overview and perspective. In C. C. Pinder & L. F. Moore (eds.), *Middle Range Theory Study of Organizations*, 1–16. Boston: Martinus Nyhoff.

Morrison, C., McGuire, E. P., Clarke, M. A. (1988) *Keys*

to W.S. Competitiveness. New York: The Conference Board Inc.

Murphy, K. R., & Saal, F. E. (1990). What should we expect from scientist-practitioners? In K. R. Murphy & F. E. Sails (eds.), *Psychology in Organizations: Integrating science and practice,* 49–66. Hillsdale, NJ: Erlbaum.

Pettigrew, A. M. (1973). Toward a political theory of organizational intervention. *Human Relations,* 28, 191–208.

Powers, D. R., Powers, M. F., Betz, F., & Aslanian, C. B. (1988). *Higher Education in Partnership with Industry.* San Francisco: Jossey-Bass.

Rowland, K. M., & Ferris, G. R. (1982). Perspectives on personnel management. In K. M. Rowland & G. R. Ferris (eds.), *Personnel Management,* 2–23. Boston: Allyn & Bacon.

Russell, J. S., Terborg, J. R., & Powers, M. L. (1985). Organizational performance and organizational level training and support. *Personnel Psychology,* 38, 849–63.

Schuler, R. S. (1990). Repositioning the human resource function: Transformation or demise? *Academy of Management Executive,* 4, 49–60.

Schuler, R. S. (1993). World class HR departments: Six critical issues. *Accounting and Business Review,* 1 (1), 43–72.

Sears, L. N., Jr. (1984). Organization and human resource professionals in transition. *Human Resource Management,* 23 (4), 409–21.

Thompson, M. (1991). Union–management relations: Recent research and theory. In R. J. Adams (ed.), *Comparative Industrial Relations,* 94–108. London: HarperCollins Academic.

Tullar, W. L. (1991). Theory development in human resource management. *Human Resource Management Review,* 1 (4), 317–23.

Wallace, M. J., Jr. (1983). Methodology, research, practice, and progression in personnel and industrial relations. *Academy of Management Review,* 8, 6–13.

Whetten, D. A. (1989). What constitutes a theoretical contribution? *Academy of Management Review,* 14 (4), 490–6.

Wright, P. M., & McMahon, G. C. (1992). Theoretical perspectives for strategic human resource management. *Journal of Management,* 18 (2), 295–320.

Part I

Perspectives on Human Resource Management

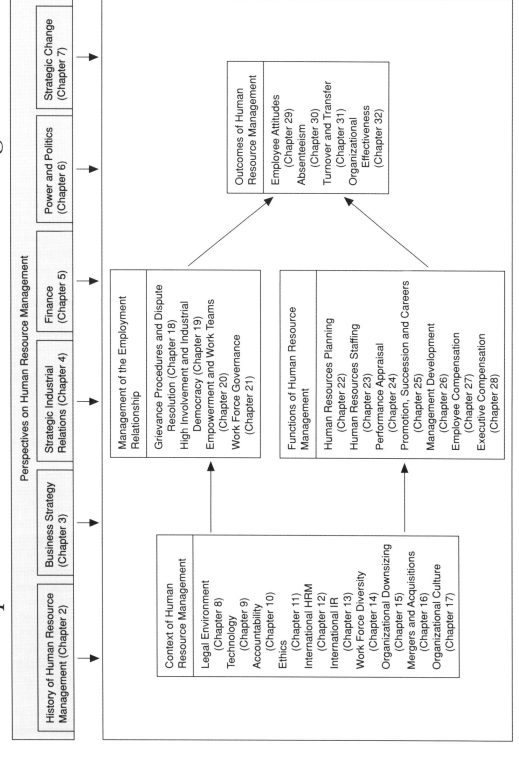

Perspectives on Human Resource Management

| History of Human Resource Management (Chapter 2) | Business Strategy (Chapter 3) | Strategic Industrial Relations (Chapter 4) | Finance (Chapter 5) | Power and Politics (Chapter 6) | Strategic Change (Chapter 7) |

Context of Human Resource Management

Legal Environment (Chapter 8)
Technology (Chapter 9)
Accountability (Chapter 10)
Ethics (Chapter 11)
International HRM (Chapter 12)
International IR (Chapter 13)
Work Force Diversity (Chapter 14)
Organizational Downsizing (Chapter 15)
Mergers and Acquisitions (Chapter 16)
Organizational Culture (Chapter 17)

Management of the Employment Relationship

Grievance Procedures and Dispute Resolution (Chapter 18)
High Involvement and Industrial Democracy (Chapter 19)
Empowerment and Work Teams (Chapter 20)
Work Force Governance (Chapter 21)

Functions of Human Resource Management

Human Resources Planning (Chapter 22)
Human Resources Staffing (Chapter 23)
Performance Appraisal (Chapter 24)
Promotion, Succession and Careers (Chapter 25)
Management Development (Chapter 26)
Employee Compensation (Chapter 27)
Executive Compensation (Chapter 28)

Outcomes of Human Resource Management

Employee Attitudes (Chapter 29)
Absenteeism (Chapter 30)
Turnover and Transfer (Chapter 31)
Organizational Effectiveness (Chapter 32)

Introduction: Perspectives on Human Resource Management

This section examines important aspects of HRM's role in high-performance organizations, which reflect considerably different concerns than have been present in earlier times. It is essential that HR and IR strategy be not only congruent with but strongly supportive of the general business strategy. Economic success in a free-market economy is measured by financial outcomes, so it is crucial that HR considers financial indicators in planning and implementing its activities. Optimal utilization of people in organizations must account for the influences of power and politics, and must recognize that organizational changes affect and are affected by its personnel.

Dulebohn, Ferris, and Stodd describe the evolution of the science and practice of human resource management from preindustrial times through the present. They describe how HRM science and practice were intertwined when the field first emerged, for a time became quite independent of each other, and today again are becoming more integrated.

Plevel, Lane, Schuler, and Nellis relate HRM activities to business strategy. They illustrate the relationship using the experience of AT&T's Global Business Communications Systems. They discuss the role of HR management in aligning people with the needs of the business, linking HR management with business strategy, and positioning the HR organization to better facilitate the preceding two activities.

Roomkin and Rosen examine strategic industrial relations, suggesting a framework for analysis that shows the interrelationship of business strategy and IR issues. Using research and case studies from several industries, they illustrate the beneficial impact on performance of the alignment of business strategy and IR policies.

Reflecting HR's growing role in business operations, Berra and Whitford assert that the successful HR manager must be fluent in the language of the business – finance. They show that understanding financial aspects of the business is important for building the effectiveness of HR, thereby enhancing its ability to add significant value to the enterprise.

Power and politics play important roles in organizational management and therefore influence the environment within which HR functions, as discussed by Ferris, Galang, Thornton, and Wayne. They point out that failure to consider the influence of power and politics can cause difficulties in carrying out HR policies, and thereby hinder HR effectiveness.

Beer, Eisenstat, and Biggadike examine HR's role in planning and implementing organizational change. Using Becton-Dickinson as an example, the authors describe its process for realigning HRM policies and practices with changes in the competitive marketplace. They argue that improving organizational alignment and adaptability is becoming the central problem for human resources.

☐ Chapter 2 ☐

The History and Evolution of Human Resource Management

James H. Dulebohn, Gerald R. Ferris, and James T. Stodd

INTRODUCTION

The field of human resource management (HRM) has emerged, developed, and evolved during the past century to represent one of the more interesting and important areas of organizational science and practice. In the first chapter, HRM was defined as the branch of organizational science that deals with the employment relationship, along with all the decisions, actions, and issues involved in that relationship. Because of its focus on the entire employment relationship, the field of HRM has not developed in isolation, but rather in the context of industrial change and economic development. As such, HRM represents a response to the dramatic and continued change that industrialization has had on society and the world of work (Miller & Coghill, 1964).

In this chapter, we review the history and evolution of the practice and science of HRM. In the first section, we describe the development of the practice of HRM as a series of eleven stages, beginning prior to the Industrial Revolution and continuing up to the present. The purpose is to provide the reader

with an understanding of the settings in which HRM practices developed, the approaches to management that contributed to HRM, and the changing roles the HRM function has occupied. In the second section, we describe the development of the science of HRM. This examination reveals that whereas the science and practice of HRM were more closely related when the field first emerged, over the years these two areas became increasingly separated and distant.

DEVELOPMENT OF THE PRACTICE OF HRM

Stage 1: Preindustrial era

The first stage is the preindustrial era, beginning around 1400 and continuing until the late 1700s. While the preindustrial period is characterized by an absence of any formal HRM function within organizations, several dramatic changes occurred during this first stage that represent seeds from which modern HRM later grew (Ling, 1965). First, there was a cessation of feudalism, the release of the laborer from the traditional serfdom relationship that bound workers to the land, and the beginning of the free employment relationship on which modern labor markets are based (Moore, 1951). Second, there was a shift from subsistence agriculture to a commercial mixed economy, the rise of the urban economy, a diffusion of economic control, and the distribution of wealth and income (Tuma, 1971). Third, there was a dramatic growth of towns and villages along with a middle class that included skilled craftsmen and merchants, who were the forerunners of entrepreneurs or factory owners (Watson, 1977).

Fourth, there was the emergence of labor specialization as part of the employment relationship. As a result of market and product expansion, craftsmen increasingly came under the service of merchants who served as middlemen. This relationship has been referred to as the domestic or putting-out system (Weber, 1927). It began when merchants began supplying craftsmen with production materials and agreed to take the finished products, and progressed to the point where the merchant controlled the production process. While the worker's dwelling remained the place of production, the putting-out system reduced the workman's productive labor to a permanent debt, and employee-type, relationship (Moore, 1951).

Stage 2: The Industrial Revolution and the factory system

The Industrial Revolution began in Great Britain in the late eighteenth century and spread to America in the early nineteenth century. Industrialization completely changed the way people earned their living. It was made possible by the replacement of human skill and effort with the rapid, exact, and indefatigable work of machines, and the replacement of human strength with inanimate sources of power.

One of the primary innovations of the Industrial Revolution was the development of the factory system. The factory was central to the process of nineteenth-century industriali-

zation and to the development of the practice of HRM. Factories were places of production based on free or wage labor and fixed capital (Weber, 1927). In general, the factory greatly expanded production and created a new class of workers and managers (Chandler, 1972). In addition, the factory system eventually led to the shift from an agriculturally based society to an industrial and manufacturing based society.

The factory resulted in dramatic changes in the organization of American industry. First, the factory system displaced and gradually replaced the self-employment household and handicraft (Chenery, 1922). Second, the factory created a class of permanent wage earners (Wera, 1921). The factory brought together many workers, who no longer could own the tools of production and because of social changes had no other way to gain a livelihood (Ware, 1924; Braverman, 1974). Third, the factory resulted in a rationalization of work and a division of labor (Weber, 1927; Hays, 1957). Production tasks were subdivided and routinized; workers became mere tenders of machines who performed specialized, repetitive, and discrete tasks that constituted only a portion of the production process.

A fourth change brought about by the factory system was the necessity of managing or supervising large numbers of workers. In the early American factories, prior to the Civil War, factory owners were usually the managers and HRM practices tended to be personal and paternalistic (Milton, 1970). As time progressed and factories began to grow in size, this highly personalized form of management was eclipsed by a laissez-faire approach to HRM that was a reflection of the ethos of the nineteenth century (Wells, 1923; Milton, 1970).

Under the laissez-faire form of management that came to dominate the factory system following the Civil War, personnel practices were autocratic, based upon a commodity concept of labor, and reflected little concern for the working conditions, safety, or job security of workers (Wera, 1921; Chenery, 1922; Weisberger, 1969). Seen as merely another factor in production, labor was purchased at terms designed to maximize the employer's profits. Consequently, there was an overall neglect of the human factor; the focus was upon materials, markets, and production (Nelson, 1975).

The entrepreneur or factory owner typically delegated management responsibility to the foreman or first-line supervisor. The foreman was responsible for successfully running the entire factory (Taylor, 1911). While the foreman's responsibilities varied depending on the type of manufacturing process, he usually exercised despotic control over the factory workers (Jacoby, 1985). In addition, the foreman was responsible for all human resource management functions: the hiring, placement, training, wage setting, grievance handling, and dismissing of workers (Nelson, 1975; Patten, 1968).

The control of workers by the foreman usually took the form of the drive system of management that was characterized by the use of force and fear (Slichter, 1919). Baron, Jennings, and Dobbin (1988, 498) described this form of early factory management as a reliance on "simple control within an industry," and an absence of rationalized employment relations (i.e., personnel practices) and production techniques (e.g., those introduced later under scientific management). This form of management characterized much of American industry up through the end of the nineteenth century, and was later viewed as unplanned, haphazard, and inefficient (Thompson, 1914).

Stage 3: The emergence of the modern corporation and managerial capitalism

The period following the Civil War and extending to the turn of the century was a period of dramatic industrial growth and organizational restructuring that set the stage for the emergence of modern HRM practice. This period witnessed a fundamental transformation of employment from being primarily agricultural to manufacturing and industry itself from being primarily small-scale, employing craftsmen, to being large-scale, employing semiskilled or unskilled operators and assemblers (Kaufman, 1993). During this time, the modern business enterprise along with managerial capitalism emerged (Chandler, 1990). The period witnessed a growth in the corporate form of organization, organizational size, the development of subdivision and departmentalization of organizational functions, the separation of the operation from the ownership of firms, and the employment of teams of salaried managers (Moore, 1951; Chandler, 1977).

Overall, an unprecedented growth of industry and the "spread of giantism," created a new order in the organization of business enterprise during this period (Scheiber, Vatter, & Faulkner, 1976, 219). The rise of the corporation was one of the revealing signs of the trend toward bigness (Weisberger, 1969; Cochran, 1944). In 1865, the typical American business was owned by an individual entrepreneur, or partnership, and had a simple organizational structure. By 1890, the dominant form of business enterprise, measured in terms of economic power and employment, was the multiunit business enterprise or giant corporation (Chandler, 1990). By 1900, corporations employed nearly 70 percent of all production workers outside of agriculture (Scheiber et al., 1976).

In spite of organizational growth and technological changes during the second half of the nineteenth century, there was not a commensurate improvement in organizational or human resource management. The focus of attention in the factory or shop was primarily given to machine processes and improvements in the size and technology of production, and not to the improvement of shop or factory management techniques (Nelson, 1980) or human methods of work

(Viteles, 1932). Most organizations continued to cling to the traditional laissez-faire form of factory management and to view labor as a commodity.

As a result, the decentralized form of factory management and the traditional delegation of responsibilities persisted. The foreman remained in control as the factory employment and production manager and "impersonality and harshness" in labor policies continued (Lescohier, 1935, 296). This continuance of traditional factory management practices contributed to low productivity and wages, extremely high rates of turnover, inefficient operations, and an increase in labor and management conflict (Slichter, 1919; Lescohier, 1935).

Concurrent with the growth and change in industry, the last several decades of the nineteenth century were characterized by economic turmoil, social upheaval, chronic unemployment, and labor unrest. First, the period experienced repeated financial panics and economic depressions. Second, the tremendous advances in industrial mechanization resulted in a dilution of workers' skills, a growth in demand for unskilled labor, and a fall in wages (Berstein, 1960). Third, there was an overabundance of workers as a result of millions of immigrants entering America from abroad and migration from rural areas to the cities, resulting in a persistent pool of unemployed workers and a continued downward spiral of market price and wages (Kaufman, 1993; Lescohier, 1935). Fourth, there was an unprecedented wave of strikes and boycotts throughout the nation, many which were spontaneous outbreaks by masses of unorganized and unskilled workers (Berstein, 1960; Perlman & Taft, 1935).

The convergence of these factors led to an increase in labor–management conflict and a dramatic increase in union membership. The organizing and bargaining efforts by the labor movement were met with a persistent adamancy by employers to refuse to recognize or negotiate with unions, and a willingness by the government to side with employers (Fossum, 1979). In spite of this, the development of HRM during the twentieth century would include a primary industrial relations (IR) component which management would use to operate in the collective bargaining framework established by the federal government through legislation.

Stage 4: Scientific management, welfare work, and industrial psychology

Scientific management and welfare work represent two separate and concurrent movements that began in the nineteenth century and, along with contributions from industrial psychology, merged around the time of World War I (WWI) to form the field of HRM (Lescohier, 1935; Eilbirt, 1959). SM and welfare work were both responses by management to worker-related problems in the factory. SM represented an effort to deal with labor and management inefficiencies primarily through the reorganization of production methods and the rationalization of work (Baron et al., 1988; Jacoby, 1985). Welfare work represented efforts to deal with labor problems by improving worker conditions (Boettiger, 1923). Industrial psychology represented the application of psychological principles towards increasing the efficiency and adjustment of the individual worker (Munsterberg, 1913).

Scientific management (SM)
During the last quarter of the nineteenth century, professional mechanical engineers emerged as important providers of technical assistance for machine production (Nadworny, 1955). Out of their ranks came a number of engineers who, under the banner of "efficiency," introduced dramatic changes that rationalized factory production and industrial management systems. These engineers viewed the traditional factory system with its decentralized and autocratic management and unsystematized methods of work as outdated,

inefficient, and incompatible with the larger more modern plants and machinery (Viteles, 1932; Nelson, 1980). Along with rationalizing production processes and redesigning complex manufacturing flows, they introduced various personnel practices to rationalize employment procedures (Baron et al., 1988). Foremost among these engineers was Frederick W. Taylor, who became the renowned father of scientific management.

Taylor began his formulation of SM while employed as an engineer at Midvale Steel Works in Philadelphia from 1878 to 1890. Taylor (1947) was concerned with worker inefficiency, "soldiering on the job," and the need for managers to gain the cooperative effort of their employees. He believed that production work needed to be systematically analyzed, studied, and improved by using the same scientific approach engineers use to design machines. With meticulous determination, Taylor began studying the elements of jobs (tasks), eliminating unnecessary motions, and timing the tasks, in an effort to discover the "one best way" and the fastest time a worker could perform a particular task (Gilbreth, 1912, 50). Time and motion study became the heart of SM and represented a way of accurately determining the amount of work a man could do.

Taylor (1947) declared that SM constituted a complete change in the mental attitude of workers and managers, not simply a set of efficiency devices, and he summarized SM as: (1) science, not the rule of thumb, (2) harmony, not discord, (3) cooperation, not individualism, and (4) maximum output, in place of restricted output. Taylor (1911, 21) stated that "what the workmen want from their employers beyond anything else is high wages, and what employers want from their workmen is a low labor cost of manufacture." He viewed workers and managers as having similar interests and mutually benefiting from increased production, and contended that the application of SM represented a partial solution of

the labor problem because it would increase production at lower cost to employers and would result in higher wages for the worker, since each worker would be compensated according to their output (Taylor, 1895; Thompson, 1914).

Time and motion study was the accurate, scientific method with which the natural laws of work could be determined (Nadworny, 1955). Taylor asserted that the exact information generated provided a reliable basis for selecting, training, evaluating, and compensating workers. The increased production, profits, and higher employee wages would result in organizational harmony. According to Taylor, SM produced the highest form of industrial democracy that ever existed since it substituted management based on exact knowledge for guesswork (Hoxie, 1915).

SM represented a new attitude toward management and Taylor's work contributed greatly to the formalization and specialization of management (Person, 1929). Taylor (1947, 7) argued that management actually "is a true science, resting upon clearly defined laws, rules, and principles as a foundation." SM introduced a new system for managing industrial enterprises and the foundational "concepts that underlie the actual management of worker and work in American industry" (Drucker, 1977, 228).

As part of SM, Taylor (1911) proposed functional management. Functional management delegated the traditional foreman's varied management responsibilities, including those related to HRM, to eight separate employees who were specialists at their functions (Gilbreth, 1912). The purpose of functional management was to enable proper management of the employee by the separation of the planning of work from its execution, and the substitution of individual judgment with rules and principles (Thompson, 1914; Person, 1929).

SM contributed to the practice of HRM in the following ways. First, Taylor's proposal for functional management called attention to the need for a separate human resource function in organizations. Second, Taylor asserted the importance and demonstrated the feasibility of job analysis as a basis for employee selection, training, job evaluation, job change, and compensation. Third, Taylor demonstrated that work and jobs can be systematically studied, analyzed, redesigned, or improved upon (Drucker, 1977). Fourth, Taylor stressed the importance of proper selection procedures and training methods. Fifth, Taylor advanced the notion of variable pay, rewarding of workers on the basis of their productivity, and the importance of using pay as a management tool. Sixth, Taylor highlighted the need for workers to be won over and led by management.

In spite of its contributions, SM had several deficiencies. Overall, SM had an excessive engineering focus on the job, to the neglect of the worker. It viewed the worker as a machine, who could adapt to the job, and saw no need to incorporate human factors in its system (Hoxie, 1915; Braverman, 1974). In addition, SM considered the worker an "economic man," who is exclusively motivated to maximize his economic gain, and therefore neglected basic social and psychological drives of employees (Beach, 1965). Further, SM represented a form of industrial autocracy and control by management over the workers: Management did all the planning of work and workers were only given voice to say yes to instructions (Yoder, 1938).

Welfare work

Some efforts were made at different times during the nineteenth and early twentieth centuries to improve both the social and working conditions of factory workers. One which became widespread during the emergence of SM was the welfare work movement (Miller & Coghill, 1964). Welfare work, like SM, was an attempt at a more systematic approach to labor problems (Nelson &

Campbell, 1972). Characterized as a unilateral endeavor by management, the popularity of welfare work grew from 1900 until WWI, at which time it was abandoned as an independent employment practice and placed under the responsibilities of personnel management (Eilbirt, 1959; Kaufman, 1993).

Welfare work was defined as representing "anything for the comfort and improvement, intellectual or social, of the employees, over and above wages paid, which is not a necessity of the industry nor required by law" (U.S. Bureau, 1919, 8). Welfare work provisions took the form of housing, schools, libraries, medical care, recreational facilities, and work-related improvements. The primary purposes of welfare work included the averting of industrial conflict and unionization, the promotion of good management and worker relations, and efforts to increase worker productivity and reduce turnover (Boettiger, 1923).

Beginning around 1900, some industries hired staff called welfare or social secretaries to administer welfare programs. The welfare secretary functioned as an intermediary between the firm and its employees and represented a rudimentary forerunner of the modern personnel administrator (Eilbirt, 1959). Often welfare secretaries' responsibilities were divided among various employment-related tasks. Based on a 1916 national field study, the U.S. Bureau of Labor Statistics (1919, 123) noted: "Very often the [welfare] secretary's sole duties are supervising the various welfare activities; in other cases the employment and welfare departments are merged into one, part of the time of the manager given to each."

Industrial psychology
Along with SM and welfare work, industrial psychology contributed to the field of HRM. Whereas SM focused on the job, industrial psychology focused on the worker and individual differences. The interest of industrial

psychology was to increase human efficiency by focusing on the maximum well-being of the worker and decreasing the physiological and psychological costs of work (Viteles, 1932; Milton, 1970).

Industrial psychology began in 1913 when Hugo Munsterberg published *Psychology and Industrial Efficiency* (Blum, 1949). Munsterberg (1913) argued for the need to establish an applied field of psychology as a counterpart to the pure science form. Munsterberg (1913) called attention to the contributions that psychology as a field of study could provide in the areas of employment testing, selection, training, and worker adjustment, efficiency, and motivation.

Others also recognized the applicability of psychology to industry. Stanley Hall, the first president of the American Psychological Association, saw the need for a journal that would focus on the applications of psychology to industry and started the *Journal of Applied Psychology* in 1917. Lillian Gilbreth, a contemporary psychologist, sought to integrate psychology with scientific management by incorporating individuality in the selection, study, and motivation of employees (Milton, 1970).

The publication of Munsterberg's book in 1913 served as a stimulus and a model for the development of industrial psychology in the United States and Europe (Viteles, 1932). Shortly after the book was published, World War I (WWI) began. While industrial psychologists had begun to develop tests prior to WWI to measure individual differences to facilitate employee selection and placement, the application of psychology to industrial problems gained acceptance as a result of the "successful use of psychology in the selection and classification of army personnel by almost every nation engaged in the war" (Viteles, 1932, 43).

After the United States became involved in the war, psychological tests were developed and administered to nearly two million American servicemen (Viteles, 1932). The military's utilization of classification tests demonstrated the usefulness of principles of industrial psychology and resulted in its acceptance, growth, and application by HRM practitioners in organizations during and following the war. Since that time, the most widely used application of industrial psychology by HRM practitioners has continued to be in the area of testing for employment, job placement, promotion, and training (Beach, 1965).

Stage 5: World War I and the emergence of the HRM profession

World War I provided conditions that resulted in the widespread recognition by American business of the need for HRM and the emergence of the field as a profession. The war brought attention to the need for "scientific personnel administration" and centralizing, under a personnel director, activities promoting the welfare and efficiency of workers (Viteles, 1932, 23). At the close of the war, the personnel or employment management department had emerged as a primary function, taking its place alongside the financial, production, and sales departments in many large as well as small organizations.

While American involvement lasted only two years, the effect of the war period – between 1915 to 1920 – on HRM was dramatic. First, during this time there was a widespread labor shortage, especially for skilled workers, caused by restrictions on immigration and workers being drawn into the war industries, the military, and government services. Labor turnover, which had been historically high, increased dramatically as a result of the increase in job opportunities for workers (Slichter, 1919). As a result, U.S. industry had to face its chronic and widespread labor turnover problem that had, since the turn of the century, been absorbed by the oversupply of workers. Second, and related, the labor shortage, accompanied by a rapid rise in wages and an increased demand for wartime production, created a need for employers to more efficiently utilize the workers that they were able to secure (Lescohier, 1935).

Third, the government established the War Industries Board that created centralized employment departments in government-run industries and set up training courses at a number of technical schools and universities to train employment managers (Bloomfield, 1919). The Board also encouraged companies in war-related industries to recognize unions, enter into collective bargaining agreements, and makes changes in the employment relationship in order to minimize strikes and production disruptions (Kaufman, 1993).

Businesses responded to the labor shortage, turnover, and labor relations problems by widely embracing PM practices. This was evident in that a substantial number of industrial firms established personnel departments between 1915 and 1920 (Jacoby, 1985). The effect of the war on the emergence of the HRM profession was summarized by *The New Republic* (1918, 102) as follows:

> *It has taken the exigencies of war to bring home to employers the imperative need for expert administration of their labor problems. The new war industries require men – skilled men in excess of the available supply. Today this expertness is being developed by high specialization by setting up a fourth major department in the factory – a personnel or employment management department to supplement the financial, production, and sales departments.*

Firms adopted functional management, which removed the hiring and firing functions from the foreman and placed them in the hands of employment departments (Eilbirt, 1959). In addition to centralizing hiring, there was an integration and expansion of former "unsystematized" HRM activities, such as welfare work, job standardization, and time study, "under the supervision of one executive who came to be known as the 'personnel manager'" (Lescohier, 1935, 325). The converging contributions of SM, welfare work,

and industrial psychology to early HRM practice were reflected in an early description of the function of PM: "to direct and coordinate human relations with a view of getting the maximum production with the minimum of effort and friction and with the proper regard for the genuine well being of the worker" (Tead & Metcalf, 1920, 2).

Although the HRM profession was recognized during the war period, it had begun to emerge prior to that time. The date marked as the beginning of the profession is 1911, when the Boston Employment Managers' Association (EMA) began (Bloomfield, 1915). The impetus came from employment managers who wanted to compare experiences and establish standards for practice (Bloomfield, 1923). Following Boston's example, EMAs were formed in other big cities throughout America.

In 1917, the National Association of Employment Managers was formed from a federation of ten city EMAs (Lescohier, 1935). The National Employment Managers' Association's second annual convention in Rochester, New York, in 1918 was attended by 800 personnel executives, received national attention, and was described as "the birth of a new profession" (National Association of Employment Managers, 1919). At the conference held two years later in 1920, approximately 3,000 personnel executives attended, indicating the phenomenal growth of the new field (Jacoby, 1985).

Although the profession was referred to by different names, the early label commonly used was "employment management," as indicated by the first professional association label. The particular focus of the profession was on the employment relation and "on the relationship between employers and workers and the labor problems that grow out of this relationship" (Kaufman, 1993, 11; Eilbirt, 1959). Finally, the Employment Management Association became the Industrial Relations Association of America in 1920, the National Personnel Association in 1922, and was renamed the American Management Association in 1923 (Kaufman, 1993).

Since its beginning as a profession in the early part of this century, different yet generally equivalent terms have been used to refer to personnel and human resource management. While the initial label was employment management, in the first university textbook on personnel administration the authors wrote that "personnel administration" is used throughout this book synonymously with "employment administration," "personnel management," "administration of human relations," and "administration of industrial relations" (Tead & Medcaff, 1920, 2). Following World War I and continuing up until the past decade, personnel administration or personnel management (PM) were used as the primary labels for the practice of HRM.

Regardless of the labels used, the initial and continuing emphasis of the field has been primarily on the management side of the employment relationship (Kaufman, 1993). The use of different terms to describe the field has been descriptive of varying activities and indicative of the changing scope of the field. The recent and widespread adoption of the term "human resource management" by both academia and business organizations, in place of personnel management, is reflective of an increased realization of the importance of the human element in organizations, and descriptive of the enlarged and increasingly significant role occupied by HRM professionals.

Stage 6: The human relations movement

An early focus of the HRM profession was labelled "human relations." While the beginning of the human relations movement is associated with the work of Harvard researchers Elton Mayo and Fritz Roethlisberger in the 1930s, a practitioner focus on human relations, characterized as "the incorporation of the human factor into SM," began during the 1920s (Kaufman, 1993, 24). This early human relations effort reflected the symbiotic combination of SM, welfare work, and elements of industrial psychology in the personnel profession. The emphasis was on increasing productivity through discovering the needs of workers, the proper way of "handling" or managing people, and increasing productivity (Bloomfield, 1923). Employment managers in general believed that conflict was not inherent in labor relations, but was an indication of poor management, and could be corrected by proper worker management techniques (Lodge, 1913; Jones, 1919; Lewisohn, 1926).

The human relations movement began as a result of a series of studies conducted at the Hawthorne facility of Western Electric in Chicago between 1924 and 1933. The purpose of the Hawthorne experiments was to ascertain the effects of illumination on workers and their output. The studies resulted in the recognition of the social function of work, the social interaction of workers, and the existence of informal organizational social systems (Roethlisberger & Dickson, 1939).

As a result of the Hawthorne experiments and the work of Mayo and Roethlisberger, the human relations movement began around 1945 and continued until the early 1960s when it was absorbed into the new discipline of organizational behavior (Kaufman, 1993). The movement viewed the worker as the most important element in business and as a complex personality that interacted in a group situation that was hard to understand (Davis, 1957). Workers were henceforth seen as having social needs and the workplace was seen as consisting of not only formal but also informal social groups, governed by group norms and attitudes, that influenced worker behaviors. Under human relations, the manager became responsible for integrating employees into the work situation in a way that would motivate them to work together cooperatively and productively, and for assisting employees to experience economic, psychological, and social satisfaction (Davis, 1957).

An assimilation of the human relations approach by HRM complemented the influences of SM, welfare work, and industrial psychology. SM focused on the requirements of the job and economic rewards as motivational elements, whereas human relations revealed the importance and frequent primacy of non-economic and social rewards as incentives (Grusky & Miller, 1981). In addition, whereas welfare work and industrial psychology provided HRM with the realization that workers have physical and psychological needs, human relations contributed the understanding that workers have social needs. Finally, human relations broadened the vision of HRM beyond the individual and job to include the work group and formal and informal social structures.

Stage 7: The "golden age" of industrial relations and the personnel management maintenance function, 1935–1970

While the formal HRM function had been enthusiastically received and established throughout American industries during and after WWI, because of economic conditions during the Great Depression, the function languished in importance for a period of time (Watson, 1977). This setback was temporary. Following the depression there was an increased need for the practice of HRM as a result of a growth in unions, federal legislation that encouraged unionization and collective bargaining, and challenges resulting from the nation's involvement in World War II. Although prior to the depression the primary attention of HRM had been directed towards PM activities, at this time there was a shift in emphasis towards the IR function of HRM.

"Golden age" of industrial relations
During the period from 1945 up to the 1970s, the primary focus of the employment relationship was on IR, and this HRM function rose in prominence. The passage of the Norris–LaGuardia Act (1932), the National

Industrial Recovery Act (1933), and the Wagner Act (1935), encouraged unionization. This New Deal legislation was rooted in the belief that there was an unequal and adversarial employment relationship that resulted in the arbitrary treatment of workers and employers' opposition to workers' attempts to organize. The Wagner Act defined the New Deal industrial relations system and "declared that the goal of public policy was to encourage the practice of collective bargaining, both to eliminate labor's inequality of bargaining power and to introduce democratic rights of independent representation and due process into industry" (Kaufman, 1993, 61). The industrial relations policies that resulted from the legislation were a product of the times, were "rooted in the mass production/natural resource economy that made the United States the world's leading industrial nation," and were designed to sustain the system and make it more equitable (Marshall, 1992, 31).

The pro-union legislation was followed by World War II, which created an extraordinary demand for labor, resulted in unprecedented union prestige, and fueled a phenomenal growth in union membership. Between 1941 and 1944, union membership grew from 8,614,000 to 12,538,900 (Berstein, 1960) and included two out of three production workers. Following WWII, unions continued to organize workers until, by the late 1950s, union membership reached its peak, at which time almost one-third of the private labor force belonged to unions (Fossum, 1979).

The IR side of HRM experienced its "golden age" between 1948 and 1958 (Kaufman, 1993). This golden age was made possible by the period of stable economic growth and unparalleled prosperity that America enjoyed following World War II and continuing up to 1970. The U.S. economy had emerged from the war with the only intact industrial infrastructure and consequently enjoyed a period of unchallenged economic hegemony during the time that other industrialized economies were rebuilt. The postwar boom, the dominance of the manufacturing sector, and the moderate competition faced by U.S. firms up until around 1970 were factors that contributed to economic stability and the continued legitimacy of New Deal industrial relations systems. The general focus of HRM was on IR because the primary need of many organizations was to operate in the collective bargaining framework of labor relations and to comply with the New Deal legislative and collective bargaining rules that had been established to govern employment policy (Kochan & Cappelli, 1984).

The personnel management (PM) maintenance function

While many firms had deprecated the personnel department during the depression because of economic necessity, government involvement in the economy during the war (e.g., federal labor allocation and wage controls) created a need for personnel departments in small and medium as well as large companies (Baron, Dobbin, & Jennings, 1986; Jacoby, 1985). According to Jacoby (1985, 260), during the war, "as practical knowledge of personnel management became a more valuable commodity, the emphasis shifted: The question was no longer whether to have a personnel department but how to operate that department." Therefore, while personnel departments existed, the PM side of HRM during the postwar period up until the 1970s generally operated as a low-profile administrative and maintenance function (Burack & Smith, 1982).

Following WWII, up to the 1970s, the PM side of HRM was reflective of business operations and was generally characterized as a "functional collection of managerial activities and practices directed at people as employees" (Mahoney & Deckop, 1986, 234). Separate management activities that were employee-oriented (e.g., recruiting, staffing, job evaluation) were clustered under PM. Although each activity had a definite function,

there was little cohesion between the activities due to the absence of an integrative purpose and objective.

Stage 8: Quality of worklife era

Beginning around the mid-1960s and continuing up through the decade of the 1970s, there was a rise in the view of the importance of human resources and a view of them as assets, not liabilities. However, this period of time, which we refer to as the Quality of Worklife era, distinguished itself as a series of efforts directed at satisfying the interests of both employees and organizations through the formulation and implementation of policies and practices which maximized organization performance and, at the same time, employee well-being. What this meant for the human resource management function was the development of programs in such areas as job design and enrichment, which, along with career planning and development, were intended to improve the psychological quality of worklife for employees, and presumably make them more committed to and satisfied with the organization. Other efforts designed to improve the quality of worklife were various forms of employee involvement or participation.

The efforts of this era were driven not only by a realization that investments in human resources were sound and should show a considerable return, but also by the changing nature of the work force. The famous General Motors Lordstown strike in 1970 demonstrated that when you have a highly educated work force being forced to work on very boring and monotonous jobs, dysfunctional behaviors will result which most certainly will be counterproductive for the organization's ability to remain effective. The work force in the 1970s not only was becoming more highly educated, but also they reflected considerably different attitudes, beliefs, and values about the role of work and organizations in their lives.

Part of these changing attitudes was reflected in increased interest in having more input and involvement in workplace practices and decisions. We began to see evidence of such programs in many different forms, but one particularly notable focus was on the nature of labor–management cooperation. For example, the ground-breaking work by Irving Bluestone and others at General Motors and the United Auto Workers in 1972 demonstrated ways that management and the union could work together collaboratively to make quality of worklife improvements. While such efforts did not proceed without difficulty, they were nonetheless monumental and of historical significance in the evolution of the field.

In many respects, the Quality of Worklife era was actively promoted and facilitated by a series of legislation passed between the mid-1960s and the mid-1970s. Fair employment practices were significantly advanced by the passage of the Civil Rights Act of 1964, with particular reference to Title VII which made it illegal to discriminate in employment decisions based on race, color, religion, sex, or national origin. The Occupational Safety and Health Act of 1970 promoted more safe and healthy workplaces, and the Employee Retirement Income Security Act of 1974 provided guidelines and regulations concerning pensions and benefits. While other pieces of legislation were passed during this era, these three Acts collectively exercised a substantial influence on both the psychological and physical quality of worklife in organizations. Furthermore, this legislation enhanced the importance and influence of the human resource management function, who were the internal experts on these matters, and thus controlled critical relationships, with federal regulatory agencies (i.e., EEOC, OSHA, ERISA) given the responsibility of monitoring organizational practices.

Stage 9: The emergence of the contemporary HRM function

Since the 1970s, the PM side of the HRM function has experienced an evolution from being a maintenance function, secondary to the IR function, to representing one of critical importance to the effectiveness of the organization. A number of environmental factors, leading to economic and structural upheaval, have resulted in this dramatic shift. Therefore, in spite of the prominence of the IR side of HRM during the initial decades of the postwar period, during that time changes began to occur that eventually resulted in a decline in the IR function and in the emergence and transformation of the PM function.

Environmental changes started to occur towards the end of the 1950s and have continued to the present which have resulted in the transformation of HRM. First, beginning in 1956, private sector unionism started to fall as a percentage of the labor force from 33 percent to around 12 percent in 1992 (Kochan, McKersie, & Cappelli, 1984; McDonald, 1992). Second, since WWII, the shift from manufacturing employment to service sector employment has continued. For instance, between 1948 and 1985, manufacturing experienced a relative decrease in employment of 9 percent while the non-government service sector, which is characteristically nonunionized, experienced an increase of 18 percent (Dulebohn, 1991). Third, since the 1960s, there has been a dramatic expansion of government regulation of the terms and conditions of employment, requirements that business have had to comply with and implement into their human resources activities (Janger, 1977).

Fourth, a number of economic changes have occurred since the late 1970s that have resulted in an erosion of both the economic hegemony and the insulated and prosperous situation that America had enjoyed during the first several decades following WWII.

These changes include a growth in international competition, domestic competition, deregulation, market pressures, technological change, and the globalization of economic activity (Kochan, Katz, & McKersie, 1986). The convergence of these factors has caused the New Deal industrial relations system to become anachronistic, and has required that "companies and countries that wish to be high-income, world-class players" adopt very different HRM policies (Marshall, 1992, 31).

In response to these challenges, companies have had to make changes that have directly affected the HRM function. First, there has been a trend by management to make strategic choices that have represented aggressive union-avoidance policies and have resulted in a decrease in union representation of their workers (Kochan et al., 1984). Second, much more reliance has been placed on the HRM "employee-relations" function and dealing with employees directly as individuals rather than on management–union relations and dealing with employees indirectly and collectively. Third, the HRM function has been called upon to foster a sense of mutuality and trust in the relations between managers and workers, to develop employees as assets with the view of increasing competitiveness, and to assist the organization's compliance with government regulations (Kochan et al., 1986; Walton, 1985; Beer & Spector, 1984).

Fourth, American companies in the late 1970s and early 1980s began to emulate the nonunionized HRM practices of successful U.S. companies such as IBM, as well as Japanese organizations. The successful application of total quality management (TQM) principles by Japanese companies contributed to the recognition that employees represent a vital organizational resource and if managed properly they can be a primary competitive advantage.

Together the changes that began to occur in the late 1950s and have continued up to the present have resulted in the transformation of the HRM function. The changes caused the displacement of the industrial relations system that appeared to function so well from 1935 up to 1970. In addition, the changes created organizational needs that required the HRM personnel function to emerge from being a low-profile and reactive maintenance activity to being a primary and strategic partner in organizations. The HRM transformation that has occurred has been such that today the HRM function is viewed as being essential for survival in today's competitive environment (Marshall, 1992).

The recent evolution of the HRM function is conveyed by the widespread use of the term HRM in place of PM. The connotation of the term HRM is distinct from PM in the following ways. First, whereas PM implies human resources as expenses, HRM indicates an emphasis on human resources as organizational assets (Lewin, 1991). The terminology, HRM, communicates a focus, not only on people as human resources, but also as resources to be managed with other organizational resources (Mahoney & Deckop, 1986). The view of employees as resources to be managed rather than expenses is indicative of the recognition that today an organization's competitive advantage is increasingly dependent on its human, rather than capital, resources (Carnevale, Gainer, & Meltzer, 1990).

Second, PM signifies a group of discrete human resources administrative subfunctions and maintenance activities that are reactive, passive, and secondary to the other significant business functions (Prewitt, 1982). HRM on the other hand indicates a proactive approach, an integration of human resource subfunctions, and an enhancement and expansion of the function, position, and strategic importance of HRM within the organization (Lewin, 1991). The growth in importance of the HRM function is evident in the fact that the top HR executive usually holds the title of vice president and reports to the chief executive officer of the company.

Stage 10: Strategic focus era

In the late 1970s, the field began to witness a considerable change in image, status, and perceived importance of the HR function in organizations. Meyer (1976) referred to HR directors as "the new corporate heroes," and he cited examples of corporate CEOs who had risen to the top ranks through the HR function. This sudden discovery of HRM as a critical function to organizational effectiveness may appear a bit surprising, yet seems to make sense when we examine other changes going on in the internal and external environments of organizations at the time. In this section, we discuss the emergence of the Strategic Focus era, which has extended from the late 1970s to the present, and thus largely concerns itself with the decade of the 1980s.

While organizations for quite some time have been concerned about business strategy, the Strategic Focus era was really initiated in the late 1970s when the principal accreditation body for business schools, the American Assembly of Collegiate Schools of Business (AACSB), mandated the teaching of business policy/strategy as a capstone or integrative course in business school curricula This event also promoted the academic study of business strategy, and suggested the importance of integrating business strategy with other areas. One of the areas that was seen as critical to merge with business strategy was human resource management, which stimulated the emergence of a new area referred to as strategic human resource management in the early 1980s. This new area deals with the integration of HRM with both strategy formulation and implementation, and it is discussed in greater detail in a later section on the academic side of human resource management.

Strategic HRM generally has referred to a long-term view of HR policy, and a simultaneous integration horizontally among the various HR functions, and a vertical integration with corporate strategic planning. Thus this integration has brought the HR function into closer contact with the top executives of the firm, and has helped to craft a role for HRM as a strategic business partner who is absolutely critical to the organization's ability to be effective and deal with key challenges and changes in the work environment.

Several specific issues have contributed to the strategic role of HRM. One is the productivity concern of U.S. organizations that emerged in the early 1980s. This resulted from the loss of ground to foreign competition, the need to operate in a global (not just a domestic) economy, and the increased recognition that a firm's competitive advantage is tied to managing human resources in a strategic way.

A second issue has been the widespread downsizing, restructuring, and redesigning of organizations. This has resulted in the old, hierarchical/pyramidal-type structures with tight controls and small spans of control giving way to flatter structures and larger spans of control. Such new structures have necessitated an increased focus on employee self-control, rather than older traditions of external control, along with more team-based work structures.

A third issue has been the need for a sound human resources strategy to effectively manage the highly diverse work force of the future. Projections suggest that the future work force will be more diverse in gender, race, ethnicity, and age, as well as in attitudes, beliefs, and values. Thus, organizations will be dealing with a different type of employee, resulting from the highly committed and solid "organization man" (Whyte, 1959) of the 1950s and 1960s being replaced by his offspring, referred to as the "new individualists" (Leinberger & Tucker, 1991), who have more self-interest than organizational interest in mind, and are not nearly as driven by the old Protestant work ethic.

Overall, the Strategic Focus era has suggested that the integration of business strategy with HRM can be an organization's competitive advantage, and thus can have bottom-line impact. We have examined the historical roots of the field of HRM, and its evolution over that time. We now turn to an examination of the HRM field today.

Stage 11: The HRM function today

The practice of HRM today is both similar and distinct to that of the past. Similarities include the continued focus of HRM on the entire employment relationship, along with all the decisions, actions, and issues involved in that relationship. In addition, while the particular roles of HRM have changed, similar to its beginning, the field has continued to provide a response to the dramatic and persistent change occurring in organizations and the employment relationship.

While similar to HRM practice of the past, the HRM function today is distinct in its involvement in meeting contemporary needs resulting from changing organizational models. Distinctions of HRM practice today include the following four features (Sisson, 1990; Blyton & Turnbull, 1992). First, HRM is characterized by the emphasis on the integration of traditional PM activities as well as HRM's involvement in overall organizational planning and change. Second, HRM today is characterized as a partner in organizational change, creator of organizational culture, and facilitator of organizational commitment and the exercise of initiative. Third, HRM is characterized by the decentralization of many of the traditional HRM activities from personnel specialists to senior line management. Fourth, as noted earlier, current HRM practice is characterized by a focus on individual employees rather than on collective management–trade union relations. In general, today's HRM function has been described as: broad and strategic; involving all managerial personnel; regarding employees

as the single most important organizational asset; being proactive in its responsibilities; and having the objective of enhancing organizational performance and meeting employee needs (Poole, 1990, 3).

In addition to the integration of traditional PM activities discussed earlier, HRM has been a partner with other management functions in the effort to respond to today's environmental challenges through organizational change. Companies in the U.S. have confronted an increasingly competitive and hostile economic environment marked by the recent convergence of economic, technological, government/legal, and international factors. Turbulence resulting from these factors has created situations which many organizations have had to struggle with to survive (Ferris, Schellenberg, & Zammuto, 1984). In an effort to cope, a majority of large U.S. firms have had to adopt and employ strategies that directly affect and involve HRM practice. These strategies have included the downsizing, restructuring, or right-sizing of organizations (Cascio, 1993), as well as adopting new employment relationships such as the utilization of contingent employees (Abraham, 1988). The effectiveness and success of these strategies has been dependent on direct HRM involvement at all levels of organizational activity and planning.

Not only have HR professionals been at the center of organizational restructuring but they also have had to facilitate organizational effectiveness in the emergent, leaner organization. The HRM function has become increasingly responsible to cultivate the requisite culture that is conducive and supportive of required behaviors. HR professionals no longer can simply be technicians proficient in the IR and PM functions of the past. Rather, they need to be architects and leaders in the development of competitive organizational social systems (Block, 1993).

The HRM function today is not only characterized as a more integrated and vital function, but holistic as well. HR practitioners of today cannot afford to only be skilled in what were once performed as independent and unrelated PM activities. Instead, they must see the forest from the trees. They must be able to build effective HRM systems in which activities such as recruitment, selection, training and development, performance evaluation, and compensation work together synergistically with a strategic focus.

Some of the specific HR responsibilities of today that relate to increasing organizational effectiveness are as follows. First, there has been a need to increase the competency and adaptability of the work force. Creating and maintaining a competitive work force and capable management team has posed new and significant challenges for HR professionals, requiring advanced skills in recruitment and selection. In addition, this has increased the necessity for effective and often intensive training and development programs. Further, new pay policies have to be developed and implemented in order to motivate employees, raise productivity, do more with less, and increase organizational performance (Schuster & Zingheim, 1992).

Second, the identification of needs and the cultivation of the requisite managerial skills also represent new challenges that the HRM function is being called on to fulfill. In addition to a competent and adaptable work force, organizational effectiveness is dependent on a new type of managerial behavior. For instance, whereas managers were once required to be independent, analytical, and decisive, the new manager needs to also have effective leadership and relational skills. The current emphasis is on collaboration, teamwork, and empowerment policies that foster employee input, all of which depend on HRM facilitation.

The new organizational structures have necessitated changes in the HR routine. Empowered managers and staff are expected to have more involvement and autonomy in traditional personnel management activities such as recruitment, selection, employee guidance and discipline, performance evaluation, even compensation. This has necessitated the decentralization of many of the traditional HRM activities from personnel specialists to senior line management. As a result, today's effective HR professional is becoming less of a "doer" and assuming more of a role that is characterized as a teacher, consultant, researcher, and systems designer. The rationale for role change is that since a number of personnel activities can be handled by plants or departments, the HR function should concentrate on utilizing the special expertise it has in the people area and in the realm of creating culture (Block, 1993).

While we have described internal functions of HRM, it is important to recognize that the HRM function of today has a direct and primary influence on the organization's external environment. With the current emphasis on customerization and service, and the fact that the policies and culture that HR professionals develop directly affect the employees, how employees are treated by the organization will impact their treatment of the organization's customers. As noted by Block (1993, 151), "Human resource practices do not impact the culture of an institution, they *are* the culture. Human resources along with financial practices are the primary messengers for communicating the kind of relationship an institution wishes to have with its customers."

HISTORY AND EVOLUTION OF THE SCIENCE OF HRM

Academic side of human resource management

The academic side of HRM started out as basically an atheoretical, problem-driven field, with very close ties to the industrial community. The emergence of HRM as an academic field began in response to HRM practioner needs. The first HRM professionals believed that they were responsible for the most important business function, and for finding solutions to critical HRM problems (e.g., turnover) (Bloomfield, 1923).

After being organized in 1911, the Boston Employment Managers' Association (EMA) recognized the need for employment managers to obtain special training (Bloomfield, 1919). Other EMAs also identified training as a primary need, and as a result, Dartmouth College started the first employment management course in 1915 (Person, 1916). During WWI, approximately a dozen other schools, including Harvard and Columbia University, began employment management courses to train employment managers, initiated by the War Industries Board (Bloomfield, 1919). These associations resulted in a number of prominent academicians, such as Harlow Person, the Director of Dartmouth's Amos Tuck School of Administration and Finance, identifying with the HRM movement (Bloomfield, 1923).

As noted, the profession of HRM began around WWI and represented the merger of SM and welfare work along with contributions from industrial and organizational psychology and later from human relations. This integration of different sources of knowledge resulted in the emerging science of HRM being characterized as multidisciplinary. As noted by Kaufman (1993, 12), the field was "not thought to qualify as an academic discipline since the study of the employment relationship, and the labor problems therein, was based largely on knowledge and theories from existing disciplines" rather than on a unique knowledge-based and theoretical framework.

Similar to Taylor, when he began studying production work, the majority of the early researchers and writers on HRM worked as industrial managers. The subjects they studied and wrote about were real problems that they confronted at their particular places of employment. The close relationship that existed between the science and practice of HRM contributed to the growth of the field and its ability to generate practical solutions to employment-related problems facing organizations (cf. Bloomfield, 1919; 1923).

During the 1920s, the number of academicians writing on HRM topics increased as schools established business and employment management programs. An examination of the HRM books and articles from that period reveals the fact that while a number of the authors were academicians, the majority still worked as employment managers (cf. Bloomfield, 1923; Berg, 1932). Similarly, many of the teachers of personnel courses in the 1920s came from the ranks of management in industry (Kaufman, 1993).

The close association between the practice and academic discipline of HRM continued until approximately 1935. At that time, the diminished importance of PM in relation to IR resulted in a shift between 1935 and 1960 in management attention from PM dealing with individual workers to industrial relations issues such as collective bargaining. PM became characterized as a maintenance, administrative, and perfunctory function, and this shift in the importance of the practice of PM was accompanied by a decreased emphasis on personnel research and the importance of PM instruction. PM courses continued to be taught at colleges and universities but they were ancillary to other business functions such as accounting, finance, and line management. This depreciation of the PM side of HRM is indicated by the fact that in 1975 it was reported that fewer than 150 of the Harvard Business School graduates were employed in personnel jobs (Foulkes, 1975).

The focus on human relations between the late 1940s through the late 1950s did contribute to the science of PM. According to Kaufman (1993), the study of human relations represented a theoretical and research focus on individual and group behavior in the work setting while personnel management, per se, had a vocational orientation and focused on specific practices related to the personnel management maintenance functions. Later in the early 1960s the academic study of human relations was absorbed into the field of organizational behavior which has made significant contributions to contemporary HRM theory and practice (Kaufman, 1993).

Similar to its beginning, the PM side of the science of HRM did not flourish as a distinct discipline between 1935 and 1960. Rather, other disciplines expanded during the postwar period from which HRM drew knowledge and theories as it began to grow in importance in the 1960s. Primary among these disciplines were social psychology, industrial psychology, human relations, and organizational behavior. The denigration of the practice of PM during this time and the lack of development as a separate discipline contributed to the erosion of close ties that originally characterized the relationship between the science and practice of PM.

During the 1960s, the academic side of PM began to undergo a transformation as the result of the development and application of theories from organizational behavior and industrial and organizational psychology to traditional personnel topics such as recruitment, selection, compensation, performance evaluation, and training (Kaufman, 1993). A catalyst to this transformation was the concurrent shift in many companies from an emphasis on IR and the emergence of PM from being a passive and reactive maintenance function, and the view of employees as personnel expenses, to the emphasis on HRM and towards approaching employees as human resources to be proactively and effectively managed (Prewitt, 1982). This change in nomenclature and perspective began first during the 1960s in organizations and did not spread to academe until a decade later (Kaufman, 1993, 121).

The current status of the science of human resource management

The recent emergence and transformation of the HRM function has been accompanied by an increased emphasis on research in the science-building approach (Kaufman, 1993). As noted, similar to its beginning, the science and practice of HRM have looked to a number of other disciplines for theory and information. Despite these contributions, the increase in HRM research, and the importance of the HRM function, the science and practice of HRM remain largely separated.

The science of HRM has historically tended to be fragmented as a field of study (Mahoney & Deckop, 1986). Until recently, the primary focus of HRM researchers has been on separate HRM activities, resulting from the vocational and maintenance focus of PM. In addition, the evolution of the field has resulted in more activities being added to the practice of HRM. Therefore, researchers' continued concentration on HRM activities has been needed and has advanced HRM practice by providing knowledge and introducing systematic methods to primary HRM functions such as employee recruitment, selection, placement, appraisal, compensation, and training (Anthony & Nicholson, 1977).

The recognition of the emerging importance and widening scope of HRM in practice has also resulted in the development of new academic perspectives of HRM. Primary has been the strategic human resource management (SHRM) perspective (Butler, Ferris, & Napier, 1991). SHRM represents an effort to link HRM activities to a firm's business strategy (Lengnick-Hall & Lengnick-Hall, 1988; Wright & Snell, 1991). The perspective is representative of the assumptions that HRM activities are organizational in scope (Schuler, 1990), HRM issues need to be considered in the formulation as well as the implementation of organizational strategy (Dyer, 1985), and HRM practice should play an integral role and impact the organization's performance and overall effectiveness (Ferris, Russ, Albanese, & Martocchio, 1990). Finally, SHRM represents a contingent approach to organizations since, "different [organizational] strategies require different behaviors and, therefore, different human resource management practices to elicit and reinforce those behaviors" (Snell, 1992, 292).

In addition to the general SHRM approach, there have been recent efforts to integrate HRM activities by placing HRM in a broader context and a higher level of analysis. First, not only has the SHRM perspective been used to relate the overall HRM function to business strategy, but also to highlight the strategic aspects of particular HR activities (Milkovich, 1988; Sonnenfeld & Peiperl, 1988), and of HRM in particular contexts (Ferris, Schellenberg, & Zammuto, 1984; Smith & Ferris, 1986; Snell, 1992; Snell & Dean, 1992). Second, other perspectives on HRM have been recently introduced including the political perspective (Ferris & Judge, 1991), the economic/utility perspective (Jones & Wright, 1992), and the international perspective (Kochan, Batt, & Dyer, 1992; Dowling & Schuler, 1990). These perspectives provide a more holistic view of HRM activities and are suggestive of the broadening nature of the field.

Continuing lack of an integrative HRM theory

In spite of these recent efforts, the academic side has continued to be characterized by an absence of an integrative theory or conceptual system of HRM (Mahoney & Deckop, 1986). The failure of HRM researchers to develop a general theory of HRM is not a recent phenomena, but has been a persistent and enduring characteristic since the atheoretical beginnings of the field. Heneman (1969) pointed out the persistent lack of a general theory in the field of HRM. He also noted that while other disciplines have studied facets of employment, the unique attribute of HRM is that its central focus is *"employment, in all its aspects (micro and macro, individual and group)"* (Heneman, 1969, 4). Based on the nature of HRM, Heneman

(1969) stressed the importance of a general theory for the field's existence, development, and usefulness.

Although the IR function of HRM made efforts to develop what have been considered general theories of industrial relations (e.g., Dunlop, 1958), the results have been judged as inadequate (Adams, 1991). Primary deficiencies of Dunlop's (1958) system, pointed out by scholars, include a failure to generate testable hypotheses, an ignorance of behavioral aspects of the employment relationship, and a portrayal of the system as static rather than dynamic (Meltz, 1991).

The historically atheoretical character of HRM, along with several other factors, has contributed to the continued lack of an integrative theory for HRM. An additional factor, previously noted, is that there has been a continued and predominant focus by HRM researchers on separate functions or activities. In addition, the primary approach to HRM research has continued to be micro-oriented, focused on the individual level of analysis, rather than macro-oriented, focused on the organizational level of analysis. Further, while the adoption and reliance on appropriate theories from other disciplines has contributed to HRM research, this practice has not encouraged the development of an integrative theory of HRM (Wallace, 1983).

Changes in HRM academic training

As noted earlier, the field of HRM has developed in response to situations. The declining emphasis on IR and growth in importance of HRM has been reflected by a shift from IR to HRM as an academic area of study. According to Beer and Spector (1984, 263), the field of HRM has been characterized by "programmatic responses to the needs and problems of whichever group(s) have the greatest influence and power." The decline in unionization, the increase in government regulation, market pressures, and the transformed role of HRM in organizations have been met by programmatic changes in academic programs, made in order to prepare students for today's HRM function.

During the 1980s, many programs in industrial relations, which had been begun following WWII, and business schools began to add HRM topics to their curricula as areas of research and teaching. The national shrinkage of private sector unionization, the growth in employment opportunities in HRM, and an increase in corporate sponsorship of HRM programs led to an increased emphasis on HRM and a de-emphasis on IR-related topics in universities and colleges. For instance, whereas during the 1960s and 1970s the majority of students attended graduate programs in labor and industrial relations programs in order to prepare for IR-related careers, since the 1980s the majority of students in these programs have been preparing for HRM careers. Changes made in these programs have included a de-emphasis on industrial and labor relations topics and labor economics, and an increased emphasis on human resources functions and psychology-oriented instruction (cf. Kochan & Cappelli, 1984). In addition, efforts have been made to shift from providing training in traditional personnel functions as separate activities to relating them, in a more holistic manner, to organizational strategy and the complex changing environment (cf. Sears, 1984).

CONCLUSION

In this chapter we have traced the history and evolution of HRM. From our discussion, several salient features that have characterized HRM are evident. We now summarize some of these prominent aspects of HRM and discuss their future implications. First, because the focus of HRM has been on the entire employee relationship, HRM has rep-

resented a response to environmental and organizational changes, beginning with the Industrial Revolution, that have radically affected aspects of the employment relationship. The field of HRM has not only developed out of changes that have occurred, but has also represented one of the primary vehicles by which organizations have dealt with these changes. The factory system, the emergence of the modern corporation, and managerial capitalism were factors that necessitated new ways of managing the employment relationship. Similarly, recent factors including global competition, the need to improve productivity, government regulation, the decline of unionization in the private sector, technological changes, and the service-oriented economy have affected the employment relationship and have required new responses from HRM.

Second, it was noted that the field of HRM was formed from the merger of scientific management, welfare work, and industrial psychology around the time of WWI. This symbiotic merger of disparate approaches to worker management has continued and is representative of the character of HRM. HRM has continued to evolve, drawing its theories and knowledge from various disciplines. As such, from its beginning to the present, HRM has been a multidisciplinary field that has represented a "cross-roads" where practioners and scholars from various disciplines meet to exchange views on various aspects of the employment relationship (Adams, 1983, 511).

Third, HRM initially emerged as a profession and a science as a result of the work of practitioners and therefore was pragmatic in nature. Challenges confronting organizations from the effects of WWI created the need for HR professionals, academic training, and research into employment problems. Consequently, the work of HRM practitioners and academicians had common objectives, and the science and practice of HRM were characterized by cooperation. Changes that occurred following 1935, including the relegation of PM to a maintenance function and the emergence of the IR side of HRM, resulted in a separation of the practice and science of HRM.

Fourth, recent challenges have resulted in both a change in the view of employees as well as the transformation of HRM to being a strategic partner in organizational performance. Today, employees are viewed as organizational assets that need to be strategically and effectively managed. Similar to the beginning of the field, HRM is increasingly being viewed as a vital and proactive organizational function. A difference, though, is that HRM's prominence is greater and its present role as a partner in the management of the firm is broader than that of the past.

The transformation and emergence of the HR function indicates the need for vehicles to bring the practice and science of HRM together. The original, close association between the science and practice of HRM enabled the field to provide solutions to problems facing organizations. Today's challenges (e.g., the changing nature of organizations through restructuring, downsizing, etc.) are greater than ever and are resulting in changes in the roles that the HR function has to fulfill. The fruitful results from the cooperation that originally existed between the science and practice of HRM suggests the appropriateness for a return to a close partnership. Perhaps the vehicles such as business–university research partnerships, discussed in Chapter 1, will contribute to this and will provide solutions to problems that will continue to confront the field.

REFERENCES

Abraham, K. G. (1988). *Restructuring the Employment Relationship: The growth of market mediated work arrangements.* Washington, D.C.: Brookings Institution.

Adams, R. R. (1983). Competing paradigms in industrial relations. *Relations Industriales*, 38 (3), 508–29.

Adams, R. J. (1991). Introduction and overview. In R. J. Adams (ed.), *Comparative Industrial Relations*, 1–9. London: HarperCollins Academic.

Anthony, W. P., & Nicholson, E. A. (1977). *Management of Human Resources: A systems approach to personnel management.* Columbus, OH: Grid Inc.

Baron, J. N., Dobbin, F. R., & Jennings, P. D. (1986). War and peace: The evolution of modern personnel administration in U.S. industry. *American Journal of Sociology*, 92, 350–83.

Baron, J. N., Jennings, P. D., & Dobbin, F. R. (1988). Mission control: The development of personnel systems in U.S. industry. *American Sociological Review*, 53, 497–514.

Beach, D. S. (1965). *Personnel: The management of people at work.* New York: Macmillan.

Beer, M., & Spector, B. A. (1984). Human resource management: The integration of industrial relations and organization development. In K. M. Rowland & G. R. Ferris (eds.), *Research in Personnel and Human Resources Management*, vol. 2, pp. 261–98. Greenwich, CT: JAI Press.

Berg, R. M. (1932). *Bibliography of Management Literature.* New York: The American Society of Mechanical Engineers.

Berstein, I. (1960). Union growth and structural cycles. In W. Galenson & S. M. Lipset (eds.), *Labor and Trade Unionism: An interdisciplinary reader.* New York: Wiley.

Block, P. (1993). *Stewardship: Choosing service over self interest.* San Francisco: Berrett-Kochler Publishers.

Bloomfield, D. (1915). The new profession of handling men. *Annals of the American Academy*, 69, 121–6.

Bloomfield, D. (ed.) (1919). The employment manager: A new profession in American industry. In D. Bloomfield (ed.), *Employment Management*, 113–17. New York: H. W. Wilson.

Bloomfield, D. (ed.) (1923). *Problems in Personnel Management.* New York: H. W. Wilson.

Blum, M. L. (1949). *Industrial Psychology and its Social Foundations.* New York: Harper.

Blyton, P., & Turnbull, P. (1992). HRM: Debates, dilemmas and contradictions. In P. Blyton & P. Turnbull (eds.), *Reassessing Human Resource Management.* London: Sage.

Boettiger, L. A. (1923). *Employee Welfare Work: A critical and historical study.* New York: Ronald Press.

Braverman, H. (1974). *Labor and Monopoly Capital.* New York: Monthly Review Press.

Burack, E. H., & Smith, R. D. (1982). *Personnel Management: A human resource system approach.* New York: Wiley.

Butler, J. E., Ferris, G. R., & Napier, N. K. (1991). *Strategy and Human Resources Management.* Cincinnati: Southwestern.

Carnevale, A., Gainer, L. J., & Meltzer, A. S. (1990). *Workplace Basics: The essential skills employers want.* San Francisco: Jossey-Bass.

Cascio, W. F. (1993). Downsizing: What do we know? What have we learned? *Academy of Management Executive*, 7 (1), 95–104.

Chandler, A. D., Jr. (1972). Anthracite coal and the beginnings of the industrial revolution in the United States. *Business History Review*, 46 (2), 141–81.

Chandler, A. D., Jr. (1977). *The Visible Hand: The managerial revolution in American business.* Cambridge, MA: Belknap.

Chandler, A. D., Jr. (1990). *Scale and Scope: The dynamics of industrial capitalism.* Cambridge, MA: Belknap.

Chenery, W. L. (1922). *Industry and Human Welfare.* New York: Macmillan.

Cochran, T. C. (1944). Business organization and the development of an industrial discipline. In H. F. Williamson (ed.), *The Growth of the American Economy,* 310–18. New York: Prentice Hall.

Davis, K. (1957). *Human Relations in Business.* New York: McGraw-Hill.

Dowling, P. J., & Schuler, R. S. (1990). *International Dimensions of Human Resource Management.* Boston: PWS-Kent.

Drucker, P. F. (1977). *People and Performance: The best of Peter Drucker on management.* New York: Harper's College Press.

Dulebohn, J. H. (1991). *A critical analysis of the theoretical background of Workforce 2000.* Unpublished manuscript, Institute of Labor and Industrial Relations, University of Illinois at Urbana-Champaign.

Dunlop, J. T. (1958). *Industrial Relations Systems.* New York: Holt.

Dyer, L. (1985). Strategic human resource management and planning. In K. M. Rowland & G. R. Ferris (eds.), *Research in Personnel and Human Resources Management,* vol. 3, pp. 1–30. Greenwich, CT: JAI Press.

Eilbirt, H. (1959). The development of personnel management in the United States. *Business History Review,* 33 (5), 345–64.

Ferris, G. R., & Judge, T. A. (1991). Personnel/human resources management: A political influence perspective. *Journal of Management,* 17, 447–88.

Ferris, G. R., Russ, G. S., Albanese, R., & Martocchio, J. J. (1990). Personnel/human resources management, unionization, and strategy determinants of organizational performance. *Human Resource Planning,* 13, 215–27.

Ferris, G. R. Schellenberg, D. A., & Zammuto, R. F. (1984). Human resource management strategies in declining industries. *Human Resource Management,* 23, 381–94.

Fossum, J. A. (1979). *Labor Relations: Development, structure, process.* Dallas, TX: Business Publications.

Foulkes, F. K. (1975). The expanding role of the personnel function, *Harvard Business Review,* 53 (2), 71–84.

Gilbreth, F. B. (1912). *Primer of Scientific Management.* New York: Van Nostrand.

Grusky, O., & Miller, G. A. (eds.) (1981). *The Sociology of Organizations.* New York: Free Press.

Hays, S. P. (1957). *The Response to Industrialism.* Chicago: University of Chicago Press.

Heneman, H. G., Jr. (1969). Toward a general conceptual system of industrial relations: How do we get there? In G. Somers (ed.), *Essays in Industrial Relations Theory,* 1–25. Ames, IA: Iowa State University Press.

Hoxie, R. F. (1915). *Scientific Management and Labor.* New York: Appleton-Century.

Jacoby, S. M. (1985). *Employing Bureaucracy: Managers, unions, and the transformation of work in American industry, 1900–1945.* New York: Columbia University Press.

Janger, A. R. (1977). *The Personnel Function: Changing objectives and organization.* New York: The Conference Board.

Jones, E. D. (1919). The new labor problem. In *Employment management,* 118–27. See Bloomfield (ed.) (1919).

Jones, G. R., & Wright, P. M. (1992). An economic approach to conceptualizing the utility of human resource management practices. In G. R. Ferris & R. M. Rowland (eds.), *Research in Personnel and Human Resources Management,* vol. 10, pp. 271–99. Greenwich, CT: JAI Press.

Kaufman, B. E. (1993). *The Origins and Evolution of the Field of Industrial Relations in the United States.* Ithaca, NY: ILR Press.

Kochan, T. A., Batt, R., & Dyer, L. (1992). International human resource studies: A framework for future research. In D. Lewin, O. S. Mitchell, & P. D. Sherer (eds.), *Research Frontiers in Industrial Relations and Human Resources,* 309–37. Madison, WI: Industrial Relations Research Association.

Kochan, T. A., & Cappelli, P. (1984). The transformation of the industrial relations and personnel function. In P. Osterman (ed.), *Internal Labor Markets,* 133–62. Cambridge, MA: MIT Press.

Kochan, T., Katz, H., & McKersie, B. (1986). *The Transformation of American Industrial Relations.* New York: Basic Books.

Kochan, T. A., McKersie, R. B., & Cappelli, P. (1984). Strategic choice and industrial relations theory, *Industrial Relations,* 23, 16–39.

Leinburger, P., & Tucker, B. (1991). *The New Individualists: The generation after the organization man.* New York: HarperCollins.

Lengnick-Hall, C. A., & Lengnick-Hall, M. L. (1988). Strategic human resources management: A review of the literature and a proposed typology. *Academy of Management Review,* 13, 454–70.

Lescohier, D. D. (1935). Working conditions. In J. R. Commons (ed.), *History of Labor in the United States, 1896–1932,* vol. 3, 3–385. New York: Macmillan.

Lewin, D. (1991). The contemporary human resource management challenge to industrial relations. In H. C. Katz (ed.), *The Future of Industrial Relations: Proceedings of the second bargaining group conference,* 82–99. Ithaca, NY: ILR Press.

Lewisohn, S. A. (1926). *The New Leadership in Industry.* New York: Dutton.

Ling, C. C. (1965). *The Management of Personnel Relations: History and origins.* Homewood, IL: Irwin.

Lodge, W. (1913). Management. *Journal of the Efficiency Society,* 3 (1), 65–74.

McDonald, C. (1992). U.S. union membership in future decades: A trade unionist's perspective. *Industrial Relations,* 31 (1), 13–30.

Mahoney, T. A., & Deckop, J. R. (1986). Evolution of concept and practice in personnel administration/human resources management (PA/HRM). *Journal of Management,* 12, 223–41.

Marshall, R. (1992). The future role of government in industrial relations. *Industrial Relations*, 31 (1), 31–49.

Meltz, N. H. (1991). Dunlop's *Industrial Relations Systems* after three decades. In R. J. Adams (ed.), *Comparative Industrial Relations*, 10–20. London: HarperCollins Academic.

Meyer, H. E. (1976). Personnel directors are the new corporate heroes, *Fortune*, 93 (2), 84–8.

Milkovich, G. T. (1988). A strategic perspective on compensation management. In G. R. Ferris & K. M. Rowland (eds.), *Research in Personnel and Human Resources Management*, vol. 6, pp. 263–88. Greenwich, CT: JAI Press.

Miller, F. B., & Coghill, M. A. (1964). Sex and the personnel manager. *Industrial and Labor Relations Review*, 18 (1), 32–44.

Milton, C. R. (1970). *Ethics & Expediency in Personnel Management: A critical history of personnel philosophy*. Columbia, SC: University of South Carolina Press.

Moore, W. E. (1951). *Industrial Relations and the Social Order*. New York: Macmillan.

Munsterberg, H. (1913). *Psychology and Industrial Efficiency*. Boston: Houghton Mifflin.

Nadworny, M. J. (1955). *Scientific Management and the Unions*. Cambridge, MA: Harvard University Press.

Nelson, D. (1975). *Managers and Workers*. Madison, WI: University of Wisconsin Press.

Nelson, D. (1980). *Frederick W. Taylor and the Rise of Scientific Management*. Madison, WI: University of Wisconsin Press.

Nelson, D., & Campbell, S. (1972). Taylorism versus welfare work in American industry: H. L. Gantt and the Bancrofts. *Business History Review*, 45 (1), 1–16.

Patten, T. H., Jr. (1968). *The Foreman: Forgotten man of management*. New York: American Management Association.

Perlman, S., & Taft, P. (1935). Labor movements. In J. Commons (ed.), *History of Labor in the United States, 1896–1932*, vol. 4. New York: Macmillan.

Person, H. S. (1916). University schools of business and the training of employment executives. *U.S. Bureau of Labor Statistics Bulletin No. 196*, 38.

Person, H. S. (1929). The new attitude toward management. In H. S. Person (ed.), *Scientific Management in American Industry*. New York: Harper.

Poole, M. (1990). Editorial: HRM in an international perspective, *International Journal of Human Resource Management*, 1 (1), 1–15.

Prewitt, L. B. (1982). The emerging field of human resources management. *Personnel Administrator*, 27 (5), 81–7.

Roethlisberger, F. J., & Dickson, W. J. (1939). *Management and the Worker*. Cambridge, MA: Harvard University Press.

Scheiber, H. N., Vatter, H. G., & Faulkner, H. (1976). *American Economic History*, 9th ed. New York: Harper & Row.

Schuler, R. S. (1990). Repositioning the human resource function: Transformation or demise? *Academy of Management Executive*, 4, 49–60.

Schuster, J. R., & Zingheim, J. K. (1992). *The New Pay*. New York: Lexington.

Sears, L. N., Jr. (1984). Organization and human resource professionals in transition. *Human Resource Management*, 23 (4), 409–21.

Sisson, K. (1990). Introducing the *Human Resource Management Journal*, *Human Resource Management Journal*, 1 (1), 1–11.

Slichter, S. H. (1919). *The Turnover of Factory Labor*. New York: Appleton.

Smith, D. S., & Ferris, G. R. (1986). Strategic human resource management and firm effectiveness in industries experiencing decline. *Human Resource Management*, 25, 441–58.

Snell, S. A. (1992). Control theory in strategic human resource management: The mediating effects of administrative information. *Academy of Management Journal*, 35, 292–327.

Snell, S. A., & Dean, J. W., Jr. (1992). Integrated manufacturing and human resource management: A human capital perspective. *Academy of Management Journal*, 35, 467–504.

Sonnenfeld, J. A., & Peiperl, M. A. (1988). Staffing policy as a strategic response: A typology of career systems. *Academy of Management Review*, 13 (4), 588–600.

Taylor, F. W. (1895). A piece rate system, being a step toward a partial solution of the labor problem. *Transactions*, 16, 856–83.

Taylor, F. W. (1911). *Shop Management*. New York: Harper.

Taylor, F. W. (1947). *Principles of Scientific Management*. New York: Harper.

Tead, O., & Metcalf, H. C. (1920). *Personnel Administration: Its principles and practice*. New York: McGraw-Hill.

The National Association of Employment Managers (1919). The National Association of Employment Managers organizes for service, *Personnel*, 1(1), 1–2.

The New Republic (1918). The rise of a new profession, *The New Republic*, 15 (186), 102–3.

Thompson, C. B. (ed.) (1914). *Scientific Management*. Cambridge, MA: Harvard University Press.

Tuma, E. H. (1971). *European Economic History: Tenth century to the present*. Palo Alto, CA: Pacific Books.

U.S. Bureau of Labor Statistics (1919). Welfare work for employees in industrial establishments in the United States. *Bulletin No. 250*, 119–23.

Viteles, M. S. (1932). *Industrial Psychology*. New York: Norton.

Wallace, M. J., Jr. (1983). Methodology, research, practice, and progression in personnel and industrial relations. *Academy of Management Review*, 8, 6–13.

Walton, R. E. (1985). The future of human resource management: An overview. In R. E. Walton & P. R. Lawrence (eds.), *HRM Trends and Challenges*, 3–11. Boston: Harvard Business School Press.

Ware, N. (1924). *The Industrial Worker 1840–1860*. Boston: Houghton Mifflin.

Watson, T. J. (1977). *The Personnel Managers*. London: Routledge & Kegan Paul.

Weber, M. (1927). *General Economic History*. New York: Greenberg.

Weisberger, B. A. (1969). *The New Industrial Society*. New York: Wiley.

Wells, L. A. (1923). *Industrial History of the United States*. New York: Macmillan.

Wera, E. (1921). *Human Engineering*. New York: Appleton.

Whyte, W. F. (1959). *Man and Organization*. Homewood, IL: Irwin.

Wright, P. M., & Snell, S. A. (1991). Toward an integrative view of strategic human resource management. *Human Resource Management Review*, 1 (4), 203–25.

Yoder, D. (1938). *Personnel and Labor Relations*. New York: Prentice Hall.

☐ Chapter 3 ☐

Business Strategy and Human Resource Management: A Profile of AT&T Global Business Communications Systems

Martin J. Plevel, Fred Lane, Randall S. Schuler, and Sandra K. Nellis

INTRODUCTION

Increasingly organizations are finding that in the context of a rapidly changing, highly competitive, global environment, it is imperative to manage all resources as effectively as possible. In this setting, the imperative of managing human resources effectively is recognized by HR professionals and line managers alike. Working together in partnership, HR professionals and line managers are addressing this imperative by integrating the management of human resources with the strategy of the business. Because this process of integration is such an extensive one, we use the example of the Global Business Communications Systems unit within AT&T to illustrate it in this chapter. We proceed under the premise that it is far easier to understand and appreciate the integration of HR and business strategy if the reader has a brief description of the business concerns and issues of AT&T and the Global Business Communications Systems unit.

A decade ago, people wondered whether AT&T could survive the rigors of competition. Today, influential people are asking whether AT&T may be the influential winner in a global contest of communications and computing as it pursues its strategy to be the world's networking leader. AT&T today has the right pieces to put together the success puzzle. It has the network in place to keep up with customers' insatiable demand for information. It has the research, development, manufacturing, sales, service, and support customers need. Over the last ten years AT&T has transformed itself into a nimble competitor, organized into more than 20 business units, each with its own special focus. The question asked by many today is: "What have been the forces within AT&T that have produced such tremendous change?"

Once again, the chapter is about principles of HR strategy with the AT&T example as a vehicle, and with a special focus on one of AT&T's business units, Global Business Communications Systems (GBCS). The relationship between the changes occurring within the business and the roles of human resource management, particularly within GBCS, are highlighted. Within AT&T and GBCS the roles of human resource management have included:

1 aligning people with the needs of the business;
2 linking human resource management with the business strategy; and
3 repositioning the human resources organization to facilitate the attainment of the first two roles.

Related theory and research

Integrating business strategy and HR is a fundamental concern of researchers and professionals alike. The concern has arisen during the past ten to fifteen years as the environment has become so much more competitive and, consequently, the need to utilize all resources effectively an imperative (Ulrich & Lake, 1990). Due to the complexity of organizations and the process of managing human resources, the task of integrating business strategy and HR has been divided into three areas: aligning people with the business; linking human resource management with the business strategy; and repositioning the human resource organization. We briefly define these areas and cite some research in the following paragraphs, using the AT&T example.

Aligning people with the needs of the business reflects several streams of work within human resource management. First, it reflects the work of Lawler, Cohen and Chang (1994) who discuss the process by which organizations identify their business priorities (people-related business issues (Schuler and Walker, 1990)) and then craft human resources programs, procedures, and practices to help implement these priorities. It reflects the work of Wright and McMahan (1992) who define these activities of linking human resource management with the goals and needs of the business as "strategic" human resource management. Their discussion of linking human resource management practices with the needs of the business using a resource-based theoretical framework is most relevant to this discussion of what happened within GBCS.

The activities within GBCS linking human resource management with the strategy of the business are rather more focused than linking with the needs of the business. Whereas the needs of the business are generated from internal and external environmental conditions (Lawler et al., 1994), the strategy of the business reflects the desires and discussion of management as to the direction of the organization (Baird & Meshoulam, 1988). This framework has been extended by Schuler (1992) who developed a 5-P model of strategic human resource management. Here the strategy of the organization is linked with several strategic human resource management activities, namely, the five P's: HR philosophy (or vision), HR policies, HR programs, HR practices, and HR processes. Within the GBCS example, these aspects of human resource management are reflected in the work of the human resources organization over the past two years.

The third role of human resource management within GBCS is that of repositioning the human resources organization (department). This involves some of the reengineering work covered by Ulrich and Lake (1990) in their discussion of organizational capability and the need to build the internal capabilities of the HR department itself. It also reflects the work of Schuler (1988) in his discussion of the repositioning of the HR department at the Swiss Bank Corporation of North America. In that discussion, the HR department was repositioned internally by restructuring the department's tasks and training the professionals to be generalists rather than specialists, and externally by identifying customers and working closely with them to develop HR products and services.

Also highlighted in this chapter are Kotter's (1990) subprocesses of adaptive change. These include:

- *Establishing direction* Developing a vision of the future, often the distant future, along with strategies for producing the changes needed to achieve that vision.

- *Aligning people* Communicating the direction to those whose cooperation may be needed so as to create coalitions that understand the vision and that are committed to its achievements.
- *Motivating and inspiring* Keeping people moving in the right direction despite major political, bureaucratic, and resource barriers to change by appealing to very basic, but often untapped, human needs, values, and emotions.

Kotter (1990) discusses these subprocesses as what leaders do to accomplish change. These adaptive changes have been accomplished within the context of AT&T, an organization which is actually going through major changes both at the corporate level and the GBCS level, namely, from regulation to deregulation and from a highly centralized functional organization to a self-sufficient decentralized business unit respectively.

While the focus of this chapter is on the relationship of business strategy and human resource management within GBCS, this can more fully be appreciated by providing a broader context. The context includes the events within AT&T and the events surrounding the creation and formation of GBCS. These are provided below, beginning with a brief description of AT&T, and followed by a description of the creation and formation of GBCS. Once in place, the roles and relationships of human resource management vis-à-vis the needs and strategy of the business are described in detail.

TRANSFORMATION AT AT&T

The employees at AT&T have experienced adaptive change as described by Kotter (1990), which has involved a complete identity change over the last ten years. AT&T has transformed itself from a monopoly that some people thought virtually guaranteed lifelong employ-ment for all of its people to a totally competitive company made up of autonomous business units.

AT&T was incorporated in 1885, but marks its beginning with Alexander Graham Bell's invention of the telephone in 1876. In its first 50 years, in addition to making telephone service available to virtually every American, AT&T established subsidiaries and allied companies in more than a dozen other countries. Before AT&T's divestiture of the Bell Telephone Companies at the end of 1983, the company had grown to more than one million employees and had become far and away the most widely held stock in America (Nadler, 1982). In 1989, the corporation went through a basic restructuring which resulted in the formation of strategic business units, each with its own culture, management structure, systems, markets, and financial accountability. The new autonomy has had profound impact on the business.

AT&T is now a global company which provides communications services and products, as well as network equipment and computer systems to businesses, consumers, telecommunications service providers, and government agencies. AT&T also offers a general purpose credit card as well as financial and leasing services. Today AT&T operates in over seventy-five countries in highly competitive, high-technology markets, with only its long distance service business still under government regulation. The basic structure of the organization is 20-plus decentralized business units. Corporate organizations and operating divisions, such as finance, law, and corporate strategic planning, support the business units, one of which is Global Business Communications Systems. AT&T has approximately 309,000 employees in 1994 with approximately 53,000 outside of the United States. See figure 3.1 for a high-level summary of AT&T's corporate structure/management system. A high-level view of AT&T's pre-1984 identity and its identity today is shown as figure 3.2.

Figure 3.1 AT&T's corporate structure

Business units – basic building blocks
• Aggregated into groups

Divisions – support the business units

AT&T's management systems

Management executive committee	Leads the development and implementation of AT&T's mission, values and strategic intent
Operations committee	Oversees execution of policies and strategies established by the management executive committee

Business-specific strategies

Today, each of AT&T's business units supports the company's global networking growth strategy. Every AT&T business unit now has two mandates. First, grow and be profitable in your own right, and second, make sure you contribute to the success of the core telecommunications network. AT&T's Multimedia Products/Services Group (MPSG) consists of businesses that offer a full line of voice, data, visual, messaging, and computing products and services. MPSG products and services add value to and through communications services. MPSG employees help customers identify their access requirements stimulating the use of AT&T's global network. MPSG businesses support AT&T's growth strategy by providing improved access through terminal devices and enhanced applications which capture more customers, expand their network needs, and strengthen existing customer relationships.

Creation and formation of GBCS

Global Business Communications Systems (GBCS) is one of the business units in the multimedia products/services group (MPSG)

at AT&T as shown in figure 3.3. GBCS was formed as a result of a merger between General Business Systems (GBS) and Business Communications Systems (BCSystems) on July 30, 1992. Both GBS and BCSystems were originally established as separate business units.

In July of 1992, the challenge of integrating GBCS was given to Jerre Stead who was originally brought into AT&T in 1991 to transform BCSystems into a global business. Stead, who had run Square D, an electrical equipment maker, was moved by AT&T chairman Robert Allen in March of 1993 to run NCR, recently renamed to AT&T Global Information Solutions, the computer company AT&T bought for $7.5 billion in stock in 1991. Patricia Russo was promoted to President of GBCS when Stead moved to NCR.

GBCS offers products and customer services to business customers of all sizes. Global in scope, its products are sold in more than 60 countries. Major products are the DEFINITY® Communications System, an all-digital private telephone switch with a capacity of 20 to 30,000 lines; Partner® and Merlin® Communications Systems – families of feature-rich phone systems for small and medium-sized businesses; the Merlin PFC™ telephone, a multiline business phone with integrated fax and copier capability; and integrated products that link telephone switches to computers for customer service and telemarketing applications.

GBCS also offers INTUITY™ Voice Processing Solutions which represent an entire family of voice and multimedia processing offers that include the INTUITY AUDIX® voice messaging solution and the INTUITY CONVERSANT® Voice Information System voice response solution; and the multilingual OVATION® voice processing system for large telecommunications service providers worldwide. In addition, GBCS also offers other emerging technologies that address business customers' computer telephone integration applications, and visual and wireless applications solutions.

45

Figure 3.2 AT&T's pre-1984 identity and its identity today

Pre-1984 identity	Identity today
One Bell system	AT&T and seven independent regional companies
One million people	Approximately 315,000 people
Regulated monopoly	Competition
Technology-driven	Market-driven
"Regulator satisfaction"	Customer satisfaction
Domestic	Global
Voice	Voice, data, image, facsimile
Stability	Constant change, mergers & acquisitions, strategic alliances
Centrally managed	Market-focused business units

Figure 3.3 AT&T groups

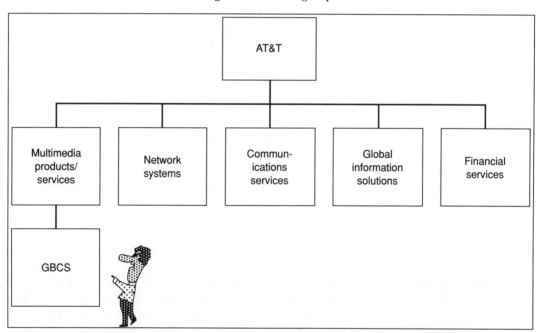

AT&T GBCS distributes products and services to small business, large business, and government customers. The GBCS marketing and strategic planning organization, which is led by Barry Karafin, has a team of managers that develops and refines market-specific strategic plans to address the needs of targeted customers.

GBCS has a strategic planning team which is responsible for developing the firm's business strategy. This strategy team works with the corporate AT&T strategic planning team, the multimedia products/services group strategic planning team and the GBCS markets, channels, and functional strategy teams.

While GBCS and AT&T's other units have, of course, had business strategies for some time, what provides distinction today is the special emphasis in GBCS on making its people the key driver for success. This new approach came along at the time that a major reengineering effort at GBCS was proving to be successful. Because of its importance in the successful transformation of GBCS and its relationship with the human resource management initiatives, this new human resources-based strategy is described here in some detail.

Reengineering for survival at Business Communications Systems

For several years, AT&T had tried to improve the lackluster performance of Business Communications Systems (BCSystems) with incremental approaches. As Jack Bucter, former President of BCSystems put it, "each year we set performance targets for the functional heads that we believed would improve the performance of the business, and each year they met those targets – but the performance of the overall business didn't improve" (Hall, Rosenthal, & Wade, 1993).

As a result, in early 1989, Bucter decided a more radical approach was needed if the business was ever to perform adequately. Since the process for selling and installing new systems was critical, he established a team dedicated to studying the current state of these processes. Once the initial data were gathered, he selected a top-performing field manager, Glenn Hazard, to lead the team in reengineering the way AT&T sold and installed PBX systems.

Glenn's team had representation from all of the relevant functions: sales, services, product management, research and development (Bell Labs), manufacturing, materials management, information systems, and training. This team was assigned to the reengineering effort full-time. The team was made aware of the seriousness of the situation, including the possibility of selling off the PBX business. As Hazard put it, "The entire team believed the future of the business was on their shoulders, and they did whatever was within their power to make the effort successful." People worked extremely long hours, often seven days a week. Some of the team members lived away from their families for extended periods of time.

Diagnostics: June, 1989 to February, 1990

Early in the data gathering and analysis phase, the reengineering team established that the scope of their effort should be broad – examining the process from the initial customer contact through selling, contracting, provisioning, installation, billing, and the collection of funds.

The diagnostic effort uncovered two difficult problems. First, the cycle time for this process was quite long, taking from three months to three years to sell and install. Through interviews of employees and customers and examining the paper trails, the team reconstructed 24 actual "projects" as a basis for the diagnostic. These projects covered not only the range of system sizes, but also different geographic areas and customer types (e.g., national, multilocation, or single site). The team identified every person involved in each of their cases, what their activities were and how much time they spent on each project. These data were confirmed by time and motion studies that were conducted at each main work center.

The second problem was that critical functions – sales and manufacturing – did not report directly to the business unit at that time. The sales function was shared with the communications services (long distance) business and manufacturing was shared with other AT&T equipment businesses. Thus, including these functions in the diagnostic was politically sensitive. Moreover, overall profit and loss responsibility was only at the presidential level. Internally focused expense-to-revenue goals at the local functional level did not provide adequate financial control or accountability.

From the initial data analysis, three important opportunities for redesign surfaced. First, there was a huge amount of work that had to be redone caused by a lack of clear roles and responsibilities in selling and provisioning a new system. Customers and the sales teams admitted that no single person had total responsibility and accountability for any specific activities in the transaction. As might be expected from this approach, actions taken upstream frequently caused unnecessary work downstream.

Rework was also caused by the manufacturing and delivery cycle. For example, the system was fully specified when the customer and the account executive agreed on a deal. However, since months or even years passed between that time and final installation, the customer's needs often changed dramatically. Despite tremendous efforts to keep the contract up to date with the customer's needs, final installations generally did not reflect what the customer wanted, which resulted in dissatisfied customers and substantial write-offs.

The second opportunity for improvement was a focus on project-level profitability. To please dissatisfied customers, sales teams did whatever they had to do to change customers' perceptions. Internal expense-to-revenue measures allowed customer satisfaction at any cost.

Finally, indirect expenses were excessive. In its case studies, the reengineering team found that headquarters and centralized support groups were extensively involved in supporting the implementation of these systems. Therefore, even when direct sales and provisioning expenses were managed well, additional overhead contributed to unprofitable sales.

Process reengineering: March, 1990 to August, 1990

Based on the diagnostics and his own experience, Hazard knew that disciplined management of all the activities needed to sell and install a system was essential for real improvement. In parallel, the business unit was successful in negotiating with AT&T executive management for a dedicated sales organization within the unit. An experienced senior manager, Patricia Russo was brought in to run the national sales organization.

The reengineering team realized that one of the vital keys to improving cost, cycle time, and customer satisfaction was to shorten the elapsed time between customer commitment and final installation. As a result, the entire process was redesigned to minimize this sub-process cycle time. Inclusion of manufacturing and material management in the project became critical because manufacturing and delivery intervals significantly influenced the total project schedule.

The new process clearly defined roles and responsibilities and standards for performance. Objectives, measurements, and rewards were changed to be customer-driven and process-oriented, rather than internally focused and functionally oriented, in order to ensure customer satisfaction and project profitability. For example, a new job (i.e., project manager) created a single point of contact, accountable for each project and its successful completion. The project manager set customer expectations around negotiated project milestones and became accountable for timely completion of activities by the project team and the customer. In support of the new process, existing systems were simplified and new systems were developed, resulting in improved response times and improved order intervals. For example, a new system was developed to help estimate project costs and to track actual costs incurred. These systems were built using the most direct approach the team could determine. Personal computers were used extensively, together with off-the-shelf software, and "intelligent front-ends" to existing systems were implemented.

In support of the reengineering effort, BCSystems reorganized the approach to centralized support and integrated the sales and provisioning responsibilities at a local branch level within a general manager–sales organization that had territory-specific profit and loss responsibility.

Piloting the new process: September, 1990 to March, 1991

A pilot was instituted in September, 1990 to determine if the process was having the impact expected, and to work out any bugs. The pilot demonstrated results that were strikingly close to those forecast by the reengineering team. The team developed tools that forecasted the resource requirements for each of the new projects. During the pilot, all but one project's resource requirements were within 5 percent of predicted levels.

Because job responsibilities and skills required changed so dramatically, substantial effort by the reengineering team, with significant support of the human resources organization, was spent developing new job descriptions, training curricula, tools, and job aids to enable people to understand and be effective in their new assignments.

Faced with communicating and managing the numerous process changes during the pilot, the team used total quality management (TQM) principles to map the new process flows from end to end. Various teams, organized around subprocesses, identified process owners, and customer–supplier inputs and outputs, and embedded formal feedback loops between process owners into the final process design to ensure continuous improvement.

Roll-out: April, 1991 to April, 1992

Management commitment, conviction, and leadership were critical to roll-out. This commitment started with the unit's top management. Based on the radical nature of the new process and the changes required, the senior leadership team had great reservations and concern about rolling out the new process.

Due to the business imperatives and the aggressive financial improvement targets established for the unit by AT&T's executive committee, Jack Bucter, president of BCS, and his senior leadership team made the decision to move forward. Pat Russo brought her field leadership team at the national sales organization together, and advised them that implementation would proceed immediately. To demonstrate unequivocal support for the new process, she made successful implementation a key performance measurement for her field managers. In the final analysis, this support was essential to successful implementation.

Results: June, 1992 to October, 1993

By the end of October, 1993 the initial implementation of the reengineered process was completely rolled out. The impact has been dramatic. Customer satisfaction has increased significantly:

- Customers' willingness to repurchase climbed from 53 percent to 82 percent.
- Customer satisfaction with project management improved to 88 percent excellent.
- Bills paid within thirty days of implementation increased from 31 percent to 71 percent.

Beyond the process changes, there has also been a dramatic change in the culture at GBCS. As Pat Russo put it, "we now have a profit focus that just did not exist before."

Keys to success

The linkage of the reengineering effort to the overall business strategy was clearly important to its success. The process was scoped out to include all of the functions important to selling and installing a PBX. The primary drivers for success included: an end-to-end process design with clearly understood objectives, measurements, and rewards; the total support of the unit's leadership team to the success of the reengineering effort; and the dedication of the reengineering team to the effort.

49

Linking the information technology (IT) strategy to the business strategy was also critical. The new IT approach provided the unit's people with the tools necessary to reduce cycle time and make informed decisions.

In addition to the obvious changes in process and systems, the reaction of the organization's culture should not be underestimated (Kotter, 1990). The breakdown of informal methods and old reward paradigms caused by reengineering heightened overall resistance to change, no matter how well planned or rational the change. Nevertheless, through the leadership of Bucter, Karafin, Russo, Hazard and the reengineering team, as well as the commitment by the national sales organization, resistance was overcome. Frequent communication at all levels was also critical. Full-time communications resources were assigned to the effort to help customers and the entire organization understand the new process. According to Hazard, to achieve business success through reengineering, it is important to keep everyone informed on all issues through constant communication.

The changes that occurred in human resource management practices when Jerre Stead joined AT&T proved to add momentum and sustain the significant improvements from reengineering success. We look at these changes now, beginning with the alignment of people with the needs of the business.

ESTABLISHING DIRECTION AND ALIGNING PEOPLE WITH THE NEEDS OF THE BUSINESS

In July, 1992, fueled by the quest to transform GBCS into the global leader in its target markets in an industry that is experiencing accelerated financial growth, the GBCS senior leadership team, referred to as the quality council, developed the GBCS pyramid. Coincident with the introduction of the

Figure 3.4   The GBCS pyramid

GBCS pyramid, the senior leadership team announced a fundamental change in the strategic focus of the unit. Previously, the strategic focus was to improve profitability by reducing costs as revenues continued to erode. The new strategic focus was to improve profitability by growing revenues in existing and new market segments while improving the basic cost structure of the unit.

The pyramid established a new framework for aligning the people with the business. It consists of a new vision, mission, values, objectives, strategic plan, tactical business plan, business processes, and management system (figure 3.4). The pyramid serves as a framework for action with a strategic long-term perspective. Its power is based on the employees (referred to as associates), who are the foundation for building all other elements of the pyramid.

The GBCS pyramid

There are several important components to the pyramid. Each is integral in aligning people to the needs of the business (Schuler, 1992).

GBCS vision

The vision represents the organization's purpose. The GBCS vision is: *To be your partner of choice – dedicated to quality, committed to your success.*

GBCS mission

The mission represents a broad plan of action for what the organization wants to do: *To be the worldwide leader in providing the highest-quality business communications products, services, and solutions.*

GBCS values

GBCS' values are used to guide decisions and behavior. They represent how the organization and its members treat customers, suppliers and other AT&T associates. The seven GBCS values are:

1 *Respect for individuals* We treat each other with respect and dignity, valuing individual and cultural differences. We communicate frequently and with candor, listening to each other, regardless of level or position.
2 *Dedication to helping customers* We truly care for each customer. We build enduring relationships by understanding and anticipating our customers' needs and by serving them better each time than the time before.
3 *Highest standards of integrity* We are honest and ethical in all our business dealings, starting with how we treat each other. We keep our promises and admit our mistakes. Our personal conduct ensures that AT&T's name is always worthy of trust.
4 *Innovation* We believe innovation is the engine that will keep us vital and growing. Our culture embraces creativity, seeks different perspectives, and risks pursuing new opportunities.
5 *Teamwork* We encourage and reward both individual and team achievements. We freely join with colleagues across organizational boundaries to advance the interest of customers and shareowners.
6 *Accountability* Each of us takes ownership for the success of GBCS. Our rewards are determined by our results.
7 *Excellence* We will be satisfied with nothing less than being the best in everything we do.

GBCS objectives

GBCS objectives reflect the quantitative commitments for the business. Each objective addresses an element of the "value equation" (figure 3.5) which represents GBCS' underlying philosophy regarding the key drivers of success and their interrelationships. Each key business objective is represented as an element of the "value equation." The "value equation" starts with associate value, the only sustainable competitive advantage (Schuler & MacMillan, 1985; Ulrich & Lake, 1990). Associate value is achieved by ensuring that all associates are continuously provided with the knowledge and have the core competencies needed to do their jobs effectively, have the ability and accountability to satisfy customers, and are extremely satisfied. Customer value is achieved by delivering value to GBCS customers. This is done by ensuring customers are provided with superior products, services, and integrated solutions by all GBCS associates taking special care to delight customers and ensure that their needs are met. Together, associate value and customer value generate profitable growth for AT&T and increase value for its shareholders. Completing the cycle, profitable growth and shareholder value produce growth in associate value, which in turn enhances customer value, and so on. At first glance, the equation seems simple. However, these are a complex set of interdependent relationships that require continuous attention to balancing all elements of the equation.

Figure 3.5   The "value equation"

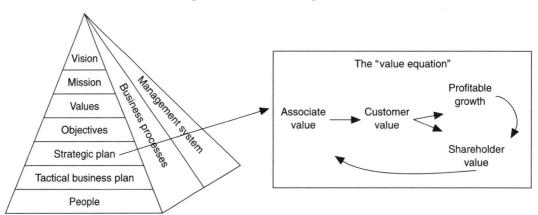

Associate value is measured by an all-associate survey which measures a person's satisfaction with various aspects of the work environment which include: job fulfillment, business direction, growth and development, management behavior, quality, and overall satisfaction. Associate value is measured by an associate satisfaction index (ASI). GBCS' objective is to increase the percentage of "extremely" and "very" satisfied associates to world-class levels in 1994.

Customer value is also measured by surveys. Customer value is determined by customers' willingness to repurchase GBCS products and services. GBCS' objective is to increase willingness to repurchase by 10 percent annually to achieve "best in class" levels by 1995.

Profitable growth and shareholder value are closely related. GBCS has designed the business structure to aggressively pursue profitable growth both domestically and globally in two ways: First, to establish strong leadership positions in new market segments such as computer–telephone integration, voice and multimedia processing, visual communications technologies and professional services, as well as to increase market share by enhancing the value of existing offers in traditional market segments. The paths to achieving these goals are identified by the GBCS strategic plan.

GBCS strategic plan

The GBCS senior leadership team has defined six key strategic business principles that guide and shape the strategic plan. These principles reflect management's overall direction for *how* to successfully achieve the business objectives with plans and actions that support those strategies. All day-to-day actions, from handling a customer's inquiry to manufacturing a system, must be performed with this strategic direction and focus in mind. The GBCS strategic business principles are:

1   Make people a key priority.
2   Win customers for life.
3   Utilize the total quality management approach to run the business.
4   Profitably grow by being the leader in customer-led applications of technology.
5   Rapidly and profitably globalize the business.
6   Be the best value supplier.

These strategic business principles serve as a guiding force to link the employees with the needs of the business by helping them understand the business direction. GBCS' strategic business goals have been successfully linked to the strategic business principles by a collaborative effort of the business leaders and the human resources leaders with their respective teams. A business strategy and planning model (figure 3.6) has been developed and serves as the driving force for the business and HR initiatives that are enabling GBCS to transform itself into a global leader in its target markets.

Tactical business plan

Whereas the strategic plan establishes a three- to five-year direction for the business to achieve its goals, the tactical plans, generally formulated around a shorter time frame, define the actions to be initiated and the objectives to be achieved in order to reach the long-term strategic goals. Consequently, all tactical plans reflect the strategic business principles. The tactical plans also incorporate end-to-end business processes and take into consideration the GBCS management system.

Business process and management system

There are two quality-related platforms that touch all parts of the pyramid – the GBCS management system and the business processes. The business processes throughout GBCS are defined and continue to be reevaluated for continuous improvement based upon total quality management (TQM). The GBCS management system is the blueprint for how the business is run. The management system provides the framework within which teams of associates systematically apply the principles of total quality management – using the Malcolm Baldrige National Quality Award criteria.

All associates within GBCS are involved in the GBCS management system. Through formal training and various learning experiences, process management teams and natural work groups are working together using a common set of tools and standards for continuous improvement. This total commitment to process improvement is the methodology that GBCS is using for achieving increased levels of associate value, customer value and financial success.

Thus far, the process and procedures by which people are aligned with the needs of the business have been described consistent with Lawler et al. (1994). As stated at the start of this chapter, aligning people with the needs of the business is one level more general than actually linking human resource management and business strategy. In the next section, linkage with business strategy is described in detail.

LINKING HUMAN RESOURCE MANAGEMENT AND BUSINESS STRATEGY

When Jerre Stead selected Fred Lane to head the BCSystems HR organization in the fall of 1991, Jerre asked his new human resources vice president to "reexamine every aspect of our people dimension." Stead emphasized the need to "engage the work force" and to create an environment that "supports our people as our only sustainable, competitive advantage."

Lane and his team tackled the task of developing a human resources strategic plan and management system that considered every aspect of worklife. The result was a comprehensive blueprint for motivating and inspiring employees as discussed by Kotter (1990) to embrace GBCS' overall business strategy. Known as the HR strategy and planning model (figure 3.7), this model provides an overall perspective on the relationships and linkages that exist today as the business continues its transformation process (Plevel, Nellis, Lane, & Schuler, 1994).

The left-hand column lists the strategic business principles discussed earlier. As shown by the arrows, these principles lead to six strategic imperatives in the human resources area. Strategic imperatives, as defined by GBCS HR, are those actions that are absolutely necessary for GBCS to achieve its business goals. Input for developing these imperatives came from external benchmarking studies, various associate forums (focus groups, surveys, training classes), interviews

Figure 3.6 GBCS business planning model

VMV	Value equation	Strategies	Business initiatives
Vision To be your partner of choice . . . dedicated to quality and committed to your success.	Associate value	1. Make people a key priority	• Recognize people as our only sustainable advantage • Foster 360-degree communication (e.g., feedback, GBCS pyramid) • Invest in training, anticipating changing needs • Evolve to an empowered, accountable culture • Value and nurture diversity
Mission To be the worldwide leader in providing the highest quality business communications products, services, and solutions.	Customer value	2. Win "customers for life"	• Serve all customers with excellence – from small locals to large multinational corporations • Emphasize strengths in sales and service • Craft service and aftermarket offers for high margins • Provide increasingly sophisticated segmentation, marketing and pricing • Drive responsibility (including P & L) to points close to customer • Serve largest part of all customers' communications needs profitably
		3. Utilize the total quality management apppoach	• Achieve industry-leading customer satisfaction, costs, profitability, share • Leverage domestic channel competitive advantage • Continue bias toward owned sales/service channels • Continue bias toward design and manufacture of core products • Source and partner where it makes sense • Own or control technology base of our core products • Achieve industry-leading manufacturing efficiency and effectiveness
Values • Respect for individuals • Dedication to helping customers • Highest standards of integrity • Innovation • Teamwork • Accountability • Excellence	Profitable growth	4. Profitably grow by being the leader in customer-led applications of technology	• Expand our core businesses • Exploit new growth opportunities • Increase application focus and provide better-offer integration • Favor internal growth over acquisitions • Slow rental erosion • Protect and grow our traditional service business
		5. Rapidly and profitably globalize	• Capitalize on non-U.S. opportunities • Provide a global product line capable of inexpensive localization • Own (partially or fully) international channels of distribution
	Shareholder value	6. Be the best *value* supplier	• Leverage market leadership to improve industry valuation • Be the price leader and be worth it!

Figure 3.7   HR strategy and planning model

GBCS business principles	GBCS HR strategic imperatives	Human resources mission	Focus areas	HR plan initiatives
Make *people* a key priority	I. Associates actively take ownership for the business success at all levels, individually and as teams by improving associate value.	To create an environment where the achievement of business goals is realized through an acceptance of individual accountability by each associate and by his/her commitment to performance excellence.	Cultural change	Learning forums such as: • Change management and you • GBCS strategy forum • PEP workshop • Quality curriculum Communication platform: • Ask the president • Answerline • All associate broadcasts • Bureaucracy busters • Associate dialogues Diversity platform: • Pluralistic leadership: Managing in a global society • Celebration of diversity • National diversity council
Use the *total quality management* approach to run our business	II. GBCS HR contributes to increased shareholder value by achieving process improvements that increase productivity and customer satisfaction.			
Rapidly and profitably globalize the business	III. Ensuring GBCS HR readiness to expand its business initiatives into global markets which requires a business partner that is sensitive to the unique needs of various cultures and people.			
Profitably grow by being the leader in customer-led applications of technology	IV. HR strategic plans and processes support and are integrated with GBCS' strategic and business planning processes so that the HR management system attracts, develops, rewards and retains associates who accept accountability for business success.		Rewards and recognition	Progress sharing plan (PSP) Special long-term plan (SLTP) recognition platform: • Partner of choice • Trailblazers • President's council • Achiever's club • Local recognition programs • Touch award
Be the *best value supplier*	V. GBCS HR provides a level of service to internal and external customers that establishes the HR organization as their value-added business partner.		Ownership	Performance excellence partnership (PEP) Associate surveys: • ASI (associate satisfaction index) • AOS (associate opinion survey) Organizational effectiveness: • Work teams • Process teams
	VI. The HR leader and team are competent to provide leadership and support to GBCS by championing HR initiatives that contribute to GBCS' success.			

with representatives of GBCS' senior leadership team, data from various consultants, and, most importantly, the business strategy.

As the arrows suggest, these imperatives shape the human resources mission, stated in the third column. To achieve that mission, Lane and his HR team determined that they would need to focus on three critical human resources areas:

1 Cultural change (CC).
2 Reward and recognition (RR).
3 Ownership (O).

These focus areas drive the development of HR's annual plan initiatives (shown in the right-hand column of figure 3.7). The primary initiatives center on performance management, recognition, and compensation practices, as well as communication programs. Of the various programs listed, consider several examples.

Performance management – performance excellence partnership

Lane and his team totally redesigned the performance management process to reflect a partnership between a supervisor (referred to as "coach") and his or her associates. Aligned with the third critical HR focus area (ownership), the process, known as performance excellence partnership (PEP), supports the GBCS value equation and serves as the foundation for aligning individual associate and team objectives, measurements, and rewards with business goals (see figure 3.8).

The GBCS quality council views PEP as a pervasive human resources practice for bringing about cultural change. The process enables a coach and associate to establish a partnership that consists of agreements regarding performance objectives, measurements, developmental needs, performance feedback, rewards, and performance reviews. PEP is based on eleven principles:

1 Mutual coach/associate partnership and accountability are essential.
2 Every associate has measurable objectives linked to the business.
3 Performance and developmental feedback are continuous and come from multiple sources.
4 Upward feedback is mandatory.
5 No direct peer-to-peer comparisons.
6 No performance ratings or forced ranking distributions.
7 Pay is for individual/team performance.
8 Demonstration of values is as important as achievement of business objectives.
9 A coach has full responsibility for salary treatment, including salary increases and lump sum bonus awards within his or her group.
10 Performance and salary review is done annually during each associate's service anniversary month.
11 The effectiveness of the PEP process is measured and improved based upon focus groups, feedback surveys, and the associate satisfaction index.

Rewards and recognition

In addition to PEP, GBCS has redesigned its compensation system to reinforce the strong link between associates' achievements and business success. The system has two components: the progress sharing plan (PSP) which now has bonuses tied to business unit performance for all associates (both management and union represented) and the special long-term plan (SLTP) for the senior and executive management teams. Both PSP and SLTP are linked to business results. SLTP has a significant linkage to associate satisfaction and customer satisfaction objective attainment to drive behaviors to achieve business success (Schuler & Jackson, 1987). See figure 3.9 for a description.

In addition to the changes in the compensation system, GBCS implemented a new

Figure 3.8 Performance excellence partnership (PEP)

Component	Purpose	HR critical focus area[a]
Objective setting	Focuses on objectives and drives performance. Must be realistic and linked to the business goals. Must be **SMART** (**S**pecific, **M**easurable, **A**chievable, **R**elevant and **T**imely). Monitored minimum of three times a year.	O
Performance feedback	Ongoing process provides valid, constructive, developmental feedback related to objective attainment. Must be **SMART** and given a minimum of three times a year.	O
Annual performance review	Focuses on achievement of objectives, how they were achieved, criticality to the business and degree of difficulty. January, 1993, GBCS converted to an AT&T service anniversary date merit review process for management associates. This reinforces objective setting as an ongoing process for the total team.	O
Upward feedback	Provides associates the opportunity to give anonymous feedback to coaches regarding specific dimensions of leadership and behavior related to values.	O
Development	Planning and implementing actions designed to enhance individual and team performance. Examples include: Training, education, task force assignments, etc.	O
Reward and recognition	Reward and recognition is a key element of PEP's success. It takes many forms such as: Non-cash awards, unique work assignments, etc. GBCS' recognition and compensation systems are specifically designed to recognize and/or pay associates for behaviors/results that are part of PEP and contribute to GBCS' success.	R

[a] CC = Cultural change; R = Rewards and recognition; O = Ownership

recognition platform to demonstrate to associates that their contributions are valued. The objective of the recognition platform is to motivate, build self-esteem, and allow the organization to identify and commend role-model behavior. Coaches are encouraged to continually make recognition an integral part of their day-to-day operations and have implemented local recognition programs in addition to the business unitwide programs. Figure 3.10 describes recognition programs for all GBCS associates. A wide variety of communications programs add support to the performance management, compensation, and recognition practices (see figure 3.11).

Getting all of these HR changes in place required substantial changes in the human resources organization. And, as was recognized at the Swiss Bank Corporation (Schuler, 1988), making changes in the HR organization itself was a useful place to begin. Therefore, this

Figure 3.9 Compensation management practices

Component	Purpose	HR critical focus area[a]
PSP for management and occupational associates	PSP supports increased associate value by providing associates the opportunity to share in earnings improvements based on achieving customer satisfaction and financial objectives.	R
SLTP for senior management team	Mirrors PSP. Has a three-year payout to establish long-term focus. Significant portion of annual variable pay tied to associate and customer satisfaction.	R

[a] CC = Cultural change; R = Rewards and recognition; O = Ownership

integral part of the GBCS transformation is described in our final section.

REPOSITIONING THE HUMAN RESOURCES ORGANIZATION

Implementing the preceding changes required new roles, new competencies, new relationships, additional resources, and new ways of operating – for both GBCS associates and the HR organization. Prior to its reorganization, GBCS human resources provided salary administration, HR information systems, staffing support, and other related administrative services. HR had to transform itself from a "provider of basic personnel services" to a strategic function, one that would be seen as adding value to the entire organization (Fitz-Enz, 1991).

With support from Jerre Stead, the human resources organization was repositioned as a key member on the senior management team and assumed the role of providing leadership on strategic human resources issues. Three areas were emphasized because of their linkage with the business strategy: diversity, labor, and HR strategic planning. The incumbents in these positions were charged with understanding how these areas could be enhanced

to strengthen GBCS' ability to achieve its business goals.

In forming the new human resources team from the former GBS and BCSystems HR organizations, the HR leadership team chose not to assign associates, by fiat, to new roles. Rather, the team asked each associate to state a job preference. The associates were told that the team would try to accommodate preferences, but that business needs would prevail in determining each person's ultimate assignment. It should be noted that 98 percent of the preferences were honored. As a result, the senior team was able to place highly skilled human resources professionals in key assignments that reflected their preferences. This enabled the organization to proceed on a transformation path with an excited, challenged, and motivated human resources staff.

The GBCS human resources organization is now made up of six teams, as shown in figure 3.12. Individuals on these teams are accountable for a wide variety of activities that support GBCS associates.

Associate services

The associate services team comprises four subteams: (1) *resource management*, which

Figure 3.10 GBCS recognition system

Program	Purpose	Eligibility[a]	Nomination process	Selection process	HR critical focus area[b]
Achievers club	Incents and recognizes associates in the NSSD, SBD and International organizations who meet the established performance criteria.	All associates in NSSD, SBD, International	Based on attainment of performance criteria.	Based on attainment of performance criteria.	R
Bureaucracy busters (BB)	Encourages associates to recommend changes to existing processes and policies that will reduce and eliminate bureaucracy.	All GBCS associates	"Proposal for accelerated action" submitted to BB coordinator. All associates may nominate.	Selection made by appropriate functional organization.	R
Partner of choice (POC)	Recognizes individuals and/or teams, who demonstrate a dedication to quality and demonstrating the values. Associates outside of GBCS are recognized if part of a GBCS team.	All GBCS associates	Nominations submitted to POC coordinator. All associates may nominate.	Selection team consists of 6 associates of all levels, from various organizations throughout the country.	R
President's council	Recognizes associates for outstanding contribution. Provides an opportunity for members to interact with the QC on initiatives affecting the value equation.	All GBCS associates	Coaches nominate.	Selection made by GBCS quality council.	R
Touch award	Honors associates for outstanding social/community contributions.	All GBCS associates	Nomination submitted to Touch coordinator. All associates may nominate.	Selection made by GBCS president's council.	R

[a] All associates, regardless of category or type, are eligible for the business unit wide recognition programs. The Achievers club and Trailblazers programs are companion programs – with the Achievers club recognizing the NSSD, SBD and International associates and Trailblazers recognizing all others.

[b] CC = Cultural change; R = Rewards and recognition; O = Ownership

Figure 3.11 Communication programs

Practice	Description	Participation[a]	Feedback mechanism	HR critical focus area[b]
Ask the president	Associates write, phone or mail questions or concerns to president of GBCS.	I/G	Acknowledgment of receipt within 24 hours. Written response from Pat Russo within 48 hours.	CC
Answerline	Associates call an 800 number with questions, issues, or requests for business-related information.	I/G	Call acknowledged within 72 hours. Written or telephone response to associate from subject expert.	CC
Chats	Small, face-to-face group meetings with business unit president and GBCS associates.	I	Associates receive immediate feedback at meeting on issues raised or questions asked. Associates provide feedback to Pat via survey following the meeting.	CC
Bureaucracy busters	All associates can submit ideas to recommend changes to existing policies or processes that will reduce or eliminate bureaucracy.	I/G	Acknowledgment of receipt within 48 hours. Written acceptance decision, share of stock award/recognition.	CC
All associate broadcasts	Video. Quarterly broadcast to all associates. Associates can view live at 60+ sites, dial-in and listen via 800 number, or view via tape after the broadcast.	I/G	Associates can call in during broadcast and ask questions. Questions are answered live if time allows. All questions and answers are published electronically after the broadcast. Associates can provide feedback via survey after the broadcast.	

Program	Description	Type[a]	Feedback/Results	Type[b]
Audio.	As-needed audio broadcasts on specific subjects. Associates dial in live via 800 number or can listen to recording for several days after initial broadcast.	I/G	Live Q & A during call. Associates can provide feedback via survey after broadcast. Trends show an increase in ask-the-president calls after each all-associates broadcast.	CC
Performance excellence partnership (PEP)	Performance and developmental initiative that ensures all associates have measurable objectives linked to GBCS business objectives.	I	Coach/associate review and revise objectives three times (minimum) per year. Objectives/accomplishments discussed in total at annual salary review. Associates provide upward feedback to coach twice a year.	O
Progress sharing plan (PSP)	Compensation plan for all GBCS associates which links pay to business results.	I	Monthly results published in *Goalposts*. Quarterly results published in *Bigger Bucks Bulletin*.	R
Recognition programs	Various programs that allow coaches and/or associates to nominate each other for performance recognition.	I/G	Peer/coach recognition; awards.	O
Associate opinion survey (AOS)	Semi-annual survey to all associates which assesses their feelings about the work climate. The associate satisfaction index (ASI) is GBCS' key measure of associate value.	I	Business unit results shared through various communication vehicles. Group results shared down to lowest level possible while still maintaining anonymity and integrity of data.	O

[a] I = Individual; G = Group
[b] CC = Cultural change; R = Rewards and recognition; O = Ownership

Figure 3.12   GBCS human resources organization chart

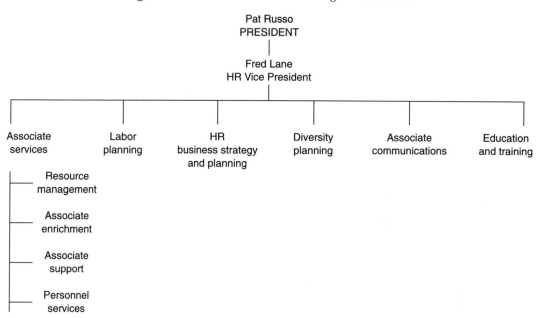

includes salary administration, compensation, and organization design; (2) *associate enrichment,* which concentrates on recognition and reward systems, quality, performance management, development, associate surveys, and work and family issues; (3) *associate support programs,* which provides expertise and support in the areas of staffing, relocation, HR information systems, and employment; and (4) *personnel services,* which works closely with GBCS HR associates in the field to design support processes and optimize delivery, maintenance, evaluation, and continuous feedback for improvement of HR programs in order to maximize their effectiveness.

GBCS has made substantial progress in developing and implementing its human resources plan initiatives. Further, every effort is being made to ensure that the operational plans which support its strategies are integrated across all functions. As a result, planning is

an integral part of the HR organization. Three teams focus on HR planning.

Labor planning

The labor planning team focuses on a partnership between the unions and GBCS management. The primary focus of this team is to jointly determine how to prepare associates for the workplace of the future, that is, to create a readiness to engage in the changing marketplace which is being driven by technological changes and new ways of working (e.g., self-managed teams).

HR business strategy and planning

The HR business strategy and planning team is responsible for ensuring that HR initiatives support the success of the business strategy. The HR strategy and planning model, discussed earlier, was developed by this team with significant support from Fred Lane, vice president of human resources.

Diversity planning

The diversity planning team ensures GBCS' constant attention to full utilization of the company's human talent. Efforts are directed at achieving awareness, understanding, and acceptance of all associates and ensuring a firm commitment to diversity throughout the organization. As part of this team's efforts, a global diversity council provides advice and counsel to associates and coaches on all issues, concerns, and opportunities related to equal opportunity and diversity. This team also develops and delivers programs, seminars, and events on matters related to EEO policy/law and valuing diversity.

Associate communications

Of the two remaining teams, the associate communications team focuses on ensuring involvement and participation from all associates by establishing multiple lines of communication with senior management. This supports one of the key themes in the new GBCS culture – that all associates have the power, protection, and permission to help GBCS improve the business.

Education and training

The education and training team focuses on developing and delivering leadership training as well as management and technical courseware and seminars for GBCS associates and customers. This team responds to the learning needs of their targeted audiences and delivers the educational experiences that will ensure their success.

SUMMARY AND CONCLUSIONS

Between 1989 and 1992, AT&T BC Systems, GBS and the merged Global Business Com-munications Systems went through tremendous change (Kotter, 1990). First, under significant financial pressure, Jack Bucter and his leadership team championed the efforts of a business reengineering team led by Glenn Hazard that radically changed the way BCSystems sold and implemented PBX systems. Next, under the direction of Jerre Stead, BCSystems was merged with GBS into GBCS. The combined leadership team formulated and launched a new vision of the business and a new strategy to align and motivate GBCS associates (Kotter, 1990) which is now being aggressively supported and refined by Pat Russo and the quality council. Under the direction of Fred Lane, the GBCS HR organization has dedicated its efforts to linking the unit's human resources efforts with the business strategy. The GBCS pyramid, the "value equation", the strategic business principles, the HR strategy and planning model, and the various HR initiatives discussed in this chapter were all critical elements in forging that linkage.

The development of the "value equation", the pyramid and the HR planning and strategy model provided important frameworks that enabled a strong alignment of the human resources efforts with the needs of the business, very consistent with the recommendations of Lawler et al. (1994) and Baird and Meshoulam (1988). These, in turn, also enabled Fred Lane and the human resources team to develop specific human resources programs and practices to link with the strategy of the business, consistent with the recommendations and findings of Schuler (1992).

But the work of Lane and his organization have gone beyond the 5-P model developed by Schuler (1992) and have enriched it substantially. The primary enrichment was the development of the concept of "associate qualities." This concept is critical for organizations in industries where there are rapidly changing customer needs due in large measure to rapid technological developments which make the development of stable job descriptions nearly impossible. In companies where jobs are more stable and limited in number it is much easier to identify the specific skills, competencies, and behaviors necessary for employees to successfully implement the business strategy. This not being the situation at GBCS, Fred Lane and his HR team developed the concept of "associate qualities." The associate qualities essentially describe the qualities associates need to have in order to implement the business strategy.

The qualities they identified are: accountability, responsibility, empowerment, and involvement. The basic GBCS human resources framework is: If the associates have these qualities, they will continuously improve their competency and work together to do their jobs, consistent with the needs of the business strategy. Whether the associates and their coaches will continue to be skilled enough to know what skills and competencies will be necessary to do their jobs with the rapid changes in the marketplace is the challenge. The existing GBCS human resources practices, which include a commitment to continuous learning, facilitate associate attainment of the needed associate qualities consistent with the needs of the business strategy (for details of this see Plevel, Nellis, Lane, & Schuler, 1994).

During the period of developing and implementing the HR strategy and planning model, Fred Lane realized that the HR organization itself needed to be repositioned and reorganized. This was done in a way that was consistent with the associate qualities identified as critical in relating HR to the business. The repositioning process created excitement in itself, thus motivating and challenging HR staff members. This repositioning was essential for the HR organization to be effective.

The overall experiences of the human resources organization at GBCS appear to confirm the frameworks previously suggested in the human resources literature and, in important ways, extend them. While this is just one case study of a very rapidly changing, high-technology firm, it seems that its experiences can provide important insights for many others.

The key lessons learned from the GBCS experience include:

- Units within larger organizations can and must change and respond to the changes of the global competitive marketplace.
- Aligning human resources with the needs of the business is necessary for successful implementation of organizational and culture change.
- Identifying specific human resource needs and competencies associated with specific business strategies is necessary for the successful implementation of business strategy.
- Developing a well-planned set of human resources plans, strategies, initiatives, programs, and practices is necessary to create the associate attributes necessary to ensure individuals are committed to behaving in ways necessary to implement the strategy and fulfill the needs of the business.
- Creating a new human resources organization, vision, mission, strategy, structure, and team of motivated and talented people is necessary in order to successfully align people with the business, link human resource management with business strategy, and develop the requisite set of human resources plans, strategies, initiatives, programs, and practices.

Challenges, of course, remain for GBCS and its effort to integrate business strategy and HR. Perhaps the most significant challenge will be the ability to retain strategic fit under conditions of constant change. AT&T and GBCS are involved in a vast, rapidly changing marketplace driven by the convergence of communications and computers and an evolving set of competitors. As such, it is likely that GBCS and other AT&T business units are also likely to change and be restructured.

The key challenge will be for GBCS to maintain the commitment to adaptive change to ensure the alignment of the people with the business strategy.

As Kotter (1990) stated, it is the responsibility of the leadership team "to energize people to overcome major obstacles toward achieving a vision, and thus to help produce the change needed to cope with a changing environment." The challenge is significant and success at GBCS in meeting that challenge will only be determined in the future.

REFERENCES

Baird, L., & Meshoulam, I. (1988). Managing two fits of strategic human resource management. *Academy of Management Review*, 13 (1), 116–28.

Fitz-Enz, J. (1991). *Human value management*. San Francisco: Jossey-Bass.

Hall, G., Rosenthal, J., & Wade, J. (1993). How to make reengineering really work. *Harvard Business Review*, Nov.-Dec., 126.

Kotter, J. (1990). *A Force for Change: How leadership differs from management*. New York: Free Press.

Lawler, E. E., Cohen, S. G., & Chang, L. (1994). Strategic human resource management. In P. Mirvis (ed.), *Strategic Human Resource Management*. San Francisco: Jossey-Bass.

Nadler, D. (1982). Interview with Charles Brown, CEO of AT&T. *Organizational Dynamics*, summer.

Plevel, M., Nellis, S., Lane, F., & Schuler, R. S. (1994). How AT&T global business communications systems is linking HR with business strategy. *Organizational Dynamics*, winter, 59–71.

Schuler, R. S. (1988). Customerizing the HR department at the Swiss Bank Corporation. *Human Resource Planning*, spring, 241–53.

Schuler, R. S. (1992). Strategic human resource management: Linking the people with the strategic needs of the business. *Organizational Dynamics*, summer, 18–32.

Schuler, R. S., & Jackson, S. E. (1987). Linking competitive strategies and human resource management practices. *Academy of Management Executive*, 1 (3), 202–19.

Schuler, R. S., & MacMillan, I. C. (1985). Gaining competitive advantage through human resource management. *Human Resource Management*, 23, 241–56.

Schuler, R. S., & Walker, J. W. (1990). Human resources strategy: Focusing on issues and actions. *Organizational Dynamics*, summer, 5–19.

Wright, P., & McMahan, G. (1992). Theoretical perspectives for strategic human resource management, *Journal of Management*, 18 (2), 295–320.

Ulrich, D., & Lake, D. (1990). *Organizational Capability*. New York: Wiley.

☐ Chapter 4 ☐

Strategic Industrial Relations

Myron Roomkin and Sherman D. Rosen

INTRODUCTION

In this chapter we deal with the efforts of employers to change their industrial relations practices in response to changing business conditions or business intentions. At such times, industrial relations is considered a strategic issue, because practices can have direct implications for the ultimate success or failure of an enterprise. The theory of strategic industrial relations is reviewed and critiqued based upon alternative explanations of change in industrial relations and the experiences of two examples, namely, the basic steel industry's relationship with the United Steelworkers, and the attempts to build cooperative labor–management relations between the Amalgamated Clothing and Textile Workers Union and both the Xerox Corporation and the men's suit manufacturing industry.

SHIFTING PATTERNS IN INDUSTRIAL RELATIONS

Industrial relations practices involving unions or the prospect of unionization can contain several strategic implications. Unions and collective bargaining have long been associated with higher costs of doing business, stemming from, among other causes, higher wages, productivity restrictions, overstaffing, and other inflexible work practices (see, e.g., Freeman & Medoff, 1984; Hirsch & Addison, 1986). Likewise, collective bargaining has been used to hinder firms from closing facilities or entering new geographic or product markets. Unions also have worked outside of collective bargaining to influence consumer choice through product boycotts or by obtaining legislation favorable to their industry or region (Delaney & Schwochau, 1993).

Practitioners, in recognition of these strategic implications, have long sought to establish an appropriate posture towards unions and unionization. For example, over forty years ago, Harbison and Coleman (1951) wrote about the "driving forces" in union–management relations, identifying several types of strategic relationships, including armed truces, working harmony, cooperation, and accommodation. Although these were often useful descriptions of existing relationships, these categories, as well as similar taxonomies, had very little predictive power. What determines the strategic posture achieved in a relationship? What determines when managers would move from an armed truce to accommodation, or vice versa? Why are some relationships cooperative and others not?

Questions like these dealing with the underlying nature of labor–management relations became very important during the 1980s. For one thing, it was the decade in which managers became highly concerned with the "strategic" implications of their responsibilities. It was a decade of strategic planning and strategic planners in both general management and functional fields, including human resource management.

But more important, even casual observation reveals that during the 1980s American industrial relations underwent enormous and sometimes contrary changes. On one hand, several long-standing bargaining adversaries sought out more cooperative relationships, frequently introducing greater degrees of employee participation and involvement at the shop floor and, in some cases, going so far as to place workers on their boards of directors. Observing these trends, *Business Week* magazine announced in 1981 the end of conflictive labor relations as we had known it since World War II and the beginning of an era of "New Industrial Relations."

However, at the same time, conflict became more commonplace in some relationships. We witnessed a growing hostility of managers to unions, declining rates of unionization, a fall in the proportion of union victories in representation elections, growth in the number of union decertification elections, greater employer militancy reflected in the growing use of striker replacements (exemplified perhaps by Reagan's firing of the air traffic controllers in 1980), and a bargaining agenda that included "take backs," two-tier wages and benefits, and other union concessions.

Clearly there were forces at work to alter relationships and the strategic posture management was taking towards unions. But the amount and diversity of change was so great, that observers wondered whether or not industrial relations had undergone a fundamental transformation. If such a transformation had in fact taken place, what type of system replaced it; does that system adequately meet the needs of workers, employers, and society; and what role should government play in this new industrial relations system?

THE TRANSFORMATION HYPOTHESIS

While the answers to the above questions are still being debated among academicians and practitioners, most people would agree that the terms of that debate have been shaped by the work of three professors from MIT, Thomas Kochan, Harry Katz, and Robert McKersie (1986). In a landmark book entitled *The Transformation of American Industrial Relations*, these authors identified the inadequacies of existing theories to explain all that was transpiring in the last decade. They introduced into the discussion the concept of *strategic choice* in the design and implementation of industrial relations policies by employers. In doing so, Kochan, Katz and McKersie (hereafter referred to as KKM) postulated the existence of a relationship between the business strategy of organizations and their industrial relations practices at a time when the human resource management function was itself developing the capacity to think and act strategically. Subsequent research went on to examine the relationship between business strategy and strategic industrial relations choices, paying particular attention to developments in the traditionally heavily unionized industries of automobile manufacturing, steel fabricating, and airlines.

The received theory of industrial relations

Until the publication of KKM's (1986) work, the received doctrine in industrial relations was that a system of workers, employers, their organizations, and specialized governmental agencies interacted in a complex environment to create a web of rules that would govern the employment relationship. This view of industrial relations as a system originated with John Dunlop's work in 1958 (reissued with new material in 1993). According to Dunlop, parties to the relationship (who Dunlop called the actors) were driven by their needs and circumstances along with the economic, social, and political contexts – what we today call the external environment of organizations (see also, Meltz, 1991).

Central to Dunlop's (1958) model is the notion that industrial relations systems evolve into a stable and stabilizing part of society. This takes place because the actors share an ideology. Ideology creates a consensus on the legitimacy of roles and goals, and places boundaries on conflict.

Stable systems also develop because the actors have the ability to adapt their relationships to the requirements of the environment. Adaptive change is seen as an important precondition for achieving a "mature" collective bargaining relationship. So strong is the association between maturity and stability that Slichter, Healy, and Livernash, wrote in their *magnum opus, The Impact of Collective Bargaining on Management* (1967, 11), that "The best goal for most firms is a stable relationship with the union on terms that permit the firm to be competitive and to adapt itself to changing conditions."

In Dunlop's (1958) terms, the American system of industrial relations, in both the unionized and nonunionized sectors, had evolved into a stable, slowly adapting institution, which was influenced heavily by the values and practices forged in the New Deal. This New Deal model featured the acceptance of unions by employers, an emphasis on maintaining industrial peace, and an acceptance of collective bargaining as the principal mechanism of employer participation and main determinant of working conditions.

Strategic choice theory

Departing from the received wisdom, KKM argued that industrial relations practices are better seen as a product of accommodation to an environment as well as the responses of organizations to those pressures. The practices of the parties may not change instantaneously. But when the parties are no longer willing to accept the old ways, or new goals are needed, change can be big and transformational.

In KKM's model (1986, 1990), American industrial relations may have looked stable for many years, but were in fact building towards a transformation which would end the old consensus. That transformation was due to the growing unwillingness of employers to recognize the inevitability of unionization, and their creation of nonunion alternatives in heavily unionized industries. In long-established bargaining relationships, the transformation meant experimentation with Quality of Worklife and Employee Involvement programs, and linking wage improvements to performance. But even more profound was the decision of employers to create a new variety of nonunionized employment built on trust between employers and employees, and a new social contract at the workplace.

This new model is best seen as a system of relationships between unions, employers, and government that operates at three levels. To paraphrase Burton's (1988) overview of this framework, at the top level, the actors decide matters of long-term strategy such as corporate investment decisions and union organizing plans. The bottom level is defined as the workplace, or shop floor. Here policies such as Employee Involvement programs are played out that affect workers, supervisors, and union representatives on a day-to-day basis. The middle tier of relationships is the traditional domain of industrial relations, typically collective bargaining activities. The central thesis of KKM is that recent changes at the top and bottom of this hierarchy have impacted significantly on the middle tier.

Figure 4.1   General framework for analyzing industrial relations issues

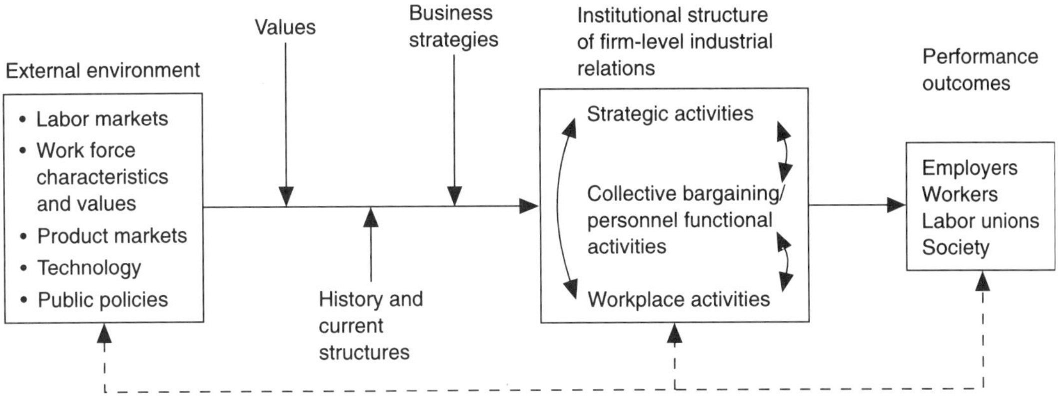

Source: Kochan, Katz, & McKersie (1994)

This three-fold conceptualization of relationships plays an important role in KKM's overall model of industrial relations, which is depicted in figure 4.1. In it, the external environment affects the institutional structure, and both factors contribute to the performance outcomes of the system. However, the environment and institutional structure are not mechanically linked to performance. Instead, the parties, particularly the employer, make choices with regard to the kind of practices they wish to follow. Because of the opportunity to select policies, KKM's model came to be known as "strategic choice" theory.

As proof of their new framework, KKM seek to explain several industrial relations developments of the past few decades. The New Deal model, according to KKM's analysis, created the middle-level practices of collective bargaining in order to address the major issues of that era (i.e., fair treatment, wage improvement, industrial peace and union legitimacy). But from the 1970s onward, environmental forces and institutional imperatives produced greater degrees of competition from domestic and international sources. Profitability in unionized firms declined, as wage increases in the unionized sector outpaced increases in the nonunionized sector.

As a consequence, unionized employers began looking for new ways to cut costs and increase profits and flexibility at the workplace.

Facing this reality in the upper tier of businesses, companies were forced to accept intentional programs of union avoidance and even deunionization. At the workplace, new programs of employee participation in management were introduced, including mechanisms for resolving workplace disputes and sharing in the financial performance of the organization.

With pressure for change coming from both the upper and lower levels of the relationship, collective bargaining was forced to accommodate. Wage and work rule concessions became commonplace. Important changes were enacted to permit more flexibility in work assignments, staffing levels, and pay systems (Piore, 1986). Collective bargaining relationships decentralized. Pattern bargaining weakened. Industrywide and multi-employer agreements, if they survived the decade, came under great pressure from employers to change. The number of work stoppages declined so dramatically that the government stopped gathering statistics on all strikes in the economy.

Perhaps the most striking changes in

labor–management relations took place at the strategic level of the relationship. Because bargaining was no longer the best way to control the effects of business decisions on unions and workers, unions sought access to boardrooms (McKersie, 1985). The unions with the greatest success in gaining entry to boardrooms were those that still had sufficient power as well as those unions in economically troubled companies or industries in which employers accepted some degree of codetermination in exchange for union cooperation and give-backs.

Elements of these new industrial relations practices also developed outside the U.S. during the past decade. In Europe and Australia, greater decentralization of wage bargaining developed (Katz, 1993), unions lost membership and market penetration in Europe and Japan, and employers nearly universally, it seemed, pursued greater flexibility in staffing and compensation. Unions, for their part, became more willing to accept variable compensation arrangements; but they also became more interested in obtaining information about businesses' performance and intentions.

Thus, it would seem that employers everywhere were more actively undertaking new directions and new practices at all levels of the relationship with unions. Behind these initiatives, KKM and others claimed, were conscious changes in business strategies and new industrial relations strategic choices.

CASE STUDIES

The following studies look at the changes in contemporary industrial relations that have taken place involving two old-line manufacturing unions – the Steelworkers Union and its relationship with employers in the basic steel industry, and the Amalgamated Clothing and Textile Workers Union (ACTWU) and its relationship with both the Xerox Corporation and employers in the men's suit manufacturing industry.

Evidence from the steel industry[1]

Big steel is one of the best places to look for signs of the transformation in American industrial relations. Organized mainly in the 1930s, unions in this industry owe much of their existence to the passage of the Wagner Act. Basic steel employers, too, owe a great deal to government, which has protected American steel manufacturers through protective trade policies and liberal enforcement of antitrust laws.

Root business strategies in the U.S. steel industry went through three phases between the 1940s and the 1990s (Hoerr, 1988). Before the 1970s, the industry exhibited the classic oligopolistic form, which allowed it to emphasize stability and shared market, even though steel firms faced increased competition from imported steel products. Between the 1970s and the mid-1980s, the central strategic problem was overcapacity as a result of declining demand for the product and rising imports. During this period, shared markets gave way to competition among the domestic producers. In the mid-1980s, bolstered by import restrictions, steel firms experienced great success, with rising profit levels and increasing sales abroad.

Industrial relations between the big steel companies and the Steelworkers Union has been highly adversarial in the long run, yet punctuated with moments of statesmanship and creative cooperation. While this industry gave us some of the longest, largest, and most frequent strikes in postwar history, the parties, especially the United Steelworkers, have recognized since 1942 that cooperative behavior would be in their interests. In 1984, National Steel Company and the Steelworkers pulled out of the coordinated bargaining committee that had traditionally negotiated industrywide agreements in this industry and set about building a new relationship. Their efforts culminated in a precedent-breaking Memorandum of Understanding on Cooperative Partnership (*Human Resource*

Management News, 1987), which expressed their agreement on the following principles:

- The recognition that their collective future depends upon a strong and economically viable company.
- Employment security, pay, and benefits depend on the ability of the company to be fully competitive with world-class competition.
- Employees are responsible and trustworthy.
- A nonautocratic management style is more appropriate and a more truly participative system should be developed.
- Where possible employees should be able to perform effectively with limited or no supervision.

Along with the demise of centralized bargaining, companies and the unions negotiated considerable reductions in labor costs as well as profit-sharing arrangements as a means of recapturing some of the lost income to employees. At the shop floor, the industry worked with the Steelworkers, under a training grant from the U.S. Department of Labor, to design and implement "labor–management participation teams" (a type of quality circle) across eight steel companies (Bernstein & Rothman, 1987).

According to Kalwa (1985), acceptance of this new relationship was a considerable transformation, driven by new strategic choices. Changes in the business environment, he argues, motivated the general managers to take control of decision making dealing with industrial relations, which was altered to emphasize company-specific and local considerations, as represented by the gradual movement away from centralized bargaining and the increase in workplace innovations. Furthermore, he points to the more active role of strategic issues as government became more involved in the industry.

Another study (Christiansen, 1983) looked at industrial relations and business strategies in three steel mills as part of a sample of nine companies in three industries. Industrial relations strategies are operationalized as being either centralized or decentralized, and business strategies are seen as seeking either low-cost operations or quality services and products. Christiansen finds that firms having consistency between their industrial relations and business strategies have improved performance, which she attributes to the purposeful pairing of the two types of strategies.

Arthur's (1992) study dealt with 30 of the 54 U.S. and Canadian minimills in operation in 1986. Minimills are the smaller, and mostly nonunion, steelmaking facilities that historically relied upon products made from melted steel and shipped to local markets, but that, during the 1980s, started serving regional markets with a greater variety of products, often fabricated in newer ways. Like Christiansen (1983), Arthur distinguishes between business strategies that seek to make the firm the lowest-cost producer of a product, and those strategies that seek to differentiate the product from others on the basis of a recognized and valued characteristic, like service, quality, shape, delivery time, and so forth. Arthur also distinguishes two types of workplace systems that could be found in these mills, the cost-reduction model, characterized by narrowly defined jobs, little employee voice, low skills requirements, and low wage rates; and the commitment maximizing model, containing broadly defined jobs, a high level of employee involvement and participation, highly skilled jobs, and high wage rates and benefits. Using regression analysis, he found that business strategy remains a significant predictor of industrial relations systems even after controlling for other relevant firm and local labor market conditions. This study is also important because it is one of the first to examine the relationship between business and industrial relations strategies in the nonunionized sector.

Roomkin and Juris (1990) contend that cooperative relationships in big steel are not new, and that the relationship has always adapted to its environment. They point to the creation during the early 1960s of the Human Relations Committee, which provided a forum for solving thorny issues away from the bargaining table, and the establishment in the early 1970s of the Experimental Negotiating Agreement, which provided for mandatory arbitration of collective bargaining disputes and a system of expedited settlement of workplace grievances. Thus, at least for the steel industry in the U.S., they argue that the old model of New Deal/adversarial union–management relations is capable of responding to the needs of the parties.

This point also is made by Adams (1988, 7) who studied steel companies in Canada. The contemporary corporation, he concludes, is "entirely capable of meeting the challenges posed by enhanced competition working from within the confines of the labor–management understandings reached in the decade after the Second World War."

Roomkin and Juris (1990) make another noteworthy point. Even though there were important differences among the strategic plans of the different steel companies, each one sought a highly similar new strategic relationship with the Steelworkers Union, one that emphasized cost reduction, productivity improvement, and workplace cooperation. Moreover, cooperation between the parties looks more like acquiescence than any fundamental shift in values or philosophy. Thus, the profit-sharing programs created in the 1980s in lieu of across-the-board wage increases were seen by managers as more of a cost-saving plan than any true shift in management philosophy.

The Amalgamated, Xerox, and the tailored clothing industry

Further insights into the possible transformation in American industrial relations can be seen in the experiences of the Amalgamated Clothing and Textile Workers Union and its relationships with two distinctly different employers: Xerox Corporation and the U.S. men's tailored clothing industry. Coincidentally, the Amalgamated's recent experiences with both cases center on Rochester, New York, the home of Xerox's main manufacturing complex in the Rochester suburb of Webster and the home of Hickey-Freeman, a maker of men's suits for executive and wealthy buyers. The union once represented numerous tailored clothing manufacturers in Rochester, but with declines in that industry, Hickey-Freeman remains the sole company under contract in Rochester and the negotiating unit at Xerox therefore has taken on increased importance for the union.

The Xerox experience

Xerox and the Amalgamated efforts at forging a new relationship have become a much discussed case study of how to develop a more cooperative workplace and to increase employee involvement within an existing collectively bargained relationship. The chronology of this development appears in the work of Cutcher-Gershenfeld (U.S. Department of Labor, 1988).

Following a period of product leadership and dramatic growth, the Xerox Corporation's share of worldwide copier revenues dropped to 41 percent in 1982 from 82 percent in 1976. Among the actions taken to stem the decline was a program to change the manufacturing environment in order to make the company more competitive on the basis of price and product quality. As part of that program, the traditional union–employer relationship was augmented by a collaborative effort designed to involve unionized workers in problem solving and decision making regarding everyday work practices. This was one of the first such programs in an existing bargaining relationship; previous efforts were mostly in new facilities or nonunionized settings.

The transformation began in the 1980 negotiations, when the parties agreed to experiment with a Quality of Worklife program (QWL). The focus at that time was on solving problems on the shop floor through group processes similar to quality circles. Initially, the union was skeptical of this approach and agreed to proceed only after receiving assurances that the program would have joint labor–management oversight, not be short lived, and would be kept separate from the traditional collective bargaining process. Consequently, after two years, over 90 problem-solving groups were established, with 25 percent of the employees in the bargaining unit volunteering to be part of the groups.

These early efforts did face some problems, however. Bidding and bumping rights in the labor agreement reduced flexibility. Layoffs tended to produce turnover in group leaders. In addition, the lengths of time required to solve problems and to implement solutions were frustrating to workers and were traceable to the difficulties teams had in getting information and access.

In 1983, an important expansion of the joint decision-making process occurred when a "study team" of workers and management was formed in response to the possibility of subcontracting. Team members were trained in group problem-solving skills, communications methods, finance, and accounting. But due to the reluctance of many managers to cooperate with the groups, they failed to reach their potential contribution. A consultant called in to help the parties find solutions identified several changes in the labor agreement pertaining to seniority, job bumping, and bidding rights. Some changes were made, but others were deferred to negotiations.

Placing the study team issues on the bargaining table was pivotal; it gave the message that the joint decision-making concept was tied into collective bargaining. The 1983 contract accepted the study team concept in exchange for a guarantee of no layoffs lasting three years for workers at the involved locations. The agreement further mandated the establishment of a study team each time subcontracting became an issue in the future; since then, several study teams have been formed.

Despite this early success, workers grew more frustrated with what they saw as inadequate communication and support from the company. Following a detailed study, 30 functional groupings of workers were designated as business area work groups (BAWGs). Supervisors were made BAWG leaders and mandatory biweekly meetings were established for the purposes of sharing information. Each BAWG, however, was free to design an appropriate method of involving workers in workplace issues. Some returned to QWL methods; others addressed issues in an ad hoc fashion; still others formed autonomous work groups.

Two other organizational transformations also occurred at Xerox. One was the establishment of strategically oriented Horizon teams, which explored future issues facing the business and the management of human resources, such as the location of a new plant. Another transformation was the establishment of a number of semiautonomous work groups, initially in areas where workers were accustomed to working independently.

In 1986 the union joined Xerox's Leadership Through Quality program, which sought to define and achieve standards of quality performance. Eventually, every manager, union official, and union member participated in quality training.

While the cooperation between Xerox and ACTWU has continued and has even expanded, the union has declined an invitation to participate in the manufacturing management operations committee. This formal role was seen as too strong a link to managerial decisions.

A key to cooperative efforts in this case has been the no-lay-off guarantee first negotiated in 1983 and included in all subsequent contracts. In the spring of 1994, the parties extended the guarantee for all 3,850 union members at the Webster manufacturing complex for a seven-year period. Under the terms of the new agreement, wage increases were limited to cost-of-living increases, capped at 6 percent annually, until 2001. The parties agreed to jointly study the reduction of costs of "low value added" jobs (e.g., cleaning, trucking, and packaging) in order to avoid subcontracting to outsiders. Moreover, at the union's suggestion, a voluntary severance package will be offered to help Xerox meet its work-force reductions (Lowe 1994).

The men's tailored clothing industry

Due to the favorable experience at Xerox, ACTWU was encouraged to seek similar innovations with other employers with which it negotiated, such as companies in the men's tailored clothing industry. Unfortunately, the union has experienced considerably less success in transforming relationships in the men's tailored clothing industry.

For decades, employment and union membership have been declining in men's clothing manufacturing. Behind this decline have been changes in consumer preferences, growing amounts of imported clothing at lower prices, and poor managerial practices. Rochester contained over a dozen big clothing manufacturers in 1930, employing over 11,000 workers, most of who were represented by the ACTWU. Today, only Hickey-Freeman (a division of Hartmarx Corporation) remains, employing less than 1,000.

In 1986, ACTWU officials approached the management of Hickey-Freeman with the suggestion that the company implement the kind of employee involvement program that was proving successful at Xerox. The union even went so far as to retain a study of the company's workplace environment from a consultant who had worked on the transformation of Xerox. The consultant's report[2] recommended establishing labor–management study teams to address the issues of training, compensation, quality, and supervisory styles. Hickey-Freeman's managers, wary of this new partnership, preferred the old ways to innovation.

At the national level, ACTWU again took the initiative in seeking a new relationship by working with the Clothing Manufacturers Association to create the National Clothing Industry Labor–Management Council, which was supposed to address long-term deficiencies in productivity.[3] But it took four years before ACTWU and the Association issued the findings of the council. When it did, the council recommended a series of steps that the parties could take to advance toward a relationship where periodic negotiations and grievance handling give way to a continuous process of joint problem-solving and union–management consultation. Among the changes it recommended were: "multiskilling" of operators in order to enhance manufacturing flexibility; alternative compensation schemes to the traditional individual piecework incentives; training for supervisors in participative leadership styles; and more employee participation and teamwork (ACTWU/CMA, 1991).

The merits of these proposals notwithstanding, the industry generally failed to follow up by producing a set of local- or areawide committees to work on the implementation of change. Resistance came mostly from the employers.

In 1991, the union made a second unsuccessful attempt to work with Hickey-Freeman to develop an employee involvement program, but it was not until 1994 that the company agreed to work on the adoption of the council's recommendations. A steering committee composed of management and union representatives is addressing the issues surrounding the introduction of teams and new compensation arrangements, such as gainsharing.

The lessons learned

The industries in these case studies range from new high technology of the second industrial revolution to one of the oldest manufacturing industries of the first. If there is a theme in these data, it is that transformation to cooperative arrangements between labor and management came about for a variety of reasons and are not just the result of management's attempt to respond to strategic necessities. Whereas Xerox took the initiative in broaching a new relationship with the Amalgamated, employers in the men's tailored clothing industry resisted the union's effort to bring similar practices to that industry. Steel companies, in several instances, were able to get the Steelworkers to accept new, innovative work practices, but frequently it was with the reluctant acceptance of the union, and achieved within the framework of their historical competitive collective bargaining relationship.

OTHER CRITICISM AND CONTROVERSIES

Without a doubt, the strategic industrial relations theory introduced by KKM and advanced by several other researchers is an important contribution to our understanding of how industrial relations practices came into being (Chelius & Dworkin, 1990). But not all academicians and practitioners have been willing to accept the fact that the long-standing New Deal model was swept away as employers pursued more appropriate business strategies. Both theoretical and methodological criticisms of the work have been offered.

Methodological limitations

As Strauss notes (1988), KKM's book is a methodological mishmash. It relies on a range of data, from impressionistic case studies and interviews to quantitative studies that fully conform to the current canons of research orthodoxy. Hildebrand (1988) refers to it as casual empiricism. As such, the work is incomplete, offering us only limited generalizability, according to Lewin (1987).

But perhaps the scientific method is not the right one with which to evaluate a work of such historical and theoretical scope. Few things in the social sciences are ever proved; it is more useful to ask whether or not the authors provide a convincing case that ties together a preponderance of the evidence. Critics contend that too much of the industrial relations developments in the past two decades is left unexplained by the strategic choice theory, and even more critically, that developments are still best understood in terms of the Dunlop (1958) concept of accommodation of all actors to their changing environment.

Integrating industrial relations and business strategies

A serious criticism of strategic choice theory has been that it fails to detail the specific linkages existing between business strategies and industrial relations practices (Roomkin & Juris, 1990). In KKM (1986) and subsequent works, we are not told which business strategies are linked unambiguously with which changes in industrial relations, or whether a particular transformation in practice might be correlated with several different strategies. Thus, for instance, Hildebrand (1988), while acknowledging that the industry pattern system in collective bargaining has collapsed, wonders why KKM's theory cannot tell us why, how, and where it has collapsed.

Business strategy as a concept

If business strategy is indeed the chief *driver* of change, the concept needs much more precision and clarity (Strauss, 1988; Roomkin & Juris, 1990). Verma (1985) notes that KKM seem to imply that any management initiative constitutes strategic thinking. For example, as Lewin (1987) notes, the decision to aggressively resist a union organizing campaign can be linked to a long-run business plan, but it also can come from the simple belief that management has a greater chance of winning if it resists.

Strauss (1988) and Thurley and Wood (1983) wonder whether strategy means a consciously developed long-run policy or one merely derived from the sum total of management's actions? Why does a company adopt a given strategy in the first place? Strategies themselves are just ideas or cognitions – that is, assessments of problems or opportunities. But ultimately, strategy produces managerial actions. As yet undetermined is the relationship between the cognitive and behavioral dimensions of strategies. Does one type of assessment imply a specific set of actions; can one type of action fit with several different strategic intentions?

Likewise, strategy is rarely self-evident or received by senior managers. Rather, it is usually a consequence of analyses that are part rational and part political. Creativity also places a large role in strategy formulation. So far, these parts of the process have not been factored into the equation completely.

Instead, strategic choice theory appears to take business strategies as an exogenous factor (see figure 4.1), as if they should be apparent to any manager facing the same set of environmental forces. These strategies, in turn, according to figure 4.1, precipitate appropriate industrial relations responses.

However, some of the more exciting developments in contemporary industrial relations have taken place when causality has flowed in the opposite direction; that is, when an industrial relations strategy has determined the business intentions of the enterprise. One example is the notion that firms seek out sustainable competitive advantages (what are called economic rents) by selecting a strategy that leverages unique, immobile, and nonreplicable resources (Peteraf, 1993). Human resources practices in general and industrial relations practices in particular are possible sources of such sustained competitive advantage. In such situations, industrial relations strategies are in fact the business strategy of the firm. Consider, for example, the efforts of unionized employees to purchase distressed companies, most notably in the case of United Airlines. Employee ownership, in many of these cases, is more than just a financial manipulation aimed at infusing capital or reducing wage costs (Davis & Weintraub, 1990). In a significant proportion of the cases, the goal is to distinguish the service or product in the marketplace with higher standards of quality or the customer's perception of more caring employees.

Another factor complicating our efforts to understand business strategy is that at any single moment managers face strategic choices in several areas of the business (e.g., finance, production, marketing, and distribution). Also, decisions affect not just the unionized or potentially unionized employees, but all other relevant stakeholders, both in- and outside the company. Thus, DeAngelo and DeAngelo (1991) found that the seven large domestic steel companies during the 1980s, who were all facing serious economic distress, not only requested wage and work rule concessions but shared the burdens with other major stakeholders as well, such as senior managers, white collar employees, and stockholders. Thus, strategic choice is not limited to industrial relations choices.

Industrial relations and human resources planning

Planning has become both an important activity and an organizing logic in the overall function of human resource management (see, for example, Fombrun, Tichy, & Devanna, 1984; Lorange & Murphy, 1983). Most strategic planning processes rest on two important tenets. First, human resources practices and policies must fit with and support the nature of the product or service (Cassell, Juris, & Roomkin, 1985). Second, human resources managers must abandon their traditional reactive role, if the function is to add value. This has placed great pressure on human resources professionals to serve as change agents and advocates for new work practices (Kochan & Dyer, 1993).

Industrial relations scholars who have been concerned about strategic choice have paid inadequate attention to the role of human resource management and human resources professionals in strategic planning. Industrial relations strategy does not stand in isolation. Rather it is one of the derived functional strategies stemming from the overall situation facing the organization and the root strategy of the business. One exception is Schuler (1989), who in a preliminary fashion has begun to integrate the strategic choice framework with a model of competitive strategy and product life-cycle analysis.

Strategic choice and new employment relationships

At the same time that union power, influence, and size were shrinking, newly innovative work practices became more commonplace. Generally called high-performance or high-commitment employment systems, the new practices typically combine many of the following elements:

- Employee involvement programs to encourage employee participation in workplace and production issues.
- Employee governance or voice in organizational matters or employee access to business decisions.
- Financial participation through compensation practices that link wages more closely to individual, group, and organizational performance.
- Greater use of teams in production, possibly including self-directed (i.e., unsupervised work groups).
- Relaxation of work rules to permit flexible staffing of assignments.
- Higher levels of investment in employee training to permit higher degrees of job security.

The debate over strategic choice theory has been whether or not the new work systems are a more logical way in which to organize the employment relationship in light of the business choices facing firms. That is to say, industrial relations and employment relations are the direct consequence of business intentions.

But there is an alternative explanation, one missed by most of the literature. Perhaps the new systems are actually the consequence of a changing definition of the firm in the last part of this century. Structurally, firms are becoming flatter and leaner. Managerially, authority and power relationships are being redefined through the decentralization of responsibility and accountability. Old notions of hierarchy and bureaucracy are being challenged. Traditional workplace practices, including unionization, are not compatible with these new types of organizations; new definitions of organization require new varieties of work systems.

Some companies have accepted this new paradigm as a logical response to competitive forces in the marketplace. However, many other companies are simply trying to stay current with changing managerial practices. In Britain, for example, Storey (1993) found that in 1986–88, firms introduced an array of far-reaching employment initiatives but without any coherent model in mind, implying a significant amount of faddism. Similar tendencies are common in the U.S. This would explain why so many companies are at least claiming to want similar employment systems, irrespective of the particular strategic circumstances they face or strategy they wish to pursue. It would also explain why so few firms actually overhaul their basic system instead of "borrowing" or "transplanting" practices selectively (Osterman, 1994).

Unions can be strategic, too

By concentrating exclusively on the role of management in shaping industrial relations practices, the proponents of strategic choice theory have accepted a rather cynical view of labor–management relations. Relations do not bend to the will of employers, even if they are stronger than unions. What are the strategic objectives of unions in the 1990s? What are the factors influencing those strategic intentions?

In fairness, most scholars and practitioners consider unions to be incapable of strategic thinking. Unions, in the conventional view, are political institutions whose leaders must respond to the short-run demands of their members, even when those demands are not in the long-term interest of the union as an organization. Rational analyses of the environment, the identification of predefined objectives, the weighing of alternative strategies – in other words, the basic elements of strategic choice – require stable leadership and clear organizational objectives.

Thus, Block (1980) found that the level of expenditures on organizing in its primary (or core) jurisdiction decreased after the union achieved a critical level of membership in that jurisdiction. Presumably, at that point union leaders would perceive a greater benefit as well as their political survival in using dues revenue to service the existing membership. In comparison, a study of union expenditures on organizing by Voos (1984) dispels the belief that unions have cut back on their efforts to bring in members. Rather than acquiescing to the heightened resistance of employers or the increased pressure of existing members for services, unions increased real organizing expenditures per union member by nearly 40 percent from the 1950s to the 1970s, according to Voos.

The latest theoretical advances on union behavior have begun to show that unions, too, can engage in strategic thinking, but we need to adopt a different definition of strategy than normally ascribed to rational organizations. Using resource dependency theory, Lawler (1990) argues that a union, like any other organization, will define its effectiveness in terms of its ability to control its external resources. As created by Pfeffer and Salancik (1978), resource dependency theory contends that an organization will form coalitions of their resource suppliers (i.e., those entities on whom they are dependent) in the face of conflicting external demands upon resources.

Employing this theory, Lawler (1990) is able to make sense of recent efforts of the American Federation of Labor–Congress of Industrial Organization to address the slide in membership of the past decade and the rising level of employer militancy. The report, *The Changing Situation of Workers and Their Unions*, prepared by the AFL-CIO's (1985) Committee on Work (subsequently called the Committee on the Evolution of Work), was an important step forward in strategic thinking for unions, insofar as it recognized the reality of external threats and laid out an action plan for the labor movement. Among the steps recommended by the AFL-CIO were the following:

1 The creation of associate memberships to permit workers to maintain a relationship with the labor movement, even though they might have lost a unionized job or the union had inadequate support among workers.
2 Improved coordination among unions in organizing campaigns.
3 Improved public and media relations.

In 1994, the Committee went so far as to endorse the concept of the high-performance work environment, and to call for new forms of worker cooperation, voice, and involvement at the workplace (AFL-CIO, 1994). Moreover, prominent trade union intellectuals and liberal economists are endorsing the concept of the transformed relationship, as evidenced by the recent treatise on labor–management cooperation by Bluestone and Bluestone (1992).

At the level of the national union, strategic planning is far from being a common practice, but indications from one study of 22 unions show that unions are recognizing the importance of taking a more systematic purposeful approach underpinning their behavior, instead of reacting to the initiatives of employers (Stratton-Devine, 1992). Such efforts, however, are still heavily influenced by political considerations, especially when it comes to questions of developing new union leaders. It is doubtful that planning in unions can be depoliticized if we are to preserve them as democratic and voluntary associations. But a little bit of planning may go a long way in helping unions to identify new distinctive competencies and services that will appeal to workers. Planning may even assist traditional unions to metamorphose into different types of institutions, ones that look more like social movements on the model of civil rights groups, or like political parties following the European model, or organized interest groups in the fashion of the American Association of Retired Persons.

IMPLICATIONS FOR PRACTITIONERS

Why should a practitioner care whether or not KKM (1986) are correct? There are several reasons.

First, there is no doubt that the initiative in shaping policies and practices towards unions, the posture of the firm towards unionization, and indeed human resource management in general have shifted to employers. In the 1950s and 1960s, the dominant defining forces were unions, collective bargaining, or the fear of unionization. In the 1970s, employment practices were more likely to

be influenced by a rising level of governmental regulation of the employment relationship. No one knows how long employers will enjoy this window of opportunity before either unions or government reassert a greater influence over practices. Indeed, new labor laws are now under consideration that will give unions greater organizing success, limit employers' ability to hire permanent replacements during work stoppages, and place restrictions on Employee Involvement programs. Less likely, but still possible, is legislation that would mandate new forms of employee representation or participation at the workplace. Thus, this is the time companies should be paying close attention to industrial relations and human resources issues.

Second, any redesign of industrial relations or human resource practices should take into account the factors mentioned in KKM's model. Business strategy may not be the sole determinant of new human resources practices, but it is certainly one of the more important criteria against which a new practice should be evaluated in any rational approach to policy. Unfortunately, as indicated above, most companies innovating in this area seem to be accepting new practices without much thought. We should not be surprised, therefore, when these practices fail to work. Thus, an important message to practitioners is: take a long hard look at what you do in industrial relations and human resource management to make sure that proposed practices are indeed your best strategic choice.

Third, more work needs to be done on the integration of business planning and industrial relations. This is true not only at the level of theory, as mentioned above, but in practice as well. With responsibility for initiating, implementing, and evaluating industrial relations having shifted to general and line managers, more work needs to be done to increase that group's knowledge of and sensitivity to human resources issues.

Fourth, with greater amounts of employee involvement at the lower tier of relationships, and new forms of employee representation at the upper tier, there is a greater need to train employees and union leaders for their new roles.

Fifth, the transformed industrial relations practices stress our current labor and employment laws almost to the breaking point. The National Labor Relations Act of 1935 was supposed to facilitate the formation of unions and conduct of collective bargaining by creating a federal regulatory framework for industrial relations. However, as unions and many academic authorities have concluded, the Act no longer achieves these goals. They are calling for labor law reform which will increase the power of unions and their ability to organize. Efforts in the 1970s to pass labor law reform ended when supporters of the changes failed to get enough votes to end debate in the Senate. A revived campaign in the 1990s may not be any more successful.

The employment laws of the U.S., however, need more than just reform, if they are to deal with new varieties of employment relationships. As noted recently by the President's Commission on the Future of Worker–Management Relations (1994), the American economy and American worker have changed greatly since the passage of the National Labor Relations Act. It may well be that the law itself is an impediment to transforming labor–management relations, because it is built on an assumption that workers and employers have conflicting interests and that only free and independent unions and collective bargaining can bridge those differences effectively. Recent decisions by the National Labor Relations Board (see for example *Electromation*[4]) have outlawed employee involvement activities in which employees and managers discuss working conditions outside of collective bargaining. Nonunionized employers and employees need at least minimal legal guidelines to better define their rights and responsibilities in the use of workers' councils or assemblies or other varieties of workplace participation, long-term financial participation schemes, and workplace dispute resolution. If we are going to create such a framework, then this is probably the right time to take a comprehensive approach to employment regulation and better coordinate the laws and agencies governing labor relations with the laws and agencies governing equal employment opportunity.

Finally, looking towards the future, we should be asking: What strategic issues are likely to affect businesses and how might they impact on the effectiveness of current practices or the need for new practices, organizations, or institutions? One such strategic issue is nearly certain to be the continued globalization in business through expanded product markets and increased foreign investments. So far, and somewhat surprisingly, labor movements in different countries have been unable and perhaps uninterested in creating multinational arrangements that would offset the bargaining power employers gain from globalized activity (Flanagan & Weber, 1974). Given the need of labor movements in several countries for more power, it is hard to imagine these unions not undertaking more transnational cooperation in organizing and bargaining.

A second trend is the long-term drive for increased productivity. No one can predict with accuracy where productivity will lag or spurt, or where the next technological breakthrough will take place. However, greater globalization will require continued efforts to control costs and produce efficiently. Flexibility in staffing, compensation, and managing human resources should continue to be an important strategic asset for companies. All the actors in the system – employers, employees, unions, and government – have an important stake in finding new ways of dealing with worker displacement and the other problems attendant upon the introduction of new technology.

NOTES

1 This section draws heavily from Roomkin and Juris (1990).
2 See *Programs for Employee and Workplace Systems of Cornell University* (1987).
3 The Bureau of Labor Statistics reports that over a 20-year period beginning in 1967, the annual rate of productivity increase in the tailored clothing industry was only 1.9 percent compared to 2.5 percent for all manufacturing combined (Seiling & Curtin 1988).
4 *Electromation, Inc. and International Brotherhood of Teamsters, Local Union 1049, AFL-CIO and "Action Committees" Party of Interest*; 309 NLRB No. 163 (1992).

REFERENCES

ACTWU/CMA National Clothing Industry Labor-Management Committee (1991). *A Strategy for Innovation.* New York: ACTWU/CMA.
AFL-CIO (1985). *The Changing Situation of Workers and their Unions.* Washington, DC: AFL-CIO.
AFL-CIO (1994). *The New American Workplace: A Labor Perspective.* Washington DC: AFL-CIO Committee on the Evolution of Work.
Adams, R. J. (1988). The "old industrial relations" and corporate competitiveness: A Canadian case, *Employee Relations*, 10, 3–7.
Arthur, J. B. (1992). The link between business strategy and industrial relations systems in American steel minimills. *Industrial and Labor Relations Review*, 45, 488–506.
Bernstein, A., & Rothman, M. (1987). Steelmakers want to make teamwork an institution, *Business Week*, May 11, 84.
Block, R. N. (1980). Union organizing and the allocation of union resources. *Industrial and Labor Relations Review*, 34, 101–13.
Bluestone, B., & Bluestone, I. (1992). *Negotiating the Future: A Labor Perspective on American Business.* New York: Basic Books.
Burton, J. F. (1988). Editor's introduction to review symposium: "Transformation of American Industrial Relations." *Industrial and Labor Relations Review*, 41, 439–42.
Cassell, F., Juris, H. A., & Roomkin, M. J. (1985). Strategic human resources planning: An orientation to the bottom line. In W. D. Guth (ed.), *Handbook of Business Strategy: 1985/1986 Yearbook*, 27/1–27/12. Boston: Warren, Gorham & Lamont.
Chelius, J., & Dworkin. J. (1990). An overview of the transformation of industrial reactions. In J. Chelius and J. Dworkin (eds.), *Reflections on the Transformation of Industrial Relations*, 1–18. Metuchen, NJ: IMLR Press/Rutgers and The Scarecrow Press.
Christiansen, E. T. (1983). Strategy, structure and labor relations performance. *Human Resource Management*, 22, 155–68.
Davis, G. M., & Weintraub, N. (1990). Labor–management relations: ESOPs in the trucking industry. In M. J.

Roomkin (ed.), *Profit Sharing and Gain Sharing*, 97–108. Metuchen, NJ: IMLR Press/Rutgers University and The Scarecrow Press.
DeAngelo, H., & DeAngelo, L. (1991). Union negotiations and corporate policy: A study of labor concessions in the domestic steel industry during the 1980s. *Journal of Financial Economics*, 30, 3–43.
Delaney, J., & Schwochau, S. (1993). Employee representation through the political process. In B. E. Kaufman & M. M. Kleiner (eds.), *Employee Representation: Alternatives and future directions*, 265–304. Madison, WI: Industrial Relations Research Association.
Dunlop, T. J. (1958). *Industrial Relations Systems.* NY: Holt, Rinehart, & Winston.
Dunlop, T. J. (1993). *Industrial Relations Systems*, rev. ed. Boston: Harvard Business School Press.
Flanagan, R. J., & Weber. A. R. (1974). *Bargaining Without Boundaries: The multinational corporation and international labor relations.* Chicago: University of Chicago Press.
Fombrun, C., Tichy, N. M., & Devanna, M. A. (1984). *Strategic Human Resource Management.* New York: Wiley.
Freeman, R. B., & Medoff, J. L. (1984). *What Do Unions Do?* New York: Basic Books.
Harbison, F. H., & Coleman. J. R. (1951). *Goals and Strategy in Collective Bargaining.* New York: Harper.
Hildebrand, G. H. (1988). Comment in "Review symposium." *Industrial and Labor Relations Review*, 41, 447.
Hirsch, B. T., & Addison, J. T. (1986). *The Economic Analysis of Unions: New approaches and evidence.* Boston: Allen & Unwin.
Hoerr, J. P. (1988). *And the Wolf Finally Came: The decline of the American steel industry.* Pittsburgh: University of Pittsburgh Press.
Human Resource Management News (1987). September 19.
Kalwa, R. W. (1985). Collective bargaining in basic steel, 1946–1983. Dissertation submitted for Ph.D. at Cornell University.
Katz, H. C. (1993). The decentralization of collective bargaining: A literature review and comparative analysis. *Industrial and Labor Relations Review*, 47, 3–22.
Kochan, T. A., & Dyer, L. (1993). Managing transformational change: The role of human resource professionals. *International Journal of Human Resource Management*, 4, 569–90.
Kochan, T. A., Katz, H. C., and McKersie, R. B. (1986). *The Transformation of American Industrial Relations.* New York: Basic Books.
Kochan, T. A., Katz, H. C., & McKersie, R. B. (1990). Strategic choice and industrial relations theory: An elaboration. In H. C. Katz (ed.), *The Future of Industrial Relations: Proceedings of the Second Bargaining Group Conference.* Ithaca, NY: ILR Press.
Kochan, T. A., Katz, H. C., & McKersie, R. B. (1994). *The Transformation of American Industrial Relations*, 2nd ed. Ithaca, NY. ILR Press.
Lawler, E. J. (1990). *Unionization and Deunionization: Strategy, tactics, and outcomes.* Columbia, SC: University of South Carolina Press.
Lewin, D. (1987). Industrial relations as a strategic variable. In M. M. Kleiner, R. N. Block, M. Roomkin,

& S. W. Salsberg (eds.), *Human Resources and the Performance of the Firm*, 1–42. Madison, WI: Industrial Relations Research Association.

Lowe, S. (1994). Deal in wings at Xerox. *Rochester Democrat & Chronicle*, May 29.

McKersie, R. B. (1985). New dimensions in industrial relations. *Proceedings of the Spring Meeting of the Industrial Relations Research Association, Detroit, Michigan*, 645–7.

Meltz, N. H. (1991). Dunlop's "Industrial Relations System" after three decades. In R. J. Adams (ed.), *Comparative Industrial Relations: Contemporary research and theory*, 10–20. London: HarperCollins Academic.

Osterman (1994). How common is workplace transformation and who adopts it? *Industrial and Labor Relations Review*, 47, 173–88.

Peteraf, M. A. (1993). The cornerstones of competitive advantage: A resource-based view. *Strategic Management Journal*, 14, 179–91.

Pfeffer, J., & Salancik, G. R. (1978). *The External Control of Organizations*. New York: Harper & Row.

Piore, M. J. (1986). Perspectives on labor market flexibility. *Industrial Relations*, 25, 146–66.

President's Commission on the Future of Worker–Management Relations (1994). *Factfinding report issued by the Commission on the Future of Worker–Management Relations*, June 2. Washington, D.C.: Bureau of National Affairs.

Programs for employee and workplace systems of Cornell University (1987). Hickey-Freeman Company, Inc.: Organizational Assessment. Unpub. manuscript, January 14.

Roomkin, M. J., & Juris, H. J. (1990). Strategy and industrial relations: An examination of the American steel industry. In J. Chelius & J. Dworkin (eds.), *Reflections on the Transformation of Industrial Relations*, 107–20.

Metuchen, NJ: IMLR Press/Rutgers University and The Scarecrow Press.

Schuler, R. S. (1989). Strategic human resource management and industrial relations. *Human Relations*, 42, 157–84.

Seiling, M. S., & Curtin, D. (1988). Patterns of productivity change in men's and boys' suits and coats. *Monthly Labor Review*, November, 25–31.

Slichter, S. H., Healy, J. J., & Livernash, E. R. (1967). *The Impact of Collective Bargaining on Management*. Washington, D.C.: The Brookings Institution.

Storey, J. (1993). The take-up of human resource management by mainstream companies: Key lessons from research. *International Journal of Human Resource Management*, 4, 529–54.

Stratton-Devine, K. (1992). Strategic human resource planning: A union perspective. *Human Resource Planning*, 15, 37–46.

Strauss, G. (1988). Comment in "Review Symposium." *Industrial and Labor Relations Review*, 41, 449–51.

The new industrial relations (1981) *Business Week*, May 11.

Thurley, K., & Wood, S. (1983). Business strategy and industrial relations strategy. In K. Thurley & S. Wood (eds.), *Industrial Relations and Management Strategy*, 197–224. Cambridge: Cambridge University Press.

U.S. Department of Labor, Bureau of Labor-Management Relations and Cooperative Programs (1988). *Tracing a Transformation in Industrial Relations: The case of Xerox Corporation and the Amalgamated Clothing and Textile Workers Union*. BLMR 123.

Verma, A. (1985). Relative flow of capital to union and nonunion plants within a firm. *Industrial Relations*, 24, 395–405.

Voos, P. B. (1984). Trends in union organizing expenditures, 1953–1977. *Industrial and Labor Relations Review*, 38, 19–30.

□ Chapter 5 □

Analytical Financial Tools and Human Resource Management

Robert L. Berra and David T. Whitford

INTRODUCTION

Traditionally, human resources (HR) managers have selected their career paths because they are people oriented rather than quantitatively inclined. They tend to enjoy interacting with individuals and resolving problems with a large human dimension. Too many HR managers are uncomfortable with balance sheets, income statements, financial ratios, or time value of money concepts. They tend to shy away from numerical involvement; this is neither necessary nor wise. The competitive, global environment in which firms operate today requires all managers, including those in HR, to understand and focus upon key business imperatives and concepts. Today's human resources managers must speak the language of their firm's line managers including the chief executive officer (CEO). They must understand the key concepts that security analysts focus upon, the factors that will determine value enhancement in security markets (Berra, 1991).

One, if not the most important, focus of the HR manager is the firm's employees. In contrast, the CEO's most important concern is the firm's shareholders. When HR people get together, their biggest complaint is that line managers do not give sufficient attention to the human dimension in their organization. On the other hand, line managers make it clear, in far too many instances, that HR managers are "touchy-feely" and appear peripheral to the mainstream of the business. This last observation unfortunately rings true in many instances and spells real trouble for the HR function. It helps explain why the CEOs at big corporations are leaning toward non-HR managers for the top HR job. The CEO wants someone who can contribute significantly to the firm's strategic business decisions, who can recommend personnel policy that is compatible with the imperatives of the company, and who can serve as an advisor in areas that go beyond HR issues. If HR executives want to impact their organizations in a significant way, they must understand what drives the business and therefore dominates the focus of the CEO (Overman, 1991).

SHARING AND UNDERSTANDING THE CEO'S FOCUS AND VISION

Why is the CEO so shareholder focused? Collectively, investors literally own the firm. Shareholders not only are concerned with the economic health of the firm today, but also they are vitally interested in the future. For publicly traded firms, stock prices and trading volume provide a daily evaluation of the firm's management team. The CEO must deal with the market's perceptions as well as economic reality. How can the CEO not only reward the firm's current shareholders but also persuade others to invest? As noted by Stewart (1991), stock prices in part reward the vision of the CEO and place a premium on those firms that consistently deliver tangible results of that vision.

If shareholders are the CEO's main concern, every employee of the firm should strive to understand how his or her job impacts upon the concerns of the firm's owners (Knight, 1992). Because the criteria used by Wall Street to assess corporate performance are much more quantitative than people-oriented, HR managers tend to lack confidence in discussing the performance benchmarks utilized by security analysts. HR managers typically do not have a high comfort level using "alphabet soup" terms like return on assets (ROA), return on equity (ROE), asset productivity, and free cash flow (Berra, 1991). That is the *bad* news. The *good* news is that this lack of confidence can be overcome through vocabulary building and practice.

This chapter has three objectives. The first is to improve the HR manager's understanding of financial statements, and to develop insights regarding the critical importance of corporate cash flows. While it is impossible to cover adequately all of the many dimensions of financial and security analysis, the second objective is to focus on a few of the most important areas. Although HR managers are responsible for administering the avalanche of early-out programs that have occurred in many U.S. corporations recently, few understand the economic criteria that the stock market uses to evaluate these decisions. The final objective of this chapter is to provide a theoretical justification for valuing these programs, and to evaluate the economic rationality of the stock market's reaction to a recent restructuring.

FINANCIAL ANALYSIS: READING BETWEEN THE LINES

The theory of finance suggests that the principal criterion for evaluating corporate performance and valuation is amazingly simple. This key criterion is cash flow (Williams, 1938; Fama & Miller, 1972). Stated differently, cash is king (Rappaport, 1986; Hackel & Livnat, 1992). Investors desire large and positive levels of net cash flow. They invest in firms that generate significantly more cash inflows than outflows. Since traditional balance sheets and income statements are prepared on an accrual accounting rather than a cash flow basis, financial analysts have developed a set of tools that provide insights and measure a firm's economic success. These tools or financial ratios evaluate the health of a firm by evaluating the determinants of the life blood of the firm, its cash flow.

Consider the financial statements for XYZ Manufacturing Inc. given in tables 5.1 and 5.2. It is important to understand exactly what these statements measure. First, the balance sheets in table 5.1 are two snapshots of the firm's assets and claims at the end of 1993 and 1992. The assets on the left-hand side of table 5.1 represent real things (i.e., cash, accounts receivable (as yet uncollected credit sales), inventories, land, and production facilities). The entries on the claims or right-hand side of table 5.1 represent obligations owed to workers, suppliers, short-term and

Table 5.1 XYZ Manufacturing Inc.: fiscal years ending December 31, 1993, and December 31, 1992 ($m.)

Assets:	1993	1992	Liabilities:	1993	1992
Cash & marketable securities	150	75	Short-term debt	1,710	1,300
Accounts receivable	2,810	2,670	Accounts payable	1,550	1,500
Inventories	2,120	1,990	Other payables	640	630
Other current assets	630	585	Total current liabilities	3,900	3,430
Total current assets	5,710	5,320	Long-term debt	2,290	1,950
			Other long-term liabilities	360	300
Net fixed assets	3,500	2,910	Total liabilities	6,550	5,680
			Shareholders' equity:		
			Common stock (100 million shares outstanding)	820	820
Other long-term assets	1,720	1,460	Retained earnings	3,560	3,190
			Total equity	4,380	4,010
Total assets	10,930	9,690	Total claims	10,930	9,690

long-term lenders, as well as the claims of the owners of the firm (i.e., its shareholders). The balance sheets provide relatively little information regarding when payment is expected from credit customers, or how soon the firm must settle up with its workers, suppliers, and lenders. However, any current asset should turn into cash within a year or less. For example, inventories will be sold, creating an account receivable which will in turn be collected within a few weeks or months. In a similar way, any current liability will be paid off within the next twelve months or less. Assets that will not turn into cash within a year or less, as well as any debt or other liability that has a maturity greater than twelve months, are referred to as long-term assets or long-term liabilities, respectively.

The shareholders' equity section of the balance sheet can be confusing. There are several reasons for this. First, accountants and financial analysts are notorious for using several different terms for the same concept. This type of term switching obfuscates something that is relatively simple and makes it appear complex. For example, the terms shareholders' equity, shareholder equity, total equity, equity, and net worth are equivalent; they are different terms for the aggregate claims of the firm's shareholders. The year-end total equity or net worth values of XYZ Manufacturing were $4.38 and $4.01 billion for 1993 and 1992, respectively.

Within the equity section of a firm's balance sheet, the common stock entries represent the net proceeds that the firm has received any time the company has issued shares. This entry indicates the number of shares that are outstanding; for XYZ Manufacturing, there are 100 million shares outstanding. The retained earnings entries indicate the cumulative net income that has been retained over the firm's history; that is, the cumulative sum of net income that has not been paid out to the shareholders in the form of dividends. It is critically important to remember that all of the entries on the right-hand or claims side of the balance sheet contain *no* money. In

85

spite of the fact that one often hears, "we'll pay for this out of retained earnings," it is impossible to write a check on the retained earnings account. Checks are drawn only on the firm's cash account, which is on the left-hand or asset side of the balance sheet. Rather than paying for an asset "out of retained earnings," checks must draw on a pool of internally generated cash flow.

Even though there is no cash in any of the liability or equity accounts, these entries convey important information to securities markets. A firm's balance sheet provides the data for calculating a variety of financial ratios such as the *debt/equity* or *debt/asset* ratio. In addition, data to calculate a company's *book value per share* and its *market to book* ratio come in part from the claims side of the balance sheet.

Both the *debt/equity* and *debt/asset* ratios measure financial leverage. Financial leverage measures the degree to which nonshareholder funds are used to finance the firm's investments. At year-end 1993, the shareholders of XYZ Manufacturing had total claims of $4.38 billion. However, these investors were able to control $10.93 billion in total assets through the use of $6.55 billion obtained from a variety of long-term and short-term liabilities (i.e., nonshareholder funds). XYZ's 1.5 *debt/equity* ratio ($6.55/$4.38 = 1.495) and the 60 percent *debt/asset* value ($6.55/$10.93 = .598) vividly portray the degree to which nonequity funds provide funding for this company's total investments.

Financial leverage, or as the Europeans prefer "gearing," allows shareholders to gain economic control of a level of total assets that exceeds the shareholders' net worth or their aggregate investment in the firm. Nonshareholder claimants such as suppliers and workers, as well as short-term and long-term lenders provide a variety of financing alternatives in the normal course of business. The level of noninterest bearing (e.g., accounts payable, wages payable, etc.) and interest bearing debt that a firm utilizes can

have a dramatic impact on the firm's shareholders. High levels of debt translate into a lower economic commitment on the part of the shareholders. In spite of this smaller total equity contribution, financial leverage allows shareholders to control a relative larger total asset and revenue base. While this creates the potential for higher rates of return for the shareholders, the inability to pay the interest on high levels of debt may result in bankruptcy and the destruction of shareholder wealth. These are the risk return trade-offs that determine how much debt a firm should employ.

Stock prices provide a daily assessment of corporate success. Consider the status of a management team of an unsuccessful firm that controls valuable assets. Because the firm's managers have been poor stewards of their shareholders' funds, the stock price of a firm in this situation will most likely be depressed. Shareholders in this type of firm have relatively few options. They can sell their shares at the depressed price and incur a loss, or they can hope for a turnaround in corporate strategy. A third alternative became quite common in the 1980s. In that era, shareholders could tender their shares to a corporate raider bent on purchasing under-valued, poorly managed firms (Shleifer & Vishny, 1988; Jensen, 1988).

Book value per share is merely the total equity or accounting net worth of the firm divided by the number of shares outstanding. For XYZ Manufacturing, the book value per share was $43.80 and $40.10 for 1993 and 1992, respectively. It is important to remember that book value per share is an accounting concept, and that the stock's current market price plays no role in determining a share's book value. As seen at the bottom of table 5.2, XYZ's stock price closed at $57.50 per share on December 31, 1993. Thus, the ratio of the company's market value per share divided by its book value per share (i.e., its *market to book* ratio at year-end 1993) was 1.32 ($57.50/$43.80 = 1.322). In the 1980s a *market*

Table 5.2 XYZ Manufacturing Inc.: operating results for the year ending December 31, 1993 ($m.) and per share data

Total revenues	11,300
Cost of goods sold	8,700
Gross profits	2,600
Selling, general and administrative expenses	830
Depreciation	470
Research and development	250
Operating income (also known as earnings before interest and taxes (EBIT))	1,050
Interest expense	400
Pretax income	650
Taxes	160
Net income	490
less: Dividends paid	120
equals: Addition to retained earnings	370
Per share data ($)	
Earnings per share (EPS)	4.90
Dividends per share (DPS)	1.20
Closing price per share (December 31, 1993)	57.50

Not all of the expenses on the income statement represent an outflow of cash; for example, depreciation of fixed assets is non-cash expense. The actual cash outflow occurs when a fixed asset is acquired. Annual depreciation expenses attempt to capture the wear and tear on fixed assets. As equipment ages, its productivity declines, and prudent management will continually upgrade fixed assets to guard against these productivity declines. These capital expenditure investments do not appear on the firm's income statement; however, they are discussed at length in the footnotes to the financial statements. Thus, if one adds back noncash expenses such as depreciation to net income, it is possible to calculate the cash flow available to fund investments in the firm's assets and/or pay dividends.

There are several additional important financial concepts included in table 5.2. These are under the "per share data" heading at the bottom of the table. Corporations have a unique governance system. Rather than one vote per shareholder, corporate charters typically call for one vote per outstanding share. A shareholder's wealth invested in a given company, as well as that shareholder's voting power, are a function of the number of shares owned. Note that XYZ's Manufacturing net income for 1993 was $490 million. As indicated in table 5.1, the firm has 100 million shares outstanding. Thus, on a per share basis, the company earned $4.90 and paid out $1.20 in dividends per share.

Also included in the per share data in table 5.2 is the closing stock price for 1993, $57.50 per share. The ratio of a firm's stock price to its *earnings per share (EPS)* is referred to as its *price/earnings (P/E) ratio*. Accordingly, XYZ's P/E ratio at year-end was approximately 12 ($57.50/$4.90 = 11.73). What accounts for differences in P/E ratios across firms and industries? The principal determinate is *growth*; firms in so-called high-tech, glamor industries, with enormous growth prospects, tend to sell at extremely high *P/E* multiples.

to book ratio significantly greater than 1.0 acted as a strong deterrent to corporate raiders. Since the demise of the junk bond-financed, hostile takeover frenzy of the 1980s, proactive corporate boards have made the job security of CEOs, whose stock prices are at or below book value, tenuous at best (Salmon, 1993; Anders, 1992; and Pound, 1992).

XYZ Manufacturing's income statement, given in table 5.2, links together the two balance sheets in table 5.1. This statement provides the results of operations for a specific period, in this instance, fiscal year 1993. Again, it is important to emphasize what the income statement presents. First, it indicates the dollar value of all sales that occurred during the period. Second, it identifies all costs associated with those sales and subtracts them to derive the firm's net income for the period.

While growth is tremendously important, other things equal, firms that perform consistently can also command a higher P/E multiple. Well managed, non-glamor firms that deliver a "three yards and a clout of dust" performance record year after year, also have above average P/E multiples, and shareholders in these firms benefit accordingly. Why? Consistent, nonvolatile performance lowers the level of risk and uncertainty to which shareholders are exposed, and the market will pay a premium for the risk reduction (Knight, 1992).

CASH IS KING

Because the vast majority of corporate revenues are generated through credit sales, there is often a striking difference between revenues and actual cash receipts. In a similar way, direct manufacturing cash purchases may also differ widely from the cost of goods sold figure on the income statement. For example, a firm that is unable to cut back its production schedule in the face of declining demand for its products, will accumulate an undesired inventory buildup. The workers who produced that inventory and the suppliers who provided production inputs want to be paid in a timely manner. An unanticipated inventory buildup, in conjunction with a potential slowdown in the collection of accounts receivable, is a surefire prescription for a corporate cash flow crisis. Unfortunately, the income statement will *not* highlight this crisis; it will only identify the costs associated with what was sold!

In order to develop an intuitive understanding regarding the corporate cash flow generating process, consider the simplistic corporate money machine depicted in figure 5.1. This octopus-like characterization is really a corporate cash flow–funds flow tank and pipeline system. Instead of single dimension figures, imagine that the lighter colored boxes are real asset tanks, and the darker colored boxes are claims tanks. These claims tanks

will not actually hold funds. Instead, when a supplier ships raw materials, the shipment flows down the funds flow pipeline and the raw materials tank begins to fill. Simultaneously, a claims marker moves upward by a corresponding dollar amount in the accounts payable tank to indicate what is owed to the supplier (i.e., the supplier's claim against the firm's assets).

Several of the components of the money machine are not rectangular, and these deserve special discussion. The cash tank is in the form of a triangle or pyramid. If cash is king (and it is), this asset box deserves a special princely structure worthy of an ancient monarch. The production process occurs in a hexagonal tank that is connected via a solid tube to the fixed asset tank. This connection is meant to represent a hydraulic interaction between production capacity and net fixed assets. This linkage attempts to capture the relationship between the level of fixed assets and production capacity. More investment creates larger production capacity. The circular figure containing sales is not a tank but a meter on the revenue pump that records the revenue-generated flow of funds (costs plus profits) that will eventually be collected from the firm's customers. If cash flow is the life blood of the firm, sales is the heart of the corporation. That is, the pump that keeps the cash flowing. Stated differently, nothing meaningful happens within a firm until something is sold.

Consider how certain transactions associated with the start-up of a manufacturing company with a single shareholder would impact this firm's cash flows. For simplicity, taxes will be omitted. The company is created when our entrepreneur purchases shares in the firm. That is, cash leaves the owner's personal checking account and is deposited in the company's checking account. Presumably, the firm has a viable product line and has identified customers for these products. Production facilities will be acquired by opening up the cash tank spigot and

Figure 5.1 The money machine

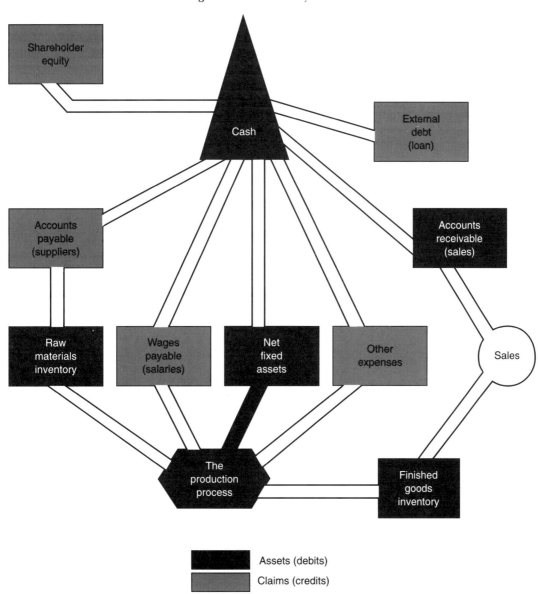

purchasing the fixed assets to be used in the manufacturing process. However, before production can begin, contracts with raw material and other suppliers must be arranged, and workers must be hired. When raw materials are received, these items flow from the supplier into the raw materials inventory tank.

As workers begin production, they transform raw materials into goods in process and finished goods inventories. Because wages and other production inputs will not be paid on a daily basis, wages and other expenses accrue, and the level of these payables increases. As the finished products are sold at a reasonable markup over production costs, revenues and the costs associated with those sales are recognized. This should generate profits, and assuming no dividend payments, an addition to retained earnings. If credit rather than cash sales generated the firm's revenues, no cash will be collected until the accounts receivable are collected. Low cash reserves in conjunction with the fact that payments for wages and suppliers are probably due before the accounts receivable will be collected, could render this undercapitalized firm insolvent. Under these circumstances, the money machine has gotten out of sync, and an additional external injection of cash from either the proceeds of an equity issue (i.e., the sale of common stock) or loan will be necessary to continue operations.

Assume that a lender is willing to provide additional liquidity by issuing a short-term loan to the firm. As operations continue, the firm should be able to repay this loan through internally generated cash flows. This results from the fact that manufacturing costs (i.e., cost of goods sold) and other expenses are more than recovered through reasonable profit margins. In this simplistic environment, synchronizing the firm's cash inflows and outflows is not a challenging task. However, as the size of the firm's revenues, assets, and employees expand, communications and coordinating mechanisms become essential. Without them, economic disasters will surely occur.

What tools are used to coordinate corporate strategy and cash flows? *Budgets!!!* They serve as the primary road map for corporate planning (Brigham & Gapenski, 1994). The budgeting process is one of, if not *the* most, critical corporate coordinating mechanism. In spite of its importance, budgeting is often viewed as a necessary evil; a process to be tolerated rather than valued. Difficulties brought on by a lack of enthusiasm for budgeting are often exacerbated by organizational provincialism. Figure 5.2 provides an overlay of organizational authority or responsibility

for various parts of the money machine. What is good for one area is often at odds with the others. For example, the purchasing department may lock in a great deal on raw materials through a bulk order. However, a sudden cash crisis may occur when the bill for six months' worth of raw materials becomes due in thirty days. Production managers are interested in long, smooth production runs, with a minimum of downtime. The marketing staff would prefer shorter, customized production runs to accommodate individual customer demand. Tough credit standards might hold down bad debt losses on credit sales in the short run, but they have the potential to stifle marketing efforts to expand the firm's customer base and exploit potentially lucrative long-run profit opportunities. Strategic success requires that every member of the management team must appreciate various organizational duties and responsibilities and the impact that they have on corporate cash flow and long-run economic viability.

TRADITIONAL TOOLS FOR EVALUATING PERFORMANCE – WHAT DO SHAREHOLDERS WANT?

In spite of a growing recognition of the importance of corporate cash flow patterns (Stewart, 1991; Rappaport, 1986), other traditional analytical techniques for evaluating corporate performance remain useful. Chief among these is ratio analysis. Financial ratios measure performance in a variety of areas. These include: *liquidity, asset productivity, financial leverage,* and *profitability.*

A popular liquidity ratio is the *current ratio,* which equals the ratio of a firm's current assets to its current liabilities. Although acceptable values for the current ratio vary from industry to industry, 2.0 is generally considered reasonably safe. Recall that current assets will eventually "turn into cash" over the next twelve months or less, while current liabilities

Figure 5.2 The money machine: an organizational context

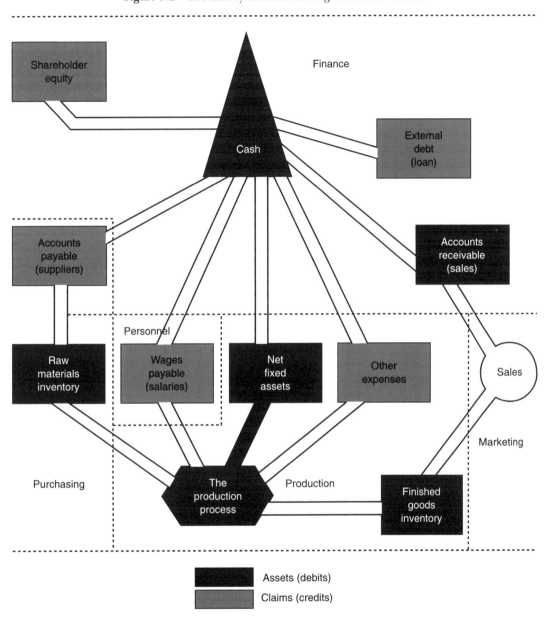

■ (black)	Assets (debits)
▨ (grey)	Claims (credits)

become due during the next year. In the context of the money machine (see figure 5.1), current assets include cash, as well as accounts receivable and inventories; that is, those assets in the pipeline flowing into the cash tank. Current liabilities are made up of those claims that flow directly from the cash tank. Thus, it is relatively easy to understand why analysts view the current ratio as a reasonable standard for evaluating a firm's ability to meet its financial obligations in a timely manner.

Rational investors do not purchase shares for charitable reasons. They seek dividend income and stock price appreciation. Stock prices directly reflect the underlying risk and return patterns inherent in strategic corporate decisions, as well as the success that the firm has had in implementing its strategies. Although the accounting return measures calculated from a firm's financial statements, and the economic returns generated by dividends and stock price changes, do not have a one-to-one relationship, they are highly correlated. Even though required returns vary across industries and firms, most risk-averse investors require a *minimum* accounting return on their equity investment (i.e., *return on equity (ROE)* of 15 to 20 percent). However, financial analysts give extraordinarily high marks to companies that consistently earn a 20 to 30 percent return on equity. These companies typically have a constantly evolving stable of dominant market share products or services. Firms with these characteristics are in an elite class among the corporations of the world.

As noted above, ROE measures the accounting rate of return that shareholders receive on their investment. A firm's total equity or net worth represents the aggregate claim of its shareholders. As "residual" claimants, shareholders earn the difference between total revenues and expenses (i.e., net income). Thus, *ROE* is defined as the ratio of *net income to shareholder equity*. Accordingly, XYZ's ROE for 1993 was 11.2 percent ($490/$4,380 = 0.1119).

Many otherwise well-informed individuals are surprised by the fact that the typical U.S. corporation earns only $5 in net income per $100 in sales, for a *profit margin* of 5 percent. The profit margin for XYZ Manufacturing in 1993 was 4.3 percent ($490/$11,300 = 0.0434). How does a profit margin of 4.3 percent generate an 11.2 percent return on equity? A clear understanding of two key factors, *return on assets (ROA)*, the ratio of *net income to total assets* as well as financial leverage, is necessary in

order to answer this question. Because the linkage between these key factors is rather technical, they are discussed separately.

The linkage development begins with return on assets; note that XYZ's ROA in 1993 was 4.5 percent ($490/$10,930 = 0.0448), just slightly above its profit margin. This increase results from the fact that XYZ's $10.93 billion asset base generated $11.3 billion in sales. During 1993, this 1.03 ($11.3/$10.93 = 1.0338) sales to total asset ratio accounted for the increase. In mathematical terms, 4.34 times 1.0338 equals 4.486 percent. Stated in nonmathematical terms, XYZ's *ROA* (net income/total assets) equals its *total asset turnover* (sales/total assets) times its *profit margin* (net income/sales).

In order to explore this relationship further, consider the following "what if" scenario. Assume that the production teams at XYZ Manufacturing made a strategic decision at the beginning of 1993 to reduce inventory levels through a *just-in-time (JIT)* inventory program. This JIT program would result in a large fraction of the firm's inventory being delivered on an "as needed" basis. The successful implementation of the program resulted in a $1,120 million decline in inventories. Had the management of XYZ been able to generate the same level of sales from a smaller total asset base, XYZ's ROA would have increased accordingly. As the excess inventory was sold, the cash generated by those sales could have been used in a variety of ways. The company could have repurchased its shares, thereby reducing its net worth by as much as $1,120 million. Alternatively, these funds could have been used to pay back short-term debt, and/or to reduce accounts payable. Assuming that the JIT program did not affect the sales and profit levels in table 5.2, XYZ's ROA would have been 5 percent [$490/($10,930 − $1,120) = 0.04995]. While this increase in ROA is relatively small, it unambiguously demonstrates that idle, unproductive assets, be they fixed plant and equipment or short-term working capital investments in accounts receivable or inventories, can be a heavy drag on a firm's ROA. Thus, well-managed companies place a heavy emphasis on efficient "asset management."

The final concept that links the interaction of a firm's profitability and asset productivity (i.e., ROA) with its accounting return on equity (ROE), is financial leverage. To see this, assume that the $1,120 million cash flow generated by XYZ's JIT inventory reduction program was used to buy back shares. If one further assumes that these shares could have been acquired for $57.50 per share, the year-end closing price, the company would have reduced its shares outstanding by 19.478 million shares ($1,120,000,000/$57.5 = 19.4783 million). Repurchasing shares with an aggregate market value of $1.12 billion (technically referred to as acquiring *treasury stock*) would have caused XYZ's shareholders equity (or net worth) to be $3,260 million rather than $4,380 million at year-end 1993. Had this happened, the company's ROE would have increased to 15 percent ($490/$3,260 = 0.1503). In contrast, if the cash flows generated by the inventory reduction had been used to reduce accounts payable, the firm's ROE would have remained at 11.2 percent ($490/$4,380 = 0.11187)! The acquisition of treasury stock resulted in a $1.12 billion cash inflow to those shareholders that tendered their shares. After this transaction, the aggregate claim of the remaining shareholders, $3,260 million, would control $9,810 ($10,930 − $1,120) million in assets. In other words, this new total asset to net worth ratio would allow the remaining shareholders to control $3 in total assets for each $1 of shareholder investment ($9,810/$3,260 = 3.009).

In addition to the improvement in ROE created by this inventory reduction–stock buyback scheme, are there other benefits or disadvantages that would result from this policy? Clearly there are. Recall that the share repurchase plan would reduce the number of shares outstanding by approximately 19.5 million shares. Thus, by December, 1993,

there would be approximately 81.5 million shares outstanding rather than 100 million. This shrinkage in shares would directly translate into a change in *earnings per share (EPS)*, and possibly even *dividends per share*. Again assuming no change in sales or net income as a result of the inventory reduction, XYZ's EPS would be $6.01 ($490/81.5 = $6.012) per share, a 22.7 percent increase over the old $4.90 level ([$6.01 − $4.90]/$4.90 = 0.22653). Further, if the company wished to maintain its $120 million aggregate dividend payout, dividends per share could be increased from $1.20 per share to $1.47 ($120/81.5 = $1.4723). Finally, if (and this is a big if) XYZ Manufacturing's P/E ratio were to remain at 11.7, the December, 1993 closing price would be $70.32 ($6.01 × 11.7 = $70.317) rather than $57.50.

If a stock repurchase strategy is as beneficial as these figures indicate, is there a downside to this type of financial policy? Without question, there is a potentially significant risk brought on by this strategy. First, if a firm's shares are "over valued," higher returns can probably be earned by investing in real projects rather than financial restructuring. Second, the relatively high level of financial leverage that this type of repurchase strategy would generate could be disastrous. Assume that an industry slump in conjunction with the inventory reduction plan resulted in a significant decline in revenues during 1994. If the decline is sharp enough, XYZ's earnings before interest and taxes might fall below the firm's interest expense. If this scenario were to occur, the company's credit rating would fall precipitously. If these conditions continued for an extended period, the company creditors might force the company into bankruptcy. There is an extremely important lesson to be learned from this exercise: *too much debt and not enough equity can be extremely dangerous to the health of the firm's employees, creditors, and shareholders*!

This final piece of the puzzle provides a simple, yet profoundly insightful tool for understanding the strategic tools available to CEOs and their management teams in generating increases in shareholder wealth. Mathematically, a firm's ROE may be decomposed into three components.

$$\text{ROE} = \frac{\text{Net income}}{\text{Sales}} \times \frac{\text{Sales}}{\text{Total assets}}$$

$$\times \frac{\text{Total assets}}{\text{Net worth}}$$

$$= \frac{\text{Net income}}{\text{Net worth}}$$

The decomposition of ROE into three primary components[1] demonstrates how a 20 percent return on equity is possible given a profit margin of 5 percent. There are a variety of operating and financing policies that could achieve this objective. In a stable industry with low sales volatility, a low level of asset productivity (i.e., sales/total assets = 1.0) in conjunction with a high degree of financial leverage (i.e., total assets/net worth = 4.0) would achieve the desired result. However, a firm in a more volatile industry may not be able to tolerate such a high degree of financial leverage. Nevertheless, the overall ROE objective could still be maintained by either increasing profitability and/or asset productivity. Although industry characteristics play an important role in determining corporate strategy, there are many alternatives available to achieve a firm's target ROE.

The data in table 5.3 provide a comparison of the profitability, asset productivity, and financial leverage policies and trade-offs across six industries. Without question, the pharmaceutical firms are the clear leaders in profit margins with an industry average of 21.1 percent. In part these high margins are attributable to pricing policies that reflect large research and development costs in conjunction with extremely high-risk and relatively short product life cycles. The telecommunications group is the next most profitable group with an average of 12.2 percent. The two least profitable groups are the retail gro-

cery and manufacturing firms, respectively. The low margins of these cyclical manufacturing firms are in large part due to a depressed farm economy, a cut back in defense expenditures and a general downsizing in this sector of the economy. In contrast, the retail grocery margins are reflective of an extremely competitive industry noted for its price competition and low margins.

Even though the grocery group ranks next to last in terms of profitability, it has the highest level of asset productivity with a total asset turnover average of 3.8 turns per year. In contrast, the three regulated telecommunications firms have an average total asset turnover of 0.45 turns. The interaction of profitability and asset productivity shifts the grocery firms from next to last in the profit margin rankings to second place based upon ROA groupings. This dramatic change in rankings is directly attributable to the grocery group's high level of asset productivity (i.e., its *total asset turnover*). Grocery stores may have low margins, but they compensate through high customer volume. In contrast, low asset productivity in the telecommunications group moves these firms from second place in the profit margin rankings to fourth place based on the ROA criterion.

The manufacturing firms, on average rank lowest based upon ROA; however, they have the highest level of financial leverage. The manufacturing firms' financial leverage amplifies the average ROA of 2.2 percent and generates an average ROE of 8.9 percent. These firms' low profit margins and ROE figures reflect the depressed economic conditions in these manufacturing firms' industries. Second and third place in the *financial leverage multiplier* (i.e., *total assets/net worth*) rankings are the telecommunications and energy firms. However, these industries' relatively low ROA generates a low ROE ranking in spite of their above average measures of financial leverage. The pharmaceutical companies on average have the most financially conservative capital structures. Notwith-

Table 5.3 Return on equity: an industry and firm comparison

Company name	Profit margin (%)	Total asset turnover	Return on total assets (%)	Financial leverage multiplier	Return on equity (%)
Abbott Labs	15.3	1.13	17.3	2.07	35.8
Eli Lilly	22.6	0.71	16.1	1.77	28.5
Merck & Co.	25.3	0.87	22.1	2.22	48.9
Pharmaceutical average	21.1	0.90	18.5	2.02	37.7
Ameritech Corporation	12.1	0.49	5.9	3.26	19.3
Pacific Telesis	11.5	0.44	5.1	2.73	13.8
Southwestern Bell	13.0	0.42	5.5	2.56	14.0
Telecommunications average	12.2	0.45	5.5	2.85	15.7
Atlantic Richfield	5.6	0.77	4.3	3.61	15.7
Exxon Corporation	4.7	1.21	5.7	2.52	14.2
Texaco Inc.	3.1	1.42	4.3	2.61	11.3
Energy average	4.5	1.13	4.8	2.91	13.7
Cummins Engine	1.8	1.68	3.0	4.45	13.4
Deere & Co.	0.7	0.83	0.5	2.61	1.4
TRW Inc.	2.0	1.52	3.1	3.85	12.0
Manufacturing average	1.5	1.34	2.2	3.64	8.9
Home Depot	5.1	1.82	9.2	1.71	15.8
Kmart Corporation	2.5	1.99	5.0	2.51	12.5
Wal-Mart Stores	3.6	2.70	9.7	2.35	22.8
Retail discount average	3.7	2.17	8.0	2.19	17.0
Albertson's Inc.	2.7	3.45	9.4	2.12	19.1
Vons Cos.	1.5	2.71	4.0	4.19	16.6
Winn-Dixie Stores	2.2	5.25	11.5	2.09	24.0
Retail grocery average	2.1	3.80	8.3	2.80	19.9

Source: December, 1993 Value Line Investment Survey

standing their low degree of financial leverage, the pharmaceutical group ranks first in terms of ROE.

The analysis shown in table 5.3 reveals a variety of factors that impact upon accounting rates of return. These include competitive and economic conditions within an industry, product risk and life cycles (particularly the pharmaceuticals), profitability–sales volume trade-offs, as well a variety of other factors. While truth does not emerge from this type of analysis, decomposition and comparisons of ROE across and within industries provide corporate stakeholders with a rich and meaningful set of evaluation measures to assess the performance of the firm and its management.

CORPORATE CASH FLOW AND MARKET VALUATION

Financial theory unambiguously states that the price of any financial asset is merely the *present value* of the *future cash flows* that one receives as the owner of that asset (Williams, 1938; Fama & Miller, 1972). Thus the theory asserts that a firm's stock price is the present value of its future dividends. This is why security analysts place such great emphasis on corporate cash flows. This present value or discounting process is referred to as the *discounted cash flow* (*DCF*) technique.

Clearly, there are many young, emerging companies that currently pay no dividends on their common stock. These firms retain all of their internally generated corporate cash flow to fund growth opportunities. As a result, the current and near-term dividend payments of these firms would equal zero. However, as growth opportunities begin to slow, these maturing corporations would initiate dividend payments, and through time, these payments typically increase.

Although it is uncommon for a firm's dividend to grow at a constant rate through time, this constant growth assumption provides a convenient way to determine the present value of all future dividend payments (Gordon, 1961; Gordon, 1962). The equation given below is often referred to as the *constant growth dividend discount model*:

$$P_0 = \frac{D_0(1 + g)}{r - g} = \frac{D_1}{r - g}$$

In this model, P_0 is the current (time zero) stock price, and D_0 is the annual (as opposed to quarterly) dividend that the firm paid last year. The dividend to be received at the end of year one, D_1, equals last year's dividend multiplied by $(1 + g)$, where g is the projected constant growth rate in dividends over the investment horizon. The r in the denominator of the terms on the right-hand side of the equation is the required market-based or economic return that an investor demands for investing in this stock. Technically, it is referred to as the *cost of equity capital* or *cost of equity*. Although this constant growth dividend stream has no maturity date, it does not have an infinitely large present value due

to the time value of money, and the fact that the cost of equity (i.e., r) will be larger than the constant growth rate, g.

To see how this constant growth dividend discount model operates, assume that an investor has a required return of 15 percent if she were to make an equity investment in the shares of CBA Inc. Last year CBA paid a $1.50 dividend per share, and this dividend is expected to grow at 10 percent forever. What is a fair price for a share of CBA's common stock? As seen below, the answer is $33.00. Again, this stock price represents the *present value* of a stream of dividends that is expected to grow at a constant rate forever.

$$P_0 = \frac{\$1.50(1.10)}{0.15 - 0.10} = \frac{\$1.65}{0.05} = \$33.00$$

With this background it is possible to begin to assess the rationality of the stock market's reaction to corporate restructurings through early-out programs (i.e., early retirement programs), as well as why security analysts tend to respond so favorably to head count reductions.

EARLY-OUTS AND CORPORATE RESTRUCTURING: AN ECONOMIC ANALYSIS

Over the last few years, almost every large U.S. corporation has announced at least one restructuring via an early-out program. In the aggregate, this has resulted in the loss of hundreds of thousands of high-paying, middle- and upper-management jobs. Corporate restructurings are so popular that it is a rare day indeed when there is *not* at least one announcement in the financial press of an early-out. Although the administration of corporate early-outs is done by human resources managers, few understand the economic rationale behind the apparent obsession that America's CEOs have with restructuring.

Recently, a large U.S. company announced the termination of 4,000 employees through early retirements and reassignments. The stock market's reaction on the day of the announcement was remarkable. That day the firm's stock price increased by slightly less than 7 percent. More dramatically, increase in the price per share resulted in a $1.024 billion increase in the aggregate value of the firm's stock, the total value of all the company's shares! The scope of the market's reaction to this restructuring was enormous; it is fair to ask if the size of this increase in market value was economically rational.

Assume that after many agonizing months, this firm's top management team concluded that it needed to reduce its work force by 4,000 workers worldwide. Because of recent increases in worker productivity and industry downsizing, these jobs would be eliminated permanently. If managed properly, this workforce reduction would not result in additional, significant decreases in revenues. And because revolutionary improvements in technology (e.g., electronic communications) permit the elimination of management layers, remaining workers will not have to work harder. While it is not possible to know with certainty what the average salary of this firm's early-out participants was last year, $50,000 appears to be a reasonable ballpark estimate. If employee benefits average 40 percent of wages, the average pretax savings would be $70,000 per worker. However, because these expenses are tax deductible, the impact of their elimination, given no change in revenue, will be diminished. Assuming a marginal corporate tax rate of 34 percent, the after-tax savings per worker would be $46,200 ($70,000 × (1 − 0.34) = $46,200). Finally, if inflation is projected to be 3 percent, and the future wages of the early-out participants were anticipated to increase 1 percent above the inflation rate, it is possible to determine the present value of removing the early-out participants from the firm's payroll.

Assume also that this company has a *cost of capital* or required return on its investments of 12 percent. This required return or *hurdle rate* is the minimum rate of return that will satisfy both the firm's shareholders and lenders. Accordingly the hurdle rate is a weighted average cost of capital that is a blend of the firm's after-tax cost of debt and required return on equity. If one is willing to accept as a first approximation that the early-out company's average wages will grow at 4 percent forever, it is possible to estimate the present value of the after-tax savings via the constant growth dividend discount model. Rather than finding the present value of a stream of dividends, the model can be used to calculate the present value of the after-tax savings per worker that results from an early-out. In other words, D_1 will be replaced by next year's after-tax savings in salary and benefits per worker, and the company's cost of capital (or hurdle rate) and growth rate in wages and benefits will play the roles of the cost of equity and constant dividend growth rate, respectively. As seen below, the present value of the average savings per worker is an extraordinary $600,600 per worker.

$$\text{Savings/worker} = \frac{\$46,200(1.04)}{0.12 - 0.04}$$

$$= \$600,600$$

The overall impact of 4,000 workers is an even more dramatic $2.4024 billion! This saving will come at a cost, however. Assuming that the package promises a lump sum of two years' salary and benefits, based upon last year's salary schedule, the after-tax cost per worker would be $92,400. The overall after-tax cost would be $369.6 million. In other words, the company is paying out $369.6 million "today," in order to "acquire" an early-out restructuring that has an after-tax present value of $2,402.4 million. Thus, the *net present value (NPV)* of this transaction would be $2.0328 billion ($2,402.4 − $369.6). If the assumptions made in valuing this transaction are correct, one would expect the aggregate market value of this firm's stock to increase by slightly over $2 billion. Stated differently, NPV measures the expected change in aggregate shareholder wealth.

This NPV estimate is full of assumptions that may or may not be realistic. For example, the 12 percent required return on assets as well as the 4 percent growth rate in wages and benefits may be too low. A 15 percent cost of capital in conjunction with a 4.5 percent wage and benefit growth rate would reduce the $2.4024 billion savings to $1.8392 billion. In addition, security analysts may assume that after a period of adjustment, many of these workers may be replaced with younger, lower-salaried workers. Conventional wisdom suggests that the company's early-out could depress employee morale and productivity in the short run. Presumably, a significant proportion of the company's early-out employees contributed to the firm's bottom line, and their contributions will be difficult to offset. Thus, the early-out program could potentially decrease revenues, or at least slow their growth significantly. The impact of these and other factors will most likely erode the $2.0328 billion NPV figure. Given the skepticism of most security analysts, the possibility of a 50 percent erosion in this $2.0328 billion NPV estimate is not out of the question. In point of fact, the actual change in market value was $1.024 billion. Accordingly, it would appear that the stock market's reaction to the restructuring was economically rational.

It is important to note, however, that other firms announcing early-out programs may not experience a similar, dramatic, and rapid rise in shareholder value. Other negative factors announced concurrently may offset the "positive" restructuring information. For example, restructuring may result in a decline in expenditures that are critical to long-run economic viability. Expense cutting can be positive, but if it reaches the future life blood of a firm's operations, serious problems can occur. Still, it is important that HR executives

understand the financial considerations that go into such decisions. It is likely that any HR department that initiated discussions of an early-out program by displaying an in-depth understanding of the financial as well as human implications of such a move, would see its own "stock" rise considerably in the eyes of the CEO and other operating managers.

CONCLUSION

Recently, Berra (1991) provided insights into what it takes to succeed as an HR professional. Two of Berra's criteria for success focused upon (1) gaining the respect of one's peers by providing meaningful inputs into corporate strategy and policy and (2) developing and maintaining a rapport with the CEO and other line managers. An inability to understand and analyze a firm's financial statements will significantly impede the attainment of Berra's criteria. In addition, Overman (1991) discussed the results of a 1989 study by the American Society for Personnel Administration (now known as the Society for Human Resource Management (SHRM)) that focused on senior level human resources professional competency. This study surveyed 23 CEOs in regard to what they want from their HR managers. These CEOs voiced universal agreement that HR professionals should possess an in-depth knowledge of the business, a strategic focus, and an understanding of finance.

The Chinese have a curse that they sometimes wish upon their enemies: "May you live in interesting times." Without ambiguity, the coming decades will be interesting for all human resources managers. Technological change will continue to accelerate. Mandated benefits and governmental regulations will not go away. The constant pressure to enhance the market value of the shareholders' investment will never subside. The HR professional plays a vital role in meshing corporate strategy with the firm's employees. If HR managers immerse themselves in their businesses and develop their analytical and financial skills, they have the potential to add significant value to the corporation in spite of these pressures. However, without the ability to communicate credibly and forcefully, using the language of Wall Street, this value enhancement will not be maximized.

NOTE

1 The decomposition of a firm's ROE is sometimes referred to as "duPont analysis" because this analytical technique was developed at E. I. duPont de Demours & Company several decades ago.

REFERENCES

Anders, G. (1992). The "barbarians" in the boardroom. *Harvard Business Review*, 70, 79–87.

Berra, R. L. (1991). What it takes to succeed at the top. *HR Magazine*, 36, 34–7.

Brigham, E. F., & Gapenski, L. C. (1994). *Financial Management Theory and Practice*. Fort Worth, TX: Dryden Press.

Fama, E. F., & Miller, M. E. (1972). *The Theory of Finance*. Hinsdale, IL: Dryden Press.

Gordon, M. J. (1961). Dividend policy, growth, and the valuation of shares. *Journal of Business*, 34, 411–33.

Gordon, M. J. (1962). *The Investment, Financing, and Valuation of the Corporation*. Homewood, IL: Irwin.

Hackel, K. S., & Livnat, J. (1992). *Cash Flow and Security Analysis*. Homewood, IL: Business One Irwin.

Jensen, M. C. (1988). Takeovers: Their causes and consequences. *Journal of Economic Perspectives*, 2, 21–48.

Knight, C. F. (1992). Emerson Electric: Consistent profits, consistently. *Harvard Business Review*, 70, 57–70.

Overman, S. (1991). What does the CEO want? *HR Magazine*, 36, 41–3.

Pound, J. (1992). Raiders, targets and politics: The history and future of American corporate control. *The Journal of Applied Corporate Finance*, 5, 6–18.

Rappaport, A. (1986). *Creating Shareholder Value: The new standard for business performance*. New York: Free Press.

Salmon, W. J. (1993). Crisis prevention: How to gear up your board. *Harvard Business Review*, 71, 68–75.

Shleifer, A., & Vishny, R. W. (1988). Value maximization and the acquisition process. *Journal of Economic Perspectives*, 2, 7–19.

Stewart, G. B., III (1991). *The Quest for Value: A guide for senior managers*. New York: HarperBusiness.

Williams, J. B. (1938). *The Theory of Investment Value*. Cambridge, MA: Harvard University Press.

☐ Chapter 6 ☐

A Power and Politics Perspective on Human Resource Management

Gerald R. Ferris, Maria Carmen Galang, Martha L. Thornton,
and Sandy J. Wayne

INTRODUCTION

As organizational scientists and practitioners, we have developed a fascination with the "machine model" of organizations, and we desperately want to believe that companies actually operate with the same degree of objectivity, rationality, and precision as a well-oiled machine. This thinking extends to human resource management (HRM) as well, and we are socialized to believe that human resources practices operate with genuinely sincere intentions to provide and gather the type of job-relevant information necessary to permit the most accurate decisions possible (Ferris & King, 1991). Thus, when errors are detected, they are assumed to be simply errors of omission caused by missed or lost information, resulting from the finite information capabilities of decision makers. However, we have come to question the validity of our "machine model," and the extent to which it portrays organizations and HRM realistically. As an alternative, or perhaps supplement to this quite rational portrayal of organizations, we might suggest that power and political dynamics are potent influences on both the formulation of HRM policies and the operation of HRM practices.

In this chapter, we introduce the power and politics perspective as a different way to view HRM in organizations. The first part draws on theory and research to examine the impact of power and politics on HRM. First, we examine power and politics at the organizational level where HRM policies and systems are formulated, and we discuss the nature of power and politics and how it influences both the development and operation of HRM systems. Then, we move down a level and discuss how both managers and their subordinates utilize power and politics within HRM systems. Next, we provide some insights from the practice of HRM, and the role played by power and politics. Finally, we attempt to provide some integration of what we know from theory and research on the power and politics perspective, with what we have observed in the practice of HRM in organizations.

THEORY AND RESEARCH ON POWER AND POLITICS IN HUMAN RESOURCE MANAGEMENT

Power and politics at the organizational level: the formation of human resources policies and systems

The nature of power and politics

Politics is not openly acknowledged in organizations, primarily because of its negative connotations. In a review of the various definitions of organizational politics, Drory and Romm (1990) noted that while there is a lack of consensus, the general view seems to be that politics involve the pursuit of ends that deviate from formal organizational goals, typically through means that are disapproved of by the organization. Of course, there are others who encourage a more neutral position. For example, Ferris, King, Judge, and Kacmar (1991) defined organizational politics very simply as the management of meaning.

Nonetheless, politics is an organizational reality and cannot be ignored (Bolman & Deal, 1991), and its neglect impedes our understanding of organizations. Much of what goes on in organizations may be better explained by utilizing a political approach (Pfeffer, 1978). This perspective questions the existence of organizational goals, and it is this notion of unitary goals and standards that underlies the negative view of politics. The political perspective recognizes instead the existence of multiple goals held by different organizational members with divergent preferences, interests, and beliefs. The ensuing conflicts among these divergent perspectives, interests, and beliefs are then resolved through the use of power and politics to influence outcomes and decisions (Pfeffer, 1978, 1981, 1989). The political analysis of organizations thus entails understanding power and its use by organizational actors (Bacharach & Lawler, 1980).

Diversity in goals among organizational members arises from sources that are both internal and external to the organization (Pfeffer, 1978, 1981). Division of labor within organizations leads to subunit goals that may conflict. Further, this differentiation results in differences in access to information and social networks, which produce identification and loyalty with the subunit. Organizational members also bring with them differences in prior socialization and training, as well as current influences from outside the organization.

Pfeffer (1981) also argues that other conditions are necessary for politics to occur. In addition to the heterogeneity in goals and beliefs among various organizational interest groups, conflicts are likewise determined by resource scarcity and interdependence among these groups. The use of politics to resolve these conflicts also depends on the importance of the issue, and distribution of power among the parties involved.

The preceding discussion serves to support the usefulness of the power and politics perspective in explaining organizational phenomena. Conflicts in preferences and beliefs among organizational members, with its corresponding use of power and politics to resolve such conflicts, can be expected in organizations. Failure to take these into consideration limits our understanding of how organizations actually operate.

The power and politics approach has been applied to human resource management, and it can be approached on two levels: the organizational level and the interpersonal level (Ferris & Judge, 1991). On the organizational level, the main concern revolves around explaining the HRM policies formulated and systems adopted by organizations, focusing on the political influences of various interest groups as the main determinant. The interpersonal level deals with influences of individual behaviors, occurring in interpersonal interactions, on decisions made and actions taken within the context of the HRM systems.

Power and politics in the formulation of human resources policies and systems

On the organizational level, power and politics is only one perspective employed to explain the existence and nature of HRM systems in organizations. Numerous factors have been identified and argued to influence HRM (e.g., Saha, 1989), and these can be classified into various theoretical perspectives. However, not one typology exists that organizes these perspectives, and it is not the intention here to do so. Some of these perspectives are described briefly to serve as contrasts to the power and politics perspective.

Jackson, Schuler, and Rivero (1989) mentioned institutional, economic, control, and political perspectives, as alternatives to the behavioral perspective they utilized in their study of 267 organizations. This behavioral approach focuses on the patterns of employee behaviors required by organizational characteristics. These patterns then determine the nature of personnel practices adopted by the organization. The organizational characteristics found to be relevant to various aspects of performance appraisal, compensation, and training were industry sector, competitive strategy, technology, and organizational structure.

Tsui and Milkovich (1987) identified three perspectives, which emphasize different sets of determinants. Organizational characteristics such as size, growth, specialization, and other internal factors have traditionally been considered the reasons for the existence of personnel activities in firms. This structural functionalism view is in contrast to the strategic contingency perspective, which attributes these developments to critical contingencies arising from the firm's environment. Such external factors as legal and union pressures thus play a significant role. A third perspective, strategic human resource management, considers both external and internal factors, in that it postulates that external influences are filtered through the firm's business strategy and introduces the notion of "fit" between human resources activities and the firm's business objectives.

Jennings (1994) provided a good review of the studies utilizing the functional or contingency, political, and cultural perspectives, as well as expanding the search for explanations beyond the organizational level of analysis to a more sociological approach. In brief, the functional or contingency perspective asserts that the need for efficiency is the driving force behind HRM, while the political view considers power and its use as the central explanatory variable, regardless of efficiency concerns. The cultural perspective draws in factors such as values, norms, and beliefs, arguing that HRM can be understood only within its cultural setting.

Broadening the political and cultural perspectives for a more sociological approach, Jennings (1994) brings in control and conflict theories and institutional theories to explain HRM. The political perspective at this more macro level employs the Marxist view of employment relations, where the inherent conflict of interests between employers and employees leads to contests for control of the labor process, which is ultimately reflected in the HRM practices in organizations. Institutional theories (Meyer & Rowan, 1977; Trice, Belasco, & Alutto, 1969) focus on societal factors and the notion of legitimacy to explain organizational structures. Through the processes of coercion, norms, and mimicry (DiMaggio & Powell, 1983), organizations adopt certain structures and practices (e.g., HRM practices) that provide the legitimacy needed to gain access to resources.

While these enumerate and discuss the different perspectives to explain HRM in organizations, these listings have not been explicitly grounded in any meaningful theoretical framework. One framework that captures the more fundamental differences of these various views is provided by Burrell and Morgan (1979), and applied by Gowler and Legge (1986) to the personnel function. Using this framework, four substantially different images of the personnel function in organizations are possible, each of which directs attention to different aspects of the function, and leads to different interpretations. The functionalist perspective, which is the dominant paradigm, views the personnel function as adaptive responses of the organization to internal and external contingencies in pursuit of organizational goals of effectiveness. The radical structuralist perspective also focuses on organizational interests, but views the personnel function as a tool to dominate and ensure the lowest possible labor costs. On the other hand, the radical humanist image portrays the personnel function as a means by which organizational members are able to realize their full potential despite the alienating effects of organizations. The personnel function within the interpretive perspective is not so much concerned with organizational interests as with how meanings of actions and events are constructed and shared with other organizational members.

All these approaches to explain HRM systems in organizations may be useful (Tsui & Milkovich, 1987), and taken together, they may provide a more complete, balanced understanding of HRM. Tsui and Milkovich (1987), for example, criticized the neglect of political pressures as an important internal factor influencing personnel activities, in the three perspectives they had identified. From an early study, Dimick and Murray (1978) proposed a model which integrates both rational and political approaches, stipulating the conditions determining when one becomes the predominant factor. Technical rationality determines the choice of personnel policies and practices, but where constraints to technical rationality exist, then influences of interest groups become more important.

Jennings (1994) also proposed the possibility of merging the political and institutional perspectives. Politics may initiate the adoption, or dominance of a new method, and its diffusion may be explained by mimetic or normative pressures, rather than the use of power and politics. Jennings, however, urged that prior to any integration, each perspective first be fully developed separately. Empirical support can then be gathered for the alternative hypotheses generated. Such an approach is also recommended by Pfeffer (1989) to provide evidence for political influences, apart from other possible explanations.

The power and politics perspective on the organizational level focuses on various interest groups as the primary determinants of HRM systems in the organization, with power and influence becoming the basis of decisions with regard to the HRM systems put in place in the organization (Pfeffer, 1989). The basic questions being asked from this perspective are who are these interest groups, what are their interests, how do these interests impact on HRM, how do they gain power and influence and become the dominant interest group, and what outcomes are derived when one interest group predominates. The power and politics perspective on the organizational level has not been fully explored, such that many of these questions remain unresolved. The discussion that follows revolves around current knowledge about these questions.

Beer, Spector, Lawrence, Mills, and Walton (1985) proposed the following as stakeholders with interest in the nature of HRM in the firm: shareholders, management, employee groups, government, the community, and unions. Empirical studies have also shown unions, personnel or human resources departments, professional, technical, and managerial employees, shareholders, and government as relevant interest groups (Pfeffer, 1989; Dimick & Murray, 1978; Edelman, 1992). Finally, vendors and customers are also now being included in the stakeholder category.

The two most often studied interest groups, unions and personnel departments, have been shown to have opposite impact on HRM systems. The presence of unions was negatively related to selectivity in hiring standards (Cohen & Pfeffer, 1986), with promotions from within (Pfeffer & Cohen, 1984), and with the proliferation of job titles (Baron & Bielby, 1986), while the presence of the personnel department was positively associated with these practices. Dimick and Murray (1978) also found that the percentage of unionized employees was negatively related to the sophistication of staffing and employment planning policies and programs. These effects of unions were attributed mainly to the value placed on seniority, and that of the personnel department to its desire to gain more power within the organization. This last argument is supported by Edelman's (1992) study which found that the nature of the organization's structural response to civil rights legislation depended on the presence of a personnel department. Where such a department existed, the organization was more likely to formulate new rules and regulations within the personnel function, and less likely to create a separate office solely for the purpose of attending to such legal requirements.

These findings are explained in terms of the interests that these groups are argued to have. Tsui (1987; Tsui & Milkovich, 1987), however, examined these interests more directly. In particular, she focused on four groups, namely, line executives, managers, professionals, and hourly employees (Tsui & Milkovich, 1987), and groups differentiated by operating or strategic level (Tsui, 1987). Her empirical studies showed not only that there were systematic differences in the preferences of various constituencies of the personnel department, but that these preferences may be in conflict. Her findings also showed that preferences of constituencies who are closer in the hierarchy are more similar.

Much more work, both theoretical and empirical, is needed that clearly delineates what these various interests are, and how they might exert competing or similar influences on HRM systems, enabling a better understanding of its nature in organizations. For example, one consequence of competing influences may be the incoherence of HRM

observed by some scholars (e.g., Blyton & Turnbull, 1992). Blyton and Turnbull described two opposing models of HRM: the Harvard model (Beer et al., 1985), which stresses the developmental aspects of HRM, and consideration of various stakeholders' interests; and the Michigan model (Fombrun, Tichy, & Devanna, 1984), emphasizing its utilitarian/instrumental functions in achieving managerial objectives. The simultaneous occurrence of both these contradictory aspects, also referred to as its soft and hard aspects respectively, may reflect the different preferences of the various groups that have a stake in HRM, and shifts in their relative influence, given the changing contingencies faced by the organization.

Power and politics are particularly salient considerations in HRM (Frost, 1989; Poole, 1990). This may be due to the difficulty in demonstrating cause-and-effect relations for HRM (Legge, 1978; Tsui, 1984). Dimick and Murray (1978) argued that this was one constraint for the use of technical rationality as a basis for making policy choices, resulting instead in political influences becoming more important determinants of such decisions. Pfeffer's (1981) model of the conditions for the use of power in organizations also includes heterogeneous beliefs about such relations. Thus, political behaviors are resorted to, especially by HR specialists, in order to convince others in the organization to accept the programs they are proposing, and to ensure support for their successful implementation (Schein, 1983; Frost, 1989). Political behaviors are also employed to influence favorable assessments of effectiveness that lead to access to resources (Tsui, 1990). In fact, because of the difficulties involved in measuring the effectiveness of the personnel function, Tsui (1984) proposed that this issue is and should ultimately be determined by the various interest groups.

The notion of groups with differing, possibly competing, interests leads to the questions of power: what determines the relative power of these groups, what are the mechanisms by which they gain power, and how is this power used to become dominant in the organization? The literature in intraorganizational power and politics provides numerous material which can be applied to HRM, although this rarely has been done. Baron, Dobbin, and Jennings (1986) and Silberman (1993) attributed the increased importance of the personnel function to societal factors such as labor shortages and government requirements, and where such factors were no longer present to provide a source of power to the personnel specialists, they turned to professionalization as a means by which to maintain their power in organizations. Russ (1987) made similar arguments in her notion of "phantom threat" and "discovered threat" for boundary-spanners like HR managers. Where critical contingencies arising from the external environment have been resolved, boundary-spanning HR managers maintain their influence by alluding to threats which in fact no longer exist, or in discovering new threats to which the organization must attend.

Legge (1978; Legge & Exley, 1975) pointed to two strategies which personnel specialists utilize in attempting to gain more power, differing on the values pursued and espoused. The conformist innovation emphasizes values that are congruent with managerial interests, such as cost effectiveness. Deviant innovation prescribes the values to which the organization must adhere. In practice, personnel specialists vacillate between these two strategies. Legge also argued that the effectiveness of the strategy depended on the economic condition of the firm. Deviant innovation can be effective where there is slack, because this allows for experimentation. Where resources are scarce, conformist innovation is more effective. Gowler and Legge (1986), however, pointed out that this strategy might backfire in that cost-effectiveness arguments also can be applied to the personnel function. In any case, they argued that a functionalist image of personnel is a useful justification for main-

taining personnel's power, thus accounting for the dominance of such an image.

Tsui's multiple constituency approach to personnel departments (1984, 1987, 1990; Tsui & Milkovich, 1987) suggested that balancing the interests of multiple constituencies, especially those who are critical, and utilizing multiple evaluation criteria would enable the personnel department to favorably influence assessments of its effectiveness, which in turn would provide the department with power and influence.

The HR department of course is not the only interest group as far as HRM is concerned, but studies that examine the other interest groups and how they are able to influence HRM systems are lacking. Nevertheless, this focus on the HR department leads to the final question of interest within the power and politics perspective, that of the consequences or outcomes when different interest groups predominate. One particular question deals with the power of the HR department, and relates it to the distinction made between *department* and *function* (Legge, 1978; Schuler, 1993). *Function* may refer narrowly to an activity, while *department* to the "institutionalized presence" in the organization. Thus, the HRM *function* may or may not be carried out by an HR *department*, or may or may not be the exclusive responsibility of the HR *department*. To illustrate, Schuler (1993) notes the international differences in the importance given to either department or function. For example, both department and function are given importance in North America, whereas in Japan, the function has long been important in organizations, while the department enjoys only a modest role. Thus, the power of the HR department is not necessary for the importance of the HRM function in the organization. However, where the HR department has achieved power and where such power is responsible for the importance of the function, would the loss of power result in the decreased importance of HRM, and would such decrease constrain the

105

organization from reaping the benefits that HRM potentially has to offer? Alternatively, where HRM has achieved significance but the HR department only has a modest role, would a gain in power make HRM less important because it might lead to line managers' abdication of this responsibility? These are some of the issues that remain to be resolved.

The discussion thus far has focused on how power and politics affects the formulation of HRM policies and systems. But power and politics also occur at the interpersonal level within HRM systems that are created by the organization. Therefore, we now turn to an examination of how power and politics play out in the interpersonal dynamics between supervisor and subordinates within HRM systems.

Power and politics in the implementation of human resources policies and practices

We saw above how power and politics influence the formulation of human resources policies through the negotiation of competing interest groups who use their position, size and influence of their coalition, and other resources to get what they want. Such power and political dynamics are indeed quite interesting, but they only tell part of the story; that is, how HR policies and systems are formulated. How these HR policies and systems are implemented and operate also bears serious consideration because power and politics are involved as well. In this section, we take a brief look at power and politics in the implementation and operation of human resources systems.

We would suggest that in much the same way that competing interest groups struggle for influence over policy formulation matters, key stakeholders compete in a similar way in gaining influence over human resources systems and decisions. In such cases, we see that human resources decision makers or raters (e.g., interviewers or managers) compete

overtly and covertly with ratees (e.g., job applicants or employees) to control the processes and outcomes of human resources systems (e.g., personnel selection, performance evaluation, promotion, etc.). In the case of raters, we find that they approach human resources systems with a variety of objectives. For example, they might approach the decision about who to hire or promote (i.e., staffing decision) from the perspective of coalition or power base building, or perpetuation of the status quo (i.e., as opposed to hiring the person with the best knowledge, skills, and abilities to perform the job). In essence, such decision makers seem to employ the criterion of "fit," and the person that is considered to fit best is the one who holds similar attitudes, beliefs, and values as the rater, or possesses other characteristics that are reflected in the dominant coalition of the organization (Judge & Ferris, 1992). Thus, such a process ensures the protection and perpetuation of the dominant coalition by promoting similarity or homogeneity. In fact, Kanter (1977) coined the term "homosocial reproduction" to reflect such organizational staffing systems. Furthermore, Longenecker, Sims, and Gioia (1987) have provided an interesting analysis of how managers use performance evaluation systems politically to satisfy their own agenda.

At the same time that raters or decision makers may approach human resources systems politically, so can ratees. In such decision-making interactions, the ratee typically operates from a position of considerably less power than the rater. However, ratees can call upon a repertoire of resources and political acumen to try to exercise control over the process and decisions. Ratees can engage in various behaviors designed to manage impressions of fit, similarity, competence, and so forth which, if executed effectively, can increase the likelihood of receiving favorable evaluations. Indeed, job applicant impression management efforts have been found to increase the evaluations made by interviewers (e.g., Fletcher, 1989; Gilmore & Ferris, 1989a, b; Kacmar, Delery & Ferris, 1992).

Although job applicants may use a variety of impression management tactics, evidence suggests that they are not equally effective. For example, Kacmar et al. (1992) examined tactics that focus on the self, such as presenting one's qualifications, and tactics that focus on the interviewer, such as compliments. The results indicated that the applicant was viewed more favorably when using self-focused tactics in comparison to other-focused tactics in the employment interview.

Similar outcomes have been found for subordinates using impression management to control the ratings they receive (e.g., Ferris, Judge, Rowland, & Fitzgibbons, 1994; Wayne & Ferris, 1990; Wayne & Kacmar, 1991). Due to the nature of jobs in organizations, it is difficult to objectively measure individual job performance. Thus, ratings are often based on a supervisor's judgments of an employee's performance, and are susceptible to subordinate influence attempts.

Theory and research on power and politics in human resource management characterizes organizations as consisting of divergent interests who compete for power and influence over the decisions, policies, and strategies that are formulated and implemented. As we saw, these competing interests can be reflected by groups or by individuals, and power and politics is played out in a variety of ways as these groups and individuals compete against each other for influence over processes and outcomes.

We now examine how the power and politics perspective can be used to better understand how the human resources department and function operate in organizations.

POWER AND POLITICS IN HUMAN RESOURCE MANAGEMENT PRACTICE

Getting HRM goals established and supported within the organization is influenced by how much power the HR unit actually has, and how the HR function is viewed by the organization. There are many ways of gaining support for goals. Obviously, one of them is ensuring that HR goals support overall corporate goals, as well as the business mission and goals of each of the units with whom the HR department is interfacing. To the extent that HR goals are in concert with the goals of these other units, then the HR department has a much greater opportunity of achieving its own objectives.

Corporate culture is also important. As long as HR objectives are consistent with corporate values, this tends to help the HR unit play from a position of greater power. Take the example of 360° evaluations of performance, whereby individuals receive evaluations from supervisors, peers, and subordinates, in addition to customers, in many cases. It does exemplify the point that what one is doing has to be in alignment with the values of the corporation. Acceptance of this latest trend in performance appraisal requires a value system that places importance on extensive feedback from many different sources.

Another important consideration is meeting the needs of the people within the organization, and insuring that these goals are in concert with organizational needs and requirements. "People" refers to the whole sphere of people within an organization. Obviously, one has to ensure that a state of equilibrium is achieved and maintained between the needs of the employee population that policies are applied to, and the needs of the organization. However, just looking at the total population is not enough. One also has to look at the specialized needs of various special interest groups because their needs must also be met within the confines of HR objectives.

There are a number of ways of determining these needs. When it comes to the needs of people as it relates to supporting their business mission and goals, one has to have a direct relationship with the key players in each one of the business units in the organization. This includes not only the HR staff in those units, if there is any, but also the unit heads or presidents. It is also helpful if the corporate HR department is represented on the corporate management committee or governing body. This allows for a two-way flow of information, and facilitates the integration of all goals; corporate, business unit, and people.

Keeping the needs of people in balance with those of the organization requires the use of multiple sources. Some sort of sounding board or listening vehicles within the organization, which actually allows one to know how the people feel who work for the company helps you do that. Again, this is dependent on the relationships one has established in the various business units to be able to obtain this kind of information access.

The power of the HR organization is based on the perceptions of business leaders throughout the corporation regarding how much value HR is adding to the achievement of their agendas. This is the bottom line. To the extent they see the HR unit as helping them meet their objectives and needs, this becomes a continuing source of power and influence for the HR organization. This is the whole notion of alignment. If the business units feel they can come to the HR department with an issue or problem, and they can sit down and discuss it, and jointly develop scenarios around that particular issue which helps the unit, then the HR department has something of value to offer. You will never be perceived as adding value unless in fact you are. Adding value is the way HR expands its influence and power.

Building relationships is the job of not one particular individual, but of all the staff in the HR department. The successes of all members add up to determining how influential the department is as a whole.

Building relationships

One strategy for achieving the perception of a "value adding" organization is establishing personal relationships at all levels throughout the business units. This allows for day-to-day contact and the opportunity to build perceptions that HR is aligned with business unit interests and is exploring how to add value to the achievement of their business goals, as opposed to pursuing a separate agenda.

The HR department has to become a support, instead of a control organization, even though there are certain functions that the HR department must oversee. And, when oversight becomes necessary, it should be done in partnership with the business units, to avoid being perceived as the third-party police. Alignment with business unit goals, and the ability to make alignment apparent is key. Without the perception of supporting business goals, there is little possibility that the HR department will be an influential part of the organization.

HR should be viewed by the organization as a problem solver. To the extent that it is not, the organization will bypass the department. When that happens, HR's role becomes much more confined and takes on more of a control function. Clearly that reduces HR's influence.

For HR to build and maintain influence, it is also important that HR maintains a high level of confidence and trust. Business units need to perceive that HR preserves their confidentiality and does not pass confidential information up in the organization.

In reviewing HR literature, it is evident certain HR departments have been able to go beyond supporting business goals, to being a meaningful partner in establishing these goals. This level of confidence and influence is not easily achieved, and must be built over time.

One way of enhancing the perceptions of business units with respect to HR's value is by directly confronting this issue. Constantly asking the unit presidents for their assessment of how the HR department, as a whole, and particular HR staff are doing in terms of adding value to their business goals, is a mechanism that can be instituted. Feedback from the individual units helps the HR department meet the needs of the business, and remain in alignment with business goals. It also keeps the HR staff always focused on adding value to the units.

The account representative concept can be used for gathering periodic feedback from the units. The account representative is in addition to all other HR staff with whom the unit relates on specific issues. In this way, several venues are created whereby dissatisfaction can be aired formally and informally.

This mechanism not only provides feedback, but it is another method of demonstrating to business units the HR department's concern for aligning with their interests, and adding value to their organizations. It demonstrates that the HR unit is concerned with providing quality service, and actively seeking feedback (positive or negative) which will allow them to ensure that high-quality standards are maintained. This also increases the confidence business units have in HR, and contributes to an effective working relationship.

External assessment enables the HR department to identify who among the staff requires development, or who may need to be replaced. More and more, HR organizations are moving towards a more professional staff with a deeper HR background and knowledge. The drawback to this approach is the danger that the HR staff will have limited knowledge and understanding of the business. Thus, there is a need to develop the HR staff's understanding of business issues as well as promoting their professional development. HR staff must be able to understand the strategic issues of the business, and how to add value to the organization.

At a point in time the HR unit may find out that some of their activities are not consistent with the organization's needs or desires, or that business units did not view them as being helpful. When that happens, one needs to be big enough to look at the situation and say: What has gone wrong? What needs to change? How do we turn this around so that we, in fact, can meet the needs of the business units? It is always a question of flexibility and evaluating the impact that HR is having on the organization.

Other strategies and tactics

Other means can be utilized to build power and influence. The HR staff has expertise, critical knowledge, skills, and abilities not found elsewhere. Indeed, such unique and critical skills and expertise will serve as a source of power and influence in the organization.

Another source of influence for HR is moving ideas laterally from one business unit to another. The corporate HR unit is typically the one that facilitates the flow of information across units. The corporate HR unit does not need to come up with all the great ideas, because there are many generated by the business units. HR can serve a valuable function of process facilitator by ensuring the lateral flow of information and ideas across units. The key is to manage this process in a way that does not appear to be forcing information upon people in a coercive way, but rather providing opportunities for information acquisition.

Similarly, the HR unit can develop external relationships with professional organizations. Attending meetings to make contact with other large companies provides some ideas that can be brought back into one's own organization. This can be another source of influence and perceived value-added. Developing external visibility also is useful because it can enhance how one is viewed internally. For example, being regarded as one of the best companies to work for is a perception that has a positive effect on the HR department.

Building relationships and adding value is a way of building one's influence base. So that when the need for support comes up, it is more likely to be given, than if those relationships had not been built. Organizations can be viewed as networks of relationships or linkages, and a unit's perceived centrality in that network contributes to its power or influence base. The foregoing discussion has proposed ways that HR can become more central in the network of relationships, and thus gain more power and influence.

An example of gaining support

One specific example of gaining support for a proposal so that it could be successful is the case of an open management staffing model. This is a system which enables all employees to have access to the job opportunities available throughout the corporation. The corporate HR staff polled all business units via electronic mail. The message sent to all units included an explanation of the open management staffing system, and why it was consistent with the culture of the organization. The units were asked whether they were in favor of moving toward the implementation of this open staffing model, and how to go about implementing the system. The responses were summarized and shared with everyone, adjustments were made to the proposed system based on business unit input, and eventually everyone agreed to go forward and discuss implementation issues.

This kind of open dialogue and input helped to build commitment to the system, because it was not seen as a corporate product or an HR product. However, not all issues can be handled in this open manner. If this had been an issue where there was to be no choice, polling the group would be inappropriate. In such cases, people should be told what will be implemented, and their role becomes one of implementation. Credibility would be undermined if the perception of choice was given when there was none.

Conversely, it is also important when there is no organizational support for a particular program, the power of corporate not be exercised. When there are a few dissenters slowing or stopping progress, then they must be influenced in a more personal way.

Position or formal power

There are some direct lines which give power and credibility within an organization, simply because of one's position in the corporate hierarchy. If one is in an organization that is highly centralized, considerable power and influence can be gained simply from where you happen to be in the organization. But in an organization which tends to be more complex and decentralized, while there is some power that can be gained from being located at the corporate headquarters and being responsible for certain functions, most power and influence is based on relationships and one's contributions, in terms of knowledge and problem solving, that helps the business units meet their missions and goals.

Building sources of power other than position power becomes necessary in a more complex, less centralized organization. Influencing people is based on knowledge, credibility, relationships, alignment with business goals, and adding value. Although one may have the power to reward and punish, relying exclusively on position power is not effective over time.

Overreliance on position power, and getting labeled as someone who is not helpful, or as someone who operates on a command-and-control methodology, causes the business units to build walls. They may close corporate HR out of their organization. Without access, HR cannot understand what is happening in the business units. To the extent that HR lacks information, influence in other areas (e.g., upwards in the organization) will also quickly diminish. It is difficult to be effective in that kind of a situation.

It is natural for business unit staffs to put up guards or shields, because they want to run their units without interference. But, transparency is necessary when the organization is highly interconnected, when the individual business units are not little smoke-stack companies which can operate independently of one another. It is healthier to have transparency so that units can know what is going on in other units and pass on useful information and ideas.

Manipulating rewards and punishments may not be the best source of power and influence. Exercising this kind of position power is the kind of thing that helps to cloud these transparent walls, and in the long run will be counterproductive.

Having the power to reward and punish is a fact of corporate life. For the HR department, that comes from having access to certain people, and being involved in decision making which affects jobs and careers. And even though this may never be employed, it is still a source of power. It influences how other people behave towards the HR staff. For example, they may hesitate to disagree with the HR unit who has this power over them because this could play out later. But it works on the HR staff as well. It is a factor that is considered in dealing with the heads of other units who are influential themselves.

Everyone has some position power, and so the issue becomes whether one is viewed as using that as a lever in a negative way, or in a useful and productive way. For example, through interactions with various people in the organization, one gets to know people with talent who could be a leader in the business. When there is an opportunity for promotion, one could use this knowledge to influence the decision. The HR department's opinions on whom to select and hire are often listened to in the organization. This is especially so when the HR unit is represented in succession planning committees.

Position power is something that can be used positively or negatively. So it is important that people use this kind of influence and power responsibly; that is, to the best advantage of the organization. This is the real key. The individual who uses power to satisfy personal needs is soon unmasked by key people in the organization, and the result is that one is viewed as being on the losing side of the ledger.

The CEO's values and perceptions

The attitude and perceptions of the chief executive officer towards the HR department is definitely an influencing factor on the power and influence held by the HR unit. Hence, the relationship with the CEO must be managed in the same way as relationships with the business units. Again, this involves being responsive to the needs of that particular individual, and that may or may not mean necessarily doing everything that the CEO wants. The HR function must be constantly aware of how it is being perceived. The knowledge by the CEO that HR is interested in adding more value, and is aligning its programs and strategies to meet the enterprise's needs, will increases the likelihood of continuing support. In addition, to the extent that he or she receives positive feedback on the HR organization from the business units, that helps to build the HR unit's influence. If feedback is negative, and the CEO already has a negative opinion, that reinforces it. The point is that HR needs to be proactive in managing the relationship with the CEO; this will contribute to their influence and power base in the organization.

In viewing the total corporate HR function, more of its time is directed to the business units than to the CEO and top corporate managers. Not surprisingly, while the HR staff spends most of its time managing relationships with the business units, the head of the HR function devotes considerably more time to working with the CEO and peer corporate executives.

INTEGRATION AND FUTURE DIRECTIONS

Thus far we have discussed how power and politics in human resource management occur at the organizational level and at the interpersonal level. To date, these two levels have been treated separately, and no attempt has been made to address how they might interrelate. We suggest, however, that the dynamics at the organizational level affect and are affected by power and politics at the interpersonal level *within* HRM systems, and we examine this notion here in order to obtain a more complete picture of the influence of power and politics in HRM.

The nature of the human resources policies and systems adopted by the organization may inadvertently influence the distribution of power and the level of politics at the interpersonal level. One way is by creating conditions that facilitate the exercise of power and politics within the organization. Ferris, Russ, and Fandt (1989) point to some of these facilitating conditions. These include situational factors such as moderate or low emotionality or task involvement, high degree of uncertainty or ambiguity, opportunities or threats which create perceptions of instrumentality of political behavior, observance of relevant others engaging in such behaviors, expections of success, and importance of the situation and its potential outcomes.

Empirical evidence for the effects of these factors has in fact been provided. Uncertainty or ambiguity was found to determine the use of social influence in organizational decision making (Pfeffer, Salancik, & Leblebici, 1976), and manipulation of information (Fandt & Ferris, 1990). Upward influence behaviors by subordinates are also affected by other situational factors such as managerial competence, warmth and support provided by the supervisor, job performance-based rewards, and fair and reasonable rules (Cheng, 1983).

Another direct way that HRM systems may inadvertently influence power and politics at the interpersonal level is by selecting people with high potential for using power and engaging in political behaviors. Individual differences such as self-monitoring, self-attention, social anxiety, Machiavellianism, and other-deception have been suggested as determinants of influence behaviors (Ferris et al., 1989; Fandt & Ferris, 1990; Deluga, 1991; House, 1988).

Of course, organizations also may deliberately influence power distribution as when empowerment programs are adopted, or when the organization is redesigned into less hierarchical structures, as a means to improve overall organizational performance. Whether the resulting redistribution of power changes the level and nature of political behaviors remains to be investigated. Thus, the possibility is suggested that organizations may adopt human resources systems that control the dysfunctional effects of power and politics in organizations, while allowing the functional aspects to transpire (House, 1988; Pfeffer, 1981).

External interest groups which have a stake in and are able to influence HRM policies and practices of the organization may likewise affect power and politics at the interpersonal level. For example, unions by directly influencing the human resources policies may indirectly influence the nature of the relationship between supervisor and subordinate. Likewise, governmental agencies in implementing employment-related laws shape these interactions. Unfortunately, the influences of these external factors on the occurrence of power and politics within the organization have not been examined.

While power and politics at the organizational level may directly or indirectly influence power and politics at the interpersonal level, the opposite effect may also occur. The effectiveness by which HRM policies and systems adopted by the organization are able to achieve the desired outcomes and satisfy the expectations of various organizational members is to some extent influenced by the level of political influence behaviors occurring at the interpersonal level. Frequently, failure to take into consideration the possible use of power and politics by individuals may account for the difficulties encountered in implementing or enforcing HR policies. Thus the way HR policies and systems are actually carried out in practice may diverge from what was intended. Power and politics that affect the implementation of HR policies and systems may bring about unexpected outcomes which hinder the effectiveness of HRM in organizations. This in turn may affect the importance given to the function, or shape the nature of the systems adopted. Unmet expectations by various interest groups may lead to their use of power and politics at a higher level, that is, influencing the formulation of HR policies and systems within the organization.

CONCLUSION

We have thus presented the power and politics perspective as an alternative and useful approach to understanding human resource management in organizations. We saw how power and politics affects the way human resources policies and systems get formulated and implemented, and we also examined the demonstration of power and politics interpersonally in day-to-day HR practices. Finally, we saw in the practice of HRM today, that power and politics is the way things often get accomplished for the HR department, which typically is in the position of attempting to influence without authority. Indeed, power and politics is a fact of organizational life, and explains much about what and how things get done. Therefore, it is useful in helping us to better understand the nature and operation of HRM in organizations today.

REFERENCES

Bacharach, S. B., & Lawler, E. J. (1980). *Power and Politics in Organizations*. San Francisco: Jossey-Bass.

Baron, J., & Bielby, W. T. (1986). The proliferation of job titles in organizations. *Administrative Science Quarterly*, 31, 561–86.

Baron, J., Dobbin, F., & Jennings, P. D. (1986). War and peace: The evolution of modern personnel administration in US industry. *American Journal of Sociology*, 92, 350–83.

Beer, M., Spector, B., Lawrence, P. R., Mills, D. Q., & Walton, R. E. (1985). *Human Resource Management: A general manager's perspective*. New York: Free Press.

Blyton, P., & Turnbull, P. (eds.) (1992). *Reassessing Human Resource Management*. London: Sage.

Bolman, L. G., & Deal, T. E. (1991). *Reframing Organizations*. San Francisco: Jossey-Bass.

Burrell, G., & Morgan, G. (1979). *Sociological Paradigms and Organizational Analysis*. London: Heinemann.

Cheng, J. L. C. (1983). Organizational context and upward influence: An experimental study of the use of power tactics. *Group and Organization Studies*, 8, 337–55.

Cohen, Y., & Pfeffer, J. (1986). Organizational hiring standards. *Administrative Science Quarterly*, 31, 1–24.

Deluga, R. J. (1991). The relationship of upward-influencing behavior with subordinate-impression management characteristics. *Journal of Applied Social Psychology*, 21, 1145–60.

DiMaggio, P. J., & Powell, W. W. (1983). The iron cage revisited: Institutional isomorphism and collective rationality in organizational fields. *American Sociological Review*, 48, 147–60.

Dimick, D. E., & Murray, V. V. (1978). Correlates of substantive policy decisions in organizations: The case of human resource management. *Academy of Management Journal*, 21, 611–23.

Drory, A., & Romm, T. (1990). The definition of organizational politics: A review. *Human Relations*, 43, 1133–54.

Edelman, L. B. (1992). Legal ambiguity and symbolic structures: Organizational mediation of civil rights law. *American Journal of Sociology*, 97, 1531–76.

Fandt, P. M., & Ferris, G. R. (1990). The management of information and impressions: When employees behave opportunistically. *Organizational Behavior and Human Decision Processes*, 45, 140–58.

Ferris, G. R., & Judge, T. A. (1991). Personnel/human resources management: A political influence perspective. *Journal of Management*, 17, 447–88.

Ferris, G. R., Judge, T. A., Rowland, K. M., & Fitzgibbons, D. E. (1994). Subordinate influence and the performance evaluation process: Test of a model. *Organizational Behavior and Human Decision Processes*, 58, 101–35.

Ferris, G. R., & King, T. R. (1991). Politics in human resources decisions: A walk on the dark side. *Organizational Dynamics*, 20, 59–71.

Ferris, G. R., King, T. R., Judge, T. A., & Kacmar, K. M. (1991). The management of shared meanings in organizations: Opportunism in the reflection of attitudes, beliefs, and values. In R. A. Giacalone & P. Rosenfeld (eds.), *Applied Impression Management: How image-making affects managerial decisions*, 41–64. Newbury Park, CA: Sage.

Ferris, G. R., Russ, G. S., & Fandt, P. M. (1989). Politics in organizations. In R. A. Giacalone & P. Rosenfeld (eds.), *Impression Management in the Organization*, 143–70. Hillsdale, NJ: Lawrence Erlbaum.

Fletcher, C. (1989). Impression management in the selection interview. In R. A. Giacalone & P. Rosenfeld (eds.), *Impression Management in the Organization*, 269–81. Hillsdale, NJ: Lawrence Erlbaum.

Fombrun, C., Tichy, N. M., & Devanna, M. A. (1984). *Strategic Human Resource Management*. New York: Wiley.

Frost, P. J. (1989). The role of organizational power and politics in human resource management. In A. N. B. Nedd, G. R. Ferris & K. M. Rowland (eds.), *International Human Resources Management*, 1–21. Supplement 1, Research in personnel and human resources management. Greenwich, CT: JAI Press.

Gilmore, D. C., & Ferris, G. R. (1989a). The effects of applicant impression management tactics on interviewer judgments. *Journal of Management*, 15, 557–64.

Gilmore, D. C., & Ferris, G. R. (1989b). The politics of the employment interview. In R. W. Eder & G. R. Ferris (eds.), *The Employment Interview: Theory, research, and practice*, 195–203. Newbury Park, CA: Sage.

Gowler, D., & Legge, L. (1986). Personnel and paradigms: Four perspectives on the future. *Industrial Relations Journal*, 17, 225–35.

House, R. J. (1988). Power and personality in complex organizations. In B. M. Staw & L. L. Cummings (eds.), *Research in Organizational Behavior*, vol. 10, pp. 305–57. Greenwich, CT: JAI.

Jackson, S. E., Schuler, R. S., & Rivero, J. C. (1989). Organizational characteristics as predictors of personnel practices. *Personnel Psychology*, 42, 727–86.

Jennings, P. D. (1994). Viewing macro HRM from without: Political and institutional perspectives. In G. R. Ferris (ed.), *Research in Personnel and Human Resources Management*, vol. 12. Greenwich, CT: JAI.

Judge, T. A., & Ferris, G. R. (1992). The elusive criterion of fit in human resources staffing. *Human Resources Planning*, 15, 47–67.

Kacmar, K. M., Delery, J. E., & Ferris, G. R. (1992). Differential effectiveness of applicant impression management tactics on employment interview decisions. *Journal of Applied Social Psychology*, 22, 1250–72.

Kanter, R. M. (1977). *Men and Women of the Corporation*. New York: Basic Books.

Legge, K. (1978). *Power, Innovation and Problem-Solving in Personnel Management*. London: McGraw-Hill.

Legge, K., & Exley, M. (1975). Authority, ambiguity and adaptation: The personnel specialists' dilemma. *Industrial Relations Journal*, 6, 51–65.

Longenecker, C. O., Sims, H. P., Jr., & Gioia, D. S. (1987). Behind the mask: The politics of employee appraisal. *Academy of Management Executive*, 1, 313–23.

Meyer, J. W., & Rowan, B. (1977). Institutionalized organizations: Formal structure as myth and ceremony. *American Journal of Sociology*, 83, 340–63.

Pfeffer, J. (1978). The micropolitics of organizations. In Marshall W. Meyer & associates (eds.), *Environments and Organizations*, 29–50. New York: Jossey-Bass.

Pfeffer, J. (1981). *Power in Organizations*. Marshfield, MA: Pitman.

Pfeffer, J. (1989). A political perspective on careers: Interests, networks, and environments. In M. G. Arthur, D. T. Hall, & B. S. Lawrence (eds.), *Handbook of Career Theory*, 380–96. New York: Cambridge University Press.

Pfeffer, J., & Cohen, Y. (1984). Determinants of internal labor markets in organizations. *Administrative Science Quarterly*, 29, 550–72.

Pfeffer, J., Salancik, G. R., & Leblebici, H. (1976). The effect of uncertainty on the use of social influence in organizational decision making. *Administrative Science Quarterly*, 21, 227–45.

Poole, M. (1990). Editorial: Human resource management in an international perspective. *International Journal of Human Resource Management*, 1, 1–15.

Russ, G. (1987). *Boundary spanning: What comes after controlling critical linkages?* Working paper, department of management, Texas A & M University.

Saha, S. K. (1989). Variations in the practice of human resource management: A review. *Canadian Journal of Administrative Science*, September, 37–45.

Schein, V. E. (1983). Strategic management and the politics of power. *Personnel Administrator*, October, 55–8.

Schuler, R. S. (1993). World class HR departments: Six critical issues. *The Singapore Accounting and Business Review*, forthcoming.

Silberman, A. (1993). *Political Behavior in Organizations: The case of the personnel managers*. Master's thesis, University of Wisconsin, Madison.

Trice, H. N., Belasco, J., & Alutto, J. A. (1969). The role of ceremonials in organizational behavior. *Industrial and Labor Relations Review*, 23, 40–51.

Tsui, A. S. (1984). Personnel department effectiveness: A tripartite approach. *Industrial Relations*, 23, 184–97.

Tsui, A. S. (1987). Defining the activities and effectiveness of the HR department: A multiple constituency approach. *Human Resource Management*, 26, 35–69.

Tsui, A. S. (1990). A multiple-constituency model of effectiveness: An empirical examination at the human resource subunit level. *Administrative Science Quarterly*, 35, 458–83.

Tsui, A. S., & Milkovich, G. T. (1987). Personnel department activities: Constituency perspectives and preferences. *Personnel Psychology*, 40, 519–37.

Wayne, S. J., & Ferris, G. R. (1990). Influence tactics, affect, and exchange quality in supervisor–subordinate interactions: A laboratory experiment and field study. *Journal of Applied Psychology*, 75, 487–99.

Wayne, S. J., & Kacmar, K. M. (1991). The effect of impression management on the performance appraisal process. *Organizational Behavior and Human Decision Processes*, 48, 70–88.

☐ Chapter 7 ☐

Strategic Change: A New Dimension of Human Resource Management

Michael Beer, Russell A. Eisenstat, and E. Ralph Biggadike

Fundamental technological, political, regulatory, and economic forces are radically changing the worldwide competitive environment. We have not seen such a metamorphosis of the economic landscape since the industrial revolution in the nineteenth century. The scope and pace of the changes over the last two decades qualify this period as a modern industrial revolution.

Michael C. Jensen, 1993

INTRODUCTION

Corporate leaders first became aware that the competitive environment was changing dramatically in the early 1980s. Though recession was the proximal cause for hard times, it soon became apparent that a paradigmatic shift in the world economy was taking place. The emergence of global markets for products and labor, deregulation, new information technology, and capital market restructuring unleashed intense competitive forces that will be reality for the foreseeable future. The scope and pace of the changes in the past decade have led Michael Jensen (1993) to compare this period to the Industrial Revolution.

Surviving in a highly competitive and turbulent environment requires managers to achieve two difficult and often conflicting goals. They must ever more tightly *align* all design elements of their organizations (i.e., structure, systems, human resources policies, and management practice) with their current business strategies. This is necessary to achieve the continuous improvements in *cost*, in the *quality* of products and customer service, and

the *speed* with which products and services reach the market. Aligning the organization with today's strategy will allow the firm to succeed against current competitors in meeting the needs of current customers. Managers must also, however, create an organization that is flexible enough to quickly *adapt* to the unpredictable and rapid changes in technology and customer needs that threaten to make current strategies and organizational forms obsolete.

The story of Apple Computer illustrates the importance, as well as the difficulties of creating an organization that is both highly aligned and adaptive (Gibbs & Beer, 1991).

Founded by Steve Jobs and Steve Wozniack in 1977, Apple invented the personal computer, the Apple II. In 1984, the Apple II was replaced by the Macintosh (Mac) and its extensions as the main product line. Ease of use and graphical interface made the Mac a success with customers. Market share in schools and with individual users grew rapidly. Extraordinary customer loyalty was developed. Once converted to the Macintosh, customers rarely switched. In 1990, Apple was a very profitable five billion dollar company, widely hailed as the most innovative in the industry.

As early as 1981, however, changes were occurring in Apple's environment that would ultimately threaten its position and demand radical change. IBM entered the market with a personal computer using a different operating system, DOS. To enter the market rapidly IBM chose a different route than Apple. It decided to open its computer architecture, inviting supplier companies to produce compatible hardware and software. Given IBM's dominant position as a mainframe supplier, the IBM personal computer quickly became the standard in the large business market. By choosing not to make its computer design proprietary, however, IBM opened the door to manufacturers of much lower-cost IBM compatible computers. In the late 1980s, IBM itself was under extreme competitive pressures as new entrants took away the dominant share of market it had gained.

By 1990, Apple was faced with a radically different competitive environment from the one in which it had emerged as a company. There were many competitors offering IBM compatible computers (using the DOS operating system) at considerable lower cost than the Macintosh. While the Mac was still a unique product and commanded customer loyalty, the development of "Windows" software by Microsoft made it possible for DOS users to attain virtually the same user-friendly features that had made the Mac II so unique for only a few hundred dollars, far less than the cost of buying a Mac. Apple, unable to penetrate the business market lost market share, its profit margin began to shrink, and it was forced to consider laying off large numbers of employees, and this despite Apple's best efforts to adapt itself.

In an effort to make Apple more business- and customer-oriented as early as 1984, Apple's board of directors hired John Scully, then the chief operating officer of PepsiCo, to take over the company from Steve Jobs,

its founder and technical guru. He installed new financial control systems, brought in top executives from the industry, and on several occasions reorganized the company. Despite these efforts, Apple lost its leadership position in the personal computer industry.

Apple's early success was due to a high level of alignment between all elements of its organization (i.e., structure, systems, human resources policies, and management practices), and between these elements and business strategy. Yet, in some ways, its very success made adapting to a changing marketplace more difficult. Highly skilled engineers were recruited and energized through a compelling vision and stock options to work 90-hour weeks in closely knit product development teams. The vision, articulated by Steve Jobs, to which the engineers became highly committed was "empowering people through technology." It facilitated the development of highly cohesive engineering teams that developed unique breakthrough products such as the Apple II and the Macintosh.

Early successes reinforced a belief among Apple's employees that the company's technology and ideas were superior and could not be matched. Deviation from its high end technology-based strategy and from its management policies stirred protest and discontent. These beliefs made changes in organizing and managing people difficult; when they were attempted they met resistance. As late in the game as 1990, rumors of layoffs triggered a failed unionization effort among Apple's engineers. Despite his position as CEO, John Scully's intention to transform Apple into a more business-driven company foundered as he increasingly sought acceptance of Apple's key opinion leaders. The culture had influenced the leader as much, if not more, than the leader had influenced the culture. Tight alignment between strategy, organization, and people had undermined the capacity of Apple to adapt.

In this chapter, we discuss what theory, research, and practice tell us about developing organizations that are both highly aligned and adaptive. A conceptual understanding of the sometimes complementary, sometimes antagonistic organizational requirements for alignment and adaptation is the first requisite, and is detailed in the next section. Next is a discussion of what we know from theory, research, and practice about changing organizations. Without an effective theory and methodology for changing the way the firm organizes and manages people, managers cannot improve either organizational alignment or adaptability. We use the Apple case to ground our discussion in both of these sections.

In the third section, we evaluate current practice in developing a more competitive organization using a set of design specifications, derived from change theory, which must be met by organizational change methods that seek to develop both an aligned and an adaptive organization. These specifications help us understand why several change methodologies used by corporations in the last 30 years failed to create realigned and adaptive organizations. Recent innovations designed to overcome these problems are described.

In the final section, we focus on an analysis of *strategic human resource management profiling* (SHRM profiling), a process for realigning an organization and its human resource management policies and practices with competitive realities developed by the authors at Becton Dickinson Company. The basis of the process is the theories and models of organizations and organization change described in the first two sections. Experience in implementing SHRM is, therefore, also a test of the theory. We end with what was leaned from five years of experience with the profiling process, and the implications for firms who want to institutionalize effective change management practice.

The idea that it is necessary to align organizations and their employees' skills and motives is at least thirty years old (Burns & Stalker, 1961; Lawrence & Lorsch, 1967).

Similarly, the theory and techniques for managing organization change embodied in the field of organization development are also approximately thirty years old (Beckhard, 1969; Lippitt, Watson, & Westerley, 1958). Yet, as the case of Apple Computer and other fallen giants such as IBM, Sears, and General Motors illustrate, the practice of maintaining organizational alignment with changing competitive realities lag far behind theory. We argue that there is a gap between theory and practice because effective methods for making the sources of misalignment (i.e., management assumptions and behavior) discussible and actionable have not been developed and/or institutionalized.

The limited conception of personnel management harbored by most human resource practitioners is also partially responsible for the gap between theory and practice. Traditional concerns about crafting and administering personnel policies that will keep employees satisfied and the company out of trouble blinds human resources practitioners to a new and urgent human resources agenda: Developing and institutionalizing a management process that will enable the corporation's business units and the firm as a whole to align and realign employee attitudes and behaviors with a continuously changing business environment.

ORGANIZATIONAL ALIGNMENT AND ADAPTABILITY: A SYSTEMS PERSPECTIVE

The word organization immediately brings to mind formal structure, the organization chart that defines the hierarchical position of people in the organization. Influenced by the organization of the military and the Church, early management scholars viewed the problem of designing an effective organization as specifying the right structure. Universal rules regarding span of control and unity of command emerged as principles of design.

Theory and research in the last several decades have shown the extreme limitations of this view. Instead, organizations are best considered as complex *open systems* (Katz & Kahn, 1978). By system, we mean that organizations consist of many interdependent parts, elements, and levels, and that changes in one aspect of an organization affect other elements. By open, we mean that organizations interact with their environment; they import human, financial, and physical resources, subject them to various transforming work processes, and produce outputs in the form of products and services, profits, and employees' attitudes and behavior. In the long run, acceptable levels of customer, shareholder, and employee satisfaction are key to providing the resources needed for the firm to continue operations.

Strategic alignment

Building on the idea of an organization as an open system, concrete and actionable models of organizational effectiveness have been developed in the last several decades. At the core of all these models is the idea of "fit" or "alignment" (Friedlander, 1971; Kotter, 1978; Beer, 1980; Waterman, Peters, & Phillips, 1980; Nadler & Tushman, 1980). These models take a contingent view of organizational design (Lawrence & Lorsch, 1967; Lorsch & Morse, 1974): That is, the design of an effective organization and its human resource management policies and practices should depend on a firm's business strategy as well as the commitment and talents of its managers and workers. This is because the behavior, motivation, and skills of employees must be appropriate for implementing the business unit's strategic task (i.e., what it must do to compete effectively). Rapidly developing innovative new products require different motivation, behavior, and skills than for pursuing ever lower cost. Thus, to realign the organization with a new strategy, managers must redesign structure, systems, human resources policies, and management practice to ensure the motivation, skills, and behavior needed to implement that strategy.

The evidence is strong that alignment leads to satisfaction of shareholders, customers, and employees, the three stakeholder groups whose support is necessary for long-term organizational survival (Denison, 1992; Kotter & Heskett, 1992). Considerable knowledge also exists about the appropriate structures, systems, policies, and practices for different competitive environments, strategies, and phases in a company's growth (Chandler, 1962; Lawrence & Lorsch, 1967; Miles & Snow, 1978; Galbraith, 1982, 1987). While this knowledge can be useful to managers, having it does not ensure the capacity of the organization to realign itself. Usually alignment results through the confluence of historical forces that lead to early success, most notably the values and beliefs of the founder. Apple Computer is the example described here, but there are many others including such well-known companies as IBM, Hewlett Packard, and UPS, and lesser known companies like Herman Miller and Lincoln Electric. Alignment ensures that the beliefs of founders about how the firm ought to be organized and managed are sustained as the firm grows. They prevent, however, awareness of the need to realign and reduce the motivation to change. For this reason, knowledge about the process for managing realignment is as important as knowledge about what patterns of organization and management typically are associated with different strategies.

Achieving alignment requires an organization's managers to accomplish three tasks:

1 Define a strategic direction that is viable given the realities of the competitive environment and the organization's human capabilities.
2 Ensure that all the elements of the organization's design are consistent with the strategy. Such a design should help to:
3 Develop the human capabilities (i.e., the

level of motivation, skills, and teamwork) required to implement the strategy, and thus meet stakeholder needs.

Organizational adaptation

Competitive advantage is sustained only if the organization is adaptive. For organizations to continue to prosper in a rapidly changing competitive environment, they must be able to make continuous modifications in their business strategies as well as in the organizational designs required to enact these strategies. Firms must move rapidly and frequently through an adaptive coping cycle (Schein, 1965). This cycle requires that managers successfully complete the following, in addition to the alignment tasks described above:

4   Accurately *sense* and *appraise* without distortion unmet stakeholder needs as well as environmental threats and opportunities before a crisis occurs.

For this fourth activity to occur, people at the organization's boundary (e.g., in sales, customer service, technical functions, etc.) must sense changes in the firm's ability to satisfy the needs of customers, employees, and shareholders. They must also accurately sense threats and opportunities created by changes in competitor behavior or technology. This information must then be transmitted rapidly to relevant parts of the firm without distortion. There, decisions must be made about the implications of these external changes for the firm's business strategy and supportive organizational design.

The implementation of these decisions requires the firm to revisit the three alignment tasks above (i.e., redefining strategy, making appropriate changes in organizational design, and developing needed human capabilities). As these changes are enacted, stakeholders' opinions about the effectiveness of the response are obtained, and the cycle is repeated. Adaptive organizations avoid crisis

through continuous implementation of this adaptive coping cycle. They possess the capacity to carry on an open and confronting dialogue with stakeholders about their satisfaction, and to involve them appropriately in redesign decisions.

A DIAGNOSTIC MODEL OF ORGANIZATIONAL ALIGNMENT AND ADAPTABILITY

For managers to ensure that the organization is aligned and adaptive, they must be able to think causally about the dynamics in their organization that account for poor performance and/or adaptability. Figure 7.1 provides a diagnostic model which managers can use to assess alignment and adaptability and improve them. It incorporates the four elements, discussed above, which managers must diagnose and act on to develop an aligned and adaptive organization (i.e., competitive strategy, human capabilities, organization design, and the capacity to sense stakeholder dissatisfaction). The model specifies from right to left:

• The three key stakeholder outcomes that managers must balance.
• The human capabilities that affect stakeholder outcomes.
• The human resources policy areas which govern the design of the organization, and therefore the level and kind of human capabilities the organization produces.
• The conditions which cause and/or must be considered in crafting human resource management policies and practices.
• The feedback loops which must be kept open to produce an adaptive organization.

We consider each of the elements in the diagnostic model in more detail below. We engage in a discussion of each element in the model moving from right to left, the

Figure 7.1 A diagnostic model of organizational effectiveness

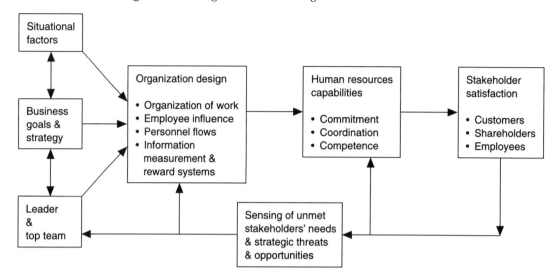

primary sequence a manager might use to diagnose why the organization is ineffective in meeting stakeholder expectations. Because the elements of the model are highly interdependent and causality is circular, a good diagnosis often demands moving out of this sequence as needed, to understand the causes of organizational ineffectiveness. The Apple case as well as research findings ground our discussion.

Organizational effectiveness depends on meeting key stakeholder needs

Over time, corporations must meet the expectations of multiple stakeholders (Beer et al., 1984). It is from these stakeholders that management draws its legitimacy, authority, and resources. The principal stakeholdes of concern are *customers*, *shareholders*, and *employees*, though others like the community and society at large must also be considered.

Most organizational effectiveness models and theories, like the model in figure 7.1, view organizations as transforming mechanisms (Beer, 1980; Nadler & Tushman, 1992).

Financial, physical, and human resources transform, through work processes, into products, profits, and employee attitudes. In the long run, acceptable levels of customer, shareholder, and employee satisfaction are key to providing the resources needed for the firm to continue operations.

In the late 1980s, Apple's stock was trading at record levels, reflecting shareholder satisfaction with its dramatically increasing sales and profits. Its customers loved the product, despite its relatively high cost, and its employees were highly committed to the vision of "empowering people through technology." Apple had managed to attract financial resources and very creative people, and to convert them into satisfied shareholders, customers, and employees.

By 1990, Apple's difficulties were reflected in lower market share, a decline in stock price, and by significant employee discontent expressed in a variety of ways including a failed unionization initiative. The causes for this shift in Apple's fortunes are in the human capabilities it produced historically, but which in 1990 were no longer sufficient to compete.

Human capabilities are key to implementing a strategy

For an organization to satisfy stakeholder needs, it must have the human capabilities that will enable it to implement its business strategy effectively. In particular, key members of the organization must be able to *coordinate* their efforts with one another, *commit* to the business strategy, and have the appropriate technical and managerial *competencies* to carry out the strategy (Beer, Spector, Lawrence, Mills, & Walton, 1984; Beer, Eisenstat, & Spector, 1990; Eisenstat & Beer, 1994). These human capabilities are discussed in greater detail below.

Coordination

Most sources of competitive advantage require efficient and effective coordination both within and between various functions (e.g., product design and development, marketing, production, selling, and customer support) in the value-creation process (Porter, 1985).

In highly uncertain and competitive environments, effective coordination is instrumental in producing superior performance in such areas as new product development and quality (Burns & Stalker, 1961; Lawrence & Lorsch, 1967; Deming, 1982). Teamwork enables the communication and reciprocity between functions needed to solve unstructured problems in a rapidly changing environment (Thompson, 1967).

If speed and low cost are necessary, it is essential that coordination be performed laterally, without resort to hierarchy. Cross-functional teams typically are the means. Relying on higher management to be the gatekeeper adds cost and slows decisions.

Commitment

Effective coordination without the intervention of hierarchy, requires commitment to the business strategy by all parts of the company as well as by labor and management.

Employees' willingness to act in the interest of the business rather than in the narrower interest of the function, technical specialty, or union becomes essential. Research demonstrates that employee initiative rather than management control is the key to effectiveness when quality, service, and productivity become important (Walton, 1985; Hackman & Oldham, 1980; Schneider, 1993; Lawler, 1986).

Competence

Competitive advantage depends on the technical competence of the organization's various functional departments such as research and development, production, or marketing. These provide the innovations in products, production, distribution, or service needed to compete. The leadership and interpersonal competence of the organization's managers will determine its ability to coordinate these activities to ensure the cost-effective and timely delivery of products and services.

1. *Distinctive competence* To compete, businesses require unique technical or functional competencies not possessed by competitors (Porter, 1985; Hamel & Prahalad, 1989). Unique competencies are fostered when functional departments (e.g., research, production, marketing, or selling) are permitted to organize and manage their people in a way that fosters different skills, motivation, and behavior from other functions, making each function distinctive (Lawrence & Lorsch, 1967).

2. *Managerial and interpersonal competence* Fostering unique and diverse competence in each functional area is the source of creative tensions that enable innovation. Coordination to overcome these tensions, however, requires skills in communication, resolving conflict, teamwork, and problem solving, and managers as well as professionals with a generalist perspective. These skills are particularly important when an organization is functioning

in a rapidly changing environment. This is because these environments usually require diverse functional competence to innovate and high levels of coordination among functional groups to respond rapidly and efficiently (Burns & Stalker, 1961; Lawrence & Lorsch, 1967). Without high levels of managerial and interpersonal competence, organizational mechanisms for coordination of such lateral teams or matrix structures fail (Davis & Lawrence, 1977: Bartlett & Ghoshal, 1990).

Apple's early success was largely due to the close match between its business strategy and its organizational capabilities. Apple's initial strategy of providing customers with uniquely usable and technologically elegant computers required high levels of technical competence in hardware and software design, high levels of commitment among engineers, and close coordination within the engineering function. Steve Jobs's vision of "empowering individuals through technology" enabled him to recruit a team of highly skilled engineers who were willing to work closely with one another for the long hours necessary to develop the Apple II and the Macintosh. Coordination of engineering with the rest of Apple was less important. Actually, the original Macintosh development group thought of themselves as a renegade organization, working in a separate building from which they flew a pirate flag. This separation was not a problem, as long as the emphasis was on innovation. The engineers didn't need marketing to tell them about the product features customers required, they were creating products for people like themselves. As a marketing manager at Apple explained: "We are what we make. I've never seen an organization where the personality of the organization is so intertwined with the personality of the product; individualistic, pure, uncompromised, ahead of everyone else, so elegant it can't fail. We are the Macintosh here."

When new competitive realities required a shift in strategy toward the rapid development of lower-cost computers for the corporate market, a new set of organizational capabilities was necessary. Inadequate teamwork between marketing and the technical function now made it impossible for Apple to succeed. Technical people were committed to technical sophistication rather than customer solutions. In 1988, they prevailed in their conflict with marketing over the inclusion of an 8 lb. battery in a new laptop. The result was a noncompetitive 22 lb. machine.

Human capabilities are shaped by multiple design levers

Coordination, commitment, and competence are shaped by *multiple* organization design levers and human resources policies ranging from formal elements such as structure and systems to informal elements such as hiring and succession practices, norms of behavior, and values. A variety of causal models have been developed (Beer, 1980; Waterman et al., 1980; Nadler & Tushman, 1980). We have chosen a four-policy framework originally developed at the Harvard Business School (Beer et al., 1984). Each area represents a domain that confronts managers with policy choices. These choices influence the amount and kind of coordination, commitment, and competence the firm will develop, and the cost effectiveness with which these capabilities are obtained. The four policy areas are defined below.

1 *Organization of work systems* The formal structure and control systems that define roles, responsibilities, and relationships to accomplish the task of the organization.
2 *Influence* The extent to which a relationship of mutual influence is established to resolve conflict in the organization horizontally (between functions, line staff, business units, and geographic regions) and vertically (between upper management and lower levels, and between management and unions).

3 *Personnel flows* The polices and practices governing employee recruitment, selection, transfer, promotion, and termination.

4 *Information, measurement, and reward systems* The kind of information made available to make decisions, the measurement systems used to judge performance, and how and what types of rewards are attached to successful performance.

Policy choices by Apple's founder, Steve Jobs, continued for too long by his successor John Scully, made Apple's distinctive competence the technical capability of its research and development function. This made Apple successful in its early years, but unresponsive to market demands for lower-cost computers in later years. Many of Apple's policies and practices sustained the power of the technical function, and prevented the development of managerial competence, coordination, and commitment to business rather than technology goals.

Until the late 1980s, Apple's hiring and promotion decisions heavily favored technical as opposed to managerial competence. The power of technical people made it difficult for marketing and production to influence the design of computers, thus increasing the cost of new products and lengthening the time it took to get new products to market. A functional structure and measurement systems discouraged coordination or commitment beyond narrow functional interests. Acting in concert, these policy choices created a pattern of inadequate coordination between functions, high commitment to technology and low commitment to business objectives, and low managerial competence. This pattern of human capabilities in turn led Apple to fail as its environment changed.

Apple Computer's loss of dominance is due to the inability of its management to realign organization with new competitive realities. The very organization that caused it to be a successful early mover in the industry prevented Apple from developing lower-cost

computers rapidly. By 1990, several different structures had been tried, though none that emphasized lateral teamwork. Measurement, reward, and personnel flow policies were not changed sufficiently to promote coordination and managerial competence. Technical people remained dominant in decisions, despite John Scully's ascendancy to the position of CEO.

Of course, a number of situational factors (e.g., the history of the organization, the characteristics of its existing work force and labor markets, and social norms and laws of the community or country) reduce the degrees of freedom managers have in changing human capabilities. That is why effective change requires early and persistent intervention over a long period of time. For example, the work force at Apple could not be fired without losing valuable technical resources and destroying commitment.

Strategy must fit the realities of the competitive environment

Businesses compete with their rivals in a number of very different ways, through providing the lowest-cost product, through beating competitors to market with new products possessing superior features, or through providing current products at superior levels of product quality and or customer service. Apple's strategy, essentially unchanged until the late 1980s, was to compete by differentiating itself through product technology, not cost, quality, or service.

Though industries differ in their competitiveness, eventually firms in most industries must reevaluate their strategy due to competitive forces unleashed in the industry (i.e., the appearance of substitute products using a different technology, suppliers who have gained power, new entrants into the market who compete with lower-cost products, and/ or enhanced power of customers) (Porter, 1985). The entry of computer manufacturers able to produce IBM-compatible DOS machines at a significantly lower cost, and the development by Microsoft Corporation of "Windows" (i.e., software that made it possible for DOS machines to provide the ease-of-use characteristics of the Macintosh) dramatically altered Apple's competitive environment. Customers could buy a computer far less expensive than the Macintosh, and for only a few hundred dollars more purchase "Windows." The Macintosh's product advantage was lost, and it had a large cost disadvantage.

Sensing unmet stakeholder needs – the key to adaptability

For an organization to be adaptive, it must obtain continuous feedback from its stakeholders, process that information non-defensively, and possess the skills at the top to lead change.

The importance of feedback

Adaptive organizations are able to respond to negative feedback from customers, employees, and shareholders by modifying their strategy and behavior. Because stakeholder satisfaction is necessary to obtain vital resources (i.e., employee effort, customer goodwill, and financial capital) their voice ultimately influences design and policy decisions. Unfortunately, stakeholder dissatisfaction does not always become known until a crisis occurs (e.g., labor unrest, a takeover effort, or a decline in market share. An effective organization, therefore, attempts to obtain ongoing *feedback* from its stakeholders about their satisfaction. If valid information is obtained and processed rapidly, without distortion, the corporation can discover how well it meets the expectations of external constituents, and what barriers employees perceive in implementing new strategies.

As the competitive environment has intensified, greater efforts are being made to solicit customer opinions (Heskett, Sasser, &

Hart, 1990). A new activism by capital markets is making companies more sensitive to shareholder value (Jensen, 1993). Employees voice their views through unions or management-inspired mechanisms such as attitude surveys, focus group interviews, and open-door policies. More and more companies are insisting, for example, that managers get the opinions of subordinates, peers, and bosses; the 360° survey as it has become known. In an era of downsizing and global competition, however, employees' power relative to customers and shareholders generally has declined.

The problem in Apple's case was not a lack of information about the changing marketplace, rather it was an inability to accurately process this information. Apple had several feedback mechanisms for identifying employee and customer concerns: for example, customer surveys and an electronic mail system that allowed employees to address top management directly. While Apple executives undoubtedly knew what was going on in the industry, they appeared unwilling and/ or unable to lead the company in a new direction. In 1988, an internal proposal for a low-cost Macintosh went unsupported and unfunded. It was not until 1990 when, forced by crisis, the 50 top executives met off-site to confront strategic issues and devastating results from an employee attitude survey. As one executive observed, "it's the first time we have really talked to each other [as a top management group] about these issues." These discussions of previously undiscussible issues led to some adjustments in strategy and organization. By 1990, however, the competitive environment had become much more difficult, and strategic options more limited.

The problem of defensiveness

Apple's failure to accurately perceive an environmental threat is not unique. It is rare that the responses of customers or employees will not raise issues about the effectiveness of the organization or its management.

Unfortunately, many internal barriers to effectiveness are not discussible. Fear of retribution, rejection, and/or concern about embarrassing others, causes those who have relevant comments to withhold them or water them down. For these reasons, lower-level managers become quite skilled at filtering threatening information. Not wanting to receive potentially painful responses, those at the top often collude with reluctant managers at lower levels to prevent an honest exchange. These defensive routines prevent organizations from changing and learning (Argyris, 1985).

Defensiveness increases when, as in Apple's case, tight alignment between business strategies, human capabilities, and design elements have allowed a firm to achieve extraordinary success in the past. These successes cause executives to develop shared assumptions about how the company ought to be organized and managed. These, in turn, create and sustain similar beliefs among lower-level managers. A strong culture emerges, and with it arrogance. When events or initiatives that challenge the validity of basic assumptions occur, they are resisted (Schein, 1985; Kotter, 1990). Because those who question assumptions are branded as disloyal, and are not promoted, the culture acts as a "drag" on efforts to change the company (Blake & Mouton, 1969).

The role of leaders in enabling and constraining adaptation

Adapting an organization's design and management practices to changes in the environment is not possible if the values of the business unit's top team are not consistent with the policies and practices demanded by the marketplace. Moreover, if adaptation requires top managers to act in ways that are inconsistent with their values, they are likely to resist that change unless they are willing and able to work through a personal change process.

Behavior at the top is important in another way as well. Unless all members of the top team accept the new strategic and organizational vision, they will be unable to lead an organization that demands high levels of coordination and commitment. Lower-level teams working across functions or business units cannot be effective unless there is agreement at the top about goals and priorities (Hackman, 1987; Nadler & Ancona, 1992; Beer et al., 1990; Beer, Eisenstat, & Biggadike, 1992; Spector & Beer, in press). Various quasi matrix structures such as cross-functional quality or product development teams, key account teams that cut across business units, and worldwide business teams demand that executives at the top not make business decisions in specific product market domains, but play a different role (i.e., attending to the external environment, choosing priorities, setting a context for teamwork, and allocating resources consistent with priorities) (Miles & Snow, 1978; Davis & Lawrence, 1977; Hackman & Oldham, 1980). Top teams in which a shared strategic vision and common assumptions about management do not exist cannot expect lower levels to work as a team. Often the struggle for power and succession within the top team prevent the development of shared vision and values (Nadler & Ancona, 1992).

Strategic adaptation and realignment at Apple Computer were blocked by a lack of consensus at the top about changes in strategy and management practice demanded by the competitive environment. A number of key executives who adhered to founder Steve Jobs's vision of Apple remained at the top long after he left the company. In 1988, Scully appointed one of these executives, Louis Gasse, to the number two position in the company. This delayed the process of knitting together a consensus at the top about a new strategic direction and the changes in organization it would demand. The 1990 offsite key executive meeting, at which strategic and management issues finally were discussed openly, did not take place until Louis Gasse was replaced by Mike Spindler, an executive who saw the need for a change in strategy and organization. Scully's delay in forging a new consensus at the top through education and/or replacement of key executives caused Apple to lose several crucial years in realigning itself.

We have described the key components in the organizational model shown in figure 7.1, and underlying principles for developing a strategically aligned and adaptive organization. The model provides a useful road map for those who are responsible for diagnosing and redesigning organizations. It is not enough, however. The turbulent environment of the 1980s has demonstrated that knowledge about how to align with new competitive realities has not found its way into practice in most companies. Like Apple Computer, many companies stumbled over the difficult problems of managing large-scale strategic and organizational change. Here, motivational and emotional issues, not rational analyses, are paramount.

MANAGING CHANGE: A COMMITMENT PERSPECTIVE

Realigning a business organization with new competitive realities involves redefining the strategy, envisioning new organizational arrangements that will align with the strategy, and a change process that moves the organization from initial awareness of the need for change through implementation of new organizational arrangements (Beckhard & Harris, 1977; Beer, 1980; Nadler, 1987).

As the case of Apple Computer amply illustrates, organizational change processes are often too slow to start, far from smooth when underway, and subject to loss of thrust and ultimate stagnation and regression, even when a newly appointed leader intends to lead a transformation. These difficulties arise

because change involves conflict between opposing forces. Change will occur when the motivation to change exceeds resistance fueled by anticipated psychological and/or economic losses. The following change formula expresses the relationship between forces that produce motivation to change and resistance forces (Beckhard & Harris, 1977; Beer, 1980; Beer, 1991):

$$Ch = (D \times M \times P) - C$$

Where:

Ch = Amount of change.
D = Dissatisfaction with the status quo.
M = Model or vision of future organizational arrangements.
P = A process for moving from the present into the future.
C = Personal cost of change to individuals and groups.

The idea that change requires motivating forces to exceed resistance forces makes an assumption about strategic realignment, one with which we think most executives agree. It is that strategic realignment ought to be carried out in a way that promotes *internal commitment* to the change (Argyris, 1970). It is possible, of course, for top executives to redefine strategy and organization at the top, and manage change by demanding compliance. Because hyper competition will demand higher levels of coordination, commitment, and competence than in the past, we assume that compliance-based strategies will not work. Such strategies cannot develop the commitment most organizations will require.

Volumes have been written about each necessary ingredient in managing change. We intend to review only the principal ideas.

Dissatisfaction with the status quo

Change requires an infusion of energy to overcome the strong beliefs and behavior established in the organization by its past successes, what we called "culture drag." Energy is mobilized by raising dissatisfaction with the status quo among key executives and opinion leaders with their performance and that of the company. When employees and groups believe that firm survival is at risk, and that they are part of the problem, energy for change is released.

A crisis in performance, such as automobile companies experienced in the early 1980s, can unleash significant amounts of energy, causing revolutionary change (Tushman & Romanelli, 1985). Unfortunately, revolutionary change is costly in economic and human terms. To avoid it, firms must anticipate the need for realignment. Proactive strategic change requires that leaders create dissatisfaction with the status quo in advance of crisis. They can do this by exposing lower levels in the organization to data from the external environment, customers, and shareholders that demonstrates the firm's vulnerability and/or declining performance. By soliciting information from lower levels about internal barriers to strategy implementation, leaders can promote their own dissatisfaction and that of their top team (Nadler, 1977). Since top management's own resistance to change is often the problem, as we saw in the case of Apple Computer, this is an essential step.

The data collection and feedback process provides the organization with information about the satisfaction of its three chief stakeholders (i.e., customers, shareholders, and employees). Thus, commitment to change is developed by amplifying and extending the sensing mechanisms shown in figure 7.1. Apple Computer's 1990 off-site conference did exactly this.

Dissatisfaction with the status quo also can be developed when a leader articulates expectations for improved performance and behavior change, and/or promotes visits to organizations that exemplify desired management practice (Beer et al., 1990; Kotter, 1990).

By creating a new standard of performance and/or behavior, these interventions produce a perceived gap between what ideally should or could be and what exists.

Model/vision of the strategically realigned organization

We stressed above that coordination, commitment, and competence are shaped by multiple aspects of the organization. Therefore, it is not surprising that organization *change programs* that address only one organizational design lever or one level of the organization have been found to be flawed. Training programs, total quality management programs, pay system changes, structural changes, culture programs, and reengineering often fail to live up to their potential (Schaffer, 1988; Beer et al., 1990). For example, 70 percent of the companies undertaking total quality management report that the results do not meet their expectations (Spector & Beer, in press). Similarly, efforts to reengineer work processes are failing despite apparent short-term performance improvements in one part of the company or one part of a cross-functional work process (Hall, Rosenthal, & Wade, 1993).

These failures to effect change occur, in part, because management does not develop a systemic, multidimensional model of the future state. Effective change in coordination, commitment, and competence requires a re-definition of roles, responsibilities, and relationships within the top team, and between interdependent functions or units. These will not occur unless the top management team specifies changes it foresees in several of the policy areas shown in figure 7.1 (Beer et al., 1990). Such a vision makes fundamental and lasting change more likely, and programmatic change less likely. Of course, difficulties confronting undiscussible issues at the top typically prevent the development of a strategically aligned organizational vision. The requirement is an effective change process that will promote dissatisfaction, and develop the strategically aligned organizational model.

PROCESS OF CHANGE

Programmatic change also occurs because top management, typically at the urging of a corporate staff function or with its willing cooperation, decides to impose on the organization its view of what needs to change (Schaffer, 1988; Beer et al., 1990).

Effective organizational change requires the leaders of a business unit to involve several levels and parts of the organization in a *process of inquiry and action focused on the key problem or strategic imperative of the business* (Beckhard & Harris, 1977; Beer, 1980; Schaffer, 1988; Beer et al., 1990; Eisenstat & Beer, 1994). Using the key strategic task or problem as the "driver" for change produces sustained motivation. Employees know that implementing business strategy is crucial for success, and they believe that programs unconnected to immediate competitive problems are much less relevant. At the same time, participation by lower levels provides leaders with valid data about problems, and with ideas about how to solve problems from those who know the most about how the organization works or doesn't work.

Participation also educates employees about the need for change and makes them aware of the personal transformation organization change will demand. Involving people in change has another advantage. It provides higher-level management with the opportunity to observe employee response to change, and then to make judgments about who is willing and able to learn new ways. Needed replacements of managers and workers can then be made more accurately and fairly, ensuring that potential resistors are unable to derail the change process. Finally, participation in change allows employees to learn how to challenge the status quo and create new ways of doing things. It leaves the

organization with a greater capacity to learn, and thus to sustain an organizational change beyond the initial change episode.

Such an involving change process requires leadership skills that go beyond traditional management skills of planning, organizing, and controlling (Kotter, 1988, 1990). Setting tough performance standards, developing trust, managing a process of involving others, envisioning the future, and confronting conflict become key leadership skills managers must possess and/or develop. Because Apple Computer did not embark on such a process until 1990, when it held its off-site key executive meeting, six years after John Scully took over the company, the company was very slow to develop dissatisfaction with the status quo and a new strategic and organizational vision.

Cost of change

The level of dissatisfaction with status quo, a compelling and systemic vision of the future, and an effective change process must exceed the level of felt loss people experience as a result of strategic realignment. Anticipated or actual loss of job security, power, relationships with coworkers, sense of competence, rewards of status, position or pay, and personal identity accompany organizational change. Change threatens the self-concept of organizational members caught up in its wake (Beer, 1991; Wiesenfeld, undated). If commitment to change is desired, ways must be found to strengthen motivation to change or reduce these felt losses. Threat to identity and self-esteem is reduced by offering those affected by change emotional support, training in new required competencies, and involvement in the change process.

Even when the entire firm could gain more than it loses, the high costs of change for particularly powerful individuals and groups can block successful adaptation. These losses often lead to defensive behavior that prevents the organization from successfully responding to potentially threatening changes in the external environment. Overcoming these defenses is essential for change to occur. A critical part of effective change management processes, then, involves the development of mechanisms that allow for the open and rational discussion of previously undiscussible issues.

THE PRACTICE OF STRATEGIC CHANGE

We can summarize our analysis of the dynamics of change by articulating a set of conditions organizational interventions must meet if they are to increase an organization's capacity for alignment and adaptation. These interventions must:

1 Ensure there is adequate energy and commitment to change through such means as:
   (a) exposing lower levels to data from the external environment while upper levels are exposed to the perceptions of lower levels about barriers to effectiveness;
   (b) raising performance standards; and
   (c) articulating and energizing strategic and organizational vision.
2 Develop a model or vision of the strategically realigned organization that is both broad (deals with all parts of the organization) and systemic (deals with all of the design levers) (Beer, 1980; Hall et al., 1993).
3 Engage individuals from all relevant parts and levels of the organization in a process of inquiry and action focused on the key problem or strategic imperative of the business (Eisenstat & Beer, 1994).
4 Ensure the reduction of organizational defensiveness so that potentially threatening information can be accurately perceived and rationally evaluated.

Unless a change process is able to satisfy all of these conditions, it is likely to fail. This is why, as we noted above, programs brought in by consultants or academics with the latest solutions rarely work (Schaffer, 1988; Beer et al., 1990; Nohria & Berkley, 1994). The substantive ideas underlying programs may be excellent (satisfying condition 2 above). Unfortunately, these design solutions or prescriptions for change are typically crafted by staff groups, academics, or consultants engaged by top management without collaboration of those who must implement them. This makes it much more difficult to develop broad commitment to change (condition 1). It also makes it less likely that the program will be tailored to address the organization's most important strategic problem, particularly if the firm has a variety of business units (condition 3). Even in those cases where a problem is strategically relevant, the lack of engagement of those who develop solutions with those who implement them makes it unlikely that organizational resistance to the proposed change will be worked through (condition 4).

The breakdown in knowledge utilization created by the gap between "men and women of knowledge who lack power and men and women of power who lack knowledge" (Bennis, 1987) has been noted by many (Bennis, Benne, & Chin, 1961; Bennis, 1987; Argyris, 1993). It is a main reason why *the practice of strategic change in organizing and managing people lags significantly behind what is known from research and theory.*

This long-standing problem in knowledge utilization led to the emergence of organization development (OD), a field practice concerned with developing more effective organizations (Beckhard, 1969; Bennis, 1969; French & Bell, 1978; Beer, 1980). Organization development focuses on process, not design solutions. Ideally, OD consultants help managers discover and define organizational problems through the data collection and diagnosis process we described above. On the basis of the diagnosis, managers redesign the organization. The OD consultant does not prescribe a solution. She or he acts as a catalyst and resource, facilitating an open discussion, helping managers find common ground, and acting as a knowledgeable resource about organizational problems and their solutions (Schein, 1988). Organization development flourished in the 1960s and 1970s in many corporations (Rush, 1973). As this brief description suggests, the practice of organizational development has done a good job of helping to address organizational defensiveness (condition 4). The emphasis on data collection also helps to develop energy for change, at least by those directly involved in the process (condition 1).

In the 1980s, however, many OD departments disappeared. One of the main reasons was that OD practice often focused on internal problems perceived by lower levels, not on the business and strategic problems perceived at the top. Interpersonal relationships, employee motivation, supervisory style, group effectiveness, and intergroup conflict became the target of change, usually with the objective of increasing commitment and moving people and groups toward more open communication, participation, and good relationships. While these change objectives are consistent with what research is beginning to show are characteristics of adaptive organizations required in today's competitive environment, OD interventions often were disconnected from business goals and strategy (condition 3). Changes might be made in dynamics of interpersonal or intergroup relationships, but the larger organizational barriers that were impeding effective strategic adaptation and realignment were apt to be untouched (condition 2). It is therefore not surprising that OD has often been perceived as concerned with people and relationships, not the business.

Some OD practice in the 1970s began to focus on the redesign of work. Based on growing understanding of how job design affects motivation, many companies undertook job enrichment programs intended to broaden jobs and give workers more auto-

nomy and responsibility (Herzberg, Mausner, & Snyderman, 1959; Hackman & Oldham, 1980). Often this involved forming work teams with considerable responsibility and authority to act. While some of these efforts succeeded, more frequently they failed (Hackman, 1975). Management practices at higher levels remained unchanged and eventually eroded intended increases in autonomy and responsibility. Again, because the organizational change process did not deal with the whole organizational system (condition 2), it was doomed to fail.

Some companies undertook to improve their human resource management practices by administering employee surveys regularly. In the best examples of this practice, the results were summarized for each subunit and fed back to the managers in charge. Then, they were required to discuss the survey data with their people, and plan change. At IBM, managers were expected to participate in this once every other year. Managers of organizational units that showed the lowest employee attitudes had to report to the CEO reasons for morale problems, and their plans for change. This practice, however, did not help IBM confront its competitive problems, formulate a new strategy, or realign the organization with new competitive realities.

The reason for the failure of survey feedback at IBM and other companies is that employee surveys typically deal with supervision and morale, not barriers to strategy implementation (condition 3). At IBM, as in other companies, such surveys are motivated by the desire to maintain a satisfied work force, not to reexamine strategy and align the organization with it. A second-order reason for the failure of surveys to stimulate realignment has to do with the feedback process. The causes of strategic alignment problems are complex, multidimensional, circular, and cultural (Schein, 1987) (condition 2). Therefore, their diagnosis is not subject to predetermined closed-end questions and scaling.

Moreover the presentation of questionnaire data often elicits an argument about the meaning of the questions and numbers, not the underlying meaning of the data. Yet we know that meaningful discussion of the data is key to understanding, commitment, and change (Klein, Kraut & Wolfson, 1971).

There are examples of individual organization development initiatives in companies that meet the four essential conditions we identified above for increasing organizational alignment and adaptability. For example, at Corning Glass Works, OD consultants helped a business unit to collect data about all aspects of the organization's alignment with strategy. Systemic redesign, to develop new products more rapidly and effectively, followed. Structure, systems staffing, and leadership style were realigned with strategy, (Beer, 1976). At Honeywell, a division experiencing competitive problems followed a similar process (Steckler & Beer, 1991).

More recently, attempts have been made to more systematically define the characteristics of interventions that facilitate ongoing organizational alignment and adaptation. Weisbord has written about "Search Conference" as well as other social technologies growing out of the sociotechnical systems movement that meet the conditions above. They develop the energy for alignment and adaptation by bringing together all relevant organizational groups around a critical organizational task in a way that encourages open communication (Weisbord, 1991).

Seeing a need for greater organizational effectiveness as the competitive environment heated up in the 1980s, a few corporations have even undertaken to institutionalize processes for strategic realignment and change. General Electric has developed the "Workout" process (Tichy & Sherman, 1993; Ashkenas & Jick, 1992). Business unit managers are expected to engage in a bottom-up change process. In large forums resembling town meetings, key members of the organization from several levels come together to surface barriers to effectiveness and engage in collective problem solving around a key business issue, or cross-functional work process. Before the meeting adjourns, the head of the business unit is expected to publicly announce whether she or he is willing to accept, reject, or defer for further study each of the recommendations developed in the Workout sessions.

The authors, in collaboration with Becton Dickinson Company, have designed a standardized process, *strategic human resource management profiling* (SHRM profiling), for diagnosing an organization's alignment with strategy, and planning change accordingly (Beer et al., 1992; Williamson & Beer, 1991). The process was designed explicitly to meet the four conditions for effective change processes listed above. It uses the systemic perspective of organizations discussed above, and a variant of the diagnostic model in figure 7.1. It is designed to produce dissatisfaction with the status quo, and a model of the future state. The authors designed the process to produce commitment to change by requiring that profilers (consultants), management, and employees work collaboratively in analyzing strategic alignment and planning change, thus overcoming the problems of knowledge utilization discussed above. By keying off strategy, the process was intended to overcome the problems with most OD practice – lack of relevance to the organization's most important business problem. By specifying a standardized process for all general managers to follow, the authors hoped to ensure a uniform high-quality change management practice that could be researched and improved. Just as important, uniformity was intended to make it easier for top management to discuss results with business unit general managers, holding them accountable for their organization's alignment and effectiveness.

While these recent developments in

organizational alignment and change methods seem quite promising, there is a need for more research on these interventions' long-term impact on organizational alignment and adaptability. In the rest of the chapter, we present a five-year progress report on the impact of SHRM profiling at Becton Dickinson.

STRATEGIC HUMAN RESOURCE MANAGEMENT AT BECTON DICKINSON

In 1988, Becton Dickinson Company, at the time a $1.5 billion dollar global, medical supply company, undertook to design a formal process by which each general manager in the company would examine the alignment of his or her organization with strategy, and plan change to realign the organization.

Strategic human resource management was undertaken by Becton Dickinson at a time of considerable strategic change. To enable the company to drive its products into global markets, it introduced a transnational organization (Bartlett & Ghoshal, 1989). Implementing this quasi worldwide matrix organization proved to be far more difficult then anticipated, however (Biggadike, 1990). At the same time, Becton Dickinson's CEO envisioned transforming the company from a medical supply company into a medical technology company. Coordination between corporate R&D and various business units and between divisional R&D and marketing, production, and selling was not effective, however, resulting in slow or a failed product development process. Finally, increasing competition in the health care industry required the company to bundle products from several divisions for key customers. They established the new supply chain staff organization, but it was running into problems coordinating with various business units. In total, the new strategies required higher levels of coordination and commitment beyond one's narrow function or unit, and different managerial competencies than previously needed.

SHRM profiling

Strategic human resource management (SHRM) profiling was envisioned to complement *strategic profiling*, a process for evaluating a business unit strategy introduced to the company in 1975 by Ray Gilmartin, an Arthur D. Little consultant at the time. After Gilmartin joined the company, strategic profiling became established practice for developing strategy. Unlike other strategic planning processes, it focuses on process not content. A "profiler" from the strategic planning department brings together the general manager of the business unit and his or her key staff, to analyze the unit's competitive environment and develop strategy. The profiler facilitates the process by posing key questions and inducing a debate within the top team. When the top team of the business unit finishes crafting their strategy, the general manager reports the result to the sector president and CEO.

Like strategic profiling, SHRM profiling is a process. A profiler from human resource or strategic planning facilitates an analysis by the top team of the extent to which the organization, human resources policies, and management practice facilitate or block implementation of the unit's key strategy. That analysis is based on interviews with employees conducted by an employee task force (ETF). A selected sample of employees in all parts of the organization are interviewed by the ETF. They are asked to identify organizational strengths, and barriers to implementing strategy. The top team is interviewed by the profiler about their effectiveness as a team, and perceptions at the top of organizational strengths and barriers. A three-day meeting follows in which are developed feedback, diagnosis, and a vision of the necessary new organizational arrangements, and a change plan. General managers must report findings and plans for change to the sector president and CEO, thus making it possible for senior management to hold general managers accountable for realignment.

SHRM profiling involves the following steps:

1 *Orientation and Planning* One-day meeting with the top team of the business unit. The team:
   (a) restates the key strategic tasks; and
   (b) appoints employee task force (ETF) to collect data about barriers to effectiveness.

2 *Data collection* The profiler trains members of the ETF to conduct interviews in all functions and several levels below the top as well in other interdependent units. Interviewees are asked to describe strengths and barriers in implementing strategic tasks defined earlier. The profiler conducts interviews with top team members about their perceptions of organizational barriers and of the top team's effectiveness.

3 *Three-day meeting to process data and plan change*:
   (a) Day 1 Feedback by ETF and profiler of their findings, and discussion of them under ground rules for open and non-defensive communication.
   (b) Day 2 Analysis of the data using the model in figure 7.1.
   (c) Day 3 Development of a vision of the organization's future state, and plans for communication and change.

4 *Top team reviews change plans with ETF*

5 *General manager reports to top management*:
   (a) ETF findings about strengths and weaknesses;
   (b) diagnosis of underlying causes;
   (c) organizational vision; and
   (d) change plan.

6 *SHRM profiling is repeated periodically.*

Assessment of SHRM profiling

Since 1988, some 14 business units and staff groups have undergone SHRM profiling, some more than once. The CEO and the top management team as well as one sector president and his division managers also have applied the process at their level. Experience with SHRM profiling has validated some of the assumptions underlying the design of the process. Also, it has identified a number of challenges organizations must meet if they are to institutionalize a process of continuous realignment aimed at making them adaptable (Beer et al., 1992; Beer, undated).

As intended, SHRM surfaced previously hidden and undiscussable problems that must be dealt with by management if the business unit is to implement strategy more effectively. Several process design elements appear to have been most critical in allowing these barriers to surface:

- The use of an employee task force composed of the organization's best people to collect data about barriers involves employees, provides valid data, and motivates the top management team to listen.
- The use of the "fishbowl" method for providing feedback enables the communication of rich information about what is effective and ineffective.
- The articulation and enforcement of ground rules for non-defensive discussion. These ground-rules reflect standard OD practice: for example, asking participants to describe others' behaviors and their consequences for the business rather than make personal attributions (Anderson, 1971; Beer, 1980).
- The focus of the meetings on strategic issues provides common ground for a searching reexamination that might otherwise be divisive and political.

In virtually all the profiles, employees perceived the following six typically undiscussable issues as barriers to strategy implementation:

1 Ineffective top team.
2 Unclear strategy and priorities.
3 Top-down management.
4 Poor vertical communication (up and down).

5 Poor interfunctional or interunit coordination.

6 Inadequate management skill and development.

We have come to regard these managerial problems as generic barriers to implementing a strategy. They are quite consistent with our organizational analysis of Apple in the 1980s. Had Apple's management been able to confront these issues, they may have been more able to realign the organization with new competitive realities. We are quite confident that these are the undiscussables that block effective strategy implementation in many companies when high levels of coordination, commitment to teamwork, and managerial competence are required.

The SHRM profiling process has helped business units at Becton Dickinson engage in a change process needed to overcome these barriers. Many have overhauled the management process at the top, and made changes in structure, systems, style, and staffing in support. The following types of organizational changes have been made:

1 Improvements in coordination:
   (a) cross-functional product teams;
   (b) improvements in product development process documentation; and
   (c) better line-staff coordination.
2 Improvements in the effectiveness of key functions (structure, staff, and style).
3 Changes in leaders' roles and behaviors:
   (a) changes in general manager's behavior;
   (b) improvements in business unit's top team process;
   (c) resource allocation process;
   (d) decision-making process and structure; and
   (e) functional managers more general management-oriented.
4 Improved vertical communication.
5 Replacement or transfer of key staff.

Given these changes, it is quite clear that where SHRM was applied, it has stimulated adaptation and strategic realignment in many of the units. While there has been variation in the amount of sustained change occurring in various business units, usually related to the general manager's leadership skills, the following quote from a general manager of one division suggests that the process was enacted in a way that is quite consistent with the four change conditions above:

SHRM allowed us to discuss that which could not be discussed before. It allowed us to discuss the undiscussable. It got things on the table that would have taken me, in a serial sense, years [to surface].

Getting feedback from employees as a mechanism is indispensable. Putting it in a strategic context is important. We were there to discuss behaviors that are consequential. The focus on strategy puts it in context. It wasn't personal. We keep coming back to the strategy. We have discovered things that are going to help us succeed or [that were] preventing us from succeeding as an organization. They are strategic issues. Delivering the goods and services to our customers better than our competitors. Once you decided that it was strategic you had to fix it or suffer the consequences of gradual loss of competitive position.

Our research leaves little doubt that SHRM profiling is a powerful process for surfacing critical barriers, and setting an agenda for strategic change. Tying the process to strategy motivates managers to confront issues and make changes. Most general managers considered it their management responsibility to address issues, even if they were personally painful. Raised expectations for change by lower-level employees, created by the public nature of the SHRM process, put general managers under pressure to respond. That pressure came from fear of a negative response to inaction, but also from a heightened awareness of how an ineffective organization might hinder strategy implementation. General managers experienced SHRM as an organizational performance appraisal that reflected on their effectiveness as managers.

Our experience with SHRM also suggests that the development of strategic alignment does not happen in a simple or a linear manner. Rather, changes appear to occur as part of an iterative learning process powered by shared experiences of failure and success. All of the units we followed over time made plans to make changes that we later learned they did not truly understand. It was not until they experienced difficulties, and had to confront the causes, that they began to fully understand the words they had spoken and put to paper in their original plans for change. In the case of SHRM, this learning crystallized in follow-up SHRM profiles, scheduled for most units at approximately two-year intervals.

Additional findings come from observing differences in levels of effectiveness between divisions, operating in two different sectors, across time. Since the SHRM profiling process was standardized, differences in response to SHRM profiling itself, as well as differences in organizational and personal change, suggest key conditions that govern success in developing strategic alignment and the capacity to adapt:

1 The skills of the leader in promoting trust, an open dialogue, and empowerment while providing unmistakable signals about the kind of business and organization she or he values certainly makes change much smoother and easier.
2 New leaders can use SHRM more easily than existing leaders, particularly if they can develop trust quickly. New general managers who led SHRM used it to begin a process of change they realized was necessary. Jack Gabarro (1987) has shown that in the first three months, managers assess their business and their key managers before taking action. Strategic human resource management provided the vehicle to do this for new general managers.

The experience of Becton Dickinson with SHRM also illuminates some of the barriers to institutionalizing processes to increase alignment and adaptation. While top managers at the corporate and divisional levels see SHRM as having contributed positively to strategic alignment, lower levels are more ambivalent, despite great energy and enthusiasm for the process just before, during, and immediately after the SHRM profiling meeting. Why?

Most general managers failed to involve employees in redesigning the organization and managing change beyond the initial data collection phase. Therefore, employees did not connect many organizational changes that occurred (see list above) with SHRM, and believe there has been little payoff for the risk they took and effort they expended. We discovered that most managers did not see the need for the continued broad employee involvement that we assumed was crucial for sustaining the energy for and commitment to change. We believe that without such commitment, employees will be reluctant to engage in SHRM in the future.

The structure of the SHRM process also seems to contribute to its episodic nature. Managers and employees seem to associate SHRM with the specifics of "the three-day meeting," where the employee task force presents back its data, and the top team works to develop a new organizational vision, not with the underlying principles of organizational change that this meeting embodies. As interventionists, most of our efforts tended to focus on making that meeting effective. We have been less involved in the ongoing day-to-day follow-up activities, where one must internalize information about a different way to achieve organizational alignment and adaptation. This is partially because of the low ratio of profilers to units being profiled, but also because virtually all general management teams have felt that implementation of SHRM results is their responsibility. As a manager in one division told us, "We like you guys to come in here with a big hammer and shake things up, but then it is our responsibility to put the pieces back together again." While we have not been involved in the "Workout" process or in Weissbord's "Search Conferences," these interventions also seem to be built around dramatic off-site events. While these events may be useful in "shaking things up," our concern is that failure to follow up adequately will unnecessarily retard the rate of progress.

Another reason for the episodic nature of SHRM may be that top management has not actively reviewed the outcome of each SHRM profile, and held managers accountable for organizational change. To do so requires that top management be willing and able to discuss the management behavior of their subordinates, something that we have found managers prefer to avoid.

Thus, SHRM has been effective as a process for raising dissatisfaction, and making organizational and management changes. We fear, however, that unless companies incorporate processes such as SHRM into the ongoing daily fabric of business (i.e., to be seen, monitored, and used by large numbers of employees) they are in danger of failing as mechanisms for ongoing realignment. The result will be an unadaptive organization.

CONCLUSIONS

The demands created by intense competition and environmental turbulence have changed the central human resource management problem for corporations. In the post World War II era, management was concerned with employee satisfaction and the reduction of conflict and disruption from unions or disgruntled employees. By offering security, firms obtained loyalty. By offering money, firms maintained satisfaction with hygiene factors,

despite considerable alienation and demotivation produced by narrow work, under involvement, and over management (Walker & Guest, 1952; Herzberg et al., 1959).

Rapid and dramatic changes in the external environment require a cross-functional perspective, and greater commitment and teamwork from employees at all levels than were required in the past. These new requirements invite far-reaching change in the internal environment of corporations. To create better value for customers and shareholders, corporations are struggling to become more effective. *The central human resources problem is becoming improving organizational alignment and adaptability.*

We believe that this forces organizations to develop an evergreen change process of data collection about undiscussable issues, an analytic framework for organizational diagnosis, a vision of the strategically realigned organization toward which they want to move, and a plan for action.

In this chapter, we have shown that the knowledge for managing such processes exists. Practice, however, is far behind, due to the inherently threatening nature of examining hidden dimensions of organization and management that may be responsible for ineffective strategy implementation. Strategic realignment requires leaders to listen to data from lower levels that challenges their approach to managing, and it requires a willingness to make adjustments to the organization and their leadership of it. If management practice is not aligned with strategy or employee expectations, feedback threatens a manager's perceptions of reality. Unless the organization can develop and sustain a dialogue about problems of alignment, it cannot become adaptive; a characteristic needed for long-term survival of the institution.

Not many executives are willing to do this unless it is demanded by crisis or by their superior, the CEO, or the board of directors. Consequently, we believe that what is necessary to sustain these processes are senior corporate managers who are both skilled and committed to rigorously reviewing inherently softer and elusive organizational and management issues. This requires treating organizational change objectives and results like financial objectives and results, holding general managers accountable for realignment of their organization and their own behavior, coaching those who need help in managing more effectively, and replacing general managers if they cannot improve their effectiveness as change leaders. Top management must recognize that developing organization's capacity to realign ensures its capacity to adapt to continual change in the competitive environment. That capability may represent the most sustainable competitive advantage.

REFERENCES

Anderson, J. (1971). *Giving and Receiving Feedback*, Note No. 9–471–067. Boston: Harvard Business School.

Ashkenas, R. N., & Jick, T. (1992). From dialogue to action in GE work out: Developmental learning in a change process. In R. Woodman & W. Pasmore (eds.), *Research in Organizational Change and Development*, vol. 6, 267–87. Greenwich, CT: JAI Press.

Argyris, C. (1970). *Intervention Theory and Method*. Reading, MA: Addison-Wesley.

Argyris, C. (1985). *Strategy, Change and Defensive Routines*. Marshfield, MA: Pitman.

Argyris, C. (1993). *Knowledge for Action: A guide to overcoming barriers to organizational change*. San Francisco: Jossey-Bass.

Bartlett, C. A., & Ghoshal, S. (1989). *Managing Across Borders: The transnational solution*. Boston: Harvard Business School.

Bartlett, C. A., & Ghoshal, S. (1990). Matrix management: Not a structure, a frame of mind. *Harvard Business Review*, July–Aug., 138–45.

Beckhard, R. (1969). *Organization Development: Strategies and models*. Reading, MA: Addison-Wesley.

Beckhard, R., & Harris, R. (1977). *Organizational Transitions: Managing complex change*. Reading, MA: Addison-Wesley.

Beer, M. (1976). *Corning Glass Works: The electronic products division (A) (B) & (C)*, Case Numbers 9–477–024, –073 & –074. Boston: Harvard Business School.

Beer, M. (1980). *Organization Change and Development: A systems view*. Santa Monica, CA: Goodyear.

Beer, M. (1991). *Leading Change*, Teaching Note No. 9–488–037. Boston, MA: Harvard Business School.

Beer, M. (undated). *Becton Dickinson: Strategic human resource profiling evaluation*. Unpublished manuscript.

Beer, M., Eisenstat, R. A., & Biggadike, E. R. (1992). *Developing an Organization Capable of Implementing and Reformulating Strategy: A preliminary test*. Working paper, Division of Research, Harvard Business School, Boston, MA.

Beer, M., Eisenstat, R. A., & Spector, B. (1990). *The Critical Path to Corporate Renewal*. Boston: Harvard Business School.

Beer, M., Spector, B., Lawrence, P. R., Mills, D. Q., & Walton, R. E. (1984). *Managing Human Assets*. New York: Free Press.

Bennis, W. (1969). *Organization Development: Its nature, origins and prospects*. Reading, MA: Addison-Wesley.

Bennis, W. (1987). Using knowledge of organizational behavior: The impossible task. In J. W. Lorsch (ed.), *Handbook of Organizational Behavior*, 29. Englewood Cliffs, NJ: Prentice Hall.

Bennis, W., Benne, K. D., & Chin, R. (1961). *The Planning of Change*. New York: Holt, Rinehart & Winston.

Biggadike, E. R. (1990). Research on managing the multinational company: A practitioner's experiences. In C. A. Bartlett, Y. Doz, & G. Hedlund (eds.), *Managing the Global Firm*, 303–25. London: Routledge.

Blake, R. R., & Mouton, J. S. (1969). *Building a Dynamic Corporation through Grid Organization Development*. Reading, MA: Addison-Wesley.

Burns, T., & Stalker, G. M. (1961). *The Management of Innovation*. London: Tavistock.

Chandler, A. (1962). *Strategy and Structure*. Cambridge, MA: MIT.

Davis, S., & Lawrence, P. R. (1977). *Matrix*. Reading, MA: Addison-Wesley.

Denison, D. (1992). *Corporate Culture and Organizational Effectiveness*. New York: Wiley.

Deming, W. E. (1982). *Out of the Crisis*. Cambridge, MA: MIT.

Eisenstat, R. A., & Beer, M. (1994). Strategic change: Realigning the organization with strategy. In L. Fahey & R. Randall (eds.), *The Portable MBA*. New York: Wiley.

French, W. L., & Bell. C. H. (1978). *Organization Development: Behavioral science interventions for organizational improvement*. Englewood Cliffs, NJ: Prentice Hall.

Friedlander, F. (1971). Congruence in organization development. *Proceedings of the Academy of Management*, 153–60. Atlanta, GA.

Gabarro, J. (1987). *The dynamics of taking charge*. Boston: Harvard Business School.

Galbraith, J. (1982). The stages of growth. *Journal of Business Strategy*, summer, 70–9.

Galbraith, J. (1987). Organization design. In J. W. Lorsch (ed.), *Handbook of Organizational Behavior*, 343–57. Englewood Cliffs, NJ: Prentice Hall.

Gibbs, M., & Beer, M. (1990). *Apple Computer: Industry, strategy and organization*, Case No. 9–491–040. Harvard Business School, Boston, MA.

Hackman, J. R. (1975). On the coming demise of job enrichment. In E. L. Cass & F. G. Simmer (eds.), *Man, Work and Society*, 97–115. New York: Van Nostrand-Reinhold.

Hackman, J. R. (1987). The design of work teams. In J. W. Lorsch (ed.), *Handbook of Organizational Behavior*, 315–43. Englewood Cliffs, NJ: Prentice Hall.

Hackman, J. R., & Oldham, G. R. (1980). *Work Redesign*. Reading, MA: Addison-Wesley.

Hall, G., Rosenthal, J., & Wade, J. (1993). How to make reengineering really work. *Harvard Business Review,* Nov.–Dec., 119–31.

Hamel, G., & Prahalad, C. K. (1989). Strategic intent. *Harvard Business Review,* May–June, 63–76.

Herzberg, F. L., Mausner, B., & Snyderman, B. (1959). *The Motivation to Work.* New York: Wiley.

Heskett, J. L., Sasser, W. E., Jr., & Hart, C. W. L. (1990). *Service Breakthroughs: Changing the rules of the game.* New York: Free Press.

Jensen, M. C. (1993). The modern industrial revolution, exit, and the failure of internal control systems. *Journal of Finance,* 48, 831–82.

Katz, D., & Kahn, R. L. (1978). *The Social Psychology of Organizations,* 2nd ed. New York: Wiley.

Kotter, J. P. (1978). *Organizational Dynamics: Diagnosis and intervention.* Reading, MA: Addison-Wesley.

Kotter, J. P. (1988). *The Leadership Factor.* New York: Free Press.

Kotter, J. P. (1990). *A Force for Change: How leadership differs from management.* New York: Free Press.

Kotter, J. P., & Heskett, J. L. (1992). *Corporate Culture and Performance.* New York: Free Press.

Klein, S. M., Kraut, A. I., & Wolfson, A. (1971). Employee reactions to attitude survey feedback: A study of the impact of structure and process. *Administrative Science Quarterly.* 16 (4), 497–514.

Lawler, E. E. (1986). *High Involvement Management: Participative strategies for improving organizational performance.* San Francisco: Jossey-Bass.

Lawrence, P. R., & Lorsch, J. W. (1967). *Organization and Environment.* Division of Research, Graduate School of Business Administration, Harvard University, Boston, MA.

Lippitt, R., Watson, S., & Westerley, B. (1958). *The Dynamics of Planned Change.* New York: Harcourt, Brace & World.

Lorsch, J. W., & Morse, (1974). *Organizations and their Members: A contingency approach.* New York: Harper Row.

Miles, R. E., & Snow, C. C. (1978). *Organization Strategy, Structure, and Process.* New York: McGraw-Hill.

Nadler, D. A. (1977). *Feedback and Organizational Development: Using data based methods.* Reading, MA: Addison-Wesley.

Nadler, D. A. (1987). The effective management of organization change. In J. W. Lorsch (ed.), *Handbook of Organizational Behavior,* 358–69. Englewood Cliffs, NJ: Prentice Hall.

Nadler, D. A., & Ancona, D. (1992). Teamwork at the top: Creating executive teams that work. In D. A. Nadler, M. S. Gerstein, & R. B. Shaw (eds.), *Organizational Architecture: Designs for changing organizations,* 209–31. San Francisco: Jossey-Bass.

Nadler, D. A., & Tushman, M. (1980). A model for diagnosing organizational behavior. *Organizational Dynamics,* 9 (2), 35–51.

Nadler, D. A., & Tushman, M. (1992). Designing organizations that have a good fit: A framework for understanding new architectures. In D. A. Nadler, M. S. Gerstein, & R. B. Shaw (eds.), *Organizational Architecture: Designs for changing organizations,* 39–56. San Francisco, CA: Jossey-Bass.

Nohria, N., & Berkley, J. D. (1994). Whatever happened to the take charge manager? *Harvard Business Review,* Jan.–Feb., 128–37.

Porter, M. E. (1985). *Competitive Advantage: Creating and sustaining superior performance.* New York: Free Press.

Rush, H. M. F. (1973). *Organization Development.* New York: The Conference Board.

Schaffer, R. (1988). *The Breakthrough Strategy.* Cambridge, MA: Ballinger.

Schein, E. H. (1965). *Organizational Psychology.* Englewood Cliffs, NJ: Prentice Hall.

Schein, E. H. (1985). *Organizational Culture and Leadership.* San Francisco: Jossey-Bass.

Schein, E. H. (1987). *The Clinical Perspective in Fieldwork.* Newbury Park, CA: Sage.

Schein, E. H. (1988). *Process Consultation: Its role in organization development,* vol. 1. Reading, MA: Addison-Wesley.

Schneider, B. (1993). The service organization: Human resource management is crucial. *Organizational Dynamics,* 21 (4), 39–52.

Spector, B., & Beer, M. (in press). Beyond TQM programs. *Journal of Change Management.*

Steckler, N., & Beer, M. (1991). *Honeywell Commercial Aviation Division (A) (B) (C),* Case Numbers 9–487–065, –066, –067. Graduate School of Business, Harvard University, Boston, MA.

Tichy, N. M. (1983). *Managing Strategic Change.* New York: Wiley.

Tichy, N. M., & Sherman, S. (1993). *Control Your Own Destiny or Someone Else Will: How Jack Welch is making G.E. the most competitive corporation.* New York: Doubleday.

Thompson, J. D. (1967). *Organizations in Action.* New York: McGraw-Hill.

Tushman, M., & Romanelli, E. (1985). Organizational evolution: A metamorphosis model of convergence and reorientation. In L. L. Cummings & B. M. Staw (eds.), *Research in Organizational Behavior,* vol. 7, pp. 171–222. Greenwich, CT: JAI Press.

Walker, C. R., & Guest, R. H. (1952). *The Man on the Assembly Line.* Boston: Harvard University Press.

Walton, R. E. (1985). From control to commitment in the workplace. *Harvard Business Review,* March–April, 76–84.

Waterman, R. H., Jr., Peters, T. J., & Phillips, J. R. (1980). Structure is not organization. *Business Horizons,* 23 (3), 14–25.

Weisbord, M. R. (1991). *Productive Workplaces: Organizing and managing for dignity, meanings, and community.* San Francisco, CA: Jossey-Bass.

Weisenfeld, B. M. (undated). A self affirmation model of reactions to change: The effects of layoffs, restructuring and outsourcing. Condensed dissertation proposal, Columbia University School of Business, New York.

Williamson, A., & Beer, M. (1991). *Becton Dickinson: Strategic human resource profiling (D) (D1),* Case Numbers 9–491–155, –156. Graduate School of Business, Harvard University, Boston, MA.

Part II

Context of Human Resource Management

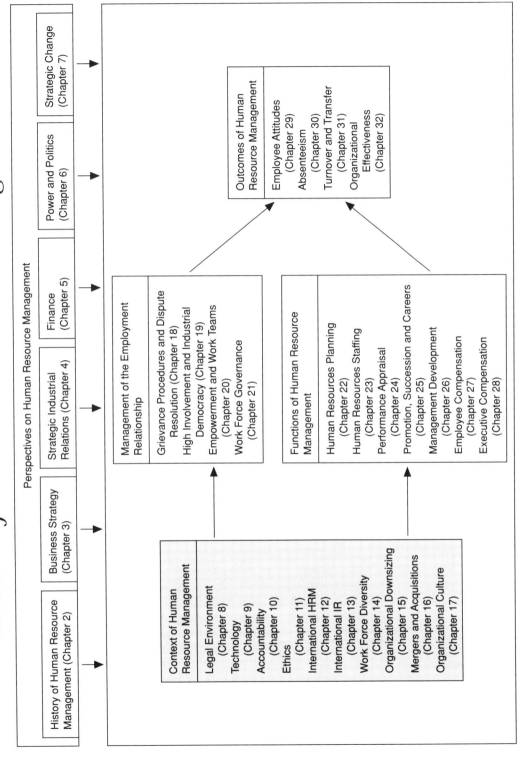

Perspectives on Human Resource Management

| History of Human Resource Management (Chapter 2) | Business Strategy (Chapter 3) | Strategic Industrial Relations (Chapter 4) | Finance (Chapter 5) | Power and Politics (Chapter 6) | Strategic Change (Chapter 7) |

Context of Human Resource Management

Legal Environment (Chapter 8)
Technology (Chapter 9)
Accountability (Chapter 10)
Ethics (Chapter 11)
International HRM (Chapter 12)
International IR (Chapter 13)
Work Force Diversity (Chapter 14)
Organizational Downsizing (Chapter 15)
Mergers and Acquisitions (Chapter 16)
Organizational Culture (Chapter 17)

Management of the Employment Relationship

Grievance Procedures and Dispute Resolution (Chapter 18)
High Involvement and Industrial Democracy (Chapter 19)
Empowerment and Work Teams (Chapter 20)
Work Force Governance (Chapter 21)

Functions of Human Resource Management

Human Resources Planning (Chapter 22)
Human Resources Staffing (Chapter 23)
Performance Appraisal (Chapter 24)
Promotion, Succession and Careers (Chapter 25)
Management Development (Chapter 26)
Employee Compensation (Chapter 27)
Executive Compensation (Chapter 28)

Outcomes of Human Resource Management

Employee Attitudes (Chapter 29)
Absenteeism (Chapter 30)
Turnover and Transfer (Chapter 31)
Organizational Effectiveness (Chapter 32)

Introduction: Context of Human Resource Management

The context of HRM is broad and multifaceted, and provides the backdrop against which we view HR functions and activities. Thus, this section examines a number of current issues that must be addressed by today's HR managers and scientists. They represent environmental aspects of the late twentieth century that have significant impacts on organizations and their employees. These influences include the economy, technology, laws, and ethics, as well as the increasing globalization of businesses. They also include demographic changes, and attempts to adapt organizational structures to deal with the new environment.

The legal context of HRM is discussed by LeRoy and Schultz. They suggest that HR legal considerations, which often are conflicting, confusing and costly, should be integrated into the general business strategy. Moreover they argue that burgeoning employment regulation, despite its good intentions, can result in a homogenization of employers and labor markets. Such mandated uniformity could seriously dilute the advantages provided by labor markets allowed to be competitive.

Snell, Pedigo, and Krawiec outline the growth of information technology in the HR field. Unfortunately, the bulk of technological innovation in HR has been directed toward routine administrative tasks, rather than using the new systems for strategic purposes. The experience of IBM is used to illustrate the successful linkage between information technology and strategic HRM.

Ferris, Mitchell, Canavan, Frink, and Hopper examine accountability in human resources systems. They note that HR accountability was shaped when the individual was key, while today it is often likely that results are produced by team efforts. This important change challenges HR scientists and practitioners to find new ways to insure that accountability remains a critical feature of HR systems.

Rosen and Juris address ethical issues faced by HR managers. The growing attention to business ethics in recent years has served to highlight the unique organizational role of the HR practitioner, who, unlike managers in other functions, has obligations to employees, shareholders, and the top management team.

The increase in international business activity has resulted in greater attention to the management of HR outside the United States. In examining international aspects of HR, Napier, Tibau, Janssens, and Pilenzo point out the pitfalls of rigidly setting policies at headquarters that are to be applied to all locations, notwithstanding significant differences in culture, custom, and laws. The international HR manager needs to have a broad perspective, with the ability and flexibility to juggle multiple constituencies, issues, and actions.

Reed, Beaumont, and Pugh review the research and practice of international industrial relations. Also, they identify global trends that will influence research and practice into the next century, and provide a case study of a Sony facility in the U.K. that illustrates the industrial relations issues in the evolving European markets.

Sessa, Jackson, and Rapini examine business responses to demographic and social changes in their chapter on workforce diversity. Managing a diverse work force, with increasing expectations of upward mobility, presents many pitfalls and opportunities. The authors use two cases, Miles Pharmaceuticals and Xerox, to illustrate the issues and the need for research on diversity intervention's impact.

Following the rapid growth of many firms in the 1980s, the 1990s has been characterized as the age of downsizing. During the latter period, many corporations have significantly reduced employment at all levels of their organizations. Whetten, Keiser, and Urban focus on the contribution of HRM to effective organizational downsizing, and also the effect of downsizing on the HRM function itself. The authors call for greater involvement of HR management as partners in the downsizing process, while recognizing the need for HR to act flexibly and adaptively in responding to its internal customers.

Mergers and acquisitions are important considerations for HR management, as Schweiger, Gosselin, and Lambertucci illustrate in their chapter titled "Preserving and Realizing Acquisition Value Through Human Resource Practices." They observe that most mergers and acquisitions leave the firm's value either lower or unchanged, then demonstrate how organizational and HR issues directly affect value creation. They also present a case study of how Molson O'Keefe successfully utilized key factors to create value in their merger.

Ulrich and LaFasto address the impact of organizational culture on human resource management, and outline what the HR manager can do to facilitate culture changes. Using examples of culture change efforts in several big corporations, the authors show that HR professionals must play a central role if culture changes are to be successfully carried out.

Chapter 8

The Legal Context of Human Resource Management: Conflict, Confusion, Cost, and Role-Conversion

Michael H. LeRoy and James M. Schultz

INTRODUCTION

Government regulation of the employment relationship has been controversial for more than a century. No issue in the 1850s and 1860s more divided the Congress and various state legislatures than slavery. Although slavery is seen as a moral issue today, it provoked debate concerning the role of federal and state powers to regulate labor markets. No American civil war over government regulation of labor markets is imminent, but numerous regulatory issues are nonetheless hotly debated.

In this chapter, we hope to stimulate practitioners to contemplate how the legal context of human resource management is changing. We also hope to encourage practitioners to integrate the legal context of human resource management as part of their general business strategy.

In addition, we intend to stimulate academic consideration of recently emerging consequences of employment regulation. Certainly much has already been debated and discussed, but often this has been accomplished without incorporating the experience of practitioners who are affected by this regulation. In addition, regulatory change is now so sweeping, and occasionally so abrupt, that it is important for the academic literature to change with new developments.

Our perspective is critical. Certainly some of the regulation we examine has led to constructive change for employees, employers, and American society. While we laud such change, our main point of departure is that the legal context of human resource management is fundamentally coercive. Whether laudatory in purpose, or laudatory in effect, employment laws are generally expressed as obligatory commands. These commands are ultimately enforced through a multitude of remedial sanctions, sometimes involving fines, monetary judgments, contract debarment, and the like.

Practitioners, therefore, *must* incorporate regulatory compliance into human resource management. In our view, practitioners need to integrate compliance in formulating business strategies, and scholars need further to examine whether regulations achieve their intended effect, and to identify unintended effects of employment regulation.

This chapter is organized around four theoretical themes. First, employers are increasingly subject to conflicting laws. This is because employment regulation now emanates from virtually all levels of government (federal, state, and sometimes municipal). Second, much employment regulation is confusing. This is due in part to vague articulation of legal duties. It is also due to increasingly technical expression of these duties. Third, employment regulation is increasingly costly. This is due in part to regulations aimed at spreading workplace risk (e.g., workers' compensation) and minimizing workplace injuries (a variety of health and safety regulations). It is also due to government's propensity to shift more responsibility from the public sector to private employers. The health care plan proposed by the Clinton administration, requiring all employers to help finance universal health insurance, illustrates this growing tendency. This kind of regulation amounts to indirect taxing and redistribution of wealth at the expense of employers. Fourth, some employment regulations not only shift costs, but result in conversion of the traditional role of employers. The gist of some employment regulation is to compel employers to perform a role, for example, immigration control, that was once exclusively exercised by public institutions.

We then relate these theoretical themes to human resource practice issues. Although our discussion relates the experience of one large employer, Walgreen Company, our goal is to select experiences that may be generalizable to most human resources practitioners, regardless of employer size or industry.

THE LEGAL CONTEXT OF HUMAN RESOURCE MANAGEMENT: A THEORETICAL PERSPECTIVE

Conflicting regulation

No single agency, branch, or level of government has exclusive jurisdiction for regulating employment. Indeed, employment regulation emanates continuously from sources as varied as the U.S. Supreme Court and Congress; Immigration and Naturalization Service, U.S. Department of Labor, and the National Labor Relations Board (NLRB); and state legislatures, agencies, courts, and city councils.

Even where subject matter seems to reside exclusively in one governmental instrumentality, other government bodies take actions that intrude on such jurisdiction. Adding to this complexity, numerous interest groups have regulatory agendas that they seek to implement through government action. When these groups find one level or branch of government uncongenial to their agenda, they shift battlegrounds to a level or branch that is more favorable. Over time, this adds to the complexity of regulation.

Taken together, these factors mean that human resource managers find themselves subject to conflicting employment regulations.

Overlapping jurisdiction

Health-benefits regulation illustrates how overlapping regulatory schemes occasionally produce conflicting regulation.

In general, states exclusively regulate insurance. However, the Employment Retirement Income Security Act (ERISA, 1988) regulates all employee benefits, including health insurance. In addition, ERISA contains a broad preemption clause, reflecting Congressional intent that federal benefits regulation displace state regulation.

Metropolitan Life Insurance Co. v. *Massachusetts* (1985) illustrates how this conflict affected employers. Massachusetts required employers who provided health insurance to include psychiatric hospitalization in their plans. This increased the cost of already expensive health insurance, leading some employers to drop all health insurance for their employees. For those employers who wanted to continue coverage, but on a less costly basis, the law seemed contrary to ERISA's general principle regulating the process of benefits administration. In contrast, Massachusetts regulated the content of benefit plans, leading to the ironic result of reducing benefits for many employees. The Supreme Court resolved this conflict by ruling that ERISA preempts state insurance law in this matter.

Striker replacement law provides another pertinent illustration. The NLRA (National Labor Relations Act, 1935), as construed in the landmark *NLRB* v. *Mackay Radio* (1937) decision, allows employers to hire permanent replacements for economic strikers. Throughout the 1980s and early 1990s, organized labor has sought federal legislation to repeal *Mackay Radio*. Failing in this effort, labor has successfully promoted passage of state labor laws that make the hiring of permanent striker replacements illegal. Minnesota's Picket Line Peace Act (1991), which adopts the language of a perennially unsuccessful Congressional bill, is a prime example. It prohibits Minnesota employers otherwise covered by the NLRA to hire a permanent striker replacement. Conflicting court rulings on the constitutionality of this law (*Midwest Motor*, 1993; *Employers Association*, 1992) have not resolved this contradiction in state and federal law.

These are only two of many federal–state conflicts in labor and employment regulation. The significance of this kind of conflict is to create uncertainty in human resource management planning, because legal rights and duties cannot be readily determined without resorting to litigation.

Concurrent jurisdiction

Another kind of regulatory conflict is produced when federal and state laws simultaneously apply. Here, the result may not be that federal law preempts state law. Instead, it may coexist with state law. Technically, this may not produce contradictory regulation, but a practitioner subject to this regime may view all this as a conflicting scheme.

Workplace safety regulation offers a good example of this phenomenon. Until recently, the conventional view was that the OSH Act (Occupational Safety and Health Act, 1988), administered by the U.S. Department of Labor, preempted most state regulation. The situation changed as federal enforcement grew lax, and a series of catastrophic accidents killed workers on the job (Getting away with murder, 1987). Local prosecutors began to try corporate officers on felony criminal charges. In a case of national significance (*Illinois* v. *Chicago Magnet Wire*, 1990), the Illinois Supreme Court ruled that OSHA did not preempt state criminal prosecution of company officials whose negligence caused serious workplace injuries.

Another important case (*Steele*, 1989) illustrates this pattern from the civil liability side of the law. The company ordered two employees to clean up toxic concentrations of spilled PCBs, without warning them or giving them appropriate protection. The employer argued that the state's workers' compensation system was the appropriate forum to redress any injury to these workers. The Ninth Circuit Court of Appeals disagreed, however, holding that the workers could go to trial on claims of employer misrepresentation of hazards in the workplace and battery.

The practical consequence here is that the workers were enabled to try their case before a jury of peers and seek punitive damages. The broader significance of the case, however, is that workers' compensation, traditionally treated as an exclusive remedial system for worker injuries, was treated as one of several remedial systems to be made simultaneously available to workers.

International Union, UAW v. *Johnson Controls* (1991) shows another aspect of concurrent jurisdiction producing regulatory conflict. An employer's policy of prohibiting women of child-bearing age from working in jobs that would expose them to lead was ruled a violation of Title VII of the 1964 Civil Rights Act. As a consequence, women were permitted to bid into higher-paying jobs that subjected

145

them to potentially harmful reproductive risks. The ruling explicitly did not shield the employer, however, from liability for creating conditions that would contribute to birth defects.

Conflicting appellate court rulings

A separate problem is created by conflicting appellate court rulings. Since federal law occupies so many employment fields, federal courts, vested with subject-matter jurisdiction, play an important role in determining regulatory policies. Where Congress or the Supreme Court definitively treats employment issues, human resources practitioners can readily identify legal boundaries. A serious problem is created, however, when Congress and the Supreme Court ignore an important employment issue. At that point, 12 U.S. courts of appeal, each exercising exclusive regional jurisdiction, become the highest-ranking lawmaking bodies. These courts, occasionally given to their own ideological proclivities, are then in position not only to render conflicting rulings, but to expound conflicting legal standards. All federal trial courts in their jurisdiction must apply these standards.

Sexual harassment demonstrates how this conflict works. When Title VII was enacted (Civil Rights Act of 1964), gender discrimination was thrown in as a last-minute amendment to the bill (*Congressional Record*, 1964). The bill nevertheless passed, without any indication of what lawmakers intended to do about gender discrimination, including the issue of sexual harassment. In this vacuum, the Equal Employment Opportunity Commission (EEOC) developed legal standards for harassment (EEOC Guidelines on Discrimination Because of Sex, 1992). Ultimately, all circuit courts of appeal reviewed this standard, and in *Meritor Savings Bank* (1986) the U.S. Supreme Court addressed some but not all sexual harassment issues. Notably, the Court did not define a standard for determining hostile-environment harassment.

The appellate courts filled this vacuum, but in contradictory fashion. Some courts required sexual harassment plaintiffs to prove psychological harm (*Rabidue*, 1986; *Vance*, 1989; *Downes*, 1985), while another used a much more liberal "reasonable victim" test (*Ellison*, 1991). These standards were widely divergent. A California employer might be liable for the persistent date-seeking conduct of a male employee, while an Illinois employer would not be liable for a male employee who touched a female coworker's breasts and buttocks.

The Supreme Court's recent decision in *Harris* (1993) only partially eliminates this conflict. Also, although sexual harassment is an important employment issue, it is only one of many treated in conflicting fashion by appellate courts. In 1994, the Supreme Court will resolve intercircuit conflicts involving the retroactive application of the 1991 Civil Rights Act (*USI*, 1993) and the definition of a supervisor under the NLRA (*NLRB* v. *Health Care Retirement Corporation of America*, 1993).

Conflicts among the circuits present planning problems for human resources practitioners who manage employees in more than one geographic area. Usually, practitioners must choose between a relatively permissive and a relatively restrictive policy. A restrictive practice, applied uniformly across circuits, may shield an employer from liability. Foregoing a more permissive policy, however, might disadvantage an employer in a circuit where a competitor, operating only in that locale, can adopt the permissive policy without creating liability. In short, conflicts among circuits have the undesirable consequence of distorting competition between employers.

Confusing regulation

While conflicting regulation produces confusion (Which set of rules applies to our situation?), confusing regulation often occurs in the absence of any conflict. Vague rules, technical rules, and rule changes are common sources of confusion for practitioners.

Vague regulation

Vague rules have unclear meanings. Occasionally, inartful drafting of a rule is the sole cause behind vagueness. More often, however, vagueness results from two other sources: political compromise that produces a regulatory scheme, or a legal tradition that favors rule flexibility.

Common law refers to judge-made law. In the U.S., this kind of law has been evolving since the colonial period. Apart from whatever employment laws Congress, federal agencies, and state legislatures create, state courts have significantly influenced employment law by modifying the employment-at-will doctrine. That common-law doctrine generally recognized an employer's unfettered right to hire or fire (as well as an employee's right to quit at will).

Recently, however, state courts have made substantial inroads on the policy their predecessors created (Leonard, 1986; Epstein, 1984). The primary vehicle for limiting an employer's right to fire at-will has been the public policy exception. In fact, there is no single public policy exception, nor a singular, concise statement of the policy. Rather, it is the cumulation of many court decisions which have cited some public policy that would be violated or contradicted if an employer were permitted to fire an employee at will. To illustrate, employers have been held to violate the public policy exception when they required an employee to commit an illegal act (*Tameny*, 1980; *Trombetta*, 1978; *Phipps*, 1987), or discharged an employee for reporting illegal conduct (*Boyle*, 1985).

Many of these decisions are defensible on their facts, but nevertheless create the overall impression that courts will interfere with an employer's right to fire whenever they please. In short, while the policy affords courts great flexibility in weighing equities of particular cases, it also has no clear boundaries.

Administrative rulings are also worded to provide for a flexible policy, but at the same time, create confusion. A recent and important NLRB decision, *E.I. du Pont de Nemours & Co.* (1993), illustrates this problem. The Board ruled that DuPont violated the NLRA's prohibition against employer domination of labor organizations by creating certain employee safety committees. The committees were unlawful because management was represented on these committees and had authority to veto employee suggestions. This probably sent a negative regulatory message to many employers who must bargain with unions, and who have some form of employee involvement programming. In *DuPont* the Board tried to reassure employers by advising them that it is lawful for employee committees to engage in brainstorming or making suggestions, because these activities do not involve decision making. This discussion is likely to be confusing for some employers, because employee involvement may fall in a gray area between making suggestions and making decisions. That area is employee *influence in decision making*, and the *DuPont* decision does not provide clear guidance concerning the legality of this level of employee input.

The Americans with Disabilities Act (1990) is a classic illustration of vague regulation produced by political compromise. Its chief architect was Senator Tom Harkin, a liberal Democrat, yet it was signed into law by a Republican president, George Bush, who freely used his veto power. Perhaps there was no veto because the legislation contained enough flexibility for employers.

The Act amounts to law by adjective. It protects "qualified individuals with a disability." *Qualified*, of course, is an indefinite modifier. Perhaps that is no problem, however, because the law states that a person is qualified if he or she can perform *essential* job functions. What is essential? That depends, although there is some presumption that employers are entitled to define the essence of job duties. A qualified individual with a disability is one who has "a major life activity that is substantially limited by a physical or mental impairment." What is a *major* life activity, and what is a *substantial* limitation? The EEOC explains these defining adjectives at length in its rules (EEOC, 1991), but not even proponents of the law would argue that these adjectives are precise. If a person is found to be a qualified individual with a disability, an employer must consider any *reasonable* accommodation that would permit the person to perform the essential job functions. Like beauty, reasonableness is in the eye of the beholder. Perhaps the law does not leave everyone to interpret subjectively, because employers may raise the defense that an accommodation presents an "undue hardship." Of course, *undue* does nothing to clarify matters. In sum, the law is long on good intentions and short on clarity.

This vagueness may have an ironic result. Not knowing whether to build more ramps or elevators first, or to redraft policies to accommodate the need for flexible assignments, employers might simply do nothing and wait to be sued. This regulatory regime is so vague that some employers might simply allow first-come, first-served litigants to establish their priorities.

Technical regulation

Technical legal expression can be a dual-edged sword, sharpening or obscuring meaning. Supreme Court Justice John Paul Stevens recently observed that "one of the contrasts between art and law is that mystery, ambiguity, and suspense are virtues in art, but not in law. . . . (R)eaders of a statute must know immediately what is intended" (Stevens, 1992, 7).

To make his point that some law is hopelessly vague and therefore confusing, he cited a technical passage in Section 1144 in the Employee Retirement Income Security Act (ERISA):

Except as provided in subsection (b) of this section, the provisions of this subchapter and subchapter III of this chapter shall supersede any and all State laws insofar as they may now or hereafter relate to any employee benefit plan described in section 1003(a) of this title and not exempt under section 1003(b) of this title (id.).

He then noted that this indecipherable section consumes 22 column inches of the dense U.S. Code.

ERISA is not the only source of technical employment regulation. Workplace safety (Air Contaminants Standard, 1989) and drug-testing regulations (Nuclear Regulatory Commission, 1989), for example, contain technically obscure language. At a philosophical level, one may lament such regulations because they discourage reasonable compliance efforts (Understanding the CFR, 1993). At a practical level, however, many employers are not content to attract attention from enforcement agencies, and therefore try to discern what these laws mean. This effort frequently means paying experts to explain what the rules are and how they apply. Technical obscurity therefore imposes a cost that does nothing to improve an employer's productivity, efficiency, or profitability.

Rule changes

Enactment of the 1991 Civil Rights Act illustrates how rule change creates regulatory confusion. In *Wards Cove Packing* v. *Atonio* (1989), the Supreme Court made proof of employment discrimination more difficult by requiring a plaintiff to demonstrate that a particular employment practice resulted in an unlawful disparate impact. The Civil Rights Act of 1991 (see Civil Rights Act of 1964, amended) overturned the burden of proof scheme in *Wards Cove.* The practical effect for practitioners was a pronounced loosening of Title VII compliance strictures in 1989, followed by a pronounced tightening of those strictures two years later.

Cost

Wages and benefits

Although the New Deal inaugurated new wage and benefit controls, this was not the first occasion for government to regulate labor markets. Colonial governments imposed strict wage controls to cope with short labor supplies (Morris, 1981). Much later, there was considerable state regulation of wages, working hours and employment of women and children (Rothstein, Knapp, & Liebman, 1991).

Nevertheless, New Deal wage and benefit legislation marked the first time that federal labor codes were imposed almost uniformly on private sector employers. FLSA (Fair Labor Standards Act of 1938, 1990) continues to regulate such matters as child labor, minimum wages, and overtime pay.

These regulations reflect good intentions to protect working people from abuse and exploitation. Nevertheless, they can be costly for some employers. No one will argue that the present minimum wage of $4.25 per hour adequately supports a worker's family. However, for some employers the minimum wage law is very costly relative to what competitors in the global economy pay for labor.

This well-intentioned law, therefore, occasionally has the effect of denying employment to workers, particularly with low skills, because employers are unwilling or unable to pay comparatively costly wages. To the extent that this law creates a structural unemployment barrier, some people are deprived of an opportunity to acquire meaningful work experience that could lead to skill development, and ultimately, a better job (Horwitz, 1993). This observation is supported by evidence that a proposed increase in the minimum wage is encouraging more employers to mechanize menial-labor processes (Horwitz, 1993).

Recently, innovations in workplace technology have combined with FLSA's overtime provision, resulting in higher employment costs for employers. The portable pager provides a good example. Some employers require workers to carry these small devices on days off, and to respond to emergency calls. Where, however, an employee's off-duty freedom is sufficiently limited (e.g., he may be told to limit his travel so that he can respond within 30 minutes to a page), he may be deemed to be working for the benefit of his employer, even though he is providing no work at all (e.g., he may be at home watching football games all weekend). Recent litigation under the overtime provisions of FLSA shows that employers may be liable for millions of dollars if use of a pager limits workers' use of off-duty time (*Local No. 169*, 1992).

Other wage and benefit legislation is very costly to employers. Employer payment of social security taxes is a prime example (Social Security Act, 1993). President Clinton's proposed health care plan would also require all employers to pay for employee health insurance. For the numerous employers who do not pay any insurance, this regulation alone would be very costly (Wessel, 1993). Still other regulation, such as the Davis-Bacon Act of 1931 (1992), is costly because it requires employers to pay above market wages.

We do not disparage any particular wage, hour, or benefit law. Our point, however, is to call attention to direct costs to employers imposed by this intricate web of regulation. In this regard, we cannot improve on Professor Richard Epstein's observation that "employers do not have an endless cornucopia to absorb such aggressive regulation" (Epstein, 1992).

For managers, it is axiomatic to incorporate these regulatory costs into their business plans. The much greater challenge, however, is to create a long-term business plan that correctly anticipates how these generally increasing costs will behave.

Safety

Apart from directly paying mandated wages and benefits, employers covered by OSHA must comply with workplace safety regulations. These regulations are voluminous, and industry- or hazard-specific.

Of course, safety regulations have the laudable purpose of protecting workers from a variety of occupational injuries and diseases. The law permits costly regulation if it can be demonstrated that such regulation benefits the health and safety of employees (The Supreme Court, 1981). Many regulations have a cost implication, however. In *American Dental Association* (1993), a court upheld a bloodborne safety regulation costing the health care industry $813 million annually, while rejecting the argument that some health care providers could not afford to comply.

There is an increasing trend toward increasingly costly safety regulation. For example, a proposed OSHA regulation aims to protect janitors from asbestos exposure (Former asbestos products, 1993). It would apply to virtually all commercial and residential buildings, and would require airtight enclosures, decontamination facilities, and air monitoring. A Brookings Institution estimate places the cost of this regulation at $7 *billion* to $12 *billion*.

A janitor's life and safety is no less precious than any other person's. There are risks, however, in all aspects of human experience, including such mundane activities as eating ordinary meals and driving vehicles within the bounds of law. At what point should the cost of regulation be given controlling weight over an uncertain prediction that such regulation will save a single life? Some workplace safety regulation appears to be premised upon safeguarding a single life, regardless of cost (*Industrial Union Department*, 1980).

Workers' compensation represents another large safety-related expense for employers, costing $70 billion in 1993 (Workers' comp, 1993). Workers' compensation costs are so significant that many employers are likely to consider strategies such as locating in low-cost states, and employing younger and presumably more healthy employees (perhaps triggering age-discrimination liability), as part of their human resources strategy.

Disability

The employment title of the Americans with Disabilities Act (ADA) became effective in July, 1992, so there is too little experience to calculate with any precision what employer costs under the law will be. Congress anticipates, however, that employers will have to bear considerable costs in accommodating protected people (House Committee on Education and Labor, 1989; Senate Committee on Labor and Human Resources, 1989).

This is due in part to the law's broad coverage, protecting an estimated 42 million people. The broad and multiple definitions of a disabled individual create the potential for most employers to consider making reasonable employment accommodations (Frierson, 1993). The EEOC's guidelines require employers to consider making workspaces more accessible, to provide assistants, to alter work schedules, and the like. Regulations shelter employers against "undue hardships." "Undue" means, however, that employers must make accommodations that are not extreme hardships, but hardships nonetheless. Courts and government agencies may lack experience to gauge what hardships are due and undue. Moreover, given the fact that the law is intended to expand employment opportunities for disabled people, and not to provide employers relief from costs, an employee bias is built into the law.

Liability

Apart from wage, benefit, and safety regulation, the growing ambit of employer liability for violating employee rights is adding to employer costs. Employers may be found liable for race and sex discrimination (Civil Rights Act, 1993), age discrimination (ADEA, 1993), benefits discrimination (ERISA, 1993), record keeping violations (Immigration

Reform and Control Act, 1993), improper use of polygraph (Employee Polygraph Protection Act, 1993), failure to provide adequate family and personal leave (Family and Medical Leave Act, 1993), retaliatory conduct (*Lingle*, 1988; *Ostrofe*, 1984), negligent hiring (*Malorney*, 1986; *Sheerin*, 1986; *Cramer*, 1985), defamation (*Lewis*, 1986), emotional distress (*English*, 1990; *Rojo*, 1989; *Johnson*, 1988; *Ford*, 1987; *Bodewig*, 1981), invasion of privacy (*Saroka*, 1992), unjust dismissal (*Gantt*, 1992; *Pierce*, 1980), insufficient notice of layoff or closing (Worker Adjustment and Retraining Notification Act, 1992), and others.

With the inexorable expansion of employer liability, beginning during the New Deal, and accelerating since the civil rights movement, compliance has become increasingly costly for employers. Ordinary experience suggests that employers hire or retain a growing number of employment professionals primarily to manage compliance. This represents a cost that does not improve an employer's productivity or efficiency.

A separate matter is the cost of awards or judgments incident to a finding of employer liability for violating a legal duty. These costs are spread much more narrowly over employers. However, they can be staggering. Recent examples include *Lucky Stores* (1993), involving a $90 million damage award against an employer for discriminating against 20,000 women; an $11.5 million whistleblower award under the False Claims Act (Naj, 1993); *Byrnes* (Jury awards $7.1 million, 1993), involving an Ohio jury award of $7.1 million against an employer found liable for age bias; *Wilson* (1991), involving a $3.4 million judgment for demoting a vice-president to warehouse janitor; *Sapporo Toyota of Los Angeles* (California jury, 1993), involving a jury award of $750,000 to an employee who was repeatedly called a "nigger" at work; and *AIC Security Investigations Ltd.* (Jury awards fired . . . director, 1993), involving a jury award of $572,000 under the ADA to a man who

was discharged after his employer learned he had terminal brain cancer. United Parcel Service recently offered to pay $12 million to settle a suit alleging that it worked delivery people off-the-clock (United Parcel, 1993). State Farm Insurance recently paid $157 million to settle a class-action sex discrimination lawsuit (State Farm Insurance, 1992), and Shoney's paid $105 million to settle a class-action race discrimination suit (Shoney's Inc., 1992). In a case involving the United Food & Commercial Workers, Nordstrom's agreed to a $15 million to $30 million settlement of FLSA overtime violations (Court approves wage, 1993).

Public sector employers are not necessarily immune from these liability problems. In *Texas Dept. of Human Services* (Texas court, 1993), an employee suing under the state's Whistleblower Act was awarded $13.5 million in damages and attorneys' fees.

Cost shifting

Several regulatory regimes discussed in this chapter are not only costly, but are cost shifting. We note this as a separate theme because this tendency is increasing, and because the rationale for cost shifting is not always based on some employment policy rationale. Increasingly, employers are subjected to new regulation simply because they are available, solvent, and in contact with most American adults.

The Americans with Disabilities Act and the administration's proposed health care plan are recent examples of sweeping regulation that redistributes social costs to employers. The ADA is a product of a peculiar period in which interest groups seek enhanced legal protection and entitlements, while few, if any, budgeting initiatives can be considered by legislatures. Congress and President Bush were persuaded that disabled people deserve substantial improvement in their living and working conditions. The employment title of the ADA assumes, however, that employers are the proper entities to subsidize this improvement. By similar thinking, proposed health care legislation assumes that all employers should pay in one fashion or another for employee health care.

It appears that employers are becoming an increasingly popular target for the subsidization of entitlements that the Congress can no longer afford because of the massive federal deficit. Just as there are limits to costs that the government can afford, there are limits to what employers can afford. Faced with shouldering more of these social costs, employers may consider relocating work and jobs as part of their business strategy. Those who cannot relocate may simply consider substituting as much labor-saving machinery as possible to reduce exposure to what amounts to per capita taxation. Or, they may raise prices.

Role conversion
Cost shifting may involve more than simply redistributing money. It often involves redefining roles and responsibilities. This is true with an increasing number of employment laws.

Proposed health care legislation not only poses more costs for employers who do not provide this benefit, it also redefines their role. As with larger employers, they are perceived to be a legitimate proxy for a government that wants to provide universal health care, but cannot itself afford it. This amounts to a form of role conversion for employers.

There is a growing and alarming regulatory trend casting employers as government proxies.

Illegal immigration was perceived to be a serious problem in the 1980s. When the federal government could not effectively secure American borders and ports, the Immigration Reform and Control Act (1992) created a legal obligation for employers to document the citizenship status of all employees. When drug laws proved ineffective, regulations were enacted directing or strongly encouraging private employers to drug-test employees (Department of Transportation, 1989; The Drug-Free Workplace Act of 1988 (1993); Drug and Alcohol Testing Act [Utah], 1992). As more children are born out of wedlock, and many young families broken by divorce, employers increasingly are the government's last resort short of prison for enforcing child support and alimony (Child Support Enforcement Amendments of 1984 (1993)). The "employer trip reduction" requirement of the 1990 Clean Air Act will begin in 1994 to make employers responsible for increasing the number of passengers per vehicle in trips between home and work. In this manner, employers are being held legally responsible for ozone depletion (Price, 1993). In addition, employers are now being targeted by proposed regulation to prohibit smoking in the workplace (Salwen, 1994).

There is almost always a good rationale for these and similar employment regulations. Quite often, however, the most compelling reason for assigning employers these regulatory roles is simply that an overwhelming majority of adult Americans work. Thus, the workplace is the most convenient and efficient place for administering a wide range of social regulation.

If regulatory trends continue, employers may be asked to collect more information about employees. This can only increase employee antagonism, by creating the perception that one's employer is a snooping agent for the state. On the other end of the spectrum, more regulations are casting employers in the role of welfare provider. It is hard to imagine any single government agency dispensing welfare while at the same time exercising police functions, but this is exactly what employment regulations are asking individual employers to do. We seriously doubt employers can perform well all the roles they are asked to play.

Table 8.1 Human resources practitioner's role matrix

	Business result of employment practice: productive	*Business result of employment practice: counterproductive*
Compliance result of employment practice: legal	Role 1: Advocate	Role 3: Lobbyist
Compliance result of employment practice: illegal	Role 2: Protector	Role 4: Whistleblower

THE LEGAL CONTEXT OF HUMAN RESOURCE MANAGEMENT: A PRACTITIONER'S PERSPECTIVE

Human resources practitioner matrix

Most human resource practitioners are not lawyers. Even those who are lawyers concern themselves ultimately with business objectives and strategies. Their legal training is applied to optimize business decisions. Regardless of his or her professional training, a human resources practitioner cannot avoid considering legal issues when making decisions or planning strategies.

To help practitioners think about their planning and decision making, we suggest the role matrix presented in table 8.1. It is too simplistic to state that businesses must choose between "right" and "wrong" employment practices. The more realistic view is that businesses are faced with opportunities to act. This leads to decision making concerning employment practices. Any action or inaction, therefore, can result in a benefit or a detriment to the business. We call these productive and counterproductive results. At the same time, business decisions affecting employment practices are legal or illegal. Our discussion concerning conflicting and confusing regulation suggests, however, that the boundary between these outcomes may be hard to determine. As the matrix shows,

all employment practice decisions produce a combination of business and compliance results.

In Role 1, a "win-win" situation exists in which compliance also helps an employer's business. Here the practitioner should be an Advocate, because advocacy of compliance is likely to enhance a business objective. In Role 2, a practitioner is faced with a situation in which an illegal practice would nevertheless be productive for the business. The practitioner's role is Protector, because of the need to prevent an employer from wrongful conduct. It is important to note that compliance in this situation ultimately results in a productive outcome for the business. In contrast, there are situations in which compliance to employment regulation is counterproductive for the business. The practitioner will be thrust into two distinct roles. In Role 3, the business pursues a legal course, notwithstanding the business-harm such compliance causes. Here the practitioner acts as Lobbyist, drawing attention to the harm regulation creates and promoting laws that would enhance business productivity. Role 4, Whistleblower, is the most difficult and controversial for practitioners. It involves situations in which the business intentionally pursues an unlawful employment practice that is counterproductive to the business.

A practitioner will only occasionally play a pure, unmixed role in making or implementing employment decisions. Quite often, the context for these decisions will require mixing a combination of these roles. Our discussion concerning conflicting regulation makes this especially likely.

Consider the conflicting employment regulation that affected Walgreen's strategy for selecting warehouse employees at a new distribution center. As part of a comprehensive business strategy to lower operating costs, Walgreen identified rising workers'-compensation costs as a general problem. Analysis showed that many claims at other centers resulted from lifting injuries. Further analysis showed that although safety training and post-injury case management were helpful in restraining costs, more effective results would be obtained by selecting and placing people who were less likely to be injured in the first place.

Walgreens also discovered an ergonomic strength test to use as a selection screen. The test measured a person's aerobic capacity (an indicator of physical endurance) and static pressure (an indicator of physical strength). Although the test was well suited to Walgreen's business objective of lowering costs, it also resulted in mostly young and male subjects scoring in the higher percentiles.

From the standpoint of employment regulation, the test was consistent with OSHA, because it would result in fewer on-the-job injuries. Importantly, however, Walgreens recognized that the test, used in isolation, would also create disparate impacts for women, older subjects, and possibly races with smaller body types. Thus, the test might place Walgreens in the position of violating several employment discrimination laws.

Faced with this conflict, Walgreens chose a balancing strategy. The company chose a low cutoff point for hiring so that the demographics of its warehouse work force would match the neighboring community. At the same time, it warned people whose test scores indicated low physical capacities of their propensity for injury, and encouraged these people to improve their physical fitness.

This strategy resulted from practitioners mixing two roles, Advocate and Protector. Obviously, the Protector role was played when potential for unlawful disparate impacts was identified and incorporated into the selection process. Once the Protector role resulted in a legally sufficient hiring cutoff, the Advocate role produced a strategy of lowering business costs and improving workplace safety through training that targeted higher-risk employees.

Role 1: Advocate

Several years before passage of the Americans with Disabilities Act, Walgreen was confronted with a labor shortage. Operations people asked for special help to find employees. Human resources saw people with disabilities as a logical solution to this problem. Research showed that people with disabilities experienced higher unemployment, but nevertheless made good employees when given the opportunity. Recently, Walgreen's findings were broadly confirmed (Disabled workers, 1993).

For Walgreens, hiring, placement, and training of disabled people began purely as a business strategy. Human resource practitioners recognized that most Walgreen managers mirrored society's general ignorance about people with disabilities. A program was developed to show managers that their drugstores could operate well when staffed with people with disabilities. Instead of communicating this view in abstract terms to managers, research was undertaken to find stores that already made productive use of people with disabilities. This resulted in a training video, to counteract existing prejudices and to begin the attitudinal shift that Walgreens needed for business reasons.

Walgreens was therefore ahead of the Americans with Disabilities Act, not because it anticipated this legislation, but because its business objectives were met by a hiring strategy that only later was reinforced by law. This coincidence between employment law and business objectives places Walgreens human resources practitioners in an Advocate role. Certainly, this role is not undiluted. Some of these practitioners have played a Protector role in revising job descriptions to reflect essential job functions. Fundamentally, however, Walgreens views the employment of people with disabilities not as a compliance issue, but as an attitude issue. The attitude filters that limited employment opportunities for these people are deeply rooted and persistent, and Walgreen's primary attention is directed to cultivating more tolerant workplace attitudes.

Role 2: Protector

Like many mass-market retailers, Walgreens operates on a small profit margin. Healthy profitability depends not only on sales, but highly efficient management. Even small changes in expenses related to sales and administration can turn a store's profit to a loss. At Walgreens, the most visible component of these expenses is payroll. Managers are constantly evaluated in their use of payroll hours and dollars. This pressure can tempt some managers to work employees off-the-clock.

Obviously, working employees off-the-clock is "good" for business profitability, but only in the narrowest sense of the word. Walgreens human resources practitioners are aware of the business pressure that may lead to this abuse, but also recognize the need to protect the company from itself. In this instance, they must therefore play a Protector role.

At Walgreens, this means more than paying lip service to the law. The Protector role requires both a proactive and reactive stance. The proactive stance requires clear communication of the employer's standards of operation. It must be clear to all what will and will not be tolerated. But there must also be an ability to react swiftly, and this entails a strong audit function.

At Walgreens, a powerful human resources information system (HRIS) is cross-linked to operational data. Dozens of human resource indicators, payroll rates, violations of time-in-grade rules, turnover rates by job codes, and reasons for terminations are constantly examined.

These data give Protectors clues to ask the right questions. Practitioners can easily identify particularly low payroll expenses. In some cases, the data may indicate superior management. In other cases, they may indicate abuse. In sum, this system allows Walgreens practitioners to identify and correct wage and hour problems very early.

Role 3: Lobbyist

Human resources practitioners are often advised not to read drafts of legislation and administrative regulations, because these drafts either do not become law or frequently change before being passed. This common advice is factually correct but strategically wrong. In an era of scarce time and resources, lobbying appears at first glance to be wasteful. This view is short-sighted, however, because most employment regulation does not have improvement of productivity or profitability as a policy goal. If human resources practitioners are unwilling to devote time to educate lawmakers, many of whom have never managed a business, how can they later complain that new laws take an unrealistic view of the business world?

Myriad employee training and licensing regulations show the need for greater lobbying. Frequently, these regulations use hours of training as a standard of employee qualification. Generally, hours of training are a false indicator of employee qualification or preparedness. In contrast, competency standards would address the lawmakers' policy goals. While there may be occasions when lawmakers consciously avoid competency standards, more likely, they focus on the time dimension because no one has explained that there is a better way to measure training.

Role 4: Whistleblower

A win-at-any-cost view took hold in various industries and businesses in the 1980s. The 1990s have brought not only more sobering business conditions, but also a sense that winning at any cost is often expensive and bad for business. This conclusion is borne out by widespread revision of business school curricula to include training in business ethics. This represents not so much a change as it does a return to good business values.

Our conception of the Whistleblower role should not be confused with instances where an aggrieved employee turns in his employer for breaking the law. Our Whistleblower is a practitioner who views his or her integration in the business operations as creating genuine accountability for the actions of the business. In large and complex organizations, rogue managers, departments, or divisions may implement an agenda that is fundamentally at cross-purposes with a business's commitment to behave legally and ethically. More than the Protector role is needed in this situation, because the deviant conduct presents a fundamental threat to the business. Our Whistleblower approaches an ultimate authority in the company to provide information, to outline the problem, and to suggest solutions.

The Whistleblower role cannot exist without a business culture that values ethical and legal conduct. Nor can it exist where the role places the practitioner at risk for casting light on situations that are likely to embarrass and frustrate wrongdoers. One way Walgreens has developed a supportive culture for the Whistleblower is to have human resources report to the chief executive officer rather than the chief operating officer. Ordinarily, when human resources disagrees with a practice or position of an operating group, its use of the Protector role is effective. This relationship not only makes possible the reporting of illegal and counterproductive employment activity to someone other than HR's own boss; its mere existence strengthens HR's hand in playing the Protector role.

CONCLUSION

Employment regulation connects theory and HR practice issues. The great volume and volatility of this regulation strains the capacity of human resources practitioners to guide employers in a lawful course. This is especially true for smaller employers, who are covered by many employment laws but who may nevertheless find legal information costs high. A legal regime that is overly complex and confusing ironically invites disobedience to the law.

Increasingly, practitioners must play a special part in this theory–practice connection because of the unique interface that is growing around their multiple roles. As Advocates and Protectors, they apply current and accurate legal information to develop business-driven employment strategies. In these roles, they seek to steer employers on a lawful and a productive course. But as our discussion of the Lobbyist indicates, the requirements of employment law are sometimes blind to business realities. Even where particular laws are not inconsistent with business, more Lobbyists are needed to inform lawmakers that the cumulative effect of administering a crushing amount of regulation is harmful. In this vein, our discussion concerning confusing and conflicting employment regulation bolsters the Lobbyist's theme of clarifying and simplifying the law.

We conclude by raising a theoretical question that reflects the experience of many practitioners. Although many employment laws are marked by good policy intentions, and are having desirable effects, is employment regulation becoming so pervasive as to homogenize employers and their labor markets? At the end of 1993, some employers consciously made themselves attractive in the labor market by offering certain health benefits. Pending health care regulation is likely, however, to take away this competitive advantage for employers. Likewise, employers who had family and medical leave policies now find themselves less differentiated than their labor market competitors since enactment of the Family and Medical Leave Act (FMLA).

We recognize that freely operating labor markets may fail to protect individuals from a kind of discrimination or exploitation that society cannot and should not tolerate. But it is also true that free labor markets also lead to the kind of personal choices and innovations that differentiates the American from the former Soviet economy. In sum, care must be taken that the rising tide of employment regulation does not wash out the positive dynamics of competitive labor markets.

REFERENCES

Age Discrimination in Employment Act, 29 U.S.C.A. §§ 621–34 (1993).

Air Contaminants Standard, 29 C.F.R. § 1910.19 (1993).

American Dental Association v. *Martin*, 984 F.2d 823 (1993).

Americans With Disabilities Act of 1990, 42 U.S.C.A. §§ 12101–213 (1993).

Bodewig v. *K-Mart Inc.*, 635 P.2d 667 (1981).

Boyle v. *Vista Eyewear Inc.*, 700 S.W.2d 859 (1985).

California jury awards Toyota employee $750,000 damages in racial harassment suit (1993). *Daily Labor Report*, July 19, A-2.

Child Support Enforcement Amendments of 1984 to the Child Support Enforcement Act of 1975, 42 U.S.C.A. §§ 651–62 (1993).

Civil Rights Act of 1964 (amended), 42 U.S.C.A. § 2000 (1993).

Congressional Record (1964), *110*, 2577–84.

Court approves wage, hour settlement by Nordstrom Inc. and UFCW (1993). *Daily Labor Report*, April 14, A-11.

Cramer v. *Housing Opportunities Commission*, 501 A.2d 25 (1985).

Davis-Bacon Act of 1931, 40 U.S.C.A. § 276 (1993).

Department of Transportation, Procedures for Workplace Drug Testing Programs, 49 C.F.R. Part 40 (1989).

Disabled workers prove productive (1993), *Job Safety & Health*, April 27, 4.

Downes v. *FAA*, 775 F.2d 288 (1985).

Drug and Alcohol Testing Act, Utah Code Ann §§ 34–38–1 to 34–38–15 (1993).

Drug-Free Workplace Act of 1988, 41 U.S.C.A. §§ 701–7 (1993).

E.I. du Pont de Nemours & Company and Chemical Workers Association Inc., 311 N.L.R.B. No. 88 (1993).

Ellison v. *Brady*, 924 F.2d 872 (1991).

Employee Polygraph Protection Act, 29 U.S.C.A. §§ 2001–9 (1993).

Employee Retirement Income Security Act of 1974, 29 U.S.C.A. § 1001 (1993).

Employers Association Inc. v. *United Steelworkers of America*, 803 F.Supp. 1558 (D.Minn. 1992).

English v. *General Electric*, 110 S.Ct. 2270 (1990).

Epstein, R. (1984). In defense of the contract at will. *University of Chicago Law Review*, 51, 947.

Epstein, R. (1992). As unions decline, labor laws constrain the job market. *The Wall Street Journal*, September 2, A11.

Equal Employment Opportunity Commission (1991). Equal Employment Opportunities For Individuals With Disabilities, 29 C.F.R. 1630.

Equal Employment Opportunity Commission (1992). Guidelines on Discrimination Because of Sex, 29 C.F.R. § 1604.11.

Fair Labor Standards Act of 1938, 29 U.S.C.A. §§ 201–19 (1993).

Family and Medical Leave Act, 29 U.S.C.A. §§ 2601–54 (1993).

Ford v. *Revlon*, Inc., 734 P.2d 580 (1987).

Former asbestos products manufacturers say OSHA rule would be most expensive ever (1993). *Daily Labor Report*, February 3, A2.

Frierson, J. (1993). Obesity as a legal disability under the ADA, Rehabilitation Act, and state handicapped employment laws, *Labor Law Journal*, 44, 286.

Gantt v. *Sentry Insurance*, 824 P.2d 680 (1992).

Getting away with murder: Federal OSHA preemption of state criminal prosecutions for industrial accidents (1987). *Harvard Law Review*, 101, 535.

Harris v. *Forklift Systems Inc.*, 114 S.Ct. 367 (1993).

Horwitz, T. (1993a). The working poor: minimum-wage jobs give many Americans only a miserable life. *The Wall Street Journal*, November 12, A1.

Horwitz, T. (1993b). Would jobs dwindle if minimum wage should be raised? *The Wall Street Journal*, November 12, A8.

House Committee on Education and Labor (1989). House Report No. 101–485, Part 2, November 9 and 14, 69.

Illinois v. *Chicago Magnet Wire*, 534 N.E.2d 962 (1989).

Immigration Reform and Control Act, 8 U.S.C.A. §§ 1324a, 1324b (1993).

Industrial Union Department v. *American Petroleum Institute*, 448 U.S. 607 (1980).

International Union, UAW v. *Johnson Controls*, 499 U.S. 187 (1991).

Johnson v. *Ramsey County*, 424 N.W.2d 800 (1988).

Jury awards fired security firm director $572,000 in first EEOC case under ADA (1993). *Daily Labor Report*, March 19, AA-1.

Jury awards $7.1 million in age bias suit by executives (1993). *Daily Labor Report*, November 3, A-5.

Leonard, A. (1986). A new common law of employment termination. *North Carolina Law Review*, 66, 631.

Lewis v. *Equitable Life Assurance Society*, 389 N.W. 876 (1986).

Lingle v. *Norge Division of Magic Chef*, 486 U.S. 399 (1988).

Local No. 169 v. *ITT Rayonier Inc.*, 971 F.2d 347 (1992).

Lucky Stores Inc. v. *U.S. Dist. Court for the Northern District of California*, 815 F.2d 571 (1993).

Malorney v. *B & L Motor Freight Inc.*, 496 N.E.2d 1086 (1986).

Meritor Savings Bank v. *Vinson*, 477 U.S. 57 (1986).

Metropolitan Life Insurance Co. v. *Massachusetts*, 471 U.S. 724 (1985).

Midwest Motor Express Inc. v. *Local 120, International Brotherhood of Teamsters*, 1993 WL 7182 (1993).

Morris, R. (1981). *Government and Labor in Early America.*

Naj, A. K. (1993). Whistle-blower at GE to get $11.5 million. *The Wall Street Journal*, April 26, A3.

National Labor Relations Act of 1935, 29 U.S.C.A. §§ 1951–69 (1935).

NLRB v. *Health Care Retirement Corp. of America*, 62 U.S.L.W. 3207 (1993).

NLRB v. *Mackay Radio*, 304 U.S. 333 (1937).

Nuclear Regulatory Commission (1989). Fitness For Duty Program, 10 C.F.R. Part 2, June 7.

Occupational Safety and Health Act, 29 U.S.C.A. § 651 (1993).

Ostrofe v. *H.S. Crocker Co.*, 670 F.2d 1378 (1984).

Phipps v. *Clark Oil & Refining Corp.*, 408 N.W.2d 569 (1987).

Picket Line Peace Act, Stat. Ann. § 179.12 (1993).

Pierce v. *Ortho Pharmaceutical Corp.*, 417 A.2d 505 (1980).

Price, D. A. (1993). Newest mandate – everyone in the carpool. *The Wall Street Journal*, November 8, A12.

Rabidue v. *Osceola Refining Co.*, 805 F.2d 611 (1986).

Raiborn, C., and D. Payne (1993). The big dark cloud of workers' compensation: does it have a silver lining? *Labor Law Journal*, 44, 554.

Rodgers, W. (1980). Benefits, costs and risks: Oversight of health and environmental decision-making. *Harvard Environmental Law Review*, 4, 191.

Rojo v. *Kliger*, 257 Cal. Rptr. 158 (1989).

Rothstein, R., Knapp, A., and Liebman, L. (1991). *Cases and Materials on Employment Law.*

Salwen, K. G. (1994). Tough new antismoking rules to be unveiled today. *The Wall Street Journal*, March 25, B1.

Saroka v. *Dayton Hudson Corp.*, 822 P.2d 1327 (1992).

Senate Committee on Labor and Human Resources (1989). Senate Report No. 101–116, August 2, 36.

Sheerin v. *Holin Co.*, 380 N.W.2d 415 (1986).

Shoney's Inc. settles 36-state job bias suit for $105 million (1992). *Daily Labor Report*, November 5, A-3.

Social Security Act, 26 U.S.C.A. § 314 (1993).

State Farm Insurance settles sex bias suit for record $157 million (1992). *Daily Labor Report*, April 29, A-12.

Steele v. *Crown-Zellerbach*, 890 F.2d 195 (1989).

Stevens, J. (1992). Dedication address. *Chicago-Kent Law Review*, 68, 5.

Tameny v. *Atlantic Richfield Co.*, 610 P.2d 1330 (1980).

Texas court upholds $13.5 million award for public sector whistleblower (1993). *Daily Labor Report*, March 23, A-1.

The Supreme Court, 1980 term (1981). *Harvard Law Review*, 91, 324.

Trombetta v. *Detroit, Toledo & Ironton Railroad*, 265 N.W.2d 385 (1978).

U.S. Congress, 100 Congressional Record 2577–2584 (1964).

USI v. *Landgraf*, 113 S.Ct. 2410 (1993).

Understanding the CFR (1993). *Job Safety & Health*, February 2, 4.

United Parcel would pay $12 million to settle unpaid overtime claims (1993). *Daily Labor Report*, November 5, A-6.

Vance v. *Southern Bell Telephone & Telegraph Co.*, 863 F.2d 1503 (1989).

Wards Cove Packing Co. v. *Atonio*, 109 S.Ct. 2115 (1989).

Wessel, D. (1993). Clinton's health plan: who wins, who loses? *The Wall Street Journal*, December 27, A1.

Wilson v. *Monarch Paper Co.*, 939 F.2d 1138 (1991).

Worker Adjustment and Retraining Notification Act, 29 U.S.C.A. §§ 2101–9 (1993).

Workers' comp: fastest growing labor cost (1993). *Daily Labor Report*, May 20, A-19.

Workers' compensation premiums up 10.8 percent in 1990, chamber reports (1993). *Daily Labor Report*, April 26, A-10.

☐ Chapter 9 ☐

Managing the Impact of Information Technology on Human Resource Management

Scott A. Snell, Patricia R. Pedigo, and George M. Krawiec

INTRODUCTION

The impact of information technology (IT) on the human resources (HR) function has been both pervasive and profound. IT encompasses a wide range of tools including hardware (from mainframes to microcomputers), software (from word-processing programs to expert systems), networks, and workstations (Scott Morton, 1991). The vast majority of firms have made at least some use of IT to transform their HR functions (Richards-Carpenter, 1991a; Kinnie & Arthur, 1993). In fact, within U.S. corporations alone, IT now represents the single largest capital expenditure, accounting for almost one-third of all capital investments (Schnitt, 1993).

Perhaps even more significant than the level of IT usage is *how* it is used within HR. IT allows us to store and retrieve large amounts of information quickly and inexpensively. We can also rapidly and accurately combine and reconfigure data to create new information. Further, we have begun to store and quickly use the judgment and decision models developed in the minds of experts, allowing us to institutionalize organizational knowledge.

With IT networks, we can communicate more easily and selectively with others in remote parts of the world, thereby allowing us to make even better use of the information at our disposal (Culnan & Markus, 1987; Rice & Blair, 1984). A recent IBM–Towers Perrin (Towers Perrin, 1992) study, "Priorities for competitive advantage," noted that IT can be a potent weapon for lowering administrative costs, increasing productivity, speeding response times, improving decision making, and enhancing customer service. Ultimately, IT can provide a data and communications platform that helps HR link and leverage the firm's human capital to achieve competitive advantage (cf. Scott Morton, 1991).

Despite the potential benefits of IT, most organizations have a fairly dismal record of turning their investments in technology into increased productivity and strategic capability (Weill & Olson, 1989). Loveman (1988), for example, found that capital expenditures on IT have historically been the least effective method for improving productivity. Kinnie and Arthurs (1993) found that, within HR, IT has been used as no more than an "electronic filing cabinet" for keeping records and processing routine administrative tasks. Furthermore the overwhelming majority of HR departments have never used their systems for strategic purposes (Richards-Carpenter, 1991b). The problem tends not to be with the availability of IT for HR application. Indeed, virtually all of the technology needed to compete in the twenty-first century is readily accessible today. Rather, the evidence suggests that senior managers do not have a workable framework that conveys how IT can be leveraged to exploit its full benefits with HR (Monsalve & Triplett, 1990).

The purpose of this chapter is to provide such a framework. In the following pages, we present our views on how managers can identify, partition, and prioritize IT applications to support their HR initiatives. In the past, we have perhaps focused too much on the technology itself and not enough on how it can be applied (cf. Schnitt, 1993). In the following sections, we describe three basic ways in which IT can impact HR. First, we discuss the *operational* impact of IT; that is, alleviating the administrative burden, reducing costs, and improving productivity internal to the HR function itself. Second, we describe the *relational* impact of IT: that is, providing managers and employees access to the HR data bases, simultaneously reducing response times, and improving service levels. Third, we discuss the *transformational* impact of IT: that is, organizing human interaction to create virtual teams and a more flexible network organization.

Throughout our discussions, we draw on existing theory and research, and combine this literature with examples of systems utilized at IBM. By integrating theory and practice we attempt to convey some of the real changes that are taking place in HR as a result of IT. While we would acknowledge that IBM represents only a single company's experiences, the examples may provide more detailed insight into the linkage between IT and HR. Most experts agree that there is a direct relationship between the systems and capabilities

afforded by IT and the way that HR operates within the firm (Broderick & Boudreau, 1992a; 1992b). Like most technological innovations in history, such as the telegraph or the assembly line, IT has changed the rules of the game within organizations (Snell & Dean, 1992). This paradigm shift has a destabilizing effect, and provides HR professionals with ample opportunity to demonstrate that they can add value to the organization in new and distinctive ways (Kinnie & Arthurs, 1993).

THE OPERATIONAL IMPACT OF IT

One of the first ways we can think about the usage of IT is improving the operational efficiency of the HR function. The strong administrative component of HR makes it a logical candidate for automation (Boudreau, 1992). Also, because cost reduction and increased productivity have been preeminent goals of HR, the focus of most IT applications has been on the internal operations of the HR function itself.

Reducing labor costs

Historically, IT has been implemented as an attempt to substitute capital for labor. Computational functions such as payroll and benefits have frequently served as the base points for IT introduction, and systems have been designed to simplify transaction processing while substantially increasing the volume of work that can be completed by one person (Zuboff, 1988). Eliminating routine clerical activities, such as data entry and control functions, has been viewed as an important method for reducing organizational overhead (cf. Schmitt, Gilliland, Landis, & Devine, 1993). In addition, IT has held promise as a labor-savings device by lowering headcount and variable transaction costs (Scott Morton, 1991).

However, in many cases, the technology has not lived up to this particular promise.

Frequently, there are no real labor savings from IT investments. Kinnie and Arthurs (1993), for example, noted that the introduction of IT brought about reduced headcount in only 19 percent of the HR departments they studied. In fact, in some 8 percent of the firms, the new systems had actually been accompanied by an increase in HR staff. Yates and Benjamin (1991) argued that, in general, the labor-savings aspect of IT is virtually always accompanied by rapid growth of the type of work the system is designed to facilitate. The typewriter, for example, was three times as fast as handwriting. Its adoption in large numbers coincided with enormous growth in all types of clerical and secretarial positions. Thus, although technology may reduce the amount of labor necessary to complete a given task, the information-handling needs tend to grow so fast that the net effect on employment per se is negligible. In our view, organizations who anticipate short-run cost reductions within HR are probably viewing the benefits of IT too narrowly.

Increasing productivity

Over the past 15 years or so, HR managers have become practically consumed with database technologies supporting their human resources information systems (HRIS). Many systems that start out as data-processing devices eventually evolve into information systems. Particularly in large companies, HR managers have discovered that having a comprehensive repository for employee data has some measurable benefits. IBM's Corporate Employee Resource Information System (CERIS), for example, ensures a standard format for nearly 600 data elements such as employee addresses, emergency contacts, education, salary history, job history, and performance data. The system processes an average of 22,000 transactions weekly, and covers nearly a half a million total employee records, approximately 150,000 of which are of currently active employees.

As HR data bases have come on-line, many executives have begun to question the basic assumptions about what personnel files need to be. Digitized image technology, for example, can eliminate the need for hard-copy files altogether (though there are some legal concerns about the elimination of hard-copy records). To eliminate paperwork, IBM's Electronic Jacket System (EJS) scans and digitizes employee records and makes the information keyword accessible (with appropriate security codes). Accompanying EJS, there is a personnel records management process that provides on-line access to all CERIS data, and an on-line placement process that maintains all of the data necessary for matching individuals and jobs.

Beyond the storage and information-handling benefits of IT, many organizations have also found that IT can be used to manipulate and reconfigure vast data bases for other administrative tasks as well (Lawler, 1992). One such application is in equal opportunity reporting. IBM's National Equal Opportunity Network (NEON) is an audit-and-edit system that automatically generates reports satisfying EEO requirements. Since its inception, NEON has saved the company approximately $5–6 million annually in processing costs, and has helped achieve a 50 percent cycle time for creating affirmative action programs. Another IBM application, the National Overtime Vacation and Absence (NOVA) system, tracks overtime, vacation and absence data, and then feeds the data to managers via an on-line system that automatically generates demographic charts and other employee information. Thus, while many automated systems were originally developed as "add-ons" to administrative data bases, the systems have substantially improved productivity within HR.

Institutionalizing organization memory

Systems such as NEON and NOVA begin to reveal that IT does not simply automate the

HR function, it also "informates" (Zuboff, 1988, 10): that is, IT systems generate large quantities of information previously unavailable to the organization. The more this type of information is available, the more managers can start asking questions about their work force. Broderick and Boudreau (1992b), for example, pointed out that managers can use decision-support systems to initiate data excursions in order to uncover trends in the data that are critical for improving productivity and work flow. As Scott Morton (1991, 11) noted:

Corporate data bases now provide an enormous reservoir of information that can be used for constructive management of the organization. Personnel records indicating who has had what job, at what salary, and with what training form the basis for understanding the skill mix in a company and help identify possible candidates for certain jobs. Thus, IT can be thought of as affecting coordination by increasing the organization's memory, thereby establishing a record that allows for the detection of patterns. Although this has been true for some time, the added power of heuristics and artificial intelligence provides important additional tools for using information.

All too often, a great deal of idiosyncratic knowledge is lost when individuals are transferred or leave an organization. This missing "human component" of an organization's memory (Huber, 1990) severely limits the ability of managers to make future decisions, and frequently means that knowledge has to be recreated somehow. Although a good deal of potential knowledge is computer-resident, we are just now beginning to effectively harness and apply the information at our disposal (cf. Johansen, 1988; Yates & Benjamin, 1991).

A logical data structure is the springboard for such applications (Herren, 1989). For example, IBM's Executive Resources Information System (EXERCIS) has been designed to identify and establish road maps for high-potential employees, thereby providing a platform for their career development and planning. Systems such as these can help HR structure information in order to forecast future career moves for key individuals, identify successors for each critical post, highlight strengths and weaknesses of key managers, and identify significant training and development needs (Richards-Carpenter, 1991a). In this way, IT can be a valuable decision-making tool that not only provides the data necessary for HR decisions, but helps to forge a pathway through that data. As Milkovich and Boudreau (1994, 256) noted, "Today the dilemma is not how to get enough data, it is how to maneuver through the sea of data and identify the most important pieces of information. The key is to focus on better decisions, not just producing data faster."

Changes in the HR function

As IT changes operations within HR, it simultaneously recasts HR from solely an administrative function to one that is more oriented toward technical/professional expertise (Parson, 1988). IT frees up HR personnel from many of the manual elements of administration, but requires that they now learn the meaning of the data generated by computer-driven processes. Further, they must ultimately determine how to organize the information into a coherent package that is usable by others (cf. Hirschorn, 1984; Zuboff, 1988). In order for organizations to take advantage of the capabilities afforded by IT, HR executives must in all likelihood support a substantial educational effort to shift the skill base of their employees. Ironically, many organizations set out into the foray of IT with the mistaken belief that automated systems can lower costs by deskilling labor. In the short run, this may be true. However, over time IT tends to result in jobs becoming more complex, dynamic, and challenging, thereby requiring more advanced technical and problem-solving skills (Snell & Dean, 1992). A recent report from the Society for Human Resource Management (SHRM)(Lawson, 1990) showed that most CEOs view in-depth technical expertise and problem-solving capabilities as the two most important capabilities of HR professionals at the operating level.

A second area where we see change is in the design of HR processes. One of the clichés about IT is that it helps us perform the wrong actions a hundred times faster (cf. Madnick, 1991). Nearly three-quarters of HR departments studied by Kinnie and Arthurs (1993) had never changed their business processes in concert with the introduction of IT. If HR departments simply "throw" computers at whatever they do manually, and never take advantage of the capabilities technology has to provide, the new system may actually rivet the old way of doing business into place, making it even more difficult to change (Schnitt, 1993). As Hammer and Champy (1993, 48) pointed out, "Automating existing processes with information technology is analogous to paving cow paths." In order to gain the improvements in productivity that most organizations seek, it is frequently necessary to reengineer the HR processes that are currently being used (cf. Madnick, 1991; Schnitt, 1993).

A third place where we can see change within HR is in the structure of the department itself. Organizational structure, in general, can be viewed as a response to limited information processing capacity (Galbraith, 1973). Centralized decision making, formalized rules and standard operating procedures are all elements of bureaucracy that are put in place to diminish information processing requirements within organizations. However, as IT increases our information processing capacity, it simultaneously allows us to reverse the effects of bureaucracy (Huber, 1990). For example, Schnitt (1993, 18) noted, "IT now makes it possible for pieces of information and even entire documents to be in many places at once, allowing different work that uses the same information to proceed ahead simultaneously." The availability of information allows us to organize with less hierarchy, and permits HR to operate as a much flatter and more flexible unit within organizations. This change is important for enhancing the service potential of HR, a topic we discuss in the next section.

THE RELATIONAL IMPACT OF IT

Whereas in the previous section we focused primarily on improving internal operations of the HR function, in this section we concentrate more on how IT influences HR's relationships with other parties within the organization. IT allows HR to enhance service to outsiders by providing line managers and employees with access to HR data bases, supporting their HR-related decisions, and increasing their ability to connect with other parts of the corporation.

Providing remote access

For the past ten to fifteen years, HR departments have devoted a great deal of time and expense stationing individuals at terminals to enter data into electronic files. The larger the organization, the more administrative burden of getting data onto the files, and the more likely it has been that editing and accuracy issues have become problematic. The solution, in many cases, has been to develop online input functions so that line managers and employees can enter, retrieve, and edit data (by themselves) from remote locations (Tinsley, 1990). IBM's CERIS system, for example, originally required that all data entries had to be handled by a trained administrator. However, with VM2CERIS, the highest volume CERIS transactions have been converted to "self-service" for managers and employees. With on-line user entry, VM2CERIS provides each employee authority over his or her data maintenance and integrity. The system validates each user's changes, and provides them with error notification and confirmation of their transactions. IBM's On-line Opinion Survey (OOS) and suggestion systems, ASAP and IDEAS, also provide real-time user entry of employee recommendations. These systems track inputs, route them to appropriate reviewers, and then follow up with feedback to the originator.

By making these systems accessible on-line, HR can eliminate waste, achieve significant improvements in data quality, and reduce the cycle time necessary for responding to customer requests. Just as automatic teller machines revolutionized the banking industry by cutting out the "middle-man," disintermediation within HR can achieve two objectives at once: reducing costs and improving service (Davidson & Davis, 1992). The Benefits Enrollment/Benefits Tracking System (BES/BTS), for example, has helped IBM lower costs (i.e., a $10–12 million projected savings), reduce administrative overhead (i.e., from a staff of over 300 to 56), improve the accuracy of benefits information, and ensure the highest levels of customer service. This system handles more than 1,200 queries daily with less than a 30-second response time. The system provides individuals with "one-stop shopping" for all benefits programs, and benefits administrators can step through a comprehensive data base of benefits information, with expert guidance and advice available whenever they need it. Using the system's hypertext search capability, administrators can query specific benefit areas that are of concern to employees. All the while, BES/BTS keeps a log of questions asked and answers given, and provides continuous real-time tracing of all benefits claims. Through IBM's information network, transactions are electronically transferred between vendors, insurance carriers, and IBM locations.

Enhancing service levels

It should be clear that on-line systems have a great potential to increase the velocity of service (Davidson & Davis, 1992). In many cases, IT enables line managers to solve their own HR-related problems. However, a valid counterargument is that IT may simply shift the burden of administration back to line personnel. If IT systems are packaged poorly, they can overload users with irrelevant and uninterpretable data (Huber, 1990). In such cases, IT inhibits rather than enhances the productivity of line management.

HR departments can avert such problems by providing decision-support systems that help line managers and employees diagnose HR-related trends before they surface as problems, perhaps even anticipating their needs in advance. IBM's Personal Data Management System (PDMS), for example, prompts managers with on-line notification of upcoming personnel actions such as performance appraisals and salary increases. The system generates summary charts on employee demographics, performance, and the like in order to simplify data analysis used for salary planning. In the not-too-distant future, speech technology may eliminate the need for keyboard strokes altogether, and users will be able to simply voice the actions they wish to undertake. These types of IT applications reinforce the idea that true customer service means helping employees do their jobs more effectively, not simply finding methods for reducing HR's workload.

IBM's On-Line Personnel Reference Library (OPRL) is further evidence that IT can be used to enhance the productivity of line personnel. OPRL provides employees with electronic access to a wide array of reference materials. Employees can use keyword searches to move through a virtual sea of information and customize their own learning process. Not surprisingly, the OPRL system dramatically reduces employee research time, not to mention the cost savings associated with producing and distributing typical hard-copy reference material. In addition, systems such as OPRL facilitate just-in-time skill development by bringing the training to the employees, rather than vice versa (Herren, 1989).

In their most advanced forms, these *performance support systems (PSS)* use artificial intelligence and hypermedia to "provide just the help a performer needs to do a job, just when the performance needs it, and in just the form in which he or she needs it" (Carr, 1992, 32). From an organizational standpoint, worldwide access to all educational and training materials encourages related business units to share the best practices and ideas, thereby facilitating continuous learning (Richards-Carpenter, 1991a).

Increasing connectivity

One of the current obstacles to further progress using IT is the need to integrate the myriad of HR systems. In many cases, IT applications have been developed in different HR areas for specialized purposes (e.g., payroll, benefits), and as a consequence, there is frequently limited coordination across the systems. Increasingly, new HR systems are being developed with an overall view of the entire system architecture (Venkatraman, 1991).

Perhaps the best example of how an integrated system would benefit HR is in the area of staffing. Particularly for multinational firms trying to coordinate activities worldwide, HR planning, recruitment, selection, and placement can be enormously unwieldy organizational activities. When employment data is not shared across interdependent business units, problems of coordination and control are exacerbated. What we have learned is that, with IT, the problems of both distance and time can shrink to near zero (Scott Morton, 1991). For example, using the Resumix application, IBM's Applicant Tracking System (ATS) supports the staffing process by tracking application information, scanning resumés, and making the information immediately accessible to line management for systematized skill searches. Resumix is a relational data-base product that provides users with search capability on a wide variety of data fields (e.g., education, training, experience, etc.) that match applicant skills with the requirements of jobs. Ultimately, systems such as Resumix will help line managers profile a vast number of employees from anywhere in the world (i.e., individuals both inside and outside the company) via an overarching network architecture.

Unfortunately, as noted earlier, most organizations have not yet integrated their HR systems to provide shared access. For some, the necessary data are decentralized in separate units throughout the corporation without any central control or communications linkage. For others, the data are centralized but inaccessible from remote locations (Broderick & Boudreau, 1992a). For each of these types of organizations, distributed data-base capability is frequently a near-term goal for HR rather than a current reality (Herren, 1989). Distributed data bases allow data to exist in multiple sites (e.g., business units), but provide a communications interface that connects users. According to Kinnie and Arthurs (1993), system integration is the most common reason cited by executives for planned technology change within HR. However, until this happens on a broader basis, companies must bear the cost of maintaining duplicate data and functions, and endure the time-consuming task of reconciling the different data files. What is certain, however, is that increasing connectivity will significantly improve coordination and planning (cf. Madnick, 1991).

Changes in the HR function

As line managers and employees gain access to HR data bases, the focus of HR shifts toward customer service. In the past, HR has had almost exclusive control over employee data because they collected it and managed it. However, in the data-based environment of IT, information is widely shared and supports a number of business applications. Now the value added by HR comes from knowledge about the data, not its ownership (Zuboff, 1988). For example, Foster and Flynn (1984, 231–2) noted that, "[F]rom the former hierarchy of position power there is developing instead a hierarchy of competency. . . . Power and resources now flow increasingly to the obvious centers of competence instead of to the traditional hierarchical loci."

By leveraging IT, HR has an opportunity to finally emerge as a power base within organizations. Instead of relegating themselves to back-room administrative routines, HR managers are in a position to provide real solutions to business problems. The ideal to be cultivated within HR is that of a "highly professional, client-oriented service" (Richards-Carpenter, 1993, 49). However, to realize this ideal, the HR staff must begin to think and act more as business partners with a more general view of what is needed for the organization to succeed (Schuler, 1990).

Within IBM, the business/service ideology has resulted in HR undergoing a complete metamorphosis. In order to reduce costs while continuing HR's dedication to quality service, IBM restructured the personnel organization to create WFS, Workforce Solutions. Since May 1992, WFS has operated as a business entity, providing a complete range of HR services to IBM business units, and to organizations outside IBM as well. The hard reality of WFS, and the point that drives its business/service philosophy, is that other divisions and organizations within IBM are free to go elsewhere for HR services if WFS cannot maintain high quality at low cost. Bringing the market pressure to bear on WFS is a fairly consequential undertaking.

The results to date have been promising. WFS is delivering HR services at lower cost than before, with an increased dedication to service quality. In addition, by exploiting the potential benefits of IT, WFS has streamlined most HR processes and consolidated a great deal of redundant activities that have been going on in separate business units. As a result of these changes, WFS has increased IBM's ability to respond to HR-related issues. The challenge now is to decrease costs further, while developing other innovative programs that support HR initiatives in the workplace.

THE TRANSFORMATIONAL IMPACT OF IT

The third way we can view the impact of IT is in how it helps transform the organization. In environments characterized by uncertainty and intense rivalry, many companies are scrambling to reinvent themselves. Global competition, faster product cycles, and the need to leverage knowledge across business units require a much more agile form of organization (Boudreau, 1992). Trends toward restructuring, reengineering, outsourcing, and strategic alliances all represent efforts by organizations to change the way they do business. IT plays a pivotal role in this transformation (McFarlan, 1984). Furthermore, while the changes are not always directed by the HR department per se, the IT applications almost always involve the management of people.

Reengineering work processes

Reengineering requires that companies rethink and fundamentally redesign the way they go about satisfying customer needs (Hammer & Champy, 1993). IT is a powerful enabler in most any company's reengineering efforts. Traditionally, organizational processes are constrained by bureaucratic precepts of division of labor, specialization, and sequential/hierarchical processing of information. However, as we have noted previously, distributed data bases and communications technology now allow information to appear in many places simultaneously (Schnitt, 1993). Decision-support systems and artificial intelligence allow generalists to do the job of experts, and front-line employees to make decisions formerly reserved for management. Each of these technology enablers allows work to be done with far less division of labor and fewer levels of hierarchy, thereby freeing up processes from the effects of bureaucracy.

Reengineering involves several HR-related changes, most of which revolve around aligning employee activities with the needs of customers (Schnitt, 1993). At IBM, "customer-aligned" employees are empowered to make commitments on behalf of the company, but to do so they must understand IBM's capabilities and be able to marshall the resources necessary to meet customer commitments. From the standpoint of HR, aligning employees with customers represents an entirely different approach to work organization, coordination, and control. In the new environment, jobs are much more flexibly designed around skills, roles, and project responsibilities rather than around stable tasks. At the extreme, employees are completely mobile, focusing on activities directed at the project or the customer, rather than on their formal departments. In fact, within IBM's New Jersey Trading Area, IT systems such as wireless communications and laptop computers now allow field personnel to link into a client-server system from remote locations. By marrying HR data bases with business data bases, IBM has essentially established an information warehouse architecture that allows employees to create a completely portable office. In addition to changes in the characteristics of jobs, this IT infrastructure even makes the location of work somewhat irrelevant (cf. Scott Morton, 1991). Mobile employees are able to spend more time working with their customers, and less time dealing with low value-added activities associated with maintaining a more traditional employment relationship.

Building virtual teams

It should be clear that reengineering tries to take advantage of two principal ingredients: a more flexible workforce and IT that allows for shared information (Hammer & Champy,

1993; Schnitt, 1993). To compete effectively, companies must be able to allocate human resources quickly, and then configure, and reconfigure, those resources to address whatever circumstances avail themselves. In a growing number of cases, this involves using virtual teams to handle special projects. These teams are typically cross-functional and, increasingly, they are transnational. That is, they are comprised of individuals from different nationalities located in different countries (Snow, Canney Davison, Hambrick, & Snell, 1993). One area where such teams are utilized within IBM is the International Airlines Solutions Centre (IASC). IASC is composed of a group of experts (i.e., some temporary, some permanent) who troubleshoot around the world for clients in the airline industry. Although IASC is headquartered outside London, its members are literally spread around the world. By using IT, virtual teams of specialists can be assembled with relatively short notice to meet the needs of any particular customer. If, for example, all members of the team are on the same communications network, a member in Paris can share information, ask for help, or work on a project with another located in Tokyo.

Staffing virtual teams, and coordinating their activities, is a formidable task, but one that is made easier by IT applications such as IBM's Opportunity Management System (OMSYS). With OMSYS, managers simply characterize a business opportunity and enter it into the system. The system then looks for requisite skilled resources and makes recommendations for building the team. OMSYS is similar to Resumix discussed earlier in that they both support relational data bases of employee skills, experience, and so forth. However, OMSYS goes a bit further in that the business opportunities drive the search, and the system creates the team.

Once virtual teams are in place, a host of IT systems, referred to collectively as "groupware," allow the teams to work together efficiently (Rockart & Short, 1991). Electronic mail, videoconferencing, and computer-to-computer links now facilitate types of collaboration that were not possible just a few years ago. For example, in cooperation with researchers at the University of Arizona, IBM developed GroupSystems, a collection of software tools that support parallel, anonymous, and collaborative group communications (McGoff, Hunt, Vogel, & Nunamaker, 1990). The capacity of IT to shrink time and distance has caused us to reexamine our definitions of the word "team." It used to be that teamwork almost always implied physical proximity of individuals. Today, groupware makes it possible for team members to coordinate both asynchronously (across time zones) and geographically (across remote locations) more easily than ever before (Rice & Blair, 1984; Tyran, Dennis, Vogel, & Nunamaker, 1992).

Creating network organizations

As virtual teams become an effective way of organizing work, they give rise to a broader form of network organization. Unlike a traditional hierarchy, a network organization is a configuration of independent business units (i.e., both inside and outside the firm) that pursue their respective specialties but form more or less permanent relationships with one another to offer a product, conduct a project, and so on. Organizational networks typically allow us to tap a wider range of resources, and frequently with greater speed (Snow & Snell, 1993).

A considerable HR challenge in a network organization is brokering talent. Both line managers and the HR department must work cooperatively to assemble the resources needed to offer a particular product or service. Staffing within a network organization may involve identifying, locating, and organizing human resources across companies and international borders, and the resultant pool of human assets may be used only temporarily; just as with a virtual team but on a larger scale.

Many of the systems discussed earlier, such as Resumix and OMSYS, can be used for these purposes. However, a more logistical problem associated with HR is assigning and tracking the activities of individuals within the network. Utilizing IT, network organizations can create horizontal and vertical working patterns on an ad hoc basis. To maintain coordination and control, while still reinforcing flexibility in the system, IBM developed its Basic Activity Reporting Tool (BART), a labor claiming system that allows individuals to document their activities in real time and establish prioritization among multiple projects. With BART, a given employee logs his or her hours against given projects, contracts, and customers. This documentation not only allows managers to track how an individual is allocating his or her time, but because each project can be given a priority weighting, it is possible to determine the value generated by each person's activities (e.g., is the person spending time on the contracts that are most important to the company). Although the system currently is used only for field personnel, it will soon be operational for tracking staff assignments as well. Eventually, the system will enable internal staffs to charge each other for skilled resources assigned to specific business opportunities.

IT applications have enormous potential for reducing transaction costs across business units and entire companies. In some cases, the systems can help different organizational units share rare talent. As Strassman (1985, 22–7) pointed out, "You cannot afford to have an expert in a very rare kidney disease on your team just in case you might need him or her some day . . . The technology allows you to have experts available electronically."

The flexibility afforded by such systems makes IT instrumental to company efforts to create the virtual corporation (Davidow & Malone, 1992). The challenge now is for the HR function to fully utilize these types of systems so that they are an integral part of the change effort, not an obstruction to it. All too often HR policies represent a microstructural artifact of the old business equation: that is, reinforcing stability and inhibiting change.

Changes in the HR function

In concert with the organizational transformation precipitated by IT, there is an ongoing transformation of the HR function itself. In an effort to increase responsiveness and flexibility, as well as reduce overhead costs, senior HR executives have taken a hard look at their core capabilities, and have begun outsourcing much of the work that was formerly done within the HR function. Contracting out peripheral areas shifts the cost structure by eliminating overhead, thus providing greater flexibility.

Theoretically, any aspect of HR can be outsourced. Potential partners include both internal line managers (who assume responsibility for staffing, training, and so forth) or external vendors (who perform tasks such as payroll, benefits administration, etc.). It is increasingly common, for example, to conduct executive education via cooperative arrangements with outside consultants, university faculty, and the like.

Looking into the future, IBM's goal is to use IT to deliver most HR services directly to employees and managers. This involves direct access through computer networks and telephone keypad access, or by highly efficient 800-number service centers – backed by expert systems and telephone technology with a small number of experts to handle complex issues and exceptional cases. As a result, the HR professional in the future will perform a consultant/facilitator role and will no longer simply dispense information or manage bureaucratic administrative processes.

Invariably the trend within many companies is toward much smaller HR staffs with HR representatives in the operating units becoming business partners and sharing actual line responsibility (cf. Keating & Jablonsky, 1990). IT enabled this transformation, and the competitive environment now demands it. As we have pointed out above, most of the administrative work that historically has been done by HR can now be done by automated systems or by managers using decision-support systems. Even standardized aspects of advice and counsel (e.g., dealing with a problem employee) increasingly can be done by expert systems and other forms of artificial intelligence. In the future, programmable solutions to recurring business problems will be systematized. The value added by HR personnel can perhaps best come from their ability to guide line managers through ill-defined or ambiguous problems related to organizational development. The last chapter of the story may be no HR function at all (cf. Schuler, 1990). This is a fairly extreme view, and one that may seem a bit unsettling. However, IT at least makes the idea plausible.

ESTABLISHING PRIORITIES FOR IT APPLICATION

We would argue that there is not, and should not be, a generic approach to IT usage within HR. IT is not a panacea, and any investment in technology should be undertaken only after judicious consideration is given to the organizational and HR contexts. Too often we become fascinated by the novelty of IT applications themselves, and forget that technology is merely a means to an end and not an end in itself. At its root, IT represents a control and coordination system. As with any such system, the best applications are those that support the desired strategy, structure, and operating philosophy of the host organization (Snell, 1992).

Aligning IT with organizational strategy

To effectively harness the potential of IT, top management should carefully assess how technology can support the existing strategy of the organization (cf. Mahmood & Soon, 1991). Ahituv and Neumann (1986), for example, noted that single-product firms with functional structures would be less likely to use distributed data bases as would conglomerates with completely autonomous divisions producing unrelated products. Logically, the level of IT decentralization would tend to be consistent with the overall structure of the organization. Similarly, Porter and Millar (1985) argued that companies competing as low-cost producers would be more likely to invest in IT applications that facilitate process efficiencies, whereas firms trying to differentiate themselves would utilize IT applications that enhance customer service. For both corporate and business-level strategies, the initial considerations for IT decisions revolve around how the technology will support the *current* competitive posture of the firm.

Perhaps more proactively, IT also can drive strategic capability. If organizations are contemplating strategic change, and technology is being positioned as a key enabler in that process, then IT should be viewed in terms of how it is used to formulate strategy (Henderson & Thomas, 1992; Rockart & Scott Morton, 1984). In volatile environments especially, strategic capability depends upon an organization's ability to rapidly reconfigure itself, allocating resources quickly, and leveraging knowledge from one arena to address problems and opportunities encountered in another (Prahalad, 1983). Our earlier discussions about network organizations exemplify how IT can be used as a platform for conceiving future courses of action.

Aligning IT with HR strategy

In addition to aligning IT with organizational strategy, top management should also carefully assess how IT applications fit with the HR strategy. Theoretically, HR strategy and company strategy can be completely different. For example, the organization as a whole may emphasize cost leadership, whereas the HR department may have decided to emphasize customer service. However, in most cases, we would expect the HR strategy to eventually fit with the organization's overall strategic posture.

The logical connection between HR strategy and IT is similar to that for organizational strategy. Broderick and Boudreau (1992b), for example, noted that IT applications that emphasize transaction processing/reporting/tracking would be most appropriate for an HR strategy that emphasizes cost control. Similarly, they noted the parallel between expert systems applications and a service-oriented HR strategy. Finally, they suggested that decision-support systems would be best used for innovation strategies within HR.

We would agree with the basic content of Broderick and Boudreau's (1992b) recommendations, and would only offer some additional insight into the processes by which executives might partition and prioritize IT applications. Regardless of the HR strategy employed, there are some basic guidelines about how to leverage IT in the delivery of HR services.

First, determine which customers (really customer "segments") within the organization the HR function is trying to serve. Even in small companies, it is usually a mistake to assume that all employees (e.g., line, staff, exempt, nonexempt, technical, professional) have the same needs from the HR department. At the risk of oversimplifying this stage of the process, we would suggest that the divergence of needs can frequently be seen in a top manager's preoccupation with cost containment, compared to a middle manager's concern with service, and rank and file employee's reliance on HR for representation. Each of these segments has a somewhat different orientation to the organization, and each requires different assistance from the HR department.

After segmenting the internal customer base, the next step is to determine what service offerings HR has at its disposal to meet each segment's needs. More to the point of IT, this process involves identifying applications of technology to HR, such as those we have discussed throughout this chapter. These IT applications represent "channels" for providing service to customers within the organization. In some cases, the technology can be adapted from one application to another in order to solve a particular customer problem. For example, electronic data interchanges (EDI) was originally designed to provide customers and suppliers access to each other's data, thereby reducing transaction costs and facilitating coordination. This particular technology has been adapted within HR to provide applicant tracking systems and labor-claiming devices. In the future, the technology may be further extended so that customers outside the organization can document, and purchase, the services of a contracted employee who has been aligned to that customer. This point is important because, as we have noted previously, IT applications originally implemented for one purpose (e.g., HRIS to lower costs), are frequently modified to perform many others (e.g., on-line query systems to support managerial decisions).

Assessing feasibility

Before making any IT decision within HR based purely on strategic criteria, top managers should also undertake a feasibility assessment to determine the realities of implementation. Although there may be a host of potentially beneficial uses of IT within HR, priority should be given to those that are technologically, economically, and organizationally feasible. Technological feasibility goes beyond the mere existence of the technology, it involves consideration of the match between IT used within HR and the level of technology adoption within the organization as a whole. A networked organization, for example, will have very different HR needs and channels than a company just beginning to utilize IT in their operations (Miles & Snow, 1986). Economic feasibility was discussed by Boudreau (1992) in terms of strict utility analyses that determine whether the investment pays for itself in terms of increased productivity, cost savings, and so forth. Justification of capital expenses is part of any business decision. Finally, organizational feasibility involves assessing the capacity of employees and management to accept various IT applications (Ahituv & Neuman, 1986). Organizational assessment often goes beyond rational decision making, and involves consideration of organizational cultures and individual work habits. Within our own organizations, we can find individuals who embrace new technology enthusiastically, while others resist it vehemently (Martocchio & Webster, 1992).

If the technological, economic, or organizational feasibility studies suggest that the company is not yet ready for a particular IT application, then HR may need to do some advance work in order to prepare the organization. Monsalve and Triplett (1990), for example, noted that HR plays a significant role in the introduction of new technology by identifying methods that minimize disruption and perceived threat among existing employees (Bostrom, Olfman, & Sein, 1990), providing guidance to ensure that the right technological skills are developed (e.g., computer literacy), identifying and evaluating the potential changes in relationships brought about by the new technology, and working with line managers to develop new structures that use the technology to improve service, increase productivity, and reduce costs throughout the company.

As we noted at the outset, the limiting factor in successful implementation of IT is not technology. Without exception, the parameters for implementation are determined by the company's ability to change the way it operates. If IT systems are simply injected into the existing organizations, they will most likely be rejected (Passino & Severance, 1990).

CONCLUSION

In this chapter we have tried to provide a framework that conveys to managers how they can leverage the benefits of IT within the HR function. First, HR can use IT to alleviate the administrative burden and improve productivity. This internal focus is clearly the most prevalent within HR, perhaps because it reinforces traditional values of cost containment and efficiency. However, exclusive reliance on such an approach may be most useful for HR in those stable and benign environments where internal processing issues constitute the greatest sources of concern (cf. Lawler, 1992).

IT can also be utilized within HR to enhance relational exchanges with internal and external stakeholders. For example, by providing others with remote access to employee data, HR functions can often reduce cycle time, increase the quality of service, and allow managers to solve more of their own HR-related problems. By using IT to "open up" the HR function, we take initial steps to recast the role of HR to that of a client-oriented service. The challenge with such an approach to IT is making certain that each separate HR function is well integrated into a common platform. Without some method of linking individual applications, the potential value of the entire system may otherwise be compromised.

Finally, IT plays an instrumental role in HR's efforts to transform organizations. Reengineering work processes, building virtual teams, creating network organizations, and the like, all require a more flexible form of organization. IT provides both the connectivity and speed necessary to identify, acquire, and allocate human resources with minimal constraint. In this setting, HR's role as organizational architect truly emerges; assembling and reassembling the particular configuration of human assets needed to capitalize on arising opportunities.

Certainly the capabilities afforded by IT are far greater than they were just a few years ago, and the potential organizational changes are so wide-sweeping that it is difficult to precisely describe the future of HR. Since IT is inherently a strategic variable, organizations are free to make choices about how they will prioritize IT applications, and how these applications will blend with other organizational systems. As in the past, our choices here will invariably effect the way we manage people.

NOTE

Research for this paper was supported by the Institute for the Study of Organizational Effectiveness, The Smeal College of Business Administration, Penn State University, University Park, PA. The authors would like to thank Gerald M. Czarnecki, Silvio A. Lanaro, James B. Thomas, and Mark Youndt for their contributions to this paper.

REFERENCES

Ahituv, N., & Neumann, S. (1986). *Principles of Information Systems for Management.* Dubuque, IA: W. C. Brown.

Bostrom, R. P. Olfman, L., & Sein, M. K. (1990). The importance of learning style in end-user training. *MIS Quarterly,* 14 (1), 101–19.

Boudreau, J. W. (1992). HRIS: Adding value, or just cutting costs? *HR Monthly,* May, 8–13.

Broderick, R., & Boudreau, J. W. (1992a). The evolution of computer use in human resource management: Interviews with ten leaders. *Human Resource Management,* 30 (4), 485–508.

Broderick, R., & Boudreau, J. W. (1992b). Human resource management information technology, and the competitive edge. *Academy of Management Executive,* 6 (2), 7–17.

Carr, C. (1992). PSS! Help when you need it. *Training and Development,* June, 31–8.

Culnan, M. J., & Markus, L. (1987). Information technologies: Electronic media and intraorganizational communication. In F. M. Jablin, L. L. Putnam, K. H. Roberts, & L. W. Porter (eds.), *Handbook of Organizational Communication,* 420–44. Beverly Hills, CA: Sage.

Davidow, W. H., & Malone, M. S. (1992). *The Virtual Corporation: Lessons from the world's most advanced companies.* New York: Harper Business.

Davidson, W. H., & Davis, S. M. (1992). Management and organization principles for the information economy. *Human Resource Management,* 29 (4), 365–83.

Foster, L. W., & Flynn, D. W. (1984). Management information technology: Its effects on organizational form and function. *Management Information Systems Quarterly*, 8, 229–36.

Galbraith, J. (1973). *Designing Complex Organizations*. Reading, MA: Addison-Wesley.

Hammer, M., & Champy, J. (1993). *Reengineering the Corporation*. New York: Harper Business.

Henderson, J. C., & Thomas, J. B. (1992). Aligning business and information technology domains: Strategic planning in hospitals. *Hospital & Health Services Administration*, 37 (1), 71–87.

Herren, L. M. (1989). The right recruitment technology for the 1990s. *Personnel Administrator*, 34 (4), 48–52.

Hirschorn, L. (1984). *Beyond Mechanization: Work and technology in a postindustrial age*. Cambridge, MA: MIT.

Huber, G. P. (1990). A theory of the effects of advanced information technologies on organizational design, intelligence, and decision making. *Academy of Management Journal*, 15 (1), 47–71.

Johansen, R. (1988). *Groupware: Computer support for business teams*. New York: Free Press.

Keating, P. J., & Jablonsky, S. F. (1990). *Changing Roles of Financial Management*. Morristown, NJ: Financial Executives Research Foundation.

Kinnie, N., & Arthurs, A. (1993). Will personnel people ever learn to love the computer? *Personnel Management*, June, 46–51.

Lawler, J. J. (1992). Computer-mediated information processing and decision making in human resource management. In G. R. Ferris & K. M. Rowland (eds.), *Research in Personnel and Human Resource Management*, vol. 10, pp. 301–44. Greenwich, CT: JAI Press.

Lawson, T. E. (1990). *The Competency Initiative: Standards of excellence for human resource executives*. SHRM Foundation, Minneapolis: Golle & Holmes Custom Education.

Loveman, G. W. (1988). An assessment of the productivity impact of information technology. Management in the 1990s Working Papers, No. 88–054. Sloan School of Management, MIT, Cambridge, MA.

McFarlan, F. W. (1984). Information technology changes the way you compete. *Harvard Business Review*, May–June, 98–103.

McGoff, C., Hunt, A., Vogel, D., & Nunamaker, J. (1990). IBM's Experiences with GroupSystems. *Interfaces*, 20 (6), 39–52.

Madnick, S. E. (1991). The information technology platform. In M. Scott Morton (ed.), *The Corporation of the 1990s: Information technology and organizational transformation*, 27–60. New York: Oxford University Press.

Mahmood, M. A., & Soon, S. K. (1991). A comprehensive model for measuring the potential impact of information technology on organizational strategic variables. *Decision Sciences*, 22 (4), 869–97.

Martocchio, J. J., & Webster, J. (1992). Effects of feedback and cognitive playfulness on performance in microcomputer software training. *Personnel Psychology*, 45, 553–78.

Miles, R. E., & Snow, C. C. (1986). Organizations: New concepts for new forms. *California Management Review*, 3, 62–73.

Milkovich G. T., & Boudreau, J. W. (1994). *Human Resource Management*. Burr Ridge, IL: Irwin.

Monsalve, M. A., & Triplett, A. (1990). Maximizing new technology. *HRMagazine*, March, 85–7.

Parsons, C. K. (1988). Computer technology: Implications for human resources management. In G. R. Ferris & K. M. Rowland (eds.), *Research in Personnel and Human Resource Management*, vol. 6, pp. 1–36. Greenwich, CT: JAI Press.

Passino, J. H., Jr., & Severance, D. G. (1990). Harnessing the potential of information technology for support of the new global organization. *Human Resource Management*, 29 (1), 69–76.

Porter, M. E., & Millar, V. E. (1985). How information gives you competitive advantage. *Harvard Business Review*, July–Aug., 149–60.

Prahalad, C. K. (1983). Developing strategic capability: An agenda for top management. *Human Resource Management*, 22, 237–54.

Rice, R. E., & Blair, H. H. (1984). *The New Media*. Beverly Hills, CA: Sage.

Richards-Carpenter, C. (1991a). Products of imagination. *Personnel Management*, January, 65–6.

Richards-Carpenter, C. (1991b). Strategic information: 1991 CIP Survey. *Personnel Management*, July, 19–22.

Richards-Carpenter, C. (1993). Loosening the purse strings. *Personnel Management*, January, 49–50.

Rockart, J. F., & Scott Morton, M. S. (1984). Implications of changes in information technology for corporate strategy. *Interfaces*, 14 (1), 84–95.

Rockart, J. F. & Short, J. E. (1991). The networked organization and the management of interdependence. In M. Scott Morton (ed.), *The Corporation of the 1990s: Information technology and organizational transformation*, 189–219. New York: Oxford University Press.

Schmitt, N., Gilliland, S. W., Landis, R. S., & Devine, D. (1993). Computer-based testing applied to selection of secretarial applicants. *Personnel Psychology*, 46, 149–65.

Schnitt, D. L. (1993). Reengineering the organization using information technology. *Journal of Systems Management*, January, 14–20, 41–2.

Schuler, R. S. (1990). Repositioning the human resource function: Transformation or demise? *Academy of Management Executive*, 4 (3), 49–60.

Scott Morton, M. S. (1991). Introduction. In M. Scott Morton (ed.), *The Corporation of the 1990s: Information technology and organizational transformation*, 61–92. New York: Oxford University Press.

Snell, S. A. (1992). Control theory in strategic human resources management: The mediating effect of administrative information. *Academy of Management Journal*, 35 (2), 292–327.

Snell, S. A., & Dean, J. W., Jr. (1992). Integrated manufacturing and human resource management: A human capital perspective. *Academy of Management Journal*, 35 (4), 467–504.

Snow, C. C., Canney Davison, S., Hambrick, D. C., & Snell, S. A. (1993). *Transnational Teams: A learning resources guide*. Final report, International Consortium for Executive Development Research, Lexington, MA.

Snow, C. C., & Snell, S. A. (1993). Staffing as strategy. In N. Schmitt and W. Borman (eds.), *Personnel Selection in Organizations*, 448–78. San Francisco: Jossey-Bass.

173

Strassman, P. (1985). Conversation with Paul Strassman. *Organization Dynamics*, 14 (2), 19–34.

Tinsley, D. B. (1990). Future flash: Computers facilitate the HR function. *Personnel*, February, 32–5.

Towers Perrin (1992). *Priorities for Competitive Advantage: An IBM–Towers Perrin study*. New York: Towers Perrin.

Tyran, C. K., Dennis, A. R., Vogel, D. R., & Nunamaker, J. F., Jr. (1992). The application of electronic meeting technology to support strategic management. *MIS Quarterly*, 16 (3), 313–34.

Venkatraman, N. (1991). IT-induced business reconfiguration. In M. Scott Morton (ed.), *The Corporation of the 1990s: Information technology and organizational transformation*, 122–58. New York: Oxford University Press.

Weill, P., & Olson, M. H. (1989). Managing investment in information technology: Mini case examples and implications. *MIS Quarterly*, 13 (1), 3–17.

Yates, J., & Benjamin, R. I. (1991). The past and present as a window on the future. In M. Scott Morton (ed.), *The Corporation of the 1990s: Information technology and organizational transformation*, 61–92. New York: Oxford University Press.

Zuboff, S. (1988). *In the Age of the Smart Machine: The future of work and power*. New York: Basic Books.

☐ Chapter 10 ☐

Accountability in Human Resources Systems

Gerald R. Ferris, Terence R. Mitchell, Patrick J. Canavan,
Dwight D. Frink, and Heidi Hopper

INTRODUCTION

To most people, the concept of accountability very simply means being held answerable for one's actions, and it is assumed to be a fundamental principle of organization. However, the media is filled with stories about various ways individuals and organizations attempt to maximize their own self-interests, which calls into question our general assumption that proper checks, balances, and indeed accountability mechanisms are present in organizations.

We have long been aware of such practices as price fixing, insider trading, and falsification of records and reports as examples of abuses carried out for either personal gain, or to increase organizational profits. More recently, we have witnessed lapses in accountability associated with human resources systems such as compensation in general, and chief executive officer (CEO) pay in particular, as well as in staffing and evaluation systems.

The prevalence of such dysfunctional behaviors in the management of human resources suggests that we need to develop a more informed understanding of accountability if we hope to design and implement mechanisms that bring about desirable and effective organizational behaviors. The purpose of this chapter is to pursue a more in-depth understanding of accountability in human resources systems. In the process, we examine theory and research on accountability (e.g., Tetlock, 1983, 1985, 1992), as well as work on control systems (e.g., Ouchi & Maguire, 1975), agency theory (e.g., Barney, 1990; Williamson, 1975), and monitoring (e.g., Larson & Callahan, 1990; Piturro, 1989), all of which emphasize ways in which employee behavior is observed, monitored, recorded, rewarded, and punished. We also examine the tensions or dilemmas that emerge and must be adequately addressed in establishing effective accountability mechanisms. Finally, we observe the nature of accountability in practice today in organizations, and we discuss future directions based on the integration of theory, research, and practice.

THE NATURE OF ACCOUNTABILITY

Accountability can be defined from an external (to the person) or internal perspective, but in either case the emphasis is on some type of external review of behavior with salient rewards and punishments contingent on that review. In many cases, it is defined as being answerable to some person or group for performing up to a particular rule or standard, or behaving in a prescribed manner. While some research focuses on organizational accountability (e.g., Dalton & Kesner, 1987; Baucus & Near, 1991; Szwajkowski, 1985), the thrust of our focus here is on individual or personal accountability.

In a general sense, personal accountability is a mechanism for enforcing organizational norms and rules as well as legal prescriptions and restraints (Tetlock, 1985, 1992). It is a link between individual employees and the organizational system to which they belong (Tetlock, Skitka, & Boettger, 1989). Working within any social system implies some regulation and control of behavior, and failure to account successfully for one's actions can lead to censure, punishment, and termination from the organization, as well as legal and financial penalties (Schlenker, 1982; Scott & Lyman, 1968; Pollack, 1990).

Externally, accountability is defined in terms of (1) a system of knowing about and evaluating someone's behavior vis-à-vis some standard, and (2) a system of rewards and punishments that are contingent upon these evaluations. Internally, accountability reflects these external conditions in the knowledge and desire to behave in such a way that the regulations, rules, and expectations will be complied with and met. Feelings of accountability reflect a desire to meet external expectations, and strong feelings of accountability are likely to have significant impacts on one's thoughts, feelings, and actions (Weigold & Schlenker, 1991).

The research on personal accountability and its influence on organizational behavior covers a wide variety of topics. For example, accountability has been shown to influence performance evaluation (Klimoski & Inks, 1990), the demonstration and effectiveness of political or influence behavior (Fandt & Ferris, 1990; Ferris & Judge, 1991), the complexity of decision strategies (McAllister, Mitchell, & Beach, 1979; Tetlock & Boettger, 1989), bargaining behavior (Pruitt, 1981), risk taking (Weigold & Schlenker, 1991), and ethical behavior (Ferris & Mitchell, 1991; Trevino, 1986; Brief, Dukerich, & Doran, 1991). We are interested in accountability in human resources systems, and we examine such systems more clearly in the next section.

ACCOUNTABILITY IN HUMAN RESOURCES SYSTEMS

In the management of the human element in organizations, there is a need to reassess the use of the model developed with manufacturing organizations as it applies to human resources decisions. In that model, materials are requisitioned according to production schedules, and bought on a market by the purchasing department. Economies of scale are used for purchases when feasible, and a rapid throughflow of resources (e.g., just-in-time management) is an objective as well. However, in dealing with human resources, planners and managers can no longer rely on simple methods of materials requisition from standard suppliers with systematic warehousing and retrieval for use when needed. The social forces and interactions inherent in dealing with people (Ferris & Mitchell, 1987) require a different set of methods and rules. Now the decisions are made concerning an element of organizations that not only has the capacity to make its own decisions, but the people making up the human element in the organization will not always have perspectives or agenda that are the same, or even compatible with the organization or its management. The fact that people are perceivers and processors of information indicates that there is a need to bring these diverse perceivers, processors, and agenda together to agree on common standards that comply with organizational, legal, and ethical guidelines. In addition, rewards for compliance and punishment for noncompliance should be part of any system of accountability. Introducing such systems provides a host of dilemmas in integrating and coordinating human resources. These dilemmas are especially relevant to the staffing, evaluation, compensation, and outflow functions of human resources systems.

Staffing

Judge and Ferris (1992) reviewed the staffing process from the perspective of organizational fit, which may be the modus operandi for most organizations. This model suggests that we select people who "fit" the organization in terms of their beliefs, values, and personality. Alternatively, one may approach the staffing function, including internal mobility, from a rational perspective, using strictly job- and task-related criteria for judgment. This model suggests that you select the person who is most likely to perform well on a particular job. In either case there must be some mechanisms in place that establish standards and support adherence to these standards before the decision criteria can be effectively set forth. Even if it were possible to minimize subjectivity in pursuit of a rational model, it seems unlikely that personal perceptions and biases could be adequately addressed without a means of holding the decision makers accountable for their decisions. Yet, Rynes and Boudreau (1986) indicated that college recruiters are not held accountable for their selection decisions, and practical experience suggests that recruiters, in general, are seldom held accountable for those they recruit. Without any such mechanism, it is conceivable that the selection process could become highly personalized, value laden, and unconstrained. An extreme example is Hollywood's notorious casting couch. Individuals using this type of method as a selection procedure are unconstrained because they are unaccountable

for the selection process, the selection decisions, or both.

There are multiple possible sources of accountability in the selection process. They include organizational policy, supervisors of both the decision makers and the employees, industry standards, professional and certifying organizations, and the legal system. Within the legal system, there are three main areas of accountability. These include the body of corporate law and regulation, licensing and certifying agencies, and civil rights and fairness laws. Typically, these provide a very loose web of constraint on selection decisions, but a web that may be tightening. In recent times, companies have been found liable for damages resulting from employees' illegal acts on the grounds that the employer should have known the employee's propensities for those acts through the selection process.

Because the selection process is the most important element in determining the composition of the human resources of an organization, it seems appropriate that the staffing decision process be subject to scrutiny to enhance the usefulness of these decisions to the organization. Accountability cannot be interpreted as a universal solution for staffing decisions, however. Gordon, Rozelle, and Baxter (1988) found increased stereotyping for laboratory experiment subjects who felt accountable for staffing decisions. The issue of both positive and negative effects of accountability is one to which we return.

Performance evaluation

There are two fundamental elements in the area of performance evaluation: the definition of performance, and the means of evaluating performance as defined. Accountability provides a means of linking these two elements, as well as providing a part of the basis by which the elements are approached. Accountability for conduct is a universally accepted norm (Tetlock, 1985, 1992), and provides the basis for social structure by seeing individuals as agents of their own actions (Cummings & Anton, 1990; Inzerilli & Rosen, 1983), and therefore subject to evaluation. Thus, performance evaluation is defined as an accountability mechanism with the basic intention of serving as a means of organizational control (Eisenhardt, 1985; Ouchi & Maguire, 1975). So, for the ratee, performance evaluation is both based on and helps define performance, and also provides information about how well standards are being met. The closeness of the linkages between the evaluations and the outcomes (rewards, punishments) of those evaluations determines the influence of accountability mechanisms upon the behavior of the ratee (Cummings & Anton, 1990).

This defining process also forms a psychological contract between the ratee and the organization that becomes a part of the basis for the employees' perceptions of organizational justice (Cummings & Anton, 1990). As a representative of the organization, the rater, as well as the organization itself as a social and legal entity, has the onus for fair evaluations, based on appropriate and useful performance criteria, and for the tightness of the linkage between the evaluation and any outcomes from that evaluation. It is therefore appropriate to insert a set of accountability mechanisms for the organization's performance evaluation system and methods.

This dual nature of organizational control and responsibility is clearly represented in the area of performance monitoring. For example, in highly computerized environments it is possible to unobtrusively monitor employees via their use of the computer networks. It is relatively simple in this type environment to impose very tight behavioral controls and very tight evaluation–outcome linkages. However, it is also possible that this may negatively influence perceptions of justice and fairness in the organization, and it also raises a series of ethical questions concerning, for example, invasion of privacy.

Accountability mechanisms seem even more important in light of the potentially ambiguous and political nature of performance evaluations in most organizations (Ferris & Judge, 1991). Two potentially biasing conditions in the performance evaluation process are subjectivity and affectivity. Subjectivity permits individual rater discretion, and affectivity (liking) may then influence performance evaluation decisions. Accountability mechanisms may be able to mitigate the biasing effects of these conditions by clarifying standards and evaluating the rater according to those standards. Two of the means for holding raters accountable are (1) to include the rating process in the raters' own performance evaluation, and (2) to provide feedback to the ratee. Klimoski and Inks (1990) found that raters modified ratings toward the ratees' expected ratings. They suggested, however, that ratings may be distorted when face-to-face feedback is expected, and that this distortion may occur in two different ways: by amount of distortion, and by direction of distortion. It is conceivable that such modifications of ratings actually may be useful in that raters' own individual biases against certain types or persons may be reduced, and also that a restriction of range in ratings may result in fewer nontask considerations influencing the ratings, thereby increasing validity. Of course, biases that are random, not monitored, or misunderstood could hardly be useful or appropriate. Two implications from this particular point are that much more research is needed in this area, and that the type of accountability mechanisms employed need to be carefully selected and implemented to match the purpose and method of the evaluation system. For example, Martell and Borg (1993) found a restriction of range in performance evaluations when a panel evaluated individuals. The question then remains regarding the accuracy and validity of the restricted-range evaluations, and whether the restricted-range evaluations were more or less useful to the particular organizational context.

178

A third means of making raters and organizations accountable for performance evaluations is to ensure tight linkages between evaluations and any outcomes from those evaluations. If goals are set, do the participants follow up on them? How tight are the linkages to compensation? Are promotion recommendations or other incentives realized?

Compensation

Perhaps no area of accountability in human resources systems has received more press than CEO compensation (Crystal, 1991; Gomez-Mejia & Balkin, 1992a). These authors suggest that the CEO compensation system is a paramount example of what can happen when there are no constraints on the decisions other than token self-justification to a board or committee, who has a vested interest in justifying the salary structure rather than monitoring it, because the members are likely CEOs themselves. A common method for establishing CEO salaries is for the CEO to hire a salary consultant who makes a market-based recommendation to the CEO, who includes the recommendation in a report to the board of directors (Crystal, 1991). The common rationale for the level of salary is that, in order to be competitive, the firm must have the very best leadership, and if the recommended salary is not paid, the CEO will leave for a better offer. We feel that this rationale is very clearly separated from any performance or other measurable criteria. That is, if the firm is doing poorly, they need a "savior" and must pay a premium for that "savior." If the firm is doing well, they need to pay a premium in order to (1) reward the leader, (2) maintain the high image appropriate for success, and (3) ensure continued success. Monks and Minow (1991) recommend stockholder groups becoming active in the calling of both the CEOs and the corporate system to account for, what some perceive to be, excessive and detrimental compensation practices. However, recent writing suggests that pay for performance is becoming a more acceptable criterion for setting CEO pay (Brown, 1992).

In other aspects of compensation, there are also movements toward increased accountability. As mentioned above, one is a clear linkage between the performance evaluation and compensation systems. This linkage has potential to impose accountability on compensation decisions for individuals. Another is the increased emphasis on linking compensation systems to strategic organizational objectives (Gomez-Mejia & Balkin, 1992a). This linkage has the potential to impose accountability on the compensation policy for the entire organization. Underlying this notion of strategy-compensation accountability linkages is the concept of responsibility for firm performance.

Compensation analysis often focuses on either market forces or equity perceptions from a general policy perspective, and sometimes includes individual performance levels or specifies a particular level within a range that is set by the above policies. Increasingly, there are attempts to institute team or group concepts into the process. Seldom, however, do we find any constituency willing to assume responsibility for firm performance. Generally, this level of accountability is reserved for coaches of athletic teams and independent business people and entrepreneurs. The highest levels of compensation accountability would include linkages between performance and compensation. It is not assumed, however, that such practices are universally beneficial. That is, accountability can potentially have adverse effects.

Human resources outflow

Within the context of outflow, there are three general areas that seem especially relevant for discussions of accountability. They are (1) the reasons or purposes for outflow decisions, (2) the sources of outflow decisions, and (3)

179

ethical and civic responsibility for outflow decisions and policies. There are three general types of outflows, which are in turn relevant to the purpose of the outflow decisions. These are quits, layoffs, and terminations.

Voluntary turnover (i.e., quits) is often examined in the context of job satisfaction (e.g., Lee & Mitchell, 1994). Accountability in this context seems useful, but might require exit interviews to determine the bases for quits. Supervisors could be held accountable for levels of turnover, if, in fact, this turnover may be indicative of inappropriate managerial actions.

As noted, accountability has been suggested as a factor involved in the demonstration and effectiveness of political behavior in organizations (Fandt & Ferris, 1990; Ferris & Judge, 1991). Politics can influence various aspects of human resources systems, including inflow, throughflow, and outflow. Layoff and termination outflow decisions have become the focus of considerable attention in recent years due to the massive downsizing of American industry, and the tightening up of equal employment opportunity law. Both of these factors have made such outflow decisions the subject of careful scrutiny. In fact, called into question has been the rational basis on which such decisions are made, and instead politics has been suggested to replace rationality as the impetus for layoff and termination decisions in many instances (Ferris, Howard, & Bergin, in press). Indeed, it has been argued that clear specification of decision criteria and the implementation of accountability mechanisms would reduce the extent to which politics could influence such human resources staffing decisions (Judge & Ferris, 1992).

THEORY AND RESEARCH RELATED TO ACCOUNTABILITY

Accountability has become one of the most frequently discussed business concepts in recent times. Given the prevalence of such issues as corporate responsibility to the environment, professional malpractice, toxic waste, pollution, insider trading, saving and loan improprieties, and so forth, it follows that calls for accountability are common. In spite of the common acceptance of the usefulness of accountability for correcting these wrongs, and the general acceptance that accountability for behavior is socially appropriate, this may be one of the least researched areas of organizational governance and social relationships. Organizational control mechanisms have been researched, however, and the theories developed concerning behavioral compliance in organizations are relevant for discussions of accountability. Three bodies of literature are especially relevant to discussions of accountability in organizations. They are agency theory, control theory, and performance monitoring.

Agency theory

Agency theory describes the relationship that exists when one person, the principal, employs another, the agent, to represent the principal's interests, usually because the agent has specialized skills, knowledge, or abilities that permit the agent to perform more effectively than the principal (Gomez-Mejia & Balkin, 1992a, b). Agency theory posits that these individuals will act in their own interests in maximizing their own utility to the extent permitted by the constraints imposed on the agent, and thus such constraints are necessary (Jensen & Meckling, 1976). The costs of these monitoring systems are borne by the owner in exchange for the increased effectiveness offered by the agency relationship.

The fundamental assumption of agency theory, that people will behave opportunistically, forms the basis of theory and recommendations. The theory assumes that there is a perpetual tension between the objectives of the owners (principals) and the managers (agents) in which the agent will continually seek means of self-advancement at the expense of the organization. The theory generally limits the potential for mutual goals, or other intrinsic motivations for compliance. Instead of capturing the complexities of interpersonal behavior in organizations, agency theory simplifies it to the point of suggesting that people are generally driven to lie, cheat, steal, and so forth, in efforts to increase self-fulfillment at others' expense (Barney, 1990).

Efforts to reduce shirking or use of organizational resources for self-serving purposes can be approached by two methods, monitoring and bonding (Eisenhardt, 1985; Gomez-Mejia & Balkin, 1992a, b; Jensen & Meckling, 1976; Ouchi & Maguire, 1975). Monitoring includes the imposition of observational methods to track agent behavior, with particular reference to their work performance. Bonding refers to mechanisms by which the agent guarantees self-limitation of self-serving behaviors (Jensen & Meckling, 1976). Monitoring is not feasible where there are high levels of ambiguity or autonomy (Gomez-Mejia & Balkin, 1992b), and in such cases, agency theory recommends incentives or rewards to elicit compliance. By taking this approach, agency theory explicitly states the necessity of accountability mechanisms, and indicates that different types of mechanisms are appropriate under different conditions. However, agency theory does not specifically address the types of accountability mechanisms, the underlying psychological mechanisms, the influence of multiple audience constituencies, or the dimensions of accountability. In short, agency theory proposes that accountability is an essential feature for the agency relationship to function, but effectively leaves the development of accountability to others.

Agency theory, like control theory described below, is generally concerned with the problem of behavioral compliance with organizational prescriptions and objectives. The theory generally describes a problem, and proposes categories of approaches to deal with the problem. It rests on the assumption of perpetual tension between the organization's and the agent's goals, and the balance of power in this tension must be maintained (Gomez-Mejia & Balkin, 1992a). In such a view, control is relatively simple in that it only requires equal force, or power, on either end of the tension to maintain appropriate behavior at an equilibrium level. Violation of this tension perspective, by altering the assumption or by increasing the complexity of the determinants of human behavior, necessarily takes the problem beyond the context of agency theory, and calls for another approach.

The direct relevance, then, of agency theory to accountability is that, first, behavioral control mechanisms are necessary in any agency relationship because behavior will otherwise be unconstrained and self-serving. Second, there are multiple methods of influencing behavior toward compliance. By not addressing the sociological or psychological aspects of behavioral intentions or controls, agency theory cannot deliver testable hypotheses regarding accountability per se. Instead, agency theory prescribes general types of mechanisms according to the levels of ambiguity or autonomy within the agency relationship. When either of these conditions are present, incentives or rewards are prescribed, and when they are absent, performance monitoring (evaluation) is recommended as the lowest cost and most effective means of behavioral control. As seen below, these prescriptions are quite similar to those proposed by organizational control theory prescriptions (Eisenhardt, 1985).

Organizational control theory

Control theory is concerned with the ways behavior is constrained or controlled in organizational settings. Based on a cybernetic model, it fundamentally asserts that standards need to be established for behavior, and the standards are enforced by rewards or sanctions, either substantive or social. The means of enforcement are dependent on contextual (i.e., product, market, and technological) conditions, and are determined by the organizational environment rather than individual concerns (Eisenhardt, 1985; Ouchi, 1977; Ouchi & Maguire, 1975). The mechanisms, or strategies, used are assigned to two categories, performance evaluations and minimizing divergence of preferences. The category of performance evaluations includes monitoring and rewarding performance. The level of difficulty of evaluating performance determines the type of control mechanism used, which is classified as either outcome-based controls or behavior-based controls (Eisenhardt, 1985; Snell, 1992). Where the processes which lead to desired outcomes are ambiguous, and neither the processes nor the outcomes are easily measured, the second category, minimizing individual divergence of preferences is used (Eisenhardt, 1985; Gomez-Mejia & Balkin, 1992a; Ouchi, 1977; Snell, 1992). Techniques for increasing homogeneity of preferences include selection, socialization, training, and other means of matching internalized behaviors with organizational objectives. From an accountability perspective, the first category calls for externally imposed accountability mechanisms, and the second category is dependent on internalized, or self-accountability, mechanisms. Ouchi and Maguire (1975) alluded to this by stating that organizations need two means of control, one for organizational needs and one for individual needs.

Like accountability, control theory is based on the assumption that people are agents of their own actions, and thus are subject to reward, sanction, or other treatment based on that agency (Tetlock, 1985, 1992). The effort, then, is to try to conform behavior to organizationally desired standards. This aspect of control theory is captured in the cybernetic concept of iterative fluctuations around the standard, much as a thermostat controls temperature by permitting fluctuations within a given range around the desired temperature. This is conceptually distinguished from

the constant-tension assumption of agency theory. In somewhat of a contrast, agency theory is less concerned with the individuals' status of self-agency, but instead sees agency relationships as characterized by divergent interests, and thus seeks to constrain behavior to a desired status, or mode, at an acceptable equilibrium.

As an alternative, some authors writing about accountability (Tetlock et al., 1989) imply the possibility of an escalation of commitment to the behavioral or decision options chosen (Staw, 1976, 1981). That is, people will internalize an action over time, and continue to behave according to that standard even when monitoring or rewards and punishments are removed. This conceptualization of accountability also corresponds with the control theory perspective that individuals' objectives are not necessarily at odds with the organizations' objectives, in contrast with agency theory (Eisenhardt, 1985). Both the accountability perspective and control theory allow variability in objectives.

Another significant departure of accountability theory from both control theory and agency theory is the role of rewards and sanctions. While the distinction may be subtle, it is nevertheless important for adequate testing of accountability hypotheses. In organization theory, rewards and sanctions are implicit (i.e., unstated) as they are inherent in performance evaluation processes (Eisenhardt, 1985). In agency theory, reward is an explicit element of agency costs (Jensen & Meckling, 1976). In both conceptualizations, the reward or sanction itself is the motivator via reinforced expectancies. In an accountability perspective, however, it is the perceptions about probabilities of outcomes, and the perceived desirability or severity of the rewards or sanctions, and what these mean to the image of self in the social context, that defines how one responds to behavioral or decision choice events (Cummings & Anton, 1990; Snell, 1992; Tetlock et al., 1989). In each case, it becomes essential to provide linkages between the behavior and outcomes for the particular outcome to have influence in the long term. However, in the accountability literature, it is the subjective variables, such as feelings about accountability (Cummings & Anton, 1990) and perceptions of audience characteristics (Tetlock et al., 1989) that are viewed as the causal variables of interest.

These three conceptualizations are useful in concert, however, because, to a large extent, they are complementary. Agency theory states that the agent will maximize his or her own utility, and mechanisms must be in place to make sure the utility of the principle and agent are similar. Control theory modifies that extreme position, suggesting the possibility of either convergent or divergent objectives, allowing internalization among the options for control mechanisms. These two perspectives, then, imply the necessity for accountability mechanisms to align the objectives and efforts of all constituencies for the overall benefit of the organization. Accountability, in turn, investigates the environment, objectives, and constituencies to determine the relationships between these elements and the behaviors and decisions that result from perceptions about these elements. An oversimplification of this conceptual relationship is that, essentially, accountability compliments agency and control theories by picking up where they leave off. The mechanisms underlying agency theory and control theory perspectives of behavioral compliance, again, are the same as those which form the basis for the accountability paradigm in that people are agents of their own actions and decisions, and are thus liable to be answerable to others for their actions and decisions. However, it is their perception of these externalities that cause their behavior. This fundamental axiom of behavior forms the basis for all social control systems.

Because of the perceptual nature of this conceptualization of accountability, this perspective suggests that the effectiveness of organizational control mechanisms hinges on the tightness of the behavior-evaluation-reward/sanction linkages, as well as the appropriateness of the rewards and sanctions for the desired outcomes. Typically, the linkage between human resource management practices and organizational outcomes is a complex one, with several other variables influencing the processes. This suggests that the relationships are messy at best, and therefore efforts to increase compliance with expectations are not nearly as effective as organizational stakeholders might wish.

Performance monitoring

A third area of study that seems relevant to accountability discussions is performance monitoring. Performance monitoring concerns the methods and sources of information gathering regarding performance (Larson & Callahan, 1990). There are three salient issues in this area of research that are notable here. One is the effect of monitoring itself, the second is the linkage between monitoring and outcomes from monitoring activities, and the third is the perceived motivations and purposes for monitoring.

Komaki (1986) found that the only significant behavioral category difference distinguishing effective managers from ineffective ones was the monitoring of work performance. One reason suggested for the increased effectiveness was that the quality of information the supervisor had was a function of this increased observation and sampling. Monitoring allowed for more accurate assessment of performance, thereby permitting the supervisor to make rewards and consequences more contingent on performance. In this scenario, an accountability perspective would suggest that workers felt accountable to their supervisor for their direct outputs, and responded with better performance.

Larson and Callahan (1990) extended this line of reasoning, arguing that there may be other motivating processes associated with monitoring that affect work productivity. They posited that Social Information Processing theory (Salancik & Pfeffer, 1978) was applicable, and that workers used the monitoring process as cues to influence their beliefs about the importance of the work, and responded favorably even without any outcomes tied to the monitoring process. In this view, the mere fact that monitoring was occurring serves to infer a higher level of importance to the monitored tasks, thus the effect was through perceptions of task importance. Ferris, Fedor, Rowland, and Porac (1985) provided support for this notion in demonstrating that monitoring by an evaluative observer increased subjects' perceptions of the significance of the task on which they were working. Here, an accountability perspective would suggest that workers were anticipating being required to defend their outputs to someone, either an external audience or themselves, and responded with more effectiveness. This perspective is more closely aligned with the social facilitation concept (Zajonc, 1965), where the presence of an evaluative observer elicits heightened awareness and subsequent output effects. It also deals with these behaviors from a more fundamental conceptualization of human nature (Tetlock, 1985, 1992; Zajonc, 1965). That is, the accountability/ social facilitation explanation provides a path to the response that is automatically processed, rather than subject to more complex controlled cognitive processing. The Social Information Processing explanation, on the other hand, implies greater cognitive effort to come to similar conclusions.

AMBIGUITIES OF ACCOUNTABILITY

So far, we have made it sound as if being held accountable in organizations is viewed as a good thing from many theoretical and practical perspectives. If we simply tell people what constitutes desired behavior, and put in place appropriate monitoring devices and rewards and punishments, functional organ-

izational behavior is sure to follow. Unfortunately, there are a number of tensions or dilemmas that arise when accountability is introduced that will need to be addressed by theory, research, and practice.

Control versus reactance

By introducing an accountability system, an organization is by definition putting limits on acceptable behavior. Controlling behavior by rules, monitoring, and rewards and punishment was an integral part of early organization theory (Barnard, 1938; Scott, 1974), and indeed has been a fundamental part of organizations.

But reactance is a natural response by individuals to controls or limitations imposed on their actions (Brehm, 1966). The notion inherent in reactance is that people attempt to restore freedom of choice where it is limited by outside forces. By prohibiting various actions that may have been acceptable in the past, there are bound to be some feelings of reactance on the part of employees. While most people will probably not rush out and engage in illegal actions or perform poorly because certain behaviors have peen prohibited or standards clarified, people may still resent the imposition of the system because it restricts their freedom and self-control.

Furthermore, such resentment can hurt organizations in other ways. For example, while some individuals might not behave unethically or perform poorly themselves, they may not report others who do. Thus, the notion of behaving correctly because one *wants to* as opposed to *has to* is an important issue to the foundations of organizational control theories, and one to which we return below.

Creativity versus conformity

A second concern is that accountability systems will limit creativity. Staw and Boettger (1990), for example, demonstrated that creative, helpful actions on the part of subordinates were inhibited when expectations about how to behave were specified as part of a formal goal-setting system. Tetlock (1983, 1985) and Schlenker (1982) have suggested that conformity and conservatism are the results of accountability, and Weigold and Schlenker (1991) found that risk taking may be reduced as well. In addition, Schnake and Dumler (1993) have suggested that accountability may inhibit people from "going the extra mile."

Apparently, making people accountable may get the explicit behavior desired, but may inhibit the divergent thinking or creativity needed for difficult problem solving. This dilemma may affect some areas (e.g., decision making) more than other areas (e.g., ethical behavior). However, as Trevino and Youngblood (1990) have shown, higher levels of moral reasoning (Kohlberg, 1969) often require complex decisions among competing alternatives based on equally attractive moral principles. Accountability may increase ethical behavior through conformity, but reduce creative problem solving and risk taking which may be needed for particularly difficult problems.

Individual values versus organizational values

Ethical dilemmas are often described as situations where individuals want to do the right thing based on their own values, but are overwhelmed by social forces to comply with the values of their boss or the prevailing culture. Brief, Dukerich, and Doran (1991) demonstrated that one's personal values were swamped by the expectations of their boss. As Pollack (1990) stated, in some cases top managers "put forth performance goals with the message 'I don't care how you do it, just do it.'" Or they implicitly encourage wrongdoing, but are protected from its consequences.

However, the opposite case is of interest as well: that is, the issue of how people behave when both managers and the prevailing culture support appropriate behavior. What do they do when accountability systems are in place? Inappropriate behavior may still occur, but in this case it will be the individual's beliefs and values that are the cause. Thus, the relevant tension here is when the individual who wants or may be inclined to do something inappropriate is confronted by a system that makes him or her accountable for their actions. The tension here is between what one wants to do based on their own beliefs and values versus the pressure brought to bear by organizational accountability.

Process versus outcome

Another distinction that is important is that in some cases people can be held accountable for outcomes while in others they are accountable for the process. For example, a sales person or customer service representative traditionally would be evaluated on outcome measures such as sales or customer complaints. In these situations, the means to the end are left unaccountable. However, one could look at other variables that are more process-oriented. The sales person could be given standards with respect to the number of cold calls made each week. The customer service representative's "friendliness" could be evaluated by having a human resources employee call in a complaint, and assess how the representative handled it.

Even in situations where there is some mechanism for process accountability for such things as values, attitudes, principles, and so forth, there is a possibility of conflict in choosing between the conditions or mechanisms of accountability. There is usually a preference for perceived objectivity in mechanisms of accountability for outcome, or performance, measures. For other types of characteristics such as effort, values, or attitudes, there may be more inherent subjectivity, and therefore ambiguity. In such cases, it is likely that the subjective variables will not be weighed as heavily as the more objective ones because they can offer alternative explanations or justifications more easily due to their ambiguity.

Supervisor versus peer versus others

The audience or constituency to which one is accountable is a critical distinction. While the organization likely has some formal, or at least semiformal, organizational control mechanisms in place, there are other audiences that are possibly more salient, as well as more influential, to the individual. Work groups and the informal organization have the capacity for enforcing behavioral norms by both overt and covert social sanctions, and indeed, we are seeing an increased organization of work at the work group or team level. Katz and Kahn (1978) suggested that one's work identity is defined by the perceived roles that accompany the position the individual occupies. These roles are defined by the interactions the individual has with the tasks, coworkers, managers, and other sources. The implication for this discussion is that these other sources of interaction have notable influences on individual behavior. While these influences may not normally be considered in discussions of accountability in organizations, this is exactly our point. Accountability is a complex concept that must include alternative sources of influence and competing constituencies if the institutional mechanisms are to be effectively understood.

Another aspect of this audience distinction in accountability is that not only are there multiple audiences, or constituencies, that will often have differing objectives, standards, and means concerning accountability, but these audiences thus compete for responsiveness from the individual. Individuals must have some sense of sensitivity to these social mechanisms in order to be effective (Schlenker & Weigold, 1989; Tetlock, 1992). This suggests that at least three different constituencies are placing accountability

demands on an individual in many circumstances; the supervisor, coworkers, and self. As mentioned above, these potentially conflicting demands may have the effect of inhibiting creativity or divergent thinking that may, in fact, be precisely what is needed for dealing with multiple constituencies and competing demands. In such instances, predictability may become very difficult at best, as one would have to predict which combination of accountability conditions or mechanisms will have the most influence, and thus be the causal agent. Of course, optimally there would be agreement between these constituencies, and there often is, otherwise the relationship between the individual and the organization would likely be severed. However, this condition can obviously not be assumed, and the dilemma regarding which constituencies will have the dominant influence (or be the most successful in influencing behavior) will invade most situations.

Compliance versus internalization

A final distinction summarizes some of the dilemmas mentioned above. Basically, we want people to behave appropriately, but we don't want to have to force them to do it. Ideally, they will do it because they want to, because it is their internal belief and value system that produces such actions.

The distinction between doing something because you are told to do it (compliance) and because you think it is the appropriate thing to do (internalization) was first articulated by Kelman (1958) and elaborated in his recent book (Kelman & Hamilton, 1989). What we want is a system of accountability that would lead to the internalization of organizationally appropriate beliefs and values. If this goal is accomplished, we would supposedly be able to remove the monitoring and checking up, as well as the rewards and punishments, and people would still behave appropriately.

In summary, accountability systems can

influence behavior. However, we would prefer systems that did not create reactance, reduce creativity, and be followed out of compliance rather than internalization. In order to develop such systems, we need to understand the psychological processes that produce feelings of accountability, and we need to explore various ways in which these feelings can be influenced. The next section discusses these topics.

TOWARD A THEORY OF ACCOUNTABILITY

Based on the foregoing issues and concerns, we have proposed a general working theory of accountability in human resources systems.

Definition

Accountability is defined as the extent to which a person's behavior is observed and evaluated by others, with important rewards and punishments being contingent upon those evaluations. There are some important components of this definition that need elaboration. First, it focuses on behavior as well as outcomes. Our concern is with both the particular actions one chooses, as well as the consequences or outcomes of those actions. Second, the focus is external. Accountability in organizations means that there is an external evaluative force (Tetlock, 1992). Internal evaluations may be important (Schlenker & Weigold, 1989), but our conceptualization of accountability in human resources systems implies an external evaluative mechanism. Third, external evaluations without contingent rewards are insufficient. Evaluation does not produce salient feelings of accountability unless important social, professional, or economic rewards are contingent upon the evaluation.

The organizational objectives are to have people behave in ways that are goal-oriented (i.e., consistent with the organization's goals), fit with the task and setting, and are appropriate, honest, and ethical. Increased accountability feelings should increase these behaviors. However, in order to achieve these objectives, we must understand the environmental or situational causes of accountability feelings, how these external factors influence cognitive processes, and the consequences of these psychological deliberations.

Causes of accountability

We believe there are three main contextual factors that increase feelings of accountability. First, there are laws, rules, and regulations. Organizations have legal constraints and prescriptions that influence the behavior of their members. These may vary from demands for data about expenditures, hiring practices, or environmental impacts to restraints on unethical behavior, such as bribes or expense account abuses. Mitchell and Scott (1990) have discussed some of these laws and rules that are external to organizations, and that prescribe appropriate behavior.

A second influence on, or cause of, accountability is the way in which an employee's behavior or performance is evaluated. When people know that their behavior is subject to, and subsequent rewards are contingent on, regular systematic evaluations, they feel more accountable. Some evaluation system characteristics that seem to increase these feelings are the frequency of evaluations, the number of evaluators, the formality of the evaluations, the strength of the linkages between the evaluation and the outcomes of the evaluation, and the openness of access to results (Mitchell, 1993).

Third, and perhaps of most importance as causes of accountability, are mechanisms of social control. These mechanisms include observability factors (e.g., monitoring, closeness of supervision), which result in evaluation apprehension (Ferris & Mitchell, 1987), as well as expectations communicated by salient others (Ferris & Judge, 1991). Accountability is significantly influenced by what others expect (Tetlock, 1985, 1992), how they gather information about fulfilling those expectations, and how they will treat us if we deviate from those expectations.

Accountability and cognitive processing

The intermediate step between the foregoing organizational or social factors that should enhance accountability, and the behavioral and organizational consequences is the cognitive processing engaged in by the individual. Whereas a number of theoretical perspectives could be used to describe these dynamics, we believe that control theory (Klein, 1989; Hyland, 1988) best captures the essence of this process. This approach suggests that people choose their behaviors based on a cybernetic-type model where there are behavioral standards, a comparison of current action against the standard, and pressure to self-correct behaviors when action-standard discrepancies occur. The literature on feedback systems (e.g., Taylor, Fisher, & Ilgen, 1984), self-assessment (e.g., Ashford, 1989), social learning (e.g., Bandura, 1988), goal setting (e.g., Locke & Latham, 1990), and decision making (e.g., Beach & Mitchell, 1990) all employ similar mechanisms to explain behavior.

From an organizational perspective, the prescriptions are clear. For a person to make both correct (i.e., externally and organizationally desired actions) and accurate assessments of their actions, they need: (1) clear standards; (2) clear and salient priorities; (3) agreement about standards; and (4) accurate and timely feedback about their behavior. To the extent that it is unclear what is expected in terms of specifying behavioral expectations, prioritizing what is important, and getting similar expectations sent from all sources, people will not feel accountable and may behave inappropriately (Baucus & Near, 1991; Grover, 1993). However, all of the above will fail unless there is also accurate and timely

feedback. One must know both the standard *and* how their behavior compares to the standard.

Accountability and attributions

Accountability deals with the pressure to justify one's decisions and actions to others. When individuals interpret these actions, they make attributional analyses regarding the causes of appropriate and inappropriate behavior. They try to determine *why* an action was taken. There has been considerable research on how this process takes place.

Attribution theory focuses on the perceived causes an individual has for his or her own behavior and performance (Heider, 1958). In achievement-related contexts, people tend to make attributions to ability/skill, luck, task difficulty, and effort as explanations for their successes and failures. For example, they might attribute their success to ability or their failure to bad luck. In the traditional measurement of attributions, individuals are asked to provide estimates of the relative contribution of each of these factors to their success or failure at a given task (Wiener, Frieze, Kukla, Reed, Rest, & Rosenbaum, 1971).

A main focus of this research has been to place these causal factors on various conceptual dimensions. Weiner's work (1980, 1985, 1986) and subsequent research suggest a conceptual framework of attributions which evolve around two main dimensions: the locus of causality (internal or external to the person) and stability (stable or unstable). Ability and effort are considered to be factors internal to the person while task difficulty and luck are considered external factors. In addition, ability and task difficulty are considered relatively stable and unchanging factors, while luck and effort are considered unstable factors.

Individuals also make attributions for controllability (felt responsibility). Weiner describes an attribution-emotion model, in which the causal attributions a person makes give rise to affective reactions, which in turn influence behavior (Weiner, 1986; Betancourt, 1990). A basic dimension of causal thinking describes the extent to which both the self and others are perceived as responsible for both positive and negative events. Attributions of responsibility (including controllability and intentionality) have a variety of motivational consequences, influencing both emotions (anger, gratitude, pity) and behaviors (altruism, aggression) (Weiner, 1991). For example, anger or pity and aggression or altruism would be emotional and behavioral responses to a failure depending upon whether one saw the person as responsible or not for the action.

We have mentioned that systems of accountability are expected to reduce the likelihood of inappropriate or unethical behavior through specific standards, and through rewards and punishments for meeting or overlooking such standards. But these systems of accountability may influence the attributions of internality or responsibility a person makes about their own and others' behavior. When accountability is high, due to organizational policy, then it is likely that attributions about actions will be external with little control (i.e., the action was chosen because of external imposition of accountability – the individuals felt like they had to do it). When there are no specific organizational guidelines about an individual's behavior, an individual will be more likely to make internal attributions with high amounts of control for their actions and decisions (i.e., the person really wanted to behave that way).

Overall, we believe that external imposition of accountability increases responsibility, decreases internality, and increases stability of attributions. More specifically, when individuals feel that they are being held accountable for their decisions and actions, they have increased attributions for responsibility, they have more external attributions for their actions (because they feel that their actions are being taken to meet external rather than internal expectations), and their actions will be more consistent over time (more stable and reliable) because the behaviors that are expected by the organization are clear and unambiguous with little room for variation.

One final issue that has received considerable attention is how different attributions are made for oneself as contrasted with making them about another person. Several researchers have described how we make attributions for the causes of others' performance (e.g., Wood & Mitchell, 1981; Weiner, 1986). When a subordinate performs poorly, performance is usually attributed to an internal cause (e.g., insufficient effort or ability), and the supervisor tends to attribute responsibility to the subordinate. In return, the subordinate may practice impression management to change this internal attribution for failure by making excuses. For example, if the subordinate gives an excuse for poor performance which is believable, the supervisor may be more likely to make an external attribution, and this external attribution leads to less punitive responses (e.g., less severe punishment). When internal attributions are made for poor performance, more punitive responses are made by the supervisor, On the other hand, when making attributions for one's own poor performance, we are likely to externalize the cause and deny responsibility. Thus an understanding of the effects of accountability will require that we know more about who is being held accountable (self, other), and the type of behavior (e.g., good or poor performance) and attribution that is made.

What this attribution research suggests is that actions are always interpreted, both by the actor and outside observers. Accountability systems are likely to produce more attributions of what we might call compliance (i.e., the person is behaving the way they are because they have to) in contrast to internalization (i.e., the person really believes what they are doing is the right thing to do, and would behave that way even if accountability was not an issue). Ideally, we would prefer the latter to the former. However, it is clear that systems of accountability work, in the sense that they reduce various kinds of illegal, unethical, or inappropriate behavior. The question we must ask is whether the introduction of such systems results in an overall benefit for the organization as well as the personal growth of employees. This is an issue to which we return later.

Consequences of accountability

The consequences of accountability (or lack of it) are significant and affect numerous areas of organizational functioning. Research has shown that accountability and ambiguity interact to affect the use of nonapproved influence tactics such as information manipulation (Fandt & Ferris, 1990). There is some indication that the unchecked acquisition of power leads to biases in performance evaluations of self and others (Kipnis, 1987). McAllister, Mitchell, and Beach (1979) demonstrated that accountability results in more analysis and thoughtful decision processes. Jones (1986) has shown that making top-level executives more accountable results in fewer lawsuits and less illegal behavior within the organization. Grover (1993) has demonstrated that ambiguity facilitates lying, and Baucus and Near (1991) have tied role ambiguity to a variety of organizational abuses (e.g., discrimination).

Thus introducing factors that increase accountability to organizational and legal standards can prevent counterproductive outcomes and increase organizational effectiveness in a number of ways. These same accountability systems, while they may create conformity to standards, may also have many negative consequences as discussed earlier in this chapter, including reactance, and lack of creativity, as well as a diminishing of organizational citizenship or prosocial behaviors (Niehoff & Moorman, 1993; Organ, 1988).

ACCOUNTABILITY IN PRACTICE

The perspective of a practitioner in human resources within a business organization is somewhat determined by the experience lived and learned by the practitioner. Pat Canavan's experience for close to the last twenty years has been in large, high-technology, multinational firms whose attention to the issue of accountability is sporadic and normally precipitated by a problem or a failure in performance. The causation of the problem or failure finds itself sorted into six categories:

1 The hybrid structures of modern, complex organizations, most frequently described as matrix structures, blur the points of accountability which are more easily found in traditional, simpler hierarchical structures.

2 The values and ethics found in the larger, progressively diverse society call into question policy descriptions of how people are expected to behave.

3 Transnational and transcultural issues of what defines appropriate behavior and what can and should be expected on the part of incumbents within the corporate culture resident in a different national culture, is as yet a very dynamic business and behavioral science issue.

4 The importance of risk taking and therefore norm changing as a highly valued entrepreneurial skill inside large organizations questions the value of compliance and conformity to organizational expectations as defined within the umbrella of accountability.

5 The rapid movement of manufacturing organizations toward empowerment and group- or team-oriented management approaches, raises the questions of individual versus group accountability. The concept of consequences for the team, both positive in terms of reward and negative in terms of evaluation and disci-

pline, are now progressively mitigated by the presence of the team as the appropriate work unit being measured.

6 Lastly, the customer has become the ultimate arbiter of what is successful performance within the organization. Certain individuals, teams, and departments are more directly associated with the response of the customer, and are therefore more easily held accountable against the ultimate metric, customer satisfaction.

Organizational structures during this century have moved away from hierarchical, pyramidal, structures, toward more flattened and matrixed organizational designs. As organizations become progressively larger in revenue, and more sensitive to the cost of management, one can expect that the current trend toward decentralization, delayering, expansion of spans of control, and the flattening of the overall structure will continue. In addition to these changes, the globalization of firms calls for the introduction of some form of regional accountability for the performance of the business in the nonhome market. Traditionally, corporations are organized around product group, function, industry segments, and/or geography. The most common modern form is some hybrid of the above. When a corporation then asks why a particular business unit is located in a particular country, or specifically why is the performance of a particular function (e.g., engineering) within a particular industry segment performing in such and such a way, this question is directed at four different spheres of the organization's matrix. Therefore, the question at a macro level of accountability becomes muddied by the evolving nature of modern organizational structures.

Also on the macro level, homogeneity of values, ethics, and rules of thumb for appropriate behavior within a corporation are also no longer widely assumed to be held in common. The movement toward diversity in the United States is translated into a variety of ethnic backgrounds, gender, and socioeconomic levels finding themselves at the board table, the management meeting, the department staff session, and the cafeteria. The maturing of organizations has evolved such that three generations may be present in many large corporations; the executive mentality having been formed in the 1950s and early 1960s, the managerial mentality formed in the late 1960s and 1970s, and the task performer and junior manager mentality formed in the 1980s. Perception of what is appropriate, how a person should be held accountable for commitment, and the nature of consequences for behavior that occurs outside of the normative umbrella for the organization are no longer easily aligned. Thus, the question of accountability as a personal experience is one that cannot be assumed to have a common language.

As an extension of the globalization of companies, the interface of national culture with corporate culture also raises new and complex issues about the basis used to evaluate others' behavior. The growth of the field of business anthropology has caused many organizations to engage in a dialogue as opposed to a definition to try to discover just what are the culture-neutral aspects of expectation, evaluation, and consequence. There is often confusion within a corporation between its corporate culture and its national culture. It is important in the discussion of accountability as a global organizational and human resources issue that this distinction gets made.

An interesting twist in the logic of accountability is brought on through organizations' need for innovation and creativity. Large corporations have a tendency toward bureaucracy, and the antidote for the ossification of the corporation is the application of supported and unsupported experimentation. The experimentation can, on a behavioral level, be labeled "norm breaking." When individuals break the norms, behave outside the expected definition of appropriateness, they run the risk of sanction and negative

191

consequence. But without this experimentation, this norm breaking and/or failure to comply, the organization will not escape the trap of entropy and continue to change, evolve, and grow. This entrepreneurial behavior, sometimes labeled "intrapreneurial," is a valued and necessary ingredient for organizational success. However, it disturbs the network of relationships and the connection between expected behavior and consequence which is the fabric of the coordinated organization. This paradox requires continuous reflection and dialogue.

Since the 1950s, there has been a steady movement toward empowerment, aided by group incentive plans, participative management programs, sensitivity training, employee involvement, the quality revolution, and borrowings from other national cultures. There is increasing recognition that much of the work in the factory, on the sales team, in the engineering laboratory, in the training organization, and countless other functional and cross-functional activity sets which comprise organizations, is conducted in that social phenomenon we call the team. The movement toward empowered work teams during the last decade has created associated human resources systems adapted and directed toward the team as opposed to the individual. Therefore, we have team goal setting, team selection processes, team compensation and incentive systems, and, possibly most importantly, team problem solving and decision making. The concept of accountability was most shaped in the era of the individual as the salient unit for organizational measurement. The individual is still the salient unit of organizational performance (i.e., it is the individual who shows up to work with a complex of willingness, abilities, and attitudes), but it is the team that embraces the tools and enacts the "units of effort" which produces the result.

In addition, this is the age of the customer. Therefore, the evaluator of behavior, the person or persons who decides and communicates whether or not what was expected has been performed, has moved outside of the organization. Only a portion of the organization's actors come in direct contact with the customer. Therefore, others in the chain providing value to the customer are evaluated by others approximate to themselves, but distant from the ultimate establisher of whether or not what was committed to has been delivered. Therefore, there is a challenge to the organization to define accountability most consistently in terms consonant with the mentality of the customer, and not consonant with the mentality only of the internal function next in the work flow. An example might be the manufacturing organization being highly concerned that the purchasing department deliver raw materials in particular orders or lots, and that they might be costed in such a way that is convenient for the manufacturing financial system. To perform against these expectations would mean that, internally, the purchasing department is being held accountable to behave in a certain way, and if it fails to do so, would be evaluated negatively by its internal client, the manufacturing organization. However, from a customer's point of view, the only relevant criteria for evaluation are simply quality of the materials supplied, the on-time delivery of those materials, and the contributing cost to the end product which must be paid for by the customer.

The above considerations try to create a schemata that indicates that there are issues as perceived from the human resources practitioner's viewpoint, living in a rapidly evolving and changing environment, that make more traditional views of accountability difficult to apply at the present time, and in the future. More flexible and more dynamic definitions of accountability, to subsume globalness, risk taking, diversity, empowered teams, customer orientation, and changing organizational structures would increase the robustness and the utility of the concept. The concept of accountability itself is extremely valuable to the practitioner because it creates a framework for consideration of the completeness and the excellence of performance.

FUTURE DIRECTIONS

Accountability is fundamental to the very nature of organizations, and indeed to the human resources systems in those organizations. But our notions about accountability were formulated based upon more traditional organizational structures and designs which are now being transformed. Organizations are different today, and they have had to change in order to be competitive and responsive to the dynamic nature of their markets and environments. Changes have taken the form of alternative structures whereby organizations have flattened out, and consist of fewer hierarchical levels. Accompanying such structural changes, we see fewer managers with increased spans of control, less individual-based and more team-based work designs, greater diversity in the work force, and all of this cast in an increasingly global economy. Furthermore we must recognize that accountability is a complex issue, with potentially both positive and negative consequences, which may occur differently at different levels in the organization. Therefore, we need to consider the challenges before us in the effective design and implementation of accountability mechanisms, particularly as they are involved in human resources systems. We highlight below several key directions for the future that blend what we have observed from theory, research, and practice on accountability.

First, we need to recognize that because we create an objective mechanism of accountability, it may not be perceived as such by the individuals or groups for whom it was designed. That is, we need to focus more on the perceptions and interpretations of accountability mechanisms by those we presume to be holding accountable, because we could create objective mechanisms that ultimately are

ineffective due to individuals and/or groups not perceiving that they are answerable for their actions.

Second, we need to better understand the social mechanisms of accountability. Human resources systems are cast within organizational environments that consist of complex social and political dynamics, and the very operation of such systems is intricately influenced by these dynamics. Thus the social and political dynamics that occur between supervisors and subordinates, and among peers are intertwined with the nature and operation of accountability mechanisms.

Third, we need to better understand the trade-offs, gains versus losses, or benefits and costs of accountability. As we discussed in this chapter, accountability can have positive as well as negative consequences determined largely by how we design and implement accountability mechanisms. We seek to achieve some degree of organizational control through the implementation of accountability mechanisms, yet, too much control may stifle the very type of innovation and creativity we need to be competitive. This is a formidable challenge, but not an insurmountable one, and as we learn more about this area, we should be able to more precisely calibrate our accountability mechanisms so that they bring about positive outcomes.

Finally, we should take a critical look at our human resources systems because we may be perpetuating the existence of old, outdated structures that no longer fit the realities of new and changing organizational environments. Let's take performance evaluation systems, for example. Advocates of total quality management approaches, such as Deming, have argued that performance evaluation is not only unnecessary, but also detrimental to organizations. We disagree with their position, but we do acknowledge that old, traditional approaches to performance evaluation which were designed for large, multilevel, pyramidal organizations may no longer be useful in our flattened-out, horizontal organizations, which are moving to more team-based work designs. Furthermore, such traditional approaches were quite static in their approach to work performance, articulating key performance dimensions that were rarely updated or changed, which also renders them outdated in many contemporary organizational contexts. In order to capture the dynamic, fluid, and rapidly changing nature of organizational environments today, we should consider performance evaluation systems that are flexible and focus on performance contracting both between employees and their supervisors as well as among members of a work team. Indeed, we see potential benefit as well in the involvement of employees, not just in the performance-contracting process, but also in the process of negotiation concerning for what they are accountable, to whom, and by when, recognizing that to an increased extent, accountability may be less to a supervisor and more to customers and/or clients. That is, not only do we believe that employees should be involved in defining performance, including the methods and measures of performance, we also believe that employees should be involved in the development and implementation of the accountability systems for their performance. Increasingly, we see these systems being customer/client-based.

These by no means exhaust all of the accountability challenges before us, but they do representatively reflect what we see as important future directions. In our opinion, accountability is an absolutely critical feature of human resources systems, and organizations overall, and it is a complex issue that requires the attention of both researchers and practitioners. If we acknowledge that our human resources are our most valuable resources, and can be our competitive advantage in the global marketplace, we need to ensure the creation of human resources systems in organizations which produce decisions and actions that maximize the potential and the well-being of our employees, and we cannot do this effectively without accountability.

REFERENCES

Ashford, S. J. (1989). Self-assessments in organizations: A literature review and integrative model. In L. L. Cummings & B. M. Staw (eds.), *Research in Organizational Behavior*, vol. 11, pp. 133–74. Greenwich, CT: JAI Press.

Bandura, A. (1988). Self regulation of motivation and action through goal systems. In V. Hamilton, G. H. Bower, & N. H. Frijida (eds.), *Cognitive Perspectives on Emotion and Motivation*, 36–61. Dordrecht, Netherlands: Kluwen Academic Publishers.

Barnard, C. I. (1938). *The Functions of the Executive.* Cambridge, MA: Harvard University Press.

Barney, J. B. (1990). The debate between traditional management theory and organizational economics: Substantive differences or intergroup conflict? *Academy of Management Review*, 15, 382–93.

Baucus, M. A., & Near, J. P. (1991). Can illegal corporate behavior be predicted? An event history analysis. *Academy of Management Journal*, 34 (1), 9–36.

Beach, L. R., & Mitchell, T. R. (1990). Image theory: A behavioral theory of decision making in organizations. In B. M. Staw & L. L. Cummings (eds.), *Research in Organizational Behavior*, vol. 12, pp. 1–41. Greenwich, CT: JAI Press.

Betancourt (1990). An attribution-empathy model of helping behavior: Behavioral intentions and judgments of help-giving. *Personality and Social Psychology Bulletin*, 16, 573–91.

Brehm, J. W. (1966). *A Theory of Psychological Reactance.* New York: Academic Press.

Brief, A. P., Dukerich, J. M., & Doran, L. I. (1991). Resolving ethical dilemmas in management: Experimental investigations of values, accountability, and choice. *Journal of Applied Psychology*, 21 (5), 380–96.

Brown, D. (1992). Can we put the brakes on CEO pay? *Management Review*, May, 10–15.

Crystal, G. S. (1991). *In Search of Excess: The overcompensation of American executives.* New York: Norton.

Cummings, L. L., & Anton, R. J. (1990). The logical and appreciative dimensions of accountability. In S. Sivastva, D. L. Cooperrider, & associates (eds.), *Appreciative Management and Leadership*, 257–86. San Francisco: Jossey-Bass.

Dalton, D. R., & Kesner, I. F. (1987). On the dynamics of corporate size and illegal activity: An empirical assessment. Paper presented at the annual meeting of the Academy of Management, New Orleans.

Eisenhardt, K. M. (1985). Control: Organizational and economic approaches. *Management Science*, 31, 134–49.

Fandt, P. M., & Ferris, G. R. (1990). The management of information and impressions: When employees behave opportunistically. *Organizational Behavior and Human Decision Processes*, 45, 140–58.

Ferris, G. R., Fedor, D. B., Rowland, K. M., & Porac, J. F. (1985). Social influence and sex effects on task performance and task perceptions. *Journal of Vocational Behavior*, 26, 66–78.

Ferris, G. R., Howard, J. L., & Bergin, T. G. (in press). Rationality and politics in organizational exit decisions.

In G. R. Ferris & M. R. Buckley (eds.), *Human Resource Management: Perspectives, context, functions, and outcomes*, 3rd ed. Boston: Allyn and Bacon.

Ferris, G. R., & Judge, T. A. (1991). Personnel/human resources management: A political influence perspective. *Journal of Management*, 17, 447–88.

Ferris, G. R., & Mitchell, T. R. (1987). The components of social influence and their importance for human resources research. In K. M. Rowland & G. R. Ferris (eds.), *Research in Personnel and Human Resources Management*, vol. 5, pp. 103–28. Greenwich, CT: JAI Press.

Ferris, G. R., & Mitchell, T. R. (1991). Personal accountability and ethical behavior in organizations. Research proposal submitted to the U.S. Army Research Institute, Washington, D.C.

Gomez-Mejia, L. R., & Balkin, D. B. (1992a). *Compensation, Organizational Strategy, and Firm Performance*. Cincinnati, OH: South-Western Publishing Co.

Gomez-Mejia, L. R., & Balkin, D. B. (1992b). Determinants of faculty pay: An agency theory perspective. *Academy of Management Journal*, 35, 921–55.

Gordon, R. A., Rozelle, R. M., & Baxter, J. C. (1988). The effect of applicant age, job level and accountability on the evaluation of job applicants. *Organizational Behavior and Human Decision Processes*, 41, 20–33.

Grover, S. L. (1993). Why professionals lie: The impact of professional role conflict on reporting accuracy. *Organizational Behavior and Human Decision Processes*, 55, 251–72.

Heider, F. (1958). *The Psychology of Interpersonal Relations*. New York: Wiley.

Hyland, M. E. (1988). Motivational control theory: An integrative framework. *Journal of Personality and Social Psychology*, 55, 642–51.

Inzerilli, G., & Rosen, M. (1983). Culture and organizational control. *Journal of Business Research*, 11, 281–92.

Jensen, M. C., & Meckling, W. H. (1976). Theory of the firm: Managerial behavior, agency costs and ownership structure. *Journal of Financial Economics*, 3, 305–60.

Jones, T. M. (1986). Corporate board structure and performance: Variations in the incidence of shareholder suits. In L. E. Preston (ed.), *Research in Corporate Social Performance and Policy*, vol. 8, pp. 345–59. Greenwich, CT: JAI Press.

Judge, T. A., & Ferris, G. R. (1992). The elusive criterion of fit in human resources staffing decisions. *Human Resource Planning*, 15, 47–67.

Katz, D., & Kahn, R. L. (1978). *The Social Psychology of Organizations*, 2nd ed. New York: Wiley.

Kelman, H. C. (1958). Compliance, identification, and internalization: Three processes of attitude change. *Journal of Conflict Resolution*, 2 (1), 51–60.

Kelman, H. C., & Hamilton, V. L. (1989). *Crimes of Obedience*. New Haven, CT: Yale University Press.

Kipnis, D. (1987). Psychology and behavioral technology. *American Psychologist*, 42, 30–6.

Klein, H. J. (1989). An integrated control theory model of work motivation. *Academy of Management Review*, 14, 150–72.

Klimoski, R., & Inks, L. (1990). Accountability forces in performance appraisal. *Organizational Behavior and Human Decision Processes*, 45, 194–208.

Kohlberg, L. (1969). State and sequence: The cognitive-developmental approach to socialization. In D. A. Goslin (ed.), *Handbook of Socialization Theory and Research*, 347–480. Chicago: Rand McNally.

Komaki, J. L. (1986). Toward effective supervision: An operant analysis and comparison of managers at work. *Journal of Applied Psychology*, 71, 270–9.

Larson, J. R., Jr., & Callahan, C. (1990). Performance monitoring: How it affects work productivity. *Journal of Applied Psychology*, 75, 530–8.

Lee, T. W., & Mitchell, T. R. (1994). An alternative approach: The unfolding model of voluntary turnover. *Academy of Management Review*, 19, 51–89.

Locke, E. A., & Latham, G. P. (1990). *A Theory of Goal Setting and Task Performance*. Englewood Cliffs, NJ: Prentice Hall.

McAllister, D. W., Mitchell, T. R., & Beach, L. R. (1979). The contingency model for the selection of decision strategies: An empirical test of the effects of significance, accountability, and reversibility. *Organizational Behavior and Human Performance*, 24, 228–44.

Martell, R. F., & Borg, M. R. (1993). A comparison of the behavioral rating accuracy of groups and individuals. *Journal of Applied Psychology*, 78, 43–50.

Mitchell, T. R. (1993). Leadership, values, and accountability. In M. M. Chemers & R. Ayman (eds.), *Leadership Theory and Research: Perspectives and directions*, 109–36. San Diego, CA: Academic Press.

Mitchell, T. R., & Scott, W. G. (1990). America's problems and needed reforms: Confronting the ethic of personal advantage. *Academy of Management Executive*, 4, 23–35.

Monks, R. A. G., & Minow, N. (1991). *Power and Accountability*. New York: HarperCollins.

Niehoff, B. P., & Moorman, R. H. (1993). Justice as a mediator of the relationship between methods of monitoring and organizational citizenship behavior. *Academy of Management Journal*, 36, 527–56.

Organ, D. W. (1988). *Organizational Citizenship Behavior: The good soldier syndrome*. Lexington, MA: Lexington Books.

Ouchi, W. G. (1977). The relationship between organizational structure and organizational control. *Administrative Science Quarterly*, 22, 95–113.

Ouchi, W. G., & Maguire, M. A. (1975). Organizational control: Two functions. *Administrative Science Quarterly*, 20, 559–69.

Piturro, M. C. (1989). Employee performance monitoring . . . or meddling? *Management Review*, May, 31–3.

Pollack, A. (1990). Whose fault scandals? Should liability end with subordinates? *New York Times*, July 30, 1–2.

Pruitt, D. (1981). *Negotiation Behavior*. New York: Academic Press.

Rynes, S., & Boudreau, J. (1986). College recruiting in large organizations: Practice, evaluation, and research implications. *Personnel Psychology*, 39, 729–57.

Salancik, G. R., & Pfeffer, J. (1978). A social information processing approach to job attitudes and job design. *Administrative Science Quarterly*, 23, 224–54.

Schlenker, B. R. (1982). Translating actions into attitudes: An identity-analytic approach to the explanation of social conduct. In L. Berkowitz (ed.), *Advances in experimental social psychology*, vol. 5, pp. 186–224. New York: Academic Press.

Schlenker, B. R., & Weigold, M. F. (1989). Self-identification and accountability. In R. A. Giacalone & P. Rosenfeld (eds.), *Impression Management in the Organization*, 21–43. Hillsdale, NJ: Lawrence Erlbaum.

Schnake, M., & Dumler, M. P. (1993). The overlooked side of organizational citizenship behavior: The impact of rewards and reward practices, or "If you want me to do that, you'll have to pay me". Paper presented at the National Meetings of the Academy of Management, Atlanta, Georgia, August.

Scott, W. G. (1974). Organization theory: A reassessment. *Academy of Management Journal*, 17, 242–54.

Scott, M., & Lyman, S. (1968). Accounts. *American Sociological Review*, 33, 46–62.

Snell, S. A. (1992). Control theory in strategic human resource management: The mediating effect of administrative information. *Academy of Management Journal*, 35, 292–327.

Staw, B. M. (1976). Knee-deep in the big muddy: A study of escalating commitment to a chosen course of action. *Organizational Behavior and Human Performance*, 16, 27–44.

Staw, B. M. (1981). The escalation of commitment to a course of action. *Academy of Management Review*, 6, 577–87.

Staw, B. M., & Boettger, R. (1990). Task revision: A neglected form of work performance. *Academy of Management Journal*, 33, 534–59.

Szwajkowski, E. (1985). Organizational illegality: Theoretical integration and illustrative application. *Academy of Management Review*, 10, 558–67.

Taylor, M. S., Fisher, C. D., & Ilgen, D. R. (1984). Individuals' reactions to performance feedback in organizations: A control theory perspective. In K. M. Rowland & G. R. Ferris (eds.), *Research in personnel and human resources management*, vol. 2, pp. 81–124. Greenwich, CT: JAI Press.

Tetlock, P. E. (1983). Accountability and complexity of thought. *Journal of Personality and Social Psychology*, 45, 285–92.

Tetlock, P. E. (1985). Accountability: The neglected social context of judgment and choice. In L. L. Cummings & B. M. Staw (eds.), *Research in organizational behavior*, vol. 7, pp. 297–332. Greenwich, CT: JAI Press.

Tetlock, P. E. (1992). The impact of accountability on judgment and choice: Toward a social contingency model. In M. P. Zanna (ed.), *Advances in Experimental Social Psychology*, vol. 25, pp. 331–77. New York: Academic Press.

Tetlock, P. E., & Boettger, R. (1989). Accountability: Social magnifier of the dilution effect. *Journal of Personality and Social Psychology*, 57, 388–98.

Tetlock, P. E., Skitka, L., & Boettger, R. (1989). Social and cognitive strategies for coping with accountability: Conformity, complexity, and bolstering. *Journal of Personality and Social Psychology*, 57, 632–40.

Trevino, L. K. (1986). Ethical decision making in organizations: A person–situation interactionist model. *Academy of Management Review*, 11, 60–617.

Trevino, L. K., & Youngblood, S. A. (1990). Bad apples in bad barrels: A causal analysis of ethical decision-making behavior. *Journal of Applied Psychology*, 75, 378–85.

Weigold, M. F., & Schlenker, B. R. (1991). Accountability and risk taking. *Personality and Social Psychology Bulletin*, 17, 25–9.

Weiner, B. (1980). *Human Motivation*. New York: Holt, Rinehart & Winston.

Weiner, B. (1985). An attributional theory of achievement motivation and emotion. *Psychological Review*, 92, 548–73.

Weiner, B. (1986). *An Attribution Theory of Motivation and Emotion*. New York: Springer-Verlag.

Weiner, B. (1991). Metaphors in motivation and attribution. *American Psychologist*, 46, 921–30.

Weiner, B., Frieze, I. H., Kukla, A., Reed, L., Rest, S., & Rosenbaum, R. M. (1971). *Perceiving the Causes of Success and Failure*. Morristown, NJ: General Learning Press.

Williamson, O. E. (1975). *Markets and Hierarchies*. New York: Free Press.

Wood, R., & Mitchell, T. R. (1981). Manager behavior in a social context: The impact of impression management on attributions and disciplinary decisions. *Organizational Behavior and Human Performance*, 28, 356–78.

Zajonc, R. B. (1965). Social facilitation. *Science*, 149, 269–74.

☐ Chapter 11 ☐

Ethical Issues in Human Resource Management

Sherman D. Rosen and Hervey A. Juris

I would rather be the man who bought the Brooklyn Bridge than the man who sold it.[1]

INTRODUCTION

The subject of ethical behavior has been with us for several millennia. There are few, if any, human resources practitioners who have not had to deal with an ethical issue at some point in their careers.

In this chapter we attempt to identify these ethical challenges and to provide a framework for dealing with them. We begin with a brief overview of business ethics which argues that the human resources manager is particularly involved because of the diverse and sometimes paradoxical role HR plays in the organization. Several schools of philosophical thought regarding ethical behavior are discussed and their relevance to the problems faced in HR assessed. It is our contention that the HR practitioner, working in the often ambiguous and sometimes chaotic business arena, needs an ethical framework more pragmatic than unbending, more immediately responsive than subject to leisurely reflection. Such a framework is to be found in the recent work of two writers, Robert C. Solomon and Laura L. Nash.

The discussion then turns to a variety of ethical situations faced by top HR executives, human resources practitioners, and line managers who deal with HR issues as a normal aspect of their job. We conclude with some concrete suggestions.

THE CURRENT STATE OF ATTENTION TO BUSINESS ETHICS

Over the last century the popular perception of business ethics has been cyclical. To some extent, attitudes have fluctuated with the economy: down during the Great Depression of the 1930s and again during the layoffs and downsizing of the late 1980s and early 1990s; and up with the growth of the 1920s, 1950s, and 1960s, and the recovery in the 1980s.

Attitudes also have fluctuated with exposés of undisciplined or unregulated abuses and excesses. These include those uncovered by the muckrakers at the beginning of the century (e.g., Sinclair, 1906; Tarbel, 1904), the stock market abuses of the 1920s that led to the formation of the SEC in the 1930s, the concerns of the sociologists in the 1950s (e.g.,

Mills, 1951, Whyte, 1956), the environmental movement, perceived excesses of the takeover binges of the 1980s, and the current concern with excessive CEO compensation in the face of continuing downsizing.

Just a generation ago there were writers who included ethical issues among the "social responsibilities of business" that were to be avoided. For them the only important objective of business was the maximization of profit. Milton Friedman (1970, 126), for example, expressed the belief that "there is one and only one social responsibility for business – to use its resources and engage in activities designed to increase its profits so long as it stays within the rules of the game. . . ." Carr (1968, 145) saw those roles as slightly different from the social norm. He likened business dealings to the bluffing of the poker player, stating that, "[Business] standards of right and wrong differ from the prevailing traditions of morality in our society. . . . [While] most businessmen are not indifferent to ethics in their private lives, . . . in their office lives they cease to be private citizens; they become game players who must be guided by a somewhat different set of ethical standards."

In more recent years ethicists have turned their attention to the micro level, where we deal with the ethical behavior of individuals in organizations, rather than the behavior of organizations or their cultures. It is at this level that human resources practitioners are playing an increasing role in moving their enterprises to an ethical way of life for the work force.

In a recent survey of over 1,000 HR practitioners, 83 percent indicated that HR personnel were responsible for providing ethical leadership and guidance in their organizations – a greater percentage than the 74 percent who indicated the "President/CEO" also filled this role (Commerce Clearing House, 1991). The assumption of ethical leadership is not an easy task. As one writer has argued, executive ranks are filled with individuals characterized as being *nonethical* instead of being *unethical*, not deliberately acting against ethical standards (Gilbreath, 1987).

The interests and activities of academics and business people have also grown in this area. In recent years the increased attention of the business press has been complemented by the establishment of publications such as *The Journal of Business Ethics* and the magazine *Business Ethics*. Concurrently there has been increased academic attention to the subject, manifested by the establishment of chairs at leading business schools (Fowler, 1992). By recent estimate 500 courses in business ethics are being offered in the U.S., with 90 percent of business schools teaching the subject; globally, there are now more than 20 units devoted to the topic (*The Economist*, 1993). A recent survey of ethics instruction in university-based industrial relations programs found 14 of 24 respondents in the U.S. and Canada – all at the graduate level – offered some form of ethics instruction. In all cases ethics issues are integrated into the course offerings; no separate courses are offered (Dibble, 1993).

Finally, the business community too has given increased attention to ethical issues. Numerous codes of ethics have been drafted and disseminated. Some firms have established "ethics offices" to deal with ethical concerns on a regular and systematic basis (Bureau of National Affairs, 1992; Gibbons, 1992; Tompkins, 1993). In addition, a growing number of firms are introducing training programs in business ethics (Myers, 1992; Hetrick, 1993).

THE SPECIAL ROLE OF THE HUMAN RESOURCES MANAGER

While ethical issues arise for many reasons, in most cases they stem from individual actions and decisions which involve a conflict between rules of human behavior and the dynamics of individuals interacting with individuals and within organizational groups.

The behavioral orientation of the HR function has in the past attracted people with a great interest in and sensitivity to the needs and aspirations of individuals. Thus, HR practitioners often have possessed a greater amount of understanding and compassion for human motivations and workplace behavior than have managers in production, finance, law, and marketing whose roles take a more aggregate view of the institution. These role differences have contributed to reactions ranging from the view that HR people are fuzzy-headed thinkers to HR as the conscience of the organization. Anthony Rucci, former senior vice president of human resources at Baxter International, suggested that HR must be the corporation's voice of compassion in dealing with people, maintaining the important values of fairness and consideration in the decision-making process (Korsvik & Juris 1990, p. 23).

Human resources practitioners, in addition to their behavioral orientation, occupy a particularly sensitive role that is different from that of managers in line functions and in other functional areas. The HR executive often walks a fine line that divides the sometimes conflicting interests of the enterprise from those of the employees. Complicating this is the fact that the top HR executive often deals directly with a boss with important influence over his or her career whose interests focus broadly on the successful performance of the enterprise and may not always be receptive to the importance of specific ethical issues raised by HR. Nor is the HR staff reporting to the top HR executive exempt from these pressures because actions of the staff – especially mid-level practitioners – reflect on the entire function.

Recent expansion of the HR role has brought another important contradictory element into play: the growing strategic involvement of the HR function (Walker, 1992; Fombrun, Tichy, & DeVanna, 1984; Fullmer, 1989). The HR leader, in occupying a strategic position in addition to the traditional administrative/operational tasks, has often become a member of the top management team forcing him or her to focus more on the integration of the strategic business issues with human resources issues (Walker, 1992). The HR leader of the 1990s and beyond needs to learn to deal with the conflict between the interests of the business, its shareholders, customers and other stakeholders and the interests of its employees.

GENERAL PHILOSOPHICAL FRAMEWORK

The ethical organization

In large part an *ethical* organization is composed of individuals who each have *values* (defined simply as ideas, qualities and opinions) that are considered worthwhile (Hodgson, 1992).

Values are derived from one's upbringing, social pressures, religion, experience, conscience, and the need to get along with others. Values engender *principles*, the standards by which individuals and corporations conduct themselves. The values of a business organization represent the coming together (sharing) by its members of these standards. Organizational principles are officially shaped by things such as: the words and actions of the founder; statements and actions of current leadership; policy statements; and codes of ethics. Often, in spite of documented principles, unwritten principles – *norms* – can vary dramatically. Thus employees may view the organization's documented principles as "what we're supposed to do" and the unwritten principles as "this is what we really do."

The width of the gap between organizational principles and norms is often directly related to integrity of leadership. Integrity of leadership has been characterized as a necessary prerequisite to an ethical organization. In such an organization the successful leader has integrated his or her values into the philosophy and day-to-day actions that communicate the principles and norms which shape ethical behavior. "The main leadership task is to energize followers' actions that support higher corporate purpose and not their own self interests" (Badaraco & Ellsworth, 1989).

Practical considerations

A representative dictionary definition of ethics is the following: "The discipline of dealing with what is good and bad and with moral duty and obligation" (Webster's Ninth New Collegiate Dictionary, 1984). This definition is correct as far as it goes, but it does little to guide the human resources practitioner in dealing with the day-to-day matters that carry ethical implications. One must go beyond the dictionary to find a framework that will help the practitioner in his or her everyday ethical challenges.

A complementary view of the ethics of management moves us from the concept of "good" and "bad" by introducing what is "right and proper and just" in the decisions and actions that affect other people (Hosmer, 1987). Here again individuals are expected to apply their own moral standards of behavior and ethical norms, beliefs, and values. However, the processes by which they are applied are as important to the resolution of ethical issues as is the recognition that a particular issue represents an ethical challenge.

Stark (1993) contends that business ethicists are only marginally influential because the leading thinkers have a grounding in moral philosophy, a discipline that adheres to the tenet of altruism. Altruism holds that one should do good simply because it is right. In application this absolutist approach could result in a conclusion that if doing something ethical leads to the disappearance of the enterprise, it is justified. Moreover business ethicists have tended to deal with "grand theorizing," asking questions such as "Is capitalism ethically justifiable?", instead

of addressing situations faced every day by managers when running a business.

In practice, an ethical approach based on moral absolutism in the day-to-day world of business is doomed to failure and frustration. In the real world managers must learn to adjust to conflicts among personal ethics, organizational espoused values and organizational norms. Actions taken to resolve ethical issues may not be effective and could have serious career implications, often more negative than positive.

In reaction to these shortcomings there has emerged in recent years a revised approach to business ethics which reflects two fundamental principles:

1 Ethics and interests can conflict.
2 In the imperfect world of mixed motives, instead of abstract distinctions between altruism and self-interest, new corporate structures, systems and decision-making processes are needed to accommodate the whole person (Stark, 1993).

Two authors, Robert C. Solomon and Laura L. Nash, have proposed orientations to ethical behavior in organizations which seem to meet these criteria.

The concept of virtue

Solomon (1992) bases his approach to business ethics on the concept of virtue as set forth by Aristotle in the *Nichomachean Ethics* over 2,300 years ago. Aristotle concluded that the end to which all human activity is directed is happiness; and happiness is attained by living a virtuous life. Moral virtue, in Aristotle's view, represents the relative mean between the extremes of excess and deficiency. In general the moral life is one of moderation in all things except virtue. Virtuous acts require conscious choice and moral purpose or motivation; people have personal moral responsibility for their actions. The achievement of moral virtue requires moral action in a social environment.

Starting with the Aristotelian concept of virtue, Solomon argues for a shift in focus from the perception of business being ruthlessly selfish and greedy to one of being a "healthy aspect of a prosperous community." He identifies and then challenges several myths:

- *The Jungle Myth* "One has to do whatever it takes to survive".
  Solomon's Reality: In the real world shared interests and mutually agreed upon rules of conduct are the norm, however competitive the industry. Business life is fundamentally cooperative involving large groups of mutually trusting networks of suppliers, customers and investors (Solomon, 1992, 26).
- *Brutal Battle Myth* The war metaphor is often used to describe business strategy and business practices.
  Solomon's Reality: "Even in the height of battle, business presupposes a certain amount of mutual trust and cooperation, the honoring of contracts, respect for the law and the rules of fair competition" (p. 28).
- *Great Machine Myth* Some people envision business as a "great machine" that treats workers like cogs on a wheel.
  Solomon's Reality: Solomon sees business as "a system of activities designed and practiced by human beings who have much to gain (and much to lose)" (p. 31).
- *Game Myth* Business is "voluntary, thrilling, challenging", focusing on winning.
  Solomon's Reality: "A focus on winning excludes productivity, service, and quality. Moreover most people in business don't see it as a game at all but rather as a way to make a living . . . [They] are not driven by overwhelming ambition, do not see all business as a challenge or the corporation as a playground, are not interested in (and are put off by) 'fast tracking' and the 'high rolling' ways of success" (p. 32).[2]

In Solomon's view ethics has ambiguous meaning: it refers to a set of theories and reflections about our behavior; and it refers to the behavior itself. He states: "How a person thinks about business – as a ruthless competition for profits or a cooperative enterprise the aim of which is the prosperity of the community – preshapes much of . . . [our] behavior and attitudes toward fellow employees or executives, competitors, customers, and the surrounding community" (p. 12). Within this context Solomon agrees with Aristotle's view of moral virtue but argues the word "moral" simply means "practical." This view, coupled with Aristotle's emphasis on moderation, leads to the conclusion that being virtuous does not involve "radical demands on our behavior." Thus a group of workable virtues for managers can be developed. These include toughness, defined as involving a "willingness to do what is necessary" and an "insistence on doing it as humanely as possible." Other managerial virtues are courage, fairness, sensitivity, honesty and gracefulness.

Nash: The covenantal ethic

The concept of the covenantal ethic is based upon the resolution of ethical issues by managers who believe that business is conducted in terms of covenants with employees, customers, suppliers, and other stakeholders (Nash, 1991). She sees three essential aspects to these covenants:

1 *Value creation* in its many forms must be the primary objective.
2 *Profit and other social returns* are not the overriding objectives of behavior but instead result from achieving other goals.
3 *Business problems* are approached more in terms of dealing with relationships than focusing on tangible products.

Within this framework Nash places emphasis on service to others, caring, and increasing a person's sense of self-worth. Basic to this approach is a view of business integrity comprised of four basic values:

1 *Honesty*, characterized as assessing and representing the business and any activity relevant to the business.
2 *Reliability*, acting consistently with one's values.
3 *Fairness*, balancing the rights of various constituencies with consistency and goodwill.
4 *Pragmatism*, "making concrete contributions to the ongoing financial and organizational health of the business."

Nash proposes three aspects of ethical problem solving for a business enterprise. First, ethical norms must be integrated with the pursuit of economic success; a legitimate return is essential but it must be accomplished with an acceptance of the enterprise's ability to create and provide value as perceived by its various constituencies. Second, there must be an other-directed attitude which addresses the needs of others as the first purpose of business thinking; the leaders of the enterprise must subordinate their self-interest to the needs of its employees, customers, and other stakeholders. Third, there must be "a capability to motivate pragmatic and competitive behavior" that is oriented toward social relationships rather than individual interests.

To be ethically effective business integrity demands that managers "walk the talk", living up to the words spoken. Nash suggests two tests to apply when facing an ethical issue:

1 Do the decisions contribute to the good reputation of the company or the manager?
2 Do the decisions promote trust?

Summary

The HR practitioner faces ethical issues in a dynamic environment that is often filled with ambiguity and pressures for prompt and timely action. In some respects the practitioner can take comfort in the laws and regulations that dominate workplace relationships. This is especially the case in areas of age, race and sex discrimination, and sexual harassment. Abuses in labor relations have also been well covered by laws and administrative regulations. However, even in these cases laws and regulations only provide a floor. Above this floor there is a considerable amount of gray area where the resolution of ethical issues is unclear. It is in this territory that values and norms come into play and a firm philosophical base is important – a base that must take into account the multiple interests of the various stakeholders in the enterprise.

We have reviewed the downside of absolutist formulations of ethical decision making and proposed two frameworks more suited to the situations that exist in business organizations – the concept of virtue and the covenantal ethic. In this next section we examine some sources of ethical dilemmas for HR people.

HUMAN RESOURCE ETHICAL SITUATIONS

There have been few surveys of HR practitioners regarding ethical issues encountered in the workplace. A recent comprehensive study was conducted in 1991 by Commerce Clearing House, Inc. (CCH), in conjunction with the Society for Human Resource Management (SHRM). Approximately 1,000 members of SHRM responded to a mail questionnaire, reporting what they considered to be the most important ethical issues, the relative severity of each problem, and the degree of success they felt would be achieved in resolving them. Table 11.1 lists the top dozen reported.

In table 11.2 appear the top functional areas where respondents reported occurrences of ethical misconduct. Ranked first was the area

Table 11.1 Top-ranked HR ethical situations

	Involve ethical considerations?	*How serious is the problem?*	*Success in resolving the problems*
Hiring, training or promotion based on favoritism (friendships or relatives)	1	1	36
Allowing differences in pay, discipline, promotion due to friendships with top management	2	1	34
Not maintaining confidentiality	3	6	27
Arrangements with vendors or consulting agencies leading to personal gain	4	9	21
Sex harassment	5	3	25
Race discrimination in recruitment or hiring	6	11	19
Sex discrimination in recruitment or hiring	7	10	22
Race harassment	8	16	15
Sex discrimination in promotion or work assignments	9	4	33
Age discrimination in recruitment or hiring	10	14	28
Retaliatory discharge	11	22	5
Sex discrimination in compensation	12	7	30

Respondents were asked to identify situations involving ethical considerations and then indicate for each one selected their view of the severity of the problem, and their success in its resolution. Thus, for example, sex harassment was the fifth most likely to have ethical implications, was the third most serious problem, and ranked 25th as most likely to be resolved.
Source: 1991 SHRM/CCH Survey

Table 11.2 Areas of ethical misconduct

Functional area	*Respondents reporting occurrence (%)*	*Respondents reporting frequent occurrence (%)*
Employment	77	16
Compensation	74	16
Labor relations	64	12
Health and safety	62	9
Generalist areas	56	4
Benefits	46	6
Training and development	45	3
Personnel research	37	2
HRIS	36	2

Source: 1991 SHRM/CCH Survey

of employment, covering all aspects of the recruitment and selection process. This was followed by compensation, labor relations, and health and safety.

In the pages that follow we discuss a number of these ethical issues plus other relevant examples, some of which have been reported by practitioners in interviews.

THE HR EXECUTIVE AND TOP MANAGEMENT

There are a number of ethical issues that usually relate only to upper levels. The most common ethical dilemmas are found in executive compensation activities.

The requests that lead to ethical problems can range from outrageous acts of greed to more mundane self-justifications based on the conclusion that "everyone is doing it." Until the recent changes in proxy reporting by the Securities and Exchange Commission, the ability to hide certain practices from public view led to numerous actions that, while legal, could be classified as residing in gray ethical neighborhoods.

As mentioned earlier, the more strategic role of the HR executive has put him or her in the middle. He or she most likely reports to the CEO, exerting influence both as a credible professional and as an advisor-consultant. Increasingly the top HR executive also deals with members of the board of directors, especially those who serve on the compensation committee. In addition, the compensation committee of many boards today acts more broadly as a human resources committee and itself calls on the human resources function for staff and consulting support. Finally, the HR executive often further increases his or her exposure to ethical dilemmas by serving as liaison between outside consultants (primarily in the area of compensation), the board, and the CEO (Baytos, 1991).

Another complication is a growing trend for compensation committees to meet directly with the HR executive, the firm's compensation consultant, or both, without the presence of the CEO. The purpose is to insure that there is a clear understanding of "responsibility . . . to the board and shareholders, not just to management" (Paulin & Cook, 1992).

While fine in theory, this ignores the fact that since the HR executive reports to the CEO on a day-to-day basis, it is practically impossible to ignore the CEO's expectations on compensation issues, particularly those that impact top management. Even in the best of relationships the CEO's outlook can differ from that of the HR executive and the board. When there is a conflict, the pressure flows from the CEO to the HR executive rather than from the board. Realistically, few CEOs would countenance for long an HR executive whose views, clearly at odds with the CEO's own, were bluntly expressed to the members of the compensation committee.

COMMONLY ENCOUNTERED SITUATIONS

One seasoned practitioner puts it this way:

> [The ethically questionable practices of certain top managers] are very subtle, reflecting self-interest and intentional manipulation of the rules for their own benefit. The individual who does this does not view it as unethical. Instead, the attitude is generally expressed this way: "I'm taking care of others at the same time . . . I'm running a multibillion dollar company that's providing tens of thousands of jobs . . . no one complains about Michael Jackson's high earnings. I bring more value than a highly paid rock singer!"

It should be noted that the reference to "taking care of others" almost always refers to the top HR executive as well as other members of the management team. This further muddies the waters for HR executives who presumably are seeking a balance between their values and growing family responsibilities.

The paragraphs that follow provide examples of issues related to cash and incentive compensation and executive prerequisites. These are areas that represent some of the most frequent ethical dilemmas posed by top management.

Cash and incentive compensation

Base salaries

The HR function (and the compensation consultant) are sometimes pressured to justify a higher level of base salary, or a higher percentage increase, than competitive practice calls for. In some cases, pressure is exerted to reevaluate the position to a higher grade for the purpose of justifying a larger than normal increase, often by "manufacturing" additional accountability. These attempts are particularly disturbing if, at the same time, increases for lower management and the rank and file are being severely restricted.

Annual incentive plans

Most short-term incentive awards are tied to the achievement of goals established (and usually agreed to by the directors) at the beginning of the plan year. While goal setting in most businesses is more an art than a science, an appropriate ethical stance would be that, once approved and announced, a goal is a goal unless extraordinary circumstances occur during the course of the year which negatively impact goal achievement. The ethical challenge is often related to the definition of "extraordinary." Some CEOs have gone to great lengths to convince their directors that events which would otherwise be considered routine were in fact "extraordinary" and not subject to management control in order that otherwise unearned management bonuses could be paid.

The human resources executive usually is responsible for the design and administration of top management incentive plans and often has input into the annual goal-setting process. In addition, the HR executive is enlisted in drafting (and sometimes presenting) the recommendations for the forthcoming year's goals and for justifying bonus targets that sometimes are not reflective of business conditions.

For example, in a firm with an equity of $2 billion, a major goal called for a 12 percent return on equity (ROE), or $240 million, as the target earnings goal for the year. In the following year, despite a restructuring charge of $500 million which reduced equity to $1.5 billion, the CEO requested his chief human resources officer to recommend to the compensation committee that the provisions of the annual incentive plan be adopted for that year without change. As a result, at a target ROE of 12 percent the company would pay the same level of bonus for attainment of $180 million in earnings, $60 million lower than the previous year. In this case the HR executive was tempted to question this windfall as being unfair to the shareholders and to the employees. That he did not reflected two contradictory feelings: his fear of losing his job and the understanding that he would benefit along with the rest of top management.

A common rationalization presented to the HR executive, when asked to bend the rules by drafting a supportive argument to the compensation committee, is management's fear that outstanding executives will leave if adequate bonuses are not paid. In some cases this occurs. In most cases this doesn't happen unless several years of payouts have been skipped by the firm in question, while competitors have continued to award bonuses to their executives.

Long-term incentive plans

Just as with annual incentive plans, many HR executives have responsibility for designing and administering the company's long-term incentive plans, often working with the chief executive officer and an outside consultant. In this role the HR executive can be enlisted in providing justifications for actions that have ethical implications, especially in situations that favor top management interests over those of other employees and investors.

Stock options, the most prevalent type of long-term incentives, are regarded by investors as the most direct link between shareholder value and executive rewards because the market determines their value to the recipient. There are two sources of ethical dilemmas in stock options: the size and the strike price.

First, the size of stock option grants to top management has ballooned in recent years. Coupled with market timing, this has led many to believe that the profits from option exercise are excessive and undeserved (Paulin and Cook, 1992). While intended as an investment vehicle to direct long-run management attention to the growth of shareholder value, there is a realization that stock acquired through the exercise of options is being treated as a trading asset. Second, some firms have engaged in the practice of canceling stock options that were granted at prices that preclude their being cashed in as trading assets. These "underwater" options were canceled long before their expiration date and immediately replaced by an identical number at the price in effect at the date of grant, making it easier for the executive to register a gain and make a profit. Recent changes in SEC reporting requirements and proposed moves by the Financial Accounting Standards Board regarding the valuation and expensing of stock options at time of grant mitigate these practices.

Executive perquisites

While perquisites represent a minor proportion of executive compensation (usually no more than 5 percent) and while recent tax law changes and proxy reporting requirements have made them less desirable, they nonetheless provide the HR executive with a disproportionate ethical headache because their cost is out of proportion to the value-added. The responsibility for administering these programs falls to the top HR executive who must live with the excesses that often are practiced. Some examples of ethically questionable practices follow.

Executive residence

The provision of a home by the firm as part of compensation for top executives is not common in the U.S., although it is in other countries. Ethical issues associated with this issue arise most often when the executive is building or has purchased a new home and has difficulty selling his current home. To overcome this obstacle the executive will ask the HR person to use the company's employee relocation program, which is designed not for this purpose, but rather to assist transferees and new hires to make a move with a minimum of financial hardship. These programs often arrange for the purchase of the transferee's old home.

There have been instances of top-level executives who were not relocating being allowed to use their company's relocation programs when a timely sale was not forthcoming or when a sale could result in a personal monetary loss. Notable in this respect was the case of Lee Iaccoca, former CEO of Chrysler Corporation, who moved to a new home after the company purchased his two current homes (Horton, 1992). Similarly, one HR executive told us of the purchase of a second home in a distant state for his company's CEO. Despite the claim that the home would be used as a conference center for company management, it served primarily as a getaway residence for the CEO and his family.

Corporate aircraft

In *Barbarians at the Gate*, a recent best-selling book, Burrough and Hellyar (1990) recounted several tales of abuse of corporate aircraft by top level managers of RJR Nabisco. The abuses usually involved personal travel at company expense. At the extreme was a story recounting the transport of the CEO's pet German

Shepherd as the sole passenger, carried on the manifest as "G. Shepherd."

In some cases, under the guise of security considerations, a firm under pressure from the CEO, will mandate that all family members ride only in corporate aircraft. According to one of the human resources managers we interviewed, his CEO was reimbursed nearly $150,000 (including gross-up to meet tax liabilities) to make him whole for the one-year cost of his and his family's travel on the corporate airplane which was taxable compensation to him.

The purpose of these examples is to show the pressures on the HR executive, as administrator of the perquisites program, to bless actions inimical to shareholder interests. A second consequence of perquisite abuse is that once they become widely known, they contribute to widening the credibility gap between top management and lower-level employees.

Club memberships

Of particular concern to HR managers required to deal with race and sex discrimination issues, are company-paid memberships in luncheon and country clubs that engage in race, ethnic, and gender discrimination. According to one human resources executive, when this inconsistency was brought to the attention of his CEO, the CEO argued that club membership was independent of workplace discrimination matters. For the HR executive, with his day-to-day involvement with the exempt and nonexempt workforce, it was not as easy to walk away from the issue.

Separation agreements

In many firms involuntary separation of top management personnel often results in disproportionately more generous severance arrangements than those granted lower-level employees. Proxy statements reveal the details for the five highest-paid employees, but arrangements often go beyond this. One frustrated practitioner stated that in his company "members of senior management take

care of each other by working out generous separation agreements."

RACE, GENDER, AGE, AND DISABILITY DISCRIMINATION

Ethical issues relating to the treatment of employees in relation to their race, ethnic origin, sex, or disability have generally been laid to rest. A framework of laws and regulations has evolved that has dramatically impacted workplace discrimination. The threat of litigation and the attendant costs have spurred employers to introduce numerous programs designed to train managers and supervisors to avoid discriminatory practices. In addition, the social environment, while not perfect, has undergone parallel change. This also improved workplace behaviors, even if they are not yet perfect.

No enterprise today would dare to publicly state that it denies minorities, women, and the disabled opportunities for employment, compensation, and advancement different from those given to white males. And increasingly employers must support their official statements with meaningful actions. Nor are employees likely to remain silent in the face of perceived discriminatory practices.

In this environment, the role of the HR function is to:

1 Monitor the principles and norms of the enterprise to insure they reflect the values of the society as expressed in its laws.
2 Monitor the selection, reward, development, and appraisal systems to insure that they are consistent with those principles and norms.
3 Vigorously pursue violations and, when necessary, vigorously work to defend the enterprise against unfounded allegations.

A demanding ethical challenge arises when there is pressure to protect the organization or an individual at the expense of someone else during an investigation. In practice, charges of discrimination and harassment often pit the accusations of the accuser and the denials of the accused against each other without clear benefit of witness or documentation, increasing the opportunity for ethical dilemmas.

EMPLOYMENT ISSUES

While discrimination and harassment situations receive the most publicity, HR practitioners are more likely to face ethical dilemmas in the areas of selection and hiring. One challenge commonly encountered is pressure to hire a long-time friend of a highly placed executive. Consider this brief example: Despite a well-established recruitment and promotion system, your supervisor calls you in to her office to tell you she thinks that "Good Ole Boy" of the XYZ Company would be terrific for the vacant division head position. "I've known Good for 20 years. He's a great guy, a great motivator, a heck of a lot of fun. I hope you'll hire him." The job Good has is a big one but with a small company. Instead of supervising a $50 million operation, he'll be expected to run a $500 million one. Also, you can immediately think of two credible candidates from within who have been identified in the company's succession plan as eligible for promotion to the position. What is right? What do you do?

Another area related to employment is that of fraudulent credentials submitted by a job applicant. One of the most common examples is that of the faked college degree. While discovery of this fabrication usually leads to the termination of the selection process, the choice becomes difficult when the applicant has a skill that is in short supply and has a proven record of success with previous employers.

The challenge is intensified in the case of an employee who has been with the firm for some time, establishes a successful record, and then is discovered to have lied about his or her educational credentials. In a 1983 study,

43 percent of mid-level executives surveyed indicated that they would overlook the deceit of a worker employed for over a year (Ricklefs, 1983).

Another employment-related ethical land mine is a request for a reference on a former employee. The fear of litigation has led to a growing tendency to limit responses to the bare facts and to make no statement regarding performance. Most corporate legal departments would strongly advise against offering any information beyond the confirmation of the dates of employment. While this is expedient for the legal department, HR people can experience considerable ethical discomfort when avoiding comment about a clear record of poor performance. Similarly, a favorable reference, motivated by compassion for a former employee with a generally undistinguished record, is equally unethical in that it misleads the prospective employer.

BENEFITS ISSUES

Employee benefits often provide considerable ethical conflicts between the real needs of individuals and the organization's need to control costs. The following represents an actual case that was decided by the U.S. Supreme Court (Gajda, 1992):

John McGann took a job with H & H Music Company. Shortly after he started he was enrolled in the H & H health plan which provided, among other things, for up to $1,000,000 of benefits while he was employed. The H & H program was "insured," in the sense that a premium was being paid to an insurance company. McGann subsequently became afflicted with AIDS and filed a claim with his employer's insurer. Soon thereafter H & H terminated its insured plan, replacing it with a self-insured plan administered by a third party. The new plan retained the $1,000,000 lifetime maximum benefit except for AIDS-related illnesses, which were capped at $5,000. Under the terms of the new plan McGann's claims in excess of $5,000 were denied.

In this case the Supreme Court held for H & H Music, stating that under existing law a self-insured employer has an absolute right to change the provisions of a benefit plan. While the reduced benefits of the new plan obviously affected McGann, the change was not considered discriminatory because it would equally affect any similarly situated claimants.[3]

There are clear ethical issues in this example. For one, cardiovascular disease imposes far greater costs on health plans than AIDS; if one wished to cut costs, one would focus on this generally costlier and more prevalent illness. Moreover, while there is no evidence that the employer was making a moral judgment, it should be noted that those afflicted with AIDS include not only homosexuals and intravenous drug users, but also young children infected through transfusion or through the mother at birth.

A contrasting situation sometimes experienced by HR executives in companies which have self-insured health plans is pressure to pay a large claim that otherwise would have been denied. This brief example summarizes the issues:

> *The dependent daughter of Sarah Walton, the firm's leading salesperson for the past three years, has a critical, life-threatening disease that has not responded to traditional treatments. Her physician recommends a new treatment which the health plan's medical advisor concludes is highly experimental with insufficient proof of success. Sarah's boss, the vice president of sales, argues that company plan should pay the estimated $100,000 cost of the procedure because Sarah is the most valuable employee in his department. "How can we treat this outstanding employee like this?"*

In this example the ethical issues relate to: management's interest in wanting to satisfy and retain a valuable employee; the interests of employees who, on the one hand, compassionately want see a fellow employee helped but, on the other hand, might view uneven application of the rules as being unfair; and the interests of the shareholders, who might take a negative view of a significant expense that is hard to justify in the cold light of day.

While health probably represents the largest benefit category for ethical challenge, other areas can bring problems. For example, managers sometimes have attempted to place a poorly performing long-time employee, with an illness which would not normally qualify, on long-term disability in lieu of termination.

The status of benefits for employees terminated in layoffs often has ethical overtones. Many HR practitioners have had to wrestle with the case of the about-to-be terminated employee who is just weeks or months from being vested in the retirement plan. Similarly, many firms raise moral issues when they reduce benefits granted to past retirees. Here the issues relate to balancing the firm's desire to control unexpectedly high costs with the breach of a promise of security in retirement as a reward for long and faithful service.

PRIVACY ISSUES

It has been asserted that all privacy issues are essentially human resources issues (Brenkert, 1981). Issues often arise in the selection process. They include, for example: the requirement for taking certain psychological tests; the validity and reliability of certain required honesty tests; the use of inappropriate and illegal application form and interview questions; and the failure to hold the results of all of these confidential (Conference Board, 1989; Linowes, 1993). They also arise during the course of employment, particularly relating to access to confidential information contained in employee records (Leonard, 1993; Smith, 1993). The following example adopted from Berenbeim (1992), is representative:

> *In 1985, Bob Spicer, a 15-year veteran salesman and a frequent winner of annual sales awards, confided to his boss that he had been drinking heavily*

209

because of depressing family problems. He was referred to the firm's employee assistance program which offered alcohol abuse counseling. Since that time Spicer's performance has been consistently superior. The high stress position of sales vice president will soon be open and Spicer has indicated his desire to be considered for it. His former boss, now the CEO, asks the VP of human resources to quietly investigate Spicer's after-work activities and also check his medical claims files, which are maintained by the firm's outside health claims administrator, to determine if Spicer's depression and alcoholism still exists. Since these records are not supposed to be available to anyone but the employee, how should the HR person proceed?

In some quarters there is growing concern over employee monitoring, particularly in the telecommunications, banking, and insurance industries. Linowes (1993) states that as many as 80 percent of the workers in these industries are subjected to telephone or computer-based monitoring. This monitoring is often surreptitious (Bureau of National Affairs, 1992), as is video surveillance in employer locker and rest rooms, usually in the course of drug investigations (Linowes, 1993). To what extent is this necessary? To what extent does it represent an invasion of privacy?

Privacy considerations have also been raised about the growing tendency to control health-related behaviors such as smoking and obesity. These can have negative effects not only on employees' health, but also on the employer's costs through absenteeism and insurance claims. There is a growing trend to prohibit smoking in the workplace. It is being resisted by advocates of smokers' rights, although this movement is being offset by the claims of deleterious effects of secondary smoke on others. In general, the issue of smoking in the workplace has been settled in many localities through local laws and ordinances, rendering the ethical issue moot. What is an issue is the extent the employer can monitor and control employee behavior outside the workplace.

Workplace privacy issues are not clear-cut in their ethical ramifications. Etzioni (1992) asserts the need for a "systematic moral and legal doctrine as to what are the rights and responsibilities of employees" when it comes to worker privacy. In the absence of that, he indicates that when "misconduct significantly affects work performance, and the employees are forewarned that certain behaviors are taboo, the corporation's needs should take precedence over the employees'."

EMPLOYEE AND LABOR RELATIONS

Employee relations situations with ethical overtones often relate to the inconsistency in the application of rules and regulations. Consider the following: The company negotiated an absence policy with the union that provided for up to five paid days off annually due to illness. This policy was extended to the nonunion office employees as well. However, while the rule was strictly enforced for bargaining unit employees, office employees were routinely paid for illness-related absences in excess of the five-day annual limit with the tacit approval of top management.

Sometimes managers insist upon exceptions to the rules for violations incurred by exceptional performers: Bill's secretary, Susan, is a young single parent, divorced and not receiving the court-ordered child support due from her ex-husband. An excellent worker, she was recently named "employee of the month". An unannounced audit reveals a $200 shortage in the petty cash account Susan is responsible for maintaining. After first denying knowledge of the missing funds, she admits to Bill that she borrowed the $200 for pressing family needs. She promises to repay the money through deductions from her pay. The company policy manual states that theft warrants termination and possible prosecution. Bill meets with the HR manager and indicates that this is the first negative in an otherwise exemplary record of performance and that Susan has proven competencies that have enhanced the performance of this department. It will be difficult to replace her. What to do?

While due process in disciplinary situations is usually clearly spelled out in union agreements, it is not as clear in nonunion situations. The question of due process is an ethical issue that has been addressed in some corporations (e.g., IBM, Federal Express, and Northrop) by the establishment of a formal grievance procedure for nonunion employees (Ewing, 1990). In some companies codes of conduct are being reviewed for their ethical ramifications, with employees being involved in the development of revised codes that reflect the culture of the enterprise while particularly emphasizing due process (Redeker, 1990; Coye & Belohlav, 1989).

Union relationships present additional ethical challenges for HR practitioners. In the CCH/SHRM survey respondents in unionized companies indicated ethical concerns in three main areas: demanding unnecessary concessions from the union; withholding information from the union; and using discipline for union and nonunion personnel inconsistently, a point we have already discussed. Does the demand for unnecessary concessions imply bad faith bargaining? Not according to the CCH study, which says that, while not illegal, such action may be unethical (Commerce Clearing House, 1991).

Withholding information usually comes in the form of bluffing in labor relations. An interesting view of the ethics of bluffing (Carson, Wokutch, & Murmann, 1982) contends that although bluffing is in effect lying, it is acceptable when the persons one is dealing with are similarly attempting to bluff or deceive. However, if one is dealing with an unusually naive or scrupulous person or group, bluffing is inappropriate.

In summary, the HR practitioner can influence the administration of the relationship between employer and employee by being knowledgeable about the ethical implications of due process, union and nonunion grievance systems, and labor negotiations. There are right and wrong ways to approach employee relations and many people agree with us the right ways are beneficial for all the stakeholders (Derber, 1958; Giacalone, Reiner, & Goodwin, 1992). As Leiserson (1938, 17–18) stated in his historic essay on the labor contract (but relevant also to the contract employers should have with all workers):

the labor contract is not a mere buying and selling contract, but a basis of human relationships on which the life purposes and happiness, liberties and opportunities of individuals, families and communities depends. . . . In apportioning rewards among workers, managers and investors, and in arranging their prerogatives, liberties, duties, and responsibilities, principles and methods must be used that are more in keeping with our professed ethical and social ideals.

RESTRUCTURING AND LAYOFFS

The restructuring activities of the past several years, and the layoffs that have resulted, cannot be considered unethical as such. While some union officials might disagree, even the export of American jobs to other countries that we see frequently in today's global economy, result in economic gain for the receiving country and jobs for its residents (Cox, 1992). Also, reductions in force due to new technologies, failure to recognize changes in the marketplace, or loss of sales to lower cost competitors, are not unethical. They may in some cases be due to incompetent management, but incompetence does not automatically equate with unethical behavior. In the past some writers have included companies that offered "lifetime employment" in the highest echelons of ethical practice. In more recent times, under intense competitive pressures and with lagging performance, these same firms have cut employees and abandoned attempts to provide jobs for life. Yet they cannot be accused of abandoning ethical principles in their struggle to survive.

However, there are ethical implications in the process by which termination decisions are made and actions taken. For example, if a restructuring requires the closing of a plant, the process by which that plant is chosen, how the news will be communicated, and the time frame for completing the layoffs are ethically important. If conducted in an atmosphere of fairness and equity with the dignity of the affected individuals in mind, the action is ethical. At best, Nash (1991) suggests that stretching the time frame for completing decision making or implementation especially be attempted.

Reductions in departmental staffing for economic reasons often result in selection methods that raise ethical issues. Consider the following: After two downsizings in the past year business conditions dictate another round of layoffs. The management committee concludes a 10 percent cut is needed and asks the HR function to design and administer a forced ranking system in each department to achieve the goal. The HR staff devises a four-point formula (one being the lowest and four being the highest) to be applied to two categories: current performance and sustained performance over the last three years. Distribution of ratings are mandated: 5 percent rated "4"; 40 percent rated "3"; 45 percent rated "2"; and 10 percent rated "1". All employees rated "1" are to be terminated. After receiving these instructions, a furious department head approaches the head of HR. She states that after the two recent cuts all of those remaining in her department were outstanding and deserved to be rated no lower than "3". "We've already reduced all the fat. Is it right to try to eliminate the remaining able performers by giving them forced low ratings?" The answer to this question is a challenge, but is probably easier to arrive at than the answer in a more common situation,

as summarized in the following (based on one suggested by Nash (1991, 214):

You, as HR manager, are aware that the market research function, which has been the subject of considerable discussion in the management committee about its value to the company, has been given a three month lease on life while its future undergoes intensive review. Your friend, a market research manager, comes to you confidentially to ask for advice. She has just been offered a job with another company and asks your advice on what she should do. You know that your friend's input on a current major project is crucial to its success and the company could not afford to lose her now. But if you shared your knowledge, she would take the offered position. On the other hand, based on past experience, there is good chance that the news of the impending review will leak within a short time.

In this brief example the manager faces the concern for a friend's welfare and a concern for the company's welfare. Where does honesty reside? What is right?

DEALING WITH ETHICAL SITUATIONS

The examples given on the foregoing pages are representative of issues facing human resources managers. They deal with relationships between HR managers and their superiors, peers, and subordinates. They also deal with relationships between one employee and another. While many ethical situations have legal implications, the issues go beyond an interest in complying with the law. More often, managers' ethical concerns focus less on legal issues than on relationships and responsibilities. In spite of this focus, the trend is toward formal ethics programs built on liability avoidance foundations.

Formal ethics programs

The genesis of the movement in large part has been the growing corporate and personal legal liability associated with organizational wrongdoing and the introduction in 1991 of new federal sentencing guidelines for convicted companies. These guidelines base penalties in part on the extent to which companies take steps to prevent misconduct. The programs being implemented emphasize reporting by employees (usually anonymously) of alleged crimes by means of telephone "hotlines" and other internal means.

This approach, commonly known as "whistleblowing", is estimated to be in place at over a hundred firms (Mason, 1994). Many of the firms adopting these programs are defense contractors, a group that has a long history of misconduct in their dealings with the federal government.

Generally, these programs are administered by corporate "ethics officers", with titles ranging from director to vice president. In some cases the top HR officer has been given the added duty of ethics officer. In one such program of a large division of a big defense contractor the VP-human resources/ethics chairs an ethics committee composed of the corporate legal counsel and representatives of the audit, facilities management, and employee relations functions. In addition, a full-time staff person investigates complaints reported on the employee hotline. The committee, meeting 2–3 times per month handles about 30 complaints a year, the majority of which are employee-relations issues related to allegations of discrimination, sexual harassment, and timecard fraud. Each case is thoroughly investigated; most are handled by the human resources department's employee-relations staff and are disposed of in a grievance procedure system that emphasizes principles of due process.

That the bulk of cases in this example relate to one employee reporting on another comes as no surprise to those who have experienced this approach. It appears to unleash personal antagonisms. Among criticisms of this approach are that an environment of mistrust is created and the fear of being reported and subsequently investigated results in a dampening of independent action, as care is taken to avoid the slightest misstep; that the reporters, even if assured anonymity – or at least confidentiality – often can be identified and harassed by the accused and their peers and superiors; and that usually the accused does not have the right to face the accuser (Mason, 1994).

One program which has received favorable attention because of its broader approach to handling ethics in the organization is the program developed by Martin Marietta Corporation (Paine, 1994). While retaining legal compliance as a critical objective, it more widely focuses on a "do it right" climate. Emphasis is on core values of honesty, fair play, quality, and environmental responsibility. Among its features are a code of conduct and ethics training for the entire work force (including a game that features 55 hypothetical cases). The program is managed by a corporate ethics officer with the assistance of ethics representatives in various locations. An ethics steering committee, composed of the president, senior executives, and two rotating employees from field locations, provides oversight.

The Martin Marietta ethics office handles employee questions and concerns about ethical situations, acting as a sounding board and providing guidance. It administers procedures for reporting and investigating ethical concerns as well as the system for disclosing violations of federal procurement law to the government. The company has twice turned itself in for improprieties connected with defense contracts, paying fines totaling $6.2 million (Hetrick, 1993).

Martin Marietta's vice president of corporate ethics does not support the idea that HR should provide ethics leadership. In his case the ethics office covers the entire organization. "Somebody needs to be watching HR" (Tompkins, 1993). In most situations, however, it is HR's role to take a leadership position (whether by choice or default). A 1991 survey of 295 personnel executives (Barnett & Cochran, 1991) shows a formal whistle-blowing policy reported by 70 percent of the respondents with three-quarters of them indicating that the HR department was the leading organizational function receiving employee charges of wrongdoing.

CONCLUSIONS

The special role of the HR function has resulted in significant exposure to ethical challenges for the HR practitioner. As the function is integrated into the strategic management of the enterprise, and the HR executive is routinely involved in processes that deal with companywide issues, the exposure to ethical issues grows.

As a result, the HR manager deals with more stakeholders than other functional managers: the interests of the company, as seen from management's perspective; the interests of the employees, where HR historically has been expected to play an advocacy role; and the interests of shareholders and other stakeholders.

This exposure is documented in the CCH/SHRM study which indicated that 83 percent of the HR respondents saw themselves as responsible for providing ethical leadership and guidance in their organization, a higher percentage than those who said their CEO provided such leadership. When asked who *should* have responsibility, 95 percent stated that HR should share it with the CEO and other top managers. This survey appears to indicate that, while HR managers are prepared to act as the "conscience" of their organizations, they feel they alone cannot fill this role. Ethical leadership is the task of all top managers, not just the HR executive.

The mantle of ethical leadership is not worn lightly and it can and does bring numerous problems. Ethical choices are often ambiguous and other managers often are not in agreement on their responses. In practice the fair and equitable answer to a problem is not necessarily in the best interests of the company. At what point do the firm's interests override the principles of the individual? In the view of the authors, HR is the only function that does not, cannot, or should not subordinate individual interests to organizational goals without at least considering the consequences.

The philosophical framework we discussed provides the HR manager with some assistance. Both Solomon and Nash move us away from moral absolutism and ask us instead to accept that ethics and interests can conflict in the imperfect world of mixed motives. Thus, the best approach to an ethical issue or dilemma is to take practicality into account and to do what is necessary in the most humane way possible (Solomon, 1992). What is necessary requires integrity practiced in an environment that subordinates self-interest to the needs of the stakeholders, while recognizing that a legitimate return is essential (Nash, 1991). "Legitimate return" must be defined by the various constituencies of the enterprise.

Nash suggests these tests when facing ethical issues:

- Do the decisions contribute to the good reputation of the company or the manager?
- Do the decisions promote trust?

In many organizations it takes a considerable amount of courage for the HR practitioner to act ethically, especially if the organization's leadership engages in unethical actions or promotes unethical behavior. The HR executive who is a member of the top management team can exert influence and sometimes bring about change in the ethical culture of the organization. However, one who expects to substantially and positively influence an organization's ethical behavior is probably doomed to disappointment. In this respect Clarence Randall, one-time chief executive of Inland Steel, put it best nearly three decades ago (Randall, 1967, 137–8):

It must be admitted . . . that not all ethical questions in business can be sharply divided between black and white. Often there is a grey area within which honorable men may differ. When the question falls in that category the junior may properly accept the judgment of his superior, and carry out his instruction. But where the action required is unqualifiedly repugnant to his own conscience he has no alternative. He must quit rather than go ahead. The consequences may be devastating in his own life. The threat to his financial security, and to the welfare of his family, may be almost beyond his power to cope. Nevertheless, the answer is clear. He must walk off the job and preserve his honor, no matter what the sacrifice.

NOTES

1 Attributed to Will Rogers in Shea (1988, 44).
2 This appears to be the weakest of Solomon's points. While a high proportion of employees view their job as "just a way to make a living," chief executives and top managers – clothed with the power and influence of their positions – are more likely to be game players who focus on winning.
3 In the opinion of some legal experts the subsequent passage of the Americans with Disabilities Act negates this decision; legal challenges are now underway.

REFERENCES

Badaracco, J. L., Jr., & Ellsworth, R. R. (1989). *Leadership and the Quest for Integrity*. Boston: Harvard Business School.

Barnett, T. R., & Cochran, D. S. (1991). Making room for the whistleblower. *HRMagazine*. January, 1991.

Baytos, L. M. (1991). Board compensation committees: Collaboration or confrontation? *Compensation and Benefits Review*, 23, May–June, 33–8.

Brenkert, G. G. (1981). Privacy, polygraphs, and work. *Business and Professional Ethics Journal*, fall, 19–35.

Berenbeim, R. E. (1992). Bad judgment or inexperience? *Across the Board*, October, 43–6.

Bureau of National Affairs (1992). Corporate ethics codes found growing, affecting human resources. *BNA's Employee Relations Weekly*, May 25, 563–4.

Burrough, B., & Hellyar, J. (1990). *Barbarians at the Gate: The fall of RJR Nabisco*. New York: Harper & Row.

Carson, T. L., Wokutch, R. E., & Murrmann, K. F. (1982). Bluffing in labor negotiations: Legal and ethical issues. *Journal of Business Ethics*, 1, 13–22.

Carr, A. Z. (1968). Is business bluffing ethical? *Harvard Business Review*. Jan.–Feb., 143–50.

Commerce Clearing House (1991). *Human Resource Management: 1991 SHRM/CCH Survey*. June 26: Commerce Clearing House Inc./Society for Human Resource Management.

Conference Board (1989). Employee privacy. New York: Research Report No. 945.

Coye, R., & Belohlav, J. (1989). Disciplining: A question of ethics? *Employee Responsibilities and Rights Journal*, 2 (3), 155–62.

Cox, C. (1992). Who cares about American workers? *Business Ethics*. March–April, 20–3.

Derber, M. (1958). *Right and Wrong in Labor Relations*. Champaign, IL: University of Illinois Institute of Labor and Industrial Relations Lecture Series No. 14.

Dibble, R. E. (1993). Ethics education in IR programs: Patterns and trends. *45th Annual Proceedings of the Industrial Relations Research Association*, 215–21.

Etzioni, A. (1992). The limits to worker privacy. *The New York Times*, December 20.

Ewing, D. W. (1990). The corporation as a just society. *Business Ethics*. March–April, 20–3.

Fombrum, C., Tichy, N., Devanna, M. A. (1984). *Strategic Human Resource Management*. New York: Wiley.

Fowler, E. M. (1992). Careers: Revamping the training of M.B.A.s. *New York Times*, April 7.

Friedman, M. (1970). The social responsibility of business is to increase its profits. *New York Times Magazine*, September 13, 32–3, 122, 124, 126.

Fullmer, W. E. (1989). Human resource management: The right hand of strategy implementation. *Human Resource Plannning*, 12 (4), 1–11.

Gajda, A. J. (1992). Health insurance after McGann. *Wall Street Journal*, November 11.

Giacalone, R. A., Reiner, M. L., & Goodwin, J. C. (1992). Ethical concerns in grievance arbitration. *Journal of Business Ethics*, 11, 267–72.

Gibbons, K. (1992). Marietta's ethics game gets gray matter going. *Washington Times*, October 19.

Gilbreath, R. S. (1987). The hollow executive. *New Management*, 4.

Hetrick, R. (1993). Martin Marietta uses game to teach corporate ethics. *The Reuters European Business Report*, March 29.

Hodgson, K. (1992). *A Rock and a Hard Place: How to make ethical decisions when the choices are tough*. New York: American Management Association.

Horton, T. R. (1992). *The CEO Paradox*. New York: American Management Association.

Hosmer, L. T. (1987). *The Ethics of Management*. Homewood, IL: Irwin.

Korsvik, W. J., & Juris, H. A. (1990). *The New Frontier in Bank Strategy: Managing people for results in turbulent times*. Homewood IL: Dow Jones Irwin.

Leiserson, W. M. (1938). *Right and Wrong In Labor Relations*. Berkeley, CA: University of California Press.

Leonard, B. (1993). The tough decision to use ethical information. *HRMagazine*. July, 72–5.

Linowes, D. F. (1993). Your personal information has gone public. *Illinois Quarterly*, Sept.–Oct., 22–4.

Mason, M. (1994). The curse of whistleblowing. *Wall Street Journal*, March 14.

Mills, C. W. (1951). *White Collar: The American middle classes*. New York: Oxford University Press.

Myers, R. N. (1992). Martin Marietta devises board game to "sell" staff on concept of ethics. *Wall Street Journal,* September 25.

Nash, L. L. (1991). *Good Intentions Aside.* Boston: Harvard University Press.

Paine, L. S. (1994). Managing organizational integrity. *Harvard Business Review.* March–April, 106–17.

Paulin, G. B., & Cook, F. W. (1992). What should be done about executive compensation? *ACA Journal,* autumn, 20–35.

Randall, C. B. (1967). *The Executive in Transition.* New York: McGraw-Hill.

Redeker, J. R. (1990). Code of conduct as corporate culture. *HRMagazine.* July, 83–7.

Ricklefs, R. (1983). Executives apply stiffer standards than public to moral dilemmas. *Wall Street Journal,* November 3.

Shea, G. F. (1988). *Practical Ethics.* New York: American Management Association.

Smith, L. (1993). What the boss knows about you. *Fortune,* August 9, 89–93.

Solomon, R. C. (1992). *Ethics and Excellence: Cooperation and integrity in business.* New York: Oxford University Press.

Stark, A. (1993). What's the matter with business ethics? *Harvard Business Review,* May–June, 1993.

Tarbel, I. M. (1904). *History of the Standard Oil Company.* New York: Phillips.

The Economist (1993). *How to be ethical and still come top.* June 5, 71.

Tompkins, N. C. (1993). Ethics officer doesn't belong in HR, say experts. *HR News, Society for Human Resource Management.* July, 8.

Walker, J. (1992). *Human Resources Strategy.* New York: McGraw-Hill.

Webster's Ninth New Collegiate Dictionary (1984). Springfield, MA: Merriam-Webster.

Whyte, W. H. (1956). *The Organization Man.* New York: Simon & Schuster.

☐ Chapter 12 ☐

Juggling on a High Wire: The Role of the International Human Resources Manager

Nancy K. Napier, Jacques Tibau, Maddy Janssens, and Ronald C. Pilenzo

INTRODUCTION

Dramatic increases in international activity in the last decade have raised attention on the management of human resources in firms operating across borders. Cross-border activity encompasses importing, exporting, and start up operations as well as alliances, mergers, and acquisitions. In such an environment, human resource management is emerging as a critical "competitive factor" (Evans, Doz, & Laurent, 1990; Schuler, Dowling, & De Cieri, 1993; Taylor, Beechler, & Napier, 1993; Teagarden, Butler, & Von Glinow, 1992) with tough questions for the international human resources (IHR) manager. What is international human resource management's (IHRM) strategic role in an organization that competes globally? What are the key components in managing IHRM? How can IHR managers design and manage IHRM activities to meet changing external and internal environments? Which IHRM activities should be coordinated worldwide and which are more appropriately done at the unit or local level? The manager must juggle IHRM issues in an increasingly unpredictable "high wire," high-stakes international environment.

Ideally, of course, managing human resources would naturally be considered in a global context. More specifically, this *Handbook* would need no separate chapter on "international human resource management." Human resources issues affecting firms operating across borders would be incorporated as a matter of course in discussions of other HRM topics. Alas, in their thinking if not their actions, many managers and scholars (at least Americans) still live in "bordered" worlds. Until we inherently think of firms in a global context, we must address explicitly the types of human resources issues facing firms that operate across borders. In this light, we explore the role of the IHR manager and the tasks and activities that (should) occur within the IHR function.

We assume that readers have some experience, or at least, interest in IHRM. Managers who encounter IHRM for the first time often have basic and technical questions (e.g., "How do I deal with immigration laws? How do I pay an expatriate? What is our tax liability?"). Such questions, while important, are beyond this chapter's scope. Instead, we offer a way to help IHR managers diagnose their firms' situations, design and manage the IHRM function, and evaluate its contribution.

Definitions

Much literature discusses IHRM in terms of how it differs from domestic HRM. Morgan (1986) discusses three factors: (1) type of employee (i.e., local nationals, expatriates, third country nationals); (2) countries of operations (i.e., host, home, other); and (3) human resources function operations (i.e., procurement, allocation, utilization). Others (e.g., Florkowski & Nath, 1990; Gronhaug & Nordhaug, 1992; Kidger, 1991) argue that IHRM differs from and is more difficult to manage than domestic HRM because of macroenvironmental factors (e.g., cultural, socioeconomic, institutional, and political dissimilarities across countries). Still others (e.g., Milliman, Von Glinow, & Nathan, 1991; Schuler et al., 1993; Taylor et al., 1993) define IHRM more at an organizational level and focus on its strategic role. For instance, Schuler et al. (1993, 422) define IHRM as, "human resource management issues, functions, and policies and practices that result from the strategic activities of multinational enterprises and that impact the international concerns and goals of those enterprises."

We sought to incorporate ideas from earlier work and input from discussions with managers in firms doing business across borders. Thus, for our discussion, IHRM comprises four critical components: (1) a firm's various environments or contexts (both inside and outside of the firm); (2) the IHRM function (i.e., activities of finding, allocating, developing, and valuing human resources, plus supporting systems and processes); (3) employees involved in work that transcends borders (i.e., mode of international interaction, level/type, and "source"), and (4) outcomes or contribution of IHRM (figure 12.1).

Together the components create a three-

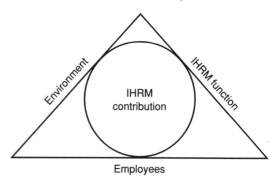

Figure 12.1 Four components of international human resource management

part framework or process of *diagnosing* organizational environments, *designing and managing* activities (of finding, allocating, developing and valuing human resources), systems, and processes in organizations that operate across borders, and *evaluating* IHRM's contribution (figure 12.2). In so doing, the IHR manager can help define and manage relationships and linkages between headquarters and units (e.g., subsidiaries, regional offices) and among subunits to enhance the overall effectiveness and efficiency of a firm (Schuler et al., 1993).

The aim of this chapter, then, is to discuss the international human resources manager's strategic role and suggest an overall approach to IHRM. The chapter comprises four main parts. The first part reviews the theory and research relating to IHRM. The second part discusses four IHRM components and presents a three-stage framework (i.e., diagnosis, design/management, evaluation). The third part illustrates the framework's ideas through an example of a Belgian multinational organization's recent experiences. Finally, the fourth part offers lessons for managers and scholars regarding IHRM.

THEORY AND RESEARCH: WHERE ARE WE NOW?

Literature on IHRM is thriving. Academic and professional books (e.g., Black, Gregersen,

Figure 12.2 International HRM framework

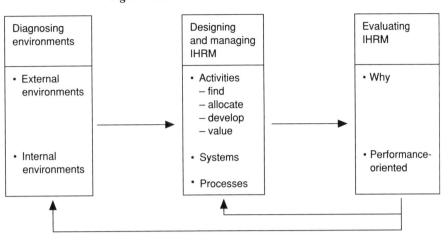

& Mendenhall, 1992a; Dowling, Schuler, & Welch, 1994), as well as literature reviews within books and journal articles have been extensive (e.g., Butler, Ferris, & Napier, 1991; McEvoy & Buller, 1993; Mendenhall & Oddou, 1985; Milliman et al., 1991; Schuler et al., 1993; Taylor & Beechler, 1993). We present a brief overview of recent literature from academic and professional sources to address interests of the dual audiences of this book and chapter. Given the volume of citations, we limited our comments to selected publications primarily between 1989 and 1993; for comprehensive reviews prior to 1989, other sources offer more detail (e.g., Dowling & Schuler, 1990; Butler et al., 1991).

Literature on IHRM has traditionally focused on several levels of analysis: (1) issues facing employees (particularly in terms of transfers overseas); (2) the IHRM function and its attendant activities; and (3) the types of factors (firm level and otherwise) that may influence IHRM. Finally, other literature discusses IHRM in various countries. In the following sections, we review briefly each category.

Employee-focused literature

Much of the (extensive) employee-focused literature examines issues relating to expat-

riate employees. The research has typically centered on American (male) managers or professionals transferred abroad: their preparation, adjustment to assignments, and issues of repatriation or return. Some work provides overall frameworks to explain employee adjustment (e.g., Black, Gregersen, & Mendenhall, 1992b; Kauppinen & Gregersen, 1993; Naumann, 1992); other research examines the reactions of expatriates to their assignments abroad (e.g., Black, 1988; Feldman & Thomas, 1992) or their return (e.g., Harvey, 1989; Napier & Peterson, 1989). Still other work examines the role that expatriates play in multinational organizations at large (e.g., Boyacigiller, 1990). Fewer investigations explore perceptions of managers from other countries or regions, including Asia (e.g., Black & Porter, 1991) and Europe (Janssens, 1993a; Scullion, 1992). Additionally, recent research examines more systematically the adjustment of spouses/partners in overseas assignments (e.g., Black & Stephens, 1989) and the issues facing selected groups of expatriates, such as women (e.g., Taylor & Napier, 1993).

Despite the plethora of recent academic and professional writing, much work on expatriates continues to support findings from earlier research (e.g., Tung, 1987) on the general lack of preparedness before assignments, the lengthy adjustment period to assignments abroad, and the difficulties and dissatisfaction of expatriates upon return from assignments (e.g., Bird & Mukuda, 1989; de Wilde, 1991; Feldman & Thomas, 1992; Harvey, 1989).

International human resource management function activities

A second large category of literature deals with the IHRM function, in terms of activities, policies and practices that firms use to manage employees. The literature typically encompasses four types of activities: finding, allocating, developing and valuing employees. *Finding* consists of planning for, recruiting, and selecting employees (e.g., Kane & Stanton, 1991; Laabs, 1991; Oddou & Mendenhall, 1991). *Allocating* includes issues relating to staffing, promoting, demoting, and transferring employees (e.g., Black & Stephens, 1989; Gregersen & Black, 1992; Kauppinen & Gregersen, 1993; Janssens, 1993a). *Developing* employees embraces policies and practices associated with preparing employees for current and future jobs in terms of formal and informal training, development programs, and career management (e.g., Evans, 1990, 1992). Finally, *valuing* employees entails appraising, rewarding, maintaining strong relations with, and assessing benefits and costs associated with employees (Janssens, 1993b; Pennings, 1993; Vance, McClaine, Boje, & Stage, 1992; Watson, 1992). The bulk of the literature dealing with the IHRM function and activities focuses on selection (i.e., criteria) and training for expatriates; more recent work examines performance appraisal and compensation issues.

Almost no literature addresses the evaluation of the IHRM function itself: that is, do the activities or the use of expatriates add value to an organization's competitiveness or effectiveness. While some scholars deal with evaluating human resources activities (e.g.,

Cascio, 1991), few deal directly with the impact or contribution of international HRM (e.g., Schuler et al., 1993; Taylor et al., 1993).

Influences on IHRM

A third category of literature places IHRM in a broader context. Several articles propose conceptual frameworks for IHRM (e.g., Dowling et al., 1994; Milliman et al., 1991; Schuler et al., 1993; Taylor et al., 1993). These models, developed by academics, generally suggest that firms and IHR managers must acknowledge the impact of external and internal influences on the way IHRM is developed and managed. Although they converge in their broader perspective for IHRM, each framework has unique elements. Dowling et al. (1994) contend that as firms grow or develop over time, they require different types of IHRM practices. Milliman et al. (1991) use organizational life cycle more specifically as a means to assess what various units will need in terms of IHRM practices. Schuler et al. (1993) stress the importance of interunit linkages as a key element of IHRM's strategic role. Finally, Taylor et al. (1993) argue for including all employees in considering IHRM issues, rather than focusing on managers and professionals, as is common in most literature.

Other work examines specific influences in the external and firm environments (Gronhaug & Nordhaug, 1992) that may indirectly affect the design and management of IHRM programs. Such "exogenous" or "external" factors (Schuler et al., 1993; Taylor et al., 1993) are ones that firms often cannot control, yet they can dramatically influence direction. Legal (e.g., Florkowski & Nath, 1990) or political (e.g., Teague, 1993) requirements can restrict, or be opportunities for (Brewster, 1993), the ways firms develop practices or interact with employees (e.g., union members). Economic health (e.g., Chiu & Levin, 1993; Greer & Ireland, 1992) or stage of economic development (e.g., Pieper,

1990) of countries in which firms operate may affect the extent to which employees seek transfer opportunities or a firm's ability to find and retain talented human resources. Culture may demand that IHRM practices be modified across countries (e.g., Schneider & De Meyer, 1991; Shore, Eagle, & Jedel, 1993; Warner, 1993). Technology (e.g., Gill, 1993) and other changes (e.g., Kanter, 1991; Stone, 1989) can influence the degree of employee participation in decision making and the types of decisions managers make about the structure and conduct of IHRM activities. Finally, industry (e.g., Bartlett & Ghoshal, 1989) may affect firms' structures and IHRM design and management.

Other literature argues that internal or "endogenous" (Schuler et al., 1993) factors also affect IHRM. Although increasing, relatively little empirical research exists specifically on whether and how firm strategy influences IHRM or, conversely, how IHRM plays a role in achieving firm strategy. Several scholars and practitioners comment on general impacts of globalization (e.g., Kanter, 1991; Lei & Slocum, 1991; Stone, 1989). Others propose conceptual models arguing that strategy (e.g., Dowling et al., 1994; Schuler et al., 1993; Taylor et al., 1993), organizational structure (e.g., Boyacigiller, 1990; Shore et al., 1993), or organizational life cycle (Milliman et al., 1991) may affect IHRM design and management. Still others, such as Teagarden et al. (1992), argue that in Mexican maquiladora firms, for example, human resources and related practices are indeed viewed as a strategic component to competitiveness.

Country or regional focused literature

A fourth category provides insights about IHRM approaches across countries. Although much work focuses on American firms, scholars and professionals increasingly examine other areas and types of firms. Some regions, and employee groups within those regions, continue to be key areas of focus, including China (e.g., Cyr & Frost, 1991; Tung, 1993; Warner, 1993), Japan (e.g., Jain, 1990; Sano, 1993), the Southeast Asian states of Singapore (e.g., Aryee, 1993; Chew & Teo, 1991) and Hong Kong (Chiu & Levin, 1993; Hildebrant & Liu, 1988), and Europe (e.g., Agres, 1991; Brewster, 1993; Courpasson & Livian, 1993; Ferner & Hyman, 1992; Maljers, 1992; Oliver & Davies, 1990; Sels, 1992, Thurley, 1990; Van den Bosch & Van Prooijen, 1992). Other areas, long neglected, are gaining notice as well. These include, for example Latin America (Grosse, 1992; Teagarden et al., 1992; Taylor & Beechler, 1993) and the Caribbean (Isaacs, 1989), Central Europe and Russia (e.g., Markoczy, 1993), and developing countries (Sadri & Williamson, 1989).

Methods

Although embryonic, IHRM literature uses an increasingly wide range of approaches to examine issues. Many scholars (e.g., Maljers, 1992; Schuler, Dowling, & De Cieri, 1992; White, 1992) and professionals (e.g., Agres, 1991; Chynoweth, 1992) use in-depth case studies to learn how firms design and manage IHRM, and other organizational functions. Other studies have surveyed individual employees (e.g., Black, 1988; Napier & Peterson, 1989) or firms. Brewster (1993) and his colleagues, for instance, surveyed over 10,000 firms throughout Europe to identify characteristics of a "European" model of HRM. Further, to compensate for the typical flaws in international research, more studies use multiple methods of data collection (e.g., surveys with interviews or case studies; Brewster, 1993; Taylor & Napier, 1993). Finally, scholars (e.g., McEvoy & Buller, 1993; Dowling et al., 1994; Schuler et al., 1993) increasingly suggest ways to conduct more systematic and integrative IHRM research. As such, future knowledge and its spread should improve (Adler & Bartholomew, 1992).

We now turn to the second part of the

chapter, where we discuss an approach that IHR managers can use to diagnose, design and manage, and evaluate IHRM.

THE ROLE OF THE INTERNATIONAL HUMAN RESOURCES MANAGER

IHRM, like other business functions, must add value to an organization. To decrease risk and enhance firm value, for instance, a chief financial officer (CFO) must understand a firm's current and intended strategy, determine what capital resources are needed, and participate in finding, allocating, developing/ investing, and assessing the return of that capital. Finally, a CFO helps manage the relationships among units to coordinate their use of financial resources. Likewise, an IHR manager will help manage costs and risks associated with international human resources while supporting overall competitive strategy. Similar to a CFO, the IHR manager will diagnose the firm's internal and external environments to understand international human resources challenges and future needs, will help find, allocate, develop, and value those human resources, and will evaluate the function's overall contribution to the firm. Finally, since IHR activities occur within units in many countries, the IHR manager and function may become a liaison among units.

This part of the chapter discusses these ideas in an IHRM context. First, we lay out four main components relating to IHRM, define them briefly, and discuss their importance. Then we explore how IHR managers can use those components in diagnosing their environments, designing and managing, and evaluating IHRM.

International human resource management components

Successful IHR managers understand and juggle at least four critical components: (1) the environments in which their organizations operate; (2) the IHRM function (i.e., activities, systems, processes); (3) the employees in their firms who are engaged in work that crosses borders; and (4) the ways that these components contribute to the firm.

Environments

Understanding the environments of firms operating across borders is critical for several reasons. First, changes in the economic, political, or related situations in a country can dramatically affect a firm's ability to conduct business. They may influence, for example, finding or placing appropriate employees in specific countries, successfully anticipating global training and development needs, or knowing which units need what types of attention.

"Environments" can range from broad external contexts (typically tied to specific countries) to ones internal to a firm (Milliman et al., 1991; Schuler et al., 1993; Taylor et al., 1993). For our discussion, we suggest four general types of environments, two "outside" and two "inside" firms (upper left corner, figure 12.3). *National level pressures* include such factors as governmental/legal, cultural, economic or labor-related aspects that ease or restrict firm operations in a given setting. The *industry pressures* include forces that move an industry toward more integration or local responsiveness, which in turn can affect the structure, functions, or market responses of firms within those industries (Bartlett & Ghoshal, 1989; Prahalad & Doz, 1987).

Firms have their own internal "environments" as well (upper left corner, figure 12.3). Units within a firm can vary in their organizational life cycle (OLC) stages (Milliman et al., 1991), which may influence the extent to which IHRM practices can and should be consistent or the amount and type of assistance that headquarters offers. Another "internal environment" is the range of specialized or distinctive *skills* within a firm that give it a competitive advantage. Identifying those

Figure 12.3 Detailed components of international HRM

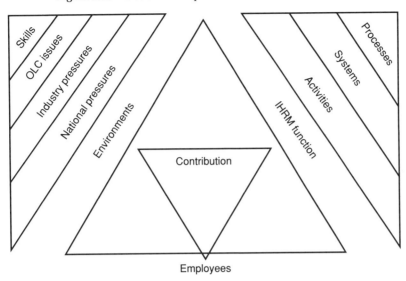

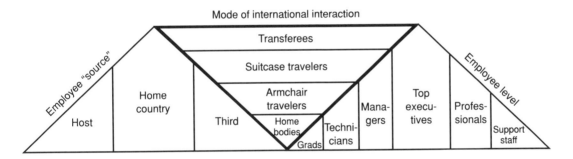

skills can affect the IHRM function and IHR manager in terms of deciding where to put efforts in finding, developing, or transferring those skills (Porter, 1990).

IHRM function

The IHRM function encompasses the "tools" or ways that IHR managers can help increase competitiveness. We include three areas: activities, systems, and processes (upper right corner, figure 12.3). *IHRM activities* are formal and informal human resources-related approaches that firms use to manage employees engaged in work that furthers the global competitiveness and other goals of a firm. In

the beginning of this part, we referred to the tasks of a chief financial officer as finding, allocating, developing or investing in, and assessing or valuing capital that a firm needs. The IHR manager designs and manages *four* similar types of activities: (1) finding qualified employees; (2) allocating them to appropriate tasks, positions, and units to enhance firm goals; (3) developing employees through such tools as career planning, or training and development programs; and (4) valuing employees to assess performance and reward their contributions.

In addition to IHRM activities, the function comprises *systems*, or tangible equipment or software that organizations use to improve performance, especially as it relates to IHRM. Two typical systems are HR information systems (HRISs) and communication networks. HRISs include information data bases that firms maintain on employees regarding technical and managerial experience, education, and the like, which can help in allocating, developing, and valuing human resources engaged in international operations. Some firms also maintain information about compensation and performance evaluation. Communication systems, particularly those developed for interaction among employees across borders (e.g., worldwide electronic mail systems) can foster integration of culture, as well as IHRM activities and practices.

Finally, IHRM *processes* are the less tangible means that firms use for integrating and improving communication and management functions across units. IHRM processes are especially important in firms operating across borders because of possible conflicts between corporate and local cultures and differences. Having a common set of values (or spoken and written language!) may, for example, help integrate employees.

Employees

Beyond the environments and the IHRM function, IHR managers juggle a third element in international HRM: the types of employees involved in international operations and their form of interaction (lower segment, figure 12.3).

Employee level/type As mentioned in the first part of the chapter, the literature has largely focused on "expatriate managers" as the main type of "international human resource" (e.g., Black, Gregersen, & Mendenhall, 1992a; Dowling et al., 1994). Taylor et al. (1993) recently questioned such emphasis and called for including all levels of employees in discussions about IHRM. We support that call and suggest that IHR managers consider what and how IHRM activities, systems, and

processes can be designed and managed for all levels and types of employees who work internationally, from top executives and mangers, to professionals and technicians, to young graduates and support personnel.

Type of interaction abroad In addition to the level or type of employee, the ways in which employees interact to conduct international business may influence the nature of IHRM activities. Employees can do their work across borders in many ways. For example, employees can be "transferees," moving for 1–5 years to another country. This group encompasses all employees who move across countries, including those who come *from* the "home" country (i.e., expatriates), those transferred *to* the home country (i.e., inpatriates), or those who move among various units other than the home country, often called "third country nationals" (Morgan, 1986). A second employee category is the "suitcase traveler," who goes from one country to another for short time periods (i.e., up to a year). To avoid high transfer costs and to handle specific challenges (e.g., transferring technical knowledge), many firms use these employees for such short-term assignments. Next, "armchair travelers" conduct international business from their home bases, with little or no travel. Such employees deal with cross-border counterparts, customers or suppliers through telephone, fax, electronic mail, or similar means. Finally, some employees (e.g., "home bodies") may have no international component to their work. Thus, as IHR managers consider what types of IHRM activities, systems, and processes are appropriate worldwide, she or he will consider whether differences by employee type are necessary.

Employee "source" Finally, although several IHR managers we have talked to (particularly in Europe) lament the notion of nationality or "source" of employee, we expect the IHR manager of the 1990s will consider it for several reasons (Dowling et al., 1994; Morgan,

1986). For example, government restrictions regarding work permits can influence finding and allocation decisions. Within Europe transfers, for instance, are simple for citizens of European Union member countries, but increasingly complex and restricted for Americans.

Contribution

A fourth component that IHR managers juggle is how to assess and show IHRM's contribution (central part, figure 12.3). Such assessment is important for several reasons. First, human resources, particularly when transferred overseas, represent a large investment for any firm. As costs are increasingly scrutinized, such expenditures will become more critical. Furthermore, if international human resources are indeed a "competitive factor," then finding, allocating, developing, and assessing them becomes that much more important.

Diagnosing environments

The academic and managerial literature on global strategy and IHRM often argues for the need for some integration or linkage across units of a firm operating across borders (e.g., Agres, 1991; Bartlett & Ghoshal, 1989; Prahalad & Doz,1987; Schuler et al., 1993). Reasons for such linkages include, for example, the gains from transferring or exchanging knowledge, the need to monitor or control activities within units, or as a way to broaden employee perspectives and enhance coordination and communication (Bartlett & Ghoshal, 1989).

A critical question then is "how much" and "what kind" of integration is appropriate. With little or no integration, a firm is simply a portfolio of disconnected units (Schuler et al., 1993). Conversely, "too much integration" can be overly complex and costly. The literature on mergers and acquisitions, for example, recommends creating relationships and linkages only on what is necessary to enhance overall effectiveness (e.g., Schweiger, Csiszar, & Napier, in press).

In this section, we examine a way for IHR managers to assess the types of relationships a firm may need among units. First, we review environmental pressures that push firms toward integration or local responsiveness (Bartlett & Ghoshal, 1989; Prahalad & Doz, 1987). Next, we discuss how managers can evaluate which units may need more attention or integration. Finally, we examine ways that IHR managers can identify which expertise areas (i.e., skills) can be driving forces behind designing and managing the IHRM function.

How much integration: pressures for integration vs. local responsiveness

This subsection has three main parts. We briefly discuss the Bartlett and Ghoshal (1989) framework and why and how we modified it for use by IHR managers, and its application in example settings.

The Bartlett and Ghoshal framework Several scholars have offered approaches to diagnosing environmental contexts (e.g., Prahalad & Doz, 1987; Porter, 1990) and the degree of integration appropriate within firms operating across borders. For this chapter, we use a framework developed by Bartlett and Ghoshal (1988, 1989) and colleagues (e.g., Ghoshal & Noria, 1989, 1993). They argue that environmental pressures will push an industry in two directions: toward more or less integration (i.e., centralization and coordination of select activities) or local responsiveness (i.e., decentralization and autonomy within units). The result is a four-cell grid (figure 12.4). Industries will tend to cluster within one cell, based upon how they (should) respond to such pressures as geographic location of suppliers or competitors, distribution costs, capital requirements and intensity, consumer demands, or standardization and transferability of production methods. When firms "match" their industry's cell in terms of

Figure 12.4   Industry category grid

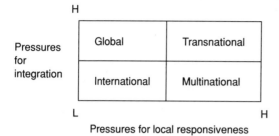

Source: Bartlett & Ghoshal (1989)

appropriate organizational structures and other arrangements, their financial performance should be higher (Ghoshal & Noria, 1993).

We adopted (and adapted) the framework for IHR managers for several reasons. First, developed and tested over a decade and reflecting input from managerial and scholarly audiences, the framework is intuitively appealing and easy for managers to apply to their own situations. Indeed, in our own research and consulting, managers could readily envision their firms' locations.

Also, the framework is not explicitly dynamic (i.e., it does not show movement or change over time within firms), yet we found managers nevertheless use it to "think" in that direction. In particular, managers can identify their firms' current positions and where they "should" be, given their industry environment. From this process, managers gain two benefits. First, if their firms are in the "wrong" cells, it helps managers see why the firm might be having difficulties. Second, the insights help managers decide how their firms might reset strategic direction. In one instance, a manager who saw his firm as being in one cell found that its environment called for another. When he realized that, he understood why his firm was struggling to integrate various activities, when it "should" have been allowing more local responsiveness.

Finally, although the framework is intended primarily for assessing pressures on industries,

we found its intuitive logic again leads managers to use it on individual units. Indeed, the framework can help managers understand why their units conflict with headquarters: if managers perceive that headquarters and the unit are at two different "positions" in the grid, their expectations differ about how much integration is appropriate.

Modifying the framework   Given our focus on IHR issues, we found a weakness of the framework to be its limited discussion about human resource management pressures and their implications. To assist the IHR manager, then, we pushed the framework two steps further. First, in addition to examining industry pressures (Bartlett & Ghoshal, 1989), we recommend that IHR managers also explore external human resources-related pressures or forces that may push industries and firms toward integration or local responsiveness. Second, we propose that managers examine human resources pressures *within* a firm for possible effects on integration.

Examples of external human resources-related pressures include: (1) existence of an available labor pool for critical skill areas; (2) government regulations regarding human resources; (3) general economic conditions (e.g., employment rate) in the countries of operation (parent country or given unit); and (4) culture in the parent or unit countries (left column, figure 12.5). In Thailand, for instance, these factors emerge in several ways. Double-digit economic growth means high demand for employees in certain skilled or professional areas (e.g., engineers, financial analysts). The labor pool is restricted, however, because of limited university slots, tremendous demand, and the tendency for many Thais to view experience at nonnational firms as short-term training before joining local companies. Hence, employee turnover is high and the capable labor pool meager. Such pressures may tend to push internationally active firms toward using transferees, and in turn, more integration and consistency of

Figure 12.5   IHRM and related factors affecting integration

Factors affecting how much to integrate	Factors affecting which units to integrate	Factors affecting what skill areas to integrate

• External
  – available labor pool
  – government restrictions
  – economic conditions
  – culture
	• Unit's willingness and ability to absorb knowledge	• Generalized skills

	• Unit's purpose
	  – start up
	  – "learning ground"
	  – strategic importance
		• Specialized skills

• Internal
  – costs/benefits of transfers
  – ability and willingness of employees to move
  – firm orientation
	• Unit's characteristics
	  – maturity
	  – need for restructuring
	  – past performance	

practices across countries. But, such actions may reduce the local unit's ability to develop its own human resources policies that would respond to market needs to find and keep local employees.

The relative condition of the economies in the headquarters and unit countries may also affect decisions on the extent and type of integration. For instance, because of the slowdown in the German economy, a German industrial chemical firm has found that home-country employees (e.g., professionals, managers and even some support staff) are increasingly willing to move. This requires more integrated IHRM activities in such areas as compensation and development, so the German transferees can eventually return successfully to Germany. Conversely, however, the Thai government works against such pressures by restricting work permits and allowable time frames for nonnationals to hold positions.

Finally, culture may affect whether and how a firm integrates IHRM practices. In Singapore, a Japanese toy manufacturing firm modified some HR activities to "fit" the local culture. Describing the approach, a manager

explained: Japanese rice is sticky, the same throughout. Chinese rice is "looser," with many different pieces. Unlike Japan, where the people (and policies) are homogeneous, Singapore has many kinds of people and cultures. He manages human resources activities the same way by modifying activities to fit the local "looser" situation.

In addition to examining external human resources pressures, we further adapted the framework to include human resources pressures *within* firms (central column, figure 12.5) that may encourage more integration or local responsiveness in IHR practices. Such pressures include, for example, the costs and benefits of employee mobility, orientation, productivity, and return of transferred employees. Given overwhelming transfer costs, which can be 2–3 times an employee's domestic salary (e.g., higher salaries and benefits, such as schooling costs), some IHR managers question the wisdom of widespread continued use of transferees. Indeed, some firms are creating single packages for newly hired staff who transfer within continental Europe, regardless of their "source." Rather than dealing with pay differences between, for example, German and British transferees, all employees receive a similar package, regardless of their source and post. Such "Eurocontracts" provide more benefits than the typical local hire, but fewer than the traditional expatriate package.

Mobility is also an issue in terms of employee ability and willingness to transfer or work across borders. Employees may (or may not) have the skills they need to succeed outside their home countries (e.g., second-language ability, cross-cultural experience and competence). Gaining such skills is time consuming, costly, and difficult for some people, even when they are technically competent. Furthermore employee unwillingness to transfer is likely to be more vexing for some firms by the year 2000. American and some German multinational firms increasingly face employees who balk at long- or short-term assignments abroad (e.g., because of dual career conflicts or school concerns). Such pressures may urge firms toward local hiring for local responsiveness in human resources activities, with perhaps some "suitcase" or "armchair traveler" support.

The length of orientation for transferees may also pressure firms toward local hiring and development or suitcase and armchair travelers. When an assignment is 2–3 years (e.g., typical in American firms) or where the culture is quite "hostile" or different from a given employee's home culture, an employee may be fully productive only toward the end of the assignment (e.g., Mendenhall & Oddou, 1985), making it difficult to justify the costs. Furthermore people insensitive to a local business environment may harm business relations and impair productivity among local employees, another force pushing to more local responsibility for human resource issues.

Finally, an "orientation" (Schuler et al., 1993) toward the use of "home country" (or other) managers in units abroad may demand more integration in planning, hiring, pay, training, or performance evaluation. One

of the American "Big Three" automobile firms, for example, has a "tradition" of using American managers in key positions abroad, meaning it also faces extra costs of integrating IHRM activities.

Applying the framework As noted earlier, the framework's four cells (figure 12.4) reflect the pressures that suggest the degree of integration or local responsiveness within firms in specific industries. For example, an *international environment*, pushing firms toward low integration and low local responsiveness, is common in industries such as machinery, printing and publishing, and paper. Such factors as relatively high product standardization and high distribution costs mean high integration would be costly; similarly, unique market demands are few, requiring little response to local needs. Such firms typically focus on domestic markets, treating international activities often as "appendages". International firms' focus, then, is on sales or exporting.

Such industries may draw upon a readily available labor force (e.g., chemical or mechanical engineers, skilled and unskilled production workers), primarily in the "home country." The aircraft manufacturer Boeing, for instance, has been a traditional international firm, partly because of its access to domestic talent, its lack of overseas production facilities (until its very recent alliance in Japan), and its focus on exporting. As a result of such a "domestic focus," Boeing has had little need for integrated IHRM activities, systems, and processes.

A *multinational environment* encourages firms to concentrate on local market concerns, with little need for extensive integration. In this environment, consumer preferences, which may vary dramatically across countries, are a primary force for decisions about structure and, ultimately, IHR needs and activities. Industries such as beverages, household appliances, retailing, and food typically fall in a multinational environment. To respond quickly to local demands, units operating in different countries demand more autonomy to develop or modify firm practices.

Given the pressure to depend upon and develop local expertise, the involvement from a parent firm (e.g., through knowledge transfer or monitoring and control) may be limited. When knowledge transfer (through transferees or "suitcase managers") does occur, it is apt to be for limited time periods. Further, the country may be developing local sources of talent and view subsidiaries as a logical employment outlet for the labor force.

A *global environment*, encouraging high integration and weak local responsiveness within firms, comprises industries such as industrial chemicals, semiconductors, standardized consumer products, and scientific instruments. Pressures pushing for integration include large capital investment requirements, worldwide product standardization, and low market demand differentiation. Gillette Company's strategy of "one (razor) blade fits all" (Uchitelle, 1994) exemplifies such an approach. Consumers need and use razor blades and fountain pens (another Gillette product) similarly worldwide. In this environment, IHR pressures for integration of certain functions (e.g., R&D) may stem from the availability of critical talent. In such a case, IHRM activities may relate primarily to a specific skill area (e.g., hiring, developing, valuing scientists).

Finally, a *transnational environment*, with industries such as automobiles, or computers, comprises forces that require high responsiveness to local market conditions *and* high integration within the firm. High capital intensity and need for economies of scale as well as a need for differentiation across geographic markets drive decisions to maximize both dimensions. A German automobile manufacturer, for example, is forced not only to adjust cars to meet local consumer demands, but also to meet "local expectations" in other areas. Customers expect to hear "German accents" in people in certain functions (e.g., sales, service). As a result, the firm continues to send German employees abroad for certain positions, even though it wants to transfer knowledge to local employees. Human resources issues may come into play here in several ways. The auto firm finds that it must "localize" servicing equipment in given countries to meet unique labor force conditions. In developing countries, equipment must be readily understood (i.e., information in the local language, more visual images instead of language in some cases), German service personnel must be able to speak the local language and understand limitations (e.g., training, experience) of employees.

While the framework suggests that industries fall within certain environments, individual *firms* do not always fall within their "correct" cells (Ghoshal & Noria, 1993). For example, another German automotive firm is undergoing a shift from being mainly "international" to more "transnational" in its orientation. Managers acknowledge that until the early 1990s, the firm was very "German" in its orientation: subsidiaries, mostly sales and service offices, were closely monitored by headquarters and staffed by Germans in key positions (e.g., country manager, technical posts). Nevertheless, the firm is being "forced" to become more "transnational" for several reasons, such as the stringent German environmental laws that compel it to seek production sites outside Germany.

Which units to integrate

Once managers have a sense of their firms' external environments and types of pressures that may affect IHR, they need to consider firm level "contexts" or environments. In the next stage of diagnosis, an IHR manager begins to assess which organizational units need greater attention or integration through transfer of knowledge, management assistance, or help in managing IHRM policies and practices (Schuler et al., 1993). We suggest that IHR managers evaluate units, drawing upon ideas from the literature on the organizational life cycle (OLC), suggested by Milliman et al. (1991).

Decisions about which units to integrate will depend on several factors (central column, figure 12.5). First, perceptions about the units' *willingness and ability* to absorb knowledge (e.g., availability of people and managers with expertise to absorb and use transferred information) may influence where and what kind of linkages are useful. For example, the relatively new Thai branch of an American financial institution must train its lending staff in the bank's credit policies. While the Thai unit staff members are willing to learn the policies, most lack the ability (i.e., expertise and previous training) to fully apply credit policies and procedures. So, while local staff members undergo training (both at headquarters and on site), the bank continues to staff key credit positions with experienced transferees from outside of Thailand.

Next, a *unit's purpose* in relation to the company as a whole may influence whether and how it needs to be integrated. Start up ventures (e.g., greenfield operations) or units "new" to the firm (e.g., joint ventures, alliances, or new acquisitions) may need more links with headquarters, at least initially. In start-ups, for instance, a unit may simply lack capable managers to run the operation (Scullion, 1992), or headquarters may want to develop more control or credibility. Thus, transferees or "suitcase managers" from a more mature unit may be used. For example, an electronics firm with a well-established regional headquarters in Belgium was responsible for building a much younger unit in France. The human resources function in France was nonexistent, leading the Belgium office to assign a "suitcase IHR manager" to the French operations on a part-time (50 percent) basis.

In other cases, units may be viewed as "learning grounds" for middle managers or high potential employees. Such units may also demand links with headquarters for certain IHR activities. A German chemical company's well-established and rapidly growing Southeast Asia divisions are viewed as a good learning ground for middle managers slated for upper-level positions. Because the Thai unit, for example, has few serious problems, transferred managers can focus on learning how markets work outside Europe and on gaining a sense of the way units work and work together outside Germany. In such cases, IHR activities such as performance evaluation or pay are integrated for such high potential employees so they can return eventually to Germany.

Finally, some units, perceived as more "strategically important," may receive more attention (and linkages) from the parent. A Japanese automobile maker operating in Europe has local managers in such "less strategic" countries as Belgium and France, but acknowledges that the larger, "more strategic" United Kingdom division will always have a Japanese general manager.

In addition to a unit's role within a firm, on site *unit characteristics* may affect expectations about the extent and type of integration needed. Such characteristics include, for example, maturity of the unit, need for restructuring, or past performance. In the example above, the IHR manager who spent 50 percent of his time developing a French unit said his initial focus was on creating very basic information about and policies for employees in the unit (i.e., when employees joined, pay and benefits data). The "link" between headquarters and the local unit can also be strong, at least during the time period needed to restructure the unit. In a British oil and chemical firm that needed to restructure and improve efficiency of certain units, a long-time employee transferred to one unit to train local staff in a new performance evaluation system that was intended to help create a new culture and way of operating. Finally, performance of the subsidiary (or head-quarters) may influence links. A European subsidiary of a Japanese firm finds its auto-nomy is increasing, partly because the unit's own performance has steadily improved but also because senior managers' attention is drawn more to domestic (i.e., Japanese) eco-nomic problems.

Areas to integrate

Once an IHR manager has a sense of *how much integration* is likely (based upon the evalua-tion of forces that push the firm toward more integration or local responsiveness) and *where there may be a need for integration* (based upon a review of the units' situations), he or she can turn to assessing *what skill areas* to focus on (right hand column, figure 12.5). Specifi-cally, the manager can identify and assess competencies which give a firm a competitive advantages.

To help IHR managers in this, we adapted Porter's (1990) ideas on the factors nations use to build competitive advantages. Porter (1990) defines generalized factors as elements such as highway systems or an educated work force; he describes specialized factors as sus-tainable bases for competitive advantage, such as people with very specialized skills, technol-ogy, or knowledge in specific fields. Likewise, for firms, "generalized factors" are readily available skills, such as skills in commonly used languages (e.g., English, German, Spanish) or expertise in international law or finance. Such skills are ones that many firms can eas-ily gain; they are necessary for successful operation but may not contribute to a firm's unique advantage. "Specialized" skills, on the other hand, might include language ability in unusual, but necessary, languages. For instance, an international American construction management firm finds itself at a loss as it begins jobs in Mongolia and the Ukraine. Most current employees have little sense of where the sites are, let alone speak the local languages! Thus to succeed in the

multi-million dollar jobs, the firm's IHR man-ager will focus on finding and developing people with the technical, language *and* cul-tural awareness skills to be able to function effectively in such remote sites.

Striking differences may exist across firms in the skills they hold or need to be com-petitive. A specialized skill for one firm may not be so for another. For example, for glo-bal industrial chemical firms, process tech-nology and research and development are specialized skills; multinational soft drink and beverage firms, on the other hand, may require specialized marketing and sales talent to address local issues. Identifying such spe-cialized factors allows an IHR manager to develop IHRM activities, systems, and pro-cesses that build on the firm's advantages.

Conclusions from diagnosis

IHR managers can receive several benefits from diagnosing their firms' contexts. First, they can be proactive in shaping their organi-zations, particularly given the important role of specialized skills for firm competitiveness. Too often, human resources managers are not strategic business players within firms. As-sessing a firm's various environments, units, and specialized skills in depth forces the IHR manager and staff to take a broader, more business-oriented view of a firm. Further, the Bartlett and Ghoshal (1989) framework allows IHR managers to identify current and possi-ble future situations in which their firms may find themselves. From such an assessment, they can begin to determine the degree to which and units where their firms and IHR activities may need to be integrated and the skill areas for focus.

Designing and managing the IHRM function

In this section, we explore IHR activities (i.e., finding, allocating, developing, and valuing human resources), and systems and processes that can support them. We define each and discuss how it may be influenced by a firm's contexts.

Finding international human resources

"Finding" refers to the tasks of planning, recruiting, and selecting human resources (at all levels) who will work internationally. These tasks will likely vary as a function of environments, characteristics of individual units, and the specialized skills that are important to a firm at a given time. For instance, the international construction management firm mentioned above (with most focus on domestic business) reflects an attitude of IHRM activities driven by a domestic focus as well. Arguing that the nature of its business prohibits long-term planning or a systematic worldwide approach regarding employees, the firm typically "finds" employees for projects, even in remote sites overseas, based on who is available or volunteers. In contrast, a retail clothing manufacturer operating in a multinational environment pushes most human resources activities and decisions to the local unit level. In its case, having local professionals and managers (particularly in marketing) who are knowledgeable about local conditions reduces the need for transferees. When the firm *does* use transferees, those people require specialized skills in cross-cultural understanding, given the subtleties likely in marketing retail products internationally. In this case, the firm uses less than 100 transferees in a firm of over 30,000 employees. Instead, the company depends heavily upon its strong corporate culture as guidance for units establishing and maintaining local practices.

A global chemical company based in the United Kingdom integrates the firm partly through extensive transfer of employees worldwide. Indeed, new hires are apt to be high-potential employees recruited with the knowledge that international transfer is probable during their careers, and are evaluated on their ability to manage abroad. Such

transfers allow employees to understand the total organization but also mean that planning, recruitment, and selection must be consistent and integrated across the firm.

Finally, a transnational electronics consumer products firm, formally based in the U.S., is moving toward a more integrated "geocentric" approach to finding employees. Managers at the firm's European headquarters in Europe, for example, already look throughout Europe for the "best person," regardless of home country. This is possible partly because individual units are maturing: five years ago the IHR staff at the regional headquarters included only British personnel; similarly, British or American staff held key positions within units in Europe. Within the last two years, as units on the continent have matured, staff from countries other than the U.K. have been promoted, both into headquarters and in local units. In addition, in such a firm with a "network" structure, with much transfer of information (and people), hiring employees who have an ability to convey and to receive specialized skills, knowledge or technology becomes part of the IHRM finding activity.

Allocating international human resources

The IHRM activity of "allocating" refers to deciding where to invest or place human resources within an organization, given the aspirations of individual employees, the immediate needs of particular units, and the overall strategic needs of the firm. As with "finding" tasks, allocation can be much influenced by national level factors, such as governmental regulations. Work permit restrictions may affect who can be transferred in or out of a country. Furthermore firms' success in allocation can rest on proper placement of people in key positions. In that light, much literature has centered on expatriates – who to transfer, assessing adjustment, and repatriation. Despite years of research and recommendations in the literature (e.g., for selecting people with cultural sensitivity), many firms apparently do not heed the advice. For example, one of the authors returned to a former employer after an absence of 20 years and discovered almost no change in how the firm chose and managed transferees. Recent research (e.g., Peterson, Sargent, Napier, & Shim, 1993) corroborates his observation.

The news is not all bad, however. Some firms have developed allocation schemes that are quite comprehensive. A global British industrial chemical firm, for example, identifies transferees based upon a worldwide career planning and performance evaluation system. The approach rates professional and managerial employees on their readiness for promotions in general, and international transfers in particular. Decisions from unit and regional levels are consolidated at headquarters to insure consistency and integration with corporate goals. In another global chemical firm, based in Germany, allocation decisions are likewise integrated worldwide. A senior management committee, meeting quarterly to review performance of transferees, plans a year in advance for each person's next move, whether "repatriation" or to another site. Both firms make such allocation decisions at headquarters to insure consistency in decisions about employees working across borders, particularly transferees.

In transnational environment firms, the allocation process will likely involve balancing the tasks of placing the right person in a job, regardless of "source," while addressing local needs. A large computer and electronics firm is developing creative approaches to such issues. After failing to find a local area network interconnect expert for Belgium, the IHR manager discovered a specialist already in one of the firm's French units. He arranged for the French expert to work part time as a "suitcase employee" on Belgian issues. Thus the firm operates more efficiently by integrating and using its resources (i.e., in this case a highly specialized skill) across borders.

Moreover in firms that are "moving" among the Bartlett and Ghoshal (1989) cells (figure 12.4), an interesting mix of approaches may develop. A Japanese automobile firm that has traditionally been "Japanese" in orientation, almost to the point of viewing itself as an "international environment" firm, is struggling to become more transnational. Japanese senior management has acknowledged, for example, that Europe is a strategic and potentially enormous market. With that has come a realization that to exploit the market, the firm must develop its human resources talent *within* Europe, rather than relying on Japanese employees. Indeed, its European allocation decisions are increasingly made with little input (at most a "review") from headquarters in Japan. Further, the Japanese human resources director in the U.K. is helping the local IHR staff build networks (i.e., within Europe and between Europe and headquarters) and create a new culture. Japanese managers recognize that the firm's corporate (heavily Japanese) culture cannot thrive in Europe, with its diverse countries and cultures, and are thus developing a "third culture:" not Japanese, not European, but a mix of the two.

Beyond the impact from the contexts, IHR managers may improve allocation decisions by considering findings from procedural justice research. Briefly, it argues that people distinguish between "fair outcomes" and "fair process" (Thibaut & Walker, 1978). They view decision making as fair when they (1) have some control over the outcome (Shapiro & Brett, 1993) and (2) are treated with respect during the process (Lind & Tyler, 1988).

Considering control and respect can help IHR managers make better allocation decisions. First, if an IHR manager has diagnosed a firm's external and internal environments, he or she should have a sense of which units need what kinds of skills. Taking the process a step further and *explaining* results of the diagnosis (i.e., allocation decisions) to unit managers and employees supports the perception that the process and outcomes are fair. Next, a two-way communication process

233

(e.g., giving managers a chance to rebut decisions) shows respect for the unit managers and allows them to exercise voice.

Developing international human resources
Developing IHR means preparing employees who work across borders (through training and development efforts) for their current and future jobs. As one IHR manager defines it, IHR development involves "building career possibilities for employees beyond the borders of their home countries." Like other IHRM activities, development should serve several groups. IHR development should help individuals achieve their personal career aspirations; it provides a way for employees to gain currently needed skills; finally, it supports an organization's long-term IHR needs. Indeed, some scholars consider development to be the "glue" that holds together a firm operating internationally (e.g., Evans, 1992).

The "glue" of IHR development may, however, differ as a function of a firm's environments, unit characteristics, or specialized skill needs. Firms in multinational or transnational environments, for instance, where local responsiveness is high, will need top managers who understand that marked differences exist in local operations. While easily said, many senior managers have difficulty understanding the concept in practice. In an American consumer electronics products firm, for example, the IHR manager in a large European subsidiary was frustrated when he received word from headquarters about an upcoming companywide program to implement "employee empowerment" and "group problem solving." The program's training approach, schedule, and expected outcomes were explicitly and carefully designed, from the perspective of a highly participative and receptive American audience. Such an approach would surely fail in France and Spain, claimed the European manager. Cultural differences on the role of employees (vs. managers) as problem solvers and the willingness to work in groups would

doom the program. Moreover the manager's assessment of the maturity of different units convinced him that several would be ill prepared to tackle an extensive training program. In his view, the senior managers and program developers themselves needed training to understand and tolerate the diversity of units outside the U.S. (Napier, Schweiger, & Kosglow, 1993).

In contrast, firms in global environments, where integration is high and local responsiveness is low, will need a pool of managers who understand how to integrate and create synergies among units. Such firms may use development efforts that help managers learn how to function in multicultural or multinational teams or language training as a way to increase trust and the ability to coordinate within the firm (Scullion, 1992).

Valuing international human resources
Valuing international human resources refers to evaluating the performance of and relationships with employees, and ways to reward individual employees, managers, and units as a result. Interestingly, though, compared to other IHRM activities, "valuing" (i.e., evaluating, rewarding, and maintaining relationships with employees) seems more "local" than other areas. Perhaps national cultures, compensation markets, or government regulations play a stronger role than in finding, allocating, or developing. Cultures may greatly affect employee perceptions about hierarchy and, consequently, their willingness to set goals (or be "given goals") in an evaluation interview. Similarly, conditions regarding pay may vary widely by country or regional markets rather than job. Salary expectations of Belgian and German employees, for example, whose "local" salaries have substantial social costs (e.g., unemployment, health care) are much greater than those of British or Spanish employees. Also, Japanese employees would traditionally expect decisions based primarily upon seniority; Americans may base decisions more on individual performance.

Finally, the government may impose regulations that affect firms' ability to work with employees. "Mitbestimmung" (codetermination) in Germany and parts of Scandinavia requires firms to establish supervisory boards, for example, comprising employee and management representatives.

Nonetheless there do appear to be some variations in "valuing" across types of firms. A global Dutch petrochemical firm, in an environment that encourages integration, uses its performance evaluation approach as its corporate "glue." By having an "excuse" to meet and discuss employee performance throughout a region, for example, the program provides an incentive for managers to build a network. A recently initiated worldwide appraisal system evaluates all employees on similar criteria for both immediate contribution or performance and longer-term potential contribution. As part of the program, IHR managers around the firm meet biannually to review employees and discuss transfers, and career directions for key employees. Regional managers meet more often and discuss specific employees, including "lower potential" ones, for possible swaps and to exchange information about policies. Even though the goals of the appraisal program are comparable across countries, some aspects of its implementation are left to local decision makers (e.g., the extent to which the employee or manager sets future goals). In addition, pay decisions, other than for "transferred" employees, are more local. Other firms use a common corporate reward philosophy but allow much local discretion. One American company used a Hay Plan Job Evaluation to set common pay levels for "global equity" (and to allow transfers), but local managers within countries set pay ranges within those levels.

A multinational environment food and beverage firm with several subsidiaries through Europe found such inconsistencies in evaluation results that it greatly simplified its system. One manager commented that while Italians rated employees generally very high, the Dutch rated employees generally very low, yielding quite different perceptions about which employees were performing better. Thus, the firm requires only that some type of evaluation be conducted within units, with little stress on the particular approach.

Finally, the European electronics firm referred to above adjusts its valuing approaches to fit its subsidiaries, depending in part on their maturity. In the new French unit, only after the first two years was an evaluation program developed. The IHR manager commented that he had to develop a payroll system, recruit top managers and key employees, establish basic administration policies and *then* he was able to help the unit create evaluation and development programs.

Although we have argued throughout for adapting IHRM activities to firm environments, the notion seems to break down with regard to managing relationships with unionized employees. Given the extensive legal restrictions in most countries for dealing with employees, most firms, regardless of other characteristics, tend to follow a "local responsiveness" approach to labor relations.

Systems

Systems encompass the tangible equipment or software that organizations use to improve performance. Two typical systems are HR information systems (HRISs) and communication networks. HRISs comprise the information data bases that firms maintain on employees relating to quantifiable information such as technical and managerial experience, education, and the like. In addition, some firms maintain information about compensation and performance evaluation. In some cases the information is developed and used locally; in other firms an overall approach and general framework is developed and modified for local use. Managers often rate equivalent employee performance differently across countries. For instance, managers in the Netherlands would give relatively lower ratings than would managers in Italy for the same level of performance.

A second common system to implement international HRM and strategy is communication networks, ranging from internal electronic mail systems to fax machines and telephones. Such systems can run into trouble when cultural practice generates resistance (e.g., French and written v. verbal communication).

Processes

Processes are the "softer," often intangible means that firms use for integrating and improving communication across units. Common values or culture is a frequently used process; interestingly, in firms where local responsiveness (and autonomy of units) is greater, a cohesive set of guiding values may be more critical than in firms where integration is more evident. Levi Strauss, an American retail clothing manufacturer in a multinational environment, consistently reinforces its corporate values as ways to help managers make decisions. For example, in this firm where diversity is valued, managers are expected to exhibit that value, even in settings where the legal requirements are less stringent than in the U.S.

Evaluating IHRM

A final component that IHR managers juggle is evaluating the function's contribution. As part of a firm's business team, an IHR manager must show awareness and understanding for the importance of evaluating IHRM. Some scholars (e.g., Cascio, 1991, who focuses on domestic human resource management activities), suggest ways to calculate costs of human resource issues or activities (e.g., turnover, health care) but do not directly relate these ideas to international settings or to the function itself. The existing literature and comments from IHR managers and our own manager co-authors lead us to conclude that the area of evaluation of IHRM is ripe for

more systematic research and practice. Few managers use methodical approaches to evaluating IHRM; almost none of the ones we have talked with over the last two years, for example, assess the "value" of their "expatriate programs." When asked how they know that the exorbitant costs (which they acknowledge) are well spent, most say they go on "faith" that the individual and the firm gain "some return" from the investment.

THE PRACTICE OF IHRM: A CASE ILLUSTRATION OF INTERBREW'S EVOLUTION

One of Europe's largest brewing firms almost fell off the high wire, while juggling IHRM issues. In 1993, Interbrew (Leuven, Belgium) produced 21 million hecolitres (5.5 billion gallons) of beer, with revenues of 69.5 billion Belgian francs ($1.9 billion). With 11,000 employees, Interbrew is Europe's fifth largest brewery and the world's seventeenth largest. It sells in fifty countries, with large operations in Belgium, France, The Netherlands, Italy, selected African countries, and Hungary. Formed from a 1988 merger of Belgium's two largest breweries (Piedboeuf and Stella Artois), it was poised to exploit European unification and an expanding global market. Even so, the company badly stumbled, before finding its footing.

Drawing on the framework's ideas, we discuss Interbrew's situation following the merger, its difficulties, and their implications for IHRM. Then, we explore how the firm has adjusted its approach to adapt to its external and internal environments.

Forcing a "global strategy"

Following the merger, senior management replaced the decentralized organizational forms in each firm with a more integrated structure. The approach sought to reduce damaging competition among units, such as one local unit that promoted its own national beers above Stella Artois, the premium beer that Interbrew wanted as its international brand.

Such problems and a new chief executive officer led to a new strategy. The CEO, a well-known automotive industry leader, moved Interbrew toward a centralized "global" orientation (e.g., international brands, acquisitions in the U.S. and South America). To enhance functional integration, for example, the sales, production, marketing, and human resources managers in individual countries reported to corporate level directors of those functions, bypassing the country managers. As a result, country managers had little formal power to enforce decisions. Furthermore they and the functional managers had to communicate almost daily with the corporate level directors. Telephone and travel costs between headquarters and the countries increased dramatically. In addition, the sheer number of decisions made at the corporate level slowed the process, frustrating corporate and country managers alike. Further, the new approach allowed for little variation in how headquarters dealt with individual units, which ranged widely in their technical sophistication and organizational life-cycle stage. The firm's IHRM activities, processes, or systems were not used deliberately to help manage the firm. Little attention was given to which areas (i.e., specialized skills) the firm should develop, since operational areas were each given relatively similar treatment.

Lastly, while there was an effort to develop a common culture and language in the combined firm, it was a "top-down" approach. It floundered since the merging firms differed extremely in corporate cultures (i.e., innovative and informal vs. conservative and hierarchical) and languages (i.e., Flemish and French). The lack of a common spoken language was particularly contentious. In Belgium, language differences have led to parallel government structures, much fighting and even threats of secession. Such disagreements emerged within the new firm, with managers and employees at times "dividing" along language lines (i.e., French vs. Flemish), which also happened to fit former company affiliations.

Reassessment and change

Two years into the global strategy, management admitted its failure and made essential adjustments. This time the strategy better matched the external environment. In addition, the IHR manager and staff have helped assess the internal environment's needs (e.g., skills, life-cycle stage) and design and manage IHRM activities, processes, and systems. As Bartlett and Ghoshal's framework (1989) suggests, the food industry is in an environment where local responsiveness is critical. As such, sales and marketing issues (i.e., taste, packaging, use of returnables) demand different approaches in each country. Furthermore, in the beer market, beers are normally brewed locally so production facilities can adjust to varying tastes. Finally, distribution issues (costs and logistical difficulties) can require on site production.

Thus Interbrew changed to a multinational approach, with a geographic, decentralized structure. Country managers regained decision-making power, and "localization" became common (i.e., management of operations by nationals), even in places like Africa. Today, country managers and most functional positions (except some brewing operations) are held by nationals.

Interbrew's specialized skills and expertise also became clear. The firm's headquarter's location, near a university with strong post-graduate programs in brewing and agricultural engineering, has allowed it to excel in that skill area. As the expertise most often sent to local production facilities, it receives much IHR attention.

The firm also began treating units according to their needs, given their OLC stages and characteristics. It identified what skills were needed where and how to transfer them. Italy, for example, was in a start-up phase in 1990–91, demanding technical assistance. Italians received training in Belgium; in addition, the local facility received some "suitcase technical experts" from Belgium.

Another "start up venture" had quite different needs. A Hungarian brewery, acquired in 1993, needed technical support and people who could manage under market privatization. In this case, two Belgian technical experts moved to Hungary for 1–3 year assignments to update the brewing capabilities. Other "suitcase travelers" (i.e., technical experts in brewing, marketing, and IHR) shuttle between Hungary and Belgium. In addition, Interbrew is training several Hungarian managers in Belgium and Hungary on corporate culture, general technical issues, and marketing and management skills. Finally, since the firm now uses English (in addition to Flemish and French) as an official language, the Hungarians are learning English.

These examples illustrate how Interbrew links and varies its approach to its units. Likewise, its approach to IHRM depends upon its environment, as well as its corporate and unit needs. Interbrew now uses mainly technical transferees and sends people in both directions (to and from headquarters). In 1993, the technical production operations in the Netherlands, Italy, and most African sites were managed by Belgian technical experts, with the expectation that locals will eventually take over. Sales and marketing are already done locally, following no single corporate approach.

After identifying the firm's environment as "multinational" and the specialized skills of importance, the IHRM group adapted activities to match corporate strategic goals. Where knowledge and expertise will be transferred to locals, for example, the recruitment process requires technical people to have proficiency in other languages (especially English), cultural adaptability (to understand and work with technicians in other countries), and a

willingness to travel or move abroad when necessary. IHRM development activities now focus on training in specialized areas (e.g., technical training in Belgium as well as in on-site local production). Because the technicians provide support in all units and very extensive support in certain units, communication ability has become very important. Communication refers both to the ability to *transfer* information (by the technician) and the ability to *receive* it (by the unit). As a result, the IHRM group provides training in communication (e.g., methods, language courses) for technicians *and* local staff operating in West and Central Europe as well as in Africa.

Valuing employees has changed to fit a multinational environment, allowing for much local control. Only two requirements hold across all units: performance appraisals are conducted at the same time of year, and each employee must have a development (i.e., career planning) interview. Otherwise, units modify the process to fit their situations.

Finally, the IHRM staff has begun to develop an information system that will allow the company to match future IHR needs with employee aspirations. The information system provides such data as technical skills, language abilities, experience in and out of the company, education and degrees, and employee development and career planning goals. Finally, the firm has begun to develop a set of common goals and values. Although they are the same throughout the company, there is now an expectation that they will be applied in ways appropriate to individual countries.

THE PRACTICE OF IHRM: LESSONS FOR MANAGERS AND SCHOLARS

Several lessons emerge from our discussion; in this last part, we examine three. First, IHRM requires an understanding of existing and developing firm environments, both inside and outside. Matching IHRM activities, processes and systems to those environments will challenge managers and scholars alike. Specifically, IHR managers should play a role in identifying appropriate activities under given conditions, developing ways to anticipate and make changes, and reconciling different perspectives (and expectations) of headquarters and units. In-depth investigation of how firms successfully take such steps is the job of scholars. At present, we have general impressions from several large firms. Clearly we need more systematic study (e.g., cases, surveys, longitudinal research).

More specifically, our discussion suggests that in most cases, even in environments where integration is high, headquarters cannot dictate completely the actions of individual units on IHRM activities. In case after case, we hear managers talk about the problems of the parent unit trying to dictate in too much detail what and how IHRM activities should be carried out. Again, the challenge is understanding the degree to which such guidance is appropriate in various situations, when and how that level of guidance will change, and what drives the change.

Finally, IHR managers must view themselves as strategic partners in firms operating internationally. Until they think of their contributions in performance terms and until they can offer value to firms in terms of their overall direction as well as the implementation (Butler, et al. 1991), their role will be minimal. Again, in concert with IHR managers, scholars can help by working to develop measures and ways of thinking about the function that are performance-oriented.

In sum, the IHR manager's task is complex, requiring skills in "juggling" multiple constituencies, issues, and actions. To succeed with such juggling, an IHR manager needs a broad perspective that is strategic and business-oriented. In addition, the manager must monitor and anticipate external change. While the challenge is daunting, it will doubtless be one of the most exciting for those who take it on.

NOTE

Several people contributed, knowingly or otherwise, to the development of this chapter. We are grateful to six, in particular. Thanks to Sully Taylor and Schon Beechler for their persistence at developing IHRM theory, Won Shim and Dick Peterson for their interview wizardry, Sumantra Ghoshal for his ideas on a beautiful June day, and Laura Farrington for her technical magic.

REFERENCES

Adler, N. J., & Bartholomew, S. (1992). Academic and professional communities of discourse: Generating knowledge of transnational human resource management. *Journal of International Business Studies*, 23 (3), 551–69.

Agres, T. (1991). Asea Brown Boveri – a model for global management. *R&D*, 33 (13), 30–4.

Aryee, S. (1993). A path-analytic investigation of three terminants of career withdrawal intentions of engineers: some HRM issues arising in a professional labour market in Singapore. *International Journal of Human Resource Management*, 4 (1), 213–30.

Bartlett, C. A., & Ghoshal, S. (1988). Organizing for worldwide effectiveness: The transnational solution. *California Management Review*, 31 (1), 54–74.

Bartlett, C. A., & Ghoshal, S. (1989). *Managing Across Borders: The transnational solution.* Boston: Harvard Business School.

Bird, A., & Mukuda, M. (1989). Expatriates in their own home: A new twist in the human resource management of Japanese MNCs. *Human Resource Management*, 28 (4), 437–53.

Black, J. S. (1988). Workrole transitions: A study of American expatriate managers in Japan. *Journal of Business Studies*, 19 (2), 277–94.

Black, J. S., Gregersen, H. B., & Mendenhall, M. E. (1992a). *Global Assignments.* San Francisco: Jossey-Bass.

Black, J. S., Gregersen, H. B., & Mendenhall, M. E. (1992b). Toward a theoretical framework of repatriation adjustment. *Journal of International Business Studies*, 23, 737–60.

Black, J. S., & Porter, L. (1991). Managerial behaviors and job performance: A successful manager in Los Angeles may not succeed in Hong Kong. *Journal of International Business Studies*, 22 (1), 99–113.

Black, J. S., & Stephens, G. K. (1989). The influence of the spouse on American expatriate adjustment and intent to stay in Pacific Rim overseas assignments. *Journal of Management*, 15 (4), 529–44.

Boyacigiller, N. (1990). The role of expatriates in the management of interdependence, complexity and risk in multinational corporations. *Journal of International Business Studies*, 21, 357–81.

Brewster, C. (1993). Developing a "European" model of human resource management. Paper presented at the Academy of International Business meetings, Hawaii.

Butler, J. E., Ferris, G. R., & Napier, N. K. (1991). *Strategy and Human Resources Management.* Cincinnati: South-Western Publishers.

239

Cascio, W. F. (1991). *Costing Human Resources: The financial impact of behavior in organizations,* 3rd ed. Boston: PWS-Kent.

Chew, I. K., & Teo, A. C. Y. (1991). Human resource practices in Singapore: A survey of local firms and MNCs. *Asia Pacific Human Resource Management,* 29 (1), 30–8.

Chiu, S., & Levin, D. A. (1993). From a labour-surplus to a labour-scare economy: Challenges to human resource management in Hong Kong. *International Journal of Human Resource Management,* 4 (1), 159–89.

Chynoweth, Emma (1992). Shell reorganizes to meet customer demands in single market. *Chemical Week,* 151 (20), 21.

Courpasson, D., & Livian, Y. (1993). Training for strategic change: Some conditions of effectiveness: A case in the banking sector in France. *International Journal of Human Resource Management,* 4 (2), 465–79.

Cyr, D. J., & Frost, P. J. (1991). Human resource management practice in China: A future perspective. *Human Resource Management,* 30 (2), 199–215.

de Wilde, J. (1991). How to train managers for going global. *Business Quarterly,* 55 (3), 41–5.

Dowling, P. J., Schuler, R. S. (1990). *International Dimensions of Human Resource Management.* Boston: PWS-Kent.

Dowling, P. J., Schuler, R. S., & Welch, D. (1994). *International Dimensions of Human Resource Management,* 2nd ed. Boston: PWS-Kent.

Evans, P. (1990). International management development and the balance between generalism and professionalism. *Personnel Management,* December, 46–50.

Evans, P. (1992). Management development as glue technology. *Human Resource Planning Journal,* 15 (1), 85–106.

Evans, P., Doz, Y., & Laurent, A. (eds.) (1990). *Human Resource Management in the International Firm.* New York: St. Martin's Press.

Feldman, D. C., & Thomas, D. C. (1992). Career management issues facing expatriates. *Journal of International Business,* 23 (2), 271–93.

Ferner, A., & Hyman, R. (1992). IR on the continent: A model of co-operation? *Personnel Management,* 24 (8), 32–4.

Florkowski, G. W., & Nath, R. (1990). MNC responses to the legal environment of international human resource management. *International Journal of Human Resource Management,* 4 (2), 303–24.

Ghoshal, S., & Nohria, N. (1989). Internal differences within multinational corporations. *Strategic Management Journal,* 10, 323–37.

Ghoshal, S., & Nohria, N. (1993). Horses for courses: Organizational firms for multinational corporations. *Sloan Management Review,* 34 (2), 23–36.

Gill, C. (1993). Technological change and participation in work organization: Recent results from a European Community survey. *International Journal of Human Resource Management,* 4 (2), 325–47.

Greer, C. R., & Ireland, T. C. (1992). Organizational and financial correlates of a "contrarian" human resource investment strategy. *Academy of Management Journal,* 35 (5), 956–84.

Gregersen, H. B., & Black, J. S. (1992). Antecedents to commitment to a parent company and a foreign operation. *Academy of Management Journal,* 35, 65–90.

Gronhaug, K., & Nordhaug, O. (1992). International human resource management: An environmental perspective. *International Journal of Human Resource Management,* 3 (1), 438–44.

Grosse, R. (1992). Competitive advantages and multinational enterprises in Latin America. *Journal of Business Research,* 25, 27–42.

Harvey, M. G. (1989). Repatriation of corporate executives: An empirical study. *Journal of International Business Studies,* 20 (1), 131–44.

Hildebrant, H. W., & Liu, J. (1988). Chinese women managers: A comparison with their U.S. and Asian counterparts. *Human Resource Management,* 27 (3), 291–314.

Isaacs, H. (1989). Human resource management in the Caribbean: Planning for the future. *Public Personnel Management,* 18 (2), 227–33.

Jain, H. C. (1990). Human resource management in selected Japanese firms, their foreign subsidiaries and locally owned counterparts. *International Labour Review,* 129 (1), 73–89.

Janssens, M. (1993a). International job transfers: Antecedents of work adjustment. Working paper. Katholieke Universiteit Leuven, Belgium.

Janssens, M. (1993b). Parent company standards as evaluation criteria of international managers' performance. Paper presented at the National Academy of Management, Atlanta, Georgia.

Kanc, R. L., & Stanton, S. (1991). Human resource planning: Where are we now? *Asia Pacific Human Resource Management,* 29 (2), 5–20.

Kanter, R. M. (1991). Transcending business boundaries: 12,000 world managers view change. *Harvard Business Review,* May–June, 151–64.

Kauppinen, M., & Gregersen, H. (1993). Towards a more comprehensive approach to expatriate adjustment research: Mode can make a difference. Paper presented at Academy of International Business meetings, Maui, Hawaii.

Kidger, P. J. (1991). The emergence of international human resource management. *International Journal of Human Resource Management,* September, 2 (2), 149–64.

Kim, W. C. & Mauborgne, R. A. (1991). Implementing global strategies: The role of procedural justice. *Strategic Management Journal,* 12, 125–43.

Kramar, R. (1992). Strategic human resource management: Are the promises fulfilled? *Asia Pacific Journal of Human Resources,* 30 (1), 1–15.

Laabs, J. J. (1991). The global talent search. *Personnel Journal,* August, 70 (8), 38–42.

Lei, D. & Slocum, J. W., Jr. (1991). Global strategic alliances: Payoffs and pitfalls. *Organizational Dynamics,* 19 (3), 44–62.

Lind, E. A. & Tyler, T. (1988). *The Social Psychology of Procedural Justice.* New York: Plenum.

McEvoy, G. M., & Buller, P. F. (1993). New directions in international human resource management research. Paper presented at the Academy of International Business meetings, Maui, Hawaii.

Maljers, F. A. (1992). Inside Unilever: The evolving transnational company. *Harvard Business Review*, 70 (5), 46–51.

Markoczy, Livia (1993). Managerial and organizational learning in Hungarian–Western mixed management organizations. *International Journal of Human Resource Management*, 4 (2), 277–304.

Mendenhall, M., & Oddou, G. (1985). The dimensions of expatriate acculturation: A review. *Academy of Management Review*, 10 (1), 39–47.

Milliman, J., Von Glinow, M. A., & Nathan, M. (1991). Organizational life cycles and strategy international human resource management in multinational companies: Implications for congruence theory. *Academy of Management Review*, 16 (2), 318–39.

Morgan, P. V. (1986). International human resource management: Factor or fiction? *Personnel Administrator*, 31 (9), 43–7.

Napier, N. K., & Peterson, R. B. (1989). Expatriate re-entry: What do repatriates have to say? *Human Resource Planning*, 14 (1), 19–28.

Napier, N. K., Schweiger, D. M., & Kosglow, J. (1993). Managing organizational diversity: Observations from cross-border acquisitions. *Human Resource Management*, 32 (4), 505–23.

Naumann, E. (1992). A conceptual model of expatriate turnover. *Journal of International Business*, 23, 499–531.

Oddou, G. R., & Mendenhall, M. K. (1991). Succession planning for the 21st century: How well are we grooming our future business leaders? *Business Horizons*, 34 (1), 26–34.

Oliver, N., & Davies, A. (1990). Adopting Japanese-style manufacturing methods: A tale of two (UK) factories. *Journal of Management Studies*, 27 (5), 555–70.

Pennings, J. M. (1993). Executive reward systems: A cross-national comparison. *Journal of Management Studies*, 30 (2), 261–80.

Peterson, R. B., Sargent, J., Napier, N. K., & Shim, W. S. (1993). International human resource management in the world's largest industrial MNCs. Paper presented at the Academy of International Business meetings, Hawaii.

Pieper, R. (Ed.) (1990). *Human Resource Management: An international comparison*. Berlin: Walter de Gruyter.

Porter, M. (1990). *The Competitive Advantage of Nations*. New York: Free Press.

Prahalad, C. K., & Doz, Y. L. (1987). *The Multinational Mission*. New York: Free Press.

Sadri, S., & Williamson, C. (1989). Management and industrial relations strategies of multinational corporations in developing countries. *Journal of Business Research*, 18 (3), 179–93.

Sano, Y. (1993). Changes and continued stability in Japanese HRM systems: Choice in the share economy. *International Journal of Human Resource Management*, 4 (1), 11–27.

Schneider, S., & De Meyer, A. (1991). Interpreting and responding to strategic issues: The impact of national culture. *Strategic Management Journal*, 12, 307–20.

Schuler, R. S., Dowling, P. J., & De Cieri, H. (1992). The formation of an international joint venture: Marley Automotive Components. *European Management Journal*, 10 (3), 304–9.

Schuler, R. S., Dowling, P. J., & De Cieri, H. (1993). An integrative framework of strategic international human resource management. *Journal of Management*, 19 (2), 419–59.

Schweiger, D. M., Csiszar, E., & Napier, N. K. (in press). A strategic approach to implementing mergers and acquisitions. In H. G. Vonkorg, A. Sinatra, & H. Singh, *Managing Corporate Acquisitions: A comparative analysis*. New York: Macmillan.

Scullion, H. (1992). Strategic recruitment and development of the "international manager": Some European considerations. *Human Resource Management*, 3 (1), 57–69.

Sels, B. (1992). The rule of pragmatism in a diverse culture. *Personnel Management*, 24 (11), 46–52.

Shapiro, D., & Brett, J. M. (1993). Comparing three processes underlying judgements of procedural justice: A filed study of mediation and arbitration. *Journal of Personality and Social Psychology*, 65, 1167–77.

Shore, L. M., Eagle, B. W. & Jedel, M. J. (1993). China–United States joint ventures: a typological model of goal congruence and cultural understanding and their importance for effective human resource management. *International Journal of Human Resource Management*, 4 (1), 67–83.

Stone, N. (1989). The globalization of Europe: An interview with Wisse Dekker. *Harvard Business Review*, 67 (3), 90–5.

Taylor, S., & Beechler, S. (1993). Human resource management system integration and adaptation in multinational firms. *Advances in International Comparative Management*, 8, 115–74.

Taylor, S., Beechler, S., & Napier, N. K. (1993). Toward an integrated theory of international human resource management. Paper presented at the Academy of International Business, Hawaii.

Taylor, S., & Napier, N. K. (1993). Successful women expatriates in Japan. Paper presented at the Academy of International Business, Hawaii.

Teagarden, M. B., Butler, M. C., & Von Glinow, M. A. (1992). Mexico's maquiladora industry: Where strategic human resource management makes a difference. *Organizational Dynamics*, 20 (3), 34–47.

Teague, Paul (1993). Towards social Europe? Industrial relations after 1992. *International Journal of Human Resource Management*, 4 (2), 349–75.

Thibaut, J., & Walker, L. (1978). *A Theory of Procedural Justice*. Hillsdale, NJ: Erlbaum.

Thurley, K. (1990). Towards a European approach to personnel management. *Personnel Management*, September, 54–7.

Tung, R. L. (1987). Expatriate assignments: Enhancing success and minimizing failure. *Academy of Management Executive*, 1 (2), 117–25.

Tung, R. L. (1993). Extended review: A comparative perspective on management and industrial training in

China. *International Journal of Human Resource Management*, 4 (1), 241–5.

Uchitelle, L. (1994). Gillette's world view: One blade fits all. *New York Times*, 3 January, C3.

Vance, C. M., McClaine, S. R., Boje, D. M., & Stage, H. D. (1992). An examination of the transferability of traditional performance appraisal principles across cultural boundaries. *Management International Review*, 32 (4), 313–26.

Van den Bosch, F. A. J., & Van Prooijen, A. A. (1992). European management: An emerging competitive advantage of European nations. *European Management Journal*, 10 (4), 445–8.

Warner, M. (1993). Human resource management "with Chinese characteristics." *International Journal of Human Resource Management*, 4 (1), 45–65.

Watson, L. I. M. (1992). Developing a Pan-European compensation and benefits package. *The Journal of European Business*, 3 (6), 21–6.

White, A. F. (1992). Organizational transformation at BP: An interview with chairman and CEO Robert Horton. *Human Resource Planning*, 15 (1), 3–14.

□ Chapter 13 □

International Industrial Relations

Thomas F. Reed, P. B. Beaumont, and Michael F. Pugh

INTRODUCTION

This chapter provides a review of research and practice in international industrial relations. After a brief overview of the field, we present a discussion of theory and research in international industrial relations: early and more recent attempts at building "grand" theories; comparative empirical studies; comparative institutional studies; and research on industrial relations within the context of multinational corporations. In the following section we explore the changing scene in international industrial relations research and practice, and present five global trends that will shape the academic and professional field not only for the remainder of this century, but also into the next century. Next comes a case study of a Sony manufacturing facility in the United Kingdom. This case study highlights the challenge of conducting industrial relations in an evolving European context. Finally, we conclude with some thoughts on future directions for both practitioners and researchers.

OVERVIEW

There is a relatively long history and tradition of international (comparative or cross-country) research in the field of industrial relations. Research along these lines has been prompted by the following kinds of issues and questions:

- Are various national systems of industrial relations exhibiting any sort of tendency to increasingly converge or diverge through time, and what are the factors involved in such processes?
- Are there "model" systems of industrial relations, some of whose features can be usefully "exported" to other systems?
- If various national systems are experiencing essentially similar problems of performance, are there any useful "best-practice" policy lessons or guidelines that can be drawn from the different attempts to cope with these difficulties?
- Do certain individual research findings transcend the particular institutional details of individual systems?

- Do multinational (transnational or international) corporations have essentially similar industrial relations arrangements in the various countries in which they are located, and do these tend to produce much the same results and outcomes in these different settings?

In view of the above list of questions, it is not surprising to find that the international industrial relations research literature (broadly defined) has basically involved four separate strands or themes of activity and concentration:

1 Attempts to build a grand, conceptual theory of industrial relations that transcends the boundaries of national systems.
2 The replication of multivariate statistical studies of certain individual issues (e.g., determinants of the level of strike activity) on data sets drawn from a number of countries.
3 A top-down, descriptive outline and discussion of the leading institutional features of different national systems, frequently centering around the convergence/divergence theme.
4 An examination of the industrial relations arrangements and practices of selected multinational corporations (MNCs) in different national settings.

However, as we see in the next section, it has been work in the latter two categories that has very largely dominated (at least in a quantitative sense) the field of international industrial relations.

THEORY AND RESEARCH IN INTERNATIONAL INDUSTRIAL RELATIONS

Grand theories

The field of industrial relations has seen periodic attempts to develop a single, grand theory of the subject area. One of the earliest, and still most widely cited, studies in this tradition is the work of John Dunlop (1958). In essence, Dunlop viewed any and all national industrial relations systems as comprising three basic groups of actors (i.e., workers and their organizations, employers and their organizations, and government bodies) who interacted in an environmental context composed of three interrelated elements: (1) technology; (2) product market (or budgetary) constraints; and (3) the power relations (and status) of the respective actors. This interaction process produced a "web of rules" to govern relationships in the workplace, and it was the task of industrial relations theory to explain how and why the web of rules varied between systems and varied over the course of time.

Although an American, Dunlop (1958) illustrated his "theory" with numerous examples drawn from countries other than the U.S. Moreover he stressed that the web of rules could be embodied in the substantive and procedural terms and conditions of collective agreements (as in the U.S. at the time), but also could be incorporated in statute law, arbitration awards, and so forth, the latter being more relevant to countries other than the United States.

Dunlop then followed up this work with a more explicit contribution to the field of international industrial relations. This particular study, undertaken with a number of colleagues (Kerr, Dunlop, Harbison, & Myers, 1960), argued that the common values and orientation of the elite decision makers in various countries were particularly important in working to produce certain similarities in industrial relations systems. Furthermore, Dunlop and his collaborators predicted that, over time, national systems would follow an increasingly convergent path because nations face common problems of industrialization.

This particular prediction has not been borne out by experience, as the members of the original research team have themselves conceded in a subsequent publication (Dunlop, Harbison, Kerr, & Myers, 1975). Indeed, it has been the divergence, rather than convergence, among national systems of industrial relations that has been emphasized by researchers in more recent years (Poole, 1986).

Nevertheless there still have appeared since the work of Dunlop proposals for single theories of industrial relations. These typically have argued the case for a particular influence or variable to constitute the central analytical core of industrial relations research across national systems. In some cases, what has been proposed is a potential dependent variable (e.g., industrial conflict or industrial democracy); in other cases, the proposal has been for focusing on an all-important, independent variable (e.g., bargaining power). In the latter category, for example, has been Clegg's (1976) comparison of a number of national industrial relations systems in which he accords key importance to the level of collective bargaining within such systems. In his view, certain leading industrial relations phenomena (e.g., the extent and nature of strike frequency, union democracy, and industrial democracy) are explicable in terms of the level at which collective bargaining is conducted in the system concerned.

More recently, Poole (1986, 198) has argued that, "attempts to establish a general inclusive comparative industrial relations theory are likely to prove fruitless . . . the optimum path for further progress would now appear to be the more precise formulation of specific theories in a series of substantive areas." In essence, Poole takes as his starting point the existing diversity of national industrial relations systems, proposes a more focused set of dependent variables (e.g., industrial conflict, industrial democracy, and the distribution of economic rewards) for analysis, and suggests the potential role(s) of differences in cultural values, ideologies, politico-economic structures, the institutional framework of industrial relations, the power

of the actors, and various temporal movements (e.g., "late development") in accounting for any observed variation. This particular framework of analysis very much seeks to incorporate into comparative studies the "strategic choice" notion that has been so prominent in recent industrial relations research in the United States (Kochan, Katz, & McKersie, 1986).

What is the current state of affairs concerning attempts to develop a larger conceptual framework of industrial relations that transcends national boundaries? Arguably, most commentators probably would support Poole's (1986) basic assessment that attempts to develop an all-embracing theory have been of relatively limited value to date. This is because such attempts have produced little more than a listing of classifications and headings that are not capable of being systematically tested and verified; in short, they are more heuristic devices than theories. Indeed, even some of the so-called middle range propositions and hypotheses in international industrial relations research seem to constitute little more than tautological statements.

Comparative empirical studies

The second strand of international industrial relations research has involved empirical models (initially developed and tested on "domestic" data) being replicated on data sets for a number of countries. This type of research has very largely involved multiple regression analysis undertaken by labor economists. Initially this line of research concentrated on attempts to explain variation over time in levels of strike activity (Hibbs, 1976), but has been extended to examinations of variations in union membership and density (Bain & Elsheikh, 1976; Freeman, 1989) and estimates of the size of union relative wage effects (Blanchflower & Freeman, 1992). This body of research has usefully indicated that certain findings and relationships appear to transcend the institutional arrangements of individual systems (whereas others do not), but can be subject to at least two important sets of criticisms:

1   Is the national systems level the appropriate level of analysis, given the extent of diversity within individual systems, and the fact that the critical levels of decision making underlying some of the variables investigated are more disaggregated ones?
2   If, as is frequently the case, differences between systems are observed, there is rarely little direct substantive explanation of why this has occurred. In short, explanations of observed differences tend to be largely ones of inference.

These two criticisms have been addressed, at least to a considerable extent, by moving away from aggregate level, multiple regression equations and making increased use of the paired comparison method, which involves selecting and studying in depth certain organizations in different societies that are matched on key variables such size, technology, and product (Sorge & Warner, 1986). This particular approach has been most recently utilized in a number of useful examinations of variation in training activity across different national systems (Daly, Hitchens, & Wagner, 1985).

Comparative institutional studies

The largest stream of international industrial relations research has been the third one, which has consisted of descriptions of the leading institutional features of different national systems. This line of research was originally driven by an interest in examining the convergence/divergence hypothesis. However, in the 1970s its focus shifted to examining the (determinants and) contribution that "corporatist" (highly centralized, tripartite) industrial relations arrangements made to the macroeconomic performance of the systems concerned (Bruno & Sachs, 1985). In the

1980s (and into the 1990s), there has been more of a return to the divergence/convergence theme, with the particular issue addressed being the role of divergent national institutional arrangements in shaping the nature of the actors' response to a reasonably common set of environmental changes (e.g., recession, restructuring, technical change) in advanced industrialized economies. For example, a recent review of industrial relations in 17 European countries highlighted the following general tendencies across systems in the 1980s (Ferner & Hyman, 1992):

- Employers seeking greater flexibility and decentralization of decision making.
- Weaker union movements, variously involving lower levels of union density and less interunion coherence.
- State initiatives to deregulate the labor market and tighten control of public expenditure.
- A weakening of corporatist industrial relations arrangements.
- A reduced overall level of strike activity.

However, the editors of the volume went on to observe (Ferner & Hyman, 1992, pp. xxx–xxxi):

> that despite common contexts and general trends, considerable variety persists. There has been convergence of systems in some respects, but increased diversity in others. This applies equally within blocs or "models" as between more disparate groups of countries . . . within individual countries, one observes patterns of change, but also of considerable continuity. Some cases – Austria, Switzerland, Luxembourg – have appeared as islands of relative stability, tranquillity even, in a turbulent sea of change. Radical transformations have been few.

In seeking to account for these observed patterns, a great deal of emphasis was placed on the role of institutions in mediating external (environmental) pressures to a greater or lesser degree with the various national systems being viewed as having institutions that were: (1) strong and inflexible (e.g., the United Kingdom and the Netherlands); (2) relatively weak (e.g., France and Italy); or (3) strong but flexible (e.g., Germany). In short, the basic messages were that diversity remains and that national institutions are important.

The vast majority of work on the institutions of national industrial relations systems has been concerned with advanced industrialized economies. This being said, the notion of "late development" (Dore, 1973) has been utilized as an explanatory device for looking at the industrial relations arrangements of developing countries. The important role of the state in the industrial relations systems of developing countries, for example, has been explained in terms of this particular notion. Furthermore, the role of the state in orchestrating a national competitive strategy based on low cost competition, including a range of measures to limit and shape union activities, has been noted in studies of individual developing countries (Ogle, 1990).

This perspective has been taken a stage further in some ongoing research concerning some Asian countries (Kurivilla, 1994). The basic question being addressed in this work is how (and in what ways) will industrial relations institutions change in order to fit with state-led development strategies that move through the various stages of import substitution, to export-led growth based on low cost competition, to export-led growth based on a more value-added response? Although emphasizing the role of the state and the national systems level, this work on developing countries is seeking to build upon some recent U.S. research (Kochan et al., 1986) that highlights the important role of the nature of competitive strategy, albeit at the individual organizational level. Research on industrial relations in developing countries also needs, relative to advanced industrialized economies, to incorporate more of a role for actors external to national systems; the International Labour Office (ILO) (Poole, 1993),

the World Bank, and the International Monetary Fund (IMF) (Kurivilla, 1994) are among the obvious candidates to include here. Finally, with the recent dramatic political changes in Eastern Europe, one is starting to see the emergence of research on industrial relations changes in former communist systems (Jürgens, Klinzing, & Turner, 1993).

At this stage, it is useful to say something about "model" industrial relations systems. What makes a system a role model for others to potentially emulate, and which particular systems have played such a role over time? According to Windmuller (1963), the three prerequisites for the industrial relations arrangements of any one country to constitute a viable model for others to potentially emulate are:

1   A fundamental consensus among the three groups of actors in the system.
2   A demonstrated capacity for high achievement or success within its own society along one or more relevant lines.
3   A willingness on the part of the model system to demonstrate or export the model to others.

Moreover it has been suggested that historically the particular countries that were cast in this "model role" position were (Kassalow, 1983): Britain (in the closing decades of the nineteenth century); Germany (before World War I); the United States (1945–60); Sweden (in the 1960s); Germany (in the 1970s); and Japan (in the 1980s). The important question of the willingness and ability to learn and adapt from the institutional practices of model systems is returned to in the final section of this chapter.

The quality of comparative national systems research has undoubtedly improved over time, with some of the research on corporatist industrial relations arrangements in the 1970s and 1980s being particularly impressive in this regard. Nevertheless concerns remain about its essentially descriptive nature, and its overwhelming concentration on formal institutional arrangements at the national level (Peterson, 1986). Various attempts have been made to address such concerns and criticisms in more recent years. For instance, most recent volumes of comparative national studies have provided tighter organizational frameworks to ensure that the individual country chapters address and present a reasonably common set of issues and material (Treu et al., 1987; Bamber & Lansbury, 1993). More notably, at the present time there are two ongoing international projects (one for Asian countries and one for countries belonging to OECD, the Organization for Economic Cooperation and Development) that are seeking to document and analyze industrial relations changes in selected industries (e.g., autos, telecommunications, steel) in light of the "strategic choice" framework of analysis (Kochan et al., 1986). These promise to be two of the more interesting studies in the field in recent times.

Studies of multinational corporations

The final stream of international industrial relations research, which has been second only (in size terms) to the national institutional approach, has concentrated on the multinational, transnational, or international corporation. The reasons for this concentration are not hard to find. According to Dicken (1992), transnational corporations are the single most important force in the modern world economy; for example, it has been estimated that some 20 to 25 percent of total world production in the world's market economies is performed by such organizations, particularly the core group of 600 such firms (Hendry, 1994).

A variety of industrial relations issues have been examined in relation to transnational corporations. Some of these issues are relatively specific to individual countries. For instance, in Britain there has been a longstanding interest in the question of whether foreign-owned subsidiaries are relatively more (or less) strike prone than domestic organizations (Hamill, 1984), a subject of rather less interest and concern in other countries. The more general themes that have characterized industrial relations research concerning multinational corporations are, first, attempts to identify the locus of industrial relations decision making: that is, which industrial relations decisions are made by management in the local subsidiaries, and which are made at corporate headquarters level? This research has been conducted via individual case studies or small-sized (convenience) samples with perhaps predictably considerable variation being apparent in the findings. However, given the limited sample sizes involved, it has been difficult to say what is "normal practice," or to identify any systematic sources of variation in the findings. The work of Hamill (1984), however, has suggested that industrial relations decision making was relatively centralized:

- the greater the degree of intersubsidiary production integration;
- in the U.S., as opposed to European-owned susidiaries;
- when the subsidiaries were greenfield sites, as opposed to well-established acquired organizations;
- when the subsidiaries' level of organizational performance was relatively poor;
- when the MNC was a significant source of operating or investment funds for the subsidiary.

A second research theme concerns the problems and difficulties that trade unions have faced or experienced when dealing with an MNC. The big issues that have been typically identified and discussed in this regard have been as follows:

1 The difficulty of identifying and gaining access to the real centers of management decision making.

2　The difficulty of identifying the ability to pay of individual subsidiaries for wage negotiation purposes because of internal transfer pricing arrangements.

3　The reduced effectiveness of industrial action due to the possibility of production switching between subsidiaries.

4　Layoffs and plant closures in individual countries in response to larger corporate-level changes and decisions that can be little influenced by the actions of the various actors in the countries concerned.

In response to such difficulties, unions have variously lobbied for changes in national-level legislation, looked to tighten the codes of conduct and guidelines issued by bodies like the OECD and the ILO, and sought to establish institutional arrangements across national boundaries. The operation of codes of conduct for MNCs and attempts to establish collective bargaining and consultative works council arrangements across national boundaries have been the subject of some research.

A third research theme has been the extent to which foreign subsidiaries conform to or diverge from the traditional industrial relations practices of the "host" national system(s). To some commentators, foreign subsidiaries in various systems have been an innovative force for constructive change (i.e., acting as potential role models) in traditional industrial relations practices, although it has to be said that the domestic union movements have not always viewed them in quite such a positive manner; the extent of nonunion operations among Japanese subsidiaries in the U.S., and among U.S. subsidiaries in the U.K., are cases in point. The role of foreign subsidiaries in importing new industrial relations practices has been discussed overwhelmingly by reference to a small number of well-known cases, although in some systems more comprehensive bodies of data are available. In Britain, for instance, one recent survey-based study (Purcell, Marginson, Edwards, & Sisson, 1987) concluded that:

1　There was little difference between foreign- and domestic-owned establishments in the matters of union recognition, collective bargaining coverage, and industrial action.

2　On the other hand, foreign-owned establishments had relatively more human resource management-type practices, a better developed industrial relations management function, and more corporate level measures to monitor and control industrial relations practices at the establishment level.

The existing body of industrial relations research concerning multinational corporations can be subject to a number of potential criticisms. First, the range of issues studied has been relatively limited, falling considerably short of the full range of industrial relations issues raised by the operation of such organizations. Second, studies that look at foreign-owned (compared to domestic-owned) establishments should, at least where sample sizes permit, take a more disaggregated approach by looking at the individual country of ownership. There is no reason, for instance, to assume that the industrial relations practices of U.S.-, German-, or Japanese-owned subsidiaries in Britain will be relatively similar. Fortunately, more disaggregated studies along these lines are beginning to emerge in some systems (Beaumont, Cressey, & Jakobsen, 1990; Wilkinson, Morris, & Munday, 1993). Finally, these studies are almost exclusively concerned with the fully owned subsidiaries of MNCs. This concentration has become much less justified in recent years as a result of the growth of new organizational forms across national boundaries, such as international joint ventures. This alternative to the more traditional foreign-owned subsidiary requires more attention from industrial relations researchers (Beaumont, 1991).

249

CHANGING INTERNATIONAL INDUSTRIAL RELATIONS RESEARCH AND PRACTICE

The previous section's review of the existing literature on international industrial relations has highlighted various weaknesses and deficiencies in the individual streams of research. At the same time, however, we noted the existence of various attempts and initiatives to remedy some of these deficiencies. This desirable trend is one we expect to see continue.

At the same time, however, researchers need to go further. This is because, at least in our judgment, international industrial relations research in the future needs to become more broad-ranging, but at the same time more focused in nature. The more broad-ranging changes we hope to see include a wider range of industrial relations issues being examined in relation to MNCs, the study of international joint-venture operations, and the movement to levels of analysis and decision making below the national systems level in comparative studies. However, at the same time we favor a more focused approach that will variously involve less grand theories, the development of more specific dependent variables, matched pairs analysis, the disaggregation of foreign ownership variables by specific country of origin, and so forth. The need for change along these lines flows from, first, our above review of existing research weaknesses and, second, changes in the international operating environment that are driving changes in individual organizations. The latter means that organizational practice is frequently in advance of industrial relations theory and research.

In our view five interrelated trends sweeping the global economy will pose significant challenges and opportunities for research and practice in international industrial relations in the twenty-first century. These trends portend an increasingly complex economic, political, institutional, and technological context for the conduct of industrial relations practice and research. Indeed, the central question for practitioners, researchers, and policy makers in the next century will be whether labor unions as we know them can remain a viable mediating institution between workers and mangers. We return to this theme at the end of the chapter.

Trend 1: Decline of unionism in industrialized nations

The 1980s was a difficult decade for unions in many industrialized nations. Eighteen of the 22 OECD countries shown in figure 13.1 (Greece and Turkey are excluded because of missing data) experienced declines in union density. Fully half of these nations experienced a decline of at least 10 percent, with New Zealand, Spain, the United States, the Netherlands, and France all reporting declines in union density in excess of 20 percent.

Each nation has its own set of factors to explain the decline in union density, but general themes run through most cases. Among these are increased international competition in product and labor markets; labor market deregulation; economic restructuring by large employers; increased employer resistance to unions; public policies and court decisions unfavorable to unions; privatization of government-controlled industries; deregulation of industries; and technological advances that make redundant certain types of labor. While the secular decline of unionism in most advanced economies is, of course, a significant trend in itself, perhaps more important is the underlying dynamics, noted below, that have contributed to this decline and will continue to exert pressure on unions in the next century.

Trend 2: Increasing competition from developing nations in product, labor, and capital markets

The most important development for international industrial relations in the early

Figure 13.1 Change in union density, 1980–88

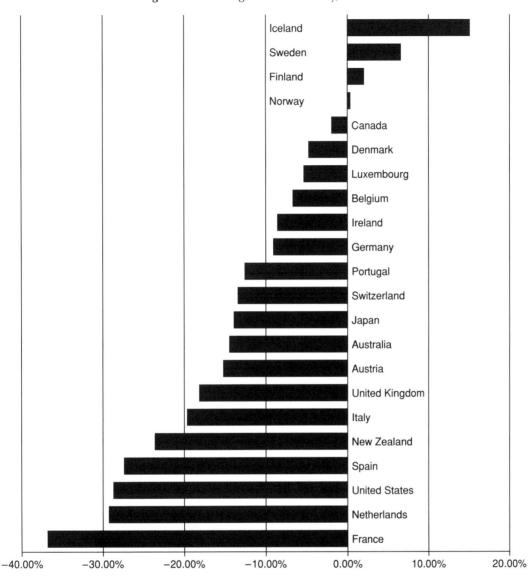

Source: OECD

twenty-first century will be the rapid growth of the emerging economies of Africa, Asia, Eastern/Central Europe, and Latin America, and the competition these nations will pose to the developed OECD nations. In 1990, developing nations accounted for about one-third of world gross domestic product (GDP).

This share of world output is expected to grow significantly as these emerging markets, freed from decades of state intervention in the economy and military control over political affairs, establish legal, political, and economic institutions that permit, legitimize, and support a market-based economy.

Figure 13.2 illustrates the rapid growth in real gross domestic product in selected emerging markets, and the relative under-performance of selected OECD nations, in 1993. These emerging markets are produc-ing extraordinary growth rates in real GDP and, according to the Organization for Eco-nomic Cooperation and Development, are expected to continue to outperform the economies of the United States and the Eu-ropean Union in 1994 and years to come. Indeed, some former colonies (e.g., Singapore and Hong Kong) have surpassed their former colonizers (the United Kingdom) in per capita gross domestic product.

While this rapid growth in real income will result in billions of new consumers of the goods and services produced by OECD economies, these emerging economies also are becoming important competitors in pro-duct, labor, and capital markets. With their relatively low wage costs and increasingly pro-ductive labor forces, many developing nations have been successful in attracting manufac-turers of both low-value-added and high-value-added products. While some of this has been new manufacturing capacity, surely a signific-ant portion of it is productive capacity trans-planted from higher-wage countries in North America, Europe, and Asia.

Even more important for the long-term competitive posture of emerging economies is the explosion of capital investment in re-cent years. Figure 13.3 illustrates a ninefold increase in net equity flows into the Pacific Rim and Latin America for the period 1986–93. Even more dramatic is the rapid pace of investment in China, both direct investment in plants and equity (share) investments in companies listed on China's stock exchanges (see figures 13.4a and 13.4b). If a series of conditions are met, including (1) sustained GDP growth that outpaces growth in OECD nations, (2) macroeconomic stability evid-enced, in part, by price and currency stabil-ity, and (3) a continuation in the trend of both individual and institutional (including

pension fund) investors committing funds to developing markets, then we expect that these emerging markets will become even more important competitors for the OECD nations and place increased downward pressure on wages and prices of certain goods and com-modities throughout the world. The increas-ing importance of less developed countries in the world economy will lead to the restruc-turing of global economic relations, and pose significant challenges to unions in OECD nations as jobs and capital are redistributed from wealthy nations to emerging markets.

Trend 3: Creation of supranational institutions and the integration of national economies into regional trading blocks

The last few decades have seen the growth and development of important supranational institutions such as the European Union, the General Agreement on Tariffs and Trade (GATT), and GATT's successor, the newly formed World Trade Organization (WTO); and the creation of regional trading blocs such as the European Community, the North American Free Trade Agreement (NAFTA) bloc, the Asia Pacific Economic Co-operation (APEC) bloc, and the various blocs of Cen-tral American and South American trading partners. If these supranational institutions and trading blocs survive the parochial inter-ests of their member parties, the impact on industrial relations will be significant.

First, supranational institutions and trad-ing blocs will reduce cross-border tariffs and structural trade barriers, thereby exposing unionized firms and workers to greater mar-ket competition. In the face of this new com-petition, unions will be less able to extract economic rents from firms and consumers. (Economic rents are "(p)ayments to a factor of production that are in excess of that amount necessary to keep it in its current employment" (Nicholson, 1978, 683).) Second, the "harmonization" of industrial relations policies within the European Union (and

Figure 13.2 Growth of real GDP, 1993

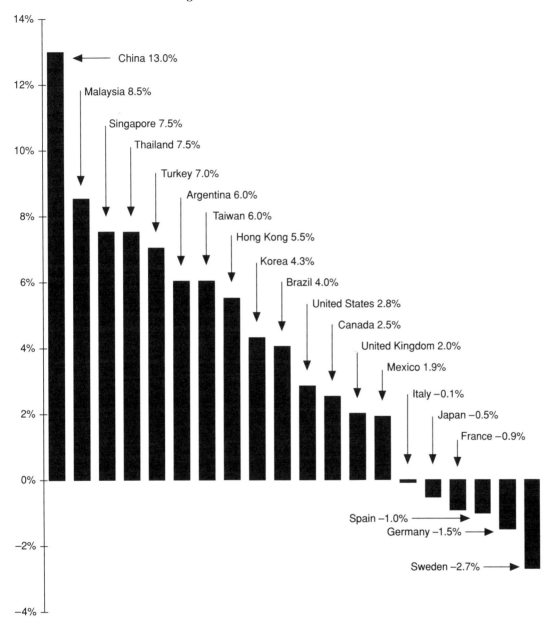

Source: *Financial Times* (1994a)

Figure 13.3 Funds invested in emerging markets

Net equity flows ($bn.)

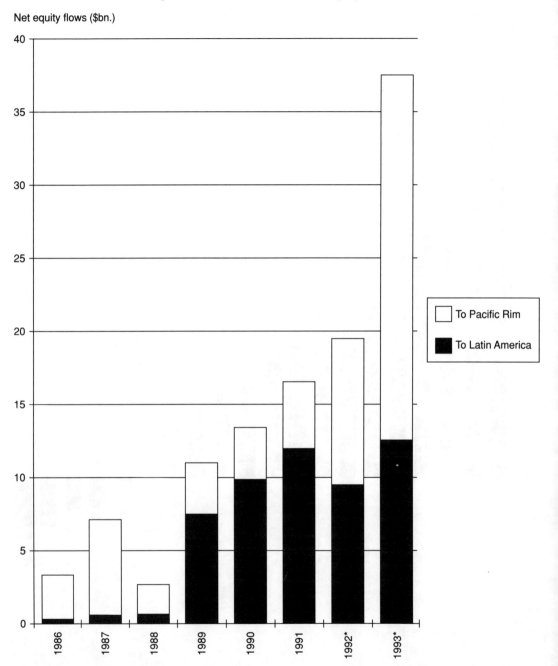

*Estimates
Source: *Financial Times* (1994b)

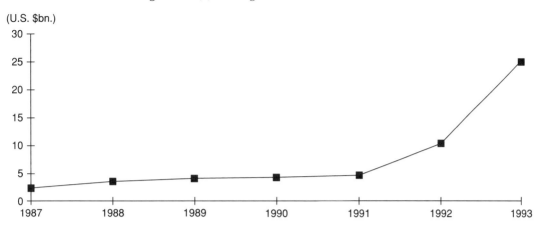

Figure 13.4(a) Foreign direct investment in China

Source: Fortune (1994)

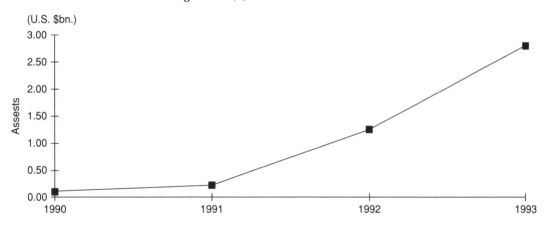

Figure 13.4(b) Growth of China funds

Source: Fortune (1994)

eventually in other trading blocs), through the use of employment law and regulation, may take from unions their raison d'être in certain circumstances. For example, health and safety regulations, dispute resolution procedures, and other concerns that unions traditionally have bargained over and helped to administer within the workplace may be supplanted by public policy emanating from Brussels (in the case of the European Union) and Texas (in the case of the labor board created by NAFTA). Thus, these supranational institutions and trading blocs not only will impact the competitive environment, but also directly affect the structure of industrial relations systems across the globe (see the case study in the next section of this chapter for an example from Europe). Third, increased labor market competition within trading blocs may lead to ethnic and racial tensions among workers. Recent reports from Luxembourg and Germany, for example, indicate growing tensions between native-born workers and guest workers from neighboring EU nations. Increased heterogeneity within work groups may make union organizing more difficult to accomplish and union solidarity more difficult to maintain.

Trend 4: Privatization and deregulation of industries

Privatization of entire industries is sweeping across Europe, Latin America, and Asia. The British government under Margaret Thatcher led the way to privatization in the 1980s, and France, Italy, and certain Eastern/Central European countries, for example, have followed suit in more recent years. In Latin America, corporations formally owned and/or dominated by national governments, such as telephone companies in Mexico, Argentina, and Brazil, and the Argentinian national petroleum company, have been privatized through initial public offerings to investors in both local and foreign stock exchanges.

The deregulation of industries, which began in the United States and the United Kingdom in the 1970s and 1980s, has gained momentum throughout the OECD as well, both as a rationalization of markets within a nation and as a response to the requirements of trading bloc treaties across national boundaries. While supranational institutions and trade agreements such as the European Union, GATT, and NAFTA will lead to *increased* regulation of certain aspects of various industries (e.g., environmental pollutants), we expect the general trend to be one of deregulation in the form of less governmental protection of favored industries.

The privatization and deregulation of industries will cause significant changes in industrial relations systems as employment levels shrink and bargaining structures change (wit-

ness the changes in the U.S. telephone industry as a result of the breakup of AT&T in the mid-1980s). While consumers will benefit from these changes, it is unclear how workers employed in these industries will benefit unless industry leaders are able to exploit new markets and/or diversification strategies. In the global arena, the movement to privatization and deregulation of industries portends significant challenges to organized labor and workplace relations as the stability of assured profit margins and increasing real income is supplanted by the turmoil of domestic and international competition.

Trend 5: Deregulation of labor markets

One of the greatest challenges facing the industrial relations systems in OECD nations is the deregulation of labor markets. This is also one of the most contentious issues. Faced with stagnating employment growth, high unemployment rates, and very expensive social safety nets that are paid for by taxes on employment, the European Union has begun exploring how greater flexibility can be introduced into its members' labor markets (Commission of the European Unions, 1993). To date, the debate has juxtaposed the traditional, highly regulated labor market (with the hope that the no growth/slow growth problem will resolve itself) with the U.S./U.K. model of labor market deregulation (which results in greater flexibility but at the cost of a large cadre of low-wage workers). A synthesis of these two strategies has not emerged and, in fact, may be impossible to achieve.

The deregulation of labor markets appears to be an inevitable consequence of the other trends discussed above. Simply stated, if product markets and capital markets become more competitive as a result of the increased competition brought about by emerging markets, regional trading blocs, and supranational institutions, then labor markets will be forced to respond or risk losing out to competitors who can offer more value for each dollar (or pound or D-mark) spent on labor.

The impact of further labor market deregulation will not be favorable to labor unions, of course. Public policies that artificially raise the cost of labor for all workers place a supportive floor or foundation beneath union-negotiated wages. Further, labor market deregulation, which complements the deregulation of industries and other pro-market policies, threatens to undermine not only workers' real wages but also the long-term stability of highly regulated labor markets.

THE PRACTICE OF INTERNATIONAL INDUSTRIAL RELATIONS

Strategy researchers have highlighted the various stages that a domestic organization can evolve through in the process of becoming internationalized (Hendry, 1994). However, what about the higher stages of internationalization whereby an organization with an existing international presence extends its operations still further into an increased number and variety of national settings? This will obviously add to the "managing complexity" theme that is so prominent in studies of the internationalization process.

In industrial relations terms, the organization concerned will face the task of having to accommodate and integrate an increasingly diverse set of national-level industrial relations practices. At the very least, this is likely to call into question the relevance and utility of a simple dichotomy between centralized (headquarters based) and decentralized (subsidiary based) decision making in industrial relations. To further complicate the picture, what if the organization finds itself in a setting where it has to respond to an external industrial relations directive from a body like the European Union? This is the focus of the case study below.

Coordinating human resources in Sony, Europe

The Sony Corporation has a number of production locations in Europe. The main ones are in the United Kingdom (currently some 5,000 employees), Germany (2,500 employees), France (2,500 employees) and Spain (2,000 employees). In the mid-1980s, a human resource (HR) management committee for Europe was established. The membership of the committee consists of seven individuals who are the leading HR specialists for the chief Sony locations (both manufacturing and sales/marketing) in Europe. The committee meets four times per year, with a further meeting in June to update representatives from the smaller Sony locations (i.e., Italy, Switzerland, and the Netherlands).

This relatively long-standing committee in Sony, Europe fits well with the argument that the sort of MNC most likely to adopt a European-wide perspective on HRM and industrial relations matters is characterized by (1) a single management structure within Europe and (2) the production of similar products in different countries for integrated production across national boundaries (Marginson, 1992). The original reason for establishing the committee was to ensure that the process of identifying individuals with high management development potential was integrated with and fitted the business needs of the organization. An important step in this process was to ensure that essentially a common (management) appraisal approach was adopted in the various European locations. This management development program typically involves an individual being on a two-year job rotation assignment in Europe, with some 20 individuals being on the program at any point in time.

This management development theme overwhelmingly dominated the agenda of the coordinating committee until the start of the 1990s. Since then a second important item has been added to the agenda, which has meant that the quarterly meetings typically last two days rather than one day as previously. This new agenda item has involved the theme of harmonization, with harmonization in certain areas of the employment package being sought both in individual countries and across Europe. These harmonization steps have resulted in significant cost savings for the corporation in a number of areas, most notably company cars, pensions policy, and insurance.

The committee has currently a third item on its agenda, namely that of formulating a response to the draft European Community (EC) directive on European works councils. Works councils, which provide certain types of representation to employees but are not affiliated with trade unions, would have the right under the EC directive to receive information from management and be consulted on certain strategic issues affecting workers. The need to take a strategic approach to this item derives from the diversity of industrial relations arrangements within the Sony Corporation in Europe. This diversity is indicated by the following:

- Two out of the three Sony plants in France are non-union.
- The leading Sony plant in Germany is unionized, but the key industrial relations decision-making body is a works council, which has strong legal underpinning for its operation.
- The Spanish plant is unionized, but is characterized by a multiunion bargaining structure.
- The leading U.K. production unit has a single union recognition agreement with a strong commitment to plant-level collective bargaining, whereas the sales/marketing set-up in the U.K. is essentially nonunion.

In view of this diversity, the coordinating committee established some 18 months ago a subcommittee to analyze the draft directive on European works councils. The subcommittee consists of the three individuals on the main committee with the most experience in dealing with unions. The initial position adopted by the subcommittee was as follows:

1 No initiative would be forthcoming from Sony until the directive was clarified.
2 In principle, they were comfortable with the notion of consultation and information sharing, but would want to ensure that any resulting arrangement did not become a vehicle for joint negotiating or bargaining.

These points have been conveyed to various bodies within individual countries and at the European-wide level within Sony. The subcommittee's deliberations also have been informed by discussions with a leading German company about their particular experience with European works councils. At the present time, the subcommittee members are much happier with the current version of the draft directive than they were with the original version.

The Sony, Europe HRM coordinating committee has evolved over time from essentially an information exchange body to one that has decison-makig authority, at least in certain selected areas. In this sense, it is instructive in two notable regards. First, it indicates that the traditional headquarters versus local subsidiary dichotomy in industrial relations decision-making terms requires some reworking and elaboration to take account of an intermediate stage of decision making (at least in some areas). Second, it suggests that discussions of the development (or not) of union–management consultation/information-sharing arrangements across national boundaries in individual organizations usefully can be informed by a prior stage of analysis: namely, whether management arrangements across national boundaries have been established.

INTEGRATION AND FUTURE DIRECTIONS

The nexus of a decline in the role and strength of certain traditional features of industrial relations systems, the impaired performance of various systems (at the individual organizational or national systems level), and the rapidly changing global economic context inevitably will generate the search for new, improved institutional arrangements to mediate and regulate workplace relations. This search process, as mentioned in an earlier section, has frequently involved seeking to learn from the practices of "model" industrial relations systems. For example, in the 1980s, U.S. managers sought to borrow certain practices, most notably quality circles, from the Japanese industrial relations system, whereas in the 1990s there is considerable practitioner, researcher, and policy-maker interest in the potential for adopting works councils from the German system. The obvious question raised, which we expect and hope to see increasingly on the agenda, is: Will such practices work equally well outside their country of origin?

To some commentators the answer to the above question is likely to be No! Such a response can be expected for at least two sets of reasons. The first set is likely to make reference to the argument of Hofstede (1983) regarding the strength of national cultures. The contention of Hofstede and others (Laurent, 1986) is that the attitudes and behavior patterns of individuals are heavily conditioned by the nature of national cultures, and that cultures vary between nations along a number of dimensions, such as:

1 The extent to which roles are based on gender.
2 The extent to which individuals relate to groups.
3 The extent to which society seeks to socialize individuals to cope with living in an uncertain environment.

4 The extent of inequalities in wealth and power.

The second argument is likely to highlight the need for a complementary ("fit") relationship between the larger external (to the individual organization) institutional context and the institutional arrangements operating in individual organizations. The contention here is that such a relationship is critical in explaining the success of institutional arrangements within organizations in the model system, but if it does not exist in the system that emulates these practices, then the results will be very different in nature.

The first argument was raised in relation to the introduction and operation of quality circles in the U.S. in the 1980s. The experience there indicated that such quality circles generally produced little bottom-line payoff and frequently did not survive the test of time. To some commentators, this would appear to reflect the fact that quality circles worked well in the group-oriented society of Japan, but would not and did not work well in the more individual-oriented society of the U.S. However, the performance of Japanese transplants in the U.S., most notably NUMMI, would appear to challenge such an interpretation. Instead, the crucial lesson that has been drawn from the Japanese transplant experience in the U.S. is that a single discrete innovation or change like quality circles will not work well in the absence of a set of complementary, supportive industrial relations changes within the organization (Kochan, Cutcher-Gershenfeld, & MacDuffie, 1989).

The second argument is likely to be raised in relation to the potential adoption of works councils in the United States. In Germany, works councils have operated very much as a joint problem-solving mechanism, whereas in the U.S. the simple transfer of works councils could see them assuming a more adversarial, arms-length bargaining role due to the lack of a supportive external (to the firm) environment. This potential difference in operation, as Freeman and Rogers (1993) noted, is likely to occur because wages and fringe benefits are set on the industry level in Germany, in contrast to the decentralized bargaining structure in the U.S. In their words (Freeman & Rogers, 1993, 45):

External guarantees – be they social benefit guarantees, centrally determined wages or rights based sanctions on job loss – in some measure render moot much intra-firm disagreement about the division of the surplus. By taking many intra-firm disputes over the surplus "off the table" these guarantees underwrite internal co-operation and flexibility toward the joint goal of improving firm performance.

As a result, Freeman and Rogers suggest that it will be essential to ensure that works councils in the U.S. not engage in wage bargaining.

Finally, the rapidly changing global economy, and the ascent of supranational institutions such as the European Union, the WTO, and trading blocs such as NAFTA and APEC, may make moot much of our concern about the features of industrial relations systems, but for very different reasons.

If the next century belongs to today's emerging markets of China, India, Southeast Asia, Latin America, Africa, and Central/Eastern Europe, then the economic supremacy of the OECD nations will be challenged. Increased competition in product, labor, and capital markets can only hurt trade unions and unionized workers, at least in the short run. Will labor unions be able to extract the economic rents that justify their existence in the context of an integrated, global economy where information, labor, products, and capital flow easily across national borders? Probably not. Alternatively, if these emerging markets are "flash-in-the-pans" (as has been the case for Latin America on a number of occasions in the twentieth century), destined for hyperinflation and economic, social, and political chaos, then unionized workers in the developed economies will be afforded a temporary reprieve from

the forces of competition, and unions may remain a viable labor market institution.

The impact of supranational institutions and regional trading blocs also must be considered. The purpose of GATT is to reduce trade barriers on a global basis; workers-as-consumers will benefit under GATT but, in a variety of industries, workers qua workers will suffer dislocations due to increased international competition.

This dilemma was highlighted in the recent meeting of GATT members in Marrakech, at which the Uruguay Round accords were signed. Prior to this meeting, the United States and France had pushed very hard for the development of international labor standards within the GATT framework. Although human rights rhetoric was employed to justify this link between trade and labor standards (Williams, 1994), it was clear to most observers that the true purpose was to ensure that relatively weaker labor standards in developing nations do not create an unfair competitive advantage for these nations (Morton, 1994). Not wanting to threaten the culmination of the Uruguay Round, France and the U.S. withdrew their demands, but with the understanding that this issue will be raised again under the auspices of the WTO.

The impact of regional trading blocs is more difficult to discern, however. Will these blocs eliminate trade barriers within the bloc, but erect barriers between the bloc and international competitors? In this case, unions may be able to extract rents in the short run, but this is not a sustainable strategy in the age of rapidly growing emerging markets and mobile capital. In the case of the European Union, the emergence and growth of a European government, headquartered in Brussels, may make unions redundant as workplace policies are promulgated on a uniform basis throughout the Community, all in the name of "harmonization." On the other hand, if regional trading blocs become building blocs of a competitive global economy, unions may be an anachronistic labor market institution relegated to the public sector and natural monopolies.

Under all of these scenarios, industrial relations practitioners and researchers face a very uncertain world. However, both will be well advised to increasingly focus on those international trends and institutions that surely will be significant influences in industrial relations systems for the rest of this century and the next.

REFERENCES

Bain, G. S., & Elsheikh, E. (1976). *Union Growth and the Business Cycle.* Oxford: Blackwell.

Bamber, G. J., & Lansbury, R. D. (eds.) (1993). *International and Comparative Industrial Relations*, 2nd ed. London: Routledge.

Beaumont, P. B. (1991). Human resource management and international joint ventures: Some evidence from Britain. *Human Resource Management Journal*, 1 (4), 90–101.

Beaumont, P. B., Cressey, P., & Jakobsen, P. (1990). Key industrial relations: West German subsidiaries in Britain. *Employee Relations*, 12 (6), 3–7.

Blanchflower, D. G., & Freeman, R. B. (1992). Unionism in the United States and other advanced OECD countries. *Industrial Relations*, 31 (1), 56–79.

Bruno, M., & Sachs, J. D. (1985). *Economics of Worldwide Stagflation.* Oxford: Blackwell.

Clegg, H. A. (1976). *Trade Unionism under Collective Bargaining.* Oxford: Blackwell.

Commission of the European Communities (1993). *Growth, Competitiveness, Employment: The challenges and ways forward into the 21st century.* White Paper, Bulletin of the European Communities, Supplement 6/93. Brussels: Commission of the European Communities.

Daly, A., Hitchens, D. M., & Wagner, K. (1985). Productivity, machinery and skills in a sample of British and German manufacturing plants. *National Institute Economic Review*, February.

Dicken, P. (1992). *Global Shift*, 2nd ed. London: Paul Chapman.

Dore, R. (1973). *British Factory, Japanese Factory: The origins of national diversity in industrial relations.* London: Allen & Unwin.

Dunlop, J. T. (1958). *Industrial Relations Systems.* New York: Holt, Rinehart & Winston.

Dunlop, J. T., Harbison, F. H., Kerr, C., & Myers, C. (1975). *Industrialism and Industrial Man Reconsidered.* New Jersey: Prentice Hall.

Ferner, A., and Hyman, R. (eds.) (1992). *Industrial Relations in the New Europe.* Oxford: Blackwell.

Financial Times (1994a). Using data from Baring Securities, February 3, 15.

Financial Times (1994b). Using OECD data, February 7, 10.

Fortune (1994). Using data from the U.S. Department of Commerce; World Bank; and Micropal Emerging Markets Monitor, March 7, 116.

Freeman, R. B. (1989). The changing status of unionism around the world. In W.-C. Huang (ed.), *Organized Labor at the Crossroads*, 111–38. Kalamazoo, MI: W. E. Upjohn Institute for Employment Research.

Freeman, R. B., & Rogers, J. (1993). Who speaks for us? Employee representation in a nonunion labor market. In B. E. Kaufman & M. M. Kleiner (eds.), *Employee Representation: Alternatives and future directions*, 13–79. Madison, WI: Industrial Relations Research Association.

Hamill, J. (1984). Labour relations decision making within multinational corporations. *Industrial Relations Journal*, 15 (2), 30–4.

Hendry, C. (1994). *Human Resource Strategies for International Growth.* London: Routledge.

Hibbs, D. A. (1976). Industrial conflict in advanced industrial societies. *American Political Science Review*, 70, 1033–58.

Hofstede, G. (1983). The cultural relativity of organizational theories. *Journal of International Business Studies*, 14 (2), 75–90.

Jürgens, U., Klinzing, L., & Turner, L. (1993). The transformation of industrial relations in Eastern Germany. *Industrial & Labor Relations Review*, 46 (2), 229–44.

Kassalow, E. M. (1983). Japan as an industrial relations model. *The Journal of Industrial Relations*, 25 (2), 201–19.

Kerr, C., Dunlop, J. T., Harbison, F., & Myers, C. A. (1960). *Industrialism and Industrial Man.* New York: Oxford University Press.

Kochan, T. A., Katz, H. C., and McKersie, R. B. (1986). *The Transformation of American Industrial Relations.* New York: Basic Books.

Kochan, T. A., Cutcher-Gershenfeld, J., & MacDuffie, J. P. (1989). Employee participation, work redesign and new technology: The implications for public policy in the 1990s. Paper prepared for the Commission on Workforce Quality and Labor Market Efficiency, US Department of Labor, May.

Kurivilla, S. (1994). Industrial relations in South East Asia. Paper presented at the winter meeting of the Industrial Relations Research Association, Boston.

Laurent, A. (1986). The cross-cultural puzzle of international human resource management. *Human Resource Management*, 25 (1), 91–102.

Marginson, P. (1992). European integration and transnational management–union relationships in the enterprise. *British Journal of Industrial Relations*, 30 (4), 529–46.

Morton, P. (1994). Squabbles hit WTO before it's even born. *Financial Post*, April 9, 5.

Nicholson, W. (1978). *Microeconomic Theory*, 2nd ed. Hinsdale, IL: Dryden Press.

Ogle, G. E. (1990). *South Korea: Dissent within the economic miracle.* London: Zed Books.

Peterson, R. B. (1986). Research design issues in comparative industrial relations. *Proceedings of the Industrial Relations Research Association*, winter, 244–51.

Poole, M. J. F. (1986). *Industrial Relations: Origins and patterns of national diversity.* London: Routledge.

Poole, M. (1993). Industrial relations: Theorizing for a global perspective. In R. J. Adams & N. M. Meltz (eds.), *Industrial relations theory*, 103–17. New Brunswick, NJ: Rutgers University Press.

Purcell, J., Marginson, P., Edwards, P., and Sisson, K. (1987). The industrial relations practices of multi-plant foreign owned firms. *Industrial Relations Journal*, 18 (2), 125–30.

Sorge, A., & Warner, M. (1986). *Comparative Factory Organization*. Aldershot: Gower.

Treu, T., et al. (1987). *Public Service Labour Relations*. Geneva: International Labour Office.

Wilkinson, B., Morris, J., & Munday, M. (1993). Japan in Wales: A new IR. *Industrial Relations Journal*, 24 (4), 273–83.

Williams, F. (1994). US waves flag for workers' rights in WTO. *Financial Times*, March 30, 5.

Windmuller, J. (1963). Model industrial relations systems. *Proceedings of the Industrial Relations Research Association*, winter.

□ Chapter 14 □

Work Force Diversity: The Good, the Bad, and the Reality

Valerie I. Sessa, Susan E. Jackson, and Darryl T. Rapini

INTRODUCTION

As we approach the beginning of a new millennium, two sets of forces are shaping and changing familiar organizational structures. First, organizations are finding that to succeed in an increasingly competitive environment, the traditional model of mass production for running business and governmental organizations no longer suffices and they must become more responsive to rapidly changing environments (Deluca & McDowell, 1992; Sayles, 1993). To do this, organizations are increasingly relying on teams composed interdepartmentally, interorganizationally, and internationally. At the same time, changing work-force demographics (e.g., Johnston & Packer, 1987) are forcing organizations to review and revise long-held beliefs and policies surrounding the people who belong to and work in these organizations. These new organizational teams combined with changing work-force demographics are bringing more and more people from diverse backgrounds (in terms of gender, race, ethnicity, religion, national origin, age, area of expertise, and many other personal characteristics) into

contact with one another. We begin this chapter with an overview of why these forces are changing organizational structures. We then describe the challenges diversity brings in terms of the assets and liabilities associated with it. Finally, we describe how two organizations – Miles Inc., Pharmaceutical Division, and the Xerox Corporation[1] – are currently addressing the challenges of managing work-force diversity.

CHANGING ORGANIZATIONAL STRUCTURES

Increasing reliance on teams

In today's business environment, many organizations are relying on teams to facilitate liaisons across departments, organizations, and countries, with the expectation that these teams will increase quality (Banas, 1988; Dumaine, 1990; Work teams, 1988), innovations (e.g., Bylinski, 1990, 72), and ultimately competitive position. These teams are comprised of members from different business or specialty backgrounds (e.g., marketing, operations, finance), different needs or motives (e.g., suppliers and customers), and different cultures (both national and organizational). Many organizations are utilizing interdepartmental teams to pursue new business strategies which emphasize quality, innovation, and speed. Work teams often bring together employees from previously segregated areas of the company, creating occupational and knowledge-based diversity. For example, research-and-design teams bring together experts with a variety of knowledge backgrounds with the expectation that combined they will produce more creative thinking and innovation. Teams also bring together employees from two or more organizations. For example, to improve the quality of their finished products, manufacturers may include their suppliers as part of a product-design team. And to ensure that the finished product appeals to their customers, they may include the end users on the team. Such teams must develop a mode of operating that fits with the differing organization cultures in which the subunits are imbedded (Hofstede, 1991; Kanter, 1989). Finally, as trade barriers are removed and competition intensifies, many U.S. companies are beginning to expand their operations to take advantage of foreign labor and consumer markets. The presence of international affiliations is likely to lead eventually to the formation of teams of people with diverse cultural backgrounds, including management teams, design teams, operations teams, and marketing teams (Adler & Ghadar, 1989; Kanter, 1991; Von Glinow & Mohrman, 1990).

The changing workforce

At the same time that organizations are relying more on teamwork, the demographics of the U.S. labor force are changing. The result is greater gender diversity, cultural diversity (including differences due to race and ethnicity), and age diversity within the newly formed teams.

Gender diversity

Women are entering the labor force in growing numbers and the work force is becoming increasingly more gender-balanced. According to government statistics, as of 1991, 46 percent of the work force was female. Furthermore, gender-based segregation in the work place is slowly declining. Government statistics show that women currently represent 41 percent of the executive, administrative, and managerial work force, although only 2.6 percent of the *Fortune 500* companies' corporate officers are women and only a handful of women have made it all the way to the top (Morrison, White, & Van Velsor, 1992). Consequently, all but the highest-level teams in organizations are likely to be characterized by gender diversity.

Many companies now realize that a corporate culture suited to an all-male work force is not as effective in this new environment. A poll of 241 *Fortune 1,000* CEOs found that nearly 80 percent said there were internal barriers that kept capable women from reaching the top (Fierman, 1990). Until companies remove these barriers, they will not be able to fully utilize the talents of nearly half the employees in their work force.

Cultural diversity

In 1987, the U.S. Department of Labor projected rapid increases in the cultural diversity of the U.S. labor supply (Johnston & Packer, 1987). Only 58 percent of the new entrants into the labor force were expected to come from the "majority" white American-born population. The remaining 42 percent were expected to be mostly immigrants (22 percent), followed by approximately equal numbers of African Americans and Hispanic Americans. Despite the fact that this will cause a more evolutionary than revolutionary change (Barnum, 1991) the work force *is* becoming more diverse. Around the world, many other countries are facing parallel changes in their work forces, although the particular ethnicities and nationalities involved differ from one country to the next.

When people with different habits and ways of viewing the world come together in the workplace, misunderstandings inevitably occur as a result of dissimilar expectations and norms. For example, employees who behave according to the adage "the squeaky wheel gets the grease" may be viewed as offensive and undesirable teammates by employees who were taught that "the nail that sticks out gets hammered down." Such misunderstandings can mean that valuable information about problems and successes is poorly transmitted or never gets used.

Age diversity

Age is affecting the work force in two ways. Descriptions of work-force demographics usually emphasize the fact that the average age of the work force is increasing. Additionally, the *distribution* of ages is changing. The shrinking rate of growth of the labor pool is pushing employers to hire at both extremes of the age distribution, with the result that both student interns and former "retirees" are being hired to fill vacant positions (Bolick & Nestleroth, 1988). Also, many companies now allow the higher educations of younger employees to substitute for the job experiences that previous cohorts of employees had to accrue to be promoted. As a result, relatively young employees are found more often in higher-level jobs. Consequently, within each level of the organizational hierarchy, age diversity is replacing the homogeneity associated with traditional age-based stratification. Employees of greatly different ages and generations are now finding themselves working side by side. These different generations differ in their values and attitudes about work (e.g., Elder, 1975; Managing generational diversity, 1991), their physical and mental functioning (Rhodes, 1983), and the everyday concerns that reflect stages in the life cycle.

The challenges of diversity

Diversity influences the organization both in the short term and in the long term. Presently, diversity is simply a fact of life that influences the recruitment, retention, motivation, and performance of today's employees. In the longer term, effectively working through diversity is an imperative for success in a highly competitive, global environment. Short-term and long-term responses to diversity must address three challenges: availability, fairness, and synergy (Jackson & Alvarez, 1992).

The availability challenge

Predictions about the future U.S. work force indicate that the skill levels needed in jobs will surpass the skill levels of the average worker. The supply of skilled labor will no longer be abundant relative to demand. In the past, employers could refuse to hire employees who were unable to work the standard workweek and punish those who were too often absent or tardy or who just simply didn't fit in. These practices controlled the diversity of the work force; selective hiring practices were used, and standard operating procedures were imposed. Those who couldn't cut it were easily replaced with someone who would readily conform. But as qualified employees become more scarce, employers can no longer say, "This is when and where you must be available for work, and this is the way we will treat you while you are here." Now they must adapt to qualified employees who say, "This is when and where the work must be available for me to do it, and this is the way I must be treated if you want me to stay."

The fairness challenge

Flexible policies and practices help employers solve the availability issue and inevitably bring them face to face with a second challenge: ensuring that all employees are treated fairly and feel that they are treated fairly. What is meant by fair treatment is no longer a simple issue. In the U.S., the issue of fair treatment of employees has been driven for many years by legal concerns. Whether a company treated employees (and job applicants) fairly was ultimately judged by the courts using technical criteria, which were negotiated by attorneys, psychologists, and psychometricians. In this context, fair treatment meant equal treatment. Supervisors and managers were admonished to act as if they were blind to differences among employees, especially if those differences might be linked to sex, race, ethnicity, age, or national origin. In the present context, fair treatment has come to mean more than just equal treatment. Now supervisors and managers are expected to treat individuals in a way best suited to those individuals (i.e., differently), so that employees *perceive* they are being treated fairly. The consequences of this paradox of similar treatment versus different treatment is that legislation developed requiring that people should not be treated differentially because of their race, sex, age, religion, or handicaps (to eliminate discrimination) in the hiring and advancement of protected classes may now be a stumbling block to economically driven attempts to make the most of each employee (Chen, 1992).

The synergy challenge
The third diversity challenge is unleashing and taking full advantage of the latent potential of diverse teams. As is discussed below, work teams can be both more productive and more creative than individuals working alone. But the same social forces that push people to reach their fullest potential can push people into unproductive and even destructive behavior patterns.

Why is diversity both an asset and a liability? The diversity discussed above has been associated with differences in values, attitudes, styles of interaction, physical and cognitive abilities, and nonwork commitments (Jackson, 1992). Both organizations and those who study

them have begun to realize that, for better or worse, diversity and thus the differences associated with diversity may change patterns of behavior established during an era when work groups were relatively homogeneous. But, at this time, no single theory explains why diversity can be both an asset and a liability. Below, we discuss theory and research that addresses why diversity may be beneficial to individuals, teams, and organizations. Then we discuss theory and research that addresses why diversity may be detrimental.

THEORY AND RESEARCH ON DIVERSITY

What's so great about diversity?: the good

Theory and research suggest that diversity in the work force may have a positive impact on the performance of individuals, teams, and organizations. Two different mechanisms may be used to explain why diversity leads to better performance. The first is based on differences in perspectives and attitudes and the second is based on differences in skills and ability.

Differences in perspectives and attitudes
Differences in demographic characteristics are associated with differences in experiences, attitudes, and perspectives of team members (e.g., Jackson, 1992). Differences in experiences and perspectives lead team members to approach problems and decisions drawing on different information, from different angles, and with different attitudes. Therefore, teams composed of team members with diverse backgrounds and characteristics would be expected to produce a wider variety of ideas, alternatives, and solutions than teams composed of people with similar demographic characteristics.

Differences in skills and ability
According to this mechanism, the presence of high-skill and high-ability members within

the team raises the performance of the whole team for two reasons. First, the team may be more likely to find the correct solution, or select the best alternative, because of the creativity, the ideational ability, the flexibility, or the divergent thinking processes of the high-ability team members themselves. Second, the presence of team members with higher skills and ability may actually stimulate other members to use divergent cognitive processes that they might not otherwise try; that is, lower-skill or lower-ability members may learn, emulate, and use the processes of the higher-skill or higher-ability members (see Nemeth, 1992 for a fuller discussion). In terms of work-force demographic diversity, there is evidence that people who are bicultural and bilingual are more able to use divergent thinking and are more flexible in their thinking (see McLeod & Lobel, 1992). Thus, performance may be improved because diverse team members add different skills and abilities; and performance may also be improved because diversity stimulates team members to consider more information and more ways of thinking about that information than they would otherwise.

Although little research has systematically tested whether, or which, of these mechanisms lead to better performance, evidence suggests that diversity in teams does have a positive impact on the performance of individuals, teams, and the organization as a whole.

Individual performance

In a program of research on minority influence,[2] Nemeth and colleagues have demonstrated that when individuals in a team are exposed to a dissenting minority, they are individually stimulated to recall more information, to use multiple strategies to problem solutions – which aids performance – and to detect correct novel solutions to problems (see Nemeth, 1992, for a review). Interestingly, these novel and correct solutions are not necessarily ever proposed by the dissenting minority. Instead, Nemeth (1992) proposes that the improved performance is a result of divergent cognitive processes that are stimulated by the minority views. Thus, the presence of team members who view the problem differently or who hold a different piece of information may stimulate others in the team to discover novel solutions that they would not have considered, thereby improving the performance of individuals.

Team performance

Basic research relating team diversity to a variety of team tasks (and conducted mostly in laboratory settings) supports the conclusion that heterogeneity improves performance in terms of creativity and decision quality of teams. This effect has been found for diversity of many types, including personality, training background, leadership abilities, attitudes (see Jackson, May, & Whitney, 1994, for a comprehensive review), ethnicity (McCleod & Lobel, 1992), and sex (Wood, 1987).

Organizational performance

Finally, a few published studies provide support for the general thesis that top-management team composition predicts strategic choices and firm performance. For example, a study of 199 top-management teams in the banking industry found that levels of organizational innovation were correlated with team heterogeneity with respect to areas of job expertise (Bantel & Jackson, 1989). Several other studies also support the general notion of a link between top-management team composition and performance (Eisenhardt & Schoonhoven, 1990; Finkelstein & Hambrick, 1990; Michel & Hambrick, 1992; Murray, 1989; Singh & Harianto, 1989; Weirsema & Bantel, 1991; Wiersema & Bird, 1993). However, a variety of organizational and environmental conditions appear to influence how and whether composition translates into performance gains (see Hambrick, 1994; Jackson, 1992).

What's the downside?: the bad

While differences among organizational and team members may prove useful in the performance of individuals, teams, and organizations, theory and research suggest that diversity has the opposite effect on job attitudes and satisfaction, communication networks, and turnover. Theory and research are based on the assumption that interpersonal similarity is one of the most important determinants of interpersonal attraction (Byrne, 1971), which in turn creates a social context for relationships among organizational members. Two theoretical perspectives – Schneider's (1987) attraction-selection-attrition (ASA) model and Pfeffer's (1983) organizational demography model – illustrate the way in which interpersonal context affects organizational behavior.

Attraction–selection–attrition model

Schneider (1987) argued that, through processes of attraction, selection, and attrition (ASA), organizations evolve toward a state of interpersonal homogeneity in terms of personality, interests, and values. A similarity → attraction effect results in people being attracted to and seeking membership in organizations whose members they believe are similar to themselves. When current members screen potential new members, they are attracted to similar others as well, so they are more likely to admit new members like themselves. After entering the organization, the new member and the more tenured members become better acquainted, and the similarity → attraction effect can again influence the feelings and behaviors of both parties. To the extent that perceived similarity is maintained, the arrangement should be judged satisfactorily. However, if the match is judged unsatisfactorily, pressures form to encourage dissimilar members to leave the organization. Over time, this homogenizing process becomes legitimized in the human resources system which allows only more homogeneity

because selection, promotion, and outflow systems ensure the status quo, leading to an organization that is more homogeneous in terms of member personality, interests, and values than would be predicted by chance. This homogeneity is manifested by and manifests itself in such areas as the organization's culture and goals.

Organizational demography theory

Closely related to Schneider's (1987) ASA model is Pfeffer's (1983) model of organizational demography. *Organizational demography,* according to Pfeffer, refers to the demographic composition of organizations. According to Pfeffer, the demographic composition of organizations influences many behavioral patterns including communications, job transfers, promotions, and turnover. Included among the dimensions of demographic composition Pfeffer considered important are age, tenure, sex, race, socio-economic background, and religion. Sociological studies and marketing research have shown that differences in people's attitudes and values are reliably associated with differences in their standing on demographic characteristics such as these. Given this evidence, the similarity effect provides a rationale for how and why the demographic composition of an organization is likely to be related to organizational phenomena.

Although there is a similarity in the phenomena and processes implicated in the ASA and organizational demography models, they come from two different perspectives. Schneider (1987) draws from the psychological perspective and emphasizes individual-level constructs of similarity and attraction, as well as individual feelings and behaviors. Pfeffer (1983), on the other hand, draws from the sociological perspective and focuses on the organizational-level constructs of homogeneity, cohesiveness, communication networks, and patterns of employee flow. The information presented below regarding job attitudes and satisfaction, communication networks, and turnover is drawn from both of these perspectives.

Job attitudes

Some evidence shows that individuals who differ from their teammates or work-unit members in sex and race are more likely to report a lower commitment to their organization, less of an intention of staying in their organization, and more absences than those who are similar to teammates in these variables. Interestingly, there is evidence that suggests that being different in sex has a more negative effect on organizational attachment for men than women and that being different in race has a more negative effect on attachment for whites than for nonwhites (Tsui, Egan, & O'Reilly, 1992); however, other evidence demonstrates that minorities are slightly less committed to the group than nonminorities (Kirchmeyer & Cohen, 1992). Additionally, the influence of team composition on attitudes has been studied in laboratory settings. In these settings, heterogeneity of teams is associated with lower cohesiveness and more negative affective reactions (see Jackson, 1992).

Networks

Diversity has long-term consequences for communication networks within the organization as well. Employees with minority status in terms of ethnicity or gender often feel they face special barriers to informal communication networks (Morrison & Von Glinow, 1990). Their reports are consistent with studies of communication patterns in work organizations, which indicate that demographic diversity is related to lower amounts of communication among coworkers. For example, a study of communication networks in five organizations found that demographic homogeneity (on dimensions of authority, education, sex, race, and organization branch) consistently characterized work-communication chains, suggesting that diversity decreases communication overall (Lincoln & Miller,

1979). Other studies of communication patterns have shown that informal networks are segregated along demographic lines (Brass, 1984); that formal and informal meetings among peers and with immediate subordinates are lower in racially diverse groups (Hoffman, 1985); and that age and tenure similarities between coworkers predict communication patterns among project teams of engineers (Ibarra, 1992, 1993; Zenger & Lawrence, 1989).

Turnover

Several studies have shown that age and tenure diversity decrease organizational commitment and increase turnover (Jackson, Brett, Sessa, Cooper, Julin, & Peyronnin, 1991; McCain, O'Reilly, & Pfeffer, 1983; O'Reilly, Caldwell, & Barnett, 1989; Wagner, Pfeffer, & O'Reilly, 1984). In addition, in top-management teams, diversity in terms of college alma mater, curriculum studied, and industry experiences is associated with higher rates of turnover (Jackson et al., 1991). This association between diversity and turnover has also been noted in non-U.S. settings (Weirsema & Bird, 1993).

THE PRACTICE OF DIVERSITY

Optimizing diversity

It appears, from the theory and research cited above, that organizations, as they deal with and change the organization to accommodate diversity, will have a difficult balancing act to perform. On the one hand, organizations might be encouraged to take full advantage of the potential benefits of the growing diversity of the work force by ensuring that work teams are composed of dissimilar employees. However, organizations that make these changes without regard to the potential detrimental effects of diversity may soon notice lower satisfaction, communication problems, and turnover, unless they undertake remedial action to solve these problems.

Ensuring a successful change effort that takes into account both the assets and liabilities of diversity is in part the responsibility of human resources professionals. They are the ones who are best able to educate business leaders about the importance of diversity and mobilize them to take both short-term and long-term action. They have available to them a wide range of tools for changing the attitudes and behaviors of their organizations' employees, including recruiting and selection methods, performance evaluation, compensation and reward systems, training and development techniques, and models for re-designing both jobs and the organization within which jobs are performed. Finally, human resources professionals are the ones with the knowledge and skills needed to analyze what their organizations need to do to respond to simultaneous changes in organizational structures and the labor market, and to develop the processes needed to deal with these.

In the remainder of this chapter, we offer guidelines and principles to human resources professionals to keep in mind as they institute changes in their organizations to maximize the potential benefits of diversity while minimizing the possible detriments. Then we present two short examples of companies engaged in processes of optimizing the diversity of their work forces. The first example is a company in the beginning of its change effort. The second example is a company which has been involved in its change effort over the past three decades. Our objective is to highlight principles of relevance and use the two companies as explanatory devices and learning tools for human resources professionals who are interested in implementing diversity programs in their organizations.

The change effort: guidelines

There are many options and choices to be made when introducing initiatives for working through diversity, but there are also a few basic principles that seem to apply for all circumstances. These principles, discussed in detail elsewhere (see Jackson, 1992) are summarized below.

Organizational assessment

Current practices and policies Before launching new diversity initiatives, the system currently in place needs to be fully understood. Otherwise, it will be difficult to foresee all of the consequences likely to follow changes in that system accurately. As a precursor to considering new initiatives, human resources professionals should investigate the organization's current practices for the purpose of analyzing why things are the way they are and which things should stay the way they are. This includes evaluating whether current practices encourage or limit diversity, understanding the forces that support the use of the organization's present system of management, and assessing which aspects of the current system are consistent with the organization's current needs.

Current work force demographics When embarking on change efforts related to diversity, human resources professionals must also understand its many dimensions in an organization. Once an awareness of the many possible types of diversity that exist has been developed, then one must learn about the nature of diversity in the organization's work force; how this diversity impacts attitudes and behaviors in the work force; and other relevant facts about diversity.

What do the numbers indicate about the backgrounds of people in the organization, and the way diversity is distributed throughout the organization? Do people with diverse backgrounds work closely together, or are they segregated into homogeneous subgroups based on occupations, hierarchical level, or geographic location? Facts such as these may be readily available in the data base of the organization's human resources information system. But if not, then some basic research may be needed.

How do the backgrounds of people relate to their attitudes and behaviors? For example, are some subgroups of employees more likely to report dissatisfaction with their coworkers or the type of supervision they receive? Are turnover patterns different among different groups of employees? Do promotion rates differ among subgroups? Is everyone equally satisfied with the career opportunities they see? Valid answers to questions such as these may be easy to obtain in organizations that routinely conduct scientifically designed employee surveys to assess attitudes. In organizations without such readily available information, however, systematic research may be needed.

What are the external resources available on work force diversity? Human resources professionals interested in undertaking a change effort in diversity should take responsibility for becoming educated about work force diversity; they should study the local labor force and projected changes in that labor force; theory and research from psychology and sociology regarding cultural differences, gender differences, age differences, intergroup relations, and teamwork; and finally, how other companies are addressing issues around diversity.

Set objectives

Once this information has been examined, the next task is to set objectives and prioritize the dimensions of diversity that are important for the organization to address. Defining clear objectives is a fundamental prerequisite to meaningful change efforts. Whether large or small, change requires time, financial and human resources, and commitments. Time, resources, and commitment are more likely to be forthcoming when everyone touched by a change effort understands what they are attempting to accomplish, and why. This happens only when objectives are clearly specified up front. In terms of diversity, the

organization might have one or several objectives. These objectives might include: social responsibility, attracting and retaining a qualified work force, facilitating teamwork, creating synergy between dispersed and diverse work units, and spanning the boundary between the organization and its markets. Which objectives are top priorities for an organization will influence the types of initiatives that are most useful.

Design interventions to fit the situation

The next step in the change effort is to design interventions that fit the situation. To do so, human resources professionals need to keep in mind who their "customers" are, whether the change should be made globally or locally, how far the change effort will extend, and the time frame for creating the change.

The customers To be effective, new initiatives require buy-in from all the relevant "customers" (Jackson, 1992). The customer metaphor emphasizes the importance of designing and delivering initiatives that the people who are affected see as valuable, are aware of, and evaluate positively. To achieve these objectives, close contact is essential. This includes contact with both primary customers, who are targeted as the direct users of a product or service, as well as secondary customers, who may not use the product directly themselves, but who are in a position to encourage or discourage direct customers' use of a product or service. For example, if flexible work schedules are the "product," primary customers would be those employees whose work schedules would be made more flexible. Secondary customers would include the managers and supervisors of these employees and, in some cases, the coworkers.

Global or local change By staying close to the customers during the change effort, it may become apparent that some changes must be introduced globally, that is, simultaneously to everyone throughout the entire organization. On the other hand, others may be effectively introduced locally to a subsection of the organization, and then, if need be, gradually spread throughout the organization. The decision to introduce an initiative globally or locally is likely to be influenced by several factors: the nature of the initiative, the design of the organization (e.g., decentralized or centralized), and how similarities and differences are distributed throughout the organization.

The boundaries of the change effort As stated above, many organizations are actively participating in new alliances with their suppliers, customers, and even their competitors. As a consequence, organizational boundaries have become more blurred. Most human resource management activities have been limited in the past to policies, programs, and practices for employees on the payroll. However, as interorganization alliances become more common, so do the pressures to extend human resource management practices beyond the organization's formal boundaries. Initiatives extending beyond organizational borders might include establishing relationships with schools (grade schools, high schools, and colleges) as well as community groups and local businesses. For example, when child-care subsidies are offered to employees, it is important that usable services are available in the local community. "Usable" implies that they are open during the hours when employees need them, that they are affordable given the size of the employer's subsidies, and that employees feel they can easily communicate with the facilities during the workday. Therefore, employers who offer child-care subsidies should consider negotiating with suppliers to ensure that the services they offer fit employees' needs.

Time frame for creating change Time is a key parameter to consider when planning any change effort. In the U.S., it is considered one of our most precious and scarce resources, so those who waste it are rightfully chastised in most organizations. One mistake is misjudging the amount of time required to carry a change effort through to a successful conclusion; unrealistic expectations for fast results may cause change efforts to be shut down prematurely. To avoid this mistake, the time requirements of new initiatives should be analyzed. Then, a decision must be made about whether the time required is affordable and fits the stated objectives.

Anticipate possible problems and be prepared to deal with them

Any new initiative can run into unanticipated problems, and diversity interventions are no exception. When organizations announce that they value differences and support diversity, they should be prepared to have employees point out contradictions between words and actions. As employees become aware that the organization is taking diversity seriously, they may be more likely to report incidents directly or indirectly related to those efforts. For example, if an organization is introducing change targeting women, more reports on sexual harassment may be brought to the surface. Second, all printed materials may come under scrutiny, from annual reports, to advertising materials, to announcements for company-sponsored social events. Other organizational activities that may suddenly be criticized include the types of clubs frequented by top-level executives, the types of community events and programs supported (or not supported) by company donations, and the types of awards offered to employees as incentives or bonuses. Finally, the change effort itself may be viewed as flawed. For example, organizations instituting awareness training programs may find that employees feel the program itself perpetuates negative stereotyping. Any organization that intends to be serious about supporting diversity should be prepared to make adjustments in many spheres of activity, including both those directly linked to diversity and those not directly linked to the diversity effort.

Institutionalize new learning

Finally, initiatives for creating organizational changes are likely to involve many different people working on many different specific projects in many different places over a long period of time. Throughout this process, a tremendous amount of knowledge and information is generated. *Recording* what has been learned is an important first step for *institutionalizing* what has been learned. Typically, standard operating procedures ensure that such systematically collected information is summarized and recorded in the form of a report. However, to institutionalize the learning, more is needed. If this information is subsequently used in making decisions about how to proceed with the initiative, the learning becomes institutionalized: that is, official policies and practices of the organization change to reflect the new information.

These four principles – organizational assessment, setting objectives and priorities, designing interventions to fit the situation, and institutionalizing learning – are used below as a framework to highlight the diversity processes in two organizations. The two examples are not meant to be evaluated, or compared and contrasted to each other; neither program of change is meant to represent "better" or "worse" processes. What these examples do represent are two companies dealing with different issues in the change process. Readers, be they students of diversity, initiators of the change effort, or those who are maintaining a long-term diversity effort, may draw from them the lessons and experiences of these companies as well as gain .ideas on how to improve and maintain their own efforts.

Examples of diversity in practice

The two companies – Miles Inc., Pharmaceutical Division, and the Xerox Corporation – were chosen as examples because they are at different stages of the change process. The first company, Miles Inc., Pharmaceutical Division, has recently begun focusing on an effort to manage diversity effectively. The company is in the midst of assessing the organization, setting objectives, and designing interventions. Managing diversity at the second company, the Xerox Corporation, arose and continues to evolve as the result of equal employment opportunity and affirmative action initiatives begun 30 years ago. Xerox is focused on continuing to institutionalize past learning, setting new objectives, and updating interventions.

Miles Inc., Pharmaceutical Division: a new initiative

Miles Inc., a North American *Fortune 100* research-based company with businesses in chemicals, health care, and imaging technology, is an independent operating company owned by Bayer AG, the German pharmaceutical and chemical company with sales of DM 42 billion and 156,000 employees worldwide. In 1993, Miles Inc.'s sales were $6.5 billion and it had 26,000 employees. Like many internationally owned companies, this European-led company has had to deal with the challenges of tailoring the company's global vision and objectives to local conditions, laws, and regulations. As a U.S. government contractor, one of these regulations includes continued compliance with Executive Orders 11,246 and 11,375 prohibiting discrimination on the basis of sex, race, color, religion, or national origin. In 1992, Helge H. Wehmeier, the new president and CEO of Miles Inc., led the senior executives in the development of a vision statement that expressed the desire to go beyond mere compliance to the Executive Orders, and to make diversity an integral part of Miles' culture. The goals of managing diversity include enhancing the company's competitive edge by attracting and retaining the best talent the labor market has to offer, and developing the skills and policies necessary to bring these diverse individuals together as a productive team.

Because of the decentralized corporate structure, the decision was made to decentralize the effort by operating division. This example targets the efforts of one of the eight Miles Inc. divisions, the pharmaceutical division, which has 6,000 employees and sales of $1.4 billion in the United States and Canada.

Immediate initiatives Both the corporation and the pharmaceutical division responded to the corporatewide diversity vision statement by immediately implementing several initiatives designed to demonstrate that they were taking diversity seriously. The first initiative to be targeted was in benefits. The division created a "family friendly benefits" concept that incorporated both corporate programs already in existence (e.g., adoption benefits, personal and family leaves, wellness programs, employee assistance programs, and flexible benefits) with new benefits (e.g., job sharing, alternate work schedules, child-care referral services, on-site degree programs, and spousal relocation assistance). This first initiative was relatively easy to implement because it was an extension of previously existing programs that management already supported. In addition, the organization responded quickly to the Americans with Disabilities Act (ADA) by redesigning facilities for access, identifying essential functions and physical requirements for all jobs, and training management on the ADA. The division participates in local ADA councils and sponsors community training and information dissemination regarding ADA.

In a third initiative, managers are held responsible for diversity management on their performance reviews and in bonus calculations. Some of the challenges the company is facing in this initiative is how to set goals to avoid the emotionally charged issues of fixed quotas and tokenism, and how to ensure that the best qualified person is hired or promoted. Fourth, the pharmaceutical division

began to advertise their seriousness toward the diversity effort through communications to employees and to the community. The goal is national recognition so that minorities and females with the needed skills will want to work for the organization, especially in the areas of science and medical research. Some examples of these activities include publicizing diversity in communications (e.g., pictures of employees include people of diverse ages, races, and sex) within as well as outside the organization, including recruiting materials, product advertising, public relations, and employee communications.

Longer-term processes At the same time that these initiatives were being put into place, the division fostered the development of a variety of employee input vehicles to help manage diversity on a longer-term basis on several levels of the organization. These employee input vehicles serve several functions in the division: They assess the current practices and policies in terms of diversity, they target and prioritize problem areas, and they communicate possible solutions to management that best fit the situation at several levels in the organization.

Several groups including the sales diversity advisory group, the two research professionals task forces, and the gay and lesbian support group discuss issues and report to line managers of particular areas and sites. Although these groups arose in a variety of ways, the company is seeking to formalize the input vehicles and has agreed to allow them to charter. Additionally, to ensure a range of opinions and perspectives, membership in some of these groups is mixed in terms of race and sex; and in some of these groups membership rotates.

Using these employee involvement groups as a model, management decided to develop a central group for the division to coordinate the specific site employee groups. This Division Diversity Advisory Group is composed of geographically and functionally diverse managers and it discusses diversity issues on a division-wide basis. The mission of this group is to recommend and review action plans for improving the pharmaceutical division's performance in hiring, promoting, and retaining employees from an increasingly diverse work force, with specific emphasis on women and minorities. The first three recommendations made by the group and adopted by management were: (1) a sexual harassment prevention education program for *all* employees; (2) a training program for all managers and supervisors designed to teach them how to manage people of diverse backgrounds; and (3) a managing diversity questionnaire to serve as a baseline and feedback tool to management regarding diversity issues in the workplace.

Managing diversity questionnaire The Division Diversity Advisory Group recognized the need for employee input at all levels and in all areas to determine where diversity issues were problematic and whether employees perceived that they were being treated fairly. Historically the company does a periodic all-employee opinion survey. As a natural extension of this method, the advisory group proposed substituting a managing diversity questionnaire for the next general opinion survey. This method had three strengths: (1) it used a method with which employees were already familiar; (2) it was an inclusive process because everyone in the division could participate; and (3) this vehicle would allow management to target and develop action plans, and to address diversity issues particularly salient and important to employees.

The company found that it could not follow the usual practice of having an outside consultant create, compile, analyze, and feedback results because too few managing diversity opinion surveys existed, nor did many consultants have adequate data bases to use for comparative norms with other companies. Instead, the division management decided to develop its own tool to be used as a baseline

measure from which it could assess its own progress at some future point. To develop the survey, the company used "meta-plan sessions," which are European developed processes using structured group problem-solving techniques. Twenty-nine meta-plan sessions of up to 25 employees per group identified and prioritized areas to address in the questionnaire. The group sessions represented a cross-section of the employees from throughout the division and were divided by race (minority and non-minority) and gender.

The survey asks questions regarding the demographics of the respondents (e.g., length of service, gender, age, family care responsibilities, job classification, job level, and department), perceived fairness in treatment of employees, career development, training, performance reviews, advancement opportunities and policies, and work scheduling and work and family programs.

Implementing a managing diversity questionnaire could include some risks for an organization. Management has to be prepared to address and deal with both perceived and real issues raised in the questionnaire. This type of method raises employee expectations, and management's timely response is critical to show its commitment. Second, there is a possibility that the survey results could be used against a company in a discrimination complaint. That is, survey results could be used as a "discoverable" document in litigation. Ironically, by trying to solicit input from employees on how to improve, a company may increase the risks that it is trying to fix or reduce.

Xerox: a company that's been there, and still is

Xerox Corporation is a *Fortune 100* company that serves a global document-processing market. The company manufactures, markets, services, and finances document-processing equipment. In 1992 the company employed approximately 100,000 people worldwide and had revenues (through sales, services, rentals, and financing) of $14.7 billion. Information presented here was gathered through interviews with Beatriz J. Vidal, manager of corporate work force diversity, and other employees and caucus members, corporate publications, and a previous case study of the diversity effort at Xerox (Sessa, 1992).

Managing diversity in the Xerox Corporation arose and continues to unfold as a natural extension of both the values of the founders of the company, and the aggressive equal employment opportunity and affirmative action measures undertaken at Xerox in the last three decades. Similar to Miles Inc., the Xerox Corporation has targeted work-force demographics on which to center its diversity efforts. Xerox first targeted African Americans in the 1960s and then women and other minorities in the 1970s. It is now expanding its scope of diversity to include global diversity, those with nontraditional sexual orientation, and Americans with disabilities. We briefly outline why and how Xerox developed a plan to balance its work force, and how that plan is working. Then, we describe how Xerox is maintaining and continuously improving its diversity program, and how it is concentrating on "managing for productivity."

Balanced work force strategy   In the early 1980s, the personnel staff at Xerox evaluated the progress of a massive affirmative action effort taken over the previous decade using numerical representation of women and minorities at the different levels of the organization and also using survey results. It found that goals that had been set for both minorities and women in nonexempt jobs and entry-level positions had been achieved. For minority males, a number of goals in middle- and upper-level grade bands had been achieved. However, goals had not been achieved for upper-level and executive positions for women. Furthermore majority males felt that they were being neglected and hurt – they felt that minorities and women were getting all the attention.

As a result of this assessment, in 1984, the company developed and implemented the balanced work force (BWF) process. The goal of BWF was to achieve and maintain equitable representation of *all* employee groups: majority females, majority males, minority males, and minority females – at all grade bands, in all functions, and in all organizations (later, as a result of input from minority caucus groups, this was changed to determine representation within various minority groups as well).

To establish this goal, both long-term ten-year goals and short-term annual targets were set using U.S. Census data and internal headcounts (Xerox subscribes to a promotion-from-within policy). Operating units were responsible for achieving BWF goals and targets, although the corporate personnel staff managed these goals at a global level. Managers were responsible for balancing their work groups, and they were evaluated in this area on their performance appraisals. In addition, managers were responsible for developing their subordinates' skills and giving them the opportunity for upward mobility to maintain the feeder base for the goals and targets at higher levels in the company. As with Miles Inc., Xerox does not and will not exclude employees from opportunities even if their representation meets or exceeds the BWF goals. The ultimate goal is to provide equal opportunity to all employees based on appropriate skills and quality of employees' contributions.

Almost one decade after starting BWF, Xerox believes that it has nearly reached a balanced work force through its aggressive measures. As of September 1993, Vidal reported that the ten-year goals that had been set for Blacks and Asians had been or were almost attained in all grade bands. With the exception of the highest two grade bands, the ten-year goals set for majority women had been or were almost attained. However, the goals set for Hispanics have not been attained at this time. Additionally, although Xerox has expanded its scope of diversity to include those with nontraditional sexual orientation and Americans with disabilities, there are no goals or annual targets established for these two groups of employees. While still concerned with improving employee representation, Xerox's focus has shifted towards how to capitalize on the benefits of diversity in terms of performance and productivity.

Managing diversity = managing for productivity: the continuing process Xerox depends on minority and women "caucus" groups to help manage diversity. However, these caucuses are different from those that arose at Miles Inc. Currently, there are six sets of caucus groups: several regional black caucuses, HAPA (Hispanic Association for Professional Advancement), an Asian caucus, several women's caucuses, and GALAXE (GAys and Lesbians At XErox). Employees with disabilities have recently developed an electronic-network support group (XED or Xerox Employees with Disabilities) to share issues, concerns, and information with both disabled and nondisabled employees. These vehicles for employee involvement in the company's effort to manage work force diversity serve several functions, including acting as a communication link between each caucus population and upper management; a vehicle for personal and professional development; a means of socializing, networking, and support; and role models for managing diversity to the majority employees. They are often the vehicle through which the corporation serves the community as well (Sessa, 1992).

The caucus groups are not an official part of the company, although all members are company employees. In fact, some of the caucus groups are incorporated and are established as separate corporate entities. The caucus groups meet on their own time, and they set their own rules, agendas, and charters. Membership in the caucus groups ranges from only a few members to as much as 40 percent to 50 percent of the population they

represent. Many of the company's initiatives for managing diversity were developed through communication with the various caucus groups.

From the founders of the corporation in the 1940s to the present, leaders of Xerox have been concerned with and have valued diversity (Sessa, 1992). Through long-term effort, equal employment, affirmative action, and BWF goals, Xerox has succeeded in creating one of the most diverse work forces in the United States. This continuing process has now evolved to emphasize managing diversity for productivity. New goals include: (1) profiting from people's differences rather than treating them as a cost or an obstacle; (2) developing diversity leadership as a keystone to building an organization which values differences; and (3) embracing a framework within which work teams can consistently perform and improve their work.

To accomplish these goals, the company is working toward removing barriers for employees so that they are unencumbered, empowered, and fully contributing. They continue to work toward a bias-free environment that respects individuals and uses differences as a leverage to productivity. As one member of GALAXE said, "This company does not tolerate harrassment or discrimination of any kind, anywhere; that will cause as quick an action as [a business crime like] embezzlement."

Rather than initiating any new programs and processes, Xerox continues to improve processes already in place. Included in the more successful processes[3] are training programs that go beyond diversity sensitivity-and-awareness training to include actual skill building; career-planning tools (e.g., the panel interview process) to ensure that qualified people will be rewarded on the basis of their performance; and performance appraisal systems for achieving BWF goals (Sessa, 1992). The company also uses total quality management (TQM) (and won the Deming prize in Japan, the Malcom Baldrige National Quality

Award in the U.S., and the European Quality Award for its efforts). The company relies extensively on internal problem-solving teams to help implement TQM.

Xerox is also putting stronger emphasis on work and family issues with the idea that different individuals and families may have different needs, and also that these needs may change over time. As a starting point for this emphasis, the company is targeting employee benefits. Through their benefits program, a series of "life cycle" benefit opportunities are being developed. Employees will be able to take advantage of these subsidy opportunities up to a total value of $10,000 over the length of their career at Xerox. So far, a child-care subsidy has been put into place. Other possible subsidies under consideration include help with first-time home buying, college tuition for dependents, non-Xerox insurance of additional dependents not already covered under Xerox benefits (e.g., elderly parents), and partial pay replacement for family-related leaves of absence. Starting in 1995, employees who retire will receive credits on the unused portion of the subsidy that will supplement their medical benefits allowance.

Other new emphases include strengthening the sexual-harassment policy by making it a stand-alone policy (previously it was a part of the nondiscrimination policy) and launching a sexual-harassment training program for all employees. Additionally, recognition and reward trips, which were traditionally only for Xerox employees and their *spouses*, are now available to employees and their *adult guests*. For many of these processes, the various caucus groups have provided the ideas and input to help put them in place.

SUMMARY AND CONCLUSIONS

In this chapter, we have discussed two forces changing and shaping organizational structures: an increasing reliance on teams and

changing work force demographics. Organization experts in both science and practice are concerned with the impact of these changes.

Although more is needed, research is demonstrating that diversity may be both beneficial in terms of improving performance at the individual, team, and organizational level but also may be problematic with respect to harnessing this diversity in a synergistic manner. Interestingly, as suggested by the organizations represented in two examples (Miles, Inc. and Xerox) practitioners may be reaching a similar conclusion: Managing diversity takes a balancing effort to improve performance while maintaining desired levels of job attitudes, satisfaction, communication, and turnover.

A goal of this chapter was to outline a few guidelines and principles needed to ensure a successful diversity change effort. These guidelines include assessing the organization and the environment, setting objectives and priorities, designing interventions to fit the particular needs of the organizations and the environment, and institutionalizing new learning. Miles Inc., Pharmaceutical Division is at a very early stage of cultural change and is currently assessing the organization and the environment to determine what the diversity issues in the organization are. This assessment can be used in the present to target problem areas and to help set objectives and priorities. The assessment can also be used in the future as a baseline against which the company can compare itself. The main lesson to be learned from the Xerox example is that organizational change is a long-term process that takes almost constant vigilance and support on many different levels of the company. Change does not happen overnight, nor does the organization remain changed without a great deal of effort over a long period of time. Xerox periodically assesses the organization (e.g., before and after BWF), sets and resets objectives (e.g., balancing the work force, managing for productivity), designs, redesigns, and improves interventions, and institutionalizes learnings.

Both companies have chosen in their change efforts to target demographic diversity in the U.S. work force. Other types of diversity that might be targeted include: occupational specialty (e.g., bringing together teams from different departments); cultural, between companies (through mergers, acquisitions, or alliances) and between countries (multinational corporations); and religion, ethnicity (other than whites, Blacks, Hispanics, and Asians), education level, tenure within the organization, level in the hierarchy, geographical location, and employment status (e.g., full-time or part-time, permanent or temporary, and exempt or nonexempt).

The activities used in these companies, and others, to manage diversity are many and varied: training and development, employee involvement teams, links with the community, different work hours and workplaces, benefits, affirmative action programs, top-management attention, public relations efforts, and alternate careers. However, the activities used need to fit the culture, the environment, and the needs of each specific company in order to work. Neither company represented here attempted to institute changes that were very different from the standard mode of operating. In most cases, they used improved, or changed processes already in existence rather than implementing totally new programs. Additionally, the employee-involvement teams evolved and function differently in the two companies.

Where do we go from here? Although scientists continue to research the influence of diversity on teams, and companies continue to develop and implement interventions, to date, there has been little systematic evaluation to determine if the diversity interventions taken in companies are having the desired effect of improving productivity while maintaining desired levels of job attitudes and satisfaction, communication, and turnover. This is an important gap between research

and practice. The research has not addressed the success of the diversity efforts taking place in organizations. In fact, many managers are unsure about what constitutes success of the diversity effort and how to measure it. When asked what indicators of success they are using, managers often respond with such answers as "Not there yet," "Too new to measure," "Statistics," "What has been accomplished so far," and "Permission to proceed" (Morrison, Ruderman, & Hughes-James, 1993).

Monitoring and evaluating a diversity intervention encompasses two dimensions: the content of the evaluation and the process. Content of the evaluation needs to include how success will be defined (in absolute terms or improvement relative to the present situation). Questions to be resolved in this area include: What indicators will be used (this may be determined by the statement of objectives)? How will the indicators be measured? When will the evaluation occur? Will the results be most useful if one considers individuals, teams, departments, or the whole organization? In terms of process, decisions need to be made regarding: Who is responsible for measuring what? Who is responsible for providing the resources needed for information collection, analysis, communication, and storage? Who has access to the results? Who is responsible for using results to guide needed adjustments? What types of records will be kept, for how long? How will the cooperation needed for all these tasks be ensured?

NOTES

1 Much of the information regarding the Xerox case was provided by Beatriz J. Vidal, manager of corporate work force diversity, human resources. Her cooperation and assistance on this project are especially appreciated.
2 Minority in this case refers to the presence of deviant opinions, perspectives, ideas, etc. in a team.
3 Xerox has also tried other processes that met with less success including sensitivity training and linking affirmative action performances of upper-level executives to the size of their bonuses (see Sessa, 1992).

REFERENCES

Adler, N., & Ghadar, F. (1991). Globalization and human resource management. In A. Rugman (ed.), *Research in Global Strategic Management: A Canadian perspective*, vol. 1, pp. 179–205. Greenwich, CT: JAI Press.

Banas, P. A. (1988). Employee involvement: A sustained labor/management initiative at the Ford Motor Company. In J. P. Campbell & R. J. Campbell (eds.), *Productivity in Organizations: New perspectives from industrial and organizational psychology*, 388–416. San Francisco: Jossey-Bass.

Bantel, K. A., & Jackson, S. E. (1989). Top management and innovations in banking: Does the composition of the top team make a difference? *Strategic Management Journal*, 10, 107–24.

Barnum, P. (1991). Misconceptions about the future U.S. work force: Implications for strategic planning. *Human Resource Planning*, 14, 209–19.

Bolick, C., & Nestleroth, S. L. (1988). *Opportunity 2000: Creative affirmative action strategies for a changing workforce.* Washington, D.C.: U.S. Government Printing Office.

Brass, D. J. (1984). Being in the right place: A structural analysis of individual influence in an organization. *Administrative Science Quarterly*, 29, 518–39.

Bylinski, G. (1990). Turning R&D into real products. *Fortune*, July 2, 72–7.

Byrne, D. (1971). *The Attraction Paradigm.* New York: Academic Press.

Chen, C. (1992). The diversity paradox. *Personnel Journal*, January, 32–6.

DeLuca, J. M., & McDowell, R. N. (1992). Managing diversity: A strategic "grass-roots" perspective. In S. E. Jackson & associates (eds.), *Working through Diversity: Human resources initiatives*, 227–47. New York: Guilford Press.

Dumaine, B. (1990). Who needs a boss? *Fortune*, May 7, 52–60.

Eisenhardt, K. M., & Schoonhoven, C. B. (1990). Organizational growth: Linking founding team, strategy, environment, and growth among U.S. semi-conductor ventures, 1978–1988. *Administrative Science Quarterly*, 35, 504–29.

Elder, G. H., Jr. (1975). Age differentiation and the life course. *Annual Review of Sociology*, 1, 165–90.

Fierman, J. (1990). Why women still don't hit the top. *Fortune*, July 30, 40–62.

Finkelstein, S., & Hambrick, D. C. (1990). Top-management-team tenure and organizational outcomes: The moderating role of managerial discretion. *Administrative Science Quarterly*, 35, 484–503.

Hambrick, D. C. (1994). Top management groups: A conceptual integration and reconsideration of the "Team" label. In B. M. Staw & L. L. Cummings (eds.), *Research in Organizational Behavior*, vol. 16, pp. 171–213. Greenwich, CT: JAI Press.

Hoffman, E. (1985). The effect of race-ratio composition on the frequency of organizational communication. *Social Psychology Quarterly*, 48, 17–26.

Hofstede, G. (1991). *Cultures and organizations.* New York: McGraw-Hill.

Ibarra, H. (1992). Homophily and differential returns: Sex differences in network structure and access in an advertising firm. *Administrative Science Quarterly*, 37, 422–47.

Ibarra, H. (1993). Personal networks of women and minorities in management: A conceptual framework. *Academy of Management Review*, 18, 57–87.

Jackson, S. E. (1992). Team composition in organizational settings: Issues in managing an increasingly diverse work force. In S. Worchel, W. Wood, and J. A. Simpson (eds.), *Group Process and Productivity*. Newbury Park, CA: Sage.

Jackson, S. E., & Alvarez, E. B. (1992). Working through diversity as a strategic imperative. In S. E. Jackson & associates (eds.), *Diversity in the Workplace: Human resources initiatives*, 13–35. New York: Guilford.

Jackson, S. E., Brett, J. F., Sessa, V. I., Cooper, D. M., Julin, J. A., & Peyronnin, K. (1991). Some differences make a difference: Individual dissimilarity and group heterogeneity as correlates of recruitment, promotions, and turnover. *Journal of Applied Psychology*, 76, 675–89.

Jackson, S. E., May, K., & Whitney, K. (1994). Diversity in decision making teams. In R. A. Guzzo & E. Salas (eds.), *Team Decision Making Effectiveness in Organizations*. San Francisco: Jossey-Bass.

Johnston, W. B., & Packer, A. H. (1987). *Workforce 2000.* Indianapolis: Hudson Institute.

Kanter, R. M. (1989). *When Giants Learn to Dance.* New York: Simon & Schuster.

Kanter, R. M. (1991). Transcending business boundaries: 12,000 world managers view change. *Harvard Business Review*, May–June, 151–64.

Kirchmeyer, C., & Cohen, A. (1992). Multicultural groups: Their performance and reactions with constructive conflict. *Group & Organization Management*, 17, 153–70.

Lincoln, J. R., & Miller, J. (1979). Work and friendship ties in organizations: A comparative analysis of relational networks. *Administrative Science Quarterly*, 24, 181–99.

McCain, B. R., O'Reilly, C. A., III, & Pfeffer, J. (1983). The effects of departmental demography on turnover. *Academy of Management Journal*, 26, 626–41.

McLeod, P. L., & Lobel, S. A. (1992). The effects of ethnic diversity on idea generation in small groups. Paper presented at the annual meetings of the Academy of Management, Las Vegas, August.

Managing generational diversity (1991). *HRMagazine*, April, 91–2.

Michel, J. G., & Hambrick, D. C. (1992). Diversification posture and top management team characteristics. *Academy of Management Journal*, 35, 9–37.

Morrison, A. M., Ruderman, M. N., & Hughes-James, M. (1993). *Making Diversity Happen: Controversies and solutions*, Report No. 320. Greensboro, NC: Center for Creative Leadership.

Morrison, A. M., & Von Glinow, M. A. (1990). Women and minorities in management. *American Psychologist*, 45, 200–8.

Morrison, A. M., White, R. P., & Van Velsor, E. (1992). *Breaking the Glass Ceiling: Can women reach the top of America's largest corporations?* New York: Addison-Wesley.

Murray, A. I. (1989). Top management group heterogeneity and firm performance. *Strategic Management Journal*, 10, special issue, 125–42.

Nemeth, C. J. (1992). Minority dissent as a stimulant to group performance. In S. Worchel, W. Wood, and J. A. Simpson (eds.), *Group Process and Productivity*. Newbury Park, CA: Sage.

O'Reilly, C. A., III, Caldwell, D. F., & Barnett, W. P. (1989). Work group demography, social integration, and turnover. *Adminstrative Science Quarterly*, 34, 21–37.

Pfeffer, J. (1983). Organizational demography. In L. L. Cummings & B. M. Staw (eds.), *Research in Organizational Behavior*, vol. 5, 299–357. Greenwich, CT: JAI Press.

Rhodes, S. R. (1983). Age-related differences in work attitudes and behavior: A review and conceptual analysis. *Psychological Bulletin*, 93, 328–67.

Sayles, L. R. (1993). *The Working Leader: The triumph of high performance over conventional management principles*. New York: Free Press.

Schneider, B. (1987). The people make the place. *Personnel Psychology*, 40, 437–53.

Sessa, V. I. (1992). Managing diversity at the Xerox corporation: Balanced workforce goals and caucus groups. In S. E. Jackson (ed.), *Diversity in the Workplace: Human resources initiatives*. New York: Guilford Press.

Singh, H., & Harianto, F. (1989). Top management tenure, corporate ownership structure and the magnitude of golden parachutes. *Strategic Management Journal*, 10, 143–56.

Tsui, A. S., Egan, T. D., & O'Reilly, C. A., III (1992). Being different: Relational demography and organizational attachment. *Administrative Science Quarterly*, 37, 549–79.

Von Glinow, M. A., & Mohrman, S. (1990). *Managing Complexity in High Technology Organizations*. New York: Oxford University Press.

Wagner, W., Pfeffer, J., & O'Reilly, C. A., III (1984). Organizational demography and turnover in top-management groups. *Adminstrative Science Quarterly*, 29, 74–92.

Wiersema, M. F., & Bantel, K. A. (1991). Top management team demography and corporate strategic change. *Academy of Management Journal*, 35, 91–121.

Wiersema, M. F., & Bird, A. (1993). Organizational demography in Japanese firms: Group heterogeneity, individual dissimilarity, and top management. *Academy of Management Journal*, 36, 996–1025.

Wood, W. (1987). Meta-analytic review of sex differences in group performance. *Psychological Bulletin*, 102, 53–71.

Work teams can rev up paper-pushers, too (1988). *Business Week*, November 28, 64–72.

Zenger, T. R., & Lawrence, B. S. (1989). Organizational demography: The differential effects of age and tenure distributions on technical communications. *Academy of Management Journal*, 2, 353–76.

☐ Chapter 15 ☐

Implications of Organizational Downsizing for the Human Resource Management Function

David A. Whetten, John D. Keiser, and Tom Urban

INTRODUCTION

There is little dispute that organizational downsizing has become a prevalent business strategy, as evidenced by reputationally stable firms such as AT&T, General Electric, Proctor & Gamble, and Kodak significantly reducing their work forces (Uchitelle, 1993). Even IBM which once argued their "no layoffs" policy was a competitive advantage (Bolt, 1985) has eliminated some 85,000 workers during the 1990s. Summarizing the extent of organizational downsizing, *Business Week*, citing Bureau of Labor Statistics data, reported 5.6 million American workers lost permanent jobs between 1987 and 1991 (Koretz, 1992).

Since the early 1980s, management researchers have produced a rich body of literature focusing on downsizing, emanating from the argument that "organizational decline" is not simply the reverse of the growth cycle (Whetten, 1980), and deserves to be examined from a unique perspective. Frequently, downsizing, with or without strategic realignment, is stimulated by a substantive decline in organizational performance (Zammuto & Cameron, 1985; Cameron, Kim, & Whetten, 1987). Yet, a decline in performance is not a necessary precondition for downsizing. Firms seeking to be more flexible, more responsive, or less bureaucratic are increasingly resorting to work-force elimination to achieve the advantages of smaller organizations (Cameron, Freeman, & Mishra, 1991).

Organizational downsizing has been examined from a variety of perspectives, including: how organizational and environmental conditions affect the intensity and direction of the downsizing efforts (DeWitt, 1993; Freeman & Cameron, 1993; Greenhalgh, Lawrence, & Sutton, 1988); the effects of downsizing from the organizational point of view (Sutton & D'Aunno, 1989; Cameron et al., 1987; Cascio, 1993; Cameron, Mishra, & Freeman, 1992); as well as from the survivors' perspective at the individual (Brockner, Grover, Reed, DeWitt, & O'Malley, 1987) and group levels (Krantz, 1985).

Prominent in the downsizing literature is a series of negative reports about its consequences, including:

1. A 1990 survey of 909 U.S. firms by Right Associates, an out-placement firm, found

that 75 percent of senior managers in downsized companies said that morale, trust, and productivity suffered after downsizing (Henkoff, 1990).

2   A survey by the Society for Human Resource Management reported that more than half of the 1,468 firms that downsized indicated that productivity had deteriorated as a result of downsizing (Henkoff, 1990).

3   Research conducted by the Wyatt consulting firm found that 71 percent of the firms involved in downsizing did so to increase productivity, but only 22 percent of those firms thought that goal had been accomplished (Bennett, 1991).

The director of research for Wyatt, John Parkington, succinctly summarized the experience of downsizing during the 1980s, "Lots of bullets were fired, but few hit their targets. Sometimes companies did it three, four, and five times, but still didn't hit their expense-reduction targets. Something is wrong" (Bennett, 1991).

Contemporaneously with the expansion of research on organizational downsizing, a new perspective emerged in the field of human resources, called strategic human resource management, which "involved linking human resource management (HRM) to firm-level outcomes with financial and strategic importance" (Butler, Ferris, & Napier, 1991). Advocates of strategic human resource management argue that effective organizational strategy development and implementation requires a central, highly proactive role for the HRM function (Lengnick-Hall & Lengnick-Hall, 1988). Inasmuch as most organizational strategic initiatives have significant implications for the amount, the type, and the configuration of its human resources, senior HRM managers need to be full partners in the strategy formulation process from its inception. Scholars writing on this subject have stressed the need to integrate HR practices with organizational strategies (Schuler

& Jackson, 1987), organizational life cycles (Millman, Von Glinow, & Nathan, 1991), and organizational characteristics (Jackson, Schuler, & Rivero, 1989). In addition, they have also stressed the key role played by the HRM function in successfully implementing strategic initiatives, especially those requiring large-scale organizational change (Ulrich and Lake, 1990).

Inevitably, as concerns about managing downsizing became more prevalent in the organizational strategy literature, strategic human resource management authors began to examine its implications for the HRM function. For example, Ferris, Schellenberg, and Zammuto (1984) developed a downsizing framework based on the rate of decline in organizational resources and the degree of qualitative change in the organization's niche. Other articles have suggested ways for HRM professionals to eliminate survivor trauma (Ropp, 1987), avoid losing highly skilled members that the organization wants to retain (Perry, 1984), and assume the role of "transition manager" during the downsizing process (Price & D'Aunno, 1984).

Unfortunately, few studies have evaluated the effect of downsizing on HRM practices, or the contributions of the HRM function to effective organizational downsizing efforts (an exception is Cook & Ferris, 1986). This is a regrettable oversight. Given the dismal success rate of downsizing initiatives, it is imperative that scholars and managers alike gain a much better understanding of the factors influencing the outcomes of a substantial downsizing initiative. One of the factors that clearly warrants investigation is the role of the HRM function. Furthermore, inasmuch as one of the primary factors impacting HRM's ability to assist senior managers effectively downsize is how the HRM staff is impacted by the downsizing initiative, it is imperative that we examine the reciprocal relationship between successful downsizing implementation and HRM capabilities, as depicted in figure 15.1.

Figure 15.1 Relationship between the effects of organizational downsizing on the HRM function and the HRM function's ability to support the organizational downsizing process

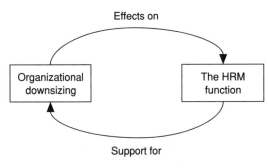

It is axiomatic to state that the impact of organizational downsizing on the HRM function affects its ability to provide the HRM services essential to the success of downsizing. However, it is not at all clear from our studies of downsizing organizations that the practical implications of this axiom are self-evident to senior managers in many firms, including some who claim to include HRM as a "strategic planning partner." Too often, decisions about what and how much to cut from the HRM function are made on the basis of what is their *share* ("We need to reduce HRM head count by X in order to reach our overall cost reduction target"), or on the basis of what is *fair* ("We must treat all the staff units the same"), rather than on the basis of what is *functional* ("What type and amount of HRM support will be required to make our downsizing plan work?"). Thus in many cases HRM staff reduction decisions suggest that tactical concerns overshadowed strategic objectives.

The most effective downsizing organizations view personnel reductions as both an "end" (increase efficiency by reducing costs) and a "means" (increase effectiveness by improving quality, time-to-market, etc.) (Cameron et al., 1991). Given the disproportionate size of nonproduction personnel in U.S. firms, compared with many of their international competitors, it is logical that downsizing plans in these organizations should disproportionately target "staff" departments (Whetten & Cameron, 1994). However, the cost of various staff functions (e.g., HRM, finance, accounting) needs to be balanced against their differential value in contributing to long-term performance-improvement plans for the operating units they serve.

Support for this position is found in the emerging literature on strategic competencies. The contribution of "intangible assets" to an organization achieving sustainable competitive advantage has been examined by a variety of organizational scholars (Coyne, 1986; Prahalad & Hamel, 1990). The basic argument is that successful organizations have a clear sense of their mission as well as what is required to compete in their chosen arena (strategic niche). A key ingredient in this strategic formula is identifying the "core competencies" required to establish and maintain a competitive edge (Ulrich & Lake, 1990). Barney (1986, 1231), for example, argues, "Our analysis suggests that strategic choices should flow mainly from the analysis of (a company's) unique skills and capabilities, rather than from the analysis of the competitive environment."

Hall (1993) differentiates between people-independent and people-dependent capabilities. The people-independent assets include such things as data bases, contracts, and trade agreements, while the people-dependent capabilities include skills, attitudes, networks, and reputations. Recently, a long-time observer of organizational downsizing, Richard Tomasko (1993), used this perspective to caution downsizing organizations to avoid losing their core competencies in the push to reduce costs. He also argued that the capabilities required to successfully downsize an organization may be quite different from those present in the predownsized organization.

There is a growing body of evidence suggesting that a large part of the explanation for the unrealized expectations of downsizing lies in how effectively human resources are managed during and after downsizing (Whetten & Cameron, 1994; Cameron et al., 1987; Cameron et al., 1992; Cascio, 1993). What is needed now is a better understanding of how the downsizing process itself impacts HRM's ability to provide the support services essential to the effective management of what is possibly the most challenging form of organizational change. To that end, the purpose of this chapter is to stimulate further thought and research on this subject by presenting a model of the organizational processes underlying the reciprocal relationship between "downsizing effects" and "HRM support" shown in figure 15.1.

Our discussion of the effects of organizational downsizing on the HRM function specifically focuses on the consequences that are most likely to impair the HRM staff's ability to successfully support the organization's downsizing/restructuring initiative. Beyond the scope of this presentation are a number of equally interesting related issues, such as, how various HRM activities are transformed by a protracted period of downsizing, how HRM career paths are altered by downsizing, and how organizational members' attitudes about the HRM function are impacted by downsizing. This analysis is informed by our examination of several HRM units in downsizing business organizations, but our models are intended to encompass a broad range of organizational circumstances. The level of analysis in this chapter is the general HRM function at the department level, rather than the individual HRM specialties. Although we use several examples involving specific HRM specialties, they are meant to illustrate general principles or propositions that are equally applicable to other specialties.

Our presentation is divided into three parts. First, we examine different approaches to organizational downsizing. Second, we focus on the specific consequences of downsizing on HRM's operating environment in terms of (1) altered client (operating unit) expectations, and (2) reduced service delivery resources. Third, we explore the combined effects of these changes on the HRM function's ability to support the downsizing initiative.

ORGANIZATIONAL DOWNSIZING STRATEGIES

Although downsizing has become a widespread practice, it is also a highly diverse practice. Several authors have proposed typologies for characterizing downsizing. Drawing on the general model of organizational change proposed by Tushman and Romanelli (1985), Freeman and Cameron (1993) distinguish between convergent and reorientation downsizing. Convergent downsizing involves shrinking the organization without making significant changes in its strategic direction. These are budget-driven efforts to reduce costs that are treated as internal, short-term adjustments. The result is that members end up "doing the same with less." Reorientation, on the other hand, involves both quantitative and qualitative changes. Plans to reduce overhead are included in a broader effort to strategically reposition the organization. Reorientation is generally stimulated by long-term dislocations in the environment, resulting from the introduction of new technology, the entry of a new form of competition, or a dramatic shift in the relevant political, economic, or social conditions.

A framework proposed by DeWitt (1993) contains similar elements. She distinguishes between two forms of downsizing (reorientation and retrenchment) and between two different sources of downsizing (an organization's domain and its structure). As in Freeman and Cameron's (1993) model, reorientation refers to broad, qualitative, changes, but DeWitt uses retrenchment, instead of convergence, to describe minor

Figure 15.2 The effects of organizational downsizing on HRM service demand and capacity

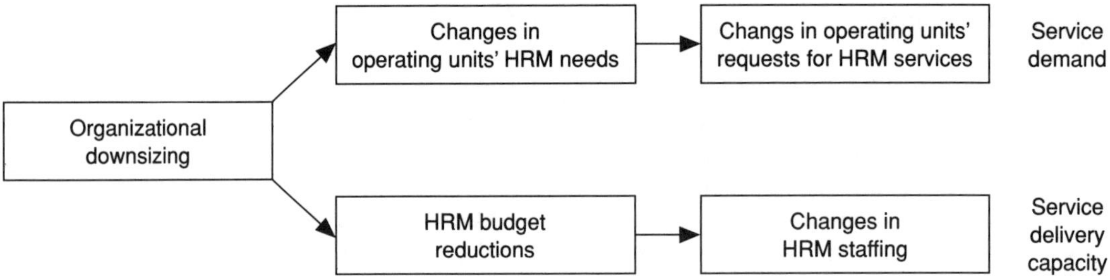

adjustments. Domain refers to an organization's competitive environment (Zammuto & Cameron, 1985), while structure pertains to the manner in which work is organized, and the formal mechanisms for facilitating internal communication and coordination (Daft, 1986). DeWitt proposes that the level of organizational decline (diminished performance) guides the downsizing choices (domain versus structure, and retrenchment versus reorientation).

In the HRM literature, Ferris et al. (1984) proposed a typology of downsizing which focuses on changes in an organization's niche. The term "niche" refers to the immediate task environment of an organization and is closely related to the concept of organizational domain used by DeWitt (1993). Ferris and his colleagues distinguish between various forms of niche change. For example, environmental conditions can change quantitatively (size) and qualitatively (shape). Either type of change can occur in small, incremental steps (continuous change), or quickly and dramatically (discontinuous change). The combination of these four characteristics of environmental change yields a typology of "environmental decline," which, as DeWitt has noted, is a good predictor of the downsizing strategy an affected organization is likely to choose. The four types of decline are: erosion (continuous and size), dissolution (discontinuous and size), contraction (continuous and shape), and collapse (discontinuous and shape).

For our purposes, the distinction between "downsizing without redesign" and "downsizing with redesign" seems most appropriate (Cameron et al., 1992). These terms capture the most common element in the current conceptualizations of downsizing, namely, quantitative versus qualitative change. Downsizing without redesign involves "right sizing" the current operations to reduce overhead. Its goal is to cut the cost of production, not to alter the form of production. When downsizing is coupled with organizational redesign, then the objectives of the change encompass qualitative transformations intended to strategically realign or restructure the organization.

DOWNSIZING'S EFFECTS ON HRM'S OPERATING ENVIRONMENT

As shown in figure 15.2, organizational downsizing has a twofold impact on the HRM function's operating environment. First, it changes the operating units' needs for HRM services. This, in turn, alters the service-request inputs entering the HRM function. Second, it reduces the HRM function's head count. This reduces the unit's ability to fill the service requests from the operating units. (Although we recognize that not all organizational downsizing results in a smaller HRM staff, for our purposes we will assume that this is the case.) When HRM units are required to simultaneously adjust to shifting demands for their services and to reduce their capacity to meet those demands, their ability to support the implementation of downsizing and redesign initiatives in operating units can be seriously impaired.

Earlier we proposed that HRM units should not be treated the same as other staff units in an organization's downsizing plan. One reason for this lies in the differences between the constituencies they serve. Tsui (1990) has used the multiple constituencies model of organizational effectiveness to examine relations between HRM units and their internal customers, or constituents. She argues that although other staff units (e.g., public relations, accounting) also serve multiple internal constituencies, the expectations expressed by the HRM unit's constituencies are more likely to be inconsistent and irreconcilable.

One reason for this is that HRM constituents represent societal, organizational, unit, and individual interests. HRM constituencies attempt to influence HRM priorities and practices citing legal restrictions, social trends, competitive pressures, company policies, operating unit priorities, employee subgroup special needs, and individual preferences. According to this line of reasoning, the more difficulty a staff unit has reconciling conflicting priorities, the more resources they require to effectively serve their constituents. By definition, downsizing exacerbates resource allocation priority conflicts stemming from the diversity of interests (Whetten, 1980). Therefore, it is to be expected that HRM units in downsizing organizations would experience greater tension than other staff functions in matching their shrinking resource pool with the conflicting demands placed on those resources by the operating units.

Layoff policy is one simple example. Various interests within an organization offer strong arguments for or against various personnel reduction alternatives. For example, "We should eliminate the poor performers so that overall organizational performance will improve." "We shouldn't use seniority-based criteria because minorities will be disproportionately affected." "We should avoid offering a voluntary early retirement package because we will likely lose valuable experience and competencies in our technical units." "All units should share the pain equally, otherwise we will have a serious morale problem in areas required to make larger-than-average cuts." "Our deteriorating financial condition is a mere symptom of what I see as a very serious fundamental strategic misalignment problem. We should examine the long-term trends in our business, decide what strategic changes are required in our organization, and then consider our cost reduction needs in the context of a general realignment plan."

Changes in the HRM services requested by the operating units in downsizing organizations actually go through two cycles of change. Their need for HRM support changes while downsizing is underway, and then again after downsizing is complete. As organizational units initiate their downsizing plans they encounter new, and often unanticipated, challenges. Typically, performance suffers due to high levels of conflict, scapegoating, resistance to change, and centralization of decision making, as well as low levels of trust, innovation, and planning (Cameron, Kim, & Whetten, 1987). These debilitating changes place extra pressure on an operating unit's management and members, and their requests for support from the HRM staff increase proportionately. After a downsizing initiative has been completed, a new set of HRM-related issues arise. For example, eliminating levels of management and empowering work teams – two popular initiatives in downsizing organizations – typically require changes in existing selection and promotion criteria, compensation systems, and training and development plans.

Changes in an operating unit's needs for HRM services can take two forms. A unit can request a different amount or level of a current service, or it can request a different type of service. For example, a downsizing sales department plagued with low morale and high stress might request more seats in an existing HRM training program on stress management. Or, an engineering department might request a new set of training and development programs designed to support self-managed work teams.

Typically, downsizing that includes redesign will produce more changes in the type of HRM services requested. Inasmuch as the operating units are undergoing a qualitative change in their operations, it is likely that their requests for HRM support will fall outside the boundaries of existing HRM programs, competencies, and experience. For example, one of the most common questions asked by line managers in these situations is, "Should we eliminate people before or after we redesign our work?" On the surface this appears to be a pretty straightforward HRM question – one that could be readily answered by drawing upon the existing HRM expertise regarding staffing, evaluating, and rewarding. However, when the experience of the HRM staff is limited to administering these functions within the context of organizational growth, they are quite often ill-prepared to evaluate the merits of the competing proposals to downsize first or to redesign first.

Managing the mandated HRM staff reductions can be equally vexing. The prevailing practice in HRM units for decades has been to respond to the changing and/or increasing needs of their customers by hiring new staff. They avoided having to choose between developing new proficiencies and eliminating old ones by increasing their overall service-delivery capacity. That form of adaptation is generally not an option in a downsizing organization (Whetten, 1987). Responding to shifting customer needs now requires HRM units to make painful prioritizing decisions, and to reevaluate role definitions and workload levels. These actions can be extremely stressful for HRM unit managers because they typically are at variance with the established personal and professional identities of the surviving HRM staff (Price & D'Aunno, 1984).

Examining the effects of different strategies for allocating mandated budget cuts has been a staple of downsizing studies for some time (Whetten & Cameron, 1994; Cameron et al., 1992). For example, the choice between across-the-board and selective-cut strategies has been shown to impact subsequent organizational performance, employee morale, interunit relations, and turnover among highly skilled members. This research provides a backdrop for examining the impact of downsizing on the HRM function.

DOWNSIZING'S EFFECTS ON HRM'S INTERNAL OPERATIONS

As shown in figure 15.3, changes in the requests for HRM services coupled with a reduction in HRM's capacity to provide services (head count) has several consequences for HRM operations. First of all, changes in the service requests from the operating units impact the HRM function's *priorities* and *practices*. While we recognize that most changes in service requests typically impact, to some extent, both HRM priorities and practices, for analytical purposes we will treat them separately.

A change in the amount of a service requested alters the HRM unit's resource allocation priorities, as reflected in the unit's *service capacities*. For example, if downsizing produces a significant increase in requests for training, or for compensation package reevaluations, or for more employee counseling, an urgent call for reinforcements is quickly sent out by the impacted area. The hard work of making tough allocation decisions involving equally legitimate and pressing needs has been characterized by one manager as, "I lay awake at nights trying to figure out how to allocate the remaining 100 staff across five service units – each of which needs at least 30 people." The difficulty of

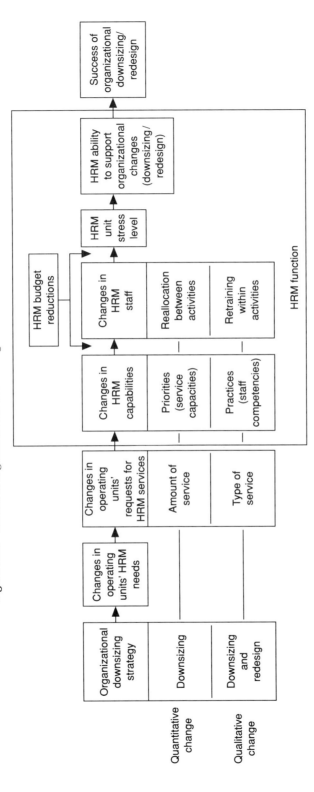

Figure 15.3 Model of organizational downsizing's effects on the HRM function

this resource reallocation task is obviously influenced by the level of changes in services required, the flexibility of the current staff resources, and the size of the reduction in HRM head count. However, in general, HRM managers in downsizing organizations experience stiff resistance to realigning staffing priorities, for a variety of reasons.

Introducing staff reallocation on the heels of staff elimination multiplies the complications of downsizing. It is challenging enough for the surviving HRM personnel to cope with the consequences of having fewer resources to do their work. Reallocation adds to this the stress of learning new jobs, working with new customers, assimilating new team members, adjusting to new bosses, moving to new locations, and so forth.

Albert's (1992) distinction between change-by-addition and change-by-subtraction highlights the challenges of managing the staff reallocation process. Reallocation is a hybrid of the two change processes (involving both subtraction and addition) which, by definition, affects at least two work teams. Subtracting a person from one team and adding that person to another team tends to be more disruptive than either subtracting or adding a person within one team. Members of the team losing the person can be expected to resist the change because of the stated or imagined implications for increasing the survivors' workload. And, members in the gaining function are often reluctant to accept the newcomer because of intraprofessional biases and prejudices ("What can someone who has been a recruiter on college campuses for 10 years possibly know about compensation?"), or suspicions about their quality ("You can bet they will only give up their rejects"). Furthermore the individuals being reassigned experience the double effects of exit and entry. They must first break established social ties, shed accepted elements of their professional identity, and reconcile themselves to losing status among coworkers based on seniority and experience. Then they must accept the

role of a trainee in the new area, work to break into established social networks, get used to the expectations of a new manager, and learn new responsibilities. Moreover having the least seniority in their new area may put them in a vulnerable position if further personnel cuts are required.

Another way of conceptualizing the impact of reallocation is to examine how much of an affected person's job is changed. When asked to describe in detail their work in a specific organization, individuals' responses fall into seven basic categories: What I do; Where I do it; When I do it; How I do it; What I get for doing it; Who I work with; Who I work for. Some combination of these attributes constitutes a person's social identity within a particular organization (Ashforth & Mael, 1989). Our interviews in downsizing organizations suggest that the larger the number of these personal identity-defining characteristics an individual is required to change at once, the more stressful the change is.

As shown in figure 15.3, a change in the type of HRM services requested alters the prevailing practice within affected HRM activities. The principal implication of changing HRM practices is the need to alter the mix of HRM *staff competencies* available to provide specific services. For example, the move to self-managed work teams often necessitates changes in training content and format. Instead of teaching general topics in open-enrollment classroom settings, HRM trainers will likely be asked to teach team-specific topics in team-restricted settings. The shift from being stand-up trainers to team developers and facilitators, may require new competencies in work group diagnosis, process consulting, meeting management, and nontraditional teaching techniques.

It is important to point out that although individual staff members who are reallocated between activity areas must be retrained, reallocation by itself does not involve introducing new skills into the HRM function. The competencies to be learned are new to the transplant but they are not new to the receiving unit. Typically, the newcomer is assigned a mentor who demonstrates effective application of existing routines and established practices. Although the identity of the new unit member is altered by the transfer, the identities of the losing and receiving work units are not affected.

This is not the case when downsizing requires changes in the type of services provided by an HRM unit. When this occurs, the identity of the HRM activity itself is altered through massive retooling and retraining. Old routines must be discarded; accepted knowledge must be discredited; new routines must be adopted; and unfamiliar knowledge must be legitimated.

The research on organizational identity helps us understand why this qualitative form of downsizing change can be extremely disruptive (Albert & Whetten, 1985; Whetten et al., 1992). Organizations (and their subunits) consist of a variety of elements that combine to constitute their unique, distinctive, and enduring identity. These include their value system, their goals, their mode of operation, and so forth. For example, an HRM unit might define itself in terms of some combination of:

1 The activities it provides (e.g., selection, training, compensation).
2 The approaches it uses in each activity area (e.g., campus recruiting, classroom instruction, work team performance incentive system).
3 The major clients, or constituencies, it serves (e.g., specific operating units, management levels, or employee groups).
4 The underlying values it espouses (e.g., HRM's position regarding the value of frequent organizational change).

When exogenous changes necessitate a fundamental transformation in a work unit's identity, the reverberating ramifications are far-reaching. Relationships must be altered,

agreements amended, expectations recalibrated, competencies learned, priorities reformulated, and plans, budgets, and schedules redone. Therefore, the more an organizational unit's identity is changed, the more time and effort it takes for a new operating steady state to be achieved (Tushman & Romanelli, 1985). Because both personal work activities and social systems are affected, qualitative changes in the type of services provided by a downsized HRM unit are generally more difficult to accommodate than are quantitative changes in the amount of services they provide.

One of the options for coping with a simultaneous increase in HRM service demand and a reduction in available HRM resources is outsourcing. The growing trend in organizations to outsource staff services, including HRM services, is especially pronounced in downsizing organizations. For example, IBM spun off its entire HRM function into a new entity called Workforce Solutions (Thornburg, 1993), and Mobil has outsourced several of its HR functions (Seeley, 1992).

Our model suggests that the decision to outsource specific HRM services as part of a downsizing strategy will be influenced by three factors:

1 The overall level of HRM staff reductions required during downsizing.
2 The degree to which changes in the amount of HRM services requested requires HRM staff reallocation.
3 The degree to which changes in the type of HRM services requested necessitates massive staff retraining.

This proposition can be represented as: *staff reductions + staff reallocations + staff retraining = pressure to outsource*. The relationship between the three factors is additive, meaning that the higher the value of each factor the greater the likelihood that outsourcing will occur.

If HRM managers decide, in principal, to consider outsourcing, our framework further suggests that the logical candidates would be those specific HRM services that combine the following attributes:

1 They are among the most labor intensive within the HRM function.
2 Requested changes in the type of services provided in this area would necessitate a significant retraining initiative (and the new competencies required are readily available from outside sources).
3 The staff currently providing these services could be reallocated to other HRM groups experiencing an increase in service demand.

Independent of our framework, outsourcing is also logical when the demand for HRM services is temporary.

Effects on the HRM staff's level of stress

As shown in figure 15.3, the combination of HRM budget cuts and changes in HRM staffing impact the stress level of unit members. Two of the most common causes of stress are role pressure and role stress (French, Caplan, & Harrison, 1982; Kahn, Wolfe, Quinn, Snoeck, & Rosenthal, 1964) associated with organizational change. The effects of change on stress are relevant for our discussion because excessive stress typically leads to absenteeism, turnover, illness, or declining productivity (Joure, Leon, & Simson, 1989), all of which interfere with the HRM function's ability to assist management in reaching their downsizing objectives.

We propose that the effects of staffing changes on HRM personnel are influenced by a combination of factors, for each form of staffing change. In response to changing demands for their services, downsized HRM departments are required to retrain their staff within a given specialty, and/or reallocate their staff across specialties. Both of these changes can vary in terms of the *degree of*

change (the extent of retraining or reallocation required) and the *scope of change* (the number of people retrained, or the number of units impacted by reallocation).

As shown in figure 15.4, HRM department managers can, at least in theory, trade off the levels of scope of change and degree of change in either retraining or reallocation in order to maintain an acceptable level of stress among the impacted staff. For example, in the case of reallocation, at the extremes the options are moving a few people among a large portion of the units (low scope, high degree), or reallocating a large portion of the people between a few units (high degree, low scope).

Taking the case of reallocation, the diagonal line in figure 15.4 represents HRM's options for managing the stress associated with internal reallocations by varying the extent of reallocation per unit (y-axis), and the number of units requiring reallocation (x-axis). Points "x^1" and "y^1" intersect on the diagonal, meaning an HRM department can maintain an acceptable level of stress by reallocating between "x^1" number of units to the extent of "y^1" portion of each unit. If the department would like to involve more units than "x^1" in the reallocation process, it must reduce the extent of reallocation per unit to less than "y^1." Conversely, if the department would like to reallocate a larger portion of the members of the affected units than level "y^1," it must select fewer than "x^1" units.

This same logic applies to retraining. The HRM department can only retrain "x^1" people to the degree "y^1" (or anywhere else along or below the diagonal) before experiencing excessive stress.

While we recognize that reallocation and retraining decisions will be heavily influenced by situation-specific requirements and constraints, consideration of how the combined levels of degree of change and scope of change impact a work unit's stress level, encourages managers to include these factors in the reallocation decision. The message of

Figure 15.4   The effect of HRM staff reductions on the HRM department's stress level

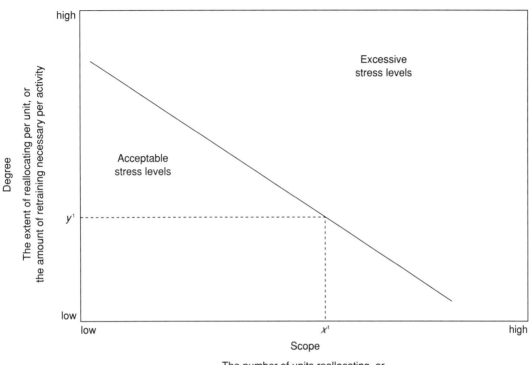

x^1 = the maximum level of the scope of reallocating or retraining, given the "y^1" level of degree of change (within acceptable stress levels)

y^1 = the maximum level of the degree of change in reallocating or retraining, given the "x^1" level of scope of change (within acceptable stress levels)

figure 15.4 is that when the combined effects of the scope and degree of change exceed an HRM unit's ability to effectively manage stress, then the HRM function's ability to provide support for the espoused objectives of the downsizing initiative will likely be compromised.

We now turn our attention to the position of the diagonal line – the amount of stress an HRM unit can effectively assimilate. There are a number of factors that affect an HRM unit's capacity for absorbing the consequences of changes in HRM service requests, including the size of the HRM staff, their level of experience, breadth of training, etc. In figure 15.5 these are combined into

HRM *resource capacity*. While a big downsizing program can affect HRM capacity in a variety of ways, the most obvious is head count reduction.

Figure 15.5 depicts the interactive effects between the level of HRM staff reductions and either staff reallocation or staff retraining on unit stress. Diagonal lines "A" and "B" signify budget/staff reductions, "A" being a modest reduction, and "B" being more severe. As reductions become more severe (with the diagonal shifting to the left), the staff's capacity for managing the stress induced by changes in the amount or type of HRM services requested decreases, as signified by the area under the diagonal. If an HRM

Figure 15.5 The effect of HRM staff reductions on the HRM department's stress level

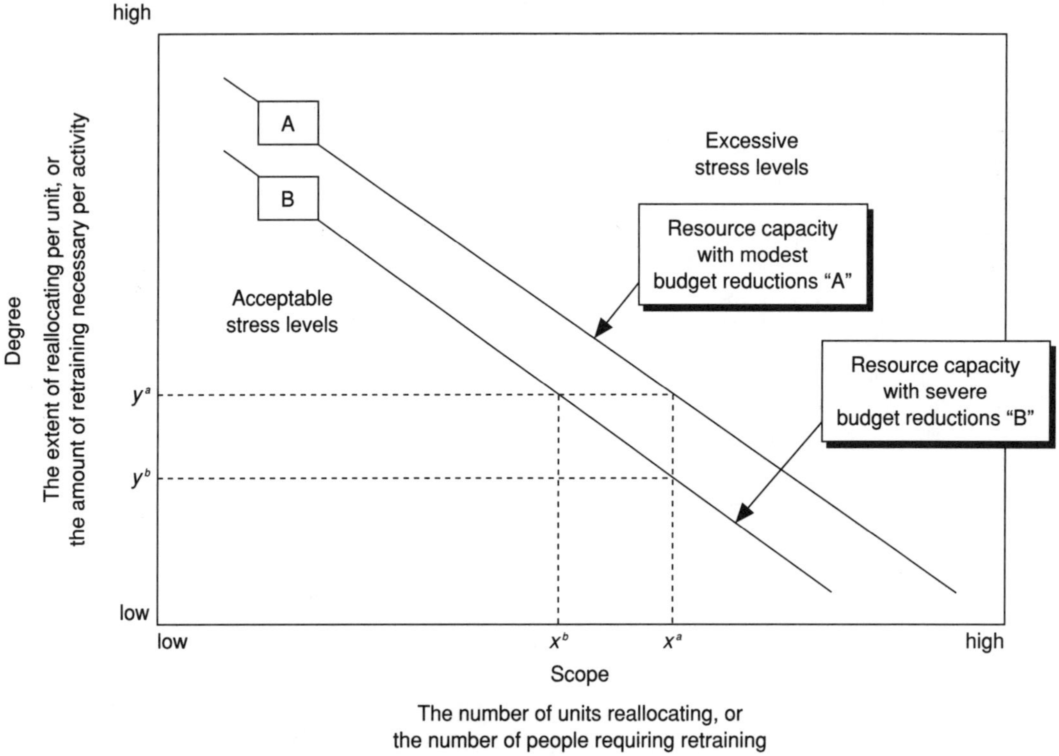

x^a = the maximum level of the scope of reallocating or retraining with budget reductions "A," given the "y^a" level of degree of change (within acceptable stress levels)

x^b = the maximum level of the scope of reallocating or retraining with budget reductions "B," given the "y^a" level of degree of change (within acceptable stress levels)

y^a = the maximum level of the degree of change in reallocating or retraining with budget reductions "A," given the "x^a" level of scope of change (within acceptable stress levels)

y^b = the maximum level of the degree of change in reallocating or retraining with budget reductions "B," given the "x^a" level of scope of change (within acceptable stress levels)

department wished to reallocate or retrain at levels "x^a" and "y^a," it could do so as long as the budget reductions were no more severe than level "A." If however, it attempted to make changes at these levels while absorbing a higher level of staff cuts ("B"), the HRM department would likely experience performance-impairing stress.

CONCLUSION

Downsizing of any type requires HRM to be a strong, competent partner in managing the process and its consequences. Despite all the talk about strategic human resource management, many organizations are only slowly incorporating HRM as full partners in the downsizing decision-making process. Indeed, probably the acid test of an organization's commitment to the ideal of making HRM a full partner in the design and implementation of strategic initiatives is how fully top management acknowledges their contribution to the expected "ends" of downsizing.

Furthermore HRM's contribution is most critical when downsizing is coupled with strategic redesign. However, because this type of downsizing places the greatest pressure on the HRM function (reduced staff coupled with qualitative changes in service requests), it also has the greatest potential to impair HRM's performance. Therefore, care must especially be exercised in this situation to protect against this unintended outcome.

To that end, our analysis suggests three general strategies for managing the potentially debilitating effects of downsizing on HRM departments. First, reduce the source of stress by negotiating reductions in the number and/or type of changes in service requests from operating units. This might take the form of working with the operating units to prioritize their proposed changes, especially those involving changes in staff competencies, and establish a realistic time frame for delivering each priority level. Alternatively, seek to transform qualitative requests into quantitative ones, for example, by proposing an increase in the capacity to teach a slightly modified course rather than developing a whole new course requiring a new form of delivery.

The second strategy focuses on preserving the HRM department's capacity to absorb the stress induced by these changes by negotiating reductions in proposed HRM staff cuts. This approach is based on the premise that effective HRM unit performance requires rough parity between its capacity and its customers' expectations. This option is particularly relevant when downsizing coupled with redesign necessitates extensive qualitative changes in the HRM function.

If the first two strategies do not yield totally satisfactory results, then the third strategy focuses on carefully planning an internal response that minimizes the effects of stress on staff performance. Following the logic of figure 15.4, this includes examining the trade-offs between the scope of change and the degree of change in retraining and/or reallocating HRM staff.

When downsizing significantly diminishes HRM staff resource capacity, causing the area beneath the diagonal in figure 15.5 to contract, opportunities for trade-offs between the scope and the degree of change decrease as well. (Naturally, as the number of people eligible for reallocation and/or retraining is reduced, so too are management's options.) Figure 15.5 graphically illustrates why the stress level in HRM units that are required to simultaneously make large personnel cuts and substantially alter their work activities often impairs their ability to effectively meet their customers' needs during or following a downsizing initiative. We contend that this significant decrement in HRM service capacity is a contributing factor to the low level of satisfaction typical of downsized organizations.

REFERENCES

Albert, S. (1992). The algebra of change. In B. M. Staw & L. L. Cummings (eds.), *Research in Organizational Behavior*, vol. 14, pp. 175–229. Greenwich, CT: JAI Press.

Albert, S., & Whetten, D. (1985). Organizational identity. In L. L. Cummings & B. M Staw (eds.), *Research in Organizational Behavior*, vol. 7, pp. 263–95. Greenwich, CT: JAI Press.

Ashforth, B. E., & Mael, F. (1989). Social identity theory and the organization. *Academy of Management Review*, 14, 20–39.

Barney, J. (1986). Strategic factor markets: Expectations, luck, and business strategy. *Management Science*, 32, 1231–41.

Bennett, A. (1991). Downsizing doesn't necessarily bring an upswing in corporate profitability. *Wall Street Journal*, June 6, B1, B4.

Bolt, J. (1985). Job security: Its time has come. In M. Beer and B. Spector (eds.), *Readings in Human Resource Management*, 288–301. New York: Free Press.

Brockner, J., Grover, S., Reed, T., DeWitt, R., & O'Malley, M. (1987). Survivors' reactions to layoffs: We get by with a little help for our friends. *Administrative Science Quarterly*, 32, 526–41.

Butler, J., Ferris, G., & Napier, N. (1991). *Strategy and Human Resource Management*. Cincinnati, OH: South-Western Publishing Co.

Cameron, K., Freeman, S., & Mishra, A. (1991). Best practices in white collar downsizing: Managing cotradictions. *Academy of Management Executive*, 5 (3), 57–73.

Cameron, K., Kim, M., & Whetten, D. (1987). Organizational effects of decline and turbulence. *Administrative Science Quarterly*, 32, 222–40.

Cameron, K., Mishra, A., and Freeman, S. (1992). Organizational downsizing. In G. P. Huber & W. H. Glick (eds.), *Organizational Change and Redesign*, 19–65. New York: Oxford University Press.

Cameron, K. S., & Whetten, D. A. (1983). *Organizational Effectiveness: A comparison of multiple models*. New York: Academic Press.

Cascio, W. F. (1993). Downsizing: What do we know? What have we learned? *Academy of Management Executive*, 7 (1), 95–104.

Cook, D. and Ferris, G. (1986). Strategic human resource management and firm effectiveness in industries experiencing decline. *Human Resource Management*, 25 (3), 441–58.

Coyne, K. P. (1986). Sustainable competitive advantage – What it is and what it isn't. *Business Horizons*, Jan.–Feb., 54–61.

Daft, R. (1986). *Organizational Theory and Design*. St. Paul, MN: West Publishing.

DeWitt, R. (1993). The structural consequences of downsizing. *Organizational Science*, 4 (1), 30–40.

Ferris, G., Schellenberg, D., & Zammuto, R. (1984). Human resource management in declining industries. *Human Resource Management*, 23 (4), 381–94.

Freeman, S., & Cameron, K. (1993). Organizational downsizing: A convergence and reorientation framework. *Organizational Science*, 4 (1), 10–29.

French, J. R. P., Jr., Caplan, R. D., & Harrison, R. V. (1982). *The Mechanisms of Job Stress and Strain*. London: Wiley.

Greenhalgh, L., Lawrence, A., & Sutton, R. (1988). Determinants of work force reduction strategies in declining organizations. *Academy of Management Review*, 13 (2), 241–54.

Hall, R. (1993). A framework linking intangible resources and capabilities to sustainable competitive advantage. *Strategic Management Journal*, 14 (8), 607–18.

Henkoff, R. (1990). Cost cutting: How to do it right. *Fortune*, April 9, 17–19.

Jackson, S., Schuler, R., & Rivero, J. (1989). Organizational characteristics as predictors of personnel practices. *Personnel Psychology*, 42, 727–86.

Joure, S. A., Leon, J. S., & Simson, D. B. (1989). The pressure cooker of work: How to deal with stress in the workplace. *Personnel Administrator*, 34, March, 92–5.

Kahn, R. L, Wolfe, D. M., Quinn, R. P., Snoeck, J. D., & Rosenthal, R. A. (1964). *Organizational Stress: Studies in role conflict and ambiguity*. London: Wiley.

Koretz, G. (1992). The white-collar jobless could really rock the vote. *Business Week*, February 28, 16.

Krantz, J. (1985). Group process under conditions of organizational decline. *Journal of Applied Behavioral Science*, 21 (1), 1–17.

Lengnick-Hall, C., & Lengnick-Hall, M. (1988). Strategic human resources management: A review of the literature and a proposed typology. *Academy of Management Review*, 13 (3), 454–70.

Millman, J., Von Glinow, M., & Nathan, M. (1991). Organizational life cycles and strategic international human resource management in multinational companies: Implications for congruence theory. *Academy of Management Review*, 16 (2), 318–39.

Perry, L. (1984). Key human resource strategies in an organization downturn. *Human Resource Management*, 23 (1), 61–75.

Prahalad, C. K., & Hamel, G. (1990). The core competence of the corporation. *Harvard Business Review*, May–June, 79–91.

Price, R., & D'Aunno, T. (1984). Managing work force reduction. *Human Resource Management*, 22 (4), 413–30.

Ropp, K. (1987). Downsizing strategies. *Personnel Administrator*, February, 61–4.

Schuler, R., & Jackson, S. (1987). Linking competitive strategies with human resource management practices. *Academy of Management Executive*, 1 (3), 207–19.

Seeley, R. S. (1992). HR redesigns to optimize effectiveness. *HRMagazine*, 37, November, 44–6.

Sutton, R., & D'Aunno, T. (1989). Decreasing organizational size: Untangling the effects of money and people. *Academy of Management Review*, 14 (2), 194–212.

Thornburg, L. (1993). IBM's agent of influence. *HRMagazine*, 38, February, 80–3.

Tomasko, R. M. (1993). Intelligent resizing: View from the top down (assessing a company's core competencies). *Management Review*, 82, May, 16–21.

Tsui, A. S. (1990). A multiple constituency model of effectiveness: An empirical examination at the human resource subunit level. *Administrative Science Quarterly*, 35, 458–83.

Tushman, M. L., & Romanelli, E. (1985). Organizational evolution: A metamorphosis model of convergence and reorientation. In L. L. Cummings & B. M. Staw (eds.), *Research in Organizational Behavior*, vol. 7, pp. 171–222. Greenwich, CT: JAI Press.

Uchitelle, L. (1993). Strong companies are joining trend to eliminate jobs. *New York Times*, July 26, 1.

Ulrich, D. and Lake, D. (1990). *Organizational Capability: Competing from the inside out*. New York: Wiley.

Whetten, D. A. (1980). Organizational decline: A neglected topic in organizational science. *Academy of Management Review*, 5, 577–88.

Whetten, D. A. (1987). Organizational growth and decline processes. *Annual Review of Sociology*, 13, 335–58.

Wetten, D. A., & Cameron, K. S. (1994). Organizational-level product initiatives: The case of downsizing. In D. H. Harris (ed.), *Organizational Linkages: Understanding the productivity paradox* (in press). Washington, D.C.: National Academy Press.

Zammuto, R., & Cameron, K. (1985). Environmental decline and organizational response. In B. M. Staw & L. L. Cummings (eds.), *Research in Organizational Behavior*, vol. 7, pp. 223–62. Greenwich, CT: JAI Press.

□ Chapter 16 □

Preserving and Realizing Acquisition Value Through Human Resources Practices

David M. Schweiger, Allain Gosselin, and Robert Lambertucci

INTRODUCTION

In spite of annual changes in the number of deals transacted, mergers and acquisitions (M & As) continue to remain a crucial part of the business landscape. However, as many executives and academic research have found (see Schweiger & Walsh, 1990 for a review of this literature), creating value for owners of the buying firm through M & As can be quite elusive; in fact most M & As either do not create value or lose value. Although there are many reasons why (see Csiszar & Schweiger, 1994), increasing attention has been given to the role of organization and human resources issues (see Haspeslagh & Jemison, 1991; Schweiger & Walsh, 1990; Buono & Bowditch, 1989 for reviews of this literature).

It is our intent in this chapter to extend our understanding of these issues and to discuss them within the framework of value creation. More specifically, we intend to demonstrate how organizational and human resources issues directly affect value creation in M & As. To accomplish this, the paper is divided into four sections. Section one presents an overview of M & A value creation, with a particular focus on the role of organization and human resources issues. Section two explores what we have learned from theory, research, and practice about these issues. However, rather than providing an exhaustive review of this literature, for it has been done elsewhere (e.g., see Buono & Bowditch, 1989; Schweiger & Walsh, 1990), we highlight key conclusions. Section three presents an illustrative case study of how Molson O'Keefe successfully handled the issues discussed in section two. Finally, section four summarizes what has been learned and what still needs to be learned.

CREATING VALUE THROUGH MERGERS AND ACQUISITIONS

Sources of value

Let us begin by defining what we mean by value. As noted by Csiszar and Schweiger (1994), for value to be created an acquisition must produce a return on capital employed that exceeds its weighted average cost of capital. As such, management must insure that it accurately understands and realizes the cash flow projections and capital investments it makes in its acquisition valuation, pricing, and negotiation. To accomplish this also requires that management understand and manage inflows and outflows of value to an acquired (and acquiring) firm that can occur during an acquisition. Therefore, depending upon the flows, value can either be created or lost. Although some of these views have been presented elsewhere (Csiszar & Schweiger, 1994), we would like to briefly review them here. An acquiring firm has an intrinsic stand-alone value prior to an acquisition. Through the process of acquisition, there are inflows and outflows that change its value, resulting in the intrinsic value of the combined firm.

Inflows of value such as the real value of the target, the positive impact (e.g., better management practices, transfer of knowledge or skills) that the buyer can bring to the target (and vice versa), and value added by combining firms (i.e., the proverbial synergies) are all sources of potential value creation. However, the overestimation of value by the target's management, the payment of acquisition premiums, restructuring costs (e.g., upgrading facilities, severance payouts), transaction costs (e.g., investment banking, legal, and consulting fees), and value leakage (e.g., loss of key employees) are all potential sources of value destruction.

How the M & A process is managed has a great bearing on whether inflows exceed outflows. There are a number of highly interrelated steps during the acquisition process that influence flows. First, the buying firm has to accurately identify, gauge, and substantiate the intrinsic value of the target, the positive impact it can have on the target (or vice versa), and the combination value. This involves sound target selection, accurate valuation, and thorough due diligence. As many who have been engaged in these activities can attest, they are inexact sciences. Valuations are often based on some future projections of discounted cash flow which require many assumptions about revenues and costs. Due diligence is often a painstaking examination of a target's strategic, financial, operational, organizational and human resources situation. These activities lead to conclusions as to whether value can be created through the acquisition, what the range of that value is, and the range of purchase price that would lead to that value.

Second, once the source of value is accurately understood, the buying firm has to capture that value through the process of bargaining and negotiation. In other words, if the buying firm agrees to a price (including transaction and restructuring costs) that exceeds the intrinsic value of the firm, the positive impact, or combination value, or if the buyer overestimates any of these, the price may be too high and value may be destroyed.

Finally, assuming the process thus far suggests that value can indeed be created, then the buying firm must be able to at least preserve its own and the target's existing intrinsic value and be able to realize, through implementation, the positive impact or combination value it hoped for. In other words, the acquisition process itself is an intervention that can affect one or both organizations and human resources in either positive or negative (i.e., value leakage) ways. For example, the loss of a key customer or research employee due to uncertainty during the acquisition negotiation can lead to the loss of intrinsic value. The failure to effectively combine (i.e., integrate) the operations of merging firms can lead to unrealized combination value, or if conflicts erupt, a loss of intrinsic value.

It is our contention that organizational and human resources issues are most germane to the preservation and realization of value. However, the highly interactive nature of all aspects of the M & A process cannot be ignored. For example, if the firm cannot implement the M & A as intended, then the usefulness of the valuation process is diminished. If the buyer overestimates combination value through poor target selection and due diligence, or negotiates poorly, and thus pays too much for a target, it cannot create value through superior implementation. Although there are many issues to consider, we will focus the remainder of this chapter on the role of organizational and human resources issues in preserving and realizing value.

Preserving value

Based on most valuation methods, preservation of value assumes that both an acquirer and a target can, at a minimum, sustain their historical cash flows or achieve the cash flows projected in their strategic or forward plans. While these assumptions seem simple enough, they may be difficult to achieve in practice. Cash flow projections, which are based on revenue and cost projections, are achieved through the continued proper utilization of both human and capital assets. Unfortunately, assumptions concerning utilization and cash flow projections are often made without regard to the short- and long-term disruptions that normally occur. Acquisition activities such as negotiations, due diligence, and closing can affect the normal operations at a time when the businesses need to operate as usual so that a determination of true intrinsic value can be made.

Value-leaking disruptions can often begin very early in the acquisition process, for example, during negotiations. Disruptions are often created by rumors (e.g., the grapevine, newspapers), uncertainty, and the concerns that stakeholders have about their future relationship with the combining organizations (e.g., see Napier, Simmons, & Stratton, 1989; Bastien, 1987; Schweiger & DeNisi, 1991). Employees are typically concerned about job security and the terms of future employment. Other stakeholders are concerned about whether existing contracts and agreements will be honored and/or improved/destroyed. While some stakeholders may not react adversely to uncertainty and rumors, many do.

Uncertainty is often triggered when stakeholders learn that an acquisition is being considered or negotiated, or due diligence is being conducted (Schweiger, Csiszar, & Napier, 1994). Although negotiations are often conducted in secret, it is often impossible for senior managers to prevent rumors, which are often negative and exaggerated, from emerging and circulating (Schweiger & DeNisi, 1991). Rumors may emerge either from sources internal or external to a firm. Obviously, the nature of the rumors and individual predispositions will influence how particular stakeholders react. Typically, however, reactions are not positive.

To combat the destructive effects of rumors and uncertainty, it is suggested that senior managers in both an acquirer and a target systematically develop and proactively execute a value preservation plan for each of their firms since value leakage does not occur only in a target (Csiszar & Schweiger, 1994). For a target, such a plan would help insure a stronger negotiating position and higher purchase price. For an acquirer it would help insure that value is not lost prior to closing. All efforts should be made by both parties to discuss such a plan early in the negotiations and perhaps formally commit to a plan in the letter of intent.

The value preservation plan should include approaches for communicating with all stakeholders, retaining key stakeholders, and interventions for managing employee trauma. Each of these is discussed briefly below.

Communications

Unfortunately, many senior managers believe that either they do not have time to communicate or that secrecy is the best method for dealing with stakeholders during acquisitions. Although it may be impossible for senior managers to completely communicate in a timely fashion (e.g., needs for secrecy, SEC or government contractor regulations), it has been suggested that legitimate attempts at honest, timely, and relevant communications may be the most effective approach for combating uncertainty and rumors and their debilitating effects (Napier et al., 1989; Bastien, 1987; Schweiger & DeNisi, 1991).

While honesty does not imply that senior managers can or should discuss every detail of an acquisition with stakeholders, it does imply, however, that they should proactively establish or enhance two-way communications, not deliberately deceive, and be realistic about the impact of an acquisition with stakeholders. Many have suggested, however, that effective firms adopt the following communication philosophy:

"If we can tell you, we will,"

"If we cannot tell you, we will tell you why (e.g., explain SEC regulations)," and

"If we do not know why, we will try and find out."

This philosophy is especially important in cases where long-term relationships (e.g., with key employees, distributors, customers) must be maintained. Since the "truth" eventually happens, lack of responsiveness to stakeholder concerns, short-term deception, excessive optimism, and speculation will eventually destroy relationships. In the end, the strength of these relationships is likely to be the most important basis for preserving value.

The most important step in developing and executing communications is to insure that senior managers take responsibility for making it happen. A sound plan will detail the messages to be communicated and time frames for communicating them, the media to be employed (e.g., employee meetings with senior managers, customer visits by senior managers, company newsletters, transition newsletters, memos, external or media relations, phone mail, fax for hard to reach or non-US locations, telephone hotlines), and the specific person or persons responsible for communicating the messages (Schweiger & Weber, 1989).

Specific communications should be dedicated to each stakeholder and their specific concerns. The media employed should be those considered most credible by the particular stakeholder. It is critical, however, that there be coordination among all media and persons responsible for communicating to insure a degree of consistency. Contradictory public information can undermine any communication effort. The best place to begin is with all members of senior management "singing from the same sheet of music."

Retaining key employees and stakeholders

Although communications may be helpful in minimizing the deleterious effects of uncertainty and rumors, they may not be sufficient to retain key employees and stakeholders who can easily sever their relationships with the involved companies, especially in cases where trust is not strong. Guarantees such as financial incentives or employment contracts may be required for key employees. For example, it has been found that it is not uncommon for employees with critical skills or knowledge to be offered bonuses (i.e., "stay packages") as inducements for remaining with their organization for a specified period of time.

Stay packages provide the organization with either time to demonstrate to employees that they have a future in the organization, to find and train adequate replacements, or eventually to eliminate jobs not needed in the long term. It is also not uncommon for key employees to be offered equity interests (even if only a "phantom" type) in the combined companies, especially in relatively small acquisitions. A central issue in awarding stay packages is whom to include and whom not to. Failure to include someone may hasten his or her departure (assuming he or she is mobile), or create jealousy and dissension. To include everyone may be very costly. In many organizations stay packages are typically awarded to people who the organization "must keep." Terms of the package will vary depending upon how important a person is (including replacement costs), organizational level, total compensation, and total available funds for such packages.

With respect to other stakeholders, either verbal or contractual assurances are likely to be needed. For example, the livelihood of key distributors and vendors, much like employees, may also be at stake during an acquisition, especially if a large percentage of their business is derived from either of the combining firms. Key customers are likely to be concerned about continuity in product availability, quality, service, etc. Failure to provide such assurances may cause them to switch to competitors. Indeed, competitors may find an acquisition an excellent time to woo customers.

Again, it is crucial that every effort be made to sustain key relationships. Whether the deal is closed or not, stakeholder relationships are the primary source of intrinsic value and may be an important source of combination value for the merging firms.

Managing employee trauma

Regardless of communications and retention agreements, many employees still may not react well to the uncertainty and rumors. It has been suggested in the literature, however, that stress reduction and change management workshops, psychological counseling, social support, and employee assistance programs help individuals cope more effectively (Marks & Cutcliffe, 1988). In sum, preserving value in both acquiring and target firms is crucial during the acquisition process, whether the deal closes or not. To assume that value will be preserved without senior management intervention, however, may be a great mistake.

Realizing value

Although sources of value creation can be identified during candidate selection, and captured during negotiations and due diligence, they can only be realized after an acquirer and a target are combined or contributions are made, and thus changes are made within one or both firms. For example, lowering cost through consolidating manufacturing facilities (i.e., economies of scale) can only be accomplished after facilities are consolidated and functioning at forecasted levels. Consolidation will likely require changes in manufacturing technology, operating procedures, and information systems; as well as the transfer, retraining, and termination of employees. Transfer of products or knowledge will only be realized when such transfer relationships are effectively working. The extent to which these changes, and others, are properly managed and executed will determine whether expected value is indeed created (Haspeslagh & Jemison, 1991; Schweiger et al., 1994; Schweiger & Walsh, 1990). The organizational change process can vary in its level of complexity and involves numerous decisions concerning the depth, location, and nature of changes, the speed of the change process, and interventions for facilitating the change process. Each of these issues is addressed below.

Depth, location and nature of changes

As most senior managers have found, organizational change can be costly, both in financial and human terms. Change often requires not only technical alterations in an organization, but political and cultural ones as well (Tichy, 1983). As such, "unnecessary" changes should be avoided in the acquisition-implementation process. In this vein, it has been suggested that firms invoke the "principle of minimum intervention" – undertake only those changes needed to create value in an acquisition: that is, focus only on those functions or activities (e.g., manufacturing, purchasing, human resources) where combination is necessary, or where a target firm needs to be changed to create value. While this principle seems somewhat obvious, regrettably it is often violated and it results in unnecessarily complex and unsuccessful acquisition implementations.

The depth, location, and nature of organizational changes will vary depending upon the sources of value creation inherent in a particular acquisition. For example, an acquisition of a small firm by a large one to gain a new technology or product may yield changes limited to only one or few functional areas and activities (e.g., R&D) in an acquirer, but may require an entire reconfiguration of a target (i.e., it is folded into the acquirer). On the other hand, a merger between two direct competitors may yield changes that cut across all the functions and activities (e.g., human resources, manufacturing, sales, legal, accounting) of both firms.

Regardless of the changes required, it is crucial that individuals responsible for identifying, gauging, and substantiating value and subsequently for realizing value have both a clear understanding of the true sources of value and the changes needed to capture them, and use their understanding to set realistic expectations and implementation priorities. It has been suggested (Haspeslagh & Jemison, 1991; Csiszar & Schweiger, 1994) that a fully integrated M & A process, from a firm's business strategy through implementation, be created. This would insure continuity of knowledge and accountability through the steps of value creation.

In addition to assessing the depth and location of changes, it is also necessary to examine the nature of the changes required. These include eliminating or shutting down units, combining units, or creating new interrelationships among units (see Schweiger et al., 1994 for a more complete discussion of these).

Speed of change process
Although there is some conjecture, one of the key issues that has not been researched is: How fast should changes be made? There are basically two schools of thought on this issue. The first suggests that changes should be made as quickly as possible, so as to minimize the employee trauma associated with prolonged uncertainty and insecurity; most employees know that "the ax is going to fall." The second suggests that a longer time frame should be employed and the firms should study and learn as much about each other as possible before changes are designed and undertaken. Intuitively, both approaches seem to make a great deal of sense. Unfortunately, the speed issue is not a simple one since there are other factors that impinge upon it.

First, the size of an acquisition and the performance expectations communicated by an acquirer's management to stockholders and bankers may influence the process. For example, small acquisitions may represent a fraction of a firm's capital commitments and may permit more patience (i.e., there is not much pressure to get an immediate return). On the other hand, a large acquisition may represent a significant capital commitment for an acquirer, be readily visible, have a potentially significant impact on its stock price, and create pressure for short-term returns (i.e., 1–2 years) to keep investors happy. In fact, some senior managers compound the pressures by creating unrealistic positive expectations for investors with respect to time frames and cash flow projections so as to gain their support for the deal. A divisional executive may do the same with respect to the CEO of a parent company (see Schweiger, Ridley, & Marini, 1992 for an example of this). When this factor becomes a driving force in acquisitions, implementation effectiveness and value realization may be severely compromised. While there is much speculation on how long it takes to implement a "large" merger, most generally agree that it takes somewhere between three and five years.

Second, and as noted earlier, due diligence is an inexact science. It is impossible to fully understand everything about a target firm prior to closing. Similar to marriage, firms learn a great deal about their partner as they live with them. This is especially the case when a firm makes acquisitions outside its areas of expertise (e.g., unrelated businesses, new countries or regions; Napier, Schweiger, & Kosglow, 1993; Haspeslagh & Jemison, 1991). While it would be desirable to simply conduct a due diligence and then design and carry out an implementation plan, events that impinge on such a plan do not operate so predictably. In many cases, the change process is incremental and experimental as the partners learn more fully about each other well after the deal is closed. The net effect is a longer, more protracted implementation process.

Third, speed of implementation may be restricted for certain types of deals. For example, in New York State, targets of hostile tender offers may have to be kept independent for a period of five years.

It is clear from the issues raised above that the implementation process should move in a purposeful fashion. Obviously, the change process can be very unsettling to an organization and create employee trauma (e.g., uncertainty, insecurity, stress) if prolonged. However, the time frame should be realistic. The greater the number and more complex the nature of the changes, the longer the implementation will likely take. The key is to implement successfully not prematurely. Regardless of the time frame, management should be realistic about the issue of time and complexity during their assessment and factor this into their cash flow projections during valuation. Failure to do so will likely lead to unmet expectations (Csiszar & Schweiger, 1994).

THEORY AND RESEARCH ON MANAGING THE IMPLEMENTATION PROCESS

There are two crucial elements in managing the implementation process. The first is to stabilize the work force during the early phases of an acquisition. The second is to manage the change process during implementation.

Stabilizing the work force

As noted in our discussion on preserving value, uncertainty and rumors are serious disruptions that can result in lower productivity and morale, and defection among key stakeholders. Such problems will continue during the implementation process as stakeholders are unsure how the change process will play out. Again, communications, stay packages and agreements such as earn-out provisions, and interventions for managing employee trauma remain important, both for preserving and realizing value during the organizational change process. Unlike the period prior to closing, however, senior management of the combined firm will have control over the activities of both firms after closing.

Managing the change process

The principal objective of the change process is to take two previously independent organizations and combine them into one organization. As our previous discussion suggests, the final form of the combined organization and the complexity of the change process will vary depending upon the sources of combination value underlying an acquisition.

There are several questions that need to be addressed during the change process. First, how will decisions concerning changes be made? Second, how will differences between organizations and units be managed, especially in cases of assimilation and innovation? Third, how will employee dislocations (e.g., terminations, transfers) be managed? Finally, how will the combined organization be rebuilt and solidified?

Change decisions

Of particular importance here is the distribution of decision-making power between combining firms and units. While it has been argued that senior managers from both firms should have equal say in such decisions, this is not always the case, especially where one firm is fully assimilated into another (Schweiger & Weber, 1989). In some cases, the senior management of a target firm often has little real power and is not retained. Even in cases where senior management is retained in a combined company, there is typically a "lesser among equals" in such decisions (Sales & Mirvis, 1984). Distribution will vary to some extent, however, depending on whether an acquiring management understands a target's business and whether a target is left to operate autonomously or not. Moreover, in some non-U.S. acquisitions, distribution becomes more complicated as other constituents such as workers' councils and employee operating boards are required by law to be involved in important decisions affecting employees.

There are advantages and disadvantages to different levels of distribution of decision-making power. When there is equal distribution, both organizations are likely to be represented better, and perhaps more fairly, in crucial decisions (e.g., employee retention, HR policies, work procedures). It is more likely to promote greater learning and understanding among members of both organizations and perhaps break down internal political and cultural sources of resistance to change. Equal distribution is also symbolic insofar as it conveys to employees that members of both organizations will be treated fairly and with respect (Schweiger et al., 1992; Marks & Mirvis, 1985; Buono & Bowditch, 1989).

This is not to imply, however, that equal distribution is always warranted. In some cases – such as when the senior management of a target has performed poorly, when employees of a target might welcome a change in senior management, when a target firm is in chaos, or when available time for implementation is limited – autocratic decisions may be very effective. In other cases, such as when the acquirer knows little about the target's business, or when intervention in the target would destroy value, it may make more sense

for a target's management to control decision making. For example, it is not uncommon for large corporations to intervene too quickly and deeply in the operations of acquired entrepreneurial firms. Often this intervention destroys the primary source of combination value.

Equal distribution may be difficult to achieve, however. First, it requires effective cooperation, conflict resolution, and sharing of power among senior managers – some things they may not be willing or have the patience to do. Second, it may require more time than autocratic decision making, something that previous expectations, or business and competitive conditions do not permit. Finally, a target's management may be weak and incapable of making proper decisions, and thus should not be involved or should be ousted.

Decision-making distribution is also an issue beyond the senior management level. Decisions concerning areas to assimilate or innovate must be made. While some of these decisions may be made by senior management, other decisions are typically delegated to functional area managers where requisite knowledge resides. Many companies create "transition" or "integration" teams to address these decisions. Typically, functional counterparts (e.g., manufacturing, R&D, HR) from each firm are assigned to these teams to conduct analyses and make recommendations concerning whether comparable units from both firms should be combined (and, if so, how), or remain independent of each other. The magnitude and complexity of the integration team process will vary depending upon the number of areas where value through combination can be achieved. Where many units are combined, an elaborate transition process will be needed, with numerous integration teams reporting to an overarching senior executive or an integration team made up of members of senior management. In cases where few units are combined, such as in the acquisition of a small firm, it may require the involvement of just a handful of managers.

Regardless of the approach chosen, careful consideration of distribution of decision making should be given very early in the acquisition process (i.e., during negotiations). While many senior managers may think these are post-closing decisions, it has been found that they are most effectively managed when they are addressed early in the acquisition process. However, regardless of how many issues are effectively negotiated early, shifts in distribution will continue as the acquisition process evolves.

An early transition team process may be an excellent vehicle for due diligence and for assessing and confirming sources of value between the combining firms. The extent to which this process can be created prior to closing, however, will be moderated by the degree of cooperation and disclosure between combining firms.

In cross-border acquisitions, national laws and cultural customs play an important role in shaping final combination decisions. In many cases, laws prevent assimilation of compensation and benefits. In some countries (e.g., England) health benefits are provided by the government, whereas in others (e.g., U.S.) they are provided by private carriers. Other issues that may impede combination include ethnic, race, and sex issues relative to work-force interaction; work ethics (e.g., Eastern vs. Western Germany), management styles, and so forth. Moreover the extent to which equal distribution of decision-making power is sought may vary by country.

Managing cultural integration

Cultural differences will become a critical issue in units that are either being combined or are forming new interrelationships with other units. Essentially, people will be required to deal with new people who are comfortable with their current ways of thinking and behaving, and who are politically vested in the status quo. The extent to which these differences are managed and resolved could ultimately determine the success of an acquisition.

During acquisitions, people often operate on barely sufficient information about their counterparts in the other firm and the other firm itself. In the absence of concrete information it is easy for people to speculate and develop inaccurate, and often negative, stereotypes about their counterparts. The net effect is potential interunit and interpersonal conflict and even hostility (i.e., the proverbial "culture clash"). When this occurs the likelihood that units are effectively combined and value is realized is greatly diminished. In fact, a recent study (Chatterjee, Lubatkin, Schweiger, & Weber, 1992) demonstrated that cultural differences among members of combining top-management teams may adversely affect the post-closing performance of acquiring firms. (It is important to note, however, that in cases where people are unimportant to the success of acquisitions, or can be easily replaced, this may be less of an issue.)

It has been suggested (Blake & Mouton, 1984; Marks, 1988; Schweiger et al., 1992; Schweiger, Ritchie, & Csiszar, 1991) that mechanisms for increasing learning and understanding between members of combining organizations can be very effective in resolving conflicts, improving decision making, developing teams, and facilitating employee adaptation. Reward systems may also prove to be a powerful mechanism for promoting cooperation. Mechanisms for increasing learning include forms of information exchange (e.g., show and tells, literature), task and socially focused offsites, intergroup mirroring and conflict resolution, and so forth. For the learning process to be effective, individuals must first be given an opportunity to learn about their counterparts, both as individuals and as employees. Such learning creates a basis by which inaccurate stereotypes, imagined differences, and thus unfounded sources of conflict are eliminated; substantive similarities and differences are better understood; and substantive differences are tolerated, utilized, or resolved. While cultural differences, politics, and conflict cannot be completely eliminated, they may be either minimized or effectively channeled.

Handling staffing and reduction in force

The extent and complexity of staffing and reductions in force will vary depending on the level of combination. Where units are combined and redundancy exists, staffing and terminations become more difficult. It is clear from our research and experience that fair, visible, and compassionate approaches to staffing and terminations are more effective in minimizing trauma (i.e., procedurally just). Staffing decisions should be based primarily on the fit between individual competencies and the transitional and future needs of the combined unit. Approaches such as favoritism and balance in numbers are often perceived by employees as inequitable and not in the best interest of the combined unit.

Competency as a basis of staffing is acceptable to most people. Moreover the approach chosen indicates to retained employees how they might be dealt with in the future and what the new culture is likely to be. It greatly influences whether key people decide to remain with the organization.

Reduction in force is often an unpleasant task. However, the methods employed for doing so can minimize the trauma associated with it. Methods that utilize voluntary turnover (e.g., attrition, early retirement) may create less trauma than those that do not. Voluntary approaches, however, can be problematic. For example, early retirement incentives may lead to over subscription. Both early retirement and attrition, may lead to the premature loss of key people needed to build a new organization.

When forced terminations are required, severance pay and extended benefits, retraining programs, outplacement assistance, internal transfers, and fair recommendations often

ease employee trauma. Typically, the depth of such services vary depending on employees' years of service and position within their firm.

Rebuilding the organization

The ultimate challenge and true source of realized value occurs when a new unified organization is built. This requires the retention of key managers and the development and solidification of a senior management team and teams within the combined units. It has been found, however, that retention and unification are ongoing challenges. They require that organizational and unit goals, strategies, cultural norms, reward systems, and so on; and that individual roles and expectations be clarified or developed, and communicated. Obviously, units that have gone through more radical changes will require more effort than those units that have not. Moreover the combination of two large firms where many, if not all, units are affected will require more effort (i.e., rebuilding the entire direction and infrastructure of the organization) than an acquisition of a small firm where few units and people are affected.

The retention of key managers and development of teams are not discrete events that occur after differences are dealt with (Schweiger et al., 1992). Actually, the nature of the relationships that are created prior to the closing and throughout the acquisition process set the stage for the rebuilding process. Old hostilities and breaches of trust cannot be healed overnight. While stay packages and the like can insure that key senior managers remain with the combined organization, they cannot insure commitment.

Team development can be facilitated through both task-oriented (e.g., problem solving) and/or interpersonally oriented (e.g., values, philosophy, individual perceptions of other members) workshops. Such workshops facilitate team interaction and help individuals learn about and interact with new and existing members. Although a great deal of learning takes place on the job, workshops can lessen

306

the time it takes for such learning to take place. As a note of caution, care should be taken not to overwhelm the organization with too many workshops and meetings. Many acquisitions require so much technical effort during the transition, that little time remains to perform the "normal" work of the organization.

Team development can also be facilitated by solidification of organizational, unit, and individual expectations. To the extent that units and individuals remain unclear about what is expected of them and how they will be rewarded both financially and nonfinancially (e.g., promotions, choice assignments), solidification and productivity will be hindered.

To summarize, creating value through combination requires that two previously independent firms be combined and changed in some fashion. In an ideal world, an acquirer would have perfect information concerning a target, know exactly where and how to document value through a combination, and simply achieve that value through a preplanned and systematic implementation. Unfortunately, we do not live in an ideal world and the process is much more complex and muddled.

While there are many factors to consider in effectively realizing value through implementation, we have attempted to isolate several key points for success based on the limited research, theory, and reported practical experience. First, implementation challenges vary depending upon the sources of value underlying an acquisition. Second, there are a number of interventions that can help facilitate implementation. Third, implementation is an evolving process that requires managers and employees to be flexible, learn, and change. Last, and most important, managers must understand the sources of value in an acquisition and intervene in the implementation process only where and when it is necessary to realize that value.

To gauge the extent to which organizations engage in the practices identified above, we examined the merger between Molson Breweries Limited and Carling O'Keefe which is discussed in the next section.

HUMAN RESOURCES ISSUES IN VALUE CREATION: THE CASE OF MOLSON O'KEEFE

Molson Breweries Limited and Carling O'Keefe were at the time of the merger two of the most important breweries in Canada. What is most interesting about this case is that they had been direct competitors for almost 150 years in a business where you have to fight long and hard to gain a single share point in the market. They had learned to distrust each other for so long that the thought of being partners was foreign to everyone. Now they had to face a new reality with the North American Free Trade Agreement (NAFTA). The main enemy was coming from the south and the American beer industry, with its unmatched competitive advantages regarding production capacity, price, and financial and marketing resources. This left Molson and Carling O'Keefe with no choice but to join forces. Besides NAFTA, a series of events, including an approaching GATT decision, also prompted the two companies to integrate their operations across Canada to become the biggest player in the Canadian beer industry with over 52 percent share of a mature market.

The following analysis will discuss the human resources (HR) interventions used to preserve and realize merger value in the main facilities of the new company in the Province of Quebec. With close to 4,000 full-time and part-time employees working in the nearby Montreal plants of each company, a complex network of company-owned or independent-distributor-operated administrative regions, including 60 warehouses located all over the territory and various union and nonunion work forces, the merger of Molson with

Carling O'Keefe represented a difficult and complex challenge with regards to HR issues.

Company backgrounds

Molson Breweries of Canada was founded in 1786 in Montreal where it still has its head office. It is the longest-established brewery in North America. At the time of the merger, Molson was also the largest brewer in Canada. In addition, it was the premier exporter of Canadian beer on the American market and one of the fifth largest exporters of beer in the world. Molson Breweries had never merged or been acquired by another company during its long history. It was a stable, mature, and profitable business. As the owner of the Montreal Canadian Hockey Club, it was also a highly visible company in Canada. The company was run in a decentralized fashion with regional administrative units having some discretion with respect to their activities. Production and distribution workers were unionized with the Teamsters, whereas clerical employees were nonunionized. Labor relations were typical of the industry – they were neither confrontational nor collaborative. Its largest brewery was located in East End Montreal.

Carling O'Keefe of Canada was founded in 1843. Its head office was in Toronto. The company had a large plant in West End Montreal. Not long before the merger, O'Keefe had been acquired by Elders IXL Limited, one of the world's largest breweries located in Australia, giving it access to a production and distribution network covering more than 80 countries. Over the recent years, Carling O'Keefe had been reorganized and restructured several times leaving the company with a lack of continuity in its management. The company was not performing well financially and, in late 1988, had to divest of some of its businesses such as the Quebec Nordiques Hockey Club and the Toronto Argonauts Football Club of the Canadian Football League. Moreover labor relations had a history of conflict and this was reflected in a labor contract containing several constraints in the flexibility of the work force. Decisions were more centralized at the head office than with Molson. On the other hand. Carling's entire office staff was unionized, as were all production, sales, and distribution staff, who were members of the UFCW.

Negotiations between the two firms were kept secret. The official announcement of the agreement of a strategic alliance between the firms came on January 18, 1989. This is when managers and employees first heard about the decision to combine, on a 50/50 basis, the North American brewing operations of both companies. But it took until July 6, 1989, almost seven months after the agreement, before the transaction was officially approved by the Bureau of Competition and Investment Policy of the Government of Canada – the bureau investigated antitrust implications of the merger. This period provided enough time for the management of both companies to develop different scenarios and prepare for the integration process.

On August 1, 1989 the new 50/50 Canadian-based partnership officially began its operations under the name of MOLSON BREWERIES. From that moment, both companies could begin the actual physical integration process. December 1991 was set as the deadline for the integration of all operations. It was believed that a year and a half was enough time to realize all the tasks and changes that were needed. Because of the many groups represented by competing unions this deadline proved to be too optimistic to determine final labor representation and had to be pushed back twice until early 1993 when the last collective agreement with the union representing employees in the sales division was signed. The actual physical and financial integration process was on target (18 months), but the overall integration took more than three years to complete because of all the labor-relations issues.

The crucial integration issue

Considering the fact that both companies had similar production, distribution, and administrative facilities, consolidation and integration of operations (i.e., combination value) quickly became the main issue. Important gains were possible with regard to cost and the utilization rate of production facilities, which was only at around 69 percent prior to the merger. An extensive rationalization program which called for the closing of seven plants across Canada and an overall 20 percent cut of the work force, from 7,000 to about 5,500, was proposed for the first two years after the merger. In the Montreal area, the Carling O'Keefe plant was to be closed in April 1991. Its operations were integrated within the Molson East End plant which was more modern and effective and also had more space for further expansion. Moreover, in the Province of Quebec, distribution facilities were consolidated by 50 percent. Over 700 jobs were cut in the process.

Shortly after the announcement of the merger, the rationalization plan was presented to employees. A generous early retirement plan and an attractive voluntary severance package were provided for those who decided to leave on their own. The voluntary merger adjustment program (MAP) was seen as a model for Canadian industry because of its extensive communication and counseling for employees. MAP was presented as a positive program for employees, providing them with new career opportunities. MAP needed to be very attractive because the working conditions in the brewing industry are superior to those of other industries. Further, Molson O'Keefe wanted ex-employees to be good ambassadors of the new company. At the national level over 1,700 employees accepted the offer to voluntarily leave the company. In fact, the program was so generous and popular that several individuals who were key to the new company accepted the severance package. This was the case for several top executives

including the likely CEO of the new company in the province of Quebec. Over 75 percent of the job cuts needed were achieved voluntarily. The situation was such that the company had to tie the severance package to specific negotiated departure dates in order to avoid the premature departure of key individuals. It also put the company in the difficult situation of having to recruit at the same time it was laying off people.

Recognizing the need to constantly improve its competitive position, Molson continued to pursue further efficiencies in addition to the more than $200 million worth of savings it had already achieved during the first two years following the merger. In 1992, the company began the second wave of cost and staff reductions. Several functions were restructured to reduce layers of management, to become more streamlined, to increase efficiency, and to improve customer service. At the same time, the company invested more than $125 million for improving production facilities.

The lingering union issue

Production employees of both companies were unionized with different unions. For almost two years, each employee group continued to be represented by its original union. As might be expected, both unions competed to be regarded as the most suitable union to represent all production employees. This "beauty contest" had a strong impact on the organizational climate on the shop floor. While relations between managers of both companies had been quite collaborative, despite the severe downsizing, it had been different at the employee level. It was obvious that some hostility between the two groups of employees would remain as long as the union issue remained unresolved. At the end of 1991, the Teamsters won a hard fought election by a small majority of 54 percent. With such a result, it was obvious that the battle between the unions would continue. An initial collective agreement was negotiated several months later in August 1992, two years after the merger. There still remain two signs that the union issue is still present. The first sign is that, not long after the new contract, union members elected an executive group originating from the rival union which had lost a few months earlier. The reason for this is that the seniority issue between the two groups of employees had not yet been resolved to the satisfaction of the former Carling group. The new company was no longer functioning with two seniority lists. The company proposed an integrated list which was presented and ratified at a union assembly as part of the acceptance of the first collective bargaining agreement. However, because it was based on the volume ratios which were upheld by the department of labor as an equitable method to staff the new brewery, the old Carling group employees, feeling disfavored, believed that resolving this sensitive issue should be the sole mandate of the new Teamsters executive.

Key HR interventions to preserve and realize acquisition value

From the start, it was recognized that HR issues were to be crucial in the success or failure of this merger. Everything had to be planned and implemented to avoid complex problems. Consequently, the HR department had become a chief player in the integration process. Here is an overview of its main activities.

Securing key talent
Soon after August 1, 1989, each company established an exhaustive inventory of its work force, describing the profile of each individual including demographics, competence and performance. This information was obviously a prerequisite to the numerous staffing decisions that had to be made in the months that followed. Special attention was given to identifying and retaining the top 10 percent of key managerial personnel that were viewed as necessary for the merger to succeed. Messages sent to these individuals were quite clear concerning the crucial role they would play in the integration of the two companies. Moreover they were offered specially developed incentive programs spread over a three-year period.

Communication
Communication had been a main concern from the very beginning. As soon as the news came out that the two companies had reached an agreement on a potential merger, every individual in both companies received a written memo explaining what was happening. Following that memo, a series of meetings were organized between management and the employees to further explain what was coming, to reassure people that they would be kept informed of new developments, and to answer questions before the rumor mill got momentum. In August of 1989, when the merger was finally approved by the Bureau of Competition and Investment Policy, a second wave of communications was directed to employees. In fact, each time that something important regarding the merger occurred, employees were formally informed prior to the general public of what was going on. As an example, a complete brochure explaining the voluntary merger adjustment program (MAP) was sent to the home of each employee, for a first reading by those most affected. A series of small group meetings were organized by the HR department to further explain the package and help employees make a sound decision. In addition to MAP a new corporate mission statement was presented to all employees.

Care was constantly taken to insure that the communication process was moving two ways. A special hot-line phone number was provided to employees who had questions regarding the impact of the merger on their benefits and working conditions. Also a new national employee newsletter, *The Molson Forum*, was launched with a large part of it reserved for questions and answers. The Quebec division launched their own *Ensemble* (Together) newspaper published quarterly as well as a memo newsflyer for topical subjects. The first attitude survey of salaried staff was also conducted two years after the merger in order to assess the extent to which the merger had affected the morale of employees. During 1992, the company's strategic direction and future plans to meet the increasingly competitive environment of the brewing industry were presented to all employees to improve their overall understanding of the business and to involve them in developing practical solutions. Several times the operations were temporarily shut down to facilitate meetings between management and employees on the three shifts and throughout the province's nine administrative regions and 35 warehouses. In addition, a new blueprint for the successful management of all Molson employees, consistent with the future challenges, was disseminated throughout the organization including vision and mission statements for managing people.

Restructuring

Because of the large overlap between the operations of the two companies, an important focus of the HR interventions was on rationalizing the work force, most particularly the management ranks. A top-down process was adopted starting with the choice of division presidents. Following their selection, they had to choose their regional vice presidents, and so on until supervisors on the shop floor were chosen. About six months after beginning the integration process, everyone in management knew where they stood.

A "zero-based staffing" approach was taken to decide staffing. All jobs were open, new criteria were established considering the requirements imposed by the new context, and every manager who had decided not to take advantage of the voluntary merger adjustment program had to go through a typical staffing process, including interviews and career as-

sessments. In a cascade of decisions, managers at each level of the hierarchy were free to choose their new subordinates from a short list prepared by the HR department without regard to the company of origin. The HR department was instrumental in ensuring the fairness of the selection process by making sure that all potential candidates available in the pool were considered and that the best candidate for the job was selected according to the criteria established at the beginning of the process. Those who had not been retained were given a "transition" status, meaning that they were to be phased out on a specific date. Obviously it was not possible to let everyone leave at the same time. Thus departures were spread out over several months, with specific dates determined based on the needs of the organization.

Following that first wave of layoffs among managers, attention turned to unionized employees. This time, selection criteria and the decision process were quite different. Since seniority was the mandatory criterion for most decisions, it was more a question of layoffs than staffing. However, in contrast with managerial ranks, it was decided from the beginning that the final composition of the unionized work force would reflect the proportion of the market share of each company. Molson was to have 58 percent of the work force and O'Keefe the remaining 42 percent. In fact, not only the total work force was to respect these proportions but also each department of the company. It was hoped that this approach provided the fairest way to reduce the head count and the best alternative to avoid unnecessary tensions between the two groups of employees. By all means, the company was careful not to exacerbate a potentially damaging "us versus them" mentality since both groups of employees had to work side by side after the integration process.

As mentioned earlier, an important part of the efforts to create a positive context around the merger was devoted to the support of those who had to be laid off. Conditions offered had to be advantageous in terms of the severance package and the delay before departure. The services of four different consulting firms specializing in career or financial counseling and job search were offered to every employee who was considering MAP or was being laid off. Career centers were established in Montreal and Quebec city and staffed with a combination of in-house specialists and external consultants providing seminars to groups or counseling to individuals including family members.

Human resource planning and development
As critical as losing key players was at the beginning, it was a unique opportunity for the company to test developmental candidates by providing reinforcement through training, developmental assignments, and, in some cases, mentorship assistance. Although the formal succession replacement system began to evolve as an "emergency plan," HR was tasked with the development of a more sophisticated skills and talents inventory reporting system originating in the division and fed into the national office. The system successfully identified individuals for key assignments in general management, offshore positions, or Molson U.S. business expansion. A key component of this HR planning process was a completely revised performance-management program based on a small number of key position objectives (KPOs) which were constantly revised between superior and subordinate. Individual performance is fed into the overall HR planning process.

Cultural integration
Culture clash was a critical concern. A conscious effort was made to create a new culture different from the ones already existing, and not to force individuals to adopt the culture of the other group. A new logo, a new uniform for employees, a challenging corporate mission emphasizing excellence, and the creation of tens of problem-solving committees all over the company are examples of actions taken to help employees acknowledge the beginning of a new company. Also, in order to limit the development of an "us vs them" mentality, several events were organized to help each group better understand the other group. Open-door visits were organized for the families of employees. Numerous formal and informal meetings were scheduled, particularly with senior staff, with the objective of putting both groups face to face and helping them verbalize their assumptions about the other group. An outside facilitator was used to help the staff. Finally, a unique "core" company-value training program was launched for all staff, supervisory, and management personnel. The cornerstones of the mandatory program were based on the company mission and values, the performance management program, and open communication.

Involvement
Significant new employee programs were introduced in response to the trauma caused by the merger. All of these activities were designed to improve employee commitment and involvement at a time when it was most needed by the company. For example, Molson Breweries Awards (MBAs), designed to reward people who demonstrated innovation and provided creative solutions, were awarded to employees. In order to facilitate team building among sales representatives who were traditionally paid on a fixed salary basis, an attractive incentive program was put in place. For nonexempt employees, including managers at all levels, a profit-sharing plan was introduced.

Partnership with unions
The merger provided an opportunity to reassess the relationship between the company and unions. A more collaborative relationship has developed. Unions are now more closely associated to the numerous changes that are taking place. Because mergers are destabilizing events in a company's life, it is a

good occasion to question fundamental things such as the way work is organized. For example, union executives were invited to accompany a delegation of managers on a visit to Miller plants in Forth Worth, Texas and Trenton, Ohio, in order to closely study their use of work teams. Other visits were conducted throughout the province of Quebec where team concepts were also being tested. This led to union endorsements to proceed broad scale with the development of self-directed work teams, comprising over 400 employees in the packaging department, and the development of several work redesign teams throughout the brewery. A further example of partnership with the union occurred recently (January 1994) when the company announced the adoption of an industry bottle. The company and the union proceeded to jointly phase out a $26 million bottle-sorting plant and to integrate 200 employees into the brewery with orientation and training provided by union and management.

Did the merger create value?

It took about three years to "officially" work out most of the changes regarding the integration of operations including the reorganization of the company. Despite the fact that it took longer than expected to get to that point all other benchmarks have been met. In addition to being the largest brewer in Canada, Molson is now also the lowest cost producer in its industry, having achieved a more efficient infrastructure of nine breweries from the original sixteen when the company was formed in August 1989. Rationalization activities have resulted in a $200 million decrease in annual operating costs compared to the situation that prevailed before the merger. Molson has maintained its dominant market position, at over 50 percent. It also has established a strong platform for growth in the United States. In attaining these results, not a single day of production was lost. Finally, a reorganization

of the company's salaried work force has resulted in a more flexible and efficient organizational structure that can better meet the challenges of the changing marketplace.

It is also important to note that an important outcome of this merger is that the most feared problems have not materialized, such as a loss of market share, a serious culture clash and the "us vs them" mentality. Differences between groups are still apparent in settings such as the cafeteria or in meetings. This indicates that the cultural integration is not yet completed.

A final consideration is that the way the merger process was managed provided an excellent basis for a whole range of changes that are now implemented in the company and which are not directly related to the merger itself. The transition structure put in place to facilitate the integration has been the springboard for technological changes, has led to the creation of task forces devoted to improving quality, and has resulted in a new partnership with the union; all are value creating outcomes for the company.

DISCUSSION AND CONCLUSION

As was mentioned in the first section of this chapter, organizations involved in a merger must face two important challenges. First, since such a dramatic event in an organization's life almost always brings a series of short- and long-term disruptions (e.g., loss of productivity, morale, and key employees), the acquiring and acquired firms must take actions to prevent and limit value leakage. The literature dealing with HR issues in M & A has emphasized the need to develop a value-preservation plan for each of the firms involved. The second challenge deals with the need to specifically develop and execute a value-creation plan mainly designed to integrate both firms and to realize the combination value expected between the two firms (Gosselin, 1987).

The Molson O'Keefe case provides an interesting illustration of how a firm involved in a successful merger managed the organizational and human resources issues to preserve and realize acquisition value. In addition, since the case addressed the merger of two large and direct competitors, with the goal of fully integrating their operations, it provided a dramatic example of a situation where the potential for value creation and destruction was particularly high. It also provided an opportunity to observe patterns of decisions and practices, and to examine them in light of what was suggested in the literature. We now discuss such observations with respect to preserving and realizing value.

The first observation that emerges from the case concerns the strategic importance given very early in the M & A process to organizational and human resources issues. Contrary to the systematic underestimation of such factors in most M & As, Molson O'Keefe considered these factors as crucial to the success or failure of the merger. This attention was given in spite of the fact that management was experiencing strong pressures to focus on financial and strategic issues. Specifically, Carling O'Keefe was experiencing severe financial problems and global pressures. Despite these pressures, they did not compromise organizational and human resources issues and were able to avoid the trap of focusing on short-term results only. Moreover the fact that the merger required the full operational and cultural integration of two close competitors who had known each other for decades can certainly explain why they gave such a high priority to these issues.

A vital concern in the case was the high potential loss of value created by the expected culture clash. As we mentioned earlier, in most M & As, people operate on barely sufficient information concerning their counterparts in the other firms and the other firm itself. For Molson O'Keefe this turned out not to be the case. Management was highly sensitive to this issue and attempted to manage it. However, this does not mean that people did not develop inaccurate and often negative stereotypes. There was a sincere concern about the development of a "superiority syndrome" or arrogance among people from Molson since they were after all financially rescuing Carling O'Keefe. If such a mentality had developed, the resulting culture clash would have endangered the long-term success of the merger. Molson O'Keefe opted for an innovative approach which called for the development of a new culture based on the best elements from each firm. Integration of cultures takes place through information exchange and increased interactions between members of both firms. Several steps were taken by Molson O'Keefe for increasing learning and understanding between members of merging organizations and avoiding excessive arrogance. These included blending the names of both firms, new logos, a challenging new strategic orientation disseminated to all employees, guided visits of both firms, and creation of joint problem-solving committees.

An implicit objective of all actions taken was to demonstrate that the merger was an alliance of two equals and not a takeover by one firm. In this regard, early in the merger, careful consideration was given to an equal distribution of power between the two new partners. Steps were taken to make sure that both firms were fairly represented in crucial decisions. For example, it was decided from the beginning that the proportion of employees coming from each firm at the end of the rationalization process would reflect their respective market share. Also, several joint transition teams, staffed by functional managers from both firms (e.g., information systems, HR), were created to analyze the way things were done in each firm and to make recommendations concerning how to combine comparable units (structure, systems, procedures). The overall objective of the teams was to manage the transition process to create a unified unit.

Complete, open, and early communications were also viewed as necessary for combating uncertainty and rumors, and their value-leaking effects. During the merging process, most employees were constantly searching their environment for information. This was why a sound communication plan was developed. The plan involved employees at all organizational levels. Two-way communications were established through a wide variety of media including employee meetings with senior managers, attitude surveys, telephone hot lines and transition newsletters. Information conveyed to people was straightforward and honest because it was believed that every employee should know where he or she stood as soon as possible. Another important aspect of the plan was the way the communication process was handled by senior managers. They were personally involved in communications and sent a signal to employees that management cares about and respects them.

Considerable attention was given to the retention of key people, including employees with critical skills or knowledge. In this case, it was necessary to not disturb production during the phasing and consolidation of plants. Stay packages were used as inducements for retaining key people for a specific period of time until the plant was completely shut down or until the organization could function without the expertise of these people. However, in contrast with communications and retention agreements, relatively less attention was given to managing employee trauma particularly for those who were not affected by layoffs. Interventions for managing merger trauma (stress management workshops, mourning/grieving, individual counseling, social support) have been limited.

It is now clear that the steps Molson O'Keefe took in order to avoid value leakage caused by the negative impacts of uncertainty, lowered employee morale, loss of productivity or high turnover were successful. But, what is often overlooked in M & As is that the disruptions they cause may create

an excellent opportunity to make profound changes that would have otherwise been difficult to realize. During M & As awareness of strategic issues facing the firm is generally high and people expect change.

Large-scale changes were begun at Molson O'Keefe and after more than four years are still taking place. In fact, people who we met in those firms mentioned that after a while it was difficult to assess the moment when the merging process ends. Such mergers between two direct competitors yield a profound revision of the structure, the culture, and the processes that cuts across all the functions and activities of both firms. Senior managers of Molson O'Keefe took the opportunity to redefine their mission and strategy, and more importantly for the first time, to begin a process of sharing their vision and values with the rest of the employees. As was suggested earlier, it is crucial that those responsible for creating value have a clear understanding of the true sources of value and the changes needed to capture them by setting realistic expectations and establishing priorities.

Restructuring and downsizing were by far the main activities undertaken to realize value. This is understandable considering the large number of redundancies that existed between the firms. Moreover, when a merger happens at the beginning of a long recession, as this one did, terminations in large numbers become difficult to avoid. Molson O'Keefe relied at first on voluntary turnover but had to consider layoffs as a last resort. As suggested in the literature, important steps were taken to ensure that layoffs were conducted in a fair and compassionate manner. Attractive severance pay, extended benefits, and outplacement assistance were offered to those who lost their jobs. When layoffs were not prevented by a labor contract, competency and performance were the formal criteria used to make layoff decisions. However, since we observed that layoffs happened in numbers proportional to the weight of each firm involved, one must conclude that balance also played some role in the decision as to who to lay off among nonexempt employees as well. In this case this criterion was important because it signaled a "merger of equals."

FINAL NOTE

Molson O'Keefe was successful in avoiding the chief sources of value destruction in a merger and on their way to realizing combination value. Management, however, had to devote considerable time and energy to make it happen by confronting critical organizational and human resources issues. Moreover they did so in a way that is consistent with recommendations in the M & A literature.

Preserving and realizing value require significant planning, listening, acting, and measuring over several years. Furthermore, by destabilizing the firms, the merger has also been the starting point of a series of radical changes that build upon the foundations provided by the early actions taken at the beginning of the 1990s. These changes will likely position Molson O'Keefe to compete more effectively in the future. People in Molson O'Keefe may not be referring as often to the merger as before, but their willingness and capacity to face the challenges ahead depend largely on how this phase in their organization's life was managed. So far little research has investigated the long-term impacts of alternative ways of preserving and realizing acquisition value for the long term. Clearly much additional work is needed in this area.

REFERENCES

Bastien, D. T. (1987). Common patterns of behavior and communication in corporate mergers and acquisitions. *Human Resource Management*, 26, 17–34.

Blake, R. R., & Mouton, J. S. (1984). *Solving Costly Organizational Conflicts: Achieving intergroup trust, cooperation, and teamwork.* San Francisco: Jossey-Bass.

Buono, A. F., & Bowditch, J. L. (1989). *The Human Side of Mergers and Acquisitions.* San Francisco: Jossey-Bass.

Chatterjee, S., Lubatkin, M., Schweiger, D. M., & Weber, Y. (1992). Cultural differences and shareholder value in related mergers: Linking equity and human capital. *Strategic Management Journal*, 13, 319–34.

Csiszar, E. N., & Schweiger, D. M. (1994). An integrative framework for creating value through acquisition. In H. E. Glass & B. N. Cavan (eds.), *Handbook of Business Strategy*, 93–115. New York: Warren, Gorham & Lamont.

Gosselin, A. (1987). Les contraintes à l'intégration des entreprises après une fusion ou une acquisition: comment 1 + 1 = 1 et 3. *Revue internationale de Gestion*.

Haspeslagh, P. C., & Jemison, D. B. (1991). *Managing Acquisitions: Creating value through corporate renewal.* New York: The Free Press.

Marks, M. L. (1988). Using I/O psychology to facilitate successful corporate mergers and acquisitions. Workshop given at the Society for Industrial/Organizational Psychology Meeting, Dallas, TX.

Marks, M. L., & Cutcliffe, J. G. (1988). Making mergers work. *Training and Development Journal*, 30–5.

Marks, M. L., & Mirvis, P. (1985). Merger syndrome: Stress and uncertainty. *Mergers and Acquisitions*, 20, 50–5.

Napier, N. K., Schweiger, D. M., & Kosglow, J. J. (1993). Managing organizational diversity: Observations from cross-border acquisitions. *Human Resource Management*, 32, 505–23.

Napier, N. K., Simmons, G., & Stratton, K. (1989). Communicating during a merger: Experience of two banks. *Human Resource Planning*. 12, 105–22.

Sales, A. L., & Mirvis, P. H. (1984). When cultures collide: Issues in acquisition. In J. R. Kimberly & R. E. Quinn (eds.), *Managing Organizational Transitions*, 107–33. Homewood, IL: Irwin.

Schweiger, D. M., Csiszar, E. N., & Napier, N. K. (1994). A strategic approach to implementing mergers and acquisitions. In G. Von Krog, A. Sinatra, and H. Singh (eds.), *The Management of Corporate Acquisitions: International perspectives*, 23–49. London: Macmillan.

Schweiger, D. M., & DeNisi, A. S. (1991). The effects of communication with employees following a merger: A longitudinal field experiment. *Academy of Management Journal*, 34, 110–35.

Schweiger, D. M., Ridley, J. R., & Marini, D. (1992). Creating one from two: The merger between Harris Semiconductor and General Electric Solid State. In S. E. Jackson (ed.), *Working through Diversity: Human resources initiatives*, 167–96. New York: Guilford Press.

Schweiger, D. M., Ritchie, M., & Csiszar, N. K. (1992). Integrating diverse workforces during an acquisition: The impact of socialization intervention on employees. Paper presented at the National Meeting of the Academy of Management, Las Vegas.

Schweiger, D. M., & Walsh, J. P. (1990). Mergers and acquisitions: An interdisciplinary view. In G. R. Ferris, & K. M. Rowland (eds.), *Research in Personnel and Human Resource Management*, vol. 8, pp. 41–107. Greenwich, CT: JAI Press.

Schweiger, D. M., & Weber, Y. (1989). Strategies for managing human resources during mergers and acquisitions: An empirical study. *Human Resources Planning*, 12, 69–86.

Tichy, N. M. (1983). *Managing Strategic Change: Technical, political and cultural dynamics.* New York: Wiley.

☐ Chapter 17 ☐

Organizational Culture and Human Resource Management

Dave O. Ulrich and Frank LaFasto

INTRODUCTION

In 1988, Jack Welch, chairman of General Electric (GE) Company, formally began the phase of his company's cultural transformation called "Workout." Workout was the culmination and evolution of Welch's commitment to transforming the General Electric Company. The explicit goal of Workout was to change the fundamental ways in which GE did business – to build into every decision and organizational act the "cultural" values of *speed, simplicity,* and *self-confidence.*

To help with this transformation, Welch assembled a highly respected group of academics and consultants to work as team leaders with assigned GE businesses and frame the cultural transformation process. The group met quarterly to plan and review the progress of the culture change effort in each GE business, and their collective experience served as the foundation for an overall GE culture change effort.

One of the discussions in an early meeting provided some interesting insights into the concept and practice of large-scale culture change in 1989. In a casual setting with about

fifteen of the team leaders, someone asked the question: "Can we name companies that have successfully completed or engaged in a culture change without a business crisis, so that we can learn from their experience and apply it to the GE context?" In the room were authors of more than twenty-five books and hundreds of articles with many years of consulting experience. Yet, when we tried to identify companies that had successfully transformed their culture, our list was very short. We could identify companies that had created new cultures (e.g., Apple, Intel, Microsoft, etc.) but, for the most part, these were companies that *started with new cultures,* not companies that had *transformed* them. We also could identify companies that had come back from the brink of disaster (e.g., Harley Davidson) to emerge as more competitive, but these companies were more turnarounds than transformations. It quickly became apparent that the concept of culture change, which was academically popularized in the 1980s (Deal & Kennedy, 1982; Schein, 1985; Martin, Feldman, Hatch, & Sitkin, 1983; Barney, 1986), had not yet fully taken hold in the business world in 1989. While academics wrote about culture change, and executives talked about it, neither group had yet fully experienced it.

Since 1989, commitment to culture change has changed dramatically. No longer is it the abstract "non-imitable competitive advantage" talked about in academic circles, but rather the heart of what many chief executives define as their primary mission. For example, in the cover story of *Fortune* (December 14, 1993), four CEOs (John F. Welch of General Electric, Lawrence Bossidy of Allied Signal, William Weiss of Ameritech, and Michael Walsh of Tenneco) talk at length about how important culture change is for their firms and how central it is to the success of their tenure as CEO. What's more, a number of consulting firms have expanded exponentially their "change management" practices (e.g., Index, Gemini, Anderson, McKenzie) in response to the many organizations attempting culture change. One consulting firm claims it will need to hire 12,000 additional consultants primarily to handle client demand for consulting advice on culture change (often called renewal, reinvention, transformation, or reengineering).

In the last few years, then, we have learned a great deal about culture change – theory and practice. In this chapter we address the question: What can human resources do to help facilitate culture change? We will explore the role of human resources (HR) at two levels: *HR practices* that might need to be modified to allow culture change to happen and *HR professionals* who need to play an activist role in order to bring about culture change. To answer our question, we will (1) review the concept and importance of culture change; (2) discuss approaches to creating culture change; (3) identify ways in which HR practices compel culture change; (4) identify roles for HR professionals in bringing about culture change; and (5) conclude with lessons learned about culture change in large complex firms.

THE CONCEPT AND IMPORTANCE OF CULTURE CHANGE

What is culture?

There are as many definitions of culture as there are writers about it.[1] Some definitions view culture as unchangeable: that is, the underlying values which are embedded and rooted in the history of the firm (Smircich, 1983); others view culture as totally malleable: that is, behaviors and practices of employees within a firm (Davis, 1984). In a simplistic way, managers who want to understand organizational culture are trying to answer the question: Why do organizations do what they do?

Cultural discussions begin with a simple premise: Organizations don't act, people do. Therefore, understanding organizational culture requires discerning the shared mind-set – or "automatic thoughts" – that individuals within the organization share (Brockbank & Ulrich, 1988; Ulrich & Lake, 1990). Automatic thoughts represent the unconscious ways individuals in organizations act and think. Simply put, they are a reflection of "the way things are done."

Automatic thoughts may be embedded in four organizational processes: work flow, communication/information flow, authority/decision-making/authority flow, and human resources flow.

Work flow refers to how work is distributed and performed within the organization. Automatic thoughts about work flow can be understood by considering the following questions:

1. Does the organization encourage work to be done by individuals or by teams? Some organizations instill automatic thoughts about individuals working independently; others attempt to build teams within divisions, across units, and across boundaries.

318

2. To what extent does the organization have the capacity to change? Some organizations respond quickly to change; some try to buffer themselves from it. Employees within the organization tend to evolve a set of automatic thoughts about how quickly changes are made. Changes may be in organization structures, reporting relationships, product developments, technologies, or working patterns. The issue is the capacity of an organization to adapt to change.

3. How does the organization deal with waste and productivity? Some organizations create automatic thoughts that accept waste and current standards of productivity as givens; others become obsessed with eliminating waste and continuously improving productivity.

4. How does the organization deal with work priorities? Some organizations try to be all things to all people for fear of excluding an individual or division. Other organizations' work processes encourage public prioritization of projects and activities.

Communication/information flow refers to how information is created and shared within the organization. It can be understood by asking the following questions:

1. How much information is shared in the organization? Some organizations are very open about their plans, directions, and processes. Other organizations keep plans numbered so no one without authorization will see them.

2. What are the information-sharing patterns within the organization? Some organizations share information one-way – from top to bottom; others develop accepted ways of sharing information that move in all directions: side to side, top to bottom, and bottom to top. The information-sharing pattern of an organization may reflect the automatic thoughts about how work gets done.

3. What is the means of communication flow? Some organizations share information primarily face to face; others use electronic mail, memos, or other secondary means. The means of information sharing often communicate how the organization gets work done.

Authority/decision-making flow deals with how decisions are made and where authority resides in the organization. It can be discerned with the following questions:

1. Where are critical decisions made in the organization – at the top or bottom levels? The location of decisions about resource allocation, strategic direction, hiring, budgets, firing, and other critical decisions are indicators of an organization's shared means for doing work. Some organizations have automatic thoughts that most, if not all, decisions are entrusted to top managers and middle managers, whereas employees are primarily responsible for making recommendations and carrying out plans. Other organizations have more distributed authority and decision making, with employees carrying more responsibility and ownership for decisions. The extent of employee participation and involvement in formulating decisions may become an automatic thought process among organizational employees.

2. What is the speed of decision making? Some organizations have automatic thoughts and accepted norms that allow decisions, once identified, to be made quickly; others take months of debate, discussion, and dialogue before arriving at a decision. Organizations are often characterized as bureaucratic or open based on this dimension.

3. How does the organization balance short- and long-term implications of decisions? Some organizations focus exclusively on short-term decisions and consequences; others primarily on the long-term. Most organizations, however, find some balance between the two.

4. How does the organization ensure accountability for decision making? Over time an organization develops expectations for

how accountable individuals are for decisions made. Some organizations absolve individuals of accountability; others emphasize it. Employees are likely to develop a set of automatic thoughts about the extent of accountability.

Human resources flow deals with how people are treated within the organization as suggested by the following questions:

1. How does the organization deal with managerial or employee failure? Does it allow for employees to take risks and fail or does it punish failure and limit risk taking? One senior manager argued convincingly that how an organization deals with managers who fail is a critical indicator of the "culture" of the organization. He contended that an organization can be too lenient and not have any consequences for failure; or be too strict and, in effect, "kill the messenger." He argued that either extreme is a strong indicator of the company's overall willingness to change and adapt to new ideas. A parallel issue to failure is success. How does an organization manage an employee's success? Does the organization reward the individual or the team? Does the organization publicize and laud success or quietly accept it as part of business practice?

2. What is the source of the organization's employee competence? Some organizations generate competence primarily by buying talent from other firms; others generate competence through training and development of their employees. The means of generating competence is often an indicator of an organization's people flow.

3. How effectively does the organization encourage and manage diversity? One critical people flow issue relates to the ways in which the organization encourages diversity. Diversity may occur in obvious areas such as race or gender, but it also may occur in issues such as cultural, global, and philosophical diversity. Some organizations try to identify diversity, then quickly eliminate it; others encourage diversity.

4. How does the organization treat individuals? Some organizations tend to treat individuals as replaceable parts, which can and should be bought or sold as commodities. Other organizations treat individuals as long-term critical investments, which should be nurtured and maintained.

5. What is the commitment of the employee to the organization and the organization to the employee? Employees have choices about what firm they join and stay with. Employee commitment to a firm may be based on some combination of economics ("this organization pays more"), relationships ("this organization is an enjoyable place to work, and I like my colleagues"), or vision ("this organization is an exciting place to be"). The basis of employee commitment indicates an underlying sense of the processes used for getting work done within the organization.

Shared mind-set about each of these four processes (and others) comes from information and behavior (see figure 17.1). Information provides employees data on what automatic thoughts are expected. The more information employees have, the more likely they are to have a shared mind-set. Information may come from a variety of sources ranging from formal HR systems to informal discussions among employees. The more credible and consistent the information, the more likely the mind-set is to be shared. At Harley Davidson, for example, when Richard Teerlink, the chairman, speaks about the importance of a learning organization, he is credible (after all, Teerlink *is* the chairman) and consistent (he constantly reiterates the same message, and he builds it into his training and performance management programs). As a result, the shared mind-set within Harley about creating a learning organization is higher than in many other organizations.

Behavior provides employees with signals as to what actions are expected. Behavior develops as employees act consistently within the shared mind-set. Action can occur through

Figure 17.1 A model for cognitive and culture change

	Causes of automatic thoughts	Automatic thoughts	Action
	• Information • Experience/behavior		
Individual issues	What information and/or behavioral experiences have we had with the activity that affect the automatic thought?	What mental images (automatic thoughts) come to mind when thinking about a particular issue?	Why do individuals do some activities with more enthusiasm than others?
Organizational issues	What information and/or behavior experiences are offered organizational stakeholders to reinforce the automatic thoughts?	What mental images (automatic thoughts) are shared among organizational stakeholders? To what extent are they shared? • Work flow • Information flow • Decision-making flow • Human resources flow Source of automatic thoughts: • Internal (among employees) • External (among customers and other stakeholders)	What unity of action exists among organizational stakeholders?

formal HR practices or informal meetings. At Harley Davidson, Rich Teerlink has institutionalized his commitment to learning through Harley University, where leadership development courses translate his values into action: through a performance effectiveness program, in which Teerlink's learning values are translated to individual performance review; and through a new organization where shared learning has become the glue that holds the organization together.

Shared mind-set may occur either inside the organization, among employees, or outside the organization, between employees and customers or suppliers. A fully shared mind-set exists when employees inside and customers or suppliers outside the organization have similar automatic thoughts about the above organizational processes. Shared mind-set may also exist at different levels of an organization. It may exist for an overall organization or for any entity within the organization (e.g., a division, business, function, etc.).

Although difficult to do, a shared mind-set may be changed through the use of information and behavior. The outcome of a shared mind-set is to change how people think and act within an organization. To change a shared mind-set, executives must send new information signals and/or change employee behavior.

Why does culture matter?

Two assumptions frame a rationale for cultural change. First, *culture affects the performance of a business* (Kotter & Heskett, 1992). If employees have a shared culture, they are more likely to be unified in their actions. Unity of action will help a business to be more focused and better able to penetrate markets, meet customer requirements, and accomplish strategic goals. In general, the more a culture is shared, the more likely the business will succeed. However, the cultural consensus and performance curve is more complex than a mere linear relationship.

In figure 17.2, we show that at times firms may have a "stronger" (more unified) culture, but their performance may actually drop (Path B), whereas other firms have a stronger culture and their performance continues to rise (Path A). The difference between firms on Path A and Path B illustrates that mere cultural consensus is not enough; it must be the *right* culture. Firms on Path B (i.e., more consensus, lower performance) may focus their culture on honoring and maintaining their traditions, not changing to new norms, focusing on internal processes, and encouraging the "one size fits all" approach. Firms on Path A (i.e., more consensus, greater performance) focus their culture on changing customer expectations, valuing diversity, reinventing the corporation, and constantly reassessing and rebuilding culture.

It is easy to identify firms that have gone down Path B: They have become stuck in their past, not renewing themselves for their future. In contrast, executives of firms on Path A are consumed with renewal, with change, and with recreation of their culture. Rich Teerlink of Harley Davidson, for example, sees as one of his primary roles creating a learning organization throughout Harley, where old values are practiced to maintain integrity with Harley's past, at the same time that new values which predict Harley's future are being learned.

Cultural unity also affects performance by focusing employees *on the right issues*. Cultural unity around the wrong values can be likened to getting to a party early, but arriving at the wrong house. When a firm's culture is aligned with the expectations of customers, then employees are focused on the right issues, and that focus will improve business performance. At Digital Equipment Corporation, the "hub" cultural statement for decades was to "value differences." This cultural hub permeated management processes. Rather than depend on rules and procedures to guide decision making, managers disagreed, debated, and explored alternatives to ensure that

Figure 17.2 Cultural unity and performance

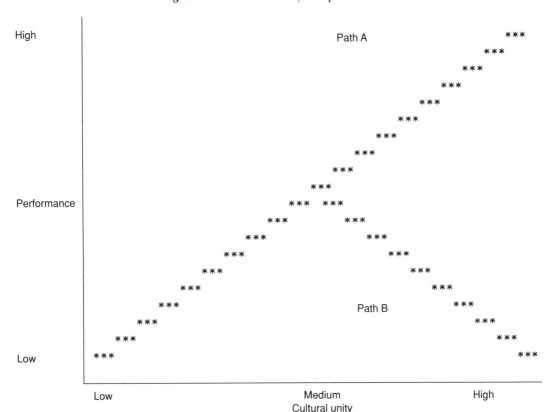

differences were valued. The "valuing differences" cultural hub worked for Digital because of the market they were in. It would not work for an organization like the Federal Aviation Administration (FAA), where the cultural hub has always been stability, precision, and rigor. The FAA culture of discipline, dedication to rules, and accuracy fits its business requirements just as Digital's more open culture suited them.

Because of the unity that comes from a strong culture, cultures become the "fingerprints" of organizations. They become the means by which employees, customers, suppliers, and investors identify organizations. For employees, the cultural fingerprint offers a sense of identity or a feeling of pride in the way they work for their company. These

fingerprints also provide an organization with marketplace acceptance. In the computer industry, for example, where cultural differentiators are equated with "brand equity," the following corporate cultures were identified:

Apple	simple . . . easy . . . friendly
Bull	challenger . . .
Fujitsu	Japanese . . . reliable . . . multiactivity
Hewlett Packard	quality . . . value
IBM	safe choice . . . tried and true
Microsoft	creative . . . easy to use . . . successful
Sun	hot . . . powerful

John Scully, who has headed up both Pepsico and Apple Computer, described Pepsico's and Apple's missions as that of creating "share of mind" not just "market share." The Apple and Pepsico cultures were created to define and distinguish their companies in the marketplace.

Cultures, or fingerprints, are unique to each firm. Competitors who try to mimic or copy cultures generally end up as also-rans with little uniqueness or identity. As businesses try to identify new ways to differentiate themselves from competitors, the cultural fingerprint becomes a viable alternative. When businesses reach technological parity, and one business can copy another's technology; when businesses reach product parity, and one business can copy another's product features; when businesses reach financial parity and one business can gain equal access to capital – then the cultural fingerprint may become a viable source of differentiation.

The second assumption about culture change is that *old ways are not new ways.* If businesses existed in static worlds, cultures could be formed and formalized. In reality, businesses exist in increasingly complex and dynamic worlds. As a result, cultures that matched old business needs must give way to cultures that reflect current market trends. The greatest challenge for company cultures is not in defining or molding them, but in being able to constantly adapt them. At Digital, for example, the "valuing differences" hub culture was viable during a dynamic and growing market. In the early 1990s, when the global computer market declined and consolidated, this "valuing differences" culture was complemented by an "accountability" focus. Robert Palmer, the chairman in 1992, encouraged all Digital employees to be "accountable" to employees, customers, and shareholders. While not denying the importance of valuing diversity and Digital's legacy, Palmer evolved the culture to changing business conditions.

A key to culture change is to recognize that

it must fit changing business requirements. New business cultures are not easy to instill. Not surprisingly, employees are much more comfortable following familiar habits. Old shoes fit better than new shoes; old work patterns are more comforting than new ones. An essential rationale for cultural change is to learn to throw away old shoes that may feel good but be doing damage to one's feet; to replace old comforting ways of work with new competitive ways of work. Just as people's attics are filled with sentimental mementos, organizations are engulfed by old cultures that feel cozy, but fail to respond to change. If they are to move forward, organizations must learn to let go of old cultures and make room for new ones.

APPROACHES TO CREATING CULTURE CHANGE

Making culture change happen has become less magical and more practical in recent years, as firms have embarked on a variety of culture change efforts. Based on the experience of a number of firms, there seem to be three types of culture change efforts (see figure 17.3). Each of these types shares information with and shapes behavior of employees in order to instill new automatic thoughts into the organization.

Top-down: directive

Action on a new culture or mind-set may be directed and driven from the top of the organization down throughout the organization. Culture change initiatives of this type are often sponsored by the senior executives, implemented through a mix of HR processes (e.g., training programs, reward or compensation programs, or corporatewide communication efforts), and cascaded throughout the organization.

Many companies use this type of culture change to implement a quality-focused culture. Baxter Healthcare Corporation, for

Figure 17.3 Types of cultural change

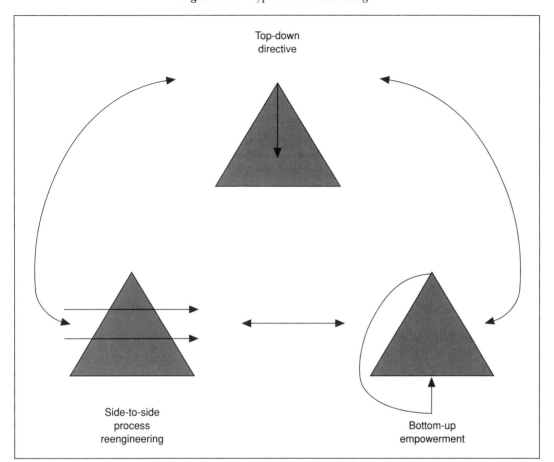

Top-down
directive

Side-to-side
process
reengineering

Bottom-up
empowerment

example, manufactures and distributes more than 120,000 health-care products – from heart valves to IV solutions – in over one hundred countries worldwide. Vernon R. Loucks, Jr., chairman and CEO, recognizes that quality is absolutely essential to the confidence customers have in Baxter – not only in terms of the product itself but in Baxter's ability as a distributor to deliver precisely the right product at the right time.

To create this high level of confidence, Loucks began a top-down quality process in the early 1980s, requiring the entire organization be trained in the quality leadership process. Since that time the concept of quality has been consistently included in Baxter's mission, its business strategies, and organizational values and practices.

A greater commitment to quality throughout the organization has become a goal at Xerox as well (Howard, 1992). Under CEO David Kearn's direction, Xerox implemented a Leadership Through Quality program. The program was cascaded throughout the organization following a L-U-T-I model: Managers at one level *L*earned the tools of quality; then *U*sed the tools in their business; then *T*aught the tools to employees the level below them; and, finally, *I*nspected to make sure that the tools were being used. In theory, no one could attend the quality program before his or her supervisor because the supervisor was the teacher of the program.

Companies continue to use the top-down directive approach to implement culture change. Boeing Corporation, for example, ran thousands of managers through a World Class Competitiveness program to communicate the changing competitive rules in the airframe business. Motorola's Six Sigma program used training and performance management initiatives to communicate the standards of its new quality-driven culture. Allied Signal's Total Quality initiative will result in all 85,000 employees being exposed to a quality framework. Pepsi's compensation program, Sharepower, ensures that every employee has some form of stock ownership in the firm as a way of increasing commitment to success.

Each of these programs attempts culture change through top-down directive initiatives. The good news about these programs is that they offer consistent, corporatewide messages about the importance of the new culture. They also institutionalize the new culture through HR practices that share information and may shape employee behavior. The challenge to these mandated initiatives is that they are often seen as isolated events in which employees are dipped in the culture for a period of time (e.g., the duration of the training) but are not fully converted to it. A series of isolated events may add up to more cynicism than culture change. In one company, middle managers who were constantly exposed to new corporate programs began to call them "AFPs" (another fine program), failing to realize that the programs were intended to change the mind-set within the company.

Top-down directives are most likely to lead to culture change when there is absolute commitment and dedication from top management; when the various programs are integrated into an overall architecture for change; and when the information from the initiatives translates to employee behavior (Howard, 1992). Top-down directives are less likely to lead to culture change when they are isolated events; when they are not clearly linked to business success; and when they are more focused on expanding minds than changing mind-sets.

Side-to-side: process reengineering

In recent years, a popular approach to culture change has focused on reengineering business processes (Hammer, 1990; Hammer & Champy, 1993). This approach focuses less on top-down directives and programs for culture change and more on examining the processes for doing work within an organization. Process reengineering begins by examining how work is done, then systematically improves the processes for doing work through streamlining operations, leveraging automation, reducing redundancies, and improving line of sight between work flow and customers.

Process reengineering has been used in a number of firms with dramatic results. Pepsico identified 16 core processes within its organization (e.g., ordering, distributing) then worked aggressively to streamline the way in which those processes were carried out. This streamlining resulted in enormous cost savings as work was done more efficiently, faster, with fewer resources, and greater customer payoff.

Process reengineering has been applied to HR processes as well as business processes. For example, in 1993, a lateral team of HR professionals at Baxter Healthcare Corporation decided to reengineer Baxter's HR systems and processes from ground zero, the goal being to place as many decisions as possible in the hands of employees and managers. A six-month effort, during which 12 members of the reengineering team devoted two full days a week to the project, resulted in the elimination of more than 150 steps from the seven main components of Baxter's human resources function:

compensation; benefits; training and development; health and safety; employee relations; staffing; and human resources information systems.

At Northern Telecom, process reengineering work has resulted in the consolidation of many HR administrative duties into a service center where employee needs are met at a high standard through a shared set of resources. This move reduced the duplication of resources, streamlined the organization, and saved money for the company while ensuring that employees (i.e., customers of the process in this case) continued to have their needs met. In another firm, it was discovered that there were 23 separate registration systems for attending training programs. Consolidating these separate systems into a single process reduced costs at the same time as it improved the efficiency of registering employees for training programs.

Process approaches to culture change assume that as processes are examined and reengineered, the new processes will bring with them a new culture or mind-set. The advantages of the process approach to culture change are that the changes should be relatively permanent; the new processes result in clear business deliverables; and the processes will force new information and behavior to occur among employees. The downside of process improvement is that to map and change even seemingly simple processes often requires an enormous amount of time and management attention. It may also take a long time for employees to see and feel the results. In addition, reengineering efforts often rely on technical experts (e.g., outside consultants) to map a process, and then improve it.

Reengineered processes lead to culture change when executives have the patience to examine and improve the processes; when the processes are clearly differentiated so that they can be improved; and when those involved in reengineering the processes have the skills and authority to make changes.

Reengineering efforts may go awry when employees lose patience in mapping processes without seeing results; when each process to be reengineered leads to an endless loop of other processes; or when those doing the reengineering have technical expertise, but lack the political sensitivity to make the change last. Just changing a process does not ensure that the culture has changed. Once the pressure for process improvement leaves, without a changed mind-set in those who are doing the new process, old processes are likely to creep back in.

Bottom-up: empowerment

A third type of culture change develops when the desired culture is quickly translated to employee action. This approach to culture change may be illustrated with a simple metaphor based on what you would do if you were going for a walk and a mosquito landed on your arm: The top-down (directive) approach to making sure that mosquitos do not attack would be to set up a government program to train people not to go where mosquitos are, to wear long-sleeve shirts, and to study the causes of the problem. The side-to-side process approach would be to reinvent and reengineer efforts to drain the swamps, spray for mosquitos, and make sure that mosquitos no longer attack. The bottom-up empowerment approach would be to kill the mosquito when it landed on your arm.

Empowerment approaches to culture change are not new, but they have received increasing attention through work in companies such as General Electric. The Workout program at General Electric lays out a desired mind-set. Jack Welch, GE's chairman, wants GE to be known for speed, simplicity, and self-confidence by customers and employees in all lines of business. To make this happen, he empowered thousands of employees to take out "low hanging fruit," or work that was counter to the new culture. For example, bureaucratic reports, meetings, approvals, and measures often were counter to the new culture. Through "town meetings," GE employees identified things they could immediately change (like killing the mosquito) to behave according to the new culture (Beatty & Ulrich, 1991).

Successful empowerment approaches to culture change are more than gripe sessions where employees come together to complain about what is wrong with the firm; they are built on the principle of "no blaming, no complaining," which means that if you don't like what is wrong, you can blame someone else or complain about it, but you have to fix it. These new approaches are more than suggestion systems in which employees offer random suggestions for improvements; they are focused on translating a specific mind-set into employee behaviors. They are more than a series of isolated discussion groups – each offering opinions about how to improve work: They are an integrated set of activities that empower employees to act based on the new culture.

In one organization an HR function applied the empowerment approach to creating a new mind-set within the function. The HR leadership council articulated the mind-set of the function, to be known as a valued partner in building organizational capability for business competitiveness. With this mind-set, the leadership team then went to groups of HR professionals and asked them to identify things they could start, stop, and continue doing to make the new mind-set a reality. These functional town meetings focused on what people could do within their own span of control to make the new mind-set real.

Empowerment approaches to culture change work when management trusts employees to make decisions relative to the new culture; when employees have not only commitment to the new culture, but the competence to deliver it; and when instant successes lead to further successes. Empowerment approaches fail when the results of a town meeting become isolated events, when the

outcomes of the town meetings do not last beyond the event itself, or when the managers who are open to new ideas in town meeting settings fail to practice the same behavior in the work setting.

Integrating the approaches to culture change

None of the three approaches to culture change is pure; no firm does one at the exclusion of the other two. However, many firms focus on one and may miss the benefits of using multiple approaches to culture change. Executives who act on new cultures may begin with any of the three approaches, but they need to quickly learn to use the other two to offer a holistic approach to instilling a new mind-set. By using all three approaches in parallel, employees receive information and shape behavior that leads to sustained culture change.

Baxter Healthcare Corporation provides a good example of a company integrating all three approaches to culture change, beginning with (a) a top-down approach to instilling quality values, strategies, and operations throughout the organization; (b) lateral team-based reengineering efforts to simplify operations, address issues, and improve quality; and (c) a bottom-up approach in which all employees are encouraged to identify and explore all quality initiatives – the goal being continuous improvement and simplification. Baxter's overall approach to quality – in product development, manufacturing, distribution, and sales to the marketplace – creates an environment in which employees are empowered to challenge the status quo in favor of quality improvement.

HUMAN RESOURCES PRACTICES AND CULTURE CHANGE

To create and sustain a culture change, HR practices must be modified. The reason why

Figure 17.4   Human resources practices, information and behavior

HR practice	Information	Behavior
Staffing	Provides employees information cues about types of employees who are valued in the organization by seeing who is hired, promoted, or outplaced.	Encourages behaviors that will be hired into the organization, be promoted through the organization, and be retained in the organization.
Development	Trains and develops employees in programs that signal which information and behavior is appropriate.	Encourages employees to behave in patterns consistent with training and development programs.
Appraisal	Standards, feedback, and processes send signals to employees about valued automatic thoughts.	Fosters behavior consistent with the standards set in the appraisal process.
Rewards	Reward processes send information cues to employees about what is valued.	Rewards favor employees who behave in ways consistent with the goals and values of the organization, so employees act in ways consistent with rewards.
Organization design	Roles, rules, policies, and other organization design issues communicate to employees what is desired.	Organizational structure predicts how employees will spend time and act within the organization.
Communications	Communications programs share with employees.	Communication programs teach employees what behaviors are important to foster and which should be stopped.

HR practices are so critical to culture change draws on our cognitive definition of culture in figure 17.2. In the logic of cognition, mindsets are created by information and behavior/ experience. In parallel, cultures are built on the information and shared experiences of employees within the firm. We believe that HR practices provide information and shape behavior and experiences of employees. By so doing, HR practices become the means whereby cultures are created and sustained. The summary of this logic is shown in figure 17.4. The following examples show how a variety of companies have used HR practices to shape their culture.

Staffing

Staffing – based on the premise that "strategy follows people" – shapes a culture by bringing new ideas and insights into the corporation. At Rubbermaid Corporation, Stanley Gault replaced 160 of 161 top positions. At Allied Signal, Larry Bossidy identified 128 key jobs in the company, then changed out 69 of those positions. In both cases, the new hires came with not only technical competence, but with a new mind-set and focus. Warren Wilhelm, then at Amoco Corporation (now at Allied Signal), described the process of filling targeted executive positions with candidates from outside the firm as "plugging your lawn" (Wilhelm, 1990). This process sends a clear message to those executives inside the firm about what it means to be successful. Over time, staffing decisions become more than messages and actually change the behavior of employees within the firm.

Baxter Healthcare's Executive Development Review (EDR) process ensures that for all senior management openings, serious management discussions occur to define what competencies are required to fill the position; what competencies exist inside the organization to meet the needs, and what processes can be used to backfill future positions. By spending time and money on the EDR process, Baxter has worked to build a strong pool of candidates from which to draw future leaders of the firm.

The most basic premise of using the staffing process as a tool for culture change is that without the right technical and cultural competencies, cultures will not sustain a change. In a popular version of this phenomenon, John Grisham's novel, *The Firm*, provides an example of a law firm that did not do an adequate job screening job candidates, ultimately leading to employee morale problems. Our colleague Steve Kerr, Clinical Professor at the University of Michigan, once said that if staffing decisions were always 100 percent correct (for the current and future technical and cultural competencies of the firm), no other HR practices would ever be necessary. Unfortunately, the percentage of correct decisions is usually much lower. Peter Drucker talks about hitting scores in the 33 percent range (Drucker, 1988), which suggests that other HR practices must come into play as well.

Development

Development attempts to sustain culture change through both individual and organizational learning. Individual learning implies that employees acquire the competencies necessary to do their work through some form of development experience. Development experiences may range from classroom training to job assignments to task force participation. From these experiences individuals may learn more about how to manage in a changing environment. At PPG, they have developed a career stages competence matrix that indicates the specific competencies an employee should have at each career stage. The competencies are tied to the core values of PPG. Employees can position themselves in the matrix and identify the competencies they need to acquire in order to be successful at their career stage. Each cell of the matrix is then tied to a development experience, either training or assignment, so that an employee can create a self-directed learning plan.

For senior executives, structured learning experiences may occur where executives' ideas and assumptions are challenged and modified over time. At Champion International, a series of three executive experiences have been designed for the top 150 executives. Over a period of about four years, all Champion executives experience six weeks of tailored executive development seminars in which a team of faculty members challenges assumptions and practices in finance, strategy, marketing, manufacturing, and human resources. The intent of these courses is to challenge current practices and to change thought processes of Champion's future executives.

Learning also occurs through development for the organization as a whole. Organizational learning occurs when ideas are generated and generalized throughout an organization (Ulrich, von Glinow, & Jick, 1993). General Electric has created a series of forums in which "best practices" are identified and shared across business unit boundaries. These workshops provide a means of sharing learning throughout the organization. Often, instead of attending as individuals, teams come to the workshops to learn the principles of a successful organization and their application to their immediate work setting.

Development builds competence in both individuals and organizations through a focus on learning. As a culture change mechanism, development experiences ensure that employees know what is expected of them and that they have the skills to deliver on the new expectations. At Digital Equipment Corporation, even in the face of economic challenges, CEO Bob Palmer is investing heavily in a development and learning agenda. This agenda will ensure that all Digital managers know what is expected of them and that they have an opportunity to acquire the skills necessary to succeed in a new culture.

Appraisal/rewards

Appraisal and rewards define the performance standards within a firm. For a cultural transformation to be sustained, managers and employees must not only experiment with new behaviors, but be rewarded for exhibiting them. Sustained culture change occurs when reward systems are modified to reinforce desired behaviors (Kerr & Slocum, 1987). There are two fundamental parts to the performance management process: appraisals that establish standards, and rewards that remunerate and award employees.

At Federal Express, a key competitive advantage is customer-perceived service quality. The company has established a service quality index that measures ten key elements of customer service and is communicated daily to all employees. Hewlett Packard measures its commitment to employee quality by assigning it as a critical corporate hoshin (pri-

ority) and using employee-attitude surveys to track progress. As Schneier, Shaw, and Beatty (1991) point out, the first step in performance management is to ensure that critical success factors are defined for successful strategy execution. They review a number of measures used by firms to drive performance: reducing the product development cycle at Rubbermaid; number of days to set up the bottling operation in a country for Coca Cola; the number of direct labor hours needed to produce a car for General Motors. Without complete, accurate, strategic, and measurable performance standards, reward systems will inevitably fail.

The second step in performance management is to make sure that rewards are linked to performance measures. Numerous types of rewards may be allocated to motivate employees. Steve Kerr describes three generic types of rewards that may be used: financial, prestige, and the work itself. Financial rewards generally include some form of profit sharing or economic sharing. To make sure that all employees were aware of and committed to firm performance, Pepsi developed a program called Sharepower in which every employee in the firm was allocated stock based on overall firm performance. Sara Lee requires that all managers own stock in the firm to ensure their commitment to the publicly traded firm as if it were a private firm. When Borg Warner went through a leveraged buyout, managers were required to acquire stock in the firm, thereby increasing their commitment to firm peformance. All of these compensation practices attempt to remunerate employees for behaving in ways that meet firm goals.

To make a culture change last long term, employees need to have incentives that reinforce new behaviors. Some of these incentives are economic, some psychic. Ameritech's "break out" program was designed to empower employees to assume more risk-taking responsibility. These actions were designed to help employees increase commitment to

Ameritech through participation in decision-making processes. Without changing reward and recognition systems, the Ameritech culture change would not be sustained.

Organization design

Organization design deals with how decisions are made, roles are fulfilled, and responsibilities allocated. Culture change often requires new organizational configurations. These configurations are based less on rules and more on responsiveness, less on span of control and more on span of commitment, less on hierarchy and more on flexibility. New organizational forms include the spider web, network organization, cluster organization, customer-focused organization, and virtual organization (Quinn, 1993; Whiteley, 1993; Davidow & Malone, 1992).

A core component of all these organizations is the ability to design and deliver work through high-performing work teams (Larson & LaFasto, 1989; Katzenbach & Smith, 1993). An excellent example of the productivity of teamwork comes from Baxter Healthcare Corporation where team selling has replaced individual selling with incredible results.

As one of the world's leading health-care companies, Baxter has more than 40 operating units, and it manufactures and distributes a line of health-care products capable of satisfying more than 70 percent of a hospitalized patient's needs. With the evolution of the health-care marketplace, it became apparent during the mid-1980s that a hospital customer required simplified access to Baxter's many products and services. As it was, sales representatives from the numerous operating units within Baxter were bumping into each other in the lobbies of hospitals. Indeed, it was not unusual to have as many as a dozen sales reps calling on the same hospital purchasing agent.

In 1987 Baxter's human resources function developed a research-based team-building process and began to introduce it throughout the organization, beginning with senior management. In 1988, human resources teamed up with corporate sales and marketing to explore the appropriateness of using teamwork as a sales strategy.

In April 1988, 120 sales reps from various divisions met at Baxter Headquarters and listened to chairman and CEO Vernon R. Loucks, Jr., talk about a changing health-care marketplace that required simplified access to Baxter by its hospital customers. The sales reps were divided into seven teams and were given teamwork training by human resources. During the remainder of 1988 these seven teams demonstrated improved sales results. By 1990 Baxter had created 90 such teamwork accounts, 10 in each of its nine U.S. geographic regions. And by 1993, sales and customer satisfaction results were so dramatic that Baxter has now redesigned its entire domestic hospital sales force into regional teams. In support of this new team-selling approach, the entire sales force of 2,200 people is provided advanced training in building collaborative teams. This training is now based on 15 years of research conducted by Baxter's HR function in conjunction with the University of Denver (LaFasto & Larson, 1993).

Another good example of the importance of teams comes from Eastman Kodak's experience in its black-and-white film division (Frangos, 1993). Kodak found that as it reshaped the organization into teams and shared responsibility, direction, and action with the teams, work performance increased dramatically. A critical part of the culture change within this Kodak division was based on the team concept of shared responsibility and accountability.

Chubb & Sons, one of the world's largest insurance brokers, has been successful for more than 100 years through a "dual accountability" organization structure. This structure was a classic matrix, incorporating both geographic (regional) and technical (underwriting) experts. As they began to face stiffer competition from direct mail insurers (e.g., USAA, Nationwide), Chubb executives realized that they would have to be even more customer-focused. As a result, they have begun to implement a customer account team structure that organizes an account team of expert resources to serve and anticipate customer demands. This structure should drive the customer-focused culture change throughout Chubb.

Communication

At the heart of all culture change efforts are communication requirements. Communication ensures that all employees not only *know*, but *feel* the importance of culture change. In every case of culture change discussed here, executives spent an enormous amount of time shaping and sharing a few simple messages. These messages indicated what the new culture was going to be, why the culture was important, and how the culture would affect individual behavior. Jack Welch (GE) constantly talks about how soft issues are critical to competitive success; Rich Teerlink (Harley Davidson) talks at length about learning; George Fisher (Motorola, now Eastman Kodak) talks about quality and customer service; Larry Bossidy (Allied Signal) preaches about profitability, people, and product mix; Vern Loucks (Baxter Healthcare) persistently reinforces the importance of respect, responsiveness, and results to Baxter's current and future success; and Bill Weiss (Ameritech) emphasizes the importance of a new cultural paradigm for competitiveness.

Multiple communication tools exist: formal speeches, videos, newsletters, management meetings, annual reports, shareholder presentations, informal employee meetings. As these communication tools focus on the new culture, changes become more understood and accepted. All of the HR tools we identified can be used for creating and sustaining culture change. They all affect information

and behavior which, in turn, shapes a new mind-set among employees (figure 17.4).

HUMAN RESOURCES PROFESSIONALS AND CULTURE CHANGE

We have discussed how HR practices may be used to shape a new culture. To leverage HR practices in this way, HR professionals must adopt new roles and responsibilities. In addition to playing new roles (Ulrich, 1994b), ways in which HR professionals may facilitate culture change have been discovered within a number of firms. Four agendas frame the roles that HR professionals may play in facilitating culture change.

Catalyst/champion/sponsor

At Rochester Telephone, a cultural transformation was necessary to compete in the changing relecommunications marketplace. To make progress in this transformation, Ronald Bittner (chairman, president, and chief executive officer) has stated a vision of being the "premier telecommunication company in the world" through products and customer focus. He has stated that "no vision can be achieved without an able and dedicated employee body. . . . We're undertaking a fresh, critical assessment of the skills and competencies each of our employees must have to move forward. Where we lack that expertise, we're committed to move it in from the outside" (Bittner, 1993). To help facilitate the cultural transformation, Bittner hired a senior HR executive, Janet Sansone, who had the explicit task of championing the change effort. Ms. Sansone's responsibility, as the senior HR executive, is to make sure that culture change is part of the discussion, that models for culture change are created and implemented, and that executive attention on culture change remains high.

At other firms, similar roles for HR executives are emerging. Senior HR executives are expected to add value by being champions of cultural change, as well as agents of change.

Facilitator

In addition to being the champion of change, HR professionals must help facilitate change. Facilitation of change was a primary role for HR professionals in GE's Workout program. Three stages of HR facilitation were defined in Workout: external support, internal transition, and management ownership.

External facilitation support occurred early in Workout activities. The external team leaders and team members helped initiate and stimulate Workout. They built relationships across levels in the organization, worked with the political backing of the CEO, and made progress framing Workout for each business. Their role was important as a catalyst for initiating Workout. However, as Workout transitioned to a more institutionalized state, the external facilitation role needed to be reduced and became replaced by internal facilitators.

HR professionals helped external facilitators. They offered technical support by helping external facilitators acquire insights into the procedures used at GE. They offered political insight by helping external facilitators understand relationships and power distribution within the business. They offered cultural and historical insights as a means of shaping external facilitator efforts, and they helped identify areas in which the previous culture was more open to change.

Internal transition facilitation occurred when GE employees assumed the responsibility for examining, managing, and implementing new work processes. Internal facilitators identified and changed work processes. They helped task forces reduce cycle time, improve engineering efforts, reduce engineering design time, and examine purchasing times. They were process observers at ongoing team meetings. They were experts in process skills.

Over time, internal facilitators replaced external facilitators. When that happened, cultural change became more owned by GE employees. HR professionals played two roles in terms of internal facilitation:

1. At times they were included in the pool of trained internal facilitators, which included talented employees from many professions (e.g., finance, engineering, marketing, research, and HR). HR professionals who had business acumen, process skills, and worked well with management teams were included in this pool.
2. HR professionals were centrally involved in the development of internal facilitator training. The training program was coordinated and designed centrally through HR professionals at GE's headquarters, and adapted and implemented locally through business unit HR professionals.

In both cases, the HR professionals were experts in designing and delivering training programs to develop a cadre of internal facilitators.

Management-owned facilitation was the end state for facilitator focus. At this step, each GE manager became his or her own facilitator. He or she had the ability to diagnose problems; implement a process to examine problems; demonstrate competence in work-flow assessment, simplification, and improvement; and build commitment among team members. When the manager became the facilitator, Workout was greatly advanced. The external and internal facilitator crutches were removed, and managers talked the Workout talk. They became owners of Workout, and Workout became an ongoing way of business.

HR professionals helped develop management competence in self-facilitation. They trained managers (again, either centrally through headquarters, and/or within each business). They were involved in selecting future managers who had facilitation competencies, and they played a key role in assessing current manager capabilities in facilitation and offering counsel and advice for improvements.

Designer

In the GE case, HR professionals played a principal role in cultural transformation by redesigning HR systems. Staffing, development, appraisal, reward, organization configuration, and communication practices were designed so that managers understood and owned the cultural transformation. Designing new systems required that HR professionals were ahead of the cultural change curve with innovative and exciting HR practices.

Demonstrator

The final and perhaps most critical role for HR professionals assisting culture change is to demonstrate the change within their own function. As Digital Equipment has undergone dramatic culture change under Bob Palmer, the vice president of HR, Richard Farrahar, worked hard to use the HR function as a leading example of reengineering and change. He spent an enormous amount of personal time dedicating senior HR talent to reengineering the HR function within Digital. By setting the example, other managers came to respect the HR function as one that "had its own house in order."

Rather than preaching culture change to the choir, HR professionals need to become part of the choir. They need to be able to live and experience firsthand the lessons of culture change.

LESSONS LEARNED

If the meetings held at GE in 1989 were reconvened in 1995, what would be the lessons learned about culture change? Given the extensive experience with culture change that many firms have had in the last five years, a number of lessons can be synthesized.

First, culture change must add value to customers. Changing the culture merely to make employees more committed is not sufficient. It must lead to a competitive position in the market by changing the identity of the firm to customers of the firm. Second, as with most lessons of business, an old concept – "equifinality" – holds (Katz & Kahn, 1978). Equifinality means that there are many ways to approach and accomplish culture change. No one has discovered a magical checklist or cookbook, but a variety of approaches have been articulated.

Third, many of the sacred truths of culture change (e.g., CEO commitment is the key; training is the key; participation is the key) are myths. As Joe Miraglia (1994) suggests, culture change has more myths than realities. It requires more than simple program solutions.

Fourth, HR professionals may play a central and critical role in culture change. Their change agenda requires new competencies and commitments, but the payoff is high. Companies that leverage HR professionals change cultures.

Fifth, many HR practices may be used to sustain and change a culture. Learning to use all the HR tools of culture change becomes an opportunity and a challenge.

Finally, it is time to build confidence in the emerging fact that culture change can and does occur. It can be defined. It can happen. It matters, however, as we indicated at the outset, that "organizations don't act; people do," making human resources an essential part of the equation.

NOTE

1 Many of these ideas are taken from Ulrich (1994a).

REFERENCES

Barney, J. (1986). Organizational culture: Can it be a source of sustained competitive advantage? *Academy of Management Review,* 11 (3), 656–65.
Beatty, R., & Ulrich, D. (1991). Reenergizing the mature organization. *Organizational Dynamics,* 20 (1), 16–30.

Bittner, R. (1993). Presentation to Goldman, Sachs, and Company at the Communacopia II Conference.

Block, P. (1993). *Stewardship: Choosing service over self-interest*. San Francisco: Berrett Koehler.

Brockbank, J. W., & Ulrich, D. (1988). Institutional antecedents of shared organizational cognitions. Working paper. Ann Arbor, MI: University of Michigan.

Davidow, W. H., & Malone, M. (1992). *The Virtual Corporation*. New York: Harper Business.

Davis, S. (1984). *Managing Corporate Culture*. Cambridge, MA: Ballinger Publishing.

Deal, T. E., & Kennedy, A. A. (1982). *Corporate Cultures: The rites and rituals of corporate life*. Reading, MA: Addison-Wesley.

Drucker, P. (1988). Management and the world's work. *Harvard Business Review*, Sept.–Oct., 65–76.

Frangos, S. (1993). *Team Zebra: How 1,500 partners revitalized Eastman Kodak's black & white film-making flow*. Essex Junction, VT: Oliver Wright.

Hammer, M. (1990). Reengineering work. *Harvard Business Review*, July–Aug.

Hammer, M., & Champy, J. (1993). *Reengineering the corporation*. New York: Harper Business.

Howard, R. (1992). The CEO as organizational architect: An interview with Xerox's Paul Aliaire. *Harvard Business Review*, Sept.–Oct., 106–23.

Katz, D., & Kahn, R. (1978). *The Social Psychology of Organizations*. New York: Wiley.

Katzenbach, J. R., & Smith, D. (1993). *The Wisdom of Teams*. Boston, MA: Harvard Business Press.

Kerr, J., & Slocum, J. W., Jr. (1987). Managing corporate culture through reward systems. *Academy of Management Executive*, 1, 99–108.

Kotter, J., & Heskett, J. (1992). *Culture and Performance*. New York: Free Press.

LaFasto, F. M. J., & Larson, C. E. (1993). *Getting Connected: Building collaborative teams*. A process for building collaboration within organizations.

Larson, C. E., & LaFasto, F. M. J. (1989). *Teamwork: What must go right/what can go wrong*. Newbury Park, CA: Sage.

Martin, J., Feldman, M. S., Hatch, M. J., Sitkin, S. B. (1983). The uniqueness paradox in organizational culture. *Administrative Science Quarterly*, 28, 438–53.

Miraglia, J. (1994). An evolutionary approach to revolutionary change and the implications for HR practice. In C. E. Schneier (ed.), *Managing Strategic Change*, New York: Human Resource Planning Society.

Quinn, J. B. (1993). *Intelligent Enterprise*. New York: Free Press.

Schein, E. G. (1985). *Organizational Culture and Leadership*. New York: Jossey-Bass.

Schneier, C. E., Shaw, D., Beatty, R. W. (1991). Performance measurement and management: A tool for strategy execution. *Human Resource Management Journal*, 30, 279–302.

Smircich, L. (1983). Concepts of culture and organizational analysis. *Administrative Science Quarterly*, 28, 339–58.

Ulrich, D. (1994a). Culture change: Will we recognize it when we see it? In C. E. Schneier (ed.), *Managing Strategic Change*. New York: Human Resource Planning Society.

Ulrich, D. (1994b). HR partnerships: From rhetoric to reality. In *Strategic Partners for High Performance*, 45–61. New York: Work in America Institute.

Ulrich, D. & Lake, D. (1990). *Organizational Capability: Competing from the inside/out*. New York: Wiley.

Ulrich, D., von Glinow, M. A., & Jick, T. (1993). High impact learning: Building and diffusing learning capability. *Organizational Dynamics*, winter, 52–66.

Whiteley, R. G. (1993). *The Customer Driven Company*. Boston: Addison-Wesley.

Wilhelm, W. (1990). Revitalizing the human resource management function in a mature, large corporation. *Human Resource Management Journal*, 29 (2), 129–44.

Part III
Management of the Employment Relationship

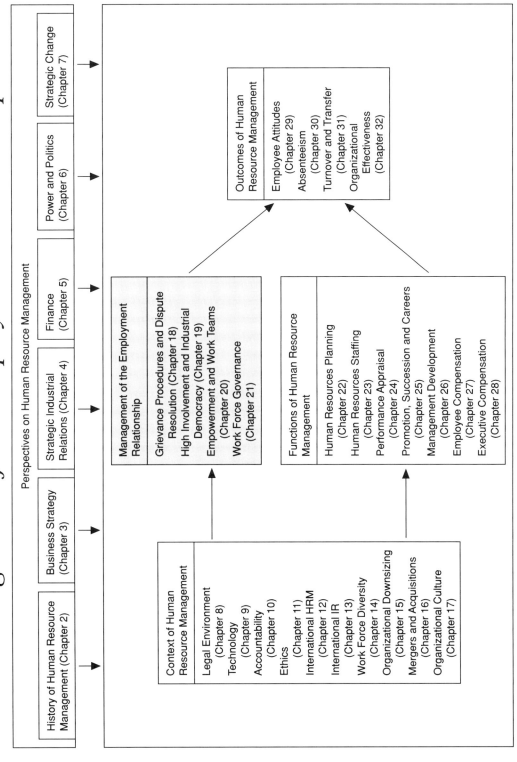

Perspectives on Human Resource Management

| History of Human Resource Management (Chapter 2) | Business Strategy (Chapter 3) | Strategic Industrial Relations (Chapter 4) | Finance (Chapter 5) | Power and Politics (Chapter 6) | Strategic Change (Chapter 7) |

Context of Human Resource Management

Legal Environment (Chapter 8)
Technology (Chapter 9)
Accountability (Chapter 10)
Ethics (Chapter 11)
International HRM (Chapter 12)
International IR (Chapter 13)
Work Force Diversity (Chapter 14)
Organizational Downsizing (Chapter 15)
Mergers and Acquisitions (Chapter 16)
Organizational Culture (Chapter 17)

Management of the Employment Relationship

Grievance Procedures and Dispute Resolution (Chapter 18)
High Involvement and Industrial Democracy (Chapter 19)
Empowerment and Work Teams (Chapter 20)
Work Force Governance (Chapter 21)

Functions of Human Resource Management

Human Resources Planning (Chapter 22)
Human Resources Staffing (Chapter 23)
Performance Appraisal (Chapter 24)
Promotion, Succession and Careers (Chapter 25)
Management Development (Chapter 26)
Employee Compensation (Chapter 27)
Executive Compensation (Chapter 28)

Outcomes of Human Resource Management

Employee Attitudes (Chapter 29)
Absenteeism (Chapter 30)
Turnover and Transfer (Chapter 31)
Organizational Effectiveness (Chapter 32)

Introduction: Management of the Employment Relationship

The effective management of the employment relationship in the future necessarily will focus on the key stakeholders in this relationship, and the relative degree of influence each can exert in work-force governance. Thus, the contributors to this section examine decision making in the workplace, and deal with significant issues concerning the roles of workers, work teams and managers in making decisions. The term "industrial democracy" is taking on new meanings in work-force governance and dispute resolution, with the arrival of empowered employees and work teams.

In the opening chapter on dispute resolution, Feuille and Hildebrand note that "grievances" are part of the natural order of things in the workplace. However, there is no natural order regarding how formal grievances are initiated, processed, and resolved. Grievance procedures are usually found in unionized firms, and still are fairly similar in general. Many large nonunion employers have adopted formal procedures also, but with much more variation in formality and the nature of the final step.

In their chapter on high involvement and industrial democracy, Landen, Bluestone, and Lawler note that there is an inevitability about democracy, and thus it is not surprising to find businesses increasingly using forms of employee involvement that transfer authority to their workers. They argue, however, that there are preferable ways of making such transfers, and examine what has been done and how it could be improved.

Liden and Tewksbury provide a framework for understanding worker empowerment, distinguishing between the empowerment of individuals and groups. They discuss the components that must be present to truly attain empowerment of individuals, and the difficulty of transitions from empowered individuals to empowered groups.

Kaufman, Lewin, and Adams address work-force governance, which they define as "the authority relations, rule-making process, and system of dispute resolution within organizations." Companies have had to adapt their governance structures to attain flexibility and accountability, as they attempt to meet increasing competition in the marketplace while maintaining fairness and equity in the workplace.

☐ Chapter 18 ☐

Grievance Procedures and Dispute Resolution

Peter Feuille and Robert L. Hildebrand

INTRODUCTION

Julie is upset that she did not receive the promotion to associate editor that she expected based on her four years of high quality work as an assistant editor, and she becomes furious when she learns that the promoted employee is somebody she trained when he was hired two years ago by her publishing company employer. She is determined to protest this obvious injustice and to demand that she be given the reward that she has earned. She is so angry that she considers filing a sex discrimination charge with the government, but she decides to hold off until she sees if she can resolve her complaint internally.

This is an example of the disagreements that arise in the workplace when employees are treated in a manner that they believe is unfair. These kinds of disagreements or conflicts are part of the natural order of things in the workplace where employees and managers have divergent interests in how scarce resources are allocated. However, there is no natural order of things regarding how these disagreements are handled. Accordingly, in this chapter we analyze how employers, employees, and employee organizations handle disagreements that result in the employee-initiated complaints that we usually call grievances. We focus on private sector workplaces with formal grievance procedures, and we draw heavily from both academic and practitioner research on workplace dispute resolution.

EMPLOYER–EMPLOYEE DISPUTES AND ORGANIZATIONAL JUSTICE

Research has documented the strong interest that employers and employees have in organizational justice, or fair treatment at work (Alexander & Ruderman, 1987; Folger & Greenberg, 1985; Fryxell & Gordon, 1989; Greenberg, 1990; Sheppard, Lewicki, & Minton, 1992). Research has shown that the perceived fairness of workplace decisions (i.e., distributive justice, or who gets what), and the perceived fairness of organizational procedures used to make these decisions (i.e., procedural justice, or how these allocation decisions are made) have important influences on employee job satisfaction. In particular, organizational procedures that give employees the opportunity to provide input into decisions that affect them are viewed as fairer than others (Folger & Greenberg, 1985; Lind & Tyler, 1988). This opportunity to be heard is generally labelled as "voice," which is a shorthand expression for the various ways that subordinates in an organization can communicate their interests upward (Greenberg & Folger, 1983), and which is usually considered as an alternative to "exit" behaviors (Hirschman, 1970). In both union and nonunion organizations, employers have increasingly given employees voice opportunities through formal human resources policies and procedures.

Some organizational procedures allow employees the opportunity to provide input into decisions as they are being made; examples include job enrichment efforts, employee participation/involvement programs, self-directed work teams, and certain kinds of performance appraisal techniques. Sheppard et al. (1992) call these "preventive voice" procedures because their focus is on soliciting or allowing employees to offer their inputs as decisions are being made. In contrast, other kinds of procedures allow employees to express their concerns about decisions already made, and grievance procedures are a prime example. Sheppard et al. call these "remedial voice" procedures because the focus is on employee objections or challenges to decisions that have already been made. As this comparison indicates, remedial voice procedures have an explicit focus on claims of improper or unfair treatment.

In the eyes of employees, especially those who file grievances, the real remedial voice value of a grievance procedure lies along two organizational justice dimensions. The first is procedural justice: Is the grievance process fair? More specifically, to what extent does the procedure offer the grievant a genuine opportunity to challenge the alleged unfair treatment and be free from retaliation for doing so? The second is distributive justice: Are grievance outcomes fair? Or, do grievance resolutions accurately reflect the pertinent grievance evidence? Our analysis provides some limited answers to these questions.

Employers have more complex and ambivalent perspectives about the emergence and resolution of grievances. Employers are concerned about organizational fairness (Greenberg, 1990), and most managers believe (at least in theory) that employees should be able to present their complaints to top management through some sort of grievance procedure (Ewing, 1971). However, most managers do not have the same positive view of internal conflict that most industrial relations/human resources (IR/HR) scholars appear to have (Baron, 1991; Dalton & Cosier, 1991). In particular, managers appear to view conflict as having more negative than positive impacts (Baron, 1991). Expressed another way, managers tend to see grievances as examples of competitive (win-lose) rather than cooperative (win-win) conflict, and grievance procedures as adversarial instead of cooperative influence mechanisms.

Managers also are concerned about the transaction cost efficiency of their decision and implementation processes across all functional organizational areas (Williamson, 1975, 1976). Managers are strongly motivated by the same concerns in the grievance arena. In other words, managerial concerns about fair treatment are balanced by managerial desires to have fewer rather than more employer–employee conflicts, and to have the grievances that do emerge handled and resolved quickly, inexpensively, and consistent with management's view of the appropriate outcome (i.e., efficiently).

One of the crucial dimensions regarding how grievances are filed and resolved is the presence or absence of a union. As we will see, grievance-processing arrangements differ dramatically across union and nonunion

341

workplaces. Indeed, these differences are so great that we need to examine union and nonunion organizations separately.

GRIEVANCE DISPUTE RESOLUTION IN THE UNIONIZED WORKPLACE

In order to understand why union–management disputes arise and how they are resolved, it is necessary to analyze the union's role in the workplace. The ostensible justification for the union's existence in any workplace is that the employer will not treat employees fairly unless the union insists upon it. Where they have representation rights, unions engage in collective bargaining negotiations with employers to seek more employee-favorable terms than the employer would otherwise provide. Unions seek to persuade employers to agree to these employee-favorable terms (higher wages, better fringes, etc.) by manipulating the employer's costs of disagreeing with the union via such tactics as (threatened or actual) strikes, slowdowns, boycotts, and so on. In other words, unions try to make it costly for the employer to say "no" to union demands. These union demands for better contract terms are pressed upon employers periodically (every two or three years or so) when the two parties negotiate a new collective bargaining agreement (or contract) to replace the contract that has expired. There is a huge body of research that indicates that unions generally have been quite successful in obtaining increased wages, fringe benefits, job security, working conditions, and employee-protective rules from employers (Kochan & Katz, 1988).

These negotiated employment terms are written down in the contract. As the above description implies, the contract is not designed to foster more efficient operations or identify new products or markets. Instead, its content consists of protections that require employers to provide employment terms that they would not ordinarily provide (e.g., fully paid health insurance, four weeks of paid

vacation), and restrictions that prevent employers from doing things that they might otherwise do (e.g., terminate an employee without just cause, promote employees without regard to seniority). Further, unions and employers generally have opposing perspectives about what these terms represent. Unions believe that these terms are the fruits of their valiant struggle with employers who are insufficiently attuned to the equity interests of employees. In contrast, employers believe that they must negotiate vigorously to protect operating efficiency from encroachment by unions who are too little concerned with the competitive realities of the marketplace. In short, in the usual union–management relationship the union's "logic of rights" is pitted against the employer's "logic of efficiency" in a competitive relationship (Friedman, 1992).

However, bounded rationality means these contract terms usually cannot be specified with the breadth and precision that will cover all contingencies that may arise (Williamson, 1975). In addition, it often is easier in negotiations to obtain mutual agreement on generally worded provisions than on clearly specified terms (Meyer & Cooke, 1988). This means that there will be situations where the contract terminology is sufficiently imprecise that more than one interpretation is arguably allowed.

This combination of contractual content and opposing perspectives means that employers and unions tend to have different incentives about how to interpret and apply the contract on a day-to-day basis. Unions typically insist on an employee-favorable interpretation of the contract's terms, for this approach will expand the range of benefits actually delivered to employees. In contrast, employers typically seek a more employer-favorable interpretation of the contract, for this approach gives employers more ability to manage the business efficiently. The following seniority versus ability grievance, which in one form or another has arisen countless times in unionized workplaces, illustrates these opposing perspectives:

> The contract provides that promotions will be awarded to the most senior employee bidding for the job, provided that "ability and qualifications are relatively equal." Jane and Jim bid for the vacant position of senior cashier at their grocery store, which would be a promotion from their current title of clerk-cashier. Jane has six years seniority, "superior" performance evaluations, and average attendance. Jim has nine years seniority, "satisfactory" evaluations, and above average attendance. The employer selects Jane for the job. The union grieves on the grounds that Jim's ability and qualifications are relatively equal with Jane's, and therefore his seniority entitles him to the position. The employer denies the grievance on the grounds that Jim's ability and qualifications are clearly inferior to Jane's, and thus Jim's seniority does not come into play.

As this example illustrates, grievances are a "naming, blaming, claiming" response (Felstiner, Abel, & Sarat, 1980) resulting from an employee or union belief that the employer has improperly interpreted the contract. Considering the nature of the contract and the parties' opposing perspectives, some amount of these grievance disputes are part of the natural order of things in a unionized workplace. What is less clear is how often these disputes will emerge, how unions and employers will process and resolve these kinds of disputes, and whose interests will prevail in these resolutions. Enter the negotiated grievance procedure.

Existence

By now it is widely known that a negotiated grievance procedure (GP) exists in almost every collective bargaining agreement in the U.S., and almost all of these grievance procedures culminate in arbitration (Bureau of National Affairs, 1989; U.S. Bureau of Labor Statistics, 1981). Indeed, grievance procedures have become one of the most stable and enduring features of U.S. union–management relationships during the past 40–50 years. This has not occurred because the government has mandated it (except for railroads and airlines, the federal government has not required grievance procedures to exist in private or public workplaces). Instead, this near-universal adoption of grievance procedures represents a voluntary union–employer quid pro quo designed to process and resolve grievances in a manner consistent with both sides' self-interest.

When collective bargaining first emerged on a large scale in the private sector during the late 1930s, the time-honored union response to an unacceptable employer decision was the strike. As union contracts became more widespread and also more complex, unions and employers eventually realized that the use of strikes (however brief) to resolve difficult grievances created too much disruption of the production process. In addition, during World War II the government had a strong national security incentive to maintain an uninterrupted production process, and the federal War Labor Board pressed unions and employers to resolve their disputes without strikes.

The result was that unions and employers contractually exchanged no-strike clauses for grievance procedures. More specifically, unions agreed to no-strike pledges, and in return employers agreed to grievance procedures that permitted union-initiated challenges to managerial actions. Most important, this quid pro quo allowed unresolved grievances to be reviewed and possibly sustained by grievance arbitrators who are jointly selected and compensated (Nolan & Abrams, 1983), and this bilateral arbitration feature is the key element of this negotiated GP system. In short, employers agreed to have their personnel decisions subject to challenge and possible reversal via the grievance procedure in return for a prohibition on work stoppages during the life of the contract. Unions and employers agreed to this arrangement because it provided for a more efficient method of grievance resolution than the use of threatened or actual work stoppages.

This union–employer grievance resolution trade-off has been one of the key success stories of American collective bargaining. In the 40–50 years since the widespread institutionalization of this trade-off in the 1940s and early 1950s, grievance strikes have diminished substantially. Instead, unions routinely use grievance and arbitration procedures for the purpose of challenging employer interpretation of the contract's terms, and the longevity of these procedures indicates that unions and employers continue to find them acceptable.

The widespread emergence of collective bargaining in government during the 1960s and 1970s also saw the widespread adoption in public sector contracts of negotiated GPs culminating in arbitration (Cleveland State University, 1990). This occurred not so much as a buy-out of the employees' right to strike, for most public employees do not have such a right (though there are exceptions in about a dozen states). Instead, these public sector GPs emerged because of union unwillingness to use employer-dominated civil service appeal procedures to process grievances and the unions' concomitant desire to mimic private sector GPs, and because of union and employer awareness that negotiated GPs provided a more efficient grievance resolution method than litigation or than the illegal grievance strikes that might sometimes occur.

In sum, formal GPs culminating in arbitration have become the norm in unionized workplaces because the union's presence created an interorganizational disputing relationship that forced the parties to find efficient methods to resolve disagreements. Unions and employers continue to view formal GPs as an acceptable way to channel contract interpretation disputes into an administratively manageable dispute resolution format while simultaneously preserving the uninterrupted functioning of the workflow process and the issuance of employee paychecks.

Operation and outcomes

Procedural characteristics

Grievance procedures exist in very diverse workplaces, and they can be expressed in quite different contract terminology. However, they usually contain the same important features:

- The procedure usually defines a grievance as a claim by an employee or the union that the employer violated the contract, which means that the union is the moving party that pushes the grievance through the procedure.
- Grievances must be expressed in writing, and managerial responses usually are given in writing (often after an oral first step).
- The procedure guarantees employees the right to be represented by the union, which means the grievant will have an advocate to press his or her claim upon management, and there usually are various procedural rules that protect the union's advocacy role.
- The procedure specifies several steps (usually about four) through which the unresolved grievance moves as it is appealed to higher levels within the company and union.
- There are explicit time limits for filing grievances and for appealing them to the next higher step.
- The prearbitration resolution of a grievance requires mutual agreement between the union and the employer, which gives the union a strong voice in prearbitration grievance resolution.
- The terminal GP step almost always is arbitration by an external arbitrator who is jointly selected and compensated by

the union and the employer, which gives the union a strong voice in the arbitrated resolution of grievances.

These procedural characteristics and assessments apply to most unionized GPs. However, these procedural dimensions tell us little about how GPs operate in practice to resolve disputes. In particular, we need to examine GP usage data to determine how effective GPs are as dispute resolution mechanisms. Lewin and Peterson (1988) specify several effectiveness dimensions that should be examined: the rate at which grievances are filed, the speed of settlement, the level (within the GP) of settlement, the arbitration rate, the perceived importance of grieved issues, and the perceived equity of grievance handling and settlement. Some of these measures deal with procedural justice (how are grievance decisions made?) and some deal with distributive justice (who prevails?). In the remainder of this section, we examine evidence that allows us to draw conclusions about some of these effectiveness dimensions.

Grievance filing

Although unionized grievance procedures may look quite similar across thousands of diverse workplaces, research indicates that in practice these procedures are used quite differently (reviews of this research can be found in Gordon & Miller (1984), Labig & Greer (1988), Lewin & Peterson (1988), and Peterson (1992)). Grievance filing rates may be the best indicator of this diversity. The standard measure is the number of grievances filed per 100 employees per year. Research indicates a large variation in this rate across workplaces (Gordon & Miller, 1984; Knight, 1986; Lewin & Peterson, 1988). For instance, a study of 1980–82 grievance activity in several dozen private and public organizations found a 15-fold variation in filing rates across these workplaces, from 1.6 to 24.9 grievances per 100 employees per year (Lewin & Peterson, 1988). These organizations existed in four

industries, and the results indicated that average filing rates were significantly higher in the surveyed steel companies than in the organizations in the other three industries (department stores, hospitals, public schools). Gordon and Miller's (1984) review found that filing rates were lower in public organizations than in private ones, with these rates ranging from one to 27 grievances per 100 employees per year. Similarly, Bemmels' (1994) survey of grievance initiation in 1,205 Canadian work groups found filing rates ranging from 0.6 (in education) to 48.2 (in railroads) grievances per 100 employees per year, with an average rate of 17. Further, this large variation in filing rates is not new (Slichter, Healy, & Livernash, 1960).

Other research has reported wide variation in filing rates within the same firm. For instance, across 18 General Motors plants in 1979, filing rates varied from 24 to 450 grievances per 100 employees (Katz, Kochan, & Gobeille, 1983). These filing rates also may vary over time in the same facilities. Lewin and Peterson's (1988) analysis found that average grievance rates declined in three of their four industries (except hospitals) during the 1980–82 period they examined (which coincided with the emergence of a severe economic recession). Even more dramatically, Ichniowski (1992) traced grievance activity in a paper mill during a change from overtly hostile union–management relations to a team-based production system (with fewer job classifications, higher pay, and explicit job security) that fostered greater cooperation. In 1983 (the last year of the "bad" system), grievances were filed at the rate of 198 grievances per 100 employees per year, and by 1985 (the second year of the "good" system), this annual filing rate had plunged to 4 (the accident and absentee rates also dropped noticeably and productivity improved substantially).

Kuch (1991) reported that unionized employees' participation in quality circles in a manufacturing plant resulted in a decline in grievance filing rates. Similarly, Katz, Kochan, and Weber (1985) found that higher levels of employee involvement in quality of work-life (QWL) programs was correlated with lower grievance filing rates across plants of one large manufacturer. Cutcher-Gershenfeld (1991) found lower rates of third- and fourth-step grievances in "transformed" (participative) work groups compared to "traditional" (adversarial) groups in a large manufacturing facility. The Cutcher-Gershenfeld (1991), Ichniowski (1992), Kuch (1991), and Katz et al. (1985) studies suggest that the adoption of employee influence mechanisms that emphasize cooperation may reduce the use of such adversarial influence vehicles as grievance procedures.

This huge variation in grievance filing rates indicates that employers and employees in some workplaces are able to develop very consistent views of how the union contract should be interpreted on a day-to-day basis, in other workplaces they develop moderate consistency, but in yet other workplaces there is considerable inconsistency. In other words, grievance disputes in unionized workplaces may be inevitable, but the rate at which they emerge certainly is not.

Why are grievances filed? Labig and Greer (1988) surveyed the grievance initiation research not long ago, and their analysis uncovered many environmental factors (economic, legal, technological, and industry characteristics), managerial factors (supervisory behaviors, management industrial relations policies), union factors (union representative behaviors, union policies), union–management interaction factors (labor relations climate, contract content), and employee dimensions (demographic characteristics, work history elements, attitudinal traits) that have been found to influence grievance-filing rates. Taken together, the studies they surveyed found a wide variety of factors that were correlated with higher or lower grievance-filing rates. However, it is very difficult to synthesize a specific explanation for griev-

ance-filing behavior from this research, for the use of noncomparable variables and work sites across this research severely limits generalizability.

For instance, there has been a great deal of research into the demographic characteristics of grievance filers compared to nonfilers (e.g., Allen & Keaveny, 1985), and a review of this research indicates that, with the possible exception of age (younger employees appear more likely to grieve than older employees; Labig & Greer, 1988), no consistent demographic portrait has emerged (Allen & Keaveny, 1985; Gordon & Miller, 1984; Labig & Greer, 1988). Some studies have looked at elements of the work environment, and it is difficult to synthesize common findings across these efforts (Labig & Greer, 1988; Labig & Helburn, 1986; Muchinsky & Maassarani, 1980; Peach & Livernash, 1974). Nelson and Reiman (1983) found that the type of technology influenced grievance-filing rates, but Bemmels, Reshef, and Stratton-Devine (1991) found that the behaviors of employees, stewards, and supervisors had more influence on grievance filing than technology and other workplace characteristics. Similarly, Bemmels (1994) found that supervisors who emphasized production rather than friendly relations with employees, and stewards who de-emphasized informal grievance resolution, contributed to higher grievance-filing rates.

Cappelli and Chauvin (1991) found that grievance rates varied directly with the size of the wage premium received by workers over alternative wages in the local labor market, and with the local unemployment rate, across plants in a large manufacturing firm. Grievance rates were higher in plants with larger wage premiums and located in areas with high unemployment, which suggests that workers are more likely to use voice when exit (quitting) is less attractive. However, Spitz (1993) found that managerial quality had a stronger influence on grievance rates in supermarkets (grievance rates were significantly lower in stores with higher-rated managers) than local wage or unemployment rates. In a study of grievance filing in public organizations where union membership was optional, Boroff (1993) found that there was a positive and strong correlation between grievance filing and being a union member. Boroff estimated that the large member/nonmember difference in filing rates was a result of the fact that employee-favorable outcomes occurred with 63 percent of the members' grievances but only 25 percent of the nonmembers' grievances.

There is evidence that the grievance procedure can be used as a battleground when union–management relations are adversarial. For instance, research has found that grievance filing rates are higher when the labor relations climate in the facility is poor (Gandz & Whitehead, 1982; Katz et al., 1983). Labig and Greer (1988) suggest that it is more likely that the grievance-filing rate is a reflection rather than a cause of an adversarial or non-cooperative relationship. Other research has found that grievance-filing rates may increase at contract negotiation time as a means of increasing the negotiating pressure on management (Kochan, Katz, & McKersie, 1986; Lewin & Peterson, 1988). In general, the evidence indicates that the grievance-filing rate often is a key indicator of the level of union–management conflict, with a high filing rate serving as a sign that the union and the employer have a highly adversarial relationship. In cooperative relationships, grievance rates tend to be much lower, largely because the parties are able to resolve their differences informally. What is less clear is why some unions and employers become embroiled in high-conflict relationships and others do not. In short, the grievance initiation research has not produced a unified explanation of grievance filing that fits all unionized workplaces, but it does indicate that there is a lot more to grievance filing than an employee's perception that he or she has been treated unfairly (see also Klass, 1989b).

What subjects are grieved? Lewin and Peterson (1988) and Bemmels (1994) confirm that grievances are filed over a very wide variety of subjects. In general, any item in the union contract can be the subject of a grievance. However, there is general agreement that discipline is the single most frequent issue grieved (Gordon & Miller, 1984; Lewin & Peterson, 1988).

Grievance processing and resolution

The available grievance processing research indicates that most grievances are resolved within the first two steps of the grievance procedure, and that most of the resolutions occur within two months of the filing date (Delaney, Lewin, & Ichniowski, 1989; Gideon & Peterson, 1979; Gordon & Miller, 1984; Knight, 1986; Lewin & Peterson, 1988; Ng & Dastmalchian, 1989). Further, these resolutions usually are achieved without outside assistance (especially from attorneys), so the out-of-pocket processing costs are low (though this ignores the cost of the employee, managerial, and union staff time devoted to grievance handling).

However, for those grievances that are arbitrated (i.e., are processed through the entire GP), the resolution process takes several additional months and is comparatively expensive. For instance, arbitration data from the Federal Mediation and Conciliation Service for the 5,500 arbitration awards issued via its auspices during fiscal 1993 show that the average arbitrator bill was $2,222 (for fees and expenses), and the average time from the grievance-filing date to the award date was 313 days (Federal Mediation and Conciliation Service, 1993). This dollar figure does not include arbitration advocacy expenses such as attorney's fees, and other data suggest that attorney representation in arbitration proceedings has become the norm (American Arbitration Association, 1993). In short, arbitration is much more efficient than strikes (or litigation) in resolving grievances, but it is quite costly compared to negotiated resolution at the prearbitration steps.

The fact that arbitration is a relatively time-consuming and expensive grievance resolution step helps explain why unions and employers use arbitration relatively sparingly. For instance, studies of union–management relationships in Canada and the U.S. have reported a variety of arbitration usage rates: 2 percent of 194 grievances were arbitrated in a Pacific Northwest pulp and paper mill (Gideon & Peterson, 1979); across several thousand grievances in eight bargaining units in the airline, basic steel, chemical, and utility industries, an average of 7 percent (within a range of 1 percent to 27 percent) were arbitrated (Knight, 1986); across several thousand grievances filed with several dozen employers in the department store, public school, hospital, and steel industries, arbitration rates averaged 9, 11, 12, and 16 percent, respectively, within very large variation across individual organizations (Lewin & Peterson, 1988); 2 percent of 1,174 grievances filed in a Canadian federal government department were arbitrated (Ng & Dastmalchian, 1989); 10 percent of 957 grievances filed in a utility were arbitrated (Todor & Owen, 1991); 4 percent of almost 5,000 grievances in nine paper mills of one company were arbitrated (Ichniowski, 1986); and 1 percent of 778 grievances in a Canadian industrial firm were arbitrated (Chaykowski, Slotsve, & Butler, 1992). In other words, even though every grievance theoretically could be arbitrated, unions and employers have learned how to resolve the vast majority of these disputes without arbitrators.

One of the key factors that drives unions and employers to some sort of prearbitration agreement with most of their grievances is their consistent estimate of how an arbitrator is likely to rule upon the grievance. It is unlikely that unions and employers, with their opposing incentives about how the contract should be interpreted, would be able to resolve 85–95 percent or more of all filed grievances unless they held generally consistent views of how most grievances would be resolved if arbitrated. As a result, arbitration's influence upon grievance resolution extends beyond the small fraction of all grievances that are arbitrated. Knight's (1986) research confirms the feedback effect that arbitration has on prearbitration grievance resolution.

Grievance outcomes

The available evidence indicates that a large proportion of all grievances filed are resolved in the employee's favor (defined as a resolution that fully or partly sustains the grievance). For instance, the proportion of employee-favorable grievance resolutions ranged from 22 percent to 70 percent across a variety of private and public workplaces in different studies (Chaykowski, Slotsve, & Butler, 1992; Dalton & Todor, 1985; Gideon & Peterson, 1979; Lewin & Peterson, 1988; Ng & Dastmalchian, 1989; Todor & Owen, 1991).

Just as there is no all-encompassing explanation of why employees file grievances, there is no single explanation for why employees prevail in some grievances and not others. One study found that grievance outcomes were influenced by the outcomes of prior grievances on the same subject, and that employee-favorable decisions were much more likely in the first two grievance steps than in the third step (Chaykowski et al., 1992). The type of issue grieved may have an influence on who prevails. For example, a study of a West Coast workplace found that the employer won about 80 percent of the grievances over sick benefits and that employees won about 85 percent of the grievances concerning performance evaluation (Dalton & Todor, 1981). Additionally, a study of a Canadian federal government department found that employees were more likely to prevail in pay and working conditions grievances and least likely to prevail in grievances over job assignments (Ng & Dastmalchian, 1989). Meyer and Cooke (1988) found that as more employees were included in a grievance, the less likely the outcome was favorable to the grievants. In their analysis of two samples of grievances, Dalton and Todor (1985) found that the gender composition of the supervisor and the union representative who processed the grievance influenced the outcome. Specifically, grievances were much less likely to be resolved in the grievant's favor when the supervisor was a woman and the union representative a man compared to the other gender compositions. In an analysis in a government organization, Klass (1989a) found that grievants with better work records and longer tenure were more likely to prevail in their grievances.

At the arbitration step, data from the American Arbitration Association for 27,000 awards issued during the 1983–93 period show that (within yearly fluctuations) employers prevail about 51 percent of the time (i.e., the grievance is denied), and that grievances are partly or fully sustained about 49 percent of the time (American Arbitration Association, 1993). If these AAA data are representative, over the long term unions and employers can expect to prevail about half the time they arbitrate. This is not an accidental result in an alternative dispute resolution (ADR) system where arbitrators usually are selected on an ad hoc basis (i.e., one case at a time, with no right to be selected again), and where the joint selection/compensation method means that arbitrators must maintain their acceptability to both sides. What may be more surprising is that some arbitrators apparently "tilt" toward unions or employers and continue to be widely used (Block & Stieber, 1987). Also, there is a only a moderate level of consistency in how different arbitrators respond to the same set of facts (Thornton & Zirkel, 1990). These findings suggest that employer and union expenditures on arbitrator search costs, which may be substantial, are rational investments.

There has not been much research that explains why unions or employers prevail at arbitration. One study of published awards found that employers were less likely to prevail in discipline awards, whereas unions were less likely to prevail in contract interpretation awards (Dilts & Deitsch, 1989). The authors' explanation was that the party with the burden of proof in these two types of arbitration cases is less likely to prevail, and this explanation is consistent with their results. An interesting and informative series of studies by Bemmels (1988a, 1988b, 1991) found that female grievants in discipline arbitration cases were significantly more likely than male grievants to have their grievances fully or partly sustained by male arbitrators. Bemmels (1990) and Thornton and Zirkel (1990) also found that most arbitrator demographic and professional characteristics were not significantly related to their decisions, which indicates that arbitral rulings cannot be predicted with easily available data.

The efficiency of arbitration and its alternatives

During the 1940s and 1950s, there was a vigorous debate in labor relations circles between the advocates of arbitration as an informal problem-solving process and those who viewed arbitration as a formal process of contractual adjudication (Nolan & Abrams, 1983). By the late 1950s, this contest had been decisively resolved in favor of the adjudicators, and nothing has occurred since then to alter this assessment. The most visible result of this adjudicative form of arbitration has been that courtroom trappings have become an integral part of the process, including the use of lawyers as advocates and arbitrators, court reporters and transcripts, subpoenas, sequestered witnesses, written briefs, written awards with lengthy opinions, and so on. Accompanying this increased formalism has been at least 40 years of continuing union and employer complaints about the cost, delay, and rigmarole associated with this "deluxe" arbitration. What has been even more notable than this continuing stream of complaints, however, is that little has been done to change the way grievance arbitration operates. This stability is eloquent testimony to the fact that arbitration is serving union and employer interests by resolving their most difficult contract interpretation disputes in a manner that is mutually acceptable.

Perhaps the two most discussed dispute resolution (DR) alternatives to adjudicatory arbitration are expedited arbitration and grievance mediation, whose speed and low cost have been hailed as providing more efficient grievance resolution. Expedited arbitration is simply a faster and cheaper method for producing an arbitrated decision. It relies on such techniques as referring selected grievances directly to arbitration (i.e., bypassing some of the grievance steps), faster hearings, an absence of lawyers, transcripts, and briefs, tight time limits for the award plus abbreviated opinions, and an arbitral fee ceiling, all to ensure that awards will be issued faster and at lower cost than in traditional arbitration. During the past 25 years, expedited arbitration received a lot of favorable publicity about its undisputed efficiency advantages (Kauffman, 1991). What is even more noteworthy, though, is the fact that this plain vanilla version of the arbitration process apparently has not been widely adopted (though most contracts provide for expedited referrals of selected grievances to arbitration).

Another alternative to traditional arbitration is grievance mediation. Spurred by the very successful use of mediation to resolve grievances in the unionized areas of the coal industry, during the 1980s grievance mediation received a great deal of favorable attention (Brett & Goldberg, 1983; Goldberg, 1982). Although mediation had been used decades ago to resolve grievances (McPherson, 1956), this technique did not become widely adopted in negotiated grievance procedures (U.S. Bureau of Labor Statistics, 1981), largely because mediation could not guarantee resolution. Instead, unions and employers placed their grievance resolution chips on arbitration.

The 1980s version of grievance mediation makes imaginative use of the threat of arbitration to assist unions and employers in resolving grievances voluntarily. In its current form, mediation operates as the penultimate step of the grievance procedure, with arbitration available if mediation is unsuccessful. This version calls for the mediator, who is also an experienced arbitrator, to hold an informal conference (not a formal hearing) with the union and the employer to discuss the grievance. If this discussion does not produce a settlement, the mediator issues an advisory opinion – on the spot – which predicts how the grievance would be decided by an arbitrator. In other words, this type of mediation is "peekaboo arbitration," in that the parties get a low-cost and nonbinding evaluation of their chances of prevailing in arbitration. This feature puts considerable pressure upon the parties, especially the party with the weaker contractual position, to reevaluate the desirability of arbitration.

This pressure is confirmed by the reports about the use of mediation, which indicate that it has successfully resolved more than three-quarters of the grievances that have been mediated, and that it has done so in a much faster and cheaper manner than traditional arbitration (Feuille, 1992). In short, mediation has been a very effective grievance resolution technique for unions and employers with high arbitration rates. What is even more noteworthy, though, is that mediation still has not been widely adopted by unions and employers in spite of the very favorable publicity it has received (Bureau of National Affairs, 1989). Whatever the specific reasons for this limited adoption (Feuille & Kolb, 1994), most unions and employers do not appear convinced that they need it. Perhaps this is ultimately a function of the fact, as seen above, that the vast majority of grievances are resolved anyway without resort to arbitration, and thus there is little pressure upon most unions and employers to adopt this incremental refinement in their grievance procedures.

Grievance procedures and public policy

One of the federal government's primary labor relations objectives over the years has been to encourage the use of procedures to absorb and resolve workplace conflict. As a result, Congress and especially the federal courts have heaped praise on negotiated grievance procedures, particularly arbitration. For instance, the U.S. Supreme Court has repeatedly said that, when unions and employers have promised to resolve grievances via arbitration and to accept the resulting awards as final and binding, they must live up to these promises even if the results are not to their liking (the 1960 *Steelworkers Trilogy* and its progeny). Further, there is nothing on the horizon to indicate any diminution in the favored public policy status of negotiated grievance procedures and arbitration. As a result, these DR procedures will continue to be the primary method by which unions and employers resolve their day-to-day disagreements over how the workplace should operate.

Consequences and impacts

Most of the research and commentary on union–management dispute resolution takes a benign view of workplace conflict. Most of the published analyses are performed by industrial relations scholars, and these individuals appear to explicitly or implicitly subscribe to the "pluralist" view of workplace disagreements. This perspective sees employers, employees, and unions as having legitimate and divergent interests, which may be summarized as the employers' efficiency interests versus the employees' equity interests as advocated by the union with its own collective institutional interests. These divergent interests in turn lead to conflict (e.g., disciplinary actions, grievances, slowdowns, strikes, etc.) over how the workplace should operate. Industrial relations scholars tend to view this conflict as constructive, in that

it indicates that these legitimately divergent views are being voiced and that neither the employer interests nor the employee interests are overwhelming the other (Feuille & Wheeler, 1981; Kochan & Katz, 1988). Human resources scholars also have come to extol the constructive effects of work-place conflict (Baron, 1991; Tjosvold, 1991). However, recent research has identified two different types of workplace impacts associated with grievance filing that are difficult to reconcile with this "conflict is good" perspective.

Productivity

Freeman and Medoff (1984) argue that grievance procedure existence, by providing an employee-voice alternative to "exit" behaviors such as quitting, results in lower quit rates and concomitantly lower employee turnover and retraining costs. Rees (1991) confirmed this proposition by finding that teacher quit rates are lower in school districts where the teacher contract provides stronger (more employee-favorable) GPs.

However, other research indicates that in unionized manufacturing plants grievance filing rates are negatively correlated with workplace productivity and/or product quality (Ichniowski, 1986; Ichniowski & Lewin, 1987; Katz et al., 1983; Katz et al., 1985; Norsworthy & Zabala, 1985). This research indicates that high levels of grievance filing are associated with reduced productivity (though Kleiner, Nickelsburg, and Pilarski (1989) argue that grievance filing rates and productivity may be positively associated under certain circumstances). It is not possible to determine to what extent this diminished productivity is the result of the "displacement effect" (i.e., employee work time diverted from production tasks to grievance processing), or the "worker reaction effect" (i.e., reduced worker effort as a reaction to the perceived unfair administration of the contract) (Ichniowski, 1986). Whatever the specific causes, high levels of formal grievance activity may be an easily observable signal that the employer–employee relationship is dysfunctional.

Grievant consequences

In theory, grievance filing should be a protected activity that does not elicit retaliation, and most grievance procedures contain no-reprisal provisions. In practice, however, grievants may be the recipient of an unfriendly postresolution managerial response. Recent research in four unionized organizations found that employees who file grievances, compared to their peers who do not file, are more likely to suffer such adverse consequences as lower performance ratings, lower promotion rates, and higher turnover in the period after they file their grievances (Lewin & Peterson, 1988). Moreover this study found that supervisors who have grievances filed against them suffer similar adverse consequences, compared with supervisors who do not have grievances filed against them. Klass and DeNisi (1989) found comparable adverse results on grievants' performance appraisals in a unionized public employer. Although these results come from only five organizations, comparable results have been found in several nonunion workplaces (as discussed later).

This research calls into question the usefulness of the prevailing exit-voice conventional wisdom about grievance procedures and their use. This received wisdom says that the exercise of voice (e.g., filing a grievance) is preferable to exit (e.g., shirking, quitting) for both employees and employers because it may result in such positive outcomes as reduced quit rates and turnover costs, enhanced job tenure and training, increased productivity, and increased employee commitment (Freeman & Medoff, 1984). The recent research on post-grievance-resolution consequences, however, suggests that an organizational reprisal perspective may be a more accurate framework through which to view grievance activity. If the results from these few analyzed

organizations are generalizable, they suggest that some managers view grievances as negative events that contribute to such unwanted outcomes as increased transaction costs and reduced productivity, rather than to such positive outcomes as reduced quit rates and enhanced commitment, and they react accordingly.

The future of unionized grievance resolution

During the 1940s and 1950s, the manner in which unions and employers resolved their day-to-day grievances changed considerably. Contract interpretation strikes became unusual and were largely replaced by grievance disputes processed through contractual grievance and arbitration procedures (Nolan & Abrams, 1983). In addition, these procedures, especially arbitration, evolved from mechanisms for informal problem-solving procedures into mechanisms for more formal contractual dispute adjudication.

However, once these grievance and arbitration procedures were in place and the parties became accustomed to using them, subsequent efforts to find more efficient methods for grievance resolution have been notable primarily for their limited adoption. In other words, once the key features of the union–employer grievance handling quid pro quo were worked out and adopted during the 1940s and 1950s, this union–management grievance accord endured largely unchanged during the ensuing years.

Further, this union–management accord has shown no signs of unraveling, even in the face of the unions' significantly declining share of the private sector workforce and the unions' substantially diminished ability during the 1980s and 1990s to conduct successful strikes (Feuille, 1994). There is some evidence that employers became more likely during the 1980s to appeal adverse arbitration awards to federal court and seek judicial rulings that these awards are null and void (Feuille & LeRoy, 1990). However, these appeals involve only a tiny fraction (1 percent or so) of all awards issued, and the courts reject most of the appeals, so arbitration remains the customary final resolution point for difficult grievances. Instead, employer attempts to avoid union-imposed grievance and arbitration procedures (and other employee-favorable elements of the union contract) appear to have taken the form of employer efforts to avoid unions altogether (Kochan et al., 1986; Lawler, 1990). Operating on a nonunion basis enables employers to unilaterally determine employment terms, including the existence and shape of grievance procedures, and in the next section we will examine how nonunion employers have done this.

GRIEVANCE DISPUTE RESOLUTION WITHOUT UNIONS

The absence of a union means that management can implement its own preferences regarding how employee complaints will be handled. These preferences usually include avoiding the "grievance" label, and instead using such names as "complaint," "appeal," "due process," "problem solving," "fair treatment," and so on in their DR procedures. The available evidence shows that although many and perhaps most nonunion employers do not provide any official complaint procedure, larger firms have been increasingly likely during the past twenty or so years to adopt formal grievance procedures (i.e., written procedures that are made known to employees and guarantee them the right to grieve). This evidence also shows that, in contrast to the union sector, these procedures are much more diverse than similar (see the review by Peterson & Lewin (1990)). However, one characteristic these nonunion procedures share is that top management usually re-

serves to itself the final decision on grievance resolution.

Existence

Periodic surveys of corporate personnel practices indicate that employers have become steadily more likely during the postwar period to provide some sort of formal grievance procedure for their nonunion employees (Feuille & Delaney, 1992). For instance, responses to six different surveys conducted during the 1977–92 period indicate that, overall, about half of the corporate respondents had a formal grievance procedure for some nonunion employees (the specific percentages ranged from 36 percent to 69 percent; Berenbeim, 1980; Chachere & Feuille, 1993; Delaney, Lewin, & Ichniowski, 1989; Edwards, 1993; Ewing, 1977; Lo Bosco, 1985). This and other research indicates that some of these procedures were companywide, others were specific to a division or facility, and some firms have more than one procedure for different employee groups or for specific types of complaints (e.g., discrimination, sexual harassment) (Chachere & Feuille, 1993; Edelman, 1990; Ewing, 1989). Because these surveys tend to oversample large firms that are more likely to have more formal personnel policies generally, and because there is some self-selection in the decision to respond, the results of these surveys almost certainly overstate the actual incidence of these formal nonunion procedures across all employers. Nevertheless, these results indicate that formal nonunion grievance procedures (or "NGPs") are becoming the norm among large employers with formal human resources policies.

Regarding the dimensions that are associated with the existence of these procedures, research invariably shows that firm size is positively and strongly correlated with the existence of a formal procedure (Chachere & Feuille, 1993; Delaney & Feuille, 1992;

Edelman, 1990). Somewhat surprisingly, this research also indicates that firms that are partly unionized are less likely to have a formal procedure for their nonunion employees than are completely nonunion firms (Berenbeim, 1980; Chachere & Feuille, 1993; Delaney & Feuille, 1992; Edelman, 1990). This finding suggests that managerial experience with unionized grievance procedures results in a reduced willingness to provide nonunion employees with a similar appeal channel.

Considering that there is no government compulsion upon employers to adopt these procedures, no union pressure to do so, and a reduced likelihood of being unionized compared to the 1940s and 1950s, the growth of these procedures during the 1970s and 1980s is rather remarkable. Some of this growth is due to employer imitation of what other employers are doing, especially as this knowledge is transmitted by HR professionals (Edelman, 1990). Some of this growth is due to employer union avoidance desires (Freeman & Kleiner, 1990), and nonunion employers are not the least bit reluctant to trumpet their union avoidance motives (Berenbeim, 1980; Freedman, 1985). However, the Chachere and Feuille (1993), Delaney and Feuille (1992), and Edelman (1990) studies suggest that this factor may deserve less weight than is commonly supposed.

Perhaps the strongest reason for the widespread emergence of these procedures is the growing desire of employees for fair treatment at work, as evidenced by their increasing willingness to seek redress in external forums when they believe they have been treated unfairly. Employees became much more willing to file discrimination complaints/lawsuits (often as a result of being terminated) and wrongful discharge lawsuits during the 1970s and 1980s (Dertouzos, Holland, & Ebener, 1988; Donohue & Siegelman, 1991; U.S. Equal Employment Opportunity Commission, 1971, 1990; Westin & Feliu, 1988). In other words, fired employees became increasingly likely to exit and then use voice.

These external complaints create the potential for very costly outcomes if employers lose. For instance, a study of 120 wrongful discharge lawsuits that were tried to a verdict in the California courts during the 1980–86 period found that employee-plaintiffs won 68 percent of the time, and the average jury verdict was $436,000 (Dertouzos, Holland, & Ebener, 1988).

Further, regardless of the outcome, the transaction costs (primarily legal fees) associated with these lawsuits and government agency complaints are high. For instance, a recent wrongful discharge lawsuit in California resulted in a verdict in the employer's favor, but the employer's legal fees exceeded one million dollars (Bureau of National Affairs, 1993). More typically, the Dertouzos et al. (1988) study found that employers spent an average of about $80,000 defending themselves in wrongful discharge trials regardless of whether they won or lost. Although these kinds of lawsuits usually are settled without trial, and thus are resolved more quickly with lower legal fees, a 1987 estimate of one employer's legal fees to win a summary judgment (i.e., a favorable judicial disposition without a trial) in a wrongful discharge lawsuit was $20,000 (Guidry & Huffman, 1990). Using information from 1980–86 California cases, Dertouzos and Karoly (1992) calculate that 95 percent of these lawsuits settle out of court at an average cost to employers of $40,000 ($25,000 to the plaintiff and $15,000 in legal fees). These figures provide an indication of how expensive it can be for employers who are on the receiving end of wrongful discharge lawsuits. Presumably, similar legal fees would be generated in discrimination lawsuits. To the extent that these kinds of disputes could be settled via an NGP and not litigated further (perhaps a heroic assumption), employers will benefit from much lower transaction costs.

In sum, we saw in the previous section that unionized employers agreed to formal GPs as a result of union pressure for a dispute resolution method that gave employees an effective way to appeal adverse treatment. There is no such collectively bargained pressure on nonunion firms. Instead, nonunion employers appear to have become more willing to impose formal GPs on themselves, primarily as a result of the individual decisions by thousands of employees to file charges and lawsuits. The large transaction costs generated by the external processing of these disputes appear to be playing a motivational role similar to the role of grievance strikes decades ago in persuading unionized employers to agree to formal GPs.

Operation and outcomes

Procedural characteristics

Nonunion grievance procedures vary widely. This variety can be seen when we consider various types of procedures on two key dimensions: the degree of formality (or the extent and specificity of the procedural rules that direct participants how to process grievances), and the degree of independence from management of the final decision maker (Aram & Salipante, 1981). The available evidence indicates that nonunion procedures, compared to unionized procedures, provide moderate levels of formality and only modest amounts of independence from management.

Perhaps the most widely mentioned type of grievance procedure is the "open door" appeal to higher management. A formal open-door procedure allows an employee to appeal an adverse decision to his or her supervisor and then up the chain of command to the higher levels of management, often with a feature that the immediate supervisor can be skipped if necessary. This type of appeal system is probably the most frequent NGP. These procedures also may be called "step review" procedures if they specify a series of precise steps through which an appeal must proceed. Some of these procedures may be quite formal, with specified steps, processing instructions for grievants and managers, forms to fill out, timelines, and so on. The unifying

element in these procedures is that management makes the final decision.

A more user-friendly approach is an "ombudsman" procedure (Rowe, 1987). In this arrangement, an ombuds office (or the human resources office may perform this service without using the ombuds label) provides a place where an employee can submit a complaint, and have the ombudsperson investigate it and try and formulate a resolution that is acceptable to the employee and management. Initial employee contacts with the ombuds office generally are confidential, though confidentiality may need to be shed in an investigation. Because the ombuds office is outside the normal chain of command, it may be a "safer" place to bring a grievance than an immediate supervisor. The ombudsperson does not have formal authority to impose a resolution to the problem. Instead, he or she serves as an investigator and mediator. This means that the success of this arrangement depends upon the communication and mediation skills of the ombudsperson rather than upon the institutional features of the procedure. Even though management still has the final authority over how the grievance will be resolved, an ombuds-type procedure provides the grievant with more grievance processing assistance than most other NGPs. There are indications that this type of procedure is becoming more frequent, with about 500 medium and large companies estimated to be using it in 1993 (Woo, 1993). Moreover an ombuds process may coexist with a more formal NGP for those grievances that the ombuds office cannot resolve.

Some nonunion procedures are identified by the nature of a specific decision step (usually the terminal step). One such category are those where a review board or panel (or "internal tribunal" (McCabe, 1988)) makes the decision about the grievance. These panels can be composed according to the employer's preferences, and there are two primary types. The first is composed exclusively or primarily of managers. The second is composed of a minority of managers and a majority of rank-and-file employees. This latter arrangement is usually called "peer review" due to the fact that the grievant's peers on the panel have control over the outcome of the grievance (Coombe, 1984; Reibstein, 1986). Another key dimension about these review panels is whether or not the panel hears face-to-face testimony from the grievant and other witnesses. In some companies these panels hear such testimony and then decide the grievance. In other companies no hearing is held. Instead, the panel reviews written information submitted about the grievance and then makes a decision (Ewing, 1989). Most of these panels serve as the final decision step, but a few procedures allow an appeal from the panel's decision (Bohlander & White, 1988).

A very small proportion of nonunion employers have multistep grievance procedures capped by arbitration. An employee who is dissatisfied with management's response to his or her grievance may appeal the matter to binding arbitration by an outside arbitrator, though some companies limit this option to certain types of grievances (particularly discharge). Most employers who provide this option also pay the arbitrator's fees and expenses (Ewing, 1989; McCabe, 1988).

Table 18.1 presents data from a 1991 survey of organizations about the procedural characteristics of their NGPs. The 111 procedures portrayed in this table represent the responses to a survey of corporations that employ alumni of a graduate IR/HR program at a large university. As the table indicates, there is considerable variation in the features contained in these procedures. For instance, most procedures can be used to grieve any work-related subject, and in most firms all employees are eligible to use the procedure, but slightly less than half of the firms require grievances to be submitted in writing. Further, half of the firms provide grievants with no rights to representation when presenting

their grievances, and most of the firms that allow representation prohibit outsiders from performing this function. Half of the firms allow grievants to call witnesses on their own behalf, but half do not. Only slightly more than half require managers to respond to grievances in writing. As the responses to these items indicate, some employers have provided considerably more procedural formality than others (see also Bohlander & White, 1988; Ewing, 1989; Lo Bosco, 1985; McCabe, 1988).

Perhaps the key dimension of interest is the nature of the final procedural step. The table's results indicate that in about 90 percent of these procedures management has reserved the final grievance decision to itself. Of these procedures 7 percent culminate in peer review panels, and 4 percent are capped by an arbitration step. In particular, the table 18.1 arbitration results are similar to the arbitration incidence results reported in other studies of employers with NGPs. For instance, a 1986–87 survey found that about 10 percent of about 450 reported NGPs ended in arbitration (Ichniowski & Lewin, 1988). Another 1986–87 survey of 78 nonunion members of the National Association of Manufacturers found that 6 of these firms (or 8 percent) provided arbitration as the final grievance step (McCabe, 1988). Another 1980s study found that 3 of 15 firms (or 20 percent) provided for arbitration of selected grievances (Ewing, 1989).

If we consider NGPs with peer review or with arbitration as the NGPs that provide considerable independence from management of the final decision maker, the results in table 18.1 and in other studies indicate that such independence is a slowly expanding idea whose time has not yet arrived in most organizations. In addition, the available information indicates that most NGPs do not provide the same level of due-process formality and grievance-processing assistance to grievants as provided in union-negotiated procedures. Considering that there is no organized collective employee voice aggressively

Table 18.1 Nonunion grievance procedure characteristics
(N = 111 organizations)

		Mean (S.D.)	Sample size
1.	Subjects which may be grieved [1–3]	2.66 (0.65)	111
	[1] Only subjects named	11	
	[2] Some exclusions	16	
	[3] All work-related	84	
2.	All employees eligible [0–1]	0.86 (0.34)	111
3.	Right to file grievances [0–1]	0.91 (0.29)	110
4.	Protect from retaliation [0–1]	0.86 (0.45)	110
5.	Must file grievances in writing [0–1]	0.44 (0.50)	111
6.	Employee time limits [0–1]	0.39 (0.49)	111
7.	Instructs how to use procedure [0–1]	0.73 (0.45)	111
8.	Series of steps [0–1]	0.85 (0.36)	111
9.	Can bypass immediate supervisor [0–1]	0.86 (0.37)	111
10.	Processing assistance provided [0–1]	0.84 (0.36)	109
11.	Employee right to be present [0–1]	0.78 (0.41)	111
12.	Employee right to representation [0–4]	1.08 (1.25)	110
	[0] No representation	55	
	[1] Another employee	9	
	[2] HR staff	36	
	[3] Outsider – not attorney	2	
	[4] Attorney	8	
13.	Right to call witnesses [0–1]	0.50 (0.50)	108
14.	Managers must respond in writing [0–1]	0.56 (0.50)	111
15.	Employer time limits for response [0–1]	0.53 (0.50)	111
16.	Final step options [1–8]	2.98 (1.68)	107
	[1] Local facility manager	24	
	[2] Senior HR manager	14	
	[3] Senior line manager	42	
	[4] Panel-managers	13	
	[5] Panel-managers (majority)/employees	3	
	[6] Panel-managers/employees (majority)	7	
	[7] Panel-peers only	0	
	[8] Outside arbitration	4	

Source: Chachere and Feuille (1993)

seeking such procedural protection in nonunion firms, this difference is not surprising.

Operation

Relatively little information is available about grievance resolution in nonunion firms. Part of this information scarcity is due to a reduced level of research attention over the years that is slowly being corrected, and another reason is the minimal grievance record keeping done in many nonunion firms. However, during the past several years some information has emerged that helps us understand how grievances are filed, processed, and resolved in nonunion firms.

Looking first at grievance-filing rates, three studies report filing rates across organizations that range from three to seven grievances per 100 employees per year (Delaney et al., 1989; Lewin, 1987, 1990). When these rates are compared with the filing rates in unionized firms presented above, they suggest that employees in nonunion firms that have formal NGPs are less than half as likely to file grievances compared to their unionized peers. However, as in the union sector, most grievances are resolved in a short period of time during the first two steps of the procedure, and only a very small fraction are appealed to the final step (Delaney et al., 1989; Ewing, 1989; Lamont, 1987; Lewin, 1987, 1990).

There is very little research that explains why nonunion employees file grievances. The filing reasons associated with the quality of the union–management relationship, the contract negotiation cycle, or with union or managerial contract administration policies are not present in the nonunion arena, and the absence of these factors may explain why grievance-filing rates are lower in nonunion than unionized firms. However, the absence of factors does not go very far in explaining why some nonunion employees grieve and most do not. One study of grievance processing in five nonunion firms found that grievants were more likely to be male, younger, less experienced, blue collar, and minority group members than nongrievants (Lewin, 1990). However, another study of a single company found that grievants were more likely to be those with longer service, and there were no gender differences (Boroff, 1990).

Boroff's (1990) study also suggests that the length of an employee's employment expectation may have a significant influence on an employee's propensity to file a grievance. Surveyed employees were asked if they had experienced unfair treatment and if they had filed a grievance. They also were asked if they expected to stay with or leave the company within the next three years. The results showed that employees who experienced unfair treatment and who expected to leave the firm were significantly more likely to file a grievance compared to employees who experienced unfair treatment and who expected

to remain with the firm. This research indicates that employees with long-term employment expectations (the "loyal" employees in Boroff's terminology) are more likely to respond to unfair treatment by remaining silent than by filing a grievance (i.e., they neither exit nor exercise voice).

We saw above that in unionized firms, a substantial share of grievances are resolved in the employee's favor, though this share varies substantially across firms. In nonunion firms, much less of this information is available. However, we can draw a tentative portrait based on results from a few studies. For instance, in three large firms grievances were resolved in the employee's favor 46, 48, and 51 percent of the time, and the probability of an employee-favorable resolution was moderately enhanced at the higher steps of the procedure (Lewin, 1987). In three metropolitan hospitals grievance resolutions favored employees 41, 48, and 54 percent of the time (Salipante & Aram, 1984). Four companies reported employee-favorable resolutions 22 to 67 percent of the time at the internal review board step, depending upon the company (Ewing, 1989).

Regarding peer review panels, one estimate is that these panels side with employees 30 to 40 percent of the time (Reibstein, 1986). Three company-specific studies confirm this estimate. For instance, an examination of peer panel decisions in two divisions of a large petrochemical company during the early 1990s found that peer panels sustained 30 percent of the 67 grievances presented to them, including 20 percent of the termination grievances (which resulted in these fired employees being reinstated with back pay) (Goulet, 1993). A study of the peer panel system at the Control Data Corporation found that these panels sustained 36 percent of the 22 grievances they decided over a three-year period (Lamont, 1987). An examination of the peer review system at the Adolph Coors Company found that 40 percent of the 89 grievances heard in one year were partly or fully sustained by these panels (Coombe, 1984). In general, the limited information available suggests that nonunion grievants prevail a significant proportion of the time.

Nonunion grievance procedures and public policy

We saw above that the federal courts have given very strong approval to the use of negotiated grievance procedures and to compliance with grievance decisions in unionized workplaces. In contrast, the current status of employment common law does not provide a clear picture of how the courts view the role of GPs in nonunion establishments. The primary legal and practical issue for employers is the extent to which the existence, use, and outcomes of an NGP either will preclude external complaints or else will be given deference in subsequent court or administrative proceedings.

Although there is variation across state and federal courts, most courts appear reluctant to adopt an official preclusion policy that prevents grievances processed through an NGP from being appealed to court and addressed on their merits. Indeed, in a well-known 1986 decision by the U.S. Supreme Court in a sexual harassment case (*Meritor Savings Bank* v. *Vinson*), the Court rejected the argument that the existence of a grievance procedure (in a nonunion firm) coupled with the plaintiff's failure to use the procedure insulates a firm from liability under the antidiscrimination laws.

However, there are numerous court decisions that indicate that judges have given employer-favorable weight to the existence and use of credible (i.e., fair) NGPs when responding to employee wrongful discharge lawsuits (Feliu, 1987; Guidry & Huffman, 1990). These decisions indicate that an NGP may not keep an employer out of court, but that the existence and use of a fair NGP will enhance the employer's chance of prevailing.

A thornier subject is how the use of NGPs generally and nonunion arbitration in particular fits into the handling of employee discrimination charges. These charges and lawsuits are filed pursuant to state or federal law, especially Title VII of the 1964 Civil Rights Act, and they have become steadily more frequent during the past 25 years. If a nonunion employee is covered by an arbitration agreement with his or her employer that encompasses employment disputes, does this arbitration arrangement mean that discrimination grievances must be arbitrated before they can be litigated? Going further, does this arbitration arrangement mean that discrimination grievances must be arbitrated and then not litigated?

In 1991, the U.S. Supreme Court sent a signal to employers and employees that arbitration may be a desirable method for resolving discrimination disputes in nonunion workplaces by answering affirmatively the first of these two questions. The Court ruled that a fired 62-year-old stockbroker, who was covered by an arbitration provision that encompassed employment disputes, could not proceed with his lawsuit against his former employer (a securities firm) in federal district court under the Age Discrimination in Employment Act (*Gilmer* v. *Interstate/Johnson Lane Corp.*). Instead, he had to take his age discrimination claim to arbitration because it was an employment dispute within the scope of the arbitration agreement. Since then, lower federal courts have ruled that employee claims of sex discrimination under Title VII must be arbitrated if the complaining employee is covered by an arbitration provision with the employer (Shearer, 1992–93). Moreover, in that same year the U.S. Congress sent a similar signal to employers by including in Section 118 of the Civil Rights Act of 1991 a provision that explicitly encouraged "the use of alternative means of dispute resolution, including . . . arbitration" to resolve disputes under this statute (which also allows for successful plaintiffs in certain cases to win damage awards in addition to lost wages). These legal developments have caused nonunion employers to look more favorably upon arbitration as a grievance resolution technique (Holmes, 1994; Lambert, 1992).

It is beyond the scope of this analysis to examine all the legal issues surrounding the use of private grievance and arbitration procedures to resolve disputes arising under discrimination statutes. From the employer perspective, probably the key unanswered question is the extent to which the use of arbitration will prevent the subsequent use of litigation to address the same claims (i.e., the second question posed above). The Supreme Court's *Gilmer* decision did not directly answer this question, and the nearest Supreme Court precedent from the unionized arena indicates that an employee who arbitrates a discrimination grievance under a union contract and loses is allowed to pursue the discrimination claim in a lawsuit pursuant to federal law (*Alexander* v. *Gardner-Denver*). Therefore, it is likely that a nonunion employee whose discrimination grievance is rejected in arbitration (or in some other type of NGP) still could pursue that same claim in a lawsuit against the employer (i.e., he or she could use the internal voice procedure and then the external voice procedure). This possibility may help explain why nonunion employers have been moving slowly to embrace arbitration rather than stampeding to adopt it in the wake of the *Gilmer* decision (Bureau of National Affairs, 1992; Lambert, 1992). Employer preferences for arbitration usually are contingent upon arbitration being used as a once-and-for-all DR procedure.

Arbitration also is at the heart of proposals for handling wrongful discharge claims by fired "at-will" employees. As seen above, these claims usually emerge as lawsuits with their large transaction costs and their potential for large verdicts in the plaintiff's favor. At the same time, employee ability to file and prevail in such lawsuits varies greatly from state to state depending upon the status of the appellate common law in each state (Koys, Briggs, & Grenig, 1987). In addition, plaintiff

attorneys are reluctant to take on these cases unless the fired employee is an "attractive" client (i.e., presents a high probability of a large recovery). In response to the situation where a few fired nonunion employees are able to win the proverbial pot of gold at the end of the wrongful discharge litigation rainbow but most are destined to suffer in silence, proposals have been put forth that would, in effect, statutorily impose an NGP upon employers and employees for the resolution of wrongful discharge claims.

For instance, in 1991 the National Conference of Commissioners on Uniform State Laws drafted and recommended that states adopt its Model Employment Termination Act (Bureau of National Affairs, 1991; Fox & Hindman, 1993). The META requires "good cause" for discharge, provides for arbitration instead of litigation to resolve termination disputes, and limits the monetary liability of employers compared with their open-ended common law exposure in a wrongful discharge lawsuit. This proposed law follows the 1987 adoption of a wrongful discharge law in Montana that contains generally similar provisions (Krueger, 1991). That law was adopted primarily because some employers supported it in the wake of expensive court verdicts won by fired employees. However, it is not clear if the litigation pressures are sufficiently strong to give employers in other states an incentive to support wrongful discharge legislation as an alternative to lawsuits, and plaintiff attorneys prefer litigation with its potential for large damage awards and contingency fees. In any case, arbitration remains at the center of the wrongful discharge DR debate.

Edwards (1993) goes further with his proposal for a statutorily-mandated system that would (1) require employers above a specified size threshold to adopt an employee handbook that would specify various employment terms; (2) make these handbooks publicly available and legally enforceable; and (3) adopt a system of mediation and arbitration to resolve all employer–employee disputes over statutory and handbook rights. If the META's method of handling wrongful discharge disputes or Edwards' wider-ranging proposal is adopted, the gap between union and nonunion voice procedures will diminish substantially.

In short, employer incentives to adopt formal NGPs, especially those with arbitration, are heavily influenced by legal developments. To date most of these developments have emanated on a case-by-case basis from the courts in the absence of explicit workplace ADR legislation.

Consequences and impacts

Productivity

There is very little research that correlates grievance procedures or grievance activity with productivity in nonunion workplaces. One study looked at the grievance situation in ten paper mills of the same company, with nine of these mills unionized and one nonunion. The nonunion mill had no grievance procedure (all nine of the unionized mills had the traditional unionized GP culminating in arbitration), and the nonunion mill was less productive than the nine unionized mills (Ichniowski, 1986). In a study of hospitals (most of which were nonunion), Spencer (1986) found that turnover of registered nurses was negatively correlated with the number of employee voice mechanisms, which included "formal grievance" and "ombudsman" procedures. These two studies do not address the productivity effects associated with grievance activity.

If we expand "productivity" to include the expenses of dispute resolution, there is no question that a formal NGP provides for a faster and cheaper method of grievance resolution than the use of such external forums as government agencies and the courts. To what extent will the presence of an NGP reduce the employer's external complaint risk? Salipante and Aram (1984) examined internal grievances and external discrimination

complaints filed during 1978–79 by nonunion employees at three metropolitan hospitals (most of the employees at these hospitals were minority and/or female). They found that the introduction and initial use of an NGP at one hospital was associated with a reduction in the rate at which external EEO charges were filed. They concluded that the NGPs in these three hospitals siphoned off and resolved some disputes that otherwise would have been filed externally, but their data indicate that some level of external complaints continued to be generated at all three hospitals.

One estimate put forward by a researcher who examined NGPs in several large firms was that the number of employee lawsuits against the employer should decline by about 5 percent per year for each year after the "establishment of a good hearing procedure and fairly widespread employee awareness of it" (Ewing, 1989, 36). This estimate is based on "what executives and attorneys told me," and not on a systematic analysis of employer grievance and litigation records. A 1984 study of eight organizations with formal NGPs reported that seven of these eight firms believed that their volume of wrongful discharge lawsuits was "significantly lower" than in other firms (Westin & Feliu, 1988, 16), but there was no information about how these studied firms arrived at this conclusion. In short, there do not appear to be any definitive studies of the extent to which the availability and use of NGPs reduces the likelihood of external complaints/lawsuits by these same employees.

Grievant consequences

Recall the research mentioned above showing that in five unionized organizations grievance filers were more likely than nonfilers to suffer adverse consequences in the period after their grievances were resolved (Lewin & Peterson, 1988; Klass & DeNisi, 1989). Other research shows similar adverse consequences for grievance filers in nonunion organizations. Compared to their peers who did not file grievances, grievants in a total of eight non-union organizations were more likely to experience such adverse consequences as lower performance ratings, lower promotion rates, and higher turnover in the period after they filed their grievances (Lewin, 1987, 1990). Similarly, the supervisors of the filers suffered similar adverse consequences compared with supervisors who did not have grievances filed against them. These field research findings have been confirmed in a laboratory study that carefully controlled employee performance to ensure that post-grievance-resolution adverse consequences were not the result of reduced performance (Carnevale, Olson, & O'Connor, 1992).

The available evidence on how grievants are treated in the period after the resolution of their grievances raises serious concern about the impact of grievance filing upon an employee's status with an employer. The available evidence is admittedly limited, but it supports the conclusion that the act of filing a grievance increases the probability of experiencing adverse consequences, and this conclusion seems valid in union and nonunion workplaces. This research confirms that employee fears of managerial retaliation for grievance filing are rational. The practical lesson from this research is that employees who experience grievable unfair treatment should try to resolve their problem informally, and if such informal resolution fails they should give careful thought to whether it is in their best interest to file and pursue a formal grievance.

DISCUSSION AND CONCLUSIONS

This analysis supports three general conclusions about the adoption and use of formal GPs in the workplace. First, management has been reluctant to adopt formal GPs unless the transaction costs associated with alternative grievance resolution methods are sufficiently high that an institutionalized remedial voice procedure is comparatively attractive. For instance, managements of unionized firms adopted GPs culminating in arbitration in preference to the use of strikes and slowdowns to resolve grievances, and managements of nonunion firms have become more willing to adopt formal GPs as a response to the increased use of external complaint forums (government agencies, courts) by individual employees. In short, the evidence suggests that managers adopt formal GPs in response to the increased likelihood that even more costly grievance resolution methods will be used.

Second, research does not provide an all-encompassing explanation about the reasons for the diverse grievance-filing and resolution behaviors across workplaces. This seems to be the result of very different research sites and research methods, especially the use of noncomparable variables. The portrait that emerges is that a host of situation-specific or idiosyncratic factors determine how often and why employees and/or unions officially protest managerial behavior. This diversity means that a unified and encompassing explanation for grievance activity and outcomes is destined to elude researchers. At the same time, this diversity requires practitioners to fully understand the workplace-specific factors that drive their own grievance systems.

Third, the manner in which GPs are adopted and grievances processed indicates that grievance resolution is not in the same category as self-managed work teams and other employee involvement programs, employee stock ownership plans, pay for performance, and other high-profile and even glamorous HRM efforts to create a more cooperative and productive employer–employee relationship. Grievance procedures are adversarial influence mechanisms, and grievances are usually viewed as competitive rather than cooperative conflict resolution episodes. Grievances often involve finger-pointing, generate hard feelings, and may interfere with productivity. Grievances also may be hazardous to the organizational careers of the grievants and their supervisors. In spite of these features, though, grievance resolution is a necessary element in an efficiently and effectively functioning organization, for there will always be some amount of disputing about how employees *are* versus *should be* treated.

Grievance resolution via unions

On the grievance disputing dimension, there are two noteworthy features associated with the presence of a union. The first is that the presence of a union usually increases the grievance dispute propensity in the workplace compared with a nonunion facility. The second is that the union uses its bargaining power to negotiate grievance procedures that give employees a much stronger channel for making their voice heard compared with their nonunion peers. In other words, the grievance dispute process occupies a much higher profile in union than in nonunion workplaces. Further, there is nothing in the well-publicized shrinkage of the private sector union density rate that diminishes this conclusion.

There is ample evidence that the manner in which unions and employers deal with each other through the grievance procedure varies substantially across workplaces and over time. However, in spite of this operational variation there is no persuasive evidence that the shape of the standard employee voice procedure in the unionized workplace will undergo any significant change in the foreseeable future. The union–management grievance-processing accord that was adopted during the 1940s and 1950s appears to be a remarkably enduring feature of U.S. collective bargaining relationships, largely because it has served the interests of unions and employers in providing a nondisruptive vehicle for resolving grievance disputes.

Perhaps the key grievance resolution feature in any union–management relationship is how to create and maintain a high-trust/low-conflict approach to grievance resolution.

Evidence shows that when union–management trust is low or absent, conflict levels generally are high, and productivity usually suffers (i.e., a low-trust/high-conflict relationship is more than merely annoying). One of the most salient conflict arenas is the grievance procedure. As a result, it is not surprising that research has consistently found a negative correlation between grievance-filing rates and productivity. What is less clear is why GPs come to be operated in a dysfunctional manner, and how unions and employers are able to change from a high-conflict to a low-conflict grievance-processing arrangement.

From a research perspective, there appear to be three useful topics for future investigation. The first is analyzing why grievances are sustained or denied. We have a very modest ability to explain why grievants prevail in some grievances and not in others. More research in this area would help increase our understanding of the distributive justice impacts of grievance procedures. The second is to continue the exploration of the grievants' post-resolution consequences that has been identified in recent research. It is disturbing that individual grievants appear to face a higher probability of adverse employment consequences as a result of grieving. Additional research would help us understand the extent and the causes of such behaviors. The third topic is the organizational impacts of grievance behaviors. This subject would profit from additional analyses of the productivity impacts of grievance behaviors, and also from more detailed investigations of the specific processes by which grievance behaviors affect the functioning of the production process.

Grievance resolution without unions

In the absence of a union, the grievance process occupies a lower profile in the workplace, and employees have a less forceful mechanism for pressing their claims of unfair treatment. Indeed, in many organizations nonunion employees have no institutional vehicle of any kind for raising these claims. At the same time, an increasing number of large nonunion firms are moving closer to the union grievance model by providing their employees with formal grievance mechanisms through which they can protest adverse treatment and seek redress from somebody other than the manager involved in the protested decision. A small share of these firms have even imposed peer review or arbitration upon themselves, and both of these decision methods offer grievants an alternative to management making the final grievance decision. In short, the past twenty-five or so years have witnessed a remarkable growth in the adoption of formal employee voice channels by nonunion firms. Much of this growth appears motivated by employer desires to avoid litigating employee complaints. Just as unionized employers came to believe that GPs with arbitration are more efficient than work disruptions as the way to resolve grievances under a collective bargaining agreement, so more and more nonunion employers are coming to believe that NGPs are more efficient than litigation as the way to resolve grievances under the implicit bargaining relationship that characterizes most nonunion employment relationships.

The results from the emerging body of research on NGPs provide ammunition to both the supporters and the skeptics of the willingness of nonunion employers to establish GPs that deliver genuine organizational justice to employees who believe that they have been treated unfairly. The supporters would insist that the existence and characteristics of these formal NGPs provide improved opportunities for the weaker party in the employment relationship – employees – to seek redress from unfair treatment, especially when compared with nonunion employees who have no access to formal complaint procedures of any kind and who therefore are at the unfettered mercy of management. Using

Greenberg's (1990) framework, the supporters would argue that this research indicates that many American employers take seriously the goal of actually being fair to employees.

In contrast, the skeptics would insist that these results indicate that large numbers of nonunion employees still have no effective remedial voice mechanism of any kind, even in many large firms that are likely to have a wide array of formal and progressive personnel policies. Further, in most of those firms with NGPs employees usually must process grievances on their own, and they must trust higher management to make a fair decision. The skeptics also would rely upon Greenberg's (1990) analysis, but they would argue that the adoption of NGPs means only that these employers are engaged in an impression management process designed to make them look fair to their employees rather than to actually be fair.

Which of these views is more accurate? The answer depends upon the benchmark used. If the NGPs portrayed in recent research are compared with the absence of any official grievance channel in most nonunion workplaces, these formal NGPs provide employees with a substantial amount of remedial voice protection. On the other hand, if these NGPs are compared with grievance procedures in unionized workplaces, these NGPs provide employees with inferior procedural and distributive justice protection. Both of these benchmarks are valid reference points. As a result, it is difficult to select one over the other.

Whichever view is adopted, it is important to develop a fuller understanding of grievance resolution in nonunion organizations. The private sector work force is now 87 percent nonunion (U.S. Bureau of Labor Statistics, 1993), but compared to what we know about remedial voice processing in the union sector, we have relatively meager knowledge of how these nonunion employees and their employers deal with employee claims of unfair treatment. Perhaps this imbalance will be remedied with additional research (see Klass & Feldman, 1993).

Two final points need to be mentioned that apply to union and nonunion workplaces. First, in keeping with the traditions of IR-HR research, this chapter has focused upon those workplace disputes and DR procedures that are visible, formal, and rational. Operationally, the disputes examined here emerge as official employer–employee conflicts and are processed through institutionalized channels for handling these conflicts. This focus ignores the private, informal, and sometimes nonrational nature of many workplace disputes and the equally private and informal manner in which these disputes are handled (Bartunek, Kolb, & Lewicki, 1992; Kolb, 1992). These informal disputes (which may have a variety of labels) are difficult to research, in large part because they leave little or no paper trail and hence are very hard to measure (i.e., these disputes do not officially exist in the organization's record-keeping system). However, the frequency of these informal disputes and private methods of handling them mean that the analysis in this chapter has not come close to exhausting the arena of workplace conflict and its resolution.

Second, during the post-World War II period there has been a steadily increasing emphasis on the formalized processing of grievance disputes. One result of this increased reliance on formal grievance procedures is the growth of a cadre of employer and employee/union advocates, government agency administrators, mediators, arbitrators, and academics (these roles often overlap) who make a comfortable living handling, deciding, and studying grievance disputes. These are the same people who produce most of the research and commentary on grievance resolution systems, and in that capacity they have a strong influence on the conventional wisdom about these systems. This received wisdom is hardly monolithic, but it emphasizes that formalized alternative dispute resolution arrangements work well in the workplace, and that there should be more of them, particularly as alternatives to work stoppages, employer domination, and litigation. Accordingly, as we continue down the workplace DR path, we may rest assured that the American workplace dispute resolution community remains vigorous in the pursuit of its professional self-interest.

REFERENCES

Alexander v. *Gardner-Denver, Inc.*, 415 U.S. 36 (1974).

Alexander, S., & Ruderman, M. (1987). The role of procedural and distributive justice in organizational behavior. *Social Justice Research*, 1, 117–98.

Allen, R. E., & Keaveny, T. J. (1985). Factors differentiating grievants and nongrievants. *Human Relations*, 38, 519–34.

American Arbitration Association (1993). *Study Time* (a quarterly newsletter for labor arbitrators), No. 4.

Aram, J. D. & Salipante, P. F., Jr. (1981). An evaluation of organizational due process in the resolution of employee/employer conflict. *Academy of Management Review*, 6, 197–204.

Baron, R. A. (1991). Positive effects of conflict: A cognitive perspective. *Employee Responsibilities and Rights Journal*, 4, 25–36.

Bartunek, J. M., Kolb, D. M., & Lewicki, R. J. (1992). Bringing conflict out from behind the scenes: Private, informal, and nonrational dimensions of conflict in organizations. In D. M. Kolb & J. M. Bartunek (eds.), *Hidden Conflict in Organizations*, 209–28. Newbury Park, CA: Sage.

Bemmels, B. (1988a). The effect of grievants' gender on arbitrators' decisions. *Industrial and Labor Relations Review*, 41, 251–62.

Bemmels, B. (1988b). Gender effects in discharge arbitration. *Industrial and Labor Relations Review*, 42, 63–76.

Bemmels, B. (1990). Arbitrator characteristics and arbitrator decisions. *Journal of Labor Research*, 11, 181–92.

Bemmels, B. (1991). Attribution theory and discipline arbitration. *Industrial and Labor Relations Review*, 44, 548–62.

Bemmels, B. (1994). The determinants of grievance initiation. *Industrial and Labor Relations Review*, 47, 285–301.

Bemmels, B., Reshef, Y., & Stratton-Devine, K. (1991). The roles of supervisors, employees, and stewards in grievance initiation. *Industrial and Labor Relations Review*, 45, 15–30.

Berenbeim, R. (1980). Nonunion complaint systems: A corporate appraisal. Conference Board Research Report No. 770. Conference Board, New York.

Block, R. N., & Stieber, J. (1987). The impact of attorneys and arbitrators on arbitration decisions. *Industrial and Labor Relations Review*, 40, 543–55.

Bohlander, G. W., & White, H. C. (1988). Building bridges: Nonunion employee grievance systems. *Personnel*, 65, 62–6.

Boroff, K. (1993). Loyalty – A correlate of exit, voice, or silence? In J. F. Burton, Jr. (ed.), *Proceedings of the Forty-Second Annual Meeting*, 307–14. Madison, WI: Industrial Relations Research Association.

Brett, J. M., & Goldberg, S. B. (1983). Grievance mediation in the coal industry: A field experiment. *Industrial and Labor Relations Review*, 37, 49–69.

Bureau of National Affairs (1989). *Collective bargaining negotiations and contracts: Basic patterns*. Washington, D.C.: BNA.

Bureau of National Affairs (1991). Draft employment termination act is approved as model law by conference of commissioners. *Daily Labor Report*, No. 154, August 9, A16.

Bureau of National Affairs (1992). Employers reluctant to embrace mandatory arbitration, survey finds. *Daily Labor Report*, No. 84, April 30, A14–A16.

Bureau of National Affairs (1993). ADR techniques gain favor in non-traditional settings. *Daily Labor Report*, No. 48, March 15, C1–C8.

Cappelli, P., & Chauvin, K. (1991). A test of an efficiency model of grievance activity. *Industrial and Labor Relations Review*, 45, 3–14.

Carnevale, P. J., Olson, J. B., & O'Connor, K. M. (1992). Reciprocity and informality in a laboratory grievance system. Unpublished paper presented at the Fifth Conference of the International Association of Conflict Management, Minneapolis. June.

Chachere, D. R., & Feuille, P. (1993). Grievance procedures and due process in nonunion workplaces. In J. F. Burton, Jr. (ed.), *Proceedings of the Forty-Fifth Annual Meeting*, 446–55. Madison, WI: Industrial Relations Research Association.

Chaykowski, R. P., Slotsve, G. A., & Butler, J. S. (1992). A simultaneous analysis of grievance activity and outcome decisions. *Industrial and Labor Relations Review*, 45, 724–37.

Cleveland State University (1990). Public sector collective bargaining agreements in major metropolitan areas. Report 9002–1. Cleveland: Industrial Relations Center, Cleveland State University. July.

Coombe, J. D. (1984). Peer review: The emerging successful application. *Employee Relations Law Journal*, 9, 659–71.

Cutcher-Gershenfeld, J. (1991). The impact on economic performance of a transformation in workplace relations. *Industrial and Labor Relations Review*, 44, 241–60.

Dalton, D. R., & Cosier, R. A. (1991). Introduction to the special issue on positive conflict. Conflict and employees: The right and processes to be heard. *Employee Responsibilities and Rights Journal*, 4, 1–5.

Dalton, D. R., & Todor, W. D. (1981). Win, lose, draw: The grievance process in practice. *Personnel Administrator*, 26, May–June, 25–9.

Dalton, D. R., & Todor, W. D. (1985). Composition of dyads as a factor in the outcomes of workplace justice: Two field assessments. *Academy of Management Journal*, 28, 704–12.

Delaney, J. T., & Feuille, P. (1992). Grievance and arbitration procedures among nonunion employers. In J. F. Burton, Jr. (ed.), *Proceedings of the Forty-Fourth Annual Meeting*, 529–38. Madison, WI: Industrial Relations Research Association.

Delaney, J. T., Lewin, D., & Ichniowski, C. (1989). Human resource policies and practices in American firms. BLMR 137. U.S. Department of Labor, Bureau of Labor-Management Relations and Cooperative Programs, Washington, D.C.

Dertouzos, J. N., Holland, E., & Ebener, P. (1988). *The Legal and Economic Consequences of Wrongful Termination*. Santa Monica, CA: Rand Corporation.

Dertouzos, J. N., & Karoly, L. A. (1992). *Labor-Market Responses to Employer Liability*. Santa Monica, CA: Rand Corporation.

Dilts, D. A., & Deitsch, C. R. (1989). Arbitration win/loss rates as a measure of arbitrator neutrality. *Arbitration Journal*, 44, September, 42–7.

Donohue, J. J., & Siegelman, P. (1991). The changing nature of employment discrimination litigation. *Stanford Law Review*, 43, 983–1033.

Edelman, L. B. (1990). Legal environments and organizational governance: The expansion of due process in the workplace. *American Journal of Sociology*, 95, 1401–40.

Edwards, R. (1993). *Rights at Work: Employment relations in the post-union era*. Washington, D.C.: Brookings Institution.

Ewing, D. W. (1971). Who wants employee rights? *Harvard Business Review*, 49, Nov.–Dec., 22–35.

Ewing, D. W. (1977). What business thinks about employee rights. *Harvard Business Review*, 55, Sept.–Oct., 81–94.

Ewing, D. W. (1989). *Justice on the Job: Resolving grievances in the nonunion workplace*. Boston: Harvard Business School.

Federal Mediation and Conciliation Service (1993). Arbitration statistics: Fiscal year 1993. Unpublished data supplied to arbitrators.

Feliu, A. G. (1987). Legal consequences of nonunion dispute-resolution systems. *Employee Relations Law Journal*, 13, 83–103.

Feuille, P. (1992). Why does grievance mediation resolve grievances? *Negotiation Journal*, 8, 131–45.

Feuille, P. (1994). Changing patterns in dispute resolution. In C. Kerr & P. Staudohar (eds.), *Labor Economics and Industrial Relations*, 475–511. Cambridge, MA: Harvard University Press.

Feuille, P., & Delaney, J. T. (1992). The individual pursuit of organizational justice: Grievance procedures in nonunion workplaces. In G. R. Ferris & K. M. Rowland (eds.), *Research in Personnel and Human Resource Management*, vol. 10, pp. 187–232. Greenwich, CT: JAI Press.

Feuille, P., & Kolb, D. M. (1994). Waiting in the wings: Mediation's role in grievance resolution. *Negotiation Journal*, 10, 249–64.

Feuille, P., & Leroy, M. (1990). Grievance arbitration appeals in the federal courts: Facts and figures. *Arbitration Journal*, 45, March, 35–47.

Feuille, P., & Wheeler, H. N. (1981). Will the real industrial relations conflict please stand up? In J. Stieber, R. M. McKersie, & D. Q. Mills (eds.), *U.S. Industrial*

Relations 1950–80: A critical assessment, 255–95. Madison, WI: Industrial Relations Research Association.

Felstiner, W. L. F., Abel, R. L., & Sarat, A. (1980). The emergence and transformation of disputes: Naming, blaming, claiming . . . *Law and Society Review*, 15, 631–54.

Folger, R., & Greenberg, J. (1985). Procedural justice: An interpretive analysis of personnel systems. In K. M. Rowland & G. R. Ferris (eds.), *Research in Personnel and Human Resource Management*, vol. 3, pp. 141–83. Greenwich, CT: JAI Press.

Fox, J. B., & Hindman, H. D. (1993). The Model Employment Termination Act: Provisions and discussion. *Employee Responsibilities and Rights Journal*, 6, 33–44.

Freedman, A. (1985). The new look in wage policy and industrial relations. Conference Board Research Report No. 865. Conference Board, New York.

Freeman, R. B., & Kleiner, M. M. (1990). The impact of new unionization on wages and working conditions. *Journal of Labor Economics*, 8, S8–S25.

Freeman, R. B., & Medoff, J. L. (1984). *What Do Unions Do?* New York: Basic Books.

Friedman, R. A. (1992). The culture of mediation: Private understandings in the context of public conflict. In D. M. Kolb & J. M. Bartunek (eds.), *Hidden Conflict in Organizations*, 143–64. Newbury Park, CA: Sage.

Fryxell, G. E., & Gordon, M. E. (1989). Workplace justice and job satisfaction as predictors of satisfaction with union and management. *Academy of Management Journal*, 32, 851–66.

Gandz, J., & Whitehead, J. D. (1982). The relationship between the industrial relations climate and grievance initiation and resolution. In B. D. Dennis (ed.), *Proceedings of the Thirty-Fourth Annual Meeting*, 320–8. Madison, WI: Industrial Relations Research Association.

Gideon, T. F., & Peterson, R. B. (1979). A comparison of alternate grievance procedures. *Employee Relations Law Journal*, 5, 222–33.

Gilmer v. *Interstate/Johnson Lane Corp.*, 111 S.Ct. 1647 (1991).

Goldberg, S. B. (1982). The mediation of grievances under a collective bargaining contract: An alternative to arbitration. *Northwestern University Law Review*, 77, 270–315.

Gordon, M. E., & Miller, S. J. (1984). Grievances: A review of research and practice. *Personnel Psychology*, 37, 117–46.

Goulet, S. L. (1993). An analysis of the impact and effects of formal nonunion grievance procedure at . . . Unpublished Master's degree tutorial. Institute of Labor and Industrial Relations, University of Illinois.

Greenberg, J. (1990). Looking fair vs. being fair: Managing impressions of organizational justice. In B. M. Staw & L. L. Cummings (eds.), *Research in Organizational Behavior*, vol. 12, pp. 111–57. Greenwich, CT: JAI Press.

Greenberg, J., & Folger, R. (1983). Procedural justice, participation, and the fair process effect in groups and organizations. In P. B. Paulus (ed.), *Basic Group Processes*, 235–56. New York: Springer-Verlag.

Guidry, G., & Huffman, G. J., Jr. (1990). Legal and practical aspects of alternative dispute resolution in nonunion companies. *Labor Lawyer*, 6, 1–48.

Hirschman, A. O. (1970). *Exit, Voice and Loyalty*. Cambridge: Harvard University Press.

Holmes, Steven A. (1994). Some workers lose right to file suit for bias at work. *New York Times*, March 18, A1.

Ichniowski, C. (1986). The effects of grievance activity on productivity. *Industrial and Labor Relations Review*, 40, 75–89.

Ichniowski, C. (1992). Human resource practices and productive labor–management relations. In D. Lewin, O. S. Mitchell, & P. D. Sherer (eds.), *Research Frontiers in Industrial Relations and Human Resources*, 239–71. Madison, WI: Industrial Relations Research Association.

Ichniowski, C., & Lewin, D. (1987). Grievance procedures and firm performance. In M. M. Kleiner, R. N. Block, M. Roomkin, & S. W. Salsburg (eds.), *Human Resources and the Performance of the Firm*, 159–93. Madison, WI: Industrial Relations Research Association.

Ichniowski, C., & Lewin, D. (1988). Characteristics of grievance procedures: Evidence from nonunion, union, and double-breasted businesses. In B. B. Dennis (ed.), *Proceedings of the Fortieth Annual Meeting*, 415–24. Madison, WI: Industrial Relations Research Association.

Katz, H. C., Kochan, T. A., & Gobeille, K. (1983). Industrial relations performance, economic performance, and QWL programs: An interplant analysis. *Industrial and Labor Relations Review*, 37, 3–17.

Katz, H. C., Kochan, T. A., & Weber, M. (1985). Assessing the effects of industrial relations systems and efforts to improve the quality of working life on organizational effectiveness. *Academy of Management Journal*, 28, 509–26.

Kauffman, N. (1991). Expedited arbitration revisited. *Arbitration Journal*, 46, September, 34–8.

Klass, B. S. (1989a). Managerial decision-making about employee grievances: The impact of the grievant's work history. *Personnel Psychology*, 42, 53–68.

Klass, B. S. (1989b). Determinants of grievance activity and the grievance system's impact on employee behavior: An integrative perspective. *Academy of Management Review*, 14, 445–58.

Klass, B. S., & DeNisi, A. S. (1989). Managerial reactions to employee dissent: The impact of grievance activity on performance ratings. *Academy of Management Journal*, 32, 705–17.

Klass, B. S., & Feldman, D. C. (1993). The evaluation of disciplinary appeals in non-union organizations. *Human Resource Management Review*, 3, 49–81.

Kleiner, M. M., Nicklesburg, G., & Pilarski, A. M. (1989). Grievances and plant performance: Is zero optimal? In B. B. Dennis (ed.), *Proceedings of the Forty-First Annual Meeting*, 172–80. Madison, WI: Industrial Relations Research Association.

Knight, T. R. (1986). Feedback and grievance resolution. *Industrial and Labor Relations Review*, 39, 585–98.

Kochan, T. A., & Katz, H. C. (1988). *Collective Bargaining and Industrial Relations*, 2nd ed. Homewood, IL: Irwin.

Kochan, T. A., Katz, H. C., & McKersie, R. B. (1986). *The Transformation of American Industrial Relations*. New York: Basic Books.

Kolb, D. M. (1992). Women's work: Peacemaking in organizations. In D. M. Kolb & J. M. Bartunek (eds.),

367

Hidden Conflict in Organizations, 63–91. Newbury Park, CA: Sage.

Koys, D., Briggs, S., & Grenig, J. (1987). State court disparity on employment-at-will. *Personnel Psychology*, 40, 565–77.

Krueger, A. B. (1991). The evolution of unjust-dismissal legislation in the United States. *Industrial and Labor Relations Review*, 44, 644–60.

Kuch, K. (1991). Quality circles in a unionized setting: Their effect on grievance rates. *Journal of Business and Psychology*, 6, 147–54.

Labig, C. E., Jr., & Greer, C. R. (1988). Grievance initiation: A literature survey and suggestions for future research. *Journal of Labor Research*, 9, 1–27.

Labig, C. E., & Helburn, I. B. (1986). Union and management policy influences on grievance initiation. *Journal of Labor Research*, 7, 269–84.

Lambert, W. (1992). Employee pacts to arbitrate sought by firms. *Wall Street Journal*, October 22, B1, B14.

Lamont, L. (1987). Control Data's review process. *Personnel*, 64, February, 7–11.

Lawler, J. J. (1990). *Unionization and Deunionization*. Columbia, SC: University of South Carolina Press.

Lewin, D. (1987). Dispute resolution in the nonunion firm: A theoretical and empirical analysis. *Journal of Conflict Resolution*, 31, 465–502.

Lewin, D. (1990). Grievance procedures in nonunion workplaces: An empirical analysis of usage, dynamics, and outcomes. *Chicago-Kent Law Review*, 66, 823–44.

Lewin, D., & Peterson, R. B. (1988). *The Modern Grievance Procedure in the United States*. New York: Quorum Books.

Lind, E. A., and Tyler, T. R. (1988). *The Social Psychology of Procedural Justice*. New York: Plenum Press.

Lo Bosco, M. (1985). Nonunion grievance procedures. *Personnel*, 62, January, 61–4.

McCabe, D. M. (1988). *Corporate Nonunion Complaint Procedures and Systems*. New York: Praeger.

McPherson, W. H. (1956). Grievance mediation under collective bargaining. *Industrial and Labor Relations Review*, 9, 200–12.

Meritor Savings Bank v. *Vinson*, 477 U.S. 57 (1986).

Meyer, D., & Cooke, W. (1988). Economic and political factors in formal grievance resolution. *Industrial Relations*, 27, 318–35.

Muchinsky, P. M., & Maassarani, M. A. (1980). Work environment effects on public sector grievances. *Personnel Psychology*, 33, 403–14.

Nelson, N. E., & Reiman, B. C. (1983). Work environment and grievance rates in a manufacturing plant. *Journal of Management*, 9, 145–58.

Ng, I., & Dastmalchian, A. (1989). Determinants of grievance outcomes: A case study. *Industrial and Labor Relations Review*, 42, 393–403.

Nolan, D. R., & Abrams, R. I. (1983). American labor arbitration: The maturing years. *University of Florida Law Review*, 35, 557–632.

Norsworthy, J. R., & Zabala, C. A. (1985). Worker attitudes, worker behavior, and productivity in the U.S. automobile industry, 1959–1976. *Industrial and Labor Relations Review*, 36, 544–57.

Peach, D. E., & Livernash, E. R. (1974). *Grievance Initiation and Resolution: A study in basic steel*. Boston: Harvard University Press.

Peterson, R. B. (1992). The union and nonunion grievance system. In D. Lewin, O. S. Mitchell, & P. D. Sherer (eds.), *Research Frontiers in Industrial Relations and Human Resources*, 131–62. Madison, WI: Industrial Relations Research Association.

Peterson, R. B., & Lewin, D. (1990). The nonunion grievance procedure: A viable system of due process? *Employee Responsibilities and Rights Journal*, 3, 1–18.

Rees, D. I. (1991). Grievance procedure strength and teacher quits. *Industrial and Labor Relations Review*, 45, 31–43.

Reibstein, L. (1986). More firms use peer review panel to resolve employees' grievances. *Wall Street Journal*, December 3, 25.

Rowe, M. P. (1987). The corporate ombudsman: An overview and analysis. *Negotiation Journal*, 3, 127–40.

Salipante, P. F., & Aram, J. D. (1984). The role of organizational procedures in the resolution of social conflict. *Human Organization*, 43, 9–15.

Shearer, R. A. (1992–93). The impact of employment arbitration agreements on sex discrimination claims: The trend toward nonjudicial resolution. *Employee Relations Law Journal*, 18, winter, 479–88.

Sheppard, B. H., Lewicki, R., & Minton, J. (1992). *Organizational Justice*. Lexington, MA: Lexington Books.

Slichter, S. H., Healy, J. J., & Livernash, E. R. (1960). *The Impact of Collective Bargaining on Management*. Washington, D.C.: Brookings Institution.

Spencer, D. G. (1986). Employee voice and employee retention. *Academy of Management Journal*, 29, 488–502.

Spitz, J. (1993). Work force response to an efficiency wage: Productivity, turnover, and the grievance rate. In J. F. Burton, Jr. (ed.), *Proceedings of the Forty-Fifth Annual Meeting*, 142–50. Madison, WI: Industrial Relations Research Association.

Thornton, R. J., & Zirkel, P. A. (1990). The consistency and predictability of grievance arbitration awards. *Industrial and Labor Relations Review*, 43, 294–307.

Tjosvold, D. (1991). Rights and responsibilities of dissent: Cooperative conflict. *Employee Rights and Responsibilities Journal*, 4, 13–23.

Todor, W. D., & Owen, C. L. (1991). Deriving benefits from conflict resolution: A macrojustice assessment. *Employee Responsibilities and Rights Journal*, 4, 37–49.

U.S. Bureau of Labor Statistics (1981). Characteristics of major collective bargaining agreements, January 1, 1980. BLS Bulletin 2095. May.

U.S. Bureau of Labor Statistics (1993). *Employment and Earnings*, 40, January, 239.

U.S. Equal Employment Opportunity Commission (1971). *5th annual report*. Washington, D.C.: U.S. Government Printing Office.

U.S. Equal Employment Opportunity Commission (1990). *Combined Annual Reports Fiscal Years 1986, 1987, 1988*. Washington, D.C.: U.S. Government Printing Office.

United Steelworkers v. American Manufacturing Co., 363 U.S. 564 (1960); *United Steelworkers v. Warrior & Gulf Navigation Co.*, 363 U.S. 574 (1960); *United Steelworkers v. Enterprise Wheel & Car Corp.*, 363 U.S. 593 (1960) (the *Steelworkers Trilogy*).

Westin, A. F., & Feliu, A. G. (1988). *Resolving Employment Disputes without Litigation.* Washington, D.C.: Bureau of National Affairs.

Williamson, O. E. (1975). *Markets and Hierarchies.* New York: Free Press.

Williamson, O. E. (1976). The economics of internal organization: Exit and voice in relation to markets and hierarchies. *American Economic Review,* 66, 369–77.

Woo, J. (1993). More businesses use ombudsmen to prevent workplace litigation. *Wall Street Journal,* February 19, B10.

Chapter 19

High Involvement Organizations and Industrial Democracy

Delmar L. Landen, Irving Bluestone, and Edward E. Lawler III

INTRODUCTION

Thirty years ago an important challenge facing the field of human resource management (HRM) was the transfer and application of scientific knowledge to the management of complex organizations. Thirty years later, this is still a challenge. In the mid-1960s, the Institute for Social Research at the University of Michigan, under the leadership of Rensis Likert, sought to respond to this dilemma by establishing the Center for the Utilization of Scientific Knowledge (CRUSK). The goal of CRUSK was to foster collaborative relationships between the HRM research community and interested organizations. The partnerships that evolved helped to define the HRM field, including organization development, organization behavior, and its more recent derivatives, employee involvement (EI), participative management, and total quality management (TQM).

Currently, similar creative efforts are working to bridge the gap between what is known about the design, organization, and management of high-performing organizations, and what is effectively being applied.

The Center for Effective Organizations at the University of Southern California, now in its fourteenth year, is one of the best examples of this type of effort. The more recently established Center for Human Resource Management at the University of Illinois is another excellent example.

Despite these notable efforts, there remains an important need to bridge the gap between what is known about management and its practice. As Bob Galvin (1989, 6), former CEO of Motorola, commented shortly after Motorola received the Malcolm Baldrige National Quality Award, "The most important thing we learned about quality is that we learned what we didn't know about what we didn't know about quality." They knew what they knew, but they didn't know what they didn't know. And that is what they learned. The field of HRM is presently faced with a similar situation. We know what we know, but we don't know what we don't know. And that is something we need to correct.

This chapter, and indeed this entire book, is intended to help all of us state more clearly some of what we know and what we need to know about HRM. Beyond this, we need to learn better how the academic and practitioner worlds can work together more effectively and push the boundaries of our knowledge beyond their present limits. This chapter starts with some things we know about organizations and their governance. Included among these initial observations are some paradoxes that center on some things that are known but not believed. Or, if believed, not practiced. Following these observations, some seemingly obvious research findings are examined. They are, nonetheless, often ignored by both researchers and practitioners. Along the way, we offer our views as to why this is the case.

One manifestation of this contradiction is the persistent separation of change efforts carried out under the banner of EI and those spearheaded by TQM advocates. Our position is that, in most respects, these two "programs" represent a common system of management, despite the fact that research shows that two-thirds of the *Fortune 1000* companies treat them as separate activities.

Paralleling this conundrum is the equally perplexing dilemma that managing and leading are not only quite different kinds of behaviors, but are qualities not subject to situational whims or dispensable in one-minute doses as promoted by those who write about leadership.

The random implementation of teams is part of this same fundamental ignorance of basic organization principles. Because teams have become the "in thing" to do, organizations are creating teams like they used to create quality circles. Our position is that teams are governed by the same principles that govern any form of workplace structure, including the total enterprise. Teams and enterprises are social inventions created to accomplish purposes which cannot be accomplished as well in other ways.

Accompanying the introduction of teams is the move toward empowerment. While practitioners speak of delegation and accountability, they also express their true intentions by saying how "we will empower them," which is simply another more subtle form of patriarchy (Block, 1993). As the saying goes, "He who empowers also unempowers." Attitudes like these are not consistent with the move toward more democratic organizations. In the context of this chapter, empowerment takes on a special meaning. To be empowered is to have the freedom and authority to act. Empowerment is extracted from the environment. Organizations of empowerment are shaped by cultures within which information, knowledge, power, and rewards are widely dispersed and individuals and teams are encouraged to be self-initiating and self-directing. Aside from assuring that voice and power are shared by everyone, feelings of pride and respect are also fundamental to democratic institutions (O'Toole, 1992).

As we seek to renew organizations, our focus must be on the future. As Russell Ackoff would advise, solving yesterday's problem only gets rid of what you don't want. It has nothing to do with getting what you do want. His advice and ours is always to start with the future. Start with what you want to create (Ackoff, l992).

This chapter concludes by proposing that the practitioner and theoretician must each adopt some of the best attributes of the other, not simply to enrich one's own capabilities, but to enhance the organizations and our profession.

SHARPENING A PERSPECTIVE

Modern thinking about employee involvement as a management strategy has its clearest and strongest roots in the writings of Likert, Argyris, and McGregor. Each wrote a seminal book over thirty years ago which helped frame the issue of employee involvement strategies. Probably the best known of these books is McGregor's (1960) which introduced the concepts of Theory X and Theory Y management. This distinguished the traditional control-oriented paradigm from the more employee-involvement-oriented approach.

Likert's (1961) writings stressed the importance of a manager's behavior and the use of groups. The work at the University of Michigan on democratic supervision helped shape the argument that leaders needed to engage in power-sharing behaviors in order to overcome resistance to change and create a world in which employees are committed to the goals of the organization while simultaneously enhancing job satisfaction and employment security.

The work of Argyris (1970) particularly focused on the impact of work structures and job structures on motivation and satisfaction. He pointed out that often the tasks that people do prevent them from having meaningful relationships with their work and work organizations, and have debilitating effects not only upon them and their performance but upon the organization and its performance.

Together, Argyris, Likert, and McGregor put in place the foundations of a paradigm of employee involvement which focuses on work design and leadership style. McGregor's work in particular generated considerable discussion, and in some cases led to small experiments in organizations. It was years later, however, before large-scale organizational change efforts resulted from his work.

Job enrichment efforts began to become popular in the mid-1960s, thanks to the work of Herzberg, Mausner, and Snyderman (1966). Also teams began to be used more frequently, particularly in Europe, partially as a result of the writings of Likert, but perhaps more directly due to the sociotechnical writings of Trist et al. (1963), Emery (1969) and others.

In trying to create more democratically managed workplaces, General Motors and some other large corporations invested in training supervisors to be more participative. Perhaps the best summary of the fit between EI theory and practice at the end of the 1960s is to say that employee involvement largely remained an evolving, relatively loosely specified paradigm that was not affecting practice in a systematic or widespread manner. Admittedly, there were interesting trials going on, but there remained a significant gap between the ideas and their application.

The rate of adoption of employee involvement increased during the 1970s and 1980s. The early 1970s saw the creation of a number of joint action union–management cooperation programs as well as the start up of a number of high-involvement or high-commitment "greenfield" plants. In many respects, these new plants were a critical part of the evolution of employee involvement. They demonstrated for the first time that business units could be run in a manner consistent with the writings of McGregor (1960) and Likert (1961). They also brought into reality the specific organizational practices that are part of the general paradigm of employee involvement. Plants such as those built by Proctor & Gamble and General Foods gained considerable national attention during the 1970s, and were acknowledged to be highly effective. In many cases, however, these new plants were encapsulated. What happened within these plants did not spread to other parts of the corporations that created them, nor to other plants being started by other organizations.

The pace of change in the area of both theory and practice picked up substantially in the 1980s. More theory developed about what contributes to an effective employee-involvement-oriented organization. More details became clear around issues of organization, the use of information technology, and the evolution of reward systems. Perhaps most importantly during the 1980s, employee involvement began to become positioned as a way for organizations to compete effectively in globally competitive markets. EI slowly became seen as a Western alternative to the Japanese approach to management, something that could truly provide a competitive advantage, and a viable replacement for the traditional command and control approach to management.

To be sure, the evolution of the employee involvement approach is still a long way from being a consistent and general replacement for the command and control management approach. Evidence from several national surveys confirms this conclusion (See e.g., Lawler, Mohrman, & Ledford, 1992). Although employee involvement has generally gained verbal acceptance as the best thing to do, the reality is that most employee involvement practiced today seems to be at a relatively low level. It involves individuals participating in problem-solving and suggestion groups, and is built on an employee involvement paradigm that is very similar to the original thinking around the human relations movement and participative supervision. The underlying assumption seems to be that it is useful to have employees make suggestions because they have knowledge about how their work is done, and potentially how it might be improved.

Most employee involvement efforts miss the idea that people throughout the organization are big stakeholders in the organization and have the right to influence strategic direction and work design decisions and to participate in the economic gains that the organization realizes. Perhaps the most viable definition of employee involvement rests on the argument that it consists of creating structures and processes that move business information, business knowledge, rewards for organizational performance, and decision-making power throughout the organization.

Using this definition of employee involvement, research suggests that EI simply has not happened in most organizational settings. Instead, organizations have moved some new information to employees and have gotten them involved in offering suggestions on improving the workplace. Thus the gap between theory and practice has narrowed for some. However, there is still an enormous gap between what is possible in employee involvement, and what, in fact, most organizations are doing. There is some reason to believe that this gap may continue to close because of the competitive pressures facing organizations. However, there is almost always a gap between new ideas about how organizations should be managed and the reality of how they are managed.

BROADENING THE CONCEPT OF QWL/EI

Aside from the likelihood that competitive pressures will serve to close the gap between theory and practice, collective bargaining will also play a significant role. Over the last fifteen years, the role of QWL/EI has been expanded to include an ever-increasing range of programs. During negotiations in auto, steel, aluminum, and related industries, old contract language was expanded and new language developed to cover a wider range of joint initiatives. In the case of GM and the UAW (1981), language was added to the contract to include the establishment of a Joint Skill Development and Training Committee and National and Local Joint Councils for Enhancing Job Security and the Competitive Edge (Pratte & Kruger, 1992). New language was introduced, such as Labor–Management Participation Teams (LMPTs) in the steel and container industries (1980), and Employee Involvement (EI) in the Ford-UAW agreement (1979). In the agreements between AT&T and the Communications Workers and the International Brotherhood of Electrical Workers (1980) the term Quality of Worklife (QWL) was broadened to take into consideration a number of joint options.

What started out as a search for ways to improve the quality of people's lives while at work evolved into a wide array of jointly designed and administered employee programs. Such programs ranged from new hire orientation to preretirement planning and included other joint efforts such as apprentice training, attendance programs, health and safety programs, and United Fund Drives (See Blue-stone & Bluestone, 1992, 161–2 for a more detailed listing).

There are almost unlimited opportunities for union–management initiatives to influence business planning and decision making. Such initiatives include the design of jobs and work systems, engineering methods, material flow, budgeting, design of new equipment and machinery, setting production schedules and contract bidding, and joint involvement in top management decision making. These and other forms of joint union–management initiatives provide the foundation for what the Bluestones call the "Enterprise Compact". (See Bluestone & Bluestone, 1992, for a full discussion of the Enterprise Compact and pp. 157–8 for a more complete listing of the kinds of joint initiatives which might be included in an Enterprise Compact.)

Research also showed that joint union–management EI efforts have yielded perform-ance improvements in the areas of quality and productivity (Cooke, 1990). The Cooke study, and similar research by Kelley and Harrison (1992), affirmed the important role that joint efforts play in achieving performance improvements otherwise not achieved in the absence of coequal processes. A 1989 U.S. Labor Department, Corporate and Labor State-of-the-Art Symposium concluded that there were six reasons why union presence in EI efforts led to desirable outcomes:

1 Unions helped weed out the bad plans up front.
2 They kept companies from reverting to old ways.
3 They provided a mechanism for address-ing a company's glitches in their EI pro-cedures without throwing out the whole participation process.
4 Unions tended to be the only practical way to give workers a meaningful voice.
5 They played a crucial role in educating workers to make informed decisions.

6 Unions provided a creative power and tension to joint efforts.

Experience and research also have shown that most participation forms start with quite limited agendas and a narrow focus. However, if the participation forms are to endure and flourish, they must be broadened to include a wider range of issues, problems, situa-tions, and goals. If the processes of involve-ment are to be enlarged to address issues of job design, work flow, work assignments, and other factors affecting the conditions in which people are working, this would suggest that where collective bargaining and employee involvement are strictly separated, the processes of collective bargaining and in-volvement must become better integrated (Cutcher-Gershenfeld, Kochan, & Verma, 1991). Moreover, if such joint efforts are to be successful, they must also meet the goals of employers, employees, and, in unionized settings, the union.

BALANCING THEORY AND PRACTICE

While new roles are emerging between the practitioner and the theoretician, much re-mains to be learned. For some managers, em-ployee motivation is still seen as giving away turkeys at Thanksgiving, monogrammed glasses for perfect attendance, and badges and balloons for "zero defects." At the same time, the scientist who is criticizing the un-tutored manager is busily writing articles on the role of the supervisory interview in employee selection and appraisals, while a good portion of the manufacturing work force is being organized into self-managing teams. According to a 1990 EI survey (Lawler et al., 1992), 47 percent of the *Fortune 1000* companies now have self-managing teams, even though the total percentage of employ-ees involved is still very low.

This dilemma is underscored by the never-ending proliferation of "programs of the month." Practitioners and academics alike bemoan this practice. However, even as this is being written, some organizations are expressing the view that TQM is passé and that reengineering is the "in thing." This aping process is fed not only by the "shoot from the hip" philosophy of some American managers, but by the promulgation of the "eight, ten or twelve points program" by some consultants.

A number of years ago, Kurt Lewin stressed the point that "There is nothing so practical as a good theory" (Weisbord, 1987). Yet, much of what goes on under the guise of EI/TQM is neither good theory nor good practice. Studies have shown that all too little attention is given to the theory and principles which underlie organization change efforts (Lawler, 1992; Wellins, Byham, & Wilson, 1991; Walton, 1987). Walton's study made clear that one of the most vital prerequisites to effective change efforts is the presence of conceptual models which align interrelated policies and integrate the interests of multiple stakeholders. This study also made it clear that technological innovation without supporting human resources innovation will not yield productivity and quality improvements equal to their technical capabilities.

While the debate about which conceptual models are most helpful will linger on for years, there is little argument among scholars that some type of model is essential. As Drucker (1990) has said, "If you don't know where you're going, any road will get you there." One example of the shortcoming of not designing and carrying out projects within the context of a conceptual model is the very early QWL "experiment" carried out at the General Motors (GM) Tarrytown Car Assembly Plant. This was the first joint Quality of Worklife (QWL) project launched in General Motors. The project involved 35 employees in the glass installation department. The overall planning for the project was carried out under the sponsorship of a local UAW-GM Union–Management Steering Committee. The aim of the project was to solve two operating problems – glass breakage and water leaks.

Prior to launching the project, considerable data were collected not only about the two problems, but also about absenteeism, grievances, discipline, suggestions, housekeeping, overall department quality, labor efficiency, and costs. In addition, a job satisfaction survey was completed by all project members.

During the 40 hours of problem-solving training, noticeable improvements were apparent in the two problems which were the targets of the study. These results were described by Guest (1979) and published by the *Harvard Business Review.*

Much was learned from the study. Aside from the reductions in glass breakage and water leaks, improvements were noted in all of the other variables measured. Absenteeism dropped sharply, as did discipline actions and grievances. Overall department quality, costs, and labor efficiency also improved, although none of these outcomes was the intended purpose of the project (Horner, 1981–82).

In the absence of a theoretical framework, it was not evident to many observers that all of these variables had a natural interdependency. The job satisfaction survey showed that the attitudes of people had much to do with their coming to work. When people didn't come to work they were disciplined. When they were disciplined, the workers filed grievances against the discipline. Moreover, in a car assembly plant the replacement worker usually cannot perform the absentee's job as well as the regular operator. Therefore, as absenteeism rose so too did the number of in-process defects. Frequently, high defects led to overtime, because that was the only way that larger numbers of repairs could be made. Extended periods of overtime invariably led to higher absenteeism. It is also important to note that a good portion of the absenteeism was due to the workers who were on disciplinary layoffs, "sent home" because they didn't come to work.

A fundamental learning from this study was that the process, the means by which people are engaged in productive activities, is the glue that grabs and holds people. Also the processes of work define and determine the outcomes of work. Moreover the quality of these processes shapes the quality of their outcomes. As has been learned repeatedly since then, *the process is the solution*. Also, it has been learned many times over that individual programs targeted at discrete problems are not the route to go. Problems are not discrete, as the Tarrytown study showed. The launching of another program is not the best route to take in efforts to deal with them. The study of vanguard organizations by O'Toole (1987) and of high-involvement organizations by Lawler (1986, 1992) shows that successful change efforts are guided by long-range strategies, incorporating a variety of initiatives and administered by knowledgeable, committed, and skilled practitioners.

Scientists must broaden their conceptual boundaries, and they must convey this understanding to the practitioner far more effectively. Practitioners must temper their inclinations to "draw, fire, aim" by creating not only a bias for action, but a bias that involves vision, strategy, and execution.

THE NATURE OF ORGANIZATIONS

Bennis (1993) predicted the decline of the bureaucracy and the inevitability of democracy almost thirty years ago. However, it has only been in recent years that the professionals in the field have said much about the "reinvention", "reengineering," and "rebirth" of the corporation, and indeed, of the government.

One of the fundamental principles about organizations is that the pieces must fit together. While this has been known for decades, it has been systematically violated. As citizens, we embrace such democratic values as equality, voice, respect, fairness, due process, assembly, and empowerment, but have created organizations based upon McGregor's (1960) Theory X assumptions. One product of this disharmony was the crises of the 1960s and 1970s regarding the "unmotivated, alienated worker," as expressed in absenteeism, turnover, sabotage, grievances, and the "problem employee." The labels used to capture this malaise were "blue collar blues," "white collar woes," and ultimately "the Lordstown Syndrome" (Gooding, 1972).

In his book, *Future Shock*, Toffler (1970) conveyed this dilemma by noting that the world is changing at exponential rates while organizations are changing at a snail's pace, if at all. Presumably the Lordstown Syndrome, characterizing the conflict between the values of American workers and the stifling effects of Taylorism, was one manifestation of this disharmony. Others, as suggested at the time by many managers, were poor quality, low productivity, and worker apathy.

Efforts to reverse the course on which our institutions were moving gave rise to job enlargement (Walker & Guest, 1952), job enrichment (Herzberg et al., 1960), survey feedback (Likert, 1967), organization development (Beckhard, 1969), and later, Quality of Worklife, first enunciated by Bluestone in 1972 (Pratte & Kruger, 1992), and Employee Involvement (Lawler, 1986).

But even under these labels, too little was being done to create the conditions which foster both democratic values and democratic practices. As O'Toole (1992) noted, "our most important institutions are unresponsive, inflexible, ineffective, and unimaginative." The tragedy of the presence of organizations of this type is not only their limiting and debilitating effects upon their members, but upon the institutions themselves. For it is precisely the quality of responsiveness, flexibility, creativity, and innovation that are needed in today's highly globalized and turbulent environment.

As Bennis (1993) noted decades ago, "Democracy is the companion of change." Certainly this is true of the larger world in which we live, as witnessed by all that has happened over the last decade in Eastern Europe and elsewhere. But it is not true for most of American business and industry.

In a May 1993 *Fortune* magazine article the author, Carol Loomis, spoke to the issue of organizations changing to keep up with society. In the article, entitled "Dinosaurs", Loomis described the plight of GM, International Business Machines (IBM) and Sears Roebuck. She asserts that the problem of these organizations is that they have gotten too big, too unresponsive, too complacent, too bureaucratic, and too arrogant. They have yet to reinvent themselves as have General Electric (GE) (Tichy & Sherman, 1993), Xerox (Kearns & Nadler, 1992) and Ford (Petersen & Hillkirk, 1991), all of whom not too many years ago were on the brink of disaster. Although one could argue that none of these reinvented organizations is a paragon of democracy, all of them are now viewed as trying to be high-involvement, high-commitment, empowered organizations, a far cry from what they were as recently as the early 1980s.

These and other organizations have learned along the way that collaborative relationships between the practitioner and the social scientist, each with their unique biases, values, knowledge, and skills, bring to the reinvention process perspectives that neither possesses independent of the other. Such partnerships also reaffirm the significant role that human resources and the broader principles of human resource management play in restructuring organizations and in revitalizing their very essence.

ADDING VALUE TO ORGANIZATIONS

A recent survey of HRM research needs conducted among a group of top-level HRM executives showed that one key priority item was to identify the ways that HRM policy and practice adds value to organizations. A second issue identified dealt with the role of HRM in influencing and/or developing business strategy. While these were conveyed as two separate issues in the survey, they most likely represent a single issue.

During the l960s, Likert (1967) argued that the causal variables of leadership, culture, and philosophy influence and alter the intervening processes of communication, decision making, coordination, control, and motivation, and they enhance and add value to such organizational outcomes as quality, efficiency, cost, morale, satisfaction, and profitability. Based on his research, Likert (1967) advised the practitioner to focus change efforts on the causal variables, since they not only define and determine the nature of the intervening processes, but are the variables that are within the immediate and direct control of all people.

This same principle and reasoning can be applied to the field of human resource management. Figure 19.1 represents a reconceptualization of Likert's (1967) earlier notion with embellishments based upon Lawler's (1986, 1992) research and writings. It suggests that HRM theories, principles, values, concepts, methods, and techniques add value to organizational processes and human capacities by means of the impact they have upon people and organizations. The intervening conditions directly influence outcomes like those flowing from the individual and the organization characteristics.

HRM brings to the strategic planning process a point of view not represented by other management disciplines. This point of view conveys a broader understanding not only of organizational outcomes, but the means by which such outcomes are influenced. Figure 19.1 also notes the natural interdependencies between individual and organizational development. It seeks to reaffirm the notion that neither individual development

Figure 19.1   The role of human resource management in adding value to people and to organizations

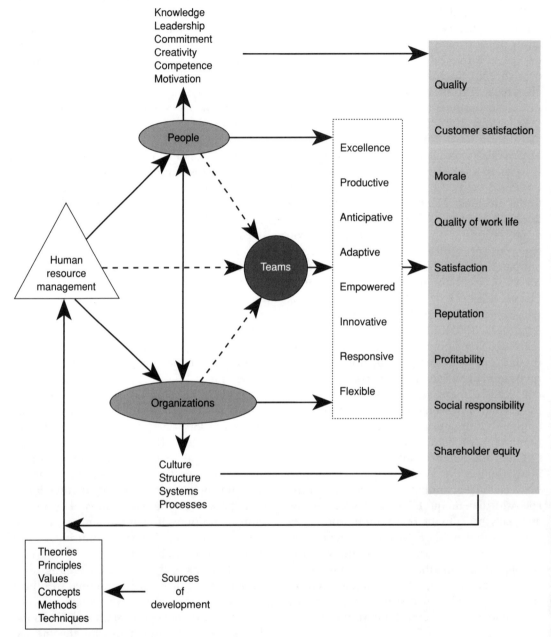

Figure 19.2 Mission–vision–philosophy model

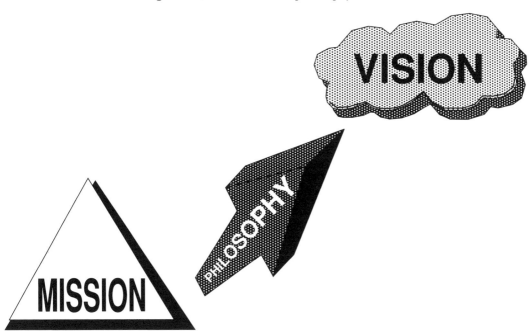

nor organizational development can occur in the absence of the other.

The model is of special significance for both the HRM practitioner and scientist because HRM brings to the process of strategic planning values which are unique to the field and vital to the success of contemporary organizations. In a large sense, the model challenges HRM practitioners to broaden the role of strategic planning to include organization planning. As the instrumentality for accomplishing business goals and objectives, the fundamental character and quality of this approach defines and determines the quality of its business accomplishments.

MISSION–VISION– PHILOSOPHY (MVP) MODEL

Strategies to manage change processes are enhanced substantially when they are integral parts of an organization's overall mission, vision, and philosophy. The MVP model (figure 19.2) also provides a conceptual framework for formulating change strategies and guiding their development and renewal. The MVP model portrays basic notions about the interdependent relationships between three key elements in the strategic planning processes: the *mission* – why do we exist; the *vision* – what do we desire; and the *philosophy* – what are the values that will guide how we manage both our mission and our vision.

The MVP model also helps in understanding how the concepts of mission, vision, and philosophy fit together, and why effective change efforts must balance each element against the others. One compelling reason for this is that an organization's future cannot be sacrificed in the pursuit of efforts to achieve today's mission; nor can today's mission be ignored because of a preoccupation with some distant future. Moreover the philosophy by which organizations are governed markedly affects their effectiveness in fulfilling their missions and in pursuing their visions.

The MVP model is patterned after one developed by Beckhard (1969). Beckhard's model, referred to as the Future State model, like the MVP model, also starts with the future. As Ackoff (1992) and Beckhard would advise, all strategic planning should start with the future – What is it that you want to create? Moreover the future is created out of actions taken in the present. DePree (1989) also counsels leaders to be conscious about the future and their visions for it as they work to accomplish today's missions.

The MVP model has a range of applications. It can be used in the start-up of new facilities, the redesign of existing ones, and in the development or restructuring of EI initiatives. Like similar design efforts, the process of engaging people in the exploration and examination of shared values and in the articulation of these values in their MVP statements, is a powerful way to build teamwork, commitment, and ownership. It is also a powerful means for people to identify those democratic values on which they wish to build their future.

In this larger context, the MVP model is at the core of a strategic planning model, the Organization Planning Model, that has been used extensively over the last two-and-a-half decades to design or redesign both small and large organizations. This model, referred to by some as the "Bull's Eye", is patterned after one developed by Walton (1974) and modified by Cherry (1982). The model had its initial applications by Walton in the design and development of the Topeka, Kansas General Foods Plant, launched in the late 1960s. Features of the model were also used in the late 1960s to bring on stream P & G's first self-managing workplaces. During the 1970s, the model was used to design over a dozen sociotechnical plants in GM, all of which were the precursors of GM's Saturn Corporation (Cherry, 1982).

ORGANIZATION PLANNING MODEL AND ITS APPLICATION

The Organization Planning Model (figure 19.3) is a conceptual framework for creating new organizations (i.e., greenfield sites), mini-enterprises, self-directing teams, the redesign of existing organizations, and the development or redevelopment of EI and or TQM strategies. The model is governed by and predicated on principles applicable to any organization. The model views organizations as systems. A system, as defined by Ackoff (1974, 13)

Is a whole that cannot be divided into its independent parts. A system consists of two or more elements, each of which satisfies three conditions:

1 *Each part can affect the behavior of the whole.*
2 *The way each element affects the whole depends on at least one other element.*
3 *Line up the elements and sub-group them in any order, and they will possess the above two elements.*

This concept of a system, and its implications for creating, governing and renewing organizations, has particular significance to the practitioners of change and the advocates of the principles and concepts of reinvention.

Earlier in the chapter, we sought to emphasize the principle of organization integrity. We also sought to make clear to both the academic and the practitioner that individual and collective efforts must be shaped and guided by theoretical frameworks which provide understanding, definition, and direction. Moreover conceptual frameworks need to enhance and enrich our ability to expand the boundaries of our knowledge and our capacity to create and foster workplaces which bring a greater measure of achievement to the organization, its members, and all other stakeholders. The Organization Planning Model starts where our understanding of organizations starts, with its core

Figure 19.3 Organization planning model

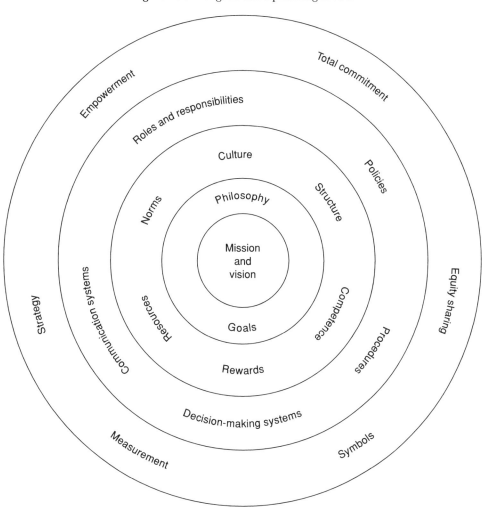

beliefs. It starts with the heart of the enterprise and the heart of the model. It starts with the MVP, the mission, vision, and philosophy, and the organization's goals. Every other element, every other part of the model, is affected by the MVP, and in turn each part affects the behavior of the whole. An organization's MVP is the litmus test against which all other elements must be gauged and judged.

When the management and Canadian Automobile Workers (CAW) were embarking on the design of a car assembly plant in Canada in the mid-1980s, they had a shared dream of creating an organization that had never been created before. As should be the case with any greenfield effort, the designers of the new enterprise were also going to bring the organization on stream, and, having done so, govern it during its early stages of development.

This joint group, of roughly fifty, met on many occasions over a two-year period. One of the group's first acts was to establish norms that would govern their relationships during the design, prestart-up, and launch of the new organization. As a guide to the group, definitions were provided for all of the terms used in the Organization Planning Model. Prior to the development of the group's norms, the following definition was reviewed and discussed:

Norms Concept

All social systems are governed by certain standards. These standards evolve over time and become the basis on which actions are based and behaviors are judged. Through the process of socialization, certain standards become normative and are preserved by group members because they reflect the group's values, desires, behavioral guidelines, and its unique quality and character.

The norms the joint union–management group established were:

- Trust
- Teamwork
- Courage
- Mutual respect
- Open communication
- Positive attitude
- Professionalism
- Integrity
- Commitment

Once having established its norms, the joint group undertook the process of defining its MVP. It started with a definition of terms, the first being the concept of a vision:

Vision Concept

A vision is a statement of what ought to be, not what is. Its role is to inspire, direct, and guide. It embodies those values that capture one's heart, one's mind, and one's soul. It is never attained; it is beyond our grasp, but within our view.

The Plant's Vision

To set the standard towards which all others will strive.

The next element of the Organization Planning Model to be defined and discussed was the mission:

Mission Concept

All organizations have a mission, the reason for their existence. A written statement of mission is essential. It serves to clarify thinking, provides a foundation for establishing goals, objectives, and plans, and to communicate to all members of the organization the function of the enterprise, its standards of performance, and a focal point for guiding individual behavior and performance.

The Plant's Mission

In our pursuit of excellence and customer satisfaction, we will dedicate ourselves to producing leading quality products.

To complete the group's MVP, the philosophy concept was presented and discussed:

The Philosophy Concept

The philosophy of an organization is a statement of beliefs and a commitment to the future. It is the basis on which policy is formulated, decisions are made, and actions are guided. An organization's philosophy conveys to people what can be expected of the organization, what is expected of them, and how the enterprise will go about the task of achieving its mission and pursuing its vision.

The Plant's Philosophy

We, the employees, will fulfill our mission by building an environment of mutual trust, respect, and involvement.

After defining the core values of the organization, the design group launched a number of subdesign groups on structure, training, human resources policy, and on each element of the Organization Planning Model. During the early meetings, the total group agreed that all subgroups, committees, task forces, and, indeed, all meetings of the overall design committee would be governed by the group's norms and MVP.

This example is particularly important because the entire process embodied the values of all participants as reflected in the group's norms and MVP. Moreover the design process was carried out consistent with the way the future plant would be operated. The group did not want to wait until the plant was up and running to exhibit the behaviors that would be vital to its future success. Their collective commitment and conviction were that the quality of the design process would define and determine the future fate of the plant. Accordingly, all meetings were seen as microcosms of how the total organization would operate in the future. As a reminder of this commitment, the norms and the plant's MVP were posted in all meeting rooms.

Over the course of two years, all the elements in figure 19.3 were addressed. Once a particular policy, system, or procedure had been developed, it was tested against the organization's norms, MVP, and all other elements in the model. While many things have happened to the plant since its highly successful launch, it continues to this day to be regarded as the parent company's "flagship" organization.

FUTURE DIRECTIONS

The title of the Bluestones' (1992) book, *Negotiating the Future,* is both an apt characterization of events that happened twenty years ago, and those likely to happen in the foreseeable future. The original QWL letter of understanding agreed to by the UAW and General Motors did indeed forecast a management movement that has swept the industrial landscape, and has been redefined many times over, and will continue to be redefined in the years ahead.

It is apparent from all that has happened in the last twenty years, and as Bennis and Slater (1964) predicted thirty years ago, there is an inevitability about democracy. Organizations are taking on cultures that proclaim and encourage democratic practices, such as those cited in the norms that people have created for themselves and their institutions. Certainly the values that are captured in the

MVP statements presented earlier provide additional testimonial to the desire of people to create and sustain organizations that are more democratic, more humane, and more effective. The models presented are predicated on the belief that people can and do make a difference. That each person is an asset, each is a leader, each is a steward (Block, 1993).

Employee involvement is a value-based philosophy about how organizations should be fashioned and governed. EI's evolving character is a product of the methods and techniques associated with its emergence and development and its philosophical underpinnings and compelling values which resonate throughout the associated developmental processes and the products of those processes.

The act of creating a future vision is as important as the vision created. Ownership, partnerships, commitment, and empowerment are the products of the act of creation along with the compelling nature of the vision itself. A vision without those defining qualities is a hollow statement more likely to breed disdain than devotion.

The models included also are intended to provide the scientist with frameworks for articulating hypotheses, organizing research findings, communicating conclusions, enlarging the body of human resources knowledge, and providing direction and guidance for others.

For the practitioner, models are fundamental to defining ultimate success. Conceptualizing what we know and identifying what we hope to do are the ingredients by which strategic initiatives are shaped and guided. As these models have suggested, shaping the fate of an organization should always start with what we are attempting to create.

The fate of an organization is also defined and shaped by the values which guide those who are its architects, leaders, and stewards. People have said, after reflecting on those characteristics associated with their best organizational experiences, that they value the qualities of open communication, mutual trust and respect, integrity, empowerment, teamwork, commitment, and courage. Also they have said that organizations with these qualities are the most effective. O'Toole (1992) has drawn the same conclusion. As he states, "Democratic organizations are more effective because they are more just." Speaking to the larger context, Halberstam (1991) says the "just and harmonious society" is, in the long run, also the strongest society. The qualities of fairness, impartiality, and equality, implicit in the word "just," are fundamentally democratic in spirit and intent.

As is true of employee involvement, democracy is not a goal, but a means to a goal. Democracy is a process by which people recognize their own potential, and gain empowerment, pride, self-respect, and dignity. It is a process within which excellence is proclaimed and practiced. Democracy is the means by which cultures of quality and excellence are defined and shaped.

Democracy flourishes only when its processes and procedures guarantee the implementation of democratic values. The essential elements driving such guarantees are employee representative systems assuring against autocratic controls and providing for involvement, commitment, and empowerment. Democracy is the means by which organizations of the future will be governed. This is not intended to be a prediction, or a forecast. It is intended to be a challenge to both the academic and the practitioner.

All people need the opportunity to demonstrate their managerial and leadership skills. It is essential that visions inspire, unite, and energize. It is also essential that involvement permeates the very essence of organizations so that the capacity to plan, organize, direct, and guide are embraced and carried out by everyone, embodying the very spirit of what we believe to be industrial democracy.

Organizations are human inventions. The organizations of the next century are already in the process of being created. Our challenge is to be certain that future creations are what we and this society value, need, and want.

REFERENCES

Ackoff, R. L. (1974). *Redesigning the Future*. New York: Wiley.

Ackoff, R. L. (1992). *Videologies: Achieving excellence through ideas, insights and innovation*. Flint, MI: GMI Engineering and Management Institute.

Argyris, C. (1970). *Intervention Theory: A behavioral approach*. Reading, MA: Addison-Wesley.

Beckhard, R. (1969). *Organization Development: Strategies and models*. Reading, MA: Addison-Wesley.

Bennis, W., & Slater, P. E. (1964). Democracy is inevitable, *Harvard Business Review*, Mar.–Apr.

Bennis, W. (1993) *Beyond Bureaucracy*. San Francisco: Jossey-Bass.

Block, P. (1993). *Stewardship*. San Francisco: Berrett-Koehler.

Bluestone, B., & Bluestone, I. (1992). *Negotiating the Future*. New York: Basic Books.

Cherry, R. L. (1982). The development of General Motors' team-based plants. In R. Zager & M. P. Rosow (eds.), *The Innovative Organization*. Elmsford, NY: Pergamon Press.

Cooke, W. N. (1990). *Labor–Management Cooperation*. Kalamazoo, MI: Upjohn Institute.

Cutcher-Gershenfeld, J., Kochan, T., & Verma, A. (1991). Recent developments in U.S. employee involvement initiatives: Erosion or diffusion. In D. Sockell, D. Lewin, and D. B. Lipsky (eds.), *Advances in Industrial and Labor Relations*. Greenwich, CT: JAI Press.

Depree, M. (1989). *Leadership is an Art*. New York: Doubleday.

Drucker, P. F. (1990). *Managing the Non-Profit Organization*. New York: HarperCollins.

Emery, F. E. (1969). *Systems Thinking*. Harmondsworth: Penguin.

Galvin, R. (1989). *Achieving Competitiveness: The human dimension*. Conference Proceedings, Champaign, IL: Institute of Labor and Industrial Relations, University of Illinois at Urbana-Champaign.

Gooding, J. (1972). *The Job Revolution*. New York: Walker.

Guest R. (1979). Quality of work life – learning from Tarrytown. *Harvard Business Review*, July–Aug., 76–87.

Halberstam, D. (1991). *The Next Century*. New York: William Morrow.

Herzberg, F., Mausner, B., & Snyderman, B. B. (1966). *Work and the Nature of Man*. Cleveland: World.

Horner, W. T. (1981–1982). A union perspective. *National Productivity Review*, 1, 1.

Kearns, D. T., & Nadler, D. A. (1992). *Prophets in the Dark*. New York: Free Press.

Kelley, M. R., & Harrison, B. (1992). Unions, technology and labor–management cooperation. In L. Mishel & P. B. Voos (eds.), *Unions and Economic Competitiveness*. Armonk, NY: Sharpe.

Lawler, E. E. (1986). *High Involvement Management*. San Francisco: Jossey-Bass.

Lawler, E. E. (1992). *The Ultimate Advantage*. San Francisco: Jossey-Bass.

Lawler, E. E., Mohrman, S. A., & Ledford, G. E. (1992). *Employee Involvement and Total Quality Management*. San Francisco: Jossey-Bass.

Likert, R. (1961). *New Patterns of Management*. New York: McGraw-Hill.

Likert, R. (1967). *The Human Organization*. New York: McGraw-Hill.

Loomis, C. J. (1993). Dinosaurs. *Fortune*, 127, 36–42.

McGregor, D. (1960). *The Human Side of Enterprise*. New York: McGraw-Hill.

O'Toole, J. (1987). *Vanguard Management*. New York: Berkley Books.

O'Toole, J. (1992). *Videologies: Achieving excellence through ideas, insights and innovation*. Flint, MI: GMI Engineering and Management Institute.

Petersen, D. R., & Hillkirk, J. (1991). *A Better Idea*. Boston: Houghton Mifflin.

Pratte, L. D., & Kruger, D. H. (1992). *The History of Contractual Provisions on Labor–Management Cooperation in the General Motors–UAW Agreements 1973–1990*. East Lansing, MI: Michigan State University.

Tichy, N. M., & Sherman, S. (1993). *Control Your Own Destiny or Someone Else Will*. New York: Currency Doubleday.

Toffler, A. (1970). *Future Shock*. New York: Random House.

Trist, E. L., Higgin, G. W., Murray, H., & Pollock, A. B. (1963). *Organizational Choice*. London: Tavistock.

U.S. Department of Labor, Bureau of Labor–Management Relations and Cooperative Programs (1989). Labor–management cooperation. *BLMR Reports*, 124, 17–20.

Walker, C., & Guest, H. R. (1952). *The Man on the Assembly Line*. Cambridge, MA: Harvard University.

Walton, R. (1974). Innovative restructuring of work. In J. Rosow (ed.), *The Worker and the Job*. Englewood Cliffs, NJ: Prentice Hall.

Walton, R. (1987). *Innovating to Compete*. San Francisco: Jossey-Bass.

Weisbord, M. R. (1987). *Productive Workplaces*. San Francisco: Jossey-Bass.

Wellins, R. S., Byham. W. C., & Wilson, J. M. (1991). *Empowered Teams*. San Francisco: Jossey-Bass.

☐ Chapter 20 ☐

Empowerment and Work Teams

Robert C. Liden and Thomas W. Tewksbury

INTRODUCTION

A dominant trend in the decade of the 1980s was the flattening of organizational hierarchies and the associated reduction of mid-level managers (Weber, 1990). And the trend is expected to continue through the 1990s. In some cases, the creation of flatter, leaner organizations has been accompanied by decentralization, the use of cross-functional teams, larger spans of control for remaining managers, and/or an expanded role in decision making and increased responsibility at lower levels of the organization.

With the trend toward flatter organizational hierarchies, many responsibilities have shifted from managers to work groups in the form of employee empowerment. Although this type of transition has been widespread, affecting many corporations, much is yet to be learned about the effects of work group empowerment on individuals, groups, and organizations. The purpose of this chapter is to provide an overview of theory, research, and practice on empowerment and the leadership of empowered work groups. Included

in our review of research are results from a recently completed field study. In our discussion of empowerment we make an important distinction between individual- and group-level empowerment.

The community psychology, mental health, and social work literatures of the 1970s and 1980s pioneered the concept of empowerment (Solomon, 1976; Rappaport, 1981). Although numerous definitions of empowerment have appeared in these fields, the central theme of most definitions has involved the transformation of powerless individuals into those who possess personal control in their lives (McWhirter, 1991). In the organizational literature, empowerment has been viewed as a set of conditions necessary for intrinsic task motivation (Conger & Kanungo, 1988), and has been defined in the as being comprised of four components (Thomas & Velthouse, 1990):

1 *Choice* Sense of personal control or influence over one's immediate work situation (Greenberger & Strasser, 1991).

2 *Competence* Self-efficacy, or the feeling

that one is capable of successfully performing a particular task or activity
(Bandura, 1982).

3 *Meaningfulness* Perception that a task or
activity is of value to oneself (cf. Hackman
& Oldham, 1976).

4 *Impact* Belief that one has an influence
on organization-level decisions or policy
making (Rotter, 1966).

However, in the published research, rarely has
more than one of the components been studied within the same investigation. Of the four
components of empowerment, by far the most
researched has been choice (Bass, 1990). A
recent empirical study involving 393 middle
managers showed that when compared with
the other three components of empowerment, the choice component was the most
critical in defining the empowerment construct (Spreitzer, 1993).

Although it has been argued that all four
components of empowerment must be realized before an individual is "truly" empowered
(Thomas & Velthouse, 1990), this remains
an empirical question. Choice appears to be
central to the concept of empowerment, and
the meaningfulness and impact "components"
may more frequently appear as outcomes of
empowerment. Similarly, competence may be
best labeled as an important precursor to
empowerment, rather than a dimension of
empowerment. This is because individuals
will not be in a position to accept the responsibility and accountability for making decisions
until they have confidence in their abilities
needed to make these decisions. Although we
agree that competence, meaningfulness, and
impact play an important role in the empowerment process, we feel that the essence
of empowerment is captured by the choice
dimension.

Previous research, some dating back to the
1930s, has addressed choice, as well as competence, meaningfulness, and impact, often
showing positive effects on outcomes such as

Figure 20.1 Degree of empowerment

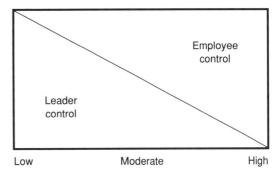

job satisfaction, individual job performance,
turnover, and organizational effectiveness. As
graphically portrayed in figure 20.1 (adapted
from Tannenbaum & Schmidt, 1958), empowerment can be conceptualized as the
amount of an individual work group member's control over work-related decisions relative to the control exerted by the formal
manager of the group. It is assumed in the
figure, based on theory and empirical research, that empowerment is a continuous
variable, with all points on the continuum
from low to high empowerment represented.
In other words, empowerment is not a dichotomous variable. Thus, throughout the
chapter, we refer to levels of empowerment,
not to an artificial dichotomy of low and high
empowerment.

Two types of empowerment are discussed
in this chapter: individual- and group-level
empowerment. *Individual-level empowerment*
refers to the degree of choice experienced
by individuals in the work setting. *Group-level
empowerment* may be defined as the amount
of choice felt by the group as a whole in
the work setting. Figure 20.1, then, may
refer either to individual or group empowerment, with level of control that the individual or group has over decision making,
relative to the formal leader, defining the
amount of choice exercised by the individual or group.

Within the available research on empowerment, a clear distinction has not been made between individual- and group-level empowerment. Often the two types of empowerment are discussed as though they are interchangeable; that what is true of individual-level empowerment is also true of group-level empowerment. We argue that these two types of empowerment are sensitive to different aspects of the situation, affect individuals in different ways, and may require different leadership behaviors.

As implied by figure 20.1, empowering individuals and work groups has important implications for leadership and management. As individuals and groups become more empowered, by definition, formal leaders maintain less control over task decisions and responsibilities of the work group. It is possible, however, for leaders to be empowered as well. Freed from day-to-day direct supervision duties, they may now become more involved in such activities as long-term planning. The role of leaders is thought to change appreciably, from controlling the activity of employees to advising and facilitating employees. However, few research studies have been conducted on the leadership of empowered individuals and groups (Manz & Sims, 1987). Leadership in empowered work settings is another issue addressed in this chapter. Related to the leadership of empowered groups, we briefly discuss the need to supplement supervisory performance evaluations with other forms of appraisal, such as peer ratings and use of group performance measures. And finally, we discuss the implementation of empowerment within the larger organizational context. We suggest that embracing empowerment across the entire organization, rather than implementing in a piecemeal fashion, substantially increases the probability that empowerment will positively influence individual attitudes and organizational effectiveness.

THEORY AND RESEARCH ON EMPOWERMENT

Although few theoretical or empirical articles in academic journals have been published on the topic of empowerment, per se, much has been written on related topics such as participative decision making, substitutes for leadership, self-leadership, intrinsic motivation, job design, democratic leadership styles, and personal control. Information gleaned from these literatures is merged with recent research that explicitly focuses on empowerment. Discussion is organized in terms of individual-level empowerment, group-level empowerment, leading empowered individuals, and leading empowered groups.

Supplementing our review of the literature are reports of findings from a recently completed field investigation of individual- and group-level empowerment (Liden, Wayne, Bradway, & Murphy, 1993a; Liden, Wayne, Bradway, & Murphy, 1994a; Liden, Wayne, Bradway, & Sparrowe, 1994b). The investigation involved 358 work group members and 60 manager/team leaders representing multiple departments of professionals in a large service sector organization. Group members responded to questionnaires, and managers/team leaders were personally interviewed. Of the 358 group members, 160 were male, 184 were female, and 14 chose not to reveal their gender. The average age of the member respondents was approximately 33 years and the average organizational tenure was 9.98 years. This investigation was preceded by a pretest and qualitative study involving 68 work group members, 19 managers, and 12 team leaders of the work groups in a service department of a large heavy-manufacturing organization (Liden, Wayne, Sparrowe, & Bradway, 1993b). The work group members responded to questionnaires, and the managers and team leaders were personally interviewed with an open-ended interview format. Of the 68 group members, 41 were male, 26 female, and one chose not to reveal his or her gender. The average age of the member respondents was 44.5, and the average tenure with the organization was 20.8 years.

Individual-level empowerment

Although the concept of empowerment received much interest and discussion among organizations during the 1980s, it really did not come to fruition on a widespread scale until the 1990s. Now many organizations have implemented empowerment concepts in at least portions of their work forces. In some cases, empowerment is implemented as a critical part of a total quality management imperative. Despite the recency of the empowerment and total quality phenomenon, the roots of empowerment can be traced to Lewin's pioneering work on participative management (Lewin, 1947; Lewin & Lippitt, 1938). Although participation in decision making is in no way synonymous with empowerment, some of what has been learned from research on participation appears to be relevant for implementing empowerment. Current and past research on individual-level empowerment is categorized according to choice, the central theme of empowerment, as well as to competence, impact, and meaningfulness.

Choice

Degree of choice in the work setting, representing the crux of empowerment, overlaps considerably with participative decision making and with autonomy from the job characteristics literature. Lewin's research (Lewin, 1947; Lewin & Lippitt, 1938) led to great interest in democracy in the workplace. Democratic work settings were characterized as involving worker influence in decision making. An extremely ambitious research program at the University of Michigan pursued the topic of employee involvement and

participation originated by Lewin and his colleagues. Out of this research came System 4 Management (Likert, 1967), touted at the time as the ideal organizational form, which was heavily based on participative decision making and extensive interaction and influence of members within work groups. Bass (1990) reported that studies on Systems 4 Management involving a wide spectrum of organizations had been conducted by 1977. For example, in a series of field experiments summarized in Katz and Kahn (1978), hierarchically structured (traditional or Systems 1) organizations were transformed such that organizational communication patterns, influence in decision making, and power were consistent with System 4 type organizations.

Reported results of these studies included significant increases in employee job satisfaction and productivity, as well as significant decreases in waste rates and absenteeism (Marrow, Bowers, & Seashore, 1967; Morse & Reimer, 1956; Seashore & Bowers, 1970). However, many researchers have concluded that these results were overinterpreted because multiple variables were manipulated at once, making it impossible to conclude that participation was actually the cause (Campbell, Dunnette, Lawler, & Weick, 1970; Lowin, 1968; Rosenberg & Rosenstein, 1980). Updated reviews of participation research have led to the same inconclusive bottom line: that participation positively affects attitudes and/or performance in some situations but not in others (Cotton, Vollrath, Froggatt, Lengnick-Hall, & Jennings, 1988; Locke, Schweiger, & Latham, 1986; Miller & Monge, 1986; Wagner & Gooding, 1987).

Although participation can be motivating for some individuals (Mitchell, 1973), one common caution with respect to participation is that it is not appropriate in all cases. For example, individuals who are apathetic, irrational, high in conformity, or not of necessary maturity may not be interested in participating in decision making (Dachler & Wilpert,

1978). It has been argued that the readiness of individuals for participation should be determined prior to implementation (Pasmore & Fagans, 1992). Although participation represents only a part of what is required for empowerment, it is possible that just as some individuals do not respond well to participation, some individuals may similarly not be interested in becoming empowered.

The amount of autonomy in deciding when and how to complete tasks, a salient ingredient in job enrichment, overlaps considerably with the choice dimension of empowerment (Hackman & Oldham, 1976). Similarly, sociologists have documented that perceptions of powerlessness in one's job contribute to feelings of alienation (Ashforth, 1989; Blauner, 1964; Shepard, 1977). Shepard (1977, 5), based on Seeman (1959), defined powerlessness as existing "when workers are unable to control their job activities," which approximates the opposite of autonomy on the job (Hackman & Oldham, 1976). It must be pointed out, however, that just as some individuals do not want to participate in decision making, some individuals do not desire an enriched job (Hackman & Oldham, 1976). This suggests that some people will not respond positively to choice or autonomy in their jobs, and more generally, may not have a desire for empowerment.

The combination of influence in decision making and autonomy results in personal control. Personal control has been defined as "an individual's beliefs, at a given point in time, in his or her ability to effect a change, in a desired direction, on the environment" (Greenberger & Strasser, 1986, 165). It has been documented that most individuals desire control, and that when employees are deprived of control by the organization, they may try to gain personal control in organizationally dysfunctional ways (Ashforth, 1989; Greenberger & Strasser, 1991). Empirical research has found personal control to be related to intrinsic task motivation (Fisher, 1978), reduced machine downtime (Wall,

Corbett, Martin, Clegg, & Jackson, 1990), job performance, and job satisfaction (Greenberger, Strasser, Cummings, & Dunham, 1989; Wall, Jackson, & Davids, 1992).

In both of our recently completed studies, work group members desired significantly greater personal control (i.e., choice) than they felt that they had now (Liden et al., 1993a, 1993b). It was also found that members reporting higher levels of current control were more desirous of greater control than were members reporting lower levels of current personal control. In other words, the more personal control members reported having currently, the more control they desired. Individuals reporting higher levels of personal control were more satisfied with their jobs, reported higher levels of organizational commitment, and expressed a stronger intention not to leave the organization. Those who reported higher levels of personal control were also rated higher on job performance by their managers or team leaders than employees with less personal control.

In addition to level of personal control, we also assessed the magnitude of the difference between perceived and desired personal control. It was found that the smaller the difference between individuals' perceived and desired control, the greater the satisfaction with work. In other words, members experiencing levels of personal control that were close to their desired amount of control were more satisfied with their work than members experiencing a large gap between their perceived and desired amount of personal control.

Competence

Before assuming high levels of personal control, individuals must have confidence in their ability to handle added responsibility accompanying increased personal control. Thus, a prerequisite of empowerment is individual self-efficacy, or confidence in being able to perform well on particular tasks (Bandura, 1982; Gist, 1987; Gist & Mitchell, 1992). Per-

390

ceptions of competence at tasks have been shown to be related to intrinsic motivation (Fisher, 1978) and to task performance in a wide variety of organizational settings (Gist & Mitchell, 1992). Perceived competence is critical with respect to an individual's desire for empowerment. If individuals are not prepared to take on higher levels of responsibility and have a fear that they will fail if given such responsibility, efforts at empowerment will not succeed (cf. Pasmore & Fagans, 1992).

Thus simply providing individuals with more responsibility and complex tasks will not be empowering unless the individuals are confident that they will succeed. In fact, the transition from a traditional hierarchical, bureaucratically structured organizational setting to a less centralized, flatter, empowered work setting typically involves a large investment in human capital. Rus (1994) noted that transforming a group of unskilled employees accustomed to responding to orders from a supervisor and making virtually no decisions on their own, to a group of empowered individuals takes from three to five years. During this period, extensive training is needed to provide individuals the competencies required of them in empowered work settings. Training required may range from basic language and math skills training to development of interpersonal and teamwork skills. Simply informing employees that they are now empowered, without providing training to develop needed skills and knowledge, will nearly always result in failure.

Although training can greatly enhance feelings of confidence and self-efficacy, actually succeeding in the use of newly acquired skills on the job acts to further enhance self-efficacy (Gist & Mitchell, 1992). Thus, even though a moderate amount of self-efficacy is needed as a prerequisite for assuming influence and control in the work setting, levels of competence and self-efficacy should increase as the result of working in an empowered setting. In this sense, competence may act

as an outcome as well as a precursor to empowerment.

Meaningfulness

When individuals are provided with influence and control over nontrivial decisions, they should view their work as being of value to the organization and/or to those outside of the organization, such as customers. The essence of meaningfulness is captured in Hackman and Oldham's (1976) "experienced meaningfulness", which is affected by the task identity, task significance, and skill variety. Individuals who: (1) know how their tasks fit into the larger scheme of things; (2) feel that the tasks they complete are significant to the organization and society; and (3) use a wide variety of skills and abilities on the job, will see their jobs as being meaningful. Similarly, sociologists have identified meaninglessness and self-estrangement as dimensions of alienation. Shepard (1977, 5), based on Seeman (1959), defined meaninglessness as existing "when workers contribute only minutely to the total product," which is essentially the opposite of Hackman and Oldham's (1976) task identity job characteristic. Self-estrangement is felt by workers who feel that society does not value their jobs, and as a result, they do not experience a sense of personal self-fulfillment. Self-estrangement is essentially the opposite of Hackman and Oldham's task significance. Thus, a critical result of working in an empowered setting is a sense that one's work has meaning to oneself and to others.

Impact

Another result of being granted personal control and influence is a sense of impact. According to Thomas and Velthouse (1990, 672), impact "refers to the degree to which behavior is seen as 'making a difference'." Impact is felt when individuals perceive that their behavior has caused, or at least influenced, important outcomes. If individuals are granted control and influence over trivial issues, a sense of impact will not result.

Conversely, the supervisor-directed behavior of a subordinate in a traditional, hierarchically structured work setting may have a great effect on important outcomes, even though the subordinate does not have choice or autonomy in executing the behavior. For control to be perceived by individuals as having impact, it must involve issues that are viewed by the individual as being significant. Individual perceptions of impact in turn tend to increase levels of intrinsic motivation (Herzberg, Mausner, & Snyderman, 1959).

In summary, empowerment has been described as being based primarily on the degree of choice, control, or influence in making salient decisions. A substantial amount of empirical research accumulating over the past 60 years has provided support for the importance of choice and control. However, a key difference exists between empowerment and previously studied constructs such as job design and participation. Dachler and Wilpert (1978, 15–16) aptly pointed out that participative decision making "seeks to increase involvement of subordinates, but only with respect to what the leader thinks is appropriate." They then asked the question, "What would participation mean if it originated at the bottom rather than being delegated or granted from above . . . ?" Empowerment provides the answer to the question they asked over 15 years ago: Individuals who are fully empowered have a say concerning *when* a decision needs to be made. They do not need to wait for a leader's approval before making a decision.

Although labeled components of empowerment by Thomas and Velthouse (1990), we feel that competence is better described as a critical prerequisite of empowerment, while meaningfulness and impact represent salient outcomes of empowerment. Choice, the opportunity to maintain influence and control, represents the core of empowerment. As a result of using influence to make important decisions, individuals should experience meaningfulness in their jobs. They should also feel that they have had an impact on others within or outside of the organization. In order for an individual to take on more responsibility by making decisions and handling more complex tasks, that individual first must have confidence in his or her skills and abilities to successfully carry out these new role demands. Without training, individuals may not gain the skill and knowledge necessary to begin tackling more challenging decisions and tasks.

Group-level empowerment

Consistent with the bureaucratic model of organization (Weber, 1947), in traditional hierarchically structured organizations, most work is accomplished at the individual level. However, accompanying the downsizing and reduction of managerial levels in many organizations over the past 10–15 years, has been greater use of groups for completing work. It is natural, then, that in many cases, empowerment has been implemented at the group level rather than at the individual level. Given this emphasis on groups in many organizations, it is somewhat surprising that virtually all of the academic research on empowerment, per se, has focused on individual-level empowerment. Although much of what has been covered with respect to individual-level empowerment should generalize to the group level, we identify where there are differences between individual- and group-level empowerment. More importantly though, we examine conflicts that may occur when attempting to empower both groups and the individual members making up those groups. As with our discussion of individual-level empowerment, group empowerment is described as being based on group choice and control. Competence is viewed as a necessary prerequisite of group empowerment, and meaningfulness and impact represent outcomes of group empowerment.

Choice

Here, we are interested in the control that the group has over the way in which it conducts its work. The previous discussion on the importance of personal control, job enrichment, and participation in individual-level choice should generalize to the group level (Hackman, 1977; Rousseau, 1977; Walton & Hackman, 1986). However, virtually no research on personal control has specifically addressed the group level, and little research has been published on group-level enrichment. Although research has been conducted on group participation in decision making (Vroom & Jago, 1978), nearly all of this research has focused on individual rather than group outcomes. The only research conducted in organizational settings that has explicitly focused on group-level choice comes from the autonomous work groups and self-managed groups literatures.

Research on autonomous work groups was initiated by Trist and his colleagues of the Tavistok Institute (Trist & Bamforth, 1951). Work groups were given substantial autonomy and decision-making power, determining such things as the group's work pace, production standards, and the way tasks were executed. Results of the early Tavistok studies suggested that relative to traditional organization of work with direct supervisory control over workers, productivity was higher, and absenteeism, turnover, and accidents lower for autonomous work groups (Trist, Higgin, Murray, & Pollock, 1963). However, much of the research on autonomous work groups was criticized, especially for its inability to make causal inferences (Lawler, 1977). More recent research with improved methods has found autonomous work groups, relative to traditional work groups, to have members who are higher in work satisfaction (Wall, Kemp, Jackson, & Clegg, 1986) and organizational commitment (Cordery, Mueller, & Smith, 1991), but absenteeism, turnover and productivity improvements have not always been replicated.

An assumption underlying research on autonomous work groups is that individual group members will experience greater personal control through the autonomy given to the group. Thus it is thought that even though not having personal responsibility for making decisions, sharing in decision making should provide the individual with greater feelings of self-determination. Results of the autonomous work group studies suggest that providing choice or control at the group level has had the effect of significantly improving individual members' attitudes and, in some cases, work behaviors. However, nearly all of the studies on autonomous work groups have involved employees who previously had worked in traditional hierarchically structured settings in which they experienced virtually no personal control. When given even a small amount of control via increased autonomy provided to the group, these employees' attitudes became much more positive. Conversely, in cases in which employees previously held substantial personal control over work-related decisions, reactions to reorganization into autonomous or self-managed groups may be negative (Manz & Angle, 1986). That is, when employees have experienced autonomy, choice, and personal control as individuals, they may perceive a loss of control when placed in a situation in which the decisions they once made as individuals are now handled collectively by the group.

The effect of group-level empowerment on group effectiveness may depend on task interdependence, which is the degree to which the group's tasks require interaction and coordination with one another. Low task interdependence describes groups in which members naturally carry out their tasks independently of one another. On the other hand, task completion requires extremely close interaction between the members of groups that are high in task interdependence. Forcing group autonomy and decision making on groups that are low in task interdependence, may lead to dysfunctional outcomes (Hackman, 1977). For example, in our study of multiple departments of a service sector organization (Liden et al., 1994a), task interdependence as rated by managers or team leaders was found to influence the association between group-level control and group effectiveness. Specifically, the relation between group control and group effectiveness was stronger for highly task interdependent groups ($r = .45$, $p < .01$) than for less task interdependent groups ($r = .02$, ns). The same effect was uncovered in open-ended interviews with managers and team leaders of the heavy manufacturing organization (Liden et al., 1993b).

Consistent with the above findings, recent research has made a distinction between work group and team (Sundstrom, DeMeuse, & Futrell, 1990). Specifically it has been argued that to qualify as a team, members must be highly dependent on one another in getting the work completed. On the other hand, task interdependence may be quite low in a traditional work group. This implies that group empowerment is appropriate for only one type of work group, one that is high in task interdependence, carrying out its work as a team.

Competence

Just as self-efficacy is a necessary prerequisite for empowerment at the individual level, group-level efficacy is essential before a group can successfully handle empowerment. At the group level, competence or group efficacy pertains to the confidence that group members have in the group being able to perform well on its tasks. Bandura (1982) introduced the notion of collective efficacy, which was later termed group potency (Shea & Guzzo, 1987). Potency deals with the extent to which members of the group are confident that

the group will be effective in reaching its objectives. Just as self-efficacy has been shown to be important with respect to individual motivation and performance, it has been argued that group member perceptions of the group's potency will be related to member motivation and group effectiveness (Bandura, 1982; Shea & Guzzo, 1987). As with individual-level empowerment, providing groups with greater control and responsibility will not result in successful outcomes unless the group is confident of its skills and abilities needed to handle the tasks or decisions at hand.

Meaningfulness

Identity and meaning of jobs are often increased with self-managed or autonomous work groups through the group decision-making process and from job rotation (Wall et al., 1986). Group members' understanding of the goals and mission of the work group is significantly enhanced when sharing in the responsibility of group decisions. Also, through job rotation, which requires learning and working on most of the jobs in the work group, each member becomes intimately familiar with the purpose and meaning of each job as well as the interrelations between jobs.

However, a potential problem with job rotation is that individuals who were in charge of a job prior to rotation may feel a loss of power and personal value when they are no longer the only person in the work unit who can handle that job. Open-ended interviews conducted with the managers and team leaders of service groups within a large manufacturing company revealed that cross-training may have the unintended effect of divesting individuals of the belief that they make a unique contribution in their work. This is to say that an individual's sense of being valued for his or her contribution may diminish when, through cross-training, it becomes evident that anyone else on the team can be expected to do the same work satisfactorily (Liden et al., 1993b).

Impact

Generalizing from the individual level to the group level, impact should be experienced when the decisions made or activities carried out are viewed as causing, or at least influencing, important outcomes. It may be more likely for individuals to perceive that they have had impact through the group than as an individual. This is because larger, more encompassing portions of work can be assigned to a group than to an individual (Hackman, 1977). Being responsible for a greater portion of the organization's work will increase the potential for that work being viewed as having an impact.

In summary, the core of group-level empowerment has been described as choice and control held by the group. The autonomous work groups literature has provided empirical support for the positive effects of choice on outcomes such as work satisfaction. A distinction was made between work groups and teams. By definition, teams are high in task interdependence. Recent research has shown that group-level empowerment is positively correlated with group effectiveness only when the group (i.e., team) is high in task interdependence. Little research explicitly focusing on competence or impact has been conducted at the group level. Although the effects of autonomous work groups on choice and meaningfulness have been demonstrated, the role of competence and impact in group-level empowerment remains an empirical question.

Leading empowered individuals

Over thirty years ago, McGregor (1960) advocated that employees would be much more inclined to meet organizational goals if allowed to determine how effort should be directed in attempting to meet the goals. Research conducted in traditional, hierarchically structured work settings, has provided support for McGregor's propositions. Leader provision of autonomy, sensitivity to subordinate needs, support, feedback, help in solving problems, and recognition of subordinate potential are related to subordinate satisfaction, productivity, and tendency not to turnover (e.g., Dansereau, Graen, & Haga, 1975; Deci, Connell, & Ryan, 1989; Ferris, 1985; Graen, Liden, & Hoel, 1982; Leana, 1986, 1987; Liden & Graen, 1980; Likert, 1967; Louis, Posner, & Powell, 1983; Scandura & Graen, 1984; Seers & Graen, 1984).

Although the aforementioned studies dealt with traditional work settings, several studies have suggested that the results might hold for relatively empowered individuals (Howell & Dorfman, 1981; Mills, 1983, Mills & Posner, 1982). In our research, group member reports of manager/ team leader concern and supporting behaviors, such as "I usually know where I stand with my manager/ team leader," "My manager/team leader recognizes my potential," and "My manager/ team leader understands my problems and needs," were found to be significantly related to individual-level job performance (Liden et al., 1994b; Liden et al., 1993). Manager/ team leader concern and supporting behaviors were shown to be positively related to choice, impact, meaningfulness, competence (Spreitzer, 1993), and personal control (Greenberger et al., 1989). We also asked questions adapted from Manz and Sims (1987) which were specifically designed to assess behaviors thought to be important in helping to empower individuals and groups. Individual reports of personal control were related to all of the "empowering" leader behaviors that we assessed, as follows:

- Leader encouragement of careful preparation for work activities.

- Leader encouragement of members setting their own goals.
- Leader encouragement of self-criticism within the group.
- Leader encouragement of praising each other for good performance.
- Leader encouragement of having a positive attitude.
- Leader encouragement to evaluate their own performance.
- Acting as a role model and inspiring members.
- Stimulating members intellectually to promote innovation.

Multiple regression results indicated that 28 percent of the variability in perceptions of individual empowerment were explained by these eight leader behaviors. It was also found that "traditional" supporting leader behaviors explained additional variance in individual personal control. Similar effects for supportive leader behaviors were found in a sample of 182 hospitality industry employees (Sparrowe, 1994).

Some organizations, including the manufacturing organization that we investigated (Liden et al., 1993b), target an eventual elimination of formal work group managers as one of the final steps of implementing empowerment. To address the desirability of removing formal managers, we conducted analyses to examine the effect of leadership on work outcomes, beyond the effects of empowerment on these outcomes. We assessed the degree of variability in work outcomes that could be explained by leader behavior after controlling for group members' reported levels of empowerment. Leader behavior explained variation in group member commitment to the organization and job performance that was not explained by empowerment. These results suggest that a replacement source for the support, feedback, and guidance provided by managers should be found before these managerial positions are eliminated.

Leading empowered groups

It has been argued that "team autonomy depends on the role of the leader and on how authority is distributed" (Sundstrom et al., 1990, 124). To be considered empowered, groups should be granted autonomy in handling the work of their groups (Hackman, 1977; Hackman & Walton, 1986). As such, the leader should take on a facilitator role, advising and guiding subordinates in handling tasks and solving problems themselves, rather than controlling and directing as in the case of large work groups operating within traditional structures (Manz & Sims, 1987). It is thought that leader attempts to take control away from group members will disrupt their work groups, and will be detrimental to work group performance. These guidelines for the management of empowered work groups remain essentially untested as few empirical studies have been conducted on the leadership of empowered work groups (e.g., Conger & Kanungo, 1988).

The reduction in the amount of direct control exerted by leaders also suggests that leaders may be less familiar with the individual work behaviors of each group member. In addition, in some organizations, group empowerment has proceeded along with reductions in managerial ranks, leaving remaining managers with responsibility for two or more work groups. Thus, performance evaluations made by managers of empowered work groups will typically be based on less information (e.g., Lord, 1985; Motowidlo, 1986). This difficulty may be exacerbated in highly task interdependent groups where individual contributions are difficult to detect (Liden & Mitchell, 1983). Because task interdependence should be more common with empowered than with traditional work groups, evaluating individual-level performance should be most difficult for leaders of empowered work groups. As a result, supervisory performance appraisals may be more prone to unfair biases as group size and degree of empowerment increases. This bias in performance evaluations may be manifested in negative group member attitudes concerning the appraisal process.

One response to the difficulties that leaders may face in evaluating individual-level job performance in large work groups is to augment appraisals to include peer evaluations (Saavedra & Kwun, 1993). Reviews of research on peer ratings have found them to be consistently valid (Mumford, 1983). Peer ratings also show promise for improving employee attitudes concerning the appraisals. For example, Mumford (1983, 874) noted that "generally, individuals who are similar to the person making the comparison will be preferred as standards for evaluation, since they provide a somewhat more precise and germane source of comparative information."

We assessed group member opinions regarding the use of peer ratings in individual performance evaluations by asking respondents, "What portion of an individual's overall performance evaluation should be based on ratings of that individual's performance made by his/her coworkers?" There was wide variation in responses to this question, with the majority of participants indicating that no more than one-third of a person's performance evaluation should be based on coworker ratings (Liden et al., 1993a, 1993b). Also, the higher the task interdependence of the group, the greater the weight that group members felt should be placed on peer evaluations relative to other performance evaluation sources.

Another approach to replacing or supplementing supervisory performance ratings is to assign a group performance evaluation to each member in the group as suggested by Hackman (1977). To examine feelings about this approach, our respondents were asked, "What portion of an individual's overall performance evaluation should be based on his or her work group's performance rating?" Operationally this involves assigning group performance ratings and/or objective data to

each member of the group as a part of each group member's individual performance rating. Respondents preferred that a greater portion of individual performance evaluations be based on group-level performance than based on peer ratings of individual performance (Liden et al., 1993a, 1993b). Also, there was a significant correlation between reported levels of empowerment and proportion of group-level performance ratings to be used in the evaluation of individual work group members. Interestingly, as group members desired more empowerment, they became more inclined to believe that group-level performance ratings should be used in assessing individual-level job performance. Also, the higher the task interdependence of the group, the more that the group members supported the use of group-level performance ratings in evaluating individuals. In summary, the greater the current and desired levels of empowerment, as well as the more highly task interdependent the work group, the more support there was for the use of group performance ratings and/or data in the evaluations of individual group members.

Related to the performance appraisal issue, it has been found that the same factors that make it difficult for leaders to evaluate individual-level performance, also may cause leaders to be less likely to reward good individual performance (e.g., Goodstadt & Kipnis, 1970). This may result in less positive subordinate perceptions of rewards. Of particular importance with respect to reward perceptions is the perceived fairness with which rewards are allocated (Folger & Konovsky, 1989; Greenberg, 1990; Kabanoff, 1991).

IMPLICATIONS FOR PRACTICE

Although few studies have been conducted on empowerment, per se, findings from research in related areas should contribute to the successful implementation of empowerment in organizations. Our review of theory and research revealed that much research related to empowerment has been conducted over the past 60 years. It behooves us to pay attention to this research, especially to guard against repeating errors of the past (Dunnette, 1966). In particular, research on participation, job enrichment, autonomous work groups, organizational change, and leadership has produced findings that appear to be relevant to empowerment efforts. For example, the following illustrate how findings from past research may generalize to the practice of empowerment. Again, we organize our discussion around the choice, competence, meaningfulness, and impact variables which depict the empowerment process:

Choice

- Past research has shown that efforts to implement participation or job enrichment must be genuine. Pseudoparticipation or pseudoenrichment in many cases will lower employee morale. It is better not to tamper with jobs at all, unless substantial changes are made so that employees actually have more responsibility and are really more involved in decision making (Hackman, 1977). Generalizing these findings to empowerment, more than lip-service must occur in order for employees to experience choice and self-determination. Provision of autonomy, personal control, and opportunities to participate in decision making must be genuine. Creating the illusion that employees are empowered when they actually are not may lead to dysfunctional outcomes, such as lower satisfaction, commitment, and performance.
- In cases in which it is not possible to substantially enrich individual jobs, group-level job redesign or enrichment may result in more positive outcomes than individual-level enrichment (Hackman, 1977). However, providing choice or au-

tonomy to work groups may result in improved group performance only for groups that are high in task interdependence. When task interdependence is low, providing choice to work groups may have no effect on group performance. In essence, group empowerment appears to be appropriate only for teams defined as highly task interdependent work groups.

- Providing choice or autonomy to work groups may have the unintended effect of removing personal control and choice from individual group members. Implementation of group-level empowerment may result in positive outcomes only for employees who previously had little personal control or autonomy.
- Successful job enrichment efforts often have the negative side effect of lower pay satisfaction (people expect more money because they are engaged in more complex tasks that require more responsibility – often handling tasks that their supervisors once held). Because empowerment efforts also involve asking people to assume more responsibility and to handle more complex and demanding tasks, it is likely that empowered individuals will also become dissatisfied with their pay.
- Job enrichment may violate labor–management contracts or civil service classifications. Similarly, empowerment efforts have been challenged by a number of unions.
- Organizational changes, such as participative decision making, tend to work best when entire systems are involved, not just the lower-level employees. It follows that empowerment may be more successful as more levels of the organization are involved in the effort. Ideally the entire organization should embrace an empowerment culture. Consistent with the total quality management approach, employees at all levels should be given the opportunity to be directly involved in providing the best possible products and services to customers.

- Traditional supportive leadership behaviors may be important even with "self-managed" workers. In other words, in the move to empowered work groups, it should not be assumed that leadership is no longer needed. Facilitating *and* supportive leadership behaviors are needed to help guide empowered groups.

Competence

- Some individuals do not have an interest in participating in decision making or do not have a desire for job enrichment. Similarly, some employees may not want to be empowered. This may be due to a lack of perceived competence for handling a more demanding job. In order to instill feelings of self-efficacy or confidence in being able to tackle job responsibilities, provision of information and training will often be needed to prepare individuals and/or groups for empowerment (Gist & Mitchell, 1992). Such training should not be limited to technical skills, but should include interpersonal and group process skills as well. However, some individuals may have the potential to learn needed skills, but simply do not want added responsibility or challenge. In these cases, it may not be feasible to retain the individual. Such individuals may disrupt empowerment efforts, especially those directed at the group level.

Meaningfulness

- For jobs of narrow scope that are difficult to transform into more meaningful jobs, group-level empowerment may allow individual members to realize greater job meaningfulness through their participation in group decisions and activities.

Impact

- As with job enrichment efforts, it is important for individuals and groups to have access to feedback on their performance. When such feedback is not available from the work itself, it should be provided by team leaders or managers. Especially for highly interdependent groups, group-level feedback needs to be available.
- To enhance teamwork, especially in highly interdependent work groups, some portion of individual performance evaluations and rewards should be based on group-level performance.

With respect to leadership, it appears that even empowered work groups benefit from the support and guidance of formal leaders, either team leaders or managers. However, leader behaviors should be limited to support and guidance, excluding directive or controlling behaviors. This implies that leaders of empowered work groups must either be trained to lead in this fashion or should be selected appropriately. For example, leaders with high needs for power (McClelland, 1971) may not be well suited for leading empowered work groups, as it may be difficult for them to relinquish power to subordinates. Stable personality traits such as need for power may be addressed only through selection, but many desired behaviors can be shaped with training (Deci et al., 1989). For example, in order for empowerment efforts to be effective, it has been suggested that leaders need to provide frequent, constructive feedback to work group members (Greenberger & Strasser, 1991). Training has been shown to significantly improve leaders' provision of self-determination and useful feedback to group members (Deci et al., 1989).

CONCLUSIONS AND SUGGESTED FUTURE DIRECTIONS

Although much is mentioned about "empowered work groups," most research focuses on individual-level empowerment. We have made what we feel is a critical distinction between individual- and group-level empowerment. An area in need of much research and practical attention is the unintended effects that group empowerment may have on individual empowerment. When individuals are unempowered before work group empowerment efforts are undertaken, there should be no problem. These employees, through shared decision making and responsibility, should experience empowerment.

However, when individuals possess substantial control over work decisions prior to the implementation of group empowerment, efforts to empower at the group level may endanger previous feelings of individual-level empowerment. Such individuals may feel that they have lost some of their previously held personal control to the group. Longitudinal research is needed to assess this issue. This research might also identify mechanisms for merging the individual- and group-levels of empowerment. And when merging these two levels of empowerment, attention needs to be paid to the structure of the group and the nature of the group's tasks. Results of our research demonstrated that group-level empowerment is not appropriate for groups that are low in task interdependence. Only when group tasks require close interaction between group members is the implementation of group empowerment appropriate. This does not mean, however, that the tasks of a work group cannot be redesigned so as to induce greater task interdependence and open the door for successful implementation of group empowerment.

Much empirical research has been conducted on variables related to or overlapping with empowerment. Although many of the findings have been positive, there has been inconsistency. For example, studies on participation, autonomous work groups, and job enrichment have not always found performance improvements. This may be attributed to a lack of attention to the larger organizational context in which change strategies have been employed (Sundstrom et al.,

1990). More attention needs to be paid to macro issues such as organizational culture, organizational structure, top-level support for change, organizational environment, types of tasks, technologies used, and clarity of communicating organizational goals to all employees.

These larger organizational issues need to be considered prior to and during efforts to implement empowerment. All members of the organization must realize that creating an empowered organization does not happen overnight. Implementation requires much hard work over several years. The decision to embrace empowerment as an imperative is generally part of an intentional shift in organizational culture. Effective transition to empowerment involves a process of migration rather than short-term pendulum swings.

A piecemeal approach to empowerment sends mixed signals throughout the organization and runs a high risk of failing to accomplish the intended outcomes. Rather, empowering an organization is a strategic initiative and calls for a well-constructed implementation plan. Two key elements are the communication of the company's intentions and the education and training necessary to prepare people to function in an empowered environment. In other words, simply issuing a proclamation saying "you are hereby empowered to conduct all of your responsibilities without stopping for approval along the way," represents irresponsible implementation.

Once the implementation of an empowerment strategy is complete, there is no turning back. Leaders who attempt to return to a directive management style will encounter strong resistance from employees who are thriving on their enriched job culture. Future hiring decisions will need to be influenced by a new applicant profile so the selection of each new employee will be compatible with the empowerment culture. And finally, employees at all levels who cling to the old culture will become dysfunctional in the new organization. Those unable to adjust will need to consider moving on to other challenges.

Some claim that empowerment is just one passing fad in a series of management fads over the years (Abrahamson, 1994). Such prophesies will no doubt be verified in organizations that adopt empowerment in small pockets, do not radically change organizational cultures and hierarchical power structures, or expect immediate results. However, when the organizational culture and restructuring needed to support and patiently nurture empowerment is developed, empowerment can succeed. Success may include higher individual, group, and organizational effectiveness as well as greater satisfaction among the organization's members and its customers.

REFERENCES

Abrahamson, E. (1994). Management fashion. Paper presented as part of a symposium at the annual meetings of the Society of Industrial and Organizational Psychologists, Nashville, Tennessee. April.

Ashforth, B. E. (1989). The experience of powerlessness in organizations. *Organizational Behavior and Human Decision Processes*, 43, 207–42.

Bandura, A. (1982). Self-efficacy mechanism in human agency. *American Psychologist*, 37, 122–47.

Bass, B. M. (1990). *Bass & Stogdill's Handbook of Leadership: Theory, research, and managerial applications.* New York: Free Press.

Blauner, R. (1964). *Alienation and Freedom: The factory worker and his industry.* Chicago: University of Chicago Press.

Campbell, J. P., Dunnette, M. D., Lawler, E. E., & Weick, K. E. (1970). *Managerial Behavior, Performance, and Effectiveness.* New York: McGraw-Hill.

Conger, J. A., & Kanungo, R. N. (1988). The empowerment process: Integrating theory and practice. *Academy of Management Review*, 13, 471–82.

Cordery, J. L., Mueller, W. S., & Smith, L. M. (1991). Attitudinal and behavioral effects of autonomous group working: A longitudinal field study. *Academy of Management Journal*, 34, 464–76.

Cotton, J. L., Vollrath, D. A., Froggatt, K. L., Lengnick-Hall, M. L., & Jennings, K. R. (1988). Employee participation: Diverse forms and different outcomes. *Academy of Management Review*, 13, 8–22.

Dachler, P., & Wilpert, B. (1978). Conceptual dimensions and boundaries of participation in organizations: A critical evaluation. *Administrative Science Quarterly*, 23, 1–39.

Dansereau, F., Graen, G., & Haga, W. (1975). A vertical dyad approach to leadership within formal organizations. *Organizational Behavior and Human Performance*, 13, 46–78.

Deci, E. L., Connell, J. P., & Ryan, R. M. (1989). Self-determination in a work organization. *Journal of Applied Psychology*, 74, 580–90.

Dunnette, M. D. (1966). Fads, fashions, and folderol in psychology. *American Psychologist*, 21, 343–52.

Ferris, G. R. (1985). Role of leadership in the employee withdrawal process: A constructive replication. *Journal of Applied Psychology*, 70, 777–81.

Fisher, C. D. (1978). The effects of personal control, competence, and extrinsic reward systems on intrinsic motivation. *Organizational Behavior and Human Performance*, 21, 273–88.

Folger, R., & Konovsky, M. (1989). Effects of procedural and distributive justice on reactions to pay raise decisions. *Academy of Management Journal*, 32, 115–30.

Gist, M. E. (1987). Self-efficacy: Implications for organizational behavior and human resource management. *Academy of Management Review*, 12, 472–85.

Gist, M. E., & Mitchell, T. R. (1992). Self-efficacy: A theoretical analysis of its determinants and malleability. *Academy of Management Review*, 17, 183–211.

Goodstadt, B., & Kipnis, D. (1970). Situational influences on the use of power. *Journal of Applied Psychology*, 54, 201–7.

Graen, G., Liden, R. C., & Hoel, W. (1982). Role of leadership in the employee withdrawal process. *Journal of Applied Psychology*, 67, 868–72.

Greenberg, J. (1990). Organizational justice: Yesterday, today, and tomorrow. *Journal of Management*, 16, 399–432.

Greenberger, D. B., & Strasser, S. (1986). Development and application of a model of personal control in organizations. *Academy of Management Review*, 11, 164–77.

Greenberger, D. B., & Strasser, S. (1991). The role of situational and dispositional factors in the enhancement of personal control in organizations. *Research in Organizational Behavior*, 13, 111–45.

Greenberger, D. B., Strasser, S., Cummings, L. L., & Dunham, R. B. (1989). The impact of personal control on performance and satisfaction. *Organizational Behavior and Human Decision Processes*, 43, 29–51.

Hackman, J. R. (1977). *Work design.* In J. R. Hackman & J. L. Suttle (eds.), *Improving Life at Work*, 96–162. Santa Monica, CA: Goodyear.

Hackman, J. R. & Oldham, G. R. (1976). Motivation through the design of work: Test of a theory. *Organizational Behavior and Human Performance*, 16, 250–79.

Hackman, J. R., & Walton, R. E. (1986). Leading groups in organizations. In P. S. Goodman and associates (eds.), *Designing effective work groups*, 72–119. San Francisco: Jossey-Bass.

Herzberg, F., Mausner, B., & Snyderman, B. B. (1959). *The Motivation to Work*, 2nd ed. New York: Wiley.

Howell, J. P., & Dorfman, P. W. (1981). Substitutes for leadership: Test of a construct. *Academy of Management Journal*, 24, 714–28.

Kabanoff, B. (1991). Equity, equality, power, and conflict. *Academy of Management Review*, 16, 416–41.

Katz, D., & Kahn, R. L. (1978). *The Social Psychology of Organizations*, 2nd ed. New York: Wiley.

Lawler, E. E. (1977). Adaptive experiments: An approach to organizational behavior research. *Academy of Management Review*, 2, 576–85.

Leana, C. R. (1986). Predictors and consequences of delegation. *Academy of Management Journal*, 29, 754–74.

Leana, C. R. (1987). Power relinquishment versus power sharing: Theoretical clarification and empirical comparison of delegation and participation. *Journal of Applied Psychology*, 72, 228–33.

Lewin, K. (1947). Frontiers in group dynamics. *Human Relations*, 1, 5–41.

Lewin, K., & Lippitt, R. (1938). An experimental approach to the study of autocracy and democracy: A preliminary note. *Sociometry*, 1, 292–300.

Liden, R. C., & Graen, G. (1980). Generalizability of the vertical dyad linkage model of leadership. *Academy of Management Journal*, 23, 451–65.

Liden, R. C., & Mitchell, T. R. (1983). The effects of group interdependence on supervisor performance evaluations. *Personnel Psychology*, 36, 289–99.

Liden, R. C., Wayne, S. J., Bradway, L., & Murphy, S. (1993a). Empowerment and effectiveness: Feedback report. Technical Report No. 3, Center for Human Resource Management, Chicago and Champaign-Urbana campuses of the University of Illinois.

Liden, R. C., Wayne, S. J., Sparrowe, R. T., & Bradway, L. (1993b). Empowerment and effectiveness: Feedback report. Technical Report No. 1, Center for Human Resource Management, Chicago and Champaign-Urbana campuses of the University of Illinois.

Liden, R. C., Wayne, S. J., Bradway, L., & Murphy, S. (1994a). A field investigation of individual empowerment, group empowerment, and task interdependence. Paper presented at the national meeting of the Academy of Management, Dallas, Texas. August.

Liden, R. C., Wayne, S. J., Bradway, L., & Sparrowe, R. T. (1994b). Leading empowered work groups. Paper presented as part of a symposium at the annual meeting of the Society of Industrial and Organizational Psychologists, Nashville, Tennessee. April.

Likert, R. (1967). *The Human Organization*. New York: McGraw-Hill.

Locke, E. A., Schweiger, D. M., & Latham, G. P. (1986). Participation in decision making: When should it be used? *Organizational Dynamics*, 14, 65–79.

Lord, R. G. (1985). An information processing approach to social perceptions, leadership, and behavioral measurement in organizations. *Research in Organizational Behavior*, 7, 87–128.

Louis, M. R., Posner, B. Z., & Powell, G. N. (1983). The availability and helpfulness of socialization practices. *Personnel Psychology*, 36, 857–66.

Lowin, A. (1968). Participative decision making: A model, literature critique, and prescriptions for research. *Organizational Behavior and Human Performance*, 3, 68–106.

McClelland, D. C. (1971). *Assessing Human Motivation*. New York: General Learning Press.

McGregor, D. M. (1960). *The Human Side of Enterprise*. New York: McGraw-Hill.

McWhirter, E. H. (1991). Empowerment in counseling. *Journal of Counseling and Development*, 69, 222–7.

Manz, C. C., & Angle, H. (1986). Can group self-management mean a loss of personal control: Triangulating a paradox. *Group & Organization Studies*, 11, 309–34.

Manz, C. C., & Sims, H. P. (1987). Leading workers to lead themselves: The external leadership of self-managing work teams. *Administrative Science Quarterly*, 32, 106–28.

Marrow, A. J., Bowers, D. G., & Seashore, S. E. (1967). *Management by Participation*. New York: Harper & Row.

Miller, K. I., & Monge, P. R. (1986). Participation, satisfaction, and productivity: A meta-analytic review. *Academy of Management Journal*, 29, 727–53.

Mills, P. K. (1983). Self-management: Its control and relationship to other organizational properties. *Academy of Management Review*, 8, 445–53.

Mills, P. K., & Posner, B. Z. (1982). The relationships among self-supervision, structure and technology in professional service organizations. *Academy of Management Journal*, 25, 437–43.

Mitchell, T. R. (1973). Motivation and participation: An integration. *Academy of Management Journal*, 16, 670–9.

Morse, N., & Reimer, E. (1956). The experimental change of a major organizational variable. *Journal of Abnormal and Social Psychology*, 52, 120–9.

Motowidlo, S. J. (1986). Information processing in personnel decisions. *Research in Personnel and Human Resource Management*, 4, 1–44.

Mumford, M. D. (1983). Social comparison theory and the evaluation of peer evaluations: A review and some applied implications. *Personnel Psychology*, 36, 867–81.

Pasmore, W. A., & Fagans, M. R. (1992). Participation, individual development and organization change: A review and synthesis. *Journal of Management*, 18, 375–97.

Rappaport, J. (1981). In praise of paradox: A social policy of empowerment over prevention. *American Journal of Community Psychology*, 9, 1–21.

Rosenberg, R. D., & Rosenstein, E. (1980). Participation and productivity: An empirical study. *Industrial and Labor Relations Review*, 33, 355–67.

Rotter, J. B. (1966). Generalized expectancies for internal versus external control of reinforcement. *Psychological Monographs*, 80 (1).

Rousseau, D. M. (1977). Technological differences in job characteristics, employee satisfaction, and motivation: A synthesis of job design research and sociotechnical systems theory. *Organizational Behavior and Human Performance*, 19, 18–42.

Rus, N. (1994). Getting started with empowered teams. Paper presented as part of a symposium at the annual meeting of the Society of Industrial and Organizational Psychologists, Nashville, Tennessee. April.

Saavedra, R., & Kwun, S. K. (1993). Peer evaluation in self-managing work groups. *Journal of Applied Psychology*, 78, 450–62.

Scandura, T. A., & Graen, G. B. (1984). Moderating effects of initial leader-member exchange status on the effects of a leadership intervention. *Journal of Applied Psychology*, 69, 428–36.

Seashore, S. E., & Bowers, D. G. (1970). The durability of organizational change. *American Psychologist*, 25, 227–33.

Seeman, M. (1959). On the meaningfulness of alienation. *American Sociological Review*, 24, 273–85.

Seers, A., & Graen, G. B. (1984). The dual attachment concept: A longitudinal investigation of the combination of task characteristics and leader-member exchange. *Organizational Behavior and Human Performance*, 33, 283–306.

Shea, G. P., & Guzzo, R. A. (1987). Groups as human resources. *Research in Personnel and Human Resource Management*, 5, 323–56.

Shepard, J. M. (1977). Technology, alienation, and job satisfaction. *Annual Review of Sociology*, 3, 1–21.

Solomon, B. B. (1976). *Black Empowerment Social Work in Oppressed Communities*. New York: Columbia University Press.

Sparrowe, R. T. (1994). Empowerment in the hospitality industry: An exploration of antecedents and outcomes. *Hospitality Management Research*.

Spreitzer, G. M. (1993). Psychological empowerment in the workplace: Construct definition, measurement, and validation. Revised version of a paper presented at the national meeting of the Academy of Management, Atlanta. August.

Sundstrom, E., DeMeuse, K. P., & Futrell, D. (1990). Work teams: Applications and effectiveness. *American Psychologist*, 45, 120–33.

Tannenbaum, R., & Schmidt, W. H. (1958). How to choose a leadership pattern. *Harvard Business Review*, 36, 95–101.

Thomas, K. W., & Velthouse, B. A. (1990). Cognitive elements of empowerment: An "interpretive" model of intrinsic task motivation. *Academy of Management Review*, 15, 666–81.

Trist, E. L., & Bamforth, K. W. (1951). Some social and psychological consequences of the long-wall method of coal getting. *Human Relations*, 4, 3–38.

Trist, E. L., Higgin, G. W., Murray, H., & Pollock, S. B. (1963). *Organizational Choice*. London: Tavistock.

Vroom, V. H., & Jago, A. G. (1978). On the validity of the Vroom–Yetton model. *Journal of Applied Psychology*, 63, 151–62.

Wagner, J. A., & Gooding, R. Z. (1987). Shared influence and organizational behavior: A meta-analysis of situational variables expected to moderate participation-outcome relationships. *Academy of Management Journal*, 30, 524–41.

Wall, D. T., Corbett, J. M., Martin, R., Clegg, C. W., & Jackson, P. R. (1990). Advanced manufacturing technology, work design, and performance: A change study. *Journal of Applied Psychology*, 75, 691–7.

Wall, D. T., Jackson, P. R., & Davids, K. (1992). Operator work design and robotics system performance: A serendipitous field study. *Journal of Applied Psychology*, 77, 353–62.

Wall, D. T., Kemp, N. J., Jackson, P. R., & Clegg, C. W. (1986). Outcomes of autonomous workgroups: A longterm field experiment. *Academy of Management Journal*, 29, 280–304.

Walton, R. E., & Hackman, J. R. (1986). Groups under contrasting management strategies. In P. S. Goodman and associates (eds.), *Designing Effective Work Groups*, 168–201. San Francisco: Jossey-Bass.

Weber, J. (1990). Farewell, fast track. *Business Week*, December 10, 192–200.

Weber, M. (1947). *The Theory of Social and Economic Organization*, trans. A. M. Enderson & T. Parsons, and ed. T. Parsons. New York: Free Press.

☐ Chapter 21 ☐

Work-Force Governance

Bruce E. Kaufman, David Lewin, and Robert G. Adams

INTRODUCTION

This chapter is devoted to the subject of work-force governance which refers to the authority relations, rule-making process, and system of dispute resolution within organizations. In earlier years research on work-force governance was largely the province of industrial relations' scholars, and was heavily oriented toward the study of unions and collective bargaining. Over the last decade, however, an increasing number of academics in the organizational and behavioral sciences have turned their attention to governance issues, reflecting the decline of the unionized sector of the economy, the emergence of a variety of alternative nonunion governance forms (e.g., work teams, peer review methods of dispute resolution), and the mounting evidence that human resources/industrial relations practices can have a significant impact on the long-term performance of firms.

In this chapter, we provide a survey of thought and research on work-force governance. The first section addresses work-force governance from the perspective of business strategy and organizational behavior, the

second from the perspective of industrial relations, and the third from the perspective of a management practitioner. In the conclusion, we then attempt to synthesize and integrate this material, ending with some thoughts on future policy and research directions.

BUSINESS STRATEGY AND ORGANIZATIONAL BEHAVIOR PERSPECTIVES

It is well recognized that work-force governance is central to the study and practice of industrial relations. Historically, the institutions of unionism and collective bargaining as mechanisms of work-force governance garnered most of the attention of researchers and practitioners. With the decline of unionism in the United States and abroad, industrial relations specialists have recently turned their attention to alternative forms of work-force governance (Kaufman & Kleiner, 1993).

In contrast, work-force governance has not been a central topic of interest in the fields of business strategy or organizational behavior. Indeed, one rarely finds an explicit treatment of work-force governance in either literatures. In both cases, issues of equity and workers' rights are treated instrumentally. That is, the firm attempts to maximize one or more measures of profitability, such as return on investment (ROI), and then adopts policies and practices to achieve the minimum amounts of equity and worker rights consistent with the profitability objective (Mahoney & Watson, 1993).

Nevertheless, both conceptually and in practice, recent developments in the fields of business strategy and organizational behavior have potentially important implications for work-force governance, which are identified and discussed below. We begin with a consideration of business strategy, followed by macroorganizational behavior, and then microorganizational behavior.

Business strategy

The key issue addressed in the business strategy literature is, "How can the firm obtain a competitive advantage in the marketplace?" In answering this question, the business strategy literature in part follows microeconomic theory in conceptualizing the firm as a profit-maximizing entity which seeks to meet customer demand by producing goods or services to the point where marginal revenue equals marginal cost. But in a purely competitive market, all firms are price takers, not price setters, so that a "strategic" initiative to obtain extra profit would seem to be misguided, indeed futile. Here, however, the business strategy literature departs from microeconomic theory in advocating the use of competitive analysis to gain a strategic market advantage or position.

In fact, the concept of competitive analysis can be said to be the central intellectual domain of the business strategy literature. Traditionally, such analysis included forecasts of customer demand for the products or services of the firm, examination of the structure of the firm's main industry, assessment of competing firms in the industry, and identification of external environmental opportunities and threats facing the firm, such as government regulation, entry and exit barriers, and technological change. This was followed by an assessment of the firm's internal organizational strengths and weaknesses, which in turn led to the identification of the resources, notably financial resources, required to implement the firm's business strategy.

While this model of business strategy has perhaps become best known through the work of Porter (1980), its origins and development lie in the work of Bain (1959), Chandler (1962) and Ansoff (1965). Chandler defined strategy as "the statement of the firm's goals and its policies and practices for achieving those goals," while Ansoff defined strategy as "the firm's mission, its concepts of business, and the scope of the product markets in which the firm participates" (Cappelli & Singh, 1992, 166). Later, Andrews (1971) expanded the definition of strategy, describing it as "the pattern of decisions in a company that determines and reveals its objectives, purposes, or goals, produces principal policies and plans for achieving these goals, and defines the range of business the company should pursue, the kind of economic and human organization it is or intends to be, and the nature of economic and noneconomic contribution it intends to make to its shareholders, employees, customers, and communities" (Cappelli & Singh, 1992, 166).

Although the literature spawned by this conceptualization of strategy has mushroomed in the last decade, the subject of work-force governance per se has received scant attention. As described shortly, however, this situation appears to be changing. In addition, there is an alternative conceptual perspective on business strategy which provides a relatively clear and direct link between human resource practices and strategy.

As suggested by Andrews (1971), it is possible to conceptualize employees as one among several constituencies or stakeholders in the firm, and to conceptualize management's main function as the weighing and balancing of multiple stakeholder interests in an internal system of *corporate governance*. Under this "balancing" approach to business strategy, it is conceivable that in certain circumstances employees will be assigned a high weight relative to other stakeholders and, consequently, that work-force governance will become more central to the strategic interests of the firm.

For example, Lewin and Sherer (1993) recently found that executives of Japanese firms operating in the U.S. systematically rank employees more highly as a stakeholder group than do executives of U.S. firms (operating in the U.S.). These rankings, in turn, were significantly positively associated with executive preferences for employee voice and representation in the enterprise – Japanese executives have stronger preferences in this regard than do U.S. executives. Earlier, Lewin and Yang (1992) found that compared to executives of U.S. firms, executives of Japanese firms assigned higher priority to human resources issues in the firm, valued human resources more highly in relation to financial resources, and believed that human resources policies and practices had a larger impact on firm performance. Thus, as a model of business strategy, stakeholder analysis seems to provide a stronger role for work-force governance than does competitive analysis and, empirically, the weight or value assigned by management to employees as stakeholders has been shown to vary across firms and national borders.

While the stakeholder model shows considerable promise as a vehicle for analyzing the strategic implications of work-force governance, events of the 1980s and early 1990s have at the same time led a number of scholars to reassess the relevance and importance of work-force governance issues for the traditional competitive analysis model of business strategy. The 1980s were characterized by a new wave of global economic competition which led firms, notably U.S. firms, to rethink their business strategies. Because so much of the new competition came from firms, especially Japanese firms, that appeared to obtain superior results from the utilization of human resources – lower labor costs, higher productivity, higher product quality, more flexible work practices, higher employee commitment, lower employee turnover – the new thinking about business strategy came to focus heavily on what may properly be called work-force governance systems. In most cases, traditional governance systems were judged to be inadequate in terms of maximization of firm performance. Consequently, and as documented by Kochan, Katz, and McKersie (1986), firms disinvested in unionized plants and invested in nonunion plants with broader jobs, more flexible work practices, and lower labor costs. Moreover, in nonunion settings, firms initiated grievance-like complaint and appeal systems as well as a variety of other alternative dispute resolution (ADR) systems. Here, work-force governance, to the extent that it exists, is governance without union representation and collective bargaining, and it is this perhaps more than anything else which most clearly signals the transformation of American industrial relations described by Kochan, Katz, and McKersie (1986).

But the shift away from unionized employment relationships and governance systems has hardly been the only strategic initiative undertaken by U.S. firms in recent years. Consider that in both unionized and nonunion settings, employers have also acted to shrink their core work forces (i.e., employees who work full-time, are covered by fringe benefit programs, and have training and promotion opportunities) and to expand their peripheral or contingent work forces.

Further, in both unionized and nonunion settings employers have increasingly been adopting team-based approaches to work based on principles of worker self-management and team monitoring of work performance. At the same time, firms have also been initiating employee compensation programs featuring variable pay arrangements, especially in the forms of profit-sharing and stock ownership plans, in which relatively more of an employee's pay is at risk than under traditional compensation programs. From the point of view of business strategy, these employee "participation" programs can be viewed in the same way in that they are all aimed at improving the performance of business enterprises. In turn, these developments provide evidence in support of the proposition that human resources practices are increasingly being linked to business strategy, and for a model that flows in a series of interconnected links from business strategy to human resources strategy to human resources practices to human resources performance to business performance (Cappelli & Singh, 1992; Lewin & Mitchell, 1994). Indeed, the relatively new field of human resources strategy focuses directly on the "fit" between human resources practices and business strategy, and conceptualizes this fit as a "dynamic capability" for enhancing business performance (Cappelli & Singh, 1992; Pfeffer, 1994; Lewin & Mitchell, 1994).

Yet even if empirical evidence supports a model of business strategy in which human resources policies and practices leverage business performance, this does not necessarily mean that work-force governance is more central to this model than to older models of business strategy. In fact, the "new thought" about business strategy and human resources strategy may well share with more traditional thinking the notion that human resources are primarily an instrument for accomplishing the goals of the firm. What is different today from before is that a work-force governance system featuring unionism, collective bargaining, individual work, full-time employment, and pay for time worked has given way to a system featuring non-represented employees without collective agreements doing team-based work with more part-time employment and a relatively greater

portion of pay at risk. In this new model of business strategy cum human resource strategy, it is an open question as to whether or not work-force governance in terms of a focus on equity in the employment relationship and worker rights occupies a more central role than it did in older models of business strategy – and this remains an open question because the basic concept of a firm appears to have changed little if at all over time.

Macroorganizational behavior

The central focus of macroorganizational behavior, or organization theory, has been on the choice and design of an organizational structure to fit an organization's strategic goals and objectives. Without question, the dominant conceptualization of the firm as an organization has been that of a hierarchy modeled on the principle of functional specialization. Today, terms such as "hierarchy" and "bureaucracy" are used largely pejoratively, but it is well to remember that Weber (1930) and others long ago advanced a positive concept of organizational hierarchy in which through centralized command, coordination, and control a hierarchy would lead to the achievement of large-scale, complex goals far more efficiently than could be done by collections of individuals or in any other organizational form. Enterprises such as General Motors, IBM, Kodak, and many others mastered the concept of hierarchy and used it to achieve preeminence in their respective industries during much of the twentieth century. From a work-force governance perspective, perhaps the leading implication of the hierarchical model of organization design was that information and communications flowed from the top to the bottom of the organization, so that workers were largely in the position of reacting to organizational directives and pronouncements.

During the 1960s and 1970s, macroorganizational behavior scholars developed more parsimonious models of organizational structure in which such variables as the geographical scope of a firm's business and the distinctiveness of its products and product markets competed with functional specialization as the basis of organizational design. Lawrence and Lorsch (1967) showed that organizational structures varied markedly according to the "differentiation" of the environments in which businesses operated, and Davis and Lawrence (1977) advocated the concept of a matrix, that is, dual reporting relationships, as the principal basis of organizational design. Out of this and other work emerged a *contingency model* of organization design in which the choice of a particular organizational structure was conceptualized as being dependent on key characteristics of the firm's environment, industry, and customers. Put differently, no longer was the single centralized command-and-control type hierarchy considered the only way to design an organizational structure for a business enterprise.

Yet, in relatively short order, the concept of a strategic business unit (SBU) emerged and was widely seized upon as the leading new basis of organizational design (Rumelt, 1984). This development in turn was strongly influenced by the merger and acquisition movement in U.S. business whereby corporate entities in effect became holding companies and operated portfolios of (often unrelated) businesses. In an SBU structure, the holding company sets financial performance objectives, but leaves the individual companies (properties) within the portfolio free to decide how to achieve these objectives.

Ironically, perhaps, none of these newer macroorganizational behavior models and practices of organizational design and structure offered a fundamentally different conception or treatment of work-force governance than that embedded in the concept of organizational hierarchy. Whether organized according to the principle of functional specialization or instead on the basis of geographical scope of the business, customer or product differentiation, or a holding company with differentiated SBUs, work-force governance remained an ancillary consideration. In all of these organizational models and forms, the underlying assumption was that managers would continue to decide how work would be done and issue orders, and workers would do the work and obey the orders. None of these models of organizational design and structure appear to have considered issues of equity and worker rights, let alone worker representation.

More redolent in its implications for work-force governance is the recent scholarly and applied work on business leadership, reengineering and organizational architecture. In this work, leaders of business enterprises are defined by some authorities (Kotter, 1990) as those who define the organization's vision, core values, and culture. From this perspective, leaders are to be distinguished from managers who attend to the operational requirements of organizational coordination and control (Nadler & Tushman, 1989).

In the mid- to late 1980s, business leaders sought to enhance organizational performance through total quality management (TQM), continuous improvement processes (CIP), and just-in-time (JIT) material, component, and final product delivery programs (Kano, 1993). The key strategic objective of these programs was to make the firm more competitive in the marketplace by developing swifter responses to customer demands and delivering higher-quality products to customers than in prior, less competitive, times. In the vernacular of this "movement," the U.S. firm of the 1980s increasingly became a "customer-driven" firm (Peters, 1990).

To implement TQM, CIP and JIT programs, however, also required a reduced emphasis on organizational hierarchy – a reduction in hierarchy or "verticality" – and an increased emphasis on worker knowledge of work processes, responsibility for work flow, and inspection-monitoring of work products. Supervision of and decision making about work, which formerly was carried out by management and its formally designated agents (supervisors), increasingly was carried out by workers themselves. Structurally, organizations became flatter as layers of management and supervision were eliminated, and workers were increasingly viewed as internal "customers" for management-initiated programs of self-management, broadened jobs, multiskilling, team-based work, flexible work arrangements, and variable pay plans. As before, this new wave of management thought did not focus explicitly or centrally on workforce governance, but it strongly suggested that workers were a relatively more important organizational stakeholder than before, that workers would deal directly with each other in self-governing teams rather than be monitored by supervisors (or represented by union steward agents), and that human resources strategy and practices were key to enhancing organizational performance.

The implications of these TQM, CIP, and JIT initiatives for work-force governance devolve largely on the *workplace* level of the modern business enterprise, rather than on the *strategy* or *policy* levels (Kochan, Katz, & McKersie, 1986). However, business reengineering focuses on the renewal and reshaping of the business enterprise as a whole through the analysis and redesign of organizational structures, decision-making processes, information flows and the jobs of managers and professionals in addition to the jobs of blue-collar and office workers. Much of the thrust of the business reengineering movement is based on information-technology and information-processing concepts and applications, and these are often proffered to business enterprises as the basis for identifying and developing the new "core competencies" which will permit them to compete effectively in the increasingly global marketplace (Prahalad & Hamel, 1990; Senge, 1990; Hammer & Champy, 1993). The business reengineering movement thus addresses itself to the strategy and policy levels as well as to

the workplace level of the enterprise, and in its organizationwide emphasis on jobs as broad collections of flexible tasks poses a strong contrast to the principles of organizational hierarchy and job specialization based on a narrow division of labor (Taylor, 1911).

The even newer organizational architecture movement goes the business reengineering movement one better, so to speak, in that it rejects the concept of a single stable organizational structure for a business. Though it too disavows the traditional concept of a hierarchical, functionally specialized organization structure for a business and favors decentralization, autonomy, and flexibility as the dominant principles of organizational design, the key insight offered by organizational architecture specialists is that a business must be prepared to reshape itself frequently and on short notice in response to changing marketplace demands (Nadler et al., 1992; Bahrami, 1992). In the extreme, there will be no permanent organizational structure for a business enterprise but, instead, a series of rapidly changing structures or "virtual organizations."

The importance of this new thought about business leadership, business reengineering, and organizational architecture for work-force governance is twofold. First, members of the "new" business enterprise will share and internalize a set of core values which are defined by senior leaders of the enterprise, and these values will in a fundamental sense "govern" the enterprise. Second, in response to marketplace demands and competitive pressures, business enterprises will often reconfigure their organizational structures so that no single, stable, permanent structure will persist over time.

Ironically, the concept of core values implies stability in the business enterprise, whereas the concept of a virtual organization implies instability. Yet the very idea of instability or rapid organizational change appears to be one of the central core values of modern business enterprises. Because some concepts and forms of work-force governance – for example, unionism, collective bargaining, codetermination, and works councils – appear to be predicated on the basis of stable organizational arrangements, they do not seem well suited to the types of business enterprises and organizational structures which presently occupy a prominent place in the macroorganizational behavior literature and which are also observed empirically. Yet, through their enhanced role as stakeholders, customers and agents of the enterprise operating in self-managed teams, performing multiple skills in flexibly designed workplaces, and having a certain share in the financial performance of the enterprise through variable pay plans, workers in modern business enterprises may well be positioned to exercise a stronger role in work-place governance than they did previously. The search for such new governance mechanisms involves considerations of microorganizational behavior, which we turn to next.

Microorganizational behavior

Historically, the diagnosis and resolution of internal organizational conflict has been a leading conceptual and empirical issue in the microorganizational behavior literature (Brown, 1986; Lewicki, Weiss, & Lewin, 1992). Much recent work has been devoted to the management of such conflict for the purposes of achieving organizational and individual goals (Lewin, 1993).

With respect to work-force governance, concepts of procedural and distributive justice are especially relevant. Procedural justice focuses on employee beliefs/perceptions/judgments about the fairness or equity of processes through which decisions are reached, whereas distributive justice focuses on employee beliefs/perceptions/judgments about the fairness or equity of the outcomes of decisions (Sheppard, Lewicki, & Minton, 1992). To illustrate, in a business enterprise that is downsizing its work force employees may perceive both the processes through which downsizing decisions are made and the outcomes of the decisions to be fair or unfair; they may judge the decision processes to be fair but the decision outcomes to be unfair; or they may judge the decision processes to be unfair but the decision outcomes to be fair. Similarly, employees make fairness judgments about management initiatives to institute self-managed teams, flexible work arrangements, and variable pay plans.

These concepts of procedural and distributive justice, which are in part grounded in traditional equity theory (Adams, 1963), are important not so much in and of themselves but because they focus attention on employee commitment/loyalty to, satisfaction with, and performance in organizations (Sheppard, Lewicki, & Minton, 1992). Thus, employees who perceive job assignment, promotion, or performance appraisal processes or outcomes to be relatively unfair are more likely to leave (quit), be dissatisfied with, and/or render poorer job performance to the organization than employees who perceive job assignment, promotion, or performance appraisal processes to be relatively fair. Hence, both procedural justice and distributive justice have potentially important behavioral outcomes for the firm (Boroff & Lewin, 1994a).

The relevance of procedural and distributive justice concepts to work-force governance rests in the recognition that a firm's set or portfolio of human resource management policies and practices can be conceived of as constituting an internal governance system. Therefore, employee beliefs, perceptions, or judgments that one or more human resources policies or practices are procedurally or distributively unfair leads to a broader judgment that the firm's internal governance is, at least in part, unfair.

In practice, firms appear to recognize this potential for perceived unfairness of the internal governance system, as reflected in their increased use of grievance-like appeal, complaint, and alternative dispute resolution

(ADR) systems and employee opinion surveys. While grievance procedures are commonplace in unionized firms, it now appears that a majority of relatively large nonunion U.S. businesses have adopted one or another type of internal dispute resolution system, and that a majority of unionized and nonunion firms conduct a periodic or annual employee opinion survey (Ichniowski & Lewin, 1988; Delaney, Lewin, & Ichniowski, 1989).

Instructively, the growth of internal dispute resolution systems and employee opinion surveys seems to have accompanied the aforementioned movement toward "flatter" organizational structures and the growth of self-managed teams, broadened jobs, flexible work practices, and variable pay arrangements. Conceptually, these participative-type human resources policies and practices are aimed largely at core workers whose commitment to the enterprise and performance on the job are important to achieving organizational performance objectives. This, in turn, requires that core workers be retained in the enterprise and that they have mechanisms in place for dealing with perceived procedural or distributive injustice – mechanisms such as grievance-like procedures and opinion surveys. From the perspective of exit-voice-loyalty theory (Hirschman, 1970; Freeman & Medoff, 1984), these grievance-like procedures and opinion surveys are adopted in the belief that they offer explicit mechanisms through which dissatisfied employees can voice their complaints rather than exit the firm.

Research on grievance and grievance-like systems has mushroomed in recent years, and the empirical findings from this research cast some doubt on the validity of the exit-voice-loyalty framework and hence on the viability of these grievance systems. For example, employee users of nonunion grievance systems, whose job performance ratings, promotion rates, and work attendance rates were not statistically different from those of nonusers in the periods prior to and during grievance system usage (grievance filing

and settlement), were found to have significantly lower performance ratings, promotion rates, and work attendance rates in the post-grievance settlement period. Further, post-grievance settlement turnover rates were significantly higher for users than for nonusers of these nonunion grievance systems. Strongly similar findings emerged from comparisons of samples of supervisors of grievance systems users and nonusers in unionized enterprises (Lewin, 1987, 1992; Boroff & Lewin, 1994b).

Research on employee responses to internal opinion surveys is relatively sparse, but there is evidence that in some countries and in some firms employee response rates to anonymous internal opinion surveys are relatively low, and that responses are biased toward the neutral midpoint of the ratings scales typically used to measure the responses to questions contained in these surveys (Lewin & Mitchell, 1994).

It is sometimes claimed that nonunion firms adopt grievance-like procedures and opinion surveys primarily to avoid unionization rather than to provide mechanisms of work-force governance (Fiorito, Lowman, & Nelson, 1987). However, the aforementioned findings about grievance procedure usage and outcomes in nonunion settings have been replicated in unionized settings (Lewin & Peterson, 1988; Boroff & Lewin, 1994a), and a recent study by Feuille and Delaney (1992) concluded that nonunion firms adopt grievance-like procedures primarily for strategic purposes. The executives of these firms indicated to the researchers that resolving intraorganizational conflicts through formal dispute resolution mechanisms helps the firms to achieve their productivity and product quality objectives.

Empirically, then, the extent to which grievance systems and employee opinion surveys are able to provide procedural or distributive justice to employees is uncertain. It may well be that in a globally competitive world with business enterprises requiring more of their employees in terms of responsibility for decision making under variable pay arrangements, and with business enterprises continuing to downsize their work forces and changing their organizational structures rapidly, the "median" employee may choose to suffer in silence and manifest loyalty to the enterprise by neither registering dissatisfaction nor leaving the firm.

Yet we are also in an era in which the idea that human resources can be used to competitive advantage by the firm has taken hold seriously in academic and practitioner circles, and in which initiatives at self-managed teams, broadened jobs, flexible work practices, and variable pay are showing considerable staying power. From this perspective, the "median" (core) worker appears to be in a more responsible job and also in a more demanding job compared to his predecessors, and the new movement toward worker participation in the enterprise should not be taken to mean that the era of work-force governance is at an end. What is dwindling, of course, is the use of unions and collective bargaining as key mechanisms of work-force governance in the U.S. and abroad, but it is well to remember that unions and bargaining are only one particular form of employee participation and governance in the enterprise. In the future, the self-managed team may constitute the primary mechanism of work-force governance in business enterprises, but other mechanisms may include associate union membership, company or voluntary unions, works council-type arrangements, codetermination, and employee ownership of the enterprise.

What is consistent in all of this is that the management-oriented literature on business strategy and organizational behavior has never treated work-force governance as a key focal issue. But surely conceptual frameworks and empirical evidence suggesting that employees are becoming a relatively more valued stakeholder in the enterprise (largely and to be sure because of their potential influence on the performance of enterprises), and the development of human resources strategy as a field of academic inquiry and practice, provide the necessary if not the sufficient conditions for those interested in work-force governance – notably industrial relations specialists – to develop the ideas upon which work-force governance mechanisms and practices can be based in modern business enterprises. In short, the demand for work-force governance is unlikely to disappear as long as there are the managed and those who manage them. Instead, it is the forms and mechanisms of work-force governance which are "up for grabs" in today's business enterprise.

THE INDUSTRIAL RELATIONS PERSPECTIVE

Work-force governance is one of the central topics of industrial relations, and for many IR scholars it effectively defines the core of the field. This is indicated by Milton Derber (1970, 7) who stated: "The view underlying this study – one held by a number of the early scholars in the field including John R. Commons and William Leiserson – perceives industrial relations as a method of government with a formal role structure, machinery for rule making and administration, and a system of due process for the orderly resolution of disputes."

Derber (1970) noted that there are a variety of forms of work-force governance. He listed the following five: autocracy, paternalism, bureaucracy, technocracy (scientific management), and democracy. Another noted IR academic, John Dunlop (1958), distinguished between four types of governance systems: dictatorial, paternal, constitutional, and worker-participative.

While IR scholars have defined the field inclusively to cover the study of all types of governance systems, both research attention and policy recommendations have favored some governance systems over others. The principal desiderata in this choice is the provision for some form of *industrial democracy* in the organization.

According to early participants in the field of industrial relations (Commons, 1921; Hicks, 1941,) the governance systems in use in pre-World War I American industry (i.e., autocracy, paternalism, technocracy) resulted in a deplorable amount of waste, conflict, and human suffering. These outcomes were inevitable, they maintained, as long as the employment relationship was of the master/servant type in which managers possessed a near-monopoly on authority and control in the plant and employees lacked both a voice in the operation of the enterprise and a system of due process for the protection of individual rights. What was the solution? The answer, according to reformers from the ranks of both management and labor, was to introduce democracy into industry.

The definition of industrial democracy varied among its adherents. For example, William Filene, a prominent Boston businessman in the early 1900s, said of it (Lauck, 1926, 59), "By industrial democracy I mean that form of industrial organization in which the employee has not only an adequate voice in the management and determination and control of work conditions, and an adequate stake in the results of work, but also, some guaranty that the management of the business shall be responsible and largely dependent for its rewards on its efficiency." Coming to it from the perspective of organized labor, the American Federation of Labor's first president, Samuel Gompers (Lauck, 1926, 58) said that, "the old political democracy is the father of the new industrial democracy. Like government, industry must guarantee equal opportunity, equal protection, equal benefits and equal rights to all."

Whatever their differences as to the conception of industrial democracy, nearly all of its proponents agreed that industrial democracy could only be realized in practice through some form of *employee representation*. By employee representation, they meant a system where individual employees select certain persons from among themselves to represent their interests and concerns to management, and where decisions about workplace matters are then determined through consultation and negotiation between management's representatives and the workers' representatives.

Benefits of employee representation

Proponents of industrial democracy believed that employee representation could materially improve industrial efficiency, workplace equity, and human well-being (see Webb & Webb, 1897; Commons, 1921; Hicks, 1941; Derber, 1970; Dickman, 1987; Kaufman, 1993; Harris, 1993). Listed below are the major defects they identified with non-democratic forms of workplace governance, and the manner in which employee representation (ER) can remedy these defects.

1. Market, legal, and ethical constraints are seen as too weak to prevent management from engaging in opportunistic behavior, such as arbitrary discipline or provision of unsafe working conditions. In reaction to management opportunism, employee work effort, collaborative behavior, and morale are harmed. ER puts a brake on management opportunism, because employees are more likely both to voice displeasure to management and to engage in a collective withdrawal of work effort (e.g., strike).
2. Individual workers suffer from an inequality of bargaining power vis-à-vis the firm due to substantial involuntary unemployment, lack of other employers in the local area, and restrictions on worker movement from one employer to another (e.g., because fringe benefits are tied to seniority), all of which tip the bargaining process in the firm's favor and

allow it to provide below-competitive wages and working conditions. ER helps equalize bargaining power to the extent that it replaces individual bargaining with some form of collective bargaining.

3. Certain aspects of working conditions (e.g., safety, sanitary conditions) are "public goods" and thus subject to the free-rider problem. The result is that they are underprovided in the workplace as each individual employee waits for someone else to speak-up to management. ER solves the public-good problem because the workers' representative has less fear than an individual worker to voice the employees' demand for improved working conditions.

4. Without some system of representation, a worker's only option for expressing dissatisfaction with undesirable working conditions is to quit the firm, leading to high costs from turnover, loss of worker experience and training, and disruption of workplace cooperation and morale. ER provides a "voice" alternative to exit and thus reduces turnover and its associated costs.

5. Lack of a formal system of employee voice also leads to inefficiencies in production as employees lack a vehicle to communicate to management information on ways to improve productivity, an incentive for doing so, and job security protections against loss of job. ER leads to greater productivity because it provides a formal system for worker participation in production, gives workers greater leverage to demand a share of increased productivity, and provides greater opportunity to obtain job security guarantees.

6. Feelings of alienation and inequity more easily develop among employees when they are not given an opportunity to provide input into decisions affecting their interests, leading to either withdrawal of effort and commitment or an increase in conflict. An ER system provides a formal mechanism for employees to have a say in organizational decision making, thus promoting greater job satisfaction, higher productivity, and reduced conflict.

7. Greater adversarialism and conflict is also caused by the absence of a formal system of dispute resolution in the firm. Without such a system, employee rights and perceptions of procedural and distributive justice are more frequently violated, leading to various forms of withdrawal behavior and conflict. An ER system ameliorates these problems to the extent that it provides for an orderly and fair basis for adjudicating disputes and providing the protection of due process in the administration of workplace justice.

8. A system of individual bargaining leads to destructive forms of competition during economic downturns as firms attempt to reduce costs and protect profits by cutting wages and labor standards. A system of ER, to the extent that it provides workers and their labor organizations with a way to take wages out of competition through collective bargaining, prevents this downward spiral and thus promotes greater macroeconomic stability, greater efficiency (because management's focus is shifted from wage cutting to methods of improved productivity and quality), and more harmonious labor–management relations.

9. As a basic principle of moral philosophy, it is unjust that people be given full democratic rights as citizens of the nation state, but then be denied many of those same rights when they agree to be an employee for a business firm. An ER system is thus desirable because it both extends representative democracy from the political sphere to the economic sphere, and contributes to the fuller development of employees as citizens and human beings.

Costs of employee representation

The purported benefits of employee representation must be weighed against the costs in determining the economic and social efficacy of industrial democracy as a form of workforce governance. At least nine different forms of cost (broadly defined) can be identified. They are:

1 Operation of an ER system entails additional administrative and resource costs, such as extra management and staff personnel, time for meetings, negotiations, and hearings, and the expenses associated with training or hiring persons skilled at dispute resolution (e.g., mediators, arbitrators).

2 To the degree that an ER system provides employees with greater collective bargaining power over wages, benefits, and work rules, it will increase the labor cost of firms.

3 An ER system may restrict management's range of options in organizing production and deploying the organization's human resources, and slow down the speed with which management can react to market changes.

4 Greater adversarialism and conflict may result from an ER system, particularly to the degree that the employees are represented by an independent labor organization that has its own mission, political agenda, and resource base.

5 Worker loyalty and attachment to the firm may be weakened to the degree that employees develop a sense of commitment to the labor organization that represents them.

6 An ER system may impede the process of microeconomic and macroeconomic adjustment to shifts in demand and supply in labor and product markets to the extent that wages or employment are rigidified, particularly if the employee representation system involves extensive pattern bargaining or industrywide bargaining.

7 The power and authority of management in the organization will be circumscribed, a factor that management will regard as a significant "cost," albeit of a nonpecuniary form.

8 An ER system may entail a loss of individual liberty for employees to the extent that a collective agreement precludes their ability to enter into mutually agreeable employment contracts with the firm, or are required to be a member of a labor organization as a condition of employment.

9 Employees' rights and welfare may also be reduced to the extent that their representative organization engages in corrupt or undemocratic practices.

Contingencies

The benefits and costs of employee representation enumerated above vary in size and significance with respect to a number of factors. Most important is the organizational form taken by the ER system.

ER systems vary along several dimensions, such as the size of the work group included, the range of issues to be jointly determined, the presence and role (if any) of a formally constituted employee organization, and the power and range of tactics given the employees and their organizations to pressure or influence management vis-à-vis the determination of the outcomes of interest. Thus, on one end of the spectrum are small subunits of a particular plant or company with a narrowly defined mission and power largely limited to providing advice to management or recommending a course of action, such as an autonomous work team, a joint labor–management safety committee, or a peer review system of dispute resolution. On the other end of the spectrum of ER systems is a highly centralized form of collective bargaining where a national or international trade union bargains an agreement covering a wide range of employment-related issues affecting hundreds of thousands of employees across numerous plants or companies, with both sides given the opportunity to resolve disputes through strike (or lockout) action. In between these polar opposites are other forms of ER, such as shop committees or "company unions," European-style works councils, and independent enterprise-based trade unions.

The benefits and costs of these alternative ER systems both tend to increase as one moves from the narrow, least powerful forms of representation to the broader, more powerful forms. A trade union, for example, will generally provide more of the nine benefits enumerated above than will a joint labor–management safety committee (e.g., the former will do a more effective job in protecting against management opportunism, in redressing labor's alleged inequality of bargaining power, in providing a formalized dispute resolution system, etc.). It is also typically the case, however, that the costs of ER will be greater with a trade union, such as from restrictive work rules, inflated labor costs, and strikes.

The optimal level of ER thus depends on a balancing of benefits and costs from alternative structural forms, a calculation that depends in part on certain additional factors noted below and on whether the calculations are made from the "private" point of view of the individual firm or the "social" point of view of the public and government policy makers.

In particular, the benefits of "stronger" ER systems are likely to appear smaller to individual firms, and the costs larger, than will be the case to policy makers. Thus, from a social point of view, collective bargaining may provide a desired stability to the wage structure and boost to consumer purchasing power, but viewed from the perspective of an individual firm this benefit generally pales in comparison to the fear that a union will raise labor costs and make the firm noncompetitive relative to lower cost, nonunion rivals. (This is to say in economics' jargon that ER has positive externalities for society.) Likewise, the dilution of management authority and power that

comes from a strong form of ER is likely to be seen by the managers of an individual firm as carrying a large "cost" in the form of reduced control and efficiency, while this same loss of managerial power and authority may appear far less threatening to policy makers who see it as a desired shift toward joint governance and democratic rights in industry. One conclusion, then, is that firms will generally desire narrower, less powerful forms of ER than will the citizenry and their elected representatives. A second is that firms will desire systems that emphasize the "voice" function of ER and minimize the bargaining or "muscle" function, as the former tends to "grow the pie" by facilitating greater information flows and employee motivation, while the latter threatens management power and fosters an adversarial struggle over "splitting the pie."

Several other contingencies should be briefly noted. One such contingency is the macroeconomic environment and, in particular, the level of unemployment in the nation. When the economy is operating close to full employment, market forces will be more effective in ensuring competitive levels of wages and working conditions and fair treatment of employees by management. At recession or depression levels of unemployment, on the other hand, the low profitability of most firms and the presence of numerous job seekers provides management with more of both a motivation and an opportunity to take unfair advantage of employees. Thus, the benefits of stronger, more centralized forms of ER typically increase with the level of unemployment. This fact helps explain, for example, why the U.S. Congress chose the depression year of 1935 to pass the National Labor Relations Act (Wagner Act), an act which sought to promote and protect trade unions and collective bargaining.

Another contingency concerns the number of firms covered by the representation system. For example, if all firms in a product market are organized by a trade union, then the union can take wages out of competition and no one firm will be at a cost disadvantage, significantly reducing the resistance of individual firms to this type of ER system. Likewise, the receptivity of firms to an ER system such as a works council is likely to be greater if all firms are mandated by law to have one, thus establishing a common competitive playing field, than if the decision for each firm is voluntary.

Yet another contingency is the structure of product and labor markets. Firms operating in monopsonistic labor markets (e.g., one-company towns) or monopolistic product markets will probably earn excess profits and, in the case of the former, will pay exploitative wage rates. In such a situation, it will probably be in the social interest to have an ER system that provides employees with more "muscle" or bargaining power. The more competitive are product and labor markets, however, the greater is the rationale for governance systems that emphasize the voice function of ER in the workplace and eschew the bargaining function, particularly over economic terms of the labor contract.

A final contingency is the nation's cultural/social system. Due to differences in social and political ethos and values, an ER system that "fits" with one nation's culture may have only a poor fit with another's. Thus, European countries seem to be more comfortable with trade unions than is the United States because of the stronger heritage in the former of class divisions and greater philosophical approval of the cartelization of markets and social regulation of business, whereas the emphasis in the U.S. on individualism and the virtues of unrestrained competition provide a more receptive political and business climate for decentralized, voluntary company-sponsored ER systems.

Developments and trends

Since the birth of industrial relations as a field of study in the early 1900s, both public policy and opinion have fluctuated markedly with regard to the relative merits of alternative forms of employee representation. During the 1920s, for example, trade union membership suffered a severe decline, while hundreds of America's largest companies established some form of employer-sponsored "company union" (Nelson, 1993). With the country's plunge into depression in the 1930s, faith in the efficacy of company unions plummeted, with a corresponding rise in public approval of collective bargaining and independent trade unions (Vittoz, 1987). The result was a meteoric rise in union membership and, as noted earlier, passage in 1935 of the Wagner Act. Not only did the Wagner Act make it public policy to promote collective bargaining, it also made illegal all forms of employer-dominated labor organizations, such as the company union.

Over the last decade, pressure has built up for reexamination and reform of the Wagner Act. An important catalyst is the dramatic decline in union density to only 12 percent of the private sector work force (implying that nearly nine out of ten private sector employees have no formal system of representation). A second factor is the growing competitiveness of product and labor markets, due to factors such as the internationalization of the economy, industry deregulation, and a heightened pace of technological change. A third is the clash between the desire of employers to establish formal plant-level organizations of employees to promote quality, safety, and involvement, and the recent (1993) *Electromation, Inc.* decision of the National Labor Relations Board that seems to imply that many such organizations are likely to be in violation of the Wagner Act's ban on employer-dominated labor organizations (Hogler, 1993).

Several lines of thought have developed in reaction to these trends and developments. One is to argue the case for expanded employee representation on the grounds that greater economic competitiveness requires more firm-level employee involvement and participation, and that these can only be gained through a formal system of ER (Marshall, 1992). A complementary argument rests on survey evidence that there is a growing "representation gap" in the nation, where this gap is the difference between the 80 percent or more of the work force that states a desire for some form of ER, and the shrinking supply of representation available through collective bargaining (Freeman & Rogers, 1993).

If one accepts these arguments for expanded ER, as do nearly all IR scholars, there then emerge at least three schools of thought on how this expanded ER should best be accomplished. One school views trade unions as the preferred form of ER and argues that the decline in union density reflects not diminished employee demand for collective bargaining but growing frustration of this demand through illegal or socially undesirable employer actions, such as intimidation of employees, refusal to bargain, extended litigation, use of high-powered "union-buster" consultants, and capital investment/disinvestment decisions (Freeman & Medoff, 1984; Greenfield & Pleasure, 1993). The solution to the representation gap, according to these IR scholars, is to strengthen the Wagner Act by expediting the representation process, increasing the penalties for unfair labor practices, and broadening the mandatory scope of bargaining and the groups of employees covered under the act (e.g., supervisors).

A second school of thought maintains that the Wagner Act should be strengthened, per the suggestions above, but that public policy should also encourage additional forms of independent representation (Weiler, 1993). According to this view, surveys reveal that most employees continue to demand some form of ER, but that a growing number do not believe that traditional-style collective bargaining meets their needs. To fill this gap, these IR scholars typically advocate that public policy

encourage all firms to establish some type of independent, European-style works council or "employee participation committee" (EPC). The EPC would not bargain over wages or other economic issues and could not strike, but management would be required to obtain the approval of the EPC before making changes in plant-level personnel policy, and to provide the EPC with data and information about the firm's strategic business plan and financial condition.

The third school of thought also favors providing more ER alternatives, but argues that the Wagner Act should be amended to relax the ban on employer-sponsored ER systems (Hogland, 1993; Estreicher, 1993). While the other schools of thought (particularly the first) oppose such a policy change for fear that employers will resurrect company unions as a manipulative device to thwart unionization, its proponents argue that competitiveness requires greater worker–management cooperation and employee involvement, and that employer-sponsored quality circles, work teams, and other such devices are a proven way to obtain more of these. From their point of view, it is short-sighted to maintain a 1930s-era prohibition on employer-sponsored forms of ER when only a distinct minority of employees have a desire for union membership, and nearly all of our principal international competitors allow more collaborative forms of worker–management decision making and problem solving.

A PRACTITIONER'S PERSPECTIVE

It is clear that all business enterprises need rules and procedures, as well as methods of resolving disputes, making decisions, and managing employees, both those who perform well and those that do not. This is equally clear to both those who advocate labor and trade unions and those who believe an enterprise can function fairly and properly protect stakeholders, without union involvement. The great historical debate has been how and by whom these required business necessities should be established and managed.

Sometimes this debate has been presented by suggesting that without unionism there is no employee involvement, participation, or fairness. The late 1980s produced such radical changes in the world of business and the ability of enterprises to prosper and survive that we have learned the issue is not that simple. In fact, we have seen a rise in processes which encourage employee involvement as union membership has declined. In the past, labor and trade union leaders were at best skeptical and at worst outright opposed to processes which provided rank and file members an opportunity to participate in the management of a business. This position came in large part from traditional union structure, which allowed input from only elected officials such as shop stewards. Others saw employee participation processes as management union-busting tactics. There were, however, a few union leaders who not only supported rank and file participation, but were strong advocates for the processes. As a result, some unions came to accept the shift to real employee participation.

There is no question that many, maybe most of the work-force governance principles as well as many pay and benefit concepts we accept and employ today in both union and non-union enterprises have evolved from the negotiating process around some bargaining table. Without the gains achieved by unions, what would the American standard of living and working conditions be today? In the extreme, the question might be, How many employees would still be working for script wages, forcing them to purchase their goods from a company store?

The current decline in union membership probably does not relate at all to a disfavor for governance principles supported by unions, but rather, it relates directly to employee concern for job security and an abundant labor market. These contributing factors to the decline of union membership in the 1980s and 1990s were often factors in union growth in the past. In most cases, poorer jobs (i.e., jobs with less pay and reduced benefits) today are not the result of a management desire for larger profits. Rather, they are necessary for survival of the enterprise.

In addition, the prounion pendulum had probably swung too far by the late 1980s. What work-force governance battles were left to fight? In the words of one long-time union official, "It's not as satisfying as it used to be. It's one thing to fight for the right of a fellow colleague to use the company's phone to call home to see if his sister-in-law survived surgery. It's another thing, and not as satisfying, to sit at a bargaining table and make speeches in favor of a sixth week of vacation." Could part of the issue be that, at least for the present, most of the great employee governance battles have already been fought?

Considering the history of trade and labor unions in the United States, would any board of directors vote to invite a union into its enterprise? Not even the most caring board with the proper focus on the value of all the stakeholders (including stockholders, employees, the community and the directors themselves) would make that choice. Today's world is more price and service competitive than ever before. Change, reengineering, cost reduction, improved productivity, and even pay and benefit reductions are most often not the means to larger profit margins. Rather, they are necessary to sustain profitability and provide for the long-term survival of the enterprise, without which there would be no work-force to govern.

All of these factors have created a focus by many employee stakeholders on keeping what they have and protecting a job. With this kind of employee concern, trade and labor unions face a tough sell. In what enterprise do employee stakeholders want to run the risk that the union's promise of better pay, benefits, and working conditions might cost jobs, maybe their own? The reduction in benefits and salaries suffered in recent years by some longer-term employees, and the part-time work and lower starting pay faced by many new employees occur most often not because of management greed, but because that is all competition and the need for survival will allow.

No explanation of work-force governance issues would be worthwhile without some discussion of how the union/nonunion debate came about in the first place. Certainly in the early days of labor and trade unionism, almost any ordinary citizen would have sided with those who supported union establishment. What work-force governance issues caused employee stakeholders to seek help by forming unions? Low pay, no benefits, unfair selection procedures, unfair demands, and management favoritism, the kind of treatment most everyone is against. Companies that managed this way opened the door and virtually asked for a new voice to help establish different and better governance principles. The governance issues were then resolved jointly between the enterprise's management and elected representatives of the newly unionized employee stakeholder.

How well did the system work? In some cases it worked well, in others it didn't. What were the factors that determined those relationships that worked and those that didn't? As with nonunion governance systems, a number of things contributed. Certainly the economy is always a factor. In very good times, almost anything works! Plenty of profits and plenty to bargain with can often make for very fine union/management relationships. More liberal rules, procedures, work rules, and benefits present no problem. In some ways, it's like the family spirit on a winning team. But what happens to the winning spirit after ten straight losses? Recent years have brought a new process to negotiations called concessionary bargaining; that is, the collective undoing of governance principles, wages, and benefits which the enterprise can no longer afford and still remain competitive. Management has found that it was much easier to give than it is to get back, and union leaders have found it very difficult to sell concessions to their members.

A critical factor in the efficiency of the system is the caliber of the people on both sides – the appointed management of the enterprise and the elected officials of the union. What is their focus? Are the governance decisions they make in the best interest of all the stakeholders? Do both sides clearly understand who the stakeholders are? Collective governing doesn't work well where one or the other party is driven entirely by political or parochial motives. We use the qualifying word "entirely" as it is a practical impossibility for either side not to be affected to some extent by political motivations and concerns. This is certainly an issue as it relates to the union official because of his or her personal reelection concerns. Trouble arises when the parties can't overcome their political differences in order to keep a proper focus on what is important to the enterprise and its stakeholders. Union members can also steer the process on a collision course when an entitlement mentality overcomes a reasonable focus or the need for the enterprise to be successful.

Except in rare circumstances, enterprises with unions in the 1990s are not able to effect change as quickly as those without. Negotiated rules and procedures just can't be adjusted as quickly as those established in other ways. Waiting for the next round of bargaining in some situations can be costly in dollars and jobs, and at the worst can be fatal for the enterprise in today's business environment. Unfortunately, the very nature of the process is too slow for the business climate of the 1990s. However, some union leaders and managements do have the appropriate stakeholder and enterprise focus to find ways to make the system continue to work.

Much has been written about the labor laws in counties other than the United States, such as Germany with its Labor Relations Act

(LRA), which provides for works councils, essentially a three-way process. One only needs to look at the economic and productivity problems of Germany in 1994 to question the success of this system as a means of work-force governance. Recently, Germany's Economic Minister, who has been very vocal and critical of German economic competitiveness, said, "We have to return to the traditional values like diligence, punctuality, and reliability."

The German LRA process, while theoretically interesting, does not seem to work very effectively in practice. Diligence, punctuality, and reliability as advocated by the German Economic Minister are not politically strong positions for the elected and politically motivated works council members to take. Again, some of the problems are closely aligned to the skills and motivations of the people involved in the codetermination process. Unlike union professionals in both the United States and Germany, the German works councils are often comprised of elected representatives who lack skills and experience in negotiating. Too many issues subject to codetermination (e.g., work rules and changes in work practices), which could and should be resolved in a timely manner by the codetermination parties, are litigated in the German labor courts because elected works council members have no motivation or incentive to make a decision that they know is correct or necessary. There is no action available to the company to force the works council members to make a decision. As a result, they commonly take the "safest" political position. It's easier to let the court resolve the issue, so that they receive no blame and maintain their personal political positions. This results in slow change, because in most cases companies must maintain the status quo until the lengthy court process is completed. Fortunately, the labor contract negotiation process for wages and benefits is different, with the unions taking the lead and the threat of a strike deadline forcing more timely resolution of issues. Even

in these negotiations, however, the works council economic committees, as the third party at the bargaining table, often slow the process.

This problem may become less of a concern in future years as many works council chairmen are taking advantage of available labor–management educational programs to advance their skills and those of the council members. It is interesting that most, if not all, of this training is paid for by the companies. Some say the companies are "providing the bullets to shoot themselves." A more positive view is that better decisions will be made more quickly, reducing the substantial costs incurred through litigation and delay. Companies are reluctant to discuss strategic issues with their works councils because they are concerned with confidentiality (despite the fact that works council members are bound by law to keep confidential company information to themselves). As a result, many issues which are subject to codetermination are actually preresolved before the works council is ever brought into the discussion. What follows is a charade, with the company trying to convince the works council that its input is really a part of the decision-making process.

As with any system, there are some outstanding works council/union/management success stories, and it cannot be denied that the system does provide a means of employee input. Unfortunately, however, as with elections and union meetings in the United States, works council meetings (to which all employee stakeholders are invited, not only council members) are often poorly attended, allowing domination by a vocal minority.

In the business world of the 1990s, an enterprise and its stakeholders are better off if the governance process can be managed without the influence of outside organizations with their own political and parochial interests. This is a tall task, however, and requires a management which is willing to do more than just listen. It must also be willing to act and to believe that its human resources are as important as any of the stakeholders. As noted in an earlier section of this chapter, Japanese firms have done just that for some time (with apparent results), and there is evidence U.S. firms are moving in the same direction – a positive development for U.S. business domestically and internationally.

Do the individual employees who produce the product and/or service on a daily basis have the skill and knowledge to make strategic and financial enterprise decisions? Probably not, but they do have the skill and knowledge to understand how large parts of the day-to-day activities should be managed. They are especially adept at solving problems and improving processes and procedures in their own areas of expertise. Well-run enterprises understand this, and they capture that skill through a variety of modern employee participation processes.

Coupled with employee involvement must come increased management emphasis on maintaining equity in the employment relationship and promoting effective two-way communication. For example, an enterprise's management faces a difficult balancing act when it comes to protecting the employees' interests with regard to wages, benefits, and rules, while at the same time considering the need for profits to provide for future growth and return on investment to the company's stockholders. Success in this effort requires effective company communication programs that help employees understand where the enterprise is going, what its problems are, what's important, and what needs to be done and why. In addition, the managers are also obligated to listen carefully to the governance issues raised by the employees. Without a union shop steward expressing his or her own interpretation of the desires of the work-force, managers must listen carefully to the employee stakeholders. They must be attuned to their concerns, willing to solve problems, and be able to communicate the rationale for their actions in response to the employee stakeholder.

As use and knowledge of employee participation techniques have advanced, a significant advantage has certainly been the reduction of the "They Syndrome." The "*They* did this – Why did *they* do that? – *They* really messed that up" attitude can be extremely destructive to the team spirit within an enterprise. As employee stakeholders gain more input to the governance process through means of employee participation that are available on a voluntary participation basis, it gets much more difficult to point a finger at the "They." As an unpublished business philosopher once said to this author, "All of a sudden people realize that *they* are the 'They'." This may be the greatest of all benefits of modern employee voluntary participation processes. When the employee stakeholders of an enterprise feel that "we" are the "They," a myriad of work-force governance concerns are more easily resolved.

CONCLUSION

We predict that work-force governance will be a big growth area in academic research and topic of public debate in the 1990s as the nation struggles to redesign business organizations and human resources practices to promote competitiveness, while at the same time protecting employee rights and advancing fairness and equity in the workplace. This chapter has highlighted several themes that will likely be center stage in this discussion. Survival of American firms in an increasingly globalized marketplace, for example, requires a governance structure that promotes flexibility, accountability, adaption to change, and employee commitment to the enterprise. At the same time, the governance system must have sufficient strength and formalization that it provides meaningful, nonthreatening opportunities for employee input into management policy and the terms and conditions of employment, safeguards employees against arbitrary or opportunistic management actions, and provides a mechanism for a fair and equitable resolution of disputes. Whether traditional union and nonunion governance systems can satisfactorily achieve these twin objectives is increasingly open to question. Hence, in the years to come, we can expect much experimentation and innovation in work-force governance, creating exciting research opportunities for academics and challenges for practitioners.

REFERENCES

Adams, J. S. (1963). Toward an understanding of equity. *Journal of Abnormal and Social Psychology*, 16 (November), 422–36.

Andrews, K. (1971). *The Concept of Corporate Strategy*. Homewood, IL: Irwin.

Ansoff, I. (1965). *Corporate Strategy*. New York: McGraw-Hill.

Bahrami, H. (1992). The emerging flexible organization: Perspectives from silicon valley. *California Management Review*, 34, summer, 33–52.

Bain, J. (1959). *Industrial Organizations*. New York: Wiley.

Boroff, K., & Lewin, D. (1994a). The relationships among loyalty, voice and intent to exit in grievance filing – a conceptual and empirical analysis. Revised Working Paper No. 211. Los Angeles, CA: Institute of Industrial Relations, UCLA.

Boroff, K., & Lewin D. (1994b). Loyalty, voice and intent to exit a union firm: A conceptual and empirical analysis. Revised Working Paper No. 268. Los Angeles, CA: Institute of Industrial Relations, UCLA.

Brown, L. D. (1986). *Managing Conflict at Organizational Interfaces*. Reading, MA: Addison-Wesley.

Cappelli, P., & Singh, H. (1992). Integrating strategic human resources and strategic management. In D. Lewin, O. S. Mitchell, & P. D. Sherer (eds.), *Research Frontiers in Industrial Relations and Human Resources*, 165–92. Madison, WI: Industrial Relations Research Association.

Chandler, A. P. (1962). *Strategy and Structure*. Cambridge, MA: MIT Press.

Commons, J. R. (1921). Industrial relations. In J. R. Commons, (ed.), *Trade Unionism and Labor Problems*, 2nd ser., 1–16. New York: Augustus Kelley.

Davis, S. M., & Lawrence, P. R. (1977). *Matrix*. Reading, MA: Addison-Wesley.

Delaney, J. T., Lewin, D., & Ichniowski, C. (1989). Human resource policies and practices in American Firms. BLMR No. 137. U.S. Department of Labor, Bureau of Labor–Management Relations and Cooperative Programs, Washington, D.C.

Derber, M. (1970). *The American Idea of Industrial Democracy*, 1865–1965. Urbana, IL: University of Illinois Press.

Dickman, H. (1987). *Industrial Democracy in America: The ideological origins of national labor relations policy*. LaSalle, IL: Open Court Press.

Dunlop, J. (1958). *Industrial Relations Systems*. New York: Holt.

Estreicher, S. (1993). Employee voice in competitive markets. *The American Prospect*, 14, summer, 48–57.

Feuille, P., & Delaney, J. T. (1992). The individual pursuit of organizational justice: Grievance procedures in nonunion workplaces. In G.R. Ferris (ed.), *Research in Personnel and Human Resource Management*, vol. 10, pp. 187–232. Greenwich, CT: JAI Press.

Fiorito, J., Lowman, C., & Nelson, F. D. (1987). The impact of human resource policies on union organizing. *Industrial Relations*, 26, spring, 113–26.

Freeman, R., & Medoff, J. (1984). *What Do Unions Do?* New York: Basic Books.

Freeman, R., & Rogers, J. (1993). Who speaks for us?: Employee representation in a nonunion labor market. In Kaufman & Kleiner (eds.), *Employee Representation*, 13–80. Madison, WI: Industrial Relations Research Association.

Greenfield, P. A., & Pleasure, R. J. (1993). Representatives of their own choosing: Finding workers' voice in the legitimacy and power of their unions. In Kaufman & Kleiner (eds.), *Employee Representation*, 169–96. Madison, WI: Industrial Relations Research Association.

Hammer, M., & Champy, J. (1993). *Reengineering the Corporation*. New York: Harper Business.

Harris, J. H. (1993). Industrial democracy and liberal capitalism. In J. H. Harris and N. Lichtenstein (eds.), *Industrial Democracy in America: The ambiguous promise*, 43–66. New York: Cambridge University Press.

Hicks, C. (1941). *My Life in Industrial Relations*. New York: Harper and Brothers.

Hirschman, A. O. (1970). *Exit, Voice and Loyalty*. Cambridge, MA: Harvard University Press.

Hogler, R. (1993). Employee involvement and electromation, inc.: An analysis and a proposal for statutory change. *Labor Law Journal*, May, 261–74.

Ichniowski, C., & Lewin, D. (1988). Characteristics of grievance procedures: Evidence from nonunion, union and double-breasted businesses. In *Proceedings of the Fortieth Annual Meeting*, 415–24. Madison, WI: Industrial Relations Research Association.

Kaufman, B. E. (1993). *The Origins and Evolution of the Field of Industrial Relations in the United States*. Ithaca, NY: ILR Press.

Kaufman, B. E., and Kleiner, M. M. (eds.) (1993). *Employee Representation: Alternatives and future directions*. Madison, WI: Industrial Relations Research Association.

Kano, N. (1993). A perspective on quality activities in American firms. *California Management Review*, 35, spring, 12–31.

Kochan, T. A., Katz, H. C., & McKersie, R. B. (1986). *The Transformation of American Industrial Relations*. New York: Basic Books.

Kotter, J. (1990). What leaders really do. *Harvard Business Review*, 67, May–June, 103–11.

Lauck, W. J. (1926). *Political and Industrial Democracy, 1776–1926*. New York: Funk & Wagnalls.

Lawrence, P. R., & Lorsch, J. W. (1967). *Organization and*

Environment: Managing Differentiation and Integration. Boston, MA: Graduate School of Business Administration, Harvard University.

Lewicki, R., Weiss, S., and Lewin, D. (1992). Models of conflict, negotiation, and third party intervention: Review and synthesis. *Journal of Organizational Behavior*, 13, 209–52.

Lewin, D. (1987). Dispute resolution in the nonunion firm: A theoretical and empirical analysis. *Journal of Conflict Resolution*, 31, September, 465–502.

Lewin, D. (1992). Grievance procedures in nonunion workplaces: An empirical analysis of usage, dynamics and outcomes. *Chicago-Kent Law Review*, 66 (3), 823–44.

Lewin, D. (1993). Conflict management and resolution in contemporary work organizations: Theoretical perspectives and empirical evidence. *Research in the Sociology of Organizations*, 12, 167–209.

Lewin, D., & Mitchell, D. J. B. (1994). *Human Resource Management: An economic approach*. Boston: PWS-Kent.

Lewin, D., & Peterson, R. B. (1988). *The Modern Grievance Procedure in the United States*. Westport, CT: Quorum.

Lewin, D., & Sherer, P. D. (1993). Does strategic choice explain senior executives preferences on employee voice and representation? In Kaufman & Kleiner (eds.), *Employee Representation*, 235–63. Madison, WI: Industrial Relations Research Association.

Lewin, D., & Yang, J. Z. (1992). HRM policies and practices of U.S. and Japanese firms operating in the U.S. In *Proceedings of the Forty-Fourth Annual Meeting*, 344–51. Madison, WI: Industrial Relations Research Association.

Mahoney, T., and Watson, M. (1993). Evolving models of work force governance: An evaluation. In Kaufman & Kleiner (eds.), *Employee Representation*, 135–68. Madison, WI: Industrial Relations Research Association.

Marshall, F. R. (1992). Work organization, unions, and economic performance. In L. Mishel & P. Voos (eds.), *Unions and Economic Performance*, 287–315. Washington, D.C.: Economic Policy Institute.

Nadler, D. A., & Tushman, M. L. (1989). Leadership for organizational change. In S. A. Mohrman, *Large Scale Organizational Change*, 100–19. San Francisco: Jossey-Bass.

Nadler, D. A., Gerstein, M. S., Shaw, R. B. & associates (1992). *Organizational Architecture: Designs for changing organizations*. San Francisco: Jossey-Bass.

Nelson, D. (1993). Employee representation in historical perspective. In B. Kaufman and M. Kleiner (eds.), *Employee Representation: Alternatives and aware directions*, 371–90. Madison, WI: Industrial Relations Research Association.

Peters, T. (1990). Get innovate or get dead: Part one. *California Management Review*, 33, fall, 9–26.

Pfeffer, J. (1994). Competitive advantage through people. *California Management Review*, 36 (winter), 9–28.

Porter, M. (1980). *Competitive Strategy*. New York: Free Press.

Prahalad, C. K., & Hamel, G. (1990). The core competence of the corporation. *Harvard Business Review*, 67, May–June, 79–91.

Rumelt, R. (1984). Toward a strategic theory of the firm. In R. Lamb (ed.), *Competitive Strategic Management*, 121–44. Englewood Cliffs, NJ: Prentice Hall.

Senge, P. (1990). *The Fifth Discipline: The art and practice of the learning organization*. New York: Doubleday Currency.

Sheppard, B., Lewicki, R. J., & Minton, J. (1992). *Organizational Justice*. Lexington, MA: Lexington Books.

Taylor, F. W. (1911). *Scientific Management*. New York: Harper.

Vittoz, S. (1987). *New Deal Labor Policy and the American Industrial Economy*. Chapel Hill, NC: University of North Carolina Press.

Webb, S., & Webb, B. (1897). *Industrial Democracy*. London: Longmans, Green.

Weber, M. (1930). *The Protestant Work Ethic and the Spirit of Capitalism*. New York: Scribner.

Weiler, P. (1993). Governing the workplace: Employee representation in the eyes of the law. In Kaufman & Kleiner (eds.), *Employee Representation*, 81–104. Madison, WI: Industrial Relations Research Association.

Part IV

Functions of Human Resource Management

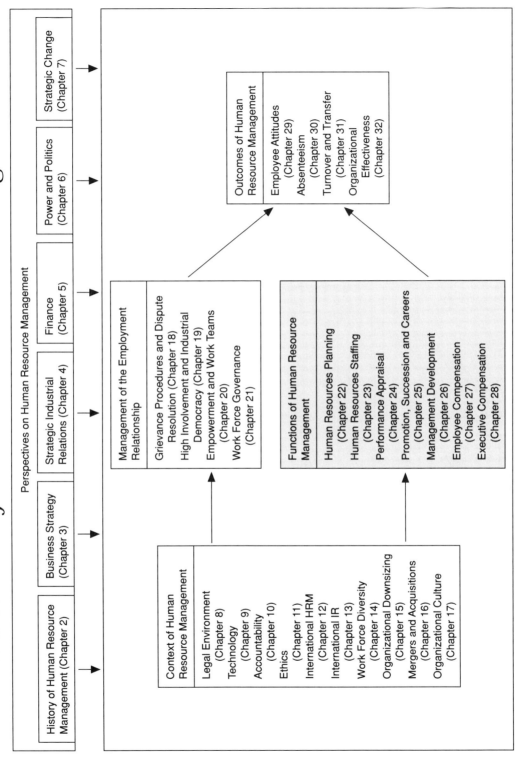

Introduction:
Functions of Human Resource
Management

This section presents the core HR functions, including planning, staffing, performance appraisal, promotion, management development, and compensation. Its purpose is to examine, from a science/practice perspective, these central functions of human resource management.

In his chapter on human resources planing, Walker makes a cogent case for the integration of HR planning with other business activities. He argues that because HR planning deals with one of the firm's critical resource needs, it must occur in the framework of the organization's general strategy. If an organization practiced completely integrated human resources planing, HR might "blend into the fabric of management and cease to exist as a staff function."

Dreher and Kendall provide an overview of human resources staffing. They argue that there is a strong relationship between staffing practices and firm success. A case study of the Associated Group provides insight into the impact of various staffing practices on a dramatic turnabout in the firm's performance.

The design, development, and implementation of performance appraisal systems are examined by Bernardin, Kane, Ross, Spina, and Johnson. They note that performance appraisals are one of the most critical yet troubling HRM functions, then provide suggestions for improving current systems. They explain how their recommendations are compatible with the "systems perspective" of Deming and others.

Forbes and Wertheim examine systems of promotion, succession, and career development. After discussing current research and practice, they conclude that current systems are often inadequate to provide the guidance needed in today's environment. Thus they identify and discuss research and practices that they feel will result in more success.

Management development systems reflect the need of firms to better identify and train individuals who can positively influence performance. Baldwin and Lawson point out that despite considerable development activity, the results have been disappointing. They argue for recognition of "the new conditions for managerial learning." These include more in-context learning, with emphasis on "articulation and evaluation of various linking contexts" that clearly relate to the key needs of the enterprise.

Gerhart, Minkoff, and Olsen discuss compensation and reward systems. They present several trade-offs in compensation practices, and argue that choices should be congruent with corporate and business strategies. In addition, they suggest that dilemmas often found in compensation programs can be alleviated by combining programs to achieve a balance of competing objectives.

Gomez-Mejia, Paulin, and Grabke focus on executive compensation issues, summarizing leading theories and discussing current program thrusts. Policy issues are emphasized. As with many other HR functions, considerable change is occurring in executive compensation, some of which is being fuelled by the emerging reform movement.

Chapter 22

The Ultimate Human Resources Planning: Integrating the Human Resources Function with the Business

James W. Walker

INTRODUCTION

As companies experience the need for change, they often apply human resource planning to define the relevant issues and develop responses to them. Broadly defined, human resources planning is the process of analyzing an organization's human resources needs under changing conditions and developing the activities necessary to satisfy these needs (Walker, 1980).

The scope and focus of such planning varies according to the issues addressed, competitive practices, the organizational context and culture, the rigor of business planning, and other factors. For some companies, human resources planning is essentially management succession and development planning. For others, it is the staffing process, including forecasting and planning for recruitment, deployment, development, and attrition of talent in relation to changing needs. Increasingly, however, it is a broader process, addressing multiple levers for increasing organizational effectiveness; for building and sustaining competitive capabilities based on the management of human

resources (Walker, 1992; Ulrich & Lake, 1990; Schuler & Walker, 1990).

In companies where competitive success requires significantly more effective management of people, human resources planning is being integrated with business planning. Managing human resources is becoming integrated with managing all resources and traditional functions, processes, and activities are being reshaped. As a result, a new paradigm is also developing for the roles and activities of the human resources staff function and its component functions.

Ideas for changes that may have seemed radical thinking just a few years ago are rapidly becoming accepted and applied as conventional today. This chapter examines the primary characteristics of the ultimate human resources planning, fully integrated with the business, as follows:

- Formulating and implementing strategies to address people-related business issues.
- Enabling managers to manage people effectively, through processes that focus on increasing organizational effectiveness.
- Redefining the human resources staff

function – its organization, roles, and capabilities.

• Defining and applying business measures of human resources effectiveness, focusing on the business impact.

There is no longer a choice. Human resources functions in a company must directly support business strategy, and the satisfaction of customer needs. At General Electric, for example, "Every effort of every man and woman in the company is focused on satisfying customers' needs. Internal functions begin to blur. Customer service? *It's not somebody's job. It's everybody's job.*" (General Electric, 1990). The traditional human resources function must give way to collaborative teamwork focusing on important people-related business issues.

RELEVANT THEORY AND RESEARCH

The published literature on human resources planning is largely prescriptive, a blend of descriptive and conceptual work. The development and integration of concepts and theory regarding human resources planning is largely an outgrowth of innovative and experimental practices in leading companies. Accordingly, the volume and quality of publications about human resources planning has developed in tandem with the evolution of company practices (Walker, 1980, 1992; Burack, 1988; Craft, 1988; Ulrich, 1986, 1987; Fombrun, Tichy, & Devanna, 1984).

This evolution is evident in articles published in journals, particularly two quarterly journals focusing on strategic human resources planning and management, *Human Resource Planning* and *Human Resource Management.* Both have published numerous case studies, results of surveys of companies, and conceptual papers. Similarly, studies reported in the biennial research symposia of The Human Resource Planning Society indicate

continuing development (Niehaus & Price, 1991).

In a benchmark project commissioned by The Human Resource Planning Society, Lee Dyer directed a series of five in-depth case studies of "real world" human resources planning processes (Dyer, 1986). The study identified and defined variations in approaches to human resources planning, whether narrow in scope (e.g., focusing on staffing) or broad in scope (comprehensive planning for managing human resources strategically). In a similarly focused study, Quinn Mills similarly found variations in planning approaches, and focused on priorities defined by top executives (Mills, 1985). Other researchers adopted a contingency approach, examining planning practices in relation to strategic objectives (Baird & Meschoulam, 1984).

As company experience has increased, research has also expanded. Recent reviews indicate a strengthening integration of human resources planning and management practices with business strategy formulation and implementation (Butler, Ferris, and Napier, 1991; Lengnick-Hall & Lengnick-Hall, 1990).

A study conducted by Towers Perrin, a management consulting firm, and sponsored by IBM, examined current and projected human resources practices of companies. The results defined a vision of human resources in the year 2000 which is:

• Responsive to a highly competitive marketplace and global business structures.
• Closely linked to business strategic plans.
• Jointly conceived and implemented by line and HR managers.
• Focused on quality, customer service, productivity, employee involvement, teamwork, and work-force flexibility.

These study findings are noteworthy in particular because of the size of the survey. The total sample size of 2,961 represents a body of opinion representing 223 of the *Fortune*

Global 500 listing of industrial companies, plus consultants, university faculty, and media respondents in twelve countries (Towers Perrin, 1990).

Many other studies have addressed needs, approaches, and results in transforming organizations with, or without, human resources staff involvement. The attention given employee involvement, customer focus, continuous quality improvement, reengineering, and other aspects of organizational change has swelled in response to growing company concerns (Kilmann, 1985; Lawler, 1981; Kotter & Heskett, 1992; Kanter, Stein, & Jick, 1992; Waterman, 1987; Mills, 1993). This literature is relevant because it defines the context for effecting change which is at the essence of human resources planning, without using traditional human resources functions as drivers of change. As human resources functions integrate with the business, organizational change and human resources studies will be indistinguishable.

FORMULATING HUMAN RESOURCES STRATEGIES

Intense global competition, rapidly changing technology, and dynamic economic and competitive conditions require companies to be adaptive and swift. Businesses today understand that rapid change is needed for sustained competitive performance, and are therefore becoming leaner, flatter, and more flexible. A *Business Week* cover article highlighted seven key elements of the "horizontal corporation", viewed as the new organizational model for companies (*Business Week*, 1993):

1 Organize around process, not tasks, functions, or departments.
2 Flatten the hierarchy, eliminate work that fails to add value, and simplify processes.
3 Use teams to manage everything and hold them accountable.
4 Let customers drive performance.
5 Reward team performance, and devel-

opment of multiple skills rather than specialization.
6 Bring employees into direct, regular contact with customers and suppliers.
7 Share information with all employees and train them to use it in their work.

All of these elements reflect changes in the management of human resources; these are business issues *and* they are people issues. Further, in this new business context, the traditional model of separate line and staff responsibilities in managing people no longer applies.

Increasingly, human resource management activities performed by managers and employees throughout an organization are vital to competitive performance. As information management, quality improvement, financial management, and other functions are becoming diffused throughout an organization, so is the management of human resources. As at General Electric, it's becoming everyone's job to build an organization that learns quickly, adapts rapidly to change, is staffed appropriately, and performs effectively.

As a result, human resources staff must be actively engaged on the management team, as full, contributing participants in the planning and implementation of necessary changes. It is not sufficient for the human resources staff to provide excellent professional services and technical expertise, generally considered its primary roles. Human resources staff need to be business-oriented, aligned with the business, and effective as consultants and business partners. Staff are increasingly expected to think and act like line managers, facilitating business change, and addressing people-related business issues.

Addressing people-related business issues

A primary way to achieve integration is to identify and address people-related issues as part of the strategic planning process and in the normal course of managing the business.

Figure 22.1   Integration of human resources in strategic management

Strategic analysis	Strategy formulation	Strategy implementation
Establish the context for strategy:	Clarify performance expectations, how we will manage in the future:	Implement processes to achieve results:
• Business context • Company strengths and weaknesses • External opportunities and threats • Sources of competitive advantage • Strategic issues	• Values, guiding principles • Business mission and vision • Objectives and priorities • Action plans • Resource allocation	• Organizational change • Performance and rewards • Strategic staffing • Learning and development • Employee relations
Identify people-related business issues	Define human resources strategies, objectives, and action plans	Implement human resource management processes

Human resources issues worthy of management attention are as integral to the success of a business as marketing, operations, technology, financial, or any other issues. Today, virtually *all* business issues have people implications; *all* human resources issues have business implications.

Strategies, including human resources strategies, may be more or less explicit, near- or long-term, general or specific, depending on the situation. They provide plans for actions that will achieve targeted results under conditions of change. Richard Pascale has defined strategy as all the things necessary for the successful functioning of an organization as an adaptive mechanism. Strategies are effective when important business issues are resolved or become less important and are replaced by new emerging issues. In this context, human resources strategies play a critical role in determining the capacity of a business to manage needed change.

Human resources staff and operating managers should work together as partners in defining and addressing business issues and their human resources implications. An opportunity for integration is lost when human resources staff independently assess people-related business issues and formulate action plans. Perversely, it becomes more difficult to achieve integration when staff is perceived to "have its own agenda," or when it views managers and employees as "arms-length" customers, rather than as partners.

Defining issues

As shown in figure 22.1, strategic management begins with strategic analysis. People-related business issues should be addressed as part of overall strategic business analysis. Strategic issues are distinct gaps between the current situation and the desired future. Hence the issues represent an opportunity for improvement or a chance to gain new competitive advantage. In a negative sense, they are problems or shortcomings that must be resolved; barriers or obstacles to performance that must be removed or avoided. Issues are sources of pain or gain.

Competitive advantage may be achieved by managing people more effectively than competitors. Of course, competitive responses may shift such practices to parity, forcing a search for new sources of advantage, or even to keep up with rapidly rising competitive standards. Among the areas typically addressed to develop competitive advantage are:

- Listening to customers and anticipating needs.
- Highly competent (with the right skills and capabilities) and stable work force.
- Enabled, empowered people.
- Effective teams and teamwork, especially across the organization.
- Open communication, networking, and sharing of information.
- Rapid, effective execution of performance objectives and plans.
- Effective use of technology to leverage talent.
- Superior utilization of talent, work flow and work design.
- Superior expense management.
- Quality management, continuous improvement.

Such challenges are compounded in multinational companies. The complexities of different cultures, work forces, legal environments, and across time zones and great travel distances, make effective teamwork, staffing, and other aspects of managing people more difficult.

Issues define the value added by the management of human resources to the business, including the value added by the human resources function. The focus on issues inherent in the business is typically very different from a focus on the human resources function and its activities. Ideally, managers identify issues within each business unit, and at each organizational level, in terms relevant to the strategic analysis supporting business planning. At each company level, the few issues that will make a critical business difference are selected to be addressed. Human resources issues of overarching importance to the businesses are identified at thc corporate level, or collectively by the business units.

Formulating strategies

Business unit managers, with human resources staff as partners, should develop long-term strategies to address important people issues. Such strategies involve multiple programs or activities and multiple functions. Human resources strategies are typically stated broadly and then translated into specific action plans; for example:

- Become the preferred employer (or employer of choice) of quality talent in the markets in which we compete for talent.
- Become an industry leader in improving teamwork and enhancing productivity.
- Establish performance management as a way of life, aligning individual and team objectives with business goals and customer requirements, evaluating results achieved, and coaching for continuous improvement.

Often companies simply identify strategic focus areas, and then address detailed planning in relation to specific initiatives. For example, companies focus on management education, valuing diversity, performance management/goal alignment, and reskilling the work force.

Strategies include achievable objectives and specific action plans (i.e., what will be done, by whom, how, when, and at what cost). Human resources integration is achieved when people-related strategies are integrated with business plans at each business level (i.e., corporate, division, unit, location). In many companies, human resources strategies are developed as separate functional plans, developed in parallel with business plans and, at best, included as a section of the business plan. The results are typically less business-relevant plans and a perceived ownership of plans by the human resources function rather than by the business management team.

433

Human resources issues and strategies need to be given sufficient "air time" for discussion in the context of operational planning and reviews, and in relation to financial, marketing, quality, service, and other business discussions. Integration suggests that there need never be a separate "human resources plan or review".

ENABLING MANAGERS TO MANAGE PEOPLE EFFECTIVELY

Managing human resources has long been considered a line management activity. Yet human resources staff have taken on more and more functions in support of managers (e.g., employee relations, sourcing and screening talent, handling performance problems and terminations, and career development). With increased support (and dependence) has often come a sense of ownership of functions, with managers and employees as *customers*. This perception has separated the human resources function, rather than integrating it with the business. Human resources staff should be considered partners in serving real customers (i.e., those people who bring revenues into the company). Accordingly, a primary emphasis of the function should be to work with managers to build and implement effective processes for staffing, learning, performance and rewards, employee relations, and achieving needed organizational change.

Redesigning human resources processes

Processes are integrated sets of activities that lead to achievement of specific targeted results. They define the roles, activities, and responsibilities of human resources staff, managers, and employees in achieving targeted outcomes or results.

To improve business results, Pepsi-Cola North America determined to turn itself "right side up" (i.e., depicted organizationally with

the customer at the top and the CEO at the bottom of the organization). It aimed to focus on the customer, empower employees, build a sense of ownership of results and values, improve processes, and flatten the organization. Critical management processes were developed as a "people management play book for coaches and performers." Each focuses on "right side up" values and behaviors which, in turn, drive increased business results.

The critical processes were grouped into three buckets: people capability (which included performance planning, appraisal, and career planning), organizational capability (which included staffing and planning, training, and organization development), and employee services and administration (which included safety, work-force diversity, dispute resolution, benefits programs and payroll processes). For each process, key line and human resources staff activities/roles, tools, and short- and long-term results were defined. Responsibility for the processes is shared as follows:

- National human resources staff are responsible for the development of the overall process and component programs.
- Business unit and local market unit staff are responsible for application of the process in the context of their business locations, including improving line management self-sufficiency and providing inputs to the process owners.
- Line managers are responsible for confirming/inputting on process design and effectiveness, and on the component programs and policies, and for executing their specific tasks within the process.

The common mission is the right *person* with the right *capability* doing the right *work* in the right *environment*. Managers and human resources staff are accountable for their "right side up" behavior, as defined in these processes.

In many leading companies, as in Pepsi, people-management processes are being re-designed (reengineered) to fit the new flexible, horizontal organization paradigm. These changes are examined in the following sections for five core processes: performance and rewards, staffing, development and learning, organizational change, and employee relations. The emerging changes represent integration of the human resources function with the business through improved alignment of practices with needs.

Performance and rewards

Companies are building a process that focuses behavior and results on business objectives and plans. Performance planning and review, which in many companies has become an institutionalized process driven by the human resources function, is being reinvented, in many ways back to its entrepreneurial origins.

The primary purpose is to help employees understand how their work affects the success of the business. Emphasis is on aligning individual and team expectations with business strategy, interpreting the relevance of business values, mission, vision, objectives, and action plans. Individuals and teams build a shared understanding of expected performance. Managers enable improved performance through coaching, providing resources such as training, and feedback on results. Performance is recognized and rewarded, but in flexible ways that fit the circumstances.

In many companies, annual salary adjustments are being handled more as adjustments for market value, especially during a period of low cost-of-living increase/inflation. Accordingly, emphasis is on contingent pay programs such as individual and team incentives, gainsharing, and profit sharing. Job evaluation is being simplified, often with fewer and broader salary bands and increased focus on linking base pay with skills and market value.

Finally, leading companies are entirely eliminating annual performance ratings, as they are no longer necessary for salary administration, and certainly not for development and performance improvement. Emphasis on pay has typically adversely influenced the quality of performance feedback, coaching, and development planning that occur in performance discussions. There is now a more positive, constructive tone in performance review. The process is driven and maintained by line managers, not by the human resources function. Performance management is integrated with the business.

Staffing

Similarly, many leading companies are building and applying processes to match talent with changing requirements. Critical skills mix and staffing issues are being faced in many companies. The response is to adopt a strategic staffing process that will guide recruiting, movement, targeted development, and separation of employees – the flow of talent in relation to future requirements.

The process typically defines future requirements, through analysis of staffing drivers, head-count changes, and capabilities required. It may involve actions to improve staffing utilization, through work flow changes, shifting work to higher value, and reassigning talent. Where requirements fluctuate, it helps balance peaks and valleys, and considers appropriate use of part-time, contract, and other contingent work force. Ultimately, it defines gaps and surpluses of talent, and required staffing actions to correct these.

While the techniques of such human resources planning have been available for decades, they are now being applied collaboratively with managers, responsible for staffing in their organizations. Their aim is to address the continual imbalance of talent supply and demand, and address staffing needs before they become crises (e.g., often requiring layoffs, aggressive recruitment or redeployment, or business plan changes). Simpler computer-based systems for such planning are available which remove much of the mystery once perceived.

Development and learning

Flexible organizations are learning organizations, placing high importance on continuous development of capabilities. Employees are challenged and enabled to learn and grow in ways that promote higher-level contribution and personal capability. Many companies believe that superior capabilities are an important source of competitive advantage and therefore are a critical management priority. Leading companies have set targets for investment in learning (e.g., 5 percent of all time should be in learning; 5–6 percent of salary budget should be expended on training and development).

Learning is built into work through challenging (and changing) tasks, through coaching by managers and peers, and through job-related development activities. Emphasis on teamwork facilitates learning by challenging employees to discover new solutions to problems and acquire new capabilities needed to implement solutions. Individuals learn readily from each other, when addressing real problems, using real data, real time. Action learning, although an approach whose wisdom has been known for decades, is now being applied in companies to accelerate learning by integrating it with real work.

Training and education continues to be important, but is increasingly focused on needs that are best addressed in this way. This requires managers and employees to identify needs and ways they may be met. Programs and courses are ideally tailored to address needs identified throughout the organization, and continually revised as needs change. This approach is far different from the traditional approach of surveying needs or interest in particular program topics, designing or acquiring programs, and offering them to prospective participants. Learning represents a participant-focused, active approach to devel-

opment. Training, education, and development represent a program-oriented, passive approach.

Interest in building a learning organization reflects a desire to integrate development and learning with the business. The role of human resources or other training staff must be to promote and support learning throughout an organization. To do this, staff must be intimately involved in the business and the learning opportunities that work provides.

Organizational change

With all of the changes occurring in businesses, the most significant people management process may be increasing organizational effectiveness, of managing organizational change itself. Companies are addressing a variety of organizational change activities, including:

- Realigning the organization structure, with wider spans and fewer levels, and balancing autonomy and integration.
- Redesigning key jobs and redefining capabilities required.
- Building effective teams and teamwork at all levels.
- Redefining the roles of managers, staff, and employees.
- Building a high-involvement organization.
- Building external alliances and networks.
- Reengineering processes, information flows, and decision making.
- Implementing continuous quality improvement as a philosophy and set of tools.

The challenge is to blend these initiatives together, as a cohesive, integrated change process. Too often, activities are implemented as independent initiatives, without necessary alignment. Consequently, the results of process reengineering as an initiative, or even continuous quality improvement, fall short of expectations.

Some organizational change processes are well integrated with the business and are models. For example, the "revolution" at General Electric was managed as a planned, three-phase process over several years: awakening, envisioning, and rearchitecting. In order to ensure continuous change, all elements were addressed. Further, as consultant Noel Tichy observed, "it is necessary to make as many people as possible agents of change. At first, you will send people to what at GE are called workout sessions; there people will learn to redefine their jobs to meet the challenges of the changing business environment, eliminating unnecessary work along the way" (Tichy & Sherman, 1993, 99).

At GE and many other companies, responsibility for managing organizational change is integrated with the business. Human resources staff participate in the process and help lead it, but it is a management process. Most importantly, there is no functional claim or domain for organizational change.

Employee relations

Even as companies radically restructure and change to become more competitive, they need to build positive employee relations. In recent years, companies have implemented massive staffing cuts, sometimes eased through early retirement programs and voluntary severance programs. At the same time, companies are reorienting employee benefits and incentives from employee retention towards facilitation of change and mobility. These changes, while necessary, have broken the implicit "social contract" with employees. As GE's Frank Doyle observed, "The best employees or prospective employees have the option to 'vote with their feet' and sell their valuable skills in a scarce market only to those companies that offer them the most voice, the best growth opportunities and appropriate rewards for their critical contributions. The burden will be on companies to attract

and retain the workers they need" (Doyle, 1992).

It is increasingly important for a company to build and apply a process that attracts, retains, and energizes its work force. Activities that may have been fragmented are brought together as a coherent employee-relations process, including:

- Communicating business vision, mission, and strategy – the imperatives for change and implications for employees.
- Clarifying and sustaining the values that define the company's desired culture and help the company make a competitive difference.
- Addressing issues relating to labor relations, equal opportunity, legal compliance, sexual harassment, and fair practice.
- Achieving and managing diversity in the work force.
- Addressing work-force issues such as work–family, workplace, health and wellness, dispute resolution/employee advocacy, policy application.

These may seem disparate topics, but they all impact employee retention, trust, and the perception that the company is a great place to work.

Pepsi-Cola, for example, calls such a process "valuing people," because this is the essential theme binding the activities together. The idea recalls the principle espoused by L. L. Bean and Bill Marriott: If you take care of your employees, they will take care of your customers. Many companies perceive that it is time to give increased attention to work-force issues, even as business-driven changes continue.

Many of these employee-relations activities have traditionally been the responsibility of the human resources function. In fact, the function is still often perceived as the champion and care provider for employees, the representative of employee interests. While

437

some activities will remain important functional services and areas of expertise, responsibility for the process should be shared with managers. Because the issues addressed are people-related business issues, the process should be integrated with the business.

REDEFINING THE HUMAN RESOURCES FUNCTION

With the integration of human resources issues with business issues and of human resources processes with management processes, it is only logical that the human resources staff function should be integrated with the business organization, rather than being a separate entity.

Companies are radically restructuring the human resources function and redefining its roles. The objectives typically cited for changes include:

- Reducing overhead expenses.
- Focusing time and resources on activities that add the greatest value to the business; reducing attention given lower-value activities.
- Aligning staff more closely with the business, as part of the management team at each level.
- Addressing important people-related business issues more effectively.

Every company staff function is subject to scrutiny with such objectives in mind. Human resources is not unique, or subject to a special purpose or calling. Like other functions, it should be organized and managed in the way the company is organized and managed. As rapid changes occur, so must the human resources function adapt and change. Some executives have suggested that their companies might even be better off without a human resources function; managers should simply be expected to do what they need to do themselves. In practice, the function would not go away, it would be integrated with the business.

Redesigning the human resources function entails choices among competing priorities. Some design factors are presented in figure 22.2. A company balances the trade-offs among factors according to business needs and circumstances. There is no single best way to organize the human resources function.

Unbundling the human resources function

While the function has evolved and changed over the decades, it is frequently still organized and managed by specialized functions, performing largely *institutional*, rather than *flexible*, roles. The human resources function in a horizontal corporation looks much different. It is unbundled into its components, and these are placed where they can perform most effectively, whether in line businesses or with external vendors.

Unbundling goes beyond merely centralizing or decentralizing human resources activities. It examines where specific activities may be best performed to support company needs. Figure 22.3 illustrates the rationale of unbundling the function, suggesting three groups of activities that may be restructured:

1 Activities that are closely aligned with business units, primarily implementation of human resources strategies and facilitation of change.
2 Activities, primarily services, that can be performed anywhere, even by external vendors.
3 Activities that address overriding company interests, such as corporate values, executive compensation and development.

As a result of unbundling, companies have created a network organization, integrated with the business.

438

Figure 22.2 Factors affecting redesign

Factor	*Result*
Need for expense reduction (fewer staff, smaller budgets)	Need for increased activities and services in priority areas
Shifting of responsibility and control to business units	Need to gain efficiencies and companywide focus through integration
Attractiveness of outsourcing to reduce staff size, improve focus of the function	Need to contain costs and retain control over quality and company focus
Opportunity to reengineer and automate processes	Cost and difficulty of implementing new technology
Importance of managing people for competitive advantage	Managers lack time, focus, or capability to assume larger roles in managing people
Need to focus on the customer, emphasize service quality and value-added	Need to view human resources function as integral part of management team, rather than a service provider
Need to integrate the function with management	Need to maintain a voice, conscience, and ombudsman for employee interests

Figure 22.3 Unbundling the human resources function

Activities aligned with business units
- Consulting on people-related business issues
- Performance and organizational effectiveness
- Employee relations
- Referral to needed technical or support services

Activities that can be anywhere
- Employee information, payroll
- Compensation and benefits
- Recruiting and employment
- Training design, technology, and delivery
- EEO and regulatory compliance
- Diversity
- Labor relations
- Medical, safety, occupational health
- Employee communications

Activities of overarching corporate interest
- Companywide values, principles, and policies
- Executive compensation
- Executive succession, staffing, and development

Organizational choices

Most companies have established *business unit human resources teams*, essentially mini-human resources functions at the plant, field region, division, or group levels. These teams go beyond merely assigning human resources representatives to client organizations; they are part of the business organizations. Staff share responsibility with line managers for implementing people-management processes. They typically have decentralized responsibility for actions and results together with line managers. They are fully attuned to the business situation and its people-related issues. Expenses are typically charged to the business unit budget, and staff typically report directly to the unit.

Sometimes staff in teams feel it is difficult to advise managers when they are part of the management team, rather than independent, "objective" professionals reporting elsewhere in the company. Challenges facing such teams include:

- Providing needed services without duplicating resources elsewhere in the company; avoiding proliferation of services and actually increasing overall expenses.
- Providing staff talent with generalist knowledge of human resources management, while also providing needed expertise relating to the unit's primary concerns (e.g., staffing, quality improvement).
- Maintaining appropriate ties with the overall human resources function, as a network.

However difficult to implement, teams are a vital element of a human resources function integrated with the business.

Central human resources staff units continue to fulfill important functions, at corporate, group, or business unit levels. They may be addressing "overarching corporate interests" such as policy matters or executive resources. They may also be providing services that are more efficiently provided centrally. The central staff may be organized by functional area, by employee groups (e.g., executives, salaried, hourly/union represented), or by strategic thrust. Pepsi-Cola's national human resources organization is aligned with the core people-management processes that they are charged with developing and maintaining (e.g., organizational capability).

Many services that are centrally provided may also be "outsourced" to *external vendors* who contend they are more cost-efficient. Superior quality services may be available to a company that lacks the scale to support internal expertise and systems. Vendors also may be more specialized and more current on innovations and leading practices. Outsourcing is expanding rapidly if for no other reason than to reduce the size of the company human resources function (to reduce the size of the apparent target). The quality of services is enhanced through use of advanced technology. Many vendors strive to provide "seamless" service, in which the company managers and employees are unaware that the service is external. Outplacement, employee assistance, recruitment/sourcing, benefits design and administration, compensation surveys and plan design, payroll, employee surveys, child care, training design and delivery, and a variety of other activities are widely outsourced.

Ironically, companies often keep these kinds of services inside, while relying on external consultants and vendors for assistance in organizational change, quality improvement, process reengineering, and management development. If organizational change is a critical lever for competitive performance, it would seem logical to bring these functions inside and contract out the other human resources functions.

If a service can be outsourced, it might be "insourced", that is, provided through a *service center*, an organizational unit dedicated to providing the service, as an internal vendor. Training centers, payroll departments, health and medical functions, and information centers are often managed as shared services or "service centers." In such situations, fees are charged for the services provided, at or above costs (hence a profit center). AT&T has a large national personnel center providing services companywide; IBM has a division, Work Force Solutions, that provides functional services to all IBM businesses in the United States. Johnson & Johnson, Hoechst-Celanese, Westinghouse, duPont, First Interstate Bancorporation, and Exxon are among other leading companies that have established service centers.

In some instances, service centers report to business units (e.g., an aerospace company division provides services to employees of all divisions in the El Segundo area), or to other company staff functions (e.g., finance). In some instances, service centers market their services externally to other companies (e.g., Bankers Trust, AT&T educational services, IBM's Work Force Solutions).

In some companies, there are pockets of human resource management resources and capabilities within business units (e.g., video production, a training facility, an extraordinary college-relations program). These may be designated as *centers of excellence* and mandated to provide services to other units across the company, perhaps with costs for services charged back. More simply, in a decentralized environment, some business units may have more expertise in labor relations, or in management development, or in gainsharing programs than others. The reliance on centers of excellence allows the company to build and utilize a network of capabilities without unnecessary duplication.

When applied together across a company, the human resources function may be organized so that it is truly integrated with the business. The activities most closely aligned with business priorities are performed within the unit. Other activities are provided in the most efficient, value-added manner. The net result is that a large, full-service, *institutional*

human resources function is increasingly hard to find.

Changing staff roles

In order to integrate the human resources function with the business, the roles of human resources staff will change, and in some ways broaden. Human resources staff perform multiple roles as business partners, as circumstances require. Studies have shown that staff need to fulfill strategic as well as operational roles to be effective business partners (Schuler, 1990; Ulrich, 1987; Ulrich & Lake, 1990). In practice, there appears to be a continuum of roles including support, service, consulting, and leadership. These multiple roles are briefly characterized in figure 22.4, with characteristics identified for support and leadership, the roles at the extremes.

While all of these roles are vital, companies are seeking to give increased emphasis to the consulting and leadership roles, which address such concerns as organizational change, while performing support and service roles at lower cost, with greater speed and greater quality. Companies estimate that their overall staff time continues to be heavily weighted toward the latter roles, an imbalance they seek to correct.

Support roles involve performing defined functions according to established standards of procedure, timing, cost, and quality. Many activities in employment, salary administration, payroll, benefits administration, training administration, EEO and legal compliance, and other functional areas require quality support work. Thanks to the use of new information, such as expert systems and direct employee dial-up or terminal access, much of this work is being automated or eliminated. Some support work is being shifted to external vendors. Functional and administrative proficiency are important capabilities.

Service roles require performance of activities to meet or exceed "client" manager or

Figure 22.4 Human resources staff roles

Support	Service	Consulting	Leadership
Respond			Initiate
Immediate impact			Future impact
Internal focus			External focus
Functional			Competitive
Efficiency			Effectiveness
Data			Concepts
Systems, technology			Process, personal interaction

employee expectations. This role requires staff to identify and assess client requirements, meet them, fix problems, and measure resulting satisfaction. Service quality is the priority, focusing on factors perceived as important by clients (e.g., dependability, accuracy, responsiveness, courtesy, competence, empathy). In addition to functional and administrative proficiency, client interaction skills and teamwork are important capabilities.

Increasingly, staff are expected to help clients define their needs, identifying and evaluating alternative actions, making choices, and implementing them effectively. Through the *consulting role*, staff add value through impartial, informed assessment and facilitation of action implementation. Important capabilities include questioning, listening, data analysis, functional/technical expertise, and project management. Consulting may be provided by business unit HR teams or by staff anywhere else in the function. Of course, many external consultants fulfill this role.

Full integration of the function occurs when human resources staff contribute directly to achieving business results, providing *leadership* on people-related issues. They do whatever it takes to address issues, taking a business perspective and acting as a member of the management team. This role benefits from functional expertise, but of greater importance are business knowledge, credible peer relationships, and the ability to develop initiatives and bring about change.

When companies bring operating managers into senior human resources positions, they are looking for consulting and leadership; however, these roles can and should be performed by staff throughout the function. Staff should be expected, enabled, and empowered to take initiatives to address business needs within their sphere of influence. Similarly, consulting and leadership roles give way to service and support when circumstances call for specific tasks to be performed. The integration of the function with the business requires a new, more flexible definition of staff roles.

Developing capabilities

All four roles require capabilities that many human resources staff have not developed. Functional expertise, while valued, is insufficient. In many companies, operating experience is becoming essential for human resources assignments. Also, companies are shaping new expectations for human resources staff, and helping individuals develop the needed capabilities.

However, at a meeting of large companies, there was agreement that perhaps only one in three current human resources professionals will successfully make the transition required for integration with the business. A third are leaving under staff reduction and retirement programs. A third will try to learn and adapt, but may not survive the function's transformation. As a result, there is considerable interest in assessing and developing human resources capabilities.

In many companies, the human resources function has been the "shoemaker's child," failing to establish and apply development practices provided to other organizational units. The applicable process includes a series of activities, such as:

- Defining required capabilities (either overall or specifically for different groups and levels), with input from clients.
- Assessing capabilities, through normal performance appraisal, development planning and review, and special (employee-initiated) multiple-input feedback.
- Including self-directed learning and "stretch initiatives" in performance plans.
- Including individuals in regular company management development programs and selected external programs matching defined needs.
- Conducting specific workshops and learning projects to meet specific needs (e.g., consulting skills, business knowledge); one company made designing and conducting such workshops a developmental project itself.
- Focusing staff conferences and planning activities on future capabilities and implications of integration with the business.
- Increasing the movement of staff into line assignments and vice versa (one company is filling 30 percent or more of professional HR positions from outside the function).

A number of large companies, including AT&T, IBM, Digital Equipment, Eastman Kodak, Prudential, and Honeywell have assigned individuals specifically to the task of planning and coordinating actions for the development of human resources staff capabilities. One way or another, capabilities will need to be developed in all human resources functions striving to integrate with the business.

APPLYING BUSINESS MEASURES TO HUMAN RESOURCES

How will the effectiveness of the human resources function be evaluated when it is integrated with the business? The ultimate measure of effectiveness is the function's impact on business performance. Yet traditional measures in human resources focus primarily on activities performed and, to a lesser extent, on the value added to the business directly as a result of these activities.

A focus on activities is appropriate, because they may yield value-added and, in turn, have a business impact. Activity measures in staffing may include colleges visited, résumés screened, candidates interviewed, rejection letters written, and referrals to line managers. In compensation, activities may include job descriptions reviewed, jobs evaluated, surveys updated, and guidelines developed. In training, activities may include programs designed, programs conducted, and number of training days completed. Within the function, adoption of new technology (e.g., information system) is an activity completed.

It is more business-relevant to measure value-added results. The focus is on outcomes or accomplishments resulting from individual and team activities. Measures typically focus on improved cost-effectiveness, but broadly address the benefit gained from an investment of time and resources to achieve certain objectives. Examples are:

- Reduced costs of hiring, relocations, terminations, turnover.
- Improved knowledge, capabilities, or performance through training.
- Improved quality of new hires.
- Increased competitiveness of compensation.

443

- Relatedness of pay to performance.
- Improved perceptions by employees in organizational surveys.
- Reduced grievances or complaints.

Value-added is the focus of attention in many human resources functions. In fact, multiple company surveys provide external benchmarks for comparison of measures, to supplement year-to-year comparison to identify improvements (Fitz-Enz, 1990).

With the integration of the function with the business, the ultimate measure is how the function contributes to the success of the organization by addressing people-related business issues. Measures may include:

- Improved management bench strength.
- Reduction of overall personnel-related costs.
- Improved account retention or customer satisfaction.
- Increased global perspective and action.
- Increased organizational flexibility, adaptivity, and change.
- Improved capability of the sales force, of research talent, etc.

To apply such measures, the management team relies on data from customers (e.g., success in the competitive marketplace), employees (e.g., surveys, feedback, retention of the best talent), and managers and executives (e.g., their performance and development). Recently, corporate directors, particularly outside directors, are providing assessments and feedback to guide improvements, including perceptions of executive performance, management depth, and strategy execution.

Business plans, including human resources strategies, should include relevant objectives or measures of impact. When important people-related issues are defined and addressed effectively, business performance will improve. In this way, the human resources function will ultimately be integrated with the business.

CONCLUSION

As the editors of this handbook have stated, the practice of human resource management has developed in the context of and as a response to structural and economic upheaval, derived from environmental and organizational changes. Practice has evolved toward a more proactive approach, an integration of human resources subfunctions, and a greater strategic business emphasis.

Theory and research in human resource management have lagged the development of practice, and this is likely to continue in an environment of rapid change. Accordingly, the focus of researchers and practitioners should be on leading-edge experimentation and innovation. Nowhere is this more evident than in the application of human resources planning to the management of needed organizational change.

The integration of the human resources function with the business will be a result of more aggressive human resources planning in companies. This begins with formulating and implementing strategies to address people-related business issues. It then requires enabling managers to manage people effectively, through processes that focus on increasing organizational effectiveness. It also requires redefining the human resources staff function, its organization, roles, and capabilities. And culminates with defining and applying business measures of human resources effectiveness, focusing on the business impact.

Human resources planning provides the facilitating process necessary to achieve integration of human resource management subfunctions with each other and with the business. To the extent that it is applied, our understanding of the mission, roles, processes, activities, and measures of the human resources function will change radically. The function may, even ideally, blend into the fabric of management and cease to exist as a separate staff function. In this way, the management of people will become integral to business performance.

REFERENCES

Baird, L., & Meschoulam, I. (1984). The HRS matrix: Managing the human resource function strategically. *Human Resource Planning*, 7 (1), 1–30.

Burack, E. H. (1988). *Creative Human Resource Planning and Applications*. Englewood Cliffs, NJ: Prentice Hall.

Business Week (1993). The horizontal corporation: It's about managing across, not up and down. December 20, 76–81.

Butler, J. E., Ferris, G. R., & Napier, N. K. (1991). *Strategy and Human Resources Management*. Cincinnati: South-Western Publishing Co.

Craft, J. (1988). Human Resource Planning and Strategy. In *Human Resource Management: Evolving Roles and Responsibilities*. Washington, D.C.: Bureau of National Affairs.

Doyle, F. P. (1992). Remarks at the Annual Conference. New York: Human Resource Planning Society.

Dyer, L. (1986). *Human Resource Planning Guide*. New York: Random House.

Fitz-Enz, J. (1990). *Human Value Management*. San Francisco: Jossey-Bass.

Fombrun, C., Tichy, N. M., & Devanna, M. A. (1984). *Strategic Human Resource Management*. New York: Wiley.

General Electric Company (1990). Letter to Shareholders, *Annual Report*.

Kanter, R. M., Stein, B. A., & Jick, T. D. (1992). *The Challenge of Organizational Change*. New York: Free Press.

Kilmann, R. H. (1985). *Beyond the Quick Fix*. San Francisco: Jossey-Bass.

Kotter, J. P., & Heskett, J. L. (1992). *Corporate Culture and Performance*. New York: Free Press.

Lawler, E. E., III (1991). *High Involvement Management*. San Francisco: Jossey-Bass.

Lengnick-Hall, C. A., & Lengnick-Hall, M. L. (1990). *Interactive Human Resource Management and Strategic Planning*. Westport, CT: Quorum.

Mills, D. Q. (1985). Planning with people in mind. *Harvard Business Review*, 63 (4), 97–105.

Mills, D. Q. (1993). *Rebirth of the Corporation*. New York: Wiley.

Niehaus, R. J., & Price, K. F. (1991). *Bottom Line Results from Strategic Human Resource Planning*. New York: Plenum.

Schuler, R. S. (1990). Repositioning the human resource function: Transformation or demise? *Academy of Management Executive*, 4 (3), 49–60.

Schuler, R. S., & Walker, J. W. (1990). Human resources strategy: Focusing on issues and actions. *Organizational Dynamics*, 19 (1), 5–19.

Tichy, N. M., & Sherman, S. (1993). *Control Your Destiny or Someone Else Will*. New York: Doubleday/Currency.

Towers Perrin (1990). *Priorities for Competitive Advantage*. New York: Towers Perrin.

Ulrich, D. (1986). Human resource planning as a competitive edge, *Human Resource Planning*. 9 (2), 41–50.

Ulrich, D. (1987). Organizational capability as a competitive advantage: Human resource professionals as strategic partners. *Human Resource Planning*, 10 (4), 169–84.

Ulrich, D., & Lake, D. (1990). *Organizational Capability*. New York: Wiley.

Walker, J. W. (1980). *Human Resources Planning*. New York: McGraw-Hill.

Walker, J. W. (1992). *Human Resource Strategy*. New York: McGraw-Hill.

Waterman, R. H., Jr. (1987). *The Renewal Factor*. New York: Bantam Books.

□ Chapter 23 □

Organizational Staffing

George F. Dreher and Daniel W. Kendall

INTRODUCTION

Employer practices designed to acquire, promote, demote, retain, and layoff employees are becoming particularly important to firms that now face global product and labor market competition. Important, as used here, relates to our belief that now, perhaps more than ever before, there is a strong relationship between staffing practice variation and firm performance. Headlines like "Kodak will cut 10,000 jobs: further hard choices likely" (Holusha, 1993), "American Airlines to cut 5,000 jobs and trim fleet" (Bryant, 1993), "Ex-workers hit back with age-bias suits" (Woo, 1992), "Workplace revolution boosts productivity at cost of job security" (Zachary & Ortega, 1993), "The BEEMER spotlight falls on Spartanburg, USA" (Templeman & Woodruff, 1992), "Why Mercedes is Alabama bound" (Woodruff & Templeman, 1993), and "Survivors of layoffs battle angst, anger, hurting productivity" (Lublin, 1993), are representative of an environment within which the need for downsizing and restructuring permeates staffing decisions among some firms while other firms build and staff completely new facilities in foreign countries. How firms manage decisions about where to build new facilities (and the resulting labor market implications associated with such decisions), how to downsize while maintaining some degree of motivation and loyalty among survivors, and how to attract, select, and retain employees possessing critical organizational skills, represent choices that can make the difference between firm success and failure.

Many excellent sources provide thorough reviews of organizational practice and the research literature devoted to staffing techniques and procedures (Gatewood & Feild, 1994; Heneman & Heneman, 1994; Schmitt & Borman, 1993). Our goal in this chapter is not to summarize this material. Instead, we provide a framework within which to consider the possibilities: that is, we discuss the staffing choices managers must make as they relate to sound management and business decisions. In addition to providing this framework, we describe how one company has managed this process while making the dramatic adjustments required to compete in an increasingly demanding business environment. We believe this offers a clear illustration of how business

Figure 23.1   Human resource management: a domain statement

Human resource activities

	Assessment/ planning	Program design	Program implementation	Program evaluation
Changing employee characteristics				
Changing reward systems and work settings				
Changing work-force composition				

(Human resource functions — vertical axis label)

conditions and resulting organizational strategies, structures, and processes influence staffing practice and policy, and how staffing practice and policy influence firm performance and survival.

STAFFING AND OTHER HUMAN RESOURCE (HR) SYSTEMS

The first step in our analysis is to present a domain statement, or a description of the possibilities. This statement goes beyond the concept of a staffing system, embedding staffing within the context of an entire HR system. The use of the term "system" is purposeful and speaks to a set of interrelated (internally consistent and externally aligned) activities that work together to accomplish particular behavioral objectives. Perhaps one of the clearest statements about the power of *systematic* managerial interventions is that of Staw (1986). He illustrates by describing individually oriented, group-oriented, and organizationally oriented management systems.

His point is that only internally congruent sets of activities are likely to affect key classes of employee behavior. For example, if the objective is to foster employee loyalty to the firm, a high degree of cooperative behavior, and behavior directed at solving organization-wide problems, the HR system should:

1   Identify and select individuals with the potential and willingness to develop skills that are specific to the company.
2   Provide long-term promotional opportunities and protected employment.
3   Use extensive organization-wide socialization and job rotation experiences to foster company and not subunit loyalty.
4   Link individual rewards to organizational performance via the use of stock options, profit sharing, and organizational bonuses.

In what follows we return to this theme as we define the attributes of a staffing *system*.

Figure 23.1 presents the dimensions of the domain statement. The figure is organized around HR functions and activities. HR functions represent three specific strategies for influencing and improving employee contributions and accomplishments. The first row of the matrix (i.e., changing employee characteristics) represents the training and development function. Employee contributions are improved over time by changing the attributes of existing employees. Employee knowledge, skills, abilities, values, expectations, and attitudes are the targets for this class of interventions.

The second row of the matrix (i.e., changing reward systems and work settings) focuses on the immediate work environment. Jobs can be designed to better utilize the knowledge, skills, and abilities of existing employees. Employee motivation can be influenced by modifying the attributes of the reward and compensation system, and employee behavior can be influenced by changing the behavior of immediate supervisors and team leaders.

Finally, the third row (i.e., changing work-force composition) represents the staffing function. Improvements in work-force contributions and productivity are achieved by systematically removing certain individuals and replacing them (or at least some of them) with individuals better suited for the objectives served by the work group or organizational unit. Staffing has to do with the utility associated with employee separations and acquisitions (Boudreau & Berger, 1985): that is, with increases or decreases in employee quality resulting from changes in work-force composition. How organizations recruit, screen, select, promote, and manage the turnover process are all components of the staffing system. Beer et al. (1985, 9) refer to this process as "managing the flow of people (at all levels) into, through, and out the organization."

STAFFING SYSTEMS

To further illustrate how staffing systems can vary across firms, consider the columns of figure 23.1. This is the same framework used by Goldstein (1974) when discussing the

components of an instructional system and, of course, can be used to describe the nature of reward systems.

While the process of assessment, design, implementation, and evaluation should be thought of as cyclical (i.e., the results of the evaluation phase become part of a new assessment phase), it is instructive to take each column in turn and describe some staffing system options. As we note again later, these options are presented in a neutral way: that is, whether or not a practice proves useful depends upon organizational circumstances and objectives.

Assessment/planning

The primary distinction here addresses an internal versus external orientation. This, of course, is an issue of focus and balance, not an issue of whether to be internal or external. The internal orientation tends to assess, review, summarize, and make estimates about the firm's internal labor market. Likely activities, processes, and measurement systems that signal an internal orientation include:

1 The preparation and maintenance of detailed position descriptions.
2 Human resources information systems that inventory the knowledge, skill, and ability (KSA) profiles of existing employees.
3 The analysis and establishment of formal career paths.
4 Analyses designed to detect KSA deficiencies among existing employees.
5 Analyses designed to detect future staffing requirements by focusing on the internal supply of and demand for labor (e.g., the calculation and use of turnover and retirement rate estimates to predict future supply).

The externally oriented planning process tends to pay more attention to the size, quality, and stability of the external labor market. The goal is to monitor the external labor market so that when a need develops, the firm can take advantage of existing opportunities. Likely processes and activities that signal an external orientation include:

1 Monitoring enrollment and curricular trends that are developing at colleges and universities that supply managerial and technical graduates.
2 Monitoring research that is descriptive of the values, needs, and skill levels of individuals comprising various regional and international labor markets.
3 The use of executive recruitment firms to learn about the availability of promising job candidates.
4 The use of newly hired employees to provide information about employment opportunities in competing companies.

Program design

After evaluating the environmental and strategic circumstances associated with the development of a staffing plan, a wide variety of choices are available to program designers. An influential article by Olian and Rynes (1984) provided perhaps the first comprehensive statement about how organizational contingencies might influence the design and ultimate effectiveness of a staffing system. We return to some of their arguments and illustrations in a subsequent section of this chapter, but note now that their work also provides useful guidance when formulating a statement about the possibilities. Where appropriate, we draw upon their original ideas.

Our discussion is organized around three basic stages of the staffing process: (1) recruitment, (2) screening/selection, and (3) retention. For each, many possible courses of action are possible.

Recruitment

Recruiting activities are designed to encourage qualified individuals to present themselves for employment. Recruiting efforts should lead not only to the identification of individuals possessing the ability and willingness to perform required job duties, but also to the identification of individuals who will accept job offers (Breaugh, 1992; Rynes & Barber, 1990). Interesting questions for employers to consider include:

1 Should the firm always attempt to recruit from within, or will external candidates be considered or even preferred?
2 What will be the defined boundaries of the external labor market? Will they be local, regional, national, or international in scope?
3 What methods and media will be used to secure applicants? Possibilities include the use of current employee referrals, public or private employment services, the use of private executive recruiters of either the retainer or contingency variety, advertising in newspapers or publications of professional societies, or campus recruiting.
4 What approaches will be taken to provide potential applicants with information about jobs, the organization, and career opportunities? Will realistic job and organizational previews be part of the recruiting strategy?

Selection criteria

Choices about selection criteria often reflect the overall theme or guiding principles that surround a company's approach to employee mobility. One of the more interesting dimensions along which companies align themselves is the *contest* versus *sponsored* mobility dimension (Rosenbaum, 1984). Sponsored mobility firms tend to segment their work force into unique opportunity structures, providing specialized training, coaching, and sponsorship to those judged to be of high potential. Thus, learning ability, aptitude, and other components of "potential" are utilized as hiring standards. Other firms may be of the contest mobility variety, whereby the goal is to encourage continuous rounds of competition. It is possible to lose early rounds of the competition and still compete in subsequent rounds. Firms of this type likely emphasize "achievement," not potential, when making hiring and promotion decisions. Contest-oriented firms pay attention to knowledge, skill, and ability as reflected in current job performance and contribution.

In addition to choices about preferred knowledge, skill, and ability profiles, firms attempt to hire, promote, and retain individuals possessing certain dispositions of the attitudinal, interest, or personality variety. Research suggests that individuals reliably differ with respect to being (1) open to new experiences, (2) assertive, gregarious, and sociable, (3) agreeable and cooperative, (4) conscientious and achievement-oriented, and (5) emotionally stable (Barrick & Mount, 1991). Firms will likely place more or less weight on attributes of this type as a function of job, group, and organizational characteristics and demands. Firms also will likely focus on the concept of employee "fit." That is, they will attempt to select individuals who will appreciate and respond positively to the unique reward system and cultural climate that has evolved to support organizational goals and objectives (Schneider, 1978).

We add, however, that the criterion of "fit" is likely to be very difficult to define and operationalize (Judge & Ferris, 1992). Our previous statement about fit focuses on identifying individuals who will respond positively to existing organizational rewards and incentives. This is very much like the concept of fit presented by Bowen, Ledford, and Nathan (1991). Their concept is at the level of person–organization fit and is based on creating congruence between the values, needs, and motives of individuals and the work-related outcomes provided by employers. However, a more complex and realistic view of how the concept of fit relates to em-

ployment decisions is that of Judge and Ferris (1992). Here the concept goes beyond person–organization fit and can include such things as the perceived similarity between job candidate and the individuals charged with making employment decisions. Appearance, personality, and value similarity between candidate and decision maker may or may not directly relate to person–organization fit. In fact, the use of the criterion of fit can depict a political rather than rational process where decision makers seek to maximize their own self-interests and organizational power while candidates use impression management techniques to secure positions of interest (Judge & Ferris, 1992).

Methods of selection

Once selection criteria have been articulated, the procedures and processes used to collect and interpret information about job candidates need to be established. Again the choices are many. The usefulness and predictive power of various selection techniques also represent topics fostering considerable empirical research. Thorough reviews of this vast literature can be found in a variety of sources (e.g., Asher & Sciarrino, 1974; Barrick & Mount, 1991; Dreher & Sackett, 1983; Gaugler et al., 1987; Ghiselli, 1973; Hunter & Hunter, 1984; Motowidlo, Dunnette, & Carter, 1990; Ones, Viswesvaran, & Schmidt, 1993; Reilly & Chao, 1982). Our purpose in this section of the chapter is not to review this literature, but to once again provide a statement about the possibilities. It is from this menu of methods that managers select appropriate techniques and processes.

One useful way to organize and categorize the long list of possibilities is to refer to figure 23.2. Selection techniques can be classified using the two dimensions of the figure. As shown, information about job candidates can come from either self-reports (candidates provide and summarize the information), or from "other" or observational sources. It also

Figure 23.2 Methods of selection

Data source	Past	Present	Future
Self-report	• Résumé • Application blank • Biodata •	• Personality test • Integrity test • •	• Situational interview • •
Observation	• Reference • Performance appraisal • Drug test •	• Work sample • Aptitude test • •	• Potential estimate • •

Time frame

is useful to consider the time period targeted for review.

First, consider types of self-reports. Self-reports of the past come in many forms. One typical self-report of the past is the résumé. Creating a résumé or responding to the questions on an application blank requires (of the job candidate) a review of past educational and work experiences. Self-reports of the present include such things as personality inventories and so-called measures of integrity and honesty. Often measurement instruments of this type ask job candidates to describe how they feel about certain social and work situations. They provide insights into their current interests, values, and needs. Finally, self-reports of the future are represented by a particular type of employment interview; the situational interview (Latham, 1989). During a situational interview, candidates are presented with realistic descriptions of situations they are likely to experience if they take a position with the interviewing firm. They then provide a self-report about how they would respond to the situation if given the chance.

Now consider some examples best classi-fied in the second row of figure 23.2. Seeking references or asking former employers or colleagues to write letters of recommendation requires the "reference" to describe the behaviors displayed and contributions made by the job candidate in the past. Observations of the present are represented by a wide range of selection techniques. For example, work samples (miniature and representative samples of work situations and processes) provide a direct measure of current work behaviors. Also, many paper-and-pencil aptitude and achievement tests fit this cell of the matrix as do certain forms of the employment interview. Interviews designed to directly sample certain skills (e.g., oral communication skills) certainly fit this category.

Finally, while trying to envision an observation of the future may seem problematic, certain sources of information marginally fit this cell of the matrix. Perhaps the best illustration is the "potential" estimate. Often, managers are asked to make predictions about how an individual will behave if given the opportunity via a promotion. They are essentially describing (predicting) situation-specific behavior of the future.

451

Employee separations

In addition to procedures and practices used to make hiring and promotion decisions, organizations also must manage the process of employee exit. A large and well-developed research literature addresses (1) the antecedents of voluntary turnover (Mobley et al., 1979), (2) the concept of an optimal turnover rate, or the rate at which the sum of retention costs and turnover costs are at a minimum (Abelson & Baysinger, 1984), and (3) the effects on survivors of organizational restructuring and downsizing (Brockner et al., 1987). Managerial action to maintain, increase, or decrease the rate of employee exit draws from a mix of HR practices. For example, the degree to which organizations are able to retain top-performing employees is likely to depend upon the design and implementation of performance contingent pay systems (Dreher, 1982). However, training, promotion and advancement, and other developmental opportunities also will influence decisions to stay or leave an employer, as will the availability and flexibility of benefit options and the opportunity to pursue interesting and challenging job assignments. Instead of discussing all aspects of the total HR system that influence this class of employee behaviors, we provide a brief discussion of one staffing system issue that currently is receiving considerable corporate attention: that is, corporate downsizing.

Over the past decade, there has been an unprecedented interest in restructuring and downsizing among U.S. corporations. The current pace of downsizing is likely to continue into the mid- and late 1990s as companies continue to eliminate excess and boost productivity in order to compete in a rapidly changing and global economy (Zachary & Ortega, 1993). When confronted with the need to reduce the work force, employers can choose from a long list of options. A few of these options are presented below:

1   One popular way to reduce staff is to offer early retirement incentives. The hope here is that a sufficiently large number of employees will "voluntarily" exit, serving to meet the downsizing targets set for each affected business unit. The other hope is that the employees choosing to leave will not be the most valued employees.
2   Staff size is reduced by utilizing a planned and involuntary layoff strategy. A variety of "selection" criteria are possible. For example, seniority rules can be applied to this type of situation. Or, it is possible to make layoff decisions based upon employee performance or the possession of critical knowledge, skills, and abilities.
3   A third strategy holds the number of employees constant, but reduces the number of hours each employee actually works. This approach is currently receiving a great deal of attention among European companies as they attempt to limit the total number of displaced workers.
4   The final option to be listed here is to hold the number of employees constant but to either introduce improved technology or modify other aspects of the HR system to meet productivity goals.

Program implementation

Programs need to be implemented with a great deal of care and thoroughness. This column of figure 23.1 does not provide as many "options" as noted for the first two columns. The liability associated with implementation failure can be great as it relates to organizational staffing. A carefully designed plan to downsize, utilizing a performance contingent layoff rule, will certainly fail if the performance measurement system is not job-related, or if managers rely on informal and potentially biased recommendations for making final employment decisions. Likewise, objective and reliable ways of scoring employment tests or interview results will fail to meet standards of fairness if raters are not properly trained and rewarded for complying with system requirements.

Program evaluation

The final column of figure 23.1 also does not suggest a wide range of options from which to choose a situation specific alternative. Instead, we argue that there are four critical criteria for evaluating the effectiveness of staffing decisions.

Strategic congruence

As noted previously, one of the earliest explicit statements about the need to integrate staffing practice with business unit or organizational strategy comes from Olian and Rynes (1984). This point has been reinforced in an influential article by Sonnenfeld and Peiperl (1988). Thus the first test of staffing system quality considers the degree to which the staffing system is congruent with and supports the overall mission of the business unit. Organizations focusing on a narrow and stable market niche (i.e., defender organizations according to the Miles and Snow (1978) typology) will strive to continuously improve the efficiency of production and distribution processes. These organizations require employees to acquire company-specific knowledge and skill, and typically find the costs of turnover to be relatively high. These firms tend to have an internal recruitment focus, seek job candidates with the potential and willingness to acquire company specific KSAs, and promote company loyalty by providing reasonably high levels of job security.

Successful firms that focus on innovation and adaptation, firms that attempt to identify and exploit new product and market opportunities (i.e., prospector organizations according to the Miles and Snow typology) need staffing systems that differ greatly from the defender. Given the need to make rapid adjustments and the need to constantly be aware of technological innovation and customer preferences, these firms are much more likely to have an external recruitment focus, value individuals with proven achievement records (in fields the prospector may have recently entered), and reject risk-averse, security-seeking job applicants.

Within-system congruence

In addition to strategic congruence, the high-quality staffing system will be congruent with the other dimensions of the HR system (e.g., training and development, rewards and compensation, and industrial relations). If recruiting and selection decisions result in a very talented but diverse work force (diverse with respect to needs, interests, and values), training and compensation practices must support and take advantage of this diversity. For example, a flexible and "at risk" benefit plan may be appropriate. Or, if the overall compensation strategy is to put considerable pay at risk via the extensive use of gainsharing or profit sharing, the selection system must identify individuals well suited for such an environment. As noted by Staw (1986), the rows of the matrix presented in figure 23.1 must be congruent. They must provide an integrated and clear statement to applicants and incumbents about what the company values, and what behaviors are to be promoted and valued.

Legal compliance

The third test of a sound staffing system is the legal test. Few areas of managerial practice have been so completely influenced by environmental events as HR practice. The scope and magnitude of the regulatory environment have led to dramatic and controversial adjustments in how HR systems are assessed, designed, implemented, and evaluated (Ledvinka & Scarpello, 1991). In the United States most employers must comply with a variety of regulations governing employment practices. These range from equal employment opportunity laws such as Title VII of the Civil Rights Act of 1964 (as amended), the Americans with Disabilities Act, and the Age Discrimination in Employment Act, to Executive Order 11246, which addresses the concept of affirmative action and the implementation of affirmative action programs (AAPs).

Value-added/cost–benefit analysis

Finally, the quality of any staffing system modification must be judged from a cost–benefit perspective (Boudreau & Berger, 1985; Cascio, 1991). Sophisticated utility models are now available to help decision makers reach informed decisions about investment options. The return on investment in a staffing or any other component of an HR system should be compared to other investment options available to the firm.

Now that we have provided a framework for describing and evaluating a staffing system, we turn to an illustration. First, we describe the strategic and structural changes that have taken place in a particular company. These changes, in turn, lead to substantial adjustments and modifications to the entire HR system. The resulting staffing system is then considered within the context of the material presented thus far in the chapter. Note that the presentation so far has focused on choices: the options available to firms. Choices about what to assess in a given situation and monitor in the environment, about how to recruit, about selection criteria, about the methods used to gather and interpret information, about how to manage the flow of employees out of the organization, and about how to implement and evaluate staffing initiatives. In what follows, we examine a sample of the choices made as this company changed its strategic direction. While this illustration focuses on executive positions of the highest level, we encourage the reader to consider staffing implications as they relate to all organizational levels.

454

STAFFING IN PRACTICE: THE ASSOCIATED GROUP

Background of the Associated Group

In 1986, the Associated Group was a company with 2,500 employees and $850 million in revenues. All employees worked in a centrally located, high-rise building in Indianapolis, Indiana. It was a company with a successful history, but a company about to experience unprecedented environmental change and competition. Built as a mutual insurance company to provide group health insurance (Blue Cross and Blue Shield indemnity coverage) to central Indiana employers, primarily in the manufacturing sector, the following problems were creating a very uncertain future for the company:

1 Large national insurers were becoming very competitive and were aggressively going after market share, particularly at the expense of regional companies.

2 Business closings and consolidations (particularly in the manufacturing sector) were causing many Indiana-based companies either to go out of business, or to move under the control of companies located elsewhere. The emerging companies typically were tied to their own insurance relationships.

3 The newer service sector employers that were creating most of the real job growth in the region were not bound to traditional insurance approaches, and being much more cost-driven, they were likely to take their business to the "lowest bidder."

4 Diversification, while seen as a necessity for survival, meant raising capital, and this was difficult for a mutual company. It could raise capital in one of two ways; by borrowing, which could jeopardize its standing with rating agencies, or by raising premiums, which had adverse effects on its owners, the policyholders.

5 The company was a one-location, one-

product, one-state organization. It was highly disciplined in servicing policyholders, but not good at quickly responding to market changes, being close to the customer, or managing costs.

6 While the company continued to maintain a large share of the Indiana market for group health insurance, reform of health care financing at the national level was receiving a lot of attention and the threat of a "one-payer" system was beginning to be taken very seriously.

7 Traditional indemnity insurance and/or self-insured programs were being recognized as part of the problem, rather than part of the solution to skyrocketing health costs. Health Maintenance Organizations (HMOs) were starting to take hold, and it was becoming clear that the traditional fee-for-service health care delivery system would be undergoing dramatic changes. The role of the insurer in this process was thus in question.

8 Health insurance underwriting cycles created a situation whereby financial performance was very cyclical; three years of underwriting losses were predictably followed by three years of underwriting profits. Such fluctuations created problems for a company that was looking for funds for expansion and diversification, since the ability to generate steady earnings growth is a key consideration for both lenders and equity investors.

It was very clear that to survive, let alone prosper, the Associated Group had to make drastic and almost immediate changes in the way it did business. To do this, a six-year strategic realignment plan was developed to address the threats noted above. A complex planning exercise led to an aggressive initiative to reengineer the corporation beginning in 1986. The strategic plan would reposition the company in the following ways:

1 Diversify beyond health insurance (while protecting the core business) into:

(a) property and casualty insurance products (traditionally, the property and casualty insurance business, while also being cyclical, has been counter-cyclical to health insurance); and

(b) health, and property and casualty (P and C) insurance brokerage (this business, while clearly related to both the health and P and C business, has tended to be much more stable because the brokers take no risk; and therefore it is much more attractive to corporate financiers because of the opportunities for steady growth in earnings).

2 Diversify geographically (beyond Indiana), with a focus on "main street" America (cities with populations of 100,000 to 1,000,000).

3 Find alternatives to borrowing, or raising premiums, for securing capital.

4 Decentralize the corporation and create small autonomous units with flat organizational structures that would be close to the customer and quick to exploit changing market opportunities.

Industry experts, regulators, and even some of the rating agencies were pessimistic when they reviewed the strategic realignment program. Among the observations:

• It was too aggressive.
• It required too many changes in the "culture" of the company, over too short a time frame.
• It required the agreement and/or approval of too many diverse organizations and constituencies, over which the Associated Group had little or no control, including lenders, rating agencies, regulators, and policyholders.
• It involved the company's management in businesses (P and C, brokerage, etc.) about which it knew very little or nothing.

Management and the board of directors of the Associated Group, while acknowledging the challenges they faced, adopted and initiated the strategic plan in January of 1986. We now provide an overview of the Associated Group in late 1993.

The Associated Group (late 1993)

Structure

A family of over 70 "three layer" (CEO/management/individual contributor) operating companies, separated both organizationally and geographically. Each operating company has its own local board of directors, a majority of whom are outsiders. The CEO of each operating company reports to the board, and is linked to the parent organization, not by a reporting relationship, but by a corporate governance system. The governance system assures a balance of autonomy for the local CEO and board on the one hand, and baseline controls for the parent organization on the other.

Size

- $3.3 billion in annual revenues.
- 12,000 employees.

Geography

- Facilities in 35 states.
- Business in 49 states.

Business portfolio

- *Health insurance* One of the foremost providers of both traditional indemnity and managed care products (Anthem Health).
- *Property and casualty insurance* The company's Shelby and Anthem Personal products cover a wide segment of both personal and commercial property and casualty products.
- *Brokerage* Acordia Inc. – a health, property, and casualty brokerage company – is the nation's seventh largest brokerage company and the ninth largest in the world. Acordia has 75 offices in 24 states.
- *Financial services* Anthem Financial is a growing regional provider of premium financing, leasing, corporate finance, and brokerage services.
- *Government contracting* The AdminaStar Companies contract with both the federal and state governments on Medicare, Medicaid, CHAMPUS, and allied contracts.

Sources of capital

In October of 1992, the company sold a portion of Acordia Inc. (the brokerage company) to the public in an offering of common stock on the New York Stock Exchange. The offering raised over $50,000,000, demonstrating that alternative sources of capital were available to a mutual company.

Compensation system

As noted in our discussion of figure 23.1, it is not appropriate to consider the attributes of a staffing system without also paying attention to other components of the entire HR system. The Associated Group views the compensation system as being central to the successful implementation of the corporate strategic plan. Thus, before reviewing staffing procedures, we provide information on this key set of HR practices.

Prior to the strategic restructuring, the pay programs at the Associated Group were very traditional and typically hierarchical. The company paid its employees well, with a highly competitive base salary and fully paid and generous array of employee benefits. While there was a performance element to the administration of annual merit reviews (base pay was reviewed and adjusted upward annually at all levels), incentive pay was limited to a small group of executives and managers. This bonus program tended to rely on a measurement system that judged performance in relation to negotiated budget targets. There were no long-term executive incentives.

The current compensation system focuses on total compensation opportunity, putting a large proportion of pay at risk. For executives and senior managers, the strategy is to pay at about the 25th percentile for base salaries, to pay at or above the mid-point for annual cash compensation at target performance (base salary plus annual incentive), and to pay up to or even above the range maximum for outstanding performance. At the senior executive level, the mix of pay is one-third base, one-third annual incentive, and one-third long-term incentive. The objective is to move all employees to some form of incentive pay (currently 95 percent of all employees are part of an incentive plan). While the proportion of pay at risk varies as a function of organization level, even the "individual contributor" level is targeted for a 10 percent pay at risk component.

Executive management (corporate staff officers and operating company CEOs) have not received annual base salary increases since 1987. Lower-level managers agreed to forego annual base adjustments beginning in 1992, in exchange for additional incentive opportunities.

All incentive plans (for all operating companies, and all levels of participation) are now keyed to actual financial performance versus outside competitive indicators *and* to the achievement of key strategic shifts. Just hitting the numbers does not yield target incentive payouts. A "no exceptions" policy on incentive targets exists. The only approval authority that can consider a request for a discretionary bonus override is the compensation committee of the board of directors.

Employees at all levels now contribute significantly to the cost of the benefits package, and executives no longer receive "perks" as a function of hierarchical level. Perks are now earned as part of the directed executive compensation (DEC) credit program. These credits, awarded on the basis of the same evaluation process used in awarding annual incentive bonuses, are then used to buy prod-

ucts and services such as financial planning, additive insurance coverage, auto purchases, and airline upgrades.

Staffing system

Changes in the company's structure, culture, and compensation practices were to have profound effects on staffing practices. The sources of candidates, the selection criteria, and the "profiles of success" that characterized the Associated Group in 1986 were a direct reflection of the culture that had evolved over many previous years. Thus, when the management team and the board of directors decided to take the company in an entirely new direction, staffing programs had to be dramatically altered.

While staffing practices at all levels changed, the focus for this discussion is on one position: that of chief executive officer for the new operating companies that were formed as a result of the strategic restructuring of the corporation. With nearly 60 of these new jobs being created by the end of 1993, and with approximately half of the positions being filled from outside recruiting sources and the other half from within, the operating company chief executive officer (OCCEO) job offers opportunity for observing just how the staffing techniques and programs had to change to mirror the more basic strategic shifts that were occurring throughout the enterprise.

In the new era of rapid strategic restructuring of the company, the hiring of key executives quickly became a critical activity. A "president's council" was established, made up of all corporate executives and all OCCEOs. Specific procedures were put in place that applied to selecting among candidates for any president's council position, including:

1   The establishment of a strategic partnership with a national executive search firm to help identify external candidates for OCCEO positions. While this partnership

did not represent an "exclusive" relationship, most positions were filled through this particular search firm. Other firms were occasionally used when there was a specific/unique skill or geographical need. The partnership executive search firm spent a great deal of time "on site," learning firsthand about the critical competencies required of OCCEOs. With a few exceptions, the searches were national in scope.

2 Selection considerations that were sharply focused on the key restructuring strategies: that is, the concentration on "Main Street American" cities, the decentralized, autonomous structure of the operating companies, and the high "at risk" nature of the compensation program.

3 The appointment of an interview panel for each position. The panel was comprised of the OCCEO's immediate superior, one or more OCCEOs from other Associated Group companies, a psychologist retained by the company, and executives representing key functional areas such as accounting, finance, marketing, law, and HR.

4 The requirement that all interviewers on each panel interview all candidates.

5 The requirement that each interviewer be given a position/skill-specific assignment and asked to report, both in narrative form and in the form of a certification, on the candidate's qualifications. Each interviewer could certify the candidate unconditionally, certify the candidate conditionally (seeking additional information), or reject the candidate.

6 The thorough reference review of all external candidates.

7 The requirement that the interview panel would meet to discuss all candidates and seek consensus on the candidate of choice.

8 Final candidate review by the CEO and the chairman of the respective operating company's board of directors.

Additionally, the Associated Group has developed constantly evolving competency profiles that are used for both internal development and for assisting outside search consultants in the identification of high-performing candidates. While these competencies change as strategic shifts occur, several core competencies have emerged. A brief description of each follows.

Strategic in focus Acts to ensure that the structure, system, business perspective, and behavior of the organization fit its strategic niche in the marketplace; ensures that the organization is optimally prepared and positioned to enact its strategy.

Information seeking/analytical Personally probes and investigates. Personally investigates and diagnoses problems to understand successes or uncover opportunities so that critical information can quickly be put to use.

Confident and disciplined self-control Takes initiative to independently move ahead into uncharted territory and trusts judgment and personal capabilities for success.

Keen interpersonal skills Understands underlying causes and predictors of behavior; develops in-depth insight into the motives and causes that underlie the behavior of others. Sees patterns or trends in others' behavior and uses this information to predict and prepare for how others usually respond.

Ability to build strategic relationships/ partnerships Purposely maintains connections and builds relationships with key others who may be critical to the future of the business (customers, brokers, insurance companies, community leaders). Understands how to select and build relationships so that they are mutually beneficial and lead to strengthened ties over time.

Ability to thrive as a team member and/or leader Acts to energize the team and organize and focus its efforts. Looks after the team's effectiveness at working together and invests time and attention to enhance team performance.

Personal involvement and directness Takes charge of the team and organization and utilizes position power for the benefit of the business. Utilizes the input and judgment of others but makes it clear that he or she will make final decisions. Takes personal ownership and responsibility for what happens in the business.

Achievement orientation Focuses on excellence, winning, and innovation. Sets demanding goals and raises the bar on an ongoing basis. Pushes for growth and expansion.

Risk orientation Willing to put pay at risk in return for the potential for very large returns. This competency creates a critical link with the compensation philosophy of the corporation.

Integrity and commitment Takes values, principles, and shared mission into account to guide and direct action. Delivers on personal or corporate commitments and obligations, even when doing so may create short-term inconveniences or problems.

The Associated Group – a summary

We have just described a company that has undergone rapid and constant change over the last eight years. It is a company that has exploited new market opportunities by following a strategy of acquisition and restructuring that focuses on geographical and business diversity. It has aggressively decentralized and created small autonomous units with flat organization structures in an attempt to be close to the customer and quick to respond to changing market opportunities.

The staffing practices observed in this company are characterized by the following:

1. Because of the premium for timely action, the company does not currently devote extensive resources to systems designed to review and assess internal staffing practice. The focus is not on preparing detailed position descriptions, the establishment of formal career paths, or the creation of a technically sophisticated HR information system. Instead, the focus is on monitoring the external environment for opportunities, companies, and talent as needed.

2. While, during the period of strategic restructuring, the corporation made use of the talent found in the executive pools of acquired companies, it also made extensive use of executive recruitment services to attract and hire external candidates possessing needed competency profiles.

3. The criteria and methods of selection used to make selection decisions at the executive level reflect a concern for proven achievement and the possession of critical knowledge, skills, and abilities (competencies). The panel interviews, structured (with interviewer assignments) to systematically cover the domain of required competencies, seem well suited for implementing a contest-mobility (not sponsored-mobility) orientation to the selection problem. Also, the concern for value/interest attributes like risk orientation and achievement orientation is congruent with strategic objectives and the corresponding pay-at-risk philosophy characterizing the Associated Group.

4. Finally, the flow of executives out of the Associated Group is largely a function of operating company performance. High performance leads to substantial financial return and likely executive retention. Again, at the level of exit, the company seems to display a contest-oriented approach to staffing.

SUMMARY AND CONCLUSIONS

In this chapter, we have attempted to provide a framework within which to consider the possibilities. Staffing practice can vary dramatically across firms. Choices made about how to acquire, promote, demote, retain, and lay off employees are likely to have profound effects upon firm performance and survival. Many excellent sources are available that provide detailed guidance related to the design, implementation, and evaluation of specific selection procedures and practices. In this chapter, we have provided a menu and an illustration of how one company selected from the long list of options. Once strategic choices have been made, we believe the technology currently exists to design and implement highly effective staffing systems. The most difficult problems (and the problems for which there are the fewest research-based solutions) appear to be at the strategic level.

REFERENCES

Abelson, M. A., & Baysinger, B. D. (1984). Optimal and dysfunctional turnover: Toward an organizational level model. *Academy of Management Review*, 9, 331–41.

Asher, J. J., & Sciarrino, J. A. (1974). Realistic work sample tests: A review. *Personnel Psychology*, 27, 519–33.

Barrick, M. R., & Mount, M. K. (1991). The big five personality dimensions and job performance: A meta-analysis. *Personnel Psychology*, 44, 1–26.

Beer, M., Spector, B., Lawrence, P. R., Mills, D. Q., & Walton, R. E. (1985). *Human Resource Management: A general manager's perspective*. New York: Free Press.

Bowen, D. E., Ledford, G. E., & Nathan, B. R. (1991). Hiring for the organization, not the job. *Academy of Management Executive*, 5, 35–51.

Boudreau, J. W., & Berger, C. J. (1985). Decision theoretic utility analysis applied to employee separations and acquisitions. *Journal of Applied Psychology*, 70, 581–612.

Breaugh, J. W. (1992). *Recruitment: Science and practice*. Boston: PWS-Kent.

Brockner, J., Grover, S., Reed, T. F., DeWitt, R. L., & O'Malley, M. (1987). Survivors' reactions to layoffs: We get by with a little help for our friends. *Administrative Science Quarterly*, 32, 526–42.

Bryant, A. (1993). American Airlines to cut 5,000 jobs and trim fleet. *New York Times*, September 15, 4–5.

Cascio, W. F. (1991). *Costing Human Resources: The financial impact of behavior in organizations*, Boston: PWS-Kent.

Dreher, G. F. (1982). The role of performance in the turnover process. *Academy of Management Journal*, 25, 137–47.

Dreher, G. F., & Sackett, P. R. (1983). *Perspectives on Employee Staffing and Selection: Readings and commentary*. Homewood, Il: Irwin.

Gatewood, R. D., & Feild, H. S. (1994). *Human Resource Selection*. Orlando, FL: Dryden Press.

Gaugler, B. B., Rosenthal, G. C., Thornton, G. C., III, & Bentson, C. (1987). Meta-analysis of assessment center validity. *Journal of Applied Psychology*, 72, 493–511.

Ghiselli, E. E. (1973). The validity of aptitude tests in personnel selection. *Personnel Psychology*, 26, 461–78.

Goldstein, I. L. (1974). *Training: Program development and evaluation*. Montery, CA: Brooks/Cole.

Heneman, H. G., & Heneman, R. L. (1994). *Staffing Organizations*. Middleton, WI: Mendota House.

Holusha, J. (1993). Kodak will cut 10,000 jobs; further hard choices likely. *New York Times*, August 19, A1, D1.

Hunter, J. E., & Hunter, R. F. (1984). Validity and utility of alternative predictors of job performance. *Psychological Bulletin*, 96, 72–95.

Judge, T. A., & Ferris, G. R. (1992). The elusive criterion of fit in human resources staffing decisions. *Human Resource Planning*, 15, 47–66.

Latham, G. P. (1989). The reliability, validity, and practicality of the situational interview. In R. W. Eder & G. R. Ferris (eds.), *The Employment Interview: Theory, research, and practice*, 169–82. Newbury Park, CA: Sage.

Ledvinka, J., & Scarpello, V. G. (1991). *Federal Regulation of Personnel and Human Resource Management*. Boston: PWS-Kent.

Lublin, J. S. (1993). Walking wounded: Survivors of layoffs battle angst, anger, hurting productivity. *Wall Street Journal*, December 6, 1, 8.

Miles, R. E., & Snow, C. C. (1978). *Organizational Strategy, Structure and Process*. New York: McGraw-Hill.

Mobley, W. H., Griffeth, H. H., Hand, H. H., & Meglino, B. M. (1979). Review and conceptual analysis of the employee turnover process. *Psychological Bulletin*, 86, 493–522.

Motowidlo, S. J., Dunnette, M. D., & Carter, G. (1990). An alternative selection procedure: A low-fidelity simulation. *Journal of Applied Psychology*, 75, 640–7.

Olian, J. D., & Rynes, S. L. (1984). Organizational staffing: Integrating practice with strategy. *Industrial Relations*, 23, 170–83.

Ones, D. S., Viswesvaran, C., & Schmidt, F. L. (1993). Comprehensive meta-analysis of integrity test validities: Findings and implications for personnel selection and theories of job performance. *Journal of Applied Psychology*, 78, 679–703.

Reilly, R. R., & Chao, G. T. (1982). Validity and fairness of some alternative employee selection procedures. *Personnel Psychology*, 35, 1–62.

Rosenbaum, J. E. (1984). *Career Mobility in a Corporate Hierarchy*. New York: Academic Press.

Rynes, S. L., & Barber, A. E. (1990). Applicant attraction strategies: An organizational perspective. *Academy of Management Review*, 15, 286–310.

Schneider, B. (1978). Person-situation selection: A review

of some ability-situation interaction research. *Personnel Psychology*, 31, 281–304.

Schmitt, N., & Borman, W. C. (1993). *Personnel Selection in Organizations*. San Francisco: Jossey-Bass.

Sonnenfeld, J. A., & Peiperl, M. A. (1988). Staffing policy as a strategic response: A typology of career systems. *Academy of Management Review*, 13, 588–600.

Staw, B. M. (1986). Organizational psychology and the pursuit of the happy/productive worker. *California Management Review*, 28, 40–53.

Templeman, J., & Woodruff, D. (1992). The BEEMER spotlight falls on Spartanburg, USA. *Business Week*, July 6, 38.

Woo, J. (1992). Ex-workers hit back with age-bias suits. *Wall Street Journal*, December 8, B1, B14.

Woodruff, D., & Templeman, J. (1993). Why Mercedes is Alabama bound. *Business Week*, October 11, 138–9.

Zachary, G. P., & Ortega, B. (1993). Age of angst: Workplace revolution boosts productivity at cost of job security. *Wall Street Journal*, March 10, A1.

☐ Chapter 24 ☐

Performance Appraisal Design, Development, and Implementation

H. John Bernardin, Jeffrey S. Kane, Susan Ross,
James D. Spina, and Dennis L. Johnson

INTRODUCTION

Performance appraisal has long been regarded as one of the most critical yet troubling areas of human resource management (Austin & Villanova, 1992; Cardy & Dobbins, 1994). While over 95 percent of companies report the use of formal systems of appraisal, most of those involved in this activity express considerable dissatisfaction with it (Bretz, Milkovich, & Read, 1992). This includes not only the people who conduct appraisals, but the people who are evaluated and the administrators of the programs as well. One manager responsible for the appraisal of ten employees at Digital Equipment Corporation put it best when he said he would rather "kick bricks with his bare feet than do performance appraisals." Appraisal systems are rarely able to deliver all of their intended benefits to organizations. In fact, some HR managers maintain that formal performance appraisal almost never delivers on any of its intended purposes. Deming, the guru of the total quality management movement, identified appraisal as one of his infamous "deadly diseases" of management (Deming, 1986), and urged

that the practice be "purged from the earth" (Scholtes, 1987, 1).

The surveys that revealed this widespread dissatisfaction were conducted with relatively large organizations (e.g., *Fortune 500* companies) which presumably have the resources to acquire the best appraisal technology available. The problem can only be worse in the vast majority of medium-sized and smaller companies which have fewer resources to devote to this activity.

The severity of the appraisal problem is also evidenced in the range of disapproval that appraisal systems receive. Three surveys shed light on the pessimism regarding performance appraisal. Kane and Kane (1988) found that the appraisal systems for each of the chief occupational types (e.g., professional, technical, administrative, etc.) were judged to be "slightly effective" or worse by anywhere from 33 percent to 55 percent of the participating *Fortune 500* organizations. This same survey found that there wasn't just one overriding problem with appraisals but rather numerous ones that have thus far resisted solution.

Two other surveys (Bernardin & Villanova, 1986; Bernardin, Stepina, & Lawther, 1990)

Table 24.1 Key points of survey results

1 The majority of people who are rated less than the highest on a rating scale disagree with the rating more than they agree (more specific performance content as a basis for the appraisal reduces this effect but a majority nonetheless still disagree with the rating more than they agree).

2 The majority of the people who disagree with the rating are less motivated and less satisfied with their jobs after the appraisal.

3 The majority of these people have "little or no idea" how to improve their performance.

4 The differences between self- and supervisory appraisals are largely a function of perceptions related to factors *perceived* to be beyond the control of the performers (i.e., performers make external attributions about less than maximal performance while observers make internal attributions).

5 Training and rating formats should concentrate on these discrepant, attributional perceptions and possible constraints on performance.

6 Managers do not perceive a strong connection between the quality of their performance appraisal activities and their own performance appraisal and merit increases.

also shed light on the extent to which raters, ratees, and administrators of performance appraisal systems are dissatisfied with the PA systems in place in their organizations. Table 24.1 summarizes the key findings.

Organizations are constantly searching for better ways to appraise performance. Pratt & Whitney (P & W), the jet engine division of United Technologies, made significant changes in its appraisal system in three consecutive years only to abandon the system for a completely different approach the very next year. Blockbuster Video substantially changed its appraisal system in consecutive years. The state of Florida installed a teacher evaluation system in 1984 and abandoned it in 1986 due to widespread discontent. International Business Machines (IBM) had to install a new system as part of a big downsizing effort

because its old, highly regarded performance appraisal system resulted in such lenient ratings that few performance distinctions could be made among the workers, and little evidence indicated that there were any unproductive workers. Ten percent of Big Blue's work force received "below satisfactory" appraisals under the new system in 1992 – the first step to termination.

A manifestation of the dissatisfaction with appraisal is the growing trend to do either formal appraisals (i.e., attaching numbers to people) or personnel comparisons only when there is a need for a personnel decision such as a promotion, a pay raise, or a termination. Some HR practitioners argue that the use of formal appraisal is actually deleterious to the essential purpose of appraisal which is performance management and performance improvement. They aver that there is little data which supports the argument that formal appraisal is required to improve performance, and plenty of evidence that employees are dissatisfied with appraisal. These arguments are frequently made in the context of team-based work or worker-involvement configurations (Moen, 1989). Deming (1986) argues that performance appraisal obfuscates systems problems within a work unit and that the variability in performance is largely a function of systems characteristics rather than individual characteristics. Managers should thus attend to improving the system so as to reduce variability in performance.

The almost universal dissatisfaction with the way in which organizations appraise employees has led to the search for alternative and better methods (e.g., Blakely, 1993; Kulik & Ambrose, 1993; Salvemini, Reilly, & Smither, 1993). This search has accelerated following the growing acceptance and implementation of the principles and practices of the managerial movement known as total quality management (TQM) (Glaser, 1993). Fundamental to TQM are the notions of continuous process improvement directed toward customer satisfaction and the involvement of employees in decision making. The latter notion, called involvement or empowerment, is commonly viewed as essential for assuring a continuous improvement orientation and the accompanying integration of organization infrastructure. It follows that employee involvement in and knowledge of processes and systems are also essential. It is necessary to go beyond the confines of the individual job description. This emerging concept may be incompatible with traditional performance appraisals which focused on individual skills and controlling individual behavior to the satisfaction of a manager or a supervisor (Scholtes, 1993).

Reengineering of operational processes to create a customer-focused organization suggests an accompanying reengineering of performance appraisal systems. Baldrige Award winners Xerox, Motorola, IBM-Rochester, and Cadillac are among those firms renovating human resources processes to accompany TQM implementation. The HR process with the most significance and the earliest one to be changed is performance appraisal (Coyle, 1991). This is followed by the re-engineering of other HR processes such as recognition, pay, education, and development.

We propose that the new trend away from appraisal is driven by experiences with essentially bad appraisal systems, and that the pessimism expressed by these practitioners is certainly justified but more a consequence of the characteristics of the appraisal systems with which they have had experience. We further propose that the effects of appraisal systems will be more positive if and when certain prescriptions are followed. We must, however, acknowledge that the data supporting our prescriptions are relatively weak at this point. We also believe (and argue) that what we recommend is compatible with the "systems perspective" of Deming and others.

The overall objective of this chapter is to provide prescriptions for improving the effectiveness of performance appraisals. These prescriptions include methods for enhancing the development, implementation, and evaluation of appraisal systems. The basis of most of our recommendations is the vast published literature on performance appraisal and our "case study" experiences with numerous organizations.

USES OF PERFORMANCE APPRAISAL

The information collected from performance appraisals is most widely used for performance management functions such as improvement, feedback, and documentation. Appraisal data are also used for staffing decisions (e.g., promotion, transfer, discharge, layoffs), compensation, training needs analysis, employee development, and research and evaluation such as test validation. Table 24.2 presents a summary of these uses, the most important of which are discussed below.

Performance management

Performance appraisal has been described as a "part of the basic managerial functions" (Cardy & Dobbins, 1994). The underlying purpose of performance management is to improve the utilization of staff resources through any of the 11 uses for appraisal presented in table 24.2. Appraisal data can reveal employees' performance weaknesses which managers can refer to when setting goals or target levels for improvements. Performance management programs may be focused at one or more of the following organizational levels: individual performers, work groups or organizational subunits, or at the entire organization. However, as we stated above, some argue that the process of formal performance appraisal which entails the assignment of a numerical rating to a person is more trouble than it is worth (e.g., Halachmi, 1993). This position is buttressed by the fact that there is no unequivocal research which shows a definitive effect for formal appraisal

Table 24.2 The many purposes of appraisal

To improve utilization of staff resources by:
1 Fostering improvements in work performance.
2 Assigning work more efficiently.
3 Meeting employees' needs for growth.
4 Assisting employees in setting career goals.
5 Recognizing potential for development to managerial positions.
6 Keeping employees advised of what is expected of them.
7 Improving job placement (i.e., effecting better employee–job matches).
8 Identifying training needs.
9 Validating selection procedures and evaluating training programs.
10 Fostering a better working relationship between subordinate and supervisor.
11 Fostering a better working relationship between work units.

To provide a basis for such personnel actions as:
1 Periodic appraisal pursuant to laws or regulations.
2 Promotion based on merit.
3 Recognition and rewards for past performance.
4 Review at completion of a probationary period.
5 Warning about unacceptable performance.
6 Layoff or termination based on merit.
7 Career development or training needs on individual basis.
8 Demotion or reduction in grade.
9 Lateral reassignment.

in the improvement or management of performance. Many practitioners and managers who have been directly involved in appraisal systems argue that the process and outcomes of formal appraisal impede the accomplishment of the objectives for which the appraisal/performance management system was established. Those who are rated tend to be preoccupied with their numerical rating and how the rating compares to ratings of others with whom they are supposed to collaborate in work. The "team" spirit of work units often suffers when the focus of appraisal is at the individual level. Practitioners also maintain

that "institutionalized" appraisal which calls for an annual appraisal of each subordinate's performance on the company appraisal form gives the appraising manager an excuse for not managing performance throughout the work period. Managers who have difficulty in providing negative feedback to subordinates are thus motivated to avoid the process if they must conform to "institutionized" appraisal requirements at the end of the calendar or fiscal year anyway. We present several recommendations later which address this problem.

Appraisal as a basis for personnel decisions

To motivate employees to improve their performance and achieve their target goals, supervisors can use incentives such as pay-for-performance programs (e.g., merit pay, incentives, bonus awards). One of the strongest compensation trends in the U.S. is toward some form of pay-for-performance system. Effective performance measurement is absolutely necessary for these systems to work (Peach & Buckley, 1993). The research in this area is not very positive either. In general, when the criteria for appraisal must be rated and not counted, the research shows that pay-for-performance systems are generally not effective (Milkovich & Wigdor, 1991; Stewart, Appelbaum, Beer, & Lebby, 1993).

Performance appraisal information is also used to make staffing decisions. These decisions involve finding employees to fill positions in the organization, or reducing the numbers of employees who exist in certain positions. Many organizations rely on performance appraisal data to decide which employees to move upwards (promote) to fill openings, and which employees to retain as a part of "downsizing" or "restructuring" effort.

One problem with relying on performance appraisal information to make decisions about job movements is that employee performance is only measured for the *current* job. If the job at the higher, lateral, or lower level is different from the employee's current job, then it may be difficult to estimate how the employee will perform on the new job. Consequently, organizations have resorted to using assessment procedures in addition to or instead of appraisal data to make staffing decisions. These assessment methods include assessment centers, paper and pencil testing, work samples, and structured interviews (e.g., Harris & Brown, 1993). Unfortunately, assessment methods have the drawback of indicating only how employees will perform when peak performance is demanded, and not how they will perform on a typical basis (Dubois, Sackett, Zedeck, & Fogli, 1993).

Most organizations focus on internal recruiting for placement to supervisory/managerial levels except the top position. Despite problems, performance appraisal still plays a significant role in the process of moving people through the organization although appraisal data are typically used only as a "first cut" in a multiple hurdle system. There is very little research which makes a "head-to-head" comparison in the predictive validity of performance appraisal versus some other method of predictive assessment such as assessment centers (e.g., McEvoy, Beatty, & Bernardin, 1987). Later in the chapter, we propose an approach for using performance appraisal as a "predictor" of future performance in another position for both internal and external hiring and retention decisions.

Many companies use performance appraisal data to make decisions about reducing the work force. In most private sector firms, appraisal information along with job needs are the only data used to determine which employees to lay off or terminate, while in unionized companies, seniority is the primary basis for making reduction-in-force decisions. Allegations of age discrimination related to employee terminations is one of the most common EEO complaints today (Hayes, 1990; Miller, Kaspin, & Schuster, 1990). As we discuss below, the process of performance appraisal falls under the close scrutiny of the courts in these and other EEO cases.

Some departments use appraisal data to determine employees' needs for training. For example, many companies now use subordinates to evaluate their supervisors or managers. The results are revealed to each manager with suggestions for specific remedial action (if needed). A growing number of companies also use 360° appraisal as a developmental tool for managers, "the practice of involving multiple raters, often including self-ratings, in the assessment of individuals" (Tornow, 1993, 211).

Research and evaluation

Appraisal data is frequently used to determine whether various human resources programs (e.g., selection, training) are effective. There are thousands of personnel selection validation projects which have used performance appraisal data as criteria in the validation effort, and numerous studies evaluating the effects of some type of training or development intervention (Daley, 1993; Nathan, Mohrman, & Milliman, 1991).

LEGAL ISSUES ASSOCIATED WITH PERFORMANCE APPRAISALS

Since performance appraisal data has been used to make many important personnel decisions (e.g., pay, promotion, selection, termination), it is understandable that it is a primary target of legal disputes involving employee charges of unfairness and bias (e.g., Ashe & McCrae, 1985, Beck-Dudley & McEvoy, 1991; Bernardin & Cascio, 1988; Murphy, Barlow, & Hatch, 1993; Schmitt, Hattrup, & Landis, 1993; Wendt, Slonaker, & Coleman, 1993). There are several legal avenues a person may pursue in the U.S. to obtain relief from discriminatory performance appraisals. The most widely used U.S. federal laws are Title VII of the Civil Rights Act and the Age

Discrimination in Employment Act. The pro-plaintiff provisions of the 1991 Civil Rights Act and the 1990 Americans with Disabilities Act (e.g., jury trials, punitive damages) give appraisal even greater importance when an employer maintains that a personnel decision was based on performance. Relatively new legal exceptions to the "employment at will" doctrine often involve performance appraisals as well (Holley & Walters, 1987). Companies also are being sued for defamation because of what is said in a performance appraisal. An employee of Hewlett-Packard, for example, sued his employer and his supervisor because the supervisor said he needed to improve his job performance in specific areas (Panaro, 1993).

Termination for cause only is the most common policy on the international scene and in organizations with collective bargaining. This termination for cause only policy puts great pressure on organizations to have effective performance appraisal systems.

There are several recommendations to assist employers in conducting fair performance appraisals and avoiding or winning legal actions. Gleaned from U.S. case law and our experiences in out-of-court settlements, these recommendations are intended as prescriptive measures that employers should take to develop fair and legally defensible performance appraisal systems (Bernardin & Cascio, 1988). Since U.S. case law and court rulings are continually updated, and obviously not applicable to other countries, this is not a guaranteed "defense-proof" listing, but rather constitutes sound personnel practices that protect the rights of both employers and employees, and enhances the effectiveness of an appraisal system regardless of the purposes for which it is used.

Legally defensible appraisal procedures

- Personnel decisions should be based on a formal, standardized performance appraisal system.
- Performance appraisal processes should be uniform for all employees within a job group, and decisions based on those performance appraisals should be monitored for differences according to the race, sex, national origin, religion, disability, or age of employees. While obtained differences as a function of any of these variables are not illegal, an organization will have more difficulty defending an appraisal system linked to personnel decisions when performance ratings are correlated with these characteristics relevant to the legal action (Murphy et al., 1993).
- Specific performance standards should be formally communicated to employees.
- Employees should be able to formally review the appraisal results.
- There should be a formal appeal process for employees to rebut rater judgments.
- Raters should be provided with written instructions or training on how to conduct appraisals in order to facilitate systematic, unbiased appraisals.
- Personnel decision makers should be informed of antidiscrimination laws and made aware of legal and illegal activity regarding decisions based on such appraisals.

Legally defensible appraisal content

- Performance appraisal content should be based on a job analysis.
- Appraisals based on employee traits should be avoided.
- Objective, verifiable performance data (e.g., sales, output, errors and other countable results) should be used whenever possible.
- Constraints on individual or unit performance which are beyond the performer's control should be considered in an appraisal to ensure that employees have equal opportunities to achieve any given critical appraisal score or performance standard.

- Specific job-related performance functions, dimensions, standards, goals or objectives, should be used rather than global measures or a single overall assessment of performance.
- Performance dimensions or objectives should be assigned weights to reflect their relative importance in calculating a composite performance score.

Legally defensible documentation of appraisal results

- A thorough written record of evidence leading to termination decisions should be maintained (e.g., performance appraisals and performance counseling to advise employees of performance deficits and to assist poor performers in making needed improvements).
- Written documentation (e.g., specific examples of behavior, results, work products) for extreme ratings should be required.
- Documentation requirements should be consistent among raters.

Legally defensible raters

- Raters should be trained in how to use the appraisal system.
- Raters must have the opportunity to observe the employee firsthand or to review important ratee performance products.
- Use of more than one rater is desirable in order to lessen the amount of influence of any one rater and to reduce the effects of biases. Peers, subordinates, customers, and clients are possible sources.

DESIGN OF AN EFFECTIVE APPRAISAL SYSTEM

The process of designing an appraisal system should ideally involve incumbents, supervisors, clients, peers, customers, and HR professionals in making decisions about each of the following issues:

- Measurement content.
- Measurement process.
- Defining the rater (i.e., who should rate performance).
- Defining the ratee (i.e., the level of performance to rate).
- Administrative characteristics.

It is a challenge to make the correct decisions since no single set of choices is optimal in all situations. The starting point should be the strategic plan of the organization and, if known, the specific purposes to be served by the system. The details of the plan should be reviewed in order to design an appraisal system consistent with the overall goals of the organization and the environment in which the organization exists. The choice of each element of an appraisal system is dependent, or *contingent*, upon the nature of the situation in which the system is to be used. The approach advocated here is to systematically assess the contingencies present in a situation, which we call a *contingency model for appraisal system design*. In the rest of this section we examine the choices that must be made for each issue.

Measurement content

In the course of designing an appraisal system there are three choices that concern the content on which performance is to be measured:

1 The focus of the appraisal.
2 Types of criteria.
3 Performance level descriptors (PLDs).

Recent reviews of the vast appraisal literature have led to some conclusions regarding the content of performance appraisal which we regard as untenable. For example, in a review of pay-for-performance systems, the National Research Council (NRC) (Milkovich & Wigdor, 1991, 3) concluded that "the search for a high degree of precision in measurement does not appear to be economically viable in most applied settings; many believe that there is little to be gained from such a level of precision." Justification for this position appears to be based on conclusions from research on rating formats and, more recently, the research on cognitive aspects of performance appraisal, almost all of which were conducted in experimental settings, conditions which do not match those the researchers typically infer and which would facilitate generalizability to the applied settings the National Research Council was supposedly addressing (Austin & Villanova, 1992; Bernardin & Villanova, 1986).

Inspired by seminal articles by Landy and Farr (1980) and Cooper (1981), research on cognitive, information processing, person perception, and memory variables apparently led to another NRC conclusion: "Whether rating traits or behaviors, raters appear to draw on trait-based cognitive models of each employee's performance . . . these general evaluations affect raters' memory for the evaluation of actual work behaviors" (Milkovich & Wigdor 1991, 67).

In fact, precision in measurement, and the "content" issue in general, has been virtually ignored in research over the last ten years, and format research conducted prior to the change in emphasis actually showed some "content" effects (Bernardin & Beatty, 1984; Bernardin & Smith, 1981). The most frequently cited article on performance appraisal through the 1980s (i.e., Landy & Farr, 1980) barely covers content issues in appraisal.

Most experts on performance appraisal take the position that, with regard to the content issue of performance appraisal, behaviors should be used in appraisal and not results or outcomes from the behaviors (e.g., DeNisi, 1992; Murphy & Cleveland, 1991; Feldman, 1992; Latham, 1986). The rationale for the position that results/outcomes should be avoided centers on problems of definition, criterion deficiency, contamination, and opportunity bias. Feldman (1992), for example,

states that "performance numbers" may be "seriously misleading or absent altogether" and "artistic or creative jobs" cannot be evaluated at all except in terms of subjective judgment. Murphy and Cleveland (1991, 92) state that "performance must ultimately be defined in terms of behaviors . . . the domain of performance is best defined as a domain of behaviors rather than a set of outcomes." Our view is that results and outcomes must be a critical component of the appraisal system, and that "outcomes" from the *customer* perspective are available for most jobs and preferable to behaviors as the focus of appraisal (Bernardin, 1992; Villanova, 1992).

Our central thesis is that performance appraisal systems based on outcomes or results defined by customers will result in more effective and "relevant" appraisal systems, based on what is generally considered to be the ultimate purpose for appraisal (i.e., to sustain or improve organizational effectiveness by meeting or exceeding customer requirements) (Beatty, 1989). Outcome measures as defined here are readily available for most jobs, the measurement of which fit an underlying theory of strategic marketing and management for service. Performance appraisal systems, like most human resources systems which are not tied to outcomes critical to external customers, are doomed to fail. We further argue that the outcome measures which are used as the basis for the appraisal of individuals or work units should be directly tied to the strategic goals of the unit and firm.

The focus on outcomes from the customer's perspective has been given impetus in recent years as the move toward integrating appraisal with strategy has been recognized as a desirable objective. Indeed, the essential balance between individual and organizational needs in the implementation of strategy is sought through the processes of performance measurement and appraisal which should be harnessed to company strategy and goals (Bower & Bartlett, 1991). Reimann (1989) concludes that this integration is frequently not achieved, particularly in long-term value creation which is an important dimension of strategy. He suggests that traditional appraisal systems are oriented toward short-term targets such as quarterly profits.

The integration of organizational functions and processes should be another goal of both strategy and the supporting management systems. The classic conflict between marketing and manufacturing is an example of where synergism is frequently lacking. One study found that agreement between these groups was significantly higher in those firms where marketing and manufacturing managers perceived that strategic plans and MBO were linked to performance appraisal (St. John, 1991).

The justification for linking strategy and appraisal has been reinforced by the accelerating movement to total quality management (TQM) where the basis of strategy is continuous improvement of all functions and processes for the purpose of customer satisfaction. Some companies are making changes to their appraisal systems to reflect this strategic movement that is supported by a culture and vision based on quality. Motorola, 3M, and duPont are among those firms that encourage a culture of innovation and expect their employees to take risks and pursue innovations (Gupta & Singhal, 1993).

Dominion Bank of Toronto, Canada designed their appraisal system to support a quality service and sales culture (Joseph, 1993). Trident Regional Health System of Charleston, South Carolina supports a total quality management strategy with an appraisal and compensation process. At Olin Corporation's research and development function the customer determines whether expectations are met or not met, and these are the only two ratings used in the appraisal process (Marien, 1992). Days Inns of America has adopted a unique organization self-appraisal by providing consumers with its hotels' quality-assurance ratings (Gillette, 1993).

A basic notion of total quality management

is the reengineering of processes for the ultimate goal of improving customer satisfaction. Xerox Canada has been a leader in getting commitment to the methodology of reengineering by tying it into the appraisal system (Barton, 1993). Another example is at Sprint Corporation where reduction of cycle time is a key focus (Moad, 1993). For example, in the information systems function, the previous output measure of lines of code per programmer hour has been changed to the average time it takes to go from conception to rollout of a new application. Outcome measures such as these are incorporated into the appraisal system.

Measurement precision is critical to the effectiveness of any appraisal system. We contend that the poor results reported above for virtually all purposes of appraisal are largely a function of a lack of precision in measuring what it is that we want to measure (i.e., performance). We must get back to basics and look at the focus of appraisal, the criteria for appraisal, the relationship of the criteria to strategic goals of the work unit or organization, and the delineation of the levels of performance. We will examine each of these next.

The focus of the appraisal

Appraisal can be either person-oriented (i.e., focusing on the person who performed the behavior) or work-oriented (i.e., focusing on the *record of outcomes* that the person achieved on the job). In order to design a system for appraising performance, it is important to first define what is meant by the term "work performance." Although job performance depends on or is a consequence of some combination of ability, effort, and opportunity, "performance" can and should be measured in terms of outcomes or results produced. Performance is defined as: The *record of outcomes* produced on a *specified job function* or activity during a *specified time period* (Bernardin & Beatty, 1984; Kane & Kane, 1993). Performance on the job as a whole would be equal to the sum (or average) of performance on the critical or essential job functions. The functions have to do with the work which is performed and *not* the characteristics of the person performing. Unfortunately, many performance appraisal systems still confuse measures of performance with measures or traits of the person, which violates the fundamental objective of performance appraisal: to evaluate performance of the person, not the person in the abstract.

Effective performance appraisal focuses on the record of outcomes and, in particular, outcomes directly linked to an organization's mission and objectives. In general, personal traits (e.g., dependability, integrity, perseverance, loyalty) should not be used when evaluating performance because such traits may foster stereotyping and other biases and are difficult to defend should litigation result. As stated in table 24.1, people who are evaluated on ambiguous criteria perceive little value in the feedback, and are often less motivated to perform well after the appraisal than before (Bernardin, 1992). Few organizations clearly define what it is they are trying to measure in work. Strategic goals are rarely carefully defined or measured (Beatty, 1989).

Strategic plans often list market standing, productivity, profitability, use of financial resources, and even public responsibility, as criteria related to their goals. A small minority carefully define the parameters for measuring these criteria, and an even smaller number link these measures up with specific individual performance content (Richards, 1986).

Even most organizations which employ some form of "management-by-objectives" (MBO), "work planning and review" (WP & R), or "standard-based" approach to appraisal, do not do an adequate job of defining "performance" (Bobko & Colella, 1994; Rodgers & Hunter, 1991). All other things being equal, the greater the specificity in the criterion definitions of "performance," the more effective the appraisal system will be, no matter what purpose it is designed to serve. In addi-

tion, the stronger the connection between the strategic goals of a division, SBU, or functional unit and these criteria, the more effective the appraisal system will ultimately be.

While many experts on performance appraisals would agree that useful, albeit deficient outcome/results measures can be derived in physical goods business for assessing worker or unit performance, most contend that such data are lacking in services (e.g., Cardy & Dobbins, 1994; Murphy & Cleveland, 1991). In services, however, many workers perform their principal functions at the same time that the service is consumed by the customer, and their performance thus directly affects customer satisfaction with the service.

We also know from the vast customer satisfaction literature that customer satisfaction is strongly related to repeat business and loyalty to the service, and that the customer is capable of distinguishing the performance of the worker from other aspects of the service provided (e.g., Band, 1991; McCune, 1989; Scherkenbach, 1985). However, the extent to which the customer is satisfied with the service cannot be separated from the performance of the service worker(s) with whom the customer interacts, since the service worker's performance is also perceived to be a component of the service. The performance of the insurance agent, the lawyer, the waiter/waitress, the customer service representative, or the trainer are thus a part of the marketing function of the organization, since buyer and seller interact directly. The service worker must be prepared to do whatever is required (within reason and cost) to meet (or exceed) the customer's requirements. For most jobs, because of the variety of ways in which job outcomes can be achieved through behaviors, a finite list of behaviors which must be exhibited is difficult (or impossible) to produce. The customer, however, by stipulating the service requirements as carefully as possible, actually participates in the design of the service product simultaneous with the production stage. The greater the degree of detail in the requirements of the customer, the greater the understanding of the criterion on the part of the service provider, and ultimately the greater the customer satisfaction. These customer requirements should define both the functions and the criteria for worker performance. This model can be adapted for internal customer requirements as well (Bernardin, 1992; Villanova, 1992).

This conceptualization of the service marketing function thus requires a performance appraisal system that is based on specific customer requirements, which should be the focus of the performer's attention. With this model of service marketing and management as a guideline, customer satisfaction with the service is a function of the representative customer requirements/expectations regarding the services. The frequency with which these requirements are met (or exceeded) for repeated or iterative functions or iterative services is the outcome measure for that particular product/service and customer combination. If practical, the product or service should be disaggregated into different job functions or subproducts/service with separate criterion measures for each constituent customer group. Table 24.3 presents a summary of the steps involved for deriving definitions of outcomes, and Villanova (1992) presents an expansion of this model tied to the strategic goals of the organization or unit.

Work in services is often performed at the same time that the service is being consumed. Employees in services who directly interact with customers are thus part of the services "product." To the extent that your stockbroker makes you feel stupid about the market when he calls with another hot tip, your view of the broker product will not be favorable. The frequency with which you feel stupid is a critical "outcome" that can and should be used to evaluate the broker along with how much stock is sold. In services, the lawyers, brokers, agents, waitresses, trainers, or professors are all part of the services product. The extent to

Table 24.3 Steps in the development of customer-based outcome measures

1 In the context of business unit performance data, benchmark data, customer-based research, and unit-level objectives, identify the products or services necessary to achieve the goals related to the requirements of the external customers.

2 Collect data on internal customer requirements and determine relationships with external customer requirements at No. 1. Develop priority list/importance weights for internal demands based on importance for external requirements. Data collection will yield customer-based appraisal methodology.

3 Consult with work unit on the products required based on unit-level goals from steps 1 and 2. The product specifications should be derived from customer-based research (i.e., customers determine the job specifications in terms of quantity, timeliness and especially quality).

4 Supervisors and subordinates consider potential constraints on attainment of required outcomes. Supervisors attend to constraints which can be eliminated and analyze organizational structure/job design characteristics in the context of customer demands (see Bernardin, 1989).

which the weighted sum total of the various parts of the "product" have met the requirements of the customer thus defines satisfaction with the "product." The manager's responsibility is to gain a clear understanding of each critical customer's requirements. This of course should include internal customers, but always with external customers as the ultimate focus (McCune, 1989). We return to this issue when we discuss the options for "rater(s)" in an appraisal system.

Types of criteria

Most appraisal systems require raters to make a single overall judgment of performance on each job function. For example, determining an overall rating for a manager's performance on "planning and organizing" would be characteristic of this approach, or making an overall rating of the extent to which the managers "organized the work schedule" is another example. There are, however, at least six criteria by which the value of performance in any work activity, function, standard or objective may be assessed (Kane & Kane, 1993). For example, raters could evaluate the "timeliness" of the manager's "planning and organizing" performance or they could rate the "quality" of that performance. Raters also could assess the "quantity" of "subordinate development," or the "quality" of the "development." These six criteria are listed and defined in table 24.4. Although all of these criteria are not relevant to every job function, a subset of them always will apply to each function, objective, or standard. The identification of the critical criteria and the weights to be applied to the performance levels defined should be directly tied to the strategic goals for the performance unit.

The human resources professional has the task of determining whether raters should assess employees' performance on each job function as a whole (i.e., considering all relevant criteria simultaneously), or whether raters should assess each relevant criterion of performance for each function separately. The overall rating approach is of course faster than making assessments on separate criteria, but has the serious drawback of requiring raters to simultaneously consider as many as six different criteria and to mentally compute their average. The probable result of all this subjective reasoning may be less accurate ratings than those done on each relevant criterion for each job activity, and less specific feedback to the performer (Martell & Borg, 1993). As we stated earlier, in general, the greater the specificity in the content of the appraisal, the more effective the appraisal system (Bernardin, 1992). One recent study of a work, planning, and review system supports this view. The greater the precision in the definition of criteria in the written perform-

Table 24.4 Criteria for assessing performance functions

1 *Quality* The degree to which the process or result of carrying out an activity approached perfection in terms of either conforming to some ideal way of performing the activity or fulfilling the activity's intended purpose.

2 *Quantity* The amount produced, expressed in such terms as dollar value, number of units, or number of completed activity cycles.

3 *Timeliness* The degree to which an activity is completed, or a result produced, at the earliest time desirable from the standpoints of both co-ordinating with the outputs of others and maximizing the time available for other activities.

4 *Cost effectiveness* The degree to which the use of the organization's resources (e.g., human, monetary, technological, material) is maximized in the sense of getting the highest gain or reduction in loss from each unit or instance of use of a resource.

5 *Need for supervision* The degree to which a performer can carry out a job function without either having to request supervisory assistance or requiring supervisory intervention to prevent an adverse outcome.

6 *Interpersonal impact* The degree to which a performer promotes feelings of self-esteem, goodwill, and cooperativeness among coworkers and subordinates.

ance standards, the more satisfied are the ratees with the process, and the greater the improvement in performance as judged by the raters (Bernardin, Hennessey, & Peyrefitte, 1994).

Performance-level descriptors (PLDs)

Work-oriented appraisal systems typically require raters to compare performance on each job function against a set of benchmarks. These benchmarks are descriptions of levels of performance, and are referred to as "anchors" or *performance level descriptors* (*PLDs*). PLDs or anchors may take three different forms: adjectives or adjective phrases;

behavioral descriptions, expectations or critical incidents; and outcomes or results produced by performing.

Adjectival benchmarks (e.g., "satisfactory," "very low," "below standard," "rarely," etc.) are generally subjective because their interpretation can mean different things to different raters. For example, one manager's definition of "below standard" may be quite different from another manager's definition. *Behavioral PLDs* or anchors consist of descriptions of the actions or behaviors taken by the person being appraised. For example, if the job function for a police officer is "crime prevention," an "effective" behavioral anchor might be "calls for assistance and clears the area of bystanders before confronting a barricaded, heavily-armed subject." An "ineffective" anchor might be "continues to write a traffic violation when hearing a report of a robbery in progress" (Landy & Goodin, 1974). Behavioral anchors are useful for developmental purposes since raters are able to give specific behavioral feedback to employees (e.g., identifying areas which need improvement). *Results-oriented PLDs* are based on outcomes produced, and may look like the "number of publications," "customer complaints," "contracts completed," "preparing and posting work schedules one week in advance of due dates," or the "number of days absent." As we stated above, results-oriented PLDs are preferable to either adjectival or behavioral PLDs when performance outcomes are important for the job and can be measured, and when an individual's contribution to the results can be clearly distinguished. Behavioral PLDs should be used if outcomes cannot be linked to a particular person or group of people.

The conceptualization of "outcome" measures we propose here includes the frequency judgment by raters/customers of the extent to which requirements were met based on clearly articulated operational definitions of the expected product and relevant criterion. The total performance score of an individual or work unit is then the sum of customer-based frequency assessments, combined with relevant results or outcome data. All of these data sources are weighted by importance for business unit objectives regarding external customer requirements (see Villanova, 1992).

Measurement process

The second set of issues to be considered when designing an appraisal system is the system's measurement process. Among the choices which must be made are the type of measurement scale, types of rating instruments, control of rating errors, accounting for situational constraints on performance, and the overall score computation method (Kamensky, 1993; Kane & Kane, 1993).

Type of measurement scale

Certain types of personnel decisions need higher levels of precision than others. For example, if the organization wants to be able to single out the highest (or lowest) performers in a group for some special recognition (discipline), then measurements at the *ordinal* level will suffice. That is, employees only need to be ranked from best to worst. Other personnel decisions (e.g., promotion decisions and identification of developmental needs) require the use of a more precise measurement scale (e.g., interval level). For example, some organizations determine promotions based to some extent on appraisal data collected across units. The extent to which an individual in one unit is judged to be superior to another in a different unit is thus needed. An interval-level scale will reveal the ranking of employees' performance as well as the actual difference in their scores (i.e., how much better one employee is compared to others). An appraisal system must be designed using a measurement scale at the needed level of precision.

Types of rating instruments

There are three basic ways in which raters can make performance assessments:

Table 24.5 Three methods of rating comparisons

1 *Comparisons among performances* Compare the performances of all ratees to each PLD for each job activity, function, or overall performance. Rater judgments may be made in one of the following ways:
   (a) Indicate which ratee in each possible *pair* of ratees performed closest to the performance level described by the PLD or attained the highest level of overall performance.
      • Illustrative method: paired comparison
   (b) Indicate how the ratees ranked in terms of closeness to the performance level described by the PLD.
      • Illustrative method: straight ranking
   (c) Indicate what percentage of the ratees performed in a manner closest to the performance level described by the PLD. (Note: the percentages have to add up to 100% for all the PLDs within each job activity/function.)
      • Illustrative method: forced distribution
2 *Comparisons among descriptors (PLDs)* Compare all the PLDs for each job activity or function and select the one (or more) that best describes the ratee's performance level. Rater judgments are made in the following way:
   (a) Indicate which of the PLDs fit the ratee's performance best (and/or worst).
      • Illustrative method: forced choice
3 *Comparisons to descriptors (PLDs)* Compare each ratee's performance to each PLD for each job activity or function. Rater judgments are made using:
   (a) Whether or not the ratee's performance matches the PLD.
      • Illustrative methods: graphic rating scales such as behaviorally anchored rating scales (BARS), management-by-objectives
   (b) The degree to which the ratee's performance matches the PLD.
      • Illustrative methods: all summated rating scales such as Behavioral Observation Scales (BOS) and Performance Distribution Assessment methods
   (c) Whether the ratee's performance was better than, equal to, or worse than that described by the PLD.
      • Illustrative method: Mixed Standard Scales

---

1 They can make comparisons among ratees' performances.
2 They can make comparisons *among* anchors or performance level descriptors (PLDs), and select the one most (or least) descriptive of the person being appraised.
3 They can make comparisons of individuals *to* anchors or performance level descriptors (PLDs).

Table 24.5 presents these three options, plus some examples of each type. Some of the most popular rating instruments representing each of these three ways are described in the next section. The essay or narrative method we discussed above does not fit into any of these

categories since this approach has no measurement process itself and, if numbers must be derived, the numbering system would then fit into one of these three categories.

Rating instruments: comparisons among ratees' performances Paired comparisons, straight ranking, and forced distribution are appraisal systems which require raters to make comparisons among ratees according to some measure of effectiveness. *Paired comparisons* require the rater to compare all possible pairs of ratees on "overall performance" or some other, usually vaguely defined standard. This task can become cumbersome for the rater as the number of employees increases and more comparisons are needed. The formula for the number of possible pairs of employees is $n(n - 1)/2$, where n = the number of employees. *Straight ranking* or rank ordering asks the rater to simply identify the "best" employee, the "second best," and so forth, until the rater has identified the worst employee. For example, the NCAA rankings in football and basketball are based on a rank ordering of the teams by coaches and the press.

Forced distribution usually presents the rater with a limited number of categories (usually five to seven) and requires (or "forces") the rater to place a designated portion of the ratees into each category. A forced distribution usually places the majority of employees in the middle category (i.e., with average ratings or raises), while fewer employees are placed in higher and lower categories. Some organizations use forced distributions to assign pay increases while others use them to assign performance ratings to ensure that raters do not assign all of their employees the most extreme (e.g., highest) possible ratings. Some organizations have adopted this approach as a part of a performance-based, downsizing effort. IBM, Xerox and Digital are examples.

Rating instruments: comparisons among performance-level descriptors The *forced choice* technique is a rating method which requires the rater to make comparisons among anchors or descriptors given for a job activity. The method is specifically designed to reduce (or eliminate) intentional rating bias where the rater deliberately attempts to rate individuals high (or low) irrespective of their performance. The rationale underlying the approach is that statements are grouped in such a way that the scoring key is not known to the rater (i.e., the way to rate higher or lower is not apparent). The most common format is a group of four statements from which the rater must select two as "most descriptive" of the person being rated. The rater is unaware of which statements (if selected) will result in higher (or lower) ratings for the ratee

because all four statements appear equally desirable or undesirable. There are usually a minimum of 20 of these groups of four statements.

While the forced choice method sounds like a good approach to alleviating deliberate rating distortion, the track record of the method when the data are used for administrative purposes is not favorable. The Michigan State Police used a forced choice instrument for less than one year before abandoning it altogether because raters hated the rating process and the hidden scoring key (King, Schmidt, & Hunter, 1980).

Rating instruments: comparisons to performance-level descriptors Methods which require the rater to make comparisons of the employee's performance to specified anchors or descriptors include: graphic rating scales, including behaviorally anchored rating scales (BARS), management by objectives (MBO), and standards-based appraisal; and summated scales, including behavioral observation scales (BOS), mixed standard scales (MSS), and performance distribution assessment (PDA).

Graphic rating scales are the most widely used type of rating format. Generally, graphic rating scales use adjectives or numbers as anchors or descriptors. One of the most heavily researched types of graphic scales is the *behaviorally anchored rating scales (BARS)*. BARS are graphic scales with specific behavioral descriptions defining various points along the scale for each dimension. One rating method for BARS asks raters to record specific observations of the employee's performance relevant to the dimension on the scale (Bernardin & Smith, 1981). The rater would then select that point along the scale which best represents the ratee's performance on that function. That point is either selected by comparing the ratee's actual observed performance to the behavioral expectations which are provided as "anchors" on the scale, or the rater simply scales the new observations and an average performance rating is

Table 24.6 Example of a summated scale

Directions Rate your manager on the way he or she has conducted performance appraisal interviews. Use the following scale to make your ratings:

Always	=	1
Often	=	2
Occasionally	=	3
Seldom	=	4
Never	=	5

1 Effectively used information about the subordinate in the discussion.
2 Skillfully guided the discussion through the problem areas.
3 Maintained control over the interview.
4 Appeared to be prepared for the interview.
5 Let the subordinate control the interview.
6 Adhered to a discussion about the subordinate's problems.
7 Seemed concerned about the subordinate's perspective of the problems.
8 Probed deeply into sensitive areas in order to gain sufficient knowledge.
9 Made the subordinate feel comfortable during discussions of sensitive topics.
10 Projected sincerity during the interview.

derived based on the mean of the newly scaled items. The new observations can be given to ratees as feedback on their performance. Research shows this approach to BARS ratings is superior to others (Bernardin & Beatty, 1984).

The method of *summated scales* is one of the oldest formats and remains one of the most popular for the appraisal of job performance. One of the most recent versions of summated scales are called behavioral observation scales (BOS) (Latham, 1986). An example of a behavioral observation scale is presented in table 24.6. For this scale, the rater is asked to indicate how frequently the ratee has performed each of the listed behaviors.

Performance distribution assessment calls for ratings of relative frequency of carefully developed performance PLDs which are scaled for effectiveness. Raters indicate the occurrence rates of the effectiveness levels achieved for each PLD (Kane, 1986). One certain advantage of the PDA approach is that the rater must consider attainable performance in the context of possible constraints on performance.

Management by objectives (MBO) is an appraisal system which calls for a comparison between specific, quantifiable target goals and the actual results achieved by an employee (Rodgers & Hunter, 1991; Epstein, 1984). MBO remains as the most popular method for the assessment of managers (Bretz et al., 1992). The measurable, quantitative goals are usually mutually agreed upon by the employee and supervisor at the beginning of an appraisal period (Bobko & Collella, 1994; Hatry, 1975). During the review period, progress towards the goals is monitored. At the end of the review period, the employee and supervisor meet to evaluate whether the goals were achieved and to decide on new goals. The goals or objectives are usually set for individual employees and differ across employees depending on the circumstances of the job. For this reason, MBO has been shown to be useful for targeting "individual" performance, yet it is less useful for making comparisons across employees (Bernardin & Beatty, 1984). This approach is used most often for supervisory and managerial personnel, although there is little practical difference between MBO, work planning and reviews systems, and standards-based approaches, which are often used for non-managerial personnel as well (Bernardin & Beatty, 1984).

Generally, the choice of a particular rating instrument seems to have relatively little effect on rating accuracy or validity with the exception being that the greater the precision in the definition of "performance" and the more specific the feedback, the more effective the appraisal system for any of the purposes we described above (Bernardin, 1992). Thus, the chief basis for selecting a particular rating instrument for use should be founded on other factors such as how well it fits with the level of precision needed. If only ordinal levels of measurement are needed, formats using comparisons among ratee performance (e.g., ranking) are adequate if performance is carefully defined as the basis for the comparisons. At the higher levels of precision (e.g., interval level), the rating instruments based on "comparison to descriptors" offer the most direct approaches to eliciting the needed rater responses. Ease of use and acceptability to raters and ratees also should be given strong consideration when choosing a rating instrument (Hartel, 1993).

Control of rating errors

Performance ratings are subject to a wide variety of inaccuracies and biases referred to as "rating errors." These errors occur in rater judgment and information processing, and can seriously affect performance appraisal results (Cardy & Dobbins, 1994). The most commonly cited rating errors include the following:

Leniency Ratings for employees are generally at the high end of the scale regardless of the actual performance of ratees. Leniency is a particularly troublesome error when ratings are used to determine a portion of compensation (Holmes, 1993). Surveys have identified leniency as the most serious problem with appraisals whenever they are linked to important decisions like compensation, promotions, or downsizing efforts (Bretz et al., 1992; Bernardin, Kane, Villanova, & Peyrefitte, 1994).

Central tendency Ratings for employees tend to be toward the center of the scale regardless of the actual performance of ratees.

Halo effect The rater allows a rating on one dimension (or an overall impression) for an employee to influence the ratings he or she assigns to other dimensions for that employee. That is, the rater inappropriately assesses ratee performance similarly across different job functions, projects, or performance dimensions (Murphy & Cleveland, 1991).

Rater affect This factor includes favoritism, stereotyping, and hostility; and excessively high or low scores given only to certain individuals or groups based on rater attitudes toward the ratee, not based on actual behaviors or outcomes (Tsui & Barry, 1986). Sex, race, age, and friendship biases are examples of this type of error which is the most common basis for lawsuits involving performance appraisals.

Primacy and recency effects When the rater's ratings are heavily influenced either by behaviors or outcomes exhibited by the ratee during the early stages of the review period (primacy) or behaviors or outcomes exhibited by the ratee near the end of the review period (recency).

Perceptual set The tendency for raters to see what they want to see or expect to see. For example, expectations of a given level of performance often affect judgments of actual performance (Hogan, 1987). Expecting low levels of performance, for example, can lead to higher judgments of performance than deserved by the actual performance. The opposite is true for an expectation of higher levels of performance. Forms of attribution bias, such as the actor-observer bias, fit into this category (Bernardin, 1989).

All of these errors can arise in two different ways: as the result of *unintentional* errors in the way people observe, store, recall, and report events, or as the result of *intentional* efforts to assign inaccurate ratings. If rating errors are *unintentional*, raters may commit them because they do not have the necessary skills to make accurate ratings, or the content of the appraisal is not carefully defined. Attempts to control unconscious, unintentional errors most often focus on rater training. Training programs to improve the rater's observational and categorization skills (called frame-of-reference training) have been shown to increase rater accuracy and consistency (Bernardin & Beatty, 1984). This training consists of creating a common frame of reference among raters in the observation process. Raters are familiarized with the rating scales, and are given opportunities to practice making ratings. Following this, they are given feedback on their practice ratings. They are also given descriptions of critical incidents of performance which illustrate outstanding, average, and unsatisfactory levels of performance on each dimension. This is done so they will know what behaviors or outcomes to consider when making their ratings (Bernardin, 1979).

A second strategy to control unintentional rating errors is to reduce the number of performance judgments a rater is required to make to try to avoid biases and errors. For example, a rating instrument using relative frequencies might pose rating questions on the form which require more objective responses, such as, "On what percent of all the times that Sue organized a meeting did she fail to contact everyone to attend the meeting?" or "On what percent of all the times that Sue organized a meeting did it begin and end on time?" The responses to these questions could then be mathematically converted into appraisal scores. Kane and Kane (1992) present a psychometric and information processing argument supporting the use of relative frequencies in appraisal and in their performance review and information standardizing method (PRISM) in particular. One additional empirical result supports the use of relative frequencies as well. Research with upward appraisal systems found that feedback from subordinates to supervisors was perceived as more useful by supervisors when the statements of managerial performance defined an outcome which required a judgment of relative frequency rather than a statement worded in a neutral manner with a rating format requiring a judgement of how effective or ineffective the supervisor was (Bernardin, Dahmus, & Redmon, 1993). For example, one statement from a Federal Aviation Administration instrument asks subordinates to indicate whether the supervisor "seeks out all necessary information needed to solve work problems." Supervisors indicated that a judgment of frequency on this type of statement (e.g., sought out the necessary information 85 percent of the time) was more instrumental in changing behavior than a mean rating of how effective (or ineffective) the supervisor was in "gathering information for subordinates."

Raters may commit rating errors *intentionally* for political reasons, or to provide certain outcomes to their employees or themselves. For example, one of the most common intentional rating errors is leniency (Holmes, 1993). Managers may assign higher ratings than an employee deserves to avoid a confrontation with the employee, to protect an employee suffering from personal problems, to acquire more recognition for the department or themselves, or to be able to reward the employee with a bonus or promotion. Although less common, managers may also intentionally assign more severe ratings than an employee deserves to motivate him or her to work harder, to teach the employee a lesson, or to build a case for firing the employee. Attempts to control intentional rating errors include: making ratings observable and provable, hiding scoring keys by using certain rating instruments (e.g., forced-choice, mixed standard scales), requiring cross-checks or reviews of ratings by other people, training raters on how to provide negative evaluations, and reducing the rater's motivation to assign inaccurate ratings. For example, the State of Virginia reduced rater motivation to rate leniently by rewarding raters for the extent to which they carefully defined "performance" for their employees, and conformed to the regulations of the rating system regarding documentation for extreme ratings.

Accounting for situational constraints on performance

As summarized in table 24.1 above, one of the main causes of perceptions of inaccurate and unfair performance appraisals is the belief by those who are rated that they are being held responsible for performance decrements that were caused by factors beyond their control. Any student who has been graded on a group project may have experienced this problem in individual appraisal. Many conditions present in the job situation or work assignment can hold a person back from performing as well as he or she could (Peters & O'Connor, 1980). Some of these constraints include: inadequate tools, lack of supplies, not enough money, too little time, lack of information, breakdowns in equipment, and not enough help from others. For example, high school teachers may be limited in the time they can allocate to teaching activities if they spend a considerable portion of their workday stopping gun fights between alleged students. However, they may still be held accountable for teaching outcomes despite these other ancillary job duties. If in a group project, one of your team members fails to retrieve vital information, the constraint could seriously hamper your ability to do your job.

Factors which hinder an employee's job performance are called *situational constraints* and are described in table 24.7. An appraisal system design should consider the effects of situational constraints so that ratees are not unfairly downgraded for these uncontrollable factors. Training programs should focus on making raters aware of potential constraints on employee performances. Research shows that this approach to appraisal training results in greater agreement in self versus supervisory appraisal (Bernardin, 1989).

Overall score computation

Once performance has been assessed on each of the job's important activities or functions,

Table 24.7 Situational constraints on performance

1 Absenteeism or turnover of key personnel.
2 Slowness of procedures for action approval.
3 Inadequate clerical support.
4 Shortages of supplies and/or raw materials.
5 Excessive restrictions on operating expenses.
6 Inadequate physical working conditions.
7 Inability to hire needed staff.
8 Inadequate performance of coworkers or personnel in other units on whom an individual's work depends.
9 Inadequate performance of subordinates.
10 Inadequate performance of managers.
11 Inefficient/unclear organizational structure or reporting relationships.
12 Excessive reporting requirements and administrative paperwork.
13 Unpredictable work loads.
14 Excessive work loads.
15 Changes in administrative policies, procedures, and/or regulations.
16 Pressures from coworkers to limit an individual's performance.
17 Unpredictable changes or additions to the types of work assigned.
18 Lack of proper equipment.
19 Inadequate communication within the organization.
20 The quality of raw materials.
21 Economic conditions (e.g., interest rates, labor availability, and costs of more basic goods and services).
22 Inadequate training.

it is usually necessary to produce an overall score reflecting the level of performance on the job as a whole. There are two primary ways of producing an overall score:

1 *Judgmental* The rater forms a subjective judgment of "overall performance," usually after completing the ratings of performance on each of the job's separate activities or functions.

2 *Mathematic* The rater, some other scorer, or a computer mathematically computes the weighted or unweighted mean of the

ratings of performance on each of the job's activities or functions.

The judgmental approach to determining an overall score is used by most organizations, but a weighted mathematic approach is more likely to accurately reflect overall performance based on all job activities or functions and in the context of strategic goals for the work unit. The question for the rater using the mathematic approach is whether to compute the overall score by equally weighting the ratings on each of the various job activities or functions, or by assigning them different weights based on their relative importance. Assuming you can derive reliable measures of importances, the latter approach is superior particularly when the importance weights are derived in the context of the unit or organization's strategic goals.

"Predictive" weights also can be derived to establish either an empirical or judgmental predictive relationship between performance on job functions across different jobs. These weighted ratings can then be used as a part of hiring, promotion, or downsizing decisions (Bernardin & Beatty, 1984). For example, subject matter experts could be used to establish a predictive matrix between functions and criteria at Job A level and different functions and criteria at Job B. A rater could then simply rate an employee on past performance and the predictive weights could then be applied to establish the predictive value of performance in Job A for performace in Job B. These data could then be used along with other data predictive of performance in Job B but not relevant to Job A. A similar procedure can be followed for organizational restructuring in which performance of certain dimensions of Job A are determined to be predictive of performance in the newly created dimensions for the restructured Job B. The weighting process for the Job A dimension ratings can then be applied to identify the people with the highest potential to perform in the new job.

The weighting approach can also be used when a company is attempting to fill a position from a pool of both internal and external candidates. A performance rating form could be prepared which requests performance data from internal and external candidates and the predictive weights could then be applied to these ratings in order to derive the predictive value of past performance in any of the relevant performance dimensions. This approach solves the problem of having performance data on internal candidates and letters of recommendation on the external candidates. The letters of recommendation can be replaced by the performance appraisal form that can be completed by the applicant, his or her boss, and/or others.

Defining the "rater"

Many organizations are concluding that the traditional boss–subordinate form of appraisal does not suit today's needs (Hartel, 1993; Tornow, 1993). The focus on individual skills and individual objectives (if any), behavioral characteristics, and rater bias does not fit the needs of the modern organization where cross-functional processes focused on customer satisfaction are required. More and more firms are moving toward some type of multiple-rater approach and most textbooks recommend it (e.g., London & Beatty, 1993; Tornow, 1993). At ARCO Transportation, the company believes that the answer is to provide each employee with more feedback, more often, and from feedback sources in addition to the one-on-one supervisory rating (Fruge & Rollins, 1993). Multiple-rater performance measurement should overcome some of the current problems such as supervisory role conflict and bias, inaccuracy, and validity (Baruch & Harel, 1993; Edwards, 1990).

The use of customers, clients, "professional shoppers," peers, and subordinates who have direct and unique knowledge of at least some aspects of the ratee's job performance will provide for a more reliable, and comprehensive assessment of performance (London & Beatty, 1993; Kaplan, 1993).

The latest trend in multirater systems is the 360° assessment (Voss, 1993). In these reviews workers get input from a variety of sources, including coworkers, customers, and their bosses (Nowack, 1993). A growing number of companies also routinely conduct formal self-appraisals and subordinate appraisals of managers and supervisors (Bernardin, 1986; Ludeman, 1993; Yammarino & Atwater, 1993).

It is generally believed that self-appraisal, combined with other rater appraisals, provides a number of advantages (Van Velsor, Taylor, & Leslie, 1993). In addition to reducing the ratee's perceived discrepancy between his or her rating and the rater's rating, the process tends to focus the individual's attention on job requirements and progress against some benchmark defined by all critical customer/raters. Moreover it provides a vehicle for rater–ratee communications. The jury is still out on the extent to which self-appraisal contributes to appraisal system effectiveness (Nilson & Campbell, 1993; Roberson, Torkel, Korsgaard, & Klein, 1993; Roberts, 1992).

One survey of 167 corporations found that the majority of the firms did not use self-evaluation in their performance appraisal process (Wells & Spinks, 1990). An alternative to self-appraisal can be some other form of employee involvement in the selection of appraisal content and particular raters (Roberson et al., 1993). At Procter & Gamble, for example, appraisers selected by the boss and the employee rate the employees' performance (Austin, 1992).

According to a recent survey by the Wyatt Co., a compensation consulting firm, 15 percent of companies surveyed reported that they used peer evaluations. Peer review is a natural accompaniment to the self-directed team. An appraisal by peers provides fast and frequent feedback from team members who are familiar with the work and the worker. Digital Equipment Corporation (DEC) uses a partnership approach that includes both self-

appraisals and ratings from peers. Typically, the appraisal includes input from every member of the employee's team. A committee made up of the individual, a chairperson, a consultant, and two coworkers reviews the appraisal with the individual (Norman & Zawacki, 1991). At Eastman Chemical Company, individual team-member reviews are conducted with the participation of the rest of the team (Austin, 1992).

Performance reviews should not only appraise past performance but should become a contract between managers and employees. Contracts might include goals for skill or career development and at least one objective or performance dimension that pertains to future team performance. The definitions of "performance level descriptors," which we described earlier, should be clarified and refined based on discussions with the ratee(s). The manager or supervisor should serve more in the role of facilitator of multirater/customer input.

The number of rater types that should be used in rating the performance of an employee depends on the number of rater types that can furnish *unique* perspectives on the performance of the ratee from a "customer" perspective. By "unique perspectives" we mean people in a position to furnish not only different information but also information processed through less severe biases. To decide how many rater types should be used and other aspects of the system, designers should address these questions:

1 Are payoffs greater than the costs (e.g., form development, rater training, additional time for administration)?
2 To what extent will operations be disrupted?
3 What is the symbolic significance of participation in the appraisal process? Are employees more satisfied with their jobs or their supervisors because they participated in the evaluation of their supervisors?

4 Can "gaming" be controlled (Bernardin & Beatty, 1987)?

5 Will users focus unduly on the system rather than the ultimate purpose for the system?

6 Will participants be satisfied with rating information and be capable of reconciling different ratings from different sources?

Conceptualizing all possible raters as all possible customers (internal and external) is a good approach to setting up a multiple-rater system (Bernardin, 1992). If only a supervisor or manager is to be used, that rater should seek performance information from all critical internal and external customers in preparation of the appraisal context prior to the start of the appraisal period, and, of course, as a part of the formal appraisal. To the extent that ratees look at the evaluator (e.g., the supervisor or manager) as the only important "customer," you have a system which can easily operate to the detriment of the organization (Bernardin, 1992; Duarte, Goodson, & Klich, 1993). The focus for both raters and ratees should be on actual internal and external customer requirements and in the context of unit/organizational strategic goals. Just as the measurement of the performance dimensions and the development of goals, objectives, or standards should have this focus, so should the identification of the sources of rating (London & Beatty, 1993; Villanova, 1992).

Defining the "ratee"

Many people assume that appraisals always focus on an *individual* level of performance. There are alternatives to using the individual as the ratee, which are becoming more common in organizations as more and more firms shift to using more self-managing teams, autonomous work groups, teamwork, and participative management to get work done. Specifically, the ratee may be defined at the individual, work group, division, or organizationwide level. It is also possible to define the ratee at multiple levels. For example, under some conditions it may be desirable to appraise performance at the work-group level for merit pay purposes, and at the individual level to identify developmental needs.

Two conditions which make it desirable to assess performance at a higher level of aggregation than the individual level are high work-group cohesiveness and difficulty in identifying individual contributions. *High work-group cohesiveness* refers to the shared feeling among work-group members that they operate as a team. Such an orientation promotes high degrees of cooperation among group members for highly interdependent tasks. Appraisals focused on individual performance may undermine the cooperative orientation needed to maintain this cohesiveness, and tend to promote individualistic or even competitive orientations. *The difficulty in identifying individual contributions* is also important to consider. In some cases, workers are so interdependent, or their individual performance is so difficult to observe or measure, that there is no choice but to focus their appraisals on performance of the higher aggregate of which they are a part. For example, to the extent that the two conditions above exist, it is advisable to consider using a higher level than the individual when evaluating performance. Instead, evaluations could be made of the group's performance, the department's, or the organization's as a whole.

Appraisal systems in the vast majority of firms have traditionally focused on the individual employee (Bretz et al., 1992). The shortcomings of this approach, such as those related to measurement content and the measurement process, have been summarized earlier in this chapter. There are the additional problems of assessing an individual's performance related to such macro issues as contribution to vision and strategy, integration of organization systems and processes, and the use of data from internal or external customers. There is little doubt that the organization of the future will continue to utilize the structural innovation of groups. Whether these groups take the form of quality circles (QCs), cross-functional teams, or self-directed work teams (SDWTs), the group is the organizational form that breaks down the hierarchical barriers of the classical pyramidal organization. Therein lies both a paradox and an opportunity. Many scholars contend that an individual appraisal system does not support the team concept and may be deleterious to the team (Rigg, 1992). Initiatives supporting teamwork will probably fail if appraisal (and compensation) is based on individual performance with no appraisal of an individual's contribution to team outcomes. Total quality management and the systems approach to organization structure cannot take hold in an organization's culture unless the values on which they are based are built into the underlying HRM activities, including performance appraisal. A logical structure would thus include an assessment of teams and/or teamwork. According to findings reported in the International Quality Study (IQS), many US companies, particularly in the automotive and computer sectors, have begun to activate the link between human resources initiatives and the reward-and-compensation infrastructure. The trend will be to rank quality and *team performance* ahead of individual performance (Benson, 1992).

The strategic change that focuses on the customer perspective requires an accompanying cultural change. The appraisal system can be an instrument for embedding this change. Consider the cultural change required when a firm moves to a team-oriented focus. Team-based performance appraisals are tangible and visible support for teamwork. These can be the vehicle for implementation of a customer-based strategy that is accompanied by a cultural change (Parker, 1992). Eastman Chemical Company illustrates how one company redesigned their appraisal system to facilitate such a change to a team-oriented focus (Joines, Quisenberry, & Sawyer, 1993).

Administrative characteristics

In any appraisal system, there are a variety of administrative decisions that must be made. These decisions include the frequency and timing of appraisals, rating medium, and method of feedback.

Frequency and timing of appraisals

This refers to the number of times per year each employee is to be formally appraised, and the time period (e.g., months) between formal appraisals. Usually, appraisals are conducted once or twice per year, with equal intervals between them (e.g., every 12 months or 6 months). Many organizations conduct appraisals as frequently as every 30 or 60 days during the first six months to one year of employment in order to monitor the performance of new employees during their probationary or orientation period.

Intervals between appraisals may be fixed (e.g., every six months, anniversary date, during the last month of fiscal year, etc.). Alternatively, intervals may be variable, and may be based on such factors as the occurrence of very poor or very high performance, consideration for a promotion, or project completion dates. Many organizations use both types of intervals: fixed for regularly occurring personnel decisions (e.g., merit pay), and variable for appraisals triggered by unusual events or performance (e.g., needs for reduction in force). A growing number of organizations now use formal appraisal only for prescribed circumstances, such as probationary evaluations and merit pay, and do not require formal evaluations unless a specific personnel action is to be taken.

Rating/data collection medium

The widespread use of desktop personal computers in the workplace has made viable the option of having raters recording performance appraisal ratings directly on computers and using the computer to record performance data. Numerous software programs are now available which provide for the entry and maintenance of appraisal data. There are several advantages to using the computer as a rating medium. The results can immediately be integrated into the computerized central personnel record systems that most organizations are now using, thereby eliminating the need for clerks to enter the data. The amount of paper that has to be generated, distributed, and filed is drastically reduced. Some computer programs also monitor rater responses for logic and completeness during the rating process. The choice of a medium depends, however, on the sophistication of the raters, availability of computers or optical scanning devices, and, of course, cost. If computers or terminals are readily available, computerized systems certainly make a great deal of sense and will ultimately prove to be cost effective.

Method of feedback
Raters should communicate appraisal results to ratees through a formal feedback meeting held between the supervisor and the employee. Feedback serves an important role both for motivational and informational purposes and for improved rater–ratee communications. For example, supportive feedback can lead to greater motivation, and feedback discussions about pay and advancement can lead to greater employee satisfaction with the process. Specific feedback is recommended instead of general feedback since it is more likely to increase an individual's performance (Ilgen, Barnes-Farrell, & McKellin, 1993; Jones et al., 1993).

The biggest hazard for the rater in providing performance feedback may be ratee reactions to the feedback. Generally, ratees believe that they have performed at higher levels than observers of their performance (Bernardin, 1989). This is especially true at the lower performance levels where there is more room for disagreement and a greater motive among ratees to engage in ego-defensive behavior. It is no wonder that raters are often hesitant about confronting poor performers with negative appraisal feedback, and may be lenient when they do. Indeed, Fisher (1979) found that raters inflated their ratings of subordinates when they were led to believe they would have to meet with the subordinate to discuss the ratings (versus raters who did not have such an obligation). Although pressure on managers to give accurate feedback may override their reluctance to give negative feedback, the pressure doesn't make the experience any more pleasant nor any less likely to evoke a leniency bias. Feedback to inform poor performers of performance deficiencies and to encourage improvement doesn't always lead to performance improvements. Many employees view their supervisors less favorably after the feedback, and feel less motivated after the appraisal (Bernardin, Stepina, & Lawther, 1990). The fear or discomfort experienced in providing negative feedback tends to differ across managers. One survey, known as the *performance appraisal discomfort scale* (*PADS*), showed that the level of discomfort felt by a rater was related to leniency of ratings (Villanova, Bernardin, Dahmus, & Sims, 1993). Rater training has been proposed to reduce the level of discomfort (Bernardin & Beatty, 1984).

To create a supportive atmosphere for the feedback meeting between the employee and supervisor, several recommendations exist. The rater should: remove distractions, avoid being disturbed, and take sufficient time in the meeting. Raters seem to have trouble adhering to these guidelines. Raters should be informal and relaxed and allow the employee the opportunity to share his or her insights. Topics that should be addressed include: praise for special assignments, the employee's own assessment of his or her performance, the supervisor's response to the employee's assessment, action plans to improve the subordinate's performance, perceived constraints on performance which require subordinate or supervisory attention, employee career aspirations, ambitions, and developmental goals. In sum, raters should

485

provide feedback which is clear, descriptive, job-related, constructive, frequent, timely, and realistic. Waiting to provide such feedback until the formal appraisal is due is one of the biggest mistakes a supervisor or manager can make. Recent research also suggests that the use of multiple raters as a basis for the appraisal increases the perceived validity and usefulness of the feedback (Bernardin, Dahmus, & Redmon, 1993).

DEVELOPING AN APPRAISAL SYSTEM

After deciding on the design of an appraisal system by making decisions about the measurement content and process, determining who should rate performance and at what level, and making necessary administrative decisions, it is time to actually develop the appraisal system. The development of an effective appraisal system consists of following seven basic steps as described below.

1. Start with a job analysis to develop customer-based outcome measures Any effort to develop an appraisal system should begin with complete information about the jobs to be appraised in the context of customer requirements. This information is typically generated through a job analysis which describes the product or service requirements as defined by all critical internal and external customers (e.g., knowledge, skills, and abilities), job content (e.g., main tasks, activities or duties), and job context features (e.g., constraints on performance, responsibilities, physical conditions). The critical incident method is one approach for the development of highly detailed appraisal data (Bownas & Bernardin, 1988).

2. Specify performance dimensions and develop performance level descriptors (PLDs) Using as much involvement by incumbents, supervisors, customers, and any other critical constituents

as possible, specify the job functions/objectives, and the criteria (e.g., quality, quantity, timeliness), relevant to each, on which employee performance is to be appraised. These function-by-criterion or objectives-by-criterion combinations will make up the system's performance dimensions. Following this, compose the necessary number of performance level descriptors (PLDs) for each performance dimension. These descriptors should be defined as specifically as possible and in the context of the unit or organization's strategic goals. Wherever possible, these descriptors should include countable results or outcomes which are important for the strategic goals of the unit or organization. Even in the case of a ranking or forced distribution, one PLD per dimension should be used (usually called a "ranking factor") which describes the standard or ideal performance on the basis of which employees are compared or ranked.

3. Scale the PLDs This is the process of determining the values to attach to each PLD. At this time, you can also have representatives of all possible rating sources determine the weights to be assigned to each performance dimension when computing an overall performance score (see step 2 of table 24.3 above). For example, raters may decide that answering phones makes up 30 percent of a clerical person's job. This factor would be assigned a weight of .30. The necessary information to compute scale values and weights is typically collected through a scaling survey questionnaire administered to both incumbents and future raters. The survey asks for opinions about the value of PLDs and the relative value of the functions. The survey approach can also be used to derive predictive weights when the appraisal data are to be used for hiring or promotional decisions. These weights can be provided by all critical customers for the position to be filled or they can be derived from criterion-related research in which performance on a particular job is regressed on to performance dimension ratings of other jobs and the regression weights are then used to weight subsequent ratings.

4. Develop rating forms or program The actual device to collect ratings or reports of performance usually is a form to be completed by the rater(s). A goal to strive for in developing either manual forms or computer-based systems is ease of use. That is, the process should be easy to understand and the rating of each performance dimension should require no more than a minute or two. Computerized appraisal which does not sacrifice content specificity is the ideal approach.

5. Develop scoring procedure In more simplistic systems, the score on each performance dimension is simply the rating that was entered and the overall score is just the average of the dimension scores. More sophisticated systems require a more involved process of hand or computer scoring. These may require development of scoring formulas, scoring sheets, procedures to submit raw ratings for scoring, and procedures to record the scores and to prepare score reports for the rater and ratee. Again, we recommend weighted scoring which can be programmed easily and much more efficiently.

6. Develop appeal process Recall our discussion of the importance of appeal processes with regard to litigation concerning appraisal. Generally, specific appeal procedures should be developed for dealing with disputed appraisal results. Disputed appraisal results may include cases of ratees disagreeing with their appraisals and cases where appraisals are challenged by the higher-level manager reviewing the ratings. For any appeal, procedures should be specified for the number of appeal stages, the composition of any arbitration panel(s), the rules of evidence, and the criteria for reaching judgments. Companies should give consideration to the use of binding arbitration provisions in lieu of litigation for all personnel decisions. The case

law on the legality on this approach to dispute resolution for EEO complaints has been supported since the related Supreme Court ruling in *Gilmer* v. *Interstate/Johnson Lane Corporation* (1991).

7. Develop rater and ratee training program and manuals Every appraisal system needs to clearly describe the duties of the raters and ratees for using the system. These may be described in written instructions on the appraisal forms or in training manuals for the rater and ratee. The rater duties refer to the process of observing performance or reviewing work products (i.e., by providing a frame of reference), preparing for the appraisal, a consideration of possible constraints on performance, the rating procedure, the scoring procedure, what to do with the completed set of ratings, and how to best provide the results to ratees.

Ratees should be made fully aware of the appraisal process through publication of a ratee manual, training, or some other communication. They should be given a description of how the appraisal system was developed, how ratees can get copies of the dimensions on which they will be appraised, how to interpret the feedback report, what the ratings will be used for in the organization, how to appeal their appraisal scores, the standards by which their appeal will be evaluated and finally judged, and the protection they have against retaliation for challenging their appraisals.

IMPLEMENTING AN APPRAISAL SYSTEM

After an appraisal system has been designed and developed, it must be implemented. The process of actually putting the system into operation consists of taking the following steps: training, integration with the organization's human resources information system (HRIS), and a pilot test.

Training

This is the most important component of a system's implementation. Separate training sessions should be held for at least three groups: raters, ratees, and all decision-makers and analysts. The training should focus on a clarification of the information provided in the manuals for raters and ratees, and should "sell" the benefits of the program to all system users including top management (Lawther et al., 1989). In addition to the "frame of reference" training we discussed earlier, the training should cover interviewing techniques, common rating errors, EEO laws, performance coaching and mentoring.

Integration with human resources information system

The results of every appraisal (whether manual or computer-based) of every employee should ideally be entered into a computerized data base. This is necessary to handle the data administration and scoring and to evaluate ratings for errors (e.g., leniency, halo, central tendency). For example, appraisal data is entered into an HRIS computer data base which is combined with other information about individuals, and work units. Appraisal data can be linked with a career ladders program as an important component of the succession planning system.

Pilot test

A final, critical step in the implementation process is a tryout of the system, or a pilot test. Given all the details involved in the design, development, and implementation of an appraisal system, it is unrealistic to expect that everything is going to run smoothly the first time the system is used. The system will have problems that can't be foreseen, and the only way to find and solve them without having to suffer minor or major disasters is to try out the system. It should be made as realistic as possible, even down to the detail of having some employees file mock appeals. Questionnaires should be distributed to raters and ratees after the process to get their reactions and to identify trouble spots. It is vital that a new appraisal system get off on the right foot. The first time it is used "for real" should leave people with a favorable impression. If it doesn't, it may lose the level of cooperation necessary to make it work effectively.

EVALUATING APPRAISAL SYSTEM EFFECTIVENESS

After an appraisal system is implemented in an organization, it should be evaluated to ensure that it is effective for meeting its intended purposes. Unfortunately, few organizations evaluate appraisal systems at this level. As with many human resources systems (e.g., training), evaluations are often not conducted at all. A comprehensive evaluation of a performance appraisal system requires the collection of several types of data including user reactions, inferential validity, discriminating power, and possible adverse impact. We review each of these measures of effectiveness next.

User reactions

It is vital to learn the attitudes and reactions of raters and ratees to an appraisal system because any system ultimately depends on them for its effectiveness. Attitudes of employees can be assessed prior to the implementation of a new system to see how receptive they may be to a pending system.

Raters' reactions are important in order to assess whether they perceive the system to be easy to use and the content representative of the important job content. Also, raters should be asked whether they feel they have been adequately trained to use the system or have been given enough time to complete appraisals. Furthermore they should be asked to indicate their commitment to making the system work. One survey, which assesses the extent to which raters perceive other raters are using the system fairly and successfully, predicted rating bias in a police department (Bernardin & Orban, 1990).

Ratee reactions to an appraisal system are important to collect since they exert powerful influences on the tendency of raters to appraise accurately. If ratees feel unfairly appraised they will probably react in a defensive or hostile fashion to raters. The raters may then assign more lenient ratings to the employees for the next appraisal session in order to avoid conflict and confrontations. This inflation will damage the accuracy of the appraisals. Generally, ratees want a system that they perceive as being fair, informative, useful, and free of bias. Their opinions on these issues should be assessed after the system has been implemented. One study found that ratees perceived that a system which formally incorporated possible constraints on employee performance was fairer than another system which did not incorporate possible constraints (Bernardin, 1989).

Inferential validity

When considering how effectively an appraisal system operates, the issue of its validity refers to accuracy. That is, the extent to which its scores correspond to the *true* levels and standings of the performances being appraised (e.g., to what degree an employee who is rated as "average" really is exhibiting "average" performance). The problem is that often we have no idea of what the "true" level of performance is. We can only rely on subjective ratings or records of performance. If we had the means of assessing "true" performance, we would be using it as our appraisal measure. Of course, performance ratings should be correlated with the extent to which strategic goals are met (or exceeded) and this determination can be made over time.

In the absence of any way to assess a system's internal validity directly, the best approach seems to be to infer validity by determining whether the appraisal system is reliable, free from bias, relevant, and has discriminant validity. The most important measure of reliability for appraisal is the extent to which independent raters agree on an evaluation. Freedom from bias is the degree to which the scores are free from evidence of errors (e.g., leniency, central tendency, halo, sexual stereotyping). Discriminant validity, related to halo effect, is the degree to which ratees are ordered differently on each performance dimension; in other words, whether the ratings on one dimension are unrelated to ratings on other dimensions. This is desirable so that each performance dimension is measuring a separate work function. Relevance is the degree to which the appraisal system encompasses all of a job's critical functions and their applicable criteria, and excludes irrelevant activities or functions. Appraisals that are relevant also weight the functions in proportion to their relative importance to effective performance and, more importantly, the strategic goals of the organization or unit.

Discriminating power

If an appraisal system is successful at differentiating ratee performances in the job(s) for which it is being used, then it is said to have discriminating power. The difficulty in assessing appraisal systems on this criterion is in defining what constitutes "success at differentiating." How much differentiation is optimal? Deming (1986), for example, would argue that all ratee variability is deleterious to organizaional effectiveness. Can we expect the distribution of ratees' scores to form a normal curve over the possible range of scores? In many cases, this may be unreasonable to expect if employees are carefully recruited, selected, and trained. The question of how much differentiation is desirable must be clearly answered before a system's discriminating power can be evaluated.

Adverse/disparate impact

This criterion focuses on the question of whether the appraisal scores of members of groups protected by laws (e.g., race, sex, age, disabilities, national origin) are significantly different from others. For example, if the performance of minority employees is evaluated significantly lower than the performance of white employees, then adverse or disparate impact may be evident if personnel decisions were made on the basis of the appraisals.

If adverse impact is found, the organization will need to do some additional checks on the appraisal system. For example, the organization should determine if the group of employees adversely effected was more likely to be given assignments that were more difficult, aversive, or subject to more extraneous constraints, or whether they received lower appraisals than they deserved based on other data. If so, then it would be unwise to continue to use the appraisal system as constituted.

If no problems are found with the system, then the appraisal system can be used even if differences are found in appraisal results as function of race, sex, age or disabilities. In general, however, personnel decisions based on appraisal systems which result in adverse impact are difficult to defend, particularly if the prescriptions we presented in the first part of this chapter are not a part of the system.

CONCLUSION

The design, development, and implementation of appraisal systems are not endeavors which can be effectively handled by following the latest fad or even by copying other organizations' systems. Instead, a new appraisal system must be considered a fundamental organizational change effort which should be pursued in the context of improving the organization's effectiveness. This means that, like any such change effort, there will be vested interests in preserving the status quo

which will be resistant to change, no matter how beneficial it may be for the organization. These sources of resistance to the change have to be identified and managed to build incentives for using a new appraisal system.

Once a well-designed system has been implemented, the work is still not done. An appraisal system has to be maintained by monitoring its operation through periodic evaluations. Only by keeping an appraisal system finely tuned will it enable managers to have a rational basis for making sound personnel decisions. Based on our review of the published literature and our own experience in organizations, we will conclude with what we regard as our most important recommendations:

1   The content or basis of performance appraisal should be a record of outcomes which are considered to be important from the perspective of all critical customers.
2   The greater the specificity in the definition of the outcome measures, the more effective the appraisal system, regardless of the purpose for which it is to serve.
3   The greater the compatibility between the strategic goals of the organization or work unit, the more effective the performance appraisal system.
4   Managers/supervisors should be conceptualized as facilitators of performance outcomes who help to define customer requirements and collect appraisal data from critical internal and external customers.
5   Multiple rater systems which include a self-appraisal component should be used whenever possible.
6   The appraisal system should formally incorporate a consideration of perceived (or actual) constraints on performance. Such constraints should be the focus of manager/supervisory attention for the next appraisal period.
7   Finally, the selection of the level of aggregation for ratee(s) should be made in the

context of the outcome measures as defined and group/unit cohesiveness.

REFERENCES

Ashe, R. L., & McRae, G. S. (1985). Performance evaluations go to court in the 1980s. *Mercer Law Review*, 36, 887–905.

Austin, N. K. (1992). Updating the performance review. *Working Woman*, 17, 32–5.

Austin, J. T., & Villanova, P. (1992). The criterion problem: 1917–1992. *Journal of Applied Psychology*, 77, 836–74.

Band, W. A. (1991). *Creating Value for Customers: Designing and implementing a total corporate strategy*. New York: Wiley.

Barton, R. S. (1993). Business process reegineering. *Business Quarterly*, 57, 101–3.

Baruch, Y., & Harel G. (1993). Multi-source performance appraisal: An empirical and methodological note. *Public Administration Quarterly*, 17, 96–111.

Beatty, R. W. (1989). Competitive human resource advantage through the strategic management of performance. *Human Resource Planning*, 12, 179–94.

Beck-Dudley, C. L., & McEvoy, G. M. (1991). Performance appraisals and discrimination suits: Do courts pay attention to validity? *Employee Responsibilities and Rights Journal*, 4, 194–263.

Benson, T. E. (1992). Quality and teamwork get a leg up. *Industry Week*, 241, 66–8.

Bernardin, H. J. (1979). The predictability of discrepancy measures in role constructs. *Personnel Psychology*, 32, 139–53.

Bernardin, H. J. (1986). Subordinate appraisal: A valuable source of information about managers. *Human Resource Management*, 25, 421–39.

Bernardin, H. J. (1989). Increasing the accuracy of performance measurement: A proposed solution to erroneous attributions. *Human Resources Planning*, 12, 239–50.

Bernardin, H. J. (1992). The "analytic" framework for customer-based performance content development and appraisal. *Human Resource Management Review*, 2, 81–102.

Bernardin, H. J., & Beatty, R. W. (1984). *Performance Appraisal: Assessing human behavior at work*. Boston: Kent-Wadsworth.

Bernardin, H. J., & Beatty, R. W. (1987). Subordinate appraisals to enhance managerial productivity. *Sloan Management Review*, 28, 63–74.

Bernardin, H. J., & Cascio, W. F. (1988). Performance appraisal and the law. In R. Schuler, S. Youngblood, & V. L. Huber (eds.), *Readings in Personnel and Human Resources Management*, 235–47. St. Paul: West Publishing.

Bernardin, H. J., Dahmus, S. A., & Redmon, G. (1993). Attitudes of first-line supervisors toward subordinate appraisals. *Human Resource Management*, 32, 315–24.

Bernardin, H. J., Hennessey, H., & Peyrefitte, J. (1994). Age, racial and gender bias as a function of the appraisal system. Paper presented at the Annual Meeting of the National Academy of Management, Dallas, TX.

Bernardin, H. J., Kane, J. S., Villanova, P., & Peyrefitte, J. (1994). The stability of leniency: Three studies. Paper presented at the Annual Meeting of the National Academy of Management, Dallas, TX.

Bernardin, H. J., & Orban, J. (1990). Leniency effect as a function of rating and format, purpose for appraisal, and rater individual differences. *Journal of Business and Psychology*, 5, 197–211.

Bernardin, H. J., & Smith, P. C. (1981). A clarification of some issues regarding the development and use of behaviorally anchored rating scales. *Journal of Applied Psychology*, 66, 458–63.

Bernardin, H. J., Stepina, L., & Lawther, W. (1990). Survey of State employees' attitudes toward performance appraisal. Report to the Florida Legislature.

Bernardin, H. J., & Villanova, P. J. (1986). Performance appraisal. In E. A. Locke (ed.), *Generalizing from Laboratory to Field Settings*, 43–62. Lexington, MA: Lexington Books.

Blakely, G. L. (1993). The effects of performance discrepancies on supervisors and subordinates. *Organization Behavior and Human Decision Processes*, 54, 57–80.

Bobko, P., & Colella, A. (1994). Employee reactions to performance standards: A review and research propositions. *Personnel Psychology*, 47, 1–36.

Bower, J. L., & Bartlett, C. (1991). *Business Policy*, 7th ed. Homewood, IL: Irwin.

Bownas, D., & Bernardin, H. J. (1988). In S. Gael (ed.), *Handbook of Job Analysis*, vol. 2, pp. 1120–37. New York: Wiley.

Bretz, R. D. Jr., Milkovich, G. T., & Read, W. (1992). The current state of performance appraisal research and practice: Concerns, directions, and implications. *Journal of Management*, 18, 321–52.

Cardy, R. L., & Dobbins, G. H. (1994). *Performance Appraisal: Alternative perspectives*. Cincinnati, OH: South-Western Publishing.

Cooper, W. H. (1981). Ubiquitous halo. *Psychological Bulletin*, 90, 218–44.

Coyle, J. (1991). Aligning human resources processes with total quality. *Employment Relations Today*, 18, 273–8.

Daley, D. M. (1993). Performance appraisal as an aid in personnel decisions: Linkages between techniques and purposes in North Carolina municipalities. *American Review of Public Administration*, 23, 201–13.

Deming, W. E. (1986). *Out of the Crisis*. Cambridge, MA: Center for Advanced Engineering Study, MIT.

DeNisi, A. S. (1992). Why analytic approaches to performance appraisal cannot work. *Human Resource Management Review*, 2, 71–80.

Duarte, N. T., Goodson, J. R., & Klich, N. R. (1993). *Journal of Organizational Behavior*, 14, 239–49.

DuBois, C. L. Z., Sackett, P. R., Zedeck, S., & Fogli L. (1993). Further exploration of typical and maximum performance criteria: Definitional issues, prediction, and white-black differences. *Journal of Applied Psychology*, 78, 205–11.

Edwards, M. R. (1990). Implementation strategies for multiple rater systems. *Personnel Journal*, 69 (9), 130, 132, 134, 137, 139.

Epstein, P. D. (1984). *Using Performance Measurement in Local Government*. New York: Van Nostrand.

Feldman, D. (1992). The case for non-analytic performance appraisal. *Human Resource Management Review*, 2, 9–35.

Fisher, C. D. (1979). Transmission of positive and negative feedback to subordinates: A laboratory investigation. *Journal of Applied Psychology*, 64, 533–40.

Fruge, M., & Rollins, T. (1993). Performance feedback – multi-source and software-assisted – increases personal and organizational success at ARCO Transportation. *Employment Relations Today*, 20, 273–86.

Gillette, B. (1993). Days basing rating system on QA scores. *Hotel & Motel Management*, 208, 4–35.

Gilmer v. *Interstate/Johnson Lane Corporation* (1991). 500 U.S. S.C. 114, L.Ed. 2d 26.

Glaser, M. (1993). Reconciliation of total quality management and traditional performance improvement tools. *Public Productivity and Management Review*, 16, 379–86.

Gupta, A. K., & Singhal, A. (1993). Managing human resources for innovation and creativity. *Research-Technology Management*, 36, 41–8.

Halachmi, A. (1993). From performance appraisal to performance targeting. *Public Personnel Management*, 22, 323–44.

Harris, M. M., & Brown, B. K. (1993). Personnel selection. In H. J. Bernardin & J. Russell (eds.), *Human Resource Management: An experiential approach*, 210–61. New York: McGraw-Hill.

Hartel, C. E. J. (1993). Rating format research revisited: Format effectiveness and acceptability depend on rater characteristics. *Journal of Applied Psychology*, 78, 212–17.

Hatry, H. P. (1975). Wrestling with police crime control productivity measurement. In J. Wolfle & J. Heaphy (eds.), *Readings on Productivity in Policing*, 86–128. Washington, D.C.: The Police Foundation.

Hayes, A. S. (1990). Layoffs take careful planning to avoid losing the suits that are apt to follow. *Wall Street Journal*, November 8, B1, B10.

Hogan, E. A. (1987). Effects of prior expectations on performance ratings: A longitudinal study. *Academy of Management Journal*, 30, 354–68.

Holley, W. H., & Walters, R. S. (1987). An employment at will vulnerability audit. *Personnel Journal*, 66, 130–9.

Holmes, B. H. (1993). The lenient evaluator is hurting your organization. *HRMagazine*, 38, 75–8.

Ilgen, D. R., Barnes-Farrell, J. L., & McKellin, D. B. (1993). Performance appraisal process research in the 1980s: What has it contributed to appraisals in use? *Organizational Behavior and Human Decision Processes*, 54, 321–68.

Joines, R. C., Quisenberry, S., & Sawyer, G. W. (1993). Business strategy drives three-pronged assessment system. *HRMagazine*, 38, 68–72.

Jones, S. D., Buerkle, M., Hall, A., Rupp, L., & Matt, G. (1993). Work group performance measurement and feedback: An integrated comprehensive system for a manufacturing department. *Group and Organization Management*, 18, 269–91.

Joseph, J. U. (1993). Harnessing human resources technologies. *Business Quarterly*, 58, 71–5.

Kamensky, J. M. (1993). Program performance measures: Designing a system to manage for results. *Public Productivity and Management Review*, 26, 395–402.

Kane, J. S. (1986). Performance distribution assessment. In R. Berk (ed.), *Performance Assessment: Methods and applications*, 237–74. Baltimore: The Johns Hopkins University Press.

Kane, J. S., & Kane, K. (1988). A survey of performance practices in *Fortune 500* companies. Unpublished manuscript.

Kane, J. S., & Kane, K. (1992). The analytic framework: The most promising approach for the advancement of performance appraisal. *Human Resource Management Review*, 2, 37–70.

Kane, J. S., & Kane, K. (1993). Performance appraisal. In H. J. Bernardin & J. Russell (eds.), *Human Resource Management: An experiential approach*, 377–404. New York: McGraw-Hill.

Kaplan, R. E. (1993). 360-Degree feedback PLUS: Boosting the power of co-worker ratings for executives. *Human Resource Management*, 32, 299–314.

King, L. M., Schmidt, F. L., & Hunter, J. E. (1980). Halo in a multidimensional forced choice performance evaluation scale. *Journal of Applied Psychology*, 65, 507–16.

Kulik, C. T., & Ambrose, M. L. (1993). Category-based and feature-based processes in performance appraisal: Integrating visual and computerized sources of performance date. *Journal of Applied Psychology*, 78, 821–30.

Landy, F. J., & Farr, J. L. (1980). Performance rating. *Psychological Bulletin*, 87, 72–107.

Landy, F. J., & Goodin, C. V. (1974). Performance appraisal. In O. G. Stahl & R. A. Staufenberger (eds.), *Personnel Administration*, North Scituate, MA: Duxbury Press.

Latham, G. P. (1986). Job performance and appraisal. In C. L. Cooper & I. Robertson (eds.), *International Review of Industrial and Organizational Psychology*, 117–55. New York: Wiley.

Lawther, W. C., Bernardin, H. J., Jennings, K., & Traynor, E. (1989). Implications of salary structure and merit pay in the fifty American states. *Review of Public Personnel Administration*, 9, 1–14.

London, M., & Beatty, R. W. (1993). 360-Degree feedback as a competitive advantage. *Human Resource Management*, 32, 353–72.

Ludeman, K. (1993). Upward feedback helps managers walk the talk. *HRMagazine*, 38, 85–93.

McCune. J. T. (1989). Customer satisfaction as a strategic weapon: Implications for performance management. *Human Resources Planning*, 12, 195–204.

McEvoy, G., Beatty, R. W., & Bernardin, H. J. (1987). Unanswered questions in assessment center research. *Journal of Business and Psychology*, 2, 97–111.

Marien, B. A. (1992). Quality in R&D: Putting TQM into the performance review process. *Research-Technology Management*, 35, 39–43.

Martell, R. F., & Borg M. R. (1993). A comparison of the behavioral rating accuracy of groups and individuals. *Journal of Applied Psychology*, 78, 43–50.

Milkovich, G. T., & Wigdor, A. K. (eds.) (1991). *Pay for Performance: Evaluating performance appraisal and merit pay*. Committee on Performance Appraisal for Merit Pay, Commission on Behavioral and Social Sciences and Education, National Research Council.

Miller, C. S. Kaspin, J. A., & Schuster, M. H. (1990). The impact of performance appraisal methods on age discrimination in employment act cases. *Personnel Psychology*, 43, 555–78.

Moad, J. (1993). New rules, new ratings as IS reengineers. *Datamation*, 39, 85–7.

Moen, R. D. (1989). The performance appraisal system: Deming's deadly disease. *Quality Progress*, November, 62–6.

Murphy, B. S., Barlow, W. E., & Hatch, D. D. (1993). Performance evaluation system – adverse age impact. *Personnel Journal*, 72, 20–3.

Murphy, K. R., & Cleveland, J. M. (1991). *Performance Appraisal: An organizational perspective*. Boston: Allyn & Bacon.

Nathan, B. R., Mohrman, A. M., & Milliman, J. (1991). Interpersonal relations as a context for the effects of appraisal interviews on performance and satisfaction: A longitudinal study. *Academy of Management Journal*, 34, 352–69.

Nilson, D., & Campbell, D. P. (1993). Self-observer rating discrepancies: Once an overrater, always an overrater? *Human Resource Management*, 32, 265–81.

Norman, C. A., & Zawacki, R. A. (1991). Team appraisals – Team approach. *Personnel Journal*, 70, 101–4.

Nowack, K. M. (1993). 360-Degree feedback: The whole story. *Training and Development*, 47, 69–72.

Panaro, G. P. (1993). Critical but honest evaluations are not defamatory. *Personnel Practice Ideas*, 9, 1–2.

Parker, G. (1992). Getting into shape. *Managing Service Quality*, 2, 251–4.

Peach, E. B., & Buckley, M. R. (1993). Pay for Performance. In H. J. Bernardin & J. Russell (eds.), *Human Resource Management: An experiential approach*, 482–515. New York: McGraw-Hill.

Peters, L. H., & O'Connor, E. J. (1980). Situational constraints and work outcomes: The influence of a frequently overlooked construct. *Academy of Management Review*, 5, 391–7.

Reimann, B. C. (1989). *Managing for Value*. Oxford, OH: The Planning Forum.

Richards, M. D. (1986). *Setting Strategic Goals and Objective*, 122–3. St. Paul: West Publishing.

Rigg, M. (1992). Reasons for removing employee evaluations from management's control. *Industrial Engineering*, 24, 17.

Roberson, L., Torkel, S., Korsgaard, A., & Klein, D. (1993). Self-appraisal and perceptions of the appraisal discussion: A field experiment. *Journal of Organizational Behavior*, 14, 129–42.

Roberts, G. E. (1992). Linkages between performance appraisal system effectiveness and rater and ratee

acceptance. *Review of Public Personnel Administration*, 12, 19–41.

Rodgers, R., & Hunter, J. E. (1991). Impact of management by objectives on organizational productivity. *Journal of Applied Psychology*, 76, 322–36.

St. John, C. H. (1991). Marketing and manufacturing agreement on goals and planned actions. *Human Relations*, 44, 211–29.

Salvemini, N. J., Reilly, R. R., & Smither, J. W. (1993). The influence of rater motivation on assimilation effects and accuracy in performance ratings. *Organizational Behavior and Human Decision Processes*, 55, 41–60.

Scherkenbach, W. W. (1985). Performance appraisal and quality: Ford's new philosophy. *Quality Progress*, 4, 40–6.

Schmitt, N., Hattrup, K., & Landis, R. S. (1993). Item bias indices based on total test score and job performance estimates of ability. *Personnel Psychology*, 46, 593–611.

Scholes, P. R. (1987). Total quality or performance appraisal: Choose one. *National Productivity Review*, 12, 349–63.

Scholtes, P. R. (1993). *An Elaboration on Deming's Teachings on Performance Appraisal*. Madison, WI: Joiner Associates Inc.

Stewart, G. B., III, Appelbaum, E., Beer, M., & Lebby, A. M. (1993). Rethink rewards. *Harvard Business Review*, 71, 37–49.

Tornow, W. W. (1993). Special issue on 360-degree feedback. *Human Resource Management*, 32, 211–19.

Tsui, A. S., & Barry, B. (1986). Interpersonal affect and rating errors. *Academy of Management Journal*, 29, 586–98.

Van Velsor, E., Taylor, S., & Leslie, J. B. (1993). An examination of the relationships among self-perception accuracy, self-awareness, gender, and leader effectiveness. *Human Resource Management*, 32, 249–63.

Villanova, P. (1992). A customer-based model for developing job performance criteria. *Human Resource Management Review*, 2, 103–14.

Villanova, P., Bernardin, H. J., Dahmus, S., & Sims, R. (1993). Rater leniency and performance appraisal discomfort. *Educational and Psychological Measurement*, 53, 789–99.

Voss, B. (1993). The 360-degree third degree. *Journal of Business Strategy*, 14, 8.

Wells, B., & Spinks, N. (1990). How companies are using employee self-evaluation forms. *Journal of Compensation & Benefits*, 6, 42–7.

Wendt, A. C., Slonaker, W. M., & Coleman, J. W. (1993). Employment discrimination is sex-blind. *SAM Advanced Management Journal*, 58, 28–33.

Yammarino, F. J., & Atwater, L.E. (1993). Understanding self-perception accuracy: Implications for human resource management. *Human Resource Management*, 32, 231–47.

☐ Chapter 25 ☐

Promotion, Succession, and Career Systems

J. Benjamin Forbes and Stanley E. Wertheim

INTRODUCTION

Promotion, succession, and career systems have a significant impact on the ability of organizations to compete effectively in today's complex and ever-changing environment. These systems are relied upon to identify and develop both the leaders needed to provide direction and the managers needed to competently operate complex organizations. They also have a significant impact on the satisfaction, organizational commitment and involvement, and motivation of all the members of the organization (Markham, Harlan, & Hackett, 1987).

Traditional promotion and succession systems are proving inadequate to provide the needed leadership as evidenced by the trend of large corporations such as IBM, Kodak, and General Motors going outside the firm for their top executives. Also the psychological contracts between employee and employer with regard to expectations for promotion and upward mobility are being torn up in the era of downsizing and delayering. Many are adapting well to this turn of events, but many others are being left bewildered and

without a clear sense of direction for their careers.

In this chapter we selectively review the theory and research on this topic. Then, we discuss practical applications of these techniques, and finally, we make recommendations for future research and for improved practice.

THEORY AND RESEARCH

Others have noted that although promotions and executive succession are critical processes for organizations and of significant concern to employees, there has been relatively little research on the topic (Ferris, Buckley, & Allen, 1992; Markham et al., 1987). However, a comprehensive review of the existing research literature on promotions may be found in Markham et al. (1987). In addition, Beatty, Schneier, and McEvoy (1987) have reviewed the executive development and management succession literature and a comprehensive study of the characteristics of top management succession systems has been reported by Friedman (1986). Our discussion of theory and research focuses on three related areas:

(1) the nature of promotion patterns or career paths within larger corporations; (2) the relationship between such patterns and corporate strategy; and (3) the promotion patterns and experiences of those who have reached the top of large corporations.

The nature of promotion patterns

Many people, including human resources managers, are not aware of the realities of career paths within large corporations. Vroom and MacCrimmon (1968) conducted a study of the promotion system in one big company. They were able to predict promotion chances based on career histories and determined that those in finance and marketing had significantly greater opportunities to move up than employees in manufacturing, and that those in personnel had very little chance for upward mobility. This information came as a shock to many in the company, including the human resources specialists.

It is commonly believed that early promotions are a critical factor in the identification and development of managers. They provide young managers with lots of early challenge and responsibility and create the experience of a cycle of success (Berlew & Hall, 1966). In the early Bell System studies (Bray, Campbell, & Grant, 1974), the positive effects of early job challenge were explained as the result of a change in the confidence and motivation of the new employees. However, an alternative explanation is that successful performance on these challenging jobs sent a positive signal to higher management about the ability of the new member, and that this signal influenced later promotion decisions (Rosenbaum, 1984). In fact, both effects are often probably in action.

The importance of early promotions was made very clear by the research of Rosenbaum (1979, 1984) who found that those who were promoted early rose to higher levels than those who were not. The first group remained in the "tournament", but those not promoted

in the early rounds were effectively eliminated from later competition. If this model accurately describes promotion patterns in most business firms, the implications for individuals and for organizations are that success in the early years is critically important – without it, the career is dead.

The ramifications may be appreciated by considering two earlier "ideal" sociological models of occupational mobility: contest and sponsored mobility (Turner, 1960). Our nation in general, and the business community in particular, values the norm of open opportunity. This is the contest mobility norm. In this system, decisions about who will move up are delayed as long as possible, and individuals are allowed maximum freedom of career mobility.

In a sponsored mobility system, decisions are made as early as possible. The advantage of this process comes from the efficiencies of specialized socialization, training, and development. Turner (1960) used the British educational system as an example of the application of this norm. Many business firms, especially those with the most sophisticated human resource management systems, such as AT&T and the Bell operating companies, have relied heavily on this model.

In the tournament system, a similar early decision is made. Here, it is based on an evaluation of early performance as reflected in promotion to a higher-level job. The model proposes that business firms initially allow all their members to compete in an open tournament. However, those who lose in the first round (by not being promoted) are eliminated from further competition. Furthermore the remaining contestants must continue to win each successive contest or they too will be eliminated. Rosenbaum's (1979) research strongly demonstrated the existence of such a system.

Rosenbaum (1984) suggested signaling theory as an explanation of the tournament pattern of mobility. This theory says that early movement is important as a criterion for later promotion because more objective standards are not available. Decision makers rely on the rate of upward mobility in relation to age or tenure as a signal of the individual's ability.

Sheridan, Slocum, Buda, and Thompson (1990) investigated the importance of early signals of employee ability and the generalizability of the tournament model. Also investigated were the effects of the "power" of the department in which the new employee started his or her career. Those who start in powerful departments have the advantage of mentors who may intercede favorably on their behalf, assist them in gaining visibility to the top managers, and provide them with important information earlier than others.

Sheridan et al. (1990) studied all employees who started a management career with a large public utility during a ten-year period. The researchers believed that a strong signal about an employee's ability would be transmitted by entrance into their first management position through the company's management trainee program. Their progress was compared to other managers who were hired from outside without a training program or were promoted into management from nonmanagement jobs. The other employees received none of the special attention given to the management trainees.

The trainees generally showed faster career mobility than the other groups. Department power affected career progress in a number of ways. Internal movements tended to be to new departments with the same level of power. Those who started in high-power departments moved more quickly and experienced greater increases in salary than those who started in the low-power functions.

The authors point out that the career management practices of this firm are consistent with their corporate strategy. This is a "steady state" firm (Kerr & Slocum, 1987) which is committed to its current business. Such firms invest heavily in management development in order to help employees understand the entire business, and to create a cohesive corporate culture through extensive socialization.

Japanese management development techniques are believed to be quite different from those found in most American firms. One characteristic of the Japanese firm is "slow evaluation and promotion" (Ouchi, 1981). This process appears similar to the contest mobility norm described earlier (i.e., everyone is in the contest for as long as possible). The "slow evaluation and promotion" system stands in stark contrast to the "fast track" mentality prevalent in U.S. organizations for quite some time.

Recent research, however, indicates that even in Japan, open contests may not reflect reality. Wakabayashi, Graen, and associates (1988) followed a group of 71 Japanese managers through their first 13 years of job tenure with "one of the leading corporations in Japan." This study clearly contradicts earlier beliefs about Japanese promotion systems. Rather than having a relatively open contest, this company, at least, used a strong tournament model with some features of the sponsored mobility approach. The timing of the first promotion (after 7 years) strongly predicted the third promotion (after 13 years). However, the information available after seven years did not predict any better than that which had been gathered in the first 3 years. This is consistent with the findings of Rosenbaum (1979). The winners are determined in the first 3 years of the competition. In fact, the fast tracks are partially set even before the contest begins, as evidenced by the impact of university ratings and assessment center potential ratings.

Lateral mobility should not be confused with upward mobility, but it is also a signal that higher-level decision makers use when deciding who to promote. Kanter (1977) described this as a factor which predicts chances of promotion in a large industrial firm. This may be because those who make such decisions see breadth of knowledge of different areas as a prerequisite for higher levels of responsibility (Kotter, 1982); or it may be that having held multiple jobs merely increases an individual's visibility within the firm.

Another variable that may act as a signal affecting chances for promotion is the functional background of the employee. Several studies have noted that firms in certain industries tend to choose their chief executives from particular functional areas (Piercy & Forbes, 1981). At a lower level, Vardi and Hammer (1977) showed that the type of job technology (i.e., long-linked, mediating, or intensive) used by rank-and-file workers within a plant affected their chances for mobility. In a comparison of managers drawn from three similar large manufacturing firms, Veiga (1985) found that career patterns were related to functional area. The fast-track managers, who moved frequently, but often laterally, were likely to be from areas representing mediating technologies like marketing and personnel, and the slow-track managers, who moved less frequently but more often vertically, were likely to be from intensive technologies like research and development and engineering.

Another study tested the tournament mobility model and also investigated two other promotion signals: breadth of experience and early functional area (Forbes, 1987). A large domestic oil company with personnel widely dispersed across the United States served as the research setting.

The results of this study offered only weak support for the tournament model of career mobility. Although early promotions were related to later attainment, strict tournament rules were not in force, because the losers (i.e., those passed over in the early periods) were later able to move up quickly. The results were more closely analogous to a horse race than to a tournament: that is, the position out of the gate had relatively little effect in comparison to position entering the home stretch.

Different mobility patterns for administrative and technical personnel may explain in part why the pattern of the early years did not always persist. Those who started in administrative positions began to move up early, but their progress seemed to level off quickly. A technical background meant a longer wait before upward movement; however, for some, this was followed by rapid promotion.

The number of different jobs, which in this study meant different functional areas or different levels of managerial responsibility, also predicted higher career attainment. This was previously noted by Kanter (1977) and, since more jobs implies less time in any one position, this finding is also consistent with the research of Sheridan and his colleagues (1990) and Veiga (1983).

In summary, the research generally supports the existence of corporate career tournaments in which early promotion is a strong predictor of later promotions. Also important are functional area and the breadth of experience that a manager has attained. One explanation for these findings is that the ambiguity involved in evaluating current managerial performance and future executive potential is so great that these surrogate signals are used instead of objective measures. The cynic might then conclude that corporate mobility is merely a matter of "being in the right place at the right time." This interpretation of the corporate promotion process has led to further elaboration of the tournament analogy (Cooper, Graham, & Dyke, 1993) and also dovetails nicely with recent discussions of and research on "politics" within human resources systems (e.g., Ferris & Judge, 1991; Ferris et al., 1992).

Noting that the field of human resource management typically assumes the rational perspective, Ferris and Judge (1991) have proposed an alternative political influence approach to understanding human resources decisions. The rational model assumes that decisions such as whom to promote should be based upon criteria such as performance or potential or fit. However, these evaluative dimensions may be socially constructed realities which lend themselves to manipulation through the skillful management of shared meaning: that is, through political influence. A number of studies have shown that performance evaluations (often a source of data to be considered in making promotion decisions) are influenced by perceptions of similarity, and may be influenced by political actions of the subordinates and for political reasons by superiors. In addition, it is generally believed that promotions are among the most political of human resources decisions (Ferris et al., 1992). Contributing to this perception is the use of sponsored mobility systems such as the "fast track" (Ferris & Judge, 1991) or mentoring programs (Markham et al., 1987). Recent studies support the role of politics in the promotion process (Ruderman, 1991), but have also found that ability and past performance are important factors (Ferris et al., 1992).

The concept of politics is one which spans levels of organizational analysis. While the previous discussion focused on the political actions of individuals, the power of various organizational units also affects the promotion process. This was noted in the Sheridan et al. (1990) study and is an explanation for the role of functional area as a factor influencing promotability (e.g., Forbes, 1987). Pfeffer's (1981) strategic contingency model of executive succession describes how different functional areas gain power as a result of their abilities to deal with critical environmental issues. He notes, however, that power may become institutionalized within one area even after the critical environmental uncertainties have shifted elsewhere. We discuss the influence of strategy on career paths further in the next section.

The big picture: promotion patterns and corporate strategy

Survey research by Ferris et al. (1992) found that organizational strategy appeared to be the significant factor driving the promotion process. A number of models exist which may further help us to understand the relationship between corporate strategy and promotion systems. Slocum and Cron (1988) focused on the two types of business strategies known as defenders and analyzers. Defenders protect their niche in relatively stable environments. Analyzers operate like defenders in some product markets but also are poised to move quickly to take advantage of new opportunities. In the defender firm there is more stability and an emphasis on carefully developing those who are in the critical areas of production and accounting/finance. These firms use extensive on-the-job training and detailed succession planning programs. They typically hire into lower-level positions and promote from within. They are likely to rely on early predictors of management potential. Although most managers move up within their functional areas, those who have been identified as high-potential employees may have the opportunity to learn various functions.

Because the analyzers are looking for new opportunities as well as trying to protect established areas, the human resources practices and career patterns are different. Some individuals are brought in at entry level and trained within specific functions, but others are recruited from outside to provide immediate expertise. The areas of marketing, engineering, and production are all important. There is more of an emphasis on movement across functions and products as a means of learning about the various departments.

The opportunities for upward mobility varied in relation to strategy within the sample of seven mature industrial products manufacturers studied by Slocum and Cron (1988). The career phenomenon of plateauing occurs when the probability of further promotion in a company becomes very low. By considering both the perceived likelihood of future promotion and the current level of performance, we may classify employees into four categories. "Stars" are employees who are

498

doing well and who are expected to continue to move up in the organization. "Comers" have been identified as having the potential to move up, but are currently performing below their potential. "Solid citizens" are performing well but are unlikely to move any farther and finally, "deadwood" are employees who are performing below standard and have little chance of moving up. Both solid citizens and deadwood are considered plateaued employees. In the defender firms, 66 percent of the employees were plateaued as compared to 27 percent in the analyzer firms. Fifty percent of the employees in the analyzers were considered comers compared to 19 percent in the defender firms and 23 percent were seen as stars in an analyzer situation in contrast to 15 percent in the defender scenario. Promotion opportunities clearly depend upon company strategy.

Promotions are part of the organization's reward system. The relationships among business strategy, reward systems, and corporate culture have been studied by Kerr and Slocum (1987). This in-depth study of 14 companies focused on their corporate growth strategies. The authors used the steady state versus evolutionary dichotomy. Steady-state firms are primarily internally focused. They may grow as the result of internally developed new products or through increased penetration of existing markets. On the other hand, evolutionary firms actively pursue new products and markets through mergers and acquisitions. Kerr and Slocum found that all but one firm with a steady-state strategy had adapted what they called a hierarchy-based reward system. All of the firms with an evolutionary strategy used a performance-based reward system.

In a hierarchy-based reward system, performance evaluation is subtle and subjective. Performance is defined qualitatively as well as quantitatively. Superiors have a great deal of control over evaluation and, consequently, mobility within the firm. A close relationship with superiors and other mentors is essential in order to be successful. The reward system motivates more cooperative effort and long-term commitment. Managers are promoted from within and promotions are often given to an employee more for developmental reasons than for business reasons. There are many lateral and diagonal moves designed to help the employee understand the whole company and build stronger internal relationships. The system performs the function of completely socializing the younger manager into a strong corporate culture.

The performance-based system is more objective. Rewards are based upon clearly defined expectations. The employee is much less dependent on the superior for evaluation or development. In fact, there is generally little concern with employee development. Socialization is not a primary purpose of the performance-based reward system. Neither cooperation with others nor learning the whole system were emphasized. Promotions were not necessarily from within – many top managers were brought in from outside. Kerr and Slocum (1987) describe the situation as a "mutually exploitive relationship."

Each reward system seems to fit the needs of the firms in which they were found. The steady state firms were mature capital-intensive operations such as aluminum, forest products, power generation, pharmaceuticals, and machine tools. It was felt that successful managers would have a long-term commitment to the firm, and be able to function well in a highly integrated organization. The hierarchy-based reward system develops such managers. The firms with an evolutionary strategy were generally conglomerates whose success depends on the management of a portfolio of businesses. In this situation, commitment to a particular business is of less value (and some might argue is actually a liability). Such firms are successful when the various businesses or divisions are given a high level of autonomy and are evaluated as objectively as possible. Loyalty and commitment are not a concern in a system where the possibility of divestment of businesses is a part of the corporate strategy. Again, the reward system promotes the type of behavior that is most compatible with the corporate strategy.

At this point, we present, in some detail, one more important conceptual system for classifying career systems. While similar to those described above, this model introduces additional categories and further refinements that may prove helpful in furthering our understanding of managerial careers. This model of career systems, developed by Sonnenfeld and Peiperl (1988), is based on two dimensions: supply flow and assignment flow. Supply flow refers to the degree to which personnel may easily move into and out of the firm. An internal supply flow implies promotion from within. External supply means that the firm actively recruits managerial and professional personnel from external sources. Assignment flow describes the bases for making job assignment and promotion decisions. These are seen within this model as being based primarily on either individual performance or on the degree of contribution to the group effort. Combining these two career properties results in four cells, some of which are very similar to the categories discussed previously. When an internal supply flow is combined with assignment based on contribution to the group, we have the career system that Sonnenfeld and Peiperl call the "club." Internal supply combined with assignment based on individual contribution is referred to as the "academy". External supply plus individual assignment criteria results in the "baseball team," and external supply with a group assignment basis is known as the "fortress."

The "club" recruits new employees primarily at the entry level and develops them slowly and carefully. The socialization of those selected into the trainee program in the public utility described by Sheridan et al. (1990) would be typical of "club" practice. There is an emphasis on fair treatment of members and loyalty to the organization is expected.

Assignments and promotions are based on contribution to the group not just individual performance. Members see their firm as providing important services – as having an important mission. Strategically, "clubs" are likely to be defenders, trying to perform efficiently and effectively within a limited domain. They are often monopolies or in regulated industries. Examples given by Sonnenfeld and Peiperl include utilities, airlines, banks, surface common carriers, as well as the military and government agencies.

Firms where internal supply flow is combined with assignment based on individual contribution are the "academies." Here the emphasis is on recruiting employees early in their career and developing them in-house. There is more emphasis on differentiating among employees based on their individual contributions, according to Sonnenfeld and Peiperl (1988). Large, well-established firms such as IBM, Kodak, and Exxon are typical examples of "academies."

Within the "academy" there are often sophisticated career development practices: assessment centers, management development programs, career tracking, sponsorship of high potential employees, and dual career ladders. The system is designed to develop and retain in-house talent. As a result, employees are oriented toward personal growth and career development.

Strategically, firms using the "academy" career system are likely to be analyzers. They are protecting established core businesses but are also constantly looking for new products and services. They try to combine stability and innovation. They need employees who are motivated to learn new things and take moderate risks while remaining loyal to the firm. Sonnenfeld and Peiperl (1988) state that the following types of firms use the "academy system": office products, pharmaceuticals, electronics, automobiles, and consumer products. The concept of tournament mobility fits nicely in this type of setting. There is an orientation toward long-term development of talented personnel. However, advancement is a function of individual performance which is evaluated on a regular basis. There are, in fact, likely to be multiple tournaments on-going in various functions and divisions. A number of forces dictate against the adher-ence to a strict tournament in which only early winners succeed. These include the nature of the business (multiple existing products or services plus the constant search for new opportunities) and the nature of the career system (long-term commitment, plus lots of lateral movement). Where more uncertainty exists early predictions are much tougher to make with any accuracy, because future needs are unknown. It is better to delay selection and develop many people and give them opportunities to prove themselves in many different settings.

The third type of career system described by Sonnenfeld and Peiperl (1988) is the "baseball team". As the name suggests, the orientation here is toward obtaining the best available talent in the labor market. These firms are looking for proven individual per-formers, and are open to external labor markets at all levels. There is little concern with employee training and development. High turnover is expected, and therefore, there is no point in succession planning. The firm is often looking for high levels of cre-ativity and innovation, and would be catego-rized stategically as a prospector. Successful employees are highly motivated people who see themselves as minor celebrities. Examples here include broadcasting, advertising, law firms, consulting firms, investment banks, and software development. The competition is very open, with employers continually searching for new talent, and at the same time dis-carding those who are no longer that useful.

The last category is the "fortress" or the "institution under siege". This organization is struggling to survive, and its needs take precedence over any individual concerns. They are hiring and firing in reaction to immediate market conditions. They may be in highly competitive businesses, or in a crisis or turnaround scenario. The firm may be reacting to a change in the external business environment, and/or may have changed its business strategy. Such reactor firms are of-ten out of control as a result of poor manage-ment or due to the nature of their business. Examples given by Sonnenfeld and Peiperl (1988) are hotels, retailing, publishing, tex-tiles, and natural resources.

The career paths of top executives

Next, we describe how these factors and others have influenced the process of succession to the top position in a large corporation: the chief executive officer. Many of the conclu-sions in this section are supported more fully by research reported in Forbes and Piercy (1991).

Although this is an oversimplification, we divide the career of a top executive into two crucial competitions. The first contest takes about 15 years and determines who will reach the threshold to top management: that is, the positions of general manager (at the division or regional level) or functional vice president (at the corporate level). This level appears to be a natural breakpoint in career progression. The salaries of senior executives take a big jump at about this point (Korn, 1988). The time taken to reach this level is a strong predictor of the time to reach the top. Those who have reached this level suddenly have much more responsibility and are much more visible to top management. They have a sub-stantial piece of the action and are now close enough to the top to be considered seriously as contenders for chief executive officer. The second important contest takes on average another 10 years, and decides who will be the leader of the entire corporation.

The early years

We define the "early years" to extend from the time the individual enters the work force

501

(at about age 24) through the time of promotion to the level of general manager or functional vice president (at about age 39). One very important signal that is typically attained before beginning the career is the level of education. We discuss this further in relation to advancement during the middle years; however, it can also affect a person's credibility from the very beginning of the career.

As discussed earlier, in some firms very early performance and promotion seem to be prerequisites for further upward mobility (tournament mobility). A study of the entire careers of chief executives revealed that, on the average, they attained their first management position after about five years; however, there was a great deal of variance about this average. It was also found that many future chief executives changed employers at least once during the first five years of their career (Forbes & Piercy, 1991).

Other signals begin to come into play as early as the first ten years of the career. Those whose functional background is related to the critical problems facing the corporation begin to move ahead. Breadth of experience is also related to upward mobility. Over two-thirds of top executives changed functional areas during years six through ten. In addition, some began to obtain more general experience and visibility through cross-functional positions, such as product or brand managers or plant managers. Breadth of experience was by far the most important variable in predicting the choice of a general manager by top executives in a policy-capturing exercise (Forbes & Piercy, 1991, chapter 4). In this study, the signals of early upward movement and functional area did not consistently influence the general management promotion decision because these signals varied with organizational strategy.

Others have shown that entering the company through a prestigious training program, and starting work in a powerful department can provide an early boost to the career

(Sheridan et al., 1990). This is also the time when a young manager may have the opportunity to be evaluated in a corporate assessment center. A positive evaluation will be a strong, long-lasting signal to promotion decision makers (Thornton & Byham, 1982). The more successful managers in the Japanese study were those with better vertical exchanges who became members of the supervisor's ingroup (Wakabayashi et al., 1988). Many of the chief executives in our CEO study (Forbes & Piercy, 1991, chapter 8) were assigned as an "assistant to" a senior manager early in their career.

Towards the end of this period, many top managers receive assignments in the international area, further increasing their breadth of experience. Also, those who reach the top are not likely to have changed employers during the last five years of the early career period. It seems that the organization is looking for evidence of loyalty and commitment among those being considered for higher level positions.

These common career events provide an opportunity for the young manager to learn more about the company, and also to begin developing important networks (Kotter, 1982, 1988). In addition, one other function is served which is equally important: These positions provide increased visibility for the young manager. He or she becomes more familiar to higher-level executives, who, in turn, become more comfortable with these people. The important career signals at this early stage seem to be telling higher management that the employee is a competent professional or manager, that he or she is trying to learn different aspects of the business, and is becoming known by others in the organization, particularly those in the upper echelons. The successful future top executive has begun to build credibility and visibility.

The middle years
The "middle years" of a top executive's career can be defined as from the time that

general management or functional vice president is reached (approximately age 39) until the time when the appointment as chief executive officer occurs (approximately age 50). This second important phase of the top executive's career has not yet been extensively researched. At this level, executives are much more visible to top-level decision makers, and decisions should be based more on direct evidence of performance. However, a great deal of subjectivity still enters into the choice of whom to promote.

Sorcher (1985, 5) boils it all down to the fundamental question: "Can he or she run things the way we want them run?" This query addresses not only bottom-line performance but also "soft" issues such as values, culture, and process, and even personal chemistry. Henry Ford's reason for firing Lee Iaccoca was simply: "Well, sometimes you just don't like somebody" (Iacocca, 1984, 127). A powerful halo surrounds the candidate with whom senior managers and directors are familiar and comfortable (Sorcher, 1985).

Kanter (1977) has observed the tendency within one large corporation for promotions to be based on personal similarity to the higher-level decision makers. This practice of "homosocial reproduction" is supported by broader studies of the backgrounds of top executives. CEOs are very likely to come from middle- or upper-class backgrounds and be the sons (very rarely the daughters) of business executives or professionals (Forbes & Piercy, 1991). They are also very well educated, with many having degrees from a small number of elite universities. However, education and socioeconomic origins seem to be somewhat compensatory factors with respect to their impact on promotability. For those with degrees from the right schools, social origins do not seem to matter; and for those of elite social background, education does not seem to be that important in predicting upward mobility (Useem & Karabel, 1986). Other studies have suggested that membership in the right clubs, religious denominations,

and political parties may affect promotion chances (Markham et al., 1987). Similar backgrounds and experiences seem to enhance credibility, familiarity, and liking.

As discussed earlier, the ambiguity and uncertainty inherent in the promotion decision opens the door to political influence at the individual level (Ferris & Judge, 1991) and to power struggles at the functional level (Pfeffer, 1981). However, there is evidence that top executive succession can be done in a logical, rational manner despite the politics. In 1981, the aristocratic, English-born, finance-oriented, CEO of General Electric, Reg Jones, chose as his successor an Irish-Catholic son of a train conductor, who was a chemical engineer, had not served in any of GE's major businesses, and who had previously acknowledged needing "improvement in handling socio-political relationships" (Tichy & Sherman, 1993). It seems that in this case, at least, the decision makers were wise enough to foresee that the organization needed considerable changes, including dismantling of the overly bureaucratic structure (much of which was created by the incumbent CEO, Jones). This was not an easy sell, however. In order to convince the board, Jones devised an elaborate "horse race," the purpose of which was to give the top decision makers time to get to know and accept this "risky maverick": Jack Welch (Vancil, 1987, 194).

PRACTICAL CONSIDERATIONS

A firm's success depends on the availability of competent human resources. Without the correct promotion and succession system in place, the firm will not be able to accomplish its strategic objectives. Therefore, it is essential that top managers and human resources professionals be aware of the strong connection between strategic planning and promotion and succession planning as described above.

One might view promotion and succession

systems as integrally linked. The first is a necessity in every organization, while the second is desirable but not always necessary. From the company perspective, promotion systems are enhanced by succession planning. If a succession system is well conceived, implemented and updated, one or more qualified candidates for promotion should be identified for any position which may be open. The higher the position in the organization hierarchy, the more valuable is succession planning and the more resources can be devoted to its implementation. An effective system should include inputs and participation by employees, line management, and the human resources function. In some cases, employees' peers may also supply inputs.

Promotion systems may take several forms but all satisfy two essential requirements. They are to fill vacancies with qualified persons and to reward good performance. Both are necessary for the success of any organization.

From the employees' perspective, the opportunity for moving up in a line of promotion should be based on length of service, or a demonstration of the ability to perform the next higher-level job, or a combination of the two. When the employees are covered by a union contract, the heavier weighting is usually given to length of service in the present position.

Where professional people are involved, it is important that the promotion ladder be divided into three to four discrete levels of experience and competence so that salary progression can take place between promotions with the additional incentive of promotional increases at periodic intervals. It is also important to follow the dual ladder principle, and provide for professional compensation on a par with managerial compensation so that outstanding professionals can be appropriately rewarded without having to become managers. This principle applies to scientists, engineers, accountants, lawyers, and salespeople, among others. It is based on the fact that not all specialists make good managers, nor are all

managers necessarily good specialists, but both are essential to a sound organization and both should be compensated appropriately.

Promotions occur when it has been determined that a position needs to be filled. The first step is the identification of the responsibilities and required qualifications for the position. The next step would be the identification of candidates. In some organizations, jobs are posted so any interested employee may apply. In others, the unit with the job opening works with Human Resources to identify candidates from within the unit or from other units. Usually the informal network of managers is also effective in identifying and screening candidates.

In some companies, employees may participate in a kind of employee opportunity program, where they make their desires for advancement known to the human resources function (HR), with or without the knowledge of their supervisor. The reason for such a discretionary program is that some supervisors may keep highly qualified employees out of the market for promotions within other areas. At the same time, some supervisors may be only too happy to offer for promotion employees whose performance is not up to par. Either of these tactics succeeds only in the short run, and the long-term result is that the supervisor is discredited.

A process used to prepare individuals for promotion, and make them visible to those outside of their immediate chain of command, is rotation of assignment. In this process, two or more employees may exchange positions for six months to a year to gain broader experience, demonstrate competence, and achieve greater visibility. The use of such techniques is expected to increase in the future as firms reduce the number of middle and general managers. This results in fewer promotional opportunities and less visibility for the employee, and fewer key positions in which to evaluate managers for further promotion.

Another effective way to identify candidates for advancement (especially at the lower levels) is to find out what they do with their own time. Outside activities provide an opportunity for employees to demonstrate initiative, responsibility, and leadership skill. Discovering these activities may provide as much information about managerial potential as on-the-job work experience. In addition, work groups generally produce informal leaders who might be identified as candidates for promotion.

Many companies use elaborate manual or computerized succession-planning systems, but these are costly and in an uncertain and discontinuous business environment they may not produce a satisfactory payback. Organizational and position restructuring make succession planning a highly speculative process. Neither the candidate nor the position may be available five or ten years from now. On the other hand, short-range succession planning or a "candidates ready in a year" plan probably makes good sense.

In selecting a candidate for promotion, as much care should be used as when the hiring decision was made. Mistakes are costly and are of two kinds. First is the promotion of someone who will fail or succeed only minimally in the new position. Second is the failure to promote someone who will perform in an outstanding manner. To minimize either of these errors, a team selection process is recommended. Involve at least three people in interviewing and making the selection. Attempt to reach a consensus, but if this is not possible, a two-out-of-three vote will usually be sufficient.

Given the importance of providing equal opportunity, the human resources function must be fully involved in the process of promotion. This will ensure not only compliance, but also provide a broader and more objective look at the candidate. HR should also have the most information available on the candidates, and is where the corporate strategic view can best be implemented.

Drawing from our review of theory and research, we must carefully consider what criteria are being used to make promotion and succession decisions. These decisions are made by human beings who often rely on a small number of simple cues or "signals". Academicians have inferred the existence of different career systems by identifying the signals used in making promotion decisions. Practitioners may change existing career systems or develop new ones by influencing the choice of these signals. For example, if decision makers, consciously or unconsciously, look for signals such as socioeconomic background, or the right education, then sponsored mobility will occur. If they believe that early performance and promotion are important indicators of ability, then we will see tournament mobility. Other signals that we have seen in the studies discussed above have included university status, assessment center evaluation, entry into a special trainee program, entry into a powerful department, early functional area, and a high level of lateral intrafirm mobility. Many of these signals are legitimate indicators of promotability. However, often career paths become institutionalized. That is, the use of a signal that seemed to make sense in the past leads to many powerful decision makers with similar backgrounds. Also, some managers may play politics and base their decisions on self-interest rather than the interest of the organization. Of course, in a changing environment this practice can be disastrous.

The recent trend of corporate boards to look outside the organization for new leadership suggests that the typical inside succession system is not working adequately. As firms face increased competition and the uncertainties of discontinuous change, many boards of directors have chosen to bypass the normal promotion and succession systems. When companies are in trouble, boards often look outside for a new CEO. This has happened recently at IBM, Kodak, and Black & Decker. The reason for this is not so much a perception of a lack of internal talent but instead the belief that the company needs new direction, vision, or even a change in its culture.

Choosing a CEO from outside the company or from another industry may seem illogical to some (e.g., many have questioned the selection of Gerstner from RJR Nabisco to head IBM) but others believe in the principle of universal management skills. That is, if a person is a skilled manager, he or she is capable of managing any organization.

Choosing an outsider as CEO causes some inevitable ripple effects. The remaining people at the next level of the organization may not fit in with the new top executive and the new culture. In addition, the CEO is likely to bring in other individuals with whom he or she has had good working relationships so as to build a firm base of support in what may be an otherwise hostile environment. Of course, this will then cause uncertainty and anxiety throughout the organization. Although sometimes outside selection is inevitable, a more flexible, more effective, internal system will usually result in a smoother transition.

RECOMMENDATIONS FOR THE FUTURE

Today, a new system for identifying and developing top management talent is desperately needed. In less volatile, less competitive times, organizations had more tolerance for poor promotion, succession, and career development systems. If the selections were not the best, the company would still survive. Today, large corporations seem to be unable to identify acceptable executive talent within the firm. At all levels the costs of incorrect promotion decisions are considerable. It has been estimated that the cost of a failed general manager is $500,000. This figure includes only the costs of selection, relocation, outplacement, and replacement of the failed executive, not the business costs of poor performance and poor morale (McCall, Lombardo, & Morrison, 1988). The total costs

would easily run into millions of dollars. Poor decisions by a CEO can jeopardize the very survival of the firm.

The traditional organization of the past was a tall, many-layered structure. Communication flows were typically up and down, mostly down. Various functional areas were isolated from one another, except when forced to interact. All important decisions were made at high levels of the firm. The larger firms adopted product divisions which were, in theory, decentralized, self-contained units. However, even here, elaborate information and control systems were designed to manage these units from the top. Internally, the organization was very efficient, but it was not particularly good at recognizing or responding to changes in the external environment.

Human resources practices evolved in this context. Top management could not possibly get to know many personnel at the lower, or even at the middle, levels of the company. Therefore, they established procedures to identify the most promising young people at the lower levels, and to develop these high potential employees. It was important to expose these future executives to a variety of functional areas, and to begin moving them up quickly so that they would soon reach a level at which meaningful decisions could be made. As a result, the most common path to the top became one that involved a fast start, breadth of experience, and often, responsibility for a division at a relatively early age. It was assumed and expected that the high-potential employees would stay with the firm throughout their entire career, so that the organization would realize a return on its substantial investment.

One problem with this traditional method is that it is based upon early identification of and commitment to a small number of serious contenders. Much is invested in these individuals. They are sponsored, mentored, and given developmental assignments, all of which is highly appropriate assuming that the very best people have been chosen. In any case, the phenomenon of the self-fulfilling prophecy begins to play a part. Both the individual and the organization become committed to seeing early predictions come true. This process can prove very costly. The company may be betting on the wrong horses; and may not discover its mistake for quite a long time. In addition, there is no way to assure that the best managers, in which you have much invested, will stay with the firm, and in today's business environment it is much less likely that they will.

Another problem with this strategy is the effect it has on those who are passed over. Motivation and productivity will fall dramatically for the employees who know that they have not won the early contests, and therefore are out of the running for higher-level positions. The problems of the plateaued mid-career employee, and the conflicts faced by women (among others) can be linked to the existence of this system (Rosenbaum, 1984).

The feasibility of an alternative system increases as we examine the direction in which business organizations are heading. In order to reduce costs, increase organizational flexibility, and improve employee involvement and motivation, many firms are moving toward flatter, less hierarchical structures. More work is being done and more decisions are being made by teams. Firms are pushing decision-making authority down to the lowest possible level, and eliminating communication barriers among the functional areas, among the remaining levels of authority, and between the firm and its environment (e.g., its customers, suppliers, communities, etc.). Many are allowing divisions, work teams, and individuals to become more autonomous than ever before.

Some fear the chaos and confusion of such organizations while others praise the simplicity. One of the latter is Jack Welch, who has transformed General Electric. According to Welch, the excessive layers of the traditional business organization just hide weaknesses and mediocrity (Tichy & Charan, 1989). Conversely, we would add, they also hide talent. In the flatter, more open organization, employees at very low levels have meaningful responsibility and can make important decisions. Everyone is more visible. It is becoming commonplace for engineers to interact with marketing managers, for production workers to communicate with customers, and for salespeople to share information with the president.

Several other factors dictate that a decisive change is needed in the way we promote and develop executives. The first is demographics. As the "baby bust" continues, business firms will have fewer younger employees from which to choose future managers. They will have larger numbers of more experienced personnel in the middle levels of the organization. There are also many more women and minorities present within the work force, and the net increase in these categories will continue to be much greater than for those who have traditionally received most of the promotions in American corporations – that is, white males (for a more detailed discussion of these trends, see Chapter 14 on workplace diversity earlier in this volume).

Future promotion practices will be further complicated by the internationalization of the business world. As American firms continue to expand abroad, more foreign-born executives are being promoted into high-ranking positions in American firms. Many American firms are being acquired by foreign owners and being managed by foreign top executives, and of course, many foreign corporations are setting up shop in the U.S. and employing American managers.

Another far-reaching set of changes involves the increased growth of small and mid-sized firms, the downsizing of larger corporations, and movement away from the practice of employees spending their entire career with one firm. Much of what has been described in this chapter relates to promotion practices within larger organizations. Smaller firms must also be more careful to promote the best candidates for managerial positions, but the critical problems may be very different and complicated by issues such as family ownership considerations. Individuals who aspire to upward mobility must be concerned not only about credibility and visibility within their own firm, but also within the industry and the broader business and nonbusiness communities.

An important supporting factor is technology. More people at lower levels will have the information and the tools to make important decisions and those at the top will have better measures of who is making the "good calls." Improved communications technology will also give more employees higher levels of visibility. However, communications must not be primarily accomplished through electronic media. Top management must make personal contact with high-performing employees in all areas of the firm. Enhanced human resources information systems will not replace personal contacts, but will supplement these with a variety of measures of performance.

Promotion systems should have as their goal the proper internal placement of all employees, so as to maximize organizational performance and individual satisfaction. We recommend a much more open contest for promotions than has ever existed before. This system should reward performance, while recognizing that performance as an individual contributor does not imply managerial ability. Better assessments of management skills and potential are needed. Decision makers must be educated so as to avoid the tendency to allow promotions to be unduly influenced by social, ethnic, or national origins, race, gender, formal education, family ties, connections, politics, or a career history that includes what were, traditionally, all the right moves. Experience would continue to be important, but the emphasis would be on the quality not the quantity of experience. This would allow the younger "baby busters" to compete with the more experienced "baby boomers." It would allow women (and men) who leave the work force and return to avoid being placed on a "mommy track."

To ensure that all management potential is identified and developed, we envision the wider application of such practices as developmental assessment centers. To avoid biasing promotion decisions, the results would be available only to the individual and to top management. The assessment center might be repeated at various points in the career, and also would be used with senior managers (White & De Vries, 1990). Positions within the organization would be evaluated with regard to their use as "assessment positions" or on-the-job assessment centers (Gaertner, 1988). The learning that comes from various types of career experiences has been identified (McCall et al., 1988). Job assignments would be based, at least partly, on the developmental needs of each individual. There would be greater use of team management and peer and subordinate evaluations. All performance evaluations would include assessments of future potential and recommendations for development. Employees should also be evaluated by outside contacts: customers, clients, suppliers, community leaders, etc.

The company would encourage new learning and development at all levels and at all ages. Formal education would be supported but not required. Cross-functional training and movement would be encouraged, but there would still be room for the functional specialist. Employees would be realistically informed of career opportunities within and outside the organization.

More entrepreneurial or "intrapreneurial" activities within the firm would be encouraged, as would involvement in community activities. These make excellent developmental and evaluative opportunities. Risk taking would be encouraged and failure tolerated. High levels of performance would be reinforced by gainsharing reward systems. Everyone would be considered a "high potential" employee.

In summary, our focus in this chapter has been on internal promotion and succession systems. However, in the future we anticipate continued movement away from the traditional promotion-from-within policy of the "academies" and "clubs," and toward the policy of selection from either within or from outside, typical of the "baseball team" (Sonnenfeld & Peiperl, 1988). More firms are feeling the need to recruit the very best talent even if it exists beyond their boundaries. Likewise, individuals may need to see themselves as "free agents," willing to move wherever the best opportunities lie. In fact, in the future, more employees will probably be turning to small and mid-size firms, and into entrepreneurial activities. Some of the concerns discussed in this chapter may be less severe in such environments but others may become more problematic unless professional human resources practices and policies are developed and applied.

This is only a vague sketch of what may appear to be a radically different approach to promotion and succession systems. Our challenge to human resources managers and to top executives is to begin to try these ideas. Discover what will work and what will not. Continually fine-tune the system. A new business world with new organizational structures and management styles requires new human resources practices.

REFERENCES

Beatty, R. W., Schneier, C. E., & McEvoy, G. M. (1987). Executive development and management succession. In K. M. Rowland & G. R. Ferris (eds.), *Research in Personnel and Human Resources Management*, vol. 5, pp. 289–322. Greenwich, CT: JAI Press.

Berlew, D. T., & Hall, D. T. (1966). The socialization of managers: Effects of expectations of performance. *Administrative Science Quarterly*, 11, 207–23.

Bray, D. W., Campbell, R. J., & Grant, D. L. (1974). *Formative Years in Business: A long-term AT&T study of managerial lives*. New York: Wiley.

Cooper, W. H., Graham, W. J., & Dyke, L. S. (1993). Tournament players. In G. R. Ferris (ed.), *Research in Personnel and Human Resources Management*, vol. 11, pp. 83–132. Greenwich, CT: JAI Press.

Ferris, G. R., Buckley, M. R., & Allen, G. M. (1992).

Promotion systems in organizations. *Human Resources Planning*, 15, 47–68.

Ferris, G. R., & Judge, T. A. (1991). Personnel/human resources management: A political perspective. *Journal of Management*, 17, 447–88.

Forbes, J. B. (1987). Early intraorganizational mobility: Patterns and influences. *Academy of Management Journal*, 30, 110–25.

Forbes, J. B., & Piercy, J. E. (1991). *Corporate Mobility and Paths to the Top: Studies for human resource and management development specialists*. Westport, CT: Quorum Books.

Friedman, S. D. (1986). Succession systems in large corporations: Characteristics and correlates of performance. *Human Resource Management*, 25, 191–213.

Gaertner, K. N. (1988). Managers' careers and organizational change. *Academy of Management Executive*, 11, 311–18.

Iacocca, L. (with W. Novak) (1984). *Iacocca: An autobiography*. New York: Bantam Books.

Kanter, R. M. (1977). *Men and Women of the Corporation*. New York: Basic Books.

Kerr, J. L., & Slocum, J. W. (1987). Managing corporate cultures through reward systems. *Academy of Management Executive*, 2, 99–108.

Korn, L. (1988). *The Success Profile*. New York: Simon & Schuster.

Kotter, J. P. (1982). *The General Managers*. New York: Free Press.

Kotter, J. P. (1988). *The Leadership Factor*. New York: Free Press.

McCall, M. W., Lombardo, M. M., & Morrison, A. M. (1988). *The Lessons of Experience: How successful executives develop on the job*. Lexington, MA: Lexington Books.

Markham W. T., Harlan, S. L., & Hackett, E. J. (1987). Promotion opportunities in organizations: Causes and consequences. In K. M. Rowland & G. R. Ferris (eds.), *Research in Personnel and Human Resources Management*, vol. 5, pp. 223–87. Greenwich, CT: JAI Press.

Ouchi, W. (1981). *Theory Z: How American business can meet the Japanese challenge*. Reading, MA: Addison-Wesley.

Piercy, J. E., & Forbes, J. B. (1981). Industry differences in chief executive officers. *MSU Business Topics*, 29, 17–29.

Pfeffer, J. (1981). *Power in Organizations*. Marshfield, MA: Pitman.

Rosenbaum, J. E. (1979). Tournament mobility: Career patterns in a corporation. *Administrative Science Quarterly*, 24, 220–41.

Rosenbaum, J. E. (1984). *Career Mobility in a Corporate Hierarchy*. Orlando, FL: Academic Press.

Ruderman, M. N. (1991). Promotion: Beliefs and reality. *Issues and Observations*, 11, 4–6.

Sheridan, J. E., Slocum, J. W., Buda, R., & Thompson, R. (1990). Effects of corporate sponsorship and departmental power on career tournaments: A study of intraorganizational mobility. *Academy of Management Journal*, 33, 578–602.

Slocum, J. W., & Cron, W. L. (1988). Business strategy, staffing, and career management issues. In M. London & E. M. Mone (eds.), *Career Growth and Human Resources Strategies*, 135–51. Westport, CT: Quorum.

Sonnenfeld, J. A., & Peiperl, M. A. (1988). Staffing policy as a strategic response: A typology of career systems. *Academy of Management Review*, 13, 588–600.

Sorcher, M. (1985). *Predicting Executive Success: What it takes to make it into senior management.* New York: Wiley.

Thornton, G. C., & Byham, W. C. (1982). *Assessment Centers and Managerial Performance.* New York: Academic Press.

Tichy, N., & Charan R. (1989). Speed, simplicity, self-confidence: An interview with Jack Welch. *Harvard Business Review*, Sept.–Oct., 112–20.

Tichy, N. M., & Sherman, S. (1993). *Control Your Destiny or Someone Else Will.* New York: Doubleday.

Turner, R. (1960). Modes of social ascent through education: Sponsored and contest mobility. *American Sociological Review*, 25, 855–67.

Useem, M., & Karabel, J. (1986). Pathways to top corporate management. *American Sociological Review*, 51, 184–200.

Vancil, R. F. (1987). *Passing the Baton: Managing the process of CEO succession.* Boston: Harvard Business School.

Vardi, Y., & Hammer, T. H. (1977). Intraorganizational mobility and career perceptions among rank and file employees in different technologies. *Academy of Management Journal*, 20, 624–35.

Veiga, J. F. (1983). Mobility influences during managerial career stages. *Academy of Management Journal*, 26, 64–85.

Veiga, J. F. (1985). To the beat of a different drummer: A comparison of managerial career paths. Paper presented at the annual meeting of The Academy of Management, San Diego, CA. August.

Vroom, V. H., & MacCrimmon, K. R. (1968). Toward a stochastic model of managerial careers. *Administrative Science Quarterly*, 13, 26–46.

Wakabayashi, M., Graen, G., Graen, M., & Graen, M. (1988). Japanese management progress: Mobility into middle management. *Journal of Applied Psychology*, 73, 217–27.

White, R. P., & DeVries, D. L. (1990). Making the wrong choice: Failure in the selection of senior-level managers. *Issues and Observations*, winter, 1–5.

☐ **Chapter 26** ☐

Management Development in a New Business Reality

Timothy T. Baldwin and Tom E. Lawson

INTRODUCTION

While it may have once been believed that effective managers are born and not made, there is now widespread agreement that management development, the complex process of enhancing individuals' effectiveness in present and future managerial roles, should be among the most important of organizational activities (Baldwin & Padgett, 1993; Bolt, 1989). Indeed, management development has become a multibillion dollar undertaking for organizations worldwide, and recent survey evidence suggests that over 90 percent of firms engage in some form of development activities for managers (Loo, 1991; Saari, Johnson, McLaughlin, & Zimmerle, 1988). The growth in organizational interest is due in large part to the harsh realities of an increasingly competitive business environment. Desperate for ways to maintain and increase competitiveness, organizations are turning to management development as a means to improve firm performance (Fulmer, 1990; Ulrich, 1989).

Interestingly, much of the existing literature on management development has lamented the *failure* of development efforts to significantly improve management skills or affect business performance (Campbell, Dunnette, Lawler, & Weick, 1970; Greiner, 1987; Hall, 1984). In fact, management development has traditionally been among the most maligned of human resources practices. As Hall (1984, 159) noted a decade ago, "if strategic human resource management is rare in contemporary organizations, then the strategic *development of managers* is virtually non-existent." Greiner (1987, 37) similarly concluded that "entertainment without development" accounts for about 75 percent of the management development budget." Indeed, the dirty little secret of management development has been that extensive organizational time and resources have been expended with little realization (or even expectation) of a value-added return. Moreover, despite the limited success of traditional development practice, the literature has been curiously sparse with respect to new approaches, refinements, and case studies of development initiatives.

In recent years, however, there has been something of a transformation of management development writing and practice. As noted earlier, the realities of global competition, downsizing, and organizational change have brought heightened interest to the management development arena. Authors now expound on the new frontiers of management development (Peters & Peters, 1990), and development as a strategy for corporate competitiveness (Bolt, 1989). In addition, organizations such as General Electric, Motorola, Northern Telecom, British Petroleum, and AT&T are striking out on their own with new and innovative approaches, and the literature is flush with accounts of such progressive organizational efforts (O'Reilly, 1993; Tichy, 1989; White, 1992).

A resounding theme in both the scholarly and popular press is that, like so many other business functions, management development must be "reengineered" if it is to truly add value in today's business context. It seems clear that sending a group of managers off to listen to management experts once a year is unlikely to effect much change in today's business context. However, less clear are the dimensions of management developmental approaches which *will* lead to greater impact. While there is a growing body of conceptual work on how managers really learn, and a burgeoning body of case studies of innovative corporate initiatives, there has been little synthesis of these bodies of literature.

The objective of this chapter is to take advantage of our academic/practitioner partnership to merge some of the recent theory and conceptual work on how managers learn with the reality of progressive management development practice. The chapter is divided into two parts. In the first part, we focus on what is known about how managers most effectively learn. A number of recent research streams have challenged conventional thinking in that regard, and our goal is to synthesize this emerging literature. Specifically, we identify three conditions for optimal management development in today's business context: (1) development in context; (2) development in collaboration; and (3) development with accountability.

In the second part, we move to a practical discussion of how these conditions for development can be translated into management development design. Specifically, we focus on describing and illustrating several innovations which reflect the new face of management development in progressive firms and embody the conditions for development described in the first part of the chapter. We conclude with some summary comments and a discussion of implications for future management development research and practice.

CONDITIONS FOR MANAGERIAL DEVELOPMENT

Development in context

Traditional management development has generally embraced a learning model whereby participants are expected to put aside their daily work for a time and go away to learn from management experts. The experts stand in front of the classroom, and present to managers what they need to know in order to be successful and effective. The logic has been to remove managers from the daily stressors and distractions of the workplace in order to provide a conducive environment for the study of general management problems and models of effective performance.

Of course, the traditional approach assumes that management development professionals are able to *predict* what business pressures and issues managers are going to face and thus are able to supply, in advance, theory that will address those issues. However, as Dixon (1993) notes, such assumptions are tenuous in a new business reality because, more than ever, managers are facing problems that are novel and for which no clear-cut answers are known. Without explicit answers, managers need to learn their way out of problems rather than applying known solutions.

Moreover a recurring theme in current literature is that development will occur best when managers attempt to deal with problems (including all the attendant stressors and distractions) in their natural managerial context. Such natural developmental contexts have at least four dimensions that distinguish them from the traditional management development model: (1) the focus is on real work; (2) problems precede theory; (3) external experts are used on a just-in-time basis; and (4) the development process is spaced to mirror the natural process of learning and growth.

Focus on real work

It is hardly controversial to suggest that development occurs primarily in response to the challenges of daily life. However, prior to recent interest in action learning (Kable, 1989; Jones, 1990; Marsick, 1990) and experience-based development (McCall, Lombardo, & Morrison, 1988), that maxim has largely been ignored in management development design. Pascale and Athos (1979) argue that one does not become an artist by "painting someone else's dots," and that intellectualizing and verbalizing will never accomplish the degree of managerial learning that experiencing, feeling, and sensing in one's own work context will. Tichy (1989) similarly contends that management is a clinical practice, and that management development therefore has to get much closer to the real world of practicing managers.

Put simply, the notion is that truly significant management development will not occur in the abstract, away from the challenges of managing the organization, because those challenges provide the essential grist for change. Even the more experiential forms of classroom training such as case studies or role plays are unlikely by themselves to provide the level of reality that is needed for significant development to occur. In such hypothetical activities the individual is not compelled to experience the frustration of failing at something he or she truly cares about, the deep concern that others will suffer for one's mistakes, the satisfaction of

completion, nor the overwhelming complexity of decisions (Dixon, 1993).

This is not to say that no deliberate action or expert input is useful or necessary to improve the learning process. Indeed, simply facing real problems is not sufficient for development to occur. Action must be accompanied by reflection on action and, indeed, some organization implementations of action learning have failed miserably because the guidance for learning from experience was insufficient (Froiland, 1994).

It should also be noted that focusing on real work does not mean the abandonment of all prior management development content and structure. It simply ensures that the focus will be on that which is most salient to the managerial population in question. Put another way, a developmental focus on real work does not preclude classroom learning or other traditional educational formats, but it does alter the reason and focus for coming together (Dixon, 1993).

Problems precede theory

Many traditional management development programs incorporate experiential exercises, preprogram assignments, and action planning. For example, managers are frequently encouraged to try out the principles they have learned back at their own work site and even sometimes to partner with another participant in an application commitment. Whatever the form, this approach represents a model whereby theory *precedes* business problems. However, consistent with the discussion above regarding real work, several recent authors have suggested that the opposite model (i.e., problems preceding theory) is more compatible with today's business reality (Dixon, 1993; Ulrich, 1989).

From the perspective of the manager and the firm, there really are no "development" problems, per se, but only *business* problems, for which management development might be one competitive strategy. The fundamental goal of management development in a new business reality is not to learn new concepts or skills, but to be more committed, more focused, and more competitive in achieving business objectives. Management development will be most successful when it is understood that the manager's prime concern is with success at managing, and that learning is a subsidiary purpose. That is, managers want to be effective, but they do not necessarily want to be learners. They may accept being a learner for some time in order to become effective, but learning itself is not the paramount goal (Mumford, 1988). Hill (1993) suggests that managers, like all human beings, are most inclined to "learn what they have to" in order to succeed in present and future roles, and therefore will be relatively inattentive to other content.

In summary, recent literature suggests that development should no longer be seen as a discrete activity that precedes the real work it is intended to shape. The old model is that first people receive training and then they go out and achieve business results. The new model suggests a reversal of that sequence whereby managers are held accountable for the achievement of business results, and then development resources are provided to facilitate and enable achievement of those results.

Assuming that problems should precede theory acknowledges that, in a changing world, it is difficult to predict what issues managers will be facing. In addition, for most real-world problems there is more than one theoretical framework which may be useful for thinking through a problem. The crucial challenge is to match development opportunities with the present problems on a more just-in-time basis.

Just-in-time experts

A problem-then-theory model is consistent with the way in which organizations are approaching problems in domains outside management development (e.g., TQM, restructuring). The movement towards empowerment in the workplace means that no longer

should managers be seeking answers solely from experts. Within the framework of management development, experts are certainly sought out and heard and their opinions considered, but managers take the responsibility for critically reflecting on the information for themselves. Experts are still needed and valued but their role is more process-oriented and directed towards facilitation rather than simply providing subject matter expertise.

Also, external expert opinion becomes only one input among many that might inform the reasoning of a manager who is dealing with a difficult issue. Ulrich (1989) has characterized much traditional development as "parade of stars training" whereby a parade of external experts are retained to present their prepackaged messages. In contrast, valuable development information might also come from peers, who may be able to help managers see themselves as others see them; customers, who may promote the examination of assumptions and foster multiple perspectives on a problem; and other stakeholders who can lend additional perspective and data to the understanding of management problems. In addition, senior managers might be asked to serve as facilitators thereby ensuring a more real work-oriented, just-in-time nature to the information.

Combining the focus on real work with a problem-then-theory model it becomes clear that management development becomes less about listening to answers from experts and more about collecting valid information from a variety of sources so that the information can be considered in terms of the local business context. The key distinction is that expertise is sought in response to problems, not in advance of them.

Spaced time frames

Traditional management development programs are bounded; they have a beginning and an end. Programs are often off-site, discrete events in a compressed time format lasting from two days to three weeks. Participants typically come, register, learn, and leave. Compressed schedules facilitate travel and minimize time away from work, which translates into allowing managers to "get it over with" and get back to work (Dixon, 1993). Although there is an increasing trend to shorten programs and accommodate the pressing demands on today's manager, the problem with compressed schedules is that they are inconsistent with the natural process of human learning and development.

It is now well documented that human development, of any kind, is a process which can only occur over time. Particularly viewed in light of fundamental changes in managerial learning strategies (e.g., action learning and collaborative teams), time is needed to act, to see the results of one's action, to talk with others, and to reflect on the action. The flow of development should match the flow of the workplace where challenges also occur over time: problems occur, get better, decline in importance then resurface, are confounded with other issues, and are sometimes resolved through no action at all. Development occurs through the challenges of real work. Thus, the schedule of a management development program must correspond to the schedule of the work world. That means a management development program may need to be spaced out over six months to a year or more.

If development is thought of as a time away from work, then management development programs that last a year long are entirely unreasonable, particularly in an era of downsized firms and increased workloads. However, the goal is to blur the distinction between program time and work time such that program time essentially *becomes* work time. In that case, spaced time frames are consistent with business flows, and therefore both are more palatable to the busy executive and ultimately more effective.

Many traditional management development programs include a kind of follow-up activity that consists of either bringing participants back together to see what they have accomplished or a phone call or a survey to check on their progress. Neither of these activities is in the spirit of spaced learning. With spaced learning, periodic meetings are a part of the learning, not a way to determine if learning occurred or to report on its results.

It should be obvious that the realities of learning in context require a different and considerably more demanding role for management development professionals. Such a perspective places particular demands on external vendors to learn the business and to partner with client firms in order to achieve a level of understanding of ongoing managerial problems and issues, to space the development activity, and to provide just-in-time expertise. But if management development is to indeed have an impact on performance, such challenges must be addressed.

Development in collaboration

Traditional management development has been a decidedly individual activity. Management development professionals have implicitly viewed the interaction between the instructor and student, and between the student and materials, as the two most important sources of development (Johnson & Johnson, 1984). By contrast, the peer interaction and group dynamics which take place have been often viewed as either irrelevant or, at best, a convenient opportunity for networking or a coincidental by-product of a developmental initiative.

Recent authors contend that the focus on individualistic learning environments is unfortunate given the research in support of collaborative learning. Although the evidence is not unequivocal, studies over the years have consistently shown that cooperative learning can produce increased learning, creative insight, higher productivity, achievement, and quality of decision making (Johnson & Johnson, 1984). Others have similarly concluded that cooperative learning is viewed positively by managers and promotes greater rapport, discussion, and enjoyment of the learning process.

Of course, the ultimate goal of management development initiatives is to enhance *individuals'* abilities and knowledge in the service of the organization. Furthermore, in a stable environment with known facts and cause–effect relationships, individual learning may be more efficient and effective than collaboration. However, most of the critical issues managers face today are matters of interpretation not fact. In equivocal situations, the validity of ideas must be tested, not by facts, but against the reasoning of others. That is, much of the learning that is critical to organizations is learning that necessitates collaboration (Dixon, 1993).

Part of the value of collaboration in learning environments is that it facilitates the validation of ideas and provides controversy to challenge ideas. A second argument for collaborative learning is that it facilitates collaborative *working*. A number of influential writers have suggested that team-based structures will be the organizational form of the future. It follows that collaborative development will help create an environment that both induces and supports collaborative working.

Of course, just bringing managers together and hoping that fruitful collaborative learning will occur is wishful thinking. Some effort must be directed toward teaching collaborative skills such as communication, trust building, decision making, and conflict management. In addition, to promote productive collaborative learning requires attention to: (1) the composition of the development group; and (2) the creation of a strong group norm of shared responsibility among development participants.

Group composition

With respect to cohort composition, traditional wisdom has been that the best developmental results are obtained when managers are comparable in experience, level, and aptitude prior to entering a program (Langer, 1979). The preference for homogeneity in group composition has been driven in part by a desire to avoid providing training at the "lowest common denominator", that is, training from which everyone, regardless of aptitude, job level, or specific assignment can learn (Feldman, 1989).

In contrast, in today's business reality, the importance of having a heterogeneous development cohort seems self-evident. Pairing managers with those from different functions and levels, subordinates, vendors, and even customers, provides an opportunity for idea exchange and facilitates networking and richer understanding of important issues and perspectives.

Productive collaborative learning also requires that the development group be kept relatively small. In this vein, Penner and Craiger (1992) point out that under most circumstances, as the size of a training group increases, individual performance declines. This decline is generally attributed to a decline in motivation which might be attributed to evaluation effects (Harkins & Szymanski, 1989). Harkins and Szymanski have proposed that the potential for evaluation of a person's performance may influence how motivated he or she is to perform well, and a key factor that will influence such an evaluation occurring is group size. More specifically, as group size increases, individual members believe that the probability their individual performance can be identified and evaluated decreases, and their motivation correspondingly drops.

Moreover, while the existence of a social facilitation effect has been well documented for many years (Cottrell, 1972), there is also evidence that, under some conditions, social interaction can be *detrimental* to motivation and performance. For example, in a study of training designed to help people interpret a financial report, Saxe (1988) found that it was *moderate* levels of interaction which led to significantly higher performance on a written achievement test as opposed to either low interaction or high interaction. This suggests that an excess of interaction may produce a form of "social loafing" or "free rider" effect whereby a person believes that since he or she is one of several people working on a task, he or she can do relatively little but still reap the benefits of the group's performance (Kerr & Bruun, 1971; Latane, Williams, & Harkins, 1979). Thus, the management and development of group norms is also crucial to the success of collaborative learning strategies.

Collaborative norms

Management development professionals have long known that dysfunctional group norms can doom the best designed development efforts. For example, Mullen and Baumeister (1987) have used the term "diving" to describe a situation in which, because of group norms, individuals are motivated to perform at less than their best. One form of diving proposed by Mullen and Baumeister can result from a group norm that discourages excellence in performance by any group member. This is essentially the rate-busting effect first recorded by Roethlisberger and Dickson (1939). The other kind of diving occurs when the group determines that excellence in performance is inappropriate for a particular individual. For example, high-status members of a team may communicate the message to other members that excellence in performance from a low-status member is not appropriate. As a result, the low-status member does not attempt to do his or her best.

In short, there is compelling evidence in favor of collaborative learning environments, but only provided that the conditions for effective collaboration are present. In traditional learning groups, members are seldom held responsible for each other's learning. For collaborative learning to work well, there must be relatively small and diverse learning cohorts, with positive group norms that support shared responsibility. Group members are accountable to provide help and encouragement to each other to ensure that all members participate fully in the assigned tasks – a type of accountability which has not characterized most traditional management development activity.

Development with accountability

To reiterate a point made earlier, development will only occur when managers are faced with issues about which they care deeply so that their intellect, beliefs, and emotions are all engaged. And there must be some risk of failure. Nonetheless, traditional management development is notable for its lack of accountability (Wexley & Baldwin, 1986). The lack of accountability and rigorous evaluation may be attributable in part to a lingering bias that learning is a "delicate flower" that can not be "forced" or even aggressively managed in the way of other types of performance. For example, while forms of goal setting, incentive compensation, and "pay at risk" are now ubiquitous in other areas of organizational life, there has been a curious reluctance to implement such strategies in conjunction with management development.

Aside from providing no evidence to facilitate program improvement and redesign, the typical absence of specific objectives and measurement may be perceived by managers as a signal of the low importance of management development to the organization. Of course, organizations today generally *pronounce* that management development is vital to their mission and future, and development expenditures have risen dramatically. However, given that research has shown that neither management pronouncements nor resources expended are among the most salient signals of the organizational importance of development initiatives, it seems plausible that managers have often not perceived that their learning and development were as important as the pronouncements would suggest (Baldwin & Magjuka, 1991).

The lack of accountability becomes of even

greater concern in collaborative learning contexts where managers may be in a position to cooperate, but may not be motivated to do so because they believe it will have little or no effect on their personal outcomes. As noted by several recent authors (e.g., Latham, 1989; Mathieu, Martineau, & Tannenbaum, 1993), Bandura's (1986) social cognitive theory provides a useful theoretical model for predicting, understanding, and increasing the motivational determinants of development effectiveness. Social cognitive theory posits reciprocal determinism among the person's cognitions, the environment, and overt behavior. Put simply, behavior influences and is influenced by both cognitive and environmental contingencies. Bandura contends that individuals regulate their behavior based on their beliefs about their ability to accomplish a task, and their beliefs about the environmental consequences of their behavior (outcome expectancies). With respect to outcome expectancies, we suspect that managers have too often been aware that they share no real responsibility for learning, and will face no posttraining evaluation regarding the application of their skills to real business issues. The result is a decline in motivation and a low yield from development initiatives.

An effective reward structure in a cooperative context could take a number of forms but has to ensure a focus on group rewards and individual accountability. As Slavin (1983) notes, the provision of rewards based on group performance creates group member norms supporting performance. That is, if group success depends on the learning performance of all the group members, group members try to make the group successful by encouraging each other to excel. Even though rewards given to groups are likely to be less finely tuned to individual performance than rewards given to individuals, group members are hypothesized to create a very sensitive and effective reward system for each other when the efforts of all group members are required for group success.

At the same time, it is crucial to not neglect the importance of individual accountability even under cooperative learning and reward conditions. That is, it may well be that working in a group under certain circumstances does increase the learning of individuals in that group more than would working in other arrangements, but it is not *necessarily* so. In either case, a measure of *group* productivity provides no evidence of this one way or the other. For example, if a group produces an excellent project report but only a few members really contributed to it, it is unlikely that the group as a whole learned more than they might have if they had to produce their own individual outcome. Therefore, while it seems entirely appropriate to link management development with business outcomes and team projects, it is important to keep in mind that all learning is ultimately an individual phenomenon, and accountability at the individual level remains important.

Mumford (1988) suggests that prior to participating in any development experience, participants implicitly ask themselves several types of questions: Do I believe this development will help me or my subordinates? Are there risks for me if I perform poorly? How does this experience relate to my job performance? Not surprisingly, the yield from development initiatives will be maximized when managers perceive that desirable outcomes (or avoidance of undesirable outcomes) are attained as a result of their full commitment to a development program.

THE NEW FACE OF MANAGEMENT DEVELOPMENT

Dissatisfied with traditional development models, and in response to the rapidly changing business environment, a number of organizations are implementing progressive innovations in the design, delivery, and evaluation of their management development. Consistent with the discussion above, recent

518

innovations in development practice are often characterized by a shift to greater degrees of learning in context, collaborative learning, and accountability. In this section, we review several recent shifts in development practice under the headings of (1) linking management development with business challenges, (2) new delivery strategies, and (3) evaluation of bottom-line payback.

Linking management development with business challenges

For management development initiatives to be effective both for the individual and the company the focus of development must be carefully linked with and orchestrated against the organization's current and unfolding business challenges and imperatives. There are currently many approaches that are appropriate for coupling management development processes with business requirements, both within multinational and U.S.-based enterprises, but the primary approaches can involve any one or a combination of the following strategies: shareholder wealth creation/economic value-added; business unit strategy; strategy implementation; core competencies and competitive capabilities; organizational transformation; and globalization forces. These approaches, moreover, ensure that "development in context" is maximized, and that executive attention and organizational resources produce widespread results. Effective management development, therefore, requires contingent integration of knowledge from many organizational fronts.

Shareholder wealth creation and economic value-added.

Many companies have recently emphasized the management of their organizations for shareholder value (Rappaport, 1992). Corporate board members are also demonstrating increasing interest in ensuring that the company formulates and implements strategies that create shareholder wealth.

One measure that is used to assess value creation is called economic value-added (EVA). EVA represents after-tax operating profit minus the total annual cost of capital. Highly regarded big corporations (e.g., Coca-Cola, AT&T, Quaker Oats, Briggs & Stratton, CSX) are employing this concept to measure an operating unit's true profitability (Walbert, 1993). Accordingly, educating middle and advanced managers in these enterprises on the conceptual and financial fundamentals of EVA, and its application within the operating context of their units, constitutes a new focus for development. AT&T, for example, benchmarks managerial and work-team performance incentives using EVA as an indicator of results.

Business unit and corporate strategy

Gaining competitive advantage represents for many organizations the key focus of operating and strategic management. Porter (1985, 1991) has defined and explicated a typology of business and corporate strategies that have been used by multinational and global corporations as a basis for gaining and sustaining long-term competitive performance. Competitive strategies can differ in a number of ways, including the extent to which companies emphasize quality enhancement, cost reduction, or innovation. Indeed, different types of competitive strategies require different types of management development practices (Mintzberg, 1994).

According to Porter (1991), the new determinants of global competitiveness within a national environment include: (1) firm strategy, structure, and rivalry; (2) factor conditions; (3) demand conditions; and (4) related and supporting industries. Companies that have used these reinforcing concepts to compete and prosper, as well as linkage mechanisms for management development, include Novo Nordisk Group, Canon, Toray, Genzyme, and Northern Telecom. Allstate Insurance has developed and implemented a program to develop managers toward understanding and applying Porter's value-chain analysis within the context of unit-specific, work-related challenges.

Strategy implementation

Many organizations have formulated and implemented management development programs, using action-learning precepts, that encompass specific organizationally based challenges that managers must confront, resolve, and implement within their unit of responsibility. The focus of this approach is to ensure commitment to and implementation of business or strategic business unit strategies. Managers, in cross-functional or project/process teams, identify specific action programs that serve to enhance and integrate individual and organizational learning via specific challenges such as effectively introducing new technology within an existing plant, maintaining high employee commitment during downsizing, and making a merger, acquisition, or strategic alliance work.

Companies that have successfully used action-learning models as part of their management development process to facilitate strategy implementation include Northern Telecom, General Electric, Cigna Corporation, and Glaxo (Bongiorno, 1993). TRW's two-week Advanced Management Program focuses on the fit between business strategy and the organization using a 360° evaluation of their leadership and management skills (Walker, 1991). General Foods has implemented a management development program that is structured into three segments (i.e., using spaced phases of learning rather than time-compressed development), and has incorporated a "renewal project" that integrates individual learning in a team activity of importance to the organization (Bolt, 1989). Volvo has been successful in activating middle management by involving them directly in the teaching process associated with action-learning methodologies (Evans, Doz, & Laurent, 1991).

Core competencies and competitive capabilities

In many organizations, the most important management development scheme arises from an analysis of and linkage with the distinctive or "core competencies" of the enterprise. Prahalad and Hamel (1990) define core competencies as the combination of individual technologies and operational skills that underlie a company's myriad product and service lines.

For example, Sony's core competence in miniaturization allows the company to make everything from the Sony Walkman to video cameras to notebook computers. Canon's core competencies in optics, imaging, and microprocessor controls have enabled it to enter markets as seemingly diverse as copiers, image scanners, cameras, and laser printers. And J. P. Morgan's scope of international thinking and work, based on established leadership in globally linked, local markets has distinguished its approach to global financial intermediation for over a century.

Within these organizations, the implicit and explicit management development implications are evident relative to organizational learning and further leveraging of competitive capabilities. In this context, advantage derives from distinctive capabilities of managers coupled with the core competencies of the business. DuPont and Campbell Soup Company, for example, have provided management development opportunities for managers to enable understanding of how to leverage core competencies. The development provides cutting-edge thinking regarding the revitalization of businesses and helps crystallize the powerfulness of core competencies as a management tool.

Organizational transformation

Driven by the need to radically transform their organizations, several CEOs of prominent multinational companies have employed management development as a pivotal organizational learning vehicle to assist in the strategic process of reinventing the organization. General Electric, Allied Signal, Ameritech, and Tenneco are all relevant company examples of how management development processes can serve as enablers to effect successful and radical organizational change (Sherman, 1993). Leadership and management development processes, instrumental in creating a shared vision of what their company should become, are most prominent in the initial stages of the transformation process. Subsequent management development focuses on competitive and customer-oriented business processes, and integrative thinking for action, within the scope of the new, reinvented business mandates. Other organizations that have used management development practices to drive turnaround and enterprise-wide transformation include British Petroleum and Conrail (Vicere, 1992).

As such, emphasis on leadership development occurs within the environment of change that requires new managerial insights, perspectives, and critical thinking skills. For example, Pepsi-Cola International developed a "multinational vocabulary" that provides a global consistency of purpose to unite and develop managers from different countries and cultures (Schuler, Fulkerson, & Dowling, 1991). The development agenda for the 1990s at Rockwell International is to expand to a concept of lifelong learning, and to make management development the catalyst for organizational change (Galbraith, 1992).

Globalization forces
During the 1990s, business enterprises will continue to address the challenge of sustaining competitiveness in an increasingly global market environment (Cavusgil, 1993). To take a leadership role, middle and advanced managers in worldwide companies need to identify those new corporate capabilities and management skills their organizations require in order to remain competitive in today's complex and diverse global arena. To compete in the more complex global environment, corporations must become "transnational", that is, able simultaneously to integrate global operations, respond to diverse local/national needs within subsidiary operations, and implement innovation rapidly around the world (Bartlett & Sumantra, 1989).

Creating and managing a transnational company presents a formidable challenge. Management development can assist in this endeavor in four ways. Many organizations: (1) involve managers around the world in a common learning experience; (2) give them a vocabulary for discussing their mutual issues; (3) present them within the same intellectual framework for thinking about the enterprise; and (4) have them all address the same crucial business issues. Worldwide organizations that have used this approach include Becton Dickinson, Corning, NEC, ABB Asea Brown Boveri Ltd., and Unilever. Johnson & Johnson recently devised and implemented a worldwide advanced management development strategy to strengthen managerial skills relative to global efficiency, local responsiveness, and worldwide learning and innovation (Conference Board, 1993). The Ericsson Group, an $8 billion Swedish telecommunications multinational, launched a management development program to meet the global business imperatives associated with strengthening linkages between country managers, product divisions, and technology centers (Evans, 1992).

The implications of these contextual and linking mechanisms are fourfold. First, top managers must assess a company's corporate intelligence in terms of connecting, sharing, and structuring management development experiences. When management development processes from previously unrelated sources and conditions are structured in a meaningful way, managers become capable of thinking thoughts and making decisions that were previously unthinkable. Second, an enterprise's management development architecture and processes must be expressed in business language, not management development terminology. Management should select and use one business development language relative to its management development philosophy and processes, and insist on its use throughout the organization. Third, senior executives should determine the highest level at which coherent institutional management behavior, facilitated through development, adds value. And fourth, once a company embarks on a management development strategy, senior executives must carefully plan the pace of its implementation. When a coherent target level for institutional managerial competence has been defined, assets for delivery can be leveraged to create economies of scope and scale. Clearly the imminent arrival of a new generation of conditions for managerial development makes linkages with business imperatives plausible.

New delivery strategies

In addition to changes in the way in which management development is tied to real work and business objectives, there have been a number of noteworthy innovations in the delivery of development. It seems that organizations are increasingly cognizant of the power of collaboration and accountability, and have moved to create delivery strategies which incorporate those concepts. In particular, a number of progressive organizational initiatives have focused on the use of cross-functional problem-solving teams as well as partnerships with academic institutions, other firms, and even customers.

Problem-solving teams

Presenting a group of managers from different functions with a specific organizational problem to address is a strategy adopted in several recent cases. For example, Whirlpool has brought together over 100 top executives

and divided them into teams to work on 15 top-priority projects selected by senior management. Each project had American and European cochairpersons, and included specific deliverables and deadlines for project completion.

Similarly, Northern Telecom, Cigna, General Electric, and other firms run programs whereby top executives are divided into teams with a specific organizational assignment. At the end of a month or so, each team is responsible for making a presentation to top managers of the firm. The managers are given access and support and are expected to make full use of any resources they need to address their respective problems.

Clearly, problem-solving teams are an explicit manifestation of collaborative learning with accountability. Learning from each other in an intense, high-visibility context is hard to duplicate in traditional classroom models, or in the daily corporate environment. Team projects lead to quicker implementation because the social pressures encourage rather than hinder application. Teams offer multiple insights on similar problems to more fully assess the means of resolving those problems. Teams make development less a single event and more an ongoing process.

Development partnerships

Another recent innovation in management development is for one or more organizations to join together, often with an educational institution, to create development experiences. For example, Indiana University and Babson University have developed partnerships whereby 6 to 10 firms cosponsor development experiences. Indiana University has also recently initiated a partnership whereby four large service firms have joined together to create development initiatives specifically targeted to the needs of service industry firms. These programs grew out of the need for a vehicle through which member companies could collaborate in the development of managers through networking, sharing "best practices," and designing programming with other firms facing similar challenges in different industries. Both universities and corporations stand to gain by developing closer links in marrying management development program design and evaluation.

Partnerships are also being forged with customers. For example, ATT, Xerox Weyerhauser, Motorola, and others have begun to use management development for stakeholders outside the company. In some cases, as many as 10 percent of all course slots are dedicated and held for customer and supplier accounts. These slots are intended for customers and suppliers to sit through and learn similar principles and concepts as those learned by employees. In other cases, programs are attended by the CEOs of important customers. By inviting these senior officers from customer firms to attend, the development experience is used to build unity of commitment between the business and its customers. Customer presence creates a different type of accountability than has characterized most development efforts.

A final partnership issue involves that between HR and top management. Traditional management development activity has been delegated and owned by the HR or organization development function. Top managers may have participated symbolically in short segments but the ownership rested with the HR group. Conversely, many firms now believe that the most successful development efforts will be those where top management assumes a primary role in design and delivery.

Several organizations are shrinking centralized departments and moving toward a decentralized form for the delivery of development efforts. As a result, responsibility for the design, production and evaluation of specific development initiatives is increasingly found at the department or business unit. Decentralized units closer to the "front" can presumably make training resource allocations that best fit their particular business needs. This structural change has helped to increase the accountability of the development function, since more scarce unit dollars are being devoted to development and the value-added (or lack thereof) of development programs is more salient to key management decision makers.

Evaluation of bottom-line results and payback

When it comes to planning and implementing management development initiatives and strategies, concentrating on "organizational impact" no longer ensures competitiveness. Relying on near-term thinking, many organizations base their management development budgets on annual projections for new initiatives that link, optimistically, with business requirements (Fuchsberg, 1993). Indeed, too many companies are squandering management attention and other resources on management development programs and processes that look like winners but fail to produce widespread, bottom-line results. Therefore, the need to evaluate management development initiatives in economic terms is becoming more apparent. In the current environment of rising costs for management development, corporate and senior line managements justifiably demand projections of expected costs and benefits of management development strategies. For many companies, human resources expenditures, which include management development, represent 18 percent to 25 percent of each revenue dollar. From that same dollar, about 4 percent to 10 percent is earmarked for capital budgeting projects. While capital budgeting expenditures are carefully examined and analyzed, the much larger human resources piece is often viewed solely as an annual expense.

As the development and productivity of managerial competence becomes a more important strategic issue for organizations, rigorous processes for calculating ongoing costs and economic and noneconomic benefits of management development programs must be devised, implemented, and monitored. Furthermore, as the management development effort in many organizations continues to expand and grow, many competing developmental programs will be proposed, and senior management and board members will continue to ask hard questions about the projected value or likely financial impact of management development investments.

Investment in management development, like any other financial decision that an organization considers, calls for an evaluation of the potential payback and the appropriate scale on which to invest. Such an evaluation, while sensible, is inherently difficult. For example, a recent survey that examined the role of development in corporate performance across 100 international companies, representing six countries, indicated that even though most companies believe that it is virtually impossible to calibrate a linkage between the money expended on leadership development and specific financial results, many are currently struggling to define a formula which can do just that (Taylor & associates, 1993).

Lawson (1993, 1994) has been involved in the custom design and implementation of return-on-investment models that determine the projected payoff from management development programs. Generally, the development of these models requires an interdisciplinary approach, one which integrates capital budgeting and financial accounting techniques with the projected utility of the management development program(s) in question (Cronshaw & Alexander, 1991). Economic factors include variable costs associated with the management development experience, accounting for corporate taxes, and discounting, or the use of net present value analysis. A study recently sponsored by British, American, and Canadian research groups offers another approach for companies to use in determining the financial effectiveness of spending on management development programs (Crawford & Webley, 1992).

Current methods used by the vast majority of big multinational corporations for measuring and accounting for both the economic and noneconomic benefits of management development are inadequate. As financial pressures become more extant, organizations will need to devise practical and valid return-on-investment measures to assess, on a pro forma basis, the projected payoff from management development initiatives. Evaluation of the benefits and the investments associated with the developmental programs is absolutely crucial to understanding how management development contributes to corporate performance.

SUMMARY AND CONCLUSIONS

The increasing complexities of operating a business under accelerating rates of change in a competitive global environment impose ever greater demands on the development of managerial talent. To gain competitive advantage, businesses have traditionally focused on technological, economic, and strategic capabilities (Porter, 1985). However, a growing body of evidence supports the positive impact of effective management on organization and subunit performance (Shipper, 1991; Day & Lord, 1988). Indeed Kotter (1988) argues that one thing that will distinguish excellent companies from the "also rans" is the amount of time and energy spent in the planning, designing, and carrying out of development activities.

However, while a considerable amount of traditional management development activity continues to go on, there is growing consensus in both the academic literature and in the business press that much of prior management development has delivered little in real value-added to the firm, and new models are required to be effective in the new business reality.

For the business practitioner, our message

is that management development initiatives must be created to embrace and exploit the conditions for managerial learning. This means that they must be conducted in context and represent an articulation and elaboration of the linking between development experiences and the company's business imperatives. It also means that more attention should be placed on arranging the learning environment in a way that it will facilitate the collaborative learning. This may mean greater use of intact work teams and task forces, and involve a greater range of collaborators and accountability in the development process. While substantial change is taking place in some quarters – and we have purposely highlighted notable examples – it is still certainly the case that much of what is discussed here probably reflects more "what should be" than "what currently is."

From a research perspective, it is an exciting time. Though new models of development are conceptually appealing, the utility of almost all management development still remains as much an article of faith as an empirical fact, and documented successes or descriptions of new approaches have been disappointingly low. Even after twenty years of perennial laments in the management development literature, it is still the case that little post-development measurement occurs. Indeed, Saari et al. (1988) summarized results from a large-scale survey of management development in 611 organizations, and concluded that few conduct any evaluation at all.

More than ever, there is a pressing need for research which attempts to systematically identify development objectives, choose an appropriate development strategy, and evaluate the outcomes to determine whether the objectives were met. It is time to move beyond research designed to show that a particular type of management development "works." Rather, we need to proceed to the more specific questions of why, when, and for whom particular development strategies are effective.

REFERENCES

Baldwin, T. T., & Magjuka, R. J. (1991). Organizational training and signals of importance: Linking pre-training perceptions to intentions to transfer. *Human Resource Quarterly*, 2, 25–36.

Baldwin, T. T., & Padgett, M. Y. (1993). Management development: A review and commentary. In C. Cooper & I. Robertson (eds.), *International Review of Industrial & Organizational Psychology*, vol. 8, pp. 35–85, London: John Wiley & Sons.

Bandura, A. (1986). *Social Foundations of Thought and Action*. Englewood Cliffs, NJ: Prentice Hall.

Bartlett, C., & Sumantra, G. (1989). *Managing Across Borders*. Cambridge, MA: Harvard Business School.

Bolt, J. F. (1989). *Executive Development: A strategy for corporate competitiveness*. New York: HarperCollins.

Bongiorno, L. (1993). Corporate America's new lesson plan. *Business Week*, October 25, 102–5.

Campbell, J. P., Dunnette, M., Lawler, E. E., & Weick, K. E., Jr. (1970). *Managerial Behavior, Performance, and Effectiveness*. New York: McGraw-Hill.

Cavusgil, S. (1993). Internationalization of business education: A challenge yet to be met. *The International Executive*, 35 (6), 469–76.

Conference Board (1993). Pushing the boundaries of management development: Best practices. Conference proceedings, New York. April.

Cottrell, N. B. (1972). Social facilitation. In C. G. McClintock (ed.), *Experimental social psychology*, 185–236. New York: Holt.

Cronshaw, S., & Alexander, R. (1991). Why capital budgeting techniques are suited for assessing the utility of personnel programs: A reply to Hunter, Schmidt, and Coggin (1988). *Journal of Applied Psychology*, 76, 454–7.

Crawford, F. W., & Webley, S. (1992). *Continuing Education and Training of the Workforce*. Issues Papers No. 1, London BC2: Needham Printers Limited.

Day, D. V., & Lord, R. G. (1988). Executive leadership and organizational performance: Suggestions for a new theory and methodology. *Journal of Management*, 14, 453–64.

Dixon, N. M. (1993). Developing managers for the learning organization. *Human Resource Management Review*, 3 (3), 243–54.

Evans, P. (1992). Management development as glue technology. *Human Resource Planning*, 15 (1), 85–106.

Evans, P., Doz, Y., & Laurent, A. (1990). *Human Resource Management in International Firms*. New York: St. Martin's.

Feldman, D. C. (1989). Socialization, resocialization and training: Reframing the research agenda. In I. Goldstein (ed.), *Training and Development in Organizations*, 376–416. San Francisco: Jossey-Bass.

Froiland, P. (1994). Action learning: Taming real problems in real time. *Training*, 34 (1), 27–34.

Fuchsberg, G. (1993). Taking Control. *Wall Street Journal*, September 10, 1.

Fulmer, R. (1990). Executive learning as a strategic weapon. *Executive Development*, 3 (3), 26–8.

Galbraith, J. (1992). Positioning human resources as a

value added function: The case of Rockwell International. *Human Resource Management*, 31 (4), 287–300.

Greiner, L. (1987). Management development. Unpublished manuscript, University of Southern California, Los Angeles.

Hall, D. T. (1984). Human resource development and organizational effectiveness. In C. Fombrun, N. Tichy, & M. Devanna (eds.), *Strategic Human Resource Management*, 159–81. New York: Wiley.

Harkins, S. G., & Szymanski, K. (1989). Social loafing and group evaluation. *Journal of Personality and Social Psychology*, 56, 934–41.

Hill, L. (1993). *Becoming a Manager: How new managers master the challenge of leadership*. New York: Penguin Books.

Johnson, D. W., & Johnson, R. T. (1984). *Cooperative Learning*. New Brighton, MN: Interaction Publishing.

Jones, M. L. (1990). Action learning as a new idea. *Journal of Management Development*, 9, 29–34.

Kable, J. (1989). Management development through action learning. *Journal of Management Development*, 8, 77–80.

Kerr, N., & Brunn, S. (1981). Ringelmann revisited: Alternative explanations for the social loafing effect. *Personality and Social Psychology*, 50, 936–41.

Kotter, J. P. (1988). *The Leadership Factor*. New York: Free Press.

Langer, E. J. (1979). The illusion of incompetence. In L. Perlmutter & R. Monty (eds.), *Choice and Perceived Control*, 301–13. Hillsdale, NJ: Lawrence Erlbaum.

Latane, B., Williams, K., & Harkins, S. (1979). Many hands make light the work: The causes and consequences of social loafing. *Journal of Personality and Social Psychology*, 37, 823–32.

Latham, G. P. (1989). Behavioral approaches to the training and learning process. In I. Goldstein (ed.), *Training and Development in Organizations*, 256–96. San Francisco: Jossey-Bass.

Lawson, T. (1993). Evaluating the financial impact of employee development initiatives. *Global Human Resource Strategies*, 2 (1), 2.

Lawson, T. (1994). Measuring the bottom-line results of human resources strategies. *Global Human Resources Strategies*, 2 (1), 2.

Loo, R. (1991). Management training in Canadian organizations. *Journal of Management Development*, 10 (5), 60–72.

McCall, M. W., Lombardo, M. M., & Morrison, A. M. (1989). *The lessons of experience: How successful executives develop on the job*. Lexington, MA: Lexington Books.

Marsick, V. (1990). Experience-based learning: Executive learning outside the classroom. *Journal of Management Development*, 9, 50–60.

Mathieu, J., Martineau, J., & Tannenbaum, S. (1993). Individual and situational influences on the development of self-efficacy: Implications for training effectiveness. *Personnel Psychology*, 46, 125–48.

Mintzberg, H. (1994). The fall and rise of strategic planning. *Harvard Business Review*, 72 (1), 107–14.

Mullen, B., & Baumeister, R. F. (1987). Group effects on self-attention and performance: Social loafing, social facilitation, and social impairment. In C. Hendrick (ed.), *Review of Personality and Social Psychology*, 189–206. Beverly Hills, CA: Sage.

Mumford, A. (1988). *Developing Top Managers*. Aldershot: Gower.

O'Reilly, B. (1993). How executives learn now. *Fortune*, April 5, 52–8.

Pascale, R., & Athos, A. (1981). *The Art of Japanese Management*. New York: Simon & Schuster.

Penner, L. A., & Craiger, J. P. (1992). The weakest link: The performance of individual team members. In R. Salas & R. Swezey (eds.), *Teams: Their training and performance*, 57–73. Norwood, NJ: Ablex.

Peters, J. L., & Peters, B. H. (1990). *New Frontiers in Management Development*. New York: Conference Board.

Porter, M. (1985). *Competitive Advantage*. New York: Free Press.

Porter, M. (1991). *The Competitive Advantage of Nations*. New York: Free Press.

Prahalad, C. K., & Hamel, G. (1990). The core competencies of the corporation. *Harvard Business Review*, 67 (3), 79–91.

Rappaport, A. (1992). CEO's and strategy: Forging a common framework. *Harvard Business Review*, 69 (3), 84–91.

Roethlisberger, F. J., & Dickson, W. J. (1939). *Management and the Worker*. Cambridge, MA: Harvard University Press.

Saari, L. M., Johnson, T. R., Mclaughlin, S. D., & Zimmerle, D. M. (1988). A survey of management training and education practices in U.S. companies. *Personnel Psychology*, 41, 731–43.

Saxe, S. (1988). Peer influence and learning. *Training and Development Journal*, 42, 40–53.

Schuler, R. S., Fulkerson, J., & Dowling, P. (1991). Strategic performance measurement and management in multinational corporations. *Human Resource Management*, 30 (2), 365–92.

Sherman, S. (1993). A master class in radical change. *Fortune*, December 13, 82–90.

Shipper, F. (1991). Mastery and frequency of managerial behaviours relative to subunit effectiveness. *Human Relations*, 44 (4), 371–88.

Slavin, R. (1983). When does cooperative learning increase student achievement? *Psychological Bulletin*, 94, 429–45.

Taylor, S., & associates (1993). Critical paths: A study of the role of executive training and development in corporate performance. Unpublished manuscript, Metaline Falls, Washington.

Tichy, N. (1989). GE's Crotonville: A staging ground for corporate revolution. *Academy of Management Executive*, 3 (2), 99–106.

Ulrich, D. (1989). Executive development as a competitive weapon. *Journal of Management Development*, 8 (5), 11–22.

Vicere, A. F. (1992). The strategic leadership imperative for executive development. *Human Resource Planning*, 15 (1), 15–31.

Walbert, L. (1993). America's best wealth creators. *Fortune*, December 27, 64–76.

Walker, J. W. (1991). *Managing Human Resources in the Information Age*. Washington, D.C.: Bureau of National Affairs.

Wexley, K. N., & Baldwin, T. T. (1986). Management development. *Journal of Management*, 12, 277–94.

White, A. F. (1992). Organizational transformation at BP: An interview with Chairman and CEO Robert Horton. *Human Resource Planning*, 15 (1), 3–14.

☐ Chapter 27 ☐

Employee Compensation: Theory, Practice, and Evidence

Barry Gerhart, Harvey B. Minkoff, and Ray N. Olsen

INTRODUCTION

As organizations continue to face mounting competitive pressures, they seek to do more with less and do it with better quality. As goals for sales volume, profits, innovation, and quality are raised, employment growth is often tightly controlled and, in many cases, substantial cuts in employment have been made. To accomplish more with fewer employees calls for effective management of human resources. Typically, the employee compensation system, the focus of this chapter, plays a principal role in efforts to manage human resources better.

Employee compensation plays such a key role because it is at the heart of the employment relationship, being of critical importance to both employees and employers. Employees typically depend on wages, salaries, and so forth to provide a large share of their income and on benefits to provide income and health security. For employers, compensation decisions influence their cost of doing business and thus their ability to sell at a competitive price in the product market. In addition, compensation decisions influence the employer's ability to compete for employees in the labor market (attract and retain), as well as their attitudes and behaviors while with the employer.

Employee compensation practices differ across employment units (e.g., organizations, business units, and facilities) on several dimensions (Gerhart & Milkovich, 1990, 1992; Gerhart, Milkovich, & Murray, 1992). The focus of the employee compensation literature has been on defining these dimensions, understanding why organizations differ on them (determinants), and assessing whether such differences have consequences for employee attitudes and behaviors, and for organizational effectiveness. In the following discussion, we briefly describe the basic dimensions of compensation and summarize some of the key theories used to explain the consequences of different compensation decisions. A discussion of pay determinants can be found in Gerhart and Milkovich (1990, 1992).

STRATEGIC PAY DIMENSIONS

Pay practices vary significantly across employing units and, to some degree, across jobs.

We discuss the form, level, structure, mix, and administration of payment systems (Gerhart & Milkovich, 1992; Heneman & Schwab, 1979; Milkovich & Newman, 1993).

First, pay can be in the form of cash or benefits (e.g., health care, retirement, paid vacation). On average, about 70 percent of payments to U.S. employees are in the form of cash, leaving 30 percent in the form of noncash and deferred cash benefits (Noe, Hollenbeck, Gerhart, & Wright, 1994). Health care has been the fastest growing benefit, and most employers describe the challenge of controlling this cost while providing quality coverage as one of their top human resource management challenges.

Second, both benefits and cash compensation can be described in terms of their level (how much). Most organizations use one or more market pay surveys to help determine what other organizations pay specific jobs in making their own pay-level decisions. More broadly, total labor costs are a function of both compensation cost per employee and total employee head count. Therefore, to assess competitiveness in the product market, organizations should not focus only on pay levels. They should compare total labor costs, and better yet, they should compare with other organizations the sort of return (or productivity) they receive in terms of profits, sales, and so forth for each dollar spent on labor costs. The now common announcements of sizable reductions in force attest to the importance of controlling labor costs. Such decisions are also sometimes driven by comparisons of revenue or profits per employee, or the ratio of sales or profits to labor costs.

Labor costs and productivity are also key factors in decisions about where to locate production. Germany's high labor costs have led to what *Business Week* described as the "exodus of German industry." German companies are moving production to lower labor cost countries, such as those in Eastern Europe and the United States.[1] BMW recently announced it would be building vehicles in South Carolina and Mercedes-Benz will produce vehicles in Alabama. Agreements such as the North American Free Trade Agreement (NAFTA) and the General Agreement on Tariffs and Trade will only reinforce the globalization of production. However, contrary to what was heard in the debate over NAFTA, labor costs will not be the determining factor in most cases, except perhaps for labor-intensive production. Labor costs as a percentage of total costs is shrinking in many cases, and other factors such as access to markets and labor-force quality will often be more important. The decision by BMW and Mercedes-Benz to build in the United States, not Mexico, is evidence of this.

Third, the structure refers to the nature of pay differentials within an employing unit. How many steps or grades are in the structure? How big are the pay differentials between different levels in the structure? Large organizations often have over twenty such levels, although many organizations have recently reduced the number of steps ("delayered"). Are employees at the same hierarchical level in different parts of the organization (e.g., different product sectors or different occupational groups) paid the same? Yet another aspect of structure is the timing of payment over employees' careers. Some organizations may bring entry level people in at a relatively high rate of pay, but then provide relatively slow pay growth, while another organization may bring employees in relatively low but offer greater opportunities for promotion and pay growth over time.

Fourth, payment systems differ in their mix (how and when cash compensation is disbursed). Some organizations pay virtually all employees a base salary that is adjusted approximately once per year through a traditional merit increase program. Merit increases become part of base salary and are supposed to depend on merit (performance), although there is a widespread belief that most employees get about the same percentage increase, regardless of their performance. As described below, an increasing number of organizations are using so-called variable pay or pay at risk, which means that some portion of employees' pay is uncertain and depends on some combination of future business unit or organization performance (e.g., profits, stock performance, productivity), group performance, and individual performance. Specific pay programs that influence pay mix are merit pay, incentive pay, gainsharing, profit sharing, and stock plans (e.g., stock options).

Fifth, pay is administered differently in different organizations. The design of pay policies differs, for example, in terms of who is involved in the process. The roles of human resources departments, line managers, and rank-and-file employees differ across situations. In some organizations, line managers may design plans, often with assistance from the human resources department. Alternatively, human resources takes the lead in other cases. Employees to be covered by a payment system are sometimes involved, and in some cases, may actually design plans for themselves.

Communication is another aspect of administration. The most technically sophisticated payment plan can generate desired employee reactions or exactly the opposite. The actual effect depends on whether the rationale for the payment plan is understood and accepted and whether employees' perceptions of the facts upon which the rationale is built (e.g., the company's financial health, the pay of employees in other jobs or organizations) are the same as the perceptions of those charged with seeing that the payment plan has the intended effects.

We focus in this chapter on cash compensation issues. Benefits warrants a chapter of its own and discussions are available elsewhere (Beam & McFadden, 1992; Gerhart & Milkovich, 1992; Noe, Hollenbeck, Gerhart, & Wright, 1994). Further, our discussion of cash compensation is mostly limited to pay-mix issues, an area that has been of great interest to organizations as they move (or consider a move) to "new" programs such as

stock plans for nonexecutives, gainsharing, and profit sharing. In the remainder of this chapter, we provide a survey of theories that have been used to study the effects of pay decisions, describe specific pay programs and their expected consequences, and review recent empirical evidence on that question.

CONSEQUENCES OF PAY DECISIONS: THEORIES

To understand what types of pay systems are most likely to be effective and how their effectiveness differs according to contingency factors such as business strategy, national culture, competitive environment, and employee characteristics, we need to have a good conceptual framework, or theory. In truth, there is as yet no grand theory of compensation that takes these contingency factors into account, although recent work by Gomez-Mejia and Balkin (1992) is promising.

In examining consequences, we need to recognize that effectiveness is a multifaceted concept that could include at a minimum, cost, productivity, innovation, quality, financial, and attitudinal dimensions. Further, the relative importance of these dimensions will vary across organizations and business units.

At the individual level of analysis, theories have been put forward to show how pay plans can be used to energize, direct, and control employee behavior. We briefly describe three such theories used in research on pay.

Reinforcement and expectancy theories

Reinforcement theory states that a response followed by a reward is more likely to recur in the future (Thorndike's Law of Effect). The implication for compensation management is that high employee performance followed by a monetary reward will make future high performance more likely. By the same token, high performance not followed by a reward will make it less likely in the future. The theory emphasizes the importance of a person actually experiencing the reward.

Like reinforcement theory, expectancy theory (Vroom, 1964) focuses on the link between rewards and behaviors (instrumentality perceptions), although it emphasizes expected (rather than experienced) rewards (i.e., incentives). Motivation is also a function of two other factors: expectancy, the perceived link between effort and performance; and valence, the expected value of outcomes (e.g., rewards). Compensation systems differ according to their impact on these motivational components. Generally speaking, pay systems differ most in their impact on instrumentality: the perceived link between behaviors and pay, also referred to in the pay literature as "line of sight." Valence of pay outcomes should remain the same under different pay systems. Expectancy perceptions often have more to do with job design and training than pay systems.

Equity theory

Equity theory suggests that employee perceptions of what they contribute to the organization, what they get in return, and how their return–contribution ratio compares to others inside and outside the organization,[2] determine how fair they perceive their employment relationship to be (Adams, 1963). Perceptions of inequity are expected to cause employees to take actions to restore equity. Unfortunately, some such actions (e.g., quitting or lack of cooperation) may not be helpful to the organization.

Two recent empirical studies provide good examples of the types of counterproductive behaviors that can occur as a result of perceived inequity. In the first study, Greenberg (1990) examined how an organization communicated pay cuts to its employees and the effects on theft rates and perceived equity. Two organization units received 15 percent across-the-board pay cuts. A third unit received no pay cut and served as a control group. The reasons for the pay cuts were communicated in different ways to the two pay-cut groups. In the "adequate explanation" pay-cut group, management provided a significant degree of information to explain its reasons for the pay cut, and also expressed significant remorse. In contrast, the "inadequate explanation" group received much less information and no indication of remorse. The control group received no pay cut (and thus no explanation).

The control group and the two pay-cut groups began with the same theft rates and equity perceptions. After the pay cut, the theft rate was 54 percent higher in the adequate explanation group than in the control group. However, in the "inadequate explanation" condition, the theft rate was 141 percent higher than in the control group. In this case, communication had a large, independent effect on employees' attitudes and behaviors.

Cowherd and Levine (1992) used a sample 102 business units in 41 corporations to examine whether the size of the pay differential between lower-level employees and top management had any impact on product quality. Cowherd and Levine suggest that individuals often compare their pay to that of people higher in the organization structure. If lower-level employees feel inequitably treated, they may seek to reduce their effort to achieve equity. Quality, in their study, was defined as customer perceptions of the quality of goods and services. They hypothesized that extrarole, or citizenship behaviors, such as freely offering to help others, following the spirit rather than letter of rules, and correcting errors that would ordinarily escape notice, would be less likely when pay differentials between hourly and top managerial employees were large. Their results supported this hypothesis, suggesting that organizations need to take care that they not forget the potential adverse motivational consequences of executive pay for the motivation of other employees.

Agency theory

Agency theory, until recently best known in the economics, finance, and law literatures, focuses on the divergent interests and goals of the organization's stakeholders, and the ways that employee compensation can be used to align these interests and goals (Eisenhardt, 1989; Fama & Jensen, 1983). Ownership and management (or control) are typically separate in the modern corporation, unlike the days when the owner and manager were often the same person. With most stockholders far removed from day-to-day operations, so-called agency costs (i.e., costs that arise from the interests of the *principals/owners* and their *agents/managers* not converging) are created. What is best for the agent/manager, may not be best for the owner.

Examples of agency costs include management spending money on perquisites (e.g., "superfluous" corporate jets) or "empire building" (acquisitions that do not add value to the company but may enhance the manager's prestige or pay) rather than seeking to maximize shareholder wealth (Lambert & Larcker, 1989). In addition, the fact that managers and shareholders may differ in their attitudes toward risk gives rise to agency costs. Shareholders can diversify their investments (and thus their risks) more easily than managers can diversify risk in their pay. As a consequence, managers may prefer relatively little risk in their pay (e.g., high emphasis on base salary, low emphasis on uncertain bonuses or incentives). Indeed, research shows that managerial compensation in manager-controlled firms is more often designed in this manner (Tosi & Gomez-Mejia, 1989). Agency costs also stem from differences in decision-making horizons. Especially where managers expect to spend little time in the job or with the organization, they may be more inclined to maximize short-run performance (and pay), perhaps at the expense of long-term success.

Agency theory is also of value in the analysis and design of nonmanagers' compensation. In this case, the divergence of interests may exist between managers (now in the role of principals) and their employees (who take on the role of agents). In designing either managerial or non-managerial compensation, the key question is, "How can such agency costs be minimized?" Agency theory says that the principal must choose a contracting scheme that helps align the interests of the agent with the principal's own interests (i.e., reduces agency costs). These contracts can be classified as either behavior-oriented (e.g., merit pay) or outcome-oriented (e.g., stock options, profit sharing, commissions).

At first blush, outcome-oriented contracts seem to be the obvious solution. If profits are high, compensation goes up. If profits go down, compensation goes down. The interests of "the firm" and employees are aligned. An important drawback, however, is that such contracts increase the amount of risk borne by the agent. Furthermore, because agents are averse to risk, they may require higher pay (a compensating wage differential) to make up for it.

Behavior-based contracts, on the other hand, do not transfer risk to the agent, and thus do not require a compensating wage differential. However, the principal must be able to monitor with little cost what the agent has done. Otherwise, the principal must either invest in monitoring/information or structure the contract so that pay is linked at least partly to outcomes.

Which type of contract should an organization use? It depends partly on the following factors (Eisenhardt, 1989):

- *Risk aversion* Risk aversion among agents makes outcome-oriented contracts more costly.
- *Outcome uncertainty* Profit is an example of an outcome. Linking pay to profits (outcome-based contract) is more costly to the extent that profits vary and so there is a risk of low profits.

- *Job programmability* As jobs become less programmable (i.e., less routine and less structured), and more difficult to monitor, outcome-oriented contracts become more likely. The increasing complexity of organizations and technology makes monitoring more difficult, and may help explain the growing use of variable pay programs (discussed below), which are examples of outcome-based contracts. Consistent with this idea, outcome-oriented contracts (e.g., profit sharing and stock plans) are more prevalent in research and development organizations, where monitoring is especially difficult (Milkovich, Gerhart, & Hannon, 1991). Pay levels are also higher, consistent with the idea that employees must be compensated for sharing more risk.
- *Measurable job outcomes* When outcomes are more measurable, outcome-oriented contracts are more likely.
- *Ability to pay* Outcome-oriented contracts contribute to higher compensation costs because of the risk premium.
- *Tradition* A tradition or custom of using (or not using) outcome-oriented contracts will make such contracts more (or less) likely.

Influences on labor-force composition

Traditionally, the theories described above have been used to understand how using pay to recognize individual contributions can influence the behaviors and attitudes of current employees, whereas pay level and benefits have been seen as a way to influence so-called membership behaviors: decisions about whether to join or remain with the organization. However, there is increasing recognition that individual pay programs may also have an effect on the nature and composition of an organization's work force (Milkovich & Wigdor, 1991; Gerhart & Milkovich, 1992). For example, it is possible that an organization that links pay to performance may attract more high performers than an organization that does not link the two. There may be a similar effect with respect to job retention.

Breaking things down further, perhaps organizations that link pay to individual performance are more likely to attract individualistic types of employees, while organizations relying more heavily on team rewards are more likely to attract more team-oriented employees. Although there is no concrete evidence of this yet, it has been found that different pay systems attract different people depending on their personality traits and values (Bretz, Ash, & Dreher, 1989; Judge & Bretz, 1992). The implication is that the design of compensation programs needs to be carefully coordinated with the business and human resources strategy.

Strategy

Moving from the individual level of analysis to the business unit and corporate level, there are theories of what corporate and pay strategies fit best together. Stage in the product life cycle (Ellig, 1981) and the degree and process of diversification (Kerr, 1985) have been raised as contingency factors in the design of pay strategies (Milkovich, 1988). Briefly, organizations (or probably more precisely, business units) may go through growth, maintenance, and decline stages, each of which calls for a different compensation strategy. For example, in the growth stage, it was recommended that there be substantial pay at risk to provide high upside earnings potential (e.g., using stock plans) to spur innovation, growth, and risk taking, combined with low fixed costs (base salary and benefits) to preserve scarce capital for investment. In the maintenance and decline stages, there would be less emphasis on pay at risk (except perhaps for more short-term focused plans), and more dollars allocated to base salary and benefits.

The literature on diversification and pay strategy suggests that single-product firms and

Table 27.1 Matching organization strategy and pay strategy

Pay strategy dimensions	Business unit strategy	
	Defenders	Prospectors
Risk sharing (variable pay)	Low	High
Time orientation	Short-term	Long-term
Pay level (short-run)	Above market	Below market
Pay level (long-run potential)	Below market	Above market
Benefits level	Above market	Below market
Centralization of pay decisions	Centralized	Decentralized
Pay unit of analysis	Job	Skills

Source: Gomez-Mejia & Balkin (1992), appendix 4b.

unrelated product firms (e.g., conglomerates) have more pay at risk than related-product firms, and pay is more decentralized and tied to business unit rather than corporate performance in the unrelated-product firms. This flexibility makes sense where each business unit has independent goals, and there is little need for coordination and thus for consistency in pay practices. From an agency theory point of view, it may be more necessary to rely on outcome-oriented contracts in unrelated-product firms because the market-specific expertise is concentrated in the business units, making it difficult for corporate headquarters to make evaluations using behavior-oriented contracts. Finally, an unrelated firm that is a result of mergers and acquisitions is more likely to have the flexibility and pay linked to unit performance than an unrelated firm that is the result of internal growth, because there is often more interdependence and interaction in the latter case (Kerr, 1985).

Gomez-Mejia and Balkin (Gomez-Mejia & Balkin, 1992; Gomez-Mejia, 1992) have summarized much of the research on these questions, and provided some of the first tests of whether firms that choose pay strategies consistent with the above frameworks actually perform better. The answer seems to be "yes." They have provided propositions about which types of pay practices are likely to be most

effective based on various strategy frameworks. For example, the Miles and Snow (1978) model classifies business units as defenders (stable markets, focus on efficiency), prospectors (focus on new markets and technologies), and analyzers, which have elements of both defenders and prospectors. According to Gomez-Mejia and Balkin, variable pay, for example, should be higher in the prospector business units than in the defender business units. Table 27.1 shows other proposed differences.

Summary

Reinforcement, expectancy, and agency theories all focus on the fact that behavior–reward contingencies can shape behaviors. However, agency theory is of particular value in studying variable pay because of its emphasis on the risk–reward trade-off, an issue that needs close attention when considering variable pay plans, and which can carry significant risk. Equity theory is also very relevant because it can be applied to just about any pay decision, because fairness is always a key concern.

Moving away from individual-level theories, life-cycle and diversification-based contingency theories suggest that pay strategies should fit with corporate strategies. The evolving empirical literature provides tentative support for many of the specific propositions.

PAY PROGRAMS

Table 27.2 summarizes the key features of some of the most widely used pay programs. Key dimensions include the payment method (whether increases roll into base salary or are paid as bonuses or equity), the frequency of payouts, the nature of the performance measure, and who is typically covered under the different plans.

In compensating employees, an organization does not have to choose one program over another. Instead, a combination of programs is often the best solution. For example, one program may foster teamwork and cooperation but not enough individual initiative. Another may do the opposite. Used in conjunction, a balance may be attained. We now turn to a discussion of some recent trends in pay and an evaluation of where such trends are likely to lead us.

Recent developments

The shift to variable pay
According to a survey of over 2,000 U.S. companies by Hewitt Associates (Tully, 1993), the percentage of companies having a variable pay policy covering all salaried employees increased from 47 percent in 1988 to 68 percent in 1993. Moreover, whereas the standard merit increase (which rolls into base salary) was larger (5 percent versus 3.9 percent) in 1988 than the merit bonus (a lump sum payment that does not become part of base salary), by 1993 the situation was reversed with the merit bonus being larger on average than the standard merit increase (5.9 percent versus 4.3 percent).

Those in the human resource management field expect the movement toward variable pay to continue. In the Workplace 2000 study conducted by Dyer and Blancero (1993), 57

human resources executives, consultants, academics, and others were asked to describe how the workplace was likely to change by the year 2000. Dyer and Blancero provided study participants the characteristics of a hypothetical service organization in 1991 and asked how it would look in the year 2000. One expectation of participants was that pay would become more variable. As table 27.3 indicates, variable pay as a percentage of total direct compensation was expected to increase significantly for each of the four occupational groups studied.

Table 27.4 provides some examples of how variable pay programs operate.

Group and organization-based variable pay
Dyer and Blancero (1993) also found a strong belief that, in the future, variable pay would be based to a lesser degree on individual performance and to a much greater degree on firm, business-unit, and work-group performance (see table 27.3). The examples in table 27.4 are consistent with this expectation. It should be noted, however, that despite these significant changes, Dyer and Blancero found that individual performance is expected to remain as the single most important determinant of variable pay for all occupational groups.

Why are organizations making greater use of variable pay, and why are they moving away from an individual focus to more of a group and organization focus? Variable pay is seen as a way of both controlling costs (especially in the case of organizationwide plans) and redirecting employee behavior.

Better cost control is expected to be gained by replacing standard merit increases with merit bonuses that are linked to firm or business-unit performance. Thus, when profits or stock returns are good, they can be shared with employees. However, when profits or stock returns are poor or nonexistent, the organization is not saddled to the same degree with high fixed labor costs.

In theory, the use of variable pay plans to

Table 27.2 Comparison of different pay programs

	Individual incentives	Merit pay	Merit bonus	Gainsharing	Profit sharing	Ownership	Skill-based pay
Payment method	Bonus	Changes in base pay	Bonus	Bonus	Bonus	Equity changes	Changes in base pay
Payout frequency	Weekly	Annually	Annually	Monthly or quarterly	Semiannually or annually	When stock sold	When skill acquired
Performance measure	Output, productivity, sales	Performance rating	Performance rating	Production or controllable costs	Profit	Stock value	Skill acquisition
Coverage	Direct labor	All employees	All employees	Production or service unit	Total organization	Total organization	All employees

Source: Adapted and extended from Lawler (1989).

Table 27.3 Variable pay as a percentage of total direct compensation: 1991 scenario and year 2000 projection

Occupational group	1991	2000	Percentage change
Executives	0.2	0.33	0.65
Managers	0.1	0.23	1.3
Professional/technical	0.1	0.18	0.8
Support	0.1	0.14	0.4

Source: Dyer & Blancero (1993).

control labor costs is fine and it even works in practice under the right conditions: namely, if employees see a compelling business need to stay competitive in this manner. However, as in the widely discussed case of the duPont Fibers division variable pay plan (Santora, 1991),[3] employee opposition to downside variability in pay when profit targets are not met can lead to such plans being discontinued as soon as the labor cost control aspect is supposed to kick in, and employees forego bonuses and receive only their (below market) base salary. This result is consistent with agency theory's prediction that outcome-oriented contracts are less successful when there is high outcome uncertainty.

Some organizations seek to avoid this "problem" by setting base pay at a higher level, and then sharing profits or stock with employees on top of their base salary during good years. These "gravy" plans do not control labor costs and, in fact, raise them. Yet, unless there is a compelling reason to believe that such pay plans significantly raise employee or organization productivity, organizations following this approach run the risk of investing extra money in the form of labor costs without realizing any return on the investment. Therefore, consistent with agency theory, employees may demand a compensating pay premium to assume risk. So, pay risk costs the organization more money, but gains in effectiveness are not certain.

Organizations that use variable pay, with or without downside risk, often believe that such plans do generate significant returns. In agency theory terms, profit-sharing, stock plans, and gainsharing are examples of outcome-based contracts that seek to align the interests of employees and management with those of owners. As such, they are expected to redirect behavior away from parochial individual goals, and more toward what it takes in terms of cooperation, commitment, and innovation to make the group, business unit, or organization a success.

A change to variable pay may be a way to send a message to employees that things are going to change in important ways and, therefore, may be helpful in supporting other significant human resources changes. For example, variable pay may support a move to a team-based organization. As another example, variable pay may help eliminate the "entitlement" mentality or culture that can result from so-called merit increase plans that (in fact) fail to differentiate between employees with different performance levels, roll the increase into base salary so the cost remains in future years, and ignore the performance of the business. With a merit bonus, the pay has to be re-earned each year. Past individual performance does not matter, and is not reflected in base salary. Therefore, employees cannot rest on their past laurels. Moreover the bonus pool may be linked to organization or business-unit profitability. Again, the idea is to align employee interests with those of the organization. In this case, the goal is to encourage continuous improvement and a forward-looking perspective.

Agency theory suggests that group and organization incentives can also contribute to greater overall levels of performance monitoring by, in effect, making each employee a principal who monitors other employees (Levine & Tyson, 1990). So, if your pay and my pay depend on what we do as a team, we will be more likely to monitor each other's performance and give feedback to one another when performance needs improvement.

Table 27.4 Examples of variable pay programs for managers

Company	Plan participants	Base pay policy	Bonus policy
Nucor Steel	14 plant managers	$80,000 to $150,000 (25% below market)	5% of every dollar earned beyond 10% return on equity goes into bonus pool. Last year, average plant manager bonus equaled base salary.
General Mills	Managers (marketing manager in this example)	$75,000 (versus $90,000 market midpoint)	$10,000 if profits growth and return on capital are at market average; up to $40,500 if profits growth and return on capital are in top 10% of market.
AT&T	80,000 middle managers and 30,000 scientists, researchers, technical employees	Between 1986 and 1989, pay raises less than one-half of competitors – move from pay leader to below midpoint	1. Individual or team bonus – pool depends in part on corporate net profitability (5% to 15% of base depending on individual/team performance). 2. Business unit net profitability (about 2% of base or less this year). 3. Corporate net profitability (7 to 11% of base).

Source: Tully (1993).

Similarly, according to equity theory, if a person feels that his or her inputs (e.g., work effort) are greater than another member of the work group, but they receive the same reward, one way to restore equity would be to encourage (or pressure) the other person to put forth more effort.

Group size, however, is a key contingency variable in discussions of the behavioral impact of group and organization variable pay plans. According to expectancy theory, the larger the number of employees covered by a pay plan, the weaker the link they see between their own performance and pay (Schwab, 1973), and thus the weaker is their motivation. Similarly, a theme from the shirking, social loafing, and free rider literatures is that individual effort decreases as the size of the group increases (Kidwell & Bennett, 1993).

The implication, therefore, is that the ability of group and organization plans to change employee behavior may be very limited in cases where large numbers of employees are covered. On this dimension, gainsharing plans, which typically cover smaller groups of employees, probably have an advantage over organizationwide plans like profit-sharing and stock-based plans. Another advantage is that the performance measures in gainsharing plans (e.g., labor costs, quality) are often more controllable, again fostering greater employee motivation to change behavior.

The trade-off, however, is that gainsharing plans can pay off big even when the company is losing money. Another difficult situation arises when management would like to bring more work into the plant, but cannot afford to because the plan payouts would become too costly. In these cases, one might say that gainsharing plans (consistent with the general history of incentive plans) sometimes "fail" because they are too "successful." The payouts of any incentive plan must walk the fine line between being too low to motivate

Table 27.5 Changes in pay to support total quantity

	Before (%)	After (%)
Performance appraisal (n = 91)		
Only supervisors as source	59	12
Peer/team appraisals	2	25
Add quality criteria/goals	–	68
Have team goals	–	41
Plan increase policies (n = 38)		
Increases tied to individual performance appraisals	88	60
Increases tied to team/organization results	8	60
Increases tied to quality results	–	49
Increases tied to skill/knowledge levels	–	33
Incentive program policies (n = 56)		
Incentives based on individual results	26	31
Incentives based on individual/team results	23	37
Incentives based on team/organization results	20	52
Salary structure policies		
Other (e.g., more pay at risk)	–	52
Fewer grades, broader range widths	–	38

n refers to the number of organizations (out of 196 total) that made changes in each pay area.
Source: Davis (1993).

employees and being too high for management to afford. Even when standards work well initially, changes in production level and technology often result in the plan being unacceptable to one party or the other. In some cases, management may choose to "buy out" employees by paying a lump sum settlement in exchange for being able to redesign the plan with different standards, especially in unionized settings. An implication is that any sort of variable pay program should have a "sunset" provision that requires evaluation of the plan after a specific number of years, to avoid having the pay program becoming irrelevant because the organization changed but the program did not.

A final reason we discuss for the growth in variable pay plans is that the increased use of total quality management (TQM) often entails a movement toward a team-based organization and empowerment of employees to go beyond their traditional roles to make decisions in a broader range of areas that are likely to have an impact on organization performance. Individual-oriented systems may not be adequate for encouraging employees to pursue broad organization goals and to engage in the cooperative team and group-based decision making necessary.

A survey conducted for the American Compensation Association (ACA) asked organizations that implemented TQM programs how their pay practices changed (Davis, 1993). As table 27.5 indicates, notable changes included less reliance on supervisors as the only source of performance appraisals, more reliance on team and organization results in setting pay, greater use of variable pay, and fewer, broader pay grades.

From an equity theory perspective, placing the entire employee population on such plans may also create a greater sense of fairness among nonexecutive employees who typically have not been covered by such plans in the past, but saw that executives were. Of course, this effect may be limited to plans where variable pay is used to provide additional upside earnings potential, as opposed to cases where it replaces a portion of base salary.

Banding, delayering, and paying the person rather than the job

In the traditional pay system, the worth of jobs is assessed on the basis of job evaluation data in combination with market survey data. Job evaluation focuses on measuring and valuing the specific characteristics and requirements of the job. Critics, however, suggest that job-based systems tend to spawn too much bureaucracy, too much emphasis by employees on doing only what is in their job description, and a lack of focus on market comparisons, which are critical for competitiveness. In addition, job levels become status indicators, which can get in the way. For example, an employee may be reluctant to accept a temporary assignment, that would be good from a developmental point of view, unless it has at least as high a job level.

There have been at least two types of responses. First, organizations like General Electric have cut levels of management and the corresponding pay grades. The goals are to improve communication and speed decisions by reducing the levels of management, and to provide wider pay grades (or bands) in order to allow more flexibility to recognize individual contributions, and to make lateral movements simpler by reducing the likelihood of a job being in a different (in this case, lower) grade (and looking like a demotion).

The participants in the Dyer and Blancero (1993) study were also asked how the number of pay levels in the hypothetical service organization would change by the year 2000. Across the four occupational groups, the 36 pay levels in 1991 were expected to decrease to 23 pay levels by 2000, a decrease of about one-fourth. Whether the hoped for advantages

of delayering and banding will offset the potential drawbacks (e.g., less opportunity for promotion) remains to be seen.

Aside from allowing more flexibility in moving employees, banding, by virtue of a greater spread between the minimum and maximum in each pay grade, is also intended to provide more opportunity to recognize individual differences in performance. So, within-level pay growth for high performers will increase, while promotion opportunities and related pay growth will decrease. It remains to be seen whether this will, on balance, be a good trade for motivational purposes. Further, banding carries the risk of becoming very expensive. Topping out of employees near the maximum would be very expensive under a banding system. Some organizations have implemented subbands or zones within bands to avoid this problem. However, one might then reasonably ask what the difference is between an old system with 30 grades and a new system with 10 bands, each with 3 subbands.

Another trend is for some organizations to move away from linking pay to job content through job evaluation, and instead pay workers for the skills they possess. Skill-based pay links pay to the breadth or depth of employee skill. The goal is to encourage learning, which in turn facilitates flexibility in work assignments and encourages learning as a way of life to help with future organization change.

Empirical evidence

Where are these recent developments in pay likely to lead us? We know that money can be a powerful motivator. Indeed, a literature review of four motivational programs (individual monetary incentives, goal-setting, job redesign, and participation in decision making) found that monetary incentives were associated with the largest average increase in physical productivity (Locke, Feren, McCaleb, Shaw, & Denny, 1980). Therefore, changes in pay practices have the potential to significantly change attitudes, behaviors, and organization functioning. The challenge, however, is to realize the potential of money as a motivator without running afoul of the many roadblocks that arise in terms of measuring performance, setting standards that are perceived as fair, and choosing the right mix of individual, group, and organization objectives to reward.

As one recent example of a variable pay program gone wrong, consider the problems Sears encountered in some of its automotive repair shops in New Jersey and California. In a State of California undercover investigation, 38 visits to 27 Sears repair shops resulted in 34 cases of unnecessary service or repair recommendations. Edward A. Brennan, the chairman of Sears, stated that "the incentive compensation program and sales goals created an environment where mistakes occurred" (Fisher, 1992). In essence, repair shop employees had been rewarded for driving revenue (i.e., selling repairs to customers). Sears subsequently changed its pay system to one that focused on "quality."

Although specific examples are useful to demonstrate specific points, what does the broader research literature tell us regarding the typical outcomes of variable pay and other pay for performance programs?

At the organization level, evidence suggests that greater emphasis on short-term bonuses and long-term incentives (relative to base pay) is associated with higher subsequent profitability, at least among top and middle-level managers (Gerhart & Milkovich, 1990). Specifically, an organization with a bonus/base ratio of 10 percent, and 28 percent of its managers eligible for long-term incentives had an average return on assets of 5.2 percent. In contrast, an organization with a 20 percent bonus to base ratio, and 48 percent of its managers eligible for long-term incentives, had an average return on assets of 7.1 percent.

The fact that organization-based bonuses and incentives work for high-level managers does not necessarily mean they will work for other types of employees, most of whom have less influence over organization performance and thus weaker instrumentality perceptions. Still, even if the motivational impact (in terms of sheer effort) of organization-based incentives is weaker for such groups, cost control and a refocusing of behavior toward broader organizational goals may still be possible with such programs.

The empirical evidence on profit-sharing plans, in fact, generally paints a positive picture, with organizations using profit sharing having higher productivity (usually defined as value-added per employee) on average than organizations that do not use profit sharing (e.g., Weitzman & Kruse, 1990; Kruse, 1993a, 1993b). Still, there has yet to be a convincing demonstration that profit-sharing actually *causes* better organization performance (Gerhart & Milkovich, 1992). It may be that organizations with higher profit levels are more likely to adopt profit-sharing plans. In addition, if a profit-sharing plan does not work out, it is likely to be discontinued. So, the only profit-sharing plans that are studied are those that have proven successful, and we do not hear about the plans that failed or needed to be replaced after they served their purpose. An organization that is deciding whether to adopt a profit-sharing plan must know how often such plans work and how often they fail or get discontinued, not just how well the successful plans work.

The evidence on stock plans is very limited, aside from the Gerhart and Milkovich (1990) study of top and middle-level managers. The evidence that is available pertains mostly to employee stock-ownership plans (ESOPs). Like profit sharing, the evidence is generally favorable (Jones & Takao, 1993; Conte & Svejnar, 1990), but the same cautions regarding causality apply. In any case, research suggests any beneficial effects of ESOPs may be stronger where employees have greater participation in making decisions, perhaps because it gives the employee a stronger feeling of ownership (Pierce, Rubinfeld, & Morgan, 1991). The costs of stock plans, especially options, may not always be obvious, but purchasing stock or issuing new stock (and the resulting dilution of the value of other shares) are costly moves. Indeed, U.S. Senator Carl Levin of Michigan introduced a bill in January 1993 that would require companies to show the granting of stock options as an expense. The Financial Accounting Standards Board (FASB) also has proposed changes to its rules in this area.

What is the evidence on gainsharing programs? Again, it is generally positive. Although the types of cautions cited above regarding causality apply, the fact that from a theoretical standpoint, gainsharing programs offer employees a better line of sight (or instrumentality) between their performance and rewards (Lawler, 1989; Schwab, 1973) suggests that the motivational impact of such programs may be stronger than is the case with organizationwide programs, like profit-sharing and stock plans. Gainsharing payouts are typically based on measures like value-added, sales value of production, or hours saved, which are more controllable by employees than profits or stock performance.

A time series study by Schuster (1983) of six gainsharing plans found substantial (around 30 percent) increases in productivity in four cases following the implementation of gainsharing. A fourth plant had an initial increase in productivity, but increases in the costs of raw materials subsequently decreased the value-added per worker, leading to no bonuses. A fifth plant, although not showing an increase in productivity, had gainsharing in place for 20 years, suggesting that the plan was working, but the productivity increase had already occurred before the study. Other studies have also found significant productivity improvements from gainsharing programs (e.g., Kaufman, 1992).

In addition to having a payout measure that is controllable, gainsharing plans often have the advantage of covering a smaller number of employees, which is also beneficial for motivation because there is less likelihood of employees "free riding" (i.e., working less hard because others will work hard). Indeed, one study estimated that a doubling of employees covered by a gainsharing plan from around 200 to 400 would reduce the expected productivity gain by almost one-half (Kaufman, 1992). The implication is that the number of employees covered can have a substantial impact on the plan's success.

The fact that gainsharing (or any pay program) has a positive impact on productivity is no guarantee that it will continue to be used. A study of a gainsharing plan at an electrical utility estimated a net savings of between $857,000 and $2 million, but the plan was discontinued since employees in other divisions (all represented by the same union) felt unfairly treated because they were not covered (Petty, Singleton, & Connell, 1992). The organization was then faced with two difficult options. First, it could include all employees under the same plan, but that would likely increase the free-rider problem and reduce the motivational impact. Second, it could have a separate plan for each division, but this could easily result in unequal payoffs to employees in different divisions, raising the same problems originally encountered with employees and the union. There would also need to be a means of preventing between-division competition. A profit-sharing or stock plan combined with gainsharing plans would be one option.

Other evidence also indicates that plans which appear to save money do not necessarily survive very long. Kaufman (1992) found that discontinued plans had improved productivity nearly as much as continuing plans. A study sponsored by the American Compensation Association (McAdams & Hawk, 1992) may shed some light on this question. They found that gainsharing plans, on average, were associated with net gains per employee of between $1,300 and $3,700 per year. Nevertheless, when asked to rate the effectiveness of gainsharing plans in improving effectiveness in areas like business performance, fostering teamwork, strengthening the pay-for-performance link, and so forth, the average effectiveness ratings all fell between 2.63 and 3.25 on a 1 (no effectiveness) to 5 (high effectiveness) scale. In other words, most respondents were pretty lukewarm about gainsharing.

Many organizations are moving to group and organization variable pay plans because they are frustrated with what they see as the failure of more traditional merit pay plans. Commonly cited problems include a lack of adequate differentiation between good and poor performers, employee and supervisor resistance, and the fact that merit increases sometimes seem to have become viewed as an entitlement by employees that is costly and does not vary with business performance.

Although there is truth to many of these assertions, one sometimes wonders if perhaps merit pay has been pronounced dead too soon. So-called studies of merit pay have often had significant limitations (see Gerhart & Milkovich, 1992). In addition, the notion that there is no merit pay is open to question.

It is common to conclude that there is no individual merit pay because raises received by good and poor performers differ by only a few percentage points. Two employees, each with a base salary of $40,000, one receiving a 5 percent increase, the other 6 percent, would receive raises differing by $400 per year before taxes, or about $8 per week. Framed this way, the difference does indeed seem small and unlikely to motivate performance.

On the other hand, the example ignores the fact that high performers are more likely to be promoted and thus will have greater earnings growth. This is part of pay-for-performance, but it may not always be communicated as well as it could. Further, even limiting one's attention to the annual increase process, it can be shown that small differences in pay raises accumulate into significant differences over time. As table 27.6 shows,

the present value (or "real" payoff) to raises higher by 1 percentage point adds up to about $76,000 over 20 years. Factoring in promotion based on performance and pay-linked benefits (e.g., retirement) would further increase the payoff to higher performers. Factoring in taxes would decrease the payoff. Would communicating the payoff to performance in this manner change the way employees react to merit pay? Our conversations with managers yielded a wide array of opinions on the matter, suggesting a good area for future research.

The empirical evidence on the effects of banding is basically nonexistent. Research on skill-based pay is just beginning to emerge. An ACA survey of organizations using skill-based pay illustrates some of the potential advantages and disadvantages. Most survey respondents felt that skill-based pay was successful in contributing to greater work-force flexibility and adaptability and in supporting work teams. However, relatively few saw any reduction in labor costs or layoffs. (Indeed, skill-based pay is thought to permit a leaner head count because of cross-training.) So, one must consider whether possible higher labor costs are justified by the advantages having to do with flexibility, adaptability, and the use of teams. Further, it must be recognized that if a plan is implemented, there are several factors that can contribute to its termination. The ACA survey found the following to be most important in terminating skill-based pay plans: inadequate management commitment, unwillingness to endure short-term implementation problems, poor plan designs that increase labor costs without providing offsetting organizational benefits, conflicts between employees included and those excluded from the plan, inadequate training opportunities, and the failure of management to require meaningful skill certifications prior to pay increases.

Only one skill-based pay study to date (Murray & Gerhart, 1994) has used objective measures of productivity and quality, a control

Table 27.6 Pay for performance: accumulations over time

		Employee 1		Employee 2	
Performance rating		Average		1 point above above average	
Annual pay growth		5%		6%	
	Year	Nominal ($)	Real ($)[a]	Nominal ($)	Real ($)[a]
	1	40,000		40,000	
	2	42,000	40,000	42,400	40,381
	3	44,100	40,000	44,944	40,766
	4	46,305	40,000	47,641	41,154
	5	48,620	40,000	50,499	41,546
	6	51,051	40,000	53,529	41,941
	7	53,604	40,000	56,741	42,341
	8	56,284	40,000	60,145	42,744
	9	59,098	40,000	63,754	43,151
	10	62,053	40,000	67,579	43,562
	11	65,156	40,000	71,634	43,977
	12	68,414	40,000	75,932	44,396
	13	71,834	40,000	80,488	44,819
	14	75,426	40,000	85,317	45,245
	15	79,197	40,000	90,436	45,676
	16	83,157	40,000	95,862	46,111
	17	87,315	40,000	101,614	46,551
	18	91,681	40,000	107,711	46,994
	19	96,265	40,000	114,174	47,441
	20	101,078	40,000	121,024	47,893
Total		1,322,638	760,000	1,471,424	836,690
Difference				148,785	76,690

[a] Using 5% discount rate.

group, and a time series before and after implementation of the plan. In a comparison of two automobile parts plants, Murray and Gerhart found that a significant increase in productivity and product quality took place in the plant that implemented skill-based pay.

Globalization and compensation

The continued globalization of markets means that we will have to increasingly consider whether the effect of different pay strategies is likely to differ from country to country, or between cultures within a country. Hofstede's (1993) work on identifying culture differences on dimensions such as power distance (i.e., the degree of inequality considered normal), individualism, masculinity, uncertainty avoidance, and short- versus long-term time orientation has been used by Hodgetts and Luthans (1993) to begin studying this question. Certain hypotheses flow readily from the national differences depicted in table 27.7.[4] Variable pay (pay at risk) may face difficulties in countries that have a high need for uncertainty avoidance such as Japan, South Korea,

Table 27.7 National culture clusters

Region or country	Power distance	Individualism	Masculinity	Uncertainty avoidance
Pacific Rim				
Hong Kong, Malaysia, Philippines, Singapore	High	Low	High	Low
Japan	High	Low	High	High
South Korea, Taiwan	High	Low	Low	High
United States, Great Britain	Low	High	High	Low

Sources: Hofstede (1993), Hodgetts & Luthans (1993).

and Taiwan. Individualistic programs such as merit pay could be a problem in cultures where collectivism is a stronger norm than individualism (e.g., the Pacific Rim countries). Still, average differences in culture are just that, averages, and should not necessarily be viewed as factors that must be taken as a given. Honda, in Japan, for example, just recently announced that it would be changing many of its managers over to a merit pay system.

On the other hand, U.S. companies that have attempted to export pay practices overseas have often encountered difficulties. Lincoln Electric, famous for its history of success using variable pay, has thus far not been successful in implementing variable pay in its overseas acquisitions. Our own experience with gainsharing plans in Western Europe has not been successful (Chilton, 1993). The cultural differences described by Hofstede and related customs are often difficult to overcome. It is probably significantly easier to implement pay practices that are not typical of a country in a greenfield setting as opposed to an acquisition. Indeed, Japanese (e.g., Honda, Nissan) and German (e.g., BMW, Mercedes-Benz) automobile plants opened in the United States have often been in greenfield sites, where the company has maximum flexibility in screening and choosing employees who will fit well with their corporate culture, human resource management, and pay philosophies.

CONCLUSION

Our goal in this chapter has been to describe the theory and practice of compensation, as well as provide an overview of recent empirical evidence on the consequences of different compensation practices. The theory section points to the many trade-offs in designing employee compensation policies. Examples of trade-offs include maximizing high individual effort versus teamwork and cooperation, controlling costs versus maximizing employee effort, and providing incentives for promotion versus producing feelings of inequity due to large pay differentials. Our message has been that the nature of such trade-offs should depend on the corporate and business strategies and that the trade-offs can be made less of a problem by combining pay programs in a way that helps balance competing objectives.

As a final comment, we would like to emphasize that, although it is important to keep abreast of what other organizations are doing (benchmarking) in the area of employee compensation, it is crucial to remember that what works for one organization may not work at all for another. Therefore, surveys of "best practices" are useful to the extent that the surveys report a diversity of best practices and the reasons why different practices are best for different organizations. The ultimate choice of a best compensation strategy rests, of course, on its fit with other human resources activities and its fit with the business strategy.

NOTES

1. Labor costs in the United States have been lower than those of Germany in recent years. However, this difference changes as currency exchange rates differ. The United States still has the highest purchasing power per capita of any country.
2. Employees may use other comparisons standards also, such as their previous or expected future jobs or cost of living.
3. Under the duPont plan, base salary was about 4 percent lower than similar employees in other divisions, unless 100 percent of the profit goal (a 4 percent increase over the previous year's profits) was reached. However, if the profit goal was exceeded, employees would earn more than similar employees in other divisions. For example, if the division reached 150 percent of the profit goal (i.e., 6 percent growth in profits), employees would receive 12 percent more than comparable employees in other divisions. In 1989, when the profit goal was exceeded, the plan seemed to work fine. However, in 1990, profits were down 26 percent from 1989, the profit goal was not met, and employees received no profit-sharing bonus. Instead, they earned 4 percent less than comparable employees in other divisions. Employees were not happy and and duPont eliminated the plan and returned to a system of fixed base salaries with no variable component.
4. Long- versus short-term orientation is not shown. Japan, Hong Kong, and China have a long-term orientation, whereas the United States has a more short-term-oriented culture.

REFERENCES

Adams, J. S. (1963). Toward an understanding of inequity. *Journal of Abnormal Psychology*, 67, 422–36.

Beam, B. T. Jr., & McFadden, J. J. (1992). *Employee benefits*. Chicago: Dearborn Financial Publishing.

Bretz, R. D., Ash, R. A., & Dreher, G. F. (1989). Do people make the place? An examination of the attraction-selection-attrition hypothesis. *Personnel Psychology*, 42, 561–81.

Chilton, K. (1993). Lincoln Electric's incentive system: Can it be transferred overseas? *Compensation and Benefits Review*, Nov.–Dec., 21–30.

Conte, M. A., & Svejnar, J. (1990). The performance effects of employee ownership plans. In A. S. Blinder (ed.), *Paying for Productivity*, 245–94. Washington, D.C.: Brookings Institution.

Cowherd, D. M., & Levine, D. I. (1992). Product quality and pay equity between lower-level employees and top management: An investigation of distributive justice theory. *Administrative Science Quarterly*, 37, 302–20.

Davis, J. H. (1993). Quality management and compensation. *ACA Journal*, autumn.

Dyer, L., & Blancero, D. (1993). Workplace 2000: A delphi study. Working paper, Center for Advanced Human Resource Studies, Cornell University, Ithaca, NY.

Eisenhardt, K. M. (1989). Agency theory: An assessment and review. *Academy of Management Review*, 14, 57–74.

Ellig, B. R. (1981). Compensation elements: Market phase determines the mix. *Compensation Review*, third quarter, 30–8.

Fama, E. F., & Jensen, M. C. (1983). Separation of ownership and control. *Journal of Law and Economics*, 26, 301–25.

Fisher, L. M. (1992). Sears auto centers to halt commissions. *New York Times*, June 23, D1.

Gerhart, B., & Milkovich, G. T. (1990). Organizational differences in managerial compensation and financial performance. *Academy of Management Journal*, 33, 663–91.

Gerhart, B., & Milkovich, G. T. (1992). Employee compensation: Research and practice. In M. D. Dunnette & L. M. Hough (eds.), *Handbook of Industrial and Organizational Psychology*, 2nd ed., 481–569. Palo Alto, CA: Consulting Psychologists Press.

Gerhart, B., Milkovich, G. T., & Murray, B. (1992). Pay, performance, and participation. In D. Lewin, O. Mitchell, & P. Sherer (eds.), *Research Frontiers in Industrial Relations*, 193–238. Madison, WI: Industrial Relations Research Association.

Gomez-Mejia, L. R. (1992). Structure and process of diversification, compensation strategy, and firm performance. *Strategic Management Journal*, 13, 381–97.

Gomez-Mejia, L. R., & Balkin, D. B. (1992). *Compensation, Organizational Strategy, and Firm Performance*. Cincinnati: South-Western.

Greenberg, J. (1990). Employee theft as a reaction to underpayment of inequity: The hidden cost of pay cuts. *Journal of Applied Psychology*, 75, 561–8.

Heneman, H. G., III, & Schwab, D. P. (1979). Work and rewards theory. In D. Yoder & H. G. Heneman, Jr. (eds.), *ASPA Handbook of Personnel and Industrial Relations*. Washington, D.C.: Bureau of National Affairs.

Hodgetts, R. M., & Luthans, F. (1993). U.S. multinationals' compensation strategies for local management: Cross-cultural implications. *Compensation & Benefits Review*, 25, Mar.–Apr., 42–8.

Hofstede, G. (1993). Cultural constraints in management theories. *Academy of Management Executive*, 7 (1), 81–94.

Jones, D. C., & Takao, K. (1993). The scope, nature, and effects of employee stock ownership plans in Japan. *Industrial and Labor Relations Review*, 46, 352–67.

Judge, T. A., & Bretz, R. D., Jr. (1992). Effect of values on job choice decisions. *Journal of Applied Psychology*, 77, 261–71.

Kaufman, R. T. (1992). The effects of Improshare on productivity. *Industrial and Labor Relations Review*, 45, 311–22.

Kerr, J. L. (1985). Diversification strategies and managerial rewards. *Academy of Management Journal*, 28, 155–79.

Kidwell, R. E., Jr., & Bennett, N. (1993). Employee

propensity to withhold effort: A conceptual model to intersect three avenues of research. *Academy of Management Review*, 18, 429–56.

Kruse, D. L. (1993a). *Profit Sharing: Does it make a difference?* Kalamazoo, MI: Upjohn Institute.

Kruse, D. L. (1993b). Does profit sharing affect productivity? Tests using panel data on profit sharing features and personnel policies. Working paper, Rutgers University, New Brunswick, NJ.

Lambert, R. A., & Larcker, D. F. (1989). Executive compensation, corporate decision-making, and shareholder wealth. In F. Foulkes (ed.), *Executive Compensation*, 287–309. Boston: Harvard Business School.

Lawler, E. E., III (1989). Pay for performance: A strategic analysis. In L. R. Gomez-Mejia (ed.), *Compensation and Benefits*. Washington, D.C.: Bureau of National Affairs.

Levine, D. I., & Tyson, L. D. (1990). Participation, productivity, and the firm's environment. In A. S. Blinder (ed.), *Paying for Productivity*. Washington, D.C.: Brookings Institution.

Locke, E. A., Feren, D. B., McCaleb, V. M., Shaw, K. N., & Denny, A. T. (1980). The relative effectiveness of four methods of motivating employee performance. In K. D. Duncan, M. M. Gruenberg, & D. Wallis (eds.), *Changes in Working Life*, 363–88. New York: Wiley.

McAdams, J. L., & Hawk, E. J. (1992). Capitalizing on human assets through permance-based rewards. *ACA Journal*, 1 (1), 60–73.

Miles, R. E., & Snow, C. C. (1978). *Organizational Strategy, Structure, and Process*. New York: McGraw-Hill.

Milkovich, G. T. (1988). A strategic perspective on compensation management. *Research in Personnel and Human Resources Management*, 6, 263–88.

Milkovich, G. T., Gerhart, B., & Hannon, J. (1991). The effects of research and development intensity on managerial compensation in large organizations. *Journal of High Technology Management Research*, 2, 133–50.

Milkovich, G. T., & Newman, J. (1993). *Compensation*, 4th ed. Homewood, IL: BPI/Irwin.

Milkovich, G. T., & Wigdor, A. K. (1991). *Pay for Performance*. Washington, D.C.: National Academy Press.

Murray, B., & Gerhart, B. (1994). Organizational outcomes from the introduction of a skill-based pay program. Working paper, Center for Advanced Human Resources Studies, Cornell University, Ithaca, NY.

Noe, R. A., Hollenbeck, J. R., Gerhart, B., & Wright, P. M. (1994). *Human Resource Management: Gaining a competitive advantage*. Burr Ridge, IL: Austen Press/Irwin.

Petty, M. M., Singleton, B., & Connell, D. W. (1992). An experimental evaluation of an organizational incentive plan in the electric utility industry. *Journal of Applied Psychology*, 77, 427–36.

Pierce, J. L., Rubenfeld, S., & Morgan, S. (1991). Employee ownership: A conceptual model of process and effects. *Academy of Management Review*, 16, 121–44.

Santora, J. E. (1991). DuPont returns to the drawing board. *Personnel Journal*, February, 34–6.

Schuster, M. (1983). The impact of union-management cooperation on productivity and employment. *Industrial and Labor Relations Review*, 36, 415–30.

Schwab, D. P. (1973). Impact of alternative compensation systems on pay valence and instrumentality perceptions. *Journal of Applied Psychology*, 58, 308–12.

Tosi, H. L., Jr., & Gomez-Mejia, L. R. (1989). The decoupling of CEO pay and performance: An agency theory perspective. *Administrative Science Quarterly*, 34, 169–89.

Tully, S. (1993). Your paycheck gets exciting. *Fortune*, November 1, 83.

Vroom, V. H. (1964). *Work and Motivation*. New York: Wiley.

Weitzman, M. L., & Kruse, D. L. (1990). Profit sharing and productivity. In A. S. Blinder (ed.), *Paying for Productivity*. Washington, D.C.: Brookings Institution.

□ **Chapter 28** □

Executive Compensation: Research and Practical Implications

Luis R. Gomez-Mejia, George Paulin, and Arden Grabke

INTRODUCTION

Executive compensation program design is a significant function of human resource management because of its direct influence on organizational strategy, employee behaviors, and firm performance. The determinants and the organizational consequences of alternative executive compensation program philosophies and approaches have been the subject of much conceptual and empirical work. Different conjectures regarding the factors that lead to the significant levels of executive compensation and the resulting performance of the firm have been made by researchers and practitioners across several disciplines, including economics, finance, psychology, sociology, and political science. The purpose of this chapter is to provide an overview of these propositions by introducing the reader to several of the leading theories with executive compensation implications.

What follows is an overview of the theories and related empirical studies that have been conducted to examine their relevance and validity. Following that is a section on the components of contemporary executive compensation programs and the policy choices faced by practitioners involved in program design and administration, including relevant references to the various theories. The chapter concludes with a section on emerging reforms and critical future issues concerning executive compensation.

LEADING THEORIES OF EXECUTIVE COMPENSATION

As previously mentioned, researchers across several disciplines have sought to explain the significant levels of executive compensation, their determinants, and their consequences. Empirical studies of executive compensation have been conducted over at least the last 70 years. Meanwhile, as executive compensation has emerged as a topic of societal, public policy, and corporate governance significance, the audience for the research has grown to include corporate management and boards, investors, and the popular business press. The theories that currently receive the most attention, although not necessarily popularly known as such, include: marginal productivity theory, governance theories of managerialism and agency theory, structural theory, human capital theory, and the symbolism theories of tournament winnings and political strategist appointments. A brief overview of each theory follows.

Marginal productivity theory

Marginal productivity theory is primarily concerned with predicting pay levels of executives. Because of the theory's origins in classical and neoclassical economics, many of its propositions about executive compensation are made within a context of analyzing the firm's ability to generate profits and maximize productive output. Two principal conclusions regarding the magnitude of executive compensation are drawn from marginal productivity theory.

The size of the executive pay package reflects the firm's net profits The purest illustration of this point is a firm where the founding entrepreneur is the sole owner and functions as chief executive officer (CEO). This individual is assumed to have had a marketable idea, used his or her resources to start the firm, and personally taken the associated risks. It is further assumed that this individual desires to achieve the highest returns on his or her investments and that, given perfect competition, this will occur when the marginal cost of production (i.e., the change in costs associated with a change in output) is equal to the market price of the product. At this point, the firm maximizes its profits and the executive maximizes his or her compensation, which is equivalent to the profits of the firm.

In practice, there are few such pure situations. Most entrepreneurs must eventually rely on outside investors for capital to grow their firms to the size of potential profit maximization. As others invest, they then share the risks and expect appropriate returns. Executive pay determination suddenly becomes more complicated as decisions must be made about what share of the profits goes to whom,

whether one party receives a bigger share of current profits as opposed to future profits, and so forth. Thus, as a practical guide, marginal productivity theory provides a rationale for the logical correlation between an executive's compensation level and the profitability of his or her firm. However, it is not a framework for determining the allocation of profits between an executive and others who invest their money or knowledge and over what future time periods.

The size of the executive pay package is proportional to the executive's marginal revenue product Here, it is assumed that the executive is hired by the firm and is paid commensurate with his or her economic contribution. The amount of compensation equals the executive's marginal revenue product, defined as the firm's net profits taking into account the executive's services, minus the net profits that would be attained if an alternative executive were hired, plus the amount that would have to be paid to the alternative executive (Roberts, 1959).

The practical implication of marginal productivity theory is that both the firm's profitability and the executive's relative economic contribution or impact are pay-level determinants. To some extent, the theory may help to explain the "star" system that has developed in the hiring of certain CEOs and other key executives. These are executives with demonstrated track records of creating shareholder value through their management skills, strategic vision, or cost-cutting expertise. Such individuals may demand and receive outsized compensation levels compared to others doing the same job because of their perceived potential to influence a firm's future profitability and value.

Governance theories

In publicly traded U.S. corporations (i.e., where the corporation's stock is listed on a stock exchange), there may be hundreds, thousands, or even millions of firm owners. For example, AT&T has an estimated 2.4 million shareholders (*Moody's Handbook of Common Stocks*, 1993–94), which is an underestimate in actuality because it does not count the individual investors in mutual funds or shares held for individuals in brokerage accounts (i.e., "street name"). It is widely held that executives should be pursuing strategies that will create long-term shareholder value, and that they should receive closely related rewards. However, because ownership often is so widely dispersed, there is little likelihood of owners convening to monitor the executive's behavior. Consequently, executives may feel free to pursue interests that do not coincide with those of the firm's owners, knowing that the owners have a limited ability to influence the executives' rewards. As a result, the executive compensation package may not be effectively linked to performance that creates or maximizes shareholder value.

Based primarily in financial economics, managerialism and agency theory are subsets of governance theory that deal with issues arising when the firm's owners are removed from the decision-making processes of the executive. Research in this area has become an important foundation for efforts to link executive rewards, particularly long-term incentives, to company stock, and to encourage executives and outside directors to own stock in their companies, which are significant executive compensation themes among publicly traded U.S. firms. Research also supports efforts by the U.S. Securities and Exchange Commission (SEC), institutional investor groups, and shareholder activists to have independent committees of public-company boards set executive pay policy on behalf of the owners. "Independent" generally means that the directors on the committee are not company employees or paid advisors, do not have overlapping board relationships (i.e., "interlocks") with company managers, and do not participate in the compensation plans that they administer.

Advocates of this theory believe that a hired executive will act in the best interests of the owners if he or she has a significant personal ownership stake. Many contemporary executive compensation programs are structured to reflect this theory by paying substantial amounts of compensation in the form of stock options, restricted stock, and other forms of stock-based rewards. A number of well-known companies have even instituted ownership guidelines stating that executives are expected to accumulate real stock holdings (i.e., actual owned shares, not outstanding options or unvested restricted shares) equivalent to specified percentages of their salaries. Examples include Chrysler, Kodak, and General Mills. Typical guideline ownership levels at large companies like those named are three-to-five times annual salary for the CEO, decreasing to one-to-two times salary for entry-level officer positions.

Managerialism

The premise underlying managerialism is that the executive's behavior is no longer constrained by the external owners, leaving less of an incentive for the executive to maximize corporate profits (Aoki, 1984; Berle & Means, 1932; Herman, 1981; Marris, 1964; Williams, 1985). The factors creating such an environment are the following: A single shareholder may not have enough at stake to launch a complaint against the executive; there are information asymmetries (i.e., the executive knows more about what is happening in the firm's internal and external environments and may use this information to his or her advantage); and it is the executive who selects those who are on the board of directors, so the board members have little incentive to discipline the executive.

The separation of ownership and control in organizations can lead to executive pay decisions that benefit the executive regardless of what the organizational outcomes and effects might be on shareholders. For example, Tosi and Gomez-Mejia (1989) found that when firms are management controlled (i.e., no single shareholder owns 5 percent or more of the company's stock), as opposed to owner-controlled, there is little variability, downside risk, and uncertainty in executive compensation amounts. In other words, an executive in such a firm is more likely to have a pay package that will increase when firm performance is good and remain at about the same level even when firm performance is poor. Furthermore an executive in such a firm is more likely to pursue activities that enhance his or her personal prestige and visibility to justify higher levels of pay, regardless of the firm's performance. For instance, executives have been found to increase firm size through corporate diversification, mergers, and acquisitions even when this has led to decreased profits (Ahimud & Lev, 1981; Kroll, Simmons, & Wright, 1990).

Management-controlled firms have also been noted to use accounting measures to determine rewards that distort the relationship between shareholder value and executive compensation (Dyl, 1989; Groff & Wright, 1989; Hunt, 1986; Larcker & Sloan, 1992; Miller & Berton, 1993). Gomez-Mejia and Balkin (1992, 165) summarized the problem of separate ownership and managerial control recognized by managerialists: "The system of governance in major corporations is devoid of checks and balances because of a fractionalized distribution of ownership, and this works to management's advantage."

Agency theory
Agency theory may be considered a theoretical extension of managerialism in that it also recognizes the problems inherent in separate ownership and managerial control; however, it goes beyond managerialism to prescribe ways to diminish the related problems. In the agency theory framework, the firm's owners are called the principals and the hired executives are called the agents. For reasons cited earlier (e.g., widely dispersed ownership making it difficult for owners to convene with

each other, the agent's superior access to information, etc.), the agent may pursue activities that benefit him or her rather than the firm's owners. This represents an "agency cost" to firm owners, which is defined specifically as the difference between net profits of the firm had the owners been the managers and the observed net profits under the agent's stewardship. Nonetheless, agency theorists posit that agency costs are a necessary evil that come with the advantages of the modern corporation such as capital availability, shared risk, and economies of scale. Agency theorists further claim that it is possible to reduce agency costs by using systems to monitor agents' behavior and incentives to align the interests of principals and their agents.

Perhaps the most commonly cited theoretical description of the monitoring process for reducing agency costs is that of Fama (1980) and Fama and Jensen (1983a, 1983b). According to these authors, a firm may be considered a "nexus of contracts," where the expected relationship between the owners and the executives is specified. These contracts simultaneously allow organizations to use the specialized knowledge of their executives and curtail executives' discretion. Contractual enforcement occurs through a decision-making process that may be broken down into four stages:

1 *Initiation stage* The executives are expected to scan the environment to identify potential opportunities and threats and generate strategic proposals for the use of existing resources.
2 *Ratification stage* The strategic proposals developed by the executives go through an approval process (normally the responsibility of the board of directors acting as representatives of the owners).
3 *Implementation stage* The strategic plan is implementated.
4 *Performance measurement stage* The owners (commonly through boards acting as their representatives) assess the contributions

made by the executives and reward them accordingly.

In summary, this four-step monitoring process allows owners to influence the performance of the executive (i.e., curtail the executive's discretion) through the use of performance criteria and evaluation.

The above process implies the use of performance-related financial incentives as a way of reducing agency costs. The intent is not on supervising the behavior of managers in the decision-making process. Rather, it is to reward them for achieving measurable results that are in the owners' best interests. Typically, these results are quantifiable. Examples are changes in stock price, return on equity, and cash flow return on investment. To be effective, it is necessary for incentives to complement, not substitute for, the monitoring activities of the owners. This means that incentives should be designed to reward the achievement of strategies that create and maximize shareholder value, under the control of independent directors representing the owners, and be an integral part of the firm's management review and control process.

Structural theory

Similar to the theories reviewed thus far, structural theory examines executive compensation at the firm level. However, rather than considering executive pay in terms of economic profits or the separation of ownership from management, structural theory focuses on the "social standards" of pay at different hierarchical levels. Based in sociology and on the work of Simon (1957), structural theory claims that organizations attempt to maintain particular salary differentials between management and subordinate levels to comply with cultural norms of proportionality. According to Simon, the norm in salary differentials between clearly differentiated hierarchical levels within a firm approximates 30 percent. This implies that executives can

expect to receive a relatively large amount of compensation in a firm that is of considerable size, and where there might be a large number of hierarchical levels. Conversely, the implication is that executive compensation levels would decline in response to the trend toward corporate "downsizing," although skeptical observers would argue that this is unlikely to actually occur.

DuPont provides an example of a practical application of structural theory. According to DuPont's SEC disclosure (1993 proxy statement), there was a general concern on the part of top management and the board compensation committee about rapidly escalating CEO compensation in large U.S. companies and "the widening divergence in CEO compensation compared to the average employee." In response, DuPont established a practice of setting the pay structure for its CEO based on an internal benchmark differential above its senior vice presidents instead of tracking CEO compensation at other companies through pay surveys. What DuPont succeeded in doing through this approach was to establish an objective rationale for setting its CEO's pay structure that reflects a theoretical hierarchical differential instead of relying primarily on competitive data.

Human capital theory

Human capital theorists examine the individual characteristics of the executive in attempting to predict pay levels (Gerhart & Milkovich, 1990). These characteristics include factors that are intrinsic to the executive such as his or her knowledge base, including education, experience, and training (Becker, 1964). According to Mincer (1975), it is possible to calculate a "rate of return" on investments made in human capital. The amount of human capital acquired by the executive at any given point determines how valuable he or she is to the firm. This, in turn, predicts how much the firm will pay for his or her services. Meanwhile, the potential value of the human capital theory would seem to diminish as executive compensation becomes increasingly performance-based, unless it can consistently predict performance outcomes through correlations with executives' personal characteristics and backgrounds.

Symbolism theories

The symbolism theories of executive compensation hypothesize that the executive's power and political influence are the primary determinants of his or her pay level. Power and politics are proposed to be of more direct importance to those who make executive pay decisions than the economic elements of firm performance and executive productivity. This is because powerful executives are likely to obtain scarce resources and successfully handle environmental uncertainties, factors that are necessary for the survival of the organization. Two symbolism theories are summarized below. The first is tournament theory, which originated in economics. The second is the political strategist theory, which has its origin in organizational psychology.

Tournament theory

As the name implies, tournament theory proposes that the amount of compensation received by executives of an organization is analogous to tournament winnings. Tournament participants are members of the organization who could eventually reach the pinnacle of the CEO position, the largest prize of all. The prospect of this prize sends powerful signals throughout the organization that by working harder and making the best possible use of one's personal talents one may, in the end, win the trophy of the number-one spot. The emphasis is not on whether an executive deserves his or her amount of compensation; rather, the focus is on the motivational properties that executive compensation levels bring to those lower in the organization.

Historically in American industry, tournament winnings were reflected in both the forms and amounts of compensation paid to executives. Although all employees received salaries, or a base wage in the case of hourly employees, and certain benefits, only the very top people were eligible for short-term incentives (e.g., annual bonuses), long-term incentives (e.g., stock options), and status-oriented perquisites (e.g., company cars, club memberships, use of company aircraft, etc.). More recently the trend has been to expand participation in both short- and long-term incentives, and for business need to determine perquisite availability as opposed to purely status considerations. Tournament winners are consequently differentiated less today in *how* they are paid and more in *how much* they are paid. Simultaneously with expanding the participation in performance-based incentives that were once limited to executives, many organizations are also differentiating the opportunities under these incentive arrangements along business unit and functional area lines. As a result of these policies, the CEO may not necessarily be the highest-paid person in the organization. The Wall Street investment banking firms are a prime example. In terms of tournament theory, the general pay-for-performance trend of the late 1980s and 1990s, if it continues, may indicate a healthy realignment of motivational priorities away from position level and status, toward individual merit and results.

Political strategist theory

Similar to tournament theory, the political strategist theory tends to ignore the rational justifications of executive compensation levels, such as those that relate pay to firm profitability, or to an executive's human capital. Attention is paid instead to the executive's ability to cater to the needs of the multiple constituents of the firm such as board members, shareholders, employees, customers, suppliers, government, and/or the general public. Based primarily on the works of Ungson and Steers (1984) and Steers and Ungson (1987), the political strategist theory proposes that the level of executive compensation can best be understood by examining how well the executive appeases these various constituent groups. Typically, these groups' needs cannot all be met at once; the executive, therefore, has to use his or her charismatic, negotiating, and consensus-building talents to convince constituents that his or her strategic agenda is best for all concerned. CEOs who possess such skills include Ross Johnson (RJR Nabisco), and Lee Iacocca (Chrysler) in the 1980s. The amount of skill the executive has in serving as political strategist, so goes the theory, determines his or her level of compensation.

Skeptical observers of U.S. executive compensation may point to the political strategist theory as support for why there was rapid escalation in outside directors' compensation accompanying the escalation in compensation of CEOs and key executives during the 1980s. They would say it was influenced by executives as a way of obtaining the directors' agreement to increase executives' pay. Likewise, they may point to the theory to explain, in part, the expansion in incentive participation as a way to temper the negative response of lower-level employees toward higher executive pay levels. In the end, these "share-the-wealth" approaches, unless justified by performance, are at the expense of shareholders who began in the 1990s to flex their political muscle, particularly with regard to executive pay issues.

Theoretical summary and empirical investigations

As should be apparent, the topic of executive compensation provides many avenues for investigation. The theories reviewed here indicate several possible perspectives including those of the firm, labor market, shareholders, and individual executives. At the level of the firm, it has been proposed that executive compensation is a function of microeconomic determinants (marginal productivity), struc-

tural factors (hierarchical levels), and symbolic/political factors (ability to pacify multiple constituents). At the level of the labor market, executive pay is said to depend on the cost of hiring the best available replacement for the current executive. At the shareholder level in management-controlled organizations, executive pay is expected to vary depending on the distribution of ownership and the monitoring/incentive mechanisms established by the firm's owners to reduce agency costs. Finally, at the individual level, an executive's pay is said to be related to his or her accumulation of learning and human capital.

Not all theoretical suppositions have received empirical support, however, primarily due to the difficulties in attempting to operationalize and test certain concepts. For example, in order to investigate the assumptions given in marginal productivity theory, one would need to know the pay requirements of an alternative executive along with how well the firm would perform under his or her leadership. There is also difficulty in trying to measure the political effectiveness of an executive when the needs and underlying perceptions of multiple constituencies need to be taken into account. Fast-changing dynamics are also a problem, including the trend toward pay-for-performance, emphasis on increasing executive and employee stock ownership, and growth in shareholder activism with executive compensation as a high-priority corporate-governance issue. Still, researchers continue to identify the significant determinants of executive compensation hypothesized in these theories.

Most empirical work has been devoted to examining the assumptions given in agency theory: namely, the testing of the proposition that an alignment of shareholder and executive interests increases the performance of the firm. A greater alignment of such interests would constitute a larger proportion of stock-based, long-term incentives relative to fixed pay (Gomez-Mejia, Tosi, & Hinkin,

1987; Tosi & Gomez-Mejia, 1989). Structural theory also has received empirical attention as researchers have attempted to test the relationship between the size of the firm (theoretically reflected in the number of hierarchical levels) and the size of the executive's pay package (Agarwal, 1981; Ciscel & Carroll, 1980; McGuire, Chiu, & Elbing, 1962; Schmidt & Fowler, 1990). Other relationships that have been examined include executive compensation levels and their associations with managerial decisions, firm diversification, environmental factors, distribution of ownership, human capital, symbolic factors, and the tax system (Gomez-Mejia & Balkin, 1992). The most salient results of this research are presented in table 28.1.

COMPONENTS OF THE EXECUTIVE COMPENSATION PROGRAM

This section reviews the principal compensation decisions and trade-offs that confront designers of executive pay programs. Many of the ideas presented here are based on the theoretical ideas and research results presented earlier, with the intent of aiding practitioners in implementing the principles that can be extrapolated from these theories and findings.

A crucial issue regarding the design of the executive compensation program is the mix of elements, or the relative importance that is placed on each component of the program. The executive's total compensation package consists of four main components: base salaries, short-term incentives, long-term incentives, and benefits/perquisites. The emphasis given to each component has significant strategic implications.

Base salaries

This is regarded as a "fixed" element of pay, meaning that it normally does not vary in relation to company performance. Because salary establishes the executive's basic standard of living, it is necessary for both high- and low-performing firms to pay at or near going market rates. These market rates are normally determined from competitive pay surveys and reflect hierarchical relationships (i.e., higher amounts for higher-level positions and vice versa).

The leading pay surveys indicate that while the geographic region is not a significant factor in salary-level competitiveness at the executive level, industry and size of the firm are. To illustrate, the Radford Associates 1993 survey of high-technology companies showed that the median salary for CEOs of firms with annual revenues of less than $40 million was $183,600, as compared to $618,000 for CEOs of firms with greater than $1 billion in annual revenues. Beneath the statistical averages, though, are wide variations related to individual performance, pay history, and experience. Differences are also related to company pay philosophy and management style.

Starting in the 1970s, when inflation was high, it became a common practice for firms to review and adjust executive salaries on an annual basis to recognize market movement and individual merit. An unfortunate side effect is that executives have generally developed an entitlement attitude toward these annual increases even when it is difficult for companies to sustain them (e.g., in a low-inflation period when higher salary costs cannot easily be passed on through higher prices or offset by productivity increases if firms already have undergone massive cost cutting). There is also the argument that executives may engage in short-term behavior that is not in the firm's best interests in the long term in order to earn larger periodic salary increases. However, any inherent tendency toward short-term reward generally should be balanced by significant long-term incentive opportunities that are discussed later.

Several structural transformations in executive salary administration began in the 1990s. First, as companies eliminated levels

Table 28.1 Empirical support for 22 propositions concerning predictors and correlates of executive pay

	Propositions	*Empirical support*
Proposition 1	Executive pay varies as a function of firm performance.	Very mixed, minimal relationships
Proposition 2	The lower the expected performance of a firm if the next best alternative executive were to be hired as a substitute for the present CEO, the higher the current CEO's pay.	Largely untested
Proposition 3	The greater the pay necessary to attract the best alternative replacement of the current CEO, the greater the compensation received by the latter.	Largely untested
Proposition 4	The greater the compensation the current CEO would receive in the open market, the higher his/her compensation.	Largely untested
Proposition 5	The more dispersed the ownership of a firm, the more executives will structure their compensation package so that their pay is flexible to move up as firm performance improves, but will not suffer if firm performance declines.	Strong
Proposition 6	The more dispersed the ownership of a firm, the less likely executives will be dismissed as firm performance declines.	Strong
Proposition 7	The more dispersed the ownership of a firm, the more likely executives will be driven to increase firm size, even if additional growth results in decreased performance.	Strong
Proposition 8	The more concentrated the ownership of a firm, the more likely executive decisions (and the CEO pay package) will have a long-term horizon.	Moderate
Proposition 9	The more concentrated the ownership of a firm, the more effective the board of directors is in disciplining executives and the lower the influence exercised by executives.	Strong
Proposition 10	Greater monitoring and incentive alignment of executives result in improved firm performance.	Moderate
Proposition 11	Greater monitoring and incentive alignment of executives leads to a greater observed linkage between executive pay and firm performance.	Moderate
Proposition 12	Increased monitoring produces higher firm performance among management-controlled firms.	Moderate
Proposition 13	Relationship between executive pay and firm performance varies by extent of diversification.	Strong
Proposition 14	Extent of division autonomy affects criteria used to reward executives.	Strong
Proposition 15	Executive pay is more strongly related to stock-related performance criteria than to accounting measures.	Negative
Proposition 16	Taller organizational structures imply more pay at the top.	Very strong
Proposition 17	Human capital plays a big role in top management's pay.	Moderate
Proposition 18	Top executive pay is used as a tournament trophy to motivate lower level managers.	Very mixed
Proposition 19	Firms compensate executives for performance over their entire tenure with the firm, not necessarily based on their most recent performance.	Moderate
Proposition 20	Executive pay reflects how well this individual fulfills his/her role as a political strategist rather than how well he/she maximizes "bottom line," objective performance criteria.	Largely untested
Proposition 21	Executive decisions are very responsive to what incumbents perceive will lead to the greatest financial reward.	Very strong
Proposition 22	Strategic rather than tax concerns drive the design of executives' pay packages.	Moderate

Source: Reprinted with permission from Gomez-Mejia & Balkin (1992).

of management, they correspondingly flattened their salary structures through what has become known as "salary banding." This is the practice of having fewer administrative ranges with wider minimum-to-maximum rates to recognize differences in individual performance. Second, a lengthening of intervals between salary increases is occurring in response to lower inflation and greater emphasis on performance-based pay elements. For executives already paid relatively high in comparison to the competitive market rate for their positions, merit increases may be 18 months to two years apart instead of the annual increases that were common. Third, although executive salaries continue to increase, the rate of increase is less than that of incentive pay elements, reflecting the pay-for-performance shift. For example, although executive salaries in a group of large U.S. companies grew at an annual rate of approximately 6.2 percent from 1984 to 1988, the value of their long-term incentive grants grew at a 14.6 percent annual rate (Paulin, 1989). A factor contributing to the escalation in CEO and key executive pay levels in the 1980s is apparent from these statistics: Although there was movement in the 1980s toward performance-based pay, it was on top of, not in lieu of, continually increasing, and some would argue already excessive, executive salaries. During the 1990s, there appears to be more of a trade-off occurring for lower-level executives and others who are being added to incentive eligibility often as a quid pro quo for higher salary increases.

Short-term incentives

The distinction between short-term incentives and long-term incentives typically is regarded to be the period for measuring performance, with short-term incentives measured for one year or less and long-term incentives measured for more than one year. Commonly, short-term incentives are awarded annually, although there are many examples of companies with quarterly plans such as 3M and Seagate Technologies. Award opportunities reflect hierarchical position relationships in most cases, with higher opportunities relative to salary for higher-level positions and vice versa. Payments normally are in cash at the end of measurement periods, but may be partly or totally in stock to encourage executive ownership, or electively or mandatorily deferred for purposes of individual tax planning or employment retention. The criticism is often heard that short-term incentives motivate decisions that maximize current results at the expense of the longer term. Yet, as is the case with the periodic merit salary increases discussed earlier, most companies effectively balance at the executive level short-term and long-term incentives (Lublin, 1994; Lopez, 1994).

Three types of short-term incentive arrangements are prevalent among U.S. companies. The first are "goal-driven" plans where a company sets target or normal award opportunities that reflect competitive amounts, such as achieving 100 percent of a goal. If there is overachievement, actual awards may range up to 150 percent to 200 percent of normal awards; conversely, such awards may drop to zero for underachievement. Performance measures may be purely financial or partly based on personal MBOs; they may be driven entirely by corporate results or weighted for business unit or individual results. In addition, financial goals may be *absolute* (e.g., a specified return on equity regardless of the difficulty or opportunity for achievement), or *relative* to internal projections (e.g., performance versus budget or business plan forecasts). Although a majority of companies probably continue to use relative internal goals based on budgets, increasingly the trend is toward absolute goals; investors are beginning to demand more consistent relationships between total annual compensation and short-term results, which they view in absolute terms related to profits and growth. Absolute goals also eliminate the classic problem of projecting lower-than-achievable performance (i.e., "sandbagging") to earn bigger awards. Nevertheless, in many cases companies cannot achieve acceptable absolute performance levels and have continued to link their goal-driven plans to internal budgets because executives believe they are entitled to receive at least some recognition via short-term awards for their efforts, regardless of company results.

The second common type of short-term incentives are "formula-driven" arrangements. Under such arrangements, executives share in a pool of funds determined from specified financial results (e.g., some percent of net profits above a threshold return on equity). Allocation of the earned pools to individual participants also may be based on formulas, or it may be wholly or partly discretionary. More of these types of plans are implemented for key executives such as those approved by shareholders at AT&T, Citicorp, J. P. Morgan, and Bank of America. It should be kept in mind in analyzing and comparing the formulas under these plans that such formulas may be serving only as shareholder safeguards to limit the maximum available awards, with different goals operating within the formulas to generate actual awards.

Finally, the third type of short-term incentive arrangements are purely discretionary plans. Here, award levels generally are determined after the fact without specified measures of goals. This is a less prevalent approach in large, mature companies, but is often used by smaller, emerging firms where annual goal setting is difficult and executive compensation programs are more informal.

Long-term incentives

As previously explained, long-term incentives generally refer to grants or awards where the payment or earnout is based on performance for a period beyond one year. The chief grant types fall into three broad categories: stock-price appreciation grants; restricted stock and restricted cash grants; and performance-based grants. Brief definitions are shown in table 28.2.

Table 28.3 shows the utilization of these various grant types by the *Fortune 200* U.S. industrial companies in 1992.

There are significantly more grant types in use than there are companies in the sample in table 28.3, reflecting the fact that most of the companies have more than one grant type in use. Among large, mature companies in the top 200, it is common to combine stock options with performance-based grants. Although the options reward for absolute stock-price growth, the performance-based grants are designed to reward strategic long-term company objectives not directly related to the stock market. Smaller companies, start-ups, and those in traditionally high-growth industries are more likely to use stock options alone. The reasons for this are higher upside reward potential related to future company growth, relatively attractive company cash flow and accounting effects, and the necessity for smaller firms to operate opportunistically to set meaningful long-term goals in awarding performance-based grants.

Stock options are by far the most prevalent grant type. Historically, they have been regarded as a direct and objective way to link executive rewards and shareholder returns. They also provide uncapped and highly leveraged incentive opportunities. In fact, the large CEO compensation levels that receive so much attention in the business press are mostly from option profits. As figure 28.1 illustrates, the highest-paid CEOs reported in *Business Week* for each of the five years from 1988–92 made an aggregate of $314.4 million. Of this amount, $302.9 (96.3 percent) was from option profits and the remaining $11.5 million (3.7 percent) was from all remaining compensation elements combined.

Even though options are commonly used, their role in executive compensation may be debated. Supporters contend that options are a reward for shareholder-value creation, but

Table 28.2 Definitions of long-term incentive grant types

Stock-price appreciation grants

Stock options Rights granted to executives to purchase shares of their company's stock at a fixed price (usually market value at the time the option is granted) for a fixed period of time (most often 10 years).

Stock appreciation rights (SARs) Rights attached to options that enable executives to receive direct payment for the related option's appreciation during the option term without exercising the option.

Stock purchases Opportunities for executives to purchase shares of their company's stock valued at market or full value at a discount price, often with the company providing financing assistance.

Restricted stock/cash grants

Restricted stock grants Grants to executives of stock or stock units subject to restrictions on transfer and risk of forfeiture until earned by continued employment.

Restricted cash grants Grants of fixed-dollar amounts (not tied to stock price) subject to transfer and forfeiture restrictions until earned by continued employment.

Performance-based grants

Performance shares/units Grants of stock, stock units, or contingent cash amounts – the full payment of which is contingent upon the company's achieving certain long-term performance goals.

Formula-value grants Rights to receive units or the gain in value of units determined by a formula rather than market value.

Dividend units Rights to receive the equivalent of the dividends paid on a specified number of company shares.

Table 28.3 1992 long-term incentive usage among top 200 industrial companies

Stock-price appreciation	
Stock options	192
SARs	24
Stock purchases	4
Restricted stock/cash	94
Performance-based	
Performance shares	47
Performance units	55
Formula value grants	3
	419

Source: Frederic W. Cook & Co., Inc. (1993)

critics contend that a large part of the rewards are from general stock market activity. Likewise, supporters of options say that executives only make money when shareholders make money, but critics say that executives too often profit simply from timing (i.e., when options are granted, exercised, and sold), and in some cases from the sheer size of their option grants. There is also potential criticism that while options are awarded ostensibly to create executive ownership, in most cases executives quickly convert their option profits to cash by selling the shares with limited ownership. There is growing sentiment that without ownership, options provide executives with the best of two worlds: upside potential on the increase in stock price on one hand, and no downside risk on the other hand.

In the early 1990s, many companies began to address these criticisms in the design of their options. Becton-Dickinson, for example, began granting "indexed" options where exercise prices were adjusted for general stock market movement. Other companies began to actively encourage or require ownership through ownership guidelines, as previously

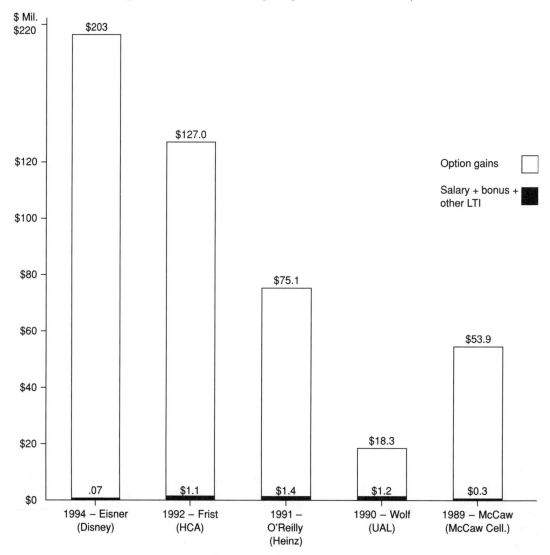

Figure 28.1 *Business Week* highest paid CEOs for selected years

mentioned, along with other methods. An example of an ownership-related design approach is the "deposit-share" option where executives are required to put owned shares on "deposit" with the company to be eligible for future option grants. General Mills, Corning, and RJR Nabisco have used this approach. The mechanics, as a general illustration, might be that the executive deposits one owned share with the company and re-

ceives two options. Another example of ownership-related option design provisions are "exercise-hold" incentives. Here, companies may grant restricted stock (see table 28.2) in a ratio of one share for every five or ten option shares exercised, with vesting of the restricted shares tied to the executives retaining the exercised option shares for specified periods of time. McKesson Corporation and Texas Instruments have used this approach.

The use of restricted stock as a long-term incentive seemed to peak in the mid- to late 1980s, although grants of this type continue to be common. Restricted stock is stock that is granted outright (i.e., no investment on the part of the executive is required), and earned at a specified future time for continued employment. Such grants became popular as employment-retention incentives, and because there was immediate real stock ownership. However, they have been widely criticized for lacking a true performance orientation because the grants still would be valuable even if stock prices declined, as long as the recipients remained in their jobs. A better role for restricted stock may be as special recognition and retention grants for down-the-line managers rather than as an executive-level, long-term incentive. Furthermore restricted stock may be effective as a form of currency in lieu of cash because of its retention and ownership characteristics. For example, Bell Atlantic and 3M have used it to pay a portion of their earned annual incentives to senior executives.

Performance-based grants are the other common form of long-term incentive, at least among more mature companies and typically as a supplement to stock options. In general, these grants are structured to provide recipients the opportunity to earn shares ("performance shares") or cash ("performance units") in the future, based on achieving preestablished, internal company financial goals. Performance-based grants were initially popularized during the prolonged bear market in the 1970s as a way to recognize strategic performance that may not be immediately reflected in stock prices. In other words, they are a way to balance the pure stock-market orientation of options.

A problem with performance-based grants has been that the definitions of strategic performance often tend to provide little more than a rationale for continuing to make long-term incentive payments when absolute financial performance or shareholder-value growth is poor, further contributing to executive entitlement. Another problem is that companies and board compensation committees have found it very difficult to identify financial performance measures that correlate directly with long-term shareholder-value creation, and to set multiyear goals for measuring performance. This has been particularly true since the 1980s, when restructuring changes, important accounting changes (e.g., FAS 89 and 106), and other extraordinary adjustments to reported earnings began to be made.

However, the problems mentioned above are not necessarily insurmountable, and performance-based grants are operating effectively in many instances where performance is measured relative to peer companies to eliminate internal goal setting, or where goals are set on an absolute basis independent of company budgets or other internal projections. Examples of the former are companies such as Amoco, J. C. Penney, and Lockheed, where performance awards have been earned based on total shareholder return versus peer companies. An example of the latter is the economic value-added ("EVA") measurement approach, where long-term incentives are paid from a specified pool generated as a percentage of the company's return on invested capital above its cost of capital. Companies that have used EVA include AT&T, Coca-Cola, and Quaker Oats (Tully, 1993).

When a company decides on which grant type(s) to use, it must keep in mind many considerations and trade-offs related to the company's stage of development and maturity, management style, business strategy, and so forth. There are also complicated technical considerations related to tax, accounting, and SEC rules which are beyond the scope of this chapter to fully review.

Benefits/perquisites

The fourth and last component of an executive's total compensation package consists of a wide variety of benefits and perquisites. Like long-term incentives, these are difficult to quantify with a high degree of reliability either because the data are not available or because it is difficult to disentangle personal from business use. The Hay Group estimates that benefits and perquisites amount to approximately one-third of the executive's annual salary (reported in McCarroll, 1993). Among *Fortune* companies, these traditionally have included company cars, company planes, country club memberships, spouse travel, chauffeur service, and home security systems (Hewitt & Associates, 1990). Often more significant to executives in terms of economic value, however, and relatively common in larger organizations, are such items as change-in-control severance agreements (i.e., "golden parachutes"), special executive retirement plans ("SERPs") where pensions are calculated using a richer formula than for nonexecutive employees, deferred compensation arrangements credited with investment returns that exceed competitive interest rates, and so forth.

From a strategic perspective, many of these special benefits may be difficult to justify. They are provided to the executive as a condition of employment related purely to job level, and they are seldom contingent on any type of performance. They are also an easy target of criticism by those who believe that executives are overpaid. For example, it is difficult for the average person on the street to understand why an executive should have a higher percentage of his or her final salary paid as a pension under a SERP when the salary itself may be in the seven-figure range.

POLICY CHOICES IN EXECUTIVE COMPENSATION PROGRAM DESIGN

Another important aspect of executive compensation concerns the policy considerations compensation professionals face when determining executive compensation philosophy and designing the executive pay programs. These policies present selections that can vary as much as or perhaps even more than the actual amounts earned under each of the four components. Drawn more heavily from the academic literature than the practitioner or popular press, the following discussion focuses on critical factors central to program design decisions.

The theoretical literature identifies four significant policy choices. They are: (1) degree of risk exposure, (2) criteria used to trigger rewards, (3) time horizon, and (4) degree of exclusivity. Each of these are discussed in turn.

Degree of risk exposure

Risk exposure addresses the extent to which the executive is forced to accept the possibility of significant financial gains or losses as a condition of employment. It is a specific case of risk aversion versus risk taking that is commonly discussed in the agency theory literature. Agency theorists argue that agents of shareholders are more risk averse than firm owners because the penalty for the executive is termination of employment if the company fails to perform profitably. An executive's job security and pay are not protected by diversification in the same way as are most shareholders' portfolios. To maintain a standard of living, an executive cannot absorb the loss of earnings to the same extent as shareholders can afford fluctuations in income. The executive's only method of spreading his or her own personal risk is through diversifying various projects or business units within the firm. As a result, agency theory would indicate that executive pay programs should be designed to induce executives to pursue riskier objectives that may prove to be in the shareholders' best interest.

Common sense dictates that greater probability of failure should be associated with greater potential reward. If risks and returns are correctly balanced, executives may be motivated to make riskier but sensible decisions that are likely to improve their income and that of shareholders. The relative risk to the executive of a firm can be analyzed along three dimensions (Ellig, 1984; Tosi & Gomez-Mejia, 1989, 1990, 1994). The first concerns how much *variability* or fluctuation in pay occurs from year to year. This dimension is lower when the pay package is designed so that a substantial portion of income is received on a stable, relatively fixed, predictable basis over time. The second dimension of risk is the *downside risk*, referring to the simultaneous potential for large gains or losses. The lower the risk exposure of the executive, the less likely it is that the executive's income will go down if performance indicators decline. The third element of risk in the executive's compensation package is the *time orientation*, or the amount of the executive's income that is tied to future performance indicators. The longer the time period under consideration, the more uncertainty faced by the firm and the greater the possibility of unforeseeable events developing that may have a negative impact on the executive's income.

An observer might conclude that a total compensation package with a higher proportion of salary and benefits/perquisites is less risky to the executive than one with a higher proportion of annual and long-term incentives, as did White and Fife (1993). Therefore, the general shift toward pay-for-performance in U.S. executive compensation should be welcomed by shareholders. But the real world of executive compensation has many subtleties. Incentive compensation arrangements may be, and often are, designed to magnify upside leverage and dampen downside risk. This is true of many companies' annual incentives and performance-based long-term grants, where earned amounts are based on internal company budgets without regard to absolute results. It is also true of stock options where there is no accompanying requirement for executives to exercise and hold company shares, and of large restricted stock grants

earned only for continued employment. Even where companies do have substantial performance-related variable compensation, they may hedge the downside to such an extent (through high salaries, SERPs, employment contracts, golden parachutes, and the like) that there is still no risk–reward symmetry. If risk is a necessary element of incentive, as theory would imply, many companies have work to do in fine-tuning their executive compensation programs. To underscore the point, one only need look at the generous treatment of CEOs who have left large companies that were regarded as underperforming under their leadership such as American Express, General Motors, IBM, Kodak, and Westinghouse.

Criteria used to trigger rewards

Here, we refer to the performance indicators firms use as the basis for determining executives' financial incentives. These criteria directly affect the risk features of the executive compensation program discussed above. The two main choices addressed in the literature concern the extent to which the performance of top executives is evaluated using objective, outcome-based, formula-driven (quantitative) procedures or subjective appraisals, inferential assessments, or other "softer" strategic, political, and organizational factors (qualitative).

Quantitative measures
The *quantitative* measures used are generally broken down into two categories: accounting-based measures or profitability indicators (e.g., earnings per share or return on equity); and stock-related indicators. The use of profitability indicators poses less compensation risk because the executive can exercise some control over them. The opposite is true for stock-related indicators because they are subject to external influences and the vagaries of the stock market.

Both types of quantitative measures are controversial. Using profitability to determine executive compensation can be criticized on the grounds that executives can internally manipulate these numbers to make themselves look good (Dyl, 1989; Groff & Wright, 1989; Hunt, 1986; Larcker & Sloan, 1992; Miller & Berton, 1993). For example, companies may set easily achievable profit targets for earning incentives; or once a company has achieved its annual profit budget and thus earned its bonuses for the year, it may start shifting profits into the next year. Conversely, using stock price to determine executive compensation can be criticized because it is sensitive to external events that may have little to do with how well a firm is being managed. It is very difficult to reliably factor out from stock-market data the extent to which the firm's stock is performing better or worse than what is "normal" or expected. An equally important issue related to quantitative measures is how goals are set in the sense of being internally or externally driven, and relative or absolute.

Qualitative measures

As the name implies, *qualitative* performance criteria require subjective judgments as to how well the executive is carrying out his or her duties. Performance assessments may incorporate a variety of intangible factors (e.g., changes in environmental conditions, market uncertainty), as opposed to relying exclusively on quantitative formulas (White & Fife, 1993). This makes it possible for an executive to be held in high regard despite poor company financial results if he or she is deemed to be accomplishing all that is feasible given internal and external constraints. In other words, qualitative performance criteria rely on behavioral and process controls that take into account "beliefs about what constitutes good performance, an awareness of other firms' performance levels, beliefs about the severity of particular organizational problems or symptoms, and attributions regarding top management's ability to alter the firm's performance" (Fredrickson, Hambrick, & Baumrin, 1988, 257).

Advantages and disadvantages of quantitative and qualitative measures

Generally, the use of qualitative performance criteria reduces the executive's risk exposure because potential problems beyond the executive's control are filtered through the informed judgment of those responsible for making performance assessments. On the other hand, this raises the possibility that the executive's pay may be decoupled from actual performance if the executive can exert undue influence on those deliberative bodies charged with the appraisals (normally board compensation committees for CEOs). Thus, an inherent problem with subjective judgments is that poor company financial performance may be "explained away" by placing blame on factors that the executive cannot control. There are also the obvious problems of fairness, agreement between sometimes conflicting parties, and the accuracy and credibility of information on which judgment is based.

It has been recommended that both quantitative and qualitative measures of performance be used in order to focus the executive's attention on the strategic goals and profitability objectives of the firm (Salter, 1973). In fact, this is how performance-related incentives most often operate in practice. At the executive level in annual incentive arrangements, quantitative measures typically are more heavily weighted (e.g., 75 percent versus 25 percent qualitative measures) to establish a pay-for-results linkage. Alternatively, an aggregate incentive pool might be generated, based on quantitative company financial measures, and allocated to participants based on qualitative measures of individual performance. However, most performance-based long-term incentives, which typically include only the most senior executives as participants, are entirely quantitative, reflecting their origin as substitutes for options.

Time horizon

The central issue, here, is how far into the future firm performance is measured when allocating financial rewards to the executive. The time horizon is important for at least three reasons. First, in theory the longer the time horizon used, the more likely the executive's pay is subject to risk because uncertainty and unpredictability increase with time. Second, if an executive's pay is subject to too much risk, he or she may be tempted to formulate long-term gaming strategies to reduce firm performance risk to a point that is harmful to shareholders. One way to accomplish this would be, for instance, to move the company into a highly speculative diversification program of mergers and acquisitions (Ahimud & Lev, 1981). Third, and perhaps most important, the long-term success of a company is not a simple composite of short-term successes. Unfortunately, what may improve the bottom line in the short run (e.g., laying off employees as a cost-cutting measure) may prove to be detrimental in the long run (e.g., lower future production capacity and reduced employee loyalty).

Ideally, executive pay should reflect a combination of short- and long-term performance. This combination is typically implemented by using incentive arrangements with different measurement periods in complementary ways. As previously mentioned, short-term incentives measure and reward performance for periods of one year or less. In contrast, performance-based long-term incentives typically run on three- to five-year measurement cycles and thus represent mid-term performance, while options generally have ten-year terms, which is about as long as most companies measure. From the executive's perspective, the uncertainty of earning long-term incentives and the whole psychology of delayed gratification tend to elevate the importance of short-term incentives in relation to long-term incentives. Companies should deal with this notion by maintaining continuity in their incentive programs through the distribution of overlapping (e.g., annual) grants of options and other long-term incentives. In this way, the real long-term nature of the incentive program comes over time not just from the measurement period represented by one grant, but by the prolonged duration of repeated grants extending out over multiyear periods.

Degree of exclusivity

"Degree of exclusivity" refers to the extent to which the executive compensation program is deliberately designed to differentiate between higher- and lower-level positions. One indicator of exclusivity is the pay differential between executives and their direct subordinates. Another indicator of exclusivity is the ratio of the executive's pay to that of the lowest-paid worker in the organization. Another related indicator of exclusivity concerns eligibility for special compensation programs (e.g., short- and long-term incentives) and benefits/perquisites. Again, firms vary widely in the degree of exclusivity reflected in their programs and the underlying reasons for it. To illustrate, it is common for smaller, growth companies in the biotechnology, computer, and electronics sectors to grant options to all employees. Egalitarianism may have something to do with this practice, but company cash flow and accounting considerations probably are the primary factors.

Among larger, mature companies where compensation in general reflects a more traditional and formal hierarchy, it has been common for only senior executives to receive option grants. In recent years, though, the trend among these firms has been to extend participation in options and other short- and long-term incentives down further in the ranks. Several such companies even have made all-employee option grants, including duPont, Merck, and Pepsico. What these practices reflect is not necessarily movement toward more egalitarian pay or organization structures, but more likely broader acceptance of pay-for-performance concepts; an attempt to substitute for higher salary increases which cannot be justified in a low-inflation period, and to control fixed salary costs; and a way to downsize organizations and eliminate some hierarchical levels and decision authority at correspondingly lower levels.

The degree of exclusivity is significant for at least three reasons. First, it reinforces a particular type of organizational structure and culture. Second, the sharp discontinuities in the earnings received by the most senior executives and their subordinates may have motivational effects related to internal competition for the CEO position. Third, special privileges and large compensation packages at the top may be intended to provide a sense of "royalty," and be used as a signaling device to reinforce a figurehead image for the CEO and other senior executives. In other words, the symbolic functions of compensation arguably may be considered as important as the substantive functions. Therefore, with the trend toward less differentiation in how executives are paid relative to others, there may be at least a partial explanation for the wider differential in how much they are paid.

EMERGING REFORMS AND CRITICAL FUTURE ISSUES

A popular consensus formed in the late 1980s was that U.S. executives often were being paid more than they deserved, and that they had too much influence on the levels of their own pay because the system of corporate governance had been co-opted by "cronyism." Evidence to support this view came primarily from research related to CEOs of large, publicly traded companies and generally led to the following five conclusions. First, the absolute numbers were staggering. For example, the CEO of Hospital Corporation of America (HCA) topped *Business Week's* list of the highest paid CEOs for 1992 at $127 million (see figure 28.1). Second, the ratios of executive pay to average employee pay were too

high, approaching average multiples of 100 : 1 between CEOs and the lowest level of employees (Beard, 1991). Third, the U.S. ratios were too high versus other industrialized nations, with comparable ratios in Japan and West Germany at 20 : 1 (Paulin, 1991). Fourth, the relationship between executive pay and company performance was weak. In other words, high executive pay levels often could not be explained by traditional profitability and stock-price indicators. For example, average CEO pay was estimated to have risen by 212 percent from 1980–90, while corporate profits were up 78 percent for the same period (Bryne, 1991). Fifth and finally, the potential for high rewards was not balanced by risk. Pay clearly increased for high levels of performance, but often did not correspondingly adjust downward with declining performance. In addition, "security-oriented" compensation provisions such as large severance benefits, SERPs, and so forth, had proliferated to the point of largely insulating most senior executives from financial risk even if they lost their jobs due to poor performance.

Abuses have not totally disappeared. However, the criticism of U.S. executive compensation levels triggered dramatic reforms beginning in the early 1990s.

New SEC proxy statement reporting requirements were adopted in 1992 and further refined in 1993. They significantly expanded the information that had to be disclosed to shareholders each year on how much the five highest-paid company "executive officers" were paid. They also required a narrative report under the signatures of board compensation committee members explaining their rationale and policies, plus a statement identifying any interlocks between management and committee members. The new disclosure requirements put the spotlight on board compensation committees, and many observers believe they have contributed to a new era of increased committee involvement and independence.

In turn, shareholder groups have been

using the disclosure information to monitor pay-for-performance within companies and demanding a more absolute relationship between annual pay levels and annual company profitability and growth; as well as between long-term incentive levels and total shareholder returns. This pressure brought to bear on companies should have the effect of increasing executive compensation risk over time.

Further reforms were introduced in the area of taxes in 1993, when rules were adopted to preclude companies from deducting annual compensation amounts for each of their top-five executives that exceeded $1 million unless they met specified requirements to designate them as "performance based." Real substance was put behind these rules when performance-based incentive deductibility became contingent on plans being administered by independent board compensation committees, and when these committees were required to disclose their policies toward pay deductibility in the proxy statements.

In the meantime, executive stock ownership has continued to gain support as a vehicle for motivating executives and balancing reward and risk. A growing number of companies have structured their executive pay programs to encourage executives to accumulate significant company ownership. Many companies have adopted executive ownership guidelines; the concept has been extended to outside directors as well at companies such as Ashland Oil, Bombay, and Gerber.

On the administrative side, more sophisticated modeling tools are being applied to estimate stock option grant values, including most notably the "Black–Scholes" and "binomial" models. These models better enable companies to compare their option grant opportunities with other companies, and to make trade-offs between options and other long-term incentive grant types and pay elements. The models also help to clarify the annualized values of long-term incentive grants, which are often confused by the business press and outside observers with option exercise profits that may represent grants made over many years, but are reported in aggregate in the year of option exercise. However, the option pricing models do not necessarily accurately reflect what an executive might be willing to pay to purchase such an option, which is different from using them as the basis for comparing grants between companies. This has sparked debate about the applicability of the models for determining an accounting expense for option grants as was proposed by the Financial Accounting Standards Board (1993).

The role of pay surveys in executive compensation is also being examined and debated. Led by board compensation committee members, there is a growing sense that the heavy reliance on pay-survey information to set executive pay levels predisposes a self-perpetuating inflationary spiral. If all companies strive to be at or above the survey averages, then the averages only can keep climbing regardless of company performance. Increasingly, pay surveys are being used as broad guidelines for determining reasonableness rather than to fine-tune individual company practices, and company economics and business strategies are becoming the primary factors shaping program design.

A myriad of executive compensation-related issues are open for further research. What are appropriate pay ratios between CEOs and entry-level employees? What is the impact of executive stock ownership on motivation and risk taking? How much stock should executives own? Should outside directors also own company stock and, if so, how much? Are traditional executive-type incentives, especially stock options, appropriate for employees further down in organizations? What should be the financial performance measures for determining executive incentives that most accurately reflect shareholders' interests? What are, and what should be, the implications of corporate downsizing on executive compensation?

These and related executive compensation issues are of great significance. They relate to broader workplace concerns involving economic fairness and equity, financial rewards as a means of monitoring behavior, and leadership by example. They have an important bearing on the future productivity and competitiveness of American business.

REFERENCES

Agarwal, N. C. (1981). Determinants of executive compensation. *Industrial Relations*, 20, 36–46.

Ahimud, Y., & Lev, B. (1981). Risk reduction as a management motive for conglomerate mergers. *Bell Journal of Economics*, 12, 605–17.

Aoki, M. (1984). *The Cooperative Game Theory of the Firm.* Oxford: Clarendon Press.

Beard, B. (1991). Companies give competition as best reason for wage increases. *Arizona Republic*, October 7, B4.

Becker, G. S. (1964). *Human Capital*, 1st ed. New York: National Bureau of Economic Research.

Berle, A., & Means, G. C. (1932). *The Modern Corporation and Private Property.* New York: Macmillan.

Bryne, J. A. (1991). The flap over executive pay. *Business Week*, June 5, 90–112.

Ciscel, D. H., & Carroll, T. M. (1980). The determinants of executive salaries: An econometric survey. *Review of Economics and Statistics*, 62, 7–13.

Dyl, E. A. (1989). Agency, corporate control and accounting methods: The LIFO–FIFO choice. *Managerial and Decision Economics*, 10 (3), 141–5.

Ellig, B. R. (1984). Incentive plans: Over the long-term. *Compensation Review*, 16 (3), 39–54.

Fama, E. F. (1980). Agency problems and the theory of the firm. *Journal of Political Economy*, 88 (2), 288–307.

Fama, E. F., & Jensen, M. C. (1983a). Separation of ownership and control. *Journal of Law and Economics*, 26, 301–24.

Fama, E. F., & Jensen, M. C. (1983b). Agency problems and residual claims. *Journal of Law and Economics*, 26, 327–49.

Financial Accounting Standards Board (1993). Accounting for stock-based compensation: Proposed statement of financial accounting standards. Financial Accounting Series No 127-C Norwalk, CT: FASB. June 3.

Frederick W. Cook & Co., Inc. (1993). *Long-term Incentive Grant Practice Among the Top-200 Fortune Industrial Companies.* New York: Frederick, W. Cook & Co., p. 5.

Fredrickson, J. W., Hambrick, D. C., & Baumrin, S. (1988). A model of CEO dismissal. *Academy of Management Review*, 13, 255–70.

Gerhart, B., & Milkovich, G. T. (1990). Organizational differences in managerial compensation and financial performance. *Academy of Management Journal*, 33, 663–91.

Gomez-Mejia, L. R., & Balkin, D. B. (1992). *Compensation,*

Organizational Strategy, and Firm Performance. Cincinnati: Southwestern Publishing.

Gomez-Mejia, L. R., Tosi, H., & Hinkin, T. (1987). Managerial control, performance, and executive compensation. *Academy of Management Journal*, 30, 51–70.

Groff, J. E., & Wright, C. J. (1989). The market for corporate control and its implications for accounting policy choice. *Advances in Accounting*, 7, 3–21.

Herman, E. S. (1981). *Corporate Control, Corporate Power.* New York: Cambridge University Press.

Hewitt & Associates, Consultants (1990). Most common perks received by top U.S. executives. Reported in *Wall Street Journal Special Report* on executive pay, April 18, R–3C.

Hunt, H. G. (1986). The separation of corporate ownership and control: Theory, evidence and implications. *Journal of Accounting Literature*, 5, 85–124.

Kroll, M., Simmons, S. A., & Wright, P. (1990). Determinants of chief executive officer compensation following major acquisitions. *Journal of Business Research*, 20, 349–66.

Larcker, D. F. & Sloan, R. G. (1992). Tracking pay for performance. *Chief Executive*, 80, 62–5.

Lopez, J. A. (1994). A better way? *Wall Street Journal*, April 13, R–6.

Lublin, J. S. (1994). Looking good: For CEOs, the pay gains haven't stopped. It's just the packaging that has changed. *Wall Street Journal*, April 13, R–6.

McCarroll, T. (1993). Rolling back executive pay. *Time*, March 1, 49–50.

McGuire, J. W., Chiu, J. S. Y., & Elbing, A. O. (1962). Executive income, sales, and profits. *American Economic Review*, 52, 753–61.

Marris, R. L. (1964). *The Economic Theory of Managerial Capitalism.* London: Macmillan.

Miller, M. W., & Berton, L. (1993). As IBM's woes grew, its accounting tactics get less conservative. *Wall Street Journal*, April 7, A–1.

Mincer, J. (1975). *Schooling, Experience and Earnings.* New York: National Bureau of Economic Research.

Moody's Handbook of Common Stocks (1993–94). Winter. New York: Moody's Investors Service Inc.

Paulin, G. B. (1989). Long-term incentives for management: An overview. *Compensation and Benefits Review*, 21 (4), 36–46.

Paulin, G. B. (1991). No let up in criticism of executive pay. *Frederick W. Cook & Co. Client Alert*, September 27, 3. New York.

Roberts, D. R. (1959). A general theory of executive compensation based on statistically tested propositions. *Quarterly Journal of Economics*, 70, 270–94.

Salter, M. S. (1973). Tailor incentive compensation to strategy. *Harvard Business Review*, 51 (2), 94–102.

Schmidt, D. R., & Fowler, K. L. (1990). Post-acquisition financial performance and executive compensation. *Strategic Management Journal*, 11 (7), 559–70.

Simon, H. A. (1957). The compensation of executives. *Sociometry*, March 20, 32–5.

Steers, R., & Ungson, G. R. (1987). Strategic issues in executive compensation decisions. In D. B. Balkin & L. R. Gomez-Mejia (eds.), *New Perspectives on Compensation*, 294–308. Englewood Cliffs, NJ: Prentice Hall.

Tosi, H. L., & Gomez-Mejia, L. R. (1989). The decoupling of CEO pay and performance: An agency theory perspective. *Administrative Science Quarterly*, 34, 169–90.

Tosi, H. L., & Gomez-Mejia, L. R. (1990). On boards and stockholder interests: The emerging debate. Unpublished technical report, University of Florida, Management Department, Gainesville.

Tosi, H. L., & Gomez-Mejia, L. R. (1994). CEO compensation monitoring and firm performance. *Academy of Management Journal*, 37 (3), 620–31.

Tully, S. (1993). The real key to creating wealth. *Fortune*, September 20, 38–50.

Ungson, G. R., & Steers, R. M. (1984). Motivation and politics in executive compensation. *Academy of Management Review*, 9 (2), 313–23.

White, W. M., & Fife, R. W. (1993). New challenges for executive compensation in the 1990s. *Compensation and Benefits Review*, 25 (1), 27–36.

Williams, M. J. (1985). Why chief executives' pay keeps rising. *Fortune*, April 1, 66–73.

Part V

Outcomes of Human Resource Management

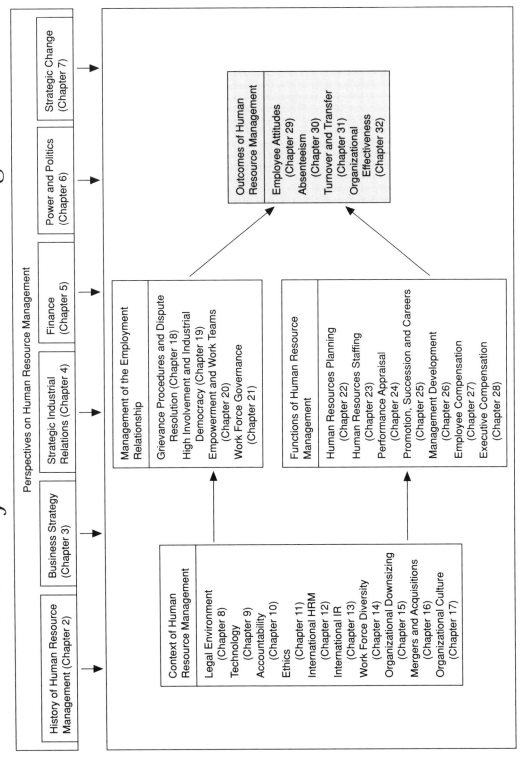

Perspectives on Human Resource Management

| History of Human Resource Management (Chapter 2) | Business Strategy (Chapter 3) | Strategic Industrial Relations (Chapter 4) | Finance (Chapter 5) | Power and Politics (Chapter 6) | Strategic Change (Chapter 7) |

Context of Human Resource Management

Legal Environment (Chapter 8)
Technology (Chapter 9)
Accountability (Chapter 10)
Ethics (Chapter 11)
International HRM (Chapter 12)
International IR (Chapter 13)
Work Force Diversity (Chapter 14)
Organizational Downsizing (Chapter 15)
Mergers and Acquisitions (Chapter 16)
Organizational Culture (Chapter 17)

Management of the Employment Relationship

Grievance Procedures and Dispute Resolution (Chapter 18)
High Involvement and Industrial Democracy (Chapter 19)
Empowerment and Work Teams (Chapter 20)
Work Force Governance (Chapter 21)

Functions of Human Resource Management

Human Resources Planning (Chapter 22)
Human Resources Staffing (Chapter 23)
Performance Appraisal (Chapter 24)
Promotion, Succession and Careers (Chapter 25)
Management Development (Chapter 26)
Employee Compensation (Chapter 27)
Executive Compensation (Chapter 28)

Outcomes of Human Resource Management

Employee Attitudes (Chapter 29)
Absenteeism (Chapter 30)
Turnover and Transfer (Chapter 31)
Organizational Effectiveness (Chapter 32)

Introduction:
Outcomes of Human Resource
Management

The preceding contexts, decisions, and activities result in a variety of consequences, some related to the organization and others not. This section examines selected outcomes that are indicators of organizational success. They include employee attitudes, specific outcomes involving absenteeism and turnover, and the general outcome of organizational effectiveness.

Judge, Hanisch, and Drankoski say that an employee's score on a valid measure of overall job satisfaction is the single most important piece of information about that person that a HR manager can have, because of bottom-line consequences and the effects on the employee. In their chapter about attitudes, they review theory and research, then examine a case study that shows how attitude research can influence business and HR decisions, and finally discuss how research and practice can be integrated.

Temporarily removing oneself from the worksite – absenteeism – is examined by Nicholson and Martocchio. They examine the research, theory, and practice of absence reduction. They argue that absence control must be congruent with business strategy, must be carried out by providing insights about it to line management, and

should be viewed as one of "many benchmarks for change and symptoms of dysfunction which need to be attended to intelligently." They conclude with a programmatic strategy for control of absence.

Permanently removing oneself or being removed from the worksite can be measured by turnover and transfer, the subject addressed by Dalton, Cairns, Canavan, Downey, Fowler, Freiwald, Johnson, King, and Lincoln. After reviewing the current state of knowledge, they assess the practical value of the information, and then they suggest fruitful areas and methods for future research. Their sub-title, "what we know is not always what we need," emphasizes their contention that cooperative work by researchers and practitioners is most likely to raise the right questions and find the best answers.

The relation of HRM to general measures of organizational effectiveness is examined by Lawler, Anderson, and Buckles. They first review the theory and research on effectiveness, and then relate it to HRM. They provide a case study of Amoco to illustrate the ideas in practice, and finally summarize the conclusions that can be drawn to date.

Chapter 29

Human Resource Management and Employee Attitudes

Timothy A. Judge, Kathy A. Hanisch, and Richard D. Drankoski

INTRODUCTION

Roznowski and Hulin (1992) recently commented that once an individual has joined an organization, his or her score on a valid measure of overall job satisfaction is the single most important piece of information a human resources manager can have about that person. Our experience with the study and practice of employee attitudes gives us little reason to disagree with their assessment. As Locke (1976) commented nearly two decades ago, job satisfaction is one of the most frequently studied concepts in the organizational sciences. Similarly, nearly all large organizations conduct attitude surveys; presumably such data are collected to influence human resources decisions.

Why are job attitudes of such central interest to researchers and practitioners? Employee attitudes (including satisfaction with work activities, coworkers, pay and benefits, supervisor(s), promotion system, working conditions, as well as other attitudes such as organizational commitment and job involvement) can have bottom-line consequences for

organizations as well as important effects on the individuals who hold these attitudes. An empirical test examining the relation between human resources programs, their impact on perceptions of organizational commitment to human resources efforts, and the latter's effect on employees' work attitudes was supported in a recent study (Kinicki, Carson, & Bohlander, 1992). Eisenberger, Fasolo, and Davis-LaMastro (1990) found that fewer absences, increased performance, greater innovation, and positive work attitudes were outcomes for those employees who perceived that the human resources department and organizational management was concerned about them. From a practical standpoint, this suggests that job satisfaction can be an important barometer of human resource management effectiveness. Job attitudes continue to be of interest to researchers for many reasons ranging from understanding their psychological causes (i.e., job attitudes are a result of interesting psychological processes) to the practical (i.e., work attitudes have pervasive influences on life attitudes, and job attitudes are related to behaviors researchers find interesting such as withdrawal decisions). Employee attitudes will undoubtedly continue to be of pervasive interest among researchers and practitioners. Unfortunately, despite this mutual interest, a considerable gap between research and practice exists in that practitioners often are not aware of the research literature and researchers often have little understanding of, or appreciation for, how attitudes are assessed and used in organizations.

Our purpose in this chapter is to provide an overview of theory, research, and practice concerning employee attitudes. We focus on job satisfaction because it is the most commonly studied job attitude. However, much of our discussion applies to other job attitudes as well and, in fact, we briefly discuss several other employee attitudes. We begin by reviewing recent theoretical advances and empirical research on the formation of job attitudes, and move to a consideration of research findings concerning the consequences of employee attitudes. We then review a research study carried out in a large U.S. organization that illustrates how research on job attitudes can be used to influence and enlighten business and human resources decisions. Finally, we conclude by discussing how theory, research, and practice can be integrated.

THEORY AND RESEARCH ON EMPLOYEE ATTITUDES

Employee attitudes and behaviors have been examined extensively in the industrial/organizational psychology, organizational behavior, and human resource management literatures. A comprehensive review of the employee-attitude literature cannot be presented here because of its voluminous nature. However, a combination and integration of the causes and consequences of employees' attitudes are discussed from the theoretical/research literature that has relevance to users of research in organizational settings.

Theoretical perspectives on employee attitudes

Locke (1976) and, more recently, Hulin (1991) summarized collectively a large amount of the literature on job satisfaction. Locke (1976) provided a historical approach to the agents (i.e., self and others (e.g., supervisors, coworkers)), events (i.e., work (e.g., task variety), rewards (e.g., promotion), and context (e.g., working conditions)) that result in job satisfaction. Job satisfaction was described by Locke as an outcome of the perception that one's job fulfills the important values that are congruent with one's needs. Consequences of employees' job satisfaction or dissatisfaction discussed by Locke (1976) included its effects on other attitudes (e.g., life satisfaction), physical and mental health, and specific organizational behaviors (e.g., absences, turnover, lateness, grievances).

Hulin (1991), in contrast, reviewed formulations of the antecedents of job satisfaction by focusing on employee inputs and organizational outcomes which consider the role of an employee's direct and opportunity costs (as a function of unemployment and available alternatives) and frames of reference (as a function of past experience and local economic conditions). His discussion of the consequences of job satisfaction involved examining general behavioral families (constructs composed of specific behaviors that reflect the same underlying behavioral tendencies). This focus on behavioral families as consequences of job attitudes is elaborated upon shortly. Although Locke and Hulin approach the topic from somewhat different directions, the two chapters are complementary and are worthwhile reading; they focus on the factors that influence employee job satisfaction, as well as the consequences of job attitudes. A book by Cranny, Smith, and Stone (1992) is a collection of chapters focusing on some of the recent work concerned with understanding job satisfaction.

The causes of job satisfaction include a

variety of aspects such as praise for accomplishments, medical benefits, good human relations skills by supervisors, competent and friendly coworkers, intrinsically interesting work, and fair pay. The specific causes relevant to employees within a given organization will vary depending on the organization, the employee, and the interaction between the two. There is, unfortunately, no single set of magic ingredients that will result every time – or even most of the time – in organizations that are staffed with satisfied employees who are at work and productive. The individual differences among employees are too prevalent to allow such a situation. From the employee's perspective, there is also, unfortunately, no perfect organization to work for that will result in him or her being constantly satisfied at work and at home, and physically and mentally healthy. What is realistic is for human resources managers to be aware of those aspects within an organization that might impact most employees' job satisfaction, and to enhance those aspects because, in the long run, the results will be fruitful for both the organization and the employee.

Thus past research has suggested that a number of factors influence job attitudes. Keeping these thoughts in mind, in the next sections the main theoretical perspectives on job attitudes are discussed. Our discussion is confined to job satisfaction because little theoretical development presently exists on other employee attitudes. Particular attention is given to the most recent and popular perspective in job satisfaction research, the dispositional approach to job satisfaction. First, however, two other dominant perspectives are reviewed, need-satisfaction models and the social information processing approach. We conclude this section with a review of the most integrative theoretical model, the interactional approach.

Need-satisfaction models

Need-satisfaction explanations of employee attitudes operate on the premise that the correspondence between the outcome desired, needed, or wanted by an individual and the outcome that is supplied by the work situation or organizational environment determines the affective employee reaction (see Locke, 1976; Stone, 1992; Lofquist & Dawis, 1969; Porter & Lawler, 1968). Those individuals, work tasks, or aspects of the working environment that are seen as facilitating an employee's attainment of desired outcomes will increase his or her job satisfaction. Conversely, those aspects or individuals that hinder the achievement of valued outcomes will lead to dissatisfaction with one or more aspects of the job. For example, a supervisor who will not respond quickly to an employee's request for needed supplies to complete a project will, most likely, lead to dissatisfaction with the employee's supervisor and perhaps work dissatisfaction. On the other hand, an employee who belongs to a union and receives a pay raise that he or she attributes to union efforts will most likely be satisfied with the union and perhaps his or her pay satisfaction will increase also.

Human resources managers need to be aware of the outcomes that employees desire and tailor those outcomes to each individual if possible. The contingencies between relevant organizational behaviors and valued employee outcomes need to be made clear to employees so that the human resources department will achieve the behaviors they want from their employees and the employees will receive their desired outcomes.

Job characteristics or the attributes of the employee's work are important variables to consider given they provide the situational perspective within which the employee makes judgments about his or her satisfaction. Research has shown that mental challenge is an important element of the factors that are related to work satisfaction and interest (Locke, 1976). Some specific work/job aspects that contain the mental challenge component include: opportunity to use one's valued skills and abilities, opportunity for new learning, being able to be creative, work variety, amount and difficulty of work, degree of responsibility, nonabitrary pressure for performance, control over work methods and pace, and job complexity (Locke, 1976). The degree of impact or effect of work attributes on an employee's satisfaction depends on whether the individual finds the work itself personally interesting and meaningful (Strong, 1943).

Social information processing

The social information processing approach is an alternative to the need-satisfaction and job characteristics approaches to job attitudes. The basic premise of the social information processing approach, as formulated by Salancik and Pfeffer (1977, 1978), is that individuals respond to social stimuli in forming job attitudes. At the extreme, the approach holds that an individual only has job attitudes when he or she is asked about them (Hulin, 1991). Proponents of this approach have criticized need-satisfaction models of job attitudes and argued that the relations between job characteristics and job attitudes are social constructions, but these criticisms have been directly addressed by Stone (1992) and Hulin (1991). It is unlikely that individuals have attitudes only when they are asked about them, and the literature on job characteristics and satisfaction has been replicated in numerous studies (Hulin, 1991; Stone, 1992). It is also probably true that social influence does play a minor role in employees' reactions to their work and organizational settings. The impact, however, is anticipated to be the greatest for new and younger employees who have not been in the work force and in an organization long enough to have preconceived ideas and past experiences about their work and organization.

Dispositional approach to job attitudes

Perhaps the most prominent area of job attitude research in the last decade has been the dispositional approach to job satisfaction. This research has been varied in its focus and methodological approach. The dispositional approach assumes that when workers are asked about their level of job satisfaction, their response depends as much on their dispositional outlook as the actual characteristics of the job. As Arvey, Carter, and Buerkley (1991) noted, the dispositional perspective assumes that a large part of job dissatisfaction is due to emotional maladjustment which is carried into prospective situations. Thus reported levels of job satisfaction (and other job attitudes) fundamentally depend on person factors such as response tendencies, cognitive styles, and emotional adjustment.

One of the earliest studies on the dispositional approach to job satisfaction was by Weitz (1952), who found a positive, significant correlation between scores on a measure of overall job satisfaction and scores on a "gripe index" thought to reflect a tendency to be critical with respect to events and objects in everyday life. Weitz's gripe index consisted of items such as one's first name, the local newspaper, and 8 1/2″ × 11″ paper. The validity of Weitz's measure in influencing job satisfaction was substantiated by Judge and Hulin (1993).

An interesting implication of Weitz's measure is the concept of *relative dissatisfaction*. Weitz argued that if two workers were equally dissatisfied with their jobs, the individual most likely to leave the organization would be the one with the *most positive* disposition (i.e., least likely to endorse items on the gripe index), because a job dissatisfied employee with a positive disposition has a high degree of relative dissatisfaction. Conversely, an employee with a relatively high degree of job dissatisfaction but a tendency to gripe about most things in his or her life is no more dissatisfied with his job than many other aspects of his or her life. Thus, this employee would be less likely to leave his or her job, despite being dissatisfied with it. A recent study supported Weitz's hypothesis in finding that the effect of job dissatisfaction on turnover decisions depended on their scores on Weitz's measure (Judge, 1993).

Other research has inferred the existence of dispositional effects on job satisfaction from stability in job attitudes without measuring dispositions directly. Staw and Ross (1985) found significant temporal and cross-situational stability in job attitudes and inferred that this was due to disposition. A somewhat similar study by Pulakos and Schmitt (1983) found that job applicants' expectations of being satisfied on a prospective job were predictive of actual satisfaction derived from the job, as measured several years later. Staw, Bell, and Clausen (1986) improved on several of the flaws in past dispositional research by measuring affective disposition directly. They found that childhood affective temperament significantly predicted job satisfaction up to thirty years after assessment. A number of other studies have linked positive (PA) and negative affectivity (NA) to measures of job satisfaction (Agho, Mueller, & Price, 1993; Butcher, Brief, & Roberson, 1993; Levin & Stokes, 1989; Watson & Slack, 1993). Perhaps the most unique research in this line of inquiry is the study by Arvey, Bouchard, Seagal, and Abraham (1989), which found significant similarity in the job satisfaction levels of identical twins reared apart. Arvey et al. (1989) interpreted this similarity to represent a genetic source of job satisfaction. A more in-depth review of these studies is beyond the scope of this chapter, but can be found in Judge (1992). In total, these studies provide a strong indication that a significant part of the variance in job satisfaction is due to affective disposition.

The dispositional approach to job satisfaction has received substantial criticism with regard to methodological issues. Arvey et al.'s (1989) study was criticized (Cropanzano & James, 1990), and then these criticisms were rebutted (Bouchard, Arvey, Keller, & Seagal, 1992), primarily on methodological grounds. The Staw and Ross (1985) study received more than its share of criticism (Gerhart, 1987;

Gutek & Winter, 1992). Davis-Blake and Pfeffer (1989) and Gerhart (1990) wrote wide-ranging critiques of the dispositional approach, again focusing largely on methodological issues. While some of these criticisms are well taken, it is not clear that the cumulative effect of these criticisms has been to severely detract from the impact of the dispositional studies (George, 1992).

Perhaps the most important area for development in dispositional research is the need to increase the theoretical underpinnings of the research (Adler & Weiss, 1988; Judge, 1992; Weiss, 1991). Because past dispositional research has provided little idea about how dispositions influence job satisfaction, this research has been characterized as a "black box" approach (Erez, 1994). Because job satisfaction is a judgment subject to cognitive and affective influences, theories from other areas of psychology may illuminate this black box. Several recent studies have helped shed light on the dispositional sources of job satisfaction. Judge and Locke (1993) and Erez (1994) found that two different types of cognitive/affective biases, dysfunctional thought processes and self-deception, were relevant to the formation of job satisfaction. Judge and Locke found that dysfunctional thought processes, manifesting such cognitive styles as perfectionism, overgeneralization, and dependence on others for approval, contributed to low levels of subjective well-being and job satisfaction. Conversely, Erez (1994) found that self-deception, a tendency to deceive oneself, contributed to positive assessments of subjective well-being and job satisfaction. The comparison of these dispositional (or quasi-dispositional) tendencies is interesting; both have been argued to be irrational tendencies, yet one represents a positive bias while the other represents a negative bias. Both of these are dispositional traits that shed light on the dispositional source of job satisfaction.

While these studies are interesting and contribute to theoretical development in this area, they do a better job of expanding the domain of dispositional attributes that may influence job satisfaction than explaining *how* dispositional states are translated into job satisfaction. A recent study is helpful in showing how dispositions may influence job satisfaction. Necowitz and Roznowski (1992) found that high NA employees were less satisfied with their jobs, were more likely to withdraw from their job, and selectively attended to the negative aspects of their jobs, more than low NA employees. The most important implication of their study is that affective disposition influences how employees process job information, and suggest that *even if job conditions are identical*, employee's dispositional tendencies influence how they perceive their work environment.

The question of the practical effects of the dispositional source of job satisfaction is not an easy one to answer. Staw and Ross (1985) suggested that the fact that there is stability in job attitudes, and the possibility that there is a dispositional source of job satisfaction, will act as "headwinds" to situational inventions (i.e., job redesign) designed to improve employee satisfaction. The assumption underlying this suggestion has been severely criticized (Gerhart, 1987, 1990), and in fact little evidence suggests that the effect of job redesign on job satisfaction depends on affective disposition (Levin & Stokes, 1989; Necowitz & Roznowski, 1992).

On the other hand, this does not mean that the dispositional source of job satisfaction is without practical implications for human resources managers. Judge's (1993) study suggested that affective disposition is an important variable in the prediction of turnover, and other research suggests that withdrawal behaviors are influenced by affective disposition (Judge & Locke, 1993; Necowitz & Roznowski, 1992). Hansen (1989) found that neuroticism (a close cousin of NA) was related to industrial accidents. Staw and Barsade (1993) found that dispositional outlook influences assessment center performance.

Thus, managers can gain greater understanding of the dissatisfaction of a particular employee, and the likely behavioral consequences resulting from that dissatisfaction, from understanding their dispositional tendencies in general. The wisdom of basing hiring decisions on affective disposition has been questioned, most notably by Davis-Blake and Pfeffer (1989). However, the fact remains that organizations are using personality measures in increasing frequency, and recent empirical data attest to the validity of such measures when properly used. For example, Tett, Jackson, and Rothstein (1991), analyzing data from nearly 500 studies, found that agreeableness was the best personality predictor of job performance (the average corrected correlation was .33). Neuroticism also was correlated with performance (the average corrected correlation was − .22).[1] This suggests, despite the concerns of others (e.g., Davis-Blake & Pfeffer, 1989), that affective disposition increasingly may be used in the selection process to realize the benefits of a productive and satisfied work force.

Interactional approach

The situational characteristics of an employee's work, job, and organization combine or interact with the employee's personal characteristics to determine his or her job attitudes. This person–environment interaction is the foundation that results in person–environment (P–E) fit. P–E fit is a theoretical approach initiated by England and Lofquist in their study of work adjustment and continues to be researched by Dawis and Weiss. The idea of an interaction between an individual and his/her environment is not new and dates back to Kantor (1924, 1926) and Lewin (1936). Past research on P–E fit involved vocational interests and occupations (Parsons, 1909; Strong, 1947) and ability requirements and occupations (Dvorak, 1935; Patterson & Darley, 1936).

P–E fit in the realm of job attitudes can be

conceptualized as the interrelationships of person variables (e.g., experience, values, disposition, personality) and environmental variables (e.g., aspects of the organization including the previously described agents and events). The interactions between the two, quite logically, are significant predictors of job attitudes (Dawis, 1992). Investigations of situational and dispositional models have rarely adequately considered the other perspective. It seems intuitively obvious that job attitudes are a function of both the job situation and context. To explain more variance in employees' attitudes, we will need to begin to examine the interaction of the two factors. Research directions on this neglected topic are expanded upon and encouraged in our call for future research in the employee-attitude area below.

Research on other employee attitudes

Organizational commitment and job involvement

Additional employee attitudes that have received a substantial amount of attention include organizational commitment and job involvement, which are two forms of work commitment. Both organizational commitment and job involvement are important because they are associated with other important organizational variables including work performance and measures of organizational withdrawal (e.g., turnover, absenteeism). Organizational commitment has been defined as consisting of two components: attitudinal and behavioral commitment. Attitudinal commitment is defined as a psychological state that reflects the strength of employee's feelings of identification and involvement with a specific organization (Porter, Steers, Mowday, & Boulian, 1974). Behavioral commitment traditionally has been defined in terms of a tendency to continue in a specific activity or course of action (Salancik, 1977); this component does not include any cognitive or attitudinal force.

More recently, Allen and Meyer (1990) conceptualized organizational commitment as a group of attitudes composed of three different components of commitment: affective, continuance, and normative. Affective commitment is similar to attitudinal commitment and refers to the emotional attachment employees feel for their organization. Continuance commitment shares some features of behavioral commitment but also reflects the employees' perceived costs of leaving the organization. Employees' feelings of obligation toward the organization defines normative commitment.

Job involvement has been defined by Lodahl and Kejner (1965) as "the degree to which a person's work performance affects his self-esteem." It has also been conceptualized by Blau (1987) as consisting of three components: self-image, a degree of participation in work, and self-esteem. Kanungo (1982) has developed a measure that assesses both job and work involvement. Job involvement is a belief that is descriptive of one's job and tends to be a function of how much the job can satisfy one's present needs. Work involvement is described as a normative belief about the value of work in one's life. This is primarily a function of one's past cultural conditioning and socialization.

Cynicism

One work-related attitude that has not received much previous research attention is cynicism. Kanter and Mirvis (1989) argued that Americans and American workers are becoming more cynical. In fact, they present data suggesting that 43 percent of all Americans could be classified as cynics of various types and argue that cynicism among American workers has increased dramatically in the last 50 years. Kanter and Mirvis lay much of the blame for the increased cynicism on the doorsteps of political institutions and businesses. While much of their analysis is rife with unsubstantiated value judgments (e.g., Republicans of the 1980s were partly responsible for the increase in cynicism, human resource management has increased exploitation and cynicism), their book does present a persuasive argument that cynicism is a work attitude with which organizations should be concerned. In order to combat increased cynicism among American workers, Kanter and Mirvis advise that organizations should consider the following:

- Foster work cultures which promote the work ethic and give workers power over their work.
- Reduce the gap between idealized and realized goals, values, and practices.
- Behave altruistically be contributing to charities and rewarding altruism.
- Manage worker expectations and provide realistic previews in the recruiting process.

As Kanter and Mirvis (1989) acknowledge, however, attempts to remove cynicism from the workplace are likely to encounter ceilings due to worker dispositions. Judge, Locke, and Durham (1994) suggested that cynicism is likely a dispositional cause of job satisfaction. Furthermore research has suggested that workers differ in the degree to which they have a trusting personality (e.g., Chun & Campbell, 1974; Rotter, 1967), which Judge et al. (1994) argued was the opposite of cynicism. This does not mean that organizations wishing to decrease the level of cynicism in the workplace face a hopeless task. Rather, organizations need to understand the dispositional tendencies of workers to make change programs more effective.

CONSEQUENCES OF EMPLOYEE ATTITUDES

Organizational withdrawal

A variety of organizational withdrawal or adaptive behaviors have been evaluated as consequences of employee attitudes or job satisfaction. Withdrawal or adaptive behaviors include behaviors employees enact to reduce their dissatisfaction with some aspect of their work or organization environment and, in effect, the behaviors help them cope with the dissatisfying situation. The relevance of withdrawal behaviors to organizational managers and employees is evident from a two-year observational study by Cherrington that found only 51 percent of employees' time was spent working (Miller, 1983). He found that the other 49 percent was allocated to coffee breaks, late starts, early departures, and personal activities. A variation of all of these behaviors could be considered as organizational withdrawal or adaptive behaviors; these types of behaviors and their antecedents have implications for organizational productivity and employee well-being (Fisher & Locke, 1992; Hanisch, 1990; Hanisch & Hulin, 1990, 1991). To begin to understand the patterns of behavior organizational employees may engage in as a result of their attitudes, a relatively new but empirically supported approach to understanding the relations between employee attitudes and behaviors is described below.

The primary focus of past employee attitude and behavior research has been on the specific negative behaviors dissatisfied employees engage in because of their detrimental effect on organizational outcomes as well as negative consequences to employees. Although examining specific behaviors may appear to be useful from a managerial perspective, there are problems when one evaluates the relations between employee attitudes and a specific behavior. Two approaches, supported in the theoretical and applied literature, are available to managers and researchers who are interested in examining the relations between employee attitudes and behaviors. The first, and most frequently examined, is the relation between a specific attitude and a specific behavior or behavioral intention (e.g. Fishbein & Ajzen, 1974). For example, if a manager is having a problem with the number of employee absences and is concerned solely with this behavior, the appropriate attitude to assess would be attitude toward being absent; this attitude could then be related to the number of employee absences (Martocchio, 1989).

A second, but quite different, approach from the same theoretical literature, is the relation between general attitudes and behavioral families or constructs. The theoretical attitude to behavior position, discussed for decades, states that there should be correspondence in terms of specificity (i.e., general attitude to general behavior family or specific attitude to specific behavior) when one evaluates attitudes and behaviors (e.g., Fishbein & Ajzen, 1974). Thurstone (1931) stated over sixty years ago that identifying an individual's general attitude toward an object only tells us the affective direction toward that object. Little can be known about the specific behavior the individual might engage in given his or her general attitude. Two individuals with the same general attitude toward an object will quite likely behave in different ways; the different behaviors will, however, accurately reflect their general attitude.

For example, two employees who are equally dissatisfied with their coworkers might express their dissatisfaction in different ways. One employee might decide to be late for work a couple of times a week while the other might decide to be absent from work every other Friday. Although both employees have the same degree of coworker dissatisfaction, they have chosen different behaviors, from a variety of choices, to adapt to their dissatisfaction. If a researcher or manager were examining the situation and was focused only on understanding why employees were absent, the information obtained would only provide part of the information; neglecting measures of lateness in this case could result in large costs to both the organization and employee. Doob (1947) summarizes this theoretical position by saying that general attitudes mediate

an entire repertoire of responses; predicting and understanding a specific behavior using a general attitude will meet with little success.

Although research has been conducted where investigators have examined the relations between a general attitude (e.g., work satisfaction) and a specific behavior (e.g., absenteeism), the level of correspondence between the attitude and behavior is deemed inappropriate by attitude researchers and theorists (e.g., Doob, 1947; Fishbein & Ajzen, 1974; Roznowski & Hanisch, 1990; Thurstone, 1931; Wicker, 1969). One cannot or should not expect to predict or understand why an individual enacts a specific behavior knowing only his or her general attitude. Knowing an individual's general attitude should allow for the prediction of behavioral families (Hanisch, 1994).

Behavioral families are constructs that are composed of individual behaviors which reflect similar behavioral tendencies toward an object or construct under investigation. The use and understanding of behavioral families in the area of employee withdrawal and adaptation has received limited attention. The recent studies that have been done have focused on empirically evaluating whether or not behavioral families exist in the organizational withdrawal arena and whether they are related to general attitudes (Hanisch, 1994; Hanisch & Hulin, 1990, 1991; Judge & Hulin, 1992; Roznowski & Hanisch, 1990). The empirical work by Hanisch (1994) and Hanisch and Hulin (1990, 1991) that found support for the relationship between general employee attitudes and organizational withdrawal was a direct response to the previously described theoretical general attitude to general behavioral family position (e.g., Doob, 1947; Fishbein & Ajzen, 1974; Roznowski & Hanisch, 1990; Thurstone, 1931).

Hanisch and Hulin (1990, 1991) have examined the general organizational withdrawal construct, which they have empirically shown to be composed of two general families of behaviors labeled *work withdrawal* and *job*

Figure 29.1   Organizational withdrawal and its components

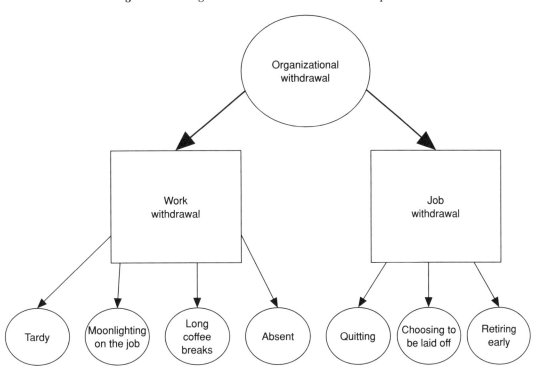

withdrawal, and its relation to general employee attitudes. Work withdrawal was defined and assessed as tendencies to avoid specific work tasks and minimize work-role inclusion; job withdrawal was defined and assessed as tendencies to remove oneself from a specific organization and its implied organizational role. Specific behaviors comprising the work withdrawal behavioral family included lateness, absenteeism, and unfavorable work behaviors (e.g., wandering around looking busy, making excuses to go somewhere to get out of work); job withdrawal was composed of turnover intentions, desire to retire, and intended retirement age. Withdrawal from a job or formal work role in a specific organization (i.e., job withdrawal) versus withdrawal or avoidance of the work tasks associated with a job or work role (i.e., work withdrawal) adequately captures the distinctions between these two general withdrawal behavioral families. Figure 29.1 displays the organiza-

tional withdrawal construct with its job and work withdrawal components and examples of their behaviors.

General employee attitudes examined by Hanisch and Hulin (1990, 1991) included work satisfaction, job importance, coworker satisfaction, pay satisfaction, health satisfaction, and retirement valence – attitudes of importance to researchers and practitioners. These attitudes were considered general in nature relative to specific attitudes that would include, for example, attitude toward quitting, attitude toward being late, and attitude toward being absent, but less general than overall job satisfaction.

The general attitude to general behavior approach, empirically supported by Hanisch and Hulin (1990, 1991), could prove to be quite useful because of the potential this line of research has for allowing a basis for generalizing to other, logically or empirically relevant, organizational attitudes and behaviors.

Examples of additional behaviors that might also be included in the work and job withdrawal behavioral families, respectively, would be leaving work early and choosing to be laid off if given the option. The variety of behaviors employees can engage in while at work as well as to remove themselves from their work tasks are numerous; there are fewer behaviors, at least intuitively, that allow employees to remove themselves from the organization or job itself. Both types of behaviors would be expected to be related to a specific attitude. If combined with other behaviors in a withdrawal behavioral family that reflect the same behavioral tendencies, they would be expected to relate to general employee attitudes. The results of the studies by Hanisch (1994) and Hanisch and Hulin (1990, 1991) suggest that individuals do not enact specific, isolated behaviors in response to negative employee attitudes or job dissatisfaction.

Judge and Hulin (1992) extended these findings by assessing constructs at an even more general level. They related overall job satisfaction and subjective well-being to a single withdrawal construct. This approach complements Hanisch and Hulin's (1990, 1991) approach in that both achieve construct correspondence at somewhat different levels of generality. Hanisch and Hulin related facets of job satisfaction to behavioral families while Judge and Hulin (1992) related overall job satisfaction to a single, general construct. Judge and Hulin found that behavioral aggregation of ten specific behaviors into a single construct resulted in a *fourfold* increase in the variance explained in withdrawal by job satisfaction and subjective well-being. Thus, similar to Hanisch and Hulin's findings, this study suggests that deeper theoretical understanding and increased behavioral prediction can be achieved by consideration of the construct of organizational withdrawal.

In summary, the results of this research, from both a theoretical as well as a practical viewpoint, discourage continued research and examination of the relations between general employee attitudes and specific withdrawal behaviors. The literature is replete with studies examining the relation between work satisfaction and absenteeism and work satisfaction and turnover (e.g., Hulin, 1991). If a significant positive relation is found between work dissatisfaction and number of absences and one attempts to reduce absences through a series of sanctions for each absence that occurs, it is likely that individuals will still be dissatisfied with their work and may engage in another behavior (e.g., being late for work, wandering around looking busy) that reflects the similar behavioral tendency as absenteeism (Rosse & Miller, 1984). This outcome would be unacceptable to managers, but this result is plausible given the empirical evidence regarding the relations between general attitudes and withdrawal behavioral families (i.e., work and job withdrawal). The relations between general attitudes and general behavioral families are substantial and document the importance of considering the multiple and patterned ways employees respond to their general attitudes.

Relationship between job satisfaction and performance

The question of whether a satisfied worker is a productive one has been debated for ages. While some early researchers in the field suggested that such a relationship existed, empirical evidence has been relatively consistent in finding a small, positive correlation between scores on a job satisfaction survey and some measure of job performance (Iaffaldano & Muchinsky, 1985). Thus it is accepted among most researchers that there is not a substantial relationship between job satisfaction and productivity (Locke, 1976). However, it is important to keep in mind that productivity is not necessarily the same as performance or value of the employee to the organization (Boudreau, Sturman, & Judge, in press). When performance or employee value is examined from a broader perspective, the effect of job satisfaction on performance must be considered in light of several other findings. First, as noted above, job attitudes have been found to predict withdrawal behaviors, which are important from both a scientific and practical point of view. Some of these withdrawal behaviors (such as absence and tardiness) are incorporated into many existing performance appraisal instruments (Bretz, Milkovich, & Read, 1992). Even those that may not be in performance appraisals have important implications for how employees are valued. Second, past research has shown that job satisfaction is related to organizational citizenship or employee helping behaviors (Bateman & Organ, 1983; Motowidlo, 1984; Smith, Organ, & Near, 1983).[2] Given the changing nature of work in organizations, citizenship behaviors increasingly are valued areas of performance from employees, and in fact may be incorporated into many definitions and measurements of performance (Organ, 1988). Thus, while satisfied employees may not be higher performers when performance is defined narrowly (e.g., in terms of productivity such as number of widgets produced per hour), the implications of having a dissatisfied work force may be substantial when one defines performance or employee value broadly. A final point on this subject is that other work attitudes besides job satisfaction are related to behavioral outcomes. For example, research has demonstrated that organizational commitment is a significant predictor of turnover (Mathieu & Zajac, 1990). Recent work on fairness or justice perceptions suggests that it influences a number of behavioral outcomes, including acceptance of job offers, turnover intentions, resolutions of disputes, survivors' reactions to layoffs, and even employee theft (Greenberg, 1990). The next section will integrate the causes and consequences of job attitudes and describe the issue of employee satisfaction from an organization directly concerned with facilitating and directing satisfied employees.

HUMAN RESOURCES PRACTICES AND EMPLOYEE ATTITUDES

Research and practice related to the understanding of employee attitudes are moving along paths that are converging. As noted earlier, recent research has suggested that it is valid and probably more useful to move beyond trying to explain specific employee behaviors (e.g., tardiness, absenteeism, grievances, turnover, etc.) as a result of identifying general employee attitudes. Rather, a shift to understanding general employee attitudes in relation to general behavior patterns appears to offer a more significant and fruitful area of study.

Similarly, organizations are rethinking why they collect data about employee attitudes, how they collect the data, the way they interpret the data, and its use as a basis for strategic human resource management planning and tactical action planning. While these organizations remain mindful of the relationship between employee attitudes and specific behaviors, their interest has moved into the realm of trying to understand the relationship between general employee attitudes and their effect on achieving more general "bottom line" outcomes; for example, achieving superior performance/financial results and employee behaviors that contribute significantly to performance, such as being more customer service-oriented. Understanding employee attitudes and shaping them (i.e., actively influencing the disposition of employees) has crossed over from being solely a tactical imperative to one which is both strategic and tactical in nature.

A new and developing paradigm of employee attitudes

Confronted with the realities of global competition, pressure on market share and profit margins, shrinking product development-to-delivery cycle times, and increasing customer demands for services or products which incorporate greater value and improved quality, companies are beginning to reconsider the role their employees play in determining the enterprise's long-term success. A newly emerging paradigm suggests that "satisfied and motivated employees" will focus their attention and energy upon meeting more completely the requirements of their customers, thereby maximizing the satisfaction of those customers. Underlying this paradigm is a belief that customer satisfaction is *the* primary determinant of whether an enterprise meets its financial objectives; in turn, employee satisfaction is regarded as a critical and necessary factor in achieving customer satisfaction.

The development of this attitude toward an organization's human resources may be traced to the implementation of total quality management (TQM) initiatives which often provided companies with the strategic framework for confronting their competition and charting the course to improved and continued financial viability. As TQM strategies have been mapped in these organizations, the integral role employees play in achieving desired and necessary outcomes, such as "getting it right the first time" and 6-sigma improvements, have been recognized. As quality has come to be understood in the broader context of demonstrating a strong commitment to satisfying the requirements of a customer, the role of the employee has taken on a deeper and broader significance. That is, in this new paradigm, all employees are required to be committed to satisfying their customers. This holds true whether those customers are internal to the organization (i.e., the next person or function to receive the output of an employee) or are external customers (i.e., the ultimate end users of the good or service provided by the enterprise). In this developing paradigm, appreciation for the relationship between employee satisfaction, customer satisfaction, and business results has a significant impact upon how organizations manage the relationship they have with their employees and how they understand, address, and influence employee attitudes.

Philosophical underpinnings of the new paradigm

In order to understand better the philosophy underlying this paradigm of employee satisfaction and motivation, it may be helpful to review the findings of a 1990 study completed by a *Fortune 25* company which examined the best practices of five multinational corporations that appear to operate with this paradigm in mind.

Each of the five companies selected for participation in this study met a number of criteria: a recognized reputation for employee satisfaction; leadership in at least one human resources management practice area (e.g., management development); achievement of financial success; an international scope of operations; having been the recipient of at least one quality award (e.g., in the United States this would be the Malcom Baldridge Quality Award); and a similar financial profile and similar number of employees as the sponsor company.

Interviews with senior human resources executives in each of the participating companies and a review of relevant documentation of values, objectives, programs, and policies resulted in the identification of ten key themes underlying the success these organizations have had in addressing employee satisfaction and motivation:

1 A fundamental belief that people are *the* primary source of competitive advantage.
2 An intense concern for employee well-being.
3 Proactive leadership and direction from the CEO level with respect to achieving high levels of employee satisfaction and motivation.
4 Line management accountability for effective people management.
5 Investment in leadership development;

at the first line level of management this means a focus on leadership dimensions such as communicating, empowering, facilitating, coaching; at higher levels, a focus on change management and "transformational leadership skills."

6   Formal encouragement of meaningful employee involvement in areas ranging from decision making to work design.

7   The use of structured communication channels to manage employee understanding of organizational values and promote desired behaviors.

8   Corporate policies, management structures and organizational processes being designed to promote employee effectiveness, rather than to control behavior.

9   People-management programs and practices that are internally aligned and mutually reinforce the enterprise's people oriented values and goals.

10 External reference points, such as employee satisfaction trends relative to external survey norms, are increasingly being used to reach a state of employee satisfaction which will support the organization's efforts to become the employer of choice.

Each of these themes contains powerful messages. Collectively they provide a strategic framework for managing the human resources of an organization and articulate the premium that must be placed on understanding and shaping employee attitudes if employees are to become, or continue to be, the company's primary source of competitive advantage.

The last theme reinforces the notion that measurement of employee attitudes is a common activity for organizations operating within the business results–customer satisfaction–employee satisfaction paradigm. Further, it strongly suggests that there is a need to collect this data so that it facilitates the internal review of existing practices, the development of new programs and processes, and comparisons, or benchmarking, against external norms.

Assessment of the current state: measuring employee attitudes

Concurrently with the benchmarking of best practices found in external organizations, the sponsor company completed two additional activities; a thorough assessment of the current state of employee satisfaction – specifically an identification of the barriers to achieving high levels of employee satisfaction – within each of the operating units within the corporation, and a critical evaluation of the utility of the diagnostic tools then being used to gather data about employee attitudes and an assessment of the long-term utility of those tools.

In order to gather data regarding root causals of employee attitudes, each operating unit reviewed the results of its most recent employee-attitude survey and, in some cases, completed employee roundtable meetings to confirm the rank-ordered contribution of specific root causes to employee dissatisfaction. Employee write-in comments gathered as part of the attitude surveys also provided additional information regarding employee perceptions.

The result of this activity was the identification of nine primary statements which were descriptive of employee attitudes at an organizationwide level. Five of the statements reflected relatively negative employee attitudes which were consistent with the need-satisfaction explanation for employee attitudes – career mobility, pay, training/development opportunities, recognition for performance, and benefits. The remaining four statements were related to the "environment" side of the equation in the interactional model of employee attitudes – management, decision making, and communication practices; staffing levels; organizational stability; and cross-functional working relationships. Although there were multiple ways that the root causes assessments were used (e.g., to help line and human resource management executives to identify priority areas of focus in strategic and tactical action planning), they also provided critical direction regarding the ongoing measurement of employee attitudes.

Assessment of current employee attitude survey processes

At the time the assessment of current employee attitudes was completed, two distinct data collection processes were being used in the sponsor company to gather attitudes about items related to employee satisfaction. One survey was designed to provide operating unit executives and first-line managers with data about the attitudes of their respective employees. It was administered by local operating units, but not on an annual basis, and did not allow for comparison to external normative data. The other survey was administered semiannually on a worldwide sampling basis and provided some comparison to a select group of outside companies on a limited number of items. However, it tended to be regarded by employees as a "corporate" survey whose results had little or no impact on subsequent actions by corporate headquarters, operating units, or first-line managers. Additionally, the survey contained questions about operational business practices, such as the effectiveness of company advertising, that tended to further cloud its purpose and value as a measurement and diagnostic tool.

As a result of this assessment of current data collection practices, a decision was made to reengineer the employee attitude survey process so that there would be a single employee-satisfaction survey administered worldwide (translated into each country's language) on an annual basis. Further, this updated survey was expected to reflect the findings of the employee-attitude root-cause assessment and to incorporate items that measured employee attitudes about related organizational practices.

The reengineered attitude survey

The redesign of the existing attitude survey was expected to examine the validity of items being asked in the current surveys and to identify a common set of core questions to be

used worldwide that would permit comparison to external in-country norms for various items and measures of overall employee satisfaction. In order to meet these requirements, a quality improvement team with representatives from international operating units and corporate headquarters completed a number of activities.

The first step in the redesign process was a statistical identification of items found in both existing employee surveys that had relatively moderate to high correlations with a summary question which asked employees to provide an assessment of their overall level of satisfaction.

The second phase involved a comparison of these items with the causes of employee dissatisfaction which were identified in the previously completed current-state root-cause analysis. This comparison identified a number of additional items to be included in the updated survey.

A third step in this process involved the identification of a vendor(s) that had the capability of supplying relevant external normative data on selected items which were to be incorporated in the survey. Not only did this activity result in identifying a supplier of this data, but the selected vendor provided additional items for inclusion in the survey, as well as nonnegotiable requirements for the wording of specific benchmark questions for which external normative data could be provided. In addition, the vendor provided specifications concerning the response scales to be used with those questions.

The fourth phase involved gathering feedback from employees and managers about the assessment of proposed items (derived from the initial three steps of this redesign process) that were to make up the survey's core set of questions. Each employee completed a premeeting questionnaire in which they evaluated the clarity of each item and its relevancy to the measurement of employee satisfaction. Employees also were asked to identify any additional topics or areas that they felt should be included in the final survey instrument. Managers, in addition to completing the clarity–relevancy evaluation were asked to provide feedback on the use of different scales (i.e., a four-point rather than a five-point scale, which included a "?" response). Also, managers were asked to identify any items they felt should not be included in an Employee Satisfaction Measurement Index. Both employees and managers met in groups with members of the corporate quality improvement team to discuss their responses to the questionnaire and to ensure that their assessments and comments were understood.

The fifth step in the redesign process involved actual completion of a potential survey, which totaled nearly a hundred items (some of which were known to be closely related in content to other items in the survey), by a sample of the organization's population. Approximately 850 employees and first- and second-level managers in each of the company's operating units, as well as employees in different functional job types, participated in the pilot delivery of the survey.

The sixth phase was an identification of the items having a relatively moderate to high correlation with an item measuring overall employee satisfaction. The quality improvement team reduced the item set which constituted the new survey core nearly in half after reviewing the results of a number of statistical analyses and making choices between items with high intercorrelations.

A final step in this process was a revalidation of this reduced set of items against the information identified in the root-cause analysis of employee dissatisfaction. The 48-item set then was adopted as the core item set used to measure employee attitudes. The updated survey was introduced for use on a worldwide basis in 1991.

Reporting survey results
Survey results for each of the 48 items are provided to immediate managers having four or more employees completing the survey. Managers can review the actual distribution of employee responses into the two negative, two positive and "?" response categories. Data is also summarized on a roll-up basis at an operating unit level. Employees have the option when completing the survey to add any write-in comments and these are transcribed verbatim and reported on an organization level that is no lower than the second level of management. By-item comparisons to external benchmarking or normative data are received at the corporate and operating unit level.

Managers receiving results for their specific work group also receive internal comparative data for each of the survey items. This provides a basis for comparing their work group's survey results with those of all employees in the operating unit who have responded to the survey. One of the significant features of the reporting process was the creation of 12-item index labeled the Immediate Manager Index. This index is considered to be the summary measurement of employees' attitudes about those items for which the manager has direct accountability.

Using measurements as the basis for action
Clearly, measuring employee attitudes is a necessary but not sufficient activity for companies pursuing the business results–customer satisfaction–employee satisfaction paradigm. A necessary next step is using the data to positively impact employee attitudes. While different organizations have different styles and approaches to communications, it is critical that the results are communicated back to employees, and especially by line management at all levels, including the CEO. As the identification of best practices noted, this type of communication underscores the importance of employee attitudes to the organization, reinforces the value placed upon employee satisfaction, and often allows for the partitioning of issues so that they may

be addressed at multiple or the most appropriate levels.

A key to taking action based on the survey results is the previously described Immediate Manager Index. Along with providing data about employee attitudes, this index provides the immediate manager with a sense of where the focus should be in order to improve employee satisfaction. However, the next activity the manager undertakes is as important as having the data about employee attitudes. It is a face-to-face group meeting with the employees in the immediate work group. In this meeting the manager works with the group to more clearly understand factors which are affecting their attitudes about a certain item(s). This dialogue is then used as the basis for the development of an action plan which is intended to address employee dissatisfaction with the item(s). Actions which the immediate manager can take, often in collaboration with the work group, represent that manager's employee-satisfaction action plan. As the benchmarking study suggested, for companies operating within this new paradigm, the immediate manager has a primary role to play in affecting employee attitudes. The feedback and action-planning activities described above reinforce that role.

Experience with using this approach of data collection, feedback, and action planning indicates that this process is most effective when action plans contain specific actions and timeframes for completion. Additionally, agreement between the manager and the work group about designated action milestones in the plan significantly contributes to the process being viewed by both managers and employees as one leading to an improvement in employee satisfaction.

Summary

At an organizational level, data collected in the process described above is being used to help shape company and human resource management policy and practices which require hard choices about the allocation of resources (e.g., in the relatively costly areas of compensation, benefits, and training and development). Using data about employee attitudes as an input into decision making has helped to ensure that the likely impact (both positive and negative) of decisions upon employee attitudes is understood consciously before the decisions are made.

In the short term, the use of surveys to help measure employee attitudes helps to provide an organization with an empirical assessment of the before and after impact of the implementation of various programs and practices. Similarly, understanding employee attitudes provides input into the strategies and tactics used to influence employee dispositions toward these programs and practices before and after they are launched. The long-term benefit to monitoring employee attitudes and acting upon the findings is expected to be improved employee satisfaction, a resulting improved likelihood that employees will be increasingly responsive to customer requirements, and an overall improvement in business results.

INTEGRATION AND FUTURE DIRECTIONS

The above comprehensive study demonstrates how job attitudes play a central role in the management of human resources in organizations. Job attitudes are caused by multiple and independent sources and the resulting consequences of these attitudes are many and varied. A great deal of research suggests that the assumptions underlying the action steps of this organization with regard to employee attitudes are well founded. For example, previous research has demonstrated a link between customer and employee satisfaction. It appears that satisfied employees are able to make their customers happy with the product or service being provided. This refers us back to the discussion of the implications of the dispositional source of job satisfaction for selection. To the extent that "positive" employees engender higher levels of customer satisfaction, the justification for using affective disposition in the selection process is increased (Judge, 1992).

Other assumptions underlying this organization's study of job attitudes also seem valid. It was assumed that financial performance depended in part on customer and employee satisfaction. Recent research also supports this assumption. Job attitudes do appear to have bottom-line consequences for organizations (Mirvis & Lawler, 1977), which may be due to their effects on withdrawal behaviors (which can be quite costly to organizations), and their effects on customer satisfaction (Brown & Mitchell, 1993). Other critical findings from the study find research support, including the effect of employee involvement and empowerment on job satisfaction (Lawler, 1986), the match between organizational and employee values leading to job satisfaction (Dawis, 1992), and the increasing frustration employees feel with their pay and promotion opportunities (Weiner, Remer, & Remer, 1992).

Of course, all is not right with the world. As in many areas of human resource management, a research–practice gap exists with respect to employee attitudes. In order to better bridge this gap, it might be useful to discuss some of the areas in which the research–practice gap is wide, and explore what can be done about it. Perhaps the most frustrating gap for both researchers and human resources professionals is the lack of translation from research findings to practice. Hundreds of studies involving job attitudes are published each year, yet these findings often do not influence human resources decisions. This lack of translation is known by most researchers and practitioners, and it is common for the researcher to blame the practitioner for his or her ignorance of the literature, and focus on practice at the expense of valid data and conclusions. On the other hand, the practitioner may bemoan the "ivory tower" focus of much academic research with little regard for practical applications, and the use of complex and arcane methodology. Below, we provide suggestions for future research and practice that may help bridge this gap.

Future job attitude research

Despite the fact that job attitudes have been heavily researched, there remain many important areas for future research. Although an exhaustive list of potentially fruitful research topics could be generated, only the most pressing areas for future research are described below. As mentioned earlier, the previous discussion of theoretical approaches to job satisfaction suggest that investigations of situational and dispositional models have rarely adequately considered the other perspective. In many ways, both streams of research have drawn unnecessary lines in the sand. It is not the case that job attitudes are solely a function of the job situation or context, but neither is it the case that all the variance in job attitudes can be explained by dispositional factors. Thus more research needs to take an integrative or interactional perspective. As noted by Terborg (1981), interactional research can take a number of different forms; all of these forms are relevant to the study of job attitudes. One form of this interaction would be where job satisfaction could be hypothesized as a function of situational and dispositional influences, with these sets of influences being independent of one another. For example, Judge and Locke (1993) included both situational (e.g., pay, intrinsic job characteristics) and dispositional (e.g., affective disposition, dysfunctional thought processes) influences on job satisfaction, but these characteristics were assumed to be relatively independent. Another interactional approach would be to assume that dispositional characteristics moderate the effect of situational factors on job satisfaction. As an example of this approach, it could be hypothesized that individuals holding a belief in the Protestant work ethic would be more satisfied in environments where the organizational culture is one of hard work, strict rules, and rigid policies, while a worker not believing in the Protestant work ethic would find such an environment aversive. There are other different possibilities that could be pursued here, but the point is that interactional research stands the greatest chance of advancing theoretical knowledge in this area.

Another prominent area for research is investigations of the effect of human resources interventions on employee attitudes. To what extent do existing, and future changes in, human resources policies and practices influence employee attitudes such as satisfaction, trust, and commitment? Research has shown that trust in management has declined in the last two decades (Milkovich & Boudreau, 1991), but the causal factors underlying this trend are unclear. Although past research has linked some interventions to job attitudes (the job redesign literature is the most notable case), more research needs to link changes in human resources practices to employee attitudes. As always, it is important that these linkages are theoretically relevant. It is likely that some human resources interventions have little effect on employee attitudes, while others may have dramatic effects on job attitudes. It is also important that job attitudes are studied at the proper level of specificity. For example, it may be more meaningful to study the effect of a change in promotion procedures on promotion satisfaction than on overall job satisfaction or, certainly, on pay or coworker satisfaction. If theoretical relevance or construct specificity considerations are ignored, insignificant results may tell us more about the weaknesses of the study than about the true relationships between human resources policies and job attitudes.

A final, related, area for future research that is important to mention is the need for future research to link job attitudes to bottom-line results. Research using a utility analysis framework has demonstrated that

human resources practices have practical, bottom-line consequences for organizations (Boudreau, 1990). However, the traditional paradigm within which utility analysis has operated has been a productivity framework, where human resources practices yield utility through their effects on employee performance or productivity. Neglected in this framework are the possible effects on employee attitudes and behaviors. Research indicates that withdrawal behaviors such as absence and turnover are costly to organizations. Failing to deliver high-quality customer service would apparently be another outcome neglected by utility analysis models. Yet, each of these outcomes likely are affected substantially by employee attitudes. Thus, future research is needed that links employee attitudes to the bottom-line through some of the mediating processes described above.

Future areas for improvement of human resources practice

The future areas of research outlined above may appear to be relevant only to academic researchers. However, these research areas have the potential to demonstrate the tangible consequences of employee attitudes. Applied research topics such as these have the potential to help bridge the gap between research and practice of employee attitudes. Further steps to bridge this gap also need to come from human resources professionals. Perhaps the most obvious step human resources professionals can take to bridge the gap between research and practice is to take affirmative steps to understand the research literature better. It is unfortunate that a voluminous, and potentially useful, literature exists on the causes, measurement, and consequences of employee attitudes, yet there is not much evidence that this research is being used to change how organizations manage employee attitudes.

Another area where the management of

employee attitudes can be improved is through investigations of the relationship between employee attitudes and customer satisfaction. Given the quality focus in most business organizations today, and given research suggesting a link between employee attitudes and customer attitudes, perhaps one of the best ways to insure that customers are satisfied is to make sure that employees are satisfied with their jobs.

Yet another important area for fruitful collaboration is conducting controlled studies. One of the most beneficial ways that this can be accomplished is through quasi-experimental designs where human resources interventions are introduced into one business unit, plant, or location, but there is also a control plant or unit that does not receive the intervention (but is similar in other ways to the unit receiving the intervention). Such designs are able to rule out many alternative explanations for any changes in attitudes that may occur as a result of the intervention. As a result, these types of studies allow researchers to isolate changes in attitudes as a function of the intervention and not due to some other factor that may have influenced attitudes at both units (e.g., companywide initiatives, company performance, economic conditions). Furthermore these designs enable pilot programs to be conducted, where the effect of human resources programs can be monitored before rolling out the program to the entire organization. Thus quasi-experimental designs offer powerful advantages and are important ways in which researchers and practitioners can collaborate in future research.

Finally, perhaps the area in which the research–practice gap can most readily be bridged is by human resources managers becoming *researchers* themselves. The research example outlined earlier that was presented as an integration of attitudinal causes and consequences suggests ways that research can reveal important and practical insights into the management of employee attitudes.

NOTES

1 Another meta-analysis on personality and job performance, published in the same journal in the same year as the Tett et al. (1991) paper (Barrick & Mount, 1991), reached different conclusions. Barrick and Mount found that conscientiousness was the best predictor of performance while agreeableness and neuroticism had much lower correlations with job performance. Various methodological and sampling differences between the two studies appear to explain the differences in the findings (Ones, Mount, Barrick, & Hunter, 1994; Tett, Jackson, Rothstein, & Reddon, 1994).

2 It should be mentioned that recent research has called into question the causal link between job satisfaction and citizenship behaviors when other factors such as task characteristics and fairness perceptions are taken into account (Farh, Podsakoff, & Organ, 1990; Konovsky & Organ, 1992; Moorman, 1991). However, the ways in which job satisfaction and citizenship behaviors might be related are complex. Potential mediating variables such as conscientiousness, mood, task perceptions, and fairness perceptions need to be modeled before it can be concluded that job satisfaction has no causal role in organizational citizenship behaviors (Johnson, 1994).

REFERENCES

Adler, S., & Weiss, H. M. (1988). Recent developments in the study of personality and organizational behavior. In C. L. Cooper & I. Robertson (eds.), *International Review of Industrial and Organizational Psychology*, vol. 3, pp. 307–30. London: Wiley.

Agho, A. O., Mueller, C. W., & Price, J. L. (1993). Determinants of employee job satisfaction: An empirical test of a causal model. *Human Relations*, 46, 1007–27.

Allen, N. J., & Meyer, J. P. (1990). The measurement and antecedents of affective, continuance, and normative commitment to the organization. *Journal of Occupational Psychology*, 63, 1–18.

Arvey, R. D., Bouchard, T. J., Seagal, N. L., & Abraham, L. M. (1989). Job satisfaction: Environmental and genetic components. *Journal of Applied Psychology*, 74, 187–92.

Arvey, R. D., Carter, G. W., & Buerkley, D. K. (1991). Job satisfaction: Dispositional and situational influences. In C. L. Cooper & I. T. Robertson (eds.), *International Review of Industrial and Organizational Psychology*, vol. 6, pp. 359–83. London: Wiley.

Barrick, M. R., & Mount, M. K. (1991). The big five personality dimensions and job performance: A meta-analysis. *Personnel Psychology*, 44, 1–26.

Bateman, T. S., & Organ, D. W. (1983). Job satisfaction and the good soldier: The relationship between affect and employee "citizenship." *Academy of Management Journal*, 26, 587–95.

Blau, G. J. (1987). Using a person-environment fit model to predict job involvement and organizational commitment. *Journal of Vocational Behavior*, 30, 240–57.

Bouchard, T. J., Arvey, R. D., Keller, L. M., & Seagal, N. L. (1992). Genetic influences on job satisfaction: A reply to Cropanzano and James. *Journal of Applied Psychology*, 77, 89–93.

Boudreau, J. W. (1990). Utility analysis for decisions in human resource management. In M. D. Dunnette & L. M. Hough (eds.), *Handbook of Industrial and Organizational Psychology*, 2nd ed., vol. 2, pp. 621–745. Palo Alto, CA: Consulting Psychologists Press.

Boudreau, J. W., Sturman, M. C., & Judge, T. A. (in press). Utility analysis: What are the black boxes, and do they affect decisions? In N. Anderson & P. Herriot (eds.), *Handbook of Selection and Appraisal*, 2nd ed. London: Wiley.

Bretz, R. D., Milkovich, G. T., & Read, W. (1992). The current state of performance appraisal research and practice: Concerns, directions, and implications. *Journal of Management*, 18, 321–52.

Brown, K. A., & Mitchell, T. R. (1993). Organizational obstacles: Links with financial performance, customer satisfaction, and job satisfaction in a service environment. *Human Relations*, 46, 725–57.

Butcher, A. H., Brief, A. P., & Roberson, L. (1993). Cookies, disposition, and job attitudes: The effects of positive mood inducing events and negative affectivity on job satisfaction in a field experiment. Paper presented at the 53rd annual meeting of the Academy of Management, Atlanta, GA.

Chun, K., & Campbell, J. (1974). Dimensionality of the Rotter interpersonal trust scale. *Psychological Reports*, 35, 1056–70.

Cranny, C. J., Smith, P. C., & Stone, E. F. (1992). *Job Satisfaction: How people feel about their jobs and how it affects their performance.* New York: Lexington Books.

Cropanzano, R., & James, K. (1990). Some methodological considerations for the behavioral genetic analysis of work attitudes. *Journal of Applied Psychology*, 75, 433–9.

Davis-Blake, A., & Pfeffer, J. (1989). Just a mirage: The search for dispositional effects in organizational research. *Academy of Management Review*, 14, 385–400.

Dawis, R. V. (1992) Person-environment fit and job satisfaction. In Cranny et al. (eds.), *Job Satisfaction*, 69–88. New York: Lexington Books.

Doob, L. W. (1947). The behavior of attitudes. *Psychological Review*, 54, 135–56.

Dvorak, B. J. (1935). Differential occupational ability patterns. *Bulletins of the Employment Stabilization Research Institute*, vol. 3. Minneapolis: University of Minnesota Press.

Eisenberger, R., Fasolo, P., & Davis-LaMastro, V. (1990). Perceived organizational support and employee diligence, commitment, and innovation. *Journal of Applied Psychology*, 75, 51–9.

Erez, A. (1994). Dispositional source of job satisfaction: The role of self-deception. Unpublished master's thesis, Cornell University, Ithaca, NY.

Farh, J., Podsakoff, P. M., & Organ, D. W. (1990). Accounting for organizational citizenship behaviors: Leader-fairness and task scope versus satisfaction. *Journal of Management*, 16, 705–21.

Fishbein, M., & Ajzen, I. (1974). Attitudes toward objects as predictors of single and multiple behavioral criteria. *Psychological Bulletin*, 81, 59–74.

Fisher, C. D., & Locke, E. A. (1992). The new look in job satisfaction research and theory. In Cranny et al. (eds.), *Job Satisfaction*, 165–94. New York: Lexington Books.

George, J. M. (1992). The role of personality in organizational life: Issues and evidence. *Journal of Management*, 18, 185–213.

Gerhart, B. (1987). How important are dispositional factors as determinants of job satisfaction? Implications for job design and other personnel programs. *Journal of Applied Psychology*, 72, 366–73.

Gerhart, B. (1990). The doubtful practical relevance of dispositional effects on job satisfaction. Working paper No. 90–06, Center for Advanced Human Resource Studies, Cornell University, Ithaca, NY.

Greenberg, J. (1990). Organizational justice: Yesterday, today, and tomorrow. *Journal of Management*, 16, 399–412.

Gutek, B. A., & Winter, S. J. (1992). Consistency of job satisfaction across situations: Fact or framing artifact? *Journal of Vocational Behavior*, 41, 61–78.

Hanisch, K. A. (1990). A causal model of general attitudes, work withdrawal, and job withdrawal, including retirement. Unpublished doctoral dissertation, University of Illinois at Urbana-Champaign.

Hanisch, K. A. (1994). Behavioral families and patterns of behavior: Matching the complexity of responses to the complexity of antecedents. Manuscript submitted for publication.

Hanisch, K. A., & Hulin, C. L. (1990). Job attitudes and organizational withdrawal: An examination of retirement and other voluntary withdrawal behaviors. *Journal of Vocational Behavior*, 37, 60–78.

Hanisch, K. A., & Hulin, C. L. (1991). General attitudes and organizational withdrawal: An evaluation of a causal model. *Journal of Vocational Behavior*, 39, 110–28.

Hansen, C. P. (1989). A causal model of the relationship among accidents, biodata, personality, and cognitive factors. *Journal of Applied Psychology*, 74, 81–90.

Hulin, C. L. (1991). Adaptation, persistence, and commitment in organizations. In M. D. Dunnette & L. M. Hough (eds.), *Handbook of Industrial and Organizational Psychology*, 2nd ed., vol. 2, pp. 445–505. Palo Alto, CA: Consulting Psychologists Press.

Iaffaldano, M. T., & Muchinsky, P. M. (1985). Job satisfaction and performance: A meta-analysis. *Psychological Bulletin*, 97, 251–73.

Johnson, D. E. (1994). Do employees use organizational citizenship behaviors as a form of influence behavior?: A discriminant validity study. Unpublished master's thesis, Cornell University, Ithaca, NY.

Judge, T. A. (1992). The dispositional perspective in human resources research. In G. R. Ferris & K. M. Rowland (eds.), *Research in Personnel and Human Resource Management*, vol. 10, pp. 31–72. Greenwich, CT: JAI Press.

Judge, T. A. (1993). Does affective disposition moderate the relationship between job satisfaction and voluntary turnover? *Journal of Applied Psychology*, 78, 395–401.

Judge, T. A., & Hulin, C. L. (1992). Job satisfaction and subjective well-being as determinants of job adaptation. *Academy of Management Best Papers Proceedings*, 222–6.

Judge, T. A., & Hulin, C. L. (1993). Job satisfaction as a reflection of disposition: A multiple-source causal analysis. *Organizational Behavior and Human Decision Processes*, 56, 388–421.

Judge, T. A., & Locke, E. A. (1993). Effect of dysfunctional thought processes on subjective well-being and job satisfaction. *Journal of Applied Psychology*, 78, 475–90.

Judge, T. A., Locke, E. A., & Durham, C. C. (1994). *The dispositional causes of job satisfaction*. Working paper, School of Industrial and Labor Relations, Cornell University.

Kantor, D. L., & Mirvis, P. H. (1989). *The Cynical Americans: Living and working in an age of discontent and disillusion*. San Francisco: Jossey-Bass.

Kantor, J. R. (1924). *Principles of Psychology*, vol. 1. Bloomington, IN: Principia Press.

Kantor, J. R. (1926). *Principles of Psychology*, vol. 2. Bloomington, IN: Principia Press.

Kanungo, R. N. (1982). Measurement of job and work commitment. *Journal of Applied Psychology*, 67, 341–9.

Kinicki, A. J., Carson, K. P., & Bohlander, G. W. (1992). Relationship between an organization's actual human resource efforts and employee attitudes. *Group & Organization Management*, 17, 135–52.

Konovsky, M. A., & Organ, D. W. (1992). Personality, satisfaction, and fairness: Sorting out their linkages with organizational citizenship behavior. Working paper No. 92-HRMG-03, A. B. Freeman School of Business, Tulane University, New Orleans, LA.

Lawler, E. E., III (1986). *High Involvement Management: Participative strategies for improving organizational performance*. San Francisco: Jossey-Bass.

Levin, I., & Stokes, J. P. (1989). Disposition approach to job satisfaction: Role of negative affectivity. *Journal of Applied Psychology*, 74, 752–8.

Lewin, K. (1936). *Principles of Topological Psychology*. New York: McGraw-Hill.

Locke, E. (1976). The nature and causes of job satisfaction. In M. D. Dunnette (ed.), *Handbook of Industrial and Organizational Psychology*, 1297–1343. New York: Wiley.

Lodahl, T. M., & Kejner, M. (1965). The definition and measurement of job involvement. *Journal of Applied Psychology*, 49, 24–33.

Lofquist, L. H., & Dawis, R. V. (1969). *Adjustment to Work*. New York: Appleton-Century-Crofts.

Martocchio, J. J. (1989). Voluntary absenteeism as reasoned action: A partial test of the Ajzen and Fishbein theory of behavioral intentions. Unpublished doctoral dissertation, Michigan State University, East Lansing, MI.

Mathieu, J. E., & Zajac, D. M. (1990). A review and meta-analysis of the antecedents, correlates, and consequences of organizational commitment. *Psychological Bulletin*, 108, 171–94.

Milkovich, G. T., & Boudreau, J. W. (1991). *Human Resource Management*, 6th ed. Homewood, IL: Irwin.

Miller, M. (1983). The "wild card" of business: How to manage the work ethic in the automated workplace. *Management Review*, 72, 8–12.

Mirvis, P. H., & Lawler, E. E., III (1977). Measuring the financial impact of employee attitudes. *Journal of Applied Psychology*, 62, 1–8.

Moorman, R. H. (1991). Relationship between organizational justice and organizational citizenship behaviors: Do fairness perceptions influence employee citizenship? *Journal of Applied Psychology*, 76, 845–55.

Motowidlo, S. J. (1984). Does job satisfaction lead to consideration and personal sensitivity? *Academy of Management Journal*, 27, 910–15.

Necowitz, L. B., & Roznowski, M. (1992). Cognitive processes underlying the negative affectivity-job satisfaction relationship. Paper presented at the 52nd annual meeting of the Academy of Management, Las Vegas, NV.

Ones, D. S., Mount, M. K., Barrick, M. R., & Hunter, J. E. (1994). Personality and job performance: A critique of the Tett, Jackson, and Rothstein (1991) meta-analysis. *Personnel Psychology*, 47, 147–56.

Organ, D. W. (1988). A restatement of the satisfaction-performance hypothesis. *Journal of Management*, 14, 547–57.

Parsons, F. (1909). *Choosing a Vocation*. Boston: Houghton.

Patterson, D. G., & Darley, J. G. (1936). *Men, Women, and Jobs*. Minneapolis, MN: University of Minnesota Press.

Porter, L., & Lawler, E. E., III (1968). *Managerial Attitudes and Performance*. Homewood, IL: Irwin-Dorsey.

Porter, L. W., Steers, R. M., Mowday, R. T., & Boulian, P. V. (1974). Organizational commitment, job satisfaction, and turnover among psychiatric technicians. *Journal of Applied Psychology*, 59, 603–9.

Pulakos, E. D., & Schmitt, N. (1983). A longitudinal study of a valence model approach for the prediction of job satisfaction of new employees. *Journal of Applied Psychology*, 68, 307–12.

Rosse, J. G., & Miller, H. E. (1984). Relationship between absenteeism and other employee behaviors. In P. S. Goodman & R. S. Atkin (eds.), *Absenteeism: New approaches to understanding, measuring, and managing employee absence*, 194–228. San Francisco: Jossey-Bass.

Rotter, J. (1967). A new scale for the measurement of interpersonal trust. *Journal of Personality*, 35, 651–65.

Roznowski, M., & Hanisch, K. A. (1990). Building systematic heterogeneity into work attitudes and behavior measures. *Journal of Vocational Behavior*, 36, 361–75.

Roznowski, M., & Hulin, C. (1992). The scientific merit of valid measures of general constructs with special reference to job satisfaction and job withdrawal. In Cranny et al. (eds.), *Job Satisfaction*, 123–63. New York: Lexington Books.

Salancik, G. R. (1977). Commitment and the control of organizational behavior and belief. In B. M. Staw & G. R. Salancik (eds.), *New Directions in Organizational Behavior*. Chicago: St. Clair Press.

Salancik, G. R., & Pfeffer, J. (1977). An examination of need-satisfaction models of job attitudes. *Administrative Science Quarterly*, 22, 427–56.

Salancik, G. R., & Pfeffer, J. (1978). A social-information processing approach to job attitudes and task design. *Administrative Science Quarterly*, 23, 224–53.

Smith, C. A., Organ, D. W., & Near, J. P. (1983). Organizational citizenship behavior: Its nature and antecedents. *Journal of Applied Psychology*, 68, 653–63.

Staw, B. M., & Barsade, S. G. (1993). Affect and managerial performance: A test of the sadder-but-wiser vs. happier-and-smarter hypotheses. *Administrative Science Quarterly*, 38, 304–31.

Staw, B. M., Bell, N. E., & Clausen, J. A. (1986). The dispositional approach to job attitudes: A lifetime longitudinal test. *Administrative Science Quarterly*, 31, 56–77.

Staw, B. M., & Ross, J. (1985). Stability in the midst of change: A dispositional approach to job attitudes. *Journal of Applied Psychology*, 70, 469–80.

Stone, E. F. (1992). A critical analysis of social information processing models of job perceptions and job attitudes. In Cranny et al. (eds.), *Job Satisfaction*, 21–52. New York: Lexington Books.

Strong, E. K., Jr. (1943). *Vocational Interests of Men and Women*. Palo Alto, CA: Stanford University Press.

Strong, E. K., Jr. (1947). *Vocational Interest Blank*. Palo Alto, CA: Stanford University Press.

Terborg, J. R. (1981). Interactional psychology and research on human behavior in organizations. *Academy of Management Review*, 6, 569–76.

Tett, R. P., Jackson, D. N., & Rothstein, M. (1991). Personality measures as predictors of job performance: A meta-analytic review. *Personnel Psychology*, 44, 703–42.

Tett, R. P., Jackson, D. N., Rothstein, M., & Reddon, J. R. (1994). Meta-analysis of personality-job performance relations: A reply to Ones, Mount, Barrick, and Hunter (1994). *Personnel Psychology*, 47, 157–72.

Thurstone, L. L. (1931). The measurement of social attitudes. *Journal of Abnormal and Social Psychology*, 26, 249–69.

Watson, D., & Slack, A. K. (1993). General factors of affective temperament and their relation to job satisfaction over time. *Organizational Behavior and Human Decision Processes*, 54, 181–202.

Weiner, A., Remer, R., & Remer, P. (1992). Career plateauing: Implications for career development. *Journal of Career Development*, 19, 37–48.

Weiss, H. M. (1991). Discussant comments. In K. James & R. Cropanzano, *Dispositions and work outcomes*. Symposium conducted at the Sixth Annual Conference of the Society for Industrial and Organizational Psychology, St. Louis, MO. April.

Weitz, J. (1952). A neglected concept in the study of job satisfaction. *Personnel Psychology*, 5, 201–5.

Wicker, A. W. (1969). Attitudes vs. actions: The relationship of verbal and overt behavioral responses to attitude objects. *Journal of Social Issues*, 25, 41–78.

Chapter 30

The Management of Absence: What Do We Know? What Can We Do?

Nigel Nicholson and Joseph J. Martocchio

INTRODUCTION

Absence is, par excellence, a pervasive "personnel problem," and one which is ubiquitous (Rhodes & Steers, 1990). Even in firms with the most primitive management systems, whether people show up to work or not is important in terms of what work gets done, by whom, and how much people are to be paid. From the earliest days of scholarship about business, absence has been seen as a management problem (Fox & Scott, 1943). There is abundant evidence that employee absenteeism leads to a number of undesired organizational outcomes, including diminished employee job performance (Bycio, 1992), a significant financial burden (Allen, 1983; Martocchio, 1992a), overstaffing to compensate for absent employees (Rhodes & Steers, 1990), and a disruption of work flow (Atkin & Goodman, 1984). Therefore, it is not hard to understand why managers and supervisors have a keen interest in minimizing levels of absenteeism. Personnel management as a functional specialism has grown during this century largely through the evolution of systems to regulate uncertainties and

variability in labor supply, remuneration, and employee relations. The maintenance of personnel records became the chief service function of its practitioners, lightening the burden which otherwise fell on line management.

This remains the case in many small- to medium-sized firms and some traditional smokestack industries. At the same time we find ourselves in a new era of personnel practice, under the aegis of human resource management (HRM), transcending the traditional reactive stance of personnel management, seeking an active developmental role in relation to the organizational culture, passing back insights and responsibilities to line management, and deploying its specialized techniques strategically in pursuit of corporate goals (Guest, 1995). The pace of this movement has been uneven, and, as a consequence, looking across the organizational landscape at the present time one finds enormous variation in the sophistication and objectives of personnel/human resource management.

Although much continues to be written about management's response to absence, surprisingly little has been said about whether the new model HRM offers a fresh approach to an old problem. Indeed, is the problem the same as it used to be? Has the nature of absence changed? Whether it has or not, there continues to be a huge volume of scholarly research on absence, and therefore a further question is whether this activity has yielded new insights into its nature which could guide HRM practice.

This, then, is the agenda for the present chapter. First, we attempt a highly condensed summary of themes in the absence literature, to identify areas of emerging consensus. Second, we examine the main current strands in absence theory. Third, we investigate the chief empirical issues of likely importance to HRM practice. Finally, we conclude with a review of how HRM practice may address these areas.

THEORY AND RESEARCH

Absence: the emerging consensus

Absence may have moved beyond the point of being "a social fact in need of a theory" (Ås, 1962), to a position of theoretical multiplicity, but not, as yet, theoretical unity (Martocchio & Harrison, 1993). Indeed, one may speculate that theoretical integration is, of necessity, elusive because of the nature of the phenomenon. Johns and Nicholson's (1982) critique of the way the field had formerly constructed absence sought to encourage new paradigms for theory, method, and research, and since their review an emerging consensus has become detectable about the nature of the phenomenon and the challenge this presents to those who would build theories about it or seek to control it. Four related elements can be identified:

1. *Absence has multiple meanings to actors and observers.* Johns (1987) contrasts these as "models" (i.e., medical, withdrawal, deviance, economic, and cultural) characterizing causal assumptions, respectively, to do with health,

disaffection, hostility, self-interest, and norms. The fact that absence has multiple and varied causes is only partly the reason for this interpretive diversity. It is also the case that the causes of absence cannot be discerned unerringly, even by absentees themselves. Therefore, these models are also attributional (i.e., a function of the values and beliefs of actors and observers) (Judge & Martocchio, 1994).

2. *Absence presents intractable problems of aligning measurement with meaning.* Various measures are incommensurate, and cannot be reliably identified with sets of causes in ways which allow variance to be partitioned and labeled in any sensible fashion, such as the widely used and abused "voluntary"/"involuntary" distinction. Typically, both researchers and practitioners have indexed absence either in terms of time lost – the volume of absence for a given period regardless of number of episodes – or in terms of frequency – the number of episodes regardless of the duration of each spell (Chadwick-Jones, Brown, Nicholson, & Sheppard, 1971) – almost always deriving these measures from personnel records (Martocchio & Harrison, 1993). However, these techniques have been found to be contaminated inasmuch as measures of purported voluntary absence spuriously assess involuntary absence, and vice versa (Hammer & Landau, 1981). Criterion contamination is exacerbated by the process of classification that takes place when the absent employee or clerk who logs absence occurrences decides how to categorize these events for inclusion in the personnel files (Atkin & Goodman, 1984; Hammer & Landau, 1981; Smulders, 1980). Conceptually, there is evidence for at least two contrasting positions: that absence is one of a "family" of equipotential behaviors representing latent underlying constructs (Hulin, 1984); and that it is highly individualized in form and expression (Hackett, Bycio, & Guion, 1989; Martocchio & Harrison, 1993; Martocchio & Judge, 1994). As we shall see, these two positions are not necessarily mutually exclusive.

3. *Absence is contextually constrained behavior.* This has two main ramifications. First, attempts to disentangle issues of meaning and measurement need to take account of the context in which the behavior is embedded. Context means several things: the structured array of possible causes such as job conditions and supervisory regimes; the nature of its consequences such as discipline or loss of pay; and the presence of normative constraints such as informal peer pressure and formal rules governing its expression. The second ramification, a corollary of the first, is that this presents a critical level-of-analysis problem (Johns, 1991). We face the conundrum that absence is highly individualized, in the sense that causes and reasons vary for the individual across time and circumstances, while at the same time it is collective behavior that is driven by social norms (Chadwick-Jones, Nicholson, & Brown, 1982). This makes it difficult to know where we should pitch our measures and apply remedies: individual, work group, division, organization, or occupational category?

4. *Absence, although defined as an employee behavior, is also a personal lifespace event.* This means that the origins of absence may lie outside the sphere of organizational action and control, in two crucial ways. First, it may reflect enduring characteristics of the individual, including various transsituational dispositions and dysfunctions (Judge & Martocchio, 1994; Martocchio & Judge, 1994). Second, it may be a chosen or enforced adjustment to nonwork events such as health hazards or domestic problems (Staw & Oldham, 1978; Steers & Rhodes, 1978). One implication of this is that absence cannot be seen solely as a dependent variable to be explained. It is not just something which "happens to" people, it is something people *do* (i.e., it is a behavior that has consequences for the person, within and outside the work sphere, in such areas as self-image, well-being, social relations, etc.). This implies that absence may reflect a changing causal dynamic. The consequences of absence at Time 1 may influence the levels of absence at Time 2 and so on, as is suggested by research revealing job attitudes to be both a *cause* and *outcome* of absence (Clegg, 1983; Tharenou, 1993).

Absence theory

For would-be theorists the challenge is apparent. No single grand theory seems plausible to encompass such a wealth of paradox and diversity. Yet the huge volume of empirical evidence of widely differing kinds provides a substantial base for mid-range theory building, to give partial or qualified accounts of absence.

Closest to attempting grand theory construction are what Martocchio and Harrison (1993) call variance theories (Mohr, 1982), which seek to identify the variables primarily predicting absence and to model how they are causally ordered (e.g., which moderate the impact of which others). The Steers and Rhodes (1978) model probably represents the paradigm example of this kind of theorizing, locating the construct "attendance motivation" as the immediate direct predictor of absence, moderated by ability to attend. Pressure to attend, job satisfaction, job situation, values and expectations, and personal characteristics are modeled as antecedents of these variables.

The model certainly summarizes much evidence in the literature by identifying variables which have been found to predict absence. But herein also lies a fatal flaw for this and other theories of its kind. There is room for debate about the generality of the predictive reliability of just about every single measurable variable in the model. Job satisfaction alone has proved a prominent source of difficulty in the literature, such is its unexpected but repeated failure to covary strongly and reliably with absence (Nicholson, Brown, & Chadwick-Jones, 1976; Hackett & Guion, 1985). There is scope for endless and fruitless debate about the sufficiency of variables included in the model, and the efficacy of attempts to augment it. Even reasonable additions such as offered by Brooke and Price (1989) lead inexorably toward unmanageable complexity and arbitrariness.

The complexity is unmanageable in the sense that to cover all contingencies amongst the array of possible predictors (i.e., all likely relationships – direct, reciprocal, mediated, etc.) is beyond the scope of available linear statistical modeling techniques. Moreover in most field settings, because absence is a low base-rate phenomenon (Hulin & Rousseau, 1980), there is just not enough variance to go around among all possible predictors. Indeed, it is difficult to imagine any circumstances under which there would be sufficient variance among all feasible independent variables to permit complete tests of these models. This kind of modeling is also doomed to failure because of arbitrariness, in the sense implied by the four points made at the start of this chapter, and especially the third point – absence is contextually constrained behavior. The thrust of these four points is that the "right" model of absence is likely to vary between settings, levels of analysis, over time, and even across individuals over time.

Nicholson's (1977) theory is open to analogous questions, insofar as it contains variance-type modeling of predictors. However, it differs in an important respect which makes it what we may term an "interpretive theory." "Attachment," a similar notion to attendance motivation, is identified as a main intervening construct, but here it is used to connote a norm of habitual attendance. This, in effect, is a decisional frame, proposing that for most people no decision is made until events or influences pass a disturbance threshold sufficient to trigger a decision to be absent. It portrays individual attendance decisions as determined by an interaction of "risk" and "susceptibility" (see figure 30.1). Risk denotes the events which may disturb the flow of regular attendance, and susceptibility is the threshold at which any disturbance will trigger absence. Note that risk embraces

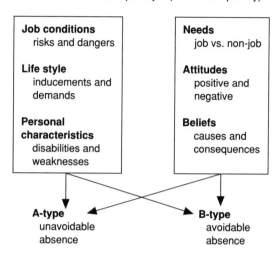

Figure 30.1 An interactionist framework

Absence = Situation × psychological state

= Risk + susceptibility + (risk × susceptibility)

both temptations and hazards, and susceptibility both attitudinal and constitutional factors. A key feature of the theory is that the same events have different risk values according to the circumstances of the individual, which means that similar appearing absences may be the consequences of quite different balances of risks and susceptibilities (i.e., a formulation which is both idiographic and interactionist). Empirical attempts to demonstrate these effects have done so with some success, though at the same time these studies point out the limitations of both idiographic and comparison group research designs to capture more variance than conventional field-based survey designs (Hackett et al., 1989; Judge & Martocchio, 1994; Martocchio & Judge, 1994; Nicholson & Payne, 1987).

This construction has two important properties which distinguish it from variance theories. First, risks and susceptibility may combine uniquely at the individual level, but they can also be expected to reflect various collective and structural elements, such as group norms, management policies, occupational conditions, cultural expectations, and so on. Some of the most common findings in the absence literature fit readily into this frame. For example, the failure of job satisfaction alone to predict absence is due to the fact that it only affects one half of the equation, susceptibility, and does so unreliably. More reliably, positive findings, such as the identification of women, younger workers, and low-job-level employees as more absence-prone can be explained through effects on both terms. Women are more at risk from domestic disturbances, and more susceptible when more tolerant norms are extended to their absence. Younger workers are more at risk from nonwork temptations, and more susceptible through weaker work attachment and financial need. Low-status workers are more at risk from health and occupational hazards, and more susceptible through lower commitment and job involvement (see figure 30.2).

Second, risks flow unpredictably and idiosyncratically for individuals over time, and the threshold at which they trigger absence can vary similarly. Combining this observation with the first point of course implies that collectively induced risks and susceptibilities are not in any absolute sense "reliable." Generalizations about the susceptibilities and risks of young, low-status, or female workers can, in effect, be seen as a portrayal of particular configurations of industrial culture during the

modern era. This implies that we should keep an open mind about the possibility that generalizations about these, and other groups, could be transient (i.e., rendered invalid by historical changes in gender roles, the work contracts of young people, and the organizational structures which define status). In passing, one may note that this point offers a significant critique of the use of meta-analytic methods to assess the "true variance" accounted for by sets of variables, since they aggregate over possibly changing history effects. However, the general point about absence theory building being made here is that interpretive models can continue to prove useful if they are able to supply a sufficiently flexible analytical frame to accommodate shifting causes and effects of absence at more than a single level of analysis. We return subsequently to consider the implications of this for human resource management.

The only other kinds of theorizing which seem likely to survive the exacting conditions we have outlined in this chapter, are those which either specify clear boundary conditions for their validity (e.g., cultural and temporal location), or which capture some situationally transcendent principle of human functioning and social life, what Martocchio and Harrison (1993) call "process" theory (Mohr, 1982). Theories meeting these conditions are clearly falsifiable in ways which variance and interpretive theories are not. For obvious reasons, attempts at this kind of theorizing are rare, but in relation to absence they do offer a way forward, so long as they do not attempt to overreach themselves by trying to account for more than specific aspects of the behavior. An example of this kind is Fichman's (1984, 1988, 1989) "dynamic motivation theory." But first we provide some background.

As previously noted, virtually all absence research has been based on variance theories. Formally, a variance theory is one that states X is a necessary and sufficient condition for the outcome Y (Mohr, 1982). In other words, Y is completely determined by X. Thus,

Figure 30.2 Some absence-prone groups

Group	Risk	Susceptibility
• Low status	• Health hazards	• Low commitment
• Young	• High competing inducements	• Low work needs
• Female	• High non-work demands	• Legitimizing beliefs

absence researchers have constructed theories with the prime objective of maximizing the variance explained in the dependent variable by the independent variables, and random variance is considered error. For example, in their meta-analysis, Hackett and Guion (1985) evaluate the integrity of the job satisfaction–absence relationship partly on the basis of variance explained.

Fichman (1991) challenged the convention that a "good" theory of absence explains all the variance by arguing that stochastic or process theories (Mohr, 1982) may be better suited for explaining absence than variance theories. Essentially, "a process theory is one that tells a little story about how something comes about, but in order to qualify as a theoretical explanation of recurrent behavior, the manner of the storytelling must conform to narrow specifications" (Mohr, 1982, 44). A process theory is defined as: (a) X is a necessary condition for Y, but not a sufficient condition; and, (b) X will cause Y stochastically. That is, whether X causes Y depends on some probabilistic process. Thus, process theories, unlike variance theories, leave residual uncertainty by construction.

An example of a process theory is Fichman's (1984, 1988, 1989) analysis of absence as the product of the dynamic operation of a set of motives, all of which are time-varying. He suggested that to explain the timing of absence and attendance, one must consider the changing strength of two sets of motives: to attend work, and to engage in activities which require absence from work. Following Atkinson and Birch (1970), he argued that unfulfilled motives increase in strength with time, and that this changing motive strength can be modeled as a set of differential equations. Thus, if all motives were internal, there were not external constraints on time allocation, and a person could act on their motives without cost, then one could construct a deterministic model of time allocation and fully explain the timing and duration of activities. However, random events such as work stop-

pages, accidents, and illness impose external constraints on time allocation.

The notion of process theories highlights the possibility of a large number of constructs which could be causes or consequences of absenteeism. Johns and Nicholson (1982) identified a number of viable constructs and suggested likely mechanisms for their effects on absenteeism. Partly stimulated by that article, there has been a flurry of new theories and hypotheses about absenteeism, including investigations of sets of explanatory constructs such as mood (George, 1989) or job satisfaction (Breaugh, 1981). Yet, one may be critical of researchers in the field for choosing to take the safest and least informative route of continuing to test those hypotheses which have been studied most often in the past.

Applications of theories established in other areas are exemplars of alternative kinds of theory building which may be able to move the field of absenteeism forward. An example is social cognitive theory (Bandura, 1991), which focuses on how individuals self-regulate beliefs about their ability and motivation. These self-regulatory systems provide the basis for purposeful action via forethought. Self-efficacy, or the judgments an individual makes about his or her capabilities to orchestrate future performance on a specific task (Gist & Mitchell, 1992), represents the key determinant of these self-management activities (Bandura, 1991). Individuals whose self-efficacy beliefs are high exert greater effort to master challenges and to initiate and persist in task-related coping efforts such as goal setting, which increase the chance of successful outcomes.

Social cognitive theory has been applied to the study of absenteeism (Frayne & Latham, 1987; Latham & Frayne, 1989). Latham and Frayne demonstrated the usefulness of self-management or self-regulatory training to improve work attendance. By relying on the premises underlying social cognitive theory, they were able to teach employees to arrange environmental contingencies, establish specific goals, and produce positive consequences for their actions that eventually led to reductions in absenteeism. In sum, Frayne and Latham successfully taught employees to manage their ability to attend work.

Another candidate for this kind of treatment is agency theory, which is widely used in industrial economics. Recently, agency theory has begun to attract attention in some areas of organizational research, such as applications of transaction cost and behavioral decision theory (Jones, 1983; Bazerman, 1994). Martocchio (1994a) has suggested how some of these ideas might be productively applied to absence.

Agency theory centers on ways to minimize the dysfunctions in the employer–employee relationship arising out of goal conflict and information asymmetry (Eisenhardt, 1989). Researchers have proposed that the problems of goal conflict and information asymmetry can be addressed through the design of the "contract" or employment practices (e.g., Jensen, 1983). Particularly relevant to absence is the notion of behavior-based contracts, which focus on the employee's behavior when that person is engaged (or is supposed to be engaged) in his or her work (Eisenhardt, 1989). In the absence domain, these contracts are known as absence control policies. Although designed to effectively manage absence frequency and duration, it may actually be the case that such policies promote absence.

Often, behavior-based contracts provide employees with a means to respond to their perceptions of goal conflict at the expense of the employer (e.g., trade-offs between work and leisure) (Youngblood, 1984). For example, Winkler (1980) studied absence as a decision that can be analyzed in terms of a work–leisure trade-off model in which individuals maximize utility subject to a budget constraint. In other words, individuals are assumed to strive toward the goal of making themselves as happy as they can, given the limited available resources (Ehrenberg & Smith, 1985). In this case, individuals would maximize their utility by taking as many paid absence days in a given period as are allowed by the organization. In addition, he proposed that an organization's absence sick-leave policy would have an effect upon the level of absence. A policy providing an individual with an allotted amount of paid absence days for illness would have both an income effect (i.e., enhancing one's wealth or income independent of the hours of work), and a substitution effect (i.e., substituting one activity for another in the direction of less work and more leisure). Organizationally sanctioned paid absence days provide individuals with income without requiring them to perform their job for a given period. A substitution effect occurs in this case because individuals are able to engage in leisure activities rather than work activities. Essentially, such a policy has fewer nonpecuniary costs than policies which require medical certification, or which do not provide paid days off. Winkler found support for his hypotheses.

Information asymmetry can be a problem for the employer in many cases. Most absence control policies distinguish between acceptable versus unacceptable reasons for absence occurrences (Ballagh, Maxwell, & Perea, 1987). Absence control policies that distinguish between licit and illicit absences require substantially more supervisory discretion in judging the acceptability of particular absence occurrences (Rhodes & Steers, 1990). Distinguishing between licit and illicit absences becomes problematic insofar as it is virtually impossible to positively identify the *true* cause of these episodes. With the exception of serious illness, it is not possible for an employer to *verify* that an absent employee is, indeed, ill (we address this matter in greater detail in the next section). However, to the degree that the absentee knows whether or not she or he is sufficiently ill to prevent attendance, one encounters the problem of information asymmetry. And to the extent that there is a tendency for employers to respond more leniently to employees who claim that their absence was the result of personal illness (Ballagh et al., 1987; Judge & Martocchio, in press; Martocchio, 1992b; Martocchio & Judge, in press), one can expect increased chances that some employees will capitalize on this information asymmetry.

Information asymmetry (and goal conflict for that matter) will be exacerbated to the extent that employees know the employers' tolerance level with regard to absences that extend beyond *explicit* organizational policy (Hill & Trist, 1955; Nicholson & Johns, 1985). Within these limits, employees may trade work for leisure with relatively minimal chance of detection and punishment, with consequent losses to the employer who stands to lose insofar as absenteeism leads to mounting fiscal costs, and disruptions to the workplace (Goodman & Atkin, 1984; Martocchio, 1992a).

Absence research

There have been enough comprehensive reviews of the absence literature for us to have no need to try to emulate or condense them here (Chadwick-Jones, Brown, & Nicholson, 1973; Goodman & Atkin, 1984; Martocchio & Harrison, 1993; Muchinsky, 1977; see also Johns, 1995 for a short summary of current knowledge). Additionally, in recent years there have been a number of meta-analyses looking at general and specific correlates of absence, including attitudes, performance, biographical variables, and turnover (Bycio, 1992; Farrell & Stamm, 1988; Hackett, 1989, 1990; Hackett & Guion, 1985; Haccoun, 1990; Martocchio, 1989; Mitra, Jenkins, & Gupta, 1992). A number of conclusions about our state of knowledge can be summarized from this huge body of empirical work.

Research results on *attitudes* show convincingly that they do not tell us the whole story about absenteeism. Work attitudes, including job satisfaction, are unreliable predictors, but are occasionally quite strong. One explanation

from attitude theory (Ajzen & Fishbein, 1980) is that for there to be a relationship between an attitude and behavior, both must correspond in terms of their levels of specificity. If one construes job satisfaction, organizational commitment, and job involvement as general attitudes and absence as a specific behavior, then one should not expect a strong relationship.

In contrast, *demographic/biographical* variables can be strong predictors of absence, though a number of other factors moderate relationships. For example, researchers have become increasingly sensitive to age-related differences in workplace outcomes, such as absenteeism (Hackett, 1990; Martocchio, 1989), because of the changing age structure of the work force (Ahlburg & Kimmel, 1986). Age and short-term absence frequency are often inversely related (e.g., Chadwick-Jones et al., 1982), though this relationship holds more strongly and reliably for men than for women (Martocchio, 1989). Moreover the nature of the age–absence relationship also depends on how physically demanding are employees' jobs.

Job conditions have complex and mixed effects, though, in general, absence is lower in more enriched and high-status positions. *Supervisory relations* are also sometimes influential, as are *work-group norms*. More widely, the *managerial regime*, and in particular how absence is treated, is an important supra-individual level of analysis influence. This can be partially subsumed under the general heading of "absence culture," denoting the array of shared values, perceptions, behavior norms, and organizational controls applying to absence (Martocchio, 1994b; Nicholson & Johns, 1985). There also has been interest in the *outcomes* of absence, with impaired job performance identified as a consistent consequence. Finally, much attention has been paid to the positive association of absence with *turnover* at individual and collective levels of analysis, with various interpretations including "withdrawal" (substitutable responses to aversive circumstances) (Rosse & Miller, 1984) and progressive quitting behavior (absence as a prelude to turnover) (Dalton & Todor, 1993).

Practitioners who look to studies of absence for information which can shed light on their practice, in effect, are concerned with two criteria for external validity: (a) the generalizability of research findings *to* particular target persons, settings, and times; and (b) generalizability of findings *across* generic types of persons, settings, and times. Generalizing *to* refers to whether the research goal was met (i.e., were the hypotheses supported or disconfirmed?). Generalizing *across* refers to whether conclusions about the effect can be stated for persons, settings, and times not sampled in the focal investigation (Cook & Campbell, 1979). The latter aspect form of external validity is of greater concern in the research literature, because of the likelihood of absence researchers framing their conclusions in ways which imply: "given these findings, we advocate this 'universal' intervention to control absence levels among all employees in all types of work organizations." Whilst rarely stated with such exaggerated force, there is nonetheless a marked tendency for researchers and practitioners to neglect important boundary characteristics related to the sample, settings, and time.

Demographics are a potentially influential source of sample-based boundary conditions. Among these, it also has been noted that most absence research has been based on samples of clerical employees or blue collar workers (Johns & Nicholson, 1982), which is understandable, given the prevalence of absence monitoring systems for these groups of employees in many organizations. Yet, these groups represent a numerically decreasing segment of the occupational continuum. More widely based strategies are needed to examine the possible causes and consequences of absence for professionals and other groups, and more broad-based sampling is needed to generalize results across cultural groups.

The final criterion to meet for externally valid conclusions is generalizability over time. It may be that the mechanisms generating absence have changed slowly over the time we have been studying them. However, with the continuing narrow range of approaches taken to absenteeism, there are still many questions to be answered about the *existence* of relationships between absence and other constructs at any time, let alone questions about the strength of those relationships and their pattern over the years.

The good news about external validity, or at least about estimating it, is that the large number of studies of absenteeism allows quantitative estimates to be calculated of the generalizability of relationships over samples, settings, and times via meta-analysis (Hunter, Schmidt, & Jackson, 1982; Martocchio, 1989), but subject to our earlier qualification that these may fail to detect history or period effects. Questions about stability over occupational groups, types of organizations, research strategies, and years of study can be answered by obtaining meta-analytic parameter estimates and credibility intervals for each of these partitions.

However, there remains one huge area of ignorance and uncertainty concerning the single most reliable predictor of absence, *ill-health*. On the surface this might seem to be less problematic than other factors we have considered, but not so. The problems of complexity and multiple determination are merely pushed back one level when we consider health, and at the center of the field we find what might be termed the black hole of absence research: minor illness. By the report of absentees and managers, minor illness accounts for the vast majority of lost time (Martocchio & Judge, 1994; Morgan & Herman, 1976; Nicholson & Payne, 1987). Unfortunately, we have almost no idea what this means and what are its causes as there has been a dearth of research on this matter. However, we can assemble pieces of evidence from various sources to form an idea of how it may be functioning as a cause of absence, and what this might imply for managerial action.

Everyday understanding of illness tends towards the fatalistic deus ex machina view, that illness constitutes a range of events visited upon us in a random, or at least in chaotically unpredictable fashion. Illness as a cause of absence is therefore an unavoidable and generally excusable hazard (Smulders, 1980). There is some support for this conjecture. Nicholson and Payne (1987) reported results of home interviews of a variety of employees who were asked to make attributions of their prior absences as well as potential future absences. They found that the vast majority of individuals attributed potential future absence to factors beyond their personal control, specifically, to illness, rather than to events within their own control, such as leisure activities. Nicholson and Payne (1987) concluded that attributing absence to medical illness reflects evolving social beliefs about what constitutes acceptable reasons for absence in a particular context, a conclusion consistent with previous research revealing medical absence to be systematically related to work and nonwork motives (Rushmore & Youngblood, 1979).

Smulders (1980) suggested that absence is one element of a "sick role" (see Parsons, 1952), a temporal process in which an individual moves from a "well" state to a state of illness, to a coping process, and finally a return to a "well" state. According to this reasoning, the absentee makes many, often unconscious, decisions to enact the "sick role" under the influence of external influences, such as the attitudes and opinions of relatives and medical professionals, and the sickness benefits offered by the employer. Employees are seen as more willing to return to his or her job when working conditions improve or upon the advice of a physician. These arguments suggest that illness will be a salient attribution about the cause of absence.

Although plausible, there are a number of alternative explanations to the social basis of "illness" absence. First, all illness has an agentic component. We are agents, albeit often unwitting, of our own illness through life-style risks, congenital incapacities, bad judgments, lowered resistance to infection, and the like (Leigh, 1986; Parkes, 1987). Some people are clearly more at risk than others, even to grave life-threatening illnesses. To this may be added that even very serious illnesses have psychogenic components, as illustrated by the link between stress and heart disease (Karasek, Baker, Marxer, Ahlbom, & Theorell, 1981). Recent research has additionally indicated that some people are at risk as "disease prone personalities" (Friedmann & Booth-Kewley, 1987).

Below the asymptote of relatively infrequent serious illness lies a much broader band of frequent minor illness, viral infections, skeletomuscular aches and pains, respiratory disorders, headaches, and digestive problems accounting for most of these. These too are agentic (e.g., alcohol hangover) and psychogenic (e.g., stress headache), and to a greater degree than for serious illness. Additionally, affecting minor illness more than serious illness, is increased uncertainty about diagnosis, attributions of cause, and behavioral responses. Nicholson and Johns (1985) discuss this as a critical aspect of the absence culture. The prevalence of deus ex machina medical reasoning not only offers illness as a self-serving justification for absence as an involuntary event, but also positively invites the framing of ambiguous states and feelings of nonsomatic origin in terms of somatic incapacity (e.g., dislike of repetitive work inducing chronic "tiredness" interpreted as viral illness).

These arguments imply that the four elements of the "emerging consensus" about the complexities and difficulties of understanding absence which we identified at the beginning of this chapter, apply equally to minor illness behavior. Minor illness has multiple meanings, is difficult to positively identify, its occurrence and significance are differentially framed by context, its origins are not confined to single lifespace domains of individuals, and its effects may be cyclical. The last of these points implies, for example, that people form views about their own health status from their prior illness experience, which may affect their future propensity to "sickness" absence, via self-attributional processes (Judge & Martocchio, 1994).

Thus far, research on absence and minor illness has done no more than identify the magnitude of the problem and its parameters (Nicholson & Payne, 1987), though new research (Harvey, 1995; Judge & Martocchio, 1994; Martocchio & Judge, 1994) is beginning to unravel some of the complexities. Harvey, in particular, drawing upon data from a large sample of public employees, has demonstrated the nonequivalence of minor illness-types as potential absence causes, and that these relationships are moderated by personal and situational factors, such as sex (i.e., men and women are differentially vulnerable to absence from varieties of minor illness). Moreover varieties of minor illness are perceived to have differing justifiability. Martocchio and Judge's work has found patterns not unlike those identified by Harvey, as well as patterns based on dispositional influences. Such findings clearly fit into the *risk × susceptibility* formulation discussed earlier, and provide further empirical confirmation of the nature of the absence culture. The research implies that the absence culture can be characterized by causal loops between the self-perceived causes of absence, the attributed reasons given for absence, and the response of managerial control systems in defining the justifiability of absence. The implication of this, and foregoing material we have considered, is that the organizational framing and treatment of absence is central to its occurrence. A potentially active stance of firms to the observation, classification, and treatment of absence for its prevention and control amounts to the human resource management of absence.

THE HUMAN RESOURCE MANAGEMENT OF ABSENCE

It has been said that absence is a lens (Johns & Nicholson, 1982) through which various organizational processes may be revealed. By the same token, HRM actions to address the issue of absence are likely to be relevant to a range of other organizational behaviors, and that effective strategic HRM will impact inter alia on absence. This implicitly is an argument for absence not to be singled out and acted upon in isolation, which invites the danger of displacing its causes into other zones (e.g., people being absent "on the job"), or for unintended and undesirable consequences to flow from management action (e.g., employees manipulating the control system) (Lawler & Rhode, 1976). A strategic approach to absence involves a programmatic awareness of its causes and conditions, the implementation of appropriate information systems, management action which addresses its systemic and cultural context, and an appreciation of how the application of familiar HRM tools may affect absence along with other employee behaviors.

This line of reasoning is supported by the widespread differences in absence at the subunit and organizational levels (Martocchio, 1994; Nicholson & Johns, 1985; Terborg, Lee, Smith, Davis, & Turbin, 1982). Organizations with strong positive and high trust cultures can be observed to enjoy low levels of largely self-managed absence, in contrast to fragmented conflictual low-trust cultures, where absence is yet another source of regular brush fires to be fought day to day. Organizations of the latter kind typically manage absence through an exclusively disciplinary frame, running the risk of the vicious cycle identified by Argyris (1964) of control mechanisms triggering dysfunctional reactions from employees which in turn evoke even firmer control mechanisms (Martocchio, 1992b; Martocchio & Judge, in press). A case reported by

Nicholson (1976) illustrated how this may apply to absence, where a company "crackdown" on absence led to a change in the distribution of absence by length and frequency so as to actually increase the total volume of absence by increasing the numbers of incidents which evaded the disciplinary system. This is not an argument for absence to be exempt from disciplinary treatment, but rather for the need for extreme care in the application of control by penalties.

The possible undesired and unintended consequences of negative reinforcement are well known (Hamner & Organ, 1978; Arvey & Ivancevich, 1980). In relation to absence, Edwards and Whitston (1989) point out that disciplinary treatments of absence may be inconsistent with and undermine management emphasis in other areas on self-discipline and high involvement. Harvey's research (Harvey & Nicholson, 1993) reveals that workers, especially those of lower status, are often strongly in favor of punitive control strategies, but with the vital qualification that they be fairly applied. Quantitative and interview data indicate that respondents, when they say this, typically mean that penalties are a deserving treatment for *other* people's absence, not their own. It is in the nature of employee attribution about absence for individuals to see their own absence as lower and more justifiable than either the evidence of records or the opinions of others would attest (Johns, in press). This poses an insoluble problem for absence control by punitive means. Disciplinary systems, usually by the agreement of employee representatives, have to be implemented as consistent, unambiguous, and transparent decision-rules, but this also makes them incapable of operationalizing the kinds of individualized discriminations which would be necessary to dispense justice "fairly" in the eyes of employees (Martocchio, 1992b; Martocchio & Judge, in press). Attempts to square this circle rely upon the ability of managers, supervisors, and human resources staff to use record systems and personal knowledge to make such discriminations, usually by classifying absence into permissible and nonpermissible categories (Conlon & Stone, 1992), and by requiring external corroboration for the former (e.g., by medical reports).

From our previous discussion, this can never achieve its objectives. If social scientists using the most sophisticated statistical and analytical tools are still unable to distinguish voluntary from involuntary absence, what hope has a first-line supervisor? Moreover, as Johns's (1994) data confirm, managers' perceptions and judgments suffer from similar distortions and biases to those of absentees. Requiring corroborative evidence of incapacity does not evade these problems, but merely buries them more deeply in the obscurity of medical etiology, and, by so doing, renders them more intractable.

Only one source of negative reinforcement seems to be a powerful and reliable source of control, without obvious and predictable undesired side effects: peer group sanction. Organizational arrangements which foster high-performance norms among cohesive work-groups support effective informal control through internalized values and responsibilities, and behavior-modifying communication between group members (Chadwick-Jones et al., 1982). These conditions cannot be created overnight, but the value of moving towards team-based cultures is being increasingly recognized in business (Hackman, 1989; Wellins, Byham, & Wilson, 1991).

Positive reinforcement strategies create fewer difficulties than most punishment strategies, but do not necessarily solve the problem. Harvey's study (Harvey & Nicholson, 1993) shows workers favor cash incentives over other methods, though there is little evidence that these have more than short-range impact at best. Scott and Markham's (1982) review of absence-control strategies makes the more general observation that there is no correspondence between managers' beliefs about the efficacy of control strategies and their actual impact. Such methods as public recognition are only rarely deployed.

In the light of our earlier discussion, one can see that managers and absentees misperceive absence levels, causes, and remedies because of the implicit models to which they adhere. Following Johns's (1987) classification, one can see people adopting either oversimplified unitary explanatory models, or switching between them to categorize and deal with different manifestations of absence. In many firms, absence is treated implicitly as either "medical" or "deviant", invoking either permission, sometimes augmented by in-house medical support, or punishment. Other agents may see the behavior as an "economic" expression of rational self-interest (leisure preference), and attempt to control it by configuring incentives and disincentives (e.g., Winkler, 1980). The "withdrawal" model recommends a "softer" approach by attempting to improve person–job fit, though this poses practical and ethical problems. Absence may be widely distributed across employees, and attempts to raise the satisfaction levels of all affected workers could prove costly and impractical. It also raises the ethical problem of appearing to reward the offender. The "cultural" model offers an even wider challenge, to shift towards a high-trust self-managed open-information environment. This is increasingly desired by companies, though not with absence control specifically in mind.

The foregoing arguments suggest, in summary, that direct control methods should reserve disciplinary treatments for only the most intractable and persistent offenders, where alternative measures, such as job switching, are unfeasible. Even in these cases though, management must be certain that they are correctly directing attention to an absence-prone person, not the victim of an absence-prone job (i.e., one in which any incumbent would find regular attendance difficult). Positive strategies should make use of information systems which raise the visibility of absence, and also allow targets to be set

and reduced absence to be rewarded with recognition. Gainsharing methods, where cost-savings from lowered absence are identified and passed on to employees also has been found to be an effective part of programmatic absence management strategies. It will be clear that a prerequisite of both positive and negative reinforcement methods is sensitive and effective absence measurement. Most companies measure absence in either rudimentary or ineffective ways (Arthur Anderson, 1991), such as gross measures of absence volume (time lost), instead of by methods, such as frequency measures, which are capable of detecting patterns with the most disruptive organizational consequences or most indicative of absence mismanagement.

All other attempts to manage absence can be said to be preventive, acting to remove the causes, rather than remedial/reactive methods which try to control outcomes. To be effective, methods need to attack both halves of the risk–susceptibility equation. Let us evaluate a range of human resources strategies and tactics by these criteria.

Selection and recruitment strategies

Selection methods may be used to screen out individuals who are disposed to high absence for reasons of personality or constitutional incapacity. This primarily addresses the susceptibility term, though absence-prone individuals may also be exposed, by habitual behaviors or endemic life-style factors, to high risk. The simplest way of rejecting such recruits is to use attendance records from previous employment as a selection criterion, since we know the best predictor of an individual's absence is their own past attendance. This is one of the ways Japanese subsidiaries in Britain have been found to secure lower absence levels than British-owned companies (Industrial Society, 1993). However, it is arguably a strategy which displaces the problem (to another firm) rather than solves it. Selection can also be used positively, to secure felicitous matching between individuals and desired company climate. Job preview methods which check the alignment of applicant style and interests with those of their likely managers and peers, reduce risk and susceptibility to the degree that they create cohesive high-performance norms.

Placement strategies

Initial job placement, and subsequent job mobility reduces risk if it helps to ensure the capacities of the worker are adapted to job demands, minimizing stress, accidents, and other hazards. Placement strategies reduce susceptibility to the degree that good person–job fit promotes attitudes and satisfactions conducive to attendance motivation.

Welfare strategies

Support systems which aim to aid the life-space adjustment of individuals beyond solely work-defined situations will operate mainly to reduce risk. Health promotion programs and employee counselling can be highly effective, and may offer the best help for many individuals with chronic dispositions toward high absence (Falkenberg, 1987; Berridge & Cooper 1993). They also act on the susceptibility term to the extent that they help to foster an ethos of caring and trust within the organization.

Socialization and resourcing strategies

Induction, formal training, and informal socialization tactics, via managers and peers, can reduce risk by helping employees to recognize and avoid work-originating hazards, and reduce susceptibility by setting desired norms and expectations. Making attendance an explicit area for attention during the joining-up phase of employment is an underused method in industry. More directly, there is also evidence for the efficacy of employee self-management training to reduce absence

(Frayne & Latham, 1987; Latham & Frayne, 1989).

Assessment and development strategies

Appraisal and promotion methods have a powerful impact on employee behavior, though they are often ineptly managed and implemented. Having absence be a focal evaluation criterion could clearly impact on susceptibility to the degree that valued career outcomes could be made contingent upon behavior. This method cannot succeed, however, when promotion is the only valued outcome and there is widespread immobility and plateauing, either through corporate delayering, downsizing, or demographic bottlenecks. Organizations typically make insufficient use of developmental strategies, such as lateral and cross-functional mobility, to avoid career frustrations and fixations (Nicholson, 1993).

Remuneration strategies

We have argued that simple direct attendance incentives may fail to have a lasting impact on susceptibility, usually because they are of insufficient magnitude to avoid habituation, or because they cannot be applied in ways which meet the requirements of positive reinforcement. They may have more symbolic recognition value, in which case a regime of high public recognition can be more directly and clearly achieved through managerial communication strategies. However, remuneration methods can make a valuable contribution to absence management when they are conceived and applied systemically, alongside other methods. Thus, cafeteria systems reinforce high involvement, as does benefit-sharing from absence reduction cost savings. An example of the latter was a firm who progressively financed their sick pay benefits out of absence saving, a method which can be seen as reconfiguring the absence culture (Personnel Management, 1993). Group payment arrangements can also send a powerful signal to reinforce team cohesiveness and performance norms, just as individual piecework systems reinforce individualized and largely uncontrollable effort-bargains. Payment systems in this sense constitute formative statements about the desired psychological contract in the firm.

Redesign strategies

Process, task, and job design are of central significance to susceptibility by virtue of their motivational properties, and to risk by virtue of the demands they impose. Although job redesign exercises have often claimed reduced absence as one of their positive outcomes, it is also conceivable that they may fail to do so because in some cases they raise risk at the same time as they lower susceptibility (e.g., by increasing role ambiguity, conflict, and workload). As with remuneration strategies, their chief benefit in relation to absence is more likely to be indirect, by moving the psychological contract in the direction of greater self-discipline, trust, and cohesive performance norms. More broadly, the redesign of sociotechnical systems can clearly impact on absence by changing the interdependence of individuals and teams. Attention to team building, work-group demography, delegated managerial authority, and other methods of increasing involvement are important here. Human resources information systems, which bring attendance into the arena of job performance, are implicated here as elsewhere.

Communications strategies

In much of what we have reviewed, consistent, and relevant information systems have been highlighted as indispensable tools to absence management. HRM has a wider base for helping to develop and communicate the core values of the organization, and reinforce desired aspects of the psychological contract. A programmatic approach to absence management which intersects with human resources

strategy more generally is necessary. Now, we develop the concluding implications for HRM of this review.

CONCLUSION AND IMPLICATIONS

As we stated in the introduction, the key themes which distinguish the function of modern HRM from its personnel management antecedents are threefold: strategic alignment, disseminated insights, and organizational development. Strategic alignment means an integrated application of the armory of HR techniques to support and help focus the more general "strategic intent" of the organization, as opposed to piecemeal find-and-fix problem-driven approaches (Gratton, 1994). Disseminated insight means HR "giving itself away," principally to line management, in the sense of helping to embed and resource the range of everyday HRM methods applicable at the workplace. Organizational development means overseeing the operation of HR information systems and communications media to help bring about envisioned organizational futures. It also means HRM specialists playing an active role in executive decision making to help effect change management and implementation.

The relevance of these points to absence should by now be plain. Strategic alignment means not trying to treat absence as an isolated aberration by single targeted methods, but to evolve simultaneously strands which will reduce risk and susceptibility in ways consistent with other ongoing organizational strategies and objectives. Disseminated insight means educating line managers toward an improved understanding of the complexities of absence, freeing them from inappropriate unitary models of cause and control, and equipping them with the information tools and resources needed to manage absence along with other performance behaviors. Organizational development means conceiving of absence as one of the many benchmarks for change and symptoms of dysfunction which need to be attended to intelligently. The literature on the management of change is also helpful in suggesting what programmatic approaches to absence control might look like. Various popular writings have drawn upon such sources to advocate absence control programs (Huczinsky & Fitzpatrick, 1989; Sargant, 1989; Rhodes & Steers, 1990). Our analysis produces a similar agenda, which can be distilled into seven elements:

1 Get into place information systems which are able to record and detect patterns of absence at different levels of analysis.
2 Use these to achieve a realistic appreciation of the causes and conditions of absence across groups and over time (i.e., how absence is contextually dependent).
3 Develop a clear view about which manifestations of absence it might be desirable and feasible to reduce.
4 Develop an action strategy which seeks to fix absence control as close as possible to the source of variance.
5 Educate managers and employees about the nature of the problem and encourage them to share responsibility for its control.
6 Operate recognition strategies which publicize achievements in absence reduction, and share the benefits of cost reduction and control.
7 Monitor and continue to manage absence actively.

In formulating any variant of this kind of programmatic control strategy, stage 3 above is a key overarching consideration. What are the feasible and desirable limits to absence control? Awareness of feasibility limits means one should always ask in any given situation what is the minimum level of absence below which it is just not possible to achieve reductions. No matter how effectively we can reduce susceptibility, we cannot create a risk-free world. Awareness of desirability limits means that a tolerant and humane regime, in

which absence for the benefit of the employee is a legitimate element of a high-trust psychological contract, may be the best of all outcomes of absence management.

REFERENCES

Ahlburg, D. A., & Kimmel, L. (1986). Human resource management implications of the changing age structure of the U.S. labor force. *Research in Personnel and Human Resources Management*, 4, 339–74.

Ajzen, I., & Fishbein, M. (1980). *Understanding Attitudes and Predicting Social Behavior*. Englewood Cliffs, NJ: Prentice Hall.

Allen, S. G. (1983). How much does absenteeism cost? *The Journal of Human Resources*, 18, 379–93.

Argyris, C. (1964). *Integrating the Individual and the Organization*. New York: Wiley.

Arthur Anderson (1991). *Absenteeism Research Survey*. Report, October. London: Arthur Anderson Consulting.

Arvey, R. D., & Ivancevich, J. M. (1980). Punishment in organizations: A review, propositions and research suggestions. *Academy of Management Review*, 5, 123–32.

Ås, D. (1962). Absenteeism – a social fact in need of a theory. *Acta Sociologica*, 6, 278–85.

Atkin, R. S., & Goodman, P. S. (1984). Methods of defining and measuring absenteeism. In Goodman and Atkin (eds.), *Absenteeism*, 47–109. San Francisco: Jossey-Bass.

Atkinson, J. W., & Birch, D. (1970). *The Dynamics of Action*. New York: Wiley.

Ballagh, J. H., Maxwell, E. B., & Perea, K. A. (1987). *Absenteeism in the Work Place*. Chicago: Commerce Clearing House.

Bandura, A. (1991). Social cognitive theory of self-regulation. *Organizational Behavior and Human Decision Processes*, 50, 248–87.

Bazerman, M. H. (1994). *Judgement in Managerial Decision Making*, 3rd ed. New York: Wiley.

Berridge, J., & Cooper, C. L. (1993). Stress and coping in UK organizations: The role of the EAP. *Work and Stress*, 7, 89–102.

Breaugh, J. A. (1981). Predicting absenteeism from prior absenteeism and work attitudes. *Journal of Applied Psychology*, 66, 555–60.

Brooke, P. P., & Price, J. L. (1989). The determinants of employee absenteeism: An empirical test of a causal model. *Journal of Occupational Psychology*, 62, 1–19.

Bycio, P. (1992). Job performance and absenteeism: A review and meta-analysis. *Human Relations*, 45, 193–220.

Chadwick-Jones, J. K., Brown, C. A., & Nicholson, N. (1973). Absence from work: Its meaning, measurement and control. *International Review of Applied Psychology*, 22, 137–55.

Chadwick-Jones, J. K., Brown, C. A., Nicholson, N., & Sheppard, C. (1971). Absence measures: Their reliability and stability in an industrial setting. *Personnel Psychology*, 24, 463–70.

Chadwick-Jones, J. K., Nicholson, N., & Brown, C. (1982). *Social Psychology of Absenteeism*. New York: Praeger.

Clegg, C. W. (1983). Psychology of employee lateness,

absence, and turnover: A methodological critique and empirical study. *Journal of Applied Psychology*, 68, 88–101.

Cook, T. D., & Campbell, D. T. (1979). *Quasi-Experimentation: Design and analysis issues for field settings*. Chicago: Rand McNally.

Conlon, E. J., & Stone, T. H. (1992). Absence schema and managerial judgement. *Journal of Management*, 18, 435–54.

Dalton, D. R., & Todor, W. D. (1993). Turnover, transfer, absenteeism: An interdependent perspective. *Journal of Management*, 19, 193–219.

Eisenhardt, K. M. (1989). Agency theory: An assessment and review. *Academy of Management Review*, 14, 57–74.

Edwards, P. K., & Whitston, C. (1989). Industrial discipline, the control of attendance, and the subordination of labour: Towards and integrated analysis. *Work, Employment & Society*, 3 (1), 1–28.

Ehrenberg, R. G., & Smith, R. S. (1985). *Modern Labor Economics*, 2nd ed. Glenview, IL: Scott, Foresman.

Falkenberg, L. (1987). Employee fitness programs: Their impact on the employee and the organization. *Academy of Management Review*, 12, 511–22.

Farrell, D., & Stamm, C. L. (1988). Meta-analysis of the correlates of employee absence. *Human Relations*, 41, 211–27.

Fichman, M. (1984). A theoretical approach toward understanding employee absence. In Goodman and Atkin (eds.), *Absenteeism*, 1–46. San Francisco, CA: Jossey-Bass.

Fichman, M. (1988). Motivational consequences of absence and attendance: Proportional hazard estimation of a dynamic motivation model. *Journal of Applied Psychology*, 73, 119–34.

Fichman, M. (1989). Attendance makes the heart grow fonder: A hazard rate approach to modeling attendance. *Journal of Applied Psychology*, 74, 325–35.

Fichman, M. (1991). Absence explanation is not explaining absence variance. Working Paper, Graduate School of Industrial Administration, Carnegie-Mellon University, Pittsburgh.

Frayne, C. A., & Latham, G. P. (1987). Application of social learning theory to employee self-management of attendance. *Journal of Applied Psychology*, 73, 387–92.

Friedmann, H. A., & Booth-Kewley, S. (1987). The "disease-prone personality": A meta-analytic view of the construct. *American Psychologist*, 42, 539–55.

Fox, J. B., & Scott, J. R. (1943). *Absenteeism: Management's problem*. Boston: Graduate School of Business Administration, Harvard University.

George, J. M. (1989). Mood and absence. *Journal of Applied Psychology*, 74, 317–24.

Gist, M. E., & Mitchell, T. R. (1992). Self-efficacy: A theoretical analysis of its determinants and malleability. *Academy of Management Review*, 17, 183–211.

Goodman, P. S. & Atkin, R. S. (eds.) (1984). *Absenteeism: New approaches to understanding, measuring and managing employee absence*. San Francisco: Jossey-Bass.

Gratton, L. (1994). Implementing strategic intent: Human resource processes as a force for change. *Business Strategy Review*, 5, 47–66.

Guest, D. (1995). Human resource management. In N. Nicholson (ed.), *Dictionary of Organizational Behavior*. Oxford: Blackwell.

Haccoun, R. R. (1990). Differential absenteeism for men and women employees: A meta-analysis. Unpublished report, University of Montreal.

Hackett, R. D. (1989). Work attitudes and employee absenteeism: A synthesis of the literature. *Journal of Occupational Psychology*, 62, 235–48.

Hackett, R. D. (1990). Age, tenure and employee absenteeism. *Human Relations*, 43, 601–19.

Hackett, R. D., Bycio, P., & Guion, R. M. (1989). An idiographic-longitudinal analysis of absenteeism among hospital nurses. *Academy of Management Journal*, 32, 424–53.

Hackett, R. D., & Guion, R. M. (1985). A re-evaluation of the absenteeism–job satisfaction relationship. *Organizational Behavior and Human Decision Processes*, 35, 340–81.

Hackman, J. R. (ed.) (1989). *Groups that Work (and those that don't): Creating conditions for effective teamwork*. San Francisco: Jossey-Bass.

Hammer, T. H., & Landau, J. C. (1981). Methodological issues in the use of absence data. *Journal of Applied Psychology*, 66, 574–81.

Hamner, C. W., & Organ, D. W. (1978). *Organizational Behavior*. Dallas: Business Publications.

Harvey, J. (1995). Perceived legitimacy of minor illness as a reason for absence. Doctoral dissertation (in preparation), University of Sheffield, UK.

Harvey, J., & Nicholson, N. (1993). Incentives and penalties as means of influencing attendance. *International Journal of Human Resources Management*, 4, 841–58.

Hill, J. M. M., & Trist, E. L. (1955). Changes in accidents and other absences with length of service. *Human Relations*, 8, 121–52.

Huczinsky, A., & Fitzpatrick, J. (1989). *Managing Absence for a Competitive Edge*. London: Pitman.

Hulin, C. L. (1984). Suggested directions for defining, measuring and controlling absenteeism. In Goodman and Atkin (eds.), *Absenteeism*, 391–420. San Francisco, CA: Jossey-Bass.

Hulin, C. L., & Rousseau, D. M. (1980) Analyzing infrequent events: Once you find them your troubles begin. In K. H. Roberts & L. Burstein (eds.), *Issues in Aggregation*, vol. 6, pp. 1–16. San Francisco: Jossey-Bass.

Hunter, J. E., Schmidt, F. L., & Jackson, G. B. (1982). *Meta-Analysis: Cumulating research findings across studies*. Beverly Hills, CA: Sage.

Industrial Society, The (1993). *Wish You Were Here*. London: The Industrial Society.

Jensen, M. (1983). Organization theory and methodology. *Accounting Review*, 56, 319–38.

Johns, G. (1987). Understanding and managing absence from work. In S. L. Dolan & R. S. Schuler (eds.), *Canadian Readings in Personnel and Human Resources Management*. St. Paul, MN: West.

Johns, G. (1991). Substantive and methodological constraints on behavior and attitudes in organizational research. *Organizational Behavior and Human Decision Processes*, 49, 80–104.

Johns, G. (1995). Absenteeism. In N. Nicholson (ed.), *Dictionary of Organizational Behavior*. Oxford: Blackwell.

Johns, G. (1994). Absenteeism estimates by employees and managers: Divergent perspectives and self-serving perceptions. *Journal of Applied Psychology*, 79, 229–39.

Johns, G., & Nicholson, N. (1982). The meanings of

absence: New strategies for theory and research. *Research in Organizational Behavior*, 4, 127–73.

Jones, G. R. (1983). Transaction costs, property rights, and organizational culture: An exchange perspective. *Administrative Science Quarterly*, 28, 454–67.

Judge, T. A., & Martocchio, J. J. (1994). Dispositional influences on attributions concerning absenteeism. Working Paper, Center for Advanced Human Resource Studies, Cornell University, Ithaca, NY.

Judge, T. A., & Martocchio, J. J. (in press). The effects of work values on absence disciplinary decisions. The role of supervisor fairness orientation. *Journal of Business and Psychology*.

Karasek, R. A., Baker, D., Marxer, F., Ahlbom, A., & Theorell, T. (1981). Job demands, job decision latitude, and cardiovascular disease: A prospective study of Swedish men. *American Journal of Public Health*, 71, 694–705.

Latham, G. P., & Frayne, C. A. (1989). Self-management training for increasing job attendance: A follow-up and replication. *Journal of Applied Psychology*, 74, 411–16.

Lawler, E. E., & Rhode, J. G. (1976). *Information and Control in Organizations*. Santa Monica, CA: Goodyear.

Leigh (1986). Correlates of work due to illness. *Human Relations*, 39, 81–100.

Martocchio, J. J. (1989). Age-related differences in employee absenteeism: A meta-analytic review. *Psychology and Aging*, 4, 409–14.

Martocchio, J. J. (1992a). The financial cost of absence decisions. *Journal of Management*, 18, 133–52.

Martocchio, J. J. (1992b). Supervisory responses to employee absenteeism: A study of supervisors' decisions. In J. F. Burton, Jr. (ed.), *Proceedings of the Forty-Fourth Annual Meetings of the Industrial Relations Research Association*, 539–48. Madison, WI: Industrial Relations Research Association.

Martocchio, J. J. (1994a). Employee absenteeism: An agency theory perspective. Working Paper, Institute of Labor and Industrial Relations, University of Illinois, Urbana, IL.

Martocchio, J. J. (1994b). The effects of absence culture on an individual's absence taking. *Human Relations*, 47, 243–62.

Martocchio, J. J., & Harrison, D. A. (1993). To be there or not to be there? Questions, theories, and methods in absenteeism research. *Research in Personnel and Human Resource Management*, 11, 259–329.

Martocchio, J. J., & Judge, T. A. (1994). A policy capturing approach to individual decisions to be absent. *Organizational Behavior and Human Decision Processes*, 57, 358–86.

Martocchio, J. J., & Judge, T. A. (in press). When we don't see eye to eye: Discrepancies in absence disciplinary decisions. *Journal of Management*.

Mitra, A., Jenkins, G. D., & Gupta, N. (1992). A meta-analytic review of the relationship between absence and turnover. *Journal of Applied Psychology*, 77, 879–89.

Mohr, L. B. (1982). *Explaining Organizational Behavior*. San Francisco: Jossey-Bass.

Morgan, L. G., & Herman, J. B. (1976). Perceived consequences of absenteeism. *Journal of Applied Psychology*, 61, 738–42.

Muchinsky, P. M. (1977). Employee absenteeism: A review of the literature. *Journal of Vocational Behavior*, 10, 316–40.

Nicholson, N. (1976). Management sanctions and absence control. *Human Relations*, 29, 139–51.

Nicholson, N. (1977). Absence behavior and attendance motivation: A conceptual synthesis. *Journal of Management Studies*, 14, 231–52.

Nicholson, N. (1993). Purgatory or place of safety? The managerial plateau and organizational agegrading, *Human Relations*, 46, 1369–89.

Nicholson, N., Brown, C. A., & Chadwick-Jones, J. K. (1976). Absence from work and job satisfaction. *Journal of Applied Psychology*, 61, 728–37.

Nicholson, N., & Johns, G. (1985). The absence culture and the psychological contract: Who's in control of absence? *Academy of Management Review*, 10, 397–407.

Nicholson, N., & Payne, R. L. (1987). Absence from work: Explanations and attributions. *Applied Psychology: An International Review*, 36, 121–32.

Parkes, K. (1987). Relative weight, smoking, and mental health as predictors of sickness and absence from work. *Journal of Applied Psychology*, 72, 275–86.

Parsons, T. (1952). The social system. London: Tavistock.

Personnel Management (1993). Link to sick pay cuts absentee rates. *Personnel Management*, April, 5.

Rhodes, S., & Steers, R. M. (1990). *Managing Employee Absenteeism*. Reading, MA: Addison-Wesley.

Rosse, J. G., & Miller, H. E. (1984). Relationship of absenteeism and other employee behaviors. In Goodman and Atkin (eds.), *Absenteeism*, 194–228. San Francisco, CA: Jossey-Bass.

Rushmore, C. H., & Youngblood, S. A. (1979). Medically-related absenteeism: Random or motivated behavior? *Journal of Occupational Medicine*, 21, 245–50.

Sargant, A. (1989). *The Missing Workforce*. London: Institute of Personnel Management.

Scott, K. D., & Markham, S. E. (1982). Absenteeism control methods: A survey of practices and results. *Personnel Administrator*, 27, 73–84.

Smulders, P. G. W. (1980). Comments on employee absence/attendance as a dependent variable in organizational research. *Journal of Applied Psychology*, 65, 368–71.

Staw, B. M., & Oldham, G. R. (1978). Reconsidering our dependent variables: A critique and empirical study. *Academy of Management Journal*, 21, 539–55.

Steers, R. M., & Rhodes, S. R. (1978). Major influences on employee attendance: A process model. *Journal of Applied Psychology*, 63, 391–407.

Terborg, J. R., Lee, T. W., Smith, F. J., Davis, G. A., & Turbin, M. S. (1982). Extension of the Schmidt and Hunter validity generalization procedure to the prediction of absenteeism behavior from knowledge of job satisfaction and organizational commitment. *Journal of Applied Psychology*, 67, 440–9.

Tharenou, P. (1993). A test of reciprocal causality for absenteeism. *Journal of Organizational Behavior*, 14, 269–87.

Wellins, R. S., Byham, W. C., & Wilson, J. M. (1991). *Empowered Teams*. San Francisco: Jossey-Bass.

Winkler, D. R. (1980). The effects of sick-leave policy on teacher absenteeism. *Industrial and Labor Relations Review*, 33, 232–40.

Youngblood, S. A. (1984). Work, nonwork, and withdrawal. *Journal of Applied Psychology*, 69, 106–7.

Chapter 31

Human Resource Management and Employee Turnover and Transfer: What We Know is Not Always What We Need

Dan R. Dalton, Douglas A. Cairns, Janet M. Canavan,
Joseph L. Downey, Allan Fowler, Gregory M. Freiwald,
Preston Johnson, Jr., Harriet F. King, and Robert W. Lincoln, Jr.

INTRODUCTION

In this chapter, we have several objectives. First, we review the current state of knowledge in the area of employee turnover and transfer. Second, we assess the practical value of such information for the human resources management (HRM) professional. Lastly, we provide a rationale and research agenda for areas which have received little or no research attention in areas that have the potential to be of decided benefit to those involved in human resource management. We organize the succeeding sections as follows: (1) the pragmatics of turnover; (2) the consequences of turnover; (3) the pragmatics of transfer; (4) the consequences of transfer; and (5) a look into the uncharted waters of turnover and transfer. Each is discussed in turn. We also occasionally provide a "management note" where it may be appropriate to underscore recent or continuing developments in the organizational environment which do not seem to be well captured by current theory and research.

THE "PRAGMATICS" OF TURNOVER

It should be noted here that, frankly, much of the extant research in turnover, and what little research there is concerning transfer, is often of little benefit to the practicing HRM professional. Such a statement is meant neither to paint all research in these areas with the same broad brush nor to criticize what may be properly referred to as basic research. Still, the veritable ocean of research which examines, for example, the individual correlates of employee turnover is less helpful, less applicable to the HRM professional.

Consider, for example, the empirical work examining whether women have a tendency to leave organizations at a greater rate than male counterparts (e.g., Light & Ureta, 1992; Miller & Wheeler, 1992; Weisberg & Kirschenbaum, 1993). Suppose it could be demonstrated that women are more likely to quit their employment than men in comparable positions. From the view of an HRM professional, what is the value of this information? Presumably no responsible organization would deliberately reduce the proportion of women hired to address this issue as to do so would constitute an egregious violation of the Civil Rights Act. Suppose it could be determined that turnover rates differ on the basis of marital status, age, religious preferences, number of dependents, or any of a myriad of such factors (see, e.g., Cotton & Tuttle, 1986; Hom, Caranikas-Walker, Prussia, & Griffeth, 1992). For an organization to act on any of this information to manage its employee turnover levels is illegal for most of these factors, and ill-advised for the balance.

Another large portion of turnover research does not rely on actual employee turnover, but on what is referred to as "intent to leave" (e.g., Dailey & Kirk, 1992; Gaertner & Nollen, 1992; Tett & Meyer, 1993; Weisberg & Kirschenbaum, 1993). There are a number of reasons for this choice, most of which are driven by methodological considerations. It may be, for example, that within the period of any study, turnover has a low base rate (i.e., relatively few employees actually quit). In that same period, though, all employees could be questioned about their intent to leave. Others would argue that actual turnover (i.e., a dichotomous variable as one either leaves or not) does not enjoy the statistical properties of intent to leave which may be scaled. Also, actual turnover often requires a longitudinal design or, failing this, the need to assess the factors associated with employees' departure retrospectively. The former is more methodologically challenging and the latter frequently subject to serious criticism.

In any case, "intent" to do something is obviously not the same as actually doing it. At the risk of some criticism for abandoning, if only briefly, our scientific rigor, the correspondence between most of our New Year's resolutions and their execution may provide some lay evidence to our suggestion. More notably, an exhaustive analysis of prior research in this area concluded that "turn-over intention is the strongest predictor of turnover; but the modest strength of the relation . . . suggests limits in intent to quit as a surrogate of turnover" (Tett & Meyer, 1993, 286; see also, Steele & Ovalle, 1984). In summary, then, HRM professionals would not, in general, be comfortable with studies relying on intent to leave as a surrogate for actual turnover.

It should be recognized here that there is near consensus on a relationship between some employee attitudes, principally job satisfaction and commitment, and employee turnover (e.g., Carsten & Spector, 1987; Cohen, 1993; Cotton & Tuttle, 1986; Hom et al., 1992; Mathieu & Zajac, 1990; Mowday, Porter, & Steers, 1982; Randall, 1990). While such relationships are generally modest, it is fair to conclude that employees characterized by low job satisfaction and low levels of commitment are more likely to leave the organization. It is satisfying, however, to note that this relationship has been generally moderated by the employment environment. Focusing on job satisfaction, for example, it has been concluded that "the relation between job satisfaction and turnover will be strong during periods of low unemployment (economic prosperity) and weak during periods of high unemployment (economic hardship). These results indicate that the job satisfaction–turnover relation became weaker as the employment level (available alternatives) decreased" (Carsten & Spector, 1987, 377).

THE CONSEQUENCES OF TURNOVER

While there are literally thousands of examples of discussion and research studies dedicated to a wide variety of predictors and implications of voluntary employee turnover (for extensive reviews see, Carsten & Spector, 1987; Cotton & Tuttle, 1986; Hom et al., 1992; Mathieu & Zajac, 1990; Mobley, 1982; Mobley,

Griffeth, Hand, & Meglino, 1979; Mowday, Porter, & Steers, 1982; Muchinsky & Tuttle, 1979; Porter & Steers, 1973; Price, 1977; Randall, 1990; Shikiar & Freudenberg, 1982; Steele & Ovalle, 1984), the overwhelming majority have a common thread. Specifically, as turnover is a dysfunctional element in most organizations, efforts and resources should be marshalled to minimize its occurrence. Such arguments are not unreasonably placed as the departure of employees at any level in the organization is, at best, an inconvenience, at worst, a disaster. At a general level, employee turnover is associated with a host of costs. These include, but are by no means limited to, separation pay, exit interviews, terminal vacation pay, certain fringe benefits, administrative costs, loss of productivity, overtime, training, recruiting, testing, and screening (see Cascio, 1991 for an excellent treatment of these issues and others).

Clearly, however, not all turnover is dysfunctional. In fact, the prevailing notion that voluntary employee turnover is largely dysfunctional has been repeatedly subject to criticism (e.g., Abelson & Baysinger, 1984; Cascio, 1991; Dalton & Kesner, 1986; Dalton, Krackhardt, & Porter, 1981; Dalton & Todor, 1979, 1982; Dalton, Todor, & Krackhardt, 1982; Staw, 1980; Staw & Oldham, 1978). In a relatively early discussion of this issue, Dalton and Todor (1979) suggested that turnover may be a strongly positive phenomenon for the organization from a variety of perspectives. That approach, however, was subject to criticism inasmuch as it did not develop a compelling rationale for the financial benefits which might be associated with reasonable levels of employee turnover.

Subsequent research (Dalton & Todor, 1982; Kesner & Dalton, 1982; Dalton & Kesner, 1986) did provide some justification for a more balanced view of employee turnover. Specifically, the positive perspective of turnover, at least under some circumstances, was buttressed by the identification of identifiable, calculable, and direct business

savings that arise as a direct function of organizational turnover. In fact, it was suggested that "responsible levels of employee turnover may be very lucrative, a veritable windfall for the organization" (Dalton & Todor, 1982: 212). Also, "this perspective [windfall account], persuasive in some cases, may actually remain substantially understated" (Dalton & Kesner, 1986: 269). Consider the rather "common-sense" elements of those arguments (see Dalton & Todor, 1993, 197–8):

- New hires are far less expensive to maintain in terms of wages and fringe benefits than more senior employees whose compensation is towards the limits of the wage progression schedule.

- Organizational contributions to, for example, state disability insurance (SDI), social security (FICA), life insurance (e.g., twice base yearly wages), and so forth are calculated from amounts earned by the employee. All contributed levels based on some proportion of wages or salary will naturally be higher for more senior employees.

- When employees not vested with ERISA benefits leave, pension payments made by the organization on their behalf are recovered.

- There are large economies regarding vacation time. Not only do more senior employees receive more vacation time (i.e., more total weeks of vacation), they are also paid substantially more for it (as a function of a higher wage rate).

- All wage differentials (e.g., shift and safety differentials) are calculated on base pay, obviously higher for more senior employees than those more newly hired.

- There are gross economies associated with absenteeism (sick leave) liability. Since its calculation is a function of base pay, "sick" senior employees are more costly than junior employees. Beyond that, employees routinely receive sick pay at a higher hour rate than they earned it. Also, when senior employees leave the organization, any liability for sick leave remaining "on the books" is recovered by the organization.

- Severance payments are usually based on seniority and/or yearly wages. Here again, any liability for severance payments (lay-offs, terminations, etc.) will be greater for the more senior employees.
- Lastly, there is a rate of return on any saved or recovered funds.

Given these considerations, it has been demonstrated that financial benefits of turnover could be substantial. For one company, the savings realized by the organization when a single person quit and was replaced by a new hire was $140,000 (Dalton & Kesner, 1986). Even these estimates may be understated. While there is no consensus regarding the use of two-tier salary schedules (e.g., Becker, 1987, 1988; Ichniowski & Delaney, 1990; Thomas & Kliener, 1992), their actual and potential impact on the economies of employee turnover is profound.

A two-tier arrangement simply provides different wage progression schedules. One range of wages applies to current employees; another range – always lower – applies to those newly hired. These arrangements greatly magnify the economies associated with employee turnover: "The amount that companies can save from such deals is hard to estimate, since *it depends on how fast current employees will be replaced by new ones*" (Flax, 1984, 75, emphasis added).

Consider the following hypothetical example (see table 31.1). Suppose that a company has a five-year wage progression schedule. First-year employees earn $10,000 per year with $5,000 increments until reaching top pay. While this is an overly simplified example as it does not include all the potential efficiencies previously noted, we hope it does capture the essence of the principle. The normal calculation (see table 31.2) of this portion of the

Table 31.1 Hypothetical wage progression schedule

Hypothetical wage progression schedule ($'000)

Entry level salary	2nd year salary	3rd year salary	4th year salary	5th year salary
10	15	20	25	30

Source: Adapted from Dalton & Todor (1993).

windfall account illustrates the economies associated with a top-pay employee leaving, replaced by a new hire.

You will have noted that from the fifth year forward, there are no further economies as the newly hired employee has progressed through the wage progression schedule and is now (like the person replaced) receiving the maximum wage rate. Accordingly, the wages "saved" by the organization are the total of the differences between a top-paid employee and the wages made as the new hire progresses through to top pay, in this hypothetical case some $50,000 dollars. The adoption of a two-tier wage schedule, however, enormously increases these savings.

Table 31.3 represents a hypothetical two-tier wage progression schedule. The schedule (A) for continuing employees is the same as the one on which we previously relied. In this case, however, Schedule B represents the second tier in which the entry level salary is lower. Obviously, employees on schedule B will never reach the top-pay level earned by employees on Schedule A.

Given this point, calculation of the economies associated with employee turnover (table 31.4) is different. Employees who quit and their replacements will not be on the same wage schedule. Accordingly, any estimate of the turnover economies must include the differences between the two wage schedules.

As noted in table 31.4, we illustrate the savings over an arbitrary ten-year period. While the savings are manifestly greater ($115,000),

Table 31.2 Windfall account savings

	Windfall account savings ($'000)		
	(A) Top wage	(B) Current wage	(A–B) Savings
1st year savings	30	10	20
2nd year savings	30	15	15
3rd year savings	30	20	10
4th year savings	30	25	5
5th year savings	30	30	0
Total savings over period			50

Source: Adapted from Dalton & Todor (1993).

Table 31.3 Hypothetical wage progression schedules: traditional and two-tier

	Hypothetical wage progression schedules: traditional and two-tier ($'000)				
	Entry level salary	2nd year salary	3rd year salary	4th year salary	5th year salary
(A) Traditional	10	15	20	25	30
(B) Two-tier	8	12	15	18	22

Source: Adapted from Dalton & Todor (1993).

Table 31.4 Windfall account savings for two-tier schedules

	Windfall account savings for two-tier schedules ($'000)		
	(A) Top wage under traditional schedule	(B) Current wage under two-tier schedule	(A–B) Savings
1st year savings	30	8	22
2nd year savings	30	12	18
3rd year savings	30	15	15
4th year savings	30	18	12
5th year savings	30	22	8
6th year savings	30	22	8
7th year savings	30	22	8
8th year savings	30	22	8
9th year savings	30	22	8
10th year savings	30	22	8
Total savings over period			115

Source: Adapted from Dalton & Todor (1993).

these estimates remain grossly underestimated. Interestingly, the actual savings are not easily calculable. Since new hires never reach pay levels afforded to departed employees, economies continue to grow for as long as newly hired individuals remain in the employ of the company.

Despite these financial implications, it would be hazardous to conclude that employee turnover is invariably beneficial to the organization. It does seem sensible to suggest, however, that employee turnover could be too low as well as too high.

> Presumably, there are high and low limits of acceptable turnover in organizations . . . the costs of having every organizational member receiving top pay, receiving maximum benefits, and being fully vested in their pension rights are enormous. Conversely, there is a level at which turnover becomes unmanageable. Naturally, this would vary from industry to industry, even subunit to subunit . . . The question, however, is subject to cost/benefit analysis. (Dalton & Todor, 1982, 217)

(See also, Abelson & Baysinger, 1984; Dalton & Todor, 1993; for outstanding utility analyses on this issue see, Boudreau, 1983; Boudreau & Berger, 1985a, b; Cascio, 1991.)

A management note

Few observers would quibble with the guidelines and suggestions provided in the prior sections. It is clear, however, that all of the research noted thus far focuses on voluntary employee turnover. In the contemporary environment, it might be properly asked why there has been no attention to that turnover which is deliberately generated by the organization (for an excellent overview, see Leana & Feldman, 1992). Table 31.5 illustrates, for example, the larger corporate layoffs reported in the last four years. These, of course, do not capture the entire magnitude of cutbacks. In fact, a recent *Business Week* (1994) cover story, "The pain of downsizing," reported that corporate America announced 615,186 layoffs

Table 31.5 The 25 largest announced layoffs since 1991

Company	Staff cutbacks
IBM	85,000
AT&T	83,500
General Motors	74,000
U. S. Postal Service	55,000
Sears	50,000
Boeing	30,000
Nynex	22,000
Hughes Aircraft	21,000
GTE	17,000
Martin-Marietta	15,000
Dupont	14,800
Eastman Kodak	14,000
Philip Morris	14,000
Procter & Gamble	13,000
Phar Mor	13,000
Bank of America	12,000
Aetna	11,800
GE Aircraft Engines	10,250
McDonnell Douglas	10,200
Bellsouth	10,200
Ford Motor	10,000
Xerox	10,000
Pacific Telesis	10,000
Honeywell	9,000
U.S. West	9,000

Source: *Business Week*, May 9, 1994, 61.

in 1993. In the first quarter of 1994, employers announced an average of more than 3,100 layoffs per day.

For many companies these patterns of involuntary reductions in force would seem to dwarf those which may have been voluntary. Yet, there is no research attention to the ramifications of this activity. Incredibly, there seems to be only one study which has systematically examined the financial impact of such cutbacks on businesses, and that for only 17 companies (Byrne, 1994). This study reported that, while there is often a short-term advantage to downsizing, gains in profit margins and return on equity are not preserved.

One study. Seventeen companies. There are

literally thousands of empirical studies addressing the impact of demographic and attitudinal variables on individual turnover, virtually all of them on voluntary turnover. Contrast that with the one study, with a sample comprised of only seventeen companies, to address the impact of millions of cutbacks on the productivity and profitability of the U.S. labor force. It is fair to say that many HRM professionals do not view that balance of research attention with favor.

A second illustration of deliberate turnover which has received very little attention (for a notable exception, see Feldman, 1994) and might be rightfully interpreted as yet another example of resizing the firm, is early retirement programs. The research that has been conducted – largely in gerontology and demography – has focused on factors which may predict why an individual might elect to accept early retirement and how that decision affects early retirees. We are aware of no research, however, which addresses whether early retirement programs, or aspects of early retirement programs are related to firm productivity or profitability. There seems to be no information on whether such programs are associated with competitive advantage within industries. Given the ubiquity of such programs, we can sympathize with the disappointment of some HRM professionals when considering the development of conceptualization and research in this area.

Employee reductions which are preceded by mergers and acquisitions may be another example of deliberately induced employee turnover. While there have been studies addressing the extent of employee turnover post-merger/acquisition (e.g., Brown & Medoff, 1988; Jensen, 1984; Walsh 1988, 1989; Walsh & Elwood, 1991) and the impact of merger/acquisition announcements on involved employees (Schweiger & DeNisi, 1991; see also, Schweiger & Walsh, 1990), we know of only one study which examined the effects of turnover on post-acquisition firm performance (Cannella & Hambrick, 1993). Once again,

this seems like so little activity in the research community based on the potential implications – and the resurgence – of merger and acquisition activity.

It isn't how many, it's who is leaving

A series of research (e.g., Dalton, Todor, & Krackhardt, 1982; Dalton, Krackhardt, & Porter, 1981; Hollenbeck & Williams, 1986; see also, Boudreau, 1983; Boudreau & Berger, 1985a, b) has concluded that the disadvantageous aspects of employee turnover – irrespective of financial considerations – are probably overstated. This perspective is founded on a simple premise: The impact of turnover depends, not on how many are leaving, but on who is leaving. It may be naive, then, to attempt to calculate the downside of employee turnover based only on the number of departures, or its percentage of the work force. Instead, the consequences of turnover probably depend on the quality and/or replaceability of those departing (see Dalton et al., 1981, 1982; and Dalton & Todor, 1993 for a discussion of the quality/replaceability distinction). Hollenbeck and Williams (1986, 606) apparently support this contention:

> *The arguments of both Dalton and Boudreau speak convincingly to the need for organizational researchers to address not just the frequency of turnover (i.e., the number), but the flow or functionality (i.e., the nature) of turnover. Both of these perspectives go beyond a consideration of the replacement costs of separations, which is the primary reason to reduce turnover frequency, and try to assess the costs (or benefits) associated with the performance differences between leavers, stayers, and replacements.*

Available research appears to sustains this perspective. Dalton et al. (1981), for example, demonstrated that 42 percent of turnover was actually beneficial to the firm. Other work has reported that 53 percent of turnover is functional (Abelson, 1987). Others, too, have empirically concluded that "not all turnover is bad for the firm" (e.g., Lucas, Parasuraman, Davis, & Enis, 1987).

A management note

This "all turnover is not the same" perspective is a potentially useful distinction. At the risk of once again surrendering our scientific rigor, this notion might be effectively captured by asking any supervisor or business owner the following questions: What percentage of those in your employ who have voluntarily left actually affected the performance of your firm or unit? Of what percentage can it honestly be said that the performance of your group deteriorated with their departure? Perhaps even more illuminating: What percentage of turnovers did you consider to be a plus for your unit? Most would agree that the departure of some employees is of decided benefit to the firm.

The available research, however, has taken but a single stride when another critical step is required. While HRM professionals probably do have some insight into the number of functional versus dysfunctional turnovers, the literature provides no guidance on how these might be separated as a practical matter. Obviously, organizations would ideally maximize their functional turnover while minimizing the dysfunctional (see Dreher, 1982; McEvoy & Cascio, 1987; Schwab, 1991 for related discussion). Our HRM professionals tell us that early retirement programs have become legendary for their inability to accomplish this. We are aware of no evidence suggesting that resizing programs have this character. Empirical inquiries of this type would be critically important to HRM professionals.

THE "PRAGMATICS" OF TRANSFER

While employee turnover remains a ubiquitous topic in organizational studies (e.g., Bernhardt & Scoones, 1993; Blau, 1993;

Cohen, 1993; Jaros, Jermier, Koehler, & Sincich, 1993; Judge, 1993; Mitra, Jenkins, & Gupta, 1992; Topel, 1993; Wiersema & Bird, 1993; Wiersema & Bantel, 1993), the issue of employee transfer is infrequently examined (see Dalton & Todor, 1987, and Dalton & Mesch, 1992 for summaries; see also, Noe, Steffy, & Barber, 1988; Nakosteen & Zimmer, 1992).

About thirty-five years ago, March and Simon (1958) suggested a model of turnover that included the possible nature of the relationship between internal mobility (transfer) and turnover. They hypothesized that an employee's perceived opportunity to transfer intraorganizationally would reduce the perceived desirability of leaving the organization. An obvious result of this proposition is that the availability of intraorganizational transfer will serve the same purpose as leaving the organization. Changing jobs (transferring) within organizations may resolve dissatisfaction with one's work as readily as changing organizations (quitting). Simply, employees may prefer to move within an organization to moving outside it.

Others recognized that transfer behavior could affect subsequent turnover (Mobley, 1977; Mobley et al., 1979). Utility analyses of employee acquisition and separation, too, acknowledge the benefits of including employee-initiated transfers (Boudreau, 1983; Boudreau & Berger, 1985a, b). Baysinger and Mobley (1984, 282–3) argue that "an increased understanding of how both internal and external alternatives influence turnover will be increasingly important." Gustafson (1982, 168) states that "In addition to their other merits, mobility programs (transfers) also may have a favorable long-term effect on resignations." Jackofsky (1984; see also Jackofsky & Peters, 1983; Anderson, Milkovich, & Tsui, 1981) noted that considering both intraorganizational as well as interorganizational employee movement should provide a more complete representation of the turnover phenomenon.

Even so, the alleged association between certain elements of transfer and turnover had not been tested empirically. Block (1978a, b) did provide indirect evidence when reporting the results that the existence of formalized transfer and promotion policies reduced voluntary employee turnover. Also, there were reports that internal mobility may be a source of increased satisfaction and commitment (Brett, 1982; Grusky, 1967; Pruden, 1973; Viega, 1981) which, derivatively, may have some potential to reduce intention to leave and perhaps turnover itself.

THE CONSEQUENCES OF TRANSFER

Dalton and Todor (1987) have provided an empirical assessment of the relationship between voluntary employee transfer and subsequent turnover. They reasoned that employees presumably attempt to transfer for some reason. Accordingly, if the employees are able to reduce these problems by transferring within the organization, they would be correspondingly less likely to quit. Conversely, employees who attempt to use the transfer option but are unsuccessful will be characterized by higher levels of turnover. In a study of two companies over a four-year period, the results were consistent with these propositions. For both companies, the highest turnover rates were associated with those individuals who requested transfers and were not accommodated. Conversely, far less turnover is evident (by a factor of over 3 in both cases) when employees are able to enjoy the transfer process.

A management note

The transfer/turnover linkage is interesting, and assuredly applicable. As noted previously, this research – apparently the only example of its kind – focuses on only half of the issue. Specifically, it does not by design address involuntary employee turnover. As the authors themselves state:

> It should also be noted that this examination focuses on voluntary internal mobility. The argument here is that employees who have the opportunity to move through the use of intraorganizational transfer are less likely to quit. While this proposition has not been subject to empirical examination, conceptual argument and related research as previously noted do provide some justification for this view. The literature does not, however, provide such a justification for employer initiated transfer. We therefore focus on that transfer activity requested by employees, not that dictated by employers. (Dalton & Todor, 1987, 707)

HRM professionals look forward to longitudinal research of the general type represented here but that address more directly employee transfer programs generated by the company. When plant closings, consolidations and related restructurings are pending, companies often offer current employees of the affected regions a right to transfer to unaffected facilities. While many would suspect that these opportunities would be met with favor, HRM professionals tell us that this is not always the case. While little research addresses these issues, it appears, in balance, that dual career issues, regional preferences, familial linkages, and other factors lead many employees to decline lateral job transfers even when such refusal results in unemployment, or subsequent employment at lesser wages, reduced benefits, and sacrificed seniority.

Our HRM professionals also tell us that intraorganizational transfers for managerial personnel, once routine, are now much more difficult to accomplish. Increasingly, even promising executives decline such placements. This tendency is particularly manifest with international assignments. We are aware of no research examining any aspect of these trends.

Given the enormous cost often associated with employer-generated transfers (e.g., moving allowances, home purchase guarantees or subsidies), certain information could be of great importance to practicing HRM professionals. How, for example, do the rates of turnover for those who have opted to transfer compare to those employees in the same organization who are employed in an unaffected area? Succinctly, are subsequent levels of turnover unusually high for those who do transfer? If so, organizations may consider the adjustment of transfer policies and its support.

Beyond this, there is another issue which appears unsettled. While it is true that the organizational literature normally extols the merits of employee-initiated, intraorganizational transfer programs, the benefits of this employee entitlement for the firm is not clear. Consider what we will refer to as the "domino effect."

Consider the following scenarios. In the first situation an employee quits – or is terminated; it makes no difference in the operation of the domino effect whether the employee voluntarily leaves the employ of the organization or otherwise. The decision is made to replace the employee – certainly nothing unusual about that course of events. The personnel division is contacted, description of the job is forwarded and so forth. Hopefully, a suitable candidate (or several) is forwarded for review. Suppose that some candidate is acceptable and is hired to replace the departed employee. This reflects a rather unimaginative scenario, repeated daily across organizations large and small.

The impact is probably rather modest. An experienced employee was lost and replaced with a new hire. Obviously, there are costs involved in such a procedure, but those costs are not of immediate issue here. The point is that *one* person was lost, and *one* person gained. Accordingly, there is only one person who will need to be trained, socialized, and whatever other processes take place so that this person can make a meaningful contribution to the organization.

Scenario two: The employee still quits. But from here, the scenario departs from the first rather substantially. In this case, no attempt is made to secure a new hire. Rather, the now open job is "up for bid." In other words, other employees are asked if they would like to be considered for the now available job – an intraorganizational transfer. This procedure, too, is not unusual. In fact, it is commonly part of a collective bargaining procedure. This process may differ slightly in its application, but its principle is straightforward. Before a new hire can be obtained, the extant employees have the right to bid for the newly opened job. The "right" to actually get such a transfer is usually based on two factors. The first is the seniority of the bidder. All other things being equal, the bidder with the most seniority – given that there were multiple bids – would get the job. The second factor is normally "on the books" but is less often seen in practice. Specifically, a successful bidder must meet some minimum performance criteria to be considered. In some cases, for example, a person could be denied a transfer because of an unacceptable attendance record.

In any case since the collective bargaining agreement contains language which provides for such transfers, the recently open job is put to bid. Consider the most simple case, one with a single bid. Mr. A quits; Ms. B bids and is transferred to Mr. A's job. There is still a problem: Someone is still required to fill the old job of Ms. B – the successful bidder. So, another iteration is necessary. Personnel is contacted and in due course another person is hired for B's job. Now, there is not just one inexperienced person as in the first scenario; rather, there are two. Ms. B is not yet familiar with her new job, the job into which she just transferred, and of course, the new hire who took B's old job will require some time to contribute at a reasonable level.

That is the most benign scenario regarding transfer. What is far more likely is something not unlike this: Mr. A quits, Ms. B transfers into A's slot, Ms. C transfers into B's slot, Mr.

D successfully transfers into C's job, and then a new hire is generated to take D's now open position. This is the nature of the "domino" effect of employee transfer. Here, one employee is not lost and replaced by another one. Rather, there are four people (B, C, D – all transfers – and the new hire), who are unfamiliar with their new job, work group, supervisor, location, and so forth.

The organizational literature provides no recognition of this phenomenon and certainly no assessment of its costs and benefits for the contemporary organization.

Perhaps a recent discussion in the *Wall Street Journal* (Templin & White, 1994) provides some illustration of the pressing nature of the "transfer" issue.

> *General Motors Corp. is hiring temporary workers to staff some factories because it is unable to move 8,300 idled workers who are receiving virtually full wages for staying put. GM is so desperate for extra hands at five plants that it is raffling off a $10,000 voucher toward a new car to entice some 1,100 idled employees . . . to attend a "jobs fair" . . . that will showcase transfer opportunities. So far, these workers, laid off since August 1992, have turned down lucrative offers elsewhere . . .*

The promise that GM's most recent three-year contract with the United Auto Workers provided the flexibility to move laid-off workers to plants where additional personnel were needed has not materialized. The corporation is paying overtime to on-site workers and hiring temporary workers – GM has declined to disclose how many temporary workers are involved – because idled workers are declining transfer opportunities. It has been estimated that GM is paying more to idled workers than the entire payroll of other members of the *Fortune 500*. While the situation at GM represents an extreme case, it does underscore the potential gravity of transfer-related concerns.

UNCHARTED WATERS OF TURNOVER AND TRANSFER

In the course of our conversations with each other a number of other issues were raised which, while relevant to turnover and transfer behavior and policies in the organization and the practice of HRM, did not seem to be in evidence in the available literature.

There was, for example, the issue of level of analysis. The great preponderance of empirical attention to turnover and transfer have been studied from the individual level of analysis. Most of the questions addressed were on the order of what are the predictors of turnover, or intent to leave, to transfer. Conspicuous in their absence are organizational studies examining the consequences of turnover and transfer on groups, subunits, and organizations. Is it true, for example, that organizations with lower levels of turnover have a competitive advantage within their industry with regard to productivity and profitability? Are stable groups more productive? More innovative?

Given the number of studies dedicated to turnover, perhaps there is a more fundamental question. As previously noted, much of the interest in turnover seems predicated on a predisposition that organizational stability is advantageous. Perhaps it is, although there is certainly little empirical evidence to bring to bear on this question. Even so, it seems curious, even contradictory, that so many organizations are pursuing strategies that seem to minimize personnel stability through an increased reliance on a nonpermanent workforce. The proliferation of part-time employees, contract employees, temporary employee services, job sharing, and similar approaches would seem to be inimicable to permanency (see Feldman & Doerpinghaus, 1992, for an excellent treatment). Is it implicitly suggested that these strategies are misguided? Whatever one's predilections may be on this matter, there is apparently no empirical evidence on which one might draw. We do not know whether firms characterized by greater reliance on these nonpermanent strategies have a competitive advantage.

Suppose stability were indicated. Does this indict what appear to be generous transfer policies by some organizations? It might be remembered that what constitutes stability from the organization's perspective (i.e., the employee did not quit) does constitute instability for any subunit to which the transferring employee reports. It also constitutes instability for the subunit from which he or she departed. Once again, the literature provides no guidance about the apparent trade-offs involved in the management of this issue.

Suppose, however, that subunit stability is less valued than organizational stability. Succinctly, the contemporary organization finds it essential to transfer its employees between responsibility centers or locations, domestic and international. Given the reticence to which we have earlier referred of many employees to accept such transfers, are modifications in employee selection indicated? Perhaps organizations should consider the hiring of nonlocals for positions for which transfers are more likely. Perhaps individuals with "track records" of multiple employers and multiple locations should be evaluated with favor. A argument could easily be marshaled to suggest that such individuals, if not predisposed to move, are certainly not systemically reticent to do so. Where the argument fails is the deficiency of support. Where is the balance between stability and willingness to relocate?

While we have noted it in previous sections, we would underscore that most research is limited to voluntary turnover and voluntary transfer. This focus results in the exclusion of a large part of organizational action in these domains. By whatever term one prefers, resizing, rightsizing, downsizing, reengineering, these restructuring efforts are involuntary from the view of most employees. A request for more research activity designed to examine this involuntary activity would seem reasonably placed.

Several of our HRM professionals evinced interest in the aftermath of the widespread restructuring of organizations that so often result in the unemployment of large portions of a company's work force. Presumably any company electing to adopt such programs does so with the belief that, on balance, the costs of such activity exceed the potential downside. A key issue raised by our HRM professionals, however, involved the consequences of these layoffs, not on those who were displaced, but on those who remained. Certainly, many of those who, as it turned out, were not involved must have had some anxiety about their possible involvement. It may be, also, that many of those who were spared had an increased work load as a function of staff reductions. The question is: What happens when the economy recovers and there is a concomitant increase in alternative job opportunities? It will be interesting to see if layoff-surviving employees have higher rates of turnover in the postsurvival, posteconomic downturn period as compared to those in equivalent positions in other companies that had no layoffs.

The dual career phenomenon, too, provides an interesting avenue of inquiry. With regard to selection, would one consider such a couple to be a threat or an opportunity? While it does seem reasonable that members of these relationships would be less likely to terminate their relationship with the company, we are unaware of any evidence directly bearing on this issue. At the same time, are members of this dual career arrangement less likely to accept company initiated transfers?

It occurs to some of us that employee turnover is not a matter of "if," but "when." At some point everyone terminates their employment with the organization, certainly some more often than others. One of the HRM professionals made a compelling point:

Often, employee turnover is a compliment to the organization from which the employee departs. What, after all, would be the point of selecting and developing a work force in which no other employer has an interest? Presumably, such a workforce could be assembled, if not respected. Is turnover, in fact, the inevitable cost of admirable HRM policies and a successful organization?

Employee turnover and transfer are not a given. Both are manageable and are, along with absenteeism, probably interdependent (Dalton & Todor, 1993). While some of the research conducted in these areas is instructive, there is much to be accomplished. We would hasten to add that it is the cooperation contemplated by those whose vision propelled the production of this book that will aid us in that quest. It should be acknowledged that it was through the interactions of the HRM professionals and the academic community that the better questions were raised in this chapter and the better insights were shared.

NOTE

I must acknowledge the complete cooperation of the Dow Chemical Company and, of course, all of those HR executives who have contributed to this manuscript. Also, very special thanks to Bob Loomis, also of the Dow Chemical Company, who not only coordinated my visit to Dow and the attendant interviews, but went well beyond any reasonable measure to make my visit both pleasant and productive.

Also, it would be inappropriate to conclude that all issues and concerns described in this article necessarily apply specifically to the Dow Chemical Company. It should also be noted that the mention of such issues and concerns does not necessarily represent the unanimous view of the HR managers at the Dow Chemical Company. The HR managers who contributed to this article often addressed issues based on their experience, not only with the Dow Chemical Company, but of the industry, other industries and companies for which they had knowledge, and whatever other contacts would be expected for professional managers in the human resources function.

REFERENCES

Abelson, M. (1987). Examination of avoidable and unavoidable turnover. *Journal of Applied Psychology*, 72, 382–6.

Abelson, M. A., & Baysinger, B. D. (1984). Optimal and dysfunctional turnover: Toward an organizational level model. *Academy of Management Review*, 9, 331–41.

Anderson, J. C., Milkovich, G. T., & Tsui, A. (1981). Intraorganizational mobility: A model and review. *Academy of Management Review*, 6, 529–38.

Baysinger, B. D., & Mobley, W. H. (1984). Employee turnover: Individual and organizational analysis. In K. M. Rowland & G. R. Ferris (eds.), *Research in Personnel and Human Resources Management*, vol. 1, pp. 269–320. Greenwich, CT: JAI Press.

Becker, B. E. (1987). Concession bargaining: The impact on shareholder equity. *Industrial & Labor Relations Review*, 40, 268–79.

Becker, B. E. (1988). Concession bargaining: The meaning of union gains. *Academy of Management Journal*, 31, 377–87.

Bernhardt, D., & Scoones, D. (1993). Promotion, turnover, and preemptive wage offers. *American Economic Review*, 83, 771–91.

Blau, G. (1993). Further exploring the relationship between job search and voluntary individual turnover. *Personnel Psychology*, 46, 313–30.

Block, R. N. (1978a). The impact of seniority provisions on the manufacturing quit rate. *Industrial Relations*, 31, 474–88.

Block, R. N. (1978b). Job change and negotiated nonwage provisions. *Industrial Relations*, 17, 296–307.

Boudreau, J. W. (1983). Effects of employee flows on utility analysis of human resource productivity improvement programs. *Journal of Applied Psychology*, 68, 396–407.

Boudreau, J. W., & Berger, C. J. (1985a). Decision-theoretic utility analysis applied to employee separations and acquisitions. *Journal of Applied Psychology*, 70, 581–612.

Boudreau, J. W., & Berger, C. J. (1985b). Toward a conceptual model of employee movement utility. In K. M. Rowland & G. R. Ferris (eds.), *Research in Personnel and Human Resource Management*, vol. 3, pp. 31–54. Greenwich, CT: JAI Press.

Brett, J. M. (1982). Job transfer and well being. *Journal of Applied Psychology*, 67, 450–63.

Brown, C., & Medoff, J. L. (1988). The impact of firm acquisitons on labor. In J. J. Auerback (ed.), *Corporate Takeovers: Causes and consequences*, 9–25. Chicago: University of Chicago Press.

Business Week (1994). The pain of downsizing. May 9, 60–9.

Byrne, A. A. (1994). There is an upside to downsizing. *Business Week*, May 9, 60–9.

Cannella, A. A., & Hambrick, D. C. (1993). Effects of executive departures on performance of acquired firms. *Strategic Management Journal*, 14, 137–52.

Carsten, J. M., & Spector, P. E. (1987). Unemployment, job satisfaction, and employee turnover: A meta-analytic test of the Muchinsky model. *Journal of Applied Psychology*, 72, 374–81.

Cascio, W. F. (1991). *Costing Human Resources: The financial impact of behavior in organizations*, 3rd ed. Boston. PWS-Kent.

Cohen, A. (1993). Organizational commitment and turnover: A meta-analysis. *Academy of Management Journal*, 36, 1140–57.

Cotton, J. L., & Tuttle, J. M. (1986). Employee turnover: A meta-analysis and review with implications for research. *Academy of Management Review*, 11, 55–70.

Dailey, R. C., & Kirk, D. J. (1992). Distributive and procedural justice as antecedents of job dissatisfaction and intent to turnover. *Human Relations*, 45, 305–17.

Dalton, D. R., & Kesner, I. F. (1986). The "windfall account" of employee turnover: Implications for two-tier salary structures. *Journal of Business Research*, 14, 269–78.

Dalton, D. R., Krackhardt, D. M., & Porter, L. W. (1981). Functional turnover: An empirical assessment. *Journal of Applied Psychology*, 66, 716–21.

Dalton, D. R., & Mesch, D. M. (1992). The impact of employee initiated transfer of absenteeism: A four-year cohort assessment. *Human Relations*, 45, 291–304.

Dalton, D. R., & Todor, W. D. (1979). Turnover turned over: An expanded and positive perspective. *Academy of Management Review*, 4, 225–36.

Dalton, D. R., & Todor, W. D. (1982). Turnover: A lucrative hard dollar phenomenon. *Academy of Management Review*, 7, 212–18.

Dalton, D. R., & Todor, W. D. (1987). The attenuating effects of internal mobility on employee turnover: Multiple field assessments. *Journal of Management*, 13, 705–11.

Dalton, D. R., & Todor, W. D. (1993). Turnover, transfer, absenteeism: An interdependent perspective. *Journal of Management*, 19, 193–220.

Dalton, D. R., Todor, W. D., Krackhardt, D. M. (1982). Turnover overstated: The functional taxonomy. *Academy of Management Review*, 7, 117–23.

Dreher, G. F. (1982). The role of performance in the turnover process. *Academy of Management Journal*, 25, 137–47.

Feldman, D. C. (1994). The decision to retire early: A review and conceptualization. *Academy of Management Review*, 19, 285–311.

Feldman, D. C., & Doerpinghaus, H. I. (1992). Patterns of part-time employment. *Journal of Vocational Behavior*, 41, 282–94.

Flax, S. (1984). Pay cuts before the job even starts. *Fortune*, 109, January, 9, 75–7.

Gaertner, K. N., & Nollen, S. D. (1992). Turnover intentions and desire among executives. *Human Relations*, 45, 447–65.

Grusky, O. (1967). Career mobility and organizational commitment. *Administrative Science Quarterly*, 10, 488–503.

Gustafson, H. W. (1982). Force-loss analysis. In W. H. Mobley, *Employee Turnover: Causes, consequences, and control*, 139–85. Reading, MA: Addison-Wesley.

Hollenbeck, J. R., & Williams, C. R. (1986). Turnover functionality versus turnover frequency: A note on work attitudes and organizational effectiveness. *Journal of Applied Psychology*, 71, 606–11.

Hom, P. W., Caranikas-Walker, F., Prussia, G. E., & Griffeth, R. W. (1992). A meta-analytical structural equations analysis of a model of employee turnover. *Journal of Applied Psychology*, 77, 890–909.

Ichniowski, K. C., & Delaney, J. T. (1990). Profitability and compensation adjustments in the retail food industry. *Industrial and Labor Relations Review*, 43, 183–202.

Jackofsky, E. F. (1984). Turnover and job performance: An integrated process model. *Academy of Management Review*, 9, 74–83.

Jackofsky, E. F., & Peters, L. H. (1983). Job turnover versus company turnover: Reassessment of the March and Simon participation hypothesis. *Journal of Applied Psychology*, 68, 490–5.

Jaros, S. J., Jermier, J. M., Koehler, J. W., & Sincich, T. (1993). Effects of continuance, affective, and moral commitment on the withdrawal process: An evaluation of eight structural equation models. *Academy of Management Journal*, 36, 951–95.

Jensen, M. C. (1984). Takeovers: Folklore and science. *Harvard Business Review*, 62, 109–21.

Judge, T. A. (1993). Does affective disposition moderate the relationship between job satisfaction and voluntary turnover? *Journal of Applied Psychology*, 78, 395–401.

Kesner, I. F., & Dalton, D. R. (1982). Turnover benefits: The other side of the "costs" coin. *Personnel*, 32, 69–76.

Leana, C. R., & Feldman, D. C. (1992). *Coping with Job Loss: How individuals, organizations, and communities respond to layoffs*. New York: Macmillan/Lexington Books.

Light, A., & Ureta, M. (1992). Panel estimates of male and female job turnover behavior: Can female nonquitters be identified? *Journal of Labor Economics*, 10, 156–81.

Lucas, G. H., Parasuraman, A., Davis, R. A., & Enis, B. (1987). An empirical study of salesforce turnover. *Journal of Marketing*, 51, 34–59.

McEvoy, G. M., & Cascio, W. F. (1987). Do good or poor performers leave? A meta-analysis of the relationship between performance and turnover. *Academy of Management Journal*, 30, 744–62.

March, J. G., & Simon, H. A. (1958). *Organizations*. New York: Wiley.

Mathieu, J. E., & Zajac, D. M. (1990). A review and meta-analysis of the antecedents, correlates, and consequences of organizational commitment. *Psychological Bulletin*, 108, 171–94.

Miller, J. G., & Wheeler, K. G. (1992). Unraveling the mysteries of gender differences in intentions to leave the organization. *Journal of Organizational Behavior*, 13, 465–78.

Mitra, A., Jenkins, G. D., & Gupta, N. (1992). A meta-analytic review of the relationship between absence and turnover. *Journal of Applied Psychology*, 77, 879–89.

Mobley, W. H. (1977). Intermediate linkages in the relationships between job satisfaction and employee turnover. *Journal of Applied Psychology*, 62, 237–40.

Mobley, W. H. (1982). *Employee Turnover: Causes, consequences, and control*. Reading, MA: Addison-Wesley.

Mobley, W. H., Griffeth, R. W., Hand, H. H., & Meglino, B. M. (1979). Review and conceptual analysis of the employee turnover process. *Psychological Bulletin*, 86, 493–522.

Mowday, R. T., Porter, L. W., & Steers, R. M. (1982). *Employee–Organization Linkages: The psychology of commitment, absenteeism, and turnover*. New York: Academic Press.

Muchinsky, P. M., & Tuttle, M. L. (1979). Employee turnover: An empirical and methodological assessment. *Journal of Vocational Behavior*, 14, 43–77.

Nakosteen, R. A., & Zimmer, M. A. (1992). Migration, age, and earnings: The special case of employee transfers. *Applied Economics*, 24, 791–802.

Noe, R. A., Steffy, B. D., & Barber, A. E. (1988). An investigation of the factors influencing employees' willingness to accept mobility opportunities. *Personnel Psychology*, 41, 559–80.

Porter, L. W., & Steers, R. M. (1973). Organizational, work, and personal factors in employee turnover and absenteeism. *Psychological Bulletin*, 80, 151–76.

Price, J. L. (1977). *The Study of Turnover*. Ames, IA: Iowa State University Press.

Pruden, H. (1973). The upward mobile, indifferent, and ambivalent typology of managers. *Academy of Management Journal*, 16, 454–64.

Randall, D. M. (1990). The consequences of organizational commitment. *Journal of Organizational Behavior*, 11, 361–78.

Schwab, D. P. (1991). Contextual variables in employee performance–turnover relationships. *Academy of Management Journal*, 34, 966–75.

Schweiger, D. M., & DeNisi, A. S. (1991). Communication with employees following a merger: A longitudinal field study. *Academy of Management Journal*, 34, 110–35.

Schweiger, D. M., & Walsh, J. P. (1990). Mergers and acquisitions: An interdisciplinary view. In K. M. Rowland & G. R. Ferris (eds.), *Research in Personnel and Human Resource Management*, vol. 8, pp. 41–107. Greenwich, CT: JAI Press.

Shikiar, R., & Freudenberg, R. (1982). Unemployment rates as a moderator of the job dissatisfaction–turnover relation. *Human Relations*, 35, 845–56.

Staw, B. M. (1980). Consequences of turnover. *Journal of Occupational Behavior*, 1, 53–273.

Staw, B. M., & Oldham, R. R. (1978). Reconsidering our dependent variables: A critique and empirical study. *Academy of Management Journal*, 21, 539–59.

Steele, R. P., & Ovalle, N. K. (1984). A review and meta-analysis of research on the relationship between behavioral intentions and employee turnover. *Journal of Applied Psychology*, 69, 673–86.

Templin, N., & White, J. B. (1994). GM goes to great lengths to match workers and work. *Wall Street Journal*, April 21, B6.

Tett, R. P., & Meyer, J. P. (1993). Job satisfaction, organizational commitment, turnover intention, and turnover: Path analyses based on meta-analytical findings. *Personnel Psychology*, 46, 259–93.

Thomas, S. L., & Kleiner, M. M. (1992). The effect of two-tier collective bargaining agreements on shareholder equity. *Industrial & Labor Relations Review*, 45, 339–51.

Topel, R. (1993). What have we learned from empirical studies of unemployment and turnover? *American Economic Review*, 83, 110–15.

Viega, J. F. (1981). Do managers on the move get anywhere? *Harvard Business Review*, 59, 20–34.

Walsh, J. P. (1988). Top management turnover following mergers and acquistions. *Strategic Management Journal*, 9, 173–83.

Walsh, J. P. (1989). Doing a deal: Merger and acquisition negotiations and the impact upon company top management turnover. *Strategic Management Journal*, 10, 307–22.

Walsh, J. P., & Elwood, J. W. (1991). Mergers, acquisitions, and pruning of managerial deadwood: An examination of the market for corporate control. *Strategic Management Journal*, 12, 201–17.

Weirsema, M., & Bird, A. (1993). Organizational demography in Japanese firms: Group heterogeneity, individual dissimilarity, and top management team turnover. *Academy of Management Journal*, 36, 996–1025.

Weirsema, M., & Bantel, K. A. (1993). Top management team turnover as an adaptation mechanism: The role of the environment. *Strategic Management Journal*, 14, 485–504.

Weisberg, J., & Kirschenbaum, A. (1993). Gender and turnover: A re-examination of the impact of sex on intent and actual job changes. *Human Relations*, 46, 987–1006.

629

☐ **Chapter 32** ☐

Human Resource Management and Organizational Effectiveness

John J. Lawler, R. Wayne Anderson, and Richard J. Buckles

INTRODUCTION

The human resource management field has undergone several profound changes over the past ten to fifteen years, many of which are documented elsewhere in this volume. Among the most significant has been the demand from top executives that human resources managers be more accountable for the policies that they recommend. The current focus on human resource management as integral to the strategic processes of firms involves viewing human resource management activities as factors of production that can be evaluated in terms of the contribution they make to the firm's profit stream (Butler, Ferris, & Napier, 1991). In other words, they must be tied to the creation of value for the organization. This is reflected, for example, in increasing expectations that human resources managers understand business and management issues beyond the conventional bounds of human resource management. Today's human resources manager needs at least a rudimentary understanding of topics such as marketing, financial analysis, and accounting to help position human resources

decisions within the firm's broader strategic context. Such accountability pressures, however, are not unique to human resource management. Other areas of management that are traditionally viewed as staff functions face similar pressures (e.g., information systems).

The notion of "effectiveness" as related to the human resources function has been explored by various authors (e.g., Galang & Ferris, in press; Tsui, 1984; Tsui, 1987; Tsui & Gomez-Mejia, 1988). One distinction is between the effectiveness of the human resource management department and the effectiveness of the overall human resource management function. The former deals with issues such as the extent to which a human resources unit succeeds in obtaining implementation of its policies, while the latter concerns the impact of those policies on organizational goal attainment. Of course, in this chapter, our concern is with effectiveness in this latter sense.

In this chapter, then, we examine the contribution of human resource management to organizational effectiveness. The chapter is organized into three main sections. We begin by exploring the theoretical relationship between three key concepts: business strategy, organizational effectiveness, and human resource management. We then review and assess the status of theory and research on the relationship between human resources strategy and practices and organizational effectiveness. The third section provides a case study of the ways in which the linkages between strategy and organizational effectiveness are envisioned in one particular company: Amoco. In the concluding section, we derive policy implications for human resources practitioners.

HUMAN RESOURCE MANAGEMENT AND ORGANIZATIONAL EFFECTIVENESS: THEORETICAL CONNECTIONS

A firm's human resources are today, more often than not, a distinguishing factor in determining whether an organization is successful. Stimulating the growth of human resources within the organization links the potential of the individual to that of the organization. Thus, the human resource manager's concern with relationships between business strategies, human performance, and organizational effectiveness is, perhaps, now more acute than at any other time in modern organizational history. It is also more complex. Traditionally, human resources approaches to organizational effectiveness emphasized behavior change efforts, yet failed to examine the organization's broader ability to achieve results.

This may be due to a number of factors, including the perception, both within and outside human resources, of the role and competency level of human resource management in the business planning process, as well as shifts in the manner in which policy and strategy are viewed and created. Because there are greater strategic role demands being made

on human resources managers and the human resources community to participate in this process, there is an emerging opportunity for human resources managers and practitioners to help define the parameters of what makes an organization perform better, and to participate in efforts to achieve greater effectiveness.

To understand this relationship better, however, will require more careful examination of: (1) the concept of organizational effectiveness; (2) the components of business strategy; and (3) the linkages among business strategy, human resources strategy, and organizational performance objectives. These relationships are summarized in figure 32.1. Our approach here builds on some of the concepts relating to business and human resources strategy developed elsewhere in this volume (see Chapters 3 and 22).

Organizational effectiveness

Efforts to define organizational effectiveness have yielded little evidence to suggest the existence of any single measure or set of measures which could be described as common to all organizations (Kirchoff, 1977). Managers rarely have either the time or the inclination to research and refine these distinctions. Practitioners see it more as a *system* of measures than as any absolute measure. Defining effectiveness is, fundamentally, an organization-specific approach. Organizational effectiveness is a set of processes, as well as a system of outcomes. Organizational effectiveness is a process in the sense that it applies management research techniques and behavioral science concepts to evaluate the strategic management process. Organizations are mechanisms of action. Therefore, it is organizational action and the consequences thereof, and not intended strategy, which determines organizational performance.

Complex organizations pursue multiple goals, and effectiveness is measured relative to a particular set of goals that are derived

Figure 32.1   Strategic human resources system

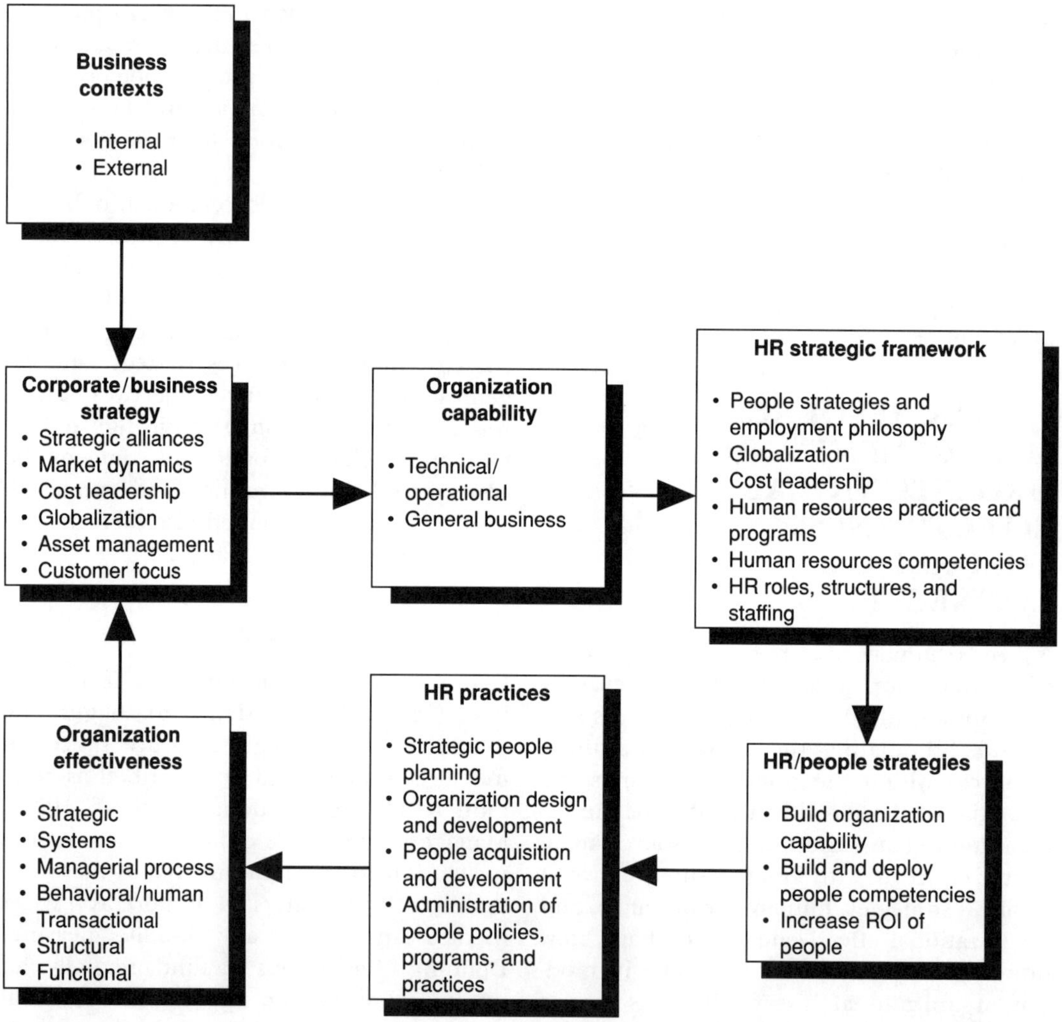

Business contexts

- Internal
- External

Corporate/business strategy
- Strategic alliances
- Market dynamics
- Cost leadership
- Globalization
- Asset management
- Customer focus

Organization capability

- Technical/ operational
- General business

HR strategic framework

- People strategies and employment philosophy
- Globalization
- Cost leadership
- Human resources practices and programs
- Human resources competencies
- HR roles, structures, and staffing

Organization effectiveness

- Strategic
- Systems
- Managerial process
- Behavioral/human
- Transactional
- Structural
- Functional

HR practices

- Strategic people planning
- Organization design and development
- People acquisition and development
- Administration of people policies, programs, and practices

HR/people strategies

- Build organization capability
- Build and deploy people competencies
- Increase ROI of people

for a specific organization under a specific set of circumstances. Organizational effectiveness, then, is also a system of outcomes that measures the degree to which an organization achieves its goals (Etzioni, 1964). Human resources managers must respond to the greater demands being placed on them to become partners in the strategic and business planning process and, as they do, the scope of their involvement in identifying and measuring indicators of organizational effectiveness will broaden. Human resource management has traditionally considered the behavioral components of organizational effectiveness. Though we do not wish to oversimplify the concept, we accept that organizational effectiveness is a combination of several measures (Cunningham, 1977).

Although their relative importance can vary from organization to organization, there are several dimensions to the effectiveness concept. Among the most significant dimensions are:

1 *Strategic* The organization's overall ability to achieve its strategic and business goals requires monitoring its use of capital and material assets. This would include measures such as return on equity (ROE), return on capital employed (ROCE), return on assets (ROA), controllable operating expenses (COE) and other financial and strategic measures.

2 *Systems* The extent to which organizational systems are linked and integrated. This might involve information systems, compensation benefits systems, and other systems (Fitz-Enz, 1984).

3 *Managerial process* The capability of management and managerial processes to obtain and distribute resources and manage the assets of the organization in carrying out goal-related tasks, such as budgeting, strategic planning or cost control. In addition, a legitimate form of measurement is an assessment of employee perceptions of managerial and organizational practices and processes.

4 *Behavioral/human resource* The organization's ability to enhance human performance and teamwork, through performance management, career management, training and development, and related activities.

5 *Transactional* The capability of the organization to seek out and engage in coalitions, alliances, joint ventures, and related activities that support business strategy.

6 *Structural* The durability and flexibility of the organization's structure for responding to a diversity of situations and events.

7 *Functional* The usefulness of the organization's activities to its client and stakeholder groups. This might include measuring such things as customer satisfaction, community awareness, supplier efforts, and environmental awareness.

Corporate/business strategy

From a practical standpoint, organizational effectiveness concerns efforts to improve or optimize organizational systems, as well as to evaluate a set of outcome indicators in a strategic system. A "strategic system" is comprised of corporate, business, and functional strategies that are created in response to a set of competitive and environmental contexts. We can generally characterize corporate and business strategy along the following dimensions:

- *Strategic alliances/joint ventures* and the emphasis management places on the importance of establishing mutually beneficial coalitions with customers, competitors, and so forth.
- *Responsiveness to market dynamics* and the needs and demands of the market place.
- *Cost leadership*, or the emphasis management places on modifying cost structures and modeling cost leadership.
- *Globalization/global expansion*, or the extent to which the organization is willing to commit time and resources to establishing an infrastructure that promotes expansion on a global scale.
- *Restructuring of the asset base* in order to take advantage of core operating competencies and human capabilities.
- *Customer focus*, or the extent to which systems have been set up and the emphasis placed on improving them in such a way that customers, both internal and external, are provided greater and greater value.

By identifying the contextual drivers of the business, management forms the basis for establishing a framework within which to create business strategies and policies. Though policy planning has a long and illustrious past, within the past fifteen years or so, there has been a shift toward what has been called *strategic management* (Hofer, Murray, Charan & Pitts, 1980; Steiner, 1979; Ansoff, 1988; Porter, 1985). This is, in fact, a paradigmatic shift. We use the term "paradigm" not to connote the methods and techniques by which policy and strategy are created but, in a more specific sense of the word as "a basic set of conceptual constructs upon which all the various theories and models in a particular field of inquiry rest" (Hofer et al., 1980). Thus, if the basic paradigm upon which a field rests changes, so must all the theories and models in the field. To that extent, we see a significant change in the way management is approaching strategy and policy.

This paradigm shift is not trivial or inconsequential in relationship to organizational effectiveness. It is, in fact, a new foundation for viewing organizational effectiveness. Strategic management is a "process that deals with fundamental organizational renewal and growth, with the development of the strategies, structures, and systems necessary to achieve such renewal and growth, and with the organizational systems needed to effectively manage the strategy formulation and implementation processes" (Hofer et al., 1980). It takes a broader view of strategy and raises two general issues for the business, both of which require members of the organization to take a systems perspective. The first reflects a relationship between strategy as a means of integrating various functional areas, and the other reflects strategy as a means for integrating the firm with its environment.

Regarding the first issue, and following Porter (1985) and Ulrich and Lake (1990), distinctions resulting in successful business strategies will depend on the extent to which functional strategies, such as human resources, are *differentiated*: that is, where requisite specialization occurs; the degree to which human resource goals, strategies, actions, and support processes are *aligned* with the strategic aspects of the business (i.e., the positioning of the organization's mission, vision, values, goals, and strategies and related parts of a system into proper relationship with one another). Successful business strategies also will depend upon how effectively human resources pol-

icies and practices are *integrated* with the business: that is, how elements or components of a system fit together in such a way that they represent a unified whole. Finally, successful strategies will depend on how well human resources systems and interrelationships within and between businesses are *linked*: that is, the point or points at which a transfer of information, energy, or materials between systems and components occurs.

As for the second issue, every organization must interact with its environment in order to survive. It imports resources, adds value to them, and exports them as products or services in exchange for additional resources. As a result, it must be capable of adapting to changing environmental conditions. The concept of *requisite variety* holds that an organizational system must maintain an adaptive capacity at least equal to that of the changing demands and circumstances of the external environment. This perspective implies the need to examine transactions with the environment and build adaptability into the organization in order to respond to both anticipated and unanticipated changes.

A system is more than a set of interdependent elements. It exchanges resources with its environment and adds value to those resources. A "system" implies that elements of the organization are interrelated and interdependent, such that changes in one element will affect other elements. Michael Porter (1985) points out that one of the keys to competitive advantage is the pursuit of what he calls horizontal strategy. This is a concept that involves optimizing the interrelationships between functional areas and operating units of the corporation in a way that minimizes conflict, takes advantage of resources available to the entire corporation, and improves linkages between systems. Attention to organizational effectiveness is, by its very nature, systemic. It is an attempt to *optimize* components in an organizational system and, thus, help produce better results for the larger organization.

Human resources managers, at all levels, in dealing with the competing demands of the day-to-day operating aspects of their jobs must also balance these against the multilevel strategic demands of the business. Thus, organizations are teleological: that is, through a hierarchy of component systems, they tend to seek *higher level goals* or *values*. These same components will then tend to proliferate and, in turn, seek higher levels of differentiation and integration (i.e., *internal elaboration*). Porter also suggests that the opposite of this, segmentation, occurs frequently in organizations because they fail to align, link, and integrate properly.

Organizational capability

A third component in this strategic system is *organizational capability*. The concept of "capability" suggests the inherent ability to perform and the concept of "organizational capability" suggests the collective ability of the organization to achieve strategy given existing business and operating conditions. Organizational capability can be any of a variety of practices and processes which allow the organization to work toward developing its internal competencies (Ulrich & Lake, 1990). Generally, however, it has to do with a more specific set of response competencies involving *asset deployment, people development, structural configurations, process capabilities, and cultural advancements* that are tied directly to the strategic goals of the business.

Human resources strategy: a framework

The principal drivers of human resources strategy are the business strategies and requisite organizational capabilities of a firm. The strategic framework for human resources and the organizational processes for managing human resources must effectively respond to the demands imposed by organizational capability, support business strategy, and result in effective measures of organization performance. At least four primary issues face the human resources manager in this regard.

First, the human resources manager must develop a framework for human resources strategy that responds to business strategy requirements. He or she must take conditions about the environment into consideration and develop the organization's employment philosophy, defining the role of human resources in the organization. Second, the human resources manager must assess the organization's capabilities around which to structure the human resources function. This includes determining how to assess organizational capabilities, identifying gaps and ways to fill them, assessing the capabilities which are required to be a leader in the human resources field, determining the relationship between organizational capabilities and pay philosophy, employee sourcing, and so forth, and organizing capabilities into career paths, succession plans, training and career development programs, and so on.

Third, the human resources manager must create a functional structure and an infrastructure by determining what arrangements best fit the organization. He or she must identify what supporting human resources practices and processes are required to allow flexibility to accommodate emerging needs and styles. Another concern is the strategic staffing philosophy (i.e., relative to number of employees, occupational mix, deployment, career versus developmental positions, job design, information systems, legal requirements, governance arrangements, etc.). In addition, the manager must seek to create an infrastructure that permits for expansion, whether globally or domestically.

Fourth, the human resources manager must develop the competencies within human resources by ascertaining those things that human resources people must do exceptionally well to support business strategies, then determining how to develop those competencies, and how much emphasis to place on cost leadership. Finally, the human resources manager must define the parameters of organizational effectiveness. Human resources managers are both strategic generalists and change agents. Thus, they are in a position to help management choose, align, and integrate effective measures based on the mission, vision, values, and goals of the organization (Fitz-Enz, 1984).

RESEARCH ON HUMAN RESOURCE MANAGEMENT AND ORGANIZATIONAL EFFECTIVENESS

We have observed above that organizational effectiveness is a multidimensional concept. At one level, however, we can differentiate between those dimensions that relate to fundamental organizational goals and those that relate to intermediate outcomes. The former are assessed by "bottom line" measures of achieved or projected levels of organizational efficiency, such as costs, profits, revenues, or return on investment. It is with respect to these effectiveness indicators that human resources managers are now most concerned when called upon to demonstrate the value of human resources practices.

Although research in human resource management has long been concerned with the relationship between employment policies and firm effectiveness, it only has been within the last decade that much research has taken place on the bottom-line consequences of employment practices. Most earlier research had been concerned with a range of intermediate outcomes, such as employee turnover, absenteeism, productivity, job satisfaction, and recruiting costs. To be sure, these may all be seen as indicators of organizational effectiveness, at least in a broader systems sense. That is, they are outcomes that contribute to the ultimate attainment of organizational goals and suggest the potential efficiency of goal attainment. However, they are not end goals and other factors may intervene, so desirable intermediate outcomes do not invariably lead to desirable levels of goal attainment.

To review and evaluate the full range of studies that have examined the relationship between human resources practices and organizational effectiveness would be a daunting task, and we certainly could not do justice to the large body of literature that exists in this area in the space available here. Consequently, we focus in on relatively recent studies (i.e., those published within the last decade); we further limit ourselves to research primarily concerned with the relationship of human resources practices to bottom-line (i.e., financial) measures of firm performance. Interested readers who wish a more extensive review of research in this area, including work relating to nonfinancial effectiveness measures, are directed to the excellent review volume edited by Kleiner, Block, Roomkin, and Salsburg (1987). In addition, other chapters in this volume consider relationships between human resource management practices and such outcomes as absenteeism (Chapter 30), employee attitudes (Chapter 29), and organizational culture and cultural change (Chapter 17).

The most significant distinction in this area of research is between normative and descriptive research. Normative approaches, such as utility analysis (Boudreau, 1991), provide techniques useful in cost–benefit analysis. Work by Flamholtz (1985) and others on "human resources accounting" links cost and financial accounting methods to human resource management. The focus is broader than utility analysis, as human resources accounting methods involve identifying an array of human resource management indicators and utilizing these as proxies for certain dimensions of organization performance. While adequate for evaluating specific programs and policies, human resources accounting and utility analysis techniques *per se* are difficult to apply in the overall evaluation of the human resource management function or its chief components. Huge amounts of data would be required, and the models are not likely to be readily portable across organizations.

In contrast to normative work, descriptive research evaluates the extent to which human resources practices contribute in reality to firm performance. Descriptive studies are usually not specific to a particular organization, and most of these studies involve sophisticated statistical analyses of firm performance measures. While not as useful in micro-level decision making as utility theory and human resources accounting, descriptive research generalizes more readily across organizational boundaries and time periods. Thus this research allows us to answer much larger questions. For example, do compensation strategies or labor relations activities generally impact a firm's bottom line?

Measurement questions

In asking whether human resources policies affect firm performance, we first need to explore the relationship between such policies and economic decision making at the level of the firm. As an example of such an exercise, Jones and Wright (1992) provide an extensive treatment of this topic, noting in particular the relationship between conventional models of firm decision making and utility theory models designed to aid decision making in the human resource management area.

Applying the logic of economic analysis to strategic decision making in the human resources area, we might consider the notion, taken from financial planning, of the internal rate of return on investment decisions. Strategic human resources decisions play out over an extended time period, so decision makers need to take into account the time value of money examining discounted cash flows. Suppose that implementation of some new human resources policy has an initial cost of *C* dollars. The policy is expected to increase profits by B_t dollars in each of the next *n* time periods.[1] The internal rate of return is defined as the discount rate (*d*) that will equate *C* with the stream of benefits:

$$C = \sum_{t=1}^{n} \frac{B_t}{(1 + d)^t}$$

In a simple model such as this, the internal rate of return can be compared to the cost of investment funds, typically taken to be the interest rate at which the firm can borrow money to finance implementation of the policy. If the interest rate is less than the internal rate of return, then the discounted benefit stream would exceed the cost of the policy and, other things being equal, the managers should choose to invest in the policy. Such a simple cost–benefit logic obviously ignores many important aspects of strategic decision making, such as intangibles and risk. Nonetheless, it provides a foundation for understanding the financial accountability pressures now confronting human resources mangers, and indicates the kind of reasoning necessary to justify substantial human resources policy initiatives.

Descriptive studies of the impact of human resources policies on firm performance begin from similar premises regarding the manner in which rational management decision making proceeds. Unfortunately, the measurement of costs and benefits is often quite difficult. Thus these studies must rely on imperfect proxies for these key variables. Cost estimates for human resources policies are not usually available. As a substitute, most research studies in this area rely on simple indicators of whether or not a given policy is present in the firm (or, if possible, the degree of implementation). These serve as independent variables in their analysis. More complicated is identifying relevant performance indicators to serve as outcome or dependent variables.

One problem in the measurement of effectiveness is that human resources policies may impact performance at various levels. First, the policy or program may impact individual workers, and effectiveness may be measured in terms of employee job satisfaction or objective behaviors, such as absenteeism and turnover rates. Policies also may be assessed in terms of intermediate outcomes, such as product quality, change in labor costs, or work-force productivity. However, the research of primary interest to us here is that which has investigated the relationship between human resources policies and bottom-line indictors of organizational performance, which normally involve some measure of the firm's overall earning power.

Studies have taken different approaches to measuring organizational financial performance. Although a wide range of indicators have been used, the most salient distinction is between research concerned with short-term versus long-term performance measures. Studies that focus on short-term measures typically utilize various accounting measures of firm performance to some fixed time period (usually one year). Accounting measures may include such measures as profits, sales, operating income growth, debt to assets, return on assets, and return on equity (McGuire, Sundgren, & Schneeweis, 1988).

The problem with short-term measures is that human resources policies, especially those assumed to have some strategic impact, are expected to have effects that play out over several years (as indicated in the preceding equation). That a relationship between human resources policies and firm performance in a particular time period is not found (or is found to be weak) may only be coincidental. For example, a firm may implement an extensive training program that may only have a payoff several years down the road. So a study linking current investment in training to current firm performance may not discern any training effects. Short-term performance measures are also subject to validity concerns, as such measures may, to some extent, be manipulated by management or affected by accounting conventions.

Long-term measures of organizational performance, while desirable, are also subject to validity concerns. One approach to creating long-term measures taken by some researchers has been to use multiyear averages for various short-term measures (e.g., a five-year moving average of return on equity). However this approach involves what may be a very arbitrary decision as to what time period constitutes the "long term." An alternative approach is to measure firm performance by the performance of the firm's shares in the stock market (at least for those companies that are publicly traded). To do so, one must assume that equity markets are reasonably efficient. That is, investors have access to important information, that they use that information in investment decisions, and that there are no constraints on the free trading of stock (e.g., there is not any "insider trading").

The advantage of a stock market based measure of firm performance is that, although it is measured in the short-term, it presumably reflects long-term factors. A stock price is assumed to reflect investors' beliefs about long-term firm performance. Thus fluctuations in stock price, or other measures derived from equity indicators, can be taken as an index of the firm's future performance potential. If this assumption is accepted, then some strategic initiative in, for example, the training area, should impact the firm's stock market performance if the move is anticipated to improve performance in the long term. There are, of course, clear problems with stock market based measures. We know "animal spirits" are at work in stock markets, so there may be considerable random noise in stock prices impacting the reliability of such measures. Even if stock market indicators do reflect anticipated long-term performance fluctuations, it seems likely that only those policies with substantial strategic impact are likely to affect such measures.

Research findings

Having examined methodological issues underlying the measurement of firm performance, we turn our attention to what empirical research has shown us to date regarding the impact of different human resources strategies and policies on organizational effectiveness. There is a very large body of literature in this area, and we present here only an overview of some of the more significant studies dealing with these topics.

Human resources strategy: a comprehensive approach

Research concerning the impact of human resources practices on firm performance approaches the problem in a couple of different ways. There are a number of studies that focus on the impact of specific human resources practices (e.g., compensation systems, labor relations policies, employment participation programs). However, another stream of analysis is concerned with overall measures of a firm's human resources strategy and its relation to firm performance. This latter line of research seems especially relevant, as it is concerned with the collective impact of many, if not all, aspects of a firm's human resources strategy. In this section, we profile research that has taken such a comprehensive approach to the evaluation of human resources strategy; the following sections review studies that center on specific human resource management practices.

The most ambitious study to date to focus on overall human resources strategy was undertaken by Delaney, Lewin, and Ichniowski (1989). They sent surveys to several thousand business units of large American corporations. The survey asked a series of questions regarding most aspects of a firm's human resource management practices, including human resources planning, training, development, evaluation, compensation, staffing, and employee involvement. The highly detailed questions were also broken down into several different employee categories (i.e., managers, professional/technical employees, clerical employees, manufacturing/production employees) and further subdivided into union and non-union categories. Unfortunately, there were some significant methodological problems with this study, the most serious being that only about 7 percent of the questionnaires were returned in a usable form. Consequently, important concerns remain as to the representativeness of the sample.

Ichniowski (1990) did further analysis with these data intended to identify underlying human resources strategies. His approach involved the use of a method known as cluster analysis. Essentially, this method was used to identify groups of firms in the sample utilizing relatively similar sets of human resources methods. Such homogeneous clusters were then defined in terms of their principal characteristics to characterize the firm's overall human resources strategy or system. Ichniowski found nine such core systems in the data that he analyzed. These ranged from fairly bureaucratic systems characteristic of, for example, unionized firms, to systems that were less structured and based on high levels of employee commitment. He then used regression analysis to determine the extent to which firms varied both with respect to employee productivity and financial performance (using a stock market based measure). This analysis showed that there was some systematic variation in both productivity and financial performance across different human resources systems. In general, Ichniowski found that more bureaucratic, union-like systems tended to have lower productivity and financial performance levels than the higher commitment systems.

More recently, Huselid (1993) has also done cross-sectional research on firm performance, endeavoring to relate a comprehensive measure of human resource management practices to firm financial performance. He constructed a human resources "sophistication" index that derives from the work of Delaney et al. (1989). There were several components to this scale and it was constructed from responses to a survey provided by senior human resources managers in several hundred firms. The scale contained a list of ten "best practices" in the human resource management area (e.g., use of employment tests, use of performance appraisals, use of promotion from within, use of quality circles or other forms of employee participation). Huselid asked the respondents the percent of employees covered by each practice in the list (further subdivided by exempt and nonexempt status). A composite sophistication index was then created by adding these responses together. He also used regression analysis to determine the impact of human resources sophistication on firm financial performance (several different indicators were used, including both stock market and accounting measures). In all instances, he found a positive and statistically significant relationship between human resource management sophistication and firm performance. In contrast to the Ichniowski (1990) study, Huselid had a much larger sample of firms and received a much higher return rate on his survey questionnaire. Consequently, some of the more significant methodological problems in the earlier study were remedied with Huselid's work.

A rather different approach to assessing the impact of human resource management methods on firm performance was taken by Abowd, Milkovich, and Hannon (1990). In contrast to the Huselid (1993) and Ichniowski (1990) studies, Abowd et al. focused on variations in a firm's stock market performance that might be related in important and public announcements by a firm relating to human resource management. Human resource management policy changes noted in *Wall Street Journal* articles were tracked in 1980 and 1987 for a group of firms. The authors then attempted to relate these announcements to changes in firm market performance, em-

ploying a method known as event analysis. The assumption here is that if human resource management practices have an impact on future firm performance, then rational investors, having knowledge of these changes, should factor such information into their evaluation of the firm and their investment decisions. The areas covered in the study included most principal human resource management functions. However, their work did not find any strong relationship between such announcements and changes in the market valuation of the firm.

Employee compensation

The largest number of published research studies in this area deals with the relationship between pay policies and firm performance. Labor costs are obviously very salient to managers and, unlike perhaps many other human resources policies, managers can readily assess the costs of different wage and salary systems. There is also an abundance of theory linking pay to performance. Much of this research concerns the relationship between pay and individual or work-group performance (Lawler, 1971). However, in recent years a range of theories have been applied to link pay policies to broader definitions of organizational performance (Gomez-Mejia & Balkin, 1992). For example, agency theory has been used to build compensation system models that, at a strategic level, relate employee rewards to stockholder wealth. Other theories Gomez-Mejia and Balkin examine in terms of compensation, employee behavior, and organizational effectiveness include behavioral decision theory (March & Simon, 1958), resource dependence theory (Pfeffer & Salancik, 1978), and the competitive strategy perspective (Porter, 1980).

Much of the research on compensation and organizational performance published up to the mid-1980s has been reviewed by Ehrenberg and Milkovich (1987). They observe that almost all of the research to that point dealing with compensation policies and financial performance concerns executive compensation. Research that had dealt with lower-level employees showed linkages to various intermediate outcomes (productivity) or specific employee behaviors (e.g., as reflected in improved performance evaluations), yet there was little research showing that pay policies for such employees related strongly to financial outcomes. Gomez-Mejia and Balkin (1992) similarly report that more recent research on pay policies and lower-level workers is still quite limited.

One study that has examined the organizational effectiveness implications of general increases in pay was conducted by Holzer (1990). He observed statistically significant relationships between increased pay and a variety of employment outcomes. For example, higher wages were associated with increased productivity, reduced job vacancies, reduced training time, and increased work experience of new hires. However, his research does not suggest that higher wages in these types of organizations are entirely offset by enhanced levels of organizational performance. His simulation work suggests that "about 46% of the higher wage premiums gained by unions and about 58% of those associated with large firms are offset by reduced costs and improved performance" (Holzer, 1990, 162-S).

In the case of executive compensation, Ehrenberg and Milkovich (1987) note that a number of studies to that point had shown a positive relationship between executive compensation and organizational performance. Other studies reviewed by these authors have shown that incentive systems for executives and so-called golden parachute agreements are also positively linked to measures of firm performance. However, Ehrenberg and Milkovich caution that correlational findings such as these have drawbacks. For example, although higher executive compensation may lead to increased organizational performance by creating incentives for executives, it might also be the case that investors in the stock market *interpret* lucrative incentive systems as a signal that the firm has resources and/or expects improved market conditions.

More recent studies also have found links between compensation policies and firm performance. Among the most interesting of these is a study by Gomez-Mejia (1992), in which the author utilizes measures of both organizational strategy and compensation strategy. In the latter case, Gomez-Mejia differentiates between "algorithmic" and "experiential" compensation strategies. The scales used to measure different aspects of a firm's compensation policies were factor analyzed to yield these two dimensions. Algorithmic strategies tend to use "mechanistic, predetermined, standardized, repetitive procedures, with minimal attention to mitigating circumstances, exceptions by rule, and external contingency factors" (Gomez-Mejia, 1992, 382). For example, algorithmic methods rely heavily on such wage-setting techniques as job evaluation. In contrast, experiential strategies are "flexible and adaptive so that these can be molded to respond to changing circumstances, factors mediating their effectiveness, sudden environmental shifts, and fluid organizational structures" (Gomez-Mejia, 1992, 382). The author then tests several propositions regarding the relationship between compensation strategy and diversification strategies. Most significant is his finding that compensation strategy *per se* is not so important in influencing firm performance. Rather, consistency between business (i.e., diversification) and compensation strategies is most important. For example, "steady state" firms have higher levels of performance when utilizing algorithmic compensation strategies, though "evolutionary" firms do better with more experiential compensation strategies.

Other fairly recent studies have explored further the relationship between compensation policies for upper-level employees and firm performance. Gerhart and Milkovich (1990) examined both the base pay and contingency pay of higher-level mangers in a large sample of organizations. They found that base pay level *per se* is not related to organizational performance. However, the higher the ratio of contingency pay (e.g., bonuses) to base pay, the higher the level of firm performance. Leonard (1990) also found that, for executives, pay level was not an important predictor of firm performance. However, contingency linkages between performance and compensation were found to lead to increases in the subsequent financial performance of the firm. Similar findings are reported in a study by Abowd (1990). In a study of CEO compensation, Zajac (1990) found that the *perception* of a linkage between personal wealth and firm performance is positively related to actual firm performance, although CEO satisfaction with pay level is not significantly related to firm performance.

Labor relations

There has also been considerable research in the area of labor relations and firm performance. An important contribution to this line of analysis was a book by Freeman and Medoff (1984) that investigated the effects of union activities on a wide range of economic outcomes. This book generated numerous studies on these topics. One limitation here is that none of this work deals specifically with the impact of employer labor relations policies *per se* on firm performance. Rather, these studies focus on effects related to the outcomes of employer actions, such as the impact of unionization or a strike. Despite these limitations, research in this area is clearly relevant to our present concerns.

There is an extensive body of research that demonstrates that unionization decreases the economic performance of firms (Addison & Hirsch, 1989; Becker & Olson, 1992). This finding is especially interesting, since another line of analysis suggests that the presence of unions increases firm productivity. Obviously, companies are engaging in human resource management or other policies that offset, to some extent, union wage gains. However, such offsetting policies are not sufficient to protect all of a firm's profit advantage. Needless to say, there is considerable variation among unionized firms, so that some subsets of these firms are able to offset most, if not all, of the union effect.

Kleiner (1990) summarizes the findings of several studies that have examined other labor relations issues in relation to firm performance, considering both productivity and stock market indicators of performance. Research has shown, for example, that the mere occurrence of a union representation election reduces shareholder equity, though the decline is greater when the union wins, rather than loses, the election (Ruback & Zimmerman, 1984). In addition, the successful negotiation of union concessions, or "give-backs," increases shareholder value (Becker, 1987), strikes reduce shareholder equity (Becker & Olson, 1986), and increased grievance activity reduces firm profits (Ichniowski, 1986).

An assessment

We have looked at a number of research studies that have endeavored to evaluate the impact of human resource management practices on the financial performance of firms. It would seem that there are several implications of this research that are especially relevant to human resource management practitioners:

1 It is fairly clear that certain human resource management practices can have a very substantial impact on firm performance. Research in the area of compensation, labor relations policies, and general human resource management strategy has been most extensive and has generated the most convincing results.

2 Much of this research answers the question: "Does this particular human resource

management practice affect firm financial performance?" Unfortunately, this does not translate readily into practice. It points the practitioner in the right direction, but does not allow her or him to estimate readily the impact of the given practice on firm performance in her or his particular organization. We need more in the way of an index that human resources mangers could use to evaluate the overall contribution of human resource management activities in their own firms. Work by Huselid (1993) helps to move the field in that direction, so that some valid and reliable yardstick may be available in the near future.

3 One area that has only been studied to a limited extent is the *interaction* of business and human resources strategy. Since human resources strategy is optimally designed to support broad strategic business objectives, we should expect that it would be the *fit* between business and human resources strategies that would be most significant in explaining firm performance. Although some studies do examine this fit issue, much more work is needed specifically in this area.

4 Another area where there is a need for greater research is in regard to the impact of *culture* on the relationship between human resource management practices and firm performance. Globalization is an important process in contemporary organizations. As we assess the impact of different human resource management practices on firm performance (or overall human resources strategy on firm performance), we must recognize that these relationships may not hold across different cultural settings. As cultural diversity becomes increasingly important within the domestic labor force, culture as a moderator of the impact of human resources strategy on firm performance becomes an even more significant issue.

HUMAN RESOURCE MANAGEMENT AND ORGANIZATIONAL EFFECTIVENESS IN PRACTICE: THE CASE OF AMOCO

We use Amoco Corporation as an example of how a company can, in practice, establish the relationships among business strategy, human resources strategy and organizational effectiveness. Amoco, a $28 billion global petrochemical company, with 46,000+ employees and headquartered in Chicago, is working to integrate business strategy and organizational performance through the effective utilization of its human resources. The petroleum and petrochemical industries are experiencing significant and fundamental change. Amoco has developed strategies for responding to these changes. Implementing them, however, will require big alterations in employee competencies, skills bases, attitudes, and behaviors as well as alignment of structure and work processes with corresponding strategies and organization capabilities. Identifying the required changes and understanding how to foster change in a cost-effective manner are the critical issues of the people component of the business strategy.

A strategic change chronology

Amoco has undergone significant strategic change since 1986. More recently, it has produced a strategic framework that represents a broad set of policies and practices to guide the company through the turbulence of the future. The most recent of these has been a radical restructuring of the corporation that has resulted in a flatter, leaner organization, one in which nearly all layers separating senior management from the business unit have been removed. The human resources function, in particular, has evolved from a reactive, administrative focus to a proactive participant in business strategy planning and execution. Some of the highlights of its development are as follows:

1986–87 An organization study identified many areas of improvement because the function was not perceived to add value to the overall success of the business.

1988–89 A strategy was developed for improving human resource management's contributions to the business by assessing existing programs and practices and comparing them with overall business requirements. Performance management and recruiting/selection were identified as critical areas for improvement, as were employee involvement, recognition and reward, compensation, executive development and education, and career management. Priorities were set and corporatewide, management-led task forces were convened to develop and implement programs in these areas.

1989–90 Senior management developed a corporatewide "change management" process, collectively known as the "Renewal Process." Renewal is defined as a broadly based, sustained effort to improve continuously the company's performance through fundamental changes in strategy, structure, processes, people, and reward systems. In figure 32.2, the Renewal Process is represented by a five-point star, where each point on the star reflects the connections and interdependencies between the main elements that lead to business effectiveness. A component of the Renewal Process was the creation, adoption, and publica-

tion of a corporate "strategic direction" consisting of mission, vision, values, goals, and strategies.

1993 A more sophisticated strategic management framework is developed. Amoco characterizes corporate and business strategy as having the elements discussed above and depicted in figure 32.1 (responsiveness to market dynamics, globalization and global expansion, customer focus, strategic alliances and joint ventures, restructuring of the asset base, cost leadership).

Teams and strategy formulation

Developing competitive strategies that also reflected common strategic elements set the stage assessing the capabilities required to carry out the business strategies. This resulted in the need for extensive revisions to Amoco's people strategies. In order to develop a support framework for the corporate strategic framework, Amoco's human resources department convened a set of cross-functional, intercompany teams, consisting of both line and support staff, to develop the people component of the corporate strategic framework. These teams developed a three-point "people strategy" based on a conceptual model consistent with figure 32.1. The work of the teams was based on the following assumptions:

1 Business strategy has three components: operating strategy, people strategy, and financial strategy.
2 Business strategies are the basis for developing people strategies.
3 The business strategy identifies the need for specific organizational capabilities and the reinforcing and building of these capabilities as the focus of the people strategy.
4 Organizational capabilities are the collective abilities of the organization required

Figure 32.2 Amoco Renewal Process

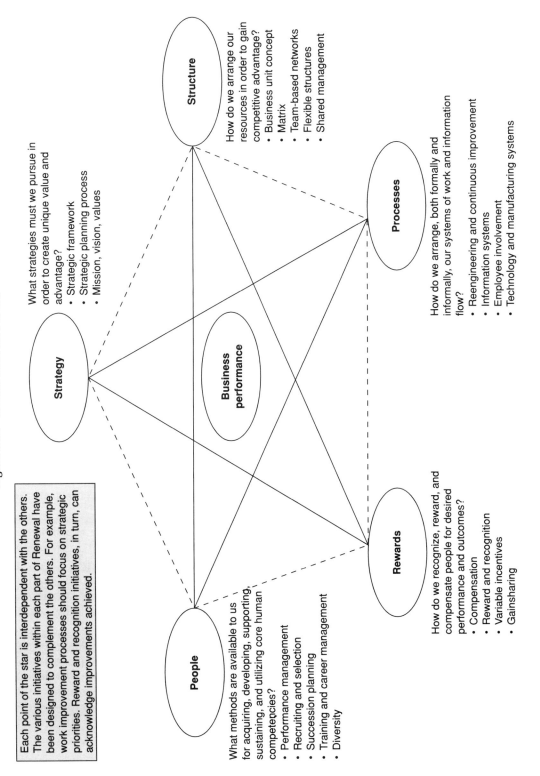

Each point of the star is interdependent with the others. The various initiatives within each part of Renewal have been designed to complement the others. For example, work improvement processes should focus on strategic priorities. Reward and recognition initiatives, in turn, can acknowledge improvements achieved.

Strategy

What strategies must we pursue in order to create unique value and advantage?
• Strategic framework
• Strategic planning process
• Mission, vision, values

Structure

How do we arrange our resources in order to gain competitive advantage?
• Business unit concept
• Matrix
• Team-based networks
• Flexible structures
• Shared management

Processes

How do we arrange, both formally and informally, our systems of work and information flow?
• Reengineering and continuous improvement
• Information systems
• Employee involvement
• Technology and manufacturing systems

Rewards

How do we recognize, reward, and compensate people for desired performance and outcomes?
• Compensation
• Reward and recognition
• Variable incentives
• Gainsharing

People

What methods are available to us for acquiring, developing, supporting, sustaining, and utilizing core human competencies?
• Performance management
• Recruiting and selection
• Succession planning
• Training and career management
• Diversity

Business performance

to accomplish strategic objectives. They are the link between the strategies and the methods of shaping the organization to achieve the strategies.

5 The operating and business units share specific common business strategies and organizational capability requirements against which the people strategy framework is developed.

6 The people strategy framework contains elements that can be customized to meet the needs of the operating and business units to better manage people and improve performance.

7 People policies, programs, and practices are the tools managers use to improve performance and execute their strategies. They must be aligned with the business strategies and supported by management as value-added activities.

A number of conclusions were reached by each of the teams and used as a basis for developing a three part people strategy. Utilizing the full talents of employees should significantly enhance Amoco's ability to execute strategy in a superior manner. Existing processes and structures limited the use of current competencies and reduced the company's speed, flexibility, and agility. Structural changes in the business environment had caused critical gaps in the capability of the organization to respond; people strategies must help to fill these gaps or the business strategies may not be successfully implemented. Motivating the work force and acquiring new talent would require a better match between the needs of employees and their business or operating unit. Balancing the needs of Amoco's diverse work force and business mix required varied approaches to pay, benefits, and related people policies and programs. Individual businesses faced different circumstances and required different people strategies and programs.

People strategy

People strategy has been designed to manage, develop and deploy people resources to support the other components of the company's business strategy. There are three basic components to Amoco's people strategy.

The first component seeks to *create the organizational capability to act quickly and decisively.* This component is designed to increase speed and decisiveness, including timely intelligence gathering, rapid information processing, decision making and disciplined execution. It requires a strengthening of business accountability for strategic and operational performance; the redesign of organizations and work processes to improve productivity and increase speed of response; the development of efficient and effective methods for rapidly processing information; and the incorporation of the ability to assess organization capability into the strategic planning process.

The second component seeks to *build and deploy critical people competencies.* This includes defining specific people competencies needed at each organizational level, developing or redeploying individuals, as appropriate, and building new competencies. The company must define core and business specific competency requirements; and it must use people policies, programs, and practices to help shape the organization and close capability gaps.

The third objective seeks to *increase the return on investment in people.* This involves clarifying goals and milestones, addressing structural and process issues, linking rewards to performance, and building the foundation for a more productive work force. This means the redesign of compensation, benefit plans, and personnel policies and programs to maximize the cost–value-added relationship; establish a work environment that enhances a more productive and empowered work force; and redefine the fundamental employment philosophy.

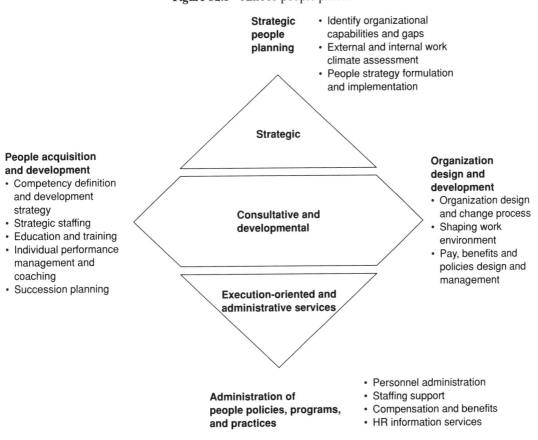

Figure 32.3 Amoco people practices

Strategic people planning
- Identify organizational capabilities and gaps
- External and internal work climate assessment
- People strategy formulation and implementation

Strategic

People acquisition and development
- Competency definition and development strategy
- Strategic staffing
- Education and training
- Individual performance management and coaching
- Succession planning

Consultative and developmental

Organization design and development
- Organization design and change process
- Shaping work environment
- Pay, benefits and policies design and management

Execution-oriented and administrative services

Administration of people policies, programs, and practices
- Personnel administration
- Staffing support
- Compensation and benefits
- HR information services

Implementation

Implementing the people strategy framework requires a collaboration between line management and HR professionals. While line managers need to be accountable for the success of their people strategies, the HR function adds value by ensuring that people policies, programs, and practices are aligned with and support those strategies. To focus emphasis and integrate human resource practices in support of the recommended people strategy framework, people practices have been grouped into four categories, as shown in figure 32.3.

Organizational effectiveness

The overall strategic plan required integration of human resource management practices as part of a coherent human resources strategy in order to complement business strategy. One outcome of this process is the assessment of organizational effectiveness. In principle, effectiveness measures can be linked back to specific human resources initiatives. The present range of measures include basic financial indicators (ROCE, ROA, and COE). But effectiveness is also measured in terms of less tangible outcomes that, nonetheless, indicate the firm's longer-term prospects.

Given the new strategies, greater options are available for systemic measures of organization effectiveness, including: strategic and financial (e.g., ROCE); systems (quality measures); managerial process (business performance plan); behavioral (team performance, individual performance; training and development); and functional (customer satisfaction, supplier quality, community awareness).

CONCLUSIONS

We have examined the interdependence of business strategy, human resources practices, and organizational effectiveness. We first considered effectiveness as it might be viewed by human resources managers, principally as an outcome of human resources practices. We then focused on theory and research that examined the relationship between human resources practices and financial indicators of organizational effectiveness. In this concluding section, we consider some of the more significant implications of what we have said, with a focus on the concerns of the practitioner.

Strategy and effectiveness concepts intertwined. Well-articulated strategic plans are driven by concepts of organizational effectiveness. The attainment of organizational effectiveness, from the perspective of the human resources manager, requires that human resources strategy complement broader business strategy. It is really the interaction of business strategy, human resources strategy, organizational capabilities, and contextual drivers that determine overall organizational effectiveness. The Amoco case provides an example of these interrelationships.

Organizational effectiveness is a multidimensional concept. There is now considerable focus on the impact of human resources practices on financial indicators of organizational effectiveness: How do human resources practices add value to the firm? However, human resources managers must continue to recognize that longer-run indicators of organizational effectiveness are also important to a firm's viability, so it is inappropriate to concentrate only on bottom-line consequences.

Human resource managers must develop appropriate indicators of nonfinancial dimensions of effectiveness. Establishing the value of human resources practices may also be accomplished by demonstrating relationships between nonfinancial effectiveness criteria and human resources strategy. Yet this demands that managers work with valid and reliable measures of these nonfinancial variables, rather than base their arguments only on anecdotal evidence.

Research on the relationship between human resources practices and organizational effectiveness is encouraging. Prior work has shown that human resources practices positively influence both financial and nonfinancial measures of organizational effectiveness. However, the research in this area is far from complete and has yet to generate tools that can be readily adapted across organizational settings to help managers assess organizational effectiveness–human resources strategy linkages.

NOTE

1   Where B_t represented the increased benefit following from the policy in time t.

REFERENCES

Abowd, J. M., Milkovich, G. T., & Hannon, J. M. (1990). Effects of human resource management decisions on shareholder value. *Industrial and Labor Relations Review*, 43, 203s–36s.

Abowd, J. M. (1990). Does performance-based managerial compensation effect corporate performance? *Industrial and Labor Relations Review*, 43, 52s–73s.

Addison, J. T., & Hirsch, B. T. (1989). Union effects on productivity, profits, and growth: Has the long run arrived? *Journal of Labor Economics*, 7, 72–105.

Ansoff, I. (1988). *The New Corporate Strategy*. New York: Wiley.

Becker, B. E. (1987). The impact of strikes on shareholder equity. *Industrial and Labor Relations Review*, 40, 268–79.

Becker, B. E., & Olson, C. A. (1986). The impact of strikes on shareholder equity. *Industrial and Labor Relations Review*, 39, 425–38.

Becker, B. E., & Olson, C. A. (1992). Unions and firm profits. *Industrial Relations*, 31, 395–415.

Boudreau, J. W. (1991). Utility analysis in human resource management decisions. In M. D. Dunnette (ed.), *Handbook of Industrial and Organizational Psychology*. Palo Alto, CA: Consulting Psychologists Press.

Butler, J. E., Ferris, G. R., & Napier, N. K. (1991). *Strategy and Human Resources Management*. Cincinnati: South-Western.

Cunningham, J. B. (1977). Approaches to the evaluation of organization effectiveness. *The Academy of Management Review*, 2, 463–74.

Delaney, J. T., Lewin, D., & Ichniowski, C. (1989). Human resource policies and practices in american firms. BLMR No. 137. U.S. Bureau of Labor–Management Relations and Cooperative Programs, Washington, D.C.

Erhenberg, R., & Milkovich, E. (1987). Compensation and firm performance. In M. Kleiner, R. Block, M. Roomkin, & S. Salsburg (eds.), *Human Resources and the Performance of the Firm*. Madison, WI: IRRA.

Etzioni, A. (1964). *Modern Organizations*. Englewood Cliffs, NJ: Prentice Hall.

Fitz-Enz, J. (1984). *How to Measure Human Resources Management*. New York: McGraw-Hill.

Flamholtz, E. (1985). *Human Resource Accounting: Advances in concepts, methods, and applications*. San Francisco: Jossey-Bass.

Freeman, R. & Medoff, J. (1984). *What Do Unions Do?* New York: Basic Books.

Galang, C., & Ferris, G. (in press). The human resources department: Its influence and effectiveness. In G. R. Ferris & M. R. Buckley (eds.), *Human Resources Management: Perspectives, context, functions, and outcomes*, 3rd ed. Boston: Allyn & Bacon.

Gerhart, B. & Milkovich, G. T. (1990). Organizational differences in managerial compensation and financial performance. *Academy of Management Journal*, 33, 663–91.

Gomez-Mejia, L. R. (1992). Structure and process of diversification, compensation strategy, and firm performance. *Strategic Management Journal*, 13, 381–97.

Gomez-Mejia, L. R., & Balkin, D. B. (1992). *Compensation, Organizational Strategy, and Firm Performance*. Cincinnati: South-Western.

Hofer, C. W., Murray, E. A., Charan, R., & Pitts, R. A. (1980). *Strategic Management: A casebook in business policy and planning*. St. Paul, MN: West Publishing.

Holzer, H. J. (1990). Wages, employer costs and employee performance in the firm. *Industrial and Labor Relations Review*, 43, 147s–64s.

Huselid, M. A. (1993). Human resource management practices and firm performance. Working paper, Institute for Management and Labor Relations, Rutgers University, New Brunswick, NJ.

Ichniowski, C. (1986). The effects of greivance activity on productivity. *Industrial and Labor Relations Review*, 40, 75–89.

Ichniowski, C. (1990). Human resource management systems and the performance of U.S. manufacturing businesses. NEBR Working Paper Series No. 3449. National Bureau of Economic Research, Cambridge, MA.

Jones, G. R., & Wright, P. M. (1992). An economic approach to conceptualizing the utility of human resource management practices. In G. Ferris & K. Rowland (eds.), *Research in Personnel and Human Resources Management*, vol. 10, pp. 271–99. Greenwich, CT: JAI Press.

Kirchoff, B. A. (1977). Organization effectiveness and policy research. *The Academy of Management Review*, 2, 347–55.

Kleiner, M. M., Block, R. N., Roomkin, M., & Salsburg, S. W. (eds.) (1987). *Human Resources and the Performance of the Firm*. Madison, WI: IRRA.

Kleiner, M. M. (1990). The role of industrial relations in firm performance. In J. A. Fossum & J. Mattson (eds.), *Employee and Labor Relations*. Washington, D.C.: BNA Press.

Lawler, E. E., III (1971). *Pay and Organizational Effectiveness: A psychological view*. New York: McGraw-Hill.

Leonard, Jonathan, S. (1990). Executive pay and firm performance. *Industrial and Labor Relations Review*, 43, 13s–29s.

McGuire, J., Sundgren, A., & Schneeweis, T. (1988). Corporate social responsibility and firm financial performance. *Academy of Management Journal*, 31, 854–72.

March, J., & Simon, H. (1958). *Organizations*. New York: Wiley.

Pfeffer, J., & Salancik, G. (1978). *The External Control of Organizations : A resource dependence perspective*. New York: Harper & Row.

Porter, M. (1980). *Competitive Strategy: Techniques for analyzing industries*. New York: Fress Press.

Porter, M. (1985). *Competitive Advantage: Creating and sustaining superior performance*. New York: The Free Press.

Ruback, R., & Zimmerman, M. B. (1984). Unionization and profitability: Evidence from the capital market. *Journal of Political Economy*, 92, 1134–57.

Steiner, G. A. (1979). *Strategic Planning: What every manager must know*. New York: Free Press.

Tsui, A. S. (1984). Personnel department effectiveness: A tripartite approach. *Industrial Relations*, 23, 184–97.

Tsui, A. S., & Gomez-Mejia, L. R. (1988). Evaluating human resource effectiveness. In L. Dyer & G. W. Holder (eds.), *Human Resource Management: Evolving roles and responsibilities*. Washington, D.C.: Bureau of National Affairs.

Ulrich, D., and Lake, D. (1990). *Organization Capability*. New York: Wiley.

Tsui, A. S. (1987). Defining the activities and effectiveness of the HR department: A multiple constituency approach. *Human Resource Management*, 26, 35–69.

Zajac, E. J. (1990). CEO selection, compensation, and firm performance: A theoretical integration and empirical analysis. *Strategic Management Journal*, 11, 217–31.

Subject Index

Note: 'n.' after a page reference indicates the number of a note on that page.

Company Index